Britannica
India & The World
CD ROM

UP-TO-DATE INFORMATION ON EVERY COUNTRY HUNDREDS OF ARTICLES PLUS DETAILED MAPS AND VIVID FLAGS ENGAGING MULTIMEDIA & RESEARCH TOOLS

Each country, dependency, and territory in the world has its own story to tell. Through detailed articles and engaging multimedia, learn what makes each place unique. Whether your interest is people and cultural life, economy and government, or society and history, this in depth look at places near and far will fascinate and educate. The World is ideal for researchers, students, travelers, and curious people everywhere.

MULTIMEDIA AND INTERESTING ARTICLES TAKE YOU ALL OVER THE WORLD
Visit places you've never been, and go back to your favorite destinations.

COLORFUL MAP AND FLAG GALLERIES
Enjoy detailed maps and vivid flags from around the world. Flag histories provide interesting explanations of the symbols, mottoes, and colors

A Workspace to save and share findings, a dictionary to look up unfamiliar terms, and other helpful tools make

ADDITIONAL HELPFUL TOOLS BONUS: 30-DAY FREE TRIAL TO BRITANNICA ONLINE PREMIUM

System Requirements
- Microsoft® Windows® XP (with SP2), Vista, 7
- Pentium III® or equivalent Processor
- 512 MB RAM (1GB recommended)
- 482 MB free hard-drive space (873 MB for Full installation)
- CD-ROM Drive
- 1024 x 768 resolution, 16-bit color
- Sound Card and speakers recommended
- Printer recommended
- Internet access recommended

Installation Instructions
1. Load the DATA DISC in your CD-ROM drive. For Windows, click Start on the Taskbar, Select Run, and use the Browse button to select install.exe on the Disc.
2. When the installation is complete, double click the Britannica program icon on your Desktop to begin. For Further information and troubleshooting information, see the readme.txt file on the Disc.

M.R.P.: Rs. 695/- (Inclusive of all Taxes)

2011

JANUARY
M	T	W	T	F	S	S
					1	2
3	4	5	6	7	8	9
10	11	12	13	14	15	16
17	18	19	20	21	22	23
24	25	26	27	28	29	30
31						

FEBRUARY
M	T	W	T	F	S	S
	1	2	3	4	5	6
7	8	9	10	11	12	13
14	15	16	17	18	19	20
21	22	23	24	25	26	27
28						

MARCH
M	T	W	T	F	S	S
	1	2	3	4	5	6
7	8	9	10	11	12	13
14	15	16	17	18	19	20
21	22	23	24	25	26	27
28	29	30	31			

APRIL
M	T	W	T	F	S	S
				1	2	3
4	5	6	7	8	9	10
11	12	13	14	15	16	17
18	19	20	21	22	23	24
25	26	27	28	29	30	

MAY
M	T	W	T	F	S	S
						1
2	3	4	5	6	7	8
9	10	11	12	13	14	15
16	17	18	19	20	21	22
23	24	25	26	27	28	29
30	31					

JUNE
M	T	W	T	F	S	S
		1	2	3	4	5
6	7	8	9	10	11	12
13	14	15	16	17	18	19
20	21	22	23	24	25	26
27	28	29	30			

JULY
M	T	W	T	F	S	S
				1	2	3
4	5	6	7	8	9	10
11	12	13	14	15	16	17
18	19	20	21	22	23	24
25	26	27	28	29	30	31

AUGUST
M	T	W	T	F	S	S
1	2	3	4	5	6	7
8	9	10	11	12	13	14
15	16	17	18	19	20	21
22	23	24	25	26	27	28
29	30	31				

SEPTEMBER
M	T	W	T	F	S	S
			1	2	3	4
5	6	7	8	9	10	11
12	13	14	15	16	17	18
19	20	21	22	23	24	25
26	27	28	29	30		

OCTOBER
M	T	W	T	F	S	S
					1	2
3	4	5	6	7	8	9
10	11	12	13	14	15	16
17	18	19	20	21	22	23
24	25	26	27	28	29	30
31						

NOVEMBER
M	T	W	T	F	S	S
	1	2	3	4	5	6
7	8	9	10	11	12	13
14	15	16	17	18	19	20
21	22	23	24	25	26	27
28	29	30				

DECEMBER
M	T	W	T	F	S	S
			1	2	3	4
5	6	7	8	9	10	11
12	13	14	15	16	17	18
19	20	21	22	23	24	25
26	27	28	29	30	31	

2012

JANUARY
M	T	W	T	F	S	S
						1
2	3	4	5	6	7	8
9	10	11	12	13	14	15
16	17	18	19	20	21	22
23	24	25	26	27	28	29
30	31					

FEBRUARY
M	T	W	T	F	S	S
		1	2	3	4	5
6	7	8	9	10	11	12
13	14	15	16	17	18	19
20	21	22	23	24	25	26
27	28	29				

MARCH
M	T	W	T	F	S	S
			1	2	3	4
5	6	7	8	9	10	11
12	13	14	15	16	17	18
19	20	21	22	23	24	25
26	27	28	29	30	31	

APRIL
M	T	W	T	F	S	S
						1
2	3	4	5	6	7	8
9	10	11	12	13	14	15
16	17	18	19	20	21	22
23	24	25	26	27	28	29
30						

MAY
M	T	W	T	F	S	S
	1	2	3	4	5	6
7	8	9	10	11	12	13
14	15	16	17	18	19	20
21	22	23	24	25	26	27
28	29	30	31			

JUNE
M	T	W	T	F	S	S
				1	2	3
4	5	6	7	8	9	10
11	12	13	14	15	16	17
18	19	20	21	22	23	24
25	26	27	28	29	30	

JULY
M	T	W	T	F	S	S
						1
2	3	4	5	6	7	8
9	10	11	12	13	14	15
16	17	18	19	20	21	22
23	24	25	26	27	28	29
30	31					

AUGUST
M	T	W	T	F	S	S
		1	2	3	4	5
6	7	8	9	10	11	12
13	14	15	16	17	18	19
20	21	22	23	24	25	26
27	28	29	30	31		

SEPTEMBER
M	T	W	T	F	S	S
					1	2
3	4	5	6	7	8	9
10	11	12	13	14	15	16
17	18	19	20	21	22	23
24	25	26	27	28	29	30

OCTOBER
M	T	W	T	F	S	S
1	2	3	4	5	6	7
8	9	10	11	12	13	14
15	16	17	18	19	20	21
22	23	24	25	26	27	28
29	30	31				

NOVEMBER
M	T	W	T	F	S	S
			1	2	3	4
5	6	7	8	9	10	11
12	13	14	15	16	17	18
19	20	21	22	23	24	25
26	27	28	29	30		

DECEMBER
M	T	W	T	F	S	S
					1	2
3	4	5	6	7	8	9
10	11	12	13	14	15	16
17	18	19	20	21	22	23
24	25	26	27	28	29	30
31						

2013

JANUARY
M	T	W	T	F	S	S
	1	2	3	4	5	6
7	8	9	10	11	12	13
14	15	16	17	18	19	20
21	22	23	24	25	26	27
28	29	30	31			

FEBRUARY
M	T	W	T	F	S	S
				1	2	3
4	5	6	7	8	9	10
11	12	13	14	15	16	17
18	19	20	21	22	23	24
25	26	27	28			

MARCH
M	T	W	T	F	S	S
				1	2	3
4	5	6	7	8	9	10
11	12	13	14	15	16	17
18	19	20	21	22	23	24
25	26	27	28	29	30	31

APRIL
M	T	W	T	F	S	S
1	2	3	4	5	6	7
8	9	10	11	12	13	14
15	16	17	18	19	20	21
22	23	24	25	26	27	28
29	30					

MAY
M	T	W	T	F	S	S
	1	2	3	4	5	6
6	7	8	9	10	11	12
13	14	15	16	17	18	19
20	21	22	23	24	25	26
27	28	29	30	31		

JUNE
M	T	W	T	F	S	S
					1	2
3	4	5	6	7	8	9
10	11	12	13	14	15	16
17	18	19	20	21	22	23
24	25	26	27	28	29	30

JULY
M	T	W	T	F	S	S
1	2	3	4	5	6	7
8	9	10	11	12	13	14
15	16	17	18	19	20	21
22	23	24	25	26	27	28
29	30	31				

AUGUST
M	T	W	T	F	S	S
			1	2	3	4
5	6	7	8	9	10	11
12	13	14	15	16	17	18
19	20	21	22	23	24	25
26	27	28	29	30	31	

SEPTEMBER
M	T	W	T	F	S	S
						1
2	3	4	5	6	7	8
9	10	11	12	13	14	15
16	17	18	19	20	21	22
23	24	25	26	27	28	29
30						

OCTOBER
M	T	W	T	F	S	S
	1	2	3	4	5	6
7	8	9	10	11	12	13
14	15	16	17	18	19	20
21	22	23	24	25	26	27
28	29	30	31			

NOVEMBER
M	T	W	T	F	S	S
				1	2	3
4	5	6	7	8	9	10
11	12	13	14	15	16	17
18	19	20	21	22	23	24
25	26	27	28	29	30	

DECEMBER
M	T	W	T	F	S	S
						1
2	3	4	5	6	7	8
9	10	11	12	13	14	15
16	17	18	19	20	21	22
23	24	25	26	27	28	29
30	31					

MANORAMA
YEARBOOK 2012

47TH

YEAR OF PUBLICATION

Malayala 🏛 Manorama

Kottayam Kozhikode Kochi Thiruvananthapuram Palakkad Kannur Kollam Thrissur
Malappuram Pathanamthitta Mumbai Chennai Bangalore Delhi Dubai Bahrain

MANORAMA
YEARBOOK 2012

Chief Editor — **Mammen Mathew**

Managing Editor — **Philip Mathew**

Editor-in-charge — **K.C. Narayanan**

Co-ordinator, Editorial Research — **V. George Mathew**

Chief Sub Editor — **Biju Mathai**

Senior Sub Editor — **C. Unnikrishna Pillai**

Sub Editor — **Kenny Jose**

Cover design: **M.M. Sabu**

Layout & Design: **P.G. Rajeev**

Contributors

APJ Abdul Kalam: Ignited Minds: The Power of the Youth (P. 24), **Ninan Koshy:** The Arab Uprising (P.164); **Dr. R.K. Pachauri:** India's Climate Change (P. 198); **Sunita Narain:** Green Growth: India's Forest Policy needs New Direction (P.234); **Dr. Vivek Menon:** Smart Environments (P. 269); **Dr. Santhosh Babu, IAS:** E-Governance: An Indian Perspective (P. 282); **B.S. Warrier:** Civil Services: a Gateway to Distinction (P.448); **Nirmala Krishnaswamy:** The International English Language Testing System (IELTS) (P. 469); **Dr. Sebastian Narively:** Scaling the Corporate Ladder - the Soft-skilled Way (P.475); **G. Parthasarathy:** Towards Normalizing Indo-Pak Relations (P. 519); **C. Sarat Chandran:** Youth Power - World's Demographic Dividend (P. 577); **Jennifer Mcintyre:** A Cybersecurity Agreement (P. 621); **Khyrunnisa A:** Indian Writing in English (P. 642); **Jacob Easow:** District Planning in India (P. 636); **Sree Sreenivasan:** Media Entrepreneurship (P. 648); **Dr. V.K. Vijayakumar:** 20 Years of Economic Reforms (P.654); **S. Bala Ravi:** Indian Agriculture at the Crossroads (P. 670); **G. Vijaya Raghavan & V.S.M. Nair:** Aadhaar: World's Most Complex Data Management System (P.786); **Prof. Joseph Mathew Palai:** 50 Great Hollywood (P.793); **Prof. P. VijayaKumar:** 50 World Classics (P. 820); **Bimal Balakrishnan, PhD:** Crisis Management (P. 915); **Dr. K.S. Parthasarathy:** Fukushima Nuclear Accident: Lessons for India (P.919) & Mayapuri Radiation Accident (P. 922); **Sunil Joseph:** Stamps for Investment (P.962); **Aakash Chopra:** What describes 'Indian Cricket' the best? (P.980); **Partab Ramchand:** Sports Arena (P. 979-1024); **Sachidananda Murthy:** A Democracy Under Pressure (P. 894); **Dr. Samuel Paul:** Corruption in India (P. 899); **R. Prasannan:** Terrorism Post-Osama (P. 903); **K.Obeidulla:** The Jasmine Revolution(P. 176); **V. George Mathew:** Quiz Show 2012 (P. 757).

Printed and published from Malayala Manorama Press, Kottayam-686 001 by Mammen Mathew, on behalf of the Malayala Manorama Co. Ltd. Chief Editor: Mammen Mathew   Managing Editor: Philip Mathew*
Reg. No. 40731/82. ISSN 0975-2250

Price Rs. 170/-

Manorama Yearbook is published as independent editions in Hindi, Tamil, Malayalam and Bengali with special focus on the relevant regions.

*Responsible for the selection of news under the PRB Act.

Circulation Offices

NEW DELHI
Malayala Manorama Co. Ltd.,
Andhra Vanitha Mandali Building
2, Azad Bhavan Road,
Indraprastha Estate,
(near ITO junction)
New Delhi -110 002.
Phone: 011-23379718,
011-23379719, 011-23379720
Fax: 011-23370020
Customer care No. 011-23379740

MUMBAI
Malayala Manorama Co. Ltd.
A-404, Marathon Innova
A Wing, 4th Floor
Off. Ganpat Rao Kadam Marg,
Lower Parel (W),
Mumbai 400 013
Phone: 022- 39495969
Fax: 022 - 24912371

KOLKATA
Malayala Manorama Co. Ltd
43/2b, Suhasini Ganguly
Sarani Marg, 1st Floor,
Bhowanipur, Kolkata- 700 025
Phone: 033-24555962
Fax- 033-24556995

CHENNAI
Malayala Manorama Co. Ltd
748, Anna Salai (Second Floor)
Chennai - 600 002.
Phone: 044-28542607
(Direct Cir) 044-28542601 to 06
Fax: 044-28542611

BANGALORE
Malayala Manorama Co. Ltd
132, 3 rd Floor Kantha Court,
Lalbagh Road,
Bangalore- 560 027
Phone: 080-22247735
Fax- 080-22247736

HYDERABAD
Malayala Manorama Co. Ltd
8-2-629/1/B, Road No.12
Banjara Hills,
Hyderabad- 500 034
Phone: 040-23314168, 23324692
Fax- 040-23322970

COIMBATORE
Malayala Manorama Co. Ltd
101, Sunshine Buildings
1056 Avinashi Road,
Coimbatore- 641 037
Phone: 0422 2245470, 0422 224
Fax: 0422 2245367

Mammen Mathew
Chief Editor

 **Manorama Yearbook**

P B No. 26 **Kottayam 686 001 Kerala India**
Phone 0481 2563646 2563656   Fax 91- 481- 562479
editorial@mm.co.in

Towards Greater Heights

I have great pleasure in presenting the 47th edition of Manorama Yearbook to our readers. The book begins with a thought–provoking article by our former President Dr. A P J Abdul Kalam on India's youth power. We draw strength from his powerful message. I believe it will inspire our youth.

Our Cover Story deals with the Arab awakening. The uprisings have caused a wave of political upheaval; leaders have been toppled. What began in Tunisia and Egypt has spread to other countries in northern Africa and West Asia. The stunning show of defiance has shocked the world. What are the dimensions of these uprisings? Is a new Arab world in the making? What is to come remains uncertain. What is certain is the overall trend towards democratisation in the Arab world.

In about 25 special articles, most of the major issues of the year have been discussed: corruption in India, the nation's performance as the world's largest democracy, the ups and downs in Indo-Pak relations and the post–Osama terrorism scenario.

India's economy has received special attention. The historic economic reforms and how they have changed India in the past two decades is the focus. Other topics of the year include the introduction of Unique Identification Authority of India (*Aadhaar*), climate change, energy challenges, power of the young generation, district planning, disaster management, 'green' growth, e-governance, digital media, Indian cricket and lessons from the Fukushima tragedy.

Our special feature this time 'Fifty World Classics' should interest readers. It has two parts: 50 immortal books and 50 great Hollywood films – books and films that have enriched and entertained the world.

Students taking competitive exams will find the following items particularly useful: the details of the new Civil Services format, the profiles of 1000 personalities, a directory of historical places, a register of records, and a quiz of 1000 questions and answers. The exhaustive coverage of current affairs - India and the world – is another informative feature. This is in addition to the updating of all regular features, done with meticulous care.

It is gratifying that Manorama Yearbook, acclaimed as a dependable source of knowledge, is being used increasingly by students, researchers, educators, executives and the general public. It is India's largest–selling reference book. Thanks to the support from users, we have been able to maintain its best seller status for years. We look forward to your comments and suggestions. They help us.

I believe the fabulous Encyclopaedia Britannica CD on India and the World that is gifted with each copy of the Yearbook will be a good companion to you.

My sincere thanks go to all our contributors, advertisers and well-wishers for their support.

I wish you a *New Year of peace*. Happy reading.

Mammen Mathew
Chief Editor

CONTENTS

1. Current Affairs

India

▶▶▶

CONTENTS

World

▶▶▶

CONTENTS

2. Events

▶▶▶

CONTENTS

3. Cover Story

4. Science World

5. Cosmos

6. Environment

CONTENTS

CONTENTS

9. World Panorama

10. Education & Career

CONTENTS

11. India

The more you care, the less you calculate.

No charges for Fund Transfer / Demand Drafts

When we give something to our customers, it's not from our bank. It's from our heart. That's why we've decided to do away with fund transfer / demand draft charges. For old customers and new customers. For old friends and new friends.

Because you mean more than your money

IDBI BANK
banking for all

CONTENTS

12. Indian Economy

 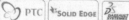

CONTENTS

13. General Knowledge

▶▶▶

CONTENTS

▶▶▶

14. Sports

People in Sports

Ignited Minds: The Power of the Youth

APJ Abdul Kalam
Former President of India

In transforming India into an economically developed nation, the youth setting a high aim is the key, followed by hard work and perseverance.

Dreams transform into thoughts
Thoughts result in action

I realize how the youth in the past have continuously contribute to the world of today in many fields. The Ignited minds of the youth contribute not just to a society that's prosperous, but also to a prosperous nation and world. Hence, I would like to discuss the topic "IGNITED MINDS: THE POWER OF THE YOUTH".

My Experience with Pramukh Swamiji Maharaj

I am reminded of my first meeting with Pramukh Swamiji Maharaj on 13 June 2001. My discussion with Swamiji on the fusion of science and spirituality and the role it could play in national development went on for an hour. I discussed with Swamiji that we were planning to establish India Vision 2020 with a mission of transforming India into an economically developed nation. Swamiji said that God's blessings are already upon the team. He shall pray that our ideas are successfully realized. May India prosper both spiritually and economically! What he wished to say was that the stronger the spiritual wealth, the stronger will become all other forms of wealth. If you increase material wealth alone, man will be lost in luxury and worldly pleasures. Spirituality will help the human being to live happily and peacefully. Prosperity of the nation with spiritual strength, is definitely the foundation for the economically developed nation.

Dr. Abdul Kalam with the youths

Youth Power

I would like to put forth that ignited minds of the youth is the most powerful resource on earth, above the earth and under it. I am convinced that the youth power, if properly directed and led, could bring about transformational changes in humanity for its progress, meeting its challenges and bringing peace and prosperity. Let us now consider two major problems the world faces: one is, out of 6.6 billion people, two–thirds of the population live below poverty line, 50% do not have access to safe drinking water, above all many do not have access to quality education. What can the youth of the world contribute to change the situation? Can every one of the educated spread literacy, at least, to five in their life? Can the youth spread the message of water conservation? Can the youth come with "out of the box solutions" for solving wa-

Youth Inspired by the Leader

> I insist that aiming small is a crime. I see youth development has multiple dimensions.

ter scarcity? I have started in my country, what is called Lead India 2020 movement. It is indeed a youth movement, with a mission for young students based on the 10–point oath which I have specially designed.

The ten–point oath given to the youth of my country conveys that the youth can make a difference in the society where they are living: in the areas of literacy, environment, social justice, minimizing rural–urban divide and work for national development, while working towards an individual goal. I insist that aiming small is a crime. I see youth development has multiple dimensions: The youth working hard on improving his knowledge with a career goal, can serve the family, can serve society, can serve the nation to which he or she belongs and can serve the humanity as a whole. All are complementary.

I realize how the contributions of the youth in the past have continuously enriched the world of today in many fields. When I am with you, I would like to recall the inspiring advice by Swami Vivekananda: "how has all the knowledge in the world been gained but by the concentration of the power of the mind? The world is ready to give up its secret if we only know, how to knock, how to give it the necessary glow. The strength and force of the glow come through concentra-

Swami Vivekanandan

tion. There is no limit to the power of the human mind. The more concentrated it is, the more power is brought to bear on one point that is the secret". Dear friends, this thought has indeed influenced my conscience and I would suggest that the education system must develop this faith among our youth and the youth should translate this faith in all their actions.

Unique You

Dear friends, Look up, what do you see: the light, the electric bulbs. Immediately, our thoughts go to the inventor *Thomas Alva Edison*, for his unique contribution

Cyclonic Hindu   Swami Vivekananda who attended the World Parliament of Religions at Chicago in 1893, made a soul-stirring speech that gave him the name 'Cyclonic Hindu' among Americans.

Edison   C V Raman

Abraham Lincoln

Recently the entire nation proudly celebrated the unique position India has achieved in world cricket. It is the result of years of nurturing talent and hard work. The country has achieved among the top positions in the world in all three major dimensions of cricket - test, one day and the 20:20 matches. Whom should we attribute this great achievement, to which has inspired the country specially the youth of India? The entire team needs appreciation including, the past teams of cricket young and experienced, the coaches and the supporting staff. Over the years many veterans have contributed to this prominent position in cricket. Of course, *Captain Mahendra Singh Dhoni* comes out clearly with the leadership quality that, "when problem occurs you become the captain of the problem, defeat the problem and succeed". I am sure that the experience of cricket will be useful to other sports and other areas of development of the country, particularly to ignite the minds of the youth.

towards the invention of the electric bulb and his electrical lighting system. When you hear the sound of aeroplane going over your house, whom do you think of? *Wright Brothers* proved that man could fly, of course at heavy risk and cost. Whom does the telephone remind you of? Of course, *Alexander Graham Bell*. When everybody considered sea travel as an experience or a voyage, a unique person was curious during his sea travel from United Kingdom to India. He was pondering why the horizon where the sky and sea meet

looks blue? His research resulted in the phenomeon of scattering of light. Of course, *Sir CV Raman* was awarded Nobel Prize. India is fortunate, the world is fortunate to have had a millennium leader of 20th century, that is Father

Graham Bell

of the Nation "*Mahatma Gandhi*" who got us freedom and also he became a great leader for South Africa's movement against apartheid. As President, *Abraham Lincoln* rallied most of the northern Democrats to the Union cause. On January 1, 1863, he issued the Emancipation Proclamation that declared forever free those slaves within the Confederacy. Lincoln is remembered for this great action throughout the world.

Mahatma Gandhi

Inventions and discoveries have emanated from creative minds that have been constantly working and imagining the outcome in the mind. With imagining and constant effort, all the forces of the universe unite behind the inspired mind, thereby leading to inventions and discoveries. The question is: are you willing to become a unique personality. Let me share an experience.

I would like to ask every one of you, one question. You want to be yourself?

| Lincoln's End | **Abraham Lincoln died on April 15, 1865 after being shot the previous day by actor John Wilkes Booth at Ford's Theatre in Washington D.C. while he was watching the comedy *Our American Cousin*.** |

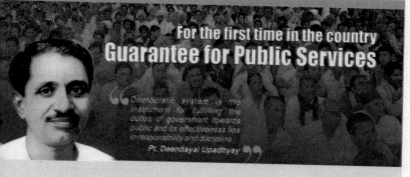

For the first time in the country
Guarantee for Public Services

"Democratic system is the instrument for fulfilling the duties of government towards public and its effectiveness lies in responsibility and discipline."
Pt. Deendayal Upadhyay

70 lac citizens benefitted in first year

- **Madhya Pradesh Public Service Guarantee Act,** is the first of its kind in the country, that gives the right to the citizens to get public services within a time-frame and also gives them the right of appeal in case of delay.

- **Shivraj Singh Chouhan, Chief Minister of Madhya Pradesh,** has embarked on a path of good governance, in which this Act is a major milestone. Ideas of Pandit Deendayal Upadhyay have been the fount from which initiatives of good governance have emanated.

- **People in Madhya Pradesh** get the services like new ration card, copy of their Khasara, new connection of electricity within stipulated time.

- **The Act** gives right to appeal if the service is not provided within stipulated time limit and also provides for penalty on the defaulting officer.

- There are now 52 services being offered to citizens within a time-frame.

Citizens have every right to get the services, given to them constitutionally. We are committed to protect the rights of citizens.

Shivraj Singh Chouhan
Chief Minister
Madhya Pradesh

Know your rights, demand your rights.
Madhya Pradesh

...sed by *Department of Public Relations, Madhya Pradesh*

Designed by Madhyam/2011

Or like everybody else?

I learnt, every youth wants to be unique, that is, YOU! But the world all around you is doing its best, day and night, to make you just "everybody else".

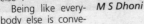
M S Dhoni

Being like everybody else is convenient at the first glance, but not satisfying in the long vision. The challenge, therefore, my young friends, is that you have to fight the hardest battle, which any human being can ever imagine to fight; and never stop fighting until you arrive at your destined place, that is, a UNIQUE YOU!

Criteria for achievement for youth

How does achievement come? There are four proven steps: having an aim in life before 20 years of age, acquiring knowledge continuously, hard work towards the aim and perseverance to defeat the problem and succeed. In this connection let me recall famous verses of 13th century Persian Sufi poet Jalaluddin Rumi:

Wings to Fly

"You were born with potential.
You were born with goodness and
trust.
You were born with ideas and dreams.
You were born with greatness.
You were born with wings.
You are not meant for crawling,
so don't, you have wings.
Learn to use them to fly."

My message to you, young friends, is that education gives you wings to fly. Achievement comes out of fire in our sub-conscious mind that "I will win". So, each one of you will have "Wings of Fire". The Wing of Fire will indeed lead to knowledge which will make you to fly as a doctor, or an engineer, or a scientist, or a teacher, or a political leader, or a bureaucrat or a diplomat or you would like to walk on the Moon and Mars or anything you want to be. I would like to assert that *"No youth today need to fear about the future".* How? The ignited mind of the youth is the most powerful resource on the earth, under the earth and above the earth.

Every youth needs to have an ethics to acquire the quality of creative leadership. If the nation needs creative leadership in all its domain, the nation has to have national ethics.

National Ethics for Sustained Growth

We need to have National ethics for sustained growth and peace. Where does it start?

* Nation has to have ethics in all its tasks, for sustained economic prosperity and peace.

> The ignited mind of the youth is the most powerful resource on the earth, under the earth and above the earth.

* If nation is to have ethics, society has to promote ethics and value system.

* If society is to have ethics and value system, families should adhere to ethics and value system;

*If families have to get evolved with ethics and value system, parenthood should have inbuilt ethics.

* Parental ethics come from great learning, value–based education and creation of clean environment that lead to righteousness in the heart.

Friends, for 21st century one of the very important business ethos will be the song "I will work with integrity and succeed with

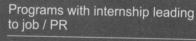

Ignited Minds

integrity". It is indeed a tough process, but only tough–minded people defeat the problem and succeed.

Conclusion

Dear friends, every one of you think of yourself, your career whether it is in science, engineering, healthcare, agriculture, arts, literature, humanities, business, management, social entrepreneurship, politics, law and executive, whatever the field that you choose, you have a responsibility to contribute and you can always say, think and act on one thing, what is that one thing – that is, the spirit of "what I can give" Under any circumstance, if everyone of you acquire the quality of saying 'What I can give', then you have arrived, we have arrived and India has arrived in realizing the Developed India vision 2020.

Finally, I would like to ask you, *what would you like to be remembered for?* You have to evolve yourself and shape your life. You should write it on a page. That page may be a very important page in the book of human history. And you will be remembered for creating that one page in the history of the nation – whether that page is the page of invention, the page of innovation or the page of discovery or the page of creating societal change or a page of removing poverty or the page of fighting injustice or planning and executing the mission of networking of rivers. I will be happy if you could write this page and mail it to me (apj@abdulkalam.com).

Now I would like to administer an oath for the youth since the planet Earth is facing many conflicts, both natural and man-made. As youth, all of you have a responsibility to work for universal harmony by ironing out all the causes of conflicts. Are you ready to repeat with me?

Oath for the Global Youth

1. I will have a goal and work hard to achieve that goal. I realize that aiming small is a crime.
2. I will always be righteous in the heart which leads to beauty in character; beauty in character brings harmony in the home, harmony in the home leads to order in the nation and order in the nation leads to peace in the world.
3. I will work with integrity and succeed with integrity.
4. I will be a good citizen, a good member of my family, a good member of the society, a good member of the nation and a good member of the world.

> As youth, all of you have a responsibility to work for universal harmony by ironing out all the causes of conflicts.

5. I will always try to save or better someone's life. Wherever I am, a thought will always come to my mind. That is "What can I give?"
6. I will always protect and enhance the dignity of every human life.
7. I will always remember that, "Let not my winged days be spent in vain".
8. I will always work for Clean Green Energy and Clean planet Earth.
9. As a youth of the Globe, I will work and work with courage to achieve success in all my tasks and enjoy the success of others.

May God bless you.

Scientist - President | **India's 11th President Dr. A.P.J. Abdul Kalam was Indian defence space scientist and scientific advisor to Defence Minister. He was honoured with Bharat Ratna in 1998. Became President in 2002.**

Part 1

Current Affairs
Pages 35 - 114

India

Indian Scientists in South Pole

The Indian Tricolour now flies high over the South Pole. Indian scientists have possibly created a world record for the shortest time taken to get to the South Pole. They achieved the feat in just eight days.

Braving temperatures as low as minus 54 degrees Celsius and navigating jagged sharp ice hills, India's first scientific expedition team to the South Pole took a different but short route to reach the earth's southernmost point.

The team led by Rasik Ravindra, director of the National Centre for Antarctic and Ocean Research (NCAOR), had left Maitri, India's second permanent research station on the Antarctica, on Nov 13, 2010 and planted the Indian flag at South Pole on Nov 22.

The eight-member team travelled 2,350 km distance (one side) between Maitri, and South Pole in arctic trucks braving the difficult weather conditions and traversing the tough terrain with snow-capped sharp razor-edged hills of 1-2 metre height.

According to Ravindra, they were asked by the Norwegian and US scientists to take a usually travelled curved route but the team decided to rather take a straight and short route to reach the southernmost tip.

The team, consisting of a geologist, glaciologist, geophysicist and a meteorologist as well as vehicle engineers, collected valuable data to study the impact of global warming on Antarctica.

The expedition travelled on four specialised arctic truck vehicles, which did face some problems due to the intense cold

Srikrishna Report on Telangana

Telengana agitators

The Srikrishna Report on Telangana Statehood has come up with six options to resolve the Telengana issue .

The six options offered by the Srikrishna report are:

1) Maintain status quo

2) Bifurcation of the State into Seemandhra and Telangana; with Hyderabad as a Union Territory and the two States developing their own capitals in due course

3) Bifurcation of State into Rayala-Telangana and coastal Andhra regions with Hyderabad being an integral part of Rayala-Telangana

4) Bifurcation of Andhra Pradesh into

Seemandhra and Telangana with enlarged Hyderabad Metropolis as a separate Union Territory

5) Bifurcation of the State into Telangana and Seemandhra according to existing boundaries with Hyderabad as the capital of Telangana and a new capital for Seemandhra.

6) Keeping the State united by simultaneously providing certain definite Constitutional/Statutory measures for socio-economic development and political empowerment of Telangana region; creation of a statutorily-empowered Telangana Regional Council.

Best option

While expressing its opinion that the first three options may not be practical, the Commission found the last option of keeping "the State united and providing constitutional/statutory measures to address the core socio-economic concerns about the development of the Telangana region," most workable in the given circumstances and in the best interest of the social and economic welfare of the people of all the three regions.

The report said, "This can be done through the establishment of a statutory and empowered Telangana Regional Council with adequate transfer of funds, functions and functionaries."

As the second best option, the Committee cited its fifth solution of bifurcation of the State into Telangana and Seemandhra according to its existing boundaries with Hyderabad as the capital of Telangana and a new capital for Seemandhra.

Death of a Music Maestro

Legendary classical singer Bhimsen Joshi passed away in Pune on January 24 after prolonged illness. Joshi, 88, was the leading exponent of the "khayal" form of singing and his renditions of devotional songs (bhajans and abhangs) mesmerised several generations of Indians through live concerts and albums and even films songs.

An artist in the Hindustani musical tradi-

Pandit Bhimsen Joshi

tion, Mr. Joshi was renowned as a master of the khayal, a genre of vocal concert music. Khayals, whose texts can range over subjects including deities, the seasons and love, are sometimes likened to Western lieder for their appearance in concert settings.

Khayals are sung in the traditional melodic modes known as ragas. They are highly improvisatory, demanding great artistry of the singer, who manipulates a song's melody, rhythm and tempo each time it is sung. The result is a rigorous yet imaginative rendition of the original song that can unspool for as long as 50 minutes.

In performance Mr. Joshi was said to have a galvanizing effect on his audiences. He had a resonant voice and formidable technique, negotiating with ease the virtuosic melodic runs that are a significant component of khayal improvisation. He embellished his singing with head, hand and bodily gestures that gathered speed along with the music.

Mr. Joshi was also known for his musical breadth. He was most closely associated with the Kirana tradition of khayal singing, which emphasizes fluidity of melody. But he also drew freely from India's many other vocal styles. As a result, his concerts had a pluralistic appeal that could transcend ethnic, linguistic, religious and class lines.

One of some 16 children of a Brahmin schoolmaster, Bhimsen Joshi was born in February 1922 at Gadag in Dharwad district of Karnataka. Captivated by music as a child, he left home very early — at 11, in many accounts — to wander the country in search

---

Governor at 29

Lord William Bentinck (born 1774) who was the British governor-general of Madras was a lieutenant colonel by age 20. He was the governor of Madras at the early age of 29. Following a mutiny, Bentinck was recalled. In 1827, he was governor-general of India.

of a guru who would teach him to sing. His father eventually found him and took him home, but over time the young Mr. Joshi apprenticed himself to a series of masters of Indian classical song. He made his first recording as a young man, and by the early 1940s was heard regularly on the radio in Mumbai. He got a boost to his career during a concert in Pune in January 1946 on the occasion of the 60th birthday of his guru, Sawai Gandharva. What distinguished him from the ordinary was his powerful voice, amazing breath control, fine musical sensibility and unwavering grasp of the fundamentals that made him the supreme Hindustani vocalist, representing a subtle fusion of intelligence and passion that imparted life and excitement to his music. In 2008 he was awarded the Bharat Ratna, the country's highest civilian honor.

Kasab Death Sentence Confirmed

The Bombay high court has confirmed the death sentence on Pakistani terrorist Ajmal Kasab on a charge, among others, of waging war against India, with regard to the November 26, 2008, attacks in Mumbai.

In its 1,208-page verdict on February 22, 2011, the court also held him responsible for the killing of senior police officials Hemant Karkare, who was the Anti-Terrorism Squad chief and was killed near Cama Hospital, along with Additional Commissioner of Police Ashok Kamte and encounter specialist Vijay Salaskar.

"There is no scope of reform or rehabilitation of the convicted-accused. This is a rarest of rare matter, so he should face capital punishment. The court cannot be more confident than it is today that death penalty must be given," said the two-judge bench of Ranjana Desai and R V More, in dismissing an appeal filed by Kasab against the death sentence imposed in May 2010 by special judge M L Tahilyani in May 2010.

Kasab was part of a two-man team with Abu Ismail, who was killed. The two together

Ajmal Kasab

killed 56 people, the judges observed.

Kasab was the only one of the 10 sent by the Lashkar-e-Toiba (LeT), a Pakistan terrorist outfit, to attack Mumbai in November 2008 who was caught alive. The official count of the people they killed was 166.

While upholding Kasab's death sentence, the HC dismissed Maharashtra government's appeal against the acquittal of Fahim Ansari and Sabauddin Ahmed. They were accused of preparing and providing with the maps of Mumbai to the LeT operatives.

The Supreme Court on Oct. 9 admitted Kasab's petition challenging his conviction and death sentence in the case. Taking cognisance of Kasab's appeal, the apex court stayed his death sentence till his petition was heard.

Union Budget for 2011-12

Finance Minister Pranab Mukherjee presented the Union Budget for the financial year 2011-12 on February 28, 2011, against the backdrop of high inflation, tight liquidity, high interest rate, industrial slowdown, delayed reforms and negative market sentiment.

Highlights of the Budget

Taxes

◆ Standard rate of excise duty held at 10 percent; no change in CENVAT rates
◆ Personal income tax exemption limit raised to ₹ 180,000 from ₹ 160,000 for individual tax payers

---

A Million Jobs

A million jobs are needed each month to sustain growth and reduce poverty in South Asia, the World Bank has said. Underemployment is spreading rampantly. Between 2000 and 2010, S. Asia created 8 lakh jobs a month.

CURRENT AFFAIRS **39**

* For senior citizens, the qualifying age reduced to 60 years and exemption limit raised to ₹ 2.50 lakh.
* Citizens over 80 years to have exemption limit of ₹ 5 lakh.
* Surcharge on domestic companies reduced to 5 percent from 7.5 percent.
* A new revised income tax return form 'Sugam' to be introduced for small tax papers.
* Minimum alternate tax to be raised to 18.5 percent from 18 percent.
* Direct tax proposals to cause 115 billion rupees in revenue loss.
* Service tax rate kept at 10 percent.
* Customs and excise proposals to result in net revenue gain of 73 billion rupees.
* Iron ore export duty raised to 20 percent .
* Nominal one per cent central excise duty on 130 items entering the tax net. Basic food and fuel and precious stones, gold and silver jewellery will be exempted.
* Peak rate of customs duty maintained at 10 per cent in view of the global economic situation.
* Basic customs duty on agricultural machinery reduced to 4.5 per cent from 5 per cent.
* Service tax widened to cover hotel accommodation above ₹ 1,000 per day.
* Service tax on air travel increased by ₹ 50 for domestic travel and ₹ 250 for international travel in economy class. On higher classes, it will be ten per cent flat.
* Electronic filing of TDS returns at source stabilised; simplified forms to be introduced for small taxpayers.

Subsidies

* Subsidy bill in 2011-12 seen at 1.44 trillion rupees
* Food subsidy bill in 2011-12 seen at 605.7 billion rupees
* Revised food subsidy bill for 2010-11 at 606 billion rupees
* Fertiliser subsidy bill in 2011-12 seen at 500 billion rupees
* Revised fertiliser subsidy bill for 2010-11 at 550 billion rupees

Pranab with the Budget Papers

* Petroleum subsidy bill in 2011-12 seen at 236.4 billion rupees
* Revised petroleum subsidy bill in 2010-11 at 384 billion rupees
* State-run oil retailers to be provided with 200 billion rupee cash subsidy in 2011-12

Fiscal Deficit

* Fiscal deficit seen at 5.1 percent of GDP in 2010-11
* Fiscal deficit seen at 4.6 percent of GDP in 2011-12
* Fiscal deficit seen at 3.5 percent of GDP in 2013-14

Spending

* Total expenditure in 2011-12 seen at 12.58 trillion rupees
* Plan expenditure seen at 4.41 trillion rupees in 2011-12, up 18.3 percent

Revenue

* Gross tax receipts seen at 9.32 trillion rupees in 2011-12
* Non-tax revenue seen at 1.25 trillion rupees in 2011-12
* Corporate tax receipts seen at 3.6 trillion rupees in 2011-12
* Tax-to-GDP ratio seen at 10.4 percent in 2011-12; seen at 10.8 percent in 2012-13
* Customs revenue seen at 1.52 trillion rupees in 2011-12
* Factory gate duties seen at 1.64 trillion rupees in 2011-12

| Castes | The word 'caste' (from the Portuguese and Spanish *casta*, meaning 'race', breed', or 'lineage') was first applied to Indian society by Portuguese travellers in the 16th century. There are about 3000 castes and more than 25,000 subcastes in India. |

◆ Service tax receipts seen at 820 billion rupees in 2011-12
◆ Revenue gain from indirect tax proposals seen at 113 billion rupees in 2011-12
◆ Service tax proposals to result in net revenue gain of 40 billion rupees in 2011-12

Growth, Inflation Expectations

◆ Economy expected to grow at 9 percent in 2012, plus or minus 0.25 percent
◆ Inflation seen lower in the financial year 2011-12

Disinvestment

◆ Disinvestment in 2011-12 seen at 400 billion rupees.
◆ Government committed to retaining 51 percent stake in public sector enterprises.

Sector Spending

◆ Allocation of more than 1.64 trillion rupees to defence sector in 2011-12.
◆ Corpus of rural infrastructure development fund raised to 180 billion rupees in 2011-12.
◆ Provision of ₹ 201.5 billion capital infusion in state-run banks in 2011-12.
◆ Allocation of 520.5 billion rupees for the education sector. ₹ 21,000 crore for Sarva Shiksha Abhiyan.
◆ Health sector allocation to be 267.6 billion rupees.
◆ ₹ 58,000 crore for Bharat Nirman; increase of ₹ 10,000 crore.
◆ Mahatma Gandhi National Rural Employment Guarantee Scheme wage rates linked to consumer price index; will rise from existing ₹ 100 per day.

Agriculture

◆ Removal of supply bottlenecks in the food sector will be in focus in 2011-12
◆ Target of credit flow to agriculture sector at 4.75 trillion rupees
◆ 3 percent interest subsidy to farmers in 2011-12

Godra train fire

Godhra Train Fire Case

A special fast track court appointed by the Gujarat High Court on the orders of the Supreme Court convicted 31 accused and acquitted 63 others in the Godhra train burning case.

Coach S-6 of the Sabarmati Express, in which 59 people, mostly 'kar sevaks' returning from Ayodhya were travelling, was burnt on February 27, 2002 at the Godhra station.

All the 31 accused were held guilty on two major counts - Section 120B (criminal conspiracy) and 302 (murder) of the Indian Penal Code.

Interestingly, even while accepting the "conspiracy" theory, the court acquitted at least two of the accused whom the police had all along maintained were among the "main conspirators." They are Moulana Umarji - who was alleged to have shouted over the public address system fitted in a nearby mosque asking the people of Godhra to rush to the railway station and "kill" kar sevaks aboard the Sabarmati Express - and Bilal Hussain Kalota, the then Congress-supported (independent) president of the Godhra municipality, who was claimed to be the main person to have collected the mob outside the rail platform to "set fire" to S-6 coach.

The owner of the Aman Guest House, Abdul Razzak Kurkur, where, according to the prosecution, a meeting was held the previous night to "hatch the conspiracy," was among the 31 convicted.

| The First Major Chess Player | Mir Sultan Khan, the first major Indian player of chess, won the All-India Championship in 1928, scoring 8.5 out of 9 points. In the next five years, he won the British Championship three times. He beat the former world champion Jose Raoul Capablanca of Cuba. |

Scam of Scams

The 2G spectrum scam invoving a battery of top politicians and bureaucrats has been labelled the biggest scam in India's history. The scam involved allegations regarding the underpricing of the 2G spectrum by the Department of Telecommunications which resulted in a heavy loss to the exchequer. The loss to the national exchequer was pegged by the government auditor at a mind-boggling ₹ 1.76 lakh crore. The 2G scam has already seen a Cabinet minister, an MP, corporate bigwigs - some of the biggest names in the telecom industry - going to jail.

A. Raja

The Controller and Auditor General of India used three different methods to assess the presumptive loss to the exchequer resulting from not auctioning 2G spectrum. The first method was based on the fact that S Tel, one of the licensees, explicitly offered to pay significantly higher license fees for the spectrum. Based on the fees offered by S Tel, the CAG estimated the loss to the exchequer at 67,364 crore .The second method was based on the price recovered by the 3G auction in 2010. The CAG reasoned that since 2G is really 2.75G (EDGE), its price should be comparable to that of 3G licenses. Based on this method, the CAG estimated the loss to the exchequer to be 176,000 crore .The third method was based on the fact that some of the licensees received FDI in the form of equity, shortly after the spectrum allocation. The CAG reasoned that this equity infusion was entirely due to the value of the allocated spectrum; this can be construed as re-sale of the spectrum by the licensee, and hence was a valid basis for assessing loss to the exchequer. Based on this method, the CAG estimated the loss to the exchequer to be anywhere between 57,666 crore (based on Etisalat's investment in Swan Telecom) and 69,626 crore (based on Telenor's investment in Unitech).

The prime accused in the case is former Telecom Minister A Raja, who the CBI has described as the mastermind of the scam. He stands accused of under-valuing spectrum as the country's Telecom Minister and selling it to companies he favoured, though they were largely ineligible for licenses to run mobile networks. Though the spectrum scam had loomed over his ministry since the sale of 2G frequency to telecom operators in 2008, it was in November 2010 that Mr Raja finally exited the government. What pushed him through the out-door was a report by the government's auditor. He had to resign in much ignominy and just two months later, on February 2 2011, he was arrested. Mr Raja faces charges of criminal conspiracy, cheating and forgery under the IPC and abuse of official position and corruption charges under the Prevention of Corruption Act.But Mr Raja claims he only followed government policy, one approved by the Prime Minister and former Finance Minister P Chidambaram. His lawyer also told the court that he might summon the PM as a witness in the case to prove that there was no loss.

The long list of the accused in the case includes DMK MP and former Tamil Nadu Chief Minister M Karunanidhi's daughter Kanimozhi, who too has been in jail since May 20 , 2011. Also in jail are former telecom secretary Siddharth Behura and Raja's former personal secretary RK Chandolia. They also face charges of conspiracy, cheating, and abusing official position.

High-profile corporate honchos facing charges in the case are - Sanjay Chandra, Former MD, Unitech Wireless; Shahid Balwa, Promoter of DB Realty and Swan Telecom; Vinod Goenka, Promoter and MD, DB Realty and Swan Telecom; Gautam Doshi, Group

Tihar Jail is not a single unit. It comprises nine prisons and houses around 12,000 inmates, although it is meant for half the number. It began with one unit in 1958, and has, since then, added separate units for political agitators, adolescents and women.

What's 2G Spectrum

It is a term used in the telecommunication sector. It is a spectrum that supports 2G technology. High bandwidth is required for this purpose.

"2G" means second-generation wireless telephone technology. 2G cellular telecom networks were commercially launched on the GSM standard in Finland in 1991.

"G" has been superseded by newer technologies, such as 2.5G, 2.75G, 3G, and 4G; however, 2G networks are still used in many parts of the world.

There are three primary benefits of 2G networks over their predecessors: phone conversations were digitally encrypted; 2G systems were significantly more efficient on the spectrum allowing for far greater mobile phone penetration levels; and 2G introduced data services for mobile, starting with SMS text messages.

MD, Anil Dhirubhai Ambani Group (ADAG); and Hari Nair and Surendra Pipara, Senior Vice Presidents, ADAG. Most face charges of cheating and criminal conspiracy. Shahid Balwa has also been charged with bribing a public servant, while Sanjay

Kanimozhi

Chandra has only been charged with criminal conspiracy. They were arrested on April 20, 2011.

Telecom companies Swan Telecom, Reliance Telecom and Unitech Wireless have been named in the chargesheet. The CBI says Swan and Unitech were granted licenses despite being ineligible.

These high profile individuals and companies were named in the first chargesheet on April 2. Then, another supplementary chargesheet was filed on April 25. This chargesheet named Ms Kanimozhi, Kalaignar TV MD Sarath Kumar, Directors of Kusegaon Fruits and Vegetables Asif Balwa and Rajeev Aggarwal, Promoter of Cineyug Films Karim Morani. They too face charges of cheating and criminal conspiracy. Kanimozhi and Sarath Kumar have also been charged with taking a bribe.

The CBI claims it has uncovered the money trail involving Swan telecom. It says Swan paid a bribe of Rs. 200 crore to DMK-owned Kalaignar TV through a maze of subsidiaries in exchange for the 2G spectrum and licenses.

Kanimozhi has been named the active brain behind Kalaignar TV. The DMK MP has denied the charges against her saying she was not involved in the day to day functioning of the channel and that the money in question was only a loan, duly returned with interest.

For its part, the Congress-party led government has publicly defended itself in the case and Kapil Sibal, who replaced A. Raja as the communication minister, has refuted the CAG reasoning. He has also justified his government's decision not to auction 2G spectrum as being in line with the policy guidelines laid down by the 10th Five-Year Plan.

Arjun Singh Passes Away

Veteran Congress leader and former Union minister Arjun Singh, who had served in various capacities including as Madhya Pradesh Chief Minister, died on March 4. He was 81.

A loyalist of the Gandhi family, Singh was vice president of the Congress under Rajiv Gandhi in the eighties and was also Governor of Punjab at the height of militancy and was instrumental in the Rajiv-Longowal accord.

Singh was a close adviser to Sonia Gandhi when she decided to enter politics and became the Congress president in 1998. He

A German Scholar of Sanskrit Theodor Benfey was a German scholar of Sanskrit and comparative linguistics, known for his edition of the ancient collection of Indian animal fables known as the *Panchatantra*. He published a Sanskrit grammar in English and a Sanskrit-English dictionary.

Timeline of 2G Scam

May 2007: A Raja takes over as Telecom Minister.

Aug 2007: Process of allotment of 2G Spectrum for telecom along with Universal Access Service (UAS) Licences initiated by the Department of Telecommunications (DoT).

Sept 25, 2007: Telecom Ministry issues press note fixing deadline for application as October 1, 2007.

Oct 1, 2007: DoT receives 575 applications for UAS licences of 46 companies.

Nov 2, 2007: The Prime Minister writes to Raja directing him to ensure allotment of 2G spectrum in a fair and transparent manner and to ensure licence fee was properly revised. Raja writes back to the Prime Minister rejecting many of his recommendations.

Nov 22, 2007: Finance Ministry writes to DoT raising concerns over the procedure adopted by it. Demand for review rejected.

Jan 10, 2008: DoT decides to issue licences on first-come-first-serve basis, preponing the cut-off date to September 25, from October 1, 2007. Later on the same day, DoT posted an announcement on its website saying those who apply between 3.30 and 4.30 pm would be issued licences in accordance with the said policy.

2008: Swan Telecom, Unitech and Tata Teleservices sell off a part of their stakes at much higher rates to Etisalat, Telenor and DoCoMo respectively.

May 19, 2009 : Another complaint was filed to the CVC by one Arun Agarwal, highlighting grant of spectrum to Swan Telecom at throw-away prices.

2009: CVC directs CBI to investigate the irregularities in allocation of 2G spectrum.

July 1, 2009: Delhi HC holds advancing of cut-off date as illegal on a petition of telecom company S-Tel.

Oct 21, 2009: CBI registers a case and files an FIR against "unknown officers of DoT and unknown private persons/companies under various provisions of

IPC and Prevention of Corruption Act.

November first week, 2010: Media publishes contents of the Comptroller and Auditor General (CAG) report on the 2G spectrum auction.

Nov 14, 2010: Raja submits his resignation.

Nov 16, 2010: CAG report on 2G spectrum allocation tabled in both houses of parliament amidst uproarious scenes.

Dec 8, 2010: The CBI raids the house of Raja and premises of former aides Siddharth Behura and R.K. Chandolia in New Delhi. It also raids houses and offices of Raja's relatives, associates and some journalists and social workers in Tamil Nadu linked to the DMK and Raja. The CBI claims recovering incriminating documents.

Dec 15, 2010: The CBI raids the houses and offices of Niira Radia, a corporate lobbyist linked with Raja. She is subsequently questioned by the CBI several times.

Feb 2, 2011: The CBI arrests Raja, Chandolia and Behura.

April 2, 2011: The CBI files charges against nine people and three firms -- Raja, Chandolia, Behura, Swan Telecom promoter Shahid Balwa, director Vinod Goenka, Unitech director Sanjay Chandra and three officials from the Reliance Anil Dhirubhai Ambani Group -- Gautam Doshi, Hari Nair and Surendra Pipara.

April 20, 2011: Special city court denies bail to Goenka, Chandra, Doshi, Nair and Pipara.

April 25, 2011: In a major embarrassment for Karunanidhi, daughter Kanimozhi named co-conspirator, along with Sharad Kumar of Kalaignar TV, Karim Morani of Cineyug Films, and Asif Balwa and Rajiv B. Agarwal of Kusegaon Realty.

May 20, 2011: Kanimozhi's bail plea rejected. She is sent to judicial custody in Tihar Jail. Sharad Kumar also sent to jail.

June 20, 2011: The Supreme Court refuses Kanimozhi's bail plea.

July 7, 2011: Maran resigns from the union cabinet.

Pratibha Patil pays tributes to Arjun Singh

was said to have been behind her unsuccessful attempt to become the prime minister after the fall of the Vajpayee government in April 1999.

Gandhi then staked her claim to form the government on the basis of support of 272 MPs but ultimately she did not have the numbers. But the political wheel turned a full circle when he lost his proximity to Sonia Gandhi and that could have played a part in not being able to realise his prime ministerial ambitions.

However, as human resource development minister in the first United Progressive Alliance government from 2004, Singh was instrumental in championing the cause of backward classes and piloted bills for ensuring reservation for them in institutions of excellence.

With failing health, Singh, who started using a wheel chair in the last years, did not make it to the Union cabinet when Dr Manmohan Singh took oath as the prime minister for a second time.

Supreme Court Allows Passive Euthanasia

In a path-breaking judgment, the Supreme Court on March 7th allowed "passive euthanasia" of withdrawing life support to patients in permanently vegetative state (PVS) but rejected outright active euthanasia of ending life through administration of lethal substances.

Refusing mercy killing of Aruna Shanbaug, lying in a vegetative state for 37 years in a Mumbai hospital, a two-judge bench of Justice Markandeya Katju and Justice Gyan Sudha Mishra, laid a set of tough guidelines under which passive euthanasia can be legalised through high court monitored mechanism.

The apex court while framing the guidelines for passive euthanasia asserted that it would now become the law of the land until Parliament enacts a suitable legislation to deal with the issue.

The bench also asked Parliament to delete Section 309 IPC (attempt to suicide) as it has become "anachronistic though it has become Constitutionally valid."

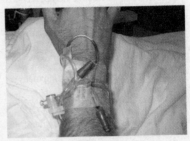

The apex court said though there is no statutory provision for withdrawing life support system from a person in a permanently vegetative state, it was of the view that "passive euthanasia" could be permissible in certain cases for which it laid down guidelines and cast the responsibility on high courts to take decisions on pleas for mercy killings.

India's Population 1.21 Billion

India's population rose to 1.21 billion people over the last 10 years, an increase by 181 million, according to the provisioal 2001 Census report. The population, which accounts for world's 17.5 per cent population, comprises 623.7 million males and 586.5 million females. China is the most populous nation acounting for 19.4 per cent of the global population.

The Bay of Bengal

The Mahanadi, Godavari, Krishna and Kaveri are large rivers on the west and the Ganga and Brahmaputra on the north that flow into the Bay of Bengal, a shallow embayment of the northeastern Indian Ocean whose area is 2,173,00 sq. km. and width 1600 km.

The population has increased by more than 181 million during the decade 2001-2011, the report said. The growth rate in 2011 is 17.64 per cent in comparison to 21.15 per cent in 2001. The 2001-2011 period is the first decade - with exception of 1911-1921- which has actually added lesser population compared to the previous decade,

Among the states and Union territories, Uttar Pradesh is the most populous state with 199 million people and Lakshadweep the least populated at 64,429.

The literacy rate has gone up from 64.83 per cent in 2001 to 74.04 per cent in 2011, showing an increase of 9.21 per cent.

However, the percentage decadal growth during 2001-2011 has registered the sharpest decline since independence ¯ a decrease of 3.90 percentage points from 21.54 to 17.64 per cent.

The Census 2011 is the 15th census of India since 1872 and conducted in two phases- houselisting and housing census (April to September 2010) and population enumeration (February 9 to 28, 2011).

The Census covered all 35 states and UTs and cost Rs 2,200 crore. 27 lakh enumerators were involved in the exercise where 8,000 metric tonnes of paper and 10,500 metric tonnes of material moved.

Kalmadi in Jail

On April 25, 2011, CBI arrested Suresh Kalmadi, former chairman of the organizing committee for the Delhi Commonwealth Games, in connection with alleged corruption and financial malpractice regarding the event held in October 2010.

Mr. Kalmadi, a ruling Congress party MP, was arrested for alleged irregularities in the Queen's Baton Relay event – equivalent to the Olympic torch relay – before the Games and also for allegedly handing out contracts to a Swiss time-keeping company that provided equipment and services at exorbitant rates, causing a huge loss to the government.

The 2010 Commonwealth Games was awarded to Delhi with great fanfare and

Suresh Kalmadi

anticipation as a way for India to show it could hold a world-class sporting event two years after Beijing hosted the Summer Olympics. It also was a rare hosting of the event by a developing nation: Mostly the Games rotate between developed countries in the British Commonwealth of nations such as Britain, Australia and Canada.

But the Games were severely marred by scandals in the run-up to the event, including allegations of corruption against the organizers and shoddy workmanship at the athletes' village and at Games venues. The Games passed without major incident though many auditoriums were very sparsely attended in the first half of the 11-day event.

Mr. Kalmadi and his team allegedly received kickbacks for twisting bidding criteria in a way that eliminated other eligible bidders and awarded the contract for time-keeping equipment to a Switzerland-based company called Swiss Timing Ltd., according to the CBI. Swiss Timing is a unit of Swatch Group and was responsible for timing events at stadiums during the Games. Mr. Kalmadi has been charged with criminal conspiracy and cheating.

Mr. Kalmadi's arrest came at a time when the Congress-led government at the Centre was deliberating over a tough anti-corruption Lokpal Bill that is expected to make graft prosecutions of officials and lawmakers more common.

Tree Planting Festival

Tree plantation as a festival (Briksharopan Utsav) was first introduced by Rabindranath Tagore at Santiniketan in 1928.

Death of a Spiritual Guru

Sathya Sai Baba, the most influential and richest in India's long line of spiritual teachers , died on April 24 at Puttaparthy. He was 84 years old.

Sai Baba was born on Nov. 23, 1926 as Sathyanarayana Raju. He reportedly performed miracles and claimed he was the reincarnation of Hindu holy man Sai Baba of Shirdi in 1940. His devotees' accounts of his childhood are filled with portents and omens, including reports of his especially charitable nature.

Sai Baba's reputation was founded largely on claims of his miraculous powers. These included the apparent ability to materialise various tokens of devotion, such as amulets, rings and pendants, out of thin air; to produce "vibhuti", or "holy" ash in prodigious amounts from his fingertips; and to manifest fully formed lingams (ellipsoids made of crystal or quartz) from his stomach by regurgitation.

Sai Baba professed that his mission was ecumenical: the emblem of his organisation

Sai Baba's body lying in state

included symbols of all the world's great faiths, but his message was essentially drawn from Hindu teachings about man and God being inseparable by virtue of the atman, or eternal soul – the "universal divine spark" which is present in all beings. The atman, he declared, "can be known only through love" – a philosophy that he distilled in the maxim: "Love all, serve all."

Sathya Sai's message and his alleged miraculous powers brought him an enormous following not only in India, but also in the West. This went far beyond the hippies and spiritual seekers who had made their way to India in the Sixties in search of enlightenment. The numerous Sai groups that proliferated in Europe, America and Australia were liberally peopled with physicians, psychologists and teachers. By the 1990s the tiny village of Puttaparthi had swollen to the size of a town and an airport was built to accommodate the growing numbers of pilgrims.

As his organisation grew, Sai Baba established an extensive network of schools and colleges throughout India, and his programme of Education in Human Values (EHV) was adopted by schools in Europe and America. The most extravagant display of his largesse was the Rayalaseema water project, inaugurated on his 70th birthday, which provided water to more than 750 villages and several towns in Andhra Pradesh.

The foundation centred on his ashram in his native village, Puttaparthi, thought to be worth Rs.40,000 crore, is devoted to building and maintaining schools, hospitals and irrigation works with a reach far beyond his own state of Andhra Pradesh.

Big Upsets in State Elections

Breaking the red citadel, Mamata Banerjee's Trinamool Congress ended the 34-year hegemony of the Left Front in West Bengal, while Jayalalithaa's AIADMK scored a landslide victory to oust DMK from power in Tamil Nadu in the elections to the State Assemblies.

Sarda Act

Age of Consent Act was modified on April 1, 1930 by raising the marriageable age of girls to 14 years and of boys to 18. This was called Sarda Act - the original bill having been introduced by Harbilas Sarda.

Congress scored a spectacular hattrick in Assam bagging a near two-third majority to retain power and managed to wrest power from the Left Democratic Front in Kerala by a wafer-thin majority but lost Puducherry to its rebel.

West Bengal

Riding a wave of change in a state where Left ideology ruled the roost for over three decades, Banerjee along with allies Congress and SUCI gave a severe trashing to the Left Front. The Banerjee-led alliance captured power with two-thirds majority by winning 227 seats in the 294 seat assembly (*for detailed party position, see pages 532-533*). Banerjee did not contest the elections.

Mamata Banerjee

The CPI(M) suffered humiliation when a number of its bigwigs, including Chief Minister Buddhadeb Bhattacharjee, bit the dust. With defeats in West Bengal and Kerala, the Left is now left with power only in Tripura.

Jayalalithaa

Tamil Nadu

Tamil Nadu lived up to its 'winner takes all' reputation as Jayalalithaa swept back to power with a landslide victory with her alliance winning 202 seats in the 234-member assembly. AIADMK on its own got 150 seats.

The DMK got 23 seats while ally Congress which contested 63 seats could manage to win only five seats.

The 2006 elections was a rare one for Tamil Nadu when for the first time it had a minority government. The DMK had then won 96 seats and the government survived on outside support from Congress and others. The AIADMK had won 61 seats in the 2006 elections.

Tarun Gogoi

Asom

Asom provided a surprisingly huge victory when Tarun Gogoi-led Congress returned to power for the third time. By bagging 78 seats the party vastly improved on its performance of 2006 when it had got just 53 seats in the 126-member assembly .

The main opposition party AGP was reduced to a rubble having won only ten seats. It had 24 seats in the earlier assembly.

Kerala

The Left Democratic Front was neck and neck in the race for power in Kerala and ultimately yielded a slender margin to the Congress-led UDF. The UDF won 72 seats, two more than the half way mark in the 140 member assembly, paving the way for a UDF ministry under chief minister Oommen Chandy. The LDF won 68 seats. Ageing

Oommen Chandy

Marxist veteran V S Achuthanandan's single-handed campaign against corruption played a leading role in curbing the UDF's tally.

The 87-year-old Chief Minister helped CPI(M) emerge as the single largest party with 45 seats against Congress' 38.

Puducherry

Puducherry broke the Congress' hold on power when it voted an alliance of N Rangasamy Congress and AIADMK which got two-thirds majority in the 30-member assembly of the Union Territory.

The NR Congress, headed by former

Pravasi Vote — For the first time in India's voting history, overseas Indian citizens were able to cast their ballot in person in the five assembly elections held in April and May 2011.

N. Rangasamy

Chief Minister N Rangasamy who had left Congress only a few months before the elections, bagged 15 seats while ally AIADMK won five seats.

The ruling Congress was reduced to seven seats, while ally DMK won two. A lone Independent was successful.

M.F. Husain Dies at 95

India's most famous artist, M.F. Husain, often referred to as the Picasso of India, died on June 10, 2011 in a London hospital. He was 95.

During his lifetime, he painted an estimated 25,000 works that in his later years were commanding record sums in keeping with his growing fame. His epic work "Mahabharata: The Battle of Ganga and Jamuna" sold at a 2008 Christie's auction for $1.6 million.

Maqbool Fida Husain was born Sept. 17, 1915, in Pandharpur in the western state of Maharashtra. His mother died while he was still a boy. At 17, he won a gold medal at an art exhibition for an oil portrait and persuaded his father to send him to art school.

Two years later, however, his father lost his job, putting an end to Husain's art studies. At 23, he got his first arts job painting cinema billboards for Bollywood. But, unable to make ends meet, he switched to designing and building toys.

During his billboard painting days in Bombay, he acquired a surrogate mother when a widow, Mehmooda Bibi, took pity on him, inviting him to eat with her family. Eventually he married her daughter, Fazila Bibi, and they had six children.

As his reputation grew throughout the 1960s and 1970s, Husain showed a talent for hyping his life and escapades, which only raised the value of his work. "Life without a bit of drama is too drab," he said on one occasion. "If I'd been in Europe, I would've been more gimmicky than Salvador Dali," he said on another.

He also explored the film medium. In 1967, his first movie, "Through the Eyes of a Painter," won the Golden Bear award at the Berlin Film Festival.

Husain's painting, with its focus on color and lines, inspired by Cubism and the art of Hindu temples, gained wide attention in the 1950s. He received national recognition for his painting "Zameen" that, instead of bemoaning rural poverty and indebtedness, was a celebration of life, a common theme in his work.

The paintings that would cause the greatest controversy and personal pain were mostly of Hindu deities. Although they were painted in the early 1970s, they didn't get much attention until 1996, when a monthly Hindi magazine, Vichar Mimansa, printed them, leading to several lawsuits by outraged conservatives. Two years later, his house was attacked by Hindu groups who vandalized several of his works.

The cases were dismissed in 2004, but two years later more controversy erupted over his "Bharatmata," or Mother India. The painting depicted a nude woman posing across a map of the country with the names of Indian states on her body, leading to legal charges that he'd "hurt the sentiments of people," prompting a warrant and his decision to turn his back on India. In his later years, he expressed a desire to return.

M.F. Husain

Husain left India in 2006, angered by Hindu hardliners who condemned his nude depictions of Hindu gods. In 2010 Husain, a Muslim, became a citizen of Qatar, divid-

---

The Forward Bloc

In 1939, Netaji Subhash Chandra Bose announced the formation of a new bloc within the Congress. It was later the 'Forward Bloc'.

reporting on the oil mafia. The oil mafia, which pilfers oil being transported and also dilutes it before sale, has been under pressure since the killing of Yashwant Sonawane in January 2011. He had also recently reported that Chhota Rajan was the mastermind behind a murder attempt on don Dawood's brother, Iqbal Kaskar, in Mumbai.

On 27 June 2011, after sixteen days of investigations, the Crime Branch declared they had cracked the case. Police officials caught seven people from different locations of India. Of which three were detained from Chembur, in Mumbai; one in Solapur; and remaining two from Rameshwaram, in Tamil Nadu. All the suspects resided in different parts of Mumbai except Satish Kalia, who settled down in Trivandrum after the birth of his daughter and cases against him were cleared. After the shootout they fled to evade arrest. All the seven suspects Rohit Thangappan Joseph alias Satish Kalia, Arun Dake, Anil Waghmode, Bablu, Sachin Gaikwad, Mangesh and Chotu were history-sheeters. The suspects were allegedly from Chhota

Jyotirmoy Dey

Rajan gang. Additional Police Commissioner (Crime) Himanshu Roy, who was supervising the case said that Chhota Rajan approached Satish Kalia who in turn organised the team to carry the shootout. Satish Kalia was the man who shot J Dey, said the police. The commissioner also added the shootout was carried out on the behest of Chhota Rajan, and the shooters were allegedly kept in dark about the profession of Jyotirmoy Dey.

A Husain Painting

ing his time between homes there and in London.

Death of a Crime Reporter

Senior journalist Jyotirmoy Dey of Mid-Day, who was known for his in-depth investigative reporting of the Mumbai underworld, was shot dead by four motorcycle-borne sharp-shooters on 11 June 2011 in Mumbai.

Dey started his journalistic career as a freelancer with *Afternoon Despatch and Courier* writing about crime in the wildlife areas. He also dabbled in photojournalism. He then started freelancing for *Mid Day* before joining them full time. He joined *Indian Express* in 1996 and soon switched to covering crime stories, especially on Mumbai underworld. In 2005, he joined *Hindustan Times*. He later re-joined *Mid Day* as crime and investigations editor.

Dey had authored two books on underworld activities, *Zero Dial: The Dangerous World of Informers* and *Khallas*. He has done many reports on underworld dons Dawood Ibrahim and Chhota Rajan.

The police believe the murder was a professional job, and may be related to his

Lord of the Riches

The discovery of mind-boggling treasures at the Padmanabha Temple in Thiruvananthapuram has catapulted it to the status of

India's richest temple. The treasures were unearthed after a direction from the Supreme Court to open the secret chambers of the temple. Sree Padmanabhaswamy Temple is one of the most famous Lord Vishnu temples of Kerala. The main temple deity, Sree Padmanabhaswamy, is a form of Vishnu in Anananthasayanam posture or in eternal sleep and so it is also known as Sree Ananda Padmanabhaswamy Temple.

The temple and its assets belong to Lord Padmanabhaswamy, and are controlled by a trust run by the Royal family. The Kerala High Court ordered the temple and its assets to be managed by the State on 31 January 2011. As trustees of the temple, the Travancore Royal family challenged the Kerala High Court's decision in the Supreme Court of India.

In June 2011, the Supreme Court directed the authorities from the archaeology department and fire services to open the secret chambers of the temple for inspection of the items kept inside. The temple has 6 vaults, labeled as A to F. While vaults A and B have been unopened over the past many years, vaults C to F have been opened from time to time. The Supreme Court had directed that "the existing practices, procedures and rituals" of the temple be followed while

Sree Padmanabhaswamy Temple

opening vaults C to F and using the articles inside. Vaults A and B shall be opened only for the purpose of making an inventory of the articles and then closed.

The review of the temple's underground vaults was undertaken by a seven-member panel appointed by the Supreme Court of India to generate an inventory, leading to the enumeration of a vast collection of articles that are traditionally kept under lock and key. A detailed inventory of the temple assets, consisting of gold, jewels, and other valuables was made.

Five Richest Temples in India

* Sree Padmanabhaswamy Temple, Thiruvananthapuram, Kerala

* Tirumala Tirupati Venkateswara Swamy Temple, Tirumala, Andhra Pradesh

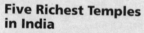

* Shirdi Saibaba Temple, Shirdi, Maharashtra

* Vaishno Devi Temple, Katra, Jammu & Kashmir

* Siddhivinayak Temple, Mumbai, Maharashtra

Pak Foreign Minister the Talk of the Town

A new young face brought hope to Pakistan's tortured relationship with India. Hina Rabbani Khar, Pakistan's 34-year old fashion-conscious and personable new foreign minister, made her first major public appearance when she held constructive talks in Delhi with her Indian counterpart, S.M.Krishna.

Appointed Pakistan's youngest foreign minister in July just a few days before her India visit, Khar spoke of a "mindset change" in both countries, and of a new generation that saw the two countries' relationship differently from past generations. "It is our desire to make the dialogue process uninterrupted and uninterruptible," she said after meeting Krishna.

The bitter relationship is maintained by people in both countries with long, sometimes life-long, memories of their three wars, one near war, near-nuclear confrontations,

Supreme Court Bans Endosulfan

The Supreme Court banned the production and use of endosulfan in the country by an important and long awaited court order on May 13, 2011. A three-Judge Bench of Chief Justice of India (CJI) S.H. Kapadia and Justices K.S. Radhakrishnan and Swatanter Kumar passed this order on a petition filed by the Democratic Youth Federation of India (DYFI). In the

Campaign against Endosulfan

petition the DYFI had urged the court to impose a ban on production and sale of endosulfan in its present form or any other derivative in the market. A 2001 study by the Centre for Science and Environment (CSE) had established the linkages between the aerial spraying of the pesticide and the growing health disorders in Kasaragod district of Kerala.

Endosulfan is a chemical pesticide (belonging to the organochlorine group), which is used against insects and mites found in vegetables, fruits, paddy, cotton, cashew, tea, coffee, tobacco and timber crops. India is the world's largest user of endosulfan producing 4,500 tonnes annually for domestic use and another 4,000 tonnes for export. Much of it is used by farmers with small and marginal holdings as endosulfan is cheap. Some 25 pesticides are banned for manufacture, import and use in India.

Hina Rabbani

and multiple deaths in both countries mostly caused by Pakistan-generated terrorism. .

Khar comes from a privileged feudal family background at the top of Pakistan's society. She is the daughter of a prominent Pakistani politician, Ghulam Noor Rabbani Khar, who persuaded her to abandon a hotel job to enter politics, and the niece of Ghulam Mustafa Khar, a former governor of the Pakistan province of Punjab. One of Mustafa Khar's ex-wives, Tehmina Durrani, described her unhappy and traumatic married life in a controversial novel, *My Feudal Lord*, that lifted the lid on Pakistani society. A review in the *Far East Economic Review* said it exposed "sex, incest, child abuse, kidnapping, sado-masochism, political betrayal and treason". Originally published in 1991 by Durrani herself, the book later became an international best-seller.

Yeddyurappa Resigns

Karnataka Chief Minister B S Yeddyurappa was forced to resign following his indictment in an illegal mining scam by the Lokayukta.

Yeddyurappa was alleged to have used his position as Chief Minister to unfairly favour his sons in the allotment of prime land in Bangalore. In response, Yeddyurappa publicly declared his assets, and then challenged the opposition and the Indian National Congress to find any "black money". However, the Karnataka Lokayukta, established by Karnataka government to investigate allegations of corruption among high level government officials investigated this case and submitted its report to the State Government and the Supreme Court .

The Lokayukta report submitted on July 27, 2011 states that there is sufficient evidence to indict Yeddyurappa and recommended his prosecution under the Prevention of Corruption Act over this land deal. It indicated that the land had been sold to South West Mining Ltd for ₹ 20 crore, as quid pro quo. The market value determined by the government for the land Yeddyurappa's family purchased was ₹ 1.4 crore when it was resold. In order to stimulate employment through private companies, state government distributed public land to private entities for mining. The allegations ranged from the land being distributed to a select few individuals with proper influence, mining and illegal transportation (without the required permit) of significantly more ore than what the private corporations disclosed to the government. The report suggested that the government was complacent about the illegal mining of 2.8 crore metric tons of iron ore from government lands without paying royalties to the government (at ₹ 16.25 per ton). According to Lokayukta finding, South West Mining Company also had donated Rs 10 crore to the Prerana Education Society, a

Sadananda Gowda being crowned by Yeddyurappa

| A Bus to Muzaffarabad | The 170-km Srinagar-Muzaffarabad bus service was a confidence building measure initiated by India and Pakistan in 2005. It facilitated the people of the divided Kashmir to come into contact wih each other for the first time in 56 years. |

trust company managed by Yeddyurappa's family members, although Yeddyurappa denied that he was a part of the trust.

In addition, Lokayukta report stated that there is sufficient evidence to indict Yeddyurappa of granting illegal mining licenses to mining companies and benefiting through them. He and his family members are also alleged to have received bribe from mining companies. The Lokayukta papers reported that a mining firm donated Rs. 10 crore to a trust owned by the CM.

The Lokayuta Report caused demands from within his party for his resignation, which he initially agreed to and then backed out of. Following the submission of the Lokayukta report, he resigned on 31 July 2011.

Narayana Murthy's Infosys Innings

Thirty years after he and his six friends got together to found the now iconic Infosys, Narayana Murthy retired on August 21, 2011, giving way to yet another veteran KV Kamath.

Employee number four at Infosys Ltd, its numero uno in every other way, N R Narayana Murthy was a legend who set standards in business in India.. He started Infosys with a paltry borrowing of Rs.10,000 from his wife and transformed it into a $6 billion revenue company with a market capitalisation of $36 billion. The founding of Infosys had an impact that has been far-reaching, across industry, across MNCs in the IT business, across geographies and indeed, for Bangalore as a city.

For industry, he raised corporate governance standards to levels that were completely new to them. Murthy recognized early on that if he had to deal with global clients, he would have to create a company that had global standards in transparency and governance. The decision to list Infosys on the Nasdaq in 1999, and thereby accept the exacting standards laid down by global stock exchanges, was a seminal moment in

Narayana Murthy

this journey. And in time, it transformed the way Indian industry looked at governance.

Infosys was also a pioneer in the use of employee stock options (ESOPs), introducing it as early as 1993. It also ensured a large public float of its shares when it listed. The wide distribution of its stocks meant that a phenomenal number of employees and ordinary shareholders could benefit from the stupendous rise in its share prices over the past decade and a half.

The IT outsourcing pioneer, together with Indian peers like TCS and Wipro, also forced global IT MNCs like IBM, HP, Accenture, Capgemini and a host of others to use India as an outsourcing destination and copy the global delivery model that the Indian companies had developed. Today, one-fifth to one-fourth of the employees of many of the global giants are based in India.

This simultaneously changed perceptions about India among citizens around the world. India is seen today as a massive bank of intelligent engineering talent, often perceived as a threat to jobs overseas. It has raised the profile of Bangalore in particular to a level that has pushed even US president Barack Obama to frequently refer to the city as an intellectual challenge to the United States.

Shammi Kapoor, India's Elvis, Dies

The veteran film star Shammi Kapoor died

Elected and Dissolved	The Bihar Assembly elected in February 2005 was dissolved three months later, even before it could be constituted. No political party was in a position to form a government. President's rule came in March and the Assembly was placed under suspended animation.

on August 14 in Mumbai, aged 79. The actor belonged to the Hindi film industry's famous family of actors which included his father, Prithviraj, and brothers Raj and Shashi Kapoor.

One of the most popular stars of his generation, he starred in hits like Junglee, *An Evening in Paris, China town* and *Kashmir Ki Kali.* During his career, he acted in more than 100 films.

A prominent star in 1950s and 1960s, fans called Kapoor the "Elvis Presley of India" for his frenetic and agile dancing in romantic hits such as 1957's *Tumsa Nahin Dekha* (You're One of a Kind) and 1959's *Dil Deke Dekho* (Give Your Heart and See).

He developed a style of his own and cinema-goers flocked to the theatres just to see the actor's antics and mannerisms.

Kapoor received a lifetime achievement prize at the International Indian Film Acad-

Shammi Kapoor

emy Awards in 2001. With his infectious on-screen persona and energy, Kapoor was considered the Indian film industry's first real star.

The actor was also a keen internet buff and amongst the first Indians to have his own website. The site profiles his famous family, who have dominated Hindi-language cinema virtually since its inception.

He also maintained Facebook and Twitter accounts, describing himself as a "Renaissance man, retired actor, computer buff".

Kiran Bedi with Anna Hazare

Jan Lokpal Bill Movement

The Jan Lokpal Bill (Citizen's ombudsman Bill) is a draft anti-corruption bill drawn up by prominent civil society activists seeking the appointment of a Jan Lokpal, an independent body that would investigate corruption cases.

The Jan Lokpal Bill, also referred to as the citizens' ombudsman bill, is intended as a more effective improvement to the original Lokpal Bill that is being proposed by the the government. The prefix 'Jan' (citizens) has been added to highlight the fact that these improvements include inputs from ordinary citizens through an activist-driven, non-governmental public consultation.

The arguments given in favour of the Jan Lokpal Bill is that if made into a law, it will create an independent ombudsman body outside government control that will have the power to register and investigate complaints against politicians and public servants without the need to get a prior approval from the government. The proponents of Jan Lokpal Bill believe that it will effectively redress citizen's grievances, protect whistle-blowers and more importantly, deter corruption.

Drafted by Justice Santosh Hegde (former Supreme Court Judge and former Lokayukta of Karnataka), Prashant Bhushan (Supreme Court Lawyer) and Arvind Kejriwal (RTI activist), the draft Bill envisages a system where a corrupt person found guilty would go to jail within two years of the complaint being made and his ill-gotten wealth being confis-

All About Anna Hazare

- Actual name - Kisan Baburao Hazare.
- Birth date - 15 June 1937.
- Unmarried.
- Born in Bhingar village in Ahmednagar district of Maharashtra to Baburao Hazare and Laxmi Bai.
- Organization - the Bhrashtachar Virodhi Jan Andolan (People's movement against Corruption).
- Began his career as a driver in the Indian Army in 1963.
- During the mid-1970s, he was involved in a road accident while driving.
- Honourably discharged from army in 1975 after completing 12 years of service.
- During his 12-year tenure as a soldier, he was posted to several places like Sikkim, Bhutan, Jammu-Kashmir, Assam, Mizoram, Leh and Ladakh.
- Gained wide acclaim for transforming his once drought-prone, impoverished village to a prosperous model village by encouraging sustainable farming and rural life as envisioned by Mahatma Gandhi.
- Was awarded the Padma Shri (1990) and Padma Bhushan (1992), the nation's fourth and third highest civilian awards respectively, for his social work.
- Lives on his pension from army service in his village.
- His campaigns are financed by voluntary donations by his supporters.
- Always seen in white clothes with a traditional Indian cap (Gandhi Topi).

cated. It also seeks power to the Jan Lokpal to prosecute politicians and bureaucrats without government permission.

Retired IPS officer Kiran Bedi and other known people like Swami Agnivesh, Sri Sri Ravi Shankar, Anna Hazare and Mallika Sarabhai are also part of the movement, called India Against Corruption. Its website describes the movement as "an expression of collective anger of people of India against corruption. We have all come together to force/request/persuade/pressurize the Government to enact the Jan Lokpal Bill. We feel that if this Bill were enacted it would create an effective deterrence against corruption."

Anna Hazare, anti-corruption crusader, went on a fast-unto-death in April, demanding that this Bill, drafted by the civil society, be adopted. Four days into his fast, the government agreed to set up a joint committee with an equal number of members from the government and civil society side to draft the Lokpal Bill together. The two sides met several times but could not agree on fundamental elements like including the PM under the purview of the Lokpal. Eventually, both sides drafted their own version of the Bill.

The government introduced its version in Parliament. Team Anna was up in arms and called the government version the "Joke Pal Bill." Anna Hazare declared that he would

A Hunger-strike	Jatindra Nath Das died in Lahore Central Jail on Sept. 13, 1929, the 63rd day of hunger-strike which he began on July 13 as a protest against the behaviour of jail authorities with the undertrial political prisoners.

begin another fast in Delhi on August 16. Hours before he was to begin his hunger strike, the Delhi Police detained and later arrested him.

The arrest resulted in huge public outcry and under pressure the government released him in the evening of 16 Aug. However, Anna Hazare refused to come out of Jail, starting his indefinite fast from Jail itself. Unwilling to use forces owing to the sensitive nature of the case, the jail authorities had no option but to let Anna spend the night inside Tihar. Later on 17 Aug, Delhi Police permitted Anna Hazare and team to use the Ramlila Maidan for the proposed fast and agitation withdrawing most of the contentious provisions they had imposed earlier. The indefinite fast and agitation began in Ramlila Maidan, New Delhi, and went on for around 288 hours (12 days from 16-August-2011 to 28-August-2011). Anna Hazare ended his 12-day fast before thousands of cheering supporters at Ramlila Maidan after parliament broadly agreed to three key demands of his civil society group to battle corruption.

The website of the India Against Corruption movement calls the Lokpal Bill of the government an "eyewash" and has on it a critique of that government Bill.

Salient Features of Jan Lokpal Bill

* An institution called Lokpal at the centre and Lokayukta in each state will be set up
* Like Supreme Court and Election Commission, they will be completely independent of the governments. No minister or bureaucrat will be able to influence their investigations.
* Cases against corrupt people will not linger on for years anymore: Investigations in any case will have to be completed in one year. Trial should be completed in next one year so that the corrupt politician, officer or judge is sent to jail within two years.
* The loss that a corrupt person caused to the government will be recovered at the

Hazare ends his fast

time of conviction.
* If any work of any citizen is not done in prescribed time in any government office, Lokpal will impose financial penalty on guilty officers, which will be given as compensation to the complainant.
* So, you could approach Lokpal if your ration card or passport or voter card is not being made or if police is not registering your case or any other work is not being done in prescribed time. Lokpal will have to get it done in a month's time. You could also report any case of corruption to Lokpal like ration being siphoned off, poor quality roads been constructed or panchayat funds being siphoned off. Lokpal will have to complete its investigations in a year, trial will be over in next one year and the guilty will go to jail within two years.
* Its members will be selected by judges, citizens and constitutional authorities and not by politicians, through a completely transparent and participatory process.
* The entire functioning of Lokpal/Lokayukta will be completely transparent. Any complaint against any officer of Lokpal shall be investigated and the officer dismissed within two months.
* CVC, departmental vigilance and anti-corruption branch of CBI will be merged into Lokpal. Lokpal will have complete powers and machinery to independently investigate and prosecute any officer, judge or politician.
* It will be the duty of the Lokpal to provide protection to those who are being

victimized for raising their voice against corruption.

The government's Lokpal Bill has kept the Prime Minister and the judiciary as well as conduct of MPs in Parliament out of the ambit of the anti-corruption watchdog. The PM, however, will come under the purview of Lokpal after he demits office.

The bill gives permission to Lokpal to probe any Union minister or officials of Group 'A' and above rank without any sanction.

According to the government's draft, the body will have a chairperson and eight members, including four judicial members - who will be former or sitting judges of Supreme Court or chief justices of the high court.

The Lok Ayuktas in the states donot come under the purview of this bill as the Centre cannot intervene in the powers of the state.

The Lokpal will have its own prosecution and investigation wing with officers and staff necessary to carry out its functions.

Bangladesh Honours Indira Gandhi

The former Prime Minister Indira Gandhi was conferred the highest Bangladesh award — the Bangladesh Swadhinata Sammanona (Bangladesh Freedom Honour) — for her outstanding contributions to Bangladesh's Liberation War. It was received by her daughter-in-law Sonia Gandhi from Bangladesh President Zillur Rahman who presented the award, the highest honour for any foreign national after 40 years of Bangladesh's independence from Pakistan.

Ms. Sonia Gandhi recalled the fond memories of her mother-in law during the tumultuous days of 1971, when the great Indian leader took a firm, principled stand to side with the oppressed people of then East Pakistan. She concluded her speech saying: "Joy Bangla, Joy Bangladesh-India Friendship."

The award included a 200 tola gold medal and a citation which read: "Ms. Indira Gandhi stood by the side of the people

Award for Indira Gandhi being received by Sonia Gandhi

of Bangladesh from the beginning of the Liberation War despite various adversities. She provided shelter to about one crore Bangladeshi refugees. She provided courage in the Liberation War by facing different diplomatic hurdles. She played a great role in freeing Bangabandhu from Pakistani jail. Her contribution to Bangladesh's Liberation War will be remembered forever."

Justice Sen Resigns

Justice Soumitra Sen of the Calcutta High Court on September 1 avoided the ignominy of becoming the first judge to be impeached

Justice Soumitra Sen

by Parliament by tendering his resignation.

53-year-old Justice Sen sent in his resignation to President Pratibha Patil five days before the Lok Sabha was to take up an impeachment motion against him. The Rajya Sabha had already passed the motion making him the first judge to have been impeached by the Upper House for misconduct.

In his letter to the President, Justice Sen said, "I am not guilty of any form of corruption."

Justice Sen was found guilty of misappropriating Rs 33.23 lakh under his custody as a court-appointed receiver in the capacity as a lawyer, and misrepresenting facts before a Calcutta court in a 1983 case.

Justice P D Dinakaran, Chief Justice of the Sikkim High Court, against whom the Rajya Sabha Chairman had set up a judicial panel to enquire into allegations of corruption, had resigned on July 29 , 2011, before impeachment proceedings could be initiated against him.

The first such case involved the impeachment motion in Lok Sabha of Justice V Ramaswami of the Supreme Court in May 1993 which fell due to lack of numbers after Congress members abstained.

Amar Singh in Cash-for-Votes Scam

Rajya Sabha MP Amar Singh was arrested in September 2011 in relation to his role in an alleged 2008 cash-for-vote scam.Mr. Singh has been accused of bribing three opposition lawmakers to support the Congress-led government in a crucial 2008 confidence vote on a nuclear deal.

Mr. Singh was arrested after a Delhi court ordered him to be sent to judicial custody. Two former members of the opposition Bharatiya Janata Party were also arrested on related charges.

Mr. Singh's arrest gave fresh credibility to the bribe allegations, which government officials had repeatedly denied. The arrest come at a bad time for the ruling Congress party, which was struggling to recover from a string of high-profile scandals that had taken a toll on party members and key allies, spurring the mass anticorruption movement led by social activist Anna Hazare.

At the time of the nuclear vote, Mr. Singh was a member of the Samajwadi party (Socialist party), a Congress ally. He has since left the party and is an independent lawmaker in the Rajya Sabha, India's upper house of Parliament.

In July 2008, the Congress-led government risked collapsing over a vote on a

Amar Singh

nuclear deal with the U.S. The nuclear deal allowed India access to nuclear technology and cheap atomic energy in exchange for allowing the United Nations to inspect some of its nuclear facilities. Several of Congress's left-wing coalition partners opposed the deal, threatening the government to lose its parliamentary majority over the issue.

The cash-for-votes allegations were first brought up by opposition politicians shortly after the nuclear vote. A parliamentary committee that looked into the issue at the time dismissed the case, citing insufficient evidence. The Congress party went on to win the general elections a year later.

The scam allegations surfaced again in March, when Web site WikiLeaks released U.S. diplomatic cables dated July 17, 2008, reporting a conversation between a Congress party official and a U.S. Embassy staff member saying four opposition MPs had been bribed to support the government in the vote. They said the MPs had been paid off for $2.5 million each. According to the cables, the U.S. Embassy official was shown "two chests containing cash" intended for pay-offs. Despite the alleged payments, the party to which the MPs belonged to – the regional Rashtriya Lok Dal party – opposed the government in the vote. The vote still passed. Reacting to the leaked cables, Prime Minister Manmohan Singh had questioned their authenticity and "absolutely and firmly" rejected the cash-for-votes allegations.

Terror Strikes Delhi

Terror struck Delhi when a powerful bomb placed in a briefcase ripped through a crowded reception area at the entrance of the Delhi High Court on 7th September,

Delhi High Court premises

killing 14 people and leaving more than 80 injured. This is the second blast outside Delhi HC since May.

The blast occurred around 10:15 am outside Gate Number 5 close to the reception area where visitors had lined up for entry passes. A group by the name Harkat-ul-Jihad claimed responsibility for the blast. The mail claimed that the blast was carried out to demand repeal of death sentence of Afzal Guru, a condemned prisoner in 2001 Parliament attack. Sources in the MHA indicate that traces of powerful explosive PETN have been traced at the blast site.

On May 25, a low-intensity explosive went off near Gate Number 7 of the Delhi High Court. Experts believe the May 25 attack may have been a dry run for a bigger attack.

Home Minister P. Chidambaram said the blast was of "high intensity" and called it a "terrorist attack". The blast also left a 3-4 feet crater at the site of the explosion. Chidambaram said it was not possible to identify the group behind the attack. The probe into the blast was handed over by government to the National Investigation Agency (NIA) whose Chief S.C. Sinha said a 20-member team headed by a DIG has been formed.

SC Breather for Narendra Modi

The Supreme Court on September 13 extricated itself from one of the country's most controversial cases, leaving it to a lower court to determine whether the chief minister of Gujarat, Narendra Modi, did enough to stop a wave of communal violence that swept the state in 2002.

A three-judge bench headed by Justice D K Jain directed the SIT, which is probing the riot cases, to submit its final report before the magistrate who was asked to decide whether to proceed against Modi and 63 others, which includes senior government officials. The bench made it clear that there was no need for it to further monitor the riot cases. The bench also comprising justices P Sathasivam and Aftab Alam said in case the magistrate decides to drop proceedings

Narendra Modi

against Modi and others, he has to hear the plea of slain MP Ehsan Jafri's widow Zakia Jafri, who had filed a complaint against the Gujarat chief minister.

The court passed the order on a petition by Zakia Jafri alleging that Modi and 62 top government officials deliberately refused to take action to contain the state-wide riots, triggered by the February 27, 2002 Godhra train carnage. Jafri, who lost her husband

Ehsan Jafri, a former Congress MP in Gulberg Housing Society massacre during riots, had told the apex court that a proper probe should be carried out by the SIT, headed by former CBI chief R K Raghavan, into her allegations of inaction and various acts of omission and commission by Modi and others after the riots.

The apex court had earlier handed over the task of probing the case to SIT which submitted its report in the court. After the SIT filed its probe report in a sealed cover, the court had also asked senior advocate Raju Ramachandran, who is assisting it as amicus curie, to analyse the SIT probe findings and file a confidential report on it. Ramachandran subsequently had submitted his report to the court, which passed the order after going through the reports by SIT and Ramachandran and referred the case back to the concerned Ahmedabad magistrate to decide the further course of action in the case.

Tremor in Sikkim

An earthquake measuring 6.9 on the Richter Scale shook Sikkim on 18 September

Sikkim Tremor

2011 killing scores of people and injuring hundreds. Strong tremors were also felt in parts of North and East India and parts of Bangladesh and Nepal, causing widespread panic. The earthquake occurred about 68 km (42 mi) northwest of Gangtok at a shallow depth of 19.7 km (12.2 mi). At its location, the continental Indian and Eurasian Plates

converge with one another along a tectonic boundary beneath the mountainous region of northeast India near the Nepalese border. Although earthquakes in this region are usually interplate in nature, preliminary data suggested the earthquake was triggered by shallow strike-slip faulting from an intraplate source within the over-riding Eurasian Plate. Initial analyses also indicated a complex origin, with the perceived tremor likely being a result of two separate events occurring close together in time at similar focal depths.

Three aftershocks, of magnitude 5.7, 5.1 and 4.6 were also felt in Sikkim, says the India Meteorological Department.

Sikkim State falls in Seismic Zone 1V of the earthquake hazard map of India, and this corresponds to High Damage Risk Zone. Seismic activity along the Himalayan arc is due to the thrusting action of Indian plate beneath the Eurasian plate. The India plate converges with Eurasia at a rate of approximately 46 mm/ year towards the north-northeast and this has resulted in the uplift of the Himalayas, the world's tallest mountain range.

Large destructive earthquakes have occured across the arc. Research as well as instrumentation indicates the possibility of large eart-quake in the near future.

A Prince Among Cricketers

Mansur Ali Khan Pataudi, one of India's greatest cricket captains ever and whose brillince and charisma inspired a generation

Pataudi's funeral procession

The Great Earthquake | **January 15, 1934 saw the greatest earthquake hitting India. The Bihar quake took a toll of 20,000 lives. Monghyr town was razed to the ground.**

Looking Ahead : The Year 2012 (India)

Presidential Election

The Election Commission of India will hold indirect 14th presidential elections

Rashtrpati Bhavan

of India in July 2012, assuming the current president completes her term of 5 years.

Legislative Assembly Elections

Multiple states of India will have elections for their legislative assemblies in 2012. The tenure of the Legislative Assemblies of the states of Manipur, Gujarat,

Uttar Pradesh Vidhansabha

Uttarakhand, Goa, Uttar Pradesh and Punjab are due to expire. The Election Commission of India (ECI) will decide on the dates of the polls.

Indian Premier League

The 2012 Indian Premier League season, abbreviated as IPL 5 or the IPL 2012, will begin on April 4 and end on May 27, 2012. It will be be the fifth season of the Indian Premier League, established by the Board of Control for Cricket in India (BCCI) in 2007. While Chennai Super Kings will compete as defending

Indian Premier League

champions, Chepauk, their home venue, is expected to host the finals.

2012 South Asian Games

The 2012 South Asian Games, officially the XII South Asian Games, is an upcoming major multi-sport event, scheduled to take place in Delhi, India in 2012. With this edition of the Games, India becomes the second country to host the Games three times (the previous editions being held in Kolkata in 1987 and Chennai in 1995), after Bangladesh. It is also the first time that Delhi will host the Games.

Best university in Latin America

On October 4th Quacquarelli Symonds, an education consultancy, published the first regional ranking of Latin American universities. The University of São Paulo (USP), the richest and biggest university in Brazil, came top.

M.A.K. Pataudi

himself as a cricketing prodigy. During his four years in the school XI he scored 2,956 runs at an overall average of 56.85. In 1959, when he was captain, he conjured 1,068 runs in the season, beating the school record established by Douglas Jardine in 1919. He also, in partnership with Christopher Snell, carried off the Public Schools Rackets championship.

In 1957, in the summer holidays, Pataudi made his first-class debut for Sussex. . Later he went up to Balliol College in Oxford, purportedly to read Arabic and French. In his first summer at Oxford he made a century (131) against Cambridge at Lord's. The next year, 1961, Pataudi, now captain of Oxford, reached his absolute peak. Against the full Yorkshire attack, which included four England bowlers, he scored 106 and 103 not out. By the end of June, with three games still to play, Pataudi was only 92 runs short of his father's record total of 1,307 runs in an Oxford season. Then he was involved in a car accident in England in which he lost an eye..

His extraordinary determination and success in overcoming the injury to his right eye led to his being appointed vice-captain for India's tour of the West Indies early in 1962. When the skipper, Nari Contractor, was laid out by a vicious delivery from Charlie Griffith in the game against Barbados, Pataudi took over and became, at 21 years and 77 days, the youngest captain in the history of Test cricket, a record that stood until 2004. He captained India to their first away series victory in New Zealand in 1968.

He scored 2,793 runs in 46 Tests at an average of 34.91 and made six centuries, the biggest of which was an unbeaten 203 against England in Delhi in 1964. As captain he led India to nine victories and suffered 19 defeats, with 19 matches drawn. Between 1957 and 1976 he played 310 first-class matches, scoring a total of 15,425 runs at an average of 33.67. A fine fielder, he took 208 catches.

Pataudi was the ninth and last Nawab of Pataudi until 1971, when the Central government abolished royal entitlements through the 26th Amendment to the Constitution. Since 2007, bilateral Test series between India and England have been contested for the Pataudi Trophy, named after his

of cricket players, passed away on September 22 aged 70 after battling a lung infection for months. The Nawab of Pataudi captained India in 40 Test matches and scored six Test centuries – all despite having only one functioning eye.

The son of the 8th Nawab of Pataudi, he was born Mohamed Mansur Ali Khan on January 5 1941 at Bhopal, of which his maternal grandfather was Nawab. His father, Iftikhar Ali Khan Pataudi, was a talented cricketer in his own right. He had scored 238 not out for Oxford against Cambridge in 1931. Subsequently he played for England against Australia on the tour of 1932-33, making a century on his Test debut in Sydney. Though plagued by ill health, he became one of the very few cricketers to play for two countries when he captained the Indians in England in 1946.

When his father died in 1952, aged only 41, Tiger, aged 11, became the 9th Nawab of Pataudi. In 1954 he went to Winchester school. At Winchester he soon established

Timeline

 ◆ **December 13, 1961:** Makes debut against England in Delhi, scores 13.
 ◆ **January 10, 1962:** Scores maiden century in his third Test, 113 against England in Chennai.
 ◆ **March 23, 1962:** Leads India in his fourth Test, in Barbados, thus becoming Test cricket's youngest captain at the age of 21.
 ◆ **February 12-13, 1964:** Scores career-best 203 not out against England in Delhi.
 ◆ **February-March 1968:** Leads India to their first overseas Test victory in Dunedin. India go on to win an away series for the first time, beating New Zealand 3-1.
 ◆ **January 23, 1975:** Plays his final Test match, scoring 9 in each innings against West Indies in Mumbai.

family for their contribution to Anglo-Indian cricket.

Pataudi was a true family man throughout his life. In 1969 he married the film star Sharmila Tagore, the great-grandniece of the poet and philosopher Rabindranath Tagore. Their son, Saif Ali Khan, is one of the heart-throbs of Bollywood. Of their two daughters, Saba is a jewellery designer, while Soha is a film actress.

New Poverty Line Draws Flak

India's Planning Commission came up with a new estimate for its own poverty line in

September. Planning Commission chairman Montek Singh Ahluwalia submitted new price data that pegged the urban poverty line at 32 rupees a day, a revision that would immediately lower the country's poor from 37% to 32% of its population . The Commission fixed the official poverty line at Rs 965 per month in urban areas and Rs 781 in rural areas. This works out to Rs 32 and and Rs 26 per day, respectively. The perceived inadequacy of these figures has led to widespread discussion and criticism in the media. In light of the controversy, it may be worth looking at where the numbers come from in the first place.

Two Measures of the BPL Population

The official poverty line is determined by the Planning Commission, on the basis of data provided by the National Sample Survey Organisation (NSSO). NSSO data is based on a survey of consumer expenditure which takes place every five years. The most recent Planning Commission poverty estimates are for the year 2004-05.

In addition to Planning Commission efforts to determine the poverty line, the Ministry of Rural Development has conducted a BPL Census in 1992, 1997, 2002, and 2011 to identify poor households. The BPL Census is used to target families for assistance through various schemes of the central government. The 2011 BPL Census was conducted along with a caste census, and was dubbed the Socio-Economic & Caste Census (SECC) 2011. Details on the methodology of SECC 2011 are available in this short Ministry of Rural Development circular.

Planning Commission Methodology

Rural and urban poverty lines were first defined in 1973-74 in terms of Per Capita Total Expenditure (PCTE). Consumption is measured in terms of a collection of goods and services known as reference Poverty Line Baskets (PLB). These PLB were determined separately for urban and rural areas and based on a per-day calorie intake of 2400 (rural) and 2100 (urban), each containing items such as food, clothing, fuel, rent, conveyance and entertainment, among others. The official poverty line is the national average expenditure per person incurred to obtain the goods in the PLB. Since 1973-74, prices for goods in the PLB have been periodically adjusted over time and across states to deduce the official poverty line.

Suresh Tendulkar

Uniform Reference Period (URP) vs Mixed Reference Period (MRP)

Until 1993-94, consumption information collected by the NSSO was based on the Uniform Reference Period (URP), which measured consumption across a 30-day recall period. That is, survey respondents were asked about their consumption in the previous 30 days. From 1999-2000 onwards, the NSSO switched to a method known as the Mixed Reference Period (MRP). The MRP measures consumption of five low-frequency items (clothing, footwear, durables, education and institutional health expenditure) over the previous year, and all other items over the previous 30 days. That is to say, for the five items, survey respondents are asked about consumption in the previous one year. For the remaining items, they are asked about consumption in the previous 30 days.

Tendulkar Committee Report

In 2009, the Tendulkar Committee Report suggested several changes to the way poverty is measured. First, it recommended a shift away from basing the PLB in caloric intake and towards target nutritional outcomes instead. Second, it recommended that a uniform PLB be used for both rural and urban areas. In addition, it recommended a change in the way prices are adjusted, and called for an explicit provision in the

PLB to account for private expenditure in health and education. For these reasons, the Tendulkar estimate of poverty for the years 1993-94 and 2004-05 is higher than the official estimate, regardless of whether one looks at URP or MRP figures. For example, while the official 1993-94 All-India poverty figure is 36 per cent (URP), applying the Tendulkar methodology yields a rate of 45.3 per cent. Similarly, the official 2004-05 poverty rate is 21.8 per cent (MRP) or 27.5 per cent (URP), while applying the Tendulkar methodology brings the number to 37.2 per cent.

L K Advani's Rath Yatra Against Corruption

Lal Krishna Advani is once again on a political yatra. It's the veteran leader's sixth 'Rath Yatra'. The 84-year-old politician went on a gruelling 38-day, 12,000-km yatra against corruption, cashing in on the Anna Hazare movement.

In 1990, Advani set out on his first Yatra, the 'Ram Rath Yatra', symbolically starting off from Somnath, Gujarat, on Sept 25,

L.K. Advani

Faster than light?

Most theorists believe that nothing can travel faster than the speed of light. In an experiment, members of the Oscillation Project with Emulsion-tRacking Apparatus (OPERA), at the European Centre for Nuclear Research (CERN) shot neutrinos out of a particle accelerator near Geneva, Switzerland, and measured how long it took the particles to travel to a neutrino detector in Gran Sasso, Italy, 732 kilometres away. The team described the unusual neutrino detection in a paper published on the research website arXiv.org. To the astonishment of the OPERA team, it was observed that Neutrinos ghostly subatomic particles, may have been travelling faster than the speed of light. Being nearly massless, neutrinos should travel at nearly the speed of light, which is approximately 299,338 kilometres a second. A nanosecond may not sound like much, but "the effect is quite large." The extra speed would mean that, over a distance of 1,000 kilometres, neutrinos travel about 20 meters farther than light travels in the same amount of time. Surprisingly, the particles appeared to have reached their destination about 60 nanoseconds faster than expected. According to Stephen Parke, head of the theoretical physics department at the U.S. government-run Fermilab near Chicago, Illinois, "If this is true, it would rock the foundations of physics."

Dave Goldberg, an astrophysicist at Philadelphia's Drexel University, suspects that if faster-than-light neutrinos did exist, they would likely have been observed in nature before now. For example, in 1987 detectors on Earth identified neutrinos and photons light particles from an exploding star. Both types of particles reached our planet at almost exactly the same instance. Goldberg's calculations show if neutrinos travel faster than light by the amount the OPERA team claims, then neutrinos from that supernova should have been detected in 1984 three years before the photons. Goldberg concedes that supernova neutrinos are less energetic and would thus be traveling slower than the neutrinos from CERN's particle accelerator. According to Goldberg, "assuming Einstein was correct, both types [of neutrinos] would be moving at something like 99.999999999% the speed of light. In other words, from a measurement point of view, they'd be going at essentially identical speeds." Goldberg agreed that physicists won't be discarding Einstein's theories anytime soon. Even if relativity turned out to be wrong. it's clearly very, very close to being right.

Even if the OPERA results are confirmed by other scientists, they wouldn't totally invalidate Einstein's theories of general and special relativity, Louis Strigari, an astrophysicist at Stanford University, stressed. Those theories still explain a remarkable range of observed phenomena in the universe. According to Strigari, "I think it's long been understood that the theories we have today aren't the full answers. If this observation holds up, then it's probably a good piece of evidence that the theories we currently have need to be reworked."

1990. By the time he reached Ayodhya on October 30, he had transformed into the political face of Hindutva. He, and the BJP, reaped rich benefits from being the right-wing hawk. The BJP rose to power in 1998-99 and Mr. Advani himself became deputy prime minister.

Indeed, every Rath Yatra, every political initiative he has undertaken since then – including travelling to Pakistan and praising Jinnah as a secular leader – has been aimed at undoing the damage of the image he acquired in 1990.

He has allowed the yatra to symbolically

Rath Yatra

tilt towards socialist leaders, choosing to start from Jai Prakash Narayan's birthplace Sitabdiara in Bihar, flagged off not by the BJP's new Hindutva poster-boy and Advani's own protégé, Gujarat chief minister Narendra Modi, but by the 'secular' Bihar chief minister Nitish Kumar. Interestingly, all along the yatra route upto Varanasi, there were not even the usual posters of either Jan Sangh founder Shyama Prasad Mukherjee or Deen Dayal Upadhyaya, although Advani did make a passing reference to the latter. Instead, Advani spoke glowingly about the socialist ideologue and leader Ram Manohar Lohia.

Political analysts say that for the common man, it has become hard to distinguish between Congress and BJP on the corruption issue. Many doubt that Mr. Advani will be able to galvanise opinion in his favour, or his party's, through the Jan Chetna Yatra. Congress sources themselves say as much, admitting that their party is scam-hit, but that despite that, "we can counter any offensive by political parties, including the BJP. What we can't counter is civil society".

India Home to Second Largest Number of Affluent People

India is home to the second largest number of affluent people with a whopping three million households which have over $1 lakh of investible funds.

According to a survey by the global market research agency TNS, while the US still is the world's most prosperous country with 31 million affluent households, India,

China and Brazil have overtaken many European countries in this measure of consumer wealth with three million affluent households each in these countries which have over $1 Lakh investible funds.

In other words, as many as 27 percent American households are affluent, while this is only 1.25 percent and 0.75 percent in regard to India and China respectively, thanks to the sheer size of their population.

Though the cut-off money is $1 lakh for all the countries it is just $40,000 in Brazil, where this 3 million households constitute five percent of the overall number of households.

However, it is Luxemburg that has the highest penetration in terms of percentage with 29 percent penetration, but in absolute numbers the number of affluent households is only 89,000, followed by the US with 27 percent penetration, Canada and Singapore 20 percent each with 2.6 million and 2,30,000 households respectively.

The study titled the TNS Global Affluent Investor Survey, is based on interviews of 12,092 affluent decision-makers across 24 markets, including the US, India, China, Canada, Brazil, France, Germany, Britain,

Symbols of Affluence

Belgium, the UAE, Israel, Hong Kong, Singapore and Australia. The online survey was carried out during May-August 2011.

The UAE and India appear in the top five countries where the affluent have over $1 million investable assets on average, alongside Singapore and Hong Kong. The only European country to feature in this top five is the Sweden, while Britain and France are the least likely in Europe to have these levels of investable assets.

The survey also finds that men are the

primary decision-makers among the affluent households in India (80 percent) and Central Europe (79 percent), but in north America this is only 45 percent.

The findings also demonstrate regional contrasts in terms of what the affluent actually invest in. While in China, India and Germany the affluent are keen investors in precious metals (35, 33, and 23 per cent of respondents respectively), this is only 3 per cent in Sweden, Norway and the Netherlands, and even lesser at 2 per cent in Denmark and Israel.

India Launches World's Cheapest Tablet Computer

India launched the world's cheapest tablet computer on October 5. Priced at around Rs. 1,200, it will now be available to students in the country as part of the government's programme to expand education through information technology.

The government is buying the first units of the lightweight touch-screen device, called Aakash, or "sky" in Hindi, for $50 each from a British company which is assembling the web-enabled devices in India.

A pilot run of 100,000 units will be given to students for free, with the first 500 handed out at the launch to a mixed response. It supports video conferencing, has two USB ports and a three-hour battery life but some users said it was slow.

India has a reputation for creating affordable products that are easy to use and sturdy enough to handle its rugged environment -- from "Tata Motors' Rs.1 lakh Nano car to generic versions of pharmaceuticals.

Two years in development, the paperback book-sized Aakash may help the government's goal of incorporating information technology in education, although critics were doubtful of its mass appeal.

Despite being a leader in software and IT services, India trails fellow BRIC nations Brazil, Russia and China in the drive to get the masses connected to the Internet and

Kapil Sibal with Aakash Tablet

mobile phones, according to a report by risk analysis firm Maplecroft.

The number of Internet users grew 15-fold between 2000 and 2010 in India, according to another recent report. Still, just 8 percent of Indians have access. That compares with nearly 40 percent in China.

The Aakash is aimed at university students for digital learning via a government platform that distributes electronic books and courses.

Testing included running video for two hours in temperatures of 48 degrees Celsius (118 degrees Fahrenheit) to mimic a northern Indian summer, said DataWind, the small London-based company that developed the tablet with the Indian Institute of Technology.

The device uses resistive LCD displays rather than a full touch screen and connects via wireless broadband. Future versions would include a mobile phone connection, making it more useful in rural areas.

Some of the mainly middle-class technology department students at the event said it needed refinement but was a good option for the poor.

Some 19 million people subscribe to mobile phones every month, making India the world's fastest growing market, but most are from the wealthier segment of the population in towns.

Warning over Metals Shortage

Geologists gathered at Fermor Meeting of the Geological Society of London, to discuss metal shortages have sounded the warning bells over shortage of some metals owing to an insatiable demand for consumer goods. According to Gawen Jenkin, geologist from the University of Leicester, mobile phones contain copper, nickel, silver, zinc, aluminium, gold, lead, manganese, palladium, platinum and tin. Besides, more than a billion people buy a mobile phone in a year which is quite a lot of metal. Then there's the neodymium in our laptop, the iron in our car, the aluminium in that soft drink can – and the list goes on. Though there's no immediate danger of 'peak metal,' but still, there will be shortages and bottlenecks of some metals like indium due to increased demand. The exploration for metals is now a key skill and it has never been a better time to become an economic geologist, working with a mining company. It is also one of the better-kept secrets of employment in a recession-hit world. Human appetite for technological goodies will be satisfied for some more time to come, and then we will have to have alternatives or forego the luxuries.

No Moderation in Inflation

The Prime Minister's Economic Advisory Council (PMEAC) citing the near double-digit inflation, has shown concern as there is no sign of moderation in the rate of price rise. It requires prompting the Reserve Bank to change its policy of monetary tightening. The situation is not at all comfortable. According to PMEAC Chairman C. Rangarajan, the overall inflation remained close to the double-digit mark, at 9.72 per cent, in September on account of costlier food products, fuel and manufactured goods. Inflation, as measured by the Wholesale

Delibrations on policy change

Price Index (WPI), stood at 9.78 per cent in August. For 10 months in a row, inflation has remained above the 9 per cent mark. According to experts, the elevated inflation level is likely to put pressure on RBI to continue with its policy of monetary tightening. The apex bank has hiked key policy rates 12 times since March 2010 to tame inflation. The bank's next monetary policy review is scheduled for October 25. During the central bank's meeting at Jaipur, RBI Governor D. Subbarao mentioned that the rate hikes has affected industrial activities, but asserted that inflation continues to remain above the comfort level of around 5 per cent. He also warned that interest rates would come down only if inflation eased. Meanwhile, in its Economic Outlook for 2011-12, the PMEAC figures show that inflation is likely to remain elevated till the third quarter of the fiscal because of high prices globally.

Bio-Diesel – an ECO-Friendly Fuel

Just as our lifestyles become more sophisticated by the day, so does the damage we do to the environment. Our every move, from watching television, to working at a computer, to taking a flight to our favourite holiday destination harms the environment in one way or the other. Air and water pollution levels are increasing world over by the day. Never before has the need to use alternative resources, such as wind, solar and nuclear energy been so high.

India is one of the largest petroleum consuming and importing countries. India imports about 70 % of its petroleum demands.

The current yearly consumption of diesel oil in India is approximately 40 million tones constituting about 40% of the total petro-product consumption. Bio-diesel can be the major replacement in terms of petro-product consumption by India which is eco-friendly too.

Bio-diesel is a clean burning, eco-friendly natural fuel obtained from tree born oil by a chemical transformation process called "Transesterification" carried out in a chemical processing plant. Transesterification is an age old chemical process and is a time tested method of transforming vegetable oils or fats into bio-diesel.

Bio-diesel is a bio-fuel produced from various feedstock's' including vegetable oils (such as oilseed, rapeseed and Soya bean), animal fats or algae. Bio-diesel can be blended with diesel for use in diesel engine vehicles. Bio-fuel – The term bio-fuel applies to any solid, liquid, or gaseous fuel produced from organic (once-living) matter. The word bio-fuel covers a wide range of products, some of which are commercially available today, and some of which are still in research and development. Bio-diesel is a fuel made from plant oils that can be used in a conventional diesel engine.

Bio-diesel, derived from the oils and fats of plants like sunflower, rape seeds, Canola or Jatropha (Bhagveranda) can be used as a substitute or an additive to diesel. As an alternative fuel bio-diesel can provide power similar to conventional diesel fuel and thus can be used in diesel engines. Bio-diesel is a renewable liquid fuel that can be produced locally thus helping reduce the country's dependence on imported crude petroleum diesel.

Bio-diesel is a safe alternative fuel to replace traditional petroleum diesel. It has high-lubricity, is a clean-burning fuel and can be a fuel component for use in existing, unmodified diesel engines. This means that no retrofits are necessary when using bio-diesel fuel in any diesel powered combustion engine. It is the only alternative fuel that offers such convenience. Bio-diesel acts like petroleum diesel, but produces less air pollution, comes from renewable sources, is biodegradable and is safer for the environment. Producing bio-diesel fuels can help create local economic revitalization

and local environmental benefits. Many groups interested in promoting the use of bio-diesel already exist at the local, state and national level.

Bio-diesel is not harmful to the environment. A vehicle tends to pollute the environment and emits harmful gasses, if injected with HSD whereas if the engine is using bio-diesel it emits no harmful gasses rather keeps the environment pollution free. Bio-diesel may not require an engine modification.

Bio-diesel can be blended with diesel so as to improve the efficiency of the engine without any hassles. Bio-diesel is cheap. Any Vehicle using Bio-diesel has very low idle starting noise. It is noted that bio-diesel has a Cetane number of over 100. Cetane number is used to measure the quality of the fuel's ignition. Bio-diesel is cost effective because it is produced locally.

As it is easy to use, bio-diesel can be used in existing engines, vehicles and infrastructure with practically no changes. Bio-diesel can be pumped, stored and burned just like petroleum diesel fuel, and can be used pure, or in blends with petroleum diesel fuel in any proportion. Power and fuel economy using bio-diesel is practically identical to petroleum diesel fuel, and year round operation can be achieved by blending with diesel fuel.

Jatropha plant

Bio-diesel provides significantly reduced emissions of carbon monoxide, particulate matter, unburned hydrocarbons, and sulfates compared to petroleum diesel fuel. Additionally, bio-diesel reduces emissions of carcinogenic compounds by as much as 85% compared with petro-diesel. When blended with petroleum diesel fuel, these emissions reductions are generally directly proportional to the amount of bio-diesel in the blend.

The existence of low volatility nature of bio-diesel, makes it easier and safe to handle than petroleum. The danger of accidental ignition increases when the fuel is being stored, transported, or transferred because of high energy content in all liquid fuels. The possibility of having an accidental ignition is related to the temperature at which the fuel will create enough vapors to ignite, known as the flash point temperature. The lower the flash point of a fuel is, the lower the temperature at which the fuel can form a combustible mixture. Bio-diesel has a flash point of over 26600F, meaning it cannot form a combustible mixture until it is heated well above the boiling point of water.

The resources that are used to produce Bio-diesel are locally available. The in-house production of Bio-diesel provides host of economic benefits for the local communities. Therefore, bio-diesel is a safe alternative fuel to replace traditional petroleum diesel.

Consumers Arise

An enlightened consumer is an empowered consumer. An aware consumer not only protects himself from exploitation but induces efficiency, transparency and accountability in the entire manufacturing and services sector. Realising the importance of consumer empowerment the Government has accorded top priority to Consumer Education, Consumer Protection and Consumer Awareness. India is a country, which has taken a lead in introducing progressive legislation for consumer protection. The most important milestone in Consumer Movement in the country has been the enactment of the Consumer Protection Act, 1986. The Act has set in motion a revolution in the field of consumer rights that perhaps cannot have a any parallel anywhere else in the World. The Act applies to all goods and services unless specially exempted by the Central Government, in all sectors whether Private, Public or Co-operative.

Basic Framework For Consumer Protection

Consumer protection initiatives by the Government hinge on 3 basic parameters. Firstly, ensuring a legal framework that comprises of Consumer Protection Act.

Secondly, evolving standards for different products to enable the consumers to make an informed choice about different products. Standards which are the essential building block for quality, play a key role in consumer protection.

Standards could be on technical requirement (specifications), improved specific standard terminology (glossary of terms), codes of practice or test methods or management systems standards. The standards are set generally by Government or inter-Governmental bodies but worldwide it is being recognised that voluntary establishment of standards plays an equally important role

for protecting consumers. Thirdly, consumer awareness and education is the main building block for consumer protection.

Consumer Protection Act, 1986

The Act enshrines all consumer rights which are internationally accepted. Under the Act, a separate three-tier quasi judicial consumer dispute redressal machinery popularly known as consumer courts or consumer forums has been set up at the national, state and district level to provide simple, speedy and inexpensive redressal to the consumer grievances against any defective

Creating consumer awareness

goods, deficiency in services including the restrictive/unfair trade practices.

Networking of Consumer

In order to establish complete interlinking of computer networking of consumer court, namely, National Commission, 35 State Commissions and 607 District Forums for its monitoring and accessing various kinds of data, the Department is moving forward to introduce computerization and networking of all consumer forums.

Initiatives Towards Consumer Awareness And Education

In a country like ours, given the scenario of economic disparity and level of education and ignorance, educating the consumers, remains a gigantic task. This calls for concerted efforts from every one. Government has taken up number of initiatives for creating consumer awareness in the country. The Consumer Awareness Scheme for the XIth Plan amounting to a total of Rs. 409 crores has been approved by the Cabinet Committee on Economic Affairs in January, 2008.

The slogan 'Jago Grahak Jago' has now become a household name as a result of the publicity campaign undertaken in the last 4 years. Through the increased thrust on consumer awareness in the XIth Five Year Plan, the Government has endeavoured to inform the common man of his rights as a consumer. As part of the consumer awareness scheme, the rural and remote areas have been given top priority.

Multi Media Publicity Campaign

Multi-media publicity campaign are being undertaken through print and electronic media on the issues that are directly relevant to the role of the Department such as ISI, Hallmark,

Labelling, MRP, Weights and Measures etc. Each advertisement is released through a network of national a well as regional newspapers throughout the country.

Simultaneously, major initiative are being launched wherein issues that have come into focus on account of new emerging areas such as telecom, real estate, credit cards, financial products, pharmaceuticals, Insurance, travel services, medicines etc. are undertaken either through joint campaigns or joint consultations with the concerned Departments.

The Department of Consumer Affairs has video spots of 30 seconds duration on various consumer related issues, which are being telecast through Cable and Satellite channels.

Special programmes have also been telecast on Lok Sabha TV and Doordarshan to highlight the issues relating to consumer awareness. Issues pertaining to rural and remote areas have been given prominence in the various advertisement spots.

Meghdoot Postcards

Consumer awareness messages are also being disseminated through Meghdoot Post cards in consultation with Department of Post to reach far-flung rural areas including North-East States. Posters carrying messages pertaining to consumer awareness have been displayed in 1.55 lakh Rural Post Offices and more than 25000 Urban Post Offices throughout the country.

National Consumer Helpline

The Department has launched a National

Help Line. The toll free number 1800-11-4000 facility is available to consumers from 9.30 A.M. to 5.30 P.M. on all the working days.

Core Centre

The Department has launched on March 15, 2005 Consumer on Line Resources and Empowerment (CORE) Centre on the website www.core.nic.in for consumer advocacy and online redressal of consumer grievances. Through the various advertisements relating to consumer awareness, adequate publicity is being given to the activities of CORE and its website so that consumers can take the help of online counselling/guidance being provided through it.

Enabling Web in 22 Indian Languages

The internet has completed 42 years of its existence on 2nd September, 2011. The generation that has not seen other means of communication than internet is grown up now. They find it easy to communicate online with their peers but when it comes to communicating with people using other Indian languages than English they find themselves clueless. Now this hindrance in communication will be over soon.

The Government committed to the goal of 'Internet for All', in close co-operation with other stakeholders has taken several steps in this direction. The World Wide Web Consortium (W3C) India Office, one of such steps, was formally launched on 6th May, 2010. A 2-day Conference on World-Wide-Web: Technology, Standards and Internationalization was held in New Delhi to mark the launching. On 15th September 2011 W3C India Office Workspace was inaugurated at Electronics Niketan, CGO Complex.

The establishment of New W3C India Office space gives it a permanent entity and would play more active and crucial role in proliferation of W3C standards among ICT industry and users to make India truly knowledge based society.

World Wide Web Consortium

World Wide Web Consortium (W3C) is an international Standards Body headquartered at Massachusetts Institute of

Technology, USA which develops Standards / Best Practices / recommendations to ensure seamless web access to all. W3C has 19 offices world-wide having the core objective of promotion, proliferation and adoption of W3C standards and its implementation according to local languages and culture. The Vision of W3C is to achieve "Web for Everyone and Web on Everything." W3C works in tandem with other standards making bodies such as UNICODE, IETF, ICANN and ISO at the international level. W3C has so far published about 183 standards for web technology and working in the future web standards. Recommendations evolved by W3C run across many technical domains.

Indian Linguistic Diversity having 22 constitutionally recognized languages and 11 complex scripts is more diverse than that of entire European Union. Apart from these 22 constitutionally recognized languages India's rich linguistic diversity boasts of 100 other major languages and 2371 dialects as per Census 2001. In India, a Language may be based on many scripts. Many languages may be based on a single script; these languages culturally differ depending on region though using same script. Even there are wide variations in the usage of the same language across various parts of the country. Linear scripts such as Roman do not change their shape hence characters juxtapose – one after another whereas Indian Languages have complex conjunct characters. Major issues related to Indian languages like orthography – spelling issues, dialect variations etc. testify that each language has its own specific requirements to be investigated carefully for enabling

W3C standards in 22 Indian Languages. Implementation of W3C standards for seamless web access across device and platforms in Indian languages makes it a gigantic and challenging task.

The Nation-Wide Flag-ship E-Governance Programme and roll-out through various national and state-wide mission mode projects and citizen services through CSCs adds a new dimension of W3C's role in India. Internationalization of W3C's standards in Indian context and their implementation addressing the complex language requirements would be a key role for W3C India. W3C India is also the national platform involving the industry, academia and users which evolve national recommendations/ guidelines from India.

W3C India Initiative will not only facilitate wider access of web by the people of this country but will also equip them to provide

locally relevant content on the internet. Such initiatives will play a great role in reducing poverty, improving health care, education, spreading good governance and addressing all local challenges in the global context.

The future internet issues need to be addressed from a holistic perspective by taking into account building blocks right from users, services and applications down to network. This requires a multi-disciplinary approach by involving innovative SMEs and develops drivers, interfaces, networks and services to support future networked society.

Participation from India is there but it is limited as some industry members are interacting with W3C on specific areas of interest to them. India need to ensure that all

her officially recognized 22 languages can be adequately represented in W3C recommendations to make Web accessible in Indian languages a reality and in view if this the role of India becomes prominent especially in the area of internationalization.

W3C India Office

W3C India Office has been set up at DIT under the aegis of Human Centered Computing Division. The Division is implementing the programme "Technology Development for Indian Languages (TDIL)". TDIL programme is engaging itself actively since 2006 with all the stakeholders in the country to work towards internationalization of W3C Recommendations.

"Enabling Web in 22 Indian languages" will accelerate the growth of Web in Indian Languages. In today's technology driven world, access to information is crucial for taking the benefits of ICT to the masses. The engagement with W3C in building all the required standards will facilitate information access on World Wide Web regardless of languages, location, ability, generation, age and income. This would prove to be a transformational step.

Yeddyurappa Surrenders

It happened two and a half months after he was forced to resign as Karnataka CM. B.S. Yeddyurappa who was confronted with an arrest warrant in a land scam case surrendered in the Special Lokayukta Court in Bangalore. The court remanded him and his close associate former Minister S.N. Krishnaiah Setty in judicial custody till Oct. 22. Yeddyurappa was taken to the Parappana Agrahara Central Prison. Mr. Setty fainted while awaiting his arrest. He was moved to the prison hospital.

After A. R. Antulay of Maharashtra, a former CM who was arrested in 1984,

Yeddyurappa being taken into custody

this was the only incident in India when a former CM was the prevention of Corruption Act.

Karnataka Governor H.R. Bhardwaj had sanctioned the prosecution of Mr. Yeddyurappa nine months ago. Yeddyurappa had been accused of being complicit in a multicrore land scam. Yeddyurappa stepped down as CM in the wake of the Lokayukta indictment in the illegal mining scam. His second term as CM began on May 30, 2008. In Nov. 2007, he took oath as CM to head the first-ever BJP-led coalition government in South India.

Slumdogs

Shocking facts about 'Indian children living in slums were revealed by Slums in India, A statistical Compendium 2011" published by the Central government.

In a country that achieved political independence some 65 years ago, about 13 per cent of the total child population of the urban areas live in slums. They number 7.6 mn. in the 26 states /UTs reporting slums.

Chandigarh gives us a dismal picture.

That is where the highest proportion of slum child population are found. It is incredible that one-fifth of the city's children live in slums. According to the data, Maharashtra has the highest slum child population with around 1.7 mn. children between 0–6 years staying in slums. U.P. has the second highest slum child population of around 0.97 mn. Andhra Pradesh (0.83 mn) M.P. (0.6 mn.), West Bengal (0.53 mn.) and Tamil Nadu (0.51 mn.) come next.

It is surprising that 1.1 of the 23 states have a more than 15 p.c. proportion of slum child population. Gujarat, Bihar, U.P., Rajasthan, Haryana and Goa fall in this category.

As for the major metros, Mumbai has 0.86 mn. children, Delhi 0.3 mn. and Kolkata 0.15 mn.

The Kochi Metro

Keralites are excited. The Kochi Metro is about to become a reality. The Centre is expected to give its approval by year-end. The note on the project has been prepared suggesting its implementation on the lines of the Chennai Metro. The system of mass rapid transport, beginning from Aluva, passing through M.G. Road and ending at Pettah would be completed in three-and-a half years' time from the day the Union Cabinet gives its nod.

The project cost has been revised by the State government to Rs. 5016 crore. It may be recalled that the cost was Rs. 1186 cr. when the project was mooted over six years ago.

The fare would be between Rs. 8 (minimum fare) and Rs. 20 (maximum). On an average, the commuters will spend less than a rupee a kilometre. The fare in Delhi is between Rs. 10 and Rs. 30.

Delhi Metro Rail Corporation is the Kochi project's consultants and executive agency. DMRC will initially operate 22 trains, each having three coaches, in Kochi.

According to Mr. E. Sreedharan, M.D. of DMRC, the number of passengers would increase at least by another 20 p.c. when the project is commissioned.

The Calcutta Metro: Work on the Metro

Railway in Calcutta started on Dec. 29, 1972. It began its first commercial run on Oct. 24, 1984 from Esplanade to Bhowanipore at 8-4 a.m. and completed the 4-km journey in less than eight minutes. Calcutta was India's first and the world's 78th city to have the underground railway. On Sept. 27, 1995, Calcutta Metro Railway ran between Dum Dum and Tollygunj - the first commercial run of the full length of 23 km.

Cabinet Okays Mining Bill

With an aim to bring in a better legislative environment for attracting investment and technology in the mining sector, the Cabinet has approved the proposal to introduce the Mines and Minerals (Development and Regulation) Bill, 2011. The bill, which must now win parliamentary approval, calls on coal miners to share a maximum 26 percent of their profits with local communities and for other miners to pay an amount equivalent to royalties.

The bill has been watered down under pressure from industry. The initial proposal said all miners should give 26 percent of profits to local communities where land acquisition is a touchy issue and many oppose natural resources being carted away by outsiders.

All coal mining companies have to share 26 percent of their profits. A part of government moves to expand social programmes for the poor, the bill seeks to simultaneously please the core support base, block flows of new recruits to a Maoist insurgency and balance modern lifestyles with traditional ways.

India's mining sector has among the worst regulatory environments and is a source for some of the country's biggest corruption scandals, at least one of which has now swept in top regional leaders of the main opposition party.

Government revenue from mining royalties now stand at Rs.40,000 crore .

India's mining sector has only opened up fully to private investors in recent years and state-run companies have lacked the funds and expertise to probe deeper than the top 50 metres or so where its iron ore and coal reserves are found.

Global mining giants BHP Billiton and Rio Tinto have only small ventures in the country. In Orissa state, Rio Tinto has been negotiating since 1995 with the state government to develop iron ore deposits in a joint venture.

While industry bodies are reconciled to sharing some profits, they have baulked at 26 percent, saying that will raise business costs too much and deter investors.

The mining ministry says that profit-sharing should make it easier for mining projects to win local approval and accelerate the pace of developments.

Labourers at a coal mine

Protests against big industrial projects are a phenomenon of the developing world from Brazil to Indonesia, and making investors plough back a portion of their income into development of local communities has been one way of dealing with resentment.

India is also trying to replace a century-old land acquisition law that seeks to placate a rural voter base worried it is being short-changed in the country's rush into modernisation.

Women Nobel Laureates

The Nobel Prizes are awarded annually by the Royal Swedish Academy of Sciences, the Swedish Academy, the Karolinska Institute, and the Norwegian Nobel Committee to individuals who make outstanding contributions in the fields of Chemistry, Physics, Literature, Peace, Physiology or Medicine and Economics. All but the economics prize were established by the 1895 will of Alfred Nobel, which dictates that the awards should be administered by the Nobel Foundation. The Nobel prize in Economics, or The Sveriges Riksbank Prize in Economic Sciences in Memory of Alfred Nobel, was established in 1968 by the Sveriges Riksbank, the central bank of Sweden, for outstanding contributions in the field of Economics.

Each prize is awarded by a separate committee; the Royal Swedish Academy of Sciences awards the Prizes in Physics, Chemistry, and Economics, the Swedish Academy awards the Prize in Literature, the Karolinska Institute awards the Prize in Physiology or Medicine, and the Norwegian Nobel Committee awards the Prize in Peace. Each recipient receives a medal, a diploma and a cash prize that has varied throughout the years. In 1901, the winners of the first Nobel Prizes were given 150,782 SEK, which is equal to 7,731,004 SEK in December 2007. In 2008, the winners were awarded a prize amount of 10,000,000 SEK. The awards are presented in Stockholm (Physics, Chemistry, Physiology or Medicine, Literature and Economics) and Oslo (Peace) in an annual ceremony on December 10, the anniversary of Nobel's death.

44 Women
Following the awards of 2011 (other than the 2011 Economics Prize), the Nobel Prize has been awarded 807 times to men and 44

times to women (there have also been 23 awards to organizations). The first woman to win a Nobel Prize was Marie Curie, who won the Nobel Prize in Physics in 1903 with her husband, Pierre Curie, and Henri Becquerel. Curie is also the only woman to have won multiple Nobel Prizes; in 1911, she won the Nobel Prize in Chemistry (and is accordingly included twice in the total figure of 44 for female laureates). Curie's daughter, Irène Joliot-Curie, won the Nobel Prize in Chemistry in 1935, making the two the only mother-daughter pair to have won Nobel Prizes. Fifteen women have won the Nobel Peace Prize, twelve women have won the Nobel Prize in Literature, ten have won the Nobel Prize in Physiology or Medicine, four have won the Nobel Prize in Chemistry, two have won the Nobel Prize in Physics and only one woman (in 2009) has won the Nobel Memorial Prize in Economic Sciences. The most Nobel Prizes awarded to women in a single year was in 2009, when five women became laureates.

Laureates are listed below, with Country and Category

1903 Marie Curie (shared with Pierre Curie and Henri Becquerel), Poland and France, Physics, "in recognition of the extraordinary services they have rendered by their joint researches on the radiation phenomena discovered by Professor Henri Becquerel"

1905 Bertha von Suttner, Austria–Hungary, Peace, Honourary President of Permanent International Peace Bureau, Bern, Switzerland; Author of Lay Down Your Arms.

1909 Selma Lagerlöf, Sweden, Literature, "in appreciation of the lofty idealism, vivid imagination and spiritual perception that characterize her writings"

1911 Marie Curie, Poland and France, Chemistry, "for her discovery of radium and polonium"

1926 **Grazia Deledda**, Italy, Literature, "for her idealistically inspired writings which with plastic clarity picture the life on her native island and with depth and sympathy deal with human problems in general"

1928 **Sigrid Undset**, Norway, Literature, "principally for her powerful descriptions of Northern life during the Middle Ages"

1931 **Jane Addams**, (shared with Nicholas Murray Butler) United States, Peace, Sociologist; International President, Women's International League for Peace and Freedom.

1935 **Irène Joliot-Curie**, (shared with Frédéric Joliot-Curie), France, Chemistry, "for their synthesis of new radioactive elements"

Irène Joliot-Curie

1938 **Pearl S. Buck**, United States, Literature, "for her rich and truly epic descriptions of peasant life in China and for her biographical masterpieces"

Pearl S. Buck

1945 **Gabriela Mistral**, Chile, Literature, "for her lyric poetry which, inspired by powerful emotions, has made her name a symbol of the idealistic aspirations of the entire Latin American world"

1946 **Emily Greene Balch**, (shared with John Raleigh Mott), United States, Peace, Formerly Professor of History and Sociology; Honorary International President, Women's International League for Peace and Freedom.

1947 **Gerty Theresa Cori**, (shared with Carl Ferdinand Cori and Bernardo Houssay), United States, Physiology or Medicine, "for their discovery of the course of the catalytic conversion of glycogen"

1963 **Maria Goeppert-Mayer**, (shared with J. Hans D. Jensen and Eugene Wigner), United States, Physics, "for their discoveries concerning nuclear shell structure"

1964 **Crowfoot Hodgk**, United Kingdom, Chemistry, "for her determinations by X-ray techniques of the structures of important biochemical substances"

1966 **Nelly Sachs**, (shared with Samuel Agnon), Sweden and Germany, Literature, "for her outstanding lyrical and dramatic writing, which interprets Israel's destiny with touching strength"

1976 **Betty Williams**, United Kingdom, Peace, Founder of the Northern Ireland Peace Movement (later renamed Community of Peace People)

1976 **Mairead Corrigan**, United Kingdom, Peace Founder of the Northern Ireland Peace Movement (later renamed Community of Peace People

1977 **Rosalyn Sussman Yalow** (shared with Roger Guillemin and Andrew Schally), United States, Physiology or Medicine, "for the development of radioimmunoassays of peptide hormones"

1979 **Mother Teresa,** India and Macedonia, Peace, Leader of Missionaries of Charity, Calcutta.

1982 **Alva Myrdal**, (shared with Alfonso García Robles), Sweden, Peace, Former Cabinet Minister; Diplomat; Writer.

1983 **Barbara McClintock**, United States, Physiology or Medicine, "for her discovery of mobile genetic elements"

1986 **Rita Levi-Montalcini**, (shared with Stanley Cohen) Italy andUnited States, Physiology or Medicine, "for their discoveries of growth factors"

1988 **Gertrude B. Elion**, (shared with James W. Black and George H. Hitchings), United States, Physiology or Medicine, "for their discoveries of important principles for drug treatment"

1991 **Nadine Gordimer**, South Africa, Literature, "who through her magnificent epic writing has - in the words of Alfred No-

Nadine Gordimer

A Commoner is Queen

King Jigme Khesar Namgyel Wangchuck of Bhutan married commoner Jetsun Pema in the state capital Thimphu on Oct. 13, 2011. The bride, 31-year old, is India-educated daughter of a pilot. She is 10-years younger than the King.

King Jigme is the youngest reigning monarch in the world.

The wedding took place at a fortress in the historic city of Punakha, 71 km from Thimphu.

Jetsun Pema is currently a student of London's Regents College.

bel - been of very great benefit to humanity"

1991 Aung San Suu Kyi, Burma, Peace, "for her non-violent struggle for democracy and human rights"

1992 Rigoberta Menchú, Guatemala, Peace, "in recognition of her work for social justice and ethno-cultural reconciliation based on respect for the rights of indigenous peoples"

1993 Toni Morrison, United States, Literature, "who in novels characterized

Rigoberta Menchú

by visionary force and poetic import, gives life to an essential aspect of American reality"

1995 Christiane Nüsslein-Volhard (shared with Edward B. Lewis and Eric F. Wieschaus), Germany, Physiology or Medicine, "for their discoveries concerning the genetic control of early embryonic development"

Toni Morrison

1996 Wisława Szymborska, Poland, Literature, "for poetry that with ironic precision allows the historical and biological context to come to light in fragments of human reality"

1997 Jody Williams, (shared with the International Campaign to Ban Landmines), United States, Peace, "for their work for the banning and clearing of anti-personnel mines"

2003 Shirin Ebadi, Iran, Peace, "for her efforts for democracy and human rights. She has focused especially on the struggle for the rights of women and children"

Shirin Ebadi

2004 Elfriede Jelinek, Austria, Literature, "for her musical flow of voices and counter-voices in novels and plays that with extraordinary linguistic zeal reveal the absurdity of society's clichés and their subjugating power"

2004 Wangari Maathai, Kenya, Peace, "for her contribution to sustainable development, democracy and peace"

2004 Linda B. Buck (shared with Richard Axel), United States, Physiology or Medicine, "for their dis-

Linda B. Buck

Doris Lessing

coveries of odorant receptors and the organization of the olfactory system"

2007 Doris Lessing, United Kingdom, Literature, "that epicist of the female experience, who with scepticism, fire and visionary power has subjected a divided civilisation to scrutiny"

2008 Françoise Barré-Sinoussi, (shared with Harald zur Hausen and Luc Montagnier), France, Physiology or Medicine, "for their discovery of human immunodeficiency virus"

2009 Elizabeth Blackburn (shared with Carol W. Greider and Jack W. Szostak), Australia and United States, Physiology or Medicine, "for the discovery of how chromosomes are protected by telomeres and the enzyme telomerase"

Elizabeth Blackburn

2009 Carol W. Greider (shared with Elizabeth Blackburn and Jack W. Szostak), United States, Physiology or Medicine, "for the discovery of how chromosomes are protected by telomeres and the enzyme telomerase"

2009 Ada E. Yonath (shared with Venkatraman Ramakrishnan and Thomas A. Steitz), Israel, Chemistry, "for studies of the structure and function of the ribosome"

Ada E. Yonath

2009 Herta Muller, Germany and Romania, Literature, "who, with the concentration of poetry and the frankness of prose, depicts the landscape of the dispossessed"

2009 Elinor Ostrom (shared with Oliver E. Williamson), United States, Economics, "for her analysis of economic governance, especially the commons"

2011 Ellen Johnson Sirleaf, Liberia, Peace, "For their non-violent struggle for the safety of women and for women's rights to full participation in peace-building work"

Leymah Gbowee and Tawakel Karman, Yemen

A Beatle Wedding

The 69-year-old former Beatle, Paul McCartney, wed his American fiancee, Nancy Shevell, 51, on October 9th at the Old Marylebone Town Hall, same London venue in which he wed his late wife Linda more than 40 years ago. It is also called the Rock-and-Roll Venue, and that's a legacy of the Beatles because Ringo Starr also got married here.

The wedding was a small family affair and the guests included brother Mike McCartney, Ringo Starr, his wife Barbara Bach and George Harrison's widow, Olivia. The day Lennon would have celebrated his 71st birthday, McCartney paid tribute to his former bandmate. He has a fortune of £495 million.

The Beatles Band comprised John Lennon, Paul McCartney, George Harison and Ringo Starr.

Elinor Ostrom

Nobel Prizes, 2011

Medicine: Dr. Bruce A. Beutler (US), Jules Hoffmann (Luxembourg-France) and Ralph Steinman (Canada) for the discovery of key secrets in 'innate' immunity. After announcement, it was known that Steiman had passed away three days ago. The committee would not name a substitute winner. They will decide what to do with the prize money.

Bruce A. Beutler   Jules Hoffmann   Ralph Steinman

Physics: Saul Perlmutter, Adam G. Riess (both of US), and Brian Schmidt (US-Australian) for discovering the accelerating expansion of the Universe. One-half of the prize of 10 mn. Swedish kronor goes to Saul Perlmutter; the other half is shared by Reiss and Schmidt.

Saul Perlmutter   Adam G. Riess   Brian Schmidt

Chemistry: Daniel Shechtman, an Israeli, won the Chemistry Nobel for discovering quasicrystals, a material in which atoms are packed together in a well-defined pattern that never repeats.

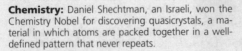

Literature: Tomas Transtromer, Swedish poet, whose work explores themes of nature, isolation and identity. Through his condensed, translucent images, he gives us fresh access to reality. There are 15 collections of poetry by him, many of which have been translated into English and 60 other languages. He has worked for much of his life as a psychologist. After a stroke in 1990, he is mostly unable to speak. A Swede has won the prize for the first time after 1974. Honorarium is $1.5 mn. (10 mn. kronor).

Daniel Shechtman   Tomas Transtromer

Economics: Thomas Sargent and Christopher Sims, both US, both 68, for their work on macro-economics and government economic policy making.

Thomas Sargent   Christopher Sims

Peace: Ellen Johnson Sirleaf and Leymeh Gbowee of Liberia and Tawakkul Karman of Yemen for their contribution to women's rights.

Ellen Sirleaf   Leymeh Gbowee   Tawakkul Karman

| Nobel for Women | This is the first time the Nobel Prize has been jointly won by three women. In 1976, two women, Betty Williams and Mairead Corrigan (N. Ireland / G. Britain), founders of the Northern Ireland Peace Movement, were jointly awarded the Peace Prize. |

Looking Ahead : The Year 2012

2012 (MMXII) will be a leap year that will start on a Sunday in the Gregorian calendar. It will be the 2012th year of the Anno Domini or Common Era designation, the 12th year of the 3rd millennium and of the 21st century; and the 3rd of the 2010s decade.

The United Nations General Assembly has declared 2012 as the International Year of Cooperatives, highlighting the contribution of cooperatives to socio-economic development, in particular recognizing their impact on poverty reduction, employment generation and social integration.

It has also been designated Alan Turing Year, commemorating the mathematician, computer pioneer, and code-breaker on the centennial of Turing's birth.

There are a variety of popular beliefs about the year 2012. These beliefs range from the spiritually transformative to the apocalyptic, and center upon various interpretations of the Mesoamerican Long Count calendar. Contemporary scientists have disputed the apocalyptic versions.

Predicted and Scheduled Events

January 13 - January 22 – The first Winter Youth Olympics will be held in Innsbruck, Austria.

Innsbruck

January 31 – 433 Eros, the second-largest Near Earth Object on record (size 13 km × 13 km × 33 km) will pass Earth at 0.1790 astronomical units (26,780,000 km; 16,640,000 mi). NASA studied Eros with the NEAR Shoemaker probe launched on February 17, 1996.

Queen Elizabeth II

February 6 – Diamond Jubilee of Queen Elizabeth II, marking the 60th anniversary of her accession to the thrones of the United Kingdom, Canada, Australia & New Zealand, and the 60th anniversary of her becoming Head of the Commonwealth.

April 17 – The United States will cede wartime control of the military of South Korea after 50 years and dissolve the Combined Forces Command. Two distinct military commands (South Korea and the United States) will operate in Korea during wartime, rather than one unified command under the

Silent Spring	Rachel Carson's book, Silent Spring, is widely credited with helping launch the environmental movement. The book published in 1962 inspired widespread public concerns with pesticides and pollution of the environment. It facilitated the ban of the pesticide DDT in 1972 in the US.

World Expo Mascots

Combined Forces Command.

May 12 - August 12 – The 2012 World Expo is to be held in Yeosu, South Korea.

May 20 – Annular solar eclipse. Path of annularity runs through the Pacific Ocean from northern China to California.

June 6 – The second and last solar transit of Venus of the century. The next pair is predicted to occur in 2117 and 2125.

Alan Turing

June 18 - June 23 – Turing Centenary Conference at the University of Cambridge, in honor of the mathematician, computer scientist, and cryptographer Alan Turing, the last day of the conference being the hundredth anniversary of his birth.

July 27 – Opening ceremony of the 2012 Summer Olympics begins in London at 19:30 UTC, 20:30 BST. London will become the first city in history to host the Olympic Games three times.

London Olympics 2012

August 12 – Closing ceremony of the 2012 Summer Olympics in London.

November 13 – Total solar eclipse (visible in Northern Australia and the South Pacific).

December 21 – The Mesoamerican Long Count calendar, notably used by the pre-Columbian Maya civilization among others, completes a "great cycle" of thirteen b'ak'tuns (periods of 144,000 days each) since the mythical creation date of the calendar's current era.

December 31 – The first commitment period of the Kyoto Protocol ends.

Dates Unknown

• China will launch the Kuafu spacecraft.

• Pleiades, a proposed supercomputer built by Intel and SGI for NASA's Ames Research Center, will be completed, reaching a peak performance of 10 Petaflops (10 quadrillion floating point operations per second).

Sequoia Supercomputer

• Sequoia, a proposed super computer built by IBM for the National Nuclear Security Administration will be completed, reaching a peak performance of 20 Petaflops.

• On the Sun, the solar maximum of Solar Cycle 24 in the 11-year sunspot cycle is forecast to occur. Solar Cycle 24 is regarded to have commenced January 2008, and on average will reach its peak of maximal sunspot activity around 2012. The period between successive solar maxima averages 11 years (the Schwabe cycle), and the previous solar maximum of Solar Cycle 23 occurred in 2000–2002. During the solar maximum the Sun's magnetic poles will reverse.

• The Kars–Tbilisi–Baku railway across the Caucasus is scheduled to be completed sometime in 2012.

In Remembrance of Jagjit Singh

Indian ghazal king Jagjit Singh who gave ghazals a new lease of life, by bringing it out of obscurity and has sang about 3000 ghazals and performed in 46 concerts. He breathed his last on Sep 23 after a brain haemorrhage. Singh, who learnt music under Pandit Chaganlal Sharma and then Ustad Jamaal Khan, rose to fame in the 1970s and 1980s with his lilting voice and refreshing style of rendering ghazals and devotional tracks. He was a Padma Bhushan recipient.

Jagjit Singh

फिल्म : प्रेमगीत (गायक जगजीत सिंह)

होंठों से छूलो तुम, मेरा गीत अमर कर दो
बन जाओ मीत मेरे मेरी प्रीत अमर कर दो

जा उस की सीमा हो, ना जनम का हो
बंधन
जब प्यार करे कोई, तो देखे केवल
मन
नई रीत चलाकर तुम ये रीत अमर कर
दो

आकाश का सूनापन, मेरे तन्हा मन में
पायल छनकाती तुम आ जाओ जीवन में
स्वरों देकर अपनी, संगीत अमर कर दो
संगीत अमर कर दो, मेरा गीत अमर कर दो

जग ने छीना मुझसे, मुझे जो भी लगा
प्यारा
सब जीत गये मुझसे, मैं हर गम से
हारा
तुम हार के दिल अपना, मेरी गीत अमर
कर दो

Early Life

Born to a Sikh couple in Rajasthan Feb 8, 1941, Singh went on to pursue a post graduation from the Kurukshetra University in Haryana. He went to Mumbai in 1965, in search of work as a singer. In 1967, he met singer Chitra and following a courtship of two years, they tied the knot. Together they came up with several hit ghazal albums like "Ecstasies", "A Sound Affair", "Passions" and "Beyond Time" and were considered a formidable husband-wife singer duo. They sang many successful duets until their only son, Vivek, died at the age of 21 in 1990. Chitra stopped singing. However, Singh continued his tryst with music - and for good. In 1987, Singh recorded the first purely digital CD album by an Indian musician, "Beyond Time".

Contribution to Bollywood

He also sang for... "Arth", "Saath Saath" and "Premgeet". He created a strong footing in films with songs like "Hontho se chhoo lo tum" ("Prem Geet"), "Tumko dekha toh yeh khayal aaya" ("Saath Saath"), "Jhuki jhuki si nazar" ("Arth"), "Hoshwalon ko" ("Sarfarosh") and "Badi nazuk hai" ("Jogger's Park").

Non-film albums

"Hope", "In Search", "Insight", "Mirage", "Visions", "Kahkashan", "Love Is Blind", "Chirag", "Sajda", "Marasim", "Face To Face", "Aaeena" and "Cry For Cry" - were successful too.

His concerts were a delight, especially when he broke into pleasant Punjabi numbers like "Saun da mahina". His heavy voice brought joy and smile to the listeners just as much tears. He had also collaborated with former Indian prime minister Atal Bihari Vajpayee in two albums, "Nayi Disha" (1999) and "Samvedna" (2002).

Besides, Krishna bhajans, Ramdhun, Shiv dhun and shabads, he has sang Christian ghazals like 'Meri rooh khuda ki pyasi he.' He faught against issues in the music industry especially for an equal percentage of royalty for singers and lyricist. Having performed with legends like Gulam Ali, the voice that won him the tag of Indian ghazal king, will remain fresh for generations to come.

World

A Call for Revolution!

The widening gap between the rich and poor fuelled a movement that had its first big international manifestation on October 15, a day that witnessed a wave of protests in several world cities. Asia, Europe, Africa and the Americas saw demonstrations against what is described as corporate greed and government cutbacks. The demonstration was inspired by America's "Occupy Wall Street" and Spains "Indignants".

Some demonstrators were wearing masks. In Madrid, people assembled for an evening rally in the Cibeles square. There was a 6-hour march from Leganes to the centre of Madrid. Zurich, Geneva, Athens, Brussels, and Sarajevo witnessed protest marches too. Free market capitalism, was the victim of attacks in Hong Kong's financial district. Demonstrators in Tokyo were furious about the Fukushima nuclear acci-

Indignant people in the West protests against financial crisis and unemployment

These targeted 951 cities in 82 countries. Rome was the chief centre. The city saw some acts of violence. Tens of thousands marched, some smashing shops and office windows. Two cars were burnt. From the Roman Forum the demonstrators moved to a square in front of St. John Lateran basilica.

A cardboard coffin was seen moving with the name of the Italian premier Silvio Berlusconi on it.

A placard said: Only One Solution: Revolution.

In London nearly 1000 people rallied in the financial district by St. Paul's Cathedral. Banners condemned Goldman Sachs: Some said 'No Cuts!'

Unemployment was the chief issue highlighted by protesters. In Paris, the movement gained support from the meeting of G20 financial powers discussing the eurozone debt crisis.

A woman during a demonstration in Marseille carried a placard which read "You are hungry? Eat a banker!"

dent. Each demonstration had a character of its own, though the general trend was one of questioning authority. In Sydney, for example, the plight of refugees and Aboriginal Australians was added to the concerns.

In Johannesburg, protesters gathered outside the Jo'burg Stock Exchange, Africa's biggest.

Organisers of the worldwide protest relied heavily on Facebook and Twitter. The entire thing reminded one of the Arab Spring.

Two Former Presidents Honoured

At the World Food Prize ceremony at the Capitol in Des Moines, Iowa in October two former Presidents were honoured. They are John Agyekum Kufuor of Ghana and Luiz Inacio Lula Da Silva of Brazil. This was a recognition of their success in tackling chronic hunger in their countries. The two leaders, through their policies, trans-

John A. Kufuor   *Lula Da Silva*

formed the lives of the poor. The World Food Prize Foundation said that the political commitment of the two put the countries concerned on track to meet or exceed the objectives of the UN Millennium Development Goals. The two leaders have, WFP said, become model examples in realising an end to hunger and poverty worldwide.

The World Food Prize was instituted in 1987 by Norman Borlaug, father of Green Revolution and Nobel Laureate. The prestigious prize has in the past been given to agricultural scientists such as M.S. Swaminathan of India. Swaminathan is the first winner of WFP Award. Muhammad Yunus, formerly of the Grameen Bank, Bangladesh was a social entrepreneur who won the Prize.

Mr. Kufuor, former President of Ghana from 2001 to 2009, helped increase the quantity and quality of food to Ghanaians. Farmers' incomes went up, and school attendance received a boost and child nutrition marked a big increase through a successful feeding programme.

Mr. Da Silva, former Brazilian President, ensured that more than 10 government ministries were focussed on the expansive Zero Hunger Programmes that gave more food to the poor, increased enrolment of primary school children and empowered the poor.

Switzerland Tops the List

Switzerland continues to be the world's most competitive country, according to the annual Global Competitiveness Report (GCR) of the World Economic Forum. The United States has fallen to the 5th position.

What has happened to Asian countries over the past five years makes the comparison interesting to student of India and China. The GCR has found that several countries in the Asian Pacific regions have made significant progress. These include China, Indonesia, Vietnam, and Sri Lanka.

China's performance has improved. It is ranked 26th thus making a gain in its score and rank since 2005. Taking India's case, one has disappointing figures. It has fallen 5 notches since last year from 51 to 56 out of 142 economies.

India's gap with China offers an interesting study. The score difference between the two has increased six-fold between 2006 and today. The gap has expanded from 0.1 to 0.6 points. GCR sees India making mediocre accomplishments in key areas.

India's infrastructure is still not up to the mark. Its supply of energy, ICT and transport is inadequate. When a country wants to do business in another country, it looks for the most advantageous factors in transport and other infrastructure. While India has made considerable progress, other countries have recorded more significant advances. When we talk of India's achievements in public health and basic education, we have several things to claim. But the fact is that the quality of India's basic education is nothing to be proud of. Nor do our public health statistics give us reason to hold our heads high.

India has dropped from rank 37 to rank 69 in the institution pillar. Our public deficit and high debt-to-GDP ratio are factors that dissuade investors. When inflation is about 10%, we are offering a discouraging picture in terms of competitiveness.

And on the corruption front our record is bad. The regulations we introduce from time to time work against our interests. One who has money to invest cannot find us very interesting people because most of us are corrupt most of the time.

No doubt figures favour China. She has risen by a notch to 26th in a year. It is one of the least indebted countries. Its savings rate is put at 53 % of GDP. In basic education and health it is doing much better than India. Business sophistication is high, measuring 37th.

Our vast domestic market is our strength. Investors are attracted by the economies of scall it offers. A new image India is trying to give shape to will, hopefully, help the country become more competitive.

Woman President for Brazil

Dilma Rousseff was elected Brazil's first female president in October 2010, defeating the opposition candidate Jose Serra by 56% to 44% in a run-off vote. She took over on 1st January 2011 from her mentor, Luiz Inacio Lula da Silva, who stepped down after two terms as the most popular president in the country's history. After taking the oath of office, Ms Rousseff promised in a speech

Dilma Rousseff

to protect the most vulnerable in Brazilian society and govern for all. She also vowed to consolidate the work of her predecessor, who she said had changed the way Brazil was governed. Brazil's economy has grown strongly in recent years, but it remains one of the most unequal societies in the world.

Ms Rousseff was appointed energy minister in President Lula's government in 2003 and served as his chief of staff from 2005 to 2010. She is known to favour a strong state role in strategic areas, including banking, the oil industry and energy.

Leading Pakistani Politician Killed

Salmaan Taseer, governor of Punjab,

Salmaan Taseer

Pakistan's most-populous province, and a member of the ruling Pakistan People's Party, was gunned down in a wealthy neighborhood of Islamabad on January 4, 2011 by a member of his security detail after speaking out against the country's controversial blasphemy laws. His attacker, Malik Mumtaz Qadri, who surrendered to police, admitted he was angered by Mr. Taseer's opposition to the blasphemy laws. Mr. Taseer had become a leading opponent of a court decision to sentence a 45-year-old Christian farm labourer, Asia Bibi, to death for blasphemy against the Prophet Muhammad.

The case attracted international attention, with Pope Benedict XVI and human-rights groups calling for her release. Mr. Taseer had attacked the court's decision and had been urging supporters on Twitter to take to the streets in protest against the blasphemy laws. His opposition had been condemned by Islamist political parties. In a Dec. 31 post on his Twitter account, a day before Islamists took to the streets across the country to demand the laws stand, Mr. Taseer wrote: "I was under huge pressure ...2 cow down b4…pressure on blasphemy. Refused. Even if I'm the last man standing."

China Overtakes Japan

In a historic shift of economic powers, China has leapfrogged over Japan to become the world's second-largest economy. Japan's government made it official on February 14th, 2011 when it said that its economy shrank at a 1.1 percent annual rate for the last three months of 2010. China's GDP, meanwhile, surged 9.8 percent. That made Japan's full-year GDP $5.47 trillion, compared with the $5.88 trillion China reported.

Both still remain considerably smaller than

When San Francisco was Shaken — San Francisco was shaken violently on April 8, 1906. On the Richter scale it was nine. The shaking lasted 47 seconds. The fires burned for three full days. 28,000 buildings were destroyed. Half the people lost their homes. By 1915 rebuilding of the city was complete.

the American economy. Japan and China combined are still worth less than the U.S.'s 2010 GDP of $14.66 trillion. But the news marks the end of an era. For nearly two generations, since overtaking West Germany in 1967, Japan stood solidly as the world's No. 2 economy. The new rankings symbolize China's rise and Japan's decline as global growth engines.

Japan has one tenth or less of China's massive population and one 25th of the latter's land area, but it has led China in its total economic output for a long period of time

Museveni Reelected President

Uganda President, Yoweri Museveni, of the ruling National Resistance Movement party won the Presidential election according to the election results declared on 20 February 2011. He defeated the opposition candidate Kizza Besigya. Yoweri Musevni won 68 percent of the votes while Kizza Besigya could manage only 26 percent of the votes. The election in Uganda was participated by 59 percent of voters. The opposition parties along with the foreign election observers alleged that the voting process was rigged in favour of Yoweri Museveni.

Museveni

Uganda is an oil-rich country with an estimated 2.5 billion barrels of oil reserves. Uganda is East Africa,s third-biggest economy after Kenya and Tanzania.

Earthquake, Tsunami and Nuclear Crisis

On March 11, 2011, an earthquake struck off the coast of Japan, churning up a devastating tsunami that caused wide scale destruction and loss of thousands of lives. Cars, ships

Japan Earthquake

and buildings were all swept away by the rampaging waters of the tsunami which struck about 400km (250 miles) north-east of Tokyo. The port city of Sendai in Miyagi prefecture was one of the worst affected. Ten metre waves struck the city deluging everything that was part of it-farmlands, cars, buildings, houses etc.

Recorded as 9.0 on the Richter scale, it was the most powerful quake ever to hit the country. As the nation struggled with a rescue effort, it also faced the worst nuclear emergency since Chernobyl; explosions and leaks of radioactive gas took place in three reactors at the Fukushima Daiichi Nuclear Power Station that suffered partial meltdowns, while spent fuel rods at another reactor overheated and caught fire, releasing radioactive material directly into the atmosphere. Japanese officials turned to increasingly desperate measures, as traces of radiation were found in Tokyo's water and in water pouring from the reactors into the ocean.

The National Police Agency has confirmed 15,787 deaths, 5,932 injured, and 4,059 people missing across eighteen prefectures. Of the 13,135 fatalities recovered by 11 April 2011, 12,143 or 92.5% died by drowning. Victims aged 60 or older accounted for 65.2% of the deaths, with 24% of total victims being in their 70s.

Adieu Liz Taylor

Dame Elizabeth Taylor, one of the 20th Century's biggest movie stars, died in Los Angeles at the age of 79. The double Oscar-winning actress had a long history of ill health and

What Causes a Tsunami?	A tsunami is a large ocean wave that is caused by sudden motion on the ocean floor. This sudden motion could be an earthquake, a powerful volcanic eruption, or an underwater landslide. The impact of a large meteorite could also cause a tsunami.

Elizabeth Taylor

was being treated for symptoms of congestive heart failure.

Taylor is iconic for being one of the most popular actresses of Hollywood's golden age. Taylor was born in London in 1932 to American parents who returned to the U.S. with World War II looming. She bounded into the spotlight at age 12 after starring in the 1944 box office sensation "National Velvet." She won acclaim as an adult with 1951's "A Place In The Sun" and went on to score best actress Oscar nominations for "Raintree County," "Cat on a Hot Tin Roof," and "Suddenly, Last Summer."

In 1963, she memorably starred in "Cleopatra." She later won Oscars for "Who's Afraid of Virginia Woolf?" and "Butterfield 8."

She was equally well-known for her glamour and film partnership with Richard Burton, one of seven husbands. She met the actor while filming 1963's *Cleopatra* - which became notorious as one of the most expensive films of all time, but which also sparked one of Hollywood's greatest romances. Taylor had already been married four times - to Conrad Hilton Jr, Michael Wilding, Michael Todd and Eddie Fisher - before she wed Burton in 1964. Their tempestuous relationship saw them divorce and remarry in 1975 before she moved on to further marriages with John W Warner and Larry Fortensky.

Beyond acting, Taylor is credited with bringing the world's attention to AIDS with her fund-raising and activism. In 1985, when Taylor's lifelong friend Rock Hudson died of AIDS, she brought national attention to the growing disease. She raised and donated millions of dollars to the cause, founding the American Foundation for AIDS Research (amfAR) and The Elizabeth Taylor AIDS Foundation.

Fidel Castro Steps Down

Former Cuban President Fidel Castro resigned his role as secretary of Cuba's Communist Party in April 2011. Castro began transferring control to his brother Raul in July 2006, when he underwent intestinal surgery, and officially stepped down as president in 2008. For the first time in more than 50 years, Fidel Castro does not hold a position in the Cuban government.

Some 1,000 delegates of Cuba's Communist Party named the ailing 84-year-old's younger brother, Raul, 79, the party's first

Fidel Castro

secretary following Castro's stepping down.

The party appointed Jose Machado Ventura, 80, as first vice president of Cuba's Council of State. Should Raul step down, Ventura would be first in line to replace him. The third spot went to Ramiro Valdes, 78. All three men fought in Cuba's 1959 revolution, which helped oust U.S.-backed dictator Fulgencio Batista and put Fidel Castro in power.

Castro and his colleagues established a communist, atheist state just 90 miles from America. He has been a thorn in the side of American presidents for more than half a century.

Prince William Marries Commoner

Prince William, second-in-line to the British throne, wed his long-term girlfriend Kate Middleton at London's Westminster Abbey on April 29, 2011 in a royal occasion of dazzling pomp and pageantry.

William, 28, and Middleton, 29, exchanged vows before nearly 2,000 guests in the abbey and a television and internet audience of millions.

| Liz Taylor and Oscar | The first three times Elizabeth Taylor was nominated, Oscar jilted her for other lead actresses. However she presented the Oscar trophy for best picture three times: "Midnight Cowboy" (1969), "The Sting" (1973) and "The Silence of the Lambs" (1991). |

Satellite Plunges into Pacific

The Upper Atmosphere Research Satellite (UARS) is the biggest NASA spacecraft to crash back to Earth, uncontrolled, since the post-Apollo, 75-ton Skylab space station and the more than 10-ton Pegasus 2 satellite, both in 1979. Skylab was about 15 times heavier than UARS. Russia's 135-ton Mir space station slammed through the atmosphere in 2001, but it was a controlled dive into the Pacific. Early on 24 September, NASA's dead six-ton UARS, launched on September 15, 1991, by the space shuttle Discovery, made its fiery death and plunged into the vast Pacific Ocean. The satellite fell sometime between 11:23 pm EDT and 1:09 am EDT.

Upper Atmosphere Research Satellite

The Immediate Factor

According to experts, a recent expansion in the Earth's atmosphere due to heating by ultraviolet radiation has been

The path of falling debris

causing UARS to fall to Earth faster than expected. The expansion increases the atmospheric drag on satellites in space, hastening re-entry. The US satellite was deployed with a mission to study the make-up of Earth's atmosphere, particularly its protective ozone layer.

Monitoring the Fall

Scientists used a specially designed camera to record the tumbling satellite through a 14-inch telescope. They identified 26 separate pieces of the satellite - representing 600 Kg, of heavy metal. The debris came down like a rain of fire. The biggest surviving chunk weighed about 200 Kgs. In 2005, NASA commanded the satel-

lite to burn its remaining fuel, lowering its orbit for an eventual suicide dive into the atmosphere. The satellite's operational orbit had an altitude of 600 kilometres.

Chances of Hurt

The US Air Force's Joint Space Operations Center and NASA reported that the 11-metre bus-sized satellite first penetrated Earth's atmosphere somewhere over the Pacific Ocean. NASA had predicted that UARS would fall over a 800-kilometre swath. So far, no one has ever been hit by a falling space junk and NASA expected that not to change. Nasa estimated earlier the chances of somebody on Earth to get hurt was 1-in-3,200. The 1 in 3,200 risk to public safety is higher than the 1 in 10,000 limit fixed earlier. Given the 7 billion people on the planet earth, any one person's odds of being

The burning debris at re-entry

struck were estimated at 1-in-22 trillion. UARS' fall was calculated to land anywhere between 57 degrees north and 57 degrees south of the equator - most of the populated world.

The Royal couple

They were formally declared married by the Archbishop of Canterbury Rowan Williams, the spiritual leader of the Church of England.

Middleton is the first "commoner" to marry a prince in proximity to the throne in over 350 years. The couple will be known as the Duke and Duchess of Cambridge.

John Paul II on Way to Sainthood

The late pope John Paul II was beatified in a three-hour ceremony on Ist May, 2011 in the biggest event hosted by the Vatican since two million people attended his funeral in 2005. The former pope is now just one stage – canonisation – away from full sainthood.

An estimated 1.5 million people flocked to St Peter's Square to watch Pope Benedict XVI declare his Polish predecessor "blessed" in a display of religious pomp watched on television and the Internet by millions around the world.

The Pope approved the beatification, the fastest in modern times, after Vatican experts ruled that the "miraculous" recovery of a French nun from Parkinson's disease was attributable to John Paul's intercession from beyond the grave. The search is now on for a

second miracle that, after scrutiny by doctors and Vatican theologians, would enable the Polish pontiff to be canonized.

John Paul's millions of admirers remember him for his charisma, his survival of an assassination attempt in 1981 and his pivotal role in challenging Communism during the Cold War.

Under normal Roman Catholic Church rules, five years must pass after a person dies before the procedure for sainthood can even begin, but the Pope can waive the five-year waiting period. Pope Benedict put John Paul II on the fast track in May 2005, just two months after his predecessor died. He was responding to the Polish pontiff's enormous popularity.

Pope John Paul II

Osama bin Laden Killed by U.S.

Osama bin Laden, the mastermind of the most devastating attack on American soil in modern times, was killed in an operation codenamed 'Operation Geronimo' by United States Navy Seals in Abbottabad, a military cantonment town not far from Islamabad on May 2, 2011.

American military and C.I.A. operatives finally cornered Bin Laden, the leader of Al Qaeda, who had eluded them for nearly a decade. The end came when U.S. forces in helicopters attacked a large walled compound where Osama and some of his family members were said to be hiding. American officials said Bin Laden resisted and was shot

Duma for 'Thought'	Before the 1905 revolution, political parties of any kind had been illegal in Russia. Russia's first truly representative legislature body convened in 1906, with 513 deputies. The name Imperial Duma came from the Russian word for 'thought'.

The International Year of Cooperatives

The United Nations General Assembly has declared 2012 as the International Year of Cooperatives, highlighting the contribution of cooperatives to socio-economic development. In adopting resolution 64/136, the Assembly noted that cooperatives impact poverty reduction, employment generation and social integration. IYC 2012 aims at giving the co-operative sector and governments a chance to: (a) increase public awareness on combining societal, economic and environmental objetives (b) promote growth and sustainability; establish appropriate policies and (c) create legacy initiatives that will go beyond 2012

What is a Cooperative?

A cooperative is an autonomous voluntary association of people who unite to meet common economic, social and cultural needs and aspirations, through a jointly owned and democratically controlled enterprise. In general, they contribute to socio-economic development. In the informal economy, workers have formed shared service cooperatives and associations to assist in their self-employment. In rural areas, savings and credit cooperatives provide access to banking services that are lacking in many communities and finance the formation of small and micro businesses, promotes inclusive finance.

The cooperative sector worldwide has about 800 million members in over 100 countries and is estimated to account for more than 100 million jobs around the world. The strength and reach of cooperatives are illustrated in the following examples: • under the umbrella of the World Council of Credit Unions, 49,000 credit unions serve 177 million members in 96 countries, and 4,200 banks under the European Association of Cooperative Banks serve 149 million clients; • agricultural cooperatives account for 80 to 99% of milk production in Norway, New Zealand and the United States; 71% of fishery production in the Republic of Korea; and 40% of agriculture in Brazil; • electric cooperatives play a key role in rural areas. In Bangladesh, rural electric cooperatives serve 28 million people. In the United States, 900 rural electric cooperatives serve 37 million people and own almost half of the electric distribution lines in the country.

Cooperatives in India

The cooperative movement in India owes its origin to agriculture and allied sectors. The number of all types of co-operatives increased from 1.81 lakh in 1950-51 to 4.53 lakh in 1996-97. The total membership of cooperative societies increased from 1.55 crore to 20.45 crore during the same period. The cooperatives are functional in various areas of the economy such as credit, production, processing, marketing, input distribution, housing, dairying and textiles. In some of the areas of their activities like dairying, urban banking and housing, sugar and handlooms, the cooperatives have achieved success to an extent but there are larger areas where they have not been so successful. The failure of cooperatives is mainly due to: dormant membership and lack of active participation of members in the management, mounting overdues in cooperative credit institution, lack of mobilisation of internal resources and over-dependence on Government assistance, lack of professional management. bureaucratic control and interference in the management, and over-politisation have proved harmful to their growth.

Osama bin Laden

in the head. He was later buried at sea.

For over two decades, Bin Laden has been Al Qaeda's leader and symbol. The death of Bin Laden marks the most significant achievement to date in Americ a's effort to defeat Al Qaeda.

The whereabouts of Ayman al-Zawahri, Al Qaeda's second-in-command, were unclear.

Bin Laden's death came nearly 10 years after Qaeda terrorists hijacked four American passenger jets, crashing three of them into the World Trade Center in New York and the Pentagon outside Washington. The fourth hijacked jet, United Flight 93, crashed into the Pennsylvania countryside after passengers fought the militants.

Harper Reelected PM

Prime Minister Stephen Harper's Conservative party recorded a decisive win in Canada's fourth federal election in seven years, taking 167 of the 308 seats in the lower chamber, the House of Commons. However, the biggest surprise was the humiliation suffered by the Liberal Party, long regarded as Canada's natural party of government. Under the ex-academic Michael Ignatieff, the Liberals slumped from 77 to 34 seats, losing several in their traditional

Stephen Harper

Ontario stronghold. The leader even failed to win his own constituency, or riding as it is called in Canada. Other shocks included the meltdown of the separatist Bloc Québécois (BQ), which lost 43 of its 47 seats. Further, the elections also produced the country's first Green MP, Elizabeth May. The election was necessitated when Mr. Harper's government was ousted by a vote of no confidence on March 26.

With this electoral outcome, Canadians will probably see more private sector involvement in their highly reputed national health service. Other likely developments are lower corporate taxes and more oil-drilling in environmentally sensitive areas. The new government may also relax some of the financial regulations that have enabled Canada to weather the global recession better than most countries.

Queen Visits Ireland

Queen Elizabeth II became the first British monarch to visit Ireland for a century when she made a historic state visit to the country in May, 2011.

Her grandfather George V was the last King to visit in 1911 before the Republic had secured independence. Relations between Westminster and Dublin have improved dramatically since the historic Good Friday Northern Ireland peace agreement in 1998 .

English monarchs dating back to Henry II had sought to add Ireland to their domain. Ireland was a running sore for English troops throughout the reign of the Tudors. James I had settled thousands of Protestants in Ulster, to the north of the island, with the result that the county is majority Protestant while the rest of Ireland is majority Catholic. That fact has complicated the bloody history of Ireland ever since.

Ireland has been the venue of numerous rebellions against Great Britain, climaxing in the Easter uprising of 1916 and the subsequent war that finally created an independent Ireland in the south, while Ulster

Olympiads

The ancient Greek Olympic Games were held every four years. The first recorded festival was held in 77 BCE. They were combined patriotic, religious and athletic festivals. The Greeks began to keep their calendar by 'Olympiads' or 4-year spans between the games.

Apple Maker Fades

Apple made technology safe for cool people—and ordinary people. It made products that worked, beautifully, without fuss and with a great deal of style. They improved markedly, unmistakably, in simplicity. For instance, press the single button on the face of the iPad and, whether you are five or 95, you can begin using it with almost no instruction. It has no manual. No geeks required.

Alma Mater: Reed College, Portland, Oregon (did only one semester) 1972.
1976: Steve, 21, started Apple, in his family-garage, with Steve Wozniak, 26, produced Apple I computer
1984: Produced Apple Macintosh
1985: Forced out of Apple; Steve launches NeXT Computers.
1986: Buys computer graphics division of Lucasfilm Ltd, Studios for $10 M,

Titan in three major industries: computers, movies and music

The Person: He was introduced to computers at the age of 12 at Hewlett Packard. He loved calligraphy. He was dyslexic. He embraced the hippie lifestyle, drugs, and Zen. He became a vegetarian. His dress code: black sweatshirt, Levi blue jeans (owns over 100), Sneaker size – 14. His Id card : Steve Jobs, Employee No. 0. He made lot of blunders that caused huge losses.
Lived: 24 Feb 1955 to 05-Oct-2011
Net Worth: $ 8.3billion
Apple Market Share - (2009) - 5.11%. Units sold in Jan 2010: 3.3 M
Positions: Chairman, Apple Inc.: Board Member of the Walt Disney and
Annual Salary as Apple CEO: $1
Annual income from Disney shares: $48 M.
Forbes rating: 136th richest man in 2010, net worth $ 5.5B
Biological mother: Joanne Schieble
Biological father: Abdulfattah Jandali, a Syrian immigrant (who never met Jobs).
Adoptive Parents: Paul and Clara Jobs
Spouse: Laurene Powell Jobs
Children: Lisa, Reed, Erin and Eve
Biological/adoptive sister: Mona/Patti

which became Pixar Animation. He was credited in Toy Story (1995) as an executive producer.
1991: Apple Powerbook released
1993: Apple Newton Messagepad introduced but failed.
1996: Apple purchases NeXT
1997: Steve returns to Apple
1998: Introduces iMac, half-egg shaped in fluroscent colours
2001: launches iBook – Apple's laptop; Introduced the hip personal music player called iPod; opens first ever Apple Store outlet.
2003: iTunes Music Store opens
2006: Mac OS X; sold Pixar to Walt Disney and became Disney's largest individual shareholder at 7% and a member of Disney's Board of Directors.
2007: launches the revolutionary smartphone –all-touch iPhone, new iMacs
2010: Apple ushers in the tablet era and redefines computing with the launch of iPad, iPhone 4 & iPad 2
2011: Steve jobs suggests Tim Cook to be the next Apple CEO and steps down; Jobs died on 05 Oct 2011

Queen Elizabeth II with Irish president Mary McAelese

remained part of Great Britain. The struggle over Ulster sparked a decades long war of terrorism and counter terrorism that led to the uneasy peace accord hammered out in the 1990s. The queen's own uncle by marriage, Lord Mountbatten, was murdered by IRA terrorists.

The queen's visit to Ireland was meant to illustrate a new, far friendlier relationship between Great Britain and Ireland. Hordes of Britons visit Ireland every year as tourists. Irish avidly watch British television and shop in British chain stores.

Mladic Arrested

After more than 15 years in hiding, onetime Bosnian Serb commander Ratko Mladic was arrested on 26 May, 2011. Mladic was the highest-ranking fugitive to remain at large after the conflicts that accompanied the breakup of Yugoslavia in the 1990s. His arrest followed a three-year investigation.

The former Yugoslav army officer was the commanding general of Bosnian Serb forces during the 1992-95 war that followed Bosnia-Herzegovina's secession from Yugoslavia. The International Criminal Tribunal for the former Yugoslavia has charged him

with leading a genocidal campaign against Bosnia's Muslim and Croat populations, including "direct involvement" in the 1995 killings of nearly 8,000 men and boys in the Muslim enclave of Srebrenica -- the worst European massacre since the Holocaust.

Mladic is accused of leading a campaign of "ethnic cleansing," widespread killing, forcible deportations, torture, forced labor and physical, psychological and sexual violence during the Bosnian war.

Mladic had been on the run since the Bosnian war ended in 1995. Mladic was the last fugitive from a triumvirate of Serbian leaders accused of genocide against Muslims and Croats as the three populations fought a brutal war over Yugoslav territory.

Former Yugoslav President Slobodan Milosevic was toppled in 2000 and sent to face charges in The Hague, but he died in 2006 while the trial was still going on. Bosnian Serb leader Radovan Karadzic was

Ratko Mladic

arrested in July 2008 and is now on trial in The Hague.

The Bosnian war was the longest of the conflicts spawned by the breakup of Yugoslavia in the early 1990s. Backed by the Milosevic government, Bosnian Serb forces seized control of more than half the country and launched a campaign against the Muslim and Croat populations.

The United Nations declared Srebrenica to be a safe haven, and tens of thousands of Bosnian Muslims flooded in, expecting protection. But a small contingent of Dutch

---

Marconi and Radio

Radio is the short form of radiotelegraphy, the age of which opened in 1901. Inventor Guglielmo Marconi picked up the first ever signal transmitted across the Atlantic Ocean. He opened the first commercial transatlantic service with stations in Ireland and Nova Scotia.

U.N. peacekeepers, lightly armed and aware that no reinforcements were coming, stood aside and allowed Mladic's troops to overrun Srebrenica, leading to the slaughter.

NATO intervened in the conflict, bombing Bosnian Serb military positions. The United States brought the leaders of the warring factions to an agreement in Dayton, Ohio, in 1995, bringing the violence to an end.

Strauss-Kahn in Sex Scandal

Dominique Strauss-Kahn, once considered a leading contender to win the French presidency in 2012, resigned as head of the International Monetary Fund after

being charged with attempting to rape a New York hotel maid.

Strauss-Kahn's risignation reshaped the race for the French presidency, eliminating President Nicolas Sarkozy's biggest rival. His resigna-

Dominique Strauss-Kahn

tion from the IMF, came more than 17 months before his term was scheduled to end.

The IMF chief was charged with criminal sexual act, attempted rape, sexual abuse, unlawful imprisonment and forcible touching, according to court papers. However, Strauss-Kahn became a free man three months after his formal indictment when a New York State Supreme Court judge ended the sexual assault case against him at the request of prosecutors, who said the hotel maid who accused the former IMF chief couldn't be trusted.

Though evidence showed Strauss-Kahn had a sexual encounter with Nafissatou Diallo in his hotel suite, prosecutors said the accuser was not credible because of lies she had told, including an earlier false rape claim.

The case drew global attention and left both the accuser and the accused with tattered reputations.

Strauss-Kahn was chosen in 2007 to a five-year IMF term in keeping with an informal agreement under which a European heads the fund while an American leads the World Bank. The World Bank saw its own chief resign when former U.S. Deputy Defense Secretary Paul Wolfowitz quit in May 2007 after controversy over his role in a pay increase for his companion.

Strauss-Kahn took the helm of the IMF in November 2007, following his loss in the primaries of his French Socialist Party ahead of the 2007 presidential elections.

Strauss-Kahn, who succeeded Spain's Rodrigo Rato, helped reshape the agency's mission and restore its relevance. When he arrived, its emergency lending dropped to $58.7 million in 2006 from $66.4 billion in 2002. Among his first moves there was to cut about 400 jobs.

The global financial panic triggered by the bankruptcy of Lehman Brothers Holdings Inc. in September 2008 restored the IMF's relevance as its emergency loans soared to a record of $91.7 billion in 2010 from $1.1 billion in 2007.

Germany to be Nuclear-free by 2022

Germany's cabinet on 6 June 2011 approved a series of laws to phase out all its nuclear plants by 2022. The measures include a massive increase of onshore and offshore wind power, the accelerated expansion of the electricity grid, and more gas-fired

Nuclear Weapons

More than 40 nations have the knowledge or technology needed to produce nuclear weapons.

generation capacity. This decision, prompted by Japan's Fukushima nuclear disaster, will make Germany the first major industrialized nation to go nuclear-free.

The cabinet agreed a gradual phase-out from nuclear power, with one of its 17 nuclear power stations each being switched off in 2015, 2017 and 2019, and three each in 2021 and 2022.

Another seven reactors, which German Chancellor Angela Merkel ordered be temporarily shut in March following the disasters at the nuclear reactors in Fukushima, Japan, are to stay switched off. An eighth plant that had been off the grid for a review will also remain shut.

People of Germany are strongly opposed to nuclear power and took to streets after Fukushima to urge the government to shut down all reactors as soon as possible.

Germany relies on nuclear power for some 23 per cent of its energy needs. Germany is determined to replace its nuclear power with renewable energy resources. In 2000 30% of electricity came from nuclear. Since then, renewables like solar and wind have expanded their share from 6.65 to 16.5%.

Now, Yinluck Shinawatra Leads Thailand

Thailand's Parliament elected Yingluck Shinawatra the country's first female prime minister, a month after her party won a landslide victory over a coalition backed by the nation's military and traditional elites. Ms. Yingluck, 44, a political novice, received 296 votes in the 500-seat Parliament, a reflection of her party's comfortable majority.

She is the youngest sister of Thaksin Shinawatra, the prime minister ousted in a 2006 military coup. Mr. Thaksin, who now lives in Dubai, evading a jail term in Thailand for abuse of power, looms large as the kingmaker and impresario of the administration and his sister's Pheu Thai Party.

Ms. Yingluck has a very hard task delivering on her party's ambitious promises: a sharp increase in the minimum wage, the construction of high-speed rail lines,

Yinluck Shinawatra

providing free tablet computers to primary school students, and revamping the country's health care system, among many others.

But her greatest challenge may be piecing together Thailand's fractured society, a task that eluded the four governments that came after the 2006 coup. Ms. Yingluck has repeatedly sought to assuage the Thai military, which increased its political clout in the years after the coup.

Pheu Thai won the July 3 election thanks to strong support from the north and northeastern parts of the country, where Mr. Thaksin's policies — universal health care, a crackdown on drugs and greater financing for local governments — proved very popular.

The losing Democrat Party is the oldest in Thailand and is generally supported by old-money business owners and the current military hierarchy. But such alliances are often fungible, and Ms. Yingluck appears to be forging her own with some members of the elite.

The victory of Ms. Yingluck and her party has nonetheless sharpened divisions between rural and urban areas and started a debate over the significance of a woman leading the country.

Ms. Yingluck is a rarity in the often macho world of Thai politics, but as someone who has never held political office before she is also one of the least experienced leaders to emerge in a major Asian country in decades.

When Pheu Thai named her as a candidate for prime minister, she was urged on by her brother. Some supporters also saw the election as a chance to send a protest message to the military and traditional elite, which had backed the departing coalition and was perceived as applying undue influence

| Morocco and AU | Morocco is not a member of the African Union. It left the OAU (former name of AU) when it admitted Western Saharan (Sahrawi) Arab Demo. Rep., a territory claimed by Morocco. |

behind the scenes.

Ms. Yingluck's professional career began at her brother's business empire — first at a company that produced telephone directories, then at AIS, the cellular phone company, and finally a real estate company. Analysts say her brother's perceived influence is likely to dog her tenure as prime minister.

Birth of a Nation

On July 9, 2011, South Sudan became the world's newest country after a tumultuous

South Sudanese
celebrate independence

independence struggle of more than 50 years that cost more than 3 million lives.

What is now South Sudan was part of the British and Egyptian condominium of Anglo-Egyptian Sudan and became part of the Republic of the Sudan when independence was achieved in 1956. Following the First Sudanese Civil War, the Southern Sudan Autonomous Region was formed in 1972 and lasted until 1983. A second Sudanese civil war soon developed and ended with the Comprehensive Peace Agreement of 2005. Later that year, southern autonomy was restored when an Autonomous Government of Southern Sudan was formed.

South Sudan has been negatively affected by the two civil wars since Sudanese independence, resulting in serious neglect, lack of infrastructural development, and major destruction and displacement. More than 2.5 million people have been killed, and more than 5 million have become externally

displaced while others have been internally displaced, becoming refugees as a result of the civil war and war-related impacts.

A referendum was held from 9 to 15 January 2011 to determine if South Sudan should declare its independence from Sudan, with 98.83% of the population voting for independence. The results for that referendum were released on 30 January 2011. Those living in the north and expatriates living overseas also voted.This led to a formal independence on 9 July, although certain disputes still remain such as sharing of the oil revenues as an estimated 80% of the oil in the nation is secured from South Sudan, which would represent amazing economic potential for one of the world's most deprived areas. The region of Abyei still remains disputed and a separate referendum will be held in Abyei on whether they want to join North or South Sudan.

South Sudan remains one of the poorest and least developed places on Earth. A girl in South Sudan is three times as likely to die in childbirth as to become literate. Even for those students who are in school, there is only one textbook for every four children. At least three-quarters of the country is illiterate, and there are significant ethnic tensions within the south. Corruption and mismanagement are huge problems in the South.

Mass Murder in Norway

The myth that the Scandinavian countries are immune to terrorism was shattered when Norway was rocked by two sequential terrorist attacks against the government and the civilian population on 22 July 2011. The first was a car bomb explosion in Oslo within Regjeringskvartalet, the executive government quarter of Norway .The car bomb was placed outside the office of Prime Minister Jens Stoltenberg and other government buildings.The explosion killed eight people and wounded several others, with more than 10 people critically injured.

The second attack occurred less than two hours later at a summer camp on the island

A Merchant of Death

Alfred Nobel was an industrialist and the inventor of dynamite. A newspaper mistakenly printed his obituary calling him a 'merchant of death'. The very much alive Nobel grew obsessed with leaving a legacy of peace. This gave rise to the birth of Nobel Prizes.

Anders Behring Breivik

of Utøya in Tyrifjorden, Buskerud. The camp was organized by AUF, the youth division of the ruling Norwegian Labour Party (AP). A gunman disguised as a policeman opened fire at the participants, killing 69 attendees.

The gunman is reported to have been armed with a handgun, an automatic weapon and a shotgun. He travelled on the ferry boat from the mainland over to that little inland island posing as a police officer, saying he was there to do research in connection with the bomb blasts.

The Norwegian Police Service arrested Anders Behring Breivik, a 32-year-old Norwegian with "right-wing sympathies" for the mass shootings on Utøya and subsequently charged him with both attacks.

U.S. Loses AAA Credit Rating

The ratings agency Standard & Poor's downgraded the U.S.'s AAA credit rating for the first time, slamming the nation's political process and criticizing lawmakers for failing to cut spending or raise revenue enough to reduce record budget deficits. The rating may be cut to AA within two years if spending reductions are lower than agreed to, interest rates rise or "new fiscal pressures" result in higher general government debt, the New York-based firm said.

Lawmakers agreed on Aug. 2 to raise the nation's $14.3 trillion debt ceiling and put in place a plan to enforce $2.4 trillion in spending reductions over the next 10 years, less than the $4 trillion S&P had said it preferred.

Moody's Investors Service and Fitch Ratings affirmed their AAA credit ratings on Aug. 2, the day President Barack Obama signed a bill that ended the debt-ceiling impasse that pushed the Treasury to the edge of default. Moody's and Fitch also said that downgrades were possible if lawmakers fail to enact debt reduction measures and the economy weakens.

Policy makers from China to Japan to Southeast Asia are lured to Treasuries as a result of efforts to stem gains in their currencies against the dollar, which would impair export competitiveness. China has accumulated $1.16 trillion in the securities and the nation's official Xinhua News Agency

said in a commentary that the U.S. must cure its "addiction" to borrowing.

S&P's action may hurt the U.S. economy over time by increasing the cost of mortgages, auto loans and other types of lending tied to the interest rates paid on Treasuries. JPMorgan Chase & Co. estimated that a downgrade would raise the nation's borrowing costs by $100 billion a year. The U.S. spent $414 billion on interest expense in fiscal 2010, or 2.7 percent of gross domestic product, according to Treasury Department data.

S&P put the U.S. government on notice on April 18 that it risked losing the AAA rating it had since 1941 unless lawmakers agreed on a plan by 2013 to reduce budget deficits and the national debt. It indicated that anything less than $4 trillion in cuts would jeopardize the rating.

The treatment of Treasuries and other

The Great Chilean Earthquake — The World's largest earthquake with an instrumentally documented magnitude occurred on May 22, 1960 near Valdivia, in southern Chile. It has been assigned a magnitude of 9.5 by the US Geological Survey. It is referred to as the "Great Chilean Earthquake".

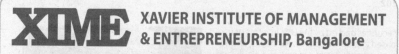

securities backed by the U.S. in terms of risk-based capital weightings for banks, savings associations, credit unions and bank and savings and loan companies won't change, the Federal Reserve and bank regulators said in a statement following the downgrade.

The U.S. currency's portion of global currency reserves dropped to 60.7 percent in the period ended March 31, from a peak of 72.7 percent in 2001, data from the International Monetary Fund in Washington show.

Riots in London

London was rocked by the worst riots in its history for decades in August , 2011. The immediate trigger for the riots was the fatal shooting by police of a 29-year-old man named Mark Duggan, an alleged crack cocaine dealer and member of the 'Star Gang'.

Duggan was shot dead during a planned arrest on 4 August 2011 on the Ferry Lane bridge, next to Tottenham Hale station. The incident was referred to the Independent Police Complaints Commission (IPCC), which is standard practice whenever a member of the public dies as a result of police action. It is not yet known why police were attempting to arrest Duggan, but the IPCC said that the planned arrest was part of Operation Trident, a unit which investigates gun crime in London. Operation Trident specialises in combating gun crime relating to the illegal drug trade. Friends and relatives of Duggan claimed that he was unarmed. The IPCC stated that Duggan was carrying a loaded handgun, and that there was no evidence that Duggan shot at the police.

Following a peaceful march on 6 August 2011 in relation to the police response to the fatal shooting of Mark Duggan, a riot began in Tottenham, North London. In the following days, rioting spread to several London boroughs and districts and eventually to some other areas of England, with the most severe disturbances outside London occurring in Bristol and cities in the Midlands and North West of England. Related localised outbreaks also occurred in many smaller towns and cities in England.

The riots were characterised by rampant looting and arson attacks of unprecedented levels. As of 15 August, about 3,100 people had been arrested, of whom more than 1,000 had been charged. There were a total 3,443 crimes across London linked to the disorder.

Five people died and at least 16 others were injured as a direct result of related violent acts. An estimated £200 million worth of property damage was incurred, and local economic activity was significantly compromised.

Police action was blamed for the initial riot, and the subsequent police reaction was criticised as being neither appropriate nor sufficiently effective. The riots have generated significant ongoing debate among political, social and academic figures about the causes and context in which they happened.

Murdoch's Media Empire in Trouble

Rupert Murdock's News International was engulfed by a huge scandal that has shaken the very foundation of his media empire. The scandal arose with the finding that The News of the World (NoW) had been illicitly hacking into the voicemail messages of prominent people to find stories. The NoW was published by News Group Newspapers, part of News International, which is a subsidiary of Rupert Murdoch's News Corporation. It admitted intercepting voicemails in April after years of rumour that the practice

Corruption Index 2010	Denmark, New Zealand and Singapore are the cleanest, according to Corruption Index 2010 released by Transparency International. Somalia is the most corrupt (1.1). Denmark scored 9.3 and India 3.3.

Rupert Murdock

was widespread, and amid intense pressure from those who believed they had been victims.

One NoW journalist, royal editor Clive Goodman, was jailed for four months in January 2007, while private investigator Glenn Mulcaire was jailed for six months, after admitting intercepting voicemail messages on royal aides' phones. Police have a list of 4,000 possible targets. Among them are celebrities, sport stars, politicians and victims of crime. They include actor Hugh Grant, publicist Max Clifford, comedian Steve Coogan, actress Sienna Miller, Lord Prescott, London Mayor Boris Johnson, football pundit Andy Gray and ex-footballer Paul Gascoigne.

The paper ceased publication on 10 July 2011 after fresh allegations that it had hacked into the voicemail messages of the murdered teenager Millie Dowler and deleted voice messages from her phone which may have led the police and her parents into believing that she was alive. The final edition signed off with headline "Thank you and goodbye" and included an apology.

Rebekah Brooks, editor of the NoW at the time of the alleged hacking of Milly Dowler's phone, was forced to resign from her job as chief executive of News International. Les Hinton, one of the top executives of Rupert Murdoch's News Corporation, also quit.

On 19 July 2011, Rupert Murdoch, James Murdoch and Rebekah Brooks gave evidence to the House of Commons Culture, Media and Sport Select Committee and denied knowing the full extent of the allegations until evidence in civil cases was requested in late 2010. Rupert Murdoch said he had "clearly" been misled by some of his staff, while James Murdoch said the company was "determined to put things right". James Murdoch also told the committee he had

not been "aware" of an email suggesting hacking went beyond a single "rogue" reporter. Two former News of the World executives later issued a statement claiming they had informed him of the email but Mr Murdoch responded by saying he stands by his testimony.

Several cases have been settled in the courts. Sienna Miller won £100,000 damages and Andy Gray received £20,000. Max Clifford brought a private case and received a reported settlement of £700,000. Other victims are awaiting the outcome of police investigations or have also launched legal action.

China's Rail Tragedy

On 23 July 2011, two high-speed trains travelling on the Yongtaiwen railway line collided on a viaduct in the suburbs of Wenzhou,

Zhejiang Province, China. The two trains derailed each other, and four cars fell off the viaduct. 40 people were killed.

Congratulatory afterglow of the successful launch of a high-speed railway between Beijing and Shanghai was still in evidence in China when the tragedy occured. The impact of the collision on the authority of the ruling Communist Party was profound. The goverment's immediate decision to freeze approval of new high-speed rail projects showed just how seriously Beijing was now taking the tragedy.

The high-speed rail project was one of the

largest recipients of the trillions of yuan made available by the Chinese government for pump-priming projects after the economic crisis of 2008. It symbolised China's success at innovation and was a leader in its efforts to modernise and showcase its engineering skills. But the project has been dogged by corruption. Rail minister Liu Zhijun was dismissed earlier amid an investigation into unspecified corruption allegations.

The government had also misjudged the public's reaction to the crash and to Beijing's inept handling of the fallout. Premier Wen Jiabao was forced into making a public statement that he was too ill to visit the accident scene. Known as "Grandpa Wen" for his comforting appearances at times of national stress, Mr Wen later promised a full and frank investigation into the crash but the damage had been done.

Violence in Karachi

Karachi, Pakistan's commercial capital, was under the grip of ethnic warfare in 2011. Karachi's ethnic wars claimed more tha 1,000 lives in the first eight months of 2011 alone. By contrast the Taliban and other religious extremists kill tiny numbers in Karachi.

A grisly new feature of the carnage was that people were not just being shot. They were being abducted and tortured; then their bullet-ridden, mutilated bodies were dumped in sacks and left in alleyways and gutters. Victims' limbs, genitals or heads were often severed. Torture cells operate across Karachi. The butchery was filmed on mobile phones and passed around, spreading the

terror further. Most victims were ordinary folk randomly targeted for their ethnicity.

A notable feature of the turf war is that each gang has the patronage of a mainstream political party, in a fight that exploded in 2008 when an election was held to end Pakistan's latest period of military rule. Political support for warring ethnic gangs means the police largely stay out of the conflict: each gang will call on political muscle if its henchmen are rounded up.

The Muttahida Qaumi Movement (MQM), a party established in the 1980s that claims to represent the Mohajirs, once had an iron grip over Karachi. That monopoly is now being challenged by the Awami National Party, which says it speaks for the ethnic Pushtun population, who migrated from the north-west of the country, and the Pakistan Peoples Party (PPP) of President Asif Zardari, which heads the ruling coalition in the capital, Islamabad. Its gang following is ethnic Baloch, from the neighbouring province of Balochistan. It is the MQM versus the rest.

The conflict's ferocity may yet threaten Pakistan's fragile return to democracy. Violence in Karachi was repeatedly used as part of the justification for toppling four national governments in the 1990s. This city of 18m people is Pakistan's economic lifeline, and the port through which most supplies reach NATO forces in Afghanistan.

For more than two decades the MQM has collected extortion money, known as bata, from businesses and homes across the city. Now, using the political backing they acquired in the 2008 election, gangsters associated with the PPP and the Awami National Party, in a loose alliance, also want their share of cash, at the heart of the conflict. Businesses now have to pay off up to three rival groups.

Famine in Somalia

A severe drought is affecting the entire East Africa region. Said to be "the worst in 60 years", the drought has caused a severe food crisis across Somalia, Ethiopia and Kenya

Novels on
Mobile
Phones
It was disclosed in 2008 that five of the ten best selling novels in Japan the previous year were written on mobile phones.

Bank with SBM
Feel the DIFFERENCE

Housing
Loan

MSME
Loan

Education
Loan

Mobile
Banking

Internet
Banking

 STATE BANK OF MYSORE
Working for a better tomorrow

www.statebankofmysore.co.in

YOUR TRUSTED BANK SINCE 1913   Toll Free No.: 1800 425 2244

Famine in Somalia

that threatens the livelihood of more than 13.3 million people. Many refugees from southern Somalia have fled to neighboring Kenya and Ethiopia, where crowded, unsanitary conditions together with severe malnutrition have led to a large number of deaths. Other countries in and around the Horn of Africa, including Djibouti, Sudan, South Sudan and parts of Uganda, are also affected by a food crisis.

On 20 July, the United Nations officially declared famine in two regions of southern Somalia, the first time a famine has been declared by the UN in nearly thirty years. Tens of thousands of people are believed to have died in southern Somalia before famine was declared. On 3 August, the UN declared famine in three other regions of southern Somalia, citing worsening conditions and inadequate humanitarian response. Famine was expected to spread across all regions of the south in the following four to six weeks. On Sept. 5, the UN added the entire Bay region in Somalia to the list of famine-stricken areas. The UN has conducted several airlifts of supplies in addition to on-the-ground assistance, but humanitarian response to the crisis has been hindered by a severe lack of funding for international aid coupled with security issues in the region.

Famine is declared when 30% of children are acutely malnourished, 20% of the population is without food, and deaths are running at two per 10,000 adults or four per 10,000 children every day. Parts of Somalia exceed these dreadful thresholds. In three provinces almost a third of people are acutely malnourished, says the UN's World Food Programme (WFP).

A New Prime Minister for Japan

Yoshihiko Noda became Japan's sixth prime minister in five years, inheriting an aging country beset with disaster recovery, nuclear crisis and economic gloom.

Yoshihiko Noda replaced Naoto Kan, who resigned after just 15 months in office with abysmal poll ratings, perpetuating the country's chronic revolving-door leadership at a time of national crisis.

Yoshihiko Noda

Noda became his centre-left party DPJ's (Democratic Party of Japan) third premier, two years to the day since it won a landslide election that ended a half-century of conservative rule — and at a time of deep voter disenchantment with all major parties.

He was elected premier by both houses of parliament a day after winning a party leadership battle that was fought along factional lines rather than on the five candidates' policy positions or their voter popularity. Noda, a 54-year-old who was relatively unknown to the electorate, conceded that, based on his looks and charisma, he would not win many votes, instead painting himself as moderate and steadfast, if a little bland.

In a display of humility, Noda stressed that he is an ordinary man without political star power or looks, and promised to be a peacemaker who will unite the deeply divided party and seek to engage the opposition.

The DPJ is deeply split between backers and enemies of scandal-tainted powerbroker Ichiro Ozawa. Noda won the poll after anti-Ozawa factions settled on him as a compromise choice to defeat their opponent's

Marriages between Cousins

Marriages between first cousins are common in some countries. Over 50 per cent marriages in Sudan and Pakistan and about one-third of weddings in Saudi Arabia are between first cousins.

candidate. The problems Noda faces would be daunting even for the boldest of leaders. The Fukushima nuclear crisis continues with its operator Tokyo Electric Power Company still struggling to bring the reactors to cold shutdown.

The radiation that has escaped from its reactors has driven more than 80,000 people from their homes, made some rural areas uninhabitable for years, and contaminated food supplies, some of which have entered the market.The disaster hit at a time when Japan, a rapidly aging society, has been stuck in cycles of slow economic growth and deflation for two decades.

The country faces a public debt mountain twice the size of the $5-trillion economy, the legacy of years of stimulus spending, and the bill is set to grow as Japan rebuilds its disaster-hit areas. On top of these woes, the economy has been hit by a strong yen, which has soared to post-war highs as a safe haven currency amid global market turmoil, hurting Japan's exporters by making their goods less competitive.

On the foreign policy front, like most of his political peers in Japan, Noda has stated his support for a strong U.S. security alliance and voiced concern about China's rising military spending and growing naval assertiveness.

September 11 Memorial

The National September 11 Memorial in New York opened to the public on September 12, 2011. The sombre memorial features twin reflecting pools that sit within the footprints of the original twin towers. The pools are nearly an acre in size and feature the largest artificial waterfalls in North America. The names of victims of both the first World Trade Center attack in 1993 and the Sept. 11, 2001, terrorist attacks are inscribed in bronze panels placed around the edge of the pools.

The memorial forms the first phase of the US$350m project of the former World Trade Center site, spearheaded by the World

September 11 Memorial

Trade Center Memorial Foundation and the Lower Manhattan Development Corporation (LMDC).

The second phase will see the opening of the 9/11 Museum, which is set to open to the public in 2012.

The US$45m Memorial Museum, designed by Davis Brody Bond architects, will cover 120,000sq ft (11,100sq m) and will be located beneath the memorial plaza.

Europe in Economic Crisis

Europe is now reeling under the pressure of a sovereig debt crisis. The crisis has grown into the biggest challenge the European Union has faced since the adoption of the euro as its single currency in 1999 . Greece, Portugal and Ireland are on life support. Italy and Spain are exhibiting worrying symptoms. Germany and France, the healthy ones, are suffering from a global economic malaise. The crisis has brought to light problems that many analysts say will require a fundamental change in the way the European Union operates.

The debt crisis first surfaced in Greece in October 2009, when the newly elected Socialist government of Prime Minister George A. Papandreou announced that his predecessor had disguised the size of the country's ballooning deficit. But the cause of the crisis goes long back , beginning with a strong euro and the very low interest rates that prevailed for much of the previous decade. The availability of easy money drove the goverment and the country's consumers to borrow money like there was no tomorrow.

BCG
Vaccination

Children in European schools had the tuberculosis vaccine made available to them in 1921. It was not administered in the US and Britain until 1940. In 40 years, more than 200 m. people worldwide had received the vaccine.

kerala
God's Own Country
www.keralatourism.org

Wake up in Malabar

...along the tiny expanse of Bekal beach, waters of Malabar lie still. Here you are just discovering the treasures of a unique theme village. Tucked in between coconut lagoons and mangroves and surrounded by tiny palm-fringed islands in Padanna is a theme village, the only one-of-its-kind in the country. Home to an oyster farm that stretches for kilometres, this village experience is perfected by huts perched on land and water as well as a wide range of ethnic delicacies. To check out the theme village and a whole range of experiences that make Malabar a unique, exotic part of God's Own Country, log on to www.keralatourism.org/malabar. You'll wake up to a new world.

To Mangalore
Kasaragod
Chandragiri Fort
Kappil Beach
Bekal Fort
Bekal Beach
Arabian Sea
Pallikara Railway Station
Theme Village Padanna
Chittari
To Calicut

Experience Malabar
| Tropical forests | Tree houses | Drive-in beach | Historic forts | Spice trails | Theme village | Temple art forms | Malabari cuisine and more

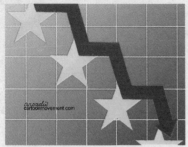

cartoonmovement.com

tensions within the union in memory, as Germany in particular has resisted aid to countries it sees as profligate, and has raised questions about whether the euro can survive as a multinational currency. It has posed great risks to many of the continent's banks, which invested heavily in government bonds, and forced deep and painful cuts in government spending that drove up unemployment and put several countries back into recession, leading a growing number of economists to call the austerity policies self-defeating.

They soon built up $400 billion in debt. In Spain and Ireland, government spending was kept under control, but easy money helped turn real-estate booms there into bubbles . In Ireland's case the process was made easier by the aggressive deregulation of its banks that helped draw investment from around the world. After the bubble burst, the Irish government made the banks' problems its own by guaranteeing all their liabilities.

After the extent of Greek debt was revealed, markets reacted by sending interest rates up not only for its debt, but also for borrowing by Spain, Portugal and Ireland.

The crisis has produced the deepest

Wikileaks Releases all US Cables Unredacted

In September 2011, Wikileaks released its entire archive of US cables uncensored. Wikileaks says all 251,287 of the leaked diplomatic cables are now online in a searchable format. The move came amid a row between Wikileaks and the *Guardian* newspaper over who was behind the earlier release of thousands of unredacted cables. Wikileaks had already published tens of thousands of the cables and planned to keep doing so until November 2011. But suddenly it decided to release all the cables unredacted

Top Revelations (India) from Wikileaks

◆ **Each Rashtriya Lok Dal (RLD) MP was paid ₹ 10 crore:** Wikileaks revealed that UPA Government gave 10 crore rupees to all the RLD MPs for gaining the trust vote over the Indo-US nuclear deal on July 22, 2008.

◆ **Sonia Gandhi's parents didn't like Rajiv:** According to the Wikileaks, Sonia Gandhi told Arnold Schwarzenegger's wife Maria Shriver in 2006 that her parents didn't like Rajiv Gandhi and that she married him against their wishes.

◆ **Hindu extremists are more dangerous than Islamic militants:** Rahul Gandhi told US Ambassador at a lunch few years ago that Hindu extremists are a bigger threat to India than Islamic terror.

◆ **Indians have 1,400 billion dollars as black money in Swiss banks:** Wikileaks report said that Indians have 1,400 billion dollars (₹ 6300000,00,00,000) in Swiss

Banks without any official record. This amount is about 13 times larger than India's foreign debt.

◆ **US embassy criticized Sonia Gandhi:** During the Indo-US Nuclear deal Sonia Gandhi was criticized sharply for not handling the opposition parties properly. Wikileaks said Sonia Gandhi was made to feel embarrassed.

◆ **Indian government was never serious in bringing Headely back to India:** Indian government was never serious in bringing David Headely back to India. 26/11 Mumbai attack's mastermind David Headely is responsible for huge loss to India.

◆ **Left parties were divided over Indo-US Nuclear deal:** Though Left parties strongly opposed the nuclear deal between India and the US, many were also supportive like Sitaram Yechury but not openly.

online. Consequentlly it began publishing its remaining cables, grouped by the country they relate to. They included 34,687 files on Iraq, 8,003 on Kuwait, 9,755 on Australia and 12,606 on Egypt.

The search database soon became overloaded, prompting Wikileaks to appeal for donations to fund additional server space. The *Guardian* said the archive contained several thousand files marked "Strictly protect," indicating US officials thought sources could be endangered if identified. Some files also name victims of sex offences, people persecuted by their governments and the locations of sensitive government installations, said the paper. In a joint statement, the *Guardian*, *El Pais, New York Times* and *Der Spiegel* said they "deplore the decision of WikiLeaks to publish the unredacted state department cables, which may put sources at risk". The papers said the decision to publish the files was made solely by Wikileaks' founder Julian Assange, who is on bail in the UK awaiting extradition to Sweden to answer allegations of rape and sexual assault.

The Wikileaks saga began at the end of 2010 after Julian Assange's organisation obtained tens of thousands of confidential

Top Revelations (World)

1. Many Middle Eastern nations are far more concerned about Iran's nuclear program than they've publicly admitted.

2. The Obama administration offered sweeteners to try to get other countries to take Guantanamo detainees, as part of its (as yet unsuccessful) effort to close the prison.

3. Afghan Vice President Ahmed Zia Massoud took $52 million in cash when he visited the United Arab Emirates in 2009, according to one cable.

4. The United States has been working to remove highly enriched uranium from a Pakistani nuclear reactor, out of concern that it could be used to build an illicit nuclear device.

American diplomatic cables. Together with a number of news organisations, Wikileaks began to release some of the documents. But the newspapers that then published them

Julian Assange

According to the Organisation for Economic Cooperation and Development (OECD), the United States now has the highest poverty rate among all the developed countries in the world. The data from the Census Bureau also indicated that the number of uninsured Americans was also on the rise, while unemployment rose from 9.3 percent to 9.6 percent.

Significantly, while lower and middle class income has fallen, the richest 5 percent in America remained relatively unbothered by the economy. The median household income, which has barely changed since 1980, fell from US$49,777 to US$49,445 in 2010. Adjusted for inflation, a middle-income family in America only earned 11 percent more in 2010 than they did in 1980, while the richest 5 percent saw their incomes surge by over 42 percent.

were absolutely clear about the need to redact references to confidential informants. A careful editorial process was conducted in those first weeks of December 2010, as newspapers filled their pages with a mass of diplomatic tittle-tattle, some of it deeply embarrassing to the US.

Wikileaks initially agreed to pass the data to several newspapers, who searched for noteworthy stories, then removed names and other sensitive data before publishing. However, it has long been known that Wikileaks lost control of the cables even before they were published and that encrypted files were circulating on the internet. It said publishing en masse was the only "internally rational action", because the *Guardian* had already made public the password used to access the encrypted data online. Wikileaks has started legal action against the paper.

US Poverty Hits Record High

46 million Americans (15.1 percent of the population) are living below the federal poverty line – the highest in percentage since 1993 and the most in absolute numbers since 1959 – according to a report released by the US Census Bureau on September 13, 2011. In 2010, 2.6 million Americans joined the ranks of individuals living below the poverty line – set at US$22,113 for a family of four and US$11,139 for an individual – raising the percentage of poor Americans from 14.3 to 15.1 percent. Broken down by state, Mississippi had the highest share of poor people, at 22.7 percent, closely followed by Louisiana, the District of Columbia, Georgia, New Mexico and Arizona. New Hampshire had the lowest poverty rate in the US at 6.6 percent.

Former Afghan Prez Rabbani Killed

Former Afghan President Burhanuddin Rabbani, the official in charge of government peace talks with the Taliban, was killed in his home on September 20, 2011 in a serious setback to efforts to reach a political solution to the 10-year-old U.S.-led war. The killing was a strong statement of Taliban opposition to peace talks, and the latest in a string of high-profile assassinations. Since Rabbani was a prominent Tajik, his killing is also likely to exacerbate ethnic divides. It was the highest profile assassination in Afghanistan since the younger half-brother of President Hamid Karzai, Ahmad Wali Karzai, was killed at his home in July by a highly trusted family security guard. It also came just a week after a deadly 20-hour siege by militants in the fortified capital.

Mr. Rabbani was a militant leader in the armed struggle against the Soviet occupation of Afghanistan from 1979-1989. His appointment as chairman of the High Peace Council, the government body in charge of peace talks, was controversial because of the brutal fight he led against the Taliban during the early 1990s when he was president of the Northern Alliance, an anti-Taliban coalition. Mr. Rabbani's government was ultimately forced from power when the Taliban took control of the capital, Kabul, in 1996.

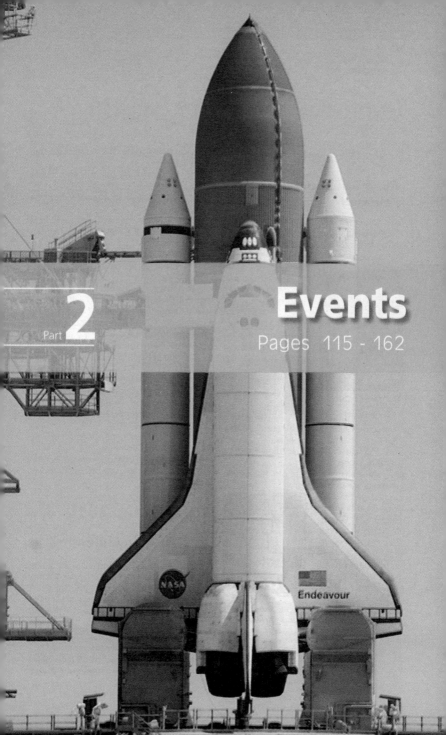

Calendar of Events, World

November 2010

Aung San Suu Kyi Released

1. A survey finds Margaret Thatcher the most influential woman • 52 die as Iraqi security forces storm a Baghdad church where militants had taken 120 people hostage •

Margaret Thatcher

Dilma Rousseff to be Brazil's first woman President • China's national census begins.

3. Nikki Haley becomes first Indian-American woman governor as she wins the race in South Carolina state • 13 blasts across Baghdad kill 76.

4. Chinese President Hu Jintao named the most powerful person in the world by *Forbes*. Obama is 2nd among 68 people.

. 7. Election in Myanmar, the first since 1990, NLD boycotts it.

9. Australians to vote on recognising Aborigines • Army-backed party USDP wins in Myanmar elections • George W. Bush's new book 'Decision Points' released.

10. Volcano death toll (Mount Merapi) in Indonesia in 191.

13. Myanmar's democracy icon Suu Kyi released from

Aung San Suu Kyi

15-year home arrest • China's Hu Jintao visits Japan.

15. Cholera death toll in Haiti soars to 900.

16. Prince William to wed girl friend Kate Middleton in April.

18. Suu Kyi terms her 7-year detention by Junta as illegal • President of Mauritius Jugnanth in India.

20. NATO summit in Lisbon.

21. Dalai Lama contemplates retirement.

23. India has 7 Golds at Asian Games against China's 165 • Nearly 380 revellers die in Cambodian festival stampede • North Korea shells a South Korean island, triggering an exchange of fire.

24. UK hit by student protests.

25. Queen Elizabeth II on a five-day state visit to the Gulf • The 29 men trapped in mine in New Zealand die.

28. Russian cargo plane crashes in Pakistan, 11 dead • North Korea places surface-to-surface missiles on launch pads in the Yellow Sea.

29. 16th FCCC conference opens in Cancun, Mexico.

30. UN Climate Change conference opens in Cancun • Russian space officials fired over failed launch.

December 2010

Landslide in Chile

01. People living with HIV: 33.3 mn. Aids-related deaths in 2009 put at 1.8 mn. • Students in London take to the street protesting plans to raise university tuition fees • Interpol calls for arrest of Wikileaks' founder Assange.

TB on the Rise

Britain is the only country in West Europe with rising rates of TB. In London cases of the disease have grown by nearly 50 p.c. since 1999. Britain has more than 9000 cases of TB diagnosed a year. London accounts for 40% of all diagnosed cases.

Ministry of Social Justice & Empowerment
Government of India

सत्यमेव जयते

Indira Gandhi National Open University
Ministry of Social Justice & Empowerment, GOI

Announce

The Establishment of Indian Sign Language Research & Training Centre (ISLRTC)

The Ministry of Social Justice and Empowerment, GOI, has approved the establishment of ISLRTC, initially on project basis for a period of five years. An autonomous Centre of the Indira Gandhi National Open University (IGNOU), the Centre will lead the way in the study, academic development, and propagation of the Indian Sign Language and in its teaching and training.

Salient Features

- IGNOU will make five acres of land available for the Centre in its Maidan Garhi campus
- The government has accorded approval for creation of 35 posts for the Centre for Departments like Sign Languages, Interpreting, Library, Documentation and Administration.
- The Centre will be established at an estimated cost of ₹44 crore over five years.
- A Committee, consisting of representatives of national-level organisations of the Deaf, will be responsible for planning and managing ISLRTC.

Objectives

- To promote the use of Indian Sign Language (ISL) in India.
- To carry out research in ISL and create linguistic record/analysis of the language.
- To carry out and promote research on bilingual approach in education of deaf children.
- To train persons in Sign linguistics and other related areas at various levels.
- To design, promote and offer programmes in ISL, interpreting and bilingual education, at various levels, through various modes including the distance mode.
- To develop and offer courses aimed at training teachers to teach ISL.

- To develop and created resources for use in teaching of ISL to children, parents, teachers and general public.
- To facilitate educational use of ISL In special schools, as the first language or medium of instruction, and in mainstream schools, as second language or as interpreter mediated language of classroom communication.
- To provide guidance in innovative education methodology for institutions providing education to the Deaf.
- To collaborate with other institutions and organisations of the Deaf to promote and propagate ISL.
- To collaborate with Universities and other educational institutions in India and abroad in sign language research, deaf and related issues.
- To produce and promote visual material in ISL story telling of both Indian and global literature and Deafness related issue.
- To create and promote literature in and about ISL.
- To facilitate PRINT AND Visual Media in promoting the use of ISL.
- To foster the development of Deaf identity and culture
- To act as a clearing house of information on ISL, Deafness, education of the hearing impaired and related areas.

CONCEPT & DESIGN: IANSPUBLISHING

03. Taliban suicide bombers kill 50 in Pakistan • Philippines overtakes India as call centre capital • Landslide buries up to 200 near Medellin in Colombia.

07. Julia Assange of Wikileaks arrested on charges of rape.

08. 83 killed in Chile prison fire • Crude oil price rises to $87.91.

10. Liu Xiabo awarded Nobel Peace Prize in absentia.

12. CEC wants opinion polls banned • 193 countries sign a new global climate regime - the Cancun Agreement • Twin 'Terror' bomb blasts rock Stockholm.

13. Iran Foreign Minister Mottaki dismissed • Ninety school children in Besancon, France held hostage by a teenager rescued.

14. Richard Holbrooke, US diplomat, is dead.

16. Nepal plane crash kills 22 • UN lifts nuclear weapons sanctions on Iraq • UK court upholds bail to Wikileaks founder Assange • Haiti cholera toll surpasses 2400.

17. EU to set up a multi-billion euro permanent financial safety net.

18. China and Pakistan sign deals worth $15 bn. • David Beckham to be honoured with lifetime achievement award at BBC Sports

Richard Holbrooke

Personality of the Year ceremony • Colombo agrees to UN Panel visit • US missiles kill 54 in Pakistan.

19. 37 dead in Bangladesh boat sinking.

20. Heavy snow paralyses air services across Europe • In Belarus, President Luckeshenki wins; mass protests against the controversial re-election • Mass hanging of 11 Sunni rebels of the Jundallah group in Iran.

22. Fresh snowfall causes further misery to passengers across Europe.

23. Julie Andrews (*The Sound of Music*) to get Grammy for life achievement at 75

Emperor Akihito and Empress

• Bomb blasts hit Swiss, Chilean embassies in Italy • Emperor Akihito is 77.

24. Oil prices hit 26-month peak • US law to hike visa fee upsets IT industry • 24,000 Vietnam workers strike at South Korean plants.

26. Ivory Coast President Gbagbo is threatened by rebel leaders • Wikileaks chief Assange signs £1.1 m autobiography deal.

28. World population to touch 7 bn. next year.

January 2011

Referendum in Sudan

01. 21 people killed as a suicide bomber blows himself up outside a Coptic church in Egypt • Russian plane bursts into flames before take off in Russia.

02. Dilma Rousseff takes charge as President of Brazil • India joins UN Security Council as a non-permanent number, after 19 years • Explosions rock Nigerian capital.

03. Visa fee hike takes effect in US • Arnold Schwarzenegger steps down as California Governor • Iraq's oil production exceeds 2.7 m. barrels a day.

04. Salman Taseer, Governor of Pakistan's Punjab province, gunned down in Islamabad, allegedly by his security guards • US not invited by Iran to tour nuclear sites.

05. China joins the world's elite club of offshore oil producers as CNOOC's output surpasses 60m. tonnes in 2010 • FAO says prices of corn, wheat and other grains can

EAST WEST
GROUP OF INSTITUTIONS

ESTD. 1968

(Recognised by Government of Karnataka) (Approved by AICTE, INC, PCI, New Delhi)
(Affiliated to Bangalore University, Rajiv Gandhi University,
Visveshwaraiah Technological University)

Late Sri. C.M. NAGARAJ
Founder

Sy No.63, 10th KM, Off Magadi Road, Near Anjananagar, Vishwaneedam P.O. Bangalore-560 091
Phone: 23286732, 23288237, 23288245, 23288899 Fax: 080-23288244, 23282825
Email: ewgi68@gmail.com; ewgi68@yahoo.co.in; Website: www.ewit.edu

ISO 9001-2000

COURSES OFFERED IN:

M.Tech.
Computer Science, Digital Electronics,
Machine Design
Civil-Structural, Civil-Geo Technical

MSc / BSc
BioTechnology-Genetics
BioChemistry-MicroBiology

MBA - MCA - BBM - BCA

B.E.
Mechanical, Civil, Computer Science,
Electrical & Electronics, Infotech,
Electronics & Communication

PharmD - Mpharm - Bpharm

BCom - BPT - BEd - BHM

POLYTECHNIC DIPLOMA
Mechanical, Civil, Mechatronics, Automobile,
Computer Science, Electrical & Electronics,
Electronics & Communication, Infotec
Commercial Practice

Dpharm - Ded - DMLT - DCT

P.U.C.
PCMB - PCME - PCMCs - CEBA

NURSING
PCBSc-M.Sc-NURSING | B.Sc - NURSING | GENERAL NURSING

UNIQUE FEATURES

◀ One among the top colleges in Bangalore and in India.
◀ Ultra modern & beautifully landscaped Wi-Fi enabled campus of 20
acres in the heart of city. ◀ Excellent infrastructure facilities & well
equipped laboratories with research facilities. ◀ State of art of teaching
with highly qualified, experienced & dedicated Teaching Fraternity.
◀ Well stacked library with online access to National & International
Journals & Magazines. ◀ Excellent students admission with consistent
result track record of rank & distinction holders. ◀ Pre-placement
training for the students to prepare them for the corporate world.
◀ 100% assured placement opportunities for the students. ◀ Tie up with Industries & MNCs for research projects
and academic upgradation and exposure from industry experts and CEO talks. ◀ Scholarships to deserved, poor &
meritorious students. ◀ Athletic arena, gymnasium and encouragement to co-curricular & extra curricular activities
for overall development of the students & staff. ◀ Regular monitoring & counseling of under performing students
through mentor system. ◀ More than half lakh Alumni Students are contributing for the development of the nation.
◀ Convenient transportation facilities, hygienic separate hostels for boys & girls, on campus food courts, Nationalized
Bank with 24 hours ATM facility. ◀ Sponsorship facilities to students and faculty for participation in national &
international conferences & symposiums.

EW-21141-FP-MM

ON CAMPUS HOSTELS WITH TIDY ROOMS & MULTI CUISINE MESS

go much higher • Ignoring threats, Pakistanis pay respects to slain Punjab Governor Salman Taseer in Lahore.

06. Hong Kong's 40 richest tycoons are all US $ billionaires again.

08. Smoking could disappear in Britain within half a century, say Citigroup researchers.

09. World's first art exchage opens in Paris, where shares of famous artworks can be bought and sold • Attempt on a US lawmaker Gabrielle Giffords' life in Tucson, Arizona kills six • 7-day Independence Referendum in Sudan begins.

10. 77 die in Iranian air crash • 2000 Haiti quake orphans reportedly sold as sex slaves • Pak Governor Taseer's assassin says he acted alone • Schools in China issue free GPS phones to boost safety.

12. Nikki Haley, Indian-American, sworn

Nikki Haley

in as the first woman Governor of South Carolina state • Australian floods; Brisbane suffers most, the worst floods in a century • Bond 23, the new James Bond film to be released in 2012, with Daniel Craig as Bond.

13. Lebanon in turmoil after government falls, Hezbellah resigns • South Sudan independence vote confirmed as valid • 360 killed in Brazil floods.

14. US likely to lift ban on ISRO, DRDO • Protesters in Tunisia demand President Ben Ali's resignation.

16. South Sudan set for nationhood • Brazil death toll is 610 • IMD says 2010 was the warmest year since 1901.

17. Tunisia: people stage rally • China says its policy that Arunachal Pradesh is a disputed area remains unchanged • 'Baby Doc', former dictator returns to Haiti after 25 years • Israel Defence Minister Ehud Barak quits Labour and forms new party 'Independence' • Chinese President Hu Jintao

in the USA.

18. Suicide bombing in Iraq kills 50.

19. A mn. people in 11 districts affected by incessant rains in Sri Lanka.

20. 50 people killed by bombs targeting Iraqi pilgrims in Karbala • A memorial for the celebrated octopus Paul unveiled in Sea

Octopus Paul

Life aquarium in Obertausen, Germany • Hu Jintao, now visiting the US, says China is willing to have dialogue on human rights.

22. Pirates hijacked 53 ships in 2010 • Irish Prime Minister Cowen quits as party leader • Mexico is the first country to use iris scans for identity cards.

Hu Jintao

24. Suicide bomber strikes at Moscow's Domodedevo airport, killing 31 and injuring 120.

26. President Obama asks US to gear up for competition from India and China • US wants defence, space collaboration with India • Davos meet opens.

27. For the third straight day, Egyptians defy police to protest against the regime of Hosni Mubarak • Yemenis stage mass demonstrations calling on President to quit.

28. Huge anti-government protest in Egypt.

30. Protests sweep through Yemen.

February

Mubarak Quits

01. Two million-strong rally in Cairo calling for an end to Mubarak regime • Oil is $100 a barrel • Jordan's King Abdullah II fires cabinet; Palestinians to hold elections • Thousands in Australia flee the path of cyclone Yasi • UN declares 2011 the Year of Forests.

King Abdullah II

02. Epic winter storm hits US, from Texas to Maine.

03. Lunar New Year begins, it is the start of the Year of the Rabbit • Egyptian Prime Minister apologises for attacks of protesters by Mubarak supporters • Jhalanath Khanal is Nepal premier • Yemeni anti-government protesters demonstrate at Sanaa varsity.

06. Communist leader Jhalanath Khanal sworn in Nepal Prime Minister.

07. Laureus Award goes to Nadal • Former Pak President Musharraf named accused in Benazir killing • Belgian runner Stefaan Engels sets new world marathon record of 2 hours and 56 minutes.

11. Egyptian President Hosni Mubarak steps down, after 18 days of mass protests.

12. Kim Clijsters regains No. 1 ranking.

13. Egypt's military suspends constitution, dissolves parliament and sets a 6-month timeframe for elections

14. Japan loses No.2 economy spot to China • Thousands of women in Italy call for Italian Prime Minister Berlusconi's

Kim Clijsters

resignation.

15. Protests and clashes in Bahrain, Yemen and Iran.

17. Opening ceremony of Cricket World Cup at Dhaka • In Bahrain, army out to quell unrest • 14 protesters killed in Libya with escalation of violence.

18. Egyptians gather in Cairo to celebrate Mubarak fall.

19. Libya's toll nears 100.

20. On the 6th day of the Libyan uprising, army opens fire on mourners, 200 dead • Thousands rally in Moroccan cities • South Africa joins BRIC grouping, which becomes BRICS • 38 killed in attack on Afghan bank.

21. Oil hits $105 on Libya violence

22. Earthquake in New Zealand kills 65, worst hit is Christchurch.

23. New Zealand quake toll is 75 and 300 are missing • Sectarian violence in Nigeria's Plateau state.

24. Crude surges to 29-month high of $112.90 as supply from Libya is reduced • Malkangiri Collector R.V. Krishna released by Maoists in Orissa • Foreigners flee from Libya • Space shuttle Discovery set to make its last mission to ISS.

26. Libyan protesters clash with government forces.

27. UN votes for curbs on Libya • Tunisia Prime Minister Ghannouchi resigns • Gadhafi's nurse Glyna returns to Ukraine.

28. Oscar awards announced: *The King's Speech* (4 Awards) is best film.

A scene from The King's Speech

No Royal Road to Geometry

The Greek mathematician Euclid known for his "Elements" on geometry founded a school in Alexandria during the reign of Ptolemy I. Asked by Ptolemy if there is a shorter way to geometry, Eculid replied, " There is no royal road to geometry."

March

Tragedy in Japan

01. Protesters block Oman port.

02. Pak minister for Minority Affairs, Shahbaz Bhatti, gunned down in Islamabad • International pressure on Gaddafi increases • Nobel Laureate Dr. Muhammad Yunus removed as Grameen Bank M.D.

04. President Obama says Gaddafi of Libya must step down from power • Egypt has a new Prime Minister: Essam Sharaf • Protests in Yemen, four killed.

05. Former Nepal Prime Minister Bhattarai passes away.

07. Fresh air strikes to ten rebel march to Tripoli • Some 10,000 houses in Christchurch, affected by a major earthquake, have to be demolished.

08. World celebrates 100th International Women's Day • Libya: people shot at sight at Zawiya • Lead poisoning kills over 400 infants in North Nigeria.

09. Qadhafi accuses the West of conspiring to usurp Libya's oil resources • 21 Catholic priests in Philadelphia suspended, for child molestation • Blast in Peshawar kills 30, injures 45.

10. Carlos slim remains the richest person in the world with $74 b. in assests • Dalai Lama to step down as the political head of Tibetan government in-exile.

11. A massive earthquake triggered by a tsunami in Japan; hunderds killed, huge damage, 8.9 magnitude, cars and boats swept away; over 45 nations offer help.

12. As death toll rises to 10,000, Japan scrambles to avert nuclear meltdown, at three earthquake hit nuclear reactors • US Geological Survey says the recent earthquake has moved Japan by about eight feet.

13. Explosion at nuclear power station at Daichi • Streets in Japan's Sendai have crumpled cars, small planes and fallen trees, triggered by the tsunami.

14. Meltdown threat after hydrogen blast at Japan's Fukushima reactor.

Fukushima

15. Bahrain placed under emergency • Fukushima nuclear power plant explodes, sending low levels of radiation floating towards Tokyo.

16. EU offers to help Japan's radiation victims • Massive crackdown in Bahrain to crush pro-democracy revolt.

17. More clashes in Yemen after protests by anti-govt. groups • People missing in Japan: 11,000.

18. UN sanctions air strikes on Libya • Libya halts military operations, as Gaddafi announces ceasefire • 30 killed in pro-democracy protest in Yemen.

21. The twin disasters projected to cost Japan $235 bn. in damages • Thousands protest in Syria • Top Yemeni General defects.

23. Elizabeth Taylor is dead.

25. Strong earthquake kills 75 in Myanmar.

28. Indo-Pak talks in New Delhi at Home Secretary level • India and Africa set $70 bn trade target.

Elizabeth Taylor

29. Sri Lanka beat New Zealand to enter World Cup semi final • Crude oil drops to $103.63 a barrel • Ricky Ponting quits as Australia's captain.

30. World Cup semi-final match between India and Pakistan in Mohali. India beats Pakistan. PMs of both countries watch the game • World Economic Forum in Davos.

The Beast | **US President Barack Obama's armoured car, The Beast, weighs seven tonnes. It can withstand a chemical attack.**

Best Sellers

Civil Services Mains Examination

April

The Wilkat Wedding

2. Power struggle in Ivory Coast kills over 1000

3. Two deadly suicide attacks near a Sufi shrine in Punjab, Pakistan • Violence kills 140 in Afghanistan's Kandahar.

4. Landslides kill 45 in Thailand • Obama announces 2012 re-election bid • 15 shot dead in Yemen protests • Hillary says Gbagbo of Ivory Coast is pushing nation to lawlessness.

5. Sangakkara steps down as captain of Sri Lanka's ODI & T20 teams • Indian Coach Gray Kirsten goes back to S. Africa • 32 dead in UN plane crash in D R Congo • Ivory Coast strongman Gbagbo is cornered in Abidjan • Mohd Yunus loses a final appeal against his sacking from Grameen Bank • Michel Martelli is Haiti's new president elect.

8. Yemeni President Saleh rejects GCC deal for his exit • In Ivory Coast, Quattara isolates Gbagbo •13 protesters killed in protests in Syria • More than 100 bodies found in the past 24 hours in western Ivory Coast.

9. Burqa ban in France goes • Libyan rebels are pushed back.

10. More than 1000 Egyptians protest in Cairo's Tahrir Square • 26 Syrian human rights activists killed • Dozens of protesters shot at in Yemen • African Union presents a blueprint for ceasefire in Libya.

11. Strong aftershock rattles Japan.

12. The two Pak expat foot soldiers Headley and Rana implicate Pak government & ISI in the 26/11 attack • Japan puts N-crisis on par with Chernobyl.

13. Egyptian leader Mubarak and two sons detained.

14. BRICS express misgivings about Nato-led air strikes in Libya • People confirmed dead in the Japanese tragedy is 13,498; people dead and missing:28,232 • NATO calls for Gaddafi to quit • Syrian Prime Minister Adel Safar forms new government.

18. Violence in Nigeria after President Jonathan heads for a victory in the election over ex-military ruler Buhari .

19. Jennifer Egan's *"A Visit from the Goon Squad"* wins Pulitzer Prize • Fidel Castro resigns; Raul Castro is new party chief.

20. Worries over US economy take gold price to $1500 /oz • Syria continues crackdown on rebels • Thousands displaced in post-election riots in Nigeria.

21. Queen Elizabeth is 85.

22. Malinga of Sri Lanka quits test cricket • Gold (Rs. 21825 for 10 gm) and silver surge to lifetime high • 20 dead in Pakistan drone attack • US authorises use of killer drones for missile strikes against Government forces in Libya.

23. Actor Lindsay Lohan sentenced in jewellery theft case is released on bail • Second day of fighting between Thai and Cambodian troops, death toll is 11.

24. Yemen protesters reject President Saleh's plan and demands his immediate departure.

25. About 500 Taliban fighters tunnel out of a prison in Afghanistan.

Obama posts online a copy of his birth certificate hoping to end the conspiracy theory among some conservatives who assert that he was not born in the US • Storms in southern US kill 128 in Alabama alone.

29. Marriage of Prince William and Kate Middleton at Westminister Abbey, London - Britain's biggest royal wedding in 30 years; 2 bn. watch event on TV • It has emerged

Prince William and Kate Middleton

that Obama's father was forced out of US for his 'playboy ways' • Prince William is made Duke of Cambridge • US tornadoes' toll is 350.

May

Osama Killed

01. Libyan leader Gaddafi escapes NATO air attack, his son and three grandchildren are killed • Pope beatifies Pope John Paul II.

02. Osama bin Laden, leader of al Qaeda terror outfit killed by US forces at Abbottabad in Pakistan • Ayman at Zawahiri, the Egyptian surgeon, likely to succeed bin Laden • Canada goes to the polls • Worldwide alert by US, Interpol.

Osama bin Laden

03. Taliban vows revenge, Zardari and army in top hit-list • Gaddafi's tanks pound rebel city Misrata, ahead of the funeral of his son killed in Nato-led air strike • Vanuatu to become the 154th number of WTO.

04. Canadian PM Stephen Harper's Conservative party wins a decisive victory in the 4th federal election in 7 years.

05. US marks 50 years since second human spaceflight • Obama says US may again carry out operations against high-profile terrorists • Iran won't use nukes against Israel, even if it obtains them.

06. Hurriyat hardliner Geelani leads prayers for Osama • Indonesian plane crashes into sea, killing all 27 passengers..

08. Sectarian violence kills 12 in Egypt.

10. Full face transplant recipient Dallas Wi s makes first public appearance.

13. Mohammed Yunus steps down from Gr neen Bank • 80 killed in Pakistan in their firs. attack to avenge Bin Laden's death.

15. IMF chief Dominique Strauss-Kahn,

Space shuttle Endeavour launched

a likely candidate for French President, arrested and charged with sexual assault on hotel maid in US.

16. Space shuttle Endeavour launched.

17. British Queen visits Irish Republic.

18. Philip Roth wins Man Booker International Prize.

19. Goof-up in India's most wanted terrorist list reported.

20. IMF chief Strauss Kahn gets bail for $1 mn., after a four-night stay in jail • NATO hits ships in Tripoli harbour • King of Bhutan announces his engagement to 20-year-old student Jetsun Pema • Train crash in South Africa's Soweto hurts 857 • India to send a revised list of fugitives to Pakistan, following the errors that crept up in the 50 most-wanted terrorist list.

21. Obama says that Pakistan's India obsession is a mistake, and that there can be more Osama-type action if required • Gunmen loyal to Yemen president Saleh in Saana besiege the UAE embassy entrapping inside envoys of US, UK, EU and four Gulf countries .

23. After a 17-hour operation, Pak security forces gain control over the Navy airbase in Karachi which came under attack by terrorists • In Iceland, the Grimsvotn volcano erupts. Domestic flights cancelled • Tornado kills 89 in Japan, Missouri, USA • Taliban leader Mullah Omar is dead, a report says.

24. Volcanic cloud over Scotland and North Ireland following eruption of Iceland's Grimsvoetn volcanco results in cancellation of 252 flights • French Finance Minister Christine Lagarde's name mentioned as new

Tepco Loss **Tokyo Electric Power Co. (Tepco) reports a loss of $15 bn. on account of the disaster at Fukushima. Its president Shimizu has resigned.**

chief • President Barack Obama in Ireland • India announces a $ 5 bn.line of credit to Africa. • NATO air strikes pound Tripoli • Obamas begin visit to Britain.

28. Interpol issues global alert for Taliban fugitives.

Jonathan Goodluck

29. Nigerian President Jonathan Goodluck is sworn in for a new term • Maltese say 'yes' to divorce.

30. Germany to shut down all its 17 nuclear power plants by 2022.

June

MF Hussain Dies in London

01. WHO warns that heavy use of mobile phone can cause cancer.

03. In Yemen, presidential palace is hit by shells, President hurt • Ratko Mladic makes his first appearance before UN judges at the Hague.

04. Ilyas Kashmiri, wanted both by India and US, reported killed in US drone attack • Pakistan hikes defence budget by Rs. 53 bn. • 19 killed in blasts in Iraq • E. coli outbreak in Germany.

06. Gary Kristen named South African coach • New Zealand cricket stalwarts Fleming and Vettori awarded the country's highest civil honours • 42 mn. people were displaced by natural disasters in 2010 • Tiger Woods tops the list of world's highest paid athletes • Nadal equals Borg's record with French Open title • 25 killed, 50 hurt in Pak blast.

09. The great Indian artist M.F. Husain, 95, dies in London • Tea Obreht wins Orange Prize for fiction.

10. WHO says the proportion of disabled people is rising and now the number stands at one billion • Croatia to join EU, membership to start by 2013.

11. Twin bomb blasts in Peshawar, 34 killed • US cuts down troops in Pakistan • Vietnam-China sea dispute escalates • Suu Kyi to deliver BBC's annual Reith lectures.

12. China to relax individual Taiwan travel ban.

13. China appears to be planning to divert Brahmputra waters from the upper reaches • Downpours in China leave 94 dead, 78 missing.

15. Ayman al-Zawahiri is the new al Qaeda chief.

16. Total lunar eclipse, the longest in 11 years • Pakistan's Gen. Kayani under pressure from colleagues for reduce ties with US • 10th anniversary of Shanghai Cooperation Organisation.

Ayman al-Zawahiri

17. OECD-FAO report says global food prices are expected to be higher in 2011-20 period compared with the previous decade • IME retains India growth at 8.2 p.c.

20. Syrian President proposes a national dialogue that will recommend sweeping reforms to change the political systems.

21. 44 die in Russian plane crash • 22 killed in Iraq blasts • Michelle Obama meets Nelson Mandela • Ex-Tunisian President Ben Ali sentenced to 35 years in prison and $ 66 m. fine after a trial in absentia • Chilean ash cloud created by Puyehve volcano grounds hundreds of flights in Australia.

22. Ban Ki-moon re-elected UN Secretary General for a second five year term.

23. Obama announces Afghan troop withdrawal.

25. Suicide blast kills 20 in Afghanistan • New York makes gay marriage legal.

26. Yemen protesters want President's sons to leave • Brazil's Jose Graziane da Silva elected FAO D-G • Russian billionaire Mikhail Prokhorov elected head of pro-business party, Just Cause • Chinese activist Hu Jia freed • Use of children as suicide bombers on the

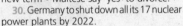

Most Dangerous for Women

According to a Thomson Reuters Foundation poll, Afghanistan, Congo and Pakistan are the most dangerous countries for women. Threats range from violence and rape to dismal healthcare.

At a time when most professional education institutions function as mere brick and mortar structures with parity courses, VIT enables its students, faculty and associates to achieve their most cherished ambitions through a solid educational system and a rich environment.

From smart classrooms with electronic white boards to sophisticated video-conferencing rooms, VIT raises the productivity of students. While the specialised research centres, a highly trained faculty and the hi-tech community spaces provide a stimulating atmosphere that nurtures fresh thinking.

That makes VIT more than just a place to learn. It gives you a chance to grow by equipping you with everything you need to achieve excellence.

International standards in education.

Intellectually stimulating environment.

Incredible placement opportunities.

VIT
Enabling
students
realise their
potential

Daniel Craig

rise in Afghanistan • Chinese PM Wen Jiabao in Britain to attend the annual UK-China Strategic Summit • Actor Daniel Craig marries actress Rachel Weisz • An Iraqi court convicts the wife of slain al-Qaeda leader Abu Ayyub al-Masri to 20 years in prison on terrorism-related charges.

27. Serena Williams knocked out of Wimbledon.

28. French Foreign Minister Christine Lagarde is the new IMF chief.

29. Battle between Nato-led forces and Taliban insurgents as the latter storm International Hotel, Kabul; 21 killed

30. Sri Lanka allows banks to transact in Chinese currency • Taiwan's former President Lee Tang-hui indicted on graft charges.

July

South Sudan is a New Nation

02. Petra Kvitova of Czech Republic is Wimbledon women's champion • Thailand goes to the polls.

03. Novak Djokovic wins Wimbledon title, beating Nadal • Yingluck Shinawatra to become Thailand's first woman PM.

05. Soil radiation in a city 60 km. from Japan's stricken nuclear plant found with caesinum contamination.

06. 197 Africans drown in the Red Sea.

08. South Sudan becomes an independent nation • World premiere of Harry Potter and the Deathly Hallows - Part 2.

11. Accident kills 53 school children in Bangladesh.

12. Afghan President Karzai's brother shot by bodyguard.

14. India to start renewable energy proj-

ects in Africa • Rebekah Brooks, resigns as chief executive of Rupert Murdoch's embattled British newspapers following the phone hacking scandal at a sunday tabloid.

15. Hillary Clinton to retire to private life after Obama's first term • Pentagon lost 24000 files to cyber attack in March.

16. Japan set to phase out nuclear power.

20. Hillary Clinton, in India, urges India to play a more assertive role in Asia-Pacific affairs .

21. Space shuttle Atlantis lands at Kennedy Space Centre in Florida after its final 13-day mission, bringing an end to the 30-year US shuttle programme.

Hillary Clinton

22. Major blasts rock Oslo, Norway's capital • 50 militants killed in Afghanistan • Heat wave kills 20 in US.

25. Oslo killing toll is 76, it is confirmed. The killer was 32-year old self-confessed Muslim-hating fundamentalist Christian,

Oslo bomb blast

Anders Behring Breivik • World Bank to provide $500 mn. to help drought victims in East Africa • Vietnam has Nguyen Tao Dung as PM.

26. 78 dead as Moroccan plane crashes into a mountain.

27. The mayor of Kandahar killed by

A 'Smart' Bandage	**Australian researchers have developed a 'smart' bandage that changes colour as a wound worsens or improves, potentially leading to the better treatment of ailments such as leg ulcers.**

suicide •US officials claim al-Qaeda is on the brink of collapse.

28. 19 die in Afghan triple blasts • Nawaz Sharif elected President of Pakistan Muslim League - Nawaz (PMLN), the country's main opposition party.

Nawaz Sharif

29. Varsity of northern Virginia's Annadale campus raided for fraud, most students from India • Drought affects 10 m. people in East Africa • South Sudan joins African Union as 54th member • Tunisia's former leader Ben Ali gets 13 years for graft change.

31. America's Ryan Lochte gets a 50th gold medal at Sanshai, matching Phelps •

Ryan Lochte

Syrian Government's crackdown kills 140 protesters.

August

Libyan Rebels take Tripoli

01. China blames Pak-trained extremists for orchestrating attacks on civilians in troubled Xinjiang province • Obama announces an eleventh hour deal with Congress to avert default on US debt payments, triggering sighs of relief around the world.

02. US Hof R passes the debt deal reached between Democrats and Republicans.

03. Obama signs debt ceiling bill.

04. Wall Street sinks on rising economic worries • UNSC condemns Syrian oppression • 58 killed in Karachi violence in five days.

05. Gaddafi's son Kham is suspected to be among those killed by NATO • Stock markets around the world tumble on grossing fears about the debts of big eurozone countries • NASA poised to launch spacecraft to Jupiter • Hillary Clinton accuses Syrian government of killing more than 2000 of its citizens during the ongoing crackdown • Viable artificial sperm created using stem cells, in USA • Chavez of Venezuela calls for divine intervention and is hopeful he will win the election next year.

08. Oil plunges below $84 • Rioting sparked by the death of an Afro-Caribbean youth in police shooting spreads across London, as youngsters go on a rampage • Rajapaksa, Sri Lankan President, goes to China, second visit in less than a year.

09. UK on high alert after three nights of riots in which shops are plundered.

10. US Fed to keep interest rates near zero for the next two years.

11. 1200 rioters held in London and other cities.

12. 600 charged with rioting in UK.

16. US is planning to withdraw from Afghanistan by 2014.

17. Economists see a 30% chance that the US will suffer another recession • IMF chief warns spending cuts will stall recovery.

18. Obama wants Syria's Asad to quit • Fresh Karachi violence kills 35.

19. Over 50 killed in Pak suicide blast.

21. Fighting rages in Tripoli, which is rocked by explosions.

22. Libyan rebels claim control of Tripoli; Gaddafi's whereabouts unknown.

23. Gold zooms to record $1917 an ounce.

24. Transitional National Council of Libya put a price of $1.67 mn. on the head of Gaddafi • China's rival to ISS, the unmanned Tiangong-1 (Heavenly Palace), the 8.5-ton test module is in final stages of preparation.

403,000 Millionaires — A study by Julius Baer group says India will have 403,000 millionaires by 2015; Asia's list will double to 2.8 m.

Steve Jobs

25. Steve Jobs resigns as Apple Computers CEO • Sri Lanka lifts emergency after 30 years.

26. All charges against former IMF chief DSK dropped • Naotokan steps down as Japanese PM • Libyan rebels shift base from Benghazi to Tripoli.

28. 4 mn. houses and businesses are without power as a result of hurricane Irene • Tony Tan is the new Singapore President • Libyan rebels close in on Gaddafi's hometown Sirte • Usain Bolt is disqualified from world 100 m. final after a false start, Jamaican Yohan Blake claims the gold in 9.92 seconds • Pakistan to confer MFN status on India this year.

29. The new Japanese PM is Yoshihiko Noda • Babu Rao Dhattarai is the next Nepal PM.

September

Denmark's First Woman PM

01. Global powers begin talks in Paris on reconstruction of Libya, Scramble for oil • London 2012 Olympics will be the first to be broadcast live in 3D.

03. Libya's links with CIA revealed - cooperation in the rendition of terror suspects for interrogation • Usain Bolt wins mens 200 m. gold at Daegu, Korea • Flavia Rennetta beats Maria Sharapova • 21 feared killed in Chile's military airplane crash • Row between Turkey and Israel over Turkey strengthening its naval forces in eastern Mediterranean escalates.

04. Anti-regime protests in Syria; 24 die in crackdown • Emergency declared in Blue Nile, Sudan • Russia introduces time zones in place of nine time belts used so far • Gaddafi believed to be hiding in Bani Walid • Gold is up, as fears of a recession in US grow • Record sale of 100,000 cars in August by BMW • $100 bn. of Libyan assets frozen under UN-EU sanctions.

07. 26 killed in bomb blast in Pakistan • Arctic sea ice melts to record low • Heavy security troops deployed outside Cairo's courthouse as Mubarak's trial is resumed • Russian plane crash kills 43, including most of a top hockey team.

10. Deadline expires for Gaddafi surrender • 163 die in Tanzania boat tragedy • Protesters storm Israeli embassy premises in Cairo; diplomatic staff flee; emergency declared in Cairo.

11. 10th anniversary of 9/11.

12. Explosion in a site that treats nuclear waste in South France • Over 100 die in Kenya pipeline fire • Samantha Stosur wins US Open • UN says at least 2600 have died during the six months of unrest that has swept Syria • Gaddafi's son Saadi flees • Sudan approves military action over the embattled state of Blue Nile bordering S. Sudan.

13. Taliban target Nato, US embassy in Kabul, 7 dead • Serbia's Novak Djokovic beats Rafael Nadal to win US Open men's singles in New York • Angola's Leila Lopez is the new Miss Universe • Moderate Islamic

Novak Djokovic

Chinese Help Gaddafi

It is revealed that China offered stock piles of weapons to prop up Gaddafi during the final months of the regime.

rule awaits Libya, say reports • BoA to slash 30,000 jobs • Floods in Pakistan kill over 200 and make 200,000 homeless.

14. US sanctions to Myanmar to continue • India pledges $ 8 m. to Somalia, Kenya and Djibouti hit by famine.

16. Denmark to have its first woman PM - Helle Thorning-Schmidt • Sirtse (Libya) under attack • Palestine to request UN for full UN membership.

Helle Thorning

17. Gaddafi loyalists stage fight-back. NTC claims UN seat • India to back Palestinian bid for UN membership.

19. VW may take over Suzuki • Yemeni forces open fire killing 26 protesters • Earthquake hits Northeast, kills 71 in Bihar, West Bengal, Sikkim, Nepal & Tibet • *Modern Family* gets five Emmys.

20. Greece avoids bond default • Afghan ex-President Rabbani assassinated • Violence rocks Saana, toll touches 60 • 57 die in China's rains and floods • Obama meets Libyan NTC head Jalid, chief Javed Nasir to Bosnia war crimes tribunal.

22. Pope says society is becoming increasingly more detached from religion • R.E.M., the rock band, has broken up after 31 years. Kenya's Edna Kiplagat wins marathon at 13th athletics world championships at

Rabbani killed

Daegu, South Korea • US warns Pakistan's ISI to cut ties with the Haqqani network.

23. Saleh is back in Yemen amid raging protest • Defiant women flout burqa ban in France.

25. Nepal flight crashes killing 19, of whom 10 are Indians.

Anwar Al Awtaki

27. Typhoon Nesat hits Manila, disrupting power supplies and normal life • Bill in US House to freeze aid to Pakistan.

30. Al-Qaeda cleric Anwar Al Awtaki killed in Yemen • Kabul is rethinking relationship with Pakistan.

October

Three Women Win Nobel Peace Prize

01. Mexico is considering temporary marriage license for 2 years • Shane Warne to marry Liz Hurley • Sumatra air crash, all 18 dead • Typhoon Nalgae lashes the Philippines.

02. Tensions mount between Afghanistan and Pakistan as Kabul says there is clear evidence of ISI hand in Rabbani murder.

03. Suu Kyi worried over violence in Myanmar • Women in Afghanistan are worried about the Taliban returning to government • Tiger Woods falls out of top 50 in world ranking • Taiwan scientists invent an 'invisible key' • Syrian dissidents establish a broad-based national council to overthrow Bashar.

04. Mogadishu car bomb kills 57 • Greeks told to tighten their belts.

05. Steve Jobs is dead • Nobel physics shared by three astronomers.

06. Sarah Palin not to run for President in 2012 • Swedish poet Tomas Transtromer wins Literature Nobel.

07. Three women, from Liberia and Yemen, win Nobel Peace Prize • Desmond Tutu is 80 • Afghan President Karzai says NATO has failed to provide Afghan with security • Paris launches electric car-sharing scheme • Syrian violence :seven killed

Suu Kyi Debuts on Film

Myanmar's pro-democracy leader Aung San Suu Kyi appears in Besson's The Lady. It was premiered at the Toronto Film Festival.

Calendar of Events, India

November 2010

2G Spectrum Scam

1. V. Anand regains his world No.1 rank, after 2 years and a month, replacing Magnus Carlsen.

4. Sonia Gandhi is No. 9 in *Forbes* 2010 list of 'world's most powerful people', and Manmohan Singh 18. • Sensex is at an all time high of 20893 • In UNDP's Human Development report 2010, India is 119th out of 169 countries surveyed.

5. Amritsar airport to be renamed after Shri Guru Ram Dass Jee.

6. Obama begins his 3-day visit to India with an announcement of business deals worth $10 b. that will create 50,000 jobs in the US.

9. CBI probe of Adarsh Housing Society scam ordered • Orissa is renamed Odisha and the language Odia.

11. In Maharashtra, Prithviraj Chauhan sworn in Chief Minister.

12. 16th Asian Games opens in Guangzhou city, China.

14. Government says exports will cross $200 bn. target for 2010-11 • Telecom Minister A. Raja re-

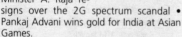

Prithviraj Chauhan

signs over the 2G spectrum scandal • Pankaj Advani wins gold for India at Asian Games.

15. Kapil Sibal given additional charge of Telecom & IT portfolio.

16. CAG reports gross irregularities in the allocation of 2G spectrum in 2008; loss to the exchequer put at Rs. 1.76 lakh crore.

20. Government files in Supreme Court affidavit on behalf of Prime Minister, that denies charges of 'inaction' on a petition seeking his sanction to prosecute the then Minister A. Raja.

22. 41st IFFI opens in Panaji.

24. Andhra Chief Minister K. Rosaiah

Nira Radia

steps down • Top LIC, bank officials arrested in a multi-million rupee bribery scam • Corporate lobbyist Nira Radia questioned by ED in 2G spectrum allocation case • Mobile Number Portability debuts, starting from Rohtak in Haryana • NRIs can now vote.

25. India opens two consulates in Sri Lanka - Jaffna and Hambantota • N. Kiran Kumar Reddy sworn is A.P. Chief Minister • Functioning of Parliament hit for 10th successive working day, as Opposition insists on a JPC for 2G spectrum case • In Bihar election, Nitish Kumar alliance has landslide victory.

26. President Pratibha Patil in Syria • No interviews of children or parents for school admissions, only a random selection process.

27. The 220-MW nuclear power plant Kaiga stage 4 project commissioned • US warns India of Wikileaks, the whistle-blowing website, which may create tension in ties with its friends.

28. India is 6th in overall medals tally at Asian Games - 14 gold, 17 silver and 33 bronze • M.S. Dhoni to set up sports academy in Jharkhand.

29. YSR Reddy's son Jagan Mohan Reddy quits Congress.

30. Government agrees to court-moni-

| Civil Aviation | India's civil aviation sector is the ninth largest in the world. It is to become the third largest market after US and China over the next ten years. |

tored probe into 2G scam • Non-Congress & non-BJP MPs seek President's intervention on 2G scam.

December

Sensex Crosses 20,000

01. Government approves Rs. 6000 cr. capital infusion in 10 PSBs.

02. BrahMos test-fired successfully • CVC P J Thomas, who says his conscience is clear, refuses to resign.

04. French President Nicolas Sarkozy in India.

06. Supreme Court issues notice to Centre and CVC, on a petition questioning P J Thomas' appointment as CVC.

08. CBI searches homes of former Telecom minister A. Raja, his close relatives and some associates

08. TRAI draws up Rs. 60,000 cr. broadband plan to reach every village by 2015.

09. CEO B.S. Lalli of Prasar Bharati indicted of financial irregularities • Forex reserves rise to $296.390 bn.

Minister A. Raja

10. Agni II Prime misfires • National Aviation Company of India Ltd. is now Air India Ltd.

12. Saina Nehwal wins Hong Kong Open, her 4th Super Series badminton title.

14. Petrol dearer by Rs.3 • Ex-CJI K.G. Balakrishnan reportedly suppressed the letter that had alleged that A. Raja had tried to influence Justice Reghupati.

15. CBI searches offices of Kanimozhi and Nira Radia.

16. Kochi to host IPL matches • India and China agree to raise bilateral trade to $100 bn. by 2015 • Hero Honda groups announce parting of ways.

17. Stone laid for Kannur international airport project • Supreme Court to take charge of the 2G Spectrum scam being investigated by CBI.

19. CMIE puts GDP growth at 9.2% in 2010-11 • 83rd plenary session of INC in New Delhi • Sachin Tendulkar is the first man to hit 50 centuries in Test matches, on the 4th day of the first Test against South Africa.

20. Onion prices skyrocket (60-70), export suspended till Jan 15 • R.K. Shetty is new IHC chief.

21. Russian President Dmitry Medvedev in India • Ghauri test fired • Sensex crosses 20,000 mark • Nira Radia grilled by CBI.

22. Parimarjan Negi, 17, is National Premier chess champion • Two Prithvi-II missiles successfully flight-tested.

23. K. Karunakaran, 93, Congress leader and Kerala CM four times, is dead • Natu-

Homage to the late K. Karunakaran

ral rubber prices at all-time high of Rs. 207 kg.

24. Life sentence awarded to physician and human rights activist Binayak Sen by a court in Raipur, for alleged links with Maoists • Raids on Suresh Kalmadi's premises.

25. ISRO's GSLV fails in its mission in the first stage.

26. Dense fog hits flights at Delhi airport • Gujjars on war path on job reservation issue.

27. Manmohan Singh tells PAC chairman he is willing to face the PAC.

28. Former CJI K.G. Balakrishnan's alleged links with Nira Radia revealed.

30. Inflation surges to 14.44 p.c. •

| India Leads in Foreign Remittances | India is the recipient of the largest volume of foreign remittances. The figue stands at Rs. 12,55,000 crores, which is about 10 per cent of the world total of remittance inflow. |

Krishna Water Disputes Tribunal II allocates highest share of water to A.P. • Srikrishna Committee on Telangana submits report.

January 2011

Bhimsen Joshi is No More

01. India and Pakistan exchange lists of their nuclear installations and facilities • Sanskriti Express, an exhibition train on Tagore, arrives in Ranchi • 2011 is Year of Chemistry.

03. Government considering the concept of having Navratna universities on the lines of the Ivy League universities • Income Tax Appellate Tribunal says in Bofors case, Quattrocchi and Win Chadha received a commission of over Rs. 412 m. Howitzer guns in 1987 • UID to replace PF A/c. No.

04. Vikram Pandit, Indian-born global

CEO of Citibank, named in an FIR accusing the bank of cheating in connection with the Rs. 300 cr. fraud at its Gurgaon branch • Sachin's 51st Test century in Cape Town • CBI firm on closing Bofors case.

Vikram Pandit

05. Suresh Kalmadi questioned by CBI • K. G. Balakrishnan's son-in-law P.V. Sreenijin resigns from Youth Congress.

06. Food inflation is 18.32% • Cold wave deaths in north India near 100.

07. Rallies in Nagaland demanding bifurcation of the State for the creation of a new state 'Frontier Nagaland'

08. Mercury plunges to -20.2°C in Leh.

09. Election Commission for urgent steps to bar criminals from contesting elections • Winter deaths in UP rise to 82 • Transgenders to be counted for the first time • Daniel Christian sets the highest bid ($900,000) in IPL player auction in Ban-

galore. Most expensive player is Gautam Gambhir at $2.4 m.

10. CAG stands by its report on 2G spectrum allocation • India's LCA Tejas gets operational clearance • Sensex tumbles 468 points on rate hike fears.

12. IndiGo orders 180 Airbus aircraft for $15.6 bn. - the largest civil aviation deal • Spot rubber is Rs. 220 a kg • Steel Plant of Rs. 697 cr. at Devali planned by Sangam Group.

13. Vigilance probe ordered against P.V. Sreenijan, son-in-law of former CJI K. G. Balakrishnan • South Africa down India by 135 runs to take 1-0 lead in the 5-match ODI series.

14.102 Sabarimala pilgrims die in stampede at Vandiperiyar, Kerala.

17. IFFCO chairman Surinder Jakhar, son of Balram Jakhar, dies in freak accident.

19. Union Council of Ministers expanded • First case of Congo virus confirmed in Ahmedabad • Sheela Thomas to become new Chairperson, Rubber Board.

20. Nationwide Mobile portability launched.

21. Governor sanctions prosecution of Chief Minister Yeddyurappa in Karnataka over allegation of denotification of land acquired by Government • Lt. Gen. P.K. Rath convicted in Sukna land scam by a court martial.

22. Amir Khan is on Berlin film festival jury.

Bhimsen Joshi

24. Pandit Bhimsen Joshi dies at 88 in Pune • Suresh Kalmadi (CGO chairman) and aide Lalit detained.

25. Padma Awards: No Bharat Ratna, 13 Padmavibhushan, 31 Padmabhushan and 84 Padma Shris.

26. 62nd Republic Day. At Delhi, Indonesian President Yudhyonomo is Chief Guest • BJP's Ekta Yatra ends after hoisting the

flag at Kathua, Jammu leaders freed.

27. Government tells SC that selection panel was unaware of chargesheet against P J Thomas, CVC • Crackdown on oil mafia in Maharashtra. Over 80,000 gazetted officers strike in protest against Collector Sonawane's killing

28. New chief of SEBI is U.K. Sinha.

30. Former Chief Minister Ashok Chavan named as one of the 13 accused in the FIR filed by CBI • India takes strong exception to radio-tagging by US of scores of Indian students duped by a sham university in California.

31. Controversy over Hasan Ali's black money • LIC crosses 2.5 crore policies target.

February

The First Container Terminal

01. Supreme Court says any steps taken by the Centre on regularisation of 2G spectrum licences will be subjected to its final orders.

02. Kerala government and Dubai sort out differences on Kochi Smart City.

05. Government sends notices to 17 account holders in a bank in Liechtenstein • IAF inducts the tactical airlift transport C-130K Super Hercules aircraft.

06. 28 Somali pirates captured off Lakshadweep.

07. CSO says Indian economy is expected to grow 8.6 p.c. during 2010-11 • Centre is reviewing the deal between ISRO and Bangalore based Devas Multimedia • RBI to issue new Rs. 10 coins.

08. Fast bowler S. Sreesanth included in World Cup squad.

09. TRAI for over

S. Sreesanth

O.N.V. Kurup

6-fold price hike for 2G licence • First day of Census 2011.

10. Prime Minister constitutes a high-level committee to review the controversial deal between Antrix Corp. and Devas Multimedia.

11. Inauguration of India's first international container transhipment terminal (ICTT) at Vallarpadom, Kerala by Prime Minister • ONV Kurup, the Malayalam poet, receives 43rd Jnanpith Award.

12. 34th National Games at Ranchi, Jharkhand.

13. Arun Shourie, former IT minister to appear before CBI in connection with the 2 G spectrum scam.

14. Karnataka High Court upholds disqualification of 5 MLAs.

15. EPFO subscribers likely to get 9.5% interest on deposit • K. Muralidharan, former KPCC President, granted re-entry to Congress • Volkswagen India rolls out 50,000th car.

17. Antrix -Devas deal aborted • Former Telecom minister A. Raja sent to Tihar jail • Naxals kidnap Malengiri (Orissa) collector.

18. R. Balakrishna Pillai, chairman of Congress's ally Kerala Congress (B) becomes the first former minister to be sent to prison for corruption in Idamalayar case.

19. The 10th World Cup begins.

21. Death penalty for terrorist Ajmal Kasab confirmed by Bombay High Court.

22. 31 convicted and 63 acquitted in Godhra train burning case.

23. Kasab (26/11 attacks) to appeal in Supreme Court • Commonwealth Games scam: Former officials Lalit Bhanot and D-G V.K. Verma, top Kalmadi aides arrested • Kerala to give rice at Rs. 2 a kg to all ration cardholders including APL cardholders • SBI plans merger of five associate banks • Lease deed signed for SmartCity Kochi project.

25. Railway budget presented by Mamata

Plastic Money

Reserve Bank of India is planning to introduce, on a pilot basis, plastic notes of Rs. 10 denomination in the jurisdiction of five out of its 22 regional offices. Replacing paper currency with plastic currency will help cut costs.

Banerjee: no ...e in fares and freights.

27. Indian: . Libya being evacuated, first batch of 500 ...rrives • Sachin becomes the first batsman ... score five hundreds • The country's first Coast Guard academy to come up at Kannur.

28. Budget presented by Pranab Mukherjee.

March

Wikileaks Expose

01. 11 convicts in Godhra train burning case given death sentence, 20 get life imprisonment • Rajya Sabha names JPC members.

02. US authorities charge former McKinsey MD Rajat Gupta with insider trading.

03. Supreme Court sets aside the appointment of P J Thomas as CVC • Bill to give child abusers 7 years in jail.

04. P.C. Chacko to head JPC for 2G spectrum scam • Arjun Singh passes away • Delhi Court discharges Quattrocchi from Bofors pay offs case.

05. DMK to pull out its ministers from UPA Government.

06. Interceptor missile testfired successfully • Varun Gandhi, BJP M.P., marries Yamini Roy Choudhury in Varanasi.

Varun Gandhi & Yamini Roy Choudhury

07. Prime Minister says CVC appointment was an error of judgement.

08. Hero to buy Honda's share in Hero Honda, in a Rs. 3841 cr. deal.

10. Lakshmi Mittal and Mukesh Ambai are 6th and 9th respectively in the top 10 Forbes' richest persons.

12. Former CVC P J Thomas to move SC seeking review of its judgement.

14. India is the largest arms importer.

16. Sadiq Batcha, associate of former Telecom miniser A. Raja, found dead.

19. Rajat Gupta, former Goldman Sachs director, sues US SEC for linking him to US's biggest insider trading scam.

20. Saina Nehwal wins first title of 2011, beating South Korean S Ji Hyun in Wilson Swiss Open.

21. Centre likely to increase D.A. by 6 p.c. • India condemns strikes on Libya.

22. Parliament proceedings stalled on Wikileaks expose on cash for - votes • Investors Warren Buffett, now in India, says he was seeking to invest in India, Brazil and China.

24. Firebrand former bureaucrat K.J. Alphons, the demolition man of Delhi, joins BJP • India estimated to see 5 p.c.

Warren Buffett

growth in farm sector in 2010-11; FM sees 9% growth.

25. Tata Motors becomes first company to make 100,000 commercial vehicles in a financial year.

28. Number of tigers in India rises to 1706, from 1411 in 2006 • Sensex breaches 19,000-mark.

29. Indian IT industry to grow at the rate of 16-18% as against global growth to rate of 4-5%.

30. Engeneering exports cross $50 bn. mark

31. According to preliminary census 2011 data, India's population is 121.02 cr., an in-

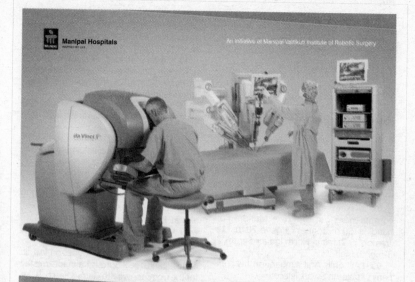

crease of 18.15 cr. from 102.87 cr. in 2001 • Gold consumption last year was 963 tonnes, demand may touch 1200 by 2020.

April

Sai Baba Passes Away

02. CBI charges A. Raja, 8 others and three companies in 2G spectrum case • India wins the World Cup beating Sri Lanka, by 6 wickets.

03. Paes and Bhupathi win their second title of the season.

04. Assam elections – I phase: 62 constituencies out of 126 • Mundra Port handled 50 m. tonnes cargo in 2010-11 • Tremors (5.7) felt in North India • Sensex at 3-month high.

05. PAC grills Anil Ambani on his company's stakes in Swan Telecom.

06. Foodgrain output in 2010-11 at 235.88 m. tonnes • Cabinet clears National Clean Energy Fund • Silver hits new high at Rs. 58,400 • Sharad Pawar quits GoM on corruption.

08. IPL season IV begins • Silver is Rs. 60,000 a kg and gold Rs. 21,275 • IPL-4 inaugurated in Chennai • Government concedes to Anna Hazare's demands to introduce in Parliament a more stringent anti-graft law, Hazare to end his fast on 9th • Kashmir leader Moulvi Shewkat Ahmad Shah killed in blast near mosque, Srinagar • Forex reserves at $305.486 bn. • Auto exports from India soar 30% in 2010-11.

11. 70% polling in Assam • Biometric PAN cards are on the way.

12. ED to attach properties of former Jharkhand CM Madhu Koda worth Rs. 130 cr.

13. General elections held in Kerala, Tamil Nadu and Puducherry • India and China agree to work towards removing all major irritants impacting bilateral relationship • Exports in 2010-11 will be in $225-230 bn. range • Sachin Tendulkar named Wisden cricketer of 2010.

16. Distribution of rice at Rs. 2 a kg. to begin on 17th.

18. Karnataka to re-impose ban on endosulfan • Rights activist Binayak Sen released on bail • Arunima Sinha, volleyball player pushed out of a train.

19. Jaitapur protest against nuke part becomes violent • Copper crash kills 17 in Arunachal.

20. SBI scraps teaser house loan scheme • PSLV-C 16 places 3 satellites in orbit.

22. Sai Baba is critically ill.

23. India's football coach Bob Houghton quits.

24. Satya Sai Baba, a cult figure with a phenomenal following across the globe, dies at 85 at Puttaparthi • Speculation on who will manage the Rs. 40,000 cr. Sai Baba Trust.

25. Kerala Chief Minister goes on fast on endosulfan issue • Suresh Kalmadi arrested for the Commonwealth Games fiasco; Rajya Sabha member Kanimozhi chargesheeted in 2G spectrum scam.

26. Wikileaks founder says there are Indian names in the Swiss bank data list • Government is pushing ahead with the Jaitapur nuclear plant project • A slipper hurled at Suresh Kalmadi being taken to a Delhi court.

27. Duncan Fletcher is appointed cricket coach • Mortal remains of spiritual guru Satya Sai Baba interred in Sai Kulwant Hall.

Satya Sai Baba

| Still Births | **India is one of the top five countries, others being Pakistan, Nigeria, China and Bangladesh representing half of all still births worldwide .** |

28. Talks fail, AI pilots' strike, flights cancelled.

30. K.V. Kamath named new chairman of Infosys • Helicopter carrying Arunachal Chief Minister Dorjee Khandu goes missing.

May

Mamata is W. Bengal CM

01. AIEEE papers leaked in UP, test postponed.

02. Delhi High Court asks striking AI pilots to end strike • Osama bin Laden is killed in Pakistan • Fund raising norms for FDI eased • The Rs.54,000 crore Posco steel plant gets final clearance from centre • Bihar Chief Minister Nitish decries change of syllabus in UPSC making English essential.

03. West Bengal phase 4 elections • RBI raises key rates 50 basis points • Savings bank rate is raised from 3.5% to 4%.

04. Body of Arunachal Pradesh Chief Minister Dorjee Khandu found after 5 days of search in Lunguthang village, 30 km, from Tawang • Hissar is 42.2°C, the hottest • Ban on general red category pesticides.

Dorjee Khandu

05. 18 held so far for using forged marksheets to procure commercial flying licences • Tagore bust unveiled in Singapore to commemorate 150th Birth anniversary of the poet.

06. K. Kanimozhi pleads ignorance of the Rs. 200cr. transfer from Dynamin Realty to Kalaignar TV • E D files charge sheet against Hassan Ali and Kashinath Tapurah • Supreme Court upholds attachment of Harshad Mehta's property • Air India pilots call off the 10-day old strike.

08. B.R. Hills and Kudremukh forests in Karnataka to become tiger reserves • Farmers' agitation, beginning in Noida, spreads • Malayalam made compulsory in schools in Kerala.

11. India releases list of 950 'most wanted fugitives' • 920 clear civil services exam.

13. Election results: AIADMK has 203 seats in 234-member Tamil Nadu assembly, Mamata Banerjee–led Trinamul Congress - Congress combine 225 / 294 in West Bengal, Tarun Gogoi's Congress has 69/126 in Assam • Public debt up 1.3% to Rs. 29.21 lakh cr. • Prime Minister returns from Kabul after 2-day visit • Supreme Court bans Endosulfan.

14. Oil firms hike petrol price by Rs. 5 a litre.

15. Oommen Chandy elected leader of the House, Kerala • In Karnataka, 11 BJP rebel MLAs support Chief Minister Reddy.

16. J. Jayalalithaa sworn in 17th Tamil Nadu

J. Jayalalithaa

Chief Minister • BJP steps up offensive against Governor Bharadwaj in Karnataka.

18. Ommen Chandy sworn in Kerala CM • Tarun Gogoi is Assom CM the third time.

20. Mamata Banerjee is sworn in West Bengal CM, the first woman to head a government • Kanimozhi, M.P. and daughter of M. Karunanidhi jailed in Tihar after bail plea in connection with 2G scam is rejected.

21. Kerala's Salim Kumar is the best film actor, both at national and state levels for his film *Adaminte Makan Abu*.

22. UPA's second anniversary celebrated • The newest communication satellite GSat-8 will be fully functional in 6 weeks.

23. UPA government defends Karnataka governor Bhardwaj.

24. It is the wealthier and more educated families in India that go for selective abortion of the second girl child, a study claims.

25. 50% concession in rail fares for women over 58 from June.

30. NCP wants Dadar station named after Ambedkar • GJM chief Bimal Gurung to

Saga-220 **Saga-220, the supercomputer at Satish Dhawan Supercomputing facility at VSSC, Thiruvananthapuram will be India's fastest supercomputer.**

India's Research Reactors

The country's first research reactor Apsara became operational on August 4, 1956 even before China or Japan built their own. The fuel was enriched uranium with cadmium as the control rods.

Cirus, formerly known as CIR, is India's second research reactor, built as a Indo-Canadian project under the Colombo Plan. This was completed on 10 July 1960. The name CIR stands for Canadian Indian Reactor and the new name Cirus is the name of the star closest to our solar system. It is a natural uranium, heavy water operated, light water cooled, high flux research reactor with a terminal power of 40 mw. It is situated at Trombay.

Zerlina is India's third research reactor. The name stands for zero energy lattice investigation nuclear assembly as it studies lattice assemblies of different kinds. The reactor attained criticality on January 14, 1961. Natural uraı.   is the fuel and heavy water the moderator.

Purnima is India's first experimental zero energy fast breeder reactor. It attained criticality on May 22, 1972. It uses plutonium oxide as fuel. Purnima is used to train personnel in the operation of plutonium fuelled fast reactors.

The Fast Breeder Test Reactor (FBTR) at Kalpakkom and the Dhruva Research Reactor at Trombay were entirely designed and built indigenously. The fast breeder reactors are more complex in technology. But they have the advantage that they produce more fuel than they consume.

A landmark in reactor technology was reached in 1984 when the small test reactor PURNIMA-II was commissioned at BARC. It was fuelled by uranium - 233 obtained from thorium abundantly found in the beach sands of Kerala.

resume talks with Mamata-led Government on Gorkhaland issue • Tax defaulters' names may be made public.

31. Angela Merkel receives Nehru Award for 2009 • Maruti may set up a unit in Gujarat.

June

Baba Ramdev's Fast

01. Controversial ministers, including Dayanidhi Maran likely to be dropped from the Cabinet • Union Ministers try to placate Baba Ramedev who insists on his indefinite fast against corruption and black money • N.D. Tiwari, former A. P. Governor, refuses to give blood sample for DNA test in a paternity suit • Bengaluru airport put on terror alert • Jayalalithaa breaks her vow and wears jewellery (ear-studs), after 14 years' gap.

02. Sania Mirza becomes the first Indian woman to enter a Grand Slam doubles final • In Karnataka, Chief Minister Yeddyurappa wins fourth trust vote • Preparations in full swing at Ramlila Grounds in Delhi where Yoga guru Baba Ramdev will begin a hunger strike against black money.

03. 20 states oppose the ban on endosulfan • Centre's talks with Baba Ramdev fail • Baba Ramdev's fast in Delhi begins • Former Haryana Chief Minister Bhajan Lall dies at 81.

05. Police crackdown on Baba Ramdev and supporters after midnight • Anna Hazare to boycott Lokpal Bill committee meeting

06. Prime Minister says crackdown on Ramdev was unfortunate but unavoidable • A street in Brampton, Canada to be named after Raj Kapoor • Kalmadi's bail plea rejected • Baba Ramdev resumes stir at Haridwar • S.C. NHRC issue notice to UPA Govt. on the police swap on Baba Ramdev's camp • No tax return for those with salary upto Rs. 5 lakh.

07. Hazare shifts fast venue from Jantar Mantar to Rajghat • P.O. Savings bank deposits to be raised from 3.50 to 4.0% • Prime Minister asks ministers to declare their assets by Aug. 31.

09. Baba Ramdev makes public details of his business empire worth over Rs. 1100 cr. • Prithvi-II tested successfully.

10. Baba Ramdev's shifted to hospital • T.H. Rana, connected with Nov. 2008 attack in Mumbai is acquitted • Forex reserves rise to $312.904 bn.

11. Veteran Bombay journalist Jyotirmoy Dey who exposed the city's underworld killed by four unidentified assassins • Forces to open up for more women.

Jyotirmoy Dey

12. Baba Ramdev ends fast on the ninth day • Police force redeployed at Posco site.

13. Union Minister J. Ramesh gives into to Kerala's Vizhinjam project, but Athirappally Hydel power project is not okayed • Supreme Court asks CBI to explain where the Rs. 200 cr., allegedly directed to KalaignarTV, has gone.

15. K.M. Chandrasekhar is Vice-Chairman of Kerala State Planning Board.

16. RBI hikes rates, EMIs to go up • Infosys Technologies renamed Infosys Ltd.

17. CBI opposes Kanimozhi bail plea • CAG

Infosys Headquarters

detects massive irregularities in the purchase of Israeli USVs worth Rs. 450 cr. • Rs. 11.56 cr. in cash, 98 kg of gold and 307 kg of silver found inside Satya Sai Baba's Yajurveda Mandir, his personal chamber • Post Office

| India's Lead in Domestic Banking | India is to become the 3rd largest domestic banking sector by 2050 after China and the US, a Pricewaterhouse Cooper's survey says. |

savings accounts to be taxed.

20. Supreme Court denies bail to Kanimozhi • Government and civil society members differ on selection of Lokpal members.

21. Monsoon to be below normal, says IMD • Government presents its draft Lokpal Bill • Naresh Chandra heads task force to review defence preparedness.

25. Fuel price hike sparks nation-wide protests • Quoting PAN is compulsory if you buy jewellery or bullion worth Rs. 5 lakh or more.

27. Ranjan Mathai is the new Foreign Secretary • Journalist Dey's murder in Mumbai was ordered by underworld don Chhota Rajan, say police • New Zealand PM John Key in India.

28. Trivandrum Padmanabha Swamy temple cellars not opened for decades, opened by an expert team.

29. UAE to open a consulate in Kerala • Opposition gains the self-financing college seat struggle in Kerala • PM says he may be brought under Lokpal.

30. Coins of 25 paise and smaller values

cease to be legal tender from July 1, 2011 • Denmark not to extradite Purulia arms drop case master-mind Kim Davy to India • Food inflation is down to 7.8 p.c. • Five more athletes including Sini Jose flunk dope test • India is the 4th largest steel producer.

July

Union Cabinet Reshuffle

02. Left wants office of Prime Minister brought under Lokpal.

03. Trivandrum Padmanabhaswamy temple's security status discussed by senior government officials, as estimates put

Padmanabhaswamy Temple

value of the treasure holdings at Rs. 1 lakh crore.

04. Telangana issue again on the boil: 10 Congress MPs and 39 MLAs and 34 TDP MLAs resign.

05. Union Minister Murli Deora offers to step down • Supreme Court says Salwa Judum is unconstitutional • Indian Railways to have its own e-ticketing soon.

06. CBI report point at Dayanidhi Maran's involvement in the 2G spectrum allocation case.

07. Union Minister Dayanidhi Maran resigns • MP Fund Allocation hiked from Rs. 2cr to Rs. 5 cr.

08. Head of Travancore's royal family informs SC they were not making any claim to the wealth and properties of Padmanab-haswamy Temple, Royal family is only the trustees.

09. Solicitor General Gopal Subramanium resigns.

10. Haryana-bound Kalka Mail derails killing 68 .

12. Union cabinet reshuffle, eight new-comers.

13. Terrorists strike: three bomb blasts in Mumbai kill 20, injure 100.

14. New Vigilance Commissioner Pradeep Kumar takes over.

15. India launches its latest communica-tion satellite GSAT-12 on board indigenous PSLV-C 17 rocket • Centre, failing to meet deadline on Endosulfan sets 3 weeks exten-

Kalka mail passenger tragedy

sion • Tata Group set to launch a house for Rs. 32,000, aimed at rural market by end of 2012.

16. Niurpama Rao appointed envoy to US.

18. Tripartite agreement for Gokhaland Territorial Administration signed.

20. Rs. 75 lakh each for Mangalore aircrash victims' families • Lokayukta recommends a probe into CM Yeddyurappa's role in illegal mining in Karnataka.

21. DRDO conducts trial of Prahaar missile.

22. Gagan Narang gets Rajiv Khel Ratna Award for 2011 • Cabinet approves BP-Reliance $72 bn. deal.

25. President Ms. Patil declares her assets – over Rs. 2.49 cr. • Bangladesh honours Indira Gandhi with the highest award.

26. Pak Foreign Minister Hina Rab-bani Khar in New Delhi.

27. Lokayukta im-plicates Yeddyurappa Government for caus-ing loss of Rs. 16,805 cr. • PMK snaps ties with DMK • S M Krishna admonishes Hina for meeting Hurriyat leader before meeting the Indian establishment.

Yeddyurappa

Gagan Narang receives the Award from the President

28. Karnataka CM Yeddyurappa agrees to resign • Cabinet approves the drafts of Lokpal Bill that doesn't include the PM or the judiciary. Anna Hazare calls it a cruel joke

and announces fast from Aug. 16.

29. Justice Dinakaran resigns • Police refuse permission to Team Anna to go on indefinite strike at Janatar Mantar d for private companies for private purposes.

August.

Anna Hazare is the Star

01. New Foreign Secretary Rajan Mathai takes charge.

02. Centre decides not to confer Padma Awards on serving bureaucrats.

03. Sadananda Gowda elected new Karnataka CM • Requests from various quarters for conferring Bharat Ratna on Sachin • Air India is in serious trouble, says PM.

04. Subsidy on diesel may be cut • Lok Pal Bill introduced in Lik Sabha; Anna Hazare burns copies of the bill • Air India to get equity infusion of Rs. 1200 cr. • Gold is Rs.24,000 per 10 grams • Sonia Gandhi in US for surgery.

05. PM is dragged to CWG mess by CAG,

Sadananda Gowda (right) taking Oath

which points to Sheila Dixit and Kalmadi in the money wasted on organising the CWG• Sensex plunges 387 points to hit a 14-month low • Commemarative stamps on Rashtrapati Bhavan issued.

07. Indian stock market among worst performers this year.

08. Gold breaches Rs. 25,000-mark per 10 gms • Sensex plunges to below 17,000 mark.

09. D. Subba Rao to be RBI governor for two more years • Kerala CM Oommen Chandy quits Vigilance portfolio • Aditya

Mehta of Mumbai clinches snooker nationals • Gold hits new peak at Rs.25,460 per 10 gm.

11. Parliament permits government to mint coins in the denomination of Rs. 1000 • Mercy petition of Rajiv killers rejected by President.

12. Rohit Nandan is new Air India chief • NIA special court awards triple life term to T. Nazeer, and double life term to Shafaz in

Tata Ace

Kozhikode twin blasts case • Tata's Nano and Ace set to roll out from new factories in Brazil, Indonesia and East Europe by 2012.

13. SBI profit halves to Rs. 1584 cr. in Q1.

14. Shammi Kapoor, veteran film actor, passes away • Assam students (AASU) begin 27-hour hunger strike protesting government failure to implement Assam accords • Anna Hazare to go ahead with his strike at Jayaprakash Nagar Park, New Delhi.

16. Anna Hazare arrested and sent to Tihar jail, later after nation-wide protest, his release is ordered, but he refuses to leave jail • Rajya Sabha wants Justice Soumitra Sen removed for corruption; impeachment motion is carried.

17. Coal India becomes the largest listed company.

18. Anna Hazare wants a revised LokPal Bill.

19. West Bengal to be renamed Paschim Banga • Gold is at a record high of Rs.

Chiranjeevi

20,520 • Sensex closes below 16000 • UP government revokes ban on the Prakash Jha - directed film *Arakashan*.

20. Film star Chiranjeevi joins Congress • Karnataka's Lokayukta to probe graft charges against Yeddyurappa.

21. Hazare says still the floor is open for talks • Rahul Dravid becomes the second highest century maker from India • NAC member Aruna Roy has described Hzare's Jan Lokpal Bill as a 'threat to democracy'.

22. On the 7th day of his fast, Anna Hazare says he would negotiate with Rahul Gandhi, PMO or Prithviraj Chauhan on Lokpal Bill • Gyanpeeth to Urdu poet Shahryar • PM writes to Anna Hazare appealing him to end his fast, and deputes FM Pranab Mukherjee to hold talks with Team Anna • 41 pilgrims killed at Nagra, UP.

23. Kanimozhi, DMK M.P., tells the court that Manmohan Singh could be called in as a witness in 2G case to prove that there is no loss to the exchequer due to spectrum allocation under former Minister A. Raja.

24. Baichung Bhutia annouces his international retirement • SC bars Tamil Nadu from repairing the Mullaperiyar dam • Amar Singh chargesheeted in the 2008 cash–for-vote scam • All party meet urges Anna Hazare to end fast (9th day now).

Baichung Bhutia

26. Three men facing death penalty for Rajiv Gandhi assassination to be hanged on Sept. 9 • Gujarat Governor appoints Retd. Justice R.A. Mehta as Lokayukta, bypassing the government • On 11th day of fast, Anna Hazare's health is

---

Workshop for Ministers — **Kerala Council of Ministers attended a workshop on state level leadership organised for them, at IIM Kozhikode on Aug. 18.**

stable • Forex reserves surge to $318.2 bn.

28. Anna Hazare ends his 12-day fast at Ramlila grounds, hailing Parliaments's nod on key elements of Jan Lokpal Bill as 'people's victory'.

30. Madras High Court stays execution of three Rajiv Gandhi killers for 8 weeks.

September

Modi Fasts

01. Enforcement Directorate books Yoga guru Ramdev for FEMA breach • Justice Soumitra Sen of Calcutta facing impeachment resigns.

03. Forex rerserves are $319.175 bn.

04. Minister Kamal Nath, with assets of Rs. 2.77 cr. is the richest in the cabinet.

05. Bellary Reddy arrested, for alleged illegal mining; 30 kg of gold and Rs. 4.5 cr. in cash seized • Manmohan Singh visits Dhaka.

06. Amar Singh, Rajya Sabha member, sent to jail for cash–for-vote scam • There is a demand for inclusion of 38 more languages in the 8th schedule.

07. 11 killed and 16 injured as briefcase bomb explodes in Delhi High Court reception

Blast in Delhi

area : Hu Ji claims responsibility • M.O.H. Farook takes over as new Kerala Governor • Amitab Bachchan to make his Hollywood debut with '*The Great Gatsby*' • Quake (4.2) shakes Delhi.

08. Sonia Gandhi returns to India after surgery • L.K. Advani to take out a yatra across the country against corruption.

10. 3000 doctors strike work in Maharashtra • B.C. Khanduri to be Uttarathand CM • India has 858.4 mn. mobile phone subscribers.

11. Dalit leader John Pandian's house arrested, a crowd goes on rampage in

Thoothukudi resulting in police firing which kills three.

12. Narinder Modi gets a respite in 2002 SC says 'no' to monitoring of the case.

13. Gujarat CM Modi to undertake a Sabbhavana Mission, with a 3-day fast • PHD Chamber study finds impact of inflation on the poor at 11.6 p.c. as compared to 7.5 p.c. for the rich • Centre warns western states of a possible terrorist attack on Mumbai airport • Indian cricket team skips ICC Annual Awards.

14. Train crash at Arakkonam kills 10 • A US Congressional report sees Modi Vs. Rahul likely for the 2014 PM • Inflation soars to

Arakkonam train crash

13-month high of 9.78% • Maharashtra government raising drinking bar age to 25 years • Telangana paralysed for 2nd day due to strike by 4 lakh government employees demanding Telangana state.

17. Modi begins 3-day fast in Ahmedabad, launching his Sabhavana mission • Ayazuddin, Azharuddin's son, injured in a road mishap dies • Congress leader Sankersingh Waghela launches a counter fast outside Sabarmati Ashram • Normality returns to Bharatpur after communal clashes kill 8 persons • Mayawati asks for quotas for minorities.

19. Narendra Modi ends his 3 day fast • Karnataka Lokayukta quits over housing plot row • BCCI terminates the contract of IPL franchise Kochi Tuskers.

20. Rupee hits new 2-year low as euro slips vs dollar • Bird flu cases in West Bengal • Over 3000 rescued in quake-hit Sikkim.

21. Disclosure of a note from a FM official in March to PMO on 2G spectrum pricing

sets off a controversy and BJP demands FM P. Chidambaram's resignation.

22. Mansur Ali Khan Pataudi, 70, passes away • Government Congress defend FM P. Chidambaram, over his stand in the 2G spectrum allocation. Opposition demands

Farewell to Nawab of Pataudi

his resignation • BSE down 707 points, after US Fed warning on the American economy • Kerala under the grip of rat fever • PM in New York, will address UN • Centre to consider repealing suicide bid as a penal offence • Government announces Rs. 50 cr. Central assistance to Sikkim .

23. Nitish Kumar to flag off Advani yatra • HC says N D Tiwari cannot be forced for DNA test but his refusal to give blood sample is proof against him • Pataudi laid to rest • Rupee at 28-month low of 49.90, Sensex falls to 16,163.

27. Union Health Minister calls the V R Krishna Iyer panel to restrict grants to those with two children 'ridiculous' • New regulation on unsolicited commercial calls and SMSes gives relief to telecom users • Planning Commission wants limit on Pharma FDI at less than 49% • JPC slams Finmin for 'suppressing' 2G facts • Ex-Advani aide S. Kulkarni arrested in cash-for-vote scam.

29. CBI gives a clean chit to Tata Teleservices in 2G case but not to Anil Ambani • Anna Hazare enters cyberworld • President to visit Switzerland and Austria .

30. J & K CM Omar apologises for revealing in Assembly names of rape victims • SC quashes bail grant to Pune stud-farm owner Hasan Ali Khan • FDI norms liberalised further • Centre to set up 6 pharma national institutes.

| Indian Rupee in SDR Basket | Montek Singh Ahluwalia, Deputy Chairman, Planning Commission, has said that Indian rupee will be the next currency to be included in the basket of SDR, in the next 10-15 years. |

**Cover
Story**

Page 163 - 192

The Arab Uprising

Dr. Ninan Koshy

There is a wave of changes in the north of Africa and West Asia. The revolts against regimes reflect a long-standing desire for freedom and economic justice.

Variously called revolution, revolt, intifada and so on, the Arab uprising, which began in Tunisia in December 2010 and then spread to other Arab nations, is a genuine expression of a long-standing desire for freedom and economic justice denied by the autocratic regimes in the region. The revolt against the regimes was not just out of economic and political grievances, but also out of a deeply rooted sense of humiliation, contempt and injustice by autocratic and self-serving regimes, felt intensely especially by the youth. The evolving situation raises several important questions. What are the common factors, if any, behind the movements? What are the possible outcomes of the demand for political reforms? How does the ongoing struggle impact the outside world and how does the outside world react? How will this affect the struggle of the Palestinian people for independent statehood?

Picture of Diversity

Answers to these questions are complex and difficult given the diversity in history, culture and politics of the different countries. The outcome of the mass protests is likely to vary in accordance with the nature and level of cohesion of the incumbent regimes and their ability to maintain their monopoly on the use of force. Despite the unpredictability of the current situation, it is clear that West Asia is experiencing a deep

Uprising in Bahrain

No.1 in Defence Expenditure | Libya recorded the highest defence expenditure in Africa. There is selective conscription for one to two years. Defence expenditure stood are $1441 mn. in 1998. This meant $238 per capita, the most in Africa, representing 5.3 percent of GDP.

Stay above the rest.

The one who stands apart is the one
who makes the difference.

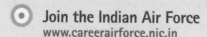

Join the Indian Air Force
www.careerairforce.nic.in

For Career Details Contact
Publicity Cell, "Disha", Air HQ(VB),
Motilal Nehru Marg, New Delhi-110106
Phone: 011-23013690
Telefax: 011-23017918
Email: career_iaf@bol.net.in

For joining as an Officer in Flying, Technical & Ground Duty Branches, please visit IAF Career website
at www.careerairforce.nic.in.

Demonstrators in Tunisia

transformation on several levels. There is no doubt that the Arab revolution sweeping the region will create a new political reality in many countries of the region. But the outcome is likely to differ. While some Arab states might be jolted into a new and fragile democratic reality, others will witness a more gradual transition or dodge the democracy trend altogether.

> The Arab uprising has been adversely affected and distorted by these regional moves and games.

Myths Demolished

Thesse revolts have immediately performed a kind of ideological house-cleaning sweeping away the wrong conceptions of a clash of civilizations that consign Arab politics to the past. They demolished the myths that Arab nationalism is dead and that alliance

with the USA guarantees regime security. The uprising began in a peaceful manner, except perhaps in Libya, but has taken a violent turn in countries like Yemen because of repression and killings by the regimes.

As protesters took to the streets from Morocco to Bahrain and violence has been engulfing Libya and Yemen, it seems self-evident that there was a powerful knock-on effect from the Tunisian and Egyptian events which overthrew autocratic regimes within a very short period. In many ways this was not surprising, given that many West Asian countries are prone to the same maladies that have plagued Egypt

Hosni Mubarak

and Tunisia. Still the Arab world is far from being a unitary bloc. Systems of government differ and not all countries share the same socio-economic grievances. Few Arab countries are also as religiously and ethnically homogenous as Tunisia and Egypt. Some harbour long-standing secessionist movements like in Yemen. These differences are likely to have an impact on the scale and shape of the uprisings as well as their results.

Manipulation and Suppression

The Arab uprising has suffered from intervention, manipulation and suppression by regional players as well as international actors. The most blatant regional intervention was of course the entry of troops from Saudi Arabia at the head of a Gulf Cooperation Council (GCC) military force into Bahrain on 14 March 2011 to put down a

Scrutiny of Ministers	**Pressure for social reforms is sweeping the Middle East. King Hamid bin Isa Al Khalifa has proposed reforms including increased scrutiny of government ministers in Bahrain. The crackdown on February protests attracted international attention.**

Uprising in Yemen

popular uprising supported by the majority Shiite population against the Sunni Bahraini monarch. Saudi officials insisted that it was Shiite Iran that was instigating the protest in Bahrain.

This has larger implications. Saudi Arabia, staunchly backed by UAE, Bahrain Kuwait and Jordan, has emerged as the principal regional rival of Iran in what Riyad and its allies are increasingly depicting as an existential conflict between West Asia's Sunni and Shiite communities. The deference shown by the West to the Saudi Kingdom, the clear leader of the region's counter-revolutionary wave is explained by a number of factors, not least of which is its role as the world's swing oil producer. Saudi Arabia is also a huge importer of US weapons.

Assistance from Qatar

But Saudi Arabia is not the only regional player that has intervened in the uprising

Angry mobs

in other countries. Qatar has been giving military and financial assistance to the rebels in Libya. It is alleged that Syrian protesters are armed and funded by some factions in Lebanon, in addition to the support by the Saudis. The Arab uprising has been adversely affected and distorted by these regional moves and games. The actions by the regional players generally suit the interests of Western powers which have militarily intervened in Libya, ostensibly to protect the civilians and are engaged in different modes of intervention in several other countries.

The Libyan case needs special treatment. Under the cover of the UN Security Council Resolution 1973 of 17 March 2011, authorizing member states to undertake "all

Uprisng in Tunisia

necessary measures" for the protection of civilians and for the enforcement of a 'no-fly zone' the NATO actually has waged a war against the Gaddafi regime. To the Western nations "all necessary measures" have come to mean only military action, excluding the range of possibilities including mediation, negotiations and diplomacy. Regime change in Libya, which NATO demanded, is not based on the UN Resolution which does not even have a reference to regime change.

Westeners Take Sides

As the military preparations of the size and magnitude employed in Libya are never improvised, there is reason to believe that the war in Libya as well as the armed in-

Women Can Vote | King Abdullah of Saudi Arabia has said that women will be allowed to vote and run as candidates for the first time, but not until 2015 municipal elections.

Efficient

Energy-efficient

CHANGING THE WAY WE USE ENERGY TODAY, FOR A BETTER TOMORROW.

It has been V-Guard's constant endeavour to reinvent itself by creating energy-efficient products that help you save more than you spend. With ingenuity at heart, V-Guard delivers technology that works to sustain energy for the uncertain tomorrow. And even with over 50 million satisfied customers, our satisfaction lies in ambitions always higher than before. Let's make the world a better place to live in.

| Refrigerator Stabilizer | Wires | Power & Control Cable | Pump | Water Heater | Fan |

| Solar Water Heater | UPS | Digital UPS & Inverter | Battery |

V-GUARD ®
The name you can trust

V-Guard Industries Ltd. Regd. Office : 33/2905 F, Vennala High School Rd., Vennala, Kochi - 682 028.
Ph.: +91 484 3005000 Fax.: 0484 3005100 E-mail: mail@vguard.in

Muammar Gaddafi

surrection against the regime was planned months prior to the Arab uprising. In Libya the Western powers have intervened in an internal conflict and taken sides in a civil war. There is reason to believe that the military action against Libya is part of a Western scheme to have control over the immense oil and natural gas reserves in that country. For the US which has denied vehemently that it harbours any strategic designs vis-à-vis Libya, the latter's criti-

> There will be a new Palestinian intifada with much of the world behind it.

cal role in facilitating China's access to its own oil and gas and the energy resources of other African countries is a key factor. The Libyan war thus fits into the US agenda to counter the growing Chinese influence in Africa. The strategic significance of the Mediterranean Sea is another important consideration for the West.

In Yemen, Bahrain, Oman, Kuwait, Saudi Arabia, Jordan, Morocco and Algeria, where there is – or there was – unrest in some form or other, Western powers are involved directly or indirectly in ensuring that the eventual outcome would be in their favour. The GCC, a grouping that is closely aligned to the US and the West, is helping them in the scheme. Even in Tuni-

sia and Egypt, the US working through individuals and groups in various institutions and segments of society, is determined to ensure that its interests and the interests of Israel will be preserved and perpetuated in the emerging political scenario. Israel and the US would prefer a government in Syria that would be more accommodative of their dominance in the region. The US's main concerns in Yemen are two–fold: counter–terrorism, especially against the al-Qaeda outfit in Yemen and the strategic port of Eden. For both the US needs a reliable ally there and a change of regime or civil war threatens US interests. The US would like to see Bahrain remain in the grip of the present rulers because the island is the home of the US Fifth Fleet. Egypt and Jordan are crucial because both have signed peace treaties with Israel.

Oil, Israel, China, geo-strategic interests, and weapons are the five reasons why the US and its Western allies are keen to shape the Arab uprising to suit their agenda. Some analysts would argue that the West is staging a "counter-revolution" to the Arab uprising, with the connivance and collusion of their Arab allies and clients.

Balance of Power

The Arab revolution is likely to change the regional balance of power decisively. The recent juxtaposition of a US-led "axis of moderation" against an Iran-led "axis of resistance" is unlikely to endure the current upheaval. Public pressure for a more independent international role and a revival of Pan-Arab cooperation is likely to

Arab thirst for democracy

No Lashes — In Sept. 2011, Saudi King Abdullah overturned a court verdict that sentenced a Saudi woman to be lashed 10 times for defying the kingdom's ban on women driving.

Morocco Demonstrators

alter the foreign policies of West Asian countries regardless of their current form of government. A return to Arab nationalism indeed seems a plausible consequence given the uprising's underlying themes of national pride and dignity. Political Islam of some shade might find a foothold in some of the states.

This transformation could skew the regional balance in favour of Iran, should it

> The contest between the USA and Iran has intensified as a result of the Arab uprising

indeed escape the crisis unscathed. The contest between the USA and Iran has intensified as a result of the Arab uprising and Iran is keen on extending its influence in the Arab world at a time when it thinks that the US influence is waning.

It appeared for a time that the focus

Libyan rebels taking control

of attention of West Asian politics shifted from the Israeli-Palestinian conflict to the wider issues raised by the uprising in various Arab states. But soon it was clear that the uprising had deep implications for the Israeli-Palestinian conflict. The Turkish President Abdulah Gul said in an op-ed article in the New York Times on April 20, 2011, with the title The Revolution's Missing Peace that the fate of the Arab world uprising will be determined by whether there is a peace between Israel and Palestinians. "Whether these uprisings lead to democracy and peace or to tyranny and conflict will depend on forging a lasting Israeli-Palestine peace agreement and a broader Israeli-Arab peace", he wrote.

Libyan rebels

Setback to US Policy

To begin with the apparent setback to the US policy in West Asia centred on Israeli security has put Israel in a vulnerable position. Israel is concerned with the future of the peace treaties, with Egypt and Jordan, which depends on the evolution of events in those countries, especially Egypt. The transitional government of Egypt has already lifted the four-year long Gaza blockade. Accustomed for decades to being at the centre of the West Asian playing field, Israel finds itself watching the regional upheaval from the sidelines, uncertain who its new friends and opponents will be and of the new rules of game.

The immediate impact of the uprising on the Palestinians was the realization that

---

Kidnapping Tourists

Yemen's rich historical heritage attracted tourists in large numbers. But the industry was hit by a spate of kidnapping of tourists by tribesmen. That was one way they could draw attention to a lack of amenities.

Reduce your carbon footprint..

...Use eco friendly Coir Products

Coir Geo textiles   Coir Pith   Coir Ply

कयर बोर्ड
Coir Board
Ministry of Micro, Small & Medium Enterprises,
Government of India

HO: Coir House, PB No.1752, M.G.Road, Kochi-682 016, Kerala, India. Ph:+91 484 2351807, Fax: 0484 2370034,
Cable: Coirboard, E-mail: coir@md2.vsnl.net.in, Website: www.coirboard.nic.in, www.coirboard.gov.in

MSME Udyamy Helpline Toll Free No. 1800-180-6763

®REFLECTIONS/CB/2011

Palestinian unity was crucial at this point of history, a realization that led to the unity agreement between Fatah and Hamas. The uprising began at a time when it had already appeared that the Palestinians were moving out of the deeply flawed US framework of peace process and seeking wider support in the international community through the UN, for early independent statehood. The uprising gave a new momentum to this initiative. If the UN recognizes a Palestinian state and the Israeli occupation continues unchanged, there will be a new Palestinian intifada with

Obama

much of the world behind it. The United States is fumbling how to sort out such a situation. The long-term implications of the Arab revolt for Israel's future are ominous which means there is imperative need for a "grand compromise" for the establishment of an independent Palestinian state.

India's Concerns

India has mainly three sets of concerns about the Arab uprising: the supply of oil from the region; the safety of Indian nationals in the countries and the larger geostrategic interests in its West Asian neighbourhood.

The new developments raise serious questions on all these. To be on the right side of history, when the Arab people are struggling for freedom and democracy, protecting these interests *Manmohan Singh* is not going to be easy. Currently Indian policy on West Asia is based on a close relationship with the US, Israel and the pro-US Arab countries. There will be changes in the policies of all these countries compelling India to revise its own policies.

(Dr. Ninan Koshy, formerly Director, Commission of the Churches on International Affairs, World Council of Churches, Geneva and formerly Visiting Fellow, Harvard Law School, Cambridge, USA)

Expatriates' Remittances | One source of foreign exchange for Syria is the expatriate Syrian workers in the Gulf countries whose remittances are equivalent to 20% of export earnings.

The Jasmine Revolution

The Arab Uprising, often referred to as Jasmine Revolution, shook the entire North Africa and West Asia. When rebellion engulfed the region, regimes collapsed and freedom won victories. A new Arab world is in the making.

Mohammed Bouazizi, a young man of 28 with some education, but no job set himself on fire in a provincial town called Sidi Bouzid in the North African country of

Tunisia on December 17, 2010. Nobody then would have thought that it was the beginning of a mass uprising against the deep rooted autocracy in the Middle East.

Bouazizi, who later succumbed to his injuries was just protesting against chronic unemployment and police harassment. He had been humiliated by a woman police constable who allegedly slapped him for selling vegetable from a cart in the town without a license. People's anger at the incident soon mingled with their bitterness at the fast deteriorating living conditions, high level corruption and lack of political freedom and grew into an unprecedented mass movement against the 23-year old dictatorship of President Zine El Abidine Ben Ali. The 65-year old despot fled the country on January 14, 2011, hardly a

Tunisia: the old order changeth

month after the self immolation of Mohammed Bouazizi.

It was the first successful demonstration of people's power in the Arab world in many years. The uprising spread like wildfire from Tunisia to other countries such as the neighbouring Libya and Egypt in North Africa as well as Yemen, and Syria in West Asia, The wave of unrest also for a while gripped some other countries like Algeria, Morocco, Jordan, Bahrain and Oman. It also had its repercussions beyond the Arab world, in Iran and even in far away China.

It came to be known as the 'Jasmine Revolution' after the national flower of Tunisia. It was also called the 'Arab Spring', a term modeled on the Prague Spring of 1968, when the people of Czechoslovakia rebelled against the communist rule and the Soviet occupation.

It was a bit surprising that the revolution in the middle east first took place in Tunisia, a country thought to be one of the most stable in the region. In fact, Tunisia lying between Algeria and Libya had rarely

Qatar Vs. Iran-Iraq	During the 80s, Qatar's status was threatened by the regional dominance of Iran and Iraq and a territorial dispute with Bahrain.

Shanthi Gears

Good gears always add into your profits

The efficiency of a gear could make or break you in your industry. That is where we step in with high quality, high precision gears, gear boxes, geared motors and gear assemblies both standard & custom built. Think gears. Think Shanthi. Because our gears won't chew into your profits.

We, at Shanthi Gears, have always endeavoured to keep pace with the evolving technologies and give highly customized solutions to industry leaders across the world because the fact remains that a machine is only as good as its gear. Ours is the only Gear Company, perhaps in the whole world, to have end-to-end facilities like castings, forgings, fabrication,heat treatment and complete gear / gear box manufacturing including hob making,

all in-house, in a built up area of one million square feet, spread over 125 acres of land.

Today, you can find that our gears are driving aircrafts, trains, tractors, compressors, cranes, elevators, conveyors and other machinery in almost every industry like cement, textile, power, steel, sugar; just to name a few.

We have brought into effect new, efficient and speedy customer support and logistics to further strengthen our customer relationship. With these additional systems, we can constantly work with our customers meeting their requirements on time, every time.

All you need is to call our Head Office or our nearest Sales Offices directly.

For any breakdown / emergency, we can do it in no time through our red channel route, by which various processes happen continuously like passing through a conveyor belt.

www.sasiads.com

SHANTHI GEARS LIMITED

304-A, Shanthi Gears Road, Singanallur, Coimbatore - 641 005. Tamilnadu. India. **Ph :** 91 - 422 - 2273722 to 34
Fax : 91 - 422 - 2273884 / 85 **E-mail :** info@shanthigears.com **Web :** www.shanthigears.com

Timeline: Tunisia

1956 : Tunisia wins independence from France with Habib Bourguiba as Prime Minister.

1957 : Tunisia becomes a republic. Bourguiba becomes President

1975 : Bourguiba becomes President-for-Life.

1987 : Bourguiba declared mentally unfit to rule. Prime Minister Zine El Abidine Ben Ali declares himself President.

2000 : Bourguiba dies.

2009 : President Ben Ali wins a fifth term in office.

2010 December: An unemployed youth Mohamed Bouazizi set himself on fire sparking violent protests against Ben Ali's dictatorship.

2011 January: Ben Ali goes into exile.

2011 June: A court in Tunisia sentences Ben Ali and wife in absentia to 35 years in jail and fined $ 66 million for embezzlement and misuse of public funds.

Tunisia, where it all started

owned half of the wealth of Tunisia.

Faced with the protests, Ben Ali again promised political reforms and at the same time tried to suppress the agitation with an iron hand. But when his troops started refusing to shoot the people he saw the writing on the wall. Along with his family he fled the country to Saudi Arabia, without even handing over power to his successor. The new Tunisian government issued an international warrant for his arrest on corruption charges. Later, a court in Tunisia sentenced Ben Ali and his wife Leila in absentia to 35 years in jail for embezzlement and misusing public funds. They were also fined $ 66 million.

Egypt

When Ben Ali fled, there were people who predicted that the next one to go would be Hosni Mubarak of Egypt. It became true in less than a month on February 11, 2011. Inspired by the successful culmina-

figured in any political developments that rocked the middle east in many years.

Tunisia which won its freedom from France in 1956 had never experienced democracy. The founding father Habib Burguiba had proclaimed himself the President of life in 1975. Ben Ali, who was Burguiba's Prime Minister staged a 'medical coup' and got Burguiba declared as senile and incapable of performing his official duties and took over power in 1987. He promised political reforms, but failed to implement them. Soon he became much more autocratic and corrupt than his predecessor. He got himself elected to the presidency five times, in polls which were widely rigged. Those who opposed were arrested and jailed. It was alleged that he and his ex-beautician wife, sons and sons in law had

Popular Uprising in Egypt

Land in Private Hands In Syria, the extensive land reform in the 1960s led to the more or less even distribution of land, which is mostly in private hands. Government controls the prices of both inputs and food.

Timeline: Egypt

Hosni Mubarak

1922 : Egypt gains independence from Britain.
1952 : Colonel Gamal Abdul Nasser leads a coup and deposes King Farouk.
1953 : Egypt becomes Republic with Muhammad Najib as President.
1956 : Nasser takes over as President. He nationalises the Suez Canal to fund the Aswan High Dam.
1956 : Britain, France and Israel invade Egypt.
1958 : Egypt and Syria join to form the United Arab Republic (UAR).
1961 : Syria withdraws from the union.
1965 : King Farouk dies in Rome.
1967 : Six-Day War. Israel captures Sinai and the Gaza Strip from Egypt, the Golan Heights from Syria and the West Bank and East Jerusalem from Jordan
1970 : Nasser dies. Vice-President Anwar al-Sadat becomes President.
1973 : Yom Kippur war. Egypt and Syria go to war with Israel to reclaim the land they lost in 1967.
1979 : Egypt signs peace treaty with Israel. In protest the Arab League expels Egypt.
1981 : President Sadat is assassinated. Vice President Hosni Mubarak takes over as President.
1989 : Egypt rejoins the Arab League.
1995 : Assassination attempt against Mubarak in Ethiopia.
2005 : President Mubarak is re-elected for a fifth consecutive term.
2007 : The ruling National Democratic Party wins most of the seats in rigged parliamentary elections.
2009 : US President Barack Obama visits Cairo and call for a new beginning between the US and the Muslim world.
2010 February : Former UN nuclear chief Mohammed ElBaradei returns to Egypt and, forms a coalition for political change.
2011 January : Protests erupt against Mubarak apparently encouraged by the Tunisian uprising. .
2011 February : Mubarak steps down and hands over power to the army council.
2011 April : Mubarak and his sons, Ala and Gamal, are arrested on charges of corruption.
2011 August : The trial of Mubarak and his sons begins.
2011 September : Mob attacks Israel's embassy in Cairo

GO OUT LEAVE EGYPT

tion of the Tunisian revolution, the Egyptian people took to the streets on January 25 demanding the exit of the octogenarian President who had been ruling the country for 30 years. Egypt had been under 'emergency law' since 1967 under which all constitutional rights were banned. The people were increasingly impoverished and at least four people had self-immolated out of desperation early in 2011.

A former commander of the Egyptian air force and later the Vice President under

Alawis and Sunnis The population of Syria is mostly Arab and Muslim, split between the majority Sunni community and others, including the Alawi, a branch of the Shiah sect. The Assad family and other Alawis control the government but most business community is Sunni.

Anwar Sadat, Mubarak came to power following the assassination of Sadat in 1981. He got himself elected to the post five times, four times by referendum and lastly by a poll in 2005 all which were widely rigged. No different was the November-December 2010 parliamentary elections in which Mubarak's National Democratic Party won all but three percent of the seats. He was pondering about running for the post again in September 2011 and simultaneously grooming his son Gamal as his successor.

He responded to the call for his resignation first by offering not to seek re-election and assuring that Gamal will not be the candidate either. But he wanted to remain in office until his current term expired in October. As protesters remained unrelenting, he appointed his trusted intelligence chief Omar Suleiman as Vice President to hold negotiations with them. Until then there

Renewed Nationalism

Violence spreads to streets

never had been a Vice President under Mubarak. He also tried to drown the agitation in blood by instigating his armed supporters to stage a counter demonstration in Tahrir Square in the capital Cairo, where the protesters had been staging mass sit-in since the first day of agitation. Several people were killed in clashes. As happened in Tunisia, the troops refused to fire on the agitators, leaving notice to Mubarak that his time was over. He stepped down on the 18th day of protests after handing over power to a group of senior military men.

As in Tunisia, the uprising in Egypt was also spontaneous and mostly without any visible leaders even though the presence of the Nobel Prize winning Dr Mohammed Elbaradei in Tahrir Square had attracted world wide attention. The former chief of the International Atomic Energy Agency wanted to inspire a peaceful transition to a more democratic regime and had been thinking of contesting the presidential election which was due in September 2011. Even he was taken by surprise by the spontaneity and enormity of the uprising.

Unlike the Tunisian dictator, Mubarak did not flee the country, but moved to the summer resort town of Sharm Al Shaik. Later he was arrested along with his two sons on charges of corruption and abuse of power. An ailing Mubarak, dressed in prison whites and lying on a hospital bed was rolled into a courtroom in August to face charges of corruption and complicity in the killing of protesters. The courtroom was housed in a police academy that once bore his name. Along with him in the cage-like dock were his two sons, Gamal and Alaa, former Interior Minister Habib el-Adly and six senior police officers.

The new government led by Field Marshal Hussein Tantawi have announced that the elections to a new parliament would be held over three rounds from November 28 to January 3. A three-round senate election will be held from January 29 to March 11. Following these elections, a committee will draft a new constitution and on the basis of which a new President will be elected.

Yemen

The third Arab nation to witness the mass unrest was Yemen, the poorest country in the middle east. Strategically located in West Asia, at the intersection of the Red Sea and the Indian Ocean, it is also politically most fragile in the region. The protests which began in February 2011 were initially against unemployment, economic hardship and corruption, but they soon grew into a movement that called for the end of the 33-year old rule of President Ali Abdullah Saleh, 69. Unlike in Tunisia and Egypt, the protests were planned and or-

Yemeni agitation

The Great Man-Made River	Libya has a major project begun in the 80s, to bring water from wells in the South to the coast. The scheme called the Great Man-Made River was planned to irrigate some 185,000 acres of land with water brought along some 4000 km. of pipes.

ganised. Opposition political parties and the tribal leaders also joined the agitation.

Saleh was just 36, when he captured power through a military coup in North Yemen in 1978 while the country was divided into two states. He became President of the unified Yemen in 1990 and was ruling the country ever since with an iron hand. Like Ben Ali and Hosni Mubarak, he was fraudulently getting elected in all the polls and was planning to run for the presidency again when his seven-year current term ends in 2013. Simultaneously he was also grooming his son Ahmed to succeed him.

As the protests grew, Saleh tried to diffuse the situation by announcing that he would not run for re-election and that he would not pass power to his son either. Later, he offered to step down and hand over power to his deputy after thirty days in return for immunity for him and his family. The deal brokered by the Gulf Cooperation Council also required the opposition to stop agitation and join a coalition with the ruling party.

But, Saleh refused to sign the deal several times at the last minute. Pitched street fighting which included artillery and mortar shelling followed between the protesters supported by powerful tribes and Saleh's armed forces. Saleh was severely injured in a rocket attack on the presidential palace in Sana'a on June 3 and was flown to the neighbouring Saudi Arabia for treatment. Also injured were the prime minister, the deputy prime minister, the parliament chief, the governor of Sana'a and a presidential aide.

Timeline : Yemen

1918 : North Yemen gains independence and is ruled by Imam Yahya.

1948 : Yahya assassinated. His son Ahmad succeeds.

1962 : Ahmad dies, succeeded by his son. Army officers seize power and declares the country as the Yemen Arab Republic.

1967 : Southern Yemen, takes the name of People's Democratic Republic of Yemen.

1978 : Ali Abdallah Saleh becomes President of North Yemen. .

1990 : Saleh takes over as President of the Unified Yemen.

1994 : Saleh declares state of emergency.

1995 - Yemen and Eritrea clash over disputed island territory.

2000 : Suicide attack against the US warship Cole in the Yemeni port of Aden kills 17 US soldiers. Al Qaeda claims responsibility.

2011 January : Demonstrations begin demanding Saleh to quit power.

2011 March : Police open fire on pro-democracy demonstrations in Sanaa, killing more than 50 people

2011 June : Saleh seriously injured in a rocket attack against the presidential compound and is flown to Saudi Arabia for treatment

2011 September : Saleh returns to Yemen from Saudi Arabia.

A Scene from Yemen

between Saleh loyalists and his armed opponents, killing many more people.

Even before the turmoil began in February, Yemen was facing several daunting security problems. It is the home of Al Qaeda in the Arabian Peninsula (AQAP), known as the most threatening branch of the global terror network. Taking advantage of the crisis, the AQAP captured control of several towns in the south where, the government troops had been battling separatists who lost a civil war in 1994. In the north, Saleh's troops had been fighting the Houthi rebels belonging to the minority Shia Zaidi sect.

Libya

The revolt against the 41-year long, capricious and autocratic rule of Muammer

Saleh's departure fuelled hopes that he would be forced to step down. The US and Saudi Arabia also tried to dissuade him from returning home in the hope of working out a peaceful transition. But, in a surprise move, Saleh returned to Sana'a in September after more than three months of medical treatment in Saudi Arabia. Defiantly he declared that he would not step down as promised earlier if his opponents were allowed to stand elections to succeed him. This sparked a new wave of violent clashes

Muammar Qaddafi in the good old days

Assad's Rule

In Syria, Hafez Assad's death marked the end of an era. He led the faction representing the Alawi community that seized power in the 1970 coup. The President exerted control through the army and the intelligence services. Syria is a centre of Arab nationalism.

Qaddafi in Libya began, in the eastern city of Bengazi on February 15, 2011. Qaddafi's attempt to suppress it using brutal force backfired and soon the rebellion engulfed the entire region. The opposition forces captured control of almost all of the fertile region including Bengazi, the second largest city in the North African country. Qaddafi deployed tanks, fighter planes and helicopter gunships against the rebels. He was also accused of employing mercenaries imported from some other African countries to shoot down his own people on the streets.

A number of ministers, diplomats, senior military officers and leaders of some of the biggest tribal groups, openly turned against Qaddafi. As the situation started threatening to become a prolonged civil war, the western powers intervened in support of the rebels. The UN Security Council in March authorised "all necessary measures" to protect the civilians from the indiscriminate use of force by the Qaddafi troops. The UN resolution was passed with Russia, China, India, Germany and Brazil abstaining. The North Atlantic Treaty Organisation (NATO) took it upon itself the implementation of the resolution and imposed a no-fly zone over the eastern region. Besides the Libyan military installations, the residential compound of Qaddafi in Tripoli also came under the NATO airstrikes. One of Qaddafi's sons, Saif-al-Arab and three of the Libyan leader's grandchildren were reportedly killed.

Marking the end of the four decade old regime of Qaddafi, the rebels at last over-

ran Tripoli and captured his headquarters at Bab al-Azizia in August. Qaddafi, along with his wife, daughters and two of his sons vanished. Gaddafi, his son Saif al-Islam, and his brother-in-law Abdullah al-Senussi have warrants against them issued by the International Criminal Court for crimes against humanity. Interpol had also issued a similar warrant against Gaddafi. Libyan rebel's National Transition Council (NTC) led by Mustafa Abdul Jalil put a price of $1.67million on the head of the former dictator.

Qaddafi a former colonel in the Libyan army was only 28 when he seized power from the pro-western King Idris in 1969.

The Qaddafi Era is Over

Colonel Muammar Gaddafi is no more. Report of the death of Libya's former dictator, after capture on Oct. 20 signalled the end of an era for the Arab world. The world now awaits to see how Libya will make a transition to a democratic, inclusive nation.

Timeline: The Rise and Fall of a Colonel

Muammar Qaddafi

1951 : Libya becomes independent under King Idris al-Sanusi.

1969 : King Idris is deposed in military coup led by Colonel Muammer Qaddafi.

1970 : Libya orders the closure of British and American airbases.

1977 : Qaddafi declares a 'people's revolution', changing the country's official name from the Libyan Arab Republic to the Great Socialist People's Libyan Arab Jamahiriyah.

1981 : US shoots down two Libyan aircraft which challenged its warplanes over the Gulf of Sirte, claimed by Libya as its territorial water.

1984 : A British policewoman is shot dead outside the Libyan embassy, in London. Britain breaks off diplomatic relations with Libya

1986 : The US bombs Libyan military facilities and residential areas of Tripoli and Benghazi. 101 people, including Qaddafi's adopted daughter are killed.

1988 : A PanAm airliner explodes over the Scottish town of Lockerbie killing 270 people. The US and Britain accuse Libya for the incident.

1992 : The UN imposes sanctions on Libya over Lockerbie bombing.

2001 : A Special Scottish court in the Netherlands sentences one of the two Libyans accused of the Lockerbie bombing to life imprisonment and acquits the other.

2002 : Libya and the US begin talks to mend relations.

2003 : Libya signs deal to compensate families of the Lockerbie bombing victims. UN Security Council votes to lift sanctions.

2006 : The US decides to restore full diplomatic ties with Libya.

2009 : Qaddafi elected chairman of the African Union.

2011 February : Protests against Qaddafi rule erupts. Authorities use aircraft to attack protestors. Many Libyan diplomats resign in protest.

2011 March : The UN Security Council authorises a no-fly zone over Libya and air strikes to protect civilians. NATO assumes command.

2011 May : International Criminal Court seeks arrest of Qaddafi for crimes against humanity.

2011 August : Rebels capture the Libyan capital Tripoli. Qaddafi flees.

2011 October 20: Muammar Gaddafi dies of wounds suffered as fighters battling to complete an eight-month-old uprising against his rule overrun his hometown Sirte.

Libya: Since 1835

In the 16th century Tripoli fell under Ottoman domination. In 1835, the country came under the direct rule of Turkey. In 1911, Italy occupied Tripoli. Turkey recognized Italian sovereignty. The Second World War saw changes. The British army expelled the Italian and their German allies. Tripolitania and Cyrenaica were placed under British and Fezzan under French, military administration. This continued until 1950.

Libya became an independent, sovereign kingdom with the former Amir of Cyrenaica, Muhammad Idris al Senussi, as King on Dec. 24, 1951. King Idris was deposed in Sept. 1969 by a group of army officers, 12 of whom formed the Revolutionary Command Council, which proclaimed the Libyan Arab Republic. The Council was chaired by Col. Muammar Qaddafi. In 1977, the RCC was superceded by a more democratic People's Congress. Qaddafi was the head of state.

Relations with the USA and other Western countries deteriorated. Throughout the 80s, Libya had constant disagreements with its neighbours. April 1987 saw the US bombing of Tripoli. This was meant to be a punishment to Qadhafi for his alleged support to international terrorism.

In 1986, a US trade embargo was enforced. In 1988 there was a bombing of a Pan Am flight over Lockerbie in Scotland. Libya refused to surrender suspects in the bombing. Sanctions were imposed by the UN in 1992. In April, 1999 Libya handed over the two suspects to be tried in the Netherlands but under Scottish law. UN agreed to lift sanctions, but the US trade embargo remained in place.

Libyan rebels

He had always been at odds with the West, especially the US. He proclaimed himself the champion of the Arab unity, but soon went on to earn the enmity of many Arab rulers as well. He was accused of sponsoring terrorism in the West and was charged with ordering the mid-air bombing of two Western passenger aircraft which killed more that 400 people. Because of these, Libya fell under long years of crippling international sanctions.

Syria

The protests against the 10-year old rule of President Bashar al Assad of Syria, began in March 2011 in the provincial town of Deraa where several school boys were jailed and tortured for scrawling anti-government graffiti on some public walls. The turmoil erupted in Deraa soon spread to several other cities including the capital Damascus and grew into a mass movement. The protesters who initially demanded the end of police brutalities, greater freedom

Timeline: Syria

1946 : Syria gains independence from France.

1947 : The Arab Socialist Baath Party is formed.

1958 : Syria and Egypt form the United Arab Republic (UAR) with Egypt's Gamal Abdul Nasser as the head.

1961 : Army officers seize power in Syria and dissolve the UAR.

1966 : Hafez al-Assad becomes Defence Minister.

1967 : Israel seizes the Golan Heights from Syria and destroy much of Syria's air force.

1970 : Hafez al-Assad overthrows President Nur al-Din al-Atasi and captures power.

1971 : Assad is elected President for a seven-year term in a plebiscite.

1973 : Syria along with Egypt go to war with Israel but fail to retake the Golan Heights.

1976 : Syrian army intervenes in the Lebanese civil war.

1982 : A Muslim Brotherhood uprising in the city of Hama is suppressed. Thousands of civilians are killed.

1994 : Assad's son Basil, who was likely to succeed his father is killed in a car accident.

2000 : Assad dies and is succeeded by his son, Bashar.

Bashar al Assad

2004 : US imposes economic sanctions on Syria over "its support to terrorism".

2005 : Syria withdraws its forces from Lebanon.

2006 : Iraq and Syria restore diplomatic relations after nearly a quarter century.

2007 : Israel carries out aerial strike against a "suspected" nuclear facility in Syria.

2010 : US renews sanctions against Syria, accusing it of supporting terrorist groups.

2011 March : Protests erupt in the southern city of Deraa.

2011 April : State of emergency in force since 1963 is lifted.

2011 May : Army tanks enter Deraa and other cities against anti-regime protests.

2011 September : Syrian death toll tops 2700, according to UN and eradication of corruption ultimately started clamouring for the outright end of Bashar's rule. The 45-year old Bashar responded first by promising political reforms and later resorted to overwhelming force in an attempt to put down the protests. Tanks were used to shoot down unarmed protesters. More than 3,000 people were killed, many more injured, and thousands detained.

The embattled Assad blamed the foreign conspirators as well as the Islamists, especially the Muslim Brotherhood for the turmoil. The Muslim Brotherhood had risen in revolt against his father, Hafez al Assad, in the city of Hama in 1982, but was ruthlessly suppressed leaving around 20,000 people dead.

Bashar, a British trained ophthalmologist came to power in 2000, after the death of his father who ruled Syria for nearly three decades. Hafez al Assad was in fact grooming his eldest son Basil to succeed him. But the death of Basil in a car accident 1994 suddenly changed Bashar's life as he was

recalled from London to Damascus. The soft-spoken Bashar had started well and kindled hope of political reforms after he released several political prisoners and eased media restrictions. But the reforms never materialised. Political parties and protests remained banned. The emergency law first imposed in 1962 was in force until it was lifted in April 2011.

As the crackdown continued, the US and the European Union stiffened economic sanctions already in place against

World's Longest-reigning Monarchs

Sl. No.	Name	Country	Length of Rule (Yrs)	Period	Age at Accession
1.	King Louis XIV	France	72	1643-1715	5
2.	King John II	Britain	71	1858 - 1929	18
3.	Emperor Franz-Josef	Austria	67	1848-1916	18
4.	Queen Victoria	Britain	63	1837-1901	18
5.	Emperor Hirohito	Japan	62	1926-1989	25
6.	Emperor K'ang His	China	61	1661-1722	8
7.	King Shobhuza II	Swaziland	60	1921-1982	22
8.	Emperor Chien Lung	China	60	1735-1796	25
9.	King Christian IV	Denmark	59	1588-1648	11
10.	King George III	Britain	59	1760-1820	22

the Bashar government. The US slapped sanctions on President Assad himself, accusing him of human rights violations. A Libya-like spectre was haunting Syria as soldiers started switching sides and joining the pro-democracy movement.

Reactions: Israel and the US

The Jasmine Revolution posed a serious challenge for the US administration, because the three countries initially affected, Tunisia, Egypt and Yemen were long under the domain of American influence. They were considered to be part of an arrangement that guaranteed the protection of the US strategic interests in the middle east. The US which used to champion the cause of democracy in the region was in fact doing the opposite by tacitly supporting the perpetuation of autocratic regimes like that of Ben Ali, Mubarak and Saleh, because it did not want to upset the status-quo. Mubarak's Egypt had been America's most powerful ally in the middle east, next only to Israel. Presence of Mubarak or his chosen successor in Cairo was also thought to be essential for the continued existence

of Egypt's peace treaty with Israel. Egypt was the first of the two Arab counties to have signed a peace accord with the Hebrew nation, the other being Jordan. The US and Israel were both worrying that in a post-Mubarak scenario, the Islamists,

Oil-rich Qatar	Oil was first discovered in 1939 and today accounts for about 90% of exports and 80% of income. Forty% of Qatar's population are Sunni Muslims, although only 25% are native Qataris, who are descended from three Bedouin tribes.

particularly the better organised Muslim Brotherhood would come to power and scrap the deal. The prospect of an alliance between them and Iran also became a nightmare for both the US and Israel.

Israel's anxiety caused by the Egyptian uprising became a reality in September when a mob broke into its embassy in Cairo and tore the Israeli flag to shreds. Israeli ambassador to Egypt along with the staff members and their families were evacuated in a special military plane. The Egyptians were protesting against the killing of six of their border guards by Israeli troops in August.

The Obama administration was keeping mum when Tunisia was in turmoil, but it could not carry on with the same policy with regard to the developments in Egypt. President Barak Obama first confined himself to urging Mubarak to initiate political reforms even when Mubarak's own army had turned against him. Ultimately, he was compelled to issue a public call for Mubarak to step down. The US was also at first reluctant to abandon President Ali Abdullah Saleh of Yemen who was considered pivotal to the American war against the Al Qaeda terrorists in that country.

But when Libya irrupted, the US and the other western nations did not wait long to ask Qaddafi to quit and declare support for the opposition forces. The US-sponsored UN Security Council resolution for imposing no-fly zone in eastern Libya and the NATO air-strikes against Qaddafi' military installations was also unprecedented in the 2011 upheaval in the middle east.

The Beginning of Constitutional Rule in Persia

What did the Middle East politics look like in early 20th century? Autocratic rule was the only thing Persia (today's Iran) had known. A beginning in constitutional government was made in 1908, when a bill of rights was drawn up. The national assembly (the Majlis) was two years old. In June 1908 the King Muhammad Ali Shah used his troops to shut down the Majlis. Martial law was imposed, and many opposition leaders executed. Though he could subdue Tehran, the capital, provinces were tough. Insurgent leaders said, "Allah has cursed tyrants". By July 1909, royalists were routed in several provincial cities. They converged on Tehran, stormed the palace and forced Muhammed Ali to take sanctuary in the Russian legation.

Twelve-year-old crown prince Ahmad Mirza was named the new Shah. The boy was terribly unhappy and wished he had gone with his parents. He even tried to escape from his palace. Within a month, the Second National Assembly was convened. It was the real beginning of constitutional rule in Persia.

Impact on Iran and China

The Jasmine Revolution for a while seemed to spread beyond the Arab heartlands as anti-government protests erupted in Iran and there was a call for agitation reverberated even in the far away China. Iran was the one middle east country which deliriously welcomed the wave of unrest in Tunisia and Egypt. The Iranian leaders even claimed that the Egyptian Revolution was inspired by their own Islamic revolution which over-

Mahmoud Ahmadinejad

threw the pro-western monarchy in 1979. This encouraged the Iranian dissidents to revive their protests against the allegedly rigged 2009 presidential elections. Riot police and plain-clothed militia fired teargas shells and wielded batons to disperse thousands of defiant protesters in Tehran, the capital. Many people including the former prime ministers Mir Hossein Mousavi and Mehdi Karroubi, who ran against President Mahmoud Ahmadinejad in the disputed election, were arrested.

An online call for a "Jasmine Revolution in China" sent jitters in Beijing in February.2011. More than 100 activists across the country were taken away by police for questioning. Many were prevented from leaving home or were missing.

Role of the Social Media

An important aspect of the Jasmine Revolution was the decisive role played by the social media network in maintaining the momentum of the uprising. When the Arabic news channel Al Jazeera and other non-state media were banned from broadcasting images of the protests, the people turned to Youtube videos and Flickr photos which allowed the people to create and broadcast their own videos and webpages. The social networking sites such as Facebook and Twitter helped them reach out to previously inaccessible audiences. The young social media activist Wael Ghonim suddenly became a hero of the Egyptian revolution.

K. Obeidullah

Marginalized Women

The first elections in the Gulf Kingdom of Saudi Arabia were held in 2005. The country's population is 27.5 mn. of whom 19 mn. are Saudis. Women's rights activists have long fought for the right to vote. Women will now be admitted to the Shura Council.

Part **4**

Science World

Pages 193 - 204

Science Scan 2012

Biped Robo Marathon

Robovie-PC, a toy-sized humanoid, 40 centimetres tall and weighing 2.4 kilograms, won the world's first full-length marathon for two-legged robots, beating its closest rival by a single second after more than two days of racing. Five bipedal machines began the non-stop 42.2-kilometre contest on a 100-metre indoor track in the western Japanese city of Osaka on Feb 24th, after greeting spectators with gestures. Robovie-PC pushed Robovie-PC Lite behind after 422 laps and crossed the line in 54 hours 57 minutes 50 seconds, one second ahead of

its rival. Their average speed was 0.77 kilometres per hour.

Metamaterial

Electrical engineers hope that man-made materials should be able to transmit power to laptops and cell phones, even cars and elevators, wirelessly. Normally, as power passes from the transmitting set to the receiving device, most of it scatters and dissipates unless the two devices are extremely close together.

According to Yaroslav Urzhumov, assistant research professor in electrical and computer engineering at Duke's Pratt School of Engineering, currently, it is possible to transmit small amounts of power over short distances, such as in radio frequency identification

devices. However, larger amounts of energy, like in lasers or microwaves, would consume anything in its path. It should be possible, now, to use metamaterials to increase the amount of power transmitted without the negative effects.

Data Transfer

The world's biggest feat in data transfer by the Karlsruhe Institute of Technology (KIT) Germany, beats its own global record of sending 10 terabits (10,000 billion bits per second) in 2010.

According to the report in the journal "Nature Photonics", Prof Jürg Leuthold, head of the Institute of Photonics and Quantum Electronics and the Institute of Microstructure Technology at KIT, attribute the astounding success to a new data process the Institute has developed, called the opto-electric decoding method, This is important if one would notice the constant growth of data volume on the internet. The challenge was to increase the process speed not only by a factor of 1,000, but by a factor of nearly a million for data processing at 26 terabits per second. In a mere second, scientists have whisked an unprecedented 26 terabits of information - the equivalent of 700 DVDs or a dizzying 26,000 billion bits - on a single laser beam across 50 km. The result shows that physical limits did not exceed even at extremely high data rates,

Uranium Analysis

Scientists of Kalpakkam-based Indira Gandhi Centre for Atomic Research in Tamil Nadu did a study on technologically important actinide

Bio Couture   A material made by the bacteria that are usually used to turn green tea into the fermented beverage kombucha - now that's what we call BioCouture. Suzanne Lee.

metals like Uranium and plutonium using Raman Spectroscopy, the first study of its kind in the world. Study of metals by Raman Spectroscopy is a challenging scientific problem due to the low penetration of laser into metals and hence low sampling volumes. According to Dr TR Ravindran of the Condensed Matter Physics Division, considering the Raman spectra of metals have not been studied widely owing to their weak spectral intensities, work on Raman Spectra of Uranium to understand its structural properties is a significant step

India to Introduce LEDs

The Bureau of Indian Standards (BIS) has finalised performance standards for light emitting diodes (LEDs) in 2011. LEDs hailed as the future lighting source are three times more efficient than compact fluorescent lamps (CFLs). Sellers claim that LEDs run for 50,000 hours. A CFL lasts 6,000 hours and an incandescent bulb has a life span of 1,200 hours. Despite these facts, LEDs account for only 8% of total lighting. LED lightings are costly. Meanwhile, the Central Institutional Mechanism (CIM), under Ministry of Power, has taken steps to reduce the cost of LEDs and distribute a free LED bulb to every family below poverty line.

Composite Oxygen Cylinders

Now, IAF and Army pilots will be able to stay airborne for longer periods. The Defence Research and Development Organisation has come up with composite oxygen cylinders that will lighten the burden of military helicopters in high-altitude areas. The oxygen cylinders now used in Chetak and Cheetah helicopters last for 20-25 minutes only. The composite oxygen cylinder weighs just one-fifth of normal cylinders but can provide oxygen supply for minimum two hours.

Developed by Defence Bio-Engineering and Electro Medical Laboratory (DEBEL), the cylinders have taken away a significant amount of weight from the choppers, increasing its weight-carrying capacity for longer durations..

CERN's LHC "Primordial Soup"

In an experiment, at CERN's Large Hadron Collider physicists from the ALICE detector team including researchers from the University of Birmingham has discovered that the very early Universe was not only very hot and dense but behaved like a hot liquid.

By accelerating and smashing together lead nuclei at the highest possible energies of over 10 trillion degrees, the ALICE experiment has generated incredibly hot and dense sub-atomic fireballs, 'recreating' the conditions that existed in the first few microseconds after the Big Bang.

According to Dr David Evans, from the University of Birmingham's School of Physics and Astronomy, and UK lead investigator at ALICE experiment, 'these first results seem to suggest that the Universe would have behaved like a super-hot liquid (primordial 'soup') known as quark-gluon plasma, immediately after the Big Bang."

The fireballs resulting from the collision only last a short time, but when the 'soup' cools down, the researchers could see thousands of particles radiating out from the fireball and draw conclusions about the soup's behaviour.

Quark-gluon plasma will help scientists understand more about the strong force and how it governs matter; the nature of the confinement of quarks – why quarks are confined in matter, such as protons; and how the Strong Force generates 98% of the mass of protons and neutrons.

The ALICE detector is placed in the LHC ring, some 100 metres underground, is 16

18 p.c. Research from US — Presently 18 per cent of the world's science research is from the United States, while 13 per cent is from China. Experts say the trend is set to be reversed in the next three years.

metres high, 26 metres long and weighs about 10,000 tons. During collisions of lead nuclei, ALICE recorded data to disk at a rate of 1.2 GBytes (two CDs) every second and wrote over two PBytes (two million GBytes) of data to disk; this is equivalent to more than three million CDs (or a stack of CDs (without boxes) several kilometres high). To process these data, ALICE will need 50,000 top-of-the-range PCs, running 24 hours a day.

WiTricity

WiTricity is commercialising a technology developed by MIT that sends power through the air (wirelessly) to run

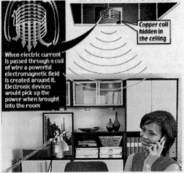

Copper coil hidden in the ceiling

When electric current is passed through a coil of wire a powerful electromagnetic field is created around it. Electronic devices would pick up the power when brought into the room

devices like laptops, DVD players, cell phones, and other common electronics. The technology involves a circuit that converts standard AC electricity to a higher frequency and feeds it to a WiTricity source. The current inside the source induces an oscilating magnetic field. The WiTricity device to be powered is tuned to the same frequency as the source and in a process called "resonant magnetic coupling," power is transferred from the source to the device. The energy of the oscillating magnetic field then induces an electrical current in the WiTricity device, lighting the bulb. WiTricity source is installed in the ceiling and each electronic product must have a WiTricity device to receive power.

Kilogramme reset

For more than 100 years, all measurements of weight have been defined in relation to a lump of metal sitting in Paris. The kilogramme is still defined as the 50 micrograms, around the weight of a mass of a piece of platinum. It's a cylinder of platinum-iridium about 39mm high, 39mm in diameter, cast by Johnson Matthey in Hatton Garden in 1879. The "international prototype" kilogramme has been at the heart of trade and scientific experiment since 1889. One problem with using a lump of metal to define such a basic quantity as kilogramme is that it is liable to change over time.

Measurements over the past century have shown that the international prototype has lost around 50 micrograms, which now experts want to get rid of. Instead, experts want to link the kilogramme to a fundamental unit of measurement in quantum physics, the Planck Constant. This redefinition would bring the kilogramme into line with the six other base units that make up the International System of Units (SI) - the metre, the second, the ampere, the kelvin, the mole and the candela. Scientists at the Royal Society in London are redefining this basic unit of measurement in terms of the fundamental constants of nature.

Pi vs. Tau

Mathematicians are campaigning for the most important number in the world to be replaced with alternate value 'tau'.

$\pi\ \pi$ Why? They claim that the number 3.14159265 - the constant which references the circumference of a circle to its diameter - is wrong and it should be replaced with tau. Tau has a value twice that of pi of 6.28. Mathematicians measure angles in radians. There are 2pi radians in a circle. That leads to all sorts of confusion. The circle has tau radians, a semicircle would have half tau, a quarter of a circle a quarter tau, and so on. Pi was first introduced in 1706 by mathematician William Jones.

| Solving Rubik's Cube Puzzle | Students at Australia's Swinburne University are confident of making a robot that could solve the Rubik's cube puzzle in less than 10 seconds. |

Radiation inside-out

Radioactivity arises naturally from the decay of particular forms of some elements, called isotopes. Some isotopes are radioactive, most are not. Nuclear radiation can be both extremely beneficial and extremely dangerous. It just depends on how it is used. X-ray machines, medical sterilization equipment and nuclear power plants all use nuclear radiation - but so do nuclear weapons.

Accidents happened at Three Mile Island (USA) and Chernobyl (Russia) nuclear power plants which released radioactive substances into the atmosphere. In the aftermath of the March 2011 earthquake and tsunami that struck Japan, a nuclear crisis occurred at Fukushima where all the 5 reactors were affected, raising fears about radiation and questions about the safety of nuclear power.

Nuclear Fall-outs

Nitrogen-16 (half-life 7 sec)- hazard only to power plant workers; Tritium or heavy hydrogen - (half-life 12 years)- collects in ground water; **Iodine 129** (half-life 15.7M yrs) & **131**-(half-life 8 days)-can be inhaled and collects in thyroid, causing cancer and other thyroid related problems; **Strontium-90** -(half-life 29 yrs)- tends to deposit in bone and bone marrow and is linked to bone cancer and lukemia.

Cesium 137- (half-life 30 yrs) - If it enters food, it can be metabolised by the human body, where it causes cancer.

Plutonium 239 (half-life 24,000 yrs)- inhalation of aerosols causes lung cancer, liver cancer and bone sarcoma.

WHO suggests that potassium iodide should be taken prior to exposure to radiation which blocks body from absorbing radioactive iodine.

Effects of Radiation:

Experts say even small radiation doses, as low as 100 millisieverts (mSv), can slightly raise cancer risks.

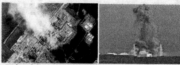

Fukushima Nuclear Fallout.

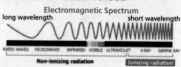

Electromagnetic Spectrum

long wavelength — short wavelength

RADIO WAVES   MICROWAVES   INFRARED   VISIBLE   ULTRAVIOLET   X-RAY   GAMMA RAY

Non-ionizing radiation   **Ionizing radiation**

Exposure in mSv

10,000- single dose, fatal within weeks; 8,000-CT scan (abdomen); **5000**-single dose, would kill half of those exposed within a month; 1,000-Single dose could cause radiation sicknesses; nausea, but not death; **700**- one mammogram; 100-1 Chest X-ray; **16.00**- CT Scan, heart; 10.00-CT Scan, full body; **2.00**- Radiation most people are exposed to per year; **0.01** - Dental X-ray; **0.0148**-Full body Airport X-ray scanner

[Smoking 1 Pack of cigarettes per day for 1-year = **80,000 mSv**]

Immediate effects

Cell damage: bleeding and fast growing cells or reduction in number of blood cells. Damage to bone marrow-blood producing cells, which also fails to produce platelets that coagulate blood.

Brain: fatigue, nausea; Hair follicle-hair loss; **Intestine lining**- Diarrhea, malnutrition; **Skin cells:** sores, peeling; **White Blood Cells and bone marrow**-Immune system failure

Later effects

DNA damage - in cell nucleus; **Egg and Sperm cells**- with damaged DNA can produce babies with birth defects; **Body cells** - cancer; develop tumours or abnormal growth; blood cell damage can lead to lukemia; **Cataracts; Anemia** and risks of infection due to loss of WBC.

Sieverts	In metric System - a radiation dose is measured in units of sieverts. Small doses such as those received from medical X-rays are measured in millisieverts (1/1000 sieverts) or microsieverts (1/1000000 sieverts).

India's Climate Change Energy Challenge

Dr. R.K. Pachauri

Director-General, The Energy & Resources Institute (TERI),
Chairman, IPCC; Director, YCEI

India shared deal with the energy challenges in terms of long term development. There is an urgent need for major shifts in energy consumption and supply in India. The democratic system can create effective response to challenges that lie ahead.

The International Energy Agency (IEA) brings out the annual World Energy Outlook, a comprehensive compilation of past energy data, analysis of the energy situation as it has emerged worldwide along with scenarios of future developments. This important publication not only presents the global scenario in respect of energy and related issues, but also looks at different regions of the world in which India is provided distinct treatment, mainly because of the importance India now occupies on the global energy scene. What is of critical importance when looking at India's place in the world are the projections of demand for oil, which continues to surge forward,

driven largely by growth in demand in the emerging markets like China and India. What is also significant is the fact that in each subsequent year the IEA has been reducing its overall demand projections for consumption of oil, even though the regional mix has been changing significantly. This downward revision in each subsequent year is the result of demand stagnation in the developed countries and more recently the impact of the economic recession that has gripped several parts of the world. It would be relevant to look at projections for oil demand by what the IEA defines as the new policies scenario. Essentially, the new policy scenario includes the effect of broad policy commitments which have been announced by different countries including national pledges to reduce greenhouse gas (GHG) emissions and in certain countries plans to phase out fossil fuel subsidies. Interestingly, the total demand projected for 2035 globally under this scenario amounts to 99 million barrels per day (mb/d). Of this the projected demand in that year for India is 7.5 mb/d as against that of China which is 15.3 mb/d. North America on the other hand shows a slight decline to 19.4 mb/d

| Deepest-Living Land Animal | Researchers at Princeton University have discovered a new worm in three South African gold mines, which they claim is the deepest-living land animal ever found on earth. The new species is Halicephalobus mephisto. |

of which the U.S. accounts for 14.9 mb/d. Hence, North America still remains the dominant consumer of oil, but China by 2035 is expected to surpass demand in the U.S. As against these projections of demand if we look at projections for supply, there is some cause for concern on account of the fact that based on information that is now available the ratio of production of oil to reserves has gone up significantly. Reserves have doubled worldwide since 1980 and have increased by one–third over the last decade. However, half the increase since 2000 is due to Canadian oil sands reserves which several groups regard as problematic on account of environmental reasons. In recent times there has been a vigorous debate on whether the world has reached peak oil production capacity. The reality is that the global oil market is certainly tight

> The reality is that the global oil market is certainly tight at this point of time and expectations make it tighter in future.

at this point of time and expectations make it tighter in future. Given the prospects of growing dependence of oil imports in India and the possibility of significant increase in oil prices worldwide, it is in India's interest to shift to other sources of energy. In a recent publication TERI has brought out the details of reserves and the potential for production of coal. The situation is certainly not comfortable because India does not have unlimited reserves of coal which could be mined to meet the growing demand. Consequently, India's dependence on coal imports is also projected to increase substantially in the future. There is, therefore, an imperative need to bring out significant improvements in the efficiency of energy consumption and a diversification and enhancement of energy supply.

The Transport Sector

One sector which needs a significant and urgent shift is the transport sector in this country. The current trend of increase in the vehicle population in the country may certainly meet consumer aspirations and the benefits of easy mobility for a population whose income is growing rapidly, but this certainly imposes a major and incalculable cost not only for this generation but for those yet to come. There is, therefore, a need for major efforts to increase public transport infrastructure and modernization of the Indian Railways so that its share of passenger and freight traffic increases over time as opposed to the trend in recent decades of perceptible decline. One projection of ownership of personal vehicles in India is a total of 708 million units by 2030 based on the growth of GDP of 6 percent per year. Consequently, the share of public transport is projected to decline from the current level of around 60 percent to 45 percent. The level of ownership of personal vehicles in India was around 70 per thousand in 2006 as compared to a little over 500 per thousand in the developed world. Aspiring to reach the same levels of ownership would be detrimental to the efficiency of energy use in this sector. Even if personal vehicle ownership keeps going up steadily, the kilometres driven per annum should go down if the consumption of petroleum products is to be kept in check. Over a period of time a major improvement in fuel efficiency of automobiles would also become imperative including a gradual shift

Moon Rock	A slice of moon rock brought back by Apollo astronauts in 1969 is sealed in a stained-glass window dedicated to scientists and technicians in the Washington Cathedral.

to hybrid and electric vehicles. Reduction in the usage of personal automobiles would come about only if consumers are provided with choices of public transport. A major effort in this direction is long overdue at the national, state and local levels. Essentially, public transport would require the creation of local capability to devise appropriate public transport systems and access to financing given the fact that public transport requires lumpy investments.

Limits on Nuclear Capacity

On the supply side, while the government plans to enhance its nuclear energy potential, there are limits on how quickly and to what extent nuclear capacity can be established. As it happens, India's trend of harnessing renewable sources of energy remains uninspiring even though the country possesses substantial resources of solar, wind and biomass energy. The large coastline that India has also provides large

> India has almost 400 million people with no access to electricity

potential for using ocean energy. However, we have not really carried out adequate research for developing technologies which can harness wave power. Another technology which has been gaining interest among visionary technologists is ocean thermal energy conversion (OTEC) for which it is estimated that the oceans around the southern tip of India and Sri Lanka provide excellent prospects.

On the 30th of June 2011, it was three years since Prime Minister Manmohan Singh announced the National Action Plan on Climate Change (NAPCC). In these three years some modest progress has been achieved, but we are nowhere close to the trajectory that is required for establishing 20,000 MW of solar capacity in the next ten years. As a short term target, the Jawaharlal Nehru National Solar Mission

targets creation of 1100 MW of grid connected solar power and 200 MW of off-grid solar power generation by the year 2030. These targets could possibly be met through current actions, but it is questionable whether they would lead to technology development and cost reductions that would facilitate achievement of the long term 2021-2022 target of 20,000 MW.

Another important development took place in May 2011, when the Intergovernmental Panel on Climate Change (IPCC) released its Special Report on Renewable Energy Sources and Climate Change Mitigation, which apart from other dimensions of renewable energy (RE) development and use worldwide, also assessed 164 scenarios with a range of global outcomes, which are expected to be achieved in the next few decades. For instance, more than half the scenarios that were examined show a contribution from RE in excess of 17 percent share of primary energy supply in 2030 rising to more than 27 percent in 2050. Scenarios with the highest RE share would reach approximately 43 percent in 2030 and 77 percent in 2050.

Energy Security

In the case of India major shifts in energy consumption and supply are urgent for reasons of ensuring higher energy security in the country. Two important factors which add further urgency to this challenge are:

1. India has almost 400 million people with no access to electricity. After almost 64 years of independence this section of

our population either lives in darkness once the sun goes down or is compelled to use polluting and inadequate sources of lighting such as kerosene, other oils and candles etc. TERI has launched a major campaign called Lighting a Billion Lives (LaBL) to provide for the systematic dissemination of solar lanterns designed and developed by TERI to provide efficient and clean lighting in homes deprived of electricity and to ensure that these are affordable and within the reach of the poorest sections of society.

2. Even though in keeping with the UN Framework Convention on Climate Change (UNFCCC) and Kyoto Protocol, the first phase of which is due to end in 2012, India is not required to commit internationally to reduction of GHGs, the pressures that are growing for India to take on binding commitments would only grow in the future and if other emerging markets such as China and Brazil accept major commitments for reduction in GHG emissions India will have to comply and respond to growing pressures for a cut in GHGs in this country as well. It is also important to keep in mind the fact that that the impact of climate changes on India is likely to be serious and, therefore, in keeping with the "common but differentiated responsibilities" defined in the UNFCCC, India would have to do something tangible both in its own interests as well as that of the global community to show that it is willing to take on part of the burden for reducing GHG emissions.

The challenge of climate change re-

quires India not only to mitigate emissions of GHGs but also adapt to impacts that the country is projected to face in the future. India has a large coastline and the problem of sea level rise would affect not only the Sundarban islands and the low lying areas in West Bengal but several other parts of the country as well. Adaptation measures may require greater attention to mangrove plantations along our coasts, proper zoning restrictions to ensure that life and property are not affected adversely through habitation in those areas which could face coastal flooding and storm surges etc.

Wealth of Biodiversity

India also has a significantly rich wealth of biodiversity. This would also be affected through the impact of climate change. In fact, the IPCC has assessed that approximately 20 to 30 percent of plant and animal species globally are likely to be at increased risk of extinction if increases in global average temperature exceed 1.5 to 2.5°C. Agricultural output is also likely to be affected in the country because the IPCC's findings indicate that globally at lower latitudes especially in seasonally dry and tropical regions crop productivity is projected to decrease for even small local temperature increases (1 to 2°C) and this could increase the risk of hunger. The IPCC also projected, the health status of millions of people is projected to be affected through, for example, increase in malnutrition, increased deaths, diseases and injury due to extreme weather events, increased burden

Mining the Moon

Indian-American Naveen Jain is behind a venture which plans to mine the moon. The Silicon Valley start-up is building robotic rovers that will search the lunar surface for precious metals and rare metallic elements.

Early Warning System

of diarrhoeal diseases, increased frequency of cardio-respiratory diseases due to higher concentration of ground level ozone in urban areas related to climate change and the altered spatial distribution of some infectious diseases.

Adaptation Measures

It is also projected that the frequency and intensity of extreme events would increase. There is now higher confidence in the projected increases in drought, heat waves and floods as well as their adverse impacts. On the basis of projections, therefore, it can be stated that adaptation measures need to be put in place which would also require some changes in governance systems. For instance, in the event of increased climate and weather–related disasters, local bodies may need to be equipped with infrastructure and equipment to deal with this effectively as well as through adequate early warning system and capacity to mount relief measures as and when required. Societies have a long record of managing the impacts of weather and climate–related events. Nevertheless, additional adaptation measures will be required to reduce the adverse impact of projected climate change and variability regardless of the scale of mitigation to be undertaken over the next two to three decades. Moreover, vulnerability to climate change can be exacerbated by other stresses. These arise from, for example, current climate hazards,

poverty and unequal access to resources, food insecurity, trends in economic globalization, conflict and incidence of diseases such as HIV and AIDS. Some planned adaptation to climate change is already occurring on a limited basis. Adaptation can reduce vulnerability especially when it is embedded within broader sectoral benefits. Hence, overall development strategy both in the centre and in the states must now come to grips with mainstreaming of climate–related actions as well as a transition to new sources of energy and higher levels of efficiency of energy use.

India, therefore, faces major long term challenges which can only be dealt with effectively if we realize the importance of longer term thinking for development. While democracies are often seen as focused only on short term measures and, therefore, ignoring longer term challenges, it is only through democratic institutions particularly through appropriate information dis-

> Additional adaptation measures will be required to reduce the adverse impact of projected climate change

semination by the media that democratic system can create effective and timely response to challenges that lie ahead. Once the response to these challenges becomes embedded in current policies, then the efforts of democratic institutions and inclusive action by every section of society can yield desirable results for the benefit not only of current generation but generations yet to come. It would be appropriate to recall Gandhiji's words, "A technological society has two choices. First it can wait until catastrophic failures expose systemic deficiencies, distortion and self-deceptions…Secondly, a culture can provide social checks and balances to correct systemic distortion prior to catastrophic failures." ∎

| Himalayas Block Birds | **Birds migrating from central Asia have found the Himalayas as a hurdle. Steppe eagles have been found frozen to death on Everests' South Col at 26,246 feet.** |

Gene Revolution

How many hours did we spend growing our food yesterday? We probably walked to the fridge or to a nearby shop. But a 100 years ago we might have worked more hours in the fields than in school or office or a factory. In the developing world, that's still the case, and food is both scarce and expensive.

Civilization advanced as we developed agriculture. Agriculture got a boost in the 1950s with new chemicals that control insects-weeds-diseases and plant breeders developing more productive varieties of grains. New improved crops and farming techniques led to much higher yields - known as the "Green Revolution." It happened at a time when the world's population was growing so fast that experts predicted massive famines. But the Green Revolution came to the rescue. India tripled the wheat grown on the same amount of land.

The world's population is growing beyond the Green Revolution's capacity to feed the people who are destroying sensitive habitats to create more farmland, which will not be enough to feed the predicted 9 billion people by 2050.

Many scientists think a new "Gene Revolution" can help both hungry humanity and the sensitive environment. The Gene Revolution uses biotechnology (BT) to create new genetically modified (GM) crops. These crops can potentially produce more food with fewer chemicals and higher nutritional value than traditional crops. Scientists think they can improve not only grains, but also the legumes, vegetables, roots, and fruits that people need for a balanced, nutritious diet.

But some people worry that these crops are not safe to eat and could cause unforeseen problems. They question whe-

ther government agencies test the products enough and whether corporate profit motives outweigh safety concerns.

Genetic Engineering

Genomics is the study of an organism's entire genetic instructions. Scientists earlier didn't know what in the tomato leaf repelled insects. With new learnings, scientists can transport DNA codes of unrelated species to get traits like disease resistance, faster growth, better flavor, nutrition, or longer shelf life. Now, plant genomics is able to give plants beneficial traits and remove genes for safer food.

PROS: Cost effective; resist pests; prosper under non-optimal conditions; environment friendly - reduce chemicals; reduce world hunger and poverty; savings in production and financial gain

CONS: This process of combining inter-species genes (recombinant DNA technology) does not have the checks and balances that are imposed by nature in traditional breeding. Without these, there is a risk of genetic instability. This means that no one can make any accurate predictions about the long term effects of GM foodstuffs on human beings and the environment. Extensive testing in this regard is either very expensive or impractical, and there is still a great deal in genetics that scientists have not properly understood.

| Achondro-plasia | Achondroplasia is a common kind of short limbed dwarfism, that affects one in 25,000 births. The average height of the person affected is 4' 2". |

BT crops

Weeds can take over a field, and to keep them out takes backbreaking work. Especially in Africa, most farmers are women, and they spend half their time weeding! The problem is hightened when there is huge crop loss due to pests. Bt crop derive its relevance in this context. Bt crop is a genetically modified organism (GMO) which has been bioengineered to resist the crop pest which causes significant damage to crops. Many nations plant Bt corn, and this corn is in use in a variety of industries. In India Bt Brinjal, Corn and Cotton are being tried. The general fear is about any adverse human health effects in the long run because scientists are trying to take advantage of toxins produced by select bacterium. The toxin, generally known as Bt, ruptures the intestines of the organisms when it is ingested. The pests typically die within two to three days of ingesting the toxin.

Topical application of this natural pesticide had some flaws, including uneven coverage and the eventual washing away of the pesticide. Therefore, researchers started to explore the idea of inserting the genes which code for the toxin directly into the genetic code of the crop, along with a section of code known as a promoter which would encourage the crop to produce the toxin, and a marker which could be used to track and identify modified crop. After some trial and error, several companies had developed Bt crops, for example, the corn has been subjected to various tests to determine whether or not it was safe. Once approved, Bt crop could be planted by farmers, along with so-called "refuge" crops of non-Bt crop. The refuge crops are used to discourage Bt resistance by providing fodder for the European corn bearer which is safe to eat. The idea is that if a few insects develop resistance, they may mate with insects who ate from the refuge crop, diluting or eliminating the resistance. By contrast, a field covered in only Bt corn would promote resistance by killing off all of the insects which were vulnerable to Bt, and

promoting the survival of resistant insects. While Bt crop clearly has some advantages, it has not been without controversy. Some researchers have raised concerns that the crop or its pollen could impact populations of other organisms. Studies have also shown in the case of Bt corn that interbreeding with regular corn creates weak amounts of the toxin in strains of corn which should not have any Bt present. Some opponents of GMOs have also argued that not enough is known about their potential impacts on human health, making them safety risks.

Discoveries Behind

The door to genetic engineering opened when scientists realized that all genes are written in the universal language of DNA. Learning to use plasmids and special "cut and paste" proteins called restriction enzymes allowed them to "edit" DNA. Now, plant genomics is cataloging genes that could give plants beneficial traits, as well as genes we could eliminate to make food safer.

Regulation

GM crops were regulated from the beginning. The safeguards requirement requires permits and testing for pest- and herbicide-resistant crops and is researching the potential problem of superweeds and superbugs. The regulating agencies generally look at the "Product, not process." It judges a plant's nutrients, not the process used to make it (genetic engineering). Companies must submit detailed safety information of field tests of GM crops to the regulating authority before introducing a new GM food. oversees field tests of GM crops.

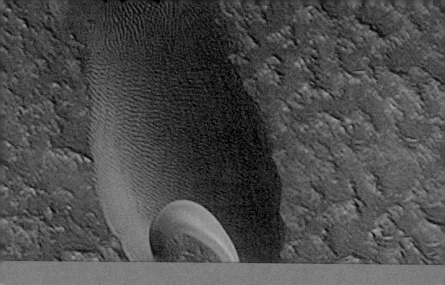

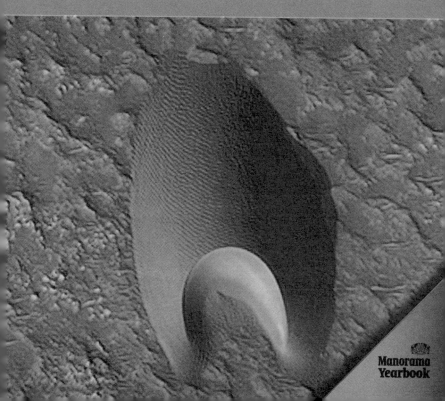

The Universe

People dreamed of spaceflight for millennia before it became reality.

Early Developments

During the millennia when space travel was only a fantasy, researchers in the sciences of astronomy, physics, chemistry, mathematics, and meteorology, developed an understanding of the solar system, the stellar universe, the atmosphere of the earth, and the probable environment in space. In the 7th and 6th centuries BC, the Greek philosophers Thales and Pythagoras noted that the earth is a sphere; in the 3d century BC the astronomer Aristarchus of Samos asserted that the earth moved around the sun. Hipparchus, another Greek, prepared information about stars and the motions of the moon in the 2nd century BC. In the 2nd century AD Ptolemy of Alexandria placed the earth at the center of the solar system in the Ptolemaic system.

Scientific Discoveries

Not until some 1400 years later did the Polish astronomer Nicolaus Copernicus systematically explain that the planets, including the earth, revolved around the sun. Later in the 16th century the observations of the Danish astronomer Tycho Brahe greatly influenced the laws of planetary motion set forth by Kepler. Galileo, Edmund Halley, Sir William Herschel, and Sir James Jeans were other astronomers who made contributions pertinent to astronautics.

In 1654 the German physicist Otto von Guericke proved that a vacuum could be maintained, refuting the old theory that nature "abhors" a vacuum. In the late 17th century Newton formulated the laws of universal gravitation and motion. Newton's laws of motion established the basic principles governing the propulsion and orbital

motion of modern spacecraft.

Even though the scientific foundations were laid in the earlier ages, space travel did not work out until the 20th century provided the actual means of rocket propulsion, guidance, and control for space vehicles.

Rocket Propulsion

The techniques of rocket propulsion also began long ago. Ancient rockets used gunpowder as fuel, very much like the present day fireworks. After the Renaissance, references were made to the proposed or actual military use of rockets in European warfare. As early as 1804 the British army put in place a rocket corps equipped with rockets that had a range of about 1830 m.

In the US, Robert Goddard, a professor of physics at Clark College (now Clark University) pioneered in rocket propulsion. He began experimenting with liquid fuels for rocketry in the early 1920s and the first successful liquid-propelled rocket was launched on March 16, 1926. World War II provided the push forward for the development of long-range suborbital rockets. The US, the Soviet Union, Great Britain, and Germany developed rockets in the same period for military purposes. The Germans

A space flight is any flight that exceeds 100 kilometres in altitude. As of March 2010, 517 humans from 38 countries have been there, 12 walked on moon. Space travellers have spent over 29000 person-days in space including over 100 person-days of space walks.

were most successful when they developed the V-2 (a liquid-propellant rocket used in the bombardment of London) at Peenemünde, a village near the Baltic coast. At the end of the war, the US Army brought back a number of the V-2s, for experimental research in vertical flights.

Space Station

Salyut and Skylab were the first spacecraft designed as space stations. Orbiting the earth for extended periods, while crews came and went on other vehicles, these space stations made possible many valuable new experiments and astronomical observations. The Soviet station, Mir, which was expected to have a useful life of 5 years, was in orbit 12 years after its launch. The long-term success of Mir led to joint efforts toward an international space station.

The Soviet Salyut 1 space station, weighing 18,600 kg, (launched on April 19, 1971) was one of the most notable flights of the Salyut/Soyuz series occurred in 1984 when cosmonauts Leonid Kizim, Vladimir Solovyov, and Oleg Atkov, spent 237 days aboard the Salyut 7 before returning to earth, the longest space flight to that date. Unused since 1986, Salyut 7 plunged to earth in February 1991.

The US Skylab program was much more ellaborate than the Soviet Salyut program. Skylab when launched on May 14, 1973 by

CONQUEST OF SPACE

YURI'S NIGHT
12 APRIL 2011
50TH ANNIVERSARY OF HUMAN SPACEFLIGHT

Following 7 test flights, several of them failures, carrying animals and equipment, the Vostok spacecraft carried a 27-year old Soviet Airforce pilot, makes history. His pressurised cabin was just 2.3 metres wide.

11 min. and 16 sec. after launch: Vostok-1's empty booster rocket ejects.

EARTH RETURN ROCKET

OPTICAL DEVICE FOR VIEWING EARTH

TANKS OF COMPRESSED OXYGEN AND NITROGEN FOR LIFE SUPPORT

Vostok 3KA-2, orbited the Earth on March 25, 1961. It carried a life-size cosmonaut mannequin and a live dog named Zvezdochka, which landed two hours after

launch in a snow-blanketed field about 1126 km from Moscow.

Three weeks later, on April 12, cosmonaut Yuri Gagarin climbed into an identical vehicle and became the first human to travel into outer space. At 0907 Moscow time Gagarin uttered the famous words "Let'S go" on the Vostok rocket, confining him in a tiny capsule, which blasted off from Tyuratam Missile Range (Baikonur Cosmodrome) Kazakhstan.

The single orbit lasted just 108 minutes and Gagarin parachuted down into a field in the Saratov region of central Russia. The architect of the Soviet space program, Sergei Korolev, tested five Vostok capsules before sending Gagarin. The world celebrated the 50th year of Yuri Gagarin's space voyage.

| The Biocon Story | **Ms. Kiran Mazumdar Shaw's Biocon Ltd. is India's first biotech company, the seventh largest biotech employer in the world and the number one biotech company in Asia in terms of revenue.** |

the Saturn 5 rocket, weighed 88,900 kg, heavier than Salyut. Skylab was a laboratory it was used to make solar-astronomical studies like long-duration medical studies of the three-man crew, multispectral observations of the earth, and variety of scientific and technological experiments, such as metallic-crystal growth in the weightless state. On July 11th 1979, during its 34,981st orbit, Skylab plunged to earth, raining fiery debris over sparsely populated western Australia and over the Indian Ocean.

The Mir space station, which the Soviets designed as a successor to the Salyut series, was launched on Feb. 20, 1986. Described by the Soviets as the core of the first permanently occupied space station, it featured six docking ports and could be operated by two cosmonauts. In 1987, Col. Yuri Romanenko spent 326 days aboard Mir. On April 12, 1987, the Soviets succeeded in docking Mir with Kvant, an 18,000-kg astrophysics module. In 1987–88, Soviet cosmonauts Vladimir Titov and Musa Manarov spent in space—366 days; in 1995 Russian cosmonaut Valery Polyakov stayed for 439 days.

International Cooperation

The US and Russian space station programs' collaboration began in 1993. In 1996 NASA and the Russian, European, Japanese, and Canadian space agencies agreed to cooperate on an International Space Station (ISS), designed to be a multinational research complex. In 1997, serious problems occurred aboard Mir. In February an air-filtering unit caught fire and burned for several minutes and the following month two oxygen generators malfunctioned. On June 25, in the worst collision in the history of human space flight, the station lost about 50% of its power supply in a crash with an unmanned cargo craft during a practice docking maneuver. In June 1998, the US space shuttle Discovery made the last scheduled shuttle mission to Mir, which was expected to remain in service through

1999. In November 1998, Russia launched the first component of the International Space Station, a propulsion and power module called Zarya. Two weeks later the US launched the space shuttle Endeavour, carrying the space station's large core unit, called Unity, which was attached to Zarya. Unity serves as the principal connector for all the parts of the station.

ISS orbits at an altitude of 350 kms approx above the Earth's surface, travelling at an average speed of 27,724 kms per hour, completing 15.7 orbits per day.

As of now, the ISS is the largest artificial satellite in Earth orbit. The ISS project is a collaboration of the space agencies like the National Aeronautics and Space Administration (NASA), Russian Federal Space Agency (RKA), Japan Aerospace Exploration Agency (JAXA), Canadian Space Agency (CSA) and European Space Agency (ESA). So far the station has been visited by astronauts from 16 different nations, and it has been the destination of six space tourists.

The Space Shuttle

In the early 1980s, the Space Transportation System (STS),(the space shuttle), became the major US space program. A multipurpose orbital-launch space plane

Enterprise

was designed to carry payloads of up to about 30,000 kg and up to 7 crew members and passengers. The upper part of the spacecraft, the orbiter stage, had a theoretical lifetime of perhaps 100 missions,

Columbia

and the winged orbiter could make unpowered landings on returning to earth. Because of the shuttle's design flexibility, satellite deployment feature and the rescue and repair of

| Cost of Space Trip | Russia is to charge $63mn. for a round trip flight on a Soyuz spacecraft to the ISI beginning in 2014. The US shuttle programme ended in 2011. |

Discovery

in-orbit satellites, its proponents saw it as a major advance in dominating space.

With the launch of the space shuttle Columbia from the Kennedy Space Center in Florida, the orbital flight test program began on April 12, 1981, is considered the first true spaceship. Over the next decade, Columbia was joined in the shuttle fleet by Challenger in 1982, Discovery in 1983, Atlantis in 1985, and Endeavour in 1991.

The early memorable flights included Mission STS-7, in 1983, whose crew included the first US woman astronaut, Sally K. Ride; Mission 41-C, in 1984, during which a satellite was retrieved, repaired, and redeployed; and Mission 51-A, in 1984, when two expensive malfunctioning satellites were retrieved and returned to earth. On Jan. 28, 1986, the shuttle Challenger was destroyed about one minute after launch because of the failure of its solid rocket boosters, in an explosion, killing all the seven astronauts

Flight Deck: Cockpit Controls

in the disaster. The shuttle launch program resumed after the disaster on Sept. 29, 1988, with the flight of Discovery and its crew of five astronauts. The success of this mission encouraged the US to resume an active launch schedule. The deployment in 1990 of the $1.5 billion Hubble Space Telescope, a daring mission to repair the malfunctioning telescope in 1993, and a servicing mission for the telescope in 1997 were notable. In 1998, were the last two scheduled shuttle missions to Mir and the deployment of the first two pieces of the International Space Station. After a series of successful missions in the late 1990s and

The 5 space shuttles

Columbia, Challenger, Discovery, Atlantis and Endeavour.
Number of launches- 135
Actual cost so far - $196bnNumber of astronauts aboard shuttle- 355
Accident- 14 - deaths (7 in Columbia in 2003; 7 in Challenger in 1986)
Cumulative time in space - 3 years, 221 days 19 hours 24 mins 43 secs - 12 days - length of final mission
Orbits of the earth
Orbits of the earth -20,958
Total distance travelled - 548 million miles

early 2000s, on Feb. 1, 2003, *Columbia* disintegrated while re-entering the earth's atmosphere. All seven astronauts on board the Columbia were killed. *Discovery* was the first space shuttle retired from NASA's fleet, after its STS-133 mission to the ISS in Feb./Mar. 2011.

Main dock of mobile launch platform

Endeavour was the second shuttle to retire after its successful 25th mission, STS-134, to the ISS in May/June 2011.

Atlantis lifted off on its final 12-day mission, STS-135, on July 8, 2011. The launch countdown was marked by tributes to the shuttle's contributions. The "closeout crew" held up high the message: " Thank you for 30 years with our nation's space shuttles!"

Atlantis

Stars

There are many millions of stars in the sky. In the whole heavens, fewer than 6000 stars are bright enough to be visible; and at any one time, less than 2500 stars are visible above the horizon.

Stars account for 98 % of the matter in a galaxy. The rest of 2% consists of interstellar or galactic gas and dust in a very attenuated form. The normal density of interstellar gas throughout the galaxy is about one-tenth of a hydrogen atom per cubic centimetre (cm³) volume.

Stars tend to form groups. **Lone stars** going on their own are the exception in the Universe. **Single stars** do not number more than 25% and **Double stars** account for some 33% of the stellar population. The rest are multiple stars. Antares in Scorpio is actually two stars. Capella and Alpha Centauri comprise 3 stars each, while Castor consists of 6 stars.

Our Solar System's place in our Milky Way Galaxy

When the hydrogen in a star is depleted, its outer regions swell and redden. This is the first sign of age. Such dying stars are called Red Giants. Our star, the Sun, is expected to turn into a red star of this type in another 5 billion years. Betelgeuse, for example, has a diameter of 480,000,000 kilometres, about 350 times the diameter of the Sun. Mira, another red giant, has a diameter of 640,000,000 kms

Black Dwarf is the tiny blackened corpse of a star like the Sun. Ultimately it disappears into the blackness of space.

White Dwarf is a tiny, dense, hot star, representing a late stage in the life of a star like the Sun. The matter in it is so incredibly dense that a single teaspoonful of it would weigh several tonnes.

Supergiants are huge stars, with all their hydrogen fuel used up in their core but continue to expand hundreds of times bigger than its original size before they finally die.

Novae and Supernovae are stars, whose brightness increases suddenly by 10 to 20 magnitudes or more and then fades gradually into normal brightness. The distinction between the two types has not been precisely explained. It would appear that they differ in degree and not in kind. The sudden increase in brightness is attributed to a partial or outright explosion. In novae, it seems that only the outer shell explodes, whereas in supernovae the entire star explodes. Novae occur more frequently than supernovae. Astronomers say that when the whole structure of the star is blown to pieces, it flares up in brilliance so that its intrinsic luminosity for the first 30 days following the explosion is equal to about 1000 million Suns in the Solar system.

Variable stars are stars that show varying degrees of luminosity. Delta Cephei, the first of this type of stars noticed in 1784 by English astronomer John Goodriche, has a regular fluctuation of brightness every 5 days and 9 hours. Stars of fluctuating luminosity, are called Cepheid Variables. In stars of this type, luminosity fluctuates between periods as small as a few hours to as long as 1000 days or more. Generally speaking, the slower the bright-dull-bright cycle, the higher the luminosity.

Quasars are powerful quasi stellar sources of radio radiations.

Pulsars are variable stars which emit regular pulses of electro-magnetic waves of very short duration.

Black Hole Strange things happen to a star at the end of its life if its mass is more than three times the mass of the Sun. Then it collapses becoming very compact. The collapse continues until the star becomes so dense that not even light escapes its gravity. Hence the object is dark and can't be viewed directly. According to General Relativity, bodies of matter curve space. If the body of matter was very dense (tons of matter packed into a small space), it convulses space into an infinitely deep chasm, called a black hole. John Wheeler, a US physicist, first used the term 'black hole' for a completely collapsed star at the Institute for Space, NY, in 1967.

Age of the Universe

The current estimate of the age of the Universe is about 13 billion years. The 60 odd-years following Hubble's original findings have seen numerous revisions of the constant. HST's main purpose was the measurement of the Hubble constant. The Hubble's constant as measured by the space telescope was on the high side implying a rather young Universe – also depending on what theoretical mode is accepted. Scientists say the Universe could be just 8 billion years old if the Hubble constant is precisely 80.

Size of the Universe

No one knows whether the Universe is finite or infinite in size. Albert Einstein described

What do we see?

All the dust-like spots we see in the picture are the stars only from our own galaxy. What lies beyond our galaxy? The Hubble Space Telescope with its camera pointed at the small block, about the 10th the size of the full

moon, which appeared to be complete black to the naked eye, with no stars visible, captured all the light it could. This is what it captured... each dot in this image is an entire galaxy. Each galaxy contains 1 trillion stars. Each star may have a system of planets. There are over 10,000 galaxies in this photo alone.

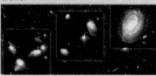

These are the most distant objects ever photographed - more than 13 billion light years away. The large galaxy picture here contains 8 times as many stars as our Milky Way Galaxy. It is so large, it technically shouldn't exist according to current physics theories.

the Universe as 'finite but unbound,' meaning that the frontiers cannot be observed even though they are definitely there.

| Black Hole: Hot or Cold | According to Stephen Hawking, the temperature of a black hole depends on its size. The smaller a black hole, the more concentrated its gravitational effects on its surroundings, and hotter the black hole appears to be. |

Some Space Facts

1. There are more than 100 billion galaxies in the universe. The largest galaxies have nearly 400 billion stars. There are an estimated 100 billion stars in the Milky Way, our galaxy. If we tried to count all the stars in just our galaxy at a rate of one star per second, it would take us about 3000 years

2. The Sun is the largest object in our solar system. It contains roughly 98% of our solar system's total mass. The surface of the Sun is 6000°C. The interior of the Sun is 15,000,000 °C. 1.3 million Earths could fit in the Sun.

3. The Moon is drifiting away from the Earth at the rate of 3.8 cm in a year. Because of this, the Earth is also slowing down. 100 years from now, the day will be 2 miliseconds longer.

4. Jupiter is the largest planet in our solar system. It is so big that all other planets could fit inside and the fastest rotating planet- 9 hrs and 55 minutes. Jupiter has 63 moons. Europa, one of the Jupiter's moons, is completely covered in ice.

5. Saturn, the second largest planet and its density is so low that it would float in water.

6. Most asteroids lie between the orbits of Mars and Jupiter. Dangerous asteroids, ones that could cause major regional or global destruction, only hit the Earth every 100,000 years on average. We can observe more than 20 million meteors every day but only 1 or 2 meteorites hit the Earth's surface each day.

7. By the most accurate definition, there are 14 known Black Holes. The closest, Cygnus X-1, is 8,000 light years. Black holes only absorb things that cross their event horizon, so they wouldn't destroy the entire universe. It's also possible for black holes to collide and merge. We can't see a blackhole, because like everything else, they also absorb light.

8. The Big Dipper is an asterism, not a constellation. The Big Dipper is actually a small part of Ursa Major. Ursa Major is the constellation. In the same way, Orion's Belt is an asterism within the Orion constellation.

9. The darkest space, with absolutely nothing around, would be about 2.7Kelvin (-270 °C). Space would be absolute zero (0Kelvin), except for background radiation which makes it ever so slightly warmer.

10. Highways, airports, dama, the pyramids, and even large vehicles have been seen by shuttle astronauts, at 217 kilometres from Earth. In fact, the Great Wall is much less visible than other things, especially things that are either reflective or a colour that contrasts the surrounding area.

Space Junk

Man-made rubbish floating in space – often litter from space exploration, including spanners, nuts, bolts, gloves and shards of space craft are what is called Space Junk.

- The majority of the space debris consist of small particles but some objects are larger, including spent rocket stages, defunct satellites and collision fragments.

- About 10 million pieces of human-made debris are estimated to be circulating in space at any one time. Out of which 22,000 human-made objects are larger than 10 centimetres across.

- Experts believe that global positioning systems, international phone connections, television signals and weather forecasts could be affected by increasing levels of space junk.

- The windows of space shuttles are often chipped by space junk when returning to earth.

- A crash between a defunct Russian Cosmos satellite and an Iridium's satellite in February 2009 left around 1,500 pieces of junk whizzing around the earth at 7.5 km a second.

- The International Space Station is fitted with special impact shield known as the Whipple Bumper, which is designed to protect the structure from damage caused by collisions with minor debris.

- As the cloud of orbiting junk shrouding the Earth grows ever denser, the most sophisticated garbage collectors of all time are taking shape. "Robotic capture" or Orbital snatch-and-grab technology to drag defunct satellites to a lower orbit to burn up on re-entry can be a reliable option in orbit.

The Solar System

Solar System means system of the Sun. All bodies under the gravitational influence of our local star, the Sun, together with the Sun, form the solar system. The largest bodies, including Earth are called planets. Often smaller cool bodies, called satellites or moons, orbit a planet. Bodies smaller than planets that orbit the Sun are classed as asteroids if they are rocky or metallic, comets if they are mostly ice and dust, and meteoroids if they are very small.

The Sun

• it is one of more than 100 billion stars in the giant spiral galaxy called the Milky Way. • is the centre of the Solar System. Its mass is about 740 times as much as that of all the planets combined. • it continuously gives off energy in several forms–visible light; invisible infrared, ultra-violet, X-rays and gamma rays, cosmic rays, radio waves and plasma. The Sun generally move in almost circular orbits around the galactic centre at an average speed of about 250 km per second. • it takes 250 million years to complete one revolution round the cen-

tre. This period is called a cosmic year. • it's energy is generated by nuclear fusion in its interior. It is calculated that the Sun consumes about 4 milliontonnes of hydrogen every second. At this rate, it is expected to burn out its stock of hydrogen in about 5 billion years and turn into a red giant.

Sunspots are dark patches noticed on the surface of the Sun. They appear dark because they are cooler (around 1500°C) than the surface of the Sun which has a temperature of about 6000°C. The largest spot ever measured (April, 1974) covered 18,130 million sq kms or approximately 0.7 % of the Sun's visible surface. The life periods of these spots also vary. They may last from a few hours to many weeks.

Polar Auroras are two auroras, the Aurora Borealis or Northern Lights and the Aurora Australis or Southern Lights. These are lights that sweep across the sky in waves or streamers or folds. They are very often multi-coloured and provide one of the finest spectacles in nature. They occur in the Arctic and the Antarctic regions respectively. The magnetosphere is the earth's mag-

Sun in 360-degree

In order to study the Sun's great explosive events that hurl billions of tonnes of charged particles at Earth, two Solar Terrestrial Relations Observatory (Stereo) satellites, were launched by NASA in 2006. It moved to either side of Sun establishing stereoscopic observing positions. Such a location in space lets scientists look at the coronal mass ejections that are thrown out of the Sun, coming our way. Thats the key to what Stereo's are all about. However, the Solar Dynamics Observatory, launched in Earth orbit a year ago, focussed on the Sun will provide the key to understand what drives the complex processes in the Sun.

You really see with these widely separated regions of the Sun's atmosphere that are

connected magnetically, showing activity at the same time, or causing activity somewhere else. These things shows us that you can't really study the Sun in great detail by looking at a bit of it, any more than you could understand the brain by le ing at a bit of it or study the Earth's regions by looking at the equator. You need this global view to really piece the jigsaw puzzle together.

Solar Statistics

Absolute Visual Magnitude	4.75
Diameter (km)	1,384,000
Rotation as seen from the Earth	
(at the Equator), days	25.38
(near the poles), days	33
Chemical Composition	
Hydrogen,	71
Helium	26.5%
Other Elements	2.5%
Age (billion years)	4.5 aprox.

* The mean distance from the Earth to the Sun (150 million km) translated into flying hours means that a jet aircraft capable of 1000 km/hr would need more than 17 years of non-stop flying to reach the Sun.

netic shield. It was at first called the Van Allen Belts after the American physicist, James Van Allen who discovered them in 1959. Van Allen's analysis of data from Explorer and Pioneer rockets found two belts of high intensity radiation in the upper atmosphere. These belts were a part of a large band of radiation called the magnetosphere. It extended far out to about 64,000 kilometres from the Earth's surface.

Extrasolar Planets

There are billions of stars and countless solar systems in our galaxy. So far Extrasolar planet hunters have found more than 565 planets orbiting more than 380 distant stars. The first planets outside our solar system were spotted in 1990, in orbit around a dying, radiation-spewing star very different from our Sun. Starting in 1995 with "51 Pegasi b" the first extrasolar, or exoplanet, discovered around a normal star, scientists have found alien worlds that are large, gassy giants and rocky.

Launch Centres

Cape Canaveral, NASA	:	Florida, USA
Baikonur Spacedrome	:	Russia
Kouro, French Guiana	:	European Space Agency
Tanegashima	:	Japan
San Marco Launch Platform	:	Kenya
Xi Chang Satellite Launch Centre	:	China
Sriharikota Launching Range	:	India
Naro Space Centre	:	Goheung, South Korea

The Hidden Zone

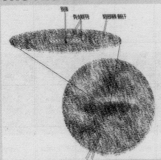

The Oort Cloud is a region beyond our Solar system - believed to be the reservoir where comets originate. Its inner edge is estimated to be 2000 - 5000 AU from the Sun. The outer edge could be halfway to the nearest star. The nearest star is 217,000AU away (39,900,000,000,000 km or distance traveled by light in 4.3 years)

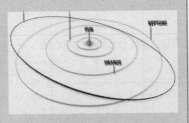

This region is at a distance traveled by light from Sun in 5 hours. Beyond these planet lies the Kuiper Belt, populated by objects composed of frozen methane, ammonia and or water ("ice")

The planets move nearly circular orbits, all lined up in a single plane called the "ecliptic". Pluto's orbit is tilted 17 degrees to the plane of the ecliptic. Other objects such as the dwarf planet Pluto, comets and steroids may have highly inclined orbits.

Waste Disposal Spacecraft from Space

The European Space Agency launched the unmanned craft, called the Johannes Kepler automated transport vehicle (ATV), in February 2011 to deliver several tons of cargo to the International Space Station, including food, supplies, fuel, and oxygen.

The glorified space freighter wasn't designed to safely return to Earth, so the space fliers on the ISS have crammed the 640-million-dollar canister with 1.3 tons of junk. Astronauts almost filled it to the brim, mostly with packing material from inside modules recently delivered to the space station, dirty clothes, food containers, broken equipment, and pretty much anything else the crew no longer wants on board. There's also containers of processed urine from the water-recycling system.

The Johannes Kepler ATV successfully undocked from the ISS on 20th June and at reentry after couple of hours it disintegrated northeast of New Zealand on 21st June.

Upon reentry, the craft put a dazzling display like that of the Jules Verne ATV, Kepler's older brother, which exploded into a shimmer on September 29, 2008.

Missions to Planets

Mercury: Mariner10, Messenger (NASA), Bepicolombo (ESA).

Venus: Mariner 2/Mariner 5 (NASA); Venera 2 To 15, Vega 1 (USSR); Magellan (NASA).

Earth- Moon: Pioneer, Luna 1 To 14 (USSR); Ranger; Zond 3to 7 (USSR); Lunar Orbiter, Surveyor, Apollo 1 to 18 (NASA); Luna Ye-8 Series (USSR); Clementine, Lunar Prospector, Smart-1, Selene (NASA); Chang'e 1 (China); Chandrayaan 1 (India)

Mars: Mariners 2 to 4 (NASA); Mars Probes (Soviet); Vikings (NASA)

Jupiter: (NASA) Pioneer 10, Pioneer 11, Voyager 1, Voyager 2, Galileo

Saturn: (NASA) The Pioneer, Voyager, Cassini, HuygenS (ESA).

Uranus: Voyager 2 (NASA)

Neptune: Voyager 2 (NASA)

SPACE SHUTTLE: (USA) Atlantis, Challenger, Columbia, Discovery, Endeavour; (USSR) Buran

Voyager 1 Probe, in July 2010 had traveled a distance traveled by light from the Sun in 16 hours (be- yond 114 AU) or 0.002 light-year. Launched in 1977, it flew past Jupiter and Saturn.

Voyager 2 Probe in July 2010 had traveled a distance traveled by light from the Sun in 13 hours (beyond 90 AU). Launched in 1977, it visited Jupiter, Saturn, Uranus, and Neptune.

Pioneer 10 Probe in July 2010 had traveled a distance traveled by light from the Sun in 14 hours (beyond 100 AU) Laun-ched in 1972, it visited Jupiter and Saturn.

Now all the 3 are headed out of the Solar System.

Solar System As We Know

PLANET SUPERLATIVES

Largest, most massive planet:	Jupiter
Fastest orbiting planet:	Mercury
Longest (synodic) day:	Mercury
Most Moons:	Jupiter
Planet with largest moon:	Jupiter
Greatest av. density:	Jupiter
Tallest mountain:	Earth
Strongest magnetic fields:	Jupiter
Most circular orbit:	Venus
Shortest (synodic) day:	Jupiter
Hottest Planet:	Venus
No Moons:	Mercury, Venus
Planet with moon with most eccentric orbit:	Neptune
Lowest av. density:	Saturn
Deepest oceans:	Jupiter
Greatest amount of liquid on the surface:	Earth

Asteroids

Over 40,000 asteroids orbiting the Sun. The asteroids, are very small bodies ranging from less than 1 to 400 kms in diameter. The name asteroid means starlike" as they appear like specks of light even in powerful telescopes. The total mass of all known asteroids, is less than that of Earth's Moon: only 26 asteroids are more than 200 km in diameter. Many asteroids occur in pairs that orbit each other and have solid bodies. Asteroids are found in several locations especially between Mars and Jupiter, but many inside the orbit of Mars are known as near-Earth asteroids. Asteroids that are thought to be larger than about 150 m in diameter that may travel as close as about 7.5 million km to Earth are called potentially hazardous objects (PHOs). There are about 300 known PHOs but none are expected to impact Earth in the foreseeable future.

Relative Size of Planets

Jupiter

Saturn

Uranus

Neptune

Mercury

Venus

Earth

Mars

THE SUN

Planet Names:

The planets were named after the Roman gods:

Mercury: god of commerce, eloquence, skill

Venus: goddess of spring, bloom, beauty

Mars: god of war

Jupiter: ruler of gods and all men

Saturn: god of agriculture

Uranus: god of heavens

Neptune: god of the sea

Mercury
Diameter: 4,849.6 km.
Density: 5.43 g/cm cube
Composition: 98% helium, 2% hydrogen
Average distance to the sun: 57.6 million km.
Time to orbit the sun: 87.97 days. Rotation: 59 days. Moons: none.

Venus
Diameter: 12032 km.
Density: 5.24 g/cm cube
Composition: CO_2 96.5%, N_2 3.5%.
Revolution: 224.70 days.
Av.distance to Sun: 107.5m. km Moons: none.

Earth
Diameter: 12739.2 km.
Density: 552 g/cm cube.
Composition: Nitrogen 78%, oxygen 21%, water 1%, argon....
Moons: 1.
Av. dist.–Sun: 149.8 m.km
Revolution: 365.30 days.
Rotation: 24 hrs (approx)

Mars
Diameter: 6,755.2 km.
Composition: CO_2 95%, 3% nitrogen, 2% argon.
Density: 3.93 g/cm cube
Av. distance to the Sun: 225.6 m. km. Revolution: 687 days.
Moons: 2. Phobos, Deimos

Jupiter
Diameter: 141,968 km..
Composition: 90% hydrogen, 10% helium
Moons: 63. (4 large ones Ganymede, Callisto, Io, Europa)
Density: 1.33 g/cm cube
Av. distance to the sun: 772.8 million km.
Revolution:11.86 years.

Saturn
Diameter: 119,296 km.
Composition: 90% hydrogen, 3% helium.
Moons: 60.
Density: 0.69 g/cm cube
Average distance to the sun: 1,417.6 million km.
Time to the orbit the sun: 29.46 years.

Uranus
Diameter: 52,096 km.
Moons: 27.
Density:1.32g/cm cube
Average distance to the Sun(km):2,852.8 million
Time to orbit the Sun: 84.01 years.
Average temperature of -2230c. It is made of mainly hydrogen and has a barren landscape apart from frozen methane clouds.

Neptune
Diameter: 49,000 km.
Atmospheric Composition: 80% hydrogen, 19% helium, 1% methane.
Moons: 13. Triton is the largest
Density: 1.64 g/cm cube
Ave distance to the sun: 4,497 million km.
Time to orbit the sun:164.80 years.

Dwarf Planets

Ceres
Ceres, discovered in 1801, the first asteroid discovered in the asteroid belt between Mars and Jupiter, to be considered as a 'planet' Mass: 0.00016 Earth masses.
Diameter: .075 Earth diameters. Orbit time: 4.6 years.
Rotation time: 9 hours.

Eris (Xena): discovered in 2005
Diameter : 2,397 kms (approx). Mass: .0027% of Earth masses. Atmospheric composition: methane and nitrogen. Eris is the largest dwarf planet in the solar system. It is slightly bigger than Pluto – an icy body that resides in the Kuiper Belt – with thousands of floating ice-balls. Moon: Dysnomia. Eris is at this time the most distant known body in the solar system. Its orbit is more eccentric and tilted than that of its neighbor Pluto. Orbit time: 557 years

Pluto: discovered –1930 by Clyde Tombaugh. Home: Kuiper Belt outside the orbit of Neptune
Moons:3. Charon, Nix, Hydra.
Diameter: 2,360 km. 0.18% of Earth
Density: 2.06 g/cm cube
Av. distance to the Sun: 5,865.6 million km. Mass: 0.002% of Earth masses
Revolution: 247.70 years.
Rotation: 6.4 days.
Atmospheric composition: methane and nitrogen.

Sun
Diameter: 1,384,000 km.
Density: 1.41 g/cm cube
Age: 4.5 billion years.
Planets: 8. Dwarf planets: 4. Pluto, Charon, Eris, Ceres
A rather ordinary, middle-age star, the gaseous sun may reach a temperature of 15.4°C million degrees celsius at its core.

Planets

The definition of planets, as accepted on 24 August 2006 is: "The IAU resolves that planets and other bodies, except satellites, in our Solar System be defined into three distinct categories in the following way:

(1) A planet is a celestial body that (a) is in orbit around the Sun, (b) has sufficient mass for its self-gravity to overcome rigid body forces so that it assumes a hydrostatic equilibrium (nearly round) shape, and (c) has cleared the neighbourhood around its orbit.

(2) A "dwarf planet" is a celestial body that (a) is in orbit around the Sun, (b) has sufficient mass for its self-gravity to overcome rigid body forces so that it assumes a hydrostatic equilibrium (nearly round) shape, (c) has not cleared the neighbourhood around its orbit, and (d) is not a satellite.

(3) All other objects, except satellites, orbiting the Sun shall be referred to as "Small Solar System Bodies".

Inner planets: Mercury, Venus, Earth and Mars. The bodies chiefly consist of iron and dense rock and are collectively called terrestrial planets (Earth–like).

Outer planets: Jupiter, Saturn, Uranus and Neptune are very big (sometimes called giant planets), with large satellite families. They are composed mostly of hydrogen, helium, ammonia and methane. These planets are called Jovian.

Meteors

As the Earth travels in its orbit around the Sun, it continually encounters meteoroids head-on. Sometimes, on a clear, dark night, an unusually large number of small meteors can be seen in rapid succession—perhaps more than 50 an hour - called a meteor shower. Because of their small size, these meteors generally burn up in the upper atmosphere and never reach the ground. Some meteor showers coincide with the passage of a comet.

Asteroids

Asteroids are smaller heavenly bodies generally found between the orbits of the planets Mars and Jupiter. They may be about 100,000 in numbers but their total mass

is only a few hundredths the mass of the Moon. They include Vesta, Eros and Icarus. Some asteroids come closer to the Earth. Apollo, even cross Earth's orbit.

Basic Facts About the Planets

Name of the Planets	Mercury	Venus	Earth	Mars	Jupiter	Saturn	Uranus	Neptune
Distance from km (millions)	57.9	108.2	149.6	227.9	778.57	1,433.53	2,872.46	4,495.1
Rotation period (days-d;hrs-h)	59 d	243 d	23.9 h	24.6 h	9.92 h	10.65 h	17.24 h	16.1 h
Orbital period (days)	88	224.7	365.256	686.98	4,331	10,747	30,589	59,800
Inclination of axis (degree)	0.01	3.39	23.45	25.19	3.13	26.73	97.77	28.32
Equatorial diameter km	4,879	12,104	12,756	6,794	142,984	120,536	51,118	49,528
In relation to Earth: Diameter	38.3%	94.9%	100%	53.3%	1,121%	945%	401%	388%
Mass (% of Earth's)	5.53	81.5	100	10.7	31,78	9,51.2	1,453.6	1,714.7
Gravity (% of Earth's)	37.8	90.7	100	37.7	236.4	91.6	88.90	112
Escape velocity km/second	4.3	10.36	11.186	5.03	59.5	35.5	21.3	23.5
Av. surface temperature ⁰C	166.9	463.9	15	-65	-110	-140	-195	-200
Planetary satellites	0	0	1	2	63	47	27	13

Venus's rotation is opposite the direction of other planets. Source: NASA: National Space Science Data

Supermoon

On March 19, in addition to being a full moon, the earth-moon distance was around 3,56,577 km, the closest in 18 years. The last time moon was closer on a full moon day was on March 8, 1993.

Moon goes round the earth in an elliptical orbit, and that makes it come close to the earth once during its orbit. The closest point, Perigee, is 3,57,00 kms. whereas at the apogee, the farthest point from earth, the distance can be about 50,000 km. This distance changes slightly every time.

The combined effects of orbital eccentricity and the sun's tides result in a substantial difference in the apparent size and brightness of the Moon at perigee and apogee. Scientists believe that such marginal increase in the tidal action is not dangerous to causing a major natural calamity.

Brush with Comet

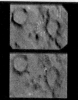

NASA's Stardust Deep Impact spacecraft marked its 12th anniversary in space on Feb. 7. Rockets were fired to direct its path toward a Feb. 14 date with Tempel 1. The spacecraft closed-on to Tempel 1, at a distance of 178 kilometers. Stardust took 72 high-resolution images of the comet and accumulated 468 kilobytes of data from the dust in its coma, the comet's atmosphere. The craft was on its extended mission of exploration called Stardust-NExT, after completing its prime mission of collecting cometary particles in 2006.

The Stardust-NExT mission met its goals, which included observing surface areas previously seen during the 2005 Deep Impact mission; imaging new terrain; and viewing the crater generated when the 2005 mission propelled an impactor at the comet.

Longer Lunar Eclipse

Lunar Eclipse of 2011, June 15

The most beautiful and the longest decadal lunar eclipse on June 15th, turned the moon bloody giving people an amazing visual enjoyment around the world. This total lunar eclipse is the first one in 2011, lasted for 100 minutes in different parts of Asia, Europe and Africa, except North America. A lunar eclipse lasted 107 minutes on July 16, 2000. The next such an eclipse is forecasted to occur only in 2141.

Green Auroras

A solar wind wreaked havoc on Earth's magnetic field in March 2011 setting off a day-long magnetic storm that sparked brilliant green auroras as seen in this shot from Poker Flat, Alaska. Sky watchers reported seeing the northern lights in Norway, Sweden, Latvia and Northern Ireland.

The polar light show starts with the ejection of charged hot gas from the sun. When this solar wind interacts with Earth's magnetic shield, high-energy particles can fall into our upper atmosphere, illuminating gas there.

Geoscience

Our understanding of the internal structure of the Earth is derived from studies of earthquakes. The shock waves sent out by an earthquake indicate the physical nature of the regions through which they pass.

Chemical Sub-division
CRUST:
  Oceanic - 7 km thick
    0-0.5 km sediments
    0.5-1 km - basalt
    1-7 km gabbro
Continental:
35 km (av.) - 80 km (under Tibet) thick
    0-1 km sediments
    1-35 km granite, gabbro
MANTLE   (2/3 of earth mass)
    Upper 35- 670 km depth
    Lower 670-2900 km depth
CORE
    Outer 2900-5170 km (liquid)
    Inner 5170-6371 km (solid)

Mechanical Sub-division
Lithosphere: rigid outer shell fragmented into plates
    Oceanic 0-65 km (basalt)
    Continental 0-120km (granite)
    Asthenosphere: 65 or 120 to 200 km molten plastic material
    Mesosphere: 200-2900 km; rigid
400 km-
670 km- no phase change below
    Outer Core: liquid

(Transition:4720-5170 km mushy)
Inner Core: solid

Lithosphere
The lithosphere is the top crust of the Earth on which our continents and ocean basins rest. It is thickest in the continental regions where it has an average thickness of 40 km and thinnest in the oceans where it may have a maximum thickness of 10 to 12 km.
Mohorovic Discontinuity: An imaginary line that separates Mantle and Crust.
Gutenberg-Wiechert Discontinuity: A separation between the Mantle and the Core.

Lithosphere forms only 3/10 of the total surface of the Earth. The rest 7/10 is taken up by the oceans.

As we see it today, the topmost portion of the land surface is sand and soil except where rocky outcrops show. All the sand and much of the soil that we see have derived from ancient rocks.

The contours of the landscape are largely conditioned by the rocky substructure of the lithosphere. Geologically speaking, all materials that make up the crust of the Earth are rocks, whether they are big granite boulders, combustible coal, soft clay or loose fragments of gravel or sand.

Rocks which form the substructure of the lithosphere may be broadly grouped into three classes:
    (i) Igneous rocks
    (ii) Sedimentary rocks and

Atmosphere > Nitrogen, Oxygen, Carbon-di-oxide

Crust > Oxygen, Silicon, Aluminium, Iron, Calcium, Sodium, Potassium, Magnesium, Quartz

Upper Mantle (asthenosphere)> Silicon di oxide, (Plastic) Magnesium oxide, Iron oxide, Aluminium, Oxygen.

Lower Mantle > Olivine, Pyroxene, Feldspar. 0C

Outer Core > Liquid Iron, Sulphur, Nickel, Oxygen.

Inner Core > Solid Iron, Nickel

Sources of Internal heat
1. Residual heat of accumulation
2. Continued trickling of heavy metals through the mantle into the core
3. Radioactive decay of long-lived radio-active isotopes.

(iii) Metamorphic rocks.

We know that the face of the Earth, that is, its visible surface has undergone radical changes in the past. Geologists explain these changes as the consequence of the cooling and contraction of the Earth, through thousands of years. This explanation seemed quite unsatisfactory to a German scientist, Alfred Wegener (1880-1930).

In 1915, Wegener published a book The Origin of Continents and Oceans in which he advanced the theory of Continental Drift. He theorised that the changes on the Earth surface were mainly due to the shifting of continents.

Plate Tectonics

Plate Tectonics tells us that it is not only the continents that are in motion, but the oceans as well. This is so, because the top crust of the Earth is not a complete single shell of granite and basalt, but a mosaic of several rigid segments, called plates. The theory of plate tectonics explains how the Earth's crust is moving in vast, rigid sections (plates) and is a modern revolution in our understanding of the planet. These plates include not only the Earth's solid upper crust, but also parts of the denser mantle below called Asthenosphere, and carry the continents and oceans on their backs like mammoth rafts. The plates with an average thickness of 100 km float on the Asthenosphere and move continuously against one another at a rate of upto 20 cm a year. Continents form only a part of the plates, the surrounding oceans form the rest of the plates. It is the plates containing both continents and oceans that move. The relation of inter-plate movement is defined by the type of plate margin: Constructive, Destructive or Conservative.

Constructive plate movement is obvious in the Atlantic Ocean. At the mid-ocean ridge, new ocean floor is continuously being produced as the Americas move further apart from Europe and Africa.

Destructive plate is found on all sides of Pacific Ocean, as the various plates slide down beneath the surrounding lithosphere.

Conservative plate movement can cause the most destructive earthquakes. It arises where adjacent plates slide past one another along transform faults, such as the San Andreas fault.

Looking at the Continents

Name	Area sq kilometres	% of Earth's area	Population Estimate (million)
Asia	43 998 000	29.5	3879
Africa	29 800 000	20.0	877
N. America	21 510 000	16.3	501
S. America**	17 598 000	11.8	379
Europe	9 699 550	6.5	727
Australia*	7 699 000	5.2	32
Antarctica	13 600 000	9.6	uninhabited

* Australia with New Zealand, Tasmania, New Guinea and the Pacific Islands, (Micronesian, Melanesian and Polynesian Islands) is called Australasia by some geographers while some others call it Oceania. ** includes Caribbean countries

Oceans of the World

Pacific	166,241,000 sq km
Atlantic	86,557,000 sq km
Indian	73,427,000 sq km
Arctic	9,485,000 sq km

Continentwise Highest Point

Continent	Peak	Height(m)
Asia	Mt. Everest	8848
Africa	Kilimanjaro	5963

Life in Space? Astronomers estimate that one star in ten is accompanied by planets. Carl Sagan said that as many as one million other civilizations, similar to ours, may exist in the Galaxy.

N. Am.	McKinley	6194
S. Am.	Aconcagua	6959
Europe	Mt. Elbrus	5633
Oceania	Puncak Jaya	4884
Antactica	Vinson Massif	4897

Continentwise Lowest Point

Continent	Peak	Depth(m)
Asia	Dead Sea	-396.8
Africa	Lake Assai	-156.1
N. Am.	Death Valley	-85.9
S. Am.	Valdes Penin	-39.9
Europe	Caspian Sea	-28.0
Oceania	Lake Eyre	-15.8

Oceans' Greatest Depths

Mariana Trench, Pacific Ocean	10920m
Puerto Rico Trench, Atlantic Ocean	8605m
Java Trench, Indian Ocean	7125m
Arctic Basin, Arctic Ocean	5122m

Major Seas

South China	2,974,600 sq km
Caribbean	2,515,900 sq km
Mediterranean	2,510,000 sq km
Bering	2,261,100 sq km
Gulf of Mexico	1,507,600 sq km
Sea of Okhotsk	1,392,100 sq km
Sea of Japan. or East Sea	1,012,900 sq km
Hudson Bay	730,100 sq km
East China	664,600 sq km
Andaman	564,900 sq km
Black	507,900 sq km
Red	453,000 sq km

Major Lakes

Caspian Sea, Asia-Europe	371,000 sq km
Superior, North America	82,100 sq km
Victoria, Africa	69,500 sq km
Huron, North America	59,600 sq km
Michigan, North America	57,800 sq km
Tanganyika, Africa	32,900 sq km
Baikal, Asia	31,500 sq km
Great Bear, North America	31,300 sq km
Aral Sea, Asia	30,700 sq km
Malawi, Africa	28,900 sq km
Great Slave, Canada	28,568 sq km
Erie, North America	25,667 sq km

Winnipeg, Canada	24,387 sq km
Ontario, North America	19,529 sq km
Balkhash, Kazakhstan	18,300 sq km

Deepest Lakes

Baikal, Russian Fed.	1620m
Tanganyika, Africa	1463m
Caspian Sea, Asia-Europe	1025m
Malawi or Nyasa, Africa	706m
Issyk-Kul, Kyrgyzstan	702m

Deepest Caves

Name	Location	Max.depth
Resseu du Foillis	France	1455
Resseu de la Pierre St.	France	1321
Snezhnaya, Caucasus	Russia	1280
Sistema Huatla	Mexico	1220

Largest Deserts of the World

Subtropical

Sahara, North Africa	9,064,650 sq. km
Arabian, Middle East	2,589,900 sq. km
Great Victoria, Australia	647,475 sq. km
Kalahari, Southern Africa	582,727 sq. km
Chihuahuan, Mexico	453,232 sq. km
Thar, India/Pakistan	453,232 sq. km
Great Sandy, Australia	388,485 sq. km
Gibson, Australia	310,788 sq. km
Sonoran, S.W. USA	310,788 sq. km
Simpson/Stony, N. Africa	145,034 sq. km
Mohave, S,W, USA	139,854 sq. km

Cool Coastal

Atacama, Chile SA	139,854 sq. km
Namib, S.W. Africa	33,668 sq. km

Cold Winter

Gobi, China	1,294,950 sq. km
Patagonian, Argentina	673,374 sq. km
Great Basin, S.W. USA	492,081 sq. km
Kara-Kum, West Asia	349,636 sq. km
Colorado, Western USA, also called the Painted Desert	336,687 sq. km
Kyzyl-Kum, West Asia	297,838 sq. km
Taklamakan, China	271,939 sq. km
Iranian, Iran	258,990 sq. km

Longest Rivers

Name	Country/ Continent	Length in kilometres
Nile	Africa	6650
Amazon	S. America	6437

Mississippi-Missouri	USA	6020
Yangtze Kiang	China	5494
Ob-Irtysh	Russia	5410
Zaire	Africa	4700
Lena	Russia	4400
Hwang Ho	China	4344
Mackenzie	Canada	4241
Mekong	Asia	4180
Niger	Africa	4180
St. Lawrence	Canada-USA	4023
Parana	S. America	4000
Yenisey	Russia	3804
Murray-Darling	Australia	3780
Volga	Russia	3690
Zambezi	Africa	3540
Maderia	S. America	3218
Purus	S. America	3200
Yukon–Teslin	Alaska-Canada	3185
Rio Grande	USA-Mexico	3040
Indus	Asia	2900
Brahmaputra (INDIA)	Asia	2900
Ganga	India	2510
Godawari	India	1450
Narmada	India	1290
Krishna	India	1290

Deep–sea Trenches

Name Deepest pt.	Length		Depth
Mariana (W. Pacific)	2250	10 924	Challenger Deep
Tonga Kermadec (S. Pacific)	2575	10 850	Vityaz 11 (Tonga)
Kuril–Kamchatka (W. Pacific)	2250	10 542	
Philippine (W. Pacific)	1350	10 539	Galathea Deep
Java-Indian (Ocean)	2250	7725	Planet Deep

Units: Length in km and depth in metres

Famous Waterfalls

Name	Country	Drop (m)
Angel	Venezuela	807
Mongefossen	Norway	774
Kukenaam	Venezuela	610
Utigard	Norway	600
Ribbon	USA	491
King George VI	Guyana	487
Roraima	Guyana	457
Upper Yosemite	USA	435
Kalambo	Tanzania–Zambia	426

Gavarnie	France	421
Tugela	S. Africa	410
Takakkaw	Canada	365

Principal Peaks

Name	Country	Height (m)
Mt. Everest*	Nepal-Tibet	8848
Everest South Summit	-	8750
K2 (Mt. Godwin)	India (POK)	8611
Kanchenjunga	Nepal-India	8598
Dhaulagiri	Nepal	8167
Nanga Parbat (Diamir)	India	8126
Annapurna	Nepal	8091
Nanda Devi	India	7817
Mt. Kamet	India	7756
Saltoro Kangri	India	7742
Gurla Mandhata	Tibet	7728
Tirich Mir	Pakistan	7700
Minya Konka	China	7690
Saser Kangiri	India	7672
Muztagh Ata	China	7546
Mt. Communism	Tajikstan	7495
Badrinath Peak	India	7138
Chomo Lhari	India-Tibet	7100
Aconcagua	Argentina	6960
Ojos del Salado	Argentina-Chile	6885
Mercedario Huascaran	Peru	6768
Liullaillaco	Chile	6723
Volcano Tupungato	Chile-Argentina	6550
Sajama Volcano	Bolivia	6520
Illimani	Bolivia	6462
Vilcanota	Peru	6300
Chimborazo	Ecuador	6267
Mt. McKinley	Alaska	6194
Cotopaxi	Ecuador	5897
Kilimanjaro	Tanzania	5895
Mt. Elbrus	Georgia	5642
Mt. Blanc	France–Italy	4807
Matterhorn	Switzerland	4478
Mt. Cook	New Zealand	3764

*[Qomolangma–feng:Chinese, Sagarmatha:Nepalese, Mi–ti gu–ti cha–pu long–na: Tibetan]. The dormant volcano Mauna Kea (on Big Island of Hawaii) could be considered the tallest mountain in the world if one measures it from its base in the Hawaiian Trough (3280 fathoms deep) to its summit, it reaches a height of 10,203m. (4205m above the msl.)

Hottest, Coldest, Driest, Wettest

Hottest Place Dallol, Denakil Depression,

Ethiopia, annual average temp. 34.4°C •
Coldest Place Plateau Station, Antarctica,
annual average temp. –56.7°C • **Wettest
Place** Mawsynram, Meghalaya 1187 cm 74-
yr. av.; (Mt. Waialeale, Hawaii Is.,1168 cm,
32-yr.av.) annual average rainfall • **Driest
Place** S. America, Atacama Desert, Chile,
0.08cm.

World's Largest Islands

Name	Area sq km	Location
Australia*	7 682 300	Indian Ocean
Greenland	2 175 600	Arctic Ocean
New Guinea	792 500	W Pacific
Borneo	725 545	Indian Ocean
Malagasy Rep.	587 000	Indian Ocean
Baffin Island	476 065	Arctic Ocean
Sumatra	427 300	Indian Ocean
Honshu	227 400	NW Pacific
Great Britain	218 041	N Atlantic
Victoria Island	217 300	Arctic Ocean
Eliesmere Island	196 236	Arctic Ocean
Celebes	189 035	Indian Ocean

* Geographically regarded as a continental land mass

Coldest in 21st Century

Air temperatures of minus 61.2 degrees Celsius were reported in the
settlement of Oimyakon in Russia's
Republic of Yakutia known as the
cold pole. Heavy frosts were reported
in neighbouring settlements as well.

The record low air temperatures of
minus 67.7 degrees Celsius were registered in Oimyakon in 1933. In the
21st century, the lowest temperature
was 64.5 degrees below zero. It was
registered in 2002.

Comparative Seismic Scale

Intensity (Mercalli)	Description	Magnitude (Ricter)	Witness Observations
I	Instrumental	1 to 2	Detected only by seismographs
II	Feeble	2 to 3	Noticed only by sensitive people
III	Slight	3 to 4	Resembling vibrations caused by heavy traffic
IV	Moderate	4	Felt by people walking; rocking free standing objects
V	Rather Strong	4 to 5	Sleepers awakened and bells ring
VI	Strong	5 to 6	Trees sway, damage from falling objects
VII	Very Strong	6	General alarm, cracking of walls
VIII	Destructive	6 to 7	Chimneys fall; some damage to buildings
IX	Ruinous	7	Ground crack; houses begin to collapse; pipes break
X	Disastrous	7 to 8	Ground badly cracked; buildings destroyed; landslides
XI	Very Disastrous	8	Few buildings remain standing; bridges and railways destroyed;water, gas, electricity, telephones disrupted
XII	Catastrophic	8 or greater	Total destruction; objects are thrown into the air, much heaving, shaking and distortion of the ground

Seismic Scale The Richter scale is a logarithmic scale, devised in 1935 by geophysicist Charles Richter, for
representing the energy released by earthquakes. A modified Mercalli scale is used to measure earthquake's
strength or its intensity.

Earthquakes and Volcanoes

The earthquakes in India are due to the drifting of the so-called Indian Plate. Scientists divide the globe into a number of major tectonic plates that drift very slowly. As these plates slide against each other a tremendous amount of energy is released causing heavy destruction.

Types: Natural Earthquakes caused by endogenic forces. (i) Volcanic-caused due to volcanic eruptions, e.g., Mt Etna. (ii) Tectonic- caused due to stress and strain along Earth's plates or dislodging of rocks during faulting. (iii) Isostatic- caused by isostatic imbalance due to sudden geological activity at a regional scale. (iv) Plutonic- earthquakes originating deep inside the earth between 250 to 650 km deep.

How do Earthquakes Occur? There are many fault-lines in the Earth's crust. A fault is where blocks of crust on either side are moving relative to one another. The typical average rate is around a millimetre per year. If this movement happened gradually it would pose few problems for people living near by. Unfortunately rocks do not behave that way. Strain builds up for decades or centuries until it reaches a critical level, and then everything gives in at once. Once a fault has given way at one point, slip movement may occur along its whole length, which may be hundreds or thousands of kilometres, though movement is usually restricted to a much shorter portion

of the whole fault. The strongest seismic waves are generated at the initial break-point. The closer to the break-point, the greater the energy and the greater the potential for destruction, especially if the break-point is near the surface. Technically, the break-point is called the earthquake focus, and the point on the surface directly above it is referred to as the epicentre. Slip further along the fault and readjustments close to the focus usually cause a series of smaller aftershocks, which continue for days (even years in extreme cases) after the initial earthquake. Such kind of energy release are called waves because of the way they move. Most of the damage caused by an earthquake is not done by the P-waves and S-waves.

These waves travel through the body of the Earth, and their energy is spread over a rapidly increasing volume as they propagate. It is other waves of the sort that travel along the surface of the ground that do most of the harm. These include up-and-down waves (like waves on the ocean) and strong side-to-side shaking waves. The P-and S-body waves travel faster than the surface waves, and, if felt, can give a few seconds (minutes, if further away) warning of the arrival of the more damaging surface waves.

When Next? Scientists can't predict earthquakes but they know in which regions earthquakes are most likely to occur. Taking

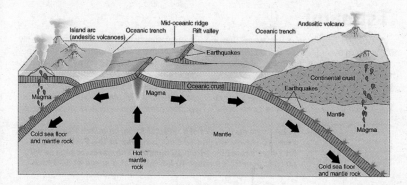

Ring of Fire

Volcanic Eruptions

Year	Volcano (place)	Deaths (approx)
79 AD	Mt. Vesuvius , Italy	16000
1586	Kelut, Indonesia	10,000
1792	Mt. Unzen, Japan	14,500
1815	Tambora, Indonesia	10,000
1883	Krakatoa, Indonesia	36,000
1902	Mt. Pelee, Martinique	28,000
1980	Mt. St. Helens, USA	57
1982	El Chichon, Mexico	1880
1985	Nevado del Ruiz,Columbia	23000
1986	Lake Nyos, Cameroon	1700
1991	Mt. Mt Pinatubo, Philipines	800

into account the speed and direction of the drift of the plates, the structure of the land masses and in particular the measurements of the tensions between different areas almost accurate probabilities can be calculated.

Volcanoes

A volcano is a mountain or hill with an opening on top known as a crater. Hot melted rock (magma), gases, ash, and other material from inside the Earth mix together a few kilometres underground, and blast out, or erupt, through the crater.

The magma is called lava when it reaches the air. Lava may be as hot as 1000 ⁰C. Gradually the lava cools and solidifies on the earth surface making new landforms. In some eruptions, huge fiery clouds rise over the mountain, and glowing rivers of lava flow down its sides.

Types of Volcanoes

Periodicity
(i) Active- that which is alive now. e.g. Etna, Stromboli, Pinatubo, etc.
(ii) Dormant- that which has not erupted for quite some time now. e.g. Vesuvius, Barren Islands.
(iii) Extinct- which has not erupted for several

centuries/millennia or may not occur in near future too.

Mode of Eruption:

(i) Central or Explosive- e.g. Hawaiian type, Vesuvius type, Pelean type, etc.
(ii) Fissure or Quite eruption: in which lava flow or flood, mud flow and fumaroles.

Ring of Fire

The hundreds of active volcanoes found on the land near the edges of the Pacific Ocean make up what is called the Ring of Fire. They mark the boundry between the plates under the Pacific Ocean and the plates under the continents around the ocean.

The Ring of Fire runs all along the west coast of South and North America, from the southern tip of Chile to Alaska. The ring also runs down the east coast of Asia, starting in the far north in Kamchatka. It extends down past Australia.

Tsunami

A tsunami is a large ocean wave that is caused by sudden motion on the ocean floor. This sudden motion could be an earthquake, a powerful volcanic eruption, or an underwater landslide. The impact of a large meteorite could also cause a tsunami. Tsunamis travel across the open ocean

at great speeds and build into large deadly waves in the shallow water of a shoreline. Most tsunamis are caused by earthquakes generated in a subduction zone, an area where an oceanic plate is being forced down into the mantle by plate tectonic forces. This friction prevents a slow and steady rate of

Tsunami in Japan	A Japanese earthquake of 9.0 Ricter Scale, on March 11th, caused tsunami waves, originated 360 km away in the Pacific Ocean, hit Tokyo's coastline within 30 minutes. The waves, as high as 9.9 metres, penetrated about 10 km inland at a speed of 500 mph.

subduction and the two plates lock 'horns.'
Accumulated Seismic Energy: As the locked plate continues to descend into the mantle the motion causes a slow distortion of the overriding plate. The result is an accumulation of energy very similar to the energy stored in a compressed spring. **Earthquake Causes Tsunami:** Energy accumulates in the overriding plate until it exceeds the frictional forces between the two stuck plates. When this happens, the overriding plate snaps back into an unrestrained position. This sudden motion is the cause of the tsunami - because it gives an enormous shove to the overlying water and inland areas of the overriding plate are suddenly lowered. **Tsunami Races Away From the Epicenter:** The moving wave begins travelling

Tsunami hitting Japan in 2011

out from where the earthquake has occurred, landward to flood the recently lowered shoreline. Tsunamis Travel Rapidly Across Ocean Basis: Tsunamis travel swiftly across the open ocean. **Tsunami "Wave Train":** Tsunamis are not single waves. Instead tsunamis are "wave trains" consisting of multiple waves.

Seasons' Mix

The earth's axis is inclined at an angle of 66.5° to the plane of its orbit. As a result of this, the earth is in different positions while revolving around the sun. During the first half of the year the northern hemisphere tilts towards the sun resulting in the season of summer in the region. During the second half of the year the southern hemisphere tilts towards the sun, and thus experiences summer and the northern hemisphere experiences winter during this period.

The Four Seasons (a) Spring When the sun is directly overhead the equator (b) Summer When the sun is directly over the tropic of Cancer—the North Temperate Zone (NTZ) experiences summer. (c) Autumn When the sun returns to the equator, the NTZ experiences the season of autumn. (d) Winter The sun is at the tropic of Capricorn and the NTZ experiences winter.

Equinoxes are dates when the nights and days are equal. During these days the sun shines directly over the equator. March 21 is called vernal equinox and September 23 is called autumnal equinox.

Solstice The time of the year when the difference between the length of days and nights is the largest is referred to as solstice. On or around June 21, the North Pole tilts towards the sun and the sun shines directly over the tropic of Cancer which is called summer solstice. On or around December 22, the earth is at the opposite end of its orbit, as a result, the South Pole tilts towards the sun and the North Pole away from it. This is called winter solstice.

Eclipses When the light of the sun or the moon is obscured by another body the sun or moon is said to be in eclipse. **Lunar Eclipse** When the earth comes between the moon and the sun, the shadow cast by the earth on the moon results in a lunar eclipse. Lunar eclipse occurs only on a full moon day but not on every full moon day. **Solar Eclipse** When the moon comes between the sun and the earth, it causes obstruction of the sun's light when viewed from the earth and is called solar eclipse. A solar eclipse occurs on a new moon day when the moon is in line with the sun.

Longest Mountain Chains	The Andes stretches 4500 miles form the world's longest mountain chain. Next come the Rockies (3100 miles), the Himalayas (2400 miles) and Australia's Great Dividing Range (2250 miles).

Atmospheric Make-up

The atmosphere is an insulating blanket protecting the Earth. It softens the intense light and heat of the Sun. Its Ozonic (O_3) layer absorbs most of the very deleterious ultraviolet rays from the Sun and thus protects living organisms from extinction.

The atmosphere is bound to the Earth by gravity. Satellites like the Moon, which have very low gravitational power, cannot and do not hold an atmosphere.

Air pressure simply means the weight of the entire air column over a given point. Air, of course, has very little weight. A litre of air weighs around 1.3 g. At the sea level, the air pressure is 1033.6 g per sq. cm. This pressure is usually described as one atmosphere.

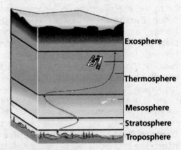

Atmospheric layers

Clouds

Clouds are made of water vapour that has evaporated from the Earth. They are very tiny droplets of microscopic size and are too light to fall down as rain. So they ride on the air waves until they condense and then fall down as rain.

Ozone Layer

According to 2006 Reports of two UN agencies, the World Meteorological Organisation (WMO) and the UN Environment Program (UNEP) , the earth's ozone layer is finally on the mend after decades of damage, i.e., recovering more slowly than experts had hoped.Over huge areas of Europe, North America and Asia in the northern hemisphere and over southern Australasia, Latin America and Africa, the layer would be back to pre-1980 levels by 2049. Over Antarctica, where so-called "ozone holes" have grown over the past 30 years, recovery was likely to be delayed until 2065. The good news is that the level of ozone-depleting substances continues

to decline from its 1992-94 peak in the troposphere and the 1990s peak in the stratosphere. The earth's atmosphere is enveloped by different layers but in the stratosphere it is covered by ozone gas. (Stratosphere extends from 12 km to 30 km above the Earth). Ozone has three oxygen atoms while oxygen has two. Ozone protects mankind from harmful radiation called ultraviolet (UV) rays from the Sun. The UV light from the Sun causes reaction leading to making and breaking of ozone oxygen. The ozone layer absorbs potentially harmful UV radiation from the Sun (at wavelengths between 240 and 320 nm). The main destroyers of the ozone are the CFCs (Choloro-fluorohydro-carbons) (from air conditioners, refrigerators, aerosols, solvents and in production of some types of packaging) and nitrogen oxides from fertilisers and aircraft emissions occurring high in the troposphere (which rise up into the stratosphere) where they are broken by UV light into chlorine (which has a very devastating effect on the ozone). One atom of chlorine can destroy over 100,000 molecules of ozone. Depletion of the ozone layer will allow UV light of the

| Animals in the Sky | There are constellations named giraffe, dragon and unicorn. Draco, the dragon, is coiled around the north pole of the sky. The unicorn is Monoceros and the giraffe Camelopardalis. |

Structure of the Atmosphere

1. Troposphere	0-10 km (poles)
	0-16 km (equator)
Tropopause	10(poles), 16(equator)
2. Stratosphere	10-16 to 50 km
Stratopause	50 km
3. Mesosphere	50-85 km
Mesopause	85 km
4. Thermosphere	85 km +
	- Ionosphere
	- Exosphere

undesirable wavelengths to penetrate the atmosphere and reach Earth's surface. This causes skin cancer, severe sunburns , cataracts, damage vegetation, crop yields and sea life, among other things.

Winds

It is the air in motion. What causes the wind is the pressure gradient, it always from high pressure area to low pressure area. Due to the Earth's rotation the wind's direction changes suddenly due to deflection. In the northern hemisphere the wind is deflected to the right and in the southern hemisphere to the left. This phenomenon is called the Ferrel's Law. The force acting behind it is Coriolis force.

Types of Winds (i) Planetary winds are those that occur at the global scale, such as the trade winds, westerlies (Roaring Forties, Furious Fifties, Shrieking-sixties),doldrums, tropical cyclones- as in India, (Typhoon-Philippines, Japan, China; Hurricane-USA, West Indies; Willy nillies- Australia), etc.

(ii) Periodic winds are those that occur at certain times during some season at specific locations, like monsoon.

(iii) Local winds develop as a result of local conditions in temperature, pressure, continentality, altitude, etc. Some examples are Tornado (velocity of >300km/hr, found in Mississippi basin-USA, Sahara-Africa; Loo in NW India and Pakistan; Mistral- originates on Alps and blows down on Mediteranean Sea; Chinook & Foehn- warm dry wind on the leeward side in USA and Switzerland respectively; Harmattan- warm dry wind blowing from NE and E to W in E Sahara (similar winds are Brickfielder- Australia, Blackroller-USA, Shamal- in Iraq and Persian gulf, Norwester- in New Zealand); Sirocco-warm dry dusty wind blowing northwards from Sahara reaching Italy, Spain, etc. Similar winds are Khamsin- Egypt, Gibli in Libya, Chilli in Tunisia, Simoon in Arabian desert); Bora- cold dry northeasterly wind blowing in Adriatic sea; Blizzard- violent, stormy, cold and powdery polar wind laden with dry snow in Siberia, Canada and USA; Purga-snow laden cold wind in Russian Tundra; Bise- cold wind in France; Laventer-strong easterly cold wind in Spain; Pampero- cold wind in Argentina's Pampas grasslands; Santa Ana- warm dry wind in USA; Tramontane-warm wind in central Europe; Yamo- warm dry wind in Japan; and Zonda-warm wind in Argentina.

(iv) Atmospheric disturbances are caused by conditions likeEl Nino, La Nina, Jetstreams (high speed wind blowing in the upper atmosphere over mid-latitudes from west).

Hurricanes

For every year, there is a pre-approved list of names for tropical storms and hurricanes. These lists are generated by the National Hurricane Center (since 1953). Since 1979, the names-list alternate between male and female. Hurricanes are named alphabetically from the list in chronological order. Thus the first tropical storm or hurricane of the year has a name that begins with "A" and the second is given the name that begins with "B." The lists contain names that begin from A to W, but exclude names that begin with a "Q" or "U." There are six lists that continue to rotate. The lists only change when there is a hurricane that is so devastating, the name is retired and another name replaces it.

The Seven Stars	The familiar shape of a saucepan of seven stars helps locate Polaris, a star very near to the north pole of the sky. During the night, all other stars appear to circle around it as the Earth turns. The seven stars make up the plough or Big Dipper.

North-East
monsoon

South-West
monsoon

El Niño

El Niño is a regularly occurring climatic feature which is a "seesaw of warm water sloshing back and forth in the Pacific Ocean" between the coast of South America and Indonesia. Usually the warm water of El Niño remains off the coast of South America for about four years and then makes its way slowly across the Pacific, back to Indonesia for another four years. Peruvian fishermen noticed that the arrival of El Niño coincided with the Christmas season so named the phenomenon after the "the baby boy" Jesus. Scientists refer to the event when warm water is in the opposite side of the ocean near Indonesia as La Niña or "the baby girl." Slow tiny waves move the warm water across the ocean during the cycle.

El Niño increases average ocean surface water temperature which causes climatic change around the world. Effects of El Niño are felt as far away from the Indian subcontinent and Pacific Ocean as Eastern Africa (there is often reduced rainfall and thus Nile River carries less water).

What is Monsoon?

In the secondary atmospheric circulation, Monsoon in itself is considered a phenomenon. Monsoon is attached to such an atmospheric circulation which reverses its flow seasonally. If this criterion of seasonal reversal is applied strictly, then only a few regions of the world have monsoon wind system. It is in Asia that monsoonal circulation is found in the ideal form. USA, Northern Australia, West Africa also has monsoon-like experiences.

Indian Monsoon The monsoon in the truest sense is observed only around the Indian Ocean. The centres of action, air masses, and the dynamics of Indian monsoon are completely different from the rest of the world monsoon systems. The peninsular shape of the country has its role, as it divides the SW monsoon flanks to the north as the Arabian Sea branch and to the east as Bay of Bengal branch.

Rain: When the SW Monsoon brings about 1 metre of average rainfall over the plains of the country as a whole, it is called normal. But there are many places such as the windward side of the Western Ghats which receive between an average of 100-250 cm of rain. At Mahabaleshwar the rainfall amounts to 650 cm and Mawsynram, on the southern slopes of Khasi-Jayantia Hills, has the unique distinction of receiving average precipitation of 965 cm, in the world.

Peculiarities of Indian monsoon are: (a) tropical location of the Indian sub-continent, (b) Himalayas–the mountain barrier to the north of the landmass, cold and dry air-mass from the Central Asian high pressure zone. It not only blocks the SW wind from crossing over to the Tibetan plateau but allows it to spread in the north Indian belt. (c) monsoon is controlled by high and low pressure centres developed over northwestern region of the Indian sub-continent, (d) It is in summer due to intense heating the high temperature (about 40 - 45°C) steepens pressure gradient over India, (e) extreme low pressure points (thermal low of upto 700 mb) that develop in the NW region, actively attract the prevailing wind from the Indian Ocean, (f) monsoon bursts over India with big turbulence, (g) Inter-tropical Convergence Zone shifts to the northern plains (about 30°N), (h) at its peak monsoon derives its strength from series of atmospheric depressions, that have their origin in the convergence zone of different air masses, (i) monsoon starts by 20th May and covers the whole country by July 15th, (j) retreating monsoon starts (also called NE monsoon) from northern regions by Sept. 1st, central India by Oct.1st, and completely by first week of November, (k) Retreat of monsoon is also accompanied by disturbances such as cyclones, causing large scale damage to life and property along the eastern coast of India.

Environmental Efforts

2011: International Year of Forests

The UN General Assembly designated 2011 the International Year of Forests to raise awareness on sustainable management, conservation and sustainable development of all types of forests. "Forests for People" was the main theme of the Year. According to World Bank estimates, more than 1.6 billion people depend on forests for their livelihoods. The forest product industry is a source of economic growth and employment, with global forest products traded internationally in the order of $270 billion. The UN's Food and Agriculture Organization (FAO) estimates that every year 130,000 km² of the world's forests are lost due to deforestation. Conversion to agricultural land, unsustainable harvesting of timber, unsound land management practices, and creation of human settlements are the most common reasons for this loss of forested areas. According to the World Bank, deforestation accounts for up to 20% of the global greenhouse gas emissions that contribute to global warming. FAO data estimates that the world's forests and forest soil store more than 1 trillion tons of carbon – twice the amount

INTERNATIONAL YEAR

found in the atmosphere. The World Bank estimates that forests provide habitats to about two-thirds of all species on earth, and that deforestation of closed tropical rainforests could account for biodiversity loss of as many as 100 species a day.

Know Your Carbon Footprint

To calculate a household's carbon footprint, log on to www.no2co2.in. The website analyses the processes and systems around us, the things we use, the food we eat, how we travel, where we stay, etc.

The International Conventions

1. UN Framework Convention on Climate Change (UNFCCC), New York, 09.05.92; Convention on Biological Diversity (CBD), Rio-de-Janeiro.

2. Cartegena Protocol on Biosafety under CBD (29.01.2000).

3. Kyoto Protocol to the UNFCCC (Kyoto, 11.12.1997); Amendment to Annex-B of the Kyoto Protocol to the UNFCCC (Nairobi, 17.11. 2006)

4. Convention on the Law of the Non-Navigational Uses of International Water courses (New York, 21.05.1997)

5. Rotterdam Convention on the Prior Informed Consent Procedure for Certain Hazardous Chemicals and Pesticides in International Trade (Rotterdam, 10.09.1998)

6. Stockholm Convention on Persistent Organic Pollutants (Stockholm, 22.05. 2001)

7. International Tropical Timber Agreement, 2006 (Geneva, 27.01.2006)

8. UN Convention on the Law of the Sea (Montego Bay, 10.12.1982)

9. UN Convention on the Law of the Sea (10.12.1982 relating to the Conservation and Management of Straddling Fish Stocks and Highly Migratory Fish Stocks (New York, 04.08.1995).

Persistent Toxic Substance Danger

Gathered in Geneva for the Fifth Conference of the Parties in April 2011, 127 nations of the world agreed to include endosulfan as an antiquated persistent insecticide, at the Stockholm Convention's list of banned substances and fixed 2012 to end its usage. But India has wrested an 11-year phase-out period till an affordable alternative is developed by the native scientists.

It is used for pulses, fruits, vegetables, mustard, sunflower, etc. Endosulfan, a DDT-era pesticide, is one of the most toxic pesticides still in use today. Each year, it took the lives of dozens of African cotton farmers until recently before being banned by most countries on the continent. Because

of its persistence, bioaccumulation, and mobility, endosulfan—travels on wind and water to places where it contaminates the environment.

India is one of the world's biggest users of endosulfan. The use of endosulfan has severely impacted the people of Kasargod district in Kerala, India, where its use on cashew plantations has left thousands suffering from birth defects, mental retardation, and cancer. This phase-out of endosulfan is an opportunity for countries to implement non-chemical alternatives to pesticides and to strengthen and expand agroecological practices. Because of its low cost and continued farmer patronage in many

places like in India, it is difficult to effect a complete ban on the substance. Indian brands cost only Rs. 290 while its alternative costs as much Rs .2000-3000.

Threats to human life: Acute Toxicity, Endocrine Disruption, Chronic Effects

Deformities in animals

Threats to environment: a wide range of insects, micro organisms, all types of animals.

Usage of Endosulfan

Total Consumption: 12 million litres

Usage - Statewise

1000 KL+ MP, AP, Maharashtra, WB, Sikkim

500KL+ Punjab, Haryana, UP, Uttrakhand, Arunachal, Asom, Nagaland, Mizoram, Manipur, Bihar, Jharkhand, Rajasthan, Gujarat, Tamil Nadu

50KL+ J&K, HP, Chhattisgarh, Odisha, Karnataka

0KL+ Kerala

Source: CropLife Survey, 2007 on Consumption of Endosulfan in India. * KL - kilo litres

---

Gravitropism	It is a natural process in a plant that is controlled by a plant hormone called Auxin. Auxins have lot of functions. When a shoot emerges from a seed, auxins cause the cells in the stem to bend upward just as it would command the roots to go downward.

Green Growth: India's Forest Policy needs New Direction

Sunita Narain

Forests have to be central to development. A proper understanding of the potential of the forest is essential.

We know we need forests for our survival. But as yet, we are still learning how we will protect, regenerate and grow forests. This is the challenge for India's environment in the years to come.

Each passing day the forestlands in India are under a big threat—not necessarily from the poor people who live in forests but from developers who want the land, minerals, water and other resources. Over time, the infrastructure imperative will take away forests, which have become the only free and available resource in the time of

> India cannot afford to set aside 22 per cent of its land, and not use it for development.

scarcity. The demand to open up forests will grow each day. Already, forestland is being lost bit by bit and all the talk about compensatory afforestation is just that—talk, not trees on the ground. In this situation we will be left with pockmarked wildlife reserves that animals and people will compete for.

It is to avoid this future that we need forests to be central to development as we reinvent it. It is in this context that we must discuss the potential of forests, both the intangible benefits of ecological security and tangible economic returns. This discussion is taboo in the forest-conservation circles,

where the country has moved from extraction to protection, without clarity about how the land will be utilised for production.

But let us also be clear that India (or for that matter any country) cannot afford to set aside 22 per cent of its land, and not use it for development. This is a message that environmentalists fighting against forest destruction are rightly reluctant to give. But it is time we changed this.

Take a look at the economic survey of the country and you will find how forests have disappeared from national accounts. There are estimates of what forests generate for the economy but no valuation of the standing forests and their role in water and soil protection, and certainly no valuation of the minor forest produce, which provides livelihood to the poor. There is no assessment of the role of forests as providers of grazing land, which in turn provide for animal care and dairying. Instead, you will see that the contribution of this sec-

Gandhiji on Prosperity	In response to a question whether he did not wish to see India reach the level of prosperity of Britain, Gandhiji said: "It took Britain half the resources of the planet to achieve this prosperity. How many planets will a country like India require?"

tor—defined as agriculture, forestry and fishing—has sharply declined each year. Its annual growth rate in 2005-06 was 5.2 per cent. By 2009-10 its growth rate turned negative. Its place has been taken by the mining and quarrying sector, which registered a growth rate of 8.7 per cent in 2009-10 against 1.3 per cent in 2005-06. In fact, forests have been blacked out in the economic assessment of the country.

Clearly, something is amiss, if we take into account the enormous potential of growing wood and non-timber products and their impact on livelihoods and economies of states. Currently, we import more and more of forest produce, from pulp to timber. It is for this reason that revenues from forests are declining in state budgets, which creates pressure for their diversion to more productive uses.

> Revenues from forests are declining in state budgets, which creates pressure for their diversion to more productive uses.

The way ahead involves three steps. One, we need to urgently value the economic potential of forests and to incorporate this into national accounts. But this valuation must go beyond carbon storage and other obvious benefits. It must take into account the million ways in which forests provide livelihood support to people.

Two, we need steps to pay for standing forests. This money must go to communities bearing the burden of conservation. The economic value of keeping forests as forests for watersheds and biodiversity has to be paid to the custodians. It will build local economies and local support for forest protection.

Three, most importantly, we have to increase the productivity of the remaining forestland. But we know that the business of cutting and planting trees that survive

cannot be successful without people who live in the forest.

Bamboo as grass

Let's take the challenge of using forests to build a green economy. One big question that was on the table last year was if bamboo was a tree or a grass. The definition makes a huge difference – if it is a grass, then it can be grown by people, harvested and sold. We know that bamboo grows like a weed and because of its high productivity and versatility of uses it has the potential of creating huge economic wealth. So if you can put bamboo in the hands of the people, to grow, to harvest and to add value, you put wealth in their hands.

But policy was reluctant to make this change. The Indian Forest Act had over time categorised bamboo as timber, which meant that the forest department had the monopoly over it. This meant those who grew bamboo in their backyard could not harvest it or transport it or indeed sell this productive grass without a number of permissions from the forest department. To get the transit pass a tree owner would have to obtain revenue records and then apply to the collector or the forest department for permission to cut. It would take up to 10 different departmental permissions and many visits to "headquarters" to get clearance. So the way out is to find a well-heeled and connected contractor, who then takes on the responsibility to pay his way through the system and facilitate the transaction. In all this, the person who grows the tree and needs the income gets shortchanged. There is no incentive to use

Sea Levels Rise Fast — Sea levels are rising fast. Scientists used fossils to reconstruct sea levels over the past two millennia on the US Atlantic coast and found they are now rising faster than at any time in the past 2,100 years. Its evident in higher temperatures and rising tides.

trees or grass as an income-generating activity. Nobody grows trees. The environment loses.

It is this that could change now. The Ministry of Environment and Forests has made it clear that the Forest Rights Act has changed the legal regime governing bamboo. This act, passed in 2006, has "vested the right of ownership, access to collect, use and dispose of minor forest product" with tribals and other traditional forest dwellers. It has also defined bamboo as a minor forest produce. The letter asks the chief ministers to direct their forest administration to treat bamboo as minor forest produce and to "respect the rights accrued to communities".

Just consider the potential. The Indian paper industry needs massive quantities of raw material and bamboo is the best pulping material. But over the years, with bamboo defined as timber, industry and forest departments have worked on contractual arrangements to get bamboo and other wood at throwaway prices. Large parts of the country's forests have been leased

> India needs roughly 1.5 million hectares of tree-bamboo land to supply raw material to the paper and pulp industry.

to the industry. This has led to deforestation and, in turn, a crippling shortage of raw material for the industry. More importantly, this policy has ended up discounting the value of trees grown by farmers. Our analysis shows that India needs roughly 1.5 million hectares of tree-bamboo land to supply raw material to the paper and pulp industry. This is a renewable raw material.

Now industry can source this from small landholders or villagers with community forest rights. It will have to pay the market value, which will increase its cost of raw material marginally. But at the same time, this buyer-seller relationship will put

money directly in the hands of people, reducing need for development assistance, which also comes at a high transactional cost. Growing trees can be a business for growth.

I call this big-ticket because this single move can rid economies across the world of the growth-without-jobs syndrome. This is the new green growth model the world is desperately seeking—creating opportunities to build economic wealth from regeneration of forests, and more importantly creating inclusive and equitable wealth and wellbeing.

Tigers: the number game is not up

Let's take another challenge: protecting tigers and other wild animals and forests. Last year, the country announced that its tiger estimation shows that tiger numbers are up -- at 1706, up from 1411 a few years ago. But does this head count mean that our strategy for tiger conservation is working?

The fact is that all previous tiger census (however flawed) had shown that the bulk of India's tigers lived not in its heavily protected and secured reserves, but in the forest habitat outside. The 1989 census found that 1327 tigers lived inside protected reserves and another 3,000 outside. The number in 2001 was some 1,500 tigers inside and as many as 2,000 outside. So, if we were to understand this trend differently, you will find that the number of tigers inside protected areas remains roughly the same over the ages-between 1400-1600. But the tigers outside the protected areas

| Light and Heat from a Lightbulb | Two per cent of the electricity used by a lightbulb is converted into light, the rest into heat. |

have disappeared or stopped being counted. This is why numbers have fallen.

This is a question that needs to be answered squarely: how many tigers can India safeguard for the future? The fact is that tigers, we know, are territorial creatures. They literally need land to roam. With the birth of a new male tiger, this search starts. Either the old tiger gives way or the male has to look for new ground. But all around our parks, forests are destroyed. We have never built a future that benefits from forest protection. In fact, people who live in lands adjoining tiger reserves will tell you that today they hate this grand animal, which kills their cattle. They have no use for the reserved-for-tiger-forest, which protects the herbivores and wild boars that destroy their growing crop. They get nothing in return for living around tiger land. They want no tigers in their land.

> Tiger conservationists will tell you each animal needs a minimum 10 sq km of territory to roam, mate and live.

This is why in the task force I chaired, post the Sariska-fiasco (when tigers had disappeared from this reserve) we had called for a different model of tiger conservation. We had explained that in the current model, even after tiger lands had been secured, there was limited space for the tiger to roam. The future numbers would be limited by the shrinking habitat.

The total area of what is called the 'core' habitat is some 17,000 sq km. Tiger conservationists will tell you each animal needs a minimum 10 sq km of territory to roam, mate and live. Add it up and you will see that's roughly why we have so many or so few tigers today.

In Kanha tiger reserve, for instance, we had seen how field managers kept a count of tiger cubs. Each year they would see cubs, but no tigers. The reason was clear:

Greenpeace

Greenpeace was founded in 1971, in Vancouver, Canada, by Jim Bohlen, Irving and Dorothy Stowe and, Paul Cote. It stands for opposing environmental abuse, saving endangered species, and increasing public awareness through direct action, lobbying, research, and innovation. Rainbow Warrior ship is used to protest since 1985. Bob Hunter, Patrick Moore and many others guided Greenpeace. Members: 3 million in about 45 nations. Volunteers: 15000. HQ: Amsterdam, Netherlands.

each year, the young tiger would move in search of territory beyond the protected, and now increasingly guarded, area. Once the outside world was forested, the tiger could expand its space. But now the forests were degraded; people were poor and angry. We called this double-jeopardy: the tigers could not move out because the forest was degraded and livestock would move in to the protected areas, also because the forest outside was degraded.

The task force recommended a different strategy for conservation, in which people who lived in the tiger's land would benefit from its protection.

But the powerful and entrenched tiger lobby mocked this strategy of coexistence, saying it was people-friendly and would destroy tiger conservation.

This is the inconvenient truth. We want tigers, but at the cost of our people. The poorest of India continue to live in the richest of tiger lands. We want tourism but for our benefits. We do not want to make people the owners, partners or indeed earners from the tourists that the tiger brings. We refuse to make peace and to grow the habitat for the tigers to roam.

This is the forest agenda for the future: let us hope we can learn to make the difference. ▪

Thunder and Lightning	**Approximately 100 lightning bolts strike the earth every second. At any given moment, there are about 1800 thunder storms happening around the world.**

Global Warming

Global warning is caused by rising levels of carbon dioxide in the atmosphere that acts as blanket to contain radiated heat and raises overall global temperatures to dangerous levels, leading to melting glaciers, rise in sea levels, unpredictable weather and changing climate patterns.

Kyoto Protocol

A protocol to the 1992 UN Framework Convention on Climate Change (UNFCCC) adopted at the 3rd session of the Conference of the Parties to the UNFCCC in 1997 in Kyoto, Japan, entered into force in 2005.

It contains legally binding commitments, in addition to those included in the UNFCCC. Most OECD countries and countries with economies in transition, agreed to control their national anthropogenic emissions of greenhouse gases (CO_2, CH4, N2O, HFCs, PFCs and SF6) at 5% below 1990 levels in the commitment period, 2008 to 2012. The protocol expires in 2012. The Intergovernmental Panel on Climate Change (IPCC) has predicted an

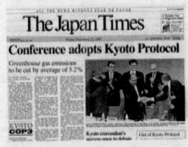

average global rise in temperature of 1.4°C to 5.8 °C between 1990 and 2100. ...if successfully and completely implemented, the Kyoto Protocol will reduce that increase by somewhere between 0.02 °C and 0.28 °C by the year 2050 *(source: Nature, October 2003).*

Copenhagen Summit

The 15th meeting of the Conference of Parties (Cop15) to UNs Framework convention on Climate change, held from 7th to the 18th of December 2009, at the Bella Centre in Copenhagen, Denmark was attended by 150 global leaders. The Conference tried to enhance emission reduction targets for the developed nations during the second commitment period of the Kyoto Protocol, which starts from 2012. It was also the conclusion of an intensive two-year negotiation process launched in 2007 under the Bali Roadmap to forge a new global agreement to tackle climate change.

Positives • Increased political awareness, public awareness and involvement • The framework for discussions on Kyoto Protocol continues meaning the protocol will survive beyond 2012 • Backs the two-track approach for talks on long-term cooperative action and on Kyoto Protocol • To keep temperature increase to below 20°C by 2050 • Scaled-up funding for poor nations, including a fast-track fund of $30 billion for 2010-2012 and US initiative to mobilise $100 billion by 2020. • Emphasises mobilisation of financial resources for supporting reforestation efforts of developing countries. • Brings in provision

| Permaculture | The term permaculture is a combination of permanent, culture and agriculture. It is basically about ensuring that the earth's limited resources are used in equitable and wise ways. The idea was developed by Bill Mollison and David Holmgren in Australia. |

COP16 Summit

COP16/CMP6 is the 16th edition of Conference of the Parties of the United Nations Framework Convention on Climate Change (COP) and the 6th Conference of the Parties serving as the meeting of the Parties to the Kyoto Protocol (CMP). The United

Nations Framework Convention on Climate Change has been signed by 195 State Parties (list) and the Kyoto Protocol has been ratified by 193 State Parties. In accordance with Article 7 of the Convention, the Conference of the Parties in its authority of the supreme body has the mandate of adopting the necessary decisions for the promotion of its effective application. The United Nations Framework Convention on Climate Change is composed of two general categories of participants: The State Parties and the observers. The observers are divided into Intergovernmental Organizations and Nongovernmental Organizations. Over a decade ago, most countries joined an international treaty -- the United Nations Framework Convention on Climate Change (UNFCCC) - to begin to consider what can be done to reduce global warming and to cope with whatever temperature increases are inevitable. More recently, a number of nations approved an addition to the treaty: the Kyoto Protocol, which has more powerful (and legally binding) measures. The UNFCCC secretariat supports all institutions involved in the climate change process, particularly the COP, the subsidiary bodies and their Bureau.

for international consultations and analysis for mitigation efforts of the emerging economies that are not financed by the developed countries.

Negatives • Division between the developed and the developing countries deepens. • No targets specified for emission cuts by developed countries and no strong commitment to reduce temperature. • No clarity on funding for mitigation and adaptation efforts of poor countries by the developed world.

Climate Change Trends

According to a research led by Deke Arnt, NOAA Climatic Data Centre's Climate Monitoring Branch, studying the effects of global warming over the past three decades, it has "already altered our planet."

The report cites recent extreme weather events in different parts of the world, including heavy rains and flooding, record heat waves and severe droughts, along with melting glaciers and sea ice.

Rising ocean surface temperatures caused by global warming have increased the temperature and moisture content of the air, setting the stage for heavier snow and rainstorms.

The report shows increase in: • Air temperature over land • Sea-surface temperature • Air temperature over oceans • Sea level • Ocean heat • Humidity and • Temperature in the troposphere, the "active-weather" layer of the atmosphere closest to the Earth's surface.

At the same time, there has been a decrease in: • Arctic sea ice • Glaciers receding even on Mt. Everest • Spring snow cover in the northern hemisphere.

An Ecological Buffer

The Hindu Kush-Himalayan range is a world heritage site for biodiversity and acts as an ecological buffer between north and south Asia. These mountains hold the water resources that form the source of life in Central Asia and for much of Asia and Eurasia.

Environmental Pollution

The word 'pollution', originally a Latin word 'pollutionem': means to make dirty.

Environmental pollution is a serious problem of the industrialised societies because people have converted the life-supporting systems of the entire living world into their own resources and have vastly disturbed the natural ecological balance. Serious degradation and depletion have been caused through overuse, misuse and mismanagement of resources to meet the human greed.

Environmental pollution is defined as the unfavourable alteration of our surroundings, wholly as a by-product of man's activities through direct or indirect efforts of changes in the physical, chemical and biological characteristics of land, air or water that harmfully affect human life or any desirable living thing. Human population explosion, rapid industrialisation, deforestation, unplanned urbanisation, scientific and technological advancement, etc. are the major causes of environment pollution.

Air Pollution: Due to air pollution, the composition of the air is changing all over the world, especially in industrialised countries. Air pollution results from gaseous emission from industry, thermal power stations, domestic combustion etc. Most of the gaseous and particulate air pollutants are products of burning of fuels. Burning of coal mainly produces carbon dioxide, sulphur dioxide and fly-ash. Lead, carbon monoxide and nitrogen oxides are added to the atmosphere from automobile exhaust.

Nitrogen oxides and sulphur dioxide together are responsible for acid rain. Carbon monoxide is highly toxic and impairs oxygen-carrying capacity of blood. Several cases of death are reported every year from carbon monoxide poisoning from gas heaters, heating devices and coal mines. Lead which is emitted by automobile is known to hamper haemoglobin formation. Compounds containing chlorine and fluorine, especially the chloroflurocarbons, are widely used as propellants and as refrigerants. They cause ozone depletion in stratosphere. Air-borne solid and liquid particulates are emitted by various industrial processes such as blasting, drilling, crushing, grinding and drying which may cause lung diseases if inhaled.

Haemoglobin is known to absorb NO_2 more easily than oxygen. About 80 to 90% NO_2 inhaled is easily absorbed into the bloodstream. This reduces the oxygen-carrying capacity of blood. NO_2 causes lung tissue to become weaker and thus causes lung cancer and emphysema (breathing problem due to the breakdown of the air sacs in the lungs, which then progressively diminishes the ability of the lungs to exchange oxygen and carbon dioxide in the blood stream). Thus, NO_2 causes bronchitis and broncho-pneumonia. In the presence of sunlight, NO_2 reacts with hydrocarbons to produce ozone, a highly toxic gas, known to cause asthma.

Water Pollution: Water pollution adversely changes the quality of water. It disturbs the balance of ecosystem and causes health hazards to humans and animals. Water becomes polluted by the presence or addition of inorganic, organic or biological substances.

Effluents from factories, paper mills, sugar mills, tanneries, urban and rural sewage are let into rivers. Water pollution also occurs due to the use of pesticides and fertilizers in agriculture. Enrichment of water

Risk of Extinction	Approximately 20-30% of species are likely to be at increased risk of extinction if warming exceeds 1.5 - 2.5 °C. A warming of about 0.2 °C per decade is projected for the next two decades.

by nutrients (esp. nitrate and phosphates) results in eutrophication of lakes and water bodies. This results in excessive growth of algae and depletion of dissolved oxygen in the lake. Oil spills from oil tankers also cause marine pollution. Various harmful chemicals like DDT can enter into the food chain through polluted water.

Noise Pollution: Noise can be defined as unwanted sound. Whether a sound is pleasant or a noise depends upon loudness, duration, rhythm and the mood of the person. The most immediate and acute effect of noise pollution is impairment of hearing, anxiety and stress and in extreme cases fright. Physiological manifestations: Increase in the rate of heart beat, constriction of blood vessels, digestive spasms and dilation of pupil of the eye. Loudness is measured in terms of decibels (dB). Just audible sound is about 10dB, a whisper is 20dB, and a normal conversation is 35-60dB. Sound beyond 80dB can be safely regarded as pollution as it harms the hearing system. WHO has fixed 45dB as the safe noise level for a city.

PM 10 and PM 2.5 : PM stands for particulate matter and the numbers 10 and 2.5 are diameter of particles in micrometer (Mm). The particles less than 10 Mm diameter which are called respirable suspended particulate matter (RSPM) can enter into human nasal tract, and particles smaller than 2.5 Mm can reach further inside up to terminal bronchi and alveoli in the lungs. It may cause serious lung diseases, tumour, cancer, etc.

Radioactive Pollution: Radioactive pollution is related to all major life supporting systems – air, water and soil. Radioactivity is a phenomenon of spontaneous emission of alpha, beta and gamma rays as a result of disintegration of atomic nuclei of some elements. Man-made sources of radiation pollution are mining and refining of radioactive material, production and explosion of nuclear weapons, nuclear power plants and fuels, and preparation of radioactive isotopes. All organisms are affected 'by ra-

Pesticide Companies in 2006

Company	Country	Sales (US$M)
1. Bayer	Germany	$6,698
2. Syngenta	Switzerland	$6,378
3. BASF	Germany	$3,849
4. Dow AgroSciences	US	$3,399
5. Monsanto	US	$3,316
6. DuPont	US	$2,154
7. MAI	Israel	$1,581
8. Sumitomo Chemical	Japan	$1,312
9. Nufarm	Australia	$1,261
10. Arytsa LifeScience	Japan	$941
11. FMC	US	$767
12. Cheminova	Denmark	$604
13. United Phosphorus	India	$477
14. Chemtura	US	$360
15. Isihara Sangyo Kaisha	Japan	$359
16. Nissan Chemical	Japan	$348
17. Sipcam-Oxon	Italy	$341
18. Kumiai Chemical	Japan	$336
19. Nippon Soda	Japan	$312
20. Nihon Nohyaku	Japan	$302

Source: Agrow 2007a

diation pollution. In high doses, radiation can cause death. Long or repeated exposure can cause cancer and leukaemia and induce mutation.

Soil pollution: The soil pollutants include pesticides, fertilisers, industrial wastes, mining wastes, salts, radioactive materials, tin, iron, lead, mercury, aluminium and plastics. Pesticides adversely affect the micro-organisms present in soil. In addition to this, pesticides enter human food chain either through plants or through water which accumulates as surface runoff or leaches down in the ground water with pesticide dissolved in it. Poisonous wastes render soil unfit for crop production. The dangerous metals like fluoride and arsenic when present in soil, contaminate not only the crops, but also ground-water.

Deforestation: Deforestation is a threat to the economy, quality of life and future of the environment. Main causes of de-

Cutting Down Trees	In developing countries, for every 10 trees cut down, only 1 tree is replanted. In Africa, the ratio is 29 to 1.

World Environment Events

Word Environment Day (WED) was started by the UN General Assembly in 1972 at the Stockholm Conference on the Human Environment. WED is commemorated each year on June 5 in a different city. Through WED, the UN stimulates worldwide awareness of the environment and enhances political attention and action. It aims to (i) give a human face to environmental issues; (ii) Empower people as active agents of sustainable and equitable development; (iii) Promote communities as central to change attitudes towards environmental issues; (iv) Advocate partnership for all nations to enjoy a safer future. WED is marked by street processions, essay and poster competitions in schools, tree planting, recycling and cleaning-up campaigns, etc. On WED, heads of State, Prime Ministers and Ministers of Environment deliver statements and commit themselves to care for the Earth. New policies and pledges are made by the government for environmental management besides signing international treaties.

Theme: A Billion Acts of Green

for the environmental movement evinced by the Billion Acts of Green campaign. The campaign aims to reach its goal before Rio+20 through its services and advocacy.

Earth Hour

Earth Hour began in Sydney, Australia, in 2007 with about two million participants. The voluntary one-hour blackout has since grown into an international event as a sign of action against global warming. While cities and famous landmarks get the most attention, families and individuals are responsible for much of Earth Hour's momentum.

Earth Day

Earth Day 2011 saw an enormous support

forestation in India are : explosion of human and livestock population, increased requirement of timber and fuel wood, expansion of agriculture land, enhanced grazing and construction of infrastructure along the mountains. Ideally 33% of land of a country must be covered by forest. Damage caused by deforestation: Intensified soil erosion, accentuated floods and drought and loss of precious wild life. India is losing about 1.5 million hectares of forest cover each year. Nearly 1% of the land surface of India is turning barren every year due to deforestation. In the Himalayan

range, rainfall has declined 3 to 4% due to deforestation.

Afforestation: It restores ecological balance of all ecosystems, maintains biological diversity, acts as catchments for soil, conserves water, prevents floods and protects lives of tribal people. So, massive afforestation programme of indigenous and exotic fast growing species would be needed for protection of forests on suitable land including wasteland. Only a massive social forestry programme can meet the demands of local people for fuel, fodder, and timber.

| Kill Camels to Cut Carbon | Australia is considering awarding carbon credits for killing feral camels to tackle climate change, suggests a paper on climate change. |

Environment Glossary

Annex 1 Countries Governments are separated into two general categories: developed countries, referred to as Annex 1 countries (who have accepted strict GHG emission reduction obligations). Developing countries are Non-Annex 1 countries who have no GHG emission reduction obligations.

Biodiversity The variety of life on Earth, including diversity at the genetic level, among species and among ecosystems and habitats. It includes diversity in abundance, distribution and in behaviour. Biodiversity also incorporates diversity of genes, other species and ecosystems.

Biofuel Fuel produced from dry organic matter or combustible oils from plants, such as alcohol from fermented sugar, black liquor from the paper manufacturing process, wood and soybean oil.

Biogas Gas, rich in methane, which is produced by the fermentation of animal dung, human sewage or crop residues in an airtight container.

Biomass Organic material, both above ground and below ground, and both living and dead, such as trees, crops, grasses, tree litter and roots.

Biome The largest unit of ecosystem classification that is convenient to recognize below the global level. Terrestrial biomes are typically based on dominant vegetation structure (such as forest and grassland). Ecosystems within a biome function in a broadly similar way, although they may have very different species composition.

Carbon Credits The concept of Carbon Credit came into existence as a result of increasing awareness of the need for pollution control. The Protocol agreed 'caps' on the maximum amount of greenhouse gases for developed and developing countries. Carbon Credits are certificates awarded to countries that successfully reduce the emissions that cause global warming.

Carbon Credits are measured in units of Certified Emission Reductions (CERs). Each CER is equivalent to one tonne of carbon dioxide reduction. India has emerged as a world leader in reduction of greenhouse gases by adopting Clean Development Mechanisms (CDMs). The idea of Carbon Credit is to allow market mechanisms to drive industrial and commercial processes in the direction of low emissions or less "carbon intensive" approaches than are used when there is no cost to emitting carbon dioxide and other Green House Gases (GHGs) into the atmosphere.

Carbon Footprint A carbon footprint is a measure of the impact our activities have on the environment, and in particular climate change. It relates to the amount of greenhouse gases produced in our day-to-day lives through burning fossil fuels for electricity, heating and transportation, etc. The carbon footprint is a measurement of all greenhouse gases in terms of tonnes or kg of CO_2 equivalent.

Green Test A green test is a test to determine whether a product is as efficient as possible in terms of energy consumption. The test focuses on certified products based on power efficiency, power usage and management, heat dissipation, cooling requirements, energy efficiency, etc.

Carbon Emission Man's development means consumption of energy producing materials which is not possible without carbon emission in most cases. According to the 2007 Summary Report by the

Flavour of Plastic	Plastic containers have been used for storing food for a while now. Research has indicated that Endocrine Disrupting Chemicals (EDC), are present in plastics. EDCs are known to cause cancer and disruption of sex hormones.

Carbon permits

Intergovernmental Panel on Climate Change, scientists reveal that the world has already burned half the fossil fuels necessary to bring about a catastrophic 2°C rise in global temperature. That is, about half a trillion tonnes of carbon has been consumed since the Industrial Revolution. Scientists believe that the total burnt amount must be kept to below a trillion tonnes. As far as current rates are concerned, that figure will be reached in 40 years. A trillion tonnes of carbon burnt would warm the globe between 1.6^0 and 2.6^0C. CO_2 may be the greatest contributor to rising global temperatures, but the next is certainly black carbon. While carbon dioxide is responsible for 40% of the earth's warming, black carbon is responsible for 12%. Black Carbon emanates from diesel engines, coal plants and cook stoves. Soot particles warm the air and melt ice.

Carbon market A set of institutions, regulations, project registration systems and trading entities that has emerged from the Kyoto Protocol. The protocol sets limits on total emissions by the world's major economies, as a prescribed number of "emission units." The protocol also allows countries that have emissions units to spare -- emissions permitted but not "used" -- to sell this excess capacity to countries that are over their targets. This is called the "carbon market," because carbon dioxide is the most widely-produced greenhouse gas, and because emissions of other greenhouse gases will be recorded and counted in terms of their "carbon dioxide equivalents."

Clean technology Manufacturing process or product technology that reduces pollution or waste, energy use or material use in comparison to the technology that it replaces. In clean as opposed to "end-of-pipe" technology, the environmental equipment is integrated into the production process.

Green tax Tax with a potentially positive environmental impact. It includes energy taxes, transport taxes, and taxes on pollution and resources. They are also called environmental taxes. Green taxes are meant to reduce environmental burden by increasing prices, and by shifting the basis of taxation from labour and capital to energy and natural resources.

Green procurement Taking environmental aspects into consideration in public and institutional procurement.

Habitat (i) The place or type of site where an organism or population naturally occurs. (ii) Terrestrial or aquatic areas distinguished by geographic, abiotic and biotic features, whether entirely natural or semi-natural.

Mitigation Structural and non-structural measures undertaken to limit the adverse impact of natural hazards, environmental degradation and technological hazards.

Sustainable development Development that meets the needs of the present generation without compromising the ability of future generations to meet their own needs.

Trophic level Successive stages of nourishment as represented by the links of the food chain. According to a grossly simplified scheme the primary producers (phytoplankton) constitute the first trophic level, herbivorous zooplankton the second trophic level and carnivorous organisms the third trophic level.

Vulnerability An intrinsic feature of people at risk. It is a function of exposure, sensitivity to impacts of the specific unit exposed (such as a watershed, island, household, village, city or country), and the ability or inability to cope or adapt.

Plasmonics

Communication systems are based on electronics or photonics. With the quest for transporting huge amounts of data at a high speed along with miniaturisation, both are facing limitations. So researchers are pioneering a new technology called 'plasmonics.'

Ozone Protection: Timeline

The ozone layer in the upper atmosphere acts like a shield-protecting life on Earth from the sun's harmful ultraviolet radiation. In 1985, scientists observed a thinning of the ozone layer over Antarctica. Since then, research has shown that ozone depletion occurs over every continent.

In 1987, world leaders signed a landmark environment treaty, the Montreal Protocol on Substances that deplete the Ozone Layer. Now, almost every country in the world has ratified the treaty and is phasing out the production and use of CFCs and other ozone-depleting substances.

1928- Scientists synthesize CFCs (Chloro-flurocarbons)

1974- Nobel prize winners Mario Molina and Sherwood Rowland discover that CFCs can break down stratospheric ozone.

1975- Scientists discover that bromine, used in fire-retarding halons and agricultural fumigants, is a potent ozone depleting substance.

1985- British Antarctic scientists agree that CFCs are depleting the stratospheric ozone layer in the northern and southern hemispheres.

2000- Japan Meteorological Agency reports the hole in the stratospheric ozone layer over the Antarctic is at its largest to date-more than twice the size of Antarctica.

2006- The ozone hole is reported to be the biggest ever, exceeding that of 2000.

2060-2075- Earliest timeframe projected for the ozone layer to recover.

Actions

1975- SC Johnson announces corporate phaseout of CFCs as aerosol product propellants.

1976- UNEP calls for an international response to the ozone issue.

Ozone hole

1978- US bans non-essential uses of CFCs as propellant in some aerosols (eg, hairsparys, deodorants, antiperspirants). Canada, Norway, and Sweden follow with a similar ban.

1981- UNEP develops a global convention to protect the ozone layer.

1987- Twenty four countries sign the Montreal Protocol on substances that deplete the ozone layer.

1989- All developed countries that are parties to the Montreal Protocol freeze production and consumption of CFCs at 1986 levels.

1990- Clean Air Act Amendments, including Title VI for Stratospheric Ozone Protection, signed into law.

1994- US eliminates production and import of halons.

1996- US eliminates production and import of CFCs, carbon tetrachoride, trichloroethane and hydrobromofluocarbons.

2002- All developing countries that are parties to the Montreal Protocol freeze methyl bromide production at 1995-1998 average levels.

2015- All developed countries to reduce consumption of hydrobromofluocarbons (HCFCs) by 90% from baseline levels.

2030-2040- All developed and developing countries that are parties to the Montreal Protocol scheduled to completely phaseout HCFCs.

BioCouture

A material made by the bacteria that are usually used to turn green tea into the fermented beverage kombucha - now that's what we call BioCouture. It can be molded and sewn into shirts and coats.

Thawing Arctic opens up new routes

Warming up of cold Arctic is the new hot in shipping circles as melting sea ice opens up prospects for trade between China and the West to move across the roof of the world. An increasing amount of seaborne traffic is beginning to move on the so-called Northern Sea Route, which traverses the Siberian coast.

The Benefits

There are also hopes of opening up more of the North West Passage above Canada. The attraction of the voyage is that it is a third of the distance of more traditional routes through the Suez Canal. This means lower C02 emissions, less fuel - and fewer pirates. Attacks on ships off Somalia and in the Gulf of Aden have become so severe that some owners already use longer sea routes around South Africa to avoid conflict.

According to Christian Bonfils, the managing director of Nordic Barents operator Nordic Bulk Carriers, it will be a saving of $180,000 in fuel costs. A Russian oil company, Novatek, is currently carrying a trial shipment of 60,000 tonnes of oil products to China via northern Siberia on the vessel Perseverance. Similarly, Norilsk Nickel, the world's largest nickel producer, has just broken new ground by carrying ore from the Arctic port of Dudinka to Rotterdam in Holland. Two tankers owned by Murmansk Shipping, the Varzuga and Indiga, loaded with 27,000 tonnes of petroleum, recently moved through the ice-thinned passage from Murniansk to Chukotka in the Russian far east. Meanwhile the Russian authorities are still trying to decide what to do about dumped radioactive materials left along the route. The Tsivolka Inlet on Novaya Zemyla has been used as a burial ground for nuclear reactors such

as the one from the first atomic-powered icebreaker, the Lenin.

Global warming is reducing the thickness and immovability of the ice but Moscow is changing too. Russia under Dmitry Medvedev is an increasingly outward-looking country. Last week in Murmansk, the Russian President signed a bilateral agreement with Norway after a 40 year row over sea boundaries. It started with arguments over fish but has become a negotiation largely driven by prospects for oil and gas in the Barents Sea and beyond.

Political and Environmental Thaw

Wider political changes are happening as the Arctic increasingly becomes a hunting ground for minerals rather than the seals of the past. Canadian and American maritime experts say two per cent of global shipping could be diverted to the Arctic by 2030, rising to five per cent by 2050. Already cruise ships are bringing tourists and income to countries such as Greenland. But they are also raising concerns about safety and pollution from oil spills. There is a widespread view that it is only a matter of time before there is an emergency: a passenger ship in trouble and potential evacuation into freezing seas. Even with the best of intentions, the wider shipping industry will have accidents. Collisions are more likely in areas of thick fog and where some navigational equipment might malfunction in extreme cold.

| The Biggest Rat | 6Kg is the weight of the world's biggest rat - roughly the weight of a small dog. Its bones were discovered by Australian archaeologists working in East Timor. |

Human Body Systems

It takes some 100 trillion cells to build a human body. There are 200 different types of these microscopic living units, each of which is highly complex. Similar cells join together to make a tissue, two or more tissues form an organ and linked organs create a system. Body systems interact to form a living human being.

Circulatory System: In the circulatory system the heart pumps blood, which travells through arteries, to all parts of the body. The blood carries the oxygen and food that the body needs to live. Veins

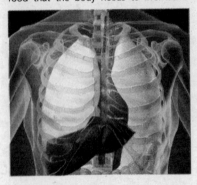

carry the blood back to the heart.

Digestive System: The digestive system moves food through parts of the body called the esophagus, stomach, and intestines. As the food passes through, some of it is broken down into tiny particles called nutrients, which the body needs. Nutrients enter the blood stream, which carries them to all parts of the body. The digestive system then changes the remaining food into waste that is eliminated from the body.

Endocrine System: The endocrine system includes glands that are needed for some body functions. There are two kinds of glands. Exocrine glands produce liquids such as sweat and saliva. Endocrine glands produce chemicals called hormones. Hormones control body functions, such as growth.

Nervous System: The nervous system enables us to feel, think, move, hear, and see. It includes the brain, the spinal cord, and nerves in all parts of the body. Nerves in the spinal cord carry signals back and forth between the brain and rest of the body. The brain tells us what to do and how to respond. It has three major parts. The cerebrum controls thinking, speech, and vision. The cerebellum is responsible for physical coordination. The brain stem controls the respiratory, circulatory, and digestive systems.

Respiratory System: The respiratory system allows us to breathe. We inhale air through nose and mouth. It goes through the windpipe (trachea) and two tubes called bronchi, to the lungs. Oxygen from the air is taken in by tiny blood vessels in the lungs. The blood then carries oxygen to the cells of the body.

Skeletal System: The skeletal system is made up of bones that hold your body upright. Some bones protect organs, like the ribs that cover the lungs.

Muscular System: Muscles are made up of elastic fibres. There are 3 types of muscles- skeletal, smooth and cardiac. The skeletal muscles help the body move. They are large muscles visible to our eyes. Smooth muscles are found in our digestive system, blood vessels, and air passages. Cardiac muscle is found only in our heart. Smooth and Cardiac muscles are involuntary muscles - they work without us knowing about them.

Reproductive System: Through the reproductive system, adult human beings procreate. Reproduction begins when sperm cell from man fertilises an egg cell from a woman.

Urinary System: This system includes kidneys, which cleans waste from the blood and regulates the water in the body.

Immune System: The Immune System protects our body from diseases by fighting against certain substances that come from outside, or antigens.

Curious Human Body Facts

The human body is a very complicated system consisting of millions of cells-organised uniquely and functioning dynamically together. The complexities can be better understood when it is highlighted. Anatomists find it useful to divide the human body into eight systems: the skeleton, the muscles, the circulatory and respiratory systems, the digestive system, the urinary system, the glandular system, the nervous system, and the skin.

Interesting Facts

- The thickness of the skin varies from 1/2 to 6 mm, depending on the area of your body.
- The four taste zones on your tongue are bitter (back), sour (back sides), salty (front sides), and sweet (front).
- One uses 14 muscles to smile and 43 to frown.
- The strongest muscle of the body is the masseter muscle, which is located in jaw.
- The small intestine is about 25 feet long.
- The large intestine is 5 feet long and 3 times wider than the small intestine.
- Most people shed 40 pounds of skin in a lifetime.
- When you sneeze, air rushes through your nose at the rate of 100mph.
- An eye lash lives about 150 days before it falls out.
- Our brain sends messages at the rate of 240 mph.
- About 400 gallons of blood flow through our kidneys in one day.
- Each of our eyes has 120 M rods, which help us see in black and white.
- Each eye has 6M cons, which help us see in colour.
- We blink our eyes about 20,000 times a day
- Our heart beats about 100,000 times a day.

- Placed end-to-end all our body's blood vessels would measure about 62,000 miles.
- The average human brain has about 100 billion nerve cells.
- The thyroid cartilage is more commonly known as the Adam's apple.
- It's impossible to sneeze with our eyes open.
- It takes the interaction of 72 different muscles to produce human speech.
- When you sneeze, all your bodily functions stop even your heart.
- Babies are born without kneecap.They don't appear till they are 2-6 years of age.
- Children grow faster in the spring season.
- Women blink twice as much as men.
- If one goes blind in one eye, that person only loses about 1/5 of vision but all of the sense of depth.
- Our eyes are always the same size from birth, but our nose and ears never stop growing.
- The length of the finger dictates how fast the fingernail grows. The nail on the middle finger grows fastest and on an average our toenails grow twice as slow as our fingernails.
- Hair is made of the same substance as fingernails.
- The nose can remember 50,000 scents.
- Similar to finger prints, everybody's tongue has a unique tongue print.
- A finger nails takes about 6 months to grow from base to tip.
- The energy used by the brain is enough to light a 25 watt bulb.
- The heart produces enough pressure to squirt blood 30 feet.
- We get a new stomach lining every 3-4 days. If we didn't, the strong acids our stomach uses to digest food would also digest our stomach.

CHROMOSOME Nucleus is the control centre of every cell. It contains 46 chromosomes which coil up tightly into an X-shape, when a cell divides. Chromosomes contain the coded instructions, called genes, for building the body's cells, tissues, organs and systems.

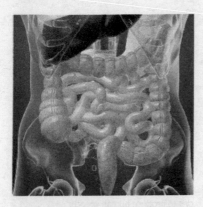

- There are about 65 muscles in our body.
- A full bladder is roughly the size of a soft ball.
- A pair of feet has 500,000 sweat glands.
- Each square inch of human skin consists of twenty feet of blood vessels.

Body Statistics

The body: has about 9.14 metres of long tube for food intake and excretion, a surface area of more than 9.29 sqm, or five times the area of the body's skin. The intestines process, at about 2.54 cm per minute, 40.64 metric tonnes of food over the course of 70 years.

Skin: 2.72 kg of skin cover the 1.85 sq.m of surface on an average adult.

DNA: Deoxyribonucleic acid, a nucleic acid, is the vital constituent of chromosomes, responsible for transmitting genetic information, in the form of genes, from parents to offspring. Each human cell contains about 2 metres of DNA supercoiled on itself such that it fits within the cell nucleus less than 10 micrometers.DNA comprises 4 bases– adenine-A, guanine-G, thymine-T, and cytosine-C, a sugar and phosphoric acid, organised in a double helix format. Within this format, A pairs only with T, and G only with C.

Bones in the body: Babies are born with over 300 bones. Many of them fuse together as we grow up - and we end up with about 206. The longest bone: The 'femur' or the thigh bone (1/4 of your height). The smallest bone: The stapes or the stirrup-bone in the middle ear - few millimetres.

More than half of an adult's 206 bones are in the hands and feet. There are 27 bones in each hand and 26 in each foot- for a total of 106.

Human Brain: The brain along with spinal cord constitutes the Nervous System. The brain consists of

(i) *Cerebrum:* The largest part of the brain consisting of two hemispheres which control voluntary actions and are the seat of intelligence, memory association, imagination and will. (ii) *Cerebellum:* The large mass having ridges and furrows attached to cerebrum, which regulates muscular movement of locomotion. (iii) *Medula Oblongata:* The lowermost part of the brain which continues as the spinal cord in the vertebral column. It controls involuntary actions.

The weight of the average human brain triples between birth and adulthood. The final weight of the brain in an adult male is about 1.4 kg (and 1.3 kg in the case of a woman) which averages about 3% of the body weight.

The brain uses about 20% of the oxygen a man breathes, 20% of calories a man takes in, and about 15% of body blood.

The brain stores information equal to 500,000 sets of the Encyclopedia Britannica. Given its compact size, efficient power consumption (equivalent to a 20-watt lightbulb) and massive storage capacity (100 trillion bits of information) it can work better than any computer. At a time our brain can retain 7 facts in the short-term memory. Neurons are the longest cells in our body- measuring 1.2m in length. Fully formed human brain contains 100 billion neurons, or nerve cells. When neuron fires off a message, it is received in one of the thousands of receptor sites in another neuron, which stops it or sends it on.

Nerves 72.418km of nerves send im-

Multitasking	According to researches, the brain actually struggles to do more than two things simultaneously. The two lobes of brain may handle two tasks at a time. More than two tasks would produce unreliable results.

pulses as rapidly as 360 km per hour. The fastest nerve impulse travels at 532 Kmph.

The Heart 27949.3 litres of blood are pumped through 96,000 km of blood vessels in a day. The hollow muscle pumps enough blood in an average lifetime to fill the fuel tanks of 56 moon rockets. Unlike other muscles, its contractions are involuntary, beginning 4 weeks after conception, before nerve cells are formed, and continue to pulse even out of body in saline solution. Muscle cells called myocytes generate a total electrical current of about 2 watts that commands the fibres to contract. Shortly after birth, those cells stop dividing.

The Blood There are about 96,000 km of blood vessels in our body. Blood comprises Plasma, RBC (red blood cells/erythrocytes), WBC (white blood cells/leukocytes) and Platelets (Thrombocytes).

Plasma is made up of 90% water, 7% proteins, and others like nutrients, salts, nitrogen waste, carbon-dioxide and hormones.

8,000,000 *RBCs* are produced in the bone marrow every second constituting 54% of hemoglobin and their count ranges between 4-6 million per cu mm.

WBC count normally ranges between 4,500 to 11,000 per cu mm

Platelets also normally count between 15,000 and 300,000 per cu mm

The Lungs Man breathes 13- 17 times a minute at rest and 80 during exercise. On an average we breathe 21600 times a day. We take in 295.261m litres in an average life span. The shock of birth causes the first breath. Muscle contracts, opening the chest and lowering interior air pressure. The baby's mouth opens in protest, air rushes in, and the newborn begins to inhale about 60 times a minute, beginning the cycle of strife and breath.The adult human lungs have an internal area of 93 m², which is 40 times the external surface of the human body.

The Liver Among some 1000 widely divergent functions, the liver regulates hormonal balance, cholesterol, blood clot-

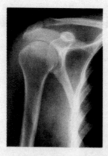

ting and poisons. The liver is the only organ that can regenerate; if as much as two thirds is removed, a whole liver can grow back.

The Alimentary System is a 9.14 metre-long tube from mouth to anus that breaks down food into particles tiny enough to pass from intestines into the bloodstream. The nutrients are then routed to the largest gland in the body, the 1.36 kg liver, to be refined into chemical and warehoused until demand soars.

Stomach: produces 2 litres of hydrochloric acid daily. 500,000 cells of stomach's inner walls are replaced every minute so that the acid does not damage the walls.

Muscles: There are 639 muscles which also account for 40% of the total body weight. The total number of muscles in the body is over 630. It takes 17 muscles to smile and 42 to stare. The largest muscle is the gluetus maximus or the buttock muscle. The smallest muscle is the stapadius muscle which controls the stapes.

The reproductive organs: A man's testes manufacture more sperm per second (about 2000) than a woman's produce eggs in a life time (about 400).

Ear Our ears can detect 1500 different tones, 350db of loudness and trace the direction of a sound within 3°.

Tongue The tongue contains more than 10,000 taste buds which are renewed weekly. It can distinguish 500 different tastes.

Nose can smell 2000-4000 different smells.

Eyes Humans can detect 10,000 colours with our eyes and a lighted candle 1.6km away. We spend 30 minutes every day being blind, the time taken for blinking.

TISSUE The lining of the small intestine has millions of microscopic finger-like projections called villi. The tissue covering villi is called columnar epithelium (orange). Its outer surface is covered with tiny microvili (green). Together this tissue provides a vast surface for absorbing food.

Fruit Juices Are Healthy: Right? Wrong

Fruit juice should not be counted as one of our five-a-day because it contains too much sugar - but dried fruit should, two new studies suggest.

Most health guidelines encourage people to consume drinks such as orange and apple juice in order to have a healthy balanced diet yet ignore dried fruits.

But the findings of two teams of UK researchers turn that advice on its head - concluding that fruit juices should be avoided and instead dried fruit consumption should be encouraged.

The first study found that even freshly squeezed fruit juices can contain as much as five teaspoons of sugar per glass because the squeezing process concentrates their sweetness. This is around two-thirds of the amount found in a can of soda and can contribute to

obesity and also disturb blood sugar levels and the body's natural metabolism.

According to researchers people are encouraged to eat whole fruits and vegetables, which have far more nutrients per calorie.

In the second study, partly conducted by the University of Leeds, researchers found that dried fruits contain just as many antioxidants, polyphenols and nutrients as normal fruit.

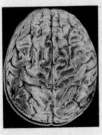

Adults blink every 4 to 6 seconds on an average

Ribs Humans usually have 12 sets of ribs, but 1 out of every 20 people is born with at least one extra.

The foot The average person will take one billion steps in his life.

Hair 1,25,000 hairs grow on the scalp, with 45 lost a day. Each follicle is capable of producing 9.14 metres in a life time.

Other Information:

Largest organ in the body: The Skin. An average man's skin if spread out, would occupy nearly 2 sq.m.

Most important organ: The pituitary gland. Controls growth, reproduction and

the working of the endocrine glands.

Some organs that never rest: The heart and the kidney.

Some organs that you can do without: Tonsils and the appendix.

Body's instant energy provider: The liver. It stores glycogen, which the body converts into glucose and burns to provide energy

Hardest substance of the body: The enamel of the teeth. By age 13, most people have 28 teeth (babies have 20). Around age 18, four more 'wisdom' teeth usually grow in to make a full set of 32 teeth.

The lighter halfmoon shape at the base of fingernails actually has a name : lunula (loon-yuh-luh)

Body cells: Two billion body cells wear out and are replaced everyday.

The outermost layer of the skin is replaced every 15 to 30 days. People who live in high altitude have 2 litres more blood than those living in lower regions.

CELLS The epithelial cells covering a villus are tightly clumped together. This organisation stops food and digestive juices leaking through to tissues below, which support these cells. As they suffer great wear and tear, epithelial cells are replaced every few days.

Human Reproduction

Sex is a phenomenon of life that sustains life forms on the planet earth. The life cycle of every living kind (a sexual population) spreads the advantageous traits in a way that it makes the next generation more capable of meeting the challenges of survival in different conditions. Sexual reproduction involves combining specialized cells (gametes) to form offspring that inherit genetic traits from both parents. Each cell has half the chromosomes of the mother and half of the father.

According to Boccadoro L., Carulli S. (2008), "Human sexuality is not simply imposed by instinct or stereotypical conducts, as it happens in animals, but it is influenced both by superior mental activity and by social, cultural, educational and normative characteristics of those places where the subjects grow up and their personality develops." Human sexuality has many aspects. It involves building up personal identity in a social evolution of individuals in a society. Sociocultural aspect casts human sexuality as a social norm under moral, ethical, philosophical and religious or spiritual framework. Medically, it deals with the physiological or even psychological aspects. Sexuality is also now viewed in the cultural, political, and legal context in a society.

The construction of sexual meanings, is an instrument by which social institutions, religion, the educational system, psychiatry, legal system, human rights, etc., control and shape human relationships. Therefore, sexuality is, generally, framed within the context of the institution of marriage. A home is an environment that provides nourishment for the growth of the young ones and guarantees mutual care and safety for all. It instills a moral obligation and individual responsibility for the part-

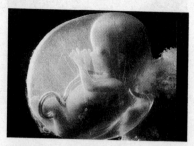

ners' sexual behaviours. In some countries, sex functions, behaviours, and feelings are expressed without any binding relationship among them. Deviant sexual practices are limited by laws in many countries. In some societies, mostly those where religion has a strong influence on social policy, marriage laws serve the purpose of encouraging people to only have sex with one partner within marriage. The underlying factor is that mature individuals engage in actions for which they own the responsibility and work towards a condition where harmony is established in the society.

Laws also ban adults from committing sexual abuse, committing sexual acts with anyone under-aged, performing sexual activities in public, and engaging in sexual activities for money (prostitution). Though these laws cover both opposite-sex sexual activities and same-sex, they may differ with regard to punishment.

Pregnancy

In medicine, pregnancy is caused by the merging of the female gamete with the male gamete, in a process referred to, as "fertilisation," or more commonly known as "conception." After the point of "fertilisation," it is referred to as an egg. The fusion of male and female gametes usu-

Genetically Identical?	Considering only the X-chromosome, the relatedness of a female to her parents stays unchanged, but to siblings, her sisters it's 3/4 (because they both inherit identical X-chromosome from their father) and to her brothers it's 1/4.

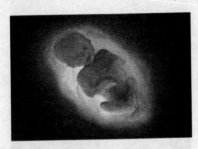

ally occurs through the act of sexual inter-course.

Embryonic Development

Human pregnancy or gestation is generally divided into 3-trimester periods. Human pregnancy averages 266 days (38 weeks) from conception, or 40 weeks from the start of the last menstrual period.

Week 1 Fertilisation. Cleavage to form a blastocyst 4-5 days after fertilization. More than 100 cells. Implantation 6-9 days after fertilisation.

Week 2 The three basic layers of the embryo develop: ectoderm, mesoderm and endoderm. *No research allowed on human embryos beyond this stage.*

Week 3 Women will not have a period. This may be the first sign that she is pregnant. Beginnings of the backbone. Neural tube develops, the beginning of the brain and spinal cord (first organs). Embryo about 2 mm long.

Week 4 Heart, blood vessels, blood and gut start forming. Umbilical cord developing. Embryo about 5 mm long.

Week 5 Brain developing. 'Limb buds', small swellings which are the beginnings of the arms and legs. Heart is a large tube and starts to beat, pumping blood. This can be seen on an ultrasound scan. Embryo about 8 mm long.

Week 6 Eyes and ears start to form.

Week 7 All major internal organs developing. Face forming. Eyes have some colour. Mouth and tongue. Beginnings of hands and feet. Fetus is 17 mm long.

By week 12 Fetus fully formed, with all organs, muscles, bones, toes and fingers. Sex organs well developed. Fetus is moving. For the rest of the gestation period, it is mainly growing in size. Fetus is 56 mm long from head to bottom. Pregnancy may be beginning to show.

By week 20 Hair beginning to grow, including eyebrows and eyelashes. Fingerprints developed. Fingernails and toenails growing. Firm hand grip. *Between 16 and 20 weeks* baby usually felt moving for first time. Baby is 160 mm long from head to bottom.

Week 24 Eyelids open. Legal limit for abortion in most circumstances.

By week 26 Has a good chance of survival if born prematurely.

By week 28 Baby moving vigorously. Responds to touch and loud noises. Swallowing amniotic fluid and urinating.

By week 30 Usually lying head down ready for birth. Baby is 240 mm from head to bottom.

40 weeks (9 months) Birth

Symptoms

Symptoms signify pregnancy. The symptoms include nausea and vomiting, excessive tiredness and fatigue, craving for certain foods not normally considered a favorite, and frequent urination particularly during night.

Medical signs associated with pregnancy include the presence of human chorionic gonadotropin (hCG) in the blood and urine, missed menstrual period, implantation bleeding that occurs at implantation of the embryo in the uterus during the 3rd or 4th week after last menstrual period, increased basal body temperature sustained for over 2 weeks after ovulation, darkening of the cervix, vagina, and vulva; softening of the vaginal portion of the cervix; softening of the uterus isthmus; and darkening of the skin in a midline of the abdomen, caused by hyperpigmentation resulting from hormonal changes, usually appearing around the middle of pregnancy.

| Breathing a day | In one day, the average person breathes out around 500 litres of the greenhouse gas CO_2 - about 1 Kg in mass. Considering the world population of 6.8 billion, their collective breathing amounts to 2500 million tonnes of CO_2 each year. |

7000 Stillborns Everyday

More than 7,200 babies are born still-born everyday across the world, 68% of them in just 10 countries including India, China and Bangladesh. Some 2.6 million stillbirths occurred, worldwide in 2009, according to the first comprehensive set of estimates published in a special series of 'The Lancet' medical journal.

Though 98 % of the stillborns occur in low and middle-income countries, high-income countries are not immune, with one in 320 babies there stillborn, a rate that has changed little in the past decade. The 5 main reasons for stillbirth are childbirth complications, maternal infections in pregnancy, maternal disorders (especially hypertension and diabetes), fetal growth restriction and congenital abnormalities.

These deaths are directly related to the lack of skilled care at this critical time nfor mothers and babies. In India, for example, rates range from 20 to 66 per 1,000 births in different states. According to Dr Flavia Bustreo, WHO's Assistant Director-General for Family and Community Health, "many stillbirth's go unrecorded, and are not seen as a major public health problem". According to an analysis to which WHO contributed in The Lancet Stillbirth Series, as many as 1.1 million stillbirths could be averted with universal coverage of the interventions.

Detection Tests

Pregnancy tests detect hormones generated by the newly formed placenta. Clinical blood and urine tests can detect pregnancy soon after implantation, which is as early as 6 to 8 days after fertilisation. Blood pregnancy tests are more accurate than urine tests. Home pregnancy tests are personal urine tests, which normally cannot detect a pregnancy until at least 12 to 15 days after fertilisation.

Contraception

Birth control is the prevention of conception or implantation of fertilised ovum or termination of pregnancy. Contraception is effective when one has the knowledge of various forms of contraceptives and their usage. It is important to educate ourselves on contraception to lead a healthy and balanced family life.

Types of contraceptives It is used as birth control methods. However, not all are equally effective. Depending on their convenience, it is for the couple to decide on the type.

Methods Natural forms (like sexual abstinence during fertile period, temperature method, mucus method, withdrawal method, rhythm method); barrier methods (like condoms - female & male, diaphragms which reduce the risk of AIDS, STDs and untimely pregnancies); Oral contraceptive pills and Intrauterine Devices (IUD); Injections; Cervical Cap; Spermicides; Film; Sponge; Sterilisation - Female (Tubectomy) - Male (Vasectomy).

Birth controll pills are oral contraceptives containing synthetic oestrogen and progesterone or synthetic progesterone alone. They are the most convenient method for all.

Sexual Orientation

They are of 3 types-heterosexual, homosexual and bisexual orientation. Individuals who do not experience sexual attraction to either sex are known as asexual. *Heterosexuality* involves individuals of opposite sexes. In India, traditionally, sexuality is allowed within marriage. There are also aberrations where people involve in sexual activity outside marriage and without any personal or social commitment. *Homosexuality* The definition of homosexuality is a preference to members of one's own sex. People who engage exclusively in same-sex sexual practices identify themselves as gay or lesbian. *Gay* refers to a man whose sexual orientation is to men. *Lesbian* refers to a woman whose sexual orientation is to women. *Bisexuals* are sexually attracted to members of both sexes. *Transsexuals*, refer to persons who is born in a particular gender but who feels himself or herself to be a member of the opposite sex.

Knowing Human diseases

A disease is a condition that impairs the proper function of the body or of one of its parts. Every living thing, both plants and animals, can succumb to disease. Hundreds of different diseases exist. Each has its own particular set of symptoms and signs, clues that enable a physician to diagnose the problem. A symptom is something a patient can detect, such as fever, bleeding, or pain. A sign is something a doctor can detect, such as a swollen blood vessel or an enlarged internal body organ. Every disease has a cause, although the causes of some remain to be discovered. Every disease also displays a cycle of onset, or beginning, course, or time span of affliction, and end, when it disappears or it partially disables or kills its victim. An epidemic disease is one that strikes many persons in a community. When it strikes the same region year after year it is an endemic disease. An acute disease has a quick onset and runs a short course. A chronic disease has a slow onset and runs sometimes years-long course. The gradual onset and long course of rheumatic fever makes it a chronic ailment.

Kinds of disease

Infectious (communicable) diseases are those that can be passed between persons such as by means of airborne droplets from a cough or sneeze. Tiny organisms such as viruses, bacteria, fungi and worms can produce infectious diseases. Whatever the causative agent, it survives in the person it infects and is passed on to another. Sometimes, a disease-producing organism gets into a person who shows no symptoms of the disease. The asymptomatic carrier can then pass the disease on to someone else without even knowing he has it.

Non-infectious (non-communicable) diseases are caused by malfunctions of the body. These include organ or tissue degeneration, erratic cell growth, and faulty blood formation and flow. Also included are disturbances of the stomach and intestine, the endocrine system, and the urinary and reproductive systems. Some diseases can be caused by diet deficiencies, lapses in the body's defence system, or a poorly operating nervous system.

Deficiency diseases due to deficiency in the diet of nutrients. They can generally be cured by providing the missing nutrients.
(a) **Protein deficiency** causes two major diseases Kwashiorkar and Marasmus.
(b) **Mineral deficiency** causes specific diseases. (i) Anaemia: Iron deficiency causes haemoglobin deficiency in blood. (ii) Goitre: Iodine deficiency causing no synthesis of thyroxine hormone of thyroid gland. (iii) Hypokalemia: potassium deficiency. (iv)

Cover Cough

Stop the spread of germs that make you and others sick

Cover your mouth and nose with a tissue when you cough or sneeze

or

Put your used tissue into the waste basket

Cough or sneeze into your upper sleeve, not your hands

Cean Hands

after coughing or sneezing

Wash hands with a soap and warm water for 20 seconds

Clean with or alcohol-based hand cleaner.

| The key to autism | Scientists at Duke University have found 'Shank 3' protein that triggers autism by stopping effective communication between brain cells. Autism is a disorder which affects the ability of children and adults to communicate and interact socially. |

Hyponatremia: Sodium deficiency causes this state of low blood pressure and loss of body weight.

(c) **Vitamin deficiency** causes a variety of diseases. (i) Night Blindness: (Vitamin A). (ii) Xerophthalmia: (dryness of eye due to lack of Vitamin A. (iii) Dermatosis: (Vitamin A). (iv) Beri-beri:(Vitamin B–thiamine). (v) Ariboflavinosis: (Vitamin B_2– riboflavin). (vi) Pellagra: (nicotinic acid/ niacin–part of B complex group). (vii) Pernicious Anaemia: (Vitamin B_{12}–Cabalamin). (viii) Scurvy: (Vitamin C –ascorbic acid). (ix) Rickets:(a disease causing disorder of calcium and phosphorus metabolism due to Vitamin D deficiency, often found in the early childhood: 6 months to 2 years. (x) Ostemalacia: (Vitamin D).

Infectious diseases are caused by various agents such as virus, bacteria, fungi and protozoa. (a) **Diseases caused by bacteria:** Cholera, Diphtheria, Tuberculosis, Leprosy, Tetanus, Typhoid, Plague, Whooping Cough, Sore Throat, Pneumonia, Bacillar dysentery, Gonorrhea, Syphilis and Botulism. (b) **Diseases caused by viruses:** Chickenpox, Measles, Poliomyletis, Rabies, Mumps, Influenza, Hepatitis, Herpes, Viral Encephalitis and AIDS. (c) **Diseases caused by fungi:** Ringworm, Athlete's foot, Dhobie itch. (d) **Diseases caused by protozoans:** Amoebiasis, Malaria, Sleeping sickness, Kalaazar, Diarrhoea, (e) **Diseases caused by worms:** Filaria, Tapeworm and Hookworm transmission.

Degenerative diseases occur due to malfunctioning of some organ or organ system in the body. They are: Heart Attack, Diabetes mellitus, Arthritis.

Eye diseases

Name of disease and symptoms: Astigmatism: Visual activity is decreased, eye strain causes headache, cylindrical lens should be used.

Cataract: Normal vision is hampered, blindness may be caused. Lens is removed and artificial lens is used.

Glaucoma: Aqueous humour pressure increases. It may cause blindness.

Dr. Death is dead

Jack Kevorkian, the retired pathologist captured the world's attention as he helped some 130 people who suffered from cancer, Lou Gehrig's disease, multiple sclerosis and paralysis, end their lives from 1990 to 1999, igniting intense debate and ending up in prison for murder, died at 83, at the William Beaumont Hospital in Michigan. Nicknamed "Dr. Death," Mr. Kevorkian catapulted into public consciousness in 1990 when he used his home made "suicide machine" in his rusted Volkswagen van to inject lethal drugs into an Alzheimer's patient who sought his help in dying.

For nearly a decade, he escaped authorities' efforts to stop him. His first four trials, all on assisted suicide charges, resulted in three acquittals and one mistrial because Michigan at the time had no law against assisted suicide. Mr. Kevorkian was stripped of his medical licence and jailed for 25-year sentence for second-degree murder, got freed in June 2007 after serving eight years and promised not assist in a suicide if he was released. Mr. Kevorkian likened himself to Martin Luther King and Mahatma Gandhi. "I put myself in my patients' place. Somebody has to do something for suffering humanity," He wrote in his 1991 book Prescription-Medicide - The Goodness of Planned Death. His life story became the subject of the 2010 HBO movie, You Don't Know Jack.

Mr. Kevorkian told a court his actions were "a medical service for an agonised human being".

Universal Blood Type	A team of Danish, English and French scientists has found a way to convert Types A, B and AB blood into Type O. The enzymatic blood conversion system enables the precise and permanent conversions of groups to enzyme converted group O (ECO)and is safe.

Sexually Transmitted Diseases

Disease	Causative organism
AIDS	HIV
Gonorrhoea	Neisseria gonoffhorae
Syphilis	Treponema pallidum
Chancroid	Haemophilus ducreyi
Granuloma	Donovania granulomatis
Trichomoniasis	Trichomonas vaginalis
Candidiasis	Candida albicans
Chlamydiasis	Chlamydia trachomatis
H.V. Vaginitis	Haemophilus vaginalis
Genital Herpes	hominis (HSV II)
Condyloma	Papilloma virus-HPV
Scabies	Sarcoptes scabieri
Pediculisis pubis	Pthius pubis
Syphilis	
Gardnerella	
Genital warts	

Hypermetropia (far sightedness): Distant objects can be seen clearly, near objects can't be seen clearly. Image formed behind retina. Biconvex lens should be used.

Strabismus (Squint): Eye ball turns to any of the sides.

Trachoma: Redness in the eye, sensation for foreign body in eye.

Cancer

Cancer is a general term used to describe over 200 individual diseases. These diseases progress differently over a period of time but share certain characteristics that include development within any tissue of a malignant growth derived from abnormalities of the host. The abnormal cells grow without any control, invade through normal tissue barriers, spread to local and distant sites within the host, and reproduce indefinitely.

Sometimes, cancer cells do not remain confined to one part of the body and penetrate and infiltrate into the adjoining tissues and dislocate their functions. Some of the cancer cells get detached from the main site of the origin and travel by blood and lymph to sites distant from the original tumour and form fresh colonies, called metastasis or secondary growth. Cells which undergo rapid, abnormal and uncontrolled growth are called neoplastic cells. The growth resulting from the division of such cells are called neoplastic growth or tumours.

Tumours are commonly classified as: (i) Benign tumours : Abnormal and persistent cell division that remains localised at the spot of origin results in the benign tumours. In some cases it can be fatal. (ii) Malignant Tumour : It first grows slowly and this state is called the latent state. The tumour later grows quickly. The cancer cells go beyond adjacent tissue and enter the blood and lymph. Once this happens, they migrate to many other sites in the body where the cancer cells continue to divide. It is metastasis.

The masses of such abnormal cells formed and spread in this way lead to the death of the host if not eradicated. The incidence of cancer is rising steadily.

Breast Cancer

It is becoming a common disease all over

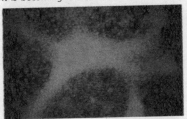

the world. It occurs in women and men. But women are more vulnerable to it. The risk of breast cancer increases with aging in women. The risk is also higher for women with a personal or family history; a long menstrual history; recent use of oral contraceptive or postmenopausal hormone replacement therapy; and no children or no live birth until age 30 or older. Other risk factors include alcohol consumption and obesity. Inherited mutations such as in the BRCA1 and BRCA2 genes greatly increase a woman's risk for breast cancer, but genetic factors account only for the 10% of the affected.

Physical symptoms include a breast lump and less commonly breast thickening, swelling, distortion or tenderness; skin irritation or dimpling; or pain, scaliness, or retraction of nipple. Breast pain is more commonly associated with benign conditions.

AIDS

The Acquired Immuno Deficiency Syndrome (AIDS) is caused by Human Immuno Deficiency Virus (HIV) which attacks human immune system, esp. lymphocytes. HIV is transmitted through blood and blood products, seminal and vaginal fluids, unprotected sex, infected blood transfusion, contaminated needles, artificial insemination, child birth to infected parents, etc. It however, does not spread by kissing, coughing, mosquito bites, food, water, working together, etc. Symptoms could be rapid weight loss, chronic diarrhoea, prolonged fever, persistent cough, herpes zoster infection, etc.

Tests like Enzyme Linked Immuno Sorbent Assay or ELISA kit, Particle Agglutination Test (PAT), Immuno Fluorescent Assay (IFA), Radio Immuno Precipitation Assay (RIPA), HIVA test, etc. are used to detect cases.

SARS

Severe Acute Respiratory Syndrome is a viral respiratory illness caused by a coronavirus, called SARS-associated coronavirus (SARS-CoV).

Symptoms: High fever (above 38°C) and

Bacterial Diseases

Disease	Causative agent
Typhoid	Salmonella typhosa
Tetanus	Clostridium tetani
Cholera	Vibrio cholerae
Syphillis	Treponema pallidum
Pneumonia	Streptococcus pneumoniae
Gonorrhoea	Nesseria gonorrhoeae
Leprosy	Mycobacterium leprae
Plague	Mucobacterium tuberculosis
Whooping cough	Berdetella pertussis
Meningitis	Meningococcus
Diptheria	Cornebacterium diptheria

cough or breathing difficulty; one or more of the following exposures during the 10 days prior to onset of symptoms; close contact (having cared for, lived with, or had direct contact with respiratory secretions or body fluids) with a person who is a suspect or probable case of SARS; travel to or living in an area with recent local transmission of SARS.

Blood Vessel Disease

Cholesterol A blood cholesterol level over 240 mg/dl (milligrams of cholesterol per deciliter of blood) approximately doubles the risk of coronary heart disease. Blood cholesterol levels between 200 and 240 mg/dl are in a zone of moderate and increasing risk. An estimated 6.5 m(10.8% of) youths aged 4-19 have levels of 200 mg/dl or higher.

Blood Pressure High blood pressure, or hypertension, affects people of all races, sexes, ethnic origins, and ages. Various causes can trigger this often symptomless disease. Since hypertension can increase one's risk for stroke, heart attack, kidney failure, and congestive heart failure, it is recommended that individuals have a blood pressure reading at least once every year. A blood pressure reading is really two measurements in one, with one written over the other, such as 122/78.

More Sleep: Good or Bad?	Studies have shown that people who sleep more than nine hours a night are at grater risk of diabetes and obesity. Oversleeping, sometimes, could be a symptom of depression.

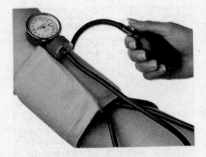

Viral Diseases

Disease and causative agent:

Acquired ImmunoDeficiency Syndrome (AIDS): Human immunodeficiency virus (HIV)

Chickenpox	Varicella herpes virus
Influenza	Orthomyxovirus
Measles (Rubeola)	Paramyxovirus
Mumps	Paramyxovirus; German
Measles	Togavirus
Pollomyelitis	Enterovirus
Rabies	Rabdovirus.

The upper number (systolic pressure) represents the amount of pressure in the blood vessels when the heart contracts (beats) and pushes blood through the circulatory system.

The lower number (diastolic pressure) represents the pressure in the blood vessels between beats, when the heart is resting. Normal blood pressure should be below 130/85 and "high normal" is between 130/85 and 139/89.

High blood pressure is divided into 4 stages, based on severity: *Stage 1 (mild)* high blood pressure ranges from 140/90 to 159/99; *Stage 2 (moderate)* is from 160/100 to 179/109; *Stage 3 (severe)* is from 180/110 to 209/119; *Stage 4 (very severe)* is 210/120 and up.

Heart Attack

Warning Signs • Uncomfortable pressure, fullness, squeezing, or pain in the centre of chest lasting 2 minutes or longer • Pain may radiate to the shoulder, arm, neck, or jaw • Sweating may accompany pain or discomfort • Nausea and vomiting also may occur • Shortness of breath, dizziness, or fainting may accompany other signs.

Stroke - Warning Signs • Sudden numbness or weakness of face, arm or leg, especially on one side of the body • Sudden confusion, trouble in speaking or understanding • Sudden trouble seeing in one or both eyes • Sudden trouble in walking, dizziness, loss of balance or coordination • Sudden severe headache with no known cause.

Genetic Disorder

(i) *ABO incompatibility*: O group mothers don't possess antigen A or B but have anti-A and anti-B antibodies. A or B group foetus in O group invites antibodies of the mother causing partial destruction of RBCs and production of bilirubin (affecting the baby with mild anaemia and jaundice). Similarly, A-group foetus in B-group moth-

Human Glands

Glands are organs of the human body that manufacture some liquid products which are secreted from the cells. There are two types of glands: (i) Ducted Glands: Ducted glands secrete their products through well-defined ducts, e.g., liver–secretes bile in the stomach; Lachrymal– tears in the eyes; Salivary– saliva in the mouth; Sweat glands in the skin–secrete sweat. (ii) Ductless Glands: Also called endocrine glands or internally secreting glands. They secrete hormones directly into the blood-stream in response to brain's instructions.

Malaria-proof
One of the best lifesaving inventions ever, the malaria-proof mosquito - genetically engineered by scientists at the University of Arizona - is immune to the Plasmodium parasite, the malaria-causing agent it transmits with its bite.

er or B-group foetus in A-group mother is attacked by antibodies of mother. ABO hemolytic (RBC-destroying) disease of new born is quite common and less severe as compared to Rh-incompatibility). (ii) *Sickle Cell anaemia*: It is due to a recessive autosomal gene (Hbs) that causes abnormalities in haemoglobin resulting in sickle of RBCs-sickle cells (rigid sickle cells obstructing capillary blood flow). (iii) *Phenylketonuria* causes deficiency of an enzyme called phenylalanine hydroxyls in liver (characterised as mental retardation, hypopigmentatiion of skin and hair, eczema, mousy odour of skin, hair and urine). (iv) *Haemophilia* a recessive trait that occurs due to absence of plasma thromboplastin or anti-haemophilia globulin. (v) *Red-Green Colour Blindness*: makes one unable to distinguish between red and green colour (predominantly in male), (vi) *Thalassemia* results from defective synthesis of sub-units of haemoglobin, (vii) *Downs' Syndrome or Mongolian Idiocy* is caused by trisomy of 21st autonomic chromosome having a total of 47 chromosomes instead of 46. It is characterised by round face, flattened nasal bridge, broad fore-head, projecting lower lip, short neck, stubby fingers, etc.

Mental Illness

Psychosis: disease of CNS. It could also be related to diabetes, hypertension, and TB. In this case the patient is unaware of the illness and refuses treatment.

Epilepsy: Seizures characterised by abnormal electrical discharge in a part of brain. Symptoms: fits of convulsions (jerk, stiffness, tongue biting, sensory changes), cry, etc.

Neurosis: The patients show excessive re-action to given stress. It involves abnormal anxiety, fear, sadness, vague aches and pains.

Schizophrenia: It is characterised by dis-organised personality (like auditory hallucinations, delusions, illogical thinking, and sense of being controlled by outside forces). Regular use of chlorpromazine and psychosocial therapy give a lot of relief.

E. coli Outbreak Caused by New Strain

The deadly E.coli outbreak that has killed 18 people and Infected over 1,600 In Europe is a completely new strain, a mutant form of two different E. coli bacteria with very aggressive genes. Almost all cases are linked to people who live In or have recently travelled to northern Germany.

Outbreak: Denmark, U.S., Norway, Netherlands, France

New strain: Contains genes from two distinct groups of enteroaggregatlve E. coli (EAEC) and entero-haemorrhaglc E. coli (EHEC)

Symptoms include bloody diarrhoea and fever

Effects: Severe infections, including haemolytlc uraemlc syndrome (HUS) - potentially lethal kidney complication which destroys red blood cells and can affect central nervous system

Contamination: Bacteria can be transferred to crops through contaminated manure, irrigation or slurry spraying, or during processing and packaging Transmission can also occur between humans

Health advice: Wash, peel or cook fruit and vegetables before eating. Wash hands regularly.

Source: WHO

Lab-Grown Lungs
It is now possible to grow new body parts in the lab. Researchers have re-created the delicate architecture of a rat lung accurately enough for it to assume 95 percent of a normal lung's inhaling and exhaling functions.

Drug Resistant Bugs

The World Health Organization focused its attention on antimicrobial resistance on World Health Day, celebrated globally on April 7. The advent of antimicrobials had led to the hope that infectious diseases might become a thing of the past.

Time has proven how misplaced this confidence was, and also demonstrated the survival skills of microbes, which should never be underestimated. It is also erroneous to suggest that super-bugs or multidrug-resistant bugs are prevalent only in developing countries but there are several superbugs that are widely prevalent in the developed world. Methicillin-resistant Staphylococcus aureus (MRSA), a bacterium responsible for several difficult-to-treat infections in humans, is one example of the superbugs that are killing thousands of people in the developed world every year.

Anti-microbial Resistance

Antimicrobial resistance (AMR) is the resistance of the micro-organism to an antimicrobial medicine to which it was earlier sensitive. AMR micro-organisms often fail to respond to standard treatment resulting in prolonged illness and higher mortality. It hampers the control of infectious diseases by reducing the effectiveness of treatment because patients remain infectious for longer and subsequently spread the resistant micro-organisms to others. Worldwide there are 440,000 MDR-TB cases annually and 150,000 deaths. Extensively drug resistant TB has been reported in 64 countries so far. Widespread resistance to chloroquine, sulfa-pyrimethamine and emergence of artemisinin resistance is seen in most malaria endemic countries. With expanded use of anti retrovirals, resistance is a concern in HIV. Methicillin Resistant Staphylococcus Aureus (MRSA) causing high percentage of hospital acquired infections is becoming more frequent. Multi-drug resistant E coli, K. pneumoniae and Enterobacter species infections are on the rise whereas Neisseria gonorrhoea and Shigella spp. infections are becoming increasingly resistant to antibiotics. WHO warns- "No action today, No cure tomorrow". The more abuse of antibiotics, the more resistance to antibiotics. Medical care would return to an age where simple infections do not respond to treatment and routine operations become life-threatening as a result of the reckless use of antibiotics.

The Superbug

The New Delhi metallo-beta-lactamase (NDM-l), also called the superbug, resistent to antibiotic, is continuing to because of worry across the world. It's the smartest gene detected in the bacterial realm, the deadliest, too. NDM-l is resistant to all known antibiotics- even carbapenem-the last resort of modem medicine. NDM 1 superbug is a piece of genetic code called 'blaNDM-1'. It basically gives them great power by producing an enzyme that helps them survive in the presence of antibiotics that would normally kill them. The resistance mechanism imparted to the bacteria by the notorious NDM-l gene is altogether a new resistance mechanism and is very powerful. Besides, NDM-l is a community-acquired resistance rather than a hospital-acquired resistance.

Most of the individual patients have direct links to India, Bangladesh or Pakistan, having been treated there for various surgeries, accidents, etc. This resistance is picked up in the community and then brought to the hospital. The problem is when an individual gets an infection such as in urinary tract, antibiotics don't work. This is more serious for vulnerable sections such as children under five years, the elderly and people who are immuno-compromised or who need to undergo surgeries.

Part **8**

Information Technology

Pages 263 - 288

Manorama Yearbook

IT Scan

India's Fastest Supercomputer

The Indian Space Research Organisation (ISRO) has built India's fastest supercomputer which can perform at 220 TeraFLOPS (Trillion Floating Point Operations Per Second). This supercomputer 'SAGA-220' (Supercomputer for Aerospace with GPU Architecture-220 TeraFLOPS) was inaugurated by ISRO Chairman K Radhakrishnan on May 2, 2011. It has been built by the Satish Dhawan Supercomputing Facility located at Vikram Sarabhai Space Centre (VSSC), Thiruvananthapuram of ISRO. The cost of building SAGA-220 is about Rs 14 crore. 'SAGA-220' is a new Graphic Processing Unit (GPU) based supercomputer. It is being used by space scientists for solving complex aerospace conditions.

Supercomputer SAGA-220

Charge Mobile Phones, Speaking

Electrical engineers at the Institute of Nanotechnology at Sungkyunkwan University in Seoul, South Korea have developed a new technique for turning sound into electricity.

The technology would also be able to harness background noise and even music to charge a phone while it is not in use. The technology uses tiny strands of zinc oxide sandwiched between two electrodes. A sound absorbing pad on top vibrates when sound waves hit it, causing the tiny zinc oxide wires to compress and release. This movement generates an electrical current that can be used to charge a battery. This is touted to be an extremely popular invention.

ICANN Opens Domain Names

Very soon, people and companies will be able to set up a website with almost any address by the end of 2012 if they have a legitimate claim to the domain name and can pay a hefty fee.

Internet Corporation for Assigned Names and Numbers (ICANN), the Internet body that oversees domain names voted to end restricting them to suffixes like .com or .gov and will receive applications for new names from Jan. 12, 2012 with the first approvals likely by the end of 2012.

The domain names could be in any characters – Cyrillic, Kanji or Devanagari for instance, for users of Russian, Japanese and Hindi.

According to Peter Dengate Thrush, ICANN Chairman, "it's the biggest change I think we have seen on the Internet, We have provided a platform for the next generation of creativity and inspiration."

The new gTLD, or generic top-level domain, programme was approved by the board of ICANN. Now, only 22 gTLDs exist – .com, .org and .info are a few examples – plus about 250 country-level domains like .uk or .cn. After the change, several hundred new gTLDs are expected to come into existence.

According to experts, corporations should be among the first to register, resulting in domain names ending in brands like .toyota, .apple or .coke. The move is seen as a big opportunity for brands to gain more control over their online presence and

Technopark — Technopark at Thirvananthapuram, the first of its kind in India, houses 100 companies that have a total of 30,000 employees.

send visitors more directly to parts of their sites -- and a danger for those who fail to take advantage. It would cost $185,000 to apply for the new domain names.

Japanese electronics giant Canon, for instance, has already made plans to apply for rights to use domain names ending with .canon. Even big cities are expected to apply such as .nyc, .london or .food could provide opportunities for many smaller businesses to grab names no longer available at the .com level -- like bicycles.london or indian.food. It's the next expansion of the Internet, it's the future of the Internet.

New Internet Address Standards

According to Christoph Meinel, Professor at Germany's Hasso Plattner Institute, because the supply of usable addresses governed by the IPv4 standard (internet protocol, version 4) has exhausted, IPv6 has now been introduced. This will allow a new way for users to get online."

Why IP addresses? In order for internet-capable devices to share information, they need a unique machine-readable address. These addresses are assigned based on a standard of internet protocols. Because humans have a hard time remembering these strings of numbers, websites are also labelled with domain names, like www.manoramaonline.com. When these addresses are typed into browsers, special servers translate them into IP addresses for the benefit of the computers.

IPv4 vs IPv6 Until recently, IP addresses had been assigned in blocks of four numbers with up to three numerals each: 217.79.215.248, for example. The new IPv6 standard will convert the numbers into a hexadecimal system. The new standard can be recognized by its eight blocks, separated by colons   01:db8:0:0:0:0:1428:57ab

Hardware change An IPv6-capable operating system is a prerequisite. Those can be found in any Windows system post Vista. There are ways to install the functionality into Windows XP systems. Mac systems starting at 10.2 and Linux, in general, support IPv6.

India's Mobile Phone Users

Once the market ruled by global brands like Nokia, Samsung and LG, the Indian mobile handset market has seen a revolution in the past few years with home grown companies giving the overseas giants a run for their money. Mobile phone users in the country – which sees some 20 million new connections joining the network every month – also have an unprecedented choice of picking their handsets from as many as 72 global and domestic players. And the price range is also wide – a plain-vanilla handset aimed at the rural market can cost as low as Rs.600.

The Indian firms Among the most visible are Spice Mobile, Micromax, Karbonn, Olive, Maxx, Lava, Videocon, Lemon, Zen, Wynncom, Techcom and T-Series.

QR Code

QR or "quick response" code, like a standard bar code, is a black and white code holding valuable information. The use of QR codes is free of any licence.
The QR code is a clearly defined ISO standard. Denso Wave owns the patent rights. Unlike bar code, QR Code is more useful because it can store (and digitally present) much more data, like URL links, geo coordinates, data or text, a phone number, product details, etc.

There are other benefits too. QR can link the user straight to a web site, jump video frames half way forward or backward, can help watch interview on YouTube. The key feature of QR Code is that many modern cell phones can scan them.Soon search engines will start recognising them. Many Android, Nokia, and Blackberry handsets come with QR code readers installed. There are many dedicated QR code readers apps, available for download Generating QR codes: There are a number of websites that will do it for free (do a web search for "QR code generator"). QR code data capacity: Numeric only=Max. 7,089 characters.

Computer Virus

Virus in computing technology is a program that has the same behavior pattern as that of a biological virus. In computing terminology it is a self-replicating/self-producing automated program. This program spreads by inserting itself into executable code or documents that are present on the computer system. This process of insertion of a virus is called infection. The file into which the code is inserted is called an infected file. Each file has an extension; document files have 'doc' as an extension. The files that are infected the most are executable files. Mostly computer virus can only affect software and cannot damage hardware.

Purpose of a Computer Virus

One may wonder why people create computer viruses and where computer viruses come from.

The virus makers have different motivating factors like: • Financial gain (employed by spammers and organized crime) • Impress peers (mostly teen hacker) • Ideological factors as freedom of knowledge or information • Technical challenge and scoring a point (I am better than the team that put your software together)

Political reasons (a means to prove a political ideology and get focus of media) • Tools to do something (schoolboy creator but this is very miniscule) • Some motives may be plain and simple revenge, cyber espionage and commercial sabotage.

Your Best Defense

The best defense against virus attacks is a good offense. Without proper protection, computer worms can spread like wildfire. From minor annoyances to major epidemics meant to cripple giant Web sites, these tenacious trespassers cost lots of money.

Some Tips to keep these Bugs at bay:

They are of two types: free software (downloadable) for individuals and owned by purchasing from the vendors.

1. Don't open any e-mail attachments that look suspicious or come from unknown senders. Be on the lookout for e-mails from people you know, but with language or style they wouldn't normally use-this should raise a red flag.

2. Install an antivirus program for VirusScan. Take the time to update the antivirus definition on the PC.

3. Go to any Security Response or Virus Information website for the latest security alerts, disinfecting instructions, and archives.

4. Stay on top of patches created by software vendors to thwart new threats and programming vulnerabilities. By registering the software after purchase, the user is notified by the maker when the updates are available. Make sure to install the necessary critical updates and fixes available through Windows Update.

5. To deal effectively with viruses, use a stable antivirus software, and follow the best practices.

Common Types of Viruses

Resident Viruses: This type of virus is a permanent which dwells in the RAM memory. From there it can interrupt all the operations corrupting files and programs that are opened, closed, copied, renamed etc. Examples include: Randex, CMJ, Meve, and MrKlunky.

Direct Action Viruses: It replicates and infects files in the directory or folder that it is in and in directories that are specified in the AUTOEXEC.BAT file PATH. This virus attacks when the computer is booted.

Overwrite Viruses: Such viruses delete the information contained in the infected files that it infects, rendering them partially or totally useless. It can be cleaned by deleting the file completely, thus losing the original content. Examples of this virus include: Way, Trj.Reboot, Trivial.88.D.

Boot Virus: It attacks the boot sector of a hard disk which is a crucial part of a disk,where information is stored together with codes that make it possible to boot (start) the computer from the disk. Examples of boot viruses include: Polyboot.B, AntiEXE.

Macro Virus: Macro viruses infect files that are created using certain applications or programs that contain macros. These mini-programs make it possible to automate repetitive actions. Examples of macro viruses: Relax, Melissa.A, Bablas, O97M/Y2K.

Directory Virus: It changes the paths that indicate the location of a file. By executing a program (file with the extension .EXE or .COM) which has been infected by a virus, we are unknowingly running the virus program, while the original file and program have been previously moved by the virus. Once infected it becomes impossible to locate the original files.

Polymorphic Virus: It encrypts or encodes itself in a different way (using differ-

Stuxnet

Iranian President Mahmoud Ahmadinejad, in 2010 September, confirmed that the nuclear facilities in Natanz, which enrich uranium had been sabotaged by a computer virus. Ahmadinejad was referring to Stuxnet, the only one-of-its-kind malware that has infected more than 30,000 computers in Iran and world over about 200,000 computers have been infected including India. Stuxnet uses near-perfect security certificates to beat anti-virus applications. It has two components a trojan (a program that acts as a benign application) and a rootkit (which allows covert access to administrator-level privileges) After accessing the destination System32\ drivers\ and hiding itself Stuxnet searches for industrial control systems connected to the computer. If it finds one it injects malicious (and invisible) codes Into the system and seizes control. If it does not. it remains inert.

According to analysts, Stuxnet sneaks into a computer through a rootkit a software that enables continued privileged access to a computer while actively hiding its presence from adminstrators by subverting standard operating system functionality. It uses "zero-day vulnerabilities in Microsoft Windows Shell" to attack the Seimen's Scada System. Once in place, the virus can replace the programmers' code and instruct the equipment what to do.

ent algorithms and encryption keys) every time they infect a system. This makes it impossible for anti-viruses to find them besides enabling them to create a large number of copies of themselves. Examples include: Elkern, Marburg, Satan Bug, and Tuareg.

File Infectors: This type of virus infects programs or executable files (files with an .EXE or .COM extension). When one of these programs is run, directly or indirectly, the virus is activated, producing the damaging effects it is programmed to carry out. The majority of existing viruses belong to this category, and can be classified depending on the actions that they carry out.

FAT Virus: The file allocation table or FAT is the part of a disk used to connect information and is a vital part of the normal functioning of the computer.

Such dangerous virus prevent access to certain sections of the disk where important files are stored. Damage caused can result in information losses from individual files or even entire directories.

Worms: Similar to a virus, it has the ability to self-replicate, and produce negative effects on a system but they are detected and eliminated by antiviruses. Examples of worms include: PSWBugbear.B, Lovgate.F, Trile.C, Sobig.D, Mapson.

Trojans or Trojan Horses: Trojans unlike viruses do not reproduce by infecting other files, nor do they self-replicate.

Logic Bombs: They are not viruses as they do not replicate. They are not even programs in their own right but rather camouflaged segments of other programs. Their aim at destroying data on the computer once certain logical conditions have been met.

Cloud Computing

The Cloud Computing is a tool that helps us share resources among the cloud service consumers, cloud partners, and cloud vendors in the cloud value chain. The resource sharing at various levels results in various cloud offerings such as infrastructure cloud (e.g. hardware, IT infrastructure management), software cloud (e.g. SaaS focusing on middleware as a service, or traditional CRM as a service), application cloud (e.g. Application as a Service, UML modeling tools as a service, social network as a service), and business cloud (e.g. business process as a service).

Google Chrome OS has initiated another revolution in the area of availing apps free for all to use and benefit.

iCloud

Steve Jobs stood up on June 6th, 2011, at an Apple keynote speech during the Apple Worldwide Developers Conference (aka WWDC) and showed Apple's brand-new service called iCloud.

This service is a "cloud" based service that allows the user, to store data for access by their Apple and non-Apple devices. This service acts as a hub for music, photos, applications, documents, eBooks (iBooks), contacts, and email and calendar data. The most basic benefit of iCloud is a free service with which one can store 5GB of data in the cloud. What the cloud represents here is an amount of server space hosted by Apple, accessible through several services including email, calendars, iTunes, the Apple App Store, and Photo Stream, amongst others in the future. The amount of space one has is not reduced by purchased music, apps, books, and photos in the Photo Stream. For music this free service is currently limited to 10 devices.

Smart Environments

Dr. Vivek Menon
Amrita School of Business, Amrita Vishwa Vidyapeetham, Kochi

According to Mark Weisaer, the most profound technologies are those that disappear. They weave themselves into the fabric of everyday life until they are indistinguishable from it. This is the essence of the fourth stage of evolution of computing environment.

The evolution of computing environments can be categorized into four eras. The first era, from the mid-1950's through the 60's was characterized by stand-alone mainframe computers. In the second era, from the 1970's through the early 1990's, computers were connected to form local-area or wide-area networks, giving rise to the concept of distributed computing. The third era began in early 1990's with the advent of mobile computing, i.e. portable computing devices such as laptop computers as well as advances in wireless networks. By allowing the end user to carry the work along with him/her, this paradigm introduced a new dimension to computing - 'any time' and 'anywhere'. Today, we are witnessing the advent of the fourth era of computing, a natural extension of mobile computing where the network is not limited to traditional computers and could potentially include almost any artefact – a device, a gadget or any object with an embedded processor providing intelligence and connectivity. This is referred to as the era of ubiquitous computing.

Ubiquitous Computing

The vision of ubiquitous computing was eloquently expressed by Mark Weiser in his seminal Scientific American (1991) article 'The Computer for the 21st century': "The most profound technologies are those that disappear. They weave themselves into the fabric of everyday life until they are indistinguishable from it." Weiser envisaged smart environments saturated with computing and communication technology and yet gracefully integrated with the human users using natural modalities such as vision, speech, gestures, and touch, rather than the traditional keyboard and mouse interfaces. This vision of ubiquitous computing (commonly referred to as pervasive computing) was far ahead of the technologies that were in existence then and attempts to realize this vision fell short of expectations. However, advances in technologies coupled with declining hardware costs over the past decade have helped us to move closer to realizing this vision.

Not Among the Best	According to C.N.R. Rao, scientist and chairman of the Scientific Advisory Council to the Prime Minister, not even a single research institute in India matches the best in the world, or MIT and Cambridge.

The ultimate goal of ubiquitous computing is to improve the human experience and quality of life by obviating the need for explicit awareness of the underlying communications and computing technologies in our daily activities. This implies that these technologies recede into the background of our lives, becoming more or less invisible, demanding little or no attention while serving the human (calm technology) and thus allowing him/her to focus on other non-trivial and non-routine tasks.

Everyday environments such as homes, offices, hospitals, malls, railway stations, airports, cities could be transformed into 'smart spaces' which could then serve their occupants better by anticipating their needs or adapting to them. A ubiquitous computing environment can also help

> A ubiquitous computing environment can also help in disaster management

in disaster management, through timely prediction, prevention, mitigation and response using a dense in situ deployment of multimodal sensors and actuators. Unlike closed-door scenarios, open scenarios introduce greater challenges and their realization is relatively difficult.

What is a Smart Environment?

A smart environment is a realization of Weiser's vision of "a physical world that is richly and invisibly interwoven with sensors, actuators, displays, and computational elements, embedded seamlessly in the everyday objects of our lives, and connected through a continuous network". As one of the key thrust areas in the pervasive computing landscape, smart environments (or smart spaces) integrate the otherwise disjoint cyber and physical worlds and thereby enable sensing and control of one world by the other. For example, computer chips

could be embedded in everyday appliances such as coffee makers, ovens, refrigerators, doors, lighting fixtures, appliances, homes, and cars (and even the human body), and networked together in order to create a smart environment conjoining the cyber and physical realms.

Illustrative Scenario. The following scenario illustrates how a small environment can enhance productivity for a busy executive:

Raj is a busy executive heading the

Chennai branch of XYZ Ltd, headquartered in Mumbai. At work, he receives a phone call from his boss in Mumbai directing him to attend an emergency meeting in Mumbai at 11.00 am the following day. After completing the call, Raj announces to his 'smart office' his intention to travel to Mumbai the next day to attend the 11.00 am meeting. In his smart office "walls have ears", and the room interprets the stated requirements spoken by Raj and initiates the process of booking his air tickets online. Meanwhile, Raj continues to work on his desktop computer and organizes the documents required for the meeting. After a few minutes, the 'smart office' announces the confirmed itinerary of his trip to Mumbai by a 7.00 am flight. Raj receives this information in his mailbox also. Subsequently, the 'smart office' carries out a web check-in for Raj on his upcoming flight and books an airport cab to pick him up from his residence at 4.30 am. Raj works late

| Methane Emissions | Agriculture accounts for around 9% of all greenhouse gas emissions in Britain. Most of this comes from sheep, cows and goats. Farming is responsible for 41% of overall methane emissions. |

into the night and finalizes the documents required for the meeting. As he is about to log off from his work computer, the 'smart office' detects the presence of updated versions of certain files required for the meeting available on the work computer and synchronizes his laptop to reflect the latest content. After a long day at work, Raj leaves for his 'smart home' and falls asleep quickly. The 'smart home' had already downloaded Raj's schedule from his mailbox and set a wake-up alarm for 4.00 am the next day after taking into consideration the time Raj usually requires to get ready and the distance to the airport . Raj is woken up by an alarm and is surprised to find that the time is already 5.00 am. What happened? The 'smart home' was constantly monitoring the flight status on the airline website and discovered a 1 hour delay in departure. Knowing that Raj slept

and translates the spoken commands to a sequence of steps that eventually result in the booking of an air ticket and the subsequent web check in. All this is achieved without any intervention or follow up from Raj thereby allowing him to be more productive at work. As he is about to log off, the 'smart office' detects the conflicting versions of files across the desktop and the laptop computers and automatically synchronizes the files, again freeing him from some mundane tasks. Back home, the flight rescheduling episode illustrates the adaptive and intelligent behaviour of smart environments. Such systems can learn the preferences of its users over time and balance them with external constraints to arrive at optimal decisions that fulfill the high level objectives of various users. The episode involving the rerouting of the cab expands the scope of smart environment applications to outdoor arenas as well. Here the entire road network of the city is fully aware of its state on a continuous basis, thereby providing timely advice to commuters regarding traffic patterns.

> A key to realizing the vision of a smart environment is the notion of "context"

late the previous night and that he normally likes to sleep a few extra minutes, the 'smart home' had reset the alarm to 5.00 am and rescheduled the cab for a pick up at 5.30 am; leaving enough time for Raj to catch his rescheduled flight of 8.00 am. En route, the 'smart cab' learns from the 'city roads monitoring system' of impending traffic delays in the normal route due to overnight construction activity. The 'smart cab' takes an alternate route suggested by the 'road monitoring system' and helps Raj to reach the airport on time. Raj feels fresh from his extra hour of sleep and impresses his boss and colleagues alike during the meeting.

As can be seen from the illustrative scenario, Raj is freed from the mundane tasks involved in managing his travel. The smart environment understands spoken language

Context Awareness

A key to realizing the vision of a smart environment is the notion of "context". Context is any information that could be used to characterize the situation of an entity like a person, place, or object and could be diverse - location, activity, time, weather, intensity of light, sound levels, health, mood, etc. to name a few. The smart environment continuously adapts to changes in various

contextual cues such as the identity of the people in the space and their number, the location within the space (bedroom, living room, office cabin, meeting room, library, etc.), activity of the user (sleeping, eating, meeting) and so on.

A majority of the existing literature is based on the traditional view of sense, reason, and act cycle. The operation of a smart environment is likened to an intelligent agent that perceives the state of an environment using a variety of sensors, reasons about the perceived state and initiates actions which in turn affect the state of the environment. While perception and actuation capabilities allow the system to be situated in the physical realm, the reasoning capabilities facilitate flexible and adaptive system behaviour in response to changes in context.

There has been a considerable interest in smart environments both in the academia and the industry. These projects have mostly focused on smart indoor environments such as smart homes and smart offices or workplaces. Some of the noted initiatives are MavHome, Aware Home, Gator Tech Smart House, The Adaptive House, Easy Living and Intelligent Home.

Identification within a Smart Environment

Identification and tracking of occupants is perhaps the most important driver for customization of services within a smart envi-

ronment. The ability to identify and track people and answer questions about their whereabouts is critical to many applications. Identification approaches vary from tag-based ones such as those involving RFID badges to those based on biometrics of the user. Tag-based methodologies tend to be obtrusive, requiring the individual to continuously wear them, however small the tag maybe. Some of the biometric techniques, such as fingerprint and iris scans, require a 'pause-and-declare' interaction with the human, making him/her aware of the technology. Audio and video based recognition techniques involving biometric modalities such as face, gait (walking style) and voice are more natural due to their similarities with recognition modalities employed by humans and hence more appropriate in smart environments.

Road Ahead

Increasing availability of computational resources at declining costs coupled with advancements in communication technologies is paving the way for greater focus on human-centered smart environments. Designing scaleable smart environments that provide personalized services to multiple occupants at acceptable levels of quality of service, after balancing their conflicting goals is indeed a challenging task. Another important challenge would be to extend the successful pilot implementations available today, albeit at a homogeneous level (such as homes, offices, automobiles) to a more heterogeneous level. This would involve generalizing the intelligent automation and decision making capabilities to facilitate seamless interaction from an individual's perspective across the diverse smart spaces that cross his daily life – smart homes, offices, vehicles, roads, hospitals, malls, airports, etc. Finally, concerns about security and privacy of inhabitants of a smart environment need to be addressed effectively in order to gain increased acceptability and adoption amongst the general public. ∎

Not Survivors, But Victims

Millions of people in Russia, Ukraine and Belarus who live in areas most-affected by fallout receive some form of compensation for the Chernobyl accident, whether they show any symptoms or not. WHO thinks such schemes have created a culture of dependency.

Kinect Thrills

Kinect is a motion sensing input device developed by Microsoft for the Xbox 360 video game console. It is based around a webcam-style add-on peripheral for the Xbox 360 console, which enables users to control and interact with the Xbox 360 without the need to touch a game controller, through a natural user interface using gestures and spoken commands.

Xbox 360 console

Xbox games products

Kinect brings games and entertainment to life in extraordinary new ways without using a controller. Imagine controlling movies and music with the wave of a hand or the sound of your voice. With Kinect, technology evaporates, letting the natural magic in all of us shine.

Kinect was launched in North America on November 4,

The fun at its height

2010, in Europe on November 10, 2010, in Australia, New Zealand and Singapore on November 18, 2010 and in Japan on November 20, 2010. Purchase options for the sensor peripheral include a bundle with the game Kinect Adventures and console bundles with either a 4 GB or 250 GBX box 360 console and Kinect Adventures.

Kinect holds the Guinness World Record of being the "fastest selling consumer electronics device". It sold an average of 133,333 units per day with a total of 8 million units in its first 60 days. 10 million units of the Kinect sensor have been shipped as of March 9, 2011.

Apple Thunders

The new ultra-high-speed computer connection introduced on Apple Mac-Book Pro laptops in 2011 is something quite amazing.The technology, called Thunderbolt, comes from Intel, and it is capable of sending two separate streams of 10 gigabits (or 800 megabytes) per second of data. That's enough to download a 20-gigabyte HD movie in 30 seconds. Thunderbolt is a new brand name for a technology called Light Peak. Light Peak transports high-speed signals between computers, displays, and peripherals.

Thunderbolt, Intel's copper wire

version of Light Peak transmits 10 gigabits per second,through electron rather than light.

The original Light Peak design put an electronic transmitter and receiver on each end of the fibre-optic cable to convert the signal into electronic form.

Switching to copper cables let Intel do the job on the cheap, but limited transmission to three metres. Fibre optics routinely carry 10 gigabits per second over kilometres.

Computer Revolution

At the heart of the computers are micro-processors. Computers are now available in all sizes, shapes and capacity, downsized, can be found in children's toys, pocket calculators, industrial robots, home appliances, etc.

Timeline

1971 Intel founded by Robert Noyce, Gordon Moore and Andy Grove introduces the world's first microprocessor called Intel 4004.

1974 Intel introduces 8080 microprocessor - was used in the first commercial PC, the Altair.

1976 Apple Computer introduces Apple I, the first single circuit board computer.

1977 Apple introduces Apple II computer with colour graphics.

1981 IBM introduces its first personal computer featuring the Intel 8088 microprocessor. It sparked the PC revolution; Shugart Associates introduced the hard drive, bringing high-capacity data storage to the PC; Adam Osborne completed the first portable computer.

1982 Lotus Development Corp. introduces Lotus 1-2-3- becomes a best seller application; GriD Systems Corp. to market the first battery-powered laptop and the portable computer industry.

1983 The IBM PC/XT establishes the IBM format PC featuring and Intel processor, Microsoft DOS and a hard drive as the popular PC platform.

1984 Apple introduces the Macintosh with a GUI making it very user friendly.

1985 Intel introduces 386 microprocessor featuring 275,000 transistors, in a 32-bit chip that brought muli-tasking capability to PC. Americal Online founded.

1987 Toshiba introduces T1000 laptops, popularised portable computing.

1988 Recordable CDs become available

1989 The PC market touches 120 million.

1990 In Geneva, Tim-Berners-Lee develops World Wide Web for distributing information by networking computers (Internet); Laptop with Windows and Intel 386SL (the first processor developed for a mobile computer)

1991 Creative Labs introduce Sound Blaster Pro board, speakers, multimedia software, available.

1993 Intel introduces Pentium processor; Microsoft introduces Windows 3.1 providing a base for consumer games and learning applications; PC games came of age with the launch of DOOM by id Software (also multiplayer version)

What is a Computer?	A computer is an electronic data processing device which can read and write, compute and compare, store and process large volumes of data with high speed, accuracy and reliability. It can interact with other devices through LAN, WiFi, Bluetooth, etc.

1994 Shipping of PCs touch 288 million, worldwide.

1995 Microsoft launches Windows 95 and its browser Internet Explorer - sold 1 million copies in the first 4 days. It pushed PCs into businesses, homes and schools. Shipping touched about 350 million.

1996 Digital Versatile Disc (DVD) debuts and is introduced on computers run on Pentium processor; the first 3d-graphics accelerators bring advanced PC gaming to home; more than 40 million people connect through Internet and $1 billion change hands online.

1997 Intel introduces Pentium-II; worldwide shipping reached 497 million; recordable and re-writable DVDs became common.

1998 Diamond Multimedia Systems pioneer portable mp3 digital music technology by introducing RIO PMP 300. PC shippment touched 590 million.

1999 Napster is founded and users started sharing music online; Intel introduces Pentium III; PC shippment reached 700 million. About 200 million internet users worldwide.

2000 Intel produces Pentium 4; by the year-end, 400 million people were using Internet.

2001 Microsoft introduces XP; half a billion people have internet access from their homes; PC shippment touched 960 million.

2002 Intel introduces Mobile Intel Pentium 4 Processor-4 enabling desktop performance in laptop; According to Gartner Dataquest, 1 billionth PC shipped.

Development Through Time

First Generation (mechanical or electromechanical)
Calculators: Difference Engine
Programmable devices: Analytical Engine
Second Generation (vacuum tube)
Calculators: IBM 604, UNIVAC 60
Programmable devices: Colossus, ENIAC, EDSAC, EDVAC, UNIVAC 1, IBM 701/702/ 650, Z22
Third Generation (discrete transistors and SSI, MSI, LSI Integrated circuits)
Mainframes: IBM7090, System360
Minicomputers: PDP-8, System 36
Fourth Generation (VLSI integrated circuits)
Microcomputer: VAX, IBM System-1
4-bit: Intel 4004/ 4040
8-bit: Intel 8008/ 8080/ Motorola 6800/ Zilog 280
16-bit: Intel8088/ Zilog Z8000
32-bit: Intel 80386/ Pentium/ Motorola 68000
64-bit: x86-64/ Power PC/ MIPS/ SPARC
Embeded: Intel 8048, 8051
Personal Computer: Desktop, Laptop, SOHO, UMPC, Tablet PC, PDA, .
Fifth Generation Presently the experimental or theoretical computing and artificial intelligence are making grounds. Some of them are Quantum computers, DNA computing, Optical computers...

2003 First ever ebook reader Sony Libre launched.
2007 Apple launches iPhone
2008 Apple appstore launched with ebooks for iPhone.

2009 Windows 7 launched. Kindle 2 launched.
2010 iPad 1,
2011 Apple iPad 2 and OS X Lion.

Touch Screen Systems

A touchscreen is basically an input device like a keyboard or mouse. It is a computer display screen that is sensitive to human touch, allowing a user to interact with the computer by touching pictures or words on the screen. It is made up of a touch sensor, a controller card, and a software driver.

Uses of Touchscreens Touch screens are used in information kiosks, computer-based training devices, and systems designed to help individuals who have difficulty manipulating a mouse or keyboard. Touchscreen systems are also used in a variety of applications, including point-of-sale systems, public information displays, industrial control systems, etc.

There are a number of types of touch screen technology: **Resistive**: A resistive touch screen panel is composed of several layers. **Surface acoustic wave**: Surface acoustic wave (SAW) technology uses ultrasonic waves that pass over the touch screen panel. **Capacitive**: Such panels are coated with indium tin oxide that conducts a continuous electrical current across

the sensor. **Infrared**: method uses an array of vertical and horizontal IR sensors that detect the interruption of a modulated light beam near the surface of the screen. **Strain gauge**: Here the screen is spring mounted on the four corners and strain gauges are used to determine deflection when the screen is touched. There are several other technologies like Optical imaging, Dispersive signal technology, Acoustic pulse recognition; Frustrated total internal reflection and Diffused laser imaging.

Android Apps

Android is the first free, open source mobile platform running on a Linux-based operating system and key mobile applications. It all started in October 2003 as Android Inc., co-founded by Andy Rubin, Rich Miner, Nick Sears and Chris White. Google bought Android as it was entering the wireless world. Android can be liberally extended to incorporate new cutting edge technologies as they emerge. Android apps (short for applications) are mobile software designed for running on the Android operating system, which is one of the most popular platforms used in cellphones, tablets and other mobile devices.

Since Android was introduced, more than 200,000 Android apps have been

developed and available for download from the Android Market—the online software store hosted by Google—but not all are free.

The best of the free ones are:

Media Player : RealPlayer / MoboPlayer
Music Player & Organizer: Astro Player
Video Sharing : YouTube
Radio Broadcasting : TuneIn Radio
Ringtone Changer : Zedge
Image Viewer : QuickPic / JustPictures!
Image Editor : Photoshop Express
Office Suite: Google Docs, Microsoft 365
E-Book Reader : Laputa Reader
Anti-malware : Lookout

Tablets

The Evolution of Tablets

1972 Dynabook Alan Kay invented the first tablet, which remained a concept.

1987 Cambridge Z88; Linus Write-Top

1990 GRIDPad 1910

1991 HP 95LX was a pocket PC with MSDOS had a keyboard.

Cambridge Z88

1992 Grid 2260

1993 Apple's Newton 6 inch PDA with type recognition; Zoomer, the palm device run on Palm OS was produced by theTandy and sold by Casio.

1999 Rocket eBook was produced by NuvoMedia

GridPad

2001 Via Tablet was the first device to be run on Windows XP TabletPC version.

2003 FSC Lifebook had the functions of notebook and touchscreen capability.

2005 Nokia 770 Internet Tablet

2006 Sony UX, Samsung Q1

2007 Kindle - Amazon's ebook with e-ink technology created a new market; Apple's iPhone replaced PDAs.

2010 iPad 1 - Apple revolutionised the device class with its tablet; Galaxy Tab ran on Android, Dell Streak, Viewsonic Viewpad, OlivePad,

2011 iPad 2; Motorolla Xoom, BlackBerry Palybook, HP TouchPad, LG Optimus, HTC Flyer.

iPad

Tablets were very much on same path in the portable computing space. while laptops, notebooks and netbooks made computers smaller and more portable, they didn't quite change the way they worked or how we used them. It was more like an adaptation to the changing needs of users. But with tablets, the keyboard and mouse are thrown out of the window in favor of multitouch interfaces. With the competition heating up, tablets now offer everything you and I need; a non-stylus based touch screen that is accurate and responsive, a fairly long battery life, portability like never before, and wireless connectivity.

Newton

While the tablet concept is a refreshing one, it also opens up many avenues for innovation in hardware components and software development. Using the tablet phenomenon as a catalyst, many other technologies have received greater prominence and exposure. Some new and many future tablets boast 3D displays and cameras, and use the latest tablet-optimized iteration of Android - version 3.0 or Honeycomb. The tech world has been captivated by the tablet phenomenon, but whether it will revolutionize portable computing or go the way of e-book readers or netbooks and decline in popularity down the line, only time will tell.

Palm Pilot

Xoom

Ban Hotmail

Russian Security Service proposes to ban Skype, Hotmail and Gmail as their unctrolled use may threaten Russia's security.

Internet Timeline

1957 In response to Russian launch of Sputnik, US created Advanced Research Projects Agency. Together with American Universities ARPAnet was brought online in 1969 (the predecessor of modern Internet)

1960 Ted Nelson created Project Xanadu and coined the term hypertext (links) in 1963.

1962 JC R Licklider introduced the idea of an 'intergalactic Network'

1974 Vint Cerf and Bob Kahn used the term "Internet" in a Transmission Control Protocol paper.

JC R Licklider

1976 Gary Thuerk sent the first spam email to 400 users of AR-PANET advertising his DEC's new range of minicomputers

1983 On Jan 1st, every machine connected to ARPANET switched to TCP/IP - which became the core of Internet.

1984 Dr. Jon Postel described his idea for .com, .org, .gov, .edu, and .mil in a series of papers in Internet Engineering Task Force.

1989 The World, an Internet Service Provider (ISO), offered the first commercial dial-up internet.

1992 Corporation for Research and Educational Networking (CERN) released the World Wide Web.

1993 1993 Marc Andreessen creates Mosaic X, a GUI for WWW, the first widely used internet browser. Later created the browser, Netscape

1994 Lycos created by Dr. Michael Loren Mauldin; Yahoo launched. Created by Jerry Yang and David Filo

1995 Pierre Omidyar released eBay (originally Auctionweb). Excite -created by Graham Spencer, Joe Kraus, Mark Van Haren, Ryan Mcintyre, Ben Lutch, Martin Reinfried. AltVista launched. Created by Louis Monler and Michael Burrows.

1996 Internet 2 released.; Hotmail launched; Ask Jeeves launched. Created by Garrett Gruener and David War

1997 Lary Page and Sergey Brin, Stanford Computer Science grads made a search

engine BackRub, which counted websites and ranked them. Later it was renamed Google. The name is derived from "googol" - a mathematical term for the number represented by the numeral 1 followed by 100 zeroes.

1998 Google Technology Incorp. founded. MSN Search launched but renamed in 2006 as Windows Live. From 2008 onwards Bing took over and Live search was discontinued.Goto.com offered advertisers the option of bidding to appear at the top of results in response to specific searches.

1999 Wi-fi, wireless internet technology standardised; Sean Fanning created Napster, at 18.

2000 The .com market collapsed after peaking 5048.62 0n the NASDAQ; GoogleAdWords launched - allowed business to place advertisements in boxes next to search results.

2001 Wikipedia launched

Total Internet Users

There are 2,095,006,005 Internet Users, as on 31 March 2011, are available today. They are detailed by geographic world regions: Africa, Asia, Europe, North America, Latin America and the Caribbean, and Oceania.

2003 Apple launched iTunes Store with 200,000 songs and within 24 hrs, a quarter of a million sold in a day; Yahoo acquired AltaVista, Inktomi, Goto, and AlltheWeb. Google launched AdSense which allowed site developers to place Google-controlled advertisements on their site and receive payments for every click on the ads.

2004 Google launched Gmail in April with 1 GB storage while Hotmail and Yahoo were offering 2 MB and 4MB respectively.

2005 YouTube launched.

2006 Dom Sagolla released Twitter; Facebookmade available for all.

2009 2009 Bing launched. Microsoft and Yahoo makes a 10-year deal to power Yahoo search engine with Bing. Google indexed 8 billion websites and processes 70.24% of web searches. ; Mobile data traffic exceeded voice traffic every single month

2011 Facebook has 750 million as actives users. Twitter in 2011 March had 200 million registered users.On a certain day, 177 million tweets were sent in a day. As on July 2011, the total number of Indexed

Webpage, according to www.worldwidewebsize.com, were 19.83 billion.

IP Counts by top 20 Countries

Total IPs in 242 Countries : 3,443,393,280

Total IPs	Country
1,527,822,162	UNITED STATES
331,813,811	CHINA
217,147,134	UNITED KINGDOM
201,822,879	JAPAN
116,060,161	GERMANY
112,222,992	KOREA, REPUBLIC OF
88,401,514	FRANCE
80,891,225	CANADA
48,678,160	ITALY
47,668,789	AUSTRALIA
45,344,129	NETHERLANDS
44,491,708	BRAZIL
38,615,128	RUSSIAN FED.
35,415,900	TAIWAN
34,796,928	INDIA
27,810,732	MEXICO
26,908,601	SPAIN
26,080,773	SWEDEN
21,596,814	SWITZERLAND
19,360,884	SOUTH AFRICA

[as on 2011-06-01]

Top Level Domains Overview

All	New	Deleted	Transferred	TLD
130,753,879	145,884	96,031	145,751	All TLDs
95,789,176	100,443	64,965	107,783	.COM
14,004,517	13,894	9,691	12,860 .	NET
9,257,856	9,554	5,774	9,068	.ORG
7,876,069	18,315	12,551	13,245	.INFO
2,105,576	1,861	1,515	1,438	.BIZ
1,720,685	1,817	1,535	1,357	.US

30 June 2011

Browsers & Search Engines

Browser is an application that lets us view the webpage and interact with it.

There are different browsers for different platforms and with multiple features.

All-Purpose Search Engines: Google, Yahoo! Search, Bing, AltaVista, search.aol, Live Search, FlixFlux, Torrentz, IceRocket, Technorati, Sphere, Lycos, Cuil, Kosmix...

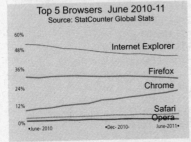

There are different kinds of search engines that specialised in searching specialised categories like Visual Search, Source Code, Shopping, School, Real Estate, Question & Answer, Books, Email, Forum, Games, Job, Legal, People, Medical, Maps, MultiMedia, News, videos, etc.

YouTube

About 36 hours of videos are uploaded every minute on YouTube, the video-sharing website owned by global search giant Google Inc. Tens of hundreds of Indian movies from the classics of 1960s to the latest ones are available on YouTube. The website is working actively to bring Hindi movies online. In 2010, 55 million people across the world watched Indian Premier League cricket live on YouTube, which points to the volume of information available online in various media formats. The amount of information being created on daily basis is mind-boggling. In 2010, 800,000 petabytes data was created. One petabyte is a million gigabytes. One would need 75 billion iPads to store this data. 100 billion non-spam e-mails and IMs (instant messages) are sent every day and 500 million people users visit various social sites.

Top 5 Browsers June 2010-11
Source: StatCounter Global Stats

- Internet Explorer
- Firefox
- Chrome
- Safari
- Opera

•June- 2010   •Dec- 2010•   June-2011•

Wikipedia

Wiki is a Hawaiian word for "quick". Wikipedia web site is based on a wiki engine, that allows users to edit the content. With the entry of Jimmy Wales, started a wiki based encyclopedia, called Wikipedia, in January 2001, just when internet junkies around the world were logging on to web 2.0. 20,000 articles were submitted by the end of the year. Total number of pages are 1.12 billion (2011 July) and articles in Aug. 2010 was 21.060.869. Other sections include Wikinews, Wikitionary (1,464,000 entries), Wikiquotes, Wikibooks, Wikiversity (open collaborative learning), Wikicommon (media), Wikisource (online library, etc. Articles: 3,684,512. Registered Users: 12,819,803. Monthly visitors 78 million

Social Networks

Email's Beginning

1962- Following Cuban missile crisis, the Pentagon initiated a program to design a network whose aim was to withstand a nuclear attack.

1965 The Massachusetts Institute of Technology (MIT) was the first to demonstrate the use of the initial email system, known as MAILBOX. This system was used to send messages to different users on the same computer.

1969 This network came to be known as the Advanced Research Projects Agency Network or ARPANET, after the program's completion

1971 Ray Tomlinson, formerly MIT, created the first email app when he patched a program called CPYNET to the existing SNDMSG. Ray's first message was "QWERTYUIOP" - the keys on the first row of a keyboard. The first mesage was sent between two computer kept next to it. He chose @ symbol to provide an addressing standard which is still in use. He is called the father of email for its invention.

1977 Ray Tomlinson sent the first network email on ARPANET. 1971 The first email sent between two computers.

1978 The first Bulletin Board Systems (BBS) exchanged data over phone lines;

the first copies of early Web browser distributed through USENET and early online Bulletin Board

1994 On of the Web's first social networking sites, GEOCITES, was founded - for users to create their own websites.

1995 Theglobe.com gave users the freedom to personalise their online experiences by publishing their own content and interacting with others with same interests.

1997 AOL instant messenger laun-ched. sixdegrees.com launched

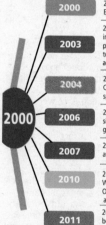

2000	2000 Microsoft introduces Entourage Mail for Mac.
2003	2003 Microsoft Outlook 2003 includes junk mail and anti-phishing filters and the ability to receive mail from multiple accounts.
2004	2004 The US Federal Trade Commission codifies email spam laws.
2006	2006 Social networking site Facebook opens to the general public.
2007	2007 Google makes Gmail available to public worldwide.
2010	2010 Outlook Mobile on Windows Phone 7 and Outlook for Mac 2011 are released.
2011	2011 Associated Press Stylebook changes "e-mail" to "email"

2011 Google + introduced with just 4 silos - Home, Photos, Circles, Sparks and Hangouts

AVERAGE SOCIAL NETWORK SEARCH INTEREST

E-Governance : An Indian Perspective

Dr. Santhosh Babu, IAS
Secretary to Government, Information Technology Department, Govt. of Tamil Nadu

Governance in India is to witness a sea change with the introduction of e-governance. It can transform the way in which interaction happens between the government and the citizen as also within the Government. It is a new experience that promises a lot to the average Indian who has been harassed for government service for generations.

What does a citizen in need of a nativity certificate do? He writes down his request on paper, takes a bus or auto, reaches the taluk office, waits there to present his application, and is told to come again after 15 days. His application is converted into a file, and the paper is sent to the Village Administrative Officer, who does a field inspection and sends his recommendation for issue or rejection of the certificate to the Revenue Inspector, who endorses the recommendation and sends the paper to the tahsildar, who then issues the certificate by putting in a series of stamps as proof of authenticity and authority. The Citizen would have, in the meantime visited the taluk office many times, to be told to come on a particular day, which again gets postponed. May be, he would by now have paid a transaction cost, a euphemism for a bribe, and then would have received the certificate. Calculate the man-hours lost to him, the transaction costs, the many trips up and down the hierarchy, and one realizes that this is the way millions of our countrymen are harassed for government

service, which is the fundamental duty of government to give and the right of the citizen to receive.

In the above interaction between the Citizen and the Government machinery, among other things three issues crop up: Firstly, for accessing any Government service, a Government office has to be visited and the request has to be given on paper. Secondly, transactions within the Government involve huge paperwork. Thirdly, the procedures adopted by the Government are cumbersome and not in tune with the changing times. This is where e-Government, a tool and its product, e-Governance, can profoundly transform the way in which interaction happens between the government and the citizen, as also the interactions within the Government. Thus, it is not just about improving delivery of services to citizens, businesses and employees; it is also about reengineering Government processes, making it more efficient, driving down costs and increasing transparency in how Government departments function. This will ultimately enable the transition of our Nation to the status of a developed nation and our society to an empowered society.

E-governance in India

While the private sector in India has adopted global best practices in corporate governance, the governance structure of the Government sector in India still remains as it was decades ago. Apart from computers being used for typing and email purposes, and many departments providing online services, a totally modern style of governance still remains elusive, as we have not gone the whole hog, happy as we have been in bringing in incremental advances. Any government office in India evokes the following feelings: place littered with files and papers, corruption, offensive, unhelpful, and de-motivated staff. The file and the 'red tape' have come to symbolize governance and the speed with which files are processed determines the speed and efficiency of governance. The file is at the heart of every government office in India, as all of them work as per the Tottenham system of administration evolved during the British times.

E-governance in India has however over the decades steadily evolved from mere computerization of Government departments to initiatives that encapsulate the finer points of governance, such as citizen-centricity, service-orientation and transparency. Initial attempts towards implementation of e-governance was with a focus on networking Government departments and developing in-house Government applications in the areas of defense, economic monitoring, planning and the deployment of Information Technology (IT) to manage data-intensive functions related to elections, census, tax administration etc. These applications during the 1970s , 1980s and early 1990s focused on the automation of internal Government functions rather than on improving citizen service delivery. The efforts of the National Informatics Centre (NIC) to connect all the district headquarters during the eighties was a very significant development. From the early nineties, IT technologies were supplemented by Information and Communication Technologies (ICT) to extend its use for wider applications in various sectors and with policy emphasis on reaching out to rural areas.

State Governments have also endeavoured to use ICT for establishing con-

> Any government office in India evokes the following feelings: place littered with files and papers, corruption, offensive, unhelpful, and de-motivated staff

nectivity, networking, setting up systems for processing information and delivering services. At a micro level this has ranged from IT automation in individual departments, electronic file handling and workflow systems, access to entitlements, public grievance systems, service delivery for high volume routine transactions such as payment of bills and taxes, to meeting poverty alleviations goals through the promotion of entrepreneurial models and provision of market information. Lessons from previous e-governance initiatives have played an important role in shaping the progressive e-governance strategy of the country. Due cognizance has been taken of the notion that to speed up e-governance implementation across the various arms of the gov-

Heart Surgery on a Dog	In 1914, at the convention of American Surgical Association, Dr. Alexis Carrel announced that he had successfully performed experimental heart surgery on a dog. He won a Nobel Prize in 1912. Heart surgery on humans began some years later.

ernment at the national, state, and local levels, a systematic approach needs to be adopted, guided by a common vision and strategy. This approach has the potential of enabling huge savings in costs through sharing of core and support infrastructure, enabling interoperability through standards, and of presenting a seamless view of government to citizens.

The National e-Governance Plan (NeGP), takes a holistic view of e-governance initiatives across the country, integrating them into a collective vision. Around this idea, a massive countrywide infrastructure reaching down to the remotest of villages is evolving, and large-scale digitization of records is taking place to enable easy, reliable access over the internet. The ultimate objective is to bring public services closer to home for the citizens, as articulated in the vision statement of NeGP. The NeGP

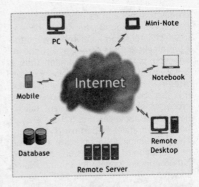

> A massive countrywide infrastructure reaching down to the remotest of villages is evolving, and large-scale digitization of records is taking place to enable easy, reliable access over the internet

seeks to create the right governance and institutional mechanisms, set up the core infrastructure and policies and implement a number of Mission Mode Projects (MMPs) at the centre, state and integrated service levels to create a citizen-centric and business-centric environment for governance.

The Framework

The framework for e-governance comprises:

Front-end delivery channels for citizens and business (State Portal, National Portal, mobile phones, home PCs, Browsing centres, integrated Common Service Centres)

Middleware (communication and secu-

rity infrastructure, gateways and integrated services facilitating integration of inter-departmental services, Data Centres)

Backend (databases of the different government agencies, service providers, state governments etc)

The Frontend

In the government there are numerous websites that provide a huge amount of information. In many of these sites there are hyperlinks for downloading application forms. But then a printout of the application form has to be taken and the same has to be sent by post, not necessarily increasing efficiency. Hence the government of India and the state governments under the NeGP has implemented the concept of a State and National portal, which means there will be just one Uniform Resource Locator (URL) that the citizen will have to remember for example HYPERLINK "http://www.tn.gov.in/"www.tn.gov.in for logging on to the Tamil Nadu state portal, or HYPERLINK "http://www.gujarat.gov.in/"www.gujarat.gov.in for logging on to the Gujarat state portal, and so on. The citizen can access information and transactional services using the State and National Portals, which will enable the citizen to apply for a service through e-forms, which can be submitted electronically along with attachments like ration card, ID card etc. The citizen will be guided through a State

| Vitamins in Foods | The presence of vitamins in foods was discovered only in 1912, though citrus fruits were known to prevent scurvy. |

Service Delivery Gateway (SSDG) to the backend application of the Government office dealing with that particular service. The service for which the request has been placed will be provided in the reverse direction, back to the citizen. The citizen will be able to access a digitally signed document. The SSDG acts as a standards based messaging switch, providing seamless interoperability and exchange of data across Government departments. SSDG acting as a nerve centre would handle large number of transactions and would help in tracking and time stamping all transactions of the Government.

The Common Service Centre (CSC) has been envisaged by the NEGP to be a 200 sqft room equipped with computers, accessories and connected to the internet, at the rate of one CSC per 6 revenue villages in the rural areas. The CSCs would provide high quality and cost-effective video, voice and data content and services in the areas of e-governance, education, health, telemedicine, entertainment as well as other private services. A highlight of the CSCs is that it will offer web-enabled e-governance services in rural areas, including application forms, certificates, and utility payments such as electricity, telephone and water bills. The scheme creates a conducive environment for the private sector and the NGOs to play an active role in implementation of the CSC Scheme, thereby becoming a partner of the government in the development of rural India. The public private partnership (PPP) model of the CSC scheme envisages a 3-tier structure consisting of the CSC operator (called Village Level Entrepreneur or VLE), the Service Centre Agency (SCA) that will be responsible for a about 500-1000 CSCs and a State Designated Agency (SDA) identified by the state government, responsible for managing implementation over the entire state.

Middleware

The State Data Centre (SDC) has been identified as one of the important elements of the core infrastructure for supporting e-governance initiatives of the National e-Governance Plan (NeGP). State Data Centres are being set up by the states to consolidate services, applications and infrastructure to provide efficient electronic delivery of G2G, G2C and G2B services. These services can be rendered by the states through common delivery platform seamlessly supported by core infrastructure for connectivity such as State Wide Area Network (SWAN) and Common Service Centre (CSC). The State Data Centre would provide many functionalities and some of the key functionalities are to function as the central repository of the state, as a Secure Data Storage, Online Delivery of Services, Citizen Information/Services Portal, State Intranet Portal, Disaster Recovery, Remote Management and Service Integration etc. SDCs would also provide better operation & management control and minimize overall cost of data management, IT resource management, deployment and other costs. Cloud computing is yet to be explored by Government agencies as a means towards reducing the costs of creating one's own data centre and subsequent issues of maintenance and sustainability.

SWAN or State Wide Area Network is an advanced telecommunication infrastructure, which is used extensively for the exchange of data and other types of information between two or more locations, separated by significant geographical distances. The medium of connectivity can be copper, optical fibre cable or wireless, as

The Coulomb	Originally, the basic unit of quantity in electricity was the coulomb. A coulomb is equal to the passage of 6.25 x 1018 electrons past a given point in an electrical system.

may be found feasible. Such wide area networks, in a way, create a highway for electronic transfer of information in the form of voice, video and data. Department of IT in Government of India is implementing the State Wide Area Network (SWAN) Scheme, envisaged to create such a connectivity in each States / union territory, to bring speed, efficiency, reliability and accountability in the overall system of Government-to-Government (G2G) functioning. In many of the states, SWAN works as a converged backbone network for voice, video and data communications. When fully implemented, SWANs across the country are expected to cover at least 50000 departmental offices through 1 million (10 lakh) route kilometres of communication links. Many states

> SWAN works as a converged backbone network for voice, video and data communications

have gone beyond the SWAN and have established horizontal connectivity to the last mile offices like Village Offices, Primary Health Centres (PHCs), Employment Exchanges etc.

The Backend

Efficient design and development of the application software for the backend is really the key to any successful e-governance initiative. Before developing an application, it is essential that a proper study of the prevailing system in the department or office be done in the form of an "As is" study, followed by a "GPR (Government Process Reengineering)" study and a "to be" study, before embarking on software development. Once the study is done and is approved by the department e-Team and the software developer, the application development can begin by following the "Software Development Lifecycle" approach.

Cloud computing and e-Governance

While e-governance has transformed the way services are provided to the citizens and brought in transparency in the government, Cloud computing is steadily yet rapidly revolutionizing the way e-governance is perceived and experienced currently. e-governance applications can assume unlimited supply of the Central Processing Unit (CPU), storage and bandwidth when operating from a Cloud. Infrastructure as a Service (IaaS) virtualizes the hardware, network and storage aspects of the data centre. Cloud offers standard Platform as a Service (PaaS) in terms of providing different kinds of systems, middleware and integration systems. And finally the Cloud offers Software as a Service (SaaS). Imagine a case of new district deciding to move to e-governance solution for some application for their citizens. The district need not purchase applications, hardware and software. They can make a request for a particular service from the Cloud provider. Instances of the required application can then be created for their use. Numerous

applications can be provided as standard services, which the departments can request for and utilise effectively.

Impacts of e-Governance

E-governance brings about two major impacts: Firstly, making the government offices work smart. Many government agencies have adopted the concept of the

| Slug & Poundal | The foot / pound / second system of reckoning includes slug and poundal. Slug is mass to which a force of 1 poundal will give an acceleration of 1 foot per second (32.17 lb). Poundal is the fundamental unit of force. |

"paperless, anytime, anywhere office" that enables files to be cleared from anywhere in the world using an Enterprise Resource Planning (ERP) based approach (examples: office of the Cabinet Secretariat, the Commerce Ministry in the Government of India, and ELCOT & TNeGA offices in Tamil Nadu). Rapid file movements within the government can enable faster service delivery to the citizen. Secondly, e-governance makes services available to the citizen at his doorstep through the internet, for instance, through the e-District project in Krishnagiri District of Tamil Nadu, citizens can apply for ten certificates from the confines of their home, browsing centre or Common Service Centre, and get a digitally signed certificate without ever visiting a Government office. These should really become the norm rather than champion driven initiatives that rarely survive once the champion moves out. Enabling orders in Government have to be concomitantly issued for making the process change legally tenable. Some of the most successful Citizen oriented e-governance projects are the Railway reservation system, MCA21 in the Ministry of Corporate Affairs, Bhoomi project in Andhra Pradesh, Akshya project in Kerala to name a few.

Challenges

The architecture and technology for e-governance initiatives should be scaleable to deal with massive amount of data over the years. Technology migration is one of the biggest challenges in e-governance application development. Moving to differ-ent versions of software and applying application and security patches is currently the key to maintaining secure data centre for e-governance. With the increasing use of Information Technology, functions in the government are now dependant on a network of critical information infrastructure. As such, any disruption of operation of information systems of critical infrastructure will have a devastating effect on citizens, economy and government services. In view of the potential impact, protection of critical information infrastructure is essential to ensure that disruptions are of minimal duration, manageable and cause the least damage possible. Thus the security of electronic transactions and storage management becomes yet another challenge. The shift from a traditional form of governance to an electronic one is challenging with

> Shift from a traditional form of governance to an electronic one is challenging with great potential for change and at the same time fraught with serious consequences

great potential for change and at the same time fraught with serious consequences. The change should take place without disturbing the system, morale of the staff or attracting a backlash from entrenched interests. The changeover should be smooth and balanced.

The mantra for e-governance should be that e-governance should minimize citizen-government office interaction, and maximize citizen-government interaction, that is the *citizen should not see the government, rather they should be able to feel the government.* The day is not far off when the web will completely become the main interface for interaction between the citizen and government. ∎

| The Calories | Heat energy is also measured using the calorie (cal), which is the energy required to increase the temperature of 1 cubic centimeter (1 ml) of water by 1 degree C. |

Unraveling 2G & 3G

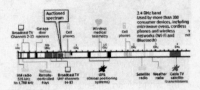

Almost all wireless technology, from cell phone to garage door openers, use radio waves to operate. Some services like TV and radio broadcasts, have exclusive use of their frequency within a geographic area. But many devices share frequencies, which can cause interference as in case of gadgets we use every day. In order to understand the technology we need to look closely at the electromagnetic spectrum, which is in fact a range of electric and magnetic waves of various wavelengths that travel at the speed of light. The spectrum comprise low frequencies, Radio frequency, Infrared, visible light, Ultraviolet, X-rays, Gamma rays and the High frequiencies. Radio waves form part of the electromagnetic spectrum range from 3kHz to 300 GHz. In India, the 2G scam centres around a small section of the radio frequency i.e., less than 2 GHz, which is basically used for Cell phone.

Frequencies are categorised as **permable range**, are considered more valuable because they can penetrate dense objects like a concrete building. Some of the examples of this category would be TV , wireless medical telemetry, Garage door, remote controlled toys, AM radio, GPS , etc. There is a **semi-permeable zone** and the frequencies can't penetrate dense objects. Its signal ranges between 2GHz and 5GHZ. Here we have consumer devices like microwave ovens, corldless phones, WiFi and Bluetooth. It is used by Satellite radio, Weather radar, Cable TV satellite transmission, etc. The third category is **Line-of-sight-zone** where signals travel long distances but could be blocked by trees and other objects. Much space in this category is reserved for military purpose, besides government needs and industrial purposes. It is used by Police radar, Satellite TV, security alarms.

2G was next technology to 1G. It used digital modulation for voice transmission instead of 1G which had analog modulation and had lower data rates for data transmission. In 2G, digital voice data can be compressed and multiplexed much more effectively than analog voice encodings through the use of various codecs, allowing more calls to be packed into the same amount of radio bandwidth.

The first major step in the evolution to 3G occurred with the introduction of General Packet Radio Service (GPRS). So the cellular services combined with GPRS became 2.5G. GPRS could provide data rates from 56 kbit/s up to 114 kbit/s. It can be used for services such as Wireless Application Protocol (WAP) access, Short Message Service (SMS), Multimedia Messaging Service (MMS), and for Internet communication services such as email and World Wide Web access. GPRS data transfer is typically charged per megabyte of traffic transferred, while data communication via traditional circuit switching is billed per minute of connection time, independent of whether the user actually is utilizing the capacity or is in an idle state.

Java Platform	**Java ME (which stands for micro-edition) still maintains the number one spot as the most popular platform for mobile browsing. This platform is in use on a large variety of devices and is rapidly losing share to both Android and the iPhone.**

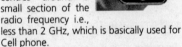

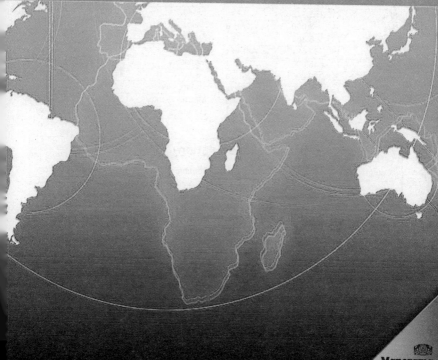

Part 9

World Panorama

Pages 289 - 446

The Biggest and The Smallest States

The Biggest

In Area

State	Area (Sq km)	Location
Russia	17,075,000	Europe-Asia
Canada	9,976,139	N. America
China	9,561,000	Asia
U.S.A.	9,372,614	N. America
Brazil	8,511,965	S. America
Australia	7,682,300	S. Pacific
India	3,287,263	Asia
Argentina	2,776,654	S. America
Kazakhstan	2,717,300	Asia
Algeria	2,381,741	Africa

In Population

State	Population	Location
China	1,341,000,000	Asia
India	1,210,193,422	Asia
USA	311,097,000	N. America
Indonesia	237,556,363	Asia
Brazil	190,732,694	S. America
Pakistan	175,646,600	Asia
Nigeria	158,259,000	Africa
Bangladesh	150,319,000	Asia
Russia	142,905,200	Europe-Asia
Japan	127,960,000	Asia

The Smallest

In Area

State	Area (sq km)	Location
Vatican City	0.44	Europe
Monaco	1.95	Europe
Nauru	21.10	S. Pacific
Tuvalu	26.00	S. Pacific
San Marino	61.00	Europe
Liechtenstein	160.00	Europe
Marshall Islands	181.00	C. Pacific
St.Kitts-Nevis	269.00	E.Caribbean
Maldives	298.00	Indian Ocean
Seychelles	308.00	indian ocean

In Population

State	Population	Location
Vatican City	800	Europe
Tuvalu	10,000	S. Pacific
Nauru	10,000	S. Pacific
Palau	21,000	W.Pacific
San Marino	31,887	Europe
Monaco	33,000	Europe
Liechtenstein	36,157	Europe
St. Kitts-Nevis	52,000	E.Caribbean
Marshal Islands	54,305	N. Pacific Ocean
Dominica	67,000	E.Caribbean

World Population-2010

Continents	Population	Continents	Population
Asia	4,164,252,000	Australia/Oceania	36,593,000
Africa	1,022,234,000	Antarctica	0
Europe	738,199,000	World	6,895,889,000
North America	542,056,000		
South America	392,555,000	Total	6,895,889,000

Biggest Country in Africa

Algeria is the biggest country in Africa, followed by Democratic Republic of Congo. Algeria became the continent's largest country after South Sudan seceded from Sudan on 9 July 2011.

Biggest Economies 2010

Rank	Country	GDP (Millions of US $)
1	United States	14,657,800
2	People's Republic of China	5,878,257
3	Japan	5,458,872
4	Germany	3,315,643
5	France	2,582,527
6	United Kingdom	2,247,455
7	Brazil	2,090,314
8	Italy	2,055,114
9	Canada	1,574,051
10	India	1,537,966
	World	62,909,274

Source: International Monetary Fund

Highest External Debt

	Feb. 2011
1. The United States of America	$14.393 trillion
2. The United Kingdom	$9.088 trillion
3. Germany	$5.028 trillion
4. France	$5.021 trillion
5. The Netherlands	$3.733 trillion
6. Spain	$2.410 trillion
7. Italy	$2.328 trillion.
8. Ireland	$2.287 trillion
9. Japan	$2.132 trillion
10. Luxembourg	$1.994 trillion

Source: World Bank

Top Recipients of Remittances 2010

India	$55 billion
China	$51 billion
Philippines	$21.3 billion
Mexico	$22.6 billion
Poland	$9.1 billion
Bangladesh	$11.1 billion
Nigeria	$10 billion
Pakistan	$9 4 billion
Morocco	$6.4 billion
Vietnam	$7.2 billion

Source: World Bank

Top Remittance– Sending Countries, 2009

	Billions of US$
United States	48.3
Saudi Arabia	26.0
Switzerland	19.6
Russian Federation	18.6
Germany	15.9
Italy	13.0
Spain	12.6
Luxembourg	10.6
Kuwait	9.9
Netherlands	8.1

Source: Development Prospects Group, World Bank

Largest Oil Reserves

Country	Proven Reserves of Oil (Billion barrels)
1. Saudi Arabia	264.5
2. Venezuela	211.2
3. Iran	137
4. Iraq	115
5. Kuwait	101.5
6. United Arab Emirates	97.8
7. Russia	77.4
8. Libya	46.4
9. Kazakhstan	39.8
10. Nigeria	37.2
World:	1526.1

Source: Statistical Review of World Energy, BP

World Official Gold Holding

(December 2010

Rank	Country/Organization	Gold(Tonnes)
1	USA	8,133.5
2	Germany	3,401.8
3	IMF	2,846.7 -
4	Italy	2,451.8
5	France	2,435.4
6	China	1,054.1
7	Switzerland	1,040.1
8	Russia	775.2

Most Densely Populated Country

The most densely populated sovereign nation is Monaco, with a population density of 16,754 people/sq.km. However, Macau in China has a population density of 18,534 people/ sq.km

9	Japan	765.2
10	Netherlands	675
11	India	614.8

Source: World Gold Council

Top Destination Countries for Refugees

	Number of Migrants (Millions)
Jordan	2.5
Pakistan	2.1
West Bank and Gaza	1.9
Syrian Arab Republic	1.6
Iran, Islamic Rep.	1.0
Germany	0.6
United States	0.6
Lebanon	0.5
Tanzania	0.5
China	0.3

Source: United Nations Population Division.

Most Visited Countries in the World 2010

Rank	Country	Visitors (Millions)
1.	France	76.8
2.	USA	59.7
3.	China	55.7
4.	Spain	52.7
5.	Italy	43.6
6.	UK	28.1
7.	Turkey	27.0
8.	Germany	26.9
9.	Malaysia	24.6
10.	Mexico	22.4
	World	940

Source : United Nations World Tourism Organization

Top Immigration Countries

	Number of Immigrants Millions
United States	42.8

Russian Federation	12.3
Germany	10.8
Saudi Arabia	7.3
Canada	7.2
United Kingdom	7.0
Spain	6.9
France	6.7
Australia	5.5
India 5.4	

Sources: Development Prospects Group, World Bank: UNPD 2009

Top Emigration Countries

	Number of Emigrants Millions
Mexico	11.9
India	11.4
Russian Federation	11.1
China	8.3
Ukraine	6.6
Bangladesh	5.4
Pakistan	4.7
United Kingdom	4.7
Philippines	4.3
Turkey	4.3

Sources: Development Prospects Group, World Bank: UNPD 2009

Top Emigration Countries of Physicians

	Thousands
India	20.3
United Kingdom	12.2
Philippines	9.8
Germany	8.8
Italy	5.8
Mexico	6.5
Spain	5.0
South Africa	4.4
Pakistan	4.4
Iran, Islamic Rep.	4.4

Source: Bhargava, Docquier, and Moullan 2010

Tiny Maldives   **The smallest country in Asia in both area and population is the Maldives.**

Nations : a Ready Reckoner

UN Members (193)*

	Country	Region	Capital	Currency
1.	Afghanistan	S.C. Asia	Kabul	Afghani
2.	Albania	S. Europe	Tirana	Lek
3.	Algeria	N. Africa	Algiers	Algerian Dinar
4.	Andorra	S. Europe	Andorra la Vella	Euro
5.	Angola	M. Africa	Luanda	readjusted Kwanza
6.	Antigua and Barbuda	Caribbean	St.John's	Eastern Caribbean Dollar
7.	Argentina	S. America	Buenos Aires	Peso
8.	Armenia	W. Asia	Yerevan	Dram
9.	Australia	Oceania	Canberra	Australian Dollar
10.	Austria	W. Europe	Vienna	Euro
11.	Azerbaijan	W. Asia	Baku	Manat
12.	Bahamas, The	Caribbean	Nassau	Bahamian dollar
13.	Bahrain	W. Asia	Manama	Bahraini Dinar
14.	Bangladesh	S.C.Asia	Dhaka	Taka
15.	Barbados	Caribbean	Bridgetown	Barbados dollar
16.	Belarus	E. Europe	Minsk	Rouble
17.	Belgium	W. Europe	Brussels	Euro
18.	Belize	C. America	Belmopan	Belize dollar
19.	Benin	W. Africa	Porto-Novo	Franc CFA
20.	Bhutan	S.C Asia	Thimphu	Ngultrum
21.	Bolivia	S. America	Sucre	Boliviano
22.	Bosnia Herzegovina	S. Europe	Sarajevo	Marka
23.	Botswana	S. Africa	Gaborone	Pula
24.	Brazil	S. America	Brasilia (Federal)	Real
25.	Brunei	S.E. Asia	Bandar Seri Begawan	Brunei dollar
26.	Bulgaria	E. Europe	Sofia	Lev
27.	Burkina Faso	W. Africa	Ouagadougou	Franc CFA
28.	Burundi	E. Africa	Bujumbura	Burundi Franc
29.	Cambodia	S.E. Asia	Phnom Penh	Riel
30.	Cameroon	M. Africa	Yaounde	Franc CFA
31.	Canada	N. America	Ottawa	Canadian dollar
32.	Cape Verde	W. Africa	Praia	Cape Verde Escudo
33.	Central African Republic	M. Africa	Bangui	Franc CFA
34.	Chad	M. Africa	N'Djamena	Franc CFA
35.	Chile	S. America	Santiago (Adm)	Peso
			Valparaiso (Leg)	Chilean peso

* South Sudan was admitted as the newest UN member on 14th July 2011. The new country is featured on page no. 428.

36.	China	E. Asia	Beijing	Renmminbi Yuan
37.	Colombia	S. America	Bogota	Colombian Peso
38.	Comoros, The	E. Africa	Moroni	Comorian Franc
39.	Congo (formerly Zaire)	M. Africa	Kinshasa	Congo Franc
40.	Congo	M. Africa	Brazzaville	Franc CFA
41.	Costa Rica -	C. America	San Jose	Costa Rican Colon
42.	Cote D' Ivoire	W. Africa	Yamoussoukro	Franc CFA (XOF)
43.	Croatia	S. Europe	Zagreb	Kuna
44.	Cuba	Caribbean	Havana	Cuban peso
45.	Cyprus	W. Asia	Nicosia	Euro
46.	Czech Republic	E. Europe	Prague	Koruna
47.	Denmark	N. Europe	Copenhagen	Danish Krone
48.	Djibouti	E.Africa	Djibouti	Djibouti Franc
49.	Dominica	Caribbean	Roseau	East Carribbean Dollar
50.	Dominican Republic	Caribbean	Santo Domingo	Peso
51.	East Timor	S.E. Asia	Dili	US Dollar
52.	Ecuador	S. America	Quito	US Dollar
53.	Egypt	N. Africa	Cairo	Egyptian Pound
54.	El Salvador	C. America	San Salvador	Colon
55.	Equatorial Guinea	M. Africa	Malabo	Franc CFA (XAF)
56.	Eritrea	E. Africa	Asmara	Nakfa
57.	Estonia	N. Europe	Tallinn	Euro
58.	Ethiopia	E. Africa	Addis Ababa	Birr
59.	Fiji Islands	Oceania	Suva	Fiji Dollar
60.	Finland	N. Europe	Helsinki	Euro
61.	France	W. Europe	Paris	Euro
62.	Gabon	M. Africa	Libreville	Franc CFA
63.	Gambia, The	W. Africa	Banjul	Dalasi
64.	Georgia	W. Asia	Tbilisi	Lari
65.	Germany	W. Europe	Berlin	Euro
66.	Ghana	W. Africa	Accra	Cedi
67.	Greece	S. Europe	Athens	Euro
68.	Grenada	Caribbean	St. George's	Eastern Carribbean Dollar
69.	Guatemala	C. America	Guatemala City	Quetzal
70.	Guinea	W. Africa	Conakry	Guinean Franc
71.	Guinea-Bissau	W. Africa	Bissau	Franc CFA
72.	Guyana	S. America	Georgetown	Guyana Dollar
73.	Haiti	Caribbean	Port-au-Prince	Gourde
74.	Honduras	C. America	Tegucigalpa	Lempira
75.	Hungary	E. Europe	Budapest	Forint
76.	Iceland	N. Europe	Reykjavik	Krona
77.	India	S.C. Asia	New Delhi	Rupee

78.	Indonesia	S.E.Asia	Jakarta	Rupiah
79.	Iran	S.C. Asia	Tehran	Rial
80.	Iraq	W. Asia	Baghdad	Iraqi Dinar
81.	Ireland	N. Europe	Dublin	Euro
82.	Israel	W. Asia	Jerusalem	Shekel
83.	Italy	S. Europe	Rome	Euro
84.	Jamaica	Caribbean	Kingston	Jamaican Dollar
85.	Japan	E. Asia	Tokyo	Yen
86.	Jordan	W. Asia	Amman	Jordan Dinar
87.	Kazakhstan	S.C. Asia	Astana	Tenge
88.	Kenya	E. Africa	Nairobi	Shilling
89.	Kiribati	Oceania	Bairiki (Tarawa)	Australian Dollar
90.	Korea, North	E. Asia	Pyongyang	Won
91.	Korea, South	E. Asia	Seoul	Won
92.	Kuwait	W. Asia	Kuwait	Kuwaiti Dinar
93.	Kyrgyzstan	S.C. Asia	Bishkek	Som
94.	Laos	S.E. Asia	Vientiane	Kip
95.	Latvia	N. Europe	Riga	Lats
96.	Lebanon	W. Asia	Beirut	Lebanese Pound
97.	Lesotho	S. Africa	Maseru	Loti
98.	Liberia	W. Africa	Monrovia	Liberian Dollar
99.	Libya	N. Africa	Tripoli	Libyan Dinar
100.	Liechtenstein	W. Europe	Vaduz	Swiss Franc
101.	Lithuania	N. Europe	Vilnius	Litas
102.	Luxembourg	W. Europe	Luxembourg	Euro
103.	Macedonia	S. Europe	Skopje	Denar
104.	Madagascar	E. Africa	Antananarivo	Ariary
105.	Malawi	E. Africa	Lilongwe	Kwacha
106.	Malaysia	S.E. Asia	Putrajaya (Adm) Kuala Lumpur (Fin.)	Ringgit
107.	Maldives	S.C. Asia	Male	Rufiyaa
108.	Mali	W. Africa	Bamako	Franc CFA
109.	Malta	S. Europe	Valletta	Euro
110.	Marshall Islands	Oceania	Majuro Atoll	US Currency
111.	Mauritania	W. Africa	Nouakchott	Ouguiya
112.	Mauritius	E. Africa	Port Louis	Mauritius Rupee
113.	Mexico	C. America	Mexico City	Mexican Peso
114.	Micronesia	Oceania	Palikir	US Currency
115.	Moldova	E. Europe	Chisinau	Leu
116.	Monaco	W. Europe	Monaco	Euro
117.	Mongolia	E. Asia	Ulan Bator	Tugrik
118.	Montenegro	S.E. Europe	Podgorica	Euro
119.	Morocco	N. Africa	Rabat	Dirham

120.	Mozambique	E. Africa	Maputo	Metical
121.	Myanmar	S.E. Asia	Yangon (Rangoon)	Kyat
122.	Namibia	S. Africa	Windhoek	Namibia Dollar
123.	Nauru	Oceania	Yaren	Australian Dollar
124.	Nepal	S.C. Asia	Kathmandu	Nepalese Rupee
125.	Netherlands, The	W. Europe	Amsterdam	Euro
126.	New Zealand	Oceania	Wellington	New Zealand Dollar
127.	Nicaragua	C. America	Managua	Cordobas
128.	Niger	W. Africa	Niamey	Franc CFA
129.	Nigeria	W. Africa	Abuja	Naira
130.	Norway	N. Europe	Oslo	Norwegian Krone
131.	Oman	W. Asia	Muscat	Rial Omani
132.	Pakistan	S.C. Asia	Islamabad	Pakistan Rupee
133.	Palau	Oceania	Melekeok	US currency
134.	Panama	C. America	Panama City	Balboa
135.	Papua New Guinea	Oceania	Port Moresby	Kina
136.	Paraguay	S. America	Asuncion	Guarani
137.	Peru	S. America	Lima	Nuevo Sol
138.	Philippines, The	S.E. Asia	Manila	Peso
139.	Poland	E. Europe	Warsaw	Zloty
140.	Portugal	S. Europe	Lisbon	Euro
141.	Qatar	W. Asia	Doha	Riyal
142.	Romania	E. Europe	Bucharest	Leu
143.	Russia	E. Europe	Moscow	Rouble
144.	Rwanda	E. Africa	Kigali	Rwanda Franc
145.	Samoa	Oceania	Apia	Tala
146.	San Marino	S. Europe	San Marino	Euro
147.	Sao Tome & Principe	M. Africa	Sao Tome	Dobra
148.	Saudi Arabia	W. Asia	Riyadh	Rial
149.	Senegal	W. Africa	Dakar	Franc CFA
150.	Serbia	S. Europe	Belgrade	Dinar
151.	Seychelles	E. Africa	Victoria	Seychelles Rupee
152.	Sierra Leone	W. Africa	Freetown	Leone
153.	Singapore	S.E. Asia	Singapore City	Singapore Dollar
154.	Slovakia	E. Europe	Bratislava	Euro
155.	Slovenia	S. Europe	Ljubljana	Euro
156.	Solomon Islands	Oceania	Honiara	Solomon Island Dollar
157.	Somalia	E. Africa	Mogadishu	Somali Shilling
158.	South Africa	S. Africa	Pretoria (Adm.) Cape Town (Leg.) Bloemfontein (Jud.)	Rand
159.	Spain	S. Europe	Madrid	Euro
160.	Sri Lanka	S.C. Asia	Colombo	Sri Lankan Rupee
161.	St. Kitts and Nevis	Caribbean	Basseterre	Carribbean dollar

162. St. Lucia	Caribbean	Castries	Carribean Dollar
163. St. Vincent and the Grenadines	Caribbean	Kingstown	East Caribbean Dollar
164. Sudan	N. Africa	Khartoum	Sudanese Pound
165. Suriname	S. America	Paramaribo	Suriname Dollar
166. Swaziland	S. Africa	Mbabane	Lilangeni
167. Sweden	N. Europe	Stockholm	Krona
168. Switzerland	W. Europe	Berne	Swiss Franc
169. Syria	W. Asia	Damascus	Syrian Pound
170. Tajikistan	S.C. Asia	Dushanbe	Somoni
171. Tanzania	E. Africa	Dodoma	Tanzanian Shilling
172. Thailand	S.E. Asia	Bangkok	Baht
173. Togo	W. Africa	Lome	Franc CFA
174. Tonga	Oceania	Nuku alofa	Paanga
175. Trinidad and Tobago	Caribbean	Port-of-Spain	Trinidad and Tobago Dollar
176. Tunisia	N. Africa	Tunis	Tunisian Dinar
177. Turkey	W. Asia	Ankara	Turkish Lira
178. Turkmenistan	S.C. Asia	Ashgabat	Manat
179. Tuvalu	Oceania	Fongafale(Funafuti)	Australian Dollar
180. Uganda	E. Africa	Kampala	Uganda Shilling
181. Ukraine	E. Europe	Kyiv	Hryvna
182. United Arab Emirates	W. Asia	Abu Dhabi	Dirham
183. United Kingdom	N. Europe	London	Pound Sterling
184. United States of America	N. America	Washington D.C.	Dollar
185. Uruguay	S. America	Montevideo	Uruguayan Peso
186. Uzbekistan	S.C. Asia	Tashkent	Som
187. Vanuatu	Oceania	Vila	Vatu
188. Venezuela	S. America	Caracas	Bolivar
189. Vietnam	S.E. Asia	Hanoi	Dong
190. Yemen	W. Asia	Sana'a	Riyal
191. Zambia	E. Africa	Lusaka	Kwacha
192. Zimbabwe	E. Africa	Harare	Zimbabwe Dollar
193. South Sudan	E. Africa	Juba	South Sudanese Pound

Non-UN Members

1.	Kosovo	Southeast Europe	Pristina	Euro
2.	Palestine*	W. Asia	Ramallah	New Shekel
3.	Sahrawi Arab Demo* Rep. (S.A.D.R.), Western Sahara	N. Africa	El-Aaiun	
4.	Turkish Cyprus	W. Asia	Nicosia	New Turkish Lira
5.	Taiwan	S. Asia	Taipei	New Taiwan Dollar
6.	Vatican City	S. Europe	Vatican City	Euro

S. Europe: Southern Europe; N. Europe: Northern Europe; E. Europe: Eastern Europe; W. Asia: Western Asia; E. Asia: Eastern Asia; S.E. Asia: South East Asia; S.C. Asia: South Central Asia; S. America: South America; N. America: North America; C. America: Central America; N.Africa: North Africa; E. Africa: East Africa; S. Africa:South Africa; M. Africa: Middle Africa.

Countries Listed By Continent

NOTE: Only UN member states are listed. In this list, countries are classified according to political criteria, using the geoscheme created by the United Nations Statistics Division.

AFRICA (54)

Algeria
Angola
Benin
Botswana
Burkina Faso
Burundi
Cameroon
Cape Verde
Central African Republic
Chad
Comoros
Congo (Dem. Rep.)
Congo, Republic of
Djibouti
Egypt
Equatorial Guinea
Eritrea
Ethiopia
Gabon
Gambia
Ghana
Guinea
Guinea-Bissau
Ivory Coast
Kenya
Lesotho
Liberia
Libya
Madagascar
Malawi
Mali
Mauritania
Mauritius
Morocco
Mozambique
Namibia
Niger
Nigeria
Rwanda
Sao Tome and Principe
Senegal
Seychelles
Sierra Leone
Somalia
South Africa
South Sudan
Sudan
Swaziland
Tanzania
Togo
Tunisia
Uganda
Zambia
Zimbabwe

ASIA (47)

Afghanistan
Armenia
Azerbaijan
Bahrain
Bangladesh
Bhutan
Brunei
Cambodia
China
Cyprus
East Timor
Georgia
India
Indonesia
Iran
Iraq
Israel
Japan
Jordan
Kazakhstan
Korea (north)
Korea (south)
Kuwait
Kyrgyzstan
Laos
Lebanon
Malaysia
Maldives
Mongolia
Myanmar
Nepal
Oman
Pakistan
Philippines
Qatar
Saudi Arabia
Singapore
Sri Lanka
Syria
Tajikistan
Thailand
Turkey
Turkmenistan
United Arab Emirates
Uzbekistan
Vietnam
Yemen

EUROPE (43)

Albania
Andorra
Austria
Belarus
Belgium
Bosnia and Herzegovina
Bulgaria
Croatia
Czech Republic
Denmark
Estonia
Finland
France
Germany
Greece
Hungary
Iceland
Ireland
Italy
Latvia
Liechtenstein
Lithuania
Luxembourg
Macedonia
Malta
Moldova
Monaco
Montenegro
Netherlands
Norway
Poland
Portugal
Romania
Russian Federation
San Marino
Serbia
Slovakia
Slovenia
Spain
Sweden
Switzerland
Ukraine
United Kingdom
Vatican City

N. AMERICA (23)

Antigua and Barbuda
Bahamas
Barbados
Belize
Canada
Costa Rica
Cuba
Dominica
Dominican Rep.
El Salvador
Grenada
Guatemala
Haiti
Honduras
Jamaica
Mexico
Nicaragua
Panama
St. Kitts & Nevis
St. Lucia
St. Vincent & the Grenadines
Trinidad & Tobago
United States

OCEANIA (14)

Australia
Fiji
Kiribati
Marshall Islands
Micronesia
Nauru
New Zealand
Palau
Papua New Guinea
Samoa
Solomon Islands
Tonga
Tuvalu
Vanuatu

S. AMERICA (12)

Argentina
Bolivia
Brazil
Chile
Colombia
Ecuador
Guyana
Paraguay
Peru
Suriname
Uruguay
Venezuela

The World Today

UN Members (193)

Note: Per capita income (p.c.i.) denotes GNI per capita as measured on purchasing power parity (PPP) dollars by IMF for the year 2010. HDI Rank denotes human development index rank as per UNDP Human Development Report 2010. For population, literacy and life expectancy, UN sources are used.

1. Afghanistan

Islamic State of Afghanistan

Capital: Kabul; **Other Large Cities:** Kandahar, Herat, Mazare-Sharif; **Currency:** Afghani; **Area:** 647,497 sq.km; **Population:** 29,117,000; **Languages:** Pushtu and Persian; **Religions:** Sunni Muslim-80%, Shia Muslim-19%; **Literacy:** 28%; **Life Expectancy:** 43.8; **p.c.i:** $ 998; **HDI rank:** 155; **Date of Independence:** 19th August 1919.

Government Type: Islamic Republic; **President:** Hamid Karzai.

History: Ahmad Shah Durranl unified the Pashtun tribes and founded Afghanistan in 1747. The country won independence from notional British control in 1919. A brief experiment in democracy ended in a 1973 coup and a 1978 Communist counter-coup. The Soviet Union invaded in 1979 to support the tottering Afghan Communist regime, touching off a long and destructive war.

The USSR withdrew in 1989 under relentless pressure by internationally supported anti-Communist mujahedin rebels. A series of subsequent civil wars saw Kabul finally fall in 1996 to the Taliban, a hardline Pakistani-sponsored movement that emerged in 1994 to end the country's civil war and anarchy. Following the 11 September 2001 terrorist attacks in the U.S., Allied, and anti-Taliban Northern Alliance military action toppled the Taliban for sheltering Osama Bin Laden. The UN-sponsored Bonn Conference in 2001 established a process for political reconstruction that included the adoption of a new constitution, a presidential election in 2004, and National Assembly elections in 2005. In December 2004, Hamid Karzai became the first democratically elected president of Afghanistan and the National Assembly was inaugurated the following December. Karzai was re-elected in November 2009 for a second term.

Economy: The principal crop is wheat. Animal husbandry is important for meat, milk and wool. Chief mineral resource: natural gas. The main industrial activity is the manufacture of woollen and cotton textiles; traditional handicrafts and woven carpets are important exports. Afghanistan produces 3400 tonnes of opium worth ($1.2b.) a year.

Mission in India: Embassy of Afghanistan, 5/50F, Shantipath, Chanakyapuri, New Delhi–110021. Tel: 26883602, 24103331, 24100412; Гax: 26875439.

  E-mail: afghanembassy@rediffrnail.com

Indian Mission in Afghanistan (Temporarily closed): Embassy of India, Malalai Wat, Shahre-Nau, Kabul, Afghanistan.

Launch-pad for Attack

In 1939 Albania was invaded by Italy. Mussolini used Albania as the launch-pad for his attack on Greece in World War II.

Tel: 00-873-763095560; Fax : 00-873-763095561.

E-mail: embassy@indembassy-kabul.com

2. Albania

Republic of Albania
(Republika e Shqi-perise)

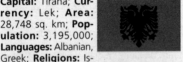

Capital: Tirana; **Currency:** Lek; **Area:** 28,748 sq. km; **Population:** 3,195,000; **Languages:** Albanian, Greek; **Religions:** Islam-70%, Christian-30%; **Literacy:** 99%; **Life Expectancy:** 76.4; **p.c.i.:** $ 7,381; **HDI rank:** 64; **Date of Independence:** 28th November, 1912.

Government Type: Parliamentary Democracy; **President:** Bamir Topi; **PM:** Sali Berisha.

History: Albania declared its independence from the Ottoman Empire in 1912, but was conquered by Italy in 1939. Communist partisans took over the country in 1944. Albania allied itself first with the USSR (until 1960), and then with China (to 1978). In the early 1990s, Albania ended 46 years of xenophobic Communist rule and established a multiparty democracy.

Economy: More than half of GDP comes from agriculture, though despite extensive terracing only around one-quarter of the country is suitable for arable farming. Important minerals: coal, oil, chrome, copper and nickel. Industries: textiles, woollen fabrics, leather goods, petrol, cement, sugar, beer and cigarettes.

Mission in India: Embassy of Albania stationed at Cairo.

3. Algeria

People's Democratic Republic of Algeria
(Al-3. Jumhuriya Al-Jaazairiya ad-Dimuqratiya ash-Shabiya)

Capital: Algiers; **Other Large Cities:** Oran, Constantine, Annaba; **Currency:** Algerian Dinar; **Area:** 2,381,741 sq.km; **Population:** 36,300,000; **Languages:** Arabic, Berber and French; **Religions:** Islam-99%; **Literacy:** 75.4%; **Life Expectancy:** 72.3; **p.c.i.:** $ 7,103; **HDI rank:** 84; **Date of Independence:** 5th July, 1962.

Government Type: Republic; **President:** Abdelaziz Bouteflika .

History: After more than a century of rule by France, Algerians fought through much of the 1950s to achieve independence in 1962. Algeria has recently emerged from a brutal conflict that followed scrapped elections in 1992. In the 1990s Algerian politics was dominated by the struggle involving the military and Islamist militants. In 1992 a general election won by an Islamist party was annulled, heralding a bloody civil war in which more than 150,000 people were slaughtered. An amnesty in 1999 led many

The Desert Desert | The Sahara Desert covers 80 per cent of Algeria. As Sahara is the Arabic for desert, it is technically called the Desert Desert.

rebels to lay down their arms.Violence has largely abated, although a state of emergency remains in place.

Economy: Agricultural products include wheat, barley, potatoes, artichokes, flax and tobacco. Fruits like dates, pomegranates and figs grow in abundance. Wine and olive oil are also produced. Chief occupation: cattle raising. Minerals: iron, zinc, mercury, copper, antimony, phosphates and petroleum. Industries: oil, light industry, food processing.

Mission in India: Embassy of the People's Democratic Republic of Algeria, E-6/5,Vasant Vihar,New Delhi-110057.Tel: 26146706, 26147036, 26147611; Fax: 26147033

E-mail: embalgindia@hotmail.com

Indian Mission in Algeria: Embassy of India, 14, Rue des Abassides, Post Box No. 108 El-Biar- 16030 Algiers, Algeria. Tel: 00-213-21–923288; Fax: 00-213-2-924011.

E-mail: indembalg@hotmail.com

4. Andorra

Principality of Andorra
(Principat d' Andorra)

Capital: Andorre-la-Vieille; **Currency:** Euro; **Area:** 464 sq.km; **Population:** 84,082; **Languages:** Catalan, French, Castilian; **Religions:**Christian-90%; **Literacy:** 100%; **Life Expectancy:** 82.51; **p.c.i:** $ 44,900; **HDI rank:** 30; **Date of Independence:** 1278 (was formed under the joined suzerainty of the French count of Foix and the Spanish bishop of Urgel).

Government Type: Parliamentary Democracy; **Head of State:** President of France and the Bishop of Urgel (Spain) as co-princes. **Head of govt:** Bartumeu Cassany.

History: The co-principality of Andorra, founded in 1278, lies in the valleys of Eastern Pyrenees, between France and Spain.

Andorra, autonomous and semi-independent, got a constitution in 1993, adopted a parliamentary system and became the 184th member of the UN. It is nominally subject to

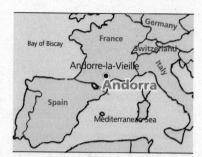

the suzerainty of France and the Bishop of Urgel in Spain. The government is carried on by a council of 28 elected members.

Economy: Tourism accounts for more than 80% of GDP. Andorra is an agricultural country. Crops: cereals, potatoes and tobacco. Products: iron, lead, alum, stone and timber.

Andorrans have the highest life expectancy in the world.

5. Angola

Republic of Angola (Republica de Angola)

Capital: Luanda; **Other Large Cities:** Huambo, Lubango; **Currency:** readjusted Kwanza; **Area:** 1,246,699 sq.km; **Population:** 18,993,000; **Languages:** Portuguese, Bantu; **Religions:** indigenous beliefs-47%, Roman Catholic-38%, Protestant-15% ; **Literacy:** 67.4%; **Life Expectancy:** 38.2; **p.c.i:** $ 6,412; **HDI rank:** 146; **Date of Independence:** 11th November, 1975.

Government Type: Republic; **President:** Jose Eduardo dos Santos; **PM:** Antonio Paulo Kassoma.

History: Angola is rebuilding the country after the end of a 27-year civil war in 2002. Fightng between the Popular Movement for Liberation of Angola(MPLA), led by Jose Eduardo Dos Santos, and then National Union for the Total Independence

---

The Motorcycle Diaries — What began as a journey to discover a homeland turned into a political odyssey for Alberto Granada and his friend Ernesto "Che" Guevara. Their journals, which became the basis for the film *The Motorcycle Diaries*, trace their political move toward Marxism.

of Angola(UNITA), led by Jonas Savimbi, followed independence from Portugal in 1975. Peace seemed imminent in 1992 when Angola held national elections, but UNITA renewed fighting after being beaten by the the MPLA at the polls. Up to 1.5 million lives have been lost in the quarter century of fighting. Savimbi's death in 2002 ended UNITA's insurgency and strengthened the MPLA's hold on power.

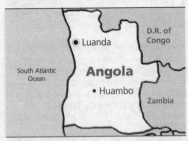

Economy: Food crops: millet, maize, bananas and cassava. Cash crops: coffee, cotton, oil palm and sisal. Industries: textiles, brewing, cement, oil refining and sugar. Producing 700,000 barrels a day, Angola is the second largest oil-producer in sub-Saharan Africa (behind Nigeria). Angola produces about one-tenth of the world's gemstones. Exports: crude petroleum, coffee, diamonds, iron ore, fish, sisal and timber.
Mission in India: Embassy of the Republic of Angola, 5/50 F, Nyaya Marg, Chanakya puri, New Delhi-110 021; Tel: 26110701, 26882680; Fax: 26110701, 24673787.
   E-mail: xietuang@del2.vsnl.net.in.
   Consulate: Mumbai: Tel:22851430/1457/6070, Fax: 22875467.
   E-mail:ambofficeluanda@netcabo.co.ao
Indian Mission in Angola: 18A Rua Marques das Minus, Caixa Postal 6040, Maculusso, Luanda, Angola. Tel: (00 2442) 392281, 371089, Fax (00 2442) 371094. E-mail: ambofficeluanda@netcabo.co.ao

6. Antigua & Barbuda

Capital: St. John's; **Currency:** East Car-

ribbean Dollar; **Area:** 442 sq km; **Population:** 89,000; **Languages:** English and Patois; **Religions:** Predominantly Protestant, some Roman Catholic; **Literacy:** 99%; **Life Expectancy:** 74.76; **p.c.i:** $ 16,566; **Date of Independence:** 1ˢᵗ Nov., 1981.
Government Type: Constitutional monarchy with UK-style Parliament; **Governor-General:** Louisse Lake-Tack; **PM:** Winston Baldwin Spencer.
History: Arawak Indians populated the islands when Columbus landed on his second voyage in 1493. Early settlements by the Spanish and French were succeeded by the English who formed a colony in 1667. Slavery, established to run the sugar plantations on Antigua, was abolished in 1834. The islands became an independent state within the British Commonwealth of Nations in 1981.

Economy: The economy is agricultural. Main exports: Sugar and sea island cotton. Tourism is a major source of income. Manufactures: garments, fans, refrigerators and rum.
Mission in India: Embassy of Antigua & Barbuda stationed at New York.

7. Argentina

Argentine Republic
(Republica Argentina)

Capital: Buenos Aires; **Other Large Cities:** Cordoba, Rosario, La Plata, Mendoza; **Cur-**

rency: Peso; **Area:** 2,766,654 sq.km; **Population:** 40,091,359; **Languages:** Spanish, Italian; **Religions:** nominally Roman Catholic-92%(less than 20% practising), Protestant-2%, Jewish-2%, other-4%;**Literacy:** 97.6%; **Life Expectancy:** 75.3; **p.c.i:** $ 15,603; **HDI rank:** 46; **Date of Independence:** 9th July, 1816 **Government Type:** Republic; **Head of State & Govt (President):** Cristina Fernandez De Kirchner.

History: In 1816, the United Provinces of the Rio Plata declared their independence from Spain. After Bolivia, Paraguay, and Uruguay went their separate ways, the area that remained became Argentina.Up until about the mid-20th century, much of Argentina's history was dominated by periods of internal political conflict between Federalists and Unitarians and between civilian and military factions. After World War II, an era of Peronist populism and direct and indirect military interference in subsequent governments was followed by a military junta that took power in 1976. Democracy returned in 1983 after a failed bid to seize the Falkland (Malvinas) Islands by force, and has persisted despite numerous challenges, the most formidable of which was a severe economic crisis in 2001-02 that led to violent public protests and the successive resignations of several presidents.

Economy: Argentina abounds in deposits of coal, lead, copper, zinc, gold, silver, sulphur and oil. Meat packing is the chief industry, with flour milling coming second. Others are chemicals, textiles, machinery, motor vehicles, paper and consumer durables. Chief crops: grains, maize, grapes, linseed, sugar, tobacco, rice, citrus fruits, livestock products. Argentina is the world's largest source of tannin.

Mission in India: Embassy of the Argentine Republic, A-2/6, Vasant Vihar, New Delhi-10057; Tel:4166 1982, 4166 1987; E-mail: eindi@mantra online.com

Indian Mission in Argentina: Embassy of India, Avenida Cordoba 950, 4th Floor, (1054) Buenos Aires, Argentina. Tel: 00-54-11-43934001, 00-54-11-43934156; Fax: 00-54-11-43934063.E-mail:indemb@indembarg.org.ar

8. Armenia

Republic of Armenia
(Haikakan Hanra-petoutioun)

Capital: Yerevan; **Other Large Cities:** Kirovakan, Kumairi; **Currency:** Dram; **Area:** 29,800 sq.km.; **Population:** 3,254,300; **Languages:** Armenian; **Religions:** Armenian Apostolic-94.7%, other Christian-4%, Yezidi-1.3%; **Literacy:** 99.7%; **Life Expectancy:** 72.0; **p.c.i:**$ 5,178; **HDI rank:** 76; **Date of Independence:** 21st September, 1991.

Government Type: Republic; **President:** Serzh Sargsian; **PM:** Tigran Sargsian.

History: Despite periods of autonomy, over the centuries Armenia came under the sway of various empires including the Roman Byzantine, Arab, Persian and Ottoman. During Word War I in the western portion of Armenia, Ottoman Turkey instituted a policy of forced resettlement coupled with other harsh pratices that resulted in an estimated 1 million Armenian deaths. The eastern area of Armenia was ceded by the Ottomans to Russia in 1828; this portion declared its independence in 1918, but was conquered by the Soviet Red Army in 1920. Armenian leaders remain preoccupied by the long conflict with Muslim Azerbaijan over Nagorno-Karabakh, a primarily Armenian populated region, assigned to Soviet Azerbaijan in the

First to Adopt Christianity	Armenia is said to be the first country in the world to make Christianity a state religion.Christianity was adopted in 301 AD as the state religion.

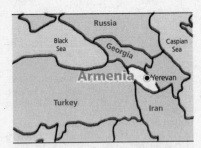

1920s by Moscow. Armenia and Azerbaijan began fighting over the area in 1988; the struggle escalated after both countries attained independence from the Soviet Union in 1991.

Economy: It is a mountainous country with very fertile soil and extensive irrigation. Important crops: Grains, potatoes, olive, almonds, grapes, cotton, dairy products. Natural resources: Copper, zinc, aluminium, molybdenum, marble, granite, cement. Industry: Chemical, cement, textiles, food industries, carpet-weaving.

Mission in India: Embassy of the Republic of Armenia, D-133, Anand Niketan, New Delhi-110021; Tel: 2411 2851, 2411 2852 Fax: 2411 2853. E-mail: armemb@vsnl.com

Indian Mission in Armenia: Embassy of India, 50/2, Dzorapi Street, Yerevan- 375019; Tel: 00-374-10-539173; Fax: 00-374-10-533984. E-mail: hoc@embassyofindia.am

9. Australia

Commonwealth of Australia

Capital: Canberra;
Other Large Cities: Sydney, Melbourne, Brisbane, Perth, Adelaide; **Currency:** Australian Dollar; **Area:** 7,682,300 sq. km; **Population:** 22,609,000; **Languages:** English and aboriginal languages; **Religions:** Catholic-25.8%, Anglican-18.7%, Uniting Church-5.7%, Presbyterian and Reformed-3%, Eastern Orthodox-2.7%, other Christian-7.9%, Buddhist-2.1%, Muslim-1.7%; **Literacy:** 99%; **Life Expectancy:** 81.2; **p.c.i:** $ 39,692; **HDI rank:** 2; **Date of Independence:** 1st January, 1901.
Government Type: Federal Parliamentary Democracy; **Governor-General:** Quentin Bryce; **PM:** Julia Gillard.

History: The first recorded European contact with Australia was in March 1606, when Dutch explorer Willem Janszoon charted the west coast of Cape York Peninsula, Queensland. Later that year, the Spanish explorer Luis Vaez de Torres sailed through the strait separating Australia and Papua New Guinea. Over the next two centuries, European explorers and traders continued to chart the coastline of Australia, then known as New Holland. In 1688, William Dampier became the first British explorer to land on the Australian coast. It was not until 1770 that another Englishman, captain James Cooke, aboard the Endeavour, extended a scientific voyage to the South Pacific in order to further chart the east coast of Australia and claim it for the British crown. Six colonies were created in the late 18th and 19th centuries; they federated and became commonwealth of Australia in 1901. The non-indigenous population at the time of Federation was 3.8 million. Half of these lived in cities, three-quarters were born in Australia, and the majority were of English, Scottish or Irish descent.

Economy: Australia is an impotant producer and exporter of wool, wheat and meat. Its mines provide minerals and metals of many

The national anthem of Australia is "Advance Australia Fair" which was composed by a Scot, Peter Dodds McCormick. A revised version of a late nineteenth century patriotic song, it was officially declared the national anthem on 19 April 1984.

Advance Australia Fair

types including coal, iron-ore, bauxite, gold, silver, lead, zinc, copper, nickel, oil and natural gas for use by local and overseas industries.

Australia has many unique plant and animal species including kangaroos, koalas, platypuses, dingos, Tasmanian devils, wombats and frilled lizards.

Australian external territories: Norfolk Island, Coral Sea Islands Territory, Territory of Ashmore and Cartier Islands, Cocos (Keeling) Island, Kiritimati (Christmas Island) and Australian Antarctic Territory, the Heard Island and Mc Donald Islands.

Mission in India: High Commission for Australia, 1/50-G, Shantipath, Chanakyapuri, New Delhi-110021. Tel: 41399900; Fax:4149 4491, 2688 7536.E-mail: austhighcom.newdelhi@dfat.gov.au

Mission in Australia: High Commission of India, 3-5, Moonah Place, Yarralumla, Canberra ACT-2600, Australia. Tel: 00-61-2-62733999; 62733774, 00-61-2-62735479 (After office hours); Fax: 00-61-2-62731308.

E-mail: is@hciindia-au.org

10. Austria

Republic of Austria (Republik Osterreich)

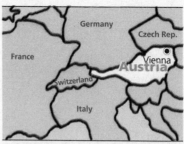

Capital: Vienna; **Other Large Cities:** Graz, Linz, Salzburg, Innsbruck; **Currency:** Euro; **Area:** 83,858 sq. km; **Population:** 8,396,760; **Languages:** German; **Religions:** Roman Catholic-73.6%, Protestant-4.7%, Islam-4.2%; **Literacy:** 99%; **Life Expectancy:** 79.8; **p.c.i:** $ 39,454; **HDI rank:** 25; **Date of Independence:** 1156.

Government Type: Federal Republic; **President:** Heinz Fischer; **Head of Govt:** Chancellor: Werner Faymann

History: Austria is no longer the dominant political force it was in Central Europe under the Hapsburg dynasty which ruled until the first world war. A republic since 1918, Austria, which was invaded by Nazi

Germany in 1938, regained full sovereignty in 1955. Austria is a federal state of nine provinces. Austria joined the EU on Jan. 1, 1995.

Economy: It depends mainly on mining, manufacturing, trade and services. Main agricultural products: livestock, forest products, grains, sugar beets, potatoes.

Mission in India: Embassy of Austria, EP-13, Chandragupta Marg, Chanakyapuri, New Delhi-110021. Tel: 26889050/049; Fax: 26886929/26886033

E-mail: new-delhi-ob@bmaa.gv.at

Indian Mission in Austria: Embassy of India and Permanent Mission of India to the UN Offices in Vienna, Kaerntnerring 2, 1010 Vienna, Austria. Tel: 00-43-1-5058666; Fax: 00-43-1-5059219

E-mail: indemb@eoivien.vienna.at; Web: www.indiaembassy.at

11. Azerbaijan

Azerbaijani Republic (Azerbaijchan Respub-likasy)

Capital: Baku; **Other Large Cities:** Gandja, Sumgait; **Currency:** Manat; **Area:** 86,600 sq.km; **Population:** 8,997,400; **Languages:** Azeri, Turkish, Russian; **Religions:** Islam-93.4%; **Literacy:** 99.5%; **Life Expectancy:** 67.5; **p.c.i:** $ 9,953; **HDI rank:** 67; **Date of Independence:** 30th August, 1991.

Government Type: Republic; **President:** Ilham Aliyev; **PM:** Artur Rasizade.

Founder of Zoroastrianism

The founder of the religion known as Zoroastrinism was born in Azerbaijan (part of the Persian Empire at the time). Zoroaster taught the existence of a single god, Ahura Mazda. His Holy Spirit was represented by fire.

History: Azerbaijan was briefly independent from 1918 to 1920; It regained its independence after the collapse of the Soviet Union in 1991.

In Jan. 90, there were violent disturbances in Baku and on the Armenian border over the enclave of Nagorno-Karabakh. Azerbaijanis are Muslims and Armenians Christians. Inside Azerbaijan is Nagorno-Karabakh, the Armenian-majority region. Inside Armenia is Nakhichevan autonomous republic, which is a part of Azerbaijan. Fighting between Azerbaijan and Armenia escalated in 1992, '93 &'94.

Economy: Azerbaijan's number one export is oil. Agricultural products: Grain, cotton, grapes, fruits, vegetables, tobacco, silk,

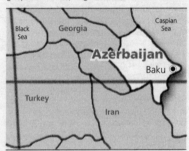

dairy products. Natural resources: oil, iron, aluminium, copper, lead, zinc, precious metals, limestone, salt. Industry: Oil, copper, chemical, building material, food, timber, textiles, fishing.

Indian Mission in Azerbaijan: Embassy of India, 31/39 Oktay Karimov Street,Ganjlik, District-Narimanov, Baku-370069, Azerbaijan. Tel:00-994-12-5646354, 5646344; Fax:00-994-12-4472572.

E-mail: eibaku.attache@azdata.net

12. The Bahamas

Commonwealth of The Bahamas

Capital: Nassau; **Currency:** Bahamian Dollar; **Area:** 13,939 sq.km; **Population:**

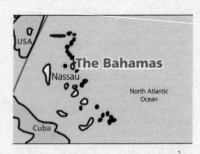

353,658; **Languages:** English, Creole; **Religions:** Christian-96.3%; **Literacy:** 95.8%; **Life Expectancy:** 73.5; **p.c.i:** $ 25,884; **HDI rank:** 43; **Date of Independence:** 10th July, 1973.

Government Type: Constitutional Parliamentary Democracy; **Governor-General:** Sir Arthur A. Foulkes; **PM:** Hubert A. Ingraham.

History: The Commonwealth of the Bahamas is an archipelago lying off the south-east coast of Florida. The Bahamas consists of more than 700 islands and over 1000 cays and rocks. Only about 30 islands are inhabited. The largest island is Andros but New Providence is the most populous. The capital Nassau is situated on this island. Eighty-five per cent of the population is Negro, the rest are Europeans.

Economy: Fishing constitutes the main occupation. Vegetables and fruits are also grown. Industries: Tourism together with tourism-driven construction and manufacturing accounts for approximately 60% of GDP. GDP by sector: agriculture (3%), industry (7%), services (90%).

13. Bahrain

State of Bahrain/Dawlat al-Bahrayn

Capital: Manama; **Currency:** Bahraini Dinar; **Area:** 669 sq. km.; **Population:** 807,000; **Languages:** Arabic, English, Farsi, Urdu; **Religions:** Islam -81.2%, Christian

---

| Land of Fire | The name for Azerbaijan derives from a word for fire. Azerbaijan has large deposits of oil and the ignition of surface oil may have led to the description of the country as the "land of fire". |

- 9%; **Literacy:** 88.8%; **Life Expectancy:** 75.6; **p.c.i:** $ 26,807; **HDI rank:** 39; **Date of Independence:** 15th August, 1971.

Government Type: Constitutional Monarchy; **Head of State:** King Hamad bin Isa Al-Khalifa; **PM:** Shaikh Khalifa bin Salman Al-Khalifa.

History: Bahrain is an Arab state comprising 33 small islands in the Arabian Gulf. Bahrain is the biggest of the islands and has lent its name to the whole archipelago. It is an independent monarchy.

Economy: Agriculture: Fruits and vegetables, alfalfa, dates, poultry. Industry: Aluminium, ship building & repairs, electronics assembly, building materials, and banking. The people enjoy a very high standard of living.

Petroleum production and refining account for about 60% of export receipts, 60% of government revenues, and 30% of GDP. A large number of exports consist of petroleum products made from refining imported crude.

Mission in India: 4,Olof Palme Marg, Vasant Vihar, New Delhi-110057;Tel:2615 4153, 2615 4154; Fax:26146731.

E-mail: bahrainembindia@yahoo.com

Consulate: 53, Maker Tower F, 5th Floor, Cuffe Parade Road, Colaba, Mumbai-400005. Tel: 2218 5856; Fax: 2218 8817

Indian Mission in Bahrain: Embassy of India, Building 182, Road 2608, Area 326, Ghudaibiya, P.O. Box No.26106, Adliya, Baharain. Tel:00-973 17712683, 17713832, 17712785; Fax:00 973 17715527.

E-mail: inderninf@batelco.com.bh

Website: http://indianembassybahrain.com

14. Bangladesh

(People's Republic of Bangladesh; Gana Prajatani Bangladesh)

Capital: Dhaka; **Other Large Cities:** Chittagong, Khulna; **Currency:** Taka; **Area:** 148,393 sq.km; **Population:** 150,319,000; **Languages:** Bangla, Chakma, Magh; **Religions:** Islam-83%, Hindu-16%; **Literacy:** 53.5%; **Life Expectancy:** 64.1; **p.c.i:** $ 1,565; **HDI rank:** 129; **Date of Independence:** 26 March 1971 is the date of independence from West Pakistan, 16 December 1971 is known as Victory Day and commemorates the official creation of the state of Bangladesh

Government Type: Parliamentary Democracy; **President:** Zillur Rahman; **PM:** Sheikh Hasina Wajed .

History: Bangladesh was formerly East Pakistan, one of the five provinces into which Pakistan was divided at its creation. East Pakistan and the four western provinces were separated by about 1,600 km of Indian territory. Although the East was more populous, government was based in West Pakistan. From the very inception of its formation, language remained the most problematic issue. Same status for Bengali language with Urdu and English was the demand and the movement involving all sections of the people of East Pakistan gave a strike call on 21 Feb, 1952. On that very day, police fired on a students' rally and several students died. Since then the day has been observed as the Language Day (Bhasa Divas).

East Pakistan became an independent entity named Bangladesh in 1971, following civil war in which India actively supported the East. Leader of this independence movement, Sheikh Mujibur Rahman became the first Prime Minister.

In January 1975 parliamentary government was replaced by a presidential form of government. Sheikh Mujib became Presi-

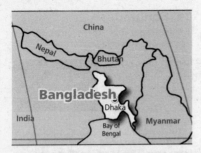

dent, assuming absolute power. In February, Bangladesh became a one-party state.

On 15 August, 1975 Sheikh Mujib and his family were assassinated in a coup. Chief of Army Staff, Major-Gen. Ziaur Rahman (Gen. Zia) took over power on 7 November, 1975. In June 1978 the country's first direct presidential election resulted in a victory for Zia, who formed a Council of Advisers. Parliamentary elections followed in February 1979 in which President Ziaur Rahman's Bangladesh Nationalist Party (BNP) won 207 of the 300 directly elective seats in the Jatiya Sangsad.

Political instability recurred, however, when Gen. Ziaur was assassinated on 30 May 1981 during an attempted military coup. The elderly Vice-President, Justice Abdus Sattar, took over as acting President but was faced with strikes and demonstrations over the execution of several officers who had been involved in the coup.

On 24 March, 1982 there was a bloodless military coup, by which Lieut. Gen. Ershad became chief martial law administrator. President Sattar was deposed. The Constitution was suspended and parliament ceased to function. Assanuddin Chowdhury was sworn in as civilian president on 27 March. Lieut. Gen. Ershad assumed the presidency on 11 Dec., 1983.

Gen. Ershad was deposed and arrested after a popular uprising in December 1990. Mr. Shahabuddin Ahmed took over as Acting President. In the general elections held in February 1991 Bangladesh National Party led by Begum Khaleda Zia won 140 seats.

Begum Zia was sworn in PM. In the general elections held in June, 1996, Awami League won 146 seats and Sheikh Hasina Wazed, daughter of the late Sheikh Mujibur Rahman, became the PM of Bangladesh. Jatiya Party quit the govt. in Mar. '98.

Economy: Although half of Bangladesh's GDP is generated through the service sector, nearly two-thirds of the people are employed in the agriculture sector, with rice as the single-most-important product. Plots of land are very small-measured in tenths of a hectare. Half the population still cannot afford to feed themselves properly.

Mission in India: High Commission for the People's Republic of Bangladesh, EP-39, Dr.S.Radhakrishnan Marg, Chankyapuri, New Delhi - 110 021. Tel: 2412 1389-94; Fax: 26878953.

E-mail: bdhcdelhi@gmail.com

Indian Mission in Bangladesh: High Commission of India. House No. 2, Road No.142, Gulshan-1, Dhaka, Bangladesh. Tel: 00-8802-9889339. E-mail: hoc@hcidhakha.org

15. Barbados

Capital: Bridgetown; **Currency:** Barbados dollar; **Area:** 430 sq km; **Population:** 257,000; **Languages:** English; **Religions:** Christian-73.6%; **Literacy:** 99.7%; **Life Expectancy:** 77.3; **p.c.i.:** $ 22,296; **HDI rank:** 42; **Date of Independence:** 30th November, 1966.

Government Type: Parliamentary Democracy; **Head of State:** Queen Elizabeth II; **Governor-General:** Sir Clifford Husbands; **PM:** Fruendel Stuart.

History: The island of Barbados is the most easterly of the Caribbean islands, lying about 400 km north east of the mainland of South America. It is included in the Windward Isles. British settlers arrived in 1627. Slavery existed until 1834. Barbados became fully self-governing within the Commonwealth on Nov. 30, 1966. In 1997, a commission

| The War of the Triple Alliance | The War of the Triple Alliance between Paraguay and the alliance of Argentina, Uruguay and Brazil (1865-1870) resulted in the loss of large areas of land as well as the lives of a very high percentage of Paraguay's soldiers. |

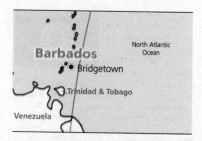

North Atlantic Ocean

Barbados

Bridgetown

Trinidad & Tobago

Venezuela

was appointed to consider abandoning all ties to Britain.

Economy: Agriculture and tourism dominate the economy of Barbados. Sugar, molasses, rum, electrical components and chemicals are major exports.

16. Belarus

(Republic of Belarus) Republika Belarus

Capital: Minsk; **Other Large Cities:** Gomel, Vitebsk; **Currency:** Rouble; **Area:** 207,600 sq.km.; **Population:** 9,481,100; **Languages:** Belorussian, Russian; **Religions:**Christian-96%; **Literacy:** 99.7%; **Life Expectancy:** 69.0; **p.c.i:** $ 13,864; **HDI rank:** 61; **Date of Independence:** 25th August, 1991.

Government Type: Republic in name, although in fact a dictatorship; **Head of State:** Aleksandr Lukashenko; **PM:** Mikhail Myasnikovich.

History: After seven decades as a constituent republic of the USSR, Belarus attained its

Sweden

Russia

Baltic Sea

Minsk

Poland

Belarus

Ukraine

independence in 1991. It has retained closer political and economic ties to Russia than any of the other former soviet republics. Russians form 13.2% of the population, Poles 4.1% and Ukrainians 2.9%.

Economy: Agriculture: Cattle-breeding for meat and dairy produce. Important products: Potato, hemp, grain, flax, fodder. Natural resources: Valuable forest land wooded with oak, elm, maple; peat deposits. Industry: motor vehicle, machine tools, agricultural machinery, peat, chemical fibre, paper, building materials, food processing, textile.

Mission in India: Embassy of the Republic of Belarus, 163, Jor Bagh, New Delhi-110 003. Tel: 2469 4518,2469 7025; Fax:2469 7029.

E-mail: india@belembassy.org

Indian Mission in Belarus: Embassy of India, Sobinova Street 63,Minsk 220040. Tel: 00-375-17-2629399, 2627739; Fax: 00-375-17-2884799, 2161896.

E-mail: amb.minsk@mea.gov.in, hoc@indemb.bn.by

17. Belgium

Kingdom of Belgium, Koninkrijk Bekgie (Dutch), Royaume de Belgique (French)

Capital: Brussels; **Other Large Cities:** Antwerp, Ghent; **Currency:** Euro; **Area:** 30,521 sq.km; **Population:** 10,827,519; **Languages:** Flemish, French and German—all official; **Religions:** Roman Catholic-75%, other (includes Protestants)-25%; **Literacy:** 99%; **Life Expectancy:** 79.4; **p.c.i:** $ 36,274; **HDI rank:** 18; **Date of Independence:** 4th October, 1830.

Government Type: Federal Parliamentary Democracy under a Constitutional Monarchy; **Head of State:** King Albert II; **PM:** Yves Letterme.

History: Belgium (in NW Europe on N. Sea) named after the Belgae, people of ancient Gaul who crossed the Rhine about the 6th

---

Country without a Government For more than a year since a general election on June 13, 2010, Belgium has had no official government. Belgium has set the world record for the country going the longest without a government in place in modern history.

dollar; **Area:** 22,965 sq. km; **Population:** 333,200; **Languages:** English, Spanish, Creole dialects; **Religions:** Christian-79%; **Literacy:** 75.1%; **Life Expectancy:** 76.1; **p.c.i:** $ 7,894; **HDI rank:** 78; **Date of Independence:** 21st September, 1981.
Government Type: Parliamentary Democracy; **Governor-General:** Colville Young; **PM:** Dean Barrow.

century B.C., has had a turbulent history. During both the World Wars it was occupied by Germany but freed itself by the end of those wars. Belgium became a Federal State in February, 1993.

Economy: Although Belgium is essentially a manufacturing country, agriculture and forestry are also very important. Industry is concentrated mainly in the populous Flemish area in the north. The main crops are oats, rye, wheat, potatoes, barley and sugar beets. Coal is the country's only important mineral. Principal industries: steel and metal products, textiles, glass, fertiliser, sugar, heavy chemicals, etc. Antwerp is the world's 4th largest port and also the world's biggest diamond-trading centre.

The European Community has its headquarters in Brussels.

Mission in India: Royal Embassy of Belgium, 50-N, Shantipath, Chanakyapuri, New Delhi-110021. Tel: 4242 8000; Telefax: 4242 8002.

E-mail:ambabel@del2.vsnl.net.in

Consulate General of Belgium in Mumbai: Morena 11, M.L. Dahanukar Marg (Carmichael Road, Mumbai-400 026; Ph: +91 22 23515186, 23521602

Indian Mission in Belgium: Embassy of India, 217-Chaussee de Vleurgat, 1050, Brussels, Belgium. Tel: 00-32-2-6409140; Fax: 00-32-2-6489638.

E-mail: hoc@indembassy.be

18. Belize

Capital: Belmopan; **Other Large Cities:** Belize City, Orange Walk; **Currency:** Belize

History: Originally a British colony, Belize was granted autonomy in 1964 and became independent in 1981. The name Belize was adopted in 1973. The original capital Belize City was laid waste by a hurricane in 1961. The capital was shifted to Belmopan, an inland town, in 1970.

Economy: Forest products, especially timber, form a major export item. Sugar, citrus fruits, corn and bananas form the major products. Maize, rice, kidney beans and sweet potatoes are the main domestic staples. Industries: Sugar, molasses, cigarettes, beer, garments, tourism. Wild life includes the curious creature manatee – an amphibian mammal– and several varieties of reptiles.

19. Benin

Republic of Benin, Republique du Benin

Capital: Porto Novo; **Other Large Cities:** Cotonou, Parakau; **Currency:** Franc CFA; **Area:** 112,622 sq.km.; **Population:** 8,778,646; **Languages:** French and Tribal di-

English in Cental America	Belize is the only country in Central America where English is the official language. Although only 4 per cent of the population speaks it as their first language, a majority speak English very well.

alects like Fon, Yoruba;
Religions: Christian-42.8%, Islam-24.4%, Vodoun-17.3%; **Literacy:** 40.5%; **Life Expectancy:** 56.7;

p.c.i: $ 1,453; **HDI rank:** 134; **Date of Independence:** 1st August, 1960.
Government Type: Republic; **Head of State & Govt (President):** Yayi Boni.

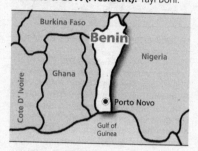

History: The People's Republic of Benin (formerly Dahomey) is located north of the Gulf of Guinea in West Africa. It is one of the smallest and most densely populated states in Africa.

The country has been plagued by coups and counter-coups. For some years Marxism-Leninism was the state ideology.

The first free presidential elections in 30 years were held in 1991.
Economy: Products: palm oil, kernels, peanuts, cotton, coffee and tobacco. Food crops: Cassava, yams, maize, sorghum. Industry: Few factories. Palm oil-processing, brewing, sugar.
Mission in India: Consulate General of Benin in New Delhi, India. Flat No.5, Sector -6, R.K. Puram Market, New Delhi, India, Tel: +91-11-2610-0114; Fax: +91-11-2610-0850; Email: sundert@ndf.vsnl.net.in

20. Bhutan

(Kingdom of Bhutan) Druk-Yul

Capital: Thimphu; **Currency:** Ngultrum; **Area:** 46,500 sq.km; **Population:** 695,822;

Languages: Dzongkha, Lhotsam (Nepali), English, Gurung, Assamese; **Religions:** Buddhist-75%, Hindu -25%; **Literacy:**

52.8%; **Life Expectancy:** 65.6; **p.c.i:** $ 5,533; **Date of Independence:** 8th August, 1949.**Government Type:** Constitutional Monarchy; **Head of State:** King Jigme Khesar Namgyel Wangchuk; **Head of Govt.:** Jigme Thinley

History: In 1865, Britain and Bhutan signed the Treaty of Sinchulu, under which Bhutan would receive an annual subsidy in exchange for ceding some border land to British India. Under British influence, a monarchy was set up in 1907; three years later, a treaty was signed whereby the British agreed not to interfere in Bhutanese internal affairs and Bhutan allowed Britain to direct its foreign affairs. This role was assumed by independent India after 1947. Two years later, a formal Indo-Bhutanese accord returned the areas of Bhutan annexed by the British, formalized the annual subsidies the country received, and defined India's responsibilities in defense and foreign relations.

King Jigme Dorji Wangchuk was succeeded in 1972 by the Western-educated 16-year-old Crown Prince, Jigme Singye Wangchuk. The new King stated his wish to maintain the Indo-Bhutan Treaty and to strengthen friendship with India.

In late 2007, after 34 years, King Wangchuk announced he was stepping down and that his son Crown Prince Jigme Khesar

Gross National Happiness	Bhutan's deveopment objective is to maximise 'Gross National Happiness'.This is based on a uniquely Bhutanese model, balancing modernization with Buddhist values.

Namgyel, would be his successor. In July 2008 a constitution was adopted that established a two-party democracy after nearly a century of absolute monarchy.

Economy: Its economy is largely a subsistence economy. People are engaged in subsistence farming; and barter is practised. Though Bhutan for long resisted the lure of tourism, it is the principal source of foreign exchange now.

Chief crops: Rice, millet, wheat, barley, maize, cardamom, potatoes, oranges, apples. Extensive and valuable forests abound.

Mission in India: Royal Bhutanese Embassy, Chandra Gupta Marg, Chanakyapuri, New Delhi-110021. Tel: 2688 9807, 2688 9809, 2688 9230; Fax: 2687 6710, 2467 4664.

E-mail: kutshabdelhi@yahoo.com, bhutanembassy_delhi@yahoo.com

Indian Mission in Bhutan: Embassy of India, India House Estate, Thimphu, Bhutan. Tel: 00-975-2-322162; Fax: 00-975-2-323195, 325341.

E-mail:hocbht@druknet.bt

21. Bolivia

(Republic of Bolivia) Republic de Bolivia

Capital: La Paz (administrative) and Sucre (judicial); **Other Large Cities:** Santa Cruz, Potosi; **Currency:** Boliviano; **Area:** 1,098,581 sq.km; **Population:** 10,426,154; **Languages:** Spanish, Quechua and Aymara; **Religions:** Roman Catholic-95%, Protestant-5%; **Literacy:** 90.7%; **Life Expectancy:** 65.6; **p.c.i:** $4,584; **HDI rank:** 95; **Date of Independence:** 6th August, 1825. **Government Type:** Republic; **Head of State & PM(President):** Juan Evo Morales.

History: Bolivia was originally part of the ancient Inca Empire . It has been named after Simon Bolivar, the famous South American fighter for freedom. Bolivia, like most Latin American states, has had a number of coups and counter-coups. It restored civilian rule

in 1982 after nearly 18 years of military regimes.

Economy: Agriculture, the mainstay of the country, engages 70 per cent of the people. Chief crops: Potatoes, sugar, coffee, corn. Tin mining was the most important industry, until 1985 when international tin market collapsed. Zinc, lead, antimony and tungsten are the other important minerals. Mining accounts for about 70% of foreign exchange earnings. Other industries: Textiles, food processing, refined petroleum. A privatisation programme affecting some 60 state-owned enterprises was launched in 1992.

Mission in India: Embassy of Bolivia stationed at New York.

22. Bosnia-Herzegovina

(Republic of Bosnia and Herzegovina) Republika Bosna i Hercegovina

Capital: Sarajevo; **Other Large Cities:** Banja Luka, Tuzla, Mostar; **Currency:** Marka; **Area:** 51,129 sq km; **Population:** 3,843,126; **Languages:** Serbo-Croatian; **Religions:** Christian-46%, Muslim-40%; **Literacy:** 96.7%; **Life Expectancy:** 74.9; **p.c.i:** $ 7,751; **HDI rank:** 68; **Date of Independence:** 1st March, 1992. **Government Type:** Federal Democratic Republic; **Presidency Chairman:** Haris Silajdzic (Bosniak):other members of the three-member presidency rotate every eight months. Presidency Member (Croat): Zeljko Komsic; Presidency Member (Serb): Nebojsa

---

El Liberator — Simon de Bolivar, born in Caracas in 1783, is known as El Liberator. Bolivar was the driving force behind ousting the Spanish from Bolivia, Colombia, Ecuador, Peru and Venezuela.

ceasefire was to come into effect but Serbs were reportedly engaged in a new 'ethnic cleansing' operation.

February 96 saw the end of the war and the fragile truce imposed by the Dayton accords was reaffirmed at a summit in Rome. In March, Sarajevo, divided by war for almost four years, was reunited as the last of five Serb areas passed to the Muslim-Croat federation. In July, UN war crimes tribunal issued arrest warrants for Bosnian Serbs' political leader Radovan Karadzic, who later agreed to step down. In Sept., elections were held for a 3-person collective presidency and for seats in a federal parliament.

Radmanovic; **Presidency Head of Govt:** Nikola Spiric.

History: The country was settled by Slavs in the 7th century. Bosnia was conquered by Turks in 1463. At the Congress of Berlin (1878), the territory was assigned to Austro-Hungarian administration under nominal Turkish suzerainty. Austria-Hungary's outright annexation in 1908 generated international tensions which contributed to the outbreak of World War I.

Croats and Muslims voted for independence in Oct. 1991. A referendum for independence was passed in Feb, 1992. A 'Serb republic' was formed in the predominantly Serb-populated Bosnian territories. Serbs' opposition to the referendum spurred violent clashes. In April, independence of the republic was recognised by U.S. and E.U. Fierce fighting continued. Serbs massacred thousands of Bosnian civilians. By mid-'94 three-fourths of Bosnia came under Serb control.

Peace talks were held but Serb-Muslim-Croat fighting continued. In '93, negotiations resumed to partition Bosnia. In July an ineffective ceasefire was in force. A peace plan authored by USA, UK, France, Germany and Russia was under consideration. NATO launched a series of massive air raids on Serbian positions and Sarajevo and in Serb-held Bosnian territory in August,'95 after the shelling of Sarajevo market by Serb gunmen.

In Sept., '95, Bosnia's warring sides decided to put an end to the three and a half-year-old war by cutting the nation into two parts: one for the rebel Serbs and the other for Muslims and the Croats. In Oct., a

Economy: Agricultural products: Wheat, maize, potatoes, plums, timber, cattle, sheep. Industry: Textiles, timber, rugs, cement, electricity, coal, steel. The war has destroyed 95% of industrial capacity.

Mission in India: Embassy of Bosnia & Herzegovina, E-9/11, Vasant Vihar, New Delhi-110 057. Tel:4166 2481; Fax: 4166 2482.

E-mail: abhind@gmail.com

23. Botswana
(Republic of Botswana)

Capital: Gaborone; **Other Large Cities:** Francistown, Lobatse; **Currency:** Pula; **Area:** 581,730 sq. km; **Population:** 1,800,098; **Languages:** English, Setswana and Sishona; **Religions:** Christian-71.6%; **Literacy:** 82.9%; **Life Expectancy:** 50.7; **p.c.i:** $ 15,449; **HDI rank:** 98; **Date of Independence:** 30th September, 1966.

Government Type: Parliamentary Republic; **Head of State & Govt (President):** Seretse Khama Ian Khama.

History: The Republic of Botswana – the land of the Batawana tribes – (formerly known as Bechuanaland) is located in Southern Africa. Most of the country is near-desert, with the Kalahari occupying the western part of the country.

Africa's Golden Boy	Once one of the world's poorest countries, Botswana now ranks among the richer middle-income ones. A lot has to do with the discovery of diamonds, of which it is the world's biggest producer.

Economy: Diamond mining accounts for more than one-third of GDP and for 70-80% of export earnings.Tourism, financial services, subsistence farming, and cattle rearing are the other key sectors. Important crops: Sorghum, corn, millet, beans. Diamonds, manganese, asbestos, coal, copper and nickel are leading mineral resources.

In Botswana, more than one in three adults aged 15-49 are infected with HIV/AIDS.

Mission in India: High Commission of the Republic of Botswana, F-8/3, Vasant Vihar, New Delhi-110057;Tel:4653 7000; Fax:4603 6191

Indian Mission in Botswana: High Commission of India, Plot 5375, President's Drive, Private Bag 249, Gaborone, Botswana. Tel: 00-267-372676; Fax: 00-267-374636.

E-mail:hicomind@info.bw

24. Brazil

(Federative Republic of Brazil) - Republica Federativa do Brasil

Capital: Brasilia; Other Large Cities : Sao Paulo, Rio de Janeiro, Belo Horizonte, Recife, Salvadore; Currency: Real; Area: 8,511,965 sq.km; Population: 190,732,694; Languages: Portuguese (official), Spanish, English, French; Religions: Roman Catholic(nominal)-73.6%, Protestant-15.4%; Literacy: 90%; Life Expectancy: 72.4; p.c.i: $

11,289; HDI rank: 73; Date of Independence: 7th September, 1822.
Government Type: Federal Republic; President: Dilma Rousseff.

History: After more than three centuries under Portuguese rule, Brazil gained its independence in 1822, maintaining a monarchical system of government until the abolition of slavery in 1888 and the subsequent proclamation of a republic by the military in 1889. Brazilian coffee exporters politically dominated the country until populist leader Getulio Vargas rose to power in 1930. By far the largest and most populous country in South America, Brazil underwent more than half a century of populist and military government until 1985, when the military regime peacefully ceded power to civilian rulers.

Economy: Around one-quarter of the labour force works in industry. The major exports of Brazil are soyabeans, sugar, coffee, iron ore, cocoa beans, maize, sisal and tobacco.

The number one coffee producer for more than a century, Brazil also leads in oranges, orange juice concentrate, alcohol, sisal, cassava and bananas. It has the planet's largest commercial cattle herd, and comes only to the United States in soya production and to India in sugar cane output.

Brazil possesses vast deposits of mineral wealth—chrome ore, iron, phosphates, uranium, manganese, copper, coal, platinum and gold. Oil is a state monopoly. The wax which is used for phonograph records and insulation is a monopoly product of the state.

Bolsa Familia

Bolsa Familia is Brazil's conditional cash-transfer programme. It ensures that poor families get cash if they send their children to school and take them for health checks.

Brazil is the only source of high grade quartz crystal in commercial quantities.

Mission in India: Embassy of Brazil, 8, Aurangzeb Road, New Delhi-110011. Tel: 91-11-2301 7301; Fax:91-11-2379 3684;

E-mail: brasindi@vsnl.com

Consulate: Mumbai:Tel:91-22-2283 4467, Fax:91-22-2283 4468 E-mail: consbrasmumbai@gmail.com

Indian Mission in Brazil: Embassy of India, SHIS QL 08, Conj. 08, Casa 01, Lago Sul, CEP- 71620 285, Brasilia DF,Brazil, Tel: 00-55-61-3248-4006 (4 lines) Fax: 00-55-61-32485486/7849.

E-mail:mailto:hoc@indianembassy.org.br
Web: www.indianembassy.org.br

25. Brunei

(Brunei Darussalam) State of Brunei Darussalam Negara Brunei Darussalam

Capital: Bander Seri Begawan (formerly called Brunei Town); **Currency:** Brunei dollar; **Area:** 5,765 sq.km; **Population:** 407,000; **Languages:** Malay, English, Chinese; **Religions:** Muslim-67%, Buddhist-13%, Christian-10%; **Literacy:** 94.9%; **Life Expectancy:** 77.1; **p.c.i:** $ 47,200; **HDI rank:** 37; **Date of Independence:** 1st January, 1984.

Government Type: Constitutional sultanate; Sultan and **PM:** Haji Hassanal Bolkiah.

History: Negara Brunei Darussalam on the northern side of the island of Borneo lies between two Malaysian territories, Sabah and

Sarawak. Brunei Malays, mostly Muslims, form more than half of the population. The Sultanate, once a powerful and independent kingdom, was annexed by Britain and was granted full internal autonomy in 1971. Became a fully sovereign and independent state on Jan. 1, 1984.

Economy: Oil and natural gas are Brunei's most valuable resources. Much of Brunei's oil comes from the offshore Ampa field. Over 40% of GDP is derived from oil and gas exports. Rice is the chief food crop. Also grown are bananas, vegetables, cassava and pepper. Other crops are coconuts, sago, cork and rubber. Rubber is an export item.

Mission in India: Brunei Darussalam High Commission, 4 Poorvi Marg, Vasant Vihar, New Delhi-110057. Tel: 2614 8340, 2614 8343; Fax: 2614 2101.

E-mail: bruneidelhi@dishnetdsl.net

Indian Mission in Brunei: High Commission of India, 'Baitussyifaa', Simpang 40-22, Jalan Sungai Akar, Bandar Seri Begawan BC 3915, Brunei Darussalam. Tel: 00-673-2-339947; Fax: 00-673-2-339783.

E-mail:hicomind@brunet.bn
Web: brunet.bn/gov/emb/india

26. Bulgaria

(Republic of Bulgaria) - Republika Bulgaria

Capital: Sofia; **Other Large Cities:** Plovdiv, Dobrich; **Currency:** Lev; **Area:** 110,912 sq km; **Population:** 7,528,103; **Languages:** Bulgarian, Turkish; **Religions:** Christian-83.8%, Muslim-12.2%; **Literacy:** 98.3%; **Life Expectancy:** 73; **p.c.i:** $ 12,052; **HDI rank:** 58; **Date of Independence:** 3rd March, 1878.

Government Type: Parliamentary Democracy; **President:** Georgi Parvanov; **PM:** Boyko Borisov .

History: Situated on the Black Sea in eastern Balkan Peninsula, Bulgaria was founded in 681. Monarchy was abolished and a people's republic was proclaimed in

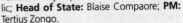

p.c.i: $ 1,341; **HDI rank:** 161; **Date of Independence:** 5th August, 1960. **Government Type:** Parliamentary Republic; **Head of State:** Blaise Compaore; **PM:** Tertius Zongo.

History: The Republic of Burkina Faso in West Africa is a landlocked state surrounded by Mali, Niger, Benin, Togo, Ghana and Cote D'Ivoire.

1946. The country's first free election after four decades of communist rule was held in 1990, and an 11-member Corporate Presidency was elected to power. In Oct. 1991, a non-communist government was elected. In Apr. '97 Bulgaria's reformist Union of Democratic Forces scored a resounding victory in parliamentary elections. The country became a member of NATO in 2003.

Economy: Principal products: Grains, tobacco, fruits, vegetables. Minerals: Coal, iron ore, copper, lead and zinc. Industry: Crude steel, pig iron, cement, chemicals, textiles, processed food.

Mission in India: Embassy of the Republic of Bulgaria, EP 16/17, Chandragupta Marg, Chana-kyapuri, New Delhi - 110021. Tel: 26115549, 26115551, 24108048; Fax: 26876190.

E-mail: bulemb@mantraonline.com

Website: www.bulgariaembindia.com

Indian Mission in Bulgaria: Embassy of India, 23, Sveti Sedmochislenitzi Street, Lozenets, Sofia 1421,Bulgaria. Tel: 00-359-2-9635675, 9635676, 9635677

E-mail: amb.sofia@mea.gov.in, hoc.sofia@mea.gov.in

Formerly a province of French West Africa called Upper Volta, the country changed its name to Burkina Faso in 1984.

Economy: It is almost exclusively an agricultural country with 80 per cent of the population dependent on agriculture. Livestock raising is highly developed. Principal crops are sorghum, millet, yams, cotton, rice, peanuts and karite. Industry is limited to local handicrafts and processed agricultural products. The country is heavily dependent on foreign aid. Some 2 million of its citizens live in nearby countries, most of them in Cote D' Ivoire and Ghana.

27. Burkina Faso

Capital: Ouagadougou; **Other Large Cities:** Koudougou,Banfora;**Currency:** Franc CFA; **Area:** 274,200 sq km; **Population:** 15,730,977; **Languages:** French and Sudanic tribal languages; **Religions:** Muslim-50%, Indigenous beliefs-40%, Christian-10%; **Literacy:** 28.7%; **Life Expectancy:** 52.3;

Mission in India: Embassy of Burkina Faso, F-3/1,Vasant Vihar, New Delhi-110 057. Tel: 2614 0641/42; Fax: 2614 0630.
E-mail: emburnd@bol.net.in

Consulate: Mumbai:Tel:23643093, Fax: 23645796.

E-mail:bhojwani@pn2.vsnl.net.in

Indian Mission in Burkina Faso: Embassy of India, No. 167, Rue Joseph Badoua, B.P. 6648, Ouagadougou- 01, Burkina Faso. Tel: +00-226-312009,00-226-314368

Highest Capital City	The world's highest "de facto" capital city is La Paz, the capital of Bolivia, which is located at an elevation of 3,660 metres above sea level.

Fax: +00-226-312012
Email: indemb@fasonet.bf

28. Burundi

(Republic of Burundi)-
Republikay' Ubu-rundi

Capital: Bujumbura;
Other Large Cities:
Kitega; **Currency:**
Burundi Franc; **Area:**
27,834 sq.km; **Popu-
lation:** 8,519,000;
Languages: French and Kirundi; **Religions:**
Christian-67%, indigenous beliefs-23%,
Muslim-10%, **Literacy:** 59.3%; **Life Expec-
tancy:** 49.6; **p.c.i:** $ 410; **HDI rank:** 166;
Date of Independence: 1st July, 1962.
Government Type: Republic; **President:**
Pierre Nkurunziza.
History: The Republic of Burundi is a small
state in east central Africa. Prior to indepen-
dence, it formed part of the Belgian-adminis-
tered UN Trust Territory of Rwanda-Urundi.

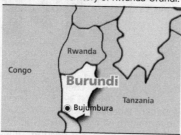

Economy: Burundi is a landlocked, resource-
poor country with an underdeveloped
manufacturing sector. The economy is
predominantly agricultural with 90% of
the population dependent on subsistence
agriculture. Economic growth depends on
coffee and tea exports, which account for
90% of foreign exchange earnings.

29. Cambodia

(Kingdom of Cambodia)
Preah Reach Ana Pak Kampuchea
Capital: Phnom-Penh; **Other Large Cities:**

Battambaug, Kam-
pong Chan; **Currency:**
Riel; **Area:** 181,035
sq km; **Population:**
13,395,682; **Languag-
es:** Khmer, French;
Religions: Buddhist-96.4%, Muslim-2.1%;
Literacy: 76.3%; **Life Expect-ancy:**
59.7; **p.c.i:** $ 2,086; **HDI rank:** 124; **Date of
Independence:** 9th November, 1953.
Government Type: Multiparty democracy
under a Constitutional Monarchy; **Head
of State:** King Norodom Sihamoni; **PM:**
Hun Sen.
History: Situated on the Indo-China Peninsula in south-east Asia, the People's Republic
of Kampuchea changed its name to the
original one Cambodia in May, 1989. For
some time–between Oct. 1970 and May
1975 – the country was also known as
Khmer Republic.

In May, 1993, the country held multi-party
elections. An interim government, was set
up by three parties, ending the 14-year reign
of the Vietnamese-installed administration.
In Sept., 1993, a new constitution was
signed, restoring Prince Sihanouk as King
of Cambodia. Khmer Rouge was outlawed
in July, 1994. They in turn, formed a provisional government.

In July 1997, second PM Hun Sen took
control of Phnom Penh and became the
supreme leader of the country. His rival, first
PM Norodom Ranariddh, fled the country.
The royalist Funcinpec party of Ranariddh
challenged the new first PM Ung Huot's election. Ranariddh was sentenced in absentia
in March to 5 years' R.I. by a military court.

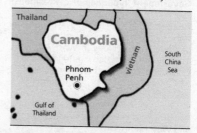

| Largest Temple | Angkor Wat, in Siem Reap, Cambodia, is the largest religious temple in the world. |

On Apr. 15, Pol Pot died. Hun Sen emerged the winner in the election of July, '98.

Economy: Cambodia is an under-developed country with 50 per cent of its land covered by virgin forests. Chief crops: Rice (occupies 90 per cent of arable land), maize, beans, black pepper, rubber. Cattle rearing and fishing are fairly well-developed. Tonle Sap is one of the world's richest sources of fresh-water fish, and most farmers are fishermen, too. The forests are rich in valuable timber. Minerals: Iron, copper, manganese and gold. Industry: Rice milling, wood and rubber.

Mission in India: Royal Embassy of Cambodia, W-112, Greater Kailash Part II, New Delhi-110 048. Tel: 2921 4435; Fax: 2921 4438.

E-mail:camboemb@bol.net.in

Indian Mission in Cambodia: Embassy of India, Villa No. 5, Street No. 466, Phnom Penh, Cambodia. Tel: 00-855-23-210912, 913; Fax: 00-855-23-213640.

E-mail:hocembindia@online.com.kh

30. Cameroon

Republic of Cameroon

Capital: Yaounde; **Other Large Cities:** Douala, Bafoussam; **Currency:** Franc CFA; **Area:** 475,442 sq.km; **Population:** 19,406,100; **Languages:** French, English; **Religions:** indigenous beliefs-40%, Christian-40%, Muslim-20%; **Literacy:** 67.9%; **Life Expectancy:** 50.4; **p.c.i.** $ 2,165; **HDI rank:** 131; **Date of Independence:** 1st January, 1960.

Government Type: Republic; **President:** Paul Biya; **PM:** Philemon Yang.

History: Situated between West and Central Africa, Cameroon was originally part of the German colony in West Africa. In 1961, British Cameroon was federated with Cameroon, forming the Federal Republic of Cameroon. In 1984, the country was renamed the Republic of Cameroon.

Cameroon has a central government and two provincial governments-East Cameroon and West Cameroon.

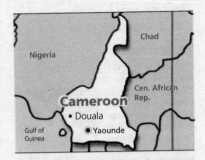

Economy: Cameroon is mainly an agricultural country raising cocoa, palm oil, coffee, rubber, groundnuts, bananas and cotton. East Cameroon is industrially developed. Major Industries are aluminium, chemicals, palm, consumer goods, crude oil, and cement.

31. Canada

Capital: Ottawa; **Other Large Cities:** Toronto, Montreal, Vancouver, Edmonton; **Currency:** Canadian dollar; **Area:** 9,976,139 sq.km; **Population:** 34,407,000; **Languages:** English, French; **Religions:** Roman Catholic-42.6%, Protestant-23.3%, Muslim-1.9%; **Literacy:** 99%; **Life Expectancy:** 80.7; **p.c.i:** $ 39,033; **HDI rank:** 8; **Date of Independence:** 1st July, 1867.

Government Type: Confederation with Parliamentary Democracy; **Head of State:** Queen Elizabeth II; **Governor-General:** David Johnston; **PM:** Stephen Harper.

History: Canada is the second-largest country in the world, but most of its territory is very sparsely settled. Canada, formerly British Colombia, was settled by Vikings in about 1000 BC. In 1497 AD, Canada was visited by Cabot.Quebec, one of the provinces in Canada was founded in 1608 by Champlain in a series of voyages he undertook to Canada. In 1774, the province of Quebec was created.

Migration of loyalists from USA after War of Independence led to division of Quebec

---

Cyrillic Alphabet | The Cyrillic alphabet originated in Bulgaria and is consequently used mostly in Slavic languages.

Mission in India: Canadian High Commission, 7/8 Shantipath, Chanakyapuri, New Delhi-110021. Tel: 4178-2000; Telefax: 4178-2020

E-mail: delhi@international.gc.ca
Web: www.india.gc.ca

Indian Mission in Canada: High Commission of India, 10, Springfield Road, Ottawa, Ontario K1M 1C9, Canada. Tel: 00-613-7443751/53; Fax: 00-613-7440913.

E-mail: hicomind@hciottawa.ca
Website: www.hciottawa.ca

into Upper and Lower Canada. In 1841, the Upper and Lower Canada reunited into Canada. And in 1867, the dominion of Canada was created by the confederation of Quebec, Ontario, Nova Scotia and New Brunswick.

Economy: Canada ranks seventh in the world in gross domestic product. The mineral industry, forest products, and agriculture have been major factors in Canada's economic development. Canada's lakes have more than 50% of the world's surface fresh water, and 75% of Canada's power needs are met by hydro-electric energy.

Agriculture's contribution to the Canadian economy averages less than 4% of both GDP and employment. Agricultural exports, led by wheat, barley, pork and horticultural products, are less than 10% of all trade. Forests cover about half of Canada's total land area. Canada is the world's leading producer of newsprint, accounting for 40% of global output.

Canada ranks first in the world in mineral exports and third in mineral production after the U.S and the states of the former Soviet Union. It is the world's largest producer of zinc, potash, uranium and nickel; the second-largest producer of asbestos, silver, titanium, gypsum and sulfur; and a leading producer of molybdenum, aluminium, cobalt, gold, led, copper, iron and platinum. Canada is a major producer of hydroelectricity, oil and gas; unlike most of its industrial partners, it is a net exporter of energy (primarily gas and electricity).

32. Cape Verde

Republic of Cape Verde/
Republica de Cabo Verde

Capital: Praia; **Currency:** Cape Verde Escudo; **Area:** 4033 sq.km; **Population:** 491,575; **Languages:** Portuguese, Crioulo; **Religions:** Christian-95%; **Literacy:** 83.8%; **Life Expectancy:** 71.7; **p.c.i:** $ 3,562; **HDI rank:** 118; **Date of Independence:** 5th July, 1975.

Government Type: Republic; **President:** Pedro Pires; **PM:** Jose Maria Neves.

History: Cape Verde is an archipelago of 15 islands in the Atlantic, 600 km west of Dakar, Senegal. Volcanic in origin, the islands are divided into two groups: Barlavento (windward) and Sotavento (leeward). Most Cape Verdeans are descendants of the first Portuguese colonists who came in 1462 and the African slaves brought in soon after.

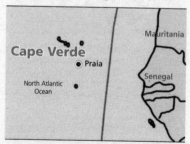

The brightest astronomical event in historic times was the supernova of 1054, which produced the Crab Nebula. The supernova was far brighter than Venus. It was bright enough to be visible in daylight and to cast a shadow at night.

Crab Nebula

Economy: Chief crops are banana, coffee, coconuts, sugarcane, maize, beans. Fishing is important. Minerals: salt.

33. Cen. African Republic

Republique Centrafricaine

Capital: Bangui; **Other Large Cities:** Bambari, Bouar; **Currency:** Franc CFA; **Area:** 622,984 sq.km; **Population:** 4,506,000; **Languages:** French and Sangho; **Religions:** Indigenous beliefs-35%, Protestant-25%, Roman Catholic-25%, Muslim-15%; **Literacy:** 48.6%; **Life Expectancy:** 44.7; **p.c.i:** $ 764; **HDI rank:** 159; **Date of Independence:** 13th August, 1960.

Government Type: Republic; **President:** Francois Bozize; **PM:** Faustin-Archange Touadera.

History: The Central African Republic lies in the heart of equatorial Africa. In 1966 Col. Jean Bedel Bokasa, Chief of Staff of the Army, ousted President David Dacko and seized control of the government.

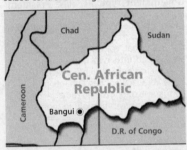

Bokasa was made President for life in 1972. In 1976, he set himself up an emperor, after the Napoleonic pattern. In 1979 a popular uprising drove him out. There was another coup in 1981. A civilian government was installed in 1993.

A government of national unity was formed in June, 1996, after an army mutiny of a month earlier was suppressed with the help of French troops. There was another mutiny in Jan. '97, which ended after French intervention.

Economy: Principal agricultural products are cotton, coffee, groundnuts and tobacco. Cotton leads in exports. Diamonds account for half of the country's export earnings. Uranium mining is becoming increasingly important. Industry: timber, textiles, light manufacturing.

34. Chad

(Republic of Chad) Republique du Tchad

Capital: N'Djamena; **Other Large Cities:** Sarh, Moundou; **Currency:** Franc CFA; **Area:** 1,284,000 sq.km; **Population:** 11,506,000; **Languages:** French, Arabic and over 100 tribal languages; **Religions:** Muslim-53.1%, Christian-34.3%; **Literacy:** 31.8%; **Life Expectancy:** 50.6; **p.c.i:** $ 1,653; **HDI rank:** 163; **Date of Independence:** 11th August, 1960.

Government Type: Republic; **President:** Idriss Deby; **PM:** Emmanuel Nadingar.

History: The Republic of Chad, a landlocked country in North Central Africa, was a province of French Equatorial Africa. The country gets its name from Lake Chad, which lies on the western border with Niger and Nigeria. Northern Muslim rebels have fought Southern Christian government and

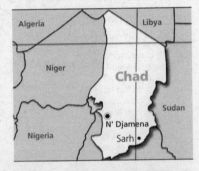

Around the Globe on a Balloon

In 1999, Brian Jones and Bertrand Piccard became the first balloonists to circumnavigate the globe non-stop taking 19 days, 21 hours and 55 minutes to travel the 29,000 miles in the balloon Breitling-Orbiter 3.

French troops since 1966. Idriss Deby took control in 1990.

Economy: The country's economy is entirely rural and based on agriculture and animal husbandry. Cotton and meat are the main exports. Cattle, sheep and camels are raised.

35. Chile

(Republic of Chile) Republica de Chile

Capital: Santiago; **Other Large Cities:** Valparaiso, Antofagasta; **Currency:** Chilean Peso; **Area:** 756,626 sq. km; **Population:** 17,211,600; **Languages:** Spanish; **Religions:** Christian-87.2%; **Literacy:** 96.5%; **Life Expectancy:** 78.6; **p.c.i:** $ 14,952; **HDI rank:** 45; **Date of Independence:** 18th September, 1810.

Government Type: Republic; **Head of State& Govt (President):** Sebastian Pinera Echenique.

History: The Republic of Chile lies on the western seaboard of South America, occupying the strip of land between Peru and Bolivia in the north to Cape Horn in the south.

It is the first South American country to elect a Marxist Govt. (under Salvador Allende in 1970) which fell in a military coup in 1973. Human rights violations marked the rule of Augusto Pinochet, removed from office in 1989. Pinochet was arrested in London in Oct. '98, but returned to Chile in March, 2000. Put under house arrest, he was declared to be unfit to stand trial in July 2001.

Economy: Though wheat, other cereals, potatoes, beans etc. are cultivated, Chile has to import about one-third of its food. It is one of world's largest producers and a leading exporter of copper. There are significant deposits of nitrate, gold, silver, lithium, molybdenum and iron ore. Oil production provides about half the oil required by the country. Exports: marine products and fruits. Thirty percent of Chile's trade is with Asian countries, 38% with EU, and the rest falls within the Americas. Industries: Fish processing, textiles, wood products.

Tierra del Fuego is the largest island in the archipelago of the same name at the southern tip of S. America. Part of the island is in Chile, part in Argentina.

Mission in India: Embassy of the Republic of Chile, 146, Jor Bagh, New Delhi-110003; Tel: 24617123, 24617165, 24617270; Telefax: 91-11-24617102.

E-mail: embchile3@vsnl.com

Indian Mission in Chile: Embassy of India, 871, Triana, Post Box No. 10433, Santigao, Chile. Tel: 00-56-2-2352005, 2352633; Fax: 00-56-2-2359607.

E-mail:chancery@embajadaindia.cl

36. China

(People's Republic of China)
Zhonghua Renmin Gonghe Guo

Capital: Beijing (Peking); **Other Large Cities:** Shanghai, Canton, Shenzhen; **Currency:** Renminbi Yuan; **Area:** 9,561,000 sq.km; **Population:** 1,341,000,000; **Languages:** Chinese (Mandarin) and other local languages; **Religions:** Officially Atheist, Buddhism, Taoism, Muslim, Christian; **Literacy:** 93.3%; **Life Expectancy:** 73; **p.c.i:** $ 7,518; **HDI rank:** 89; **Date of Independence:** 221 BC (unification under the Qin or Ch'in Dynasty); 1st January, 1912 (Qing Dynasty replaced by a Republic); 1st October 1949 (People's Republic established)

Government Type: Communist state; **President:** Hu Jintao; **PM:** Wen Jiabao.

Tiger Moms

Amy Chua, a Chinese-American law lecturer, has whipped up a storm with her book *Battle Hymn of the Tiger Mother*. She argues that "Chinese parents raise such stereotypically successful kids', because "Chinese mothers are superior".

History: The most populous country in the world and the third largest in area, China is made up of 22 provinces, 5 autonomous regions and four municipalities. It occupies most of the habitable mainland of East Asia. Two-thirds of the territory is mountainous or desert; only one-tenth is cultivated. The eastern half of China is one of the world's best-watered lands. Three great river systems (the Chang or Yangtze, Huang or Yellow and Xi) provide water for the farmlands.

Following internal conflicts after World War II involving the Kuomintang, Communists and other factions, China came under the domination of Communist armies. The People's Republic of China was proclaimed in Peking on October 1, 1949, under Mao Tse-Tung. The Kuomin-tang govt. moved to Taiwan, Dec. 8, 1949. Mao died in 1976 and Deng Xiaoping succeeded him as the 'paramount leader' of China. Deng died in 1997 and Jiang Zemin came to power.

On Oct. 26, 1971 China was admitted a member of the UN, displacing Nationalist China (Taiwan).

Student uprising in 1989 for political reform and liberalisation was put down by the government. Tiananmen Square, outside the Great Hall of the People, was the main scene of the demonstrations. It is estimated that 5000 people died and 10,000 were injured. China released its top dissident leader Wang Dan in Apr. 98.

Economy: China is essentially an agricultural country. The main crops are rice, tea, tobacco, sugarcane, jute, soya, groundnut and hemp. The main forest products are teak and ting oil. Among the principal industries are cotton and woollen mills, iron, leather and electrical equipments. The chief minerals are coal, manganese, iron ore, gold, copper, lead, zinc, silver, tungsten, mercury, antimony and tin. Petroleum industry is steadily growing.

In late 1978, the Chinese leadership began moving the economy from a Soviet-style centrally planned economy to a more market-oriented system. The result has been a quadrupling of GDP since 1978.

Tibet: One of the five autonomous regions, Tibet is a thinly populated region of high plateaus and massive mountains. Capital is Lhasa, and population about 2.44m., of whom 500,000 are Chinese. China installed a Communist govt. in 1953, revising the theocratic Lamaist Buddhist rule. There was an uprising in 1959. It was crushed, and Buddhism was almost totally suppressed. The Dalai Lama and 100,000 Tibetans fled to India.

Chinese rule over Tibet is controversial. Human rights groups accuse the authorities of the systematic destruction of Tibetan Buddhist culture and the persecution of monks loyal to the Dalai Lama, the exiled spiritual leader who is campaigning for autonomy within China.

Mission in India: Embassy of the People's Republic of China, 50-D, Shantipath, Chanakyapuri, New Delhi-110021. Tel: 2611 2345; Fax:2688 5486.

E-mail:chinaemb_in@mfa.gov.cn

Indian Mission in China: Embassy of India, 1, Ritan Dong Lu, Beijing 100600, China. Tel: 00-86-10-65321908; Fax: 00-86-10-65324684.

E-mail:webmaster@indianembassy.org.cn

Hong Kong

Hong Kong became a Special Administrative Region of China on July 1, '97 when the colony was handed over by Britain, which ruled it for 156 years.

Capital: Victoria; **Currency:** Hong Kong dollar; **Area:** 1071 sq.km; **Population:** 7,061,200; **Languages:** English and Can-

Russia
Mongolia
Great Wall of China
Beijing
Sea of Japan
China
Tibet
Shanghai
India
Shenzhen
Hong Kong
Macao

China's Box-office Gold

China's biggest domestic box-office hit to date is a freewheeling romp full of sex, violence, and humour. *Let the Bullets Fly*, directed by Jiang Wen, tells the brutally comic tale of a bandit facing off with the local strongman for control of a provincial town.

tonese; **Religions:** Confucianism and Buddhism; **Life Expectancy:** 82.2; **Literacy:** 94.6%; **p.c.i:** $ 45,277; **HDI rank:** 21; **Date of Independence:** Special Administrative region of China.
Government Type: Limited Democracy; **Chief Executive:** Donald Tsang.

Lying along the south east coast of China, at the mouth of the Canton river, Hong Kong comprises Hong Kong island, Kowloon Peninsula, the New Territories and over 230 small islands. Hong Kong became a British colony in 1843. The New Territories were acquired by Britain in 1898 by lease for 99 years. By an agreement reached in 1984, China recovered sovereignty over Hong Kong in July 1997.

The population is almost entirely Chinese with a sprinkling of other nationalities. It is one of the world's greatest transhipment ports.
Indian Mission in Hong Kong: Consulate General of India, 16-D United Centre, 95, Queensway, Hong Kong. Tel: 00-852-25284028, 25272275; Fax: 00-852-28664124.

E-mail:cg@indianconsulate.org.uk/consular@indianconsulate.org.hk

Web: www.indianconsulate.org.hk

Macao

Capital: Macao; **Currency:** Macanese pataca; **Area:** 15.5 sq.km; **Population:** 542,200; **Languages:** Portuguese and Cantonese; **Religions:** Confucianism; **Life Expectancy:** 80.7; **Literacy:** 91.3%; **p.c.i:** $ 30,000.
Chief Executive: Fernando Chui Sai-on.

Macao or Macau is a former Portuguese territory in South China, at the mouth of the Canton river. The territory consists of the Macao peninsula and the adjoining islands of Taipa and Coloane. Portugal granted it broad autonomy in 1976. As per the agreement between Portugal and China, Macao reverted to China on Dec. 20, 1999. China has permitted Macao to continue as an independent territory mainly because of the big entrepot trade it commands. Macao is a free market for gold and an infamous centre of smuggling and gambling. China has pledged to Portugal that it will implement the 'one country two systems' principle in Macao.

The population is almost entirely Chinese. Industry, once restricted to matches and fireworks, now includes plastics, textiles, cameras, binoculars and such other consumer items. Cultivation is sparse. Only rice and vegetables are grown. Macao has an important fishing industry.

37. Colombia

(Republic of Colombia)
Republica de Colombia

Capital: Bogota;
Other Large Cities: Medellin, Cartagena;
Currency: Colombian Peso; **Area:** 1,139,000 sq. km;
Population: 45,920,000; **Languages:** Spanish; **Religions:** Roman Catholic-90%; **Literacy:** 92.7%; **Life Expectancy:**72.9; **p.c.i:** $ 9,445; **HDI rank:** 79; **Date of Independence:** 20th July, 1810.
Government Type: Republic; **Head of State & Govt (President):** Juan Manuel Santos.
History: Colombia was discovered by Alonso de Ojeda in 1499. It was once a part of the South American Spanish Empire. In 1819, Simon Bolivar, the first President, broke the hold of Spain. Bolivar united New Granada, as it was called, with Venezuela and Ecuador in the Greater Colombia Confederation in

1819. Venezuela and Ecuador broke away in 1929-30, and Panama withdrew in 1903.

Economy: Colombia is the largest producer and exporter of mild coffee. Other products are bananas, fresh flowers, cotton fibre, sugar, rice, tobacco, maize and wheat. The country is the world's leading producer of emeralds (50% world output) and is a substantial producer of platinum and gold; it holds the largest coal reserves in Latin America, rich nickel deposits and natural gas fields.

Industries include textiles, cement, motor vehicles, beverages, food products, chemicals and non-metallic minerals.

Mission in India: Embassy of Colombia, 3 Palam Marg, First Floor, Vasant Vihar, New Delhi-110 057; Tel:4166 2103, 4166 2105; Fax: 4166 2104

E-mail: edelhi@minrelext.gov.in

Indian Mission in Colombia: Embassy of India, Avenida Calle 116,No. 7-15, Int. 2,Off. 301, Torre Cusezar,Santa Barbara, Bogota D.C.,Colombia. Tel: 00-57-1-6373259/ 279/ 280/ 289, Fax: 00-57-1-6373451/ 516.E-mail:hoc.bogota@mea.gov.in, indembog@cable.net.co

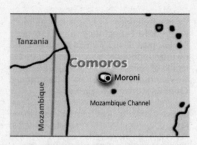

moroe, Anjouan and Moheli—and a number of islets and coral reefs. With neighbouring Mayotte, they were attached to Madagascar from 1914 to 1947, when the four islands became a French Overseas Territory. In a 1974 referendum, the three islands voted for independence while Mayotte voted to remain French.

Economy: Agriculture is the mainstay of the economy. (Vanilla, copra, perfume plants, fruits). Industry: Perfumes.

Mission in India: Hon. Consul General: K.L. Ganju, 27-28 G. Floor, Double Storey, New Rajinder Nagar, New Delhi - 110060; Tel: 2874 1319/2874 1328. e-mail: klganju@hotmail.com

38. The Comoros

(Federal Islamic Republic of the Comoros) Jumhuriyat al-Qumer al-Itthadiyah al-Islamiyah

Capital: Moroni; **Other Large Cities:** Fomboni, Mutsamudu; **Currency:** Comorian Franc; **Area:** 1862 sq.km; **Population:** 691,000; **Languages:** Arabic and Comoran; **Religions:** Islam-98%; **Literacy:** 75.1%; **Life Expectancy:** 65.2; **p.c.i:** $ 1,176; **HDI rank:** 140; **Date of Independence:** 6th July, 1975.

Government Type: Republic; **Head of State (President):** Ikililou Dhoinine.

History: The Comoro Islands lie at the northern end of the Mozambique Channel, between Africa and Madagascar. The archipelago consists of 3 islands—Grande-Co-

39. Congo, D.R. of (Formerly Zaire)

Democratic Republic of the Congo

Capital: Kinshasa; **Other Large Cities:** Lubumbashi, Kananga; **Currency:** Congolese Franc; **Area:** 2,344,885 sq km; **Population:** 67,827,000; **Languages:** French, Kiswahili, Lingala and other African languages; **Religions:** Roman Catholic-50%,Protestant-20%, Kimbanguist-10%, Muslim-10%; **Literacy:** 67.2%; **Life Expectancy:** 46.5; **p.c.i:** $ 340; **HDI rank:** 168; **Date of Independence:** 30th June, 1960.

Government Type: Republic; **President:** Gen. Joseph Kabila. **PM:** Adolphe Muzito.

History: The history of DR Congo has been one of civil war and corruption. After inde-

Vaccine for Malaria

Manuel Elkin Patarroyo is a Colombian who developed a vaccine for malaria. He donated the rights for the vaccine to the World Health Organization.

Franc CFA; **Area:** 342,000 sq km; **Population:** 3,759,000; **Languages:** French, Lingala, Congo, Teke; **Religions:** Christian-50%, animist-48%, Muslim-2%; **Literacy:** 81.1%; **Life Expectancy:** 55.3; **p.c.i:** $4,487; **HDI rank:** 126; **Date of Independence:** 15th August 1960 **Government Type:** Republic; **President:** Gen. Denis Sassou Nguesso.

pendence in 1960, the country immediately faced an army mutiny and an attempt at secession by its mineral-rich province of Katanga. A year later, its prime minister, Patrice Lumumba, was seized and killed by troops loyal to army chief Joseph Mobutu. In 1965 Mobutu seized power, later renaming the country Zaire and himself Mobutu Sese Seko. He turned Zaire into a springboard for operations against Soviet-backed Angola and thereby ensured US backing. But he also made Zaire synonymous with corruption. After the Cold War, Zaire ceased to be of interest to the US.

Economy: The major assets of Congo are her copper mines and the diamond deposits. The country is rich in other minerals like cobalt (60% of world reserves), cadmium, manganese, zinc and uranium. The forests abound in high class wood like mahogany, ebony and teak. Principal agricultural products are coffee, palm oil, rubber, sugarcane, maize, rice, cassava and plantains. Main manufactures are tobacco, textiles, wood products, metal items, building materials, foodstuffs and beverages.

Mission in India: Embassy of the Democratic Republic of Congo, B-2/6, Vasant Vihar, New Delhi-110057. Tel: 4166 0976.

E-mail: CongoEmbassy@yahoo.co.in

40. Congo

(Republic of the Congo)
Republique du Congo

Capital: Brazzaville; **Other Large Cities:** Pointe-Noire, Loubomo; **Currency:**

History: Formerly part of the French Equatorial Africa, the Republic of Congo in West Central Africa became autonomous within the French Community in 1958 and fully independent in Aug. 1960. In 1963, the country adopted a Marxist-Leninist stance. In 1969, a new constitution was promulgated. Marxism was renounced in 1990. A democratically elected government came into office in 1992.

In June 97, fighting broke out between armed forces backing President Lissouba and his once marxist predecessor Denis Sassou Nguesso. Troops loyal to the latter took control of Brazzaville in October.

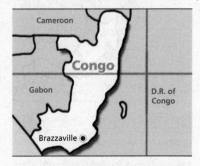

Economy: Agriculture: Palm oil and kernels, cassava, cocoa, coffee, tobacco. Industry: Processed foods, textiles, cement, metal industries. Main exports: timber, diamonds, palm oil, crude petroleum, sugar and groundnuts.

Mission in India: Embassy of the Republic of Congo stationed at Beijing.

41. Costa Rica

(Republic of Costa Rica)
Republica de Costa Rica

Capital: San Jose;
Other Large Cities:
Alajuela, Cartago;
Currency: Costa Rica
n Colon; **Area:** 51,100

sq.km; **Population:**
4,563,538; **Languages:** Spanish, English;
Religions: Christian-87.3%-92%; **Literacy:**
95.9%; **Life Expectancy:** 78.8; **p.c.i:** $
10,732; **HDI rank:** 62; **Date of Independence:** 15th September 1821.
Government Type: Democratic Republic;
Head of State & Govt (President): Laura
Chinchilla Miranda.

The Republic of Costa Rica (the Rich
Coast) is a Central American state. It lies
between Nicaragua and Panama.
History: For nearly three centuries Costa
rica formed part of the Spanish American
dominion.

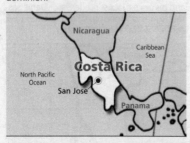

Economy: The country is mainly agricultural.
Coffee is the most important product, accounting for about half the exports. Other
crops include banana, sugar, cocoa, cotton.
Bananas, cocoa, cattle and, recently, sugar
are exported. In recent years there has been
a shift towards high-tech exports like computer chips and services. Now Costa Rica is
the largest exporter of technology goods
per capita in Latin America. After abolishing its army nearly half a century ago, the
country has pumped large sums of money
into education, creating a highly skilled
workforce that reflects a population with a
95% literacy rate.

Industry: Pharmaceuticals, furniture,
aluminium, textiles, tourism. People enjoy a
relatively high standard of living. 93%
have electricity. Silicon processors have brought prosperity to Costa Rica in recent
years.

Mission in India: Hon. Consulate General of Costa Rica, D-388 Defence Colony,
New Delhi-110 024. Tel:24625670; Fax:
23327231;

E-mail: bradynd@de12.vsnl.net.in

42.Cote D' Ivoire (Ivory Coast)

(Republique de la Cote d'Ivoire)

Capital: Yamoussoukro (official), Abidjan(de
facto); **Other Large
Cities:** Bouake; **Currency:** Franc CFA;
Area: 322,462 sq.km.;

Population: 21,571,000; **Languages:**
French and Tribal; **Religions:** Muslim-38.6%,
Christian-32.8%, Indigenous-11.9%.
The majority of foreigners (migratory
workers) are Muslim-70% and Christian
(20%); **Literacy:** 48.7%; **Life Expectancy:**
48.3; **p.c.i:** $ 1,686; **HDI rank:** 149; **Date
of Independence:** 7th August, 1960.
Government Type: Republic; **President:**
Alassane Ouattara; **PM:** Guillaume Soro.

Cote D'Ivoire in Western Africa is bordered
by Mali and Burkina Faso in the north, Ghana
in the east, the Gulf of Guinea in the south,
and Liberia and Guinea in the west.
History: The Republic of Ivory Coast, once
an overseas territory of France, became independent on August 7, 1960. From 1986,
the French version of the name became the
only correct title. There are about 60 ethnic
groups, the principal being the Baule, the
Bete and the Senufo. General Robert Guei
seized power in Dec, 1999. There was a coup
attempt in 2002. A peace agreement was
signed in 2003, but there was trouble again.
A power-sharing plan was arrived at in Mar.

Some Like it Hot	Vinegar, hot peppers and salt are the three ingredients of Tabasco sauce. Every drop of the sauce is aged, distilled and bottled on Louisiana's Avery Island since Edmund McIlhenny came up with the recipe in 1868.

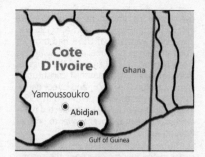

03, and ceasefire signed in May.

Economy: Agriculture, forestry and fishing employ 90 per cent of the population. Cote D'Ivoire is world's largest cocoa producer, the third most important coffee producer and the most important African producer of timber. Sugar, cotton, bananas and pineapples are other important crops. Industrialisation has developed rapidly since independence, particularly food processing, textiles and saw mills. Important minerals: Diamonds and manganese.

Mission in India: Embassy of Cote D' Ivoire,B-9/6,Vasant Vihar,New Delhi-110 057. Tel: 4604 3000.

E-mail: embassy@amb2ci-inde.org

Indian Mission in Cote D'Ivoire (Ivory Coast): Embassy of India, Villa/Lot No. 2728, ILot 229, 7eme Tranche,II-Plateaux - Angre Abidjan 06 B.P. 318,Abidjan 06,Cote d'Ivoire. Tel: 00-225-22423769, 22427079; Fax: 00-225-22426649.

E-mail:indemabj@afnet.net

43. Croatia

(Republic of Croatia) Republika Hrvatska

Capital: Zagreb; **Other Large Cities:** Zagreb, Split; **Currency:** Kuna; **Area:** 56,538 sq. km; **Population:**

4,425,747; **Languages:** Serbo-Croatian; **Religions:** Christian-92.6%, Muslim-1.3%; **Literacy:** 98.7%; **Life Expectancy:** 75.7; **p.c.i:** $ 17,608; **HDI rank:** 51; **Date of**

Independence: 25th June, 1991.

Government Type: Presidential/Parliamentray Democracy; **President:** Ivo Josipovic ; **PM:** Jadranka Kosor.

History: Former Yugoslavia's second largest republic, Croatia in S.E. Europe, has an extensive Adriatic coastline.

Croats migrated to their present territory in the 6th century. Croatia was united with Hungary in 1091. In 1918, Croatia became a part of the new Kingdom of Serbs, Croats and Slovenes, which was renamed Yugoslavia in 1929. Croatia then became one of the six 'Socialist Republics' constituting the Yugoslav federation. On June 25, 1991, Croatia declared independence. Serbs rebelled, sparking a 7 month-long civil war. The Krajina and other predominantly Serb areas proclaimed the desire for union with Serbia. UN peace-keeping mission arrived at the beginning of 1992. European Community (EC) recognised Croatia on January 15, 1992. Fighting between ethnic Serbs and Croats continued. A ceasefire with Serb rebels forming a self-declared republic of Krajina was agreed to in March,1994. In Aug, '96, Croatia and Serbia agreed to resume normal diplomatic ties after years of hostility. Croatia joined NATO's extended family in May, 2000.

Ethnic breakdown: Croats–75%; Serbs–12%; others–13%.

Economy: Agricultural products: Wheat, maize, potatoes, olives, plums, livestock, timber. Industry: Textiles, chemicals, coal, lignite, cement, sugar, steel, plastics, textiles.

Mission in India: Embassy of the Republic of Croatia, A-15, West End, New Delhi-110 021. Tel: 4166 3101; Fax: 2411 6873

E-mail:croemb.new-delhi@mvpei.hr

Indian Mission in Croatia: Embassy of India, Embassy of India,Kulmerska 23A, 10000 Zagreb, Croatia. Tel: 00-385-1-4873239/40/41; Fax: 00-385-1-4817907.

E-mail:embassy.india@zg.htnet.hr

44. Cuba

(Republic of Cuba) Republica de Cuba

Capital: Havana; **Other Large Cities:** Santiago de Cuba, Santa Clara; **Currency:** Cuban Peso; **Area:** 110,922 sq.km; **Population:** 11,240,841; **Languages:** Spanish; **Religions:** Nominally 85% Roman Catholic before Castro assuming power; **Literacy:** 99.8%; **Life Expectancy:** 78.3; **p.c.i :** $ 9,700; **Date of Independence:** 20th May, 1902. **Government Type:** Communist State; **Head of State & Govt (President):** Raul Castro Ruz.

History: Cuba, the largest island in the Greater Antilles group is known as the Pearl of the Caribbean Sea. It is formed by two main islands - the island of Cuba and the Isle of Youth- and more than 4000 keys and small isles.

Columbus discovered Cuba in 1492 and Spain ruled it for four centuries.

In 1959 Dr. Fidel Castro overthrew General Batista, the dictatorial president and took over power. Emigres made an unsuccessful invasion at the Bay of Pigs in Apr. 1961. In 1962 USA learned that USSR had brought nuclear missiles to Cuba. After a warning from President J.F. Kennedy, the missiles were removed. A communist constitution came into force in 1976, and direct parliamentary elections were permitted in 1992. In Jan. '98, Fidel Castro was re-elected president. Castro handed over power to brother Raul on July 31, 2006.

Economy: Cuba is the largest producer of sugar in the world. Tobacco is the second largest crop. Cattle, poultry and fishing have become important in recent years. Cuba is rich in nickel deposits.

Mission in India: Embassy of the Republic of Cuba,W-124 A, Greater Kailash-I, New Delhi-110 048. Tel: 2924 2467,2924 2468; Fax:2923 2469.

E-mail: embcuind@del6.vsnl.net.in

Indian Mission in Cuba: Embassy of India, No. 202, Calle 21, Esquina a 'K',Vedado, Havana, Cuba. Tel: 00-53-7-8333777, 8333169, 551700; Fax: 001-8146801064, 00-53-7-8333287.

E-mail:hoc@indembassyhavana.cu

45. Cyprus

(Republic of Cyprus) Kypriaki Dimokratia (Greek)/Kibiris Cumhuriyeti (Turkish)

Capital: Nicosia; **Other Large Cities:** Limassol, Larnanca; **Currency:** Euro; **Area:** 9,251 sq.km; **Population:** 801,851; **Languages:** Greek, Turkish and English; **Religions:** Greek Orthodox-78%, Muslim-18%, other (includes Maronite and Amenian Apostolic) 4%; **Literacy:** 97.7%; **Life Expectancy:** 79; **p.c.i :** $ 28,045; **HDI rank:** 35; **Date of Indepe dence:** 16th August, 1960. **Government Type:** Republic; **President:** Demetris Christofias.

History: The Republic of Cyprus lies in the North Eastern corner of the East Mediterranean basin, at the meeting point of three

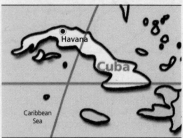

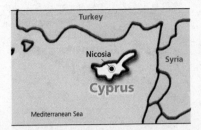

continents—Europe, Asia and Africa. In 1974 it was invaded by Turkey and nearly 40% of its territory is still under Turkish occupation. A Turkish Cypriot Federated State was proclaimed in 1975 and in 1983 the state unilaterally proclaimed itself as the 'Turkish Republic of Northern Cyprus' (TRNC). In 1994, informal talks were held between the Presidents of Cyprus and TRNC but no progress was made. In Aug '96, violence jolted Cypriots on both sides. UN attempts to reunify Cyprus have not been successful.

Economy: The healthy climate and the natural beauty of the island make it an ideal place for tourists.

Cyprus is mainly an agricultural island. Main agricultural exports are: potatoes, grapes, carrots, fresh vegetables, citrus, milk. Main industrial exports are: readymade clothing, footwear, cement, travel goods, plastic products, water pumps, furniture, cosmetics, etc.

Mission in India: High Commission of the Republic of Cyprus, 67, Jor Bagh, New Delhi-110 003. Tel: 2469 7503, 2469 7508; Fax: 2462 8828.

E-mail:cyprus@del3.vsnl.net.in

Web: www.cyprushedelhi.com

Indian Mission in Cyprus: High Commission of India, 3, Indira Gandhi Street, Montparnasse Hill, P.O. Box 25544, Engomi, 2413 Nicosia, Cyprus. Tel: 00-357-2-351741, 351170; Fax: 00-357-2-350402.

E-mail: hcoffice@cytanet.com.cy

46. Czech Republic

(Ceska Republika)

Capital: Prague; **Other Large Cities:** Brno, Ostrava; **Currency:** Koruna; **Area:** 78,864 sq km; **Population:** 10,515,818; **Languages:** Czech; **Religions:** Roman Catholic-26.8%, Protestant-2.1%, other-3.3%, unspecified-8.8%, unaffiliated-59%; **Literacy:** 99%; **Life Expectancy:** 76.5; **p.c.i:** $ 24,987; **HDI rank:** 28; **Date of Independence:** 1st January, 1993.

Government Type: Parliamentary Democracy; **President:** Vaclav Klaus; **PM:** Petr Necas.

History: The Czech Republic and Slovakia became independent states when the Czech and Slovak Federal Republic (Czechoslovakia) was dissolved.

Czechoslovakia, a republic landlocked in Central Europe, was composed of 64% Czechs and 31% Slovaks. The Czechoslovak Socialist Republic was established in January 1969 as a federal state of two nations of equal rights. In 1990, the country changed its name to the Czech and Slovak Federative Republic and dropped 'socialist' to symbolise its departure from the communist past. Disputes between the two regions over post-

communist reforms turned the union bitter. In June, 1992 the 74-year old federation's Czech and Slovak regions agreed to part.

Economy: Agriculture: Sugarbeet, wheat, potatoes, barley, maize, rye. Industry: Pig iron, crude steel, rolled steel products, cement, paper, sulphuric acid, synthetic fibres, sugar, beer, armaments, cars. Minerals: Coal, caolin, uranium.

Mission in India: Embassy of the Czech

Mendel's Birthplace	Gregor Johann Mendel, the biologist and botanist who established the basis of modern genetics , was born in Hyncice in the present-day Czech Republic

Republic, 50-M, Niti Marg, Chanakyapuri, New Delhi-110 021, Tel: 2611 0205, 2611 0318, 2611 0382, 2688 6218; Fax: 91-11-2688 6221.

E-mail: newdelhi@embassy.mzv.cz
Web: mfa.cz/newdelhi

Indian Mission in Czech Republic: Embassy of India, Milady Horakove 60/93,170 00, Prague 7,Czech Republic. Tel: 00-420-2-57533; Fax:00-420-2-57533378, 57533285.

E-mail: india@india.cz, hoc@india.cz

47. Denmark

(Kingdom of Denmark)
Kongeriget Danmark

Capital: Copenhagen; **Other Large Cities:** Odense, Alborg, Randers; **Currency:** Danish Krone; **Area:** 43,074 sq km; **Population:** 5,560,628; **Languages:** Danish; **Religions:** Evangelical Lutheran-95%, other Christian(includes Protestant and Roman Catholic) 3%, Muslim-2%; **Literacy:** 99%; **Life Expectancy:** 78.3; **p.c.i:** $ 36,764; **HDI rank:** 19; **Date of Independence:** Denmark was first organised as a unified state in the 10th century. In 1849, Denmark became a Constitutional Monarchy.

Government Type: Constitutional Monarchy; **Head of State:** Queen Margrethe II; **PM:** Lars Loekke Rasmussen.

History: Denmark, the smallest of the Scandinavian countries, is situated in northern Europe between the North Sea and the Baltic Sea. It comprises the peninsula of Jutland, the Islands of Zealand, Funen and Bornholm and 480 smaller islands. No one in Denmark is more than 52 km from the sea. No wonder that the Danes were Vikings a few generations ago.

Denmark is a constitutional monarchy, the Queen and the Parliament (Folketing) jointly holding legislative powers.

Economy: About 62 per cent of the land is under cultivation. Denmark is one of the largest exporters of dairy products. Fishing forms an important occupation. Denmark is famous for its co-operative institutions. The first co-operative society was established in 1866. Shipbuilding, machinery of different types, textiles, furniture, iron and steel-ware account for a major portion of industry. Danish exports include stylish furniture, the hi-fi equipment of Bang & Olufsen, and the ubiquitous plastic Lego bricks. Carlsberg beer is one of the world's most venerable brands.

Mission in India: Royal Danish Embassy, 11-Aurangzeb Rd., New Delhi-110011. Tel: 4209 0700, 4209 0751(Visa); Telefax: 2379 2019, 2379 2891.

E-mail: delamb@um.dk

Indian Mission in Denmark: Embassy of India, Vangehusvej 15, 2100 Copenhagen, Denmark. Tel: 00-45-39299201, 39182888, 39182995; Telefax: 00-45-39270218.

E-mail:indemb@email.dk

Outlying Territories of Denmark

The Faeroe Islands

Capital: Torshavn; **Area:** 1399 sq.km; **Population:** 48,585
PM: Kaj Leo Johannessen.

The islands, in the North Atlantic, are mountainous and of volcanic origin. The islands have been represented in the Dan-

---

Prague Spring

In 1968 Alexander Dubcek's government tried to introduce a more liberal form of communism - this was known as the "Prague Spring". In August the USSR occupied Czechoslovakia and removed Dubcek and other government leaders from office.

ish Parliament since 1851. They are self-governing in most matters.

Only 2% of the surface is cultivated. Grazing is the mainstay of the economy. Deep sea fishing is the most important sector.

Greenland

Capital: Nuuk (Godthaab); **Area:** 2,175,600 sq.km; **Population:** 56,452.
PM: Kuupik Kleist.

The world's largest island, Greenland lies between the North Atlantic and the Polar Sea. Over 80% of the area is ice-capped.

A Danish possession since 1380, Greenland became an integral part of the Danish Kingdom in 1953. In 1979 home rule was won by Greenland. With this, Greenlandic place names came into official use. Greenland is now Kalaallit Nunaat. The capital is Nuuk (old one Gothab). Full internal self-government was attained in Jan., 1981.

Fish is the main product of the island. Greenland is the world's only source of natural cryolite, important in making aluminium.

48. Djibouti

(Republic of Djibouti) Jumhouriyya Djibouti

Capital: Djibouti; **Currency:** Djibouti Franc; **Area:** 21,783 sq.km; **Population:** 879,000; **Languages:** French, Arabic, Affar, Issa; **Religions:** Islam-94%, Christian-6%; **Literacy:** 70.3%; **Life Expectancy:** 54.8; **p.c.i:** $ 2,553; **HDI rank:** 147; **Date of Independence:** 27th June, 1977.

Government Type: Republic; **President:** Ismail Omar Guelleh; **PM:** Mohamed Dileita Dileita

History: Djibouti was first known as French Somaliland and then as the French Territory of Afars and Issas. Lying between Ethiopia and Somalia and looking out on the Red Sea and the Gulf of Aden, the state is of extreme strategic importance.

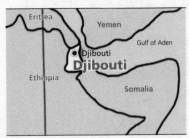

Economy: The land is economically poor, being mostly volcanic desert with scattered plateaus and highlands. Agriculture is possible only in restricted areas with irrigation facilities. Goats, sheep and camels form the major wealth of the state. Salt is a major product. Huge salt deposits are found in the lakes of Alol and Assal. Trade is almost entirely based in the capital Djibouti. French aid as well as assistance from Arab countries is the mainstay of the economy.

Mission in India: Honorary Consulate 3, Aurangzeb Lane, New Delhi-110011; Tel: 23011642/648; Telefax: 23011634.

E-mail: djibouti@spectranet.com

Indian Mission: Honorary Consulate of India, P.B.No.171, Djibouti. Tel:+253-350142; Fax:+253-351778

49. Dominica

(Commonwealth of Dominica)

Capital: Roseau; **Currency:** East Caribbean dollar; **Area:** 750 sq km; **Population:** 67,000; **Languages:** English and French Patois; **Religions:** Christian-90.9%; **Literacy:** 88%; **Life Expectancy:** 75.55; **p.c.i:** $ 10,456; **Date of Independence:** 3rd November, 1978

Government Type: Parliamentary Democracy; **President:** Nicholas J.O. Liverpool; **PM:** Roosevelt Skerrit.

History: Commonwealth of Dominica lies in the Lesser Antilles in Eastern Caribbean. Once a British protectorate, it assumed the

Baltic Sea States	Russia is a member of the Council of the Baltic Sea States. Other members are Denmark, Estonia, Finland, Germany, Iceland, Latvia, Lithuania, Norway, Poland, Sweden, and the European Commission.

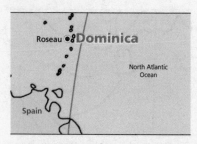

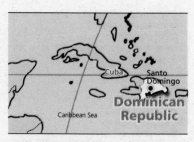

status of a British Associate State in 1967.

The island is volcanic in origin and largely mountainous with numerous thermal springs. The population includes Negroes, Mulattoes, Carib Indians and Europeans.

Economy: Exports include bananas, cocoa, copra and fruits. Tourism is an important industry.

Mission in India: Honorary Consulate of Commonwealth of Dominica, 283, Gulmohar Enclave, New Delhi-110049; Tel: 2686 2595; Fax:011-2651 0860.

E-mail:dominica_ shukla@vsnl.net

50. Dominican Republic

(Republica Dominica)

Capital: Santo Domingo; **Other Large Cities:** La Vega, San Pedro; **Currency:** Dominican Peso; **Area:** 48,442 sq km; **Population:** 9,378,818; **Languages:** Spanish; **Religions:** Roman Catholic-95%, other-5%; **Literacy:** 89.1%; **Life Expectancy:** 72.2; **p.c.i:** $ 8,647; **HDI rank:** 88; **Date of Independence:** 27th February, 1844.

Government Type: Democratic Republic; Head of State & Govt (President): Leonel Fernandez.

History: The Dominican Republic in the West Indies occupies the eastern two-thirds of Hispaniola, the second largest island of the Greater Antilles. Originally under Spain, the Dominican Republic became independent in 1844. The population is mainly composed of a mixed race of European (Span-

ish) and African blood.

Economy: The state is predominantly agricultural. The most important crops are sugarcane, coffee, cocoa, tobacco and rice. Industry: Sugar refining, textiles, cement.

51. East Timor

(Democratic Republic of East Timor)

Capital: Dili; **Area:** 14,874 sq km; **Population:** 1,171,000; **Languages:** Tetum & Portuguese (official), English and Bahasa Indonesian (working languages); **Religions:** Roman Catholic-98%, Muslim-1%, Protestant-1%, **Literacy:** 50.1%; **Life Expectancy:** 60.8; **p.c.i:** $ 2,663; **HDI rank:** 120; **Date of Independence:** 20th May, 2002.

Government Type: Republic; **President:** Jose Ramos Horta; **PM:** Kay Rala Xanana Gusmao

History: At midnight on May 19, 2002 East Timor became an independent country, after 450 years of Portuguese rule, 24

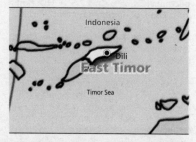

of brutal Indonesian occupation and two-and-a-half under the supervision of the UN. East Timor became a member of the United Nations in Sept. 2002.

Economy: East Timor's economy is dominated by agriculture with 75% of the country's population engaging in this activity. The major agricultural products are sweet potatoes and corn along with cash crops – especially coffee. Farmers on the coastal plains also grow rice and plantation crops such as rubber, tobacco, and coconuts. In addition, the forests yield many kinds of timber, including sandal wood.

52. Ecuador

(Republic of Ecuador) Republica del Ecuador

Capital: Quito; **Other Large Cities:** Guaya quil, Cuenca; **Currency:** US dollar; **Area:** 283,561 sq km; **Population:** 14,306,000; **Languages:** Spanish, Quechuan and tribal dialects; **Religions:** Roman Catholic-95%; Others -5%, **Literacy:** 91%; **Life Expectancy:** 75; **p.c.i:** $ 7,951; **HDI rank:** 77; **Date of Independence:** 24th May, 1822

Government Type: Republic; **Head of State & Govt (President):** Rafael Correa Delgado.

History: Ecuador lies on the west coast of South America. A part of the great Inca Empire, Ecuador came under Spanish rule in 1533.

Some 40% of the population is Amerindian. Guayaquil is the chief seaport and

airport. The Galapagos islands (the home of huge tortoises) belong to Ecuador.

Economy: Ecuador is the world's largest exporter of bananas. Sugarcane, African palm, cacao, balsawood (world's largest exporter), rice and coffee are grown.

Industry: Food processing, wood products, textiles, sugar. Silver ore is now the chief mineral product. There are large deposits of copper, gold and zinc. The production of petroleum is increasing. The so-called 'Panama' hats made of Tequila straw are made in Ecuador.

53. Egypt

(Arab Republic of Egypt)
Jumhuriyah Misr al-Arabiya

Capital: Cairo; **Other Large Cities:** Alexandria, Giza; **Area:** 997,677 sq.km; **Population:** 80,030,000; **Languages:** Arabic, English; **Religions:** Muslim (mostly Sunni)-90%, Coptic-9%, other Christian-1%; **Literacy:** 66.4%; **Life Expectancy:** 71.3; **Currency:** Egyptian Pound; **p.c.i:** $ 6,367; **HDI rank:** 101; **Date of Independence:** 28th February, 1922.

Government Type: Republic; **President:** vacant; **PM:** Essam Sharaf.

Egypt, traditionally known as the Gift of the Nile, occupies north east Africa.

History: Egypt has one of the oldest civilisations in the world, its recorded history going back to more than 5000 B.C. In 1922 Egypt became an independent monarchy and in 1953 a republic. The early years were dominated by Gamal Abdel Nasser. Nasser was replaced on his death in 1970 by Anwar Ali Sadat. Sadat was assassinated in 1981 and was replaced by Hosni Mubarek .

Egypt merged with Syria in 1958 to form United Arab Republic; Syria broke away from the union in 1961.

Economy: The main agricultural area is Lower Egypt which covers the delta of the Nile. Crops are cotton, onions, wheat,

| Most Populous City in Africa | Cairo in Egypt is Africa's most populated city with an estimated 17 million residents living in the metropolitan area. |

maize, millet, rice, sugarcane and fruits of various kinds. Industry: Textiles, chemicals, petrochemicals, food processing, cement. Exports are cotton, rice, mineral products, textiles, refrigerators, tyres, cement and electrical instruments.

Mission in India: Embassy of the Arab Republic of Egypt, 1/50–M, Niti Marg, Chanakyapuri, New Delhi-110021. Tel: 26114096/97; Fax: 91-11-26885355.

E-mail: india_emb@mfa.gov.eg

Indian Mission in Egypt: Embassy of India, 5 Aziz Abaza Street, Zamalek, P.O. Box No.718, Cairo 11211, Egypt. Tel: 00-20-2-7360052, 7356053; Fax: 00-20-2-7364038.

E-mail:embassy@indembcairo.com

54. El Salvador

(Republic of El Salvador)
Republica do El Salvador

Capital: San Salvador; **Other Large Cities:** Santa Ana, San Maguel; **Currency:** Salvadoran colon; **Area:** 21,393 sq.km; **Population:** 6,194,000; **Languages:** Spanish; **Religions:** Roman Catholic-57.1%; Protestant-21.2%; **Literacy:** 82%; **Life Expectancy:** 71.9; **p.c.i:** $ 7,442; **HDI rank:** 90; **Date of Independence:** 15th September, 1821.

Government Type: Republic; **Head of State & Govt (President):** Mauricio Funes Cartagena.

History: El Salvador is the smallest and the most densely populated of the Central American States and the only one without an Atlantic coast line.

A 12-year civil war that killed 75,000 people ended in 1992. In 1998 Hurricane Mitch killed 200 and made 30,000 homeless. In 2001, earthquakes and drought caused heavy damage.

Economy: The country is predominantly agricultural. The principal crop is coffee which accounts for one half of exports. Other products are cotton, maize and sugar. Fisheries are being developed and figure prominently in the export list. Industry: Food & beverages, textiles, petroleum products.

55. Equatorial Guinea

(Republic of Equatorial Guinea)
Republica de Guinea Ecuatorial

Capital: Malabo; **Other Large Cities:** Bata; **Currency:** Franc CFA; **Area:** 28,051 sq.km; **Population:** 693,000; **Languages:** Spanish, Fang, Bubi and pidgin English; **Religions:** Nominally Christian and predominantly Roman Catholic, pagan practices; **Literacy:** 87%; **Life Expectancy:** 51.6; **p.c.i:** $ 18,387; **HDI rank:** 117; **Date of Independence:** 12th October, 1968.

Government Type: Republic; **President:** Brig-Gen. Teodoro Obiang Nguema Mbasogo; **PM:** Ignacio Milan Tang.

GDP per Person Equatorial Guinea had the fastest growth in GDP per head between 2001 and 2010. Azerbaijan and Turkenistan had the next fastest growth rates.

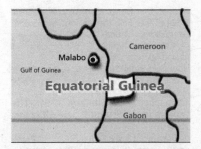

History: Equatorial Guinea, formerly Spanish Guinea, comprises the islands of Fernando Po (now Bioko), Corcisco, Great Elobey, Little Elobey, and Annoban and the mainland territory of Rio Muni on the west coast of Africa. In 1975, almost all place names were changed by President Macias Nguema. The capital Santa Isabel thus became Malabo. Macias Nguema was ousted by his nephew, Mbasogo on Sept. 29, 1979. Constitutional rule was resumed in 1982.

Economy: The discovery and exploitation of large oil reserves have contributed to dramatic economic growth in recent years. Forestry, farming and fishing are also major components of GDP. Coffee is cultivated upto 900 m and cocoa upto 600 m unit. There are also forests of ebony, mahogany and oak. Other products are cocoa, coffee, timber, palm oil and bananas. The country is heavily dependent on foreign aid.

Mission in India: Embassy of the Republic of Equatorial Guinea stationed at Beijing.

56. Eritrea

(State of Eritrea)

Capital: Asmara; Other Large Cities: The Ports of Massawa and Assab; Currency: Nakfa; Area: 117,600 sq. km; Population: 5,224,000; Languages: Tigrinya Arabic and several other local languages; Religions: Muslim, Coptic Christian, Roman Catholic, Protestant; Literacy: 64.2%; Life Expectancy: 58; p.c.i: $ 676;

Date of Independence: 24th May, 1993.
Government Type: Transitional Government; Head of State & Govt (President): Isaias Afworki.

History: Eritrea, until recently the northern- most province of Ethiopia, is situated on the African shore of the Red Sea. In 1890, it became an Italian colony but Italy lost the colony to a British invasion force in 1941. After World War II, a U.N. resolution made Eritrea an autonomous, self-governing region of Ethiopia, apparently against the wishes of most of Eritrea's population. In 1962 Ethiopian emperor Haile Selassie formally annexed Eritrea. Beginning in the mid-60's the province was repeatedly torn by fighting between the Eritrean Liberation Front (ELF) and other groups like Eritrean People's Liberation Front (EPLF) advocating secession from Ethiopia, and the Ethiopian army. Africa's longest civil war of 31 years ended in 1993.

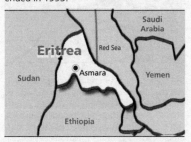

Economy: Agriculture: Sorghum, livestock including camels and goats, Red Sea fishing. Minerals: Gold, copper, potash, iron ore. Exports: Hides, salt, cement, gum arabic.
Mission in India: Hon. Consulate of Eritrea, B-8/14, Vasant Vihar, New Delhi-110 057. Tel: 26140830; Telefax: 91-11-26141067.

57. Estonia

(Republic of Estonia)/Esti Vabariik

Capital: Tallinn; Other Large Cities: Tartu, Kohtla-Jarve; Currency: Euro; Area: 45,100 sq.km; Population: 1,340,122; Languages: Estonian; Religions: Chris-

---

Most Violent Region on Earth The countries known as "the northern triangle" of the Central American isthmus form what is now the most violent region on earth. El Salvador, Guatemala and Honduras, along with Jamaica and Venezuela, suffer the world's highest murder rates.

tian: 27.8%; **Literacy:** 99.8%; **Life Expectancy:** 71.4; **p.c.i:** $ 18,274; **HDI rank:** 34; **Date of Independence:** 20th August, 1991.

Government Type: Parliamentary Republic; **Head of State:** Toomas Hendrik Ilves; **PM:** Andrus Ansip.

History: Estonia seceded from Soviet Union and attained independence in 1991, 50 years after the three Baltic states of Estonia, Latvia and Lithuania were annexed by Stalin's USSR. The first free elections in over 50 years were held in Sept. '92.

Economy: Agriculture and dairy farming are the major occupations. Some 22% of the territory is covered by forests, which provide fuel and raw material for Industires. Agricultural products: Grain, potatoes, vegetables, dairy products. Natural resources: Shale deposits, timber, peat, phosphorites. Industry: Ship-building, furniture, match & pulp, leather, garments, agricultural machinery, electric motors.

Mission in India: Honorary Consulate General of the Republic of Estonia, A-11, Kailash Colony, First Floor, New Delhi-110048; Tel: 2923 9808; Fax: 2923 2575.

58. Ethiopia

(Federal Democratic Republic of Ethiopia)/Ye Etiyop'iya Hezbawi Dimokrasiyawi Republick

Capital: Addis Ababa; **Other Large Cities:** Gondar, Dire Dawa; **Currency:** Birr; **Area:** 1,221,900 sq.km; **Population:**79,455,634;

Languages: Amharic, Oromigna, Tigrigna and 60 other small languages; **Religions:** Christian 60.8%, Muslim-32.8%, traditional 4.6%, other-1.8%; **Literacy:** 35.9%; **Life Expectancy:** 52.9; **p.c.i:** $ 1,018; **HDI rank:** 157.

Government Type: Federal Republic; **President:** Girma Woldegiorgis; **PM:** Meles Zenawi.

History: Black Africa's oldest state formerly known as Abyssinia. A mountainous country in north-east Africa, it has a colourful history. The Ethiopian emperors claimed descent from King Solomon and the famous Queen of Sheba. The last Emperor of Ethiopia Haile Sellasie I was deposed by armed marxist forces which took over the govt. in 1974. Opposition to this goverment mounted in 1991 and marxist leader Mengistu Haile Mariam had to flee the country. A new government consisting of various groups was formed by the Ethiopian Revolutionary Democratic Front, an umbrella group of six rebel armies. Eritrea, a province on the Red Sea, declared its independence in 1993.

May, 1995 saw the birth of a new Federal Democratic Republic of Ethiopia after four years of transitional rule. The new constitution divides Ethiopia into nine ethnically distinct regions, which have the right to secede through a popular referendum.

There was an undeclared war between

Ethiopia and Eritrea (May-June, 1998) over an area on the border between the two. Efforts by OAU didn't yield much. Fighting resumed in 1999 and 2000. Thousands died on both sides. In Dec. the two countries formally ended the war, with an accord signed in Algiers, but tensions continued.

Economy: Ethiopia's economy is based on agriculture, which accounts for half of GDP, 60% of exports, and 80% of total employment. The agricultural sector suffers from frequent drought and poor cultivation practices. Coffee is the most important export. Other important exports include qat, live animals, hides, and gold.

Mission in India: Embassy of the Federal Democratic Republic of Ethiopia, 7/50-G, Satya Marg, Chanakyapuri, New Delhi-110021. Tel: 26119513, 26119514; Fax: 26875731.

E-mail: delethem@yahoo.com

Indian Mission in Ethiopia: Embassy of India, Arada Kifle Ketema,Kebele-14, H.No. 224,Post Box No. 528,Addis Ababa, Ethiopia. Tel: 00-251-11-1235538 /39/40/41; Fax: 00-251-11-1235547, 1235548.

E-mail: hoc.addisababa@mea.gov.in, rajdut@ethionet.et (Chancery)

59. Fiji

(Republic of the Fiji Islands)

Capital: Suva; **Other Large Cities:** Lautoka, Nadi; **Currency:** Fijian dollar; **Area:** 18,376 sq.km; **Population:** 854,000; **Languages:** English, Fijian and Hindi; **Religions:** Christian-64.5%, Hindu-27.9%, Muslim-6.3%; **Literacy:** 94.4%; **Life Expectancy:** 68.8; **p.c.i:** $ 4,450; **HDI rank:** 86; **Date of Independence:** 10th October, 1970.

Government Type: Republic; **President:** Ratu Epeli Nailatikau; **PM:** Laisenia Qarase.

Fiji consists of 332 islands and islets in western S. Pacific, lying 1750 km. north of New Zealan

History: These islands came under British rule in 1874. From 1879, indentured In-

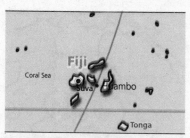

dian labour was imported into the islands to work on European sugar plantations. Their descendants now form about half of the population. Melanesians, the original inhabitants, make up 43 per cent, the rest being made up of Europeans, Chinese and others. On Oct. 10, 1970 Britain granted independence to Fiji.

Economy: Fiji is a famous tourist centre with 3,00,000 to 4,00,000 tourists annually. Its major products are agricultural. Sugar and coconuts form 90 per cent of the total exports. Rice and ginger are grown too. Mining is limited and industries are (sugar refining, light industry and tourism) growing. Gold is mined on Viti Levu, and is another major export.

Mission in India: Fiji High Commi-ssion, N-87, Panchsheel Park,New Delhi-110 017. Tel: 41751092/93; Fax: 41751095

Indian Mission in Fiji: High Commission of India, Level 7, LICI Building, Butt. Street, P.O. Box 471, Suva, Fiji Islands. Tel: 00-679-3301125; Fax: 00-679-3301032.

E-mail:hicomindsuva@is.com.fj

60. Finland

(Republic of Finland)/Suomen Tasavalta

Capital: Helsinki; **Other Large Cities:** Tampere, Espoo; **Currency:** Euro; **Area:** 338,000 sq.km.; **Population:** 5,379,900; **Languages:** Finnish and Swedish; **Religions:** Lutheran Church of Finland-82.5%, Orthodox Church-1.1%, other Christian-1.1%,others-0.1%,None-15.1%;**Literacy:**

99%; **Life Expectancy:** 79.3; **p.c.i:** $ 34,401;
HDI rank: 16; **Date of Independence:** 6th
December, 1917.

Government Type: Republic; **President:**
Ms. Tarja Halonen; **PM:** Mari Kiviniemi.

History: The Republic of Finland is a Baltic
State, which once formed part of the Russian Empire. Finland has more than 20,000
lakes. 62% of the population live in urban
areas.

Economy: The most important rural activity is forestry. Finland's vast forests of pine,
spruce, and birch support a number of major industries. The extensive pulp and paper
sector is responsible for around one-quarter
of world paper exports. Other industries are
shipbuilding, metals, machinery, textiles,
leather and chemicals. Chief agricultural
crops are grains, potatoes and dairy products. Finland joined the EU on Jan. 1, 1995.

Mission in India: Embassy of Finland, E-3,
Nyaya Marg, Chanakyapuri, New Delhi -
110021. Tel: 41497500; Fax: 41497555

E-mail: sanomat.nde@formin.fi

Consulate: Mumbai, Tel: 6639 0033, Fax:
6639 0044,

E-mail: finconsmumbai@shrenuj.com

Calcutta: Tel:2287 4328, 2290 1960 Fax:
2287 4329.

E-mail: mpc@cal.vsnl.net.in;

Chennai: Tel:28524141,Fax:28521253.

E-mail: siva _holdings@vsnl.net

Indian Mission in Finland: Embassy of
India, Satamakatu 2 A 8, 00160, Helsinki,
Finland. Tel: 00-358-9-2289910; Fax: 00-
358-9-6221208.Email:indianembassy@indianembassy.fi

61. France
(French Republic)/Republique Francaise

Capital: Paris; **Other
Large Cities:** Marseilles, Lyons, Strasbourg;
Currency: Euro; **Area:**
543,965 sq.km; **Population:** 65,821,885;
Languages: French and regional dialects; **Religions:** Roman Catholic-83%-88%, Protestant-2%, Jewish 1%, Muslim-5%-10%, un
affiliated-4%; **Literacy:** 99%; **Life Expectancy:** 80.7; **p.c.i:** $ 34,092; **HDI rank:** 14;
Date of Independence: 486 (Unification
by Clovis).

Government Type: Republic; **President:**
Nicolas Sarkozy. **PM:** Francois Fillon.

History: France, the largest country in
western Europe, lies between three big nations-Spain, Germany and Italy. The island
of Corsica-the birthplace of Napoleon-
forms an integral part of France. The French
Revolution (1789-1793) made France, once
a grand monarchy, a republic. Since then republican and imperial forms of government
followed one after another until the Fifth
Republic. The French Community came into
being in 1958 under President Charles de
Gaulle. France is a member of the European
Union.

Economy: The country is the largest food
producer and exporter in Western Europe.
Main crops: Grains, maize, rice, fruits, vegetables, wine, potatoes, livestock and dairy
products. Among manufactured products,
the most important are chemicals, silk, cot-

| Gift of the French People | The Statue of Liberty was presented to the American people by the people of France on 4th July 1884 and shipped to the US in early 1885. Frederic Auguste Bartholdi was its sculptor and Gustave Eiffel its structural engineer. |

ton textiles, automobiles, aircraft, ships, precision instruments, electronic equipment, perfumes and wines.

Overseas Departments: French Guiana, Guadeloupe, Martinique, Reunion.

Overseas Territories: French Polynesia, French Southern and Antarctic Lands, New Caledonia and dependencies, Wallis and Futuna Islands. Overseas departments elect representatives to the National Assembly and the administrative organisation of mainland France applies to them. The administrative organisation of overseas territories includes a locally elected government.

Territorial collectivities: St. Pierro and Miquelon; Mayotte.

Mission in India: Embassy of France, 2/50-E, Shantipath, Chanakyapuri, New Delhi-110021. Tel: 2419 6100; Fax: 2419 6119.

Consulate General of France: Hoechst House, 7th Floor, Nariman Point (next to NCPA), Mumbai-400 021. Ph: 0091-22-56694000; Web: www.consulfrance-bombay.org.

Indian Mission in France: Embassy of India, 5, Rue Alfred Dehodencq, 75016 Paris, France. Tel: 00-33-1-40507070; Fax: 00-33-1-40500996.

E-mail: eiparis.admin@wanadoo.fr

62. Gabon

(Gabonese Republic)
Republique Gabonaise

Capital: Libreville; **Other Large Cities:** Port- Gentil, Masuku; **Currency:** Franc CFA; **Area:** 267,667; **Population:** 1,501,000;

Languages: French and Bantu dialects; **Religions:** Christian-55%-75%; **Literacy:** 86.2%; **Life Expectancy:** 56.7; **p.c.i:** $14,865; **HDI rank:** 93; **Date of Independence:** 17th August, 1960.

Government Type: Republic; **President:** Ali Bongo Ondimba; **PM:** Paul Biyoghe .

History: The Gabon Republic is situated on the western coast of central Africa. Formerly a province of French Equatorial Africa, Gabon attained independence in 1960.

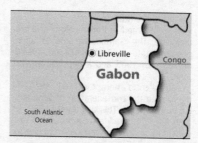

Economy: Gabon is one of the most prosperous black African countries. Most of the country is covered by a dense tropical forest. Chief crops are cocoa, coffee, rice, peanuts, sugarcane. The economy, traditionally dependent on forestry, is now dominated by mining. The manganese deposit at Moanda in the south is one of the world's richest deposits. Crude oil production is already the fifth highest in Africa. Uranium, gold and iron ore are also mined. Industry: Processing of food, timber and textiles

Mission in India: Embassy of Gabon stationed at Tokyo.

63. The Gambia

(Republic of The Gambia)

Capital: Banjul; **Other Large Cities:** Serrekunda, Farafenni; **Currency:** Dalasi; **Area:** 11,295 sq.km; **Population:** 1,751,000;

Languages: English and Mandinka, Wolof; **Religions:** Muslim-90%, Christian-8%, Indigenous beliefs-2%; **Literacy:** 42.5%; **Life Expectancy:** 59.4; **p.c.i:** $ 1,972; **HDI rank:** 151; **Date of Independence:** 18th February, 1965

Government Type: Republic; **Head of State& Govt:** Lt.Yahya Jammeh.

The Gambia, the smallest African country, is a narrow strip of land in West Africa, extending inland from the Atlantic Ocean for about 30 miles on either side of the Gambia River and surrounded on three sides by Senegal. Nearly half the inhabitants belong to the Mandingo tribe.

History: Formerly a British colony and protectorate, the Gambia became an independent state within the Commonwealth on Feb. 18, 1965 and a Republic in April 1970.

After a coup attempt in 1981, the Gambia formed the confederation of Senegambia with Senegal. This lasted until 1989.

In July, '94, a military coup ousted President Dawda Jawara, who was in power for

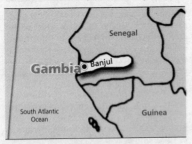

24 years. In Aug. '96, voters approved a constitution paving the way for a return to democracy. The 2-year-old ban on political parties was lifted.

Economy: Peanuts are the main crop, along with rice and palm kernels. Textiles, food and manufactured goods are significant items of import. Tourism is the biggest foreign exchange earner.

Mission in India: Honorary Consulate General of the Republic of Gambia, B-11, May Fair Garderns, New Delhi-110 016; Tel: 26860285; Fax: 91-24532503.

E-mail: kvachani @hotmail.com

64. Georgia

(Republic of Georgia)
Sakaratvelos Respublica

Capital: Tbilisi (Tiflis); Other Large Cities: Kutaisi, Batumi; Currency: Lari; Area: 69,700 sq.km; Population: 4,436,000; Languages: Georgian, Russian; Religions:

Christian - 88.6%, Islam - 9.9%; Literacy: 100%; Life Expectancy: 74; p.c.i: $5,057; HDI rank: 89; Date of Independence: 9th April, 1991

Government Type: Republic; President: Mikhail Saakashvili; PM: Nikoloz Gilauri.

History: Georgia, a former Soviet republic, is bordered by the Black Sea, Turkey, Armenia and Azerbaijan.

Georgia has a fine climate and is known for its natural wealth, variety and beauty. It has the largest manganese mines in the world.

Georgia includes the Autonomous Republics of Abkhasia and Adjaria and the former Autonomous Region of South Ossetia.

Economy: Agriculture: Tea, citrus fruits, grapes, grain, vegetables, potatoes, silk, tobacco, bamboo, eucalyptus. Natural resources: Manganese, coal, baryta, oil, marble, iron. Industry: Food processing, tea, brewery, textile, chemical fibres, paper and metallurgy.

Georgia was admitted to the UN as the 179th member in July, 1992 – the last of the former Soviet republics to join the world organisation.

Mission in India: Honorary Consulate of Georgia, 19 DDA, Community Centre, Zamrudpur, Kailash colony Ext., New Delhi-110 048; Tel: 26431015; Fax: 26447864.

E-mail:georgiaconsulate@rediffmail.com

65. Germany

(Federal Republic of Germany)
Bundes-republik Deutschland

Capital: Berlin; Other Large Cities: Ham-

I am a Berliner

During a visit to Germany in 1963 President John F. Kennedy was greeted with rapturous approval when he said "Ich bin ein Berliner". Later, this caused some amusement for although the translation is "I am a Berliner", a Berliner is also a type of doughnut.

burg, Munich, Cologne, Frankfurt, Leipzig; **Currency:** Euro; **Area:** 357,020 sq.km.; **Population:** 81,802,000;

Languages: German; **Religions:** Protestant-34%, Roman Catholic-34%, Muslim-3.7%, unaffiliated or others-28.3%; **Literacy:** 99%; **Life Expectancy:** 79.4; **p.c.i:** $ 35,930; **HDI rank:** 10; **Date of Independence:** 3rd October, 1990 (date of unification of West Germany and East Germany) **Government Type:** Federal Republic; **President:** Christian Wulff; **Head of Govt:** Chancellor Angela Merkel.

History: Germany since 1871 had been a nation united in one country of numerous states which had a common language and traditions. Since World War II, until 1990, it had been split in two parts: Federal Republic of Germany (West Germany) and German Democratic Republic (East Germany). The merger of the two Germanys took place on Oct. 3, 1990 and the first all-German elections since 1937 were held on Dec. 2, 1990.

The Federal Republic is made up of 16 Lander (States). The Bundestag (Federal Diet) is the supreme legislative body. With the addition of 144 members of the East German Volkskammer, the total membership rose to 663 in 1990

Economy: Of the land 48% is used for agriculture and 29% is wooded. Chief crops: Grains, potatoes, sugar beets. Major mineral resources: Lignite, coal, iron and copper ores and potash. Industry: Steel, ships, vehicles, machinery, coal and chemicals.

Mission in India: Embassy of the Federal Republic of Germany, No.6/50-G, Chanakyapuri, New Delhi-110 021. Tel: 44199199, 26871831;Telefax: 26873117.

E-mail:info@new-delhi.diplo.de

Indian Mission in Germany: Embassy of India, Tiergartenstrasse 17, 10785 Berlin, Germany. Tel: 00-49-30-257950 ; Fax: 00-49-30-25795102 .

E-mail:chancery@indianembassy.de

66. Ghana

(Republic of Ghana)

Capital: Accra; **Other Large Cities:** Kumasi, Takoradi; **Currency:** Cedi; **Area:** 238,537 sq. km; **Population:** 24,233,431; **Langua**

ges: English (official language) and eight major national languages; **Religions:** Christian-68.8%, Muslim-15.9%, traditional - 8.5%; **Literacy:** 65%; **Life Expectancy:** 60;**p.c.i:** $ 1,609; **HDI rank:** 130; **Date of Independence:** 6th March, 1957.

Government Type: Constitutional Democracy; **President (Head of State & Govt):** John Evans Atta Mills.

History: Dr. Kwame Nkrumah was the first President. Coups occurred in 1966, 1972, 1978, 1979 and 1981. A new pluralistic democratic constitution was approved in 1992.

Ghana was the first place in sub-Saharan Africa where Europeans arrived to trade - first in gold, later in slaves. It was also the

Media Baron's Roots

Robert Maxwell was born Jan Ludvik Hoch (1923) in Czechoslovakia. Hoch was a Jew who fought the Nazis through the Czech Resistance Movement. Hoch changed his name to Robert Maxwell and went on to become one of the most powerful media owners in the UK.

first black African nation in the region to achieve independence from a colonial power, in this instance Britain.

Economy: Ghana is primarily an agricultural country which held position as world's leading producer of cocoa for long. Other crops: kolanuts, palm products, bananas, coffee, maize and rubber. Exports: Timber, gold, diamonds, manganese, bauxite and cocoa. Industry: Aluminium and light industry. Gold and cocoa production, and individual remittances are major sources of foreign exchange.

Mission in India: Ghana High Commission, 50-N, Satya Marg, Chanakyapuri, New Delhi-110021. Tel:26883315, 26883298, 26883338; Telefax: 26883202.

E-mail: ghcindia@vsnl.net

Indian Mission in Ghana: High Commission of India, No.9, Ridge Road, Roman Ridge, P.O. Box CT-5708, Accra, Ghana. Tel: 00-233-21-775601, 775602; Fax: 00-233-21-772176.

E-mail- indiahc@ncs.com.gh

67. Greece

(Hellenic Republic) Elliniki Dimokratia

Capital: Athens; **Other Large Cities :** Thesaloniki, Salonika, Larissa; **Currency:** Euro; **Area:** 131,990 sq.km; **Population:** 11,306,183; **Languages:** Greek; **Religions:** Greek Orthodox (Christian)- 98%, Muslim-1.3%, others-0.7%; **Literacy:** 97.1%; **Life Expectancy:** 79.5; **p.c.i:** $ 28,833; **HDI rank:** 22; **Date of Independence:** 1829.

Government Type: Parliamentary Republic; **President:** Karolos Papoulias; **PM:** Georgios Papandreou.

History: Greece or the Hellenic Republic, on the Mediterranean Sea, occupies the southern end of the Balkan Peninsula in south-east Europe. Ancient Greece's achievements in art, architecture, science, mathematics, philosophy, drama, literature and democracy were unparalleled. The country reached the peak of its glory in the 5th century B.C.

Politically independent till the 1st century B.C., the Greeks succumbed to Roman might in the latter half of that century. Later they came under Byzan-tine and Ottoman empires. In 1830, Greece regained its freedom as a monarchic state. After many vicissitudes of fortune, monarchy was abolished in 1974, since then Greece has been a republic. Greece is a member of the European Union.

Numerous islands constitute about one-fifth of total area, of which the largest is Crete.

Economy: Greece, though till recently an agricultural country, has now developed industrially. In merchant shipping, Greece owns a surprisingly big tonnage. Tourism is Greece's biggest industry. Others: Textiles, chemicals, metals, wine, food processing, cement. Chief crops: Wheat, sugar beet, grapes, other fruits, milk, olive oil, cotton.

Mission in India: Embassy of Greece, EP-32, Dr.S.Radhakrishnan Marg, Chanakyapuri, New Delhi-110021. Tel: 26880700, Telefax: 26888010; E-mail:gremb.del@mfa.grt; Web : www.greeceinindia.com

Indian Mission in Greece: Embassy of India, 3, Kleanthous Street, 10674 Athens, Greece. Tel: 00-30-1-7216227, 7216481; Fax: 00-30-210 7235458 & 210 7211252.

E-mail:indembassy@ath.forthnet.gr

68. Grenada

Capital: St. George's; **Currency:** East Caribbean dollar; **Area:** 344 sq.km; **Popula-

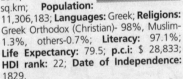

Oracle of Delphi — Delphi was one of the most important religious sites of Ancient Greece and sacred to Apollo. The Oracle at Delphi was consulted by visitors from all over Greece, seeking advice on the future.

tion: 104,000; **Languages:** English and French-African patois; **Religions:** Roman Catholic- 53%, Anglican- 13.8%, other Protes-tant- 33.2%; **Literacy:** 96%; **Life Expectancy:** 68.7; **p.c.i:** $ 10,881; **Date of Independe-nce:** 7th February, 1974

Government Type: Parliamentary Democracy; **Gov.Gen.:** Carlyle Arnold Glean; **PM:** Tillman Thomas.

History: Grenada is an island country in the West Indies. It is the most southerly island of the Windward Islands chain and includes Southern Grenadines (islands), the largest of which is Carriacou.

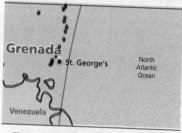

The population is of mixed origin: European, Negro and Carib Indians.

Economy: Tourism is a growing industry but agriculture dominates the economy. Grenada is known as the 'Spice Island' and is the world leader in the production of nutmeg and mice. Other major agricultural products are cocoa, bananas and tropical fruit and vegetables.

Mission in India: Honorary Consulate of Grenada, 12, Sunder Nagar, New Delhi-110 003. Tel: 24354512; Fax: 23328307.

E-mail: skkandhari@vsnl.net

69. Guatemala

(Republic of Guatemala)
Republica de Guatemala

Capital: Guatemala City; **Other Large Cities:** Escuintla, Peurto Barrios; **Curren-**

cy: Quetzal; **Area:** 108,889 sq.km; **Population:** 14,361,666; **Languages:** Spanish and Indian dialects; **Religions:** Roman Catholic, Protestant, Indigenous Mayan beliefs; **Literacy:** 73.2%; **Life Expectancy:** 70.3; **p.c.i:** $ 4,871; **HDI rank:** 116; **Date of Inde-pendence:** 15th September, 1821.

Government Type: Constitutional Democratic Republic; **President:** Alvaro Colom Caballeros.

History: Guatemala, a republic, is the northernmost and the third largest of the five central American states and has the largest population.

After remaining as a Spanish colony for about three centuries (1524 –1821), Guatemala became a republic in 1839. Guatemala's claims to British Honduras (Belize) led to the rupture of diplomatic relations with Britain in 1963. More than 100,000 people have been killed in civil wars since 1961.

Economy: The soil is very fertile. Agriculture is the most important occupation. Principal crop is coffee. Other important export items are bananas, cotton, gum, sugar, maize, tobacco, fruits and beef. Industry: Food and

beverages, textiles, tyres, construction materials, tobacco and chemicals.

Indian Mission in Guatemala: Honorary Consulate of India, P.O. Box No. 886, Via 4,5-52, Zone4, Esquina 6a-Avenida, Guatemala City, Gautemala. Tel: 00-502-2-310404; Fax: 00-502-2-325365.

70. Guinea

(Republic of Guinea)
Republique de Guinee

Capital: Conakry; **Other Large Cities:** Kankan, Kindia; **Currency:** Guinean Franc; **Area:** 245,857 sq.km; **Population:** 10,324,000 **Languages:** French and 8 national languages; **Religions:** Muslim- 85%, Christian-8%, indigenous belifes- 7%; **Literacy:** 29.5% (in French); **Life Expectancy:** 56; **p.c.i:** $ 1,056; **HDI rank:** 156; **Date of Independence:** 2nd October, 1958.
Government Type: Republic; **President:** Alpha Conde. **PM:** Mohamed Said Fofana.
History: Guinea is a former French overseas territory on the Atlantic coast of West Africa.

Under the constitution of the Fifth (French) Republic, Guinea voted for secession and proclaimed itself an independent republic in 1958. The first President was Sekou Toure. The army mutiny of Feb. 1996 was suppressed by President Conte.
Economy: Subsistence agriculture supports 80% of the population. Main crops are cassava, plantains, sugarcane, bananas and palm kernels. It exports coffee, honey, bananas, palm kernels, iron and aluminium ore. Guinea has probably the world's largest deposit of bauxite.
Mission in India: Embassy of Guinea stationed at Moscow.

71. Guinea-Bissau

(Republic of Guinea-Bissau)
Republica da Guine-Bissau

Capital: Bissau; **Currency:** Franc CFA; **Area:** 36,125 sq.km; **Population:** 1,647,000; **Languages:** Crioulo, Portuguese and tribal languages; **Religions:** indigenous beliefs-40%, Muslim-50%, Christian-10%; **Literacy:** 64.6%; **Life Expectancy:** 46.4; **p.c.i:** $ 1,082; **HDI rank:** 164; **Date of Independence:** 24th September, 1973.
Government Type: Republic; **President:** Malam Bacai Sanha; **PM:** Carlos Gomes Junior.
History: Guinea-Bissau, formerly Portuguese Guinea, is on the Atlantic coast of West Africa. The land is part plain and part plateau.

Guinea-Bissau unilaterally declared independence in 1973. Portugal recognised its independence in 1974. Joao Bernardo Vieira who seized power in 1980, was elected in 1989 and re-elected in 1994. A civil war was triggered by an army uprising in June, 1998 and Vieira was toppled. There was a military coup in 2003.

In May '97, Guinea-Bissau joined the French Franc Zone.

Economy: The main occupation is agriculture. Swamp rice (grown in the coastal plains), coconuts, cassava, sweet potatoes and maize form the important food crops.

The Bauhaus The Bauhaus, a school of design founded in the early twentieth century in Germany, had a strong influence over art, architecture and product design. Its founder's aim was to bring together architecture, sculpture and painting.

The cash crops are groundnuts, coconuts and palm oil. Cattle raising is widespread. Industry: Food processing, beer and soft drinks.

72. Guyana

(Co-operative Republic of Guyana)

Capital: Georgetown; **Other Large Cities:** Linden, New Amsterdam; **Currency:** Guyana dollar; **Area:** 214,969 sq.km; **Population:** 784,894; **Languages:** English, Hindi, Urdu, Creole; **Religions:** Hindu-28.4%, Pentecostal-16.9%, Roman Catholic-8.1%, Anglican-6.9%, Seventh Day Adventist-5%, Muslim-7.2%; **Literacy:** 99%; **Life Expectancy:** 66.8; **p.c.i:** $ 6,893; **HDI rank:** 104; **Date of Independence:** 26th May, 1966.

Government Type: Republic; **President:** Bharrat Jagdeo; **PM:** Samuel Hinds

Guyana (former British Guiana) lies on the north east coast of South America.

History: Guyana became a British colony in 1814 and an independent sovereign state within the Commonwealth of Nations in 1966.

Economy: The economy is based on agriculture. (Sugarcane, rice, coconuts and citrus). Sugar, rice and bauxite are the main exports. There are considerable deposits of gold and diamonds. Dense tropical forests cover much of the land.

Industry: Mining and Textiles
Mission in India: High Commission of the Republic of Guyana B 3/20 Vasant Vihar, New Delhi 110057. Tele: 011-4166 9717, 4166 9718; Fax: 011-4166 9714. Email: hcommguy.del@gmail.com.
Indian Mission in Guyana: High Commission of India, 307 Church Street, Queenstown, P.O. Box No. 101148, Georgetown, Guyana. Tele: 00-592-2263996, 2268965, 2263240; Fax: 00-592-2257012.
E-mail: hicomind@guyana.net.gy

73. Haiti

(Republic of Haiti) Republique d' Haiti

Capital: Port-au-Prince; **Currency:** Gourde; **Area:** 27,750 sq.km; **Population:** 10,085,214; **Languages:** French (official), and Creole; **Religions:** Roman Catholic-80%, Protestant-16%; **Literacy:** 62.1%; **Life Expectancy:** 60.9; **p.c.i:** $ 1,121; **HDI rank:** 145; **Date of Independence:** 1st January, 1804.

Government Type: Republic; **President:** Rene Preval; **PM:** Jean-Max Bellerive.

History: Haiti is part of the West Indies known as Hispaniola in the Atlantic lying between Cuba on the west and Puerto Rico on the east

A 28-year dictatorship by the Duvalier family ended in Feb. 1986. By mid-1990, there had been five governments. Father Jean Bertrand Aristide was elected President in Dec. 1990 but was deposed in a coup and

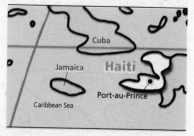

exiled in Sept. '91. The UN imposed a worldwide oil, arms and financial embargo on Haiti in June, 1993. Aristide returned to Haiti and was restored in office in Oct.'94. A U.N. peacekeeping force took over responsibility for Haiti in March, '95. Aristide transferred power to his elected successor Rene Preval in Feb. '96. He was back in power in November 2000.

Economy: Chief agricultural products: Coffee, sugar, bananas, rice, cocoa, tobacco, sisal and cotton. Industry: Sugar refining, textiles and cement. Bauxite is the chief mineral exported. Tourism is Haiti's second largest source of foreign exchange.

Indian Mission in Haiti: Honorary Consulate of India, C/o. Hnadal & Fils, 199, Rue Du Magasin de L'Etat, P.O.Box No.633, Port-au-Prince (Republic of Haiti). Tel: 00-(509) 222310; Fax: 00-(509) 238489.

74. Honduras

(Republic of Honduras)
Republic de Honduras

Capital: Tegucigalpa D.C.; **Currency:** Lempira; **Area:** 112,088 sq.km; **Population:** 8,215,313; **Languages:** Spanish and some Indian dialects; **Religions:** Roman Catholic-97%, Protestant-3%; **Literacy:** 83.6%; **Life Expectancy:** 70.2; **p.c.i:** $ 4,404; **HDI rank:** 106; **Date of Independence:** 15th September, 1821.
Government Type: Democratic Constitutional Republic; **President:** Porfirio Lobo Sosa.

History: Formerly a Spanish colony, Honduras has gone through a series of dictatorships, military juntas, coups and counter-coups.

Economy: Honduras is one of the poorest countries in the western hemisphere. The chief crop is bananas which constitute 65 per cent of the country's exports. Coffee, cotton, maize and tobacco are also grown. Timber is abundant and cattle raising is a major occupation. Industry: Textiles, wood products, cigars, beer and cement.

75. Hungary

(Republic of Hungary) Magyar Koztarsasag

Capital: Budapest; **Other Large Cities:** Miskolc, Debrecen; **Currency:** Forint; **Area:** 93,033 sq. km; **Population:** 10,014,324; **Languages:** Hungarian (Magyar); **Religions:** Roman Catholic-51.9%, Calvinist-15.9%; **Literacy:** 99.4%; **Life Expectancy:** 73.3; **p.c.i:** $ 18,815; **HDI rank:** 36; **Date of Independence:** 1001 (Date of unification by King Stephen I).
Government Type: Parliamentary Democracy; **President:** Pal Schmitt; **PM:** Viktor Orban

History: Hungary had a stormy history being successively overrun by Huns, Magyars, Turks, Hungarians and Austrians. Hungary became an independent republic in 1918 and the Hungarian Socialist Republic in 1919. In 1990, Hungary embraced democracy and market economy. The last Soviet

Cause of World War 1 | The immediate cause of the First World War (1914-18) was the assassination in Sarajevo of Archduke Franz Ferdinand, the Habsburg heir to the Austrian-Hungarian throne.

troops left Hungary in June, 1991. In July '97, NATO invited Hungary to become a full member of the alliance within two years. The country joined NATO in March '99.

Economy: The private sector accounts for more than 80% of GDP. Hungary exports engineering products, machine tools, motor vehicles and electrical and electronic goods. Chief imports are iron ore, coal, crude oil and consumer goods. More than 97 per cent of agricultural land is collectivised. Vineyards occupy around 186,000 hectares. Other crops: Grains, sunflowers, potatoes and sugar beets.

Mission in India: Embassy of the Republic of Hungary, 2/50 M, Niti Marg, Chanakyapuri, New Delhi-110021. Tel: 26114737; Teleax: 26886742.

E-mail: huembde12@vsnl.com

Indian Mission in Hungary: Embassy of India, Buzavirag utca 14, 1025 Budapest, Hungary. Tel: 00-36-1-3257742, 3257743; Fax: 00-36-1-3257745.

E-mail:chancery@indembassy.hu
Webset: www.indianembassy.hu

76. Iceland

(Republic of Iceland) Lyoveldio Island

Capital: Reykjavik; **Currency:** Krona; **Area:** 102,846 sq. km; **Population:** 318,452; **Languages:** Icelandic; **Religions:** Lutheran Church of Iceland -80.7%, Roman Catholic-2.5%; **Literacy:** 99%; **Life Expectancy**: 81.8; **p.c.i:** $ 36,681; **HDI rank:** 17; **Date of Independence:** 17th June, 1944.

Government Type: Constitutional Republic; **President:** Olafur Ragnar Grimsson; **PM:** Johanna Sigurdardottir.

History: The people of Iceland are the descendants of the dare-devil Vikings of Norway. After having been independent till the 13th century it became part of Norway, and then passed under Danish rule. In 1941 the Althing (the world's oldest surviving parliament) voted for complete independence

and a republic was formed on June 17, 1944. Iceland's language has maintained its purity for 1000 years.

Iceland remains outside the EU but, although it has no armed forces, it is a member of Nato. In 1985 it declared itself a nuclear-free zone.

Economy: Less than one per cent of Iceland's territory is arable. Potatoes, turnips and hay are the major crops. Fishing industry is highly developed. It accounts for 75% of export earnings, 20% of GDP and engages one-seventh of the work force. Exports: Marine products and aluminium. Iceland taps thermal and hydro power for energy-hungry industries.

Mission in India: Embassy of Iceland,11, Aurangzeb Road, New Delhi,-110021.Tel: 4353 0300; Fax:4240 3001.

Consulates: Consulate General, 'Speedbird House', 41/2 M, Connaught Circus, New Delhi-110 001. Tel: 23417122; Fax: 23416275.

E-mail: khemka@13.vsnl.net.in
E-mail: Khemka@de13.vsnl.net.in

Indian Mission in Iceland: Honorary Consulate General of India, Solvallagate 48, 101, Reykjavik, Iceland. P.O. Box No. 678, 121 Reykjavik. Tel: 00-354-1-28255; Fax: 00-354-1-625010.

77. India

Capital: New Delhi; **Other Large Cities:** Mumbai, Kolkata, Chennai; **Currency:** Rupee; **Area:** 3,287,263

Keeping Sidewalks Warm **Reykjavik, the capital of Iceland, has sidewalks that are heated by geothermal heat in the winter. Maybe this takes care of snow-shoveling...**

sq.km.; **Population:** 1,210,193,422; **Languages:** Hindi (official), English, 18 officially recognised languages; **Religions:** Hindu-80.5%, Muslim-13.4%, Christian- 2.3%, Sikh-1.9%, other 1.8%, unspecified 0.1%; **Literacy:** 74.4%; **Life Expec-tancy:** 64.7; **p.c.i:** $3,290; **HDI rank:** 119; **Date of Independence:** 15th August, 1947. **Government Type:** Federal Republic; **President:** Smt. Pratibha Patil; **PM:** Dr. Manmohan Singh.

For details see Part- Eight, India

78. Indonesia

(Republic of Indonesia) Republik Indonesia

Capital: Jakarta; **Other Large Cities:** Surabaya, Bandung; **Currency:** Rupiah; **Area:** 1,904,569 sq. km; **Population:** 237,556,363; **Languages:** Bahasa Indonesian, Dutch, English, Javanese and other Austronesian languages; **Religions:** Muslim-86.1%, Protestant-5.7%, Roman Catholic-3%, Hindu-1.8%, other or unspecified 3.4%; **Literacy:** 92%; **Life Expectancy:** 70.7; **p.c.i:** $ 4,380; **HDI rank:** 108; **Date of Independence:** 17th August, 1945. **Government Type:** Republic; **Head of State & Govt (President):** Susilo Bambang Yudhoyono.

History: Formerly the Dutch East Indies, the Republic of Indonesia, the biggest Islamic nation, is an archipelago state consisting of about 13,500 (6000 inhabited) islands extending some 5150 km. along the

Equator in the Indian and Pacific Oceans.

The largest islands of the archipelago are Sumatra, Java, Kalimantan (Indonesian Borneo), Sulavesi and Irian Java.

The islands were made an integral part of the Netherlands Kingdom in 1922. During World War II, Indonesia was under Japanese military occupation. On Aug. 17, 1945, Indonesia proclaimed independence from the Dutch.

After a war of independence, the Netherlands transferred sovereignty to Indonesia on December 27, 1949. A republic was declared August 17, 1950, with Dr.Sukarno as president. Gen. Suharto, head of the army was named President in 1968.

Economy: One of the world's richest countries in natural resources, Indonesia has vast supplies of tin, oil and fairly big deposits of bauxite, copper, nickel, gold and silver. Agriculture is the main occupation of the people. Crops include rice, tobacco, coffee, rubber, cassava, maize, pepper, kapok, coconut, palm oil, tea and sugarcane. Food processing, textiles, paper, cement, automobile & cycle assembly works and chemicals factories have developed.

Mission in India: Embassy of the Republic of Indonesia,50-A,Chanakyapuri, New Delhi- 110021. Tel: 26118642-45; Fax: 26874402, 26886763, 26888279.

E-mail:iembassy@giasd101.vsnl.net.in

Consulate General of the Republic of Indonesia: 19, Altamount Road, Cumballa Hill, Mumbai-400 026; Ph: 91-22-23868678, 23800940; E-mail: kjrimumb@bom3. vsnl.net.in

Indian Mission in Indonesia: Embassy of India, S-1, Jalan H.R. Rasuna Said, Kuningan, Jakarta-12950, Indonesia. Tel: 00-62-21-5204150, 5204152; Fax: 00-62-21-5204160.

E-mail: admjkt@net-zap.com

79. Iran

(Islamic Republic of Iran) Jomhori-e-Islami-e-Iran

Capital: Teheran; **Other Large Cities:** Esfahan, Mashad; **Currency:** Rial; **Area:**

1,648,000sq.km; **Population:** 75,078,000; **Languages:** Persian (Farsi), Turk, Kurdish, Arabic; **Religions:**
Shi'a Muslim-89%, Sunni Muslim-9%, Zoroastrian, Jewish, Christian and Baha'i-2%; **Literacy:** 82.3%; **Life Expectancy:** 71; **p.c.i:** $ 11,024; **HDI rank:** 70; **Date of Independence:** 1st April, 1979.
Government Type: Islamic Republic; **President:** Mahmud Ahmadi-Nejad.

History: Iran, formerly Persia, lies between Caspian Sea and the Persian Gulf and consists of a central plateau surrounded by mountains. A popular revolution of Islamic character swept the long-ruling Shah Mohammed Reza Pahlavi from power and installed a strict clerical leadership under Ayatollah Ruhollah Khomeini, spiritual leader of the Shia Muslim community.

Iran is a country of great antiquity, celebrated alike for its culture and military valour.

Economy: Agriculture employs 30% of the labour force. The chief products are wheat, barley, rice, fruits (largest producer of dates),wool and sugar beets. Iran is one of the biggest oil-producing regions in the Middle East. It owns 7.5% of total world oil reserves and 15% of global gas deposits. Emeralds and other gems are found in Khorassan and Kerman. Persian carpets, made on handlooms are famous. Other industries: Textiles, cement, processed foods, steel and copper fabrication.

Mission in India: Embassy of the Islamic Republic of Iran, No. 5, Barakhamba Road, New Delhi-110001. Tel: 23329600-02; Fax: 23325493, 23713704 (Armed Forces).
E-mail:info@iran-embassy.org.in
Consulate General of The Islamic Republic of Iran: "Swapnalok", First Floor, 47, Nepean Sea Road, Mumbai-400 026; Ph: 022-2363 0073,2363 4102,2363 1029.
Indian Mission in Iran: Embassy of India, No. 46, Mir-Emad St.,Corner of 9th Street, Dr. Beheshti Avenue,P.O. Box No. 15875-4118,Tehran, Iran. Tel: 00-98-21 88755103-5; Fax: 00-98-21-88755973, 88745557.
E-mail: hoc.tehran@mea.gov.in

80. Iraq

(Republic of Iraq) al Jumhoriya al 'Iraqia

Capital: Baghdad; Other Large Cities: Basra, Mosul; **Currency:** Dinar; **Area:** 438,446sq.km; **Population:** 31,467,000;
Languages: Arabic (official) and Kurdish; **Religions:** Muslim-97% (Shi'a-60-65%, Sunni-32-37%), Christian or other-3%; **Literacy:** 74%; **Life Expectancy:** 59.5; **p.c.i:** $ 3,599; **Date of Independence:** 3rd October, 1932.
Government Type: Transitional Government; **Govt.:** The country is under U.S. control; **President:** Jalal Talabani; **P.M:** Nuri al-Maliki.

History: Iraq in the Middle East, is the mo-

World's Most Beautiful City	It was China's Hangzhou, which Marco Polo called the world's most beautiful city. The renowned 14th century Moroccan explorer Ibn Batuta said it was "the biggest city I have ever seen on the face of the earth."

dern name for Mesopotamia (Meso-middle, Potamia-rivers), the land lying between the two great rivers, Euphrates and Tigris.

Iraq is one of the most ancient countries of the world and has produced a culture– the Mesopotamian Civilisation – which has influenced European and Asian civilisations.

An international crisis was sparked when Iraq overran Kuwait in Aug., 1990. A US-led coalition beat Iraq in Feb, 1991. An estimate puts casualties at 85,000.

Economy: Three quarters of the population depend on agriculture for their living. Chief products: Wheat, barley, rice, dates (largest exporter), cotton, sugarcane, livestock. Petroleum is the most important sector of the economy. Iraq occupies the fifth place among oil-producing countries. Industry: Petrochemicals, textiles, oil refining and cement.

Mission in India: Embassy of the Republic of Iraq, B-5/8, Vasant Vihar, New Delhi-110057. Tel: 26149085; Telefax: 26149076.

Indian Mission in Iraq: Embassy of India, House No.6, Zokak No. 25, Mohalla 306, Hay Al Magrib, P.O. Box-4114, Adhamiya, Baghdad, Iraq. Tel: 00-914-1-4228419, 5417377, 5435776; Fax: 00-914-1-4228419, 5417377, 5435776; E-mail: eoibaghdad@yahoo.com

81. Ireland

(Republic of Ireland) Eire

Capital: Dublin; **Other Large Cities:** Cork, Limerick; **Currency:** Euro; **Area:** 70,282 sq.km; **Population:** 4,470,700; **Languages:** Irish and English; **Religions:** Roman Catholic-87.4%, Church of Ireland-2.9%; **Literacy:** 99%; **Life Expectancy:** 78.9; **p.c.i:** $ 38,685; **HDI rank:** 5; **Date of Independence:** 6th December, 1921.

Government Type: Republic; **President:** Mrs. Mary McAleese; **PM:** Enda Kenny.

Ireland or Eire, the Emerald Isle, is an island in the N. Atlantic lying west of Great Britain.

The independent state of Ireland consists of only 26 counties out of the 32 that make up the whole island. The 6 remaining counties form the area known as Northern Ireland which is directly administered by the United Kingdom.

History: Ireland emerges in history with the coming of St. Patrick in A.D. 432 and the spread of Christianity. An invasion led by Norman barons during the 12th century led to a period of almost eight centuries of British rule in Ireland. In 1921 Great Britian recognised Ireland as a more or less independent unit within the Commonwealth and the country became known as the Irish Free State. In 1932 the Fianna Fail party under Eamon de Valera came to power and gradually removed the last vestiges of allegiance to the British Crown. In 1937, a new constitution was adopted which made Ireland effectively a republic. In 1949 Ireland formally declared itself a Republic and ceased to be a member of the Commonwealth. Ireland is a member of the EU.

In 1993, the Irish and British governments made a peace plan to resolve the Northern Ireland issue. Much of it was rejected by Sinn Fein, the political wing of the Irish Republican Army (IRA), an extremist group working for the unification of Ireland. On Aug. 31, 1994, IRA announced ceasefire and said it would use only political means to achieve unification. When peace talks lagged, it resumed the terror campaign in Feb. '96. In 1997, Sinn Fein

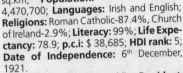
The Sound of Music

The classic film *The Sound of Music* is based on the true story of the Von Trapp family and their escape from Nazi Austria. Julie Andrews nearly turned down the role of Maria von Trapp fearing the character was too similar to her role in *Mary Poppins*.

won a seat in Ireland's parliament for the first time since 1981. On July 20, IRA declared 'unequivocal' ceasefire.

Ireland is the birthplace of many famous English-language writers, among them W.B. Yeats, James Joyce, Samuel Beckett, Oscar Wilde and George Bernard Shaw.

Economy: Ireland had formerly a mainly agricultural economy. Chief crops: Grains, potatoes, sugar beets, vegetables, fruits. In recent decades industrial output has expanded rapidly due to increased foreign investment. Ireland now has affiliates of more than 1,000 foreign companies employing more than 90,000 workers.

Mission in India: Embassy of Ireland, 230 Jor Bagh, New Delhi-110003. Tel: 24626733, 24629135(Visa); Fax: 24697053.

E-mail: newdelhiembassy@dfa.ie

Indian Mission in Ireland: Embassy of India, 6, Leeson Park, Dublin-6, Ireland. Tel: 00-353-1-4970843, 4970959; Fax: 00-353-1-4978074.

E-mail: indembassy@eircom.net

82. Israel

(State of Israe l) Medinat Israel

Capital: Jerusalem;
Other Large Cities: Tel Aviv, Haifa; **Currency:** New Shekel; **Area:** 20,772 sq.km; **Population:** 7,708,400;
Languages: Hebrew (official) and Arabic; **Religions:** Jewish-76.4%, Muslim-16%, Christian-2.1%, Druze-1.6%, unspeciifed-3.9%; **Literacy:** 97.1%; **Life Expectancy:** 80.7; **p.c.i:** $ 29,404; **HDI rank:** 15; **Date of Independence:** 14th May, 1948
Government Type: Parliamentary Democracy; **President:** Shimon Peres **PM:** Binjamin Netanyahu.

History: The division of the former British mandate of Palestine and the creation of the state of Israel have been at the centre of Middle Eastern conflicts for the past sixty years.

The creation of Israel was the culmination of the Zionist movement, whose aim

was a homeland for Jews scattered all over the world following the Diaspora. After the Nazi Holocaust, pressure grew for the international recognition of a Jewish state, and in 1948 Israel came into being.

Much of the history of the region since that time has been one of conflict between Israel on one side and Palestinians, represented by the Palestine Liberation Organisation, and Israel's Arab neighbours, on the other. Hundreds of thousands of Palestinians were displaced, and several wars were fought involving Egypt, Jordan, Syria and Lebanon.

Palestinians in the West Bank, including east Jerusalem, have lived under Israeli occupation since 1967. The settlements that Israel has built in the West Bank are home to around 400,000 people and are deemed to be illegal under international law, although Israel disputes this.

Israel evacuated its settlers from the Gaza Strip in 2005 and withdrew its forces, ending almost four decades of military occupation. However, after the militant Islamic group Hamas seized control of Gaza in June 2007, Israel intensified its economic blockade of the Strip.

In 1979 Egypt and Israel signed a peace agreement, but it wasn't until the early 1990s, after years of an uprising known as the intifada, that a peace process began with the Palestinians. Despite the handover of Gaza and parts of the West Bank to Palestinian control, a "final status" agreement has yet to be reached.

The main stumbling blocks include the status of Jerusalem and the fate of Palestinian refugees and Jewish settlements.

Economy: Kibbutzim (collective cultivation), irrigation schemes and reclamation of desert-land formed the main feature of agricultural development. Citrus fruits are the main exports. Wine-making is an extensive industry. In diamond-cutting, Israel comes next only to Belgium. Other industries are textiles, electronics, machinery, processed foods and chemicals.

Gaza Strip: Area- 363 sq.km; Pop-1,054,200. Agreements between Israel and PLO in 1993 and '94 provided for interim self-rule in Gaza. Israel is in control of security, while Palestinian Authority is responsible for civil govt. Most inhabitants are Palestinian Arabs.

West Bank: Area- 5,879 sq. km; Pop.-1,557,000. Palestinian Authority administers several major cities, but Israel retains control over much land. In '94, Jericho was given to Palestinian control. Self-rule was expanded in '95. In '97 there was agreement on partial pullout from Hebron.

Mission in India: Embassy of Israel, 3, Aurangzeb Road, New Delhi-110 011; Tel: (011)3041 4500; Fax: (011)3041 4555.

E-mail: info@newdelhi.mfa.gov.il

Indian Mission in Israel: Embassy of India, 140 Hayarkon Street, P.O Box 3368, Tel Aviv 61033, Israel. Tel: 00-972-3-5291999; Fax: 03-5291953.

E-mail: indemtel@indembassy.co.il

83. Italy

(Italian Republic) Republica Italiana

Capital: Rome; **Other Large Cities:** Milan, Naples, Turin, Florence; **Currency:** Euro; **Area:** 301,278 sq.km.; **Population:** 60,605,053; **Languages:** Italian; **Religions:** Roman Catholic-90% (about one-third practising), other-10% (includes many Protestant and Jewish communities and a growing Muslim immigrant community); **Literacy:** 98.9%; **Life Expectancy:** 80.5; **p.c.i:** $ 29,418; **HDI rank:** 23; **Date of Independence:** 17th March, 1861.

Government Type: Republic; **President:** Giorgio Napolitano; **PM:** Silvio Berlusconi.

History: Italy, once the headquarters of the great Roman Empire, disintegrated into many petty states during the latter Middle Ages. Modern Italy began to develop when King Victor Emmanuel II of Savioa became ruler.

On April 28, 1945 Benito Mussolini, the Fascist dictator, was put to death. Consequent on a referendum on June 2, 1946, Italy voted for a Republic. The king laid down his kingship. Italy is a member of the European Union.

The art works of Botticelli, Leonardo da Vinci, Michelangelo, Tintoretto and Caravaggio, the operas of Verdi and Puccini, the cinema of Federico Fellini, the architecture of Venice, Florence and Rome are just a fraction of Italy's treasures from over the centuries.

Economy: Since World War II, Italy has revolutionised agricultural production. The chief crops are grapes, wheat, sugarbeet, fruits and vegetables. Italy is among the highly industrialised countries of the world, main products being steel, machinery, electrical, mechanical and electronic gadgets, automobiles, chemicals, cement, textiles and shoes. Italy is world's largest jewellery maker. Tourism is an important source of revenue, providing employment and an influx of foreign currency.

Mission in India: Embassy of Italy, 50-E, Chandragupta Marg, Chanakyapuri, New

The "Three Fountains"

Known as the "Three Fountains," Dante Alighieri (1265-1321), Francesco Petrarch (1304-1374), and Giovanni Boccaccio (1313-1375) are arguably the three most famous Italian authors of all time.

Delhi-110021. Tel: 26114355, 26114359; Telefax: 26873889.

E-mail:ambasciata.newdelhi@esteri.it

Indian Mission in Italy: Embassy of India, Via XX Settembre, 5, 00187, Rome, Italy. Tel: 00-39-06-4884642 to 45; Fax: 00-39-06-4819539.

E-mail:admin.wing@indianembassy.it

Ivory Coast

(See under Cote D'Ivoire)

84. Jamaica

Capital: Kingston; **Currency:** Jamaican dollar; **Area:** 11,425 sq.km; **Population:** 2,730,000; **Languages:** English and Jamaican Creole; **Religions:** Protestant-62.5%, Roman Catholic-2.6%, others including some spiritual cults-34.9%; **Literacy:** 86%; **Life Expectancy:** 72.6; **p.c.i:** $ 8,811; **HDI rank:** 80; **Date of Independence:** 6th August, 1962.

Government Type: Constitutional Parliamentary Democracy; **Gov.Gen.:** Dr.Patrick L.Allen; **PM:** Bruce Golding.

Jamaica, an island in the Greater Antilles group of the West Indies, is situated in the Caribbean Sea, 144 km south of Cuba.

History: Jamaica was visited by Columbus in 1494 and ruled by Spain till 1655 when Britain occupied it. On August 6, 1962 Jamaica became fully independent and a member of the Commonwealth. About 75% of the population is of African ethnic origin.

Known for its strong sense of self identity expressed through its music, food and rich cultural mix, Jamaica's influence extends far beyond its shores.

Economy: The economy is heavily dependent on services,which account for more than 60% of GDP. Jamaica derives most of its foreign exchange from tourism, remittances, and bauxite/alumina. The dominant crop is sugar, with molasses and rum as important by-products. Bananas, citrus fruits and coconuts are also grown. Jamaica is the world's second largest producer of bauxite and alumina. Other industries are cement, tobacco, consumer goods and tourism.

Mission in India: Embassy of Jamaica stationed at Ottawa

Indian Mission in Jamaica: High Commission of India, 27, Seymour Avenue, P.O. Box No. 446, Kingston-6, Jamaica.Tel:00-1 -876-9273114, 9274270; Fax: 00-1-876-9782801, 9780359.

E-mail:hicomindkin@cwjamaica.com

85. Japan

(Nippon)

Capital: Tokyo; **Other Large Cities:** Yokohama, Osaka, Saporo, Kyoto, Hiroshima; **Currency:** Yen; **Area:** 377,765 sq.km; **Population:** 127,960,000; **Languages:** Japanese; **Religions:** Shinto and Buddhism-84%, others-16% (including Christian-2%); **Literacy:** 99%; **Life Expectancy:** 82.6; **p.c.i:** $ 33,828; **HDI rank:** 11; **Date of Independence:** 660 B.C.

Government Type: Parliamentary Democracy; **Head of State:** Emperor Akihito; **PM:** Naoto Kan.

History: Legend has it that the Japanese Empire was founded by Emperor Jimmu in 660 B.C. In A.D. 1868 Emperor Meiji united the whole of Japan under his rule. Japan had little trade relations with foreign countries until 1871 when it entered into a trade treaty with USA. After the feudal system was abolished, westernisation set

Parmesan Cheese

Parmesan cheese originated in the area around Parma, Italy. Italians also created many other cheeses, including gorgonzola, mozzarella, provolone, and ricotta. No one knows when the pizza was invented, but the people of Naples made it popular.

in. In 1952, Japan regained its sovereignty. Japan's victory in the Russo-Japanese War of 1904-05 raised her prestige among European powers.

Economy: Rice, the staple food of Japan, is cultivated in half the area of arable land. Other crops are wheat, barley, potatoes and tobacco. Japan, one of the most industrially advanced countries of the world, is a leader in technology and the world's second richest country. The principal industries are automobiles, iron and steel, chemicals, textiles (cotton, wool, silk and synthetics), fishing, ceramics, precision instruments, fertilisers, machinery and shipbuilding.

Mission in India: Embassy of Japan, 50-G Shantipath, Chanakyapuri, New Delhi - 110 021. Tel: 26876581, 26876564; Fax: 26885587.

E-mail: jpembjic@bol.ne.in

Web: www.japan-emb.org.in

Cultural & Information Centre, 32-Ferozeshah Road, New Delhi-110 001. Tel: 3329803; Fax:371-2124

Indian Mission in Japan: Embassy of India, 5-7-2, Kojimachi MT 31 Building, Chiyoda-ku, Tokyo-102-0083,Japan. Tel: 00-81-3-32622391to 97; Fax: 00-81-3-32344866.

E-mail: indembjp@gol.com

86. Jordan

(Hashemite Kingdom of Jordan) al Mamlaka al Urduniya al Hashemiyah

Capital: Amman; **Other Large Cities:**

Zarka, Irbid, Salt; **Currency:** Jordan Dinar; **Area:** 89,287 sq.km; **Population:** 6,472,000; **Languages:** Arabic and English; **Religions:** Sunny Muslim-92%, Christian-6%, others-2%; **Literacy:** 91.1%; **Life Expectancy:** 72.5; **p.c.i:** $ 5,658; **HDI rank:** 82; **Date of Independence:** 25th May, 1946.

Government Type: Constiitutional Monarchy; **Head of State:** King Abdullah II; **PM:** Marouf al-Bakhit.

History: A constitutional monarchy in southwest Asia, Jordan was popularly known as Trans-Jordan till 1949, when the popular name was changed to the Hashemite Kingdom of Jordan. The population is chiefly Arab of whom the majority are Muslims.

Economy: Jordan is largely desert but the western portion is fertile and produces citrus fruits, wheat, barley, lentils and water melons. Phosphate and potash make up the country's most important export item, but tourism remains its main foreign exchange earner.

Textiles, cement, food-processing, petroleum products, iron and fertiliser are major industries.

Mission in India: Embassy of the Hashemite Kingdom of Jordan, 30, Golf Links, New Delhi-110 003; Tel:24653318, 24653099; Fax: 24653353.

E-mail:jordan@jordanembassyindia.org

Indian Mission in Jordan: Embassy of India, Jabal Ammn, 1st Circle, Post Box 2168,

| The Roman Empire | At its height in A.D. 117, the Roman Empire stretched from Portugal in the West to Syria in the east, and from Britain in the North to the North African deserts across the Mediterranean. It covered 2.3 million miles and had a population of 120 million people. |

Amman, Jordan. Tel: 00-962-6-4622098, 4637262; Fax: 00-962-6-4659540.

E-mail: itm.amman@mea.gov.in

87. Kazakhstan

(Republic of Kazakhstan)
Kazak Respubli-kasy

Capital: Astana (also known as Akmola); **Other Large Cities:** Karaganda, Chimkent; **Currency:** Teng-eS; **Area:** 2,717,300 sq.km; **Population:** 16,433,000; **Languages:** Kazakh, Russian, German; **Religions:** Muslim-47%, Russian Orthodox-44%, Protestant-2%, others-7%; **Literacy:** 99.6%; **Life Expectancy:** 67; **p.c.i:** $ 12,401; **HDI rank:** 66; **Date of Independence:** 16th December, 1991.

Government Type: Republic; **President:** Nursultan A. Nazarbayev; **PM:** Karim Masimov.

History: The second largest former Soviet Republic is an ethnically diverse country whose population includes over hundred nationalities.

Economy: Agriculture: Grain, sugar beet, potatoes, vegetables, meat, milk, eggs, cotton. Natural resources: Half of former Soviet Union's total deposits of copper, lead and zincare are in Kazakhstan. Other minerals: coal, tungsten, oil, nickel, chromium, molybdenum, manganese. Kazakhistan has the second largest oil field in the world in Kasagan, and sits on an estimated 3 billion tonnes of oil and 2 trillion tonnes of gas.

Main industries: Iron ore, sulphuric acid, agricultural machinery, ferroconcrete, knitwear, footwear, hosiery.

Mission in India: Embassy of the Republic of Kazakhstan, 61, Poorvi Marg, Vasant Vihar, New Delhi-110 057; Tel: 4600 7710,4600 7700; Telefax: 4600 7701.

E-mail: office@kazembassy.in

Indian Mission in Kazakhstan: Embassy of India, Kaskad Business Centre, 5th Floor, 6/1 Kabanbai Batyr Avenue, Astana, Kazakhstan Tel: 00-7-7172-925700/701/ 702/ 703, 242257; Fax: 00-7-7172-925716/ 717.

E-mail: hoc.astana@mea.gov.in

88. Kenya

(Republic of Kenya) Jamhuriya Kenya

Capital: Nairobi; **Other Large Cities:** Mombasa, Kisumu; **Currency:** Shilling; **Area:** 582,646 sq.km; **Population:** 38,610,097; **Languages:** Kiswahili, English, Kikuyu and several other local languages; **Religions:** Protestant-45%, Roman Catholic-33%, Indigenous beliefs-10%, Muslim-10%, others-2%; **Literacy:** 73.6%; **Life Expectancy:** 54.1; **p.c.i:** $ 1,784; **HDI rank:** 128; **Date of Independence:** 12th December, 1963.

Government Type: Republic; **President:** Mwai Kibaki.

History: Founding president and liberation struggle icon Jomo Kenyatta led Kenya from independence in 1963 until his death in 1978, when president Daniel Arap Moi took power in a constitutional succession. The country was a de facto one-party state from 1969 until 1982 when the ruling Kenya African National Union(KANU) made itself the sole legal party in Kenya. President Moi stepped down in 1992 following fair and peaceful elections.

Economy: The chief cash crops are coffee, tea, sisal, cereals, wattle and pyrethrum. Kenya has a significant dairy industry. Mineral industries are being organised. Other industries include textiles, consumer goods

30,000 Hiroshimas — The magnitude 9.0 earthquake that hit Japan on March 11, 2011 was the largest ever in the country's history. It was equivalent in power to 30,000 Hiroshimas.

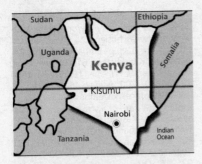

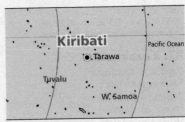

and processed foods. Major exports are tea, coffee, horticulture, petroleum products and cement.

Mission in India: High Commission of Kenya, 34, Paschimi Marg, Vasant Vihar, New Delhi - 110 057. Tel: 2614 6537/38, 26146540; Fax: 2614 6550.

E-mail: info@kenyahicom-delhi.com

Indian Mission in Kenya: High Commission of India, Jeewan Bharati Building, Harambee Avenue, P.O. Box 30074, Nairobi, Kenya. Tel: 00-254-2-222566, 222567, 224500, 225180; Fax: 00-254-2-316242. E-mail: hcinfo@wananchi.com, conshci@iconnect.co.ke

89. Kiribati

(Republic of Kiribati) Ribaberikin Kiribati

Capital: Tarawa; **Currency:** Australian dollar; **Area:** 861 sq. km; **Population:** 100,000; **Languages:** Gilbertese and English; **Religions:** Roman Catholic-52%, Protestant (Congregational)-40%; **Life Expectancy:** 63.22; **p.c.i:** $ 6,181; **Date of Independence:** 12th July, 1979.
Government Type: Republic; **Head of State and Govt.:** Anote Tong.
History: Gilbert islands, till recently a British colony, became independent under the name Kiribati (pronounced Kiribas) in July, 1979.
Economy: These islands, spread over a

vast area in South West Pacific, number around 33. All islands except Ocean Island (Banaba) are low atolls with coconuts, pandanus and bread fruit forming the main vegetation. The population is Micronesian and Polynesian. Agriculture and fishing are the main occupations. Ocean Island has high grade phosphate deposits which are being mined and exported. Copra is the other major export item.

90. Korea (North)

(Democratic People's Republic of Korea) Chosun Minchuchui Inmin Konghwaguk

Capital: Pyongyang; **Other Large Cities:** Hamhung, Chongjin; **Currency:** Won; **Area:** 120,538 sq.km; **Population:** 23,991,000; **Languages:** Korean; **Religions:** Traditionally Buddhist and Confucianist, some Christian and syncretic Chondogyo (Religion of the Heavenly Way); **Literacy:** 99%; **Life Expectancy:** 67.3; **p.c.i:** $ 1,700; **Date of Independence:** 15th August, 1945.
Government Type: Communist State; **President:** Marshal Kim Jong Il; **PM:** Choe Yong Rim.

The Democratic People's Republic of Korea occupies the northern part of the Korean peninsula.

History: During the Second World War, America occupied South Korea, and Russia North Korea. At the Potsdam Conference, the 38th parallel of latitude was recognised as the line of division between the occupation areas of Russia and America. South

| How to Pronounce Kenya? | The only country that has changed the pronunciation of its name is Kenya. While it was formerly pronounced "KEEN-ya", the name is now pronounced "KEN-ya", like the last name of leader Jomo Kenyatta was pronounced. |

91. Korea (South)

(Republic of Korea) Taehan Min'guk

Capital: Seoul; **OtherLargeCities:** Pusan, Inchon; **Currency:** Won; **Area:** 98,859 sq.km; **Population:** 48,988,833; **Languages:** Korean; **Religions:** Christian-26.3%, Buddhist-23.2%, other or unknown-1.3%, none- 49.3%; **Literacy:** 99%; **Life Expectancy:** 78.6; **p.c.i:** $ 27,791; **HDI rank:** 12; **Date of Independence:** 15th August, 1945.

Government Type: Republic; **President:** Lee Myung-bak; **PM:** Kim Hwang-sik.

History: The Republic of Korea, for-mally proclaimed on August 15, 1948, forms the southern part of the Korean peninsula. The period 1950-53 saw the Korean War, a tragic experience for the entire Korean people.

In 1991, the prime ministers of North and South Korea signed a declaration of non-aggression and reconciliation.

Economy: Chief crops are rice, wheat, barley, potatoes and vegetables. Fish is both an export item and a source of food. There are substantial coal deposits. Other minerals include iron, tungsten, graphite and fluorite. Has made big leaps in industry - textiles, electronics, steel, petrochemicals, ships and motor vehicles.

Koreans formed the Republic of Korea in May, 1948. North Korea was formed into the Democratic People's Republic of Korea on Sept. 9, 1948. North Korean army attacked S. Korea in June, 1950, initiating the Korean War. U.S. and other western nations, with U.N. backing, supported the south. China sent an army across the border. The war ended in an armistice (July 1953) leaving Korea divided by a 'no-man's land' along the 38th parallel. Kim II Sung, who ruled Korea since 1948 died in July, 1994.

Economy: All industries are nationalised. Agriculture is collectivised. Chief crops: rice, maize, potatoes. Industrial development has concentrated on heavy industry, electricity, metallurgy, machinery and chemicals. The country is rich in coal and iron and many non-ferrous metals and hydro-electric power. It is one of the five leading countries of the world in the production of tungsten, graphite and magnetite.

Mission in India: Embassy of the Democratic People's Republic of Korea, E-455, Greater Kailash, Part-II, New Delhi - 110 048. Tel: 2123 9644, Telefax: 2223 9645.

Indian Mission in Korea (Democratic People's Republic): Embassy of India, 6, Munsudong, Taehek Street, District Daedonggang, Pyong-yang, DPR Korea. Tel: 00-850-2-3817274, 3817215; Fax: 00-850-2-3817619; Email: indemhoc@di.chesin.com

Mobile Money Kenya has one of the highest rates of mobile-phone penetration in Africa, dominated by MPESA, the biggest network of mobile-phone-based money transfer. Kenyans transferred some $7 billion, the equivalent of 20% of GDP, via their mobile phones in 2010.

Mission in India: Embassy of the Republic of Korea, 9, Chandragupta Marg, Chanakyapuri Extn., New Delhi - 110 021 Tel: 4200 7000; Fax: 26884840.

E-mail : india@mofat.go.kr

Indian Mission in Korea: Embassy of India, 37-3, Hannam-dong, Yongsanku, Seoul 140210, Republic of Korea. Tel: 00-82-2-798 4257/7984268; Fax: 00-82-2-7969534; Email: hoc.seoul@mea.gov.in

92. Kuwait

(State of Kuwait) Dowlat al-Kuwait

Capital: Kuwait City; **Other Large Cities:** Hawalli, as-Salimiya; **Currency:** Kuwaiti dinar; **Area:** 17,818 sq. km; **Population:** 3,051,000; **Languages:** Arabic and English; **Religions:** Islam-75%; **Literacy:** 94.5%; **LifeExpectancy:** 77.6; **p.c.i:** $38,293; **HDI rank:** 47; **Date of Independence:** 19th June 1961. **Government Type:** Constitutional Monarchy; **President:** Amir Sabah al-Ahmed al-Jabir al-Sabah; **PM:** Nasir Muhammed al-Ahmad al Sabah.

History: Kuwait, a small Arab state, is on the north western coast of the Persian Gulf between Iraq and Saudi Arabia. There are 9 islands off the coast of Kuwait. Rate of growth of population is 3.33%. More than 125 nationalities live in Kuwait.

One of the richest oil nations of the world, Kuwait was traditionally under the rule of the Al-Sabah dynasty founded in 1756. In 1961, when Kuwait achieved full

independence, Iraq claimed the territory as part of Iraq. Finally in August 1990 Iraq led by Saddam Hussein occupied Kuwait until it was expelled by a US-led coalition in Operation Desert Storm.

Economy: Kuwait is a small, relatively open economy with proved crude oil reserves of about 104 billion barrels – 10% of world reserves. Petroleum accounts for nearly half of GDP, 95% of export revenue, and 80% of government income. Kuwait's climate limits agricultural development. Consequently with the exception of fish, it depends almost wholly on food imports. Other products: fertilisers, chemicals, building materials, shrimp.

Mission in India: Embassy of the State of Kuwait, 5-A, Shantipath, Chanakyapuri, New Delhi - 110021. Tel: 24100791; Fax: 26873516

Indian Mission in Kuwait: Embassy of India, Diplomatic Enclave, Arabian Gulf Street, P.O. Box. No. 1450-Safat, 3015-Safat, Kuwait. Tel: 00-965-22530600 /12/13, 22527246, 22523568, 2530616; Fax: 00-965-22546958, 22571192.

E-mail: amboffice@indembkwt.org, contact@indembkwt.org

Website: www.indembkwt.org

93. Kyrgyzstan

(Republic of Kyrgyzstan)
Kyrgyz Respubli-kasy

Capital: Bishkek; **Currency:** Som; **Area:** 198,500 sq.km; **Population:** 5,418,300; **Languages:** Kirghyz, Russian; **Religions:** Muslim-75%, Russian Orthodox-20%, others-5%; **Literacy:** 99.3%; **Life Expectancy:** 65.9; **p.c.i:** $ 2,162; **HDI rank:** 109; **Date of Independence:** 31st August, 1991. **Government Type:** Republic; **President:** Roza Otunbayeva.

History: Kyrgyzstan is situated on the Tien-Shan mountains.

Economy: Agriculture: Kyrgyzstan is famed

Longest Railway Tunnel	The 33-mile Seikan Tunnel that links Honshu to Hokkaido under the Tsugaru Strait is both the world's longest and the deepest operational rail tunnel in the world, although the Gotthard Base Tunnel in Switzerland will be longer when it opens to traffic in 2017.

History: Laos–Lao People's Democratic Republic–occupies a strategic position in south east Asia. A French protectorate since 1893, Laos became an inde-pendent sovereign state within the French Union in 1949. Conflicts among neutralist, communist and conservative factions created a chaotic political situation.

In the 1980s, Vietnamese aid - military and financial - was the chief support. Since 1988, investment from Thailand and USA has been substantial. In 1997, Laos was admitted to ASEAN.

for its livestock breeding. Bee-keeping is well-developed. Products: Grain, cotton, potatoes, vegetables, fruit, meat, milk, eggs, wool, tobacco.

Industry: Sugar, food, cotton, wool, tanning, flour mills, tobacco, timber, textile, engineering, metallurgy, oil and mining.

Mission in India: Embassy of the Kyrgyz Republic, C-93, Anand Niketan, New Delhi-110021; Tel: 24108008; Fax: 24108009.

E-mail: kyrgyzembassy@yandex.ru

Indian Mission in Kyrgyzstan: Embassy of India, 164-A, Chui (Prospect), Bishkek-720001, Kyrgyzstan. Tel: 00-996-312-210863; Fax: 00-996-312-660708, 210849

E-mail: indembas@ infotel.kg

94. Laos

(Lao People's Democratic Republic)
Sathala-nalat Paxathipatai Paxaxon Lao

Capital: Vientiane; **Other Large Cities:** Savannakhet, Pakse; **Currency:** Kip; **Area:** 236,800 sq.km; **Population:** 6,230,200;

Languages: Lao, Tribal, English, French; **Religions:** Buddhist-67%, Christian-1.5%, other and unspecified-31.5%; **Literacy:** 68.7%; **Life Expectancy:** 64.4; **p.c.i:** $ 2,435; **HDI rank:** 122; **Date of Independence:** 19th July, 1949.

Government Type: Communist State; **President:** Lt.Gen. Choummali Saignason; **PM:** Thongsing Thammavong

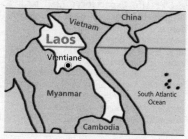

Economy: The chief products are rice, maize, tobacco, cotton. Major industrial products: Tin, timber, textiles.

Mission in India: Embassy of the Lao P.D.R., A 104/7, Parmanand Estate, Maharani Bagh, New Delhi-110 065; Tel:4132 7352; Fax:4132 7353.

E-mail: laosemb_delhi@hotmail.com

Indian Mission in Lao P.D.R.: Embassy of India, 002, Ban Wat-Nak,Thadeua Road, KM 3, Sisattanak District, Vientiane, Lao, PDR. Tel: 00-856-21-352301-04; Fax: 00-856-21-352300. E-mail: indiaemb@laotel.com

95. Latvia

(Republic of Lativia) Latvijas Republika

Capital: Riga; **Other Large Cities:** Dauga-vpils, Liepaja; **Currency:** Lats; **Area:** 63,700 sq. km; **Population:** 2,229,500; **Languages:** Latvian, Lithu-

Tyre; **Currency:** Lebanese Pound; **Area:** 10,400 sq.km; **Population:** 4,255,000; **Languages:** Arabic, French & English; **Religions:** Muslim-59.7%, Christian-39%, Jewish; **Literacy:** 89.6%; **Life Expectancy:** 72; **p.c.i:** $ 15,331; **Date of Independence:** 22nd November, 1943.

Government Type: Republic; **President:** Michel Suleiman; **PM:** Saad Hariri.

History: The Republic of Lebanon occupies a strip of land along the Mediterranean coast between Syria and Israel.

anian, Russian; **Religions:** Lutheran, Roman Catholic, Russian Orthodox; **Literacy:** 99.8%; **Life Expectancy:** 72.7; **p.c.i:** $ 14,330; **HDI rank:** 48; **Date of Independence:** 21st August, 1991.

Government Type: Parliamentary Democracy; **Head of State:** Valdis Zatlers; PM: Valdis Dombrovskis.

History: Latvia has the Baltic sea on the north and west. Neighbours are Estonia, Lithuania, Byelorussia and Russia. Latvia seceded from Soviet Union and attained independence in August, 1991, after having attempted to establish independence in 1990.

Latvia continues a pro-western foreign policy; It was largely cut off from the western world during 50 years of Soviet rule.

Economy: Crops: oats, barley, rye, potatoes, flax, sugarbeet, meat, milk and eggs. Cattle breeding and dairy farming are chief occupations. Natural resources: peat, briquettes and gypsum. Industry: Electric railway passenger cars and long-distance telephone exchanges (the main producer of these in former Soviet Union), paper and woollen goods, sawn timber, mineral fertilisers, hosiery, garments, leather footwear, chemical fibre, buses and radio receivers.

Mission in India: Hon. Consulate General of Republic of Latvia, 114, Sunder Nagar, New Delhi-110 003; Telefax: 011-43600600.

96. Lebanon

(Republic of Lebanon)
al-Jumhouriya al-Lubnaniya

Capital: Beirut; **Other Large Cities:** Sidon,

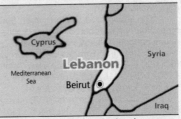

According to constitutional conventions, the Maronite Christians and Sunni Muslims shared power. However, because of the 16-year-old civil war between the Christians (30%) and Muslims (70%) there has been no stable administration. Terrorist bombings were common in 1983; so was kidnapping of foreign nationals by Islamic militants in the 1980s.

Economy: Lebanon produces olive oil, grain and fruits. The chief industries are oil refining, food processing, textiles, chemicals and cement.

Mission in India: Embassy of Lebanon, H-1, Anand Niketan, New Delhi-110021. Tel: 24110919 & 24111415, Telefax: 24110818.

E-mail: lebemb@airtelmail.in

Indian Mission in Lebanon: Embassy of India, 31, Kantari Street, Sahmarani Building, P.O. Box No. 113-5240 (Hamra) 11-1764, Beirut, 1107-2090. Tel: 00-961-1-373539, 372619; Fax: 00-961-1-373538.

E-mail: hoc.beirut@mea.gov.in

Haven for African Slaves	Liberia was founded as a voluntary haven for freed American slaves. The land was purchased from tribal chiefs in 1822 by the American Colonization Society, the price including a box of beads, three pairs of shoes, a box of soap, a barrel of rum, and 12 spoons.

97. Lesotho

(Kingdom of Lesotho)

Capital: Maseru; **Currency:** Loti; **Area:** 30,355 sq.km; **Population:** 2,084,000; **Languages:** English and Sesotho; **Religions:** Christian-80%, indigenous beliefs-20%; **Literacy:** 82.2%; **Life Expectancy:** 42.6; **p.c.i:** $ 1,266; **HDI rank:** 141; **Date of Independence:** 4th October, 1966. **Government Type:** Parliamentary Constitutional Monarchy; **Head of State:** King Letsie III; **PM:** Pakalitha Mosisili.

History: The Kingdom of Lesotho is an enclave within the Republic of South Africa. Lesotho was a British protectorate under the name Basutoland. It became independent as Lesotho on Oct. 4, 1966. King Moshoeshoe II died in a car accident in January, 1996.

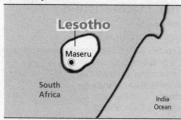

Economy: Crops: maize, grains, peas, beans. Livestock-raising is important activity. Livestock, diamonds, wool and mohair are the main exports. Industry: Food processing. Most of Lesotho's GNP is provided by citizens working in S. Africa.

Mission in India: High commission of the Kingdom of Lesotho, B-8/19, Vasant Vihar, New Delhi-110057.Tel:4166 0713; Telefax: 2614 1636; E-mail: lesothonewdelhi@airtelbroadband.in

98. Liberia

(Republic of Liberia)

Capital: Monrovia; **Other Large Cities:** Buchanan; **Currency:** Liberian dollar; **Area:** 111,369 sq.km; **Population:** 4,102,000;

Languages: English and tribal dialects; **Religions:** Indigenous beliefs-40%, Christian-40%, Muslim-20%; **Literacy:** 56%; **Life Expectancy:** 45.7; **p.c.i:** $ 396; **HDI rank:** 162; **Date of Independence:** 26th July, 1847. **Government Type:** Republic; **President & PM:** Ellen Johnson - Sirleaf.

History: Liberia lies on the Atlantic coast of Africa. It was founded in 1822 in order to settle freed American slaves in West Africa.

Economy: About 90 per cent of the population is engaged in agriculture, much of it at subsistence level. Main crops are cassava, coffee, rice, cocoa and palm oil. Iron ore and rubber are the main exports. Industry: Food processing, mining.

Civil strife that broke out in Dec. '89 tore the country apart making it the most violent country in the region. About half the population became refugees as a result of the Civil War, which claimed 150,000 lives.

In 1994, a 17-member coalition transition government was instituted. Factional fighting continued. The leaders signed about a dozen peace accords, only to resume fighting. Monrovia descended into chaos and bloodshed in 1996. Ruth Perry led a transitional government in Sept. '96, becoming modern Africa's first female head of state.

In July '97, Charles Taylor, a warlord who

Least Populous City in Africa Maseru, the capital of the Kingdom of Lesotho, has a population of around 14,000.

launched a civil war eight years ago to oust dictator Samuel Doe, won 75% of the presidential vote, and came to power, pledging to build a new country and apologising for the past bloodshed and violence.

Mission In India: Honorary Consulate General. Mohan House, Zamrudpur Community Centre, Kailash Colony Extn. New Delhi- 110 048. Tel: 264333135; Fax: 26460191

99. Libya

(Socialist People's Libyan Arab Jamahiriya) al-Jamahiriyah al-Arabiya al-Libya al-Shabiya al-Ishtirakiya

Capital: Tripoli; **Other Large Cities:** Benghazi, Misurata; **Currency:** Libyan Dinar; **Area:** 1,759,540 sq. km; **Population:** 6,546,000; **Languages:** Arabic; **Religions:** Sunni Muslim-97%; **Literacy:** 86.8%; **Life Expectancy:** 74; **p.c.i:** $ 14,878; **HDI rank:** 53; **Date of Independence:** 24th December, 1951. **Government Type:** Military Dictatorship; **President:** Col. Muammar El-Gaddafi; **PM:** al-Baghdadi Ali al-Mahmudi.

History: An Arab state on the Mediterranean coast of North Africa, Libya changed its name to 'The Socialist People's Libyan Arab Jamahiriya' in 1977. 'Jamahiriya' means 'State of the masses'.

Formerly an Italian colony, Libya became an independent state in 1951. The king was deposed in 1969.

Economy: The main agricultural products are wheat, barley, dates, olives, almond and citrus fruits. Fishing, tobacco processing, dyeing and weaving, handicrafts and petroleum are the important industries. Oil was discovered in 1957 and today Libya is one of the leading producers of oil.

Libya is the only country with a single-coloured flag.

Mission in India: People's Bureau of the Great Socialist People's Libyan Arab Jamahiriya, 22, Golf Links, New Delhi - 110003. Tel: 24697717, 24697771; Telefax: 24633005.

E-mail:libya_bu_ind@yahoo.com

Indian Mission in Libya: Embassy of India, Nafleen Area, Near Fashloom Roundabout, P.O. Box No. 3150, Tripoli, Libya. Tel: 00-218-21- 3409288/89; Fax: 00-218-21-3409282, 3404843.

E-mail:indembtrip@hotmail.com, commercial_indembtrip@yahoo.com

100. Liechtenstein

(Principality of Liechtenstein)
Furstentum Liechtenstein

Capital: Vaduz; **Other Large Cities:** Sachaan; **Currency:** Swiss Franc; **Area:** 160sq.km; **Population:** 36,157; **Languages:** German; **Religions:** Roman Catholic-79.81%, Protestant-7%, unknown-10.6%, others-6.2%; **Literacy:** 100%; **Life Expectancy:** 80.06; **p.c.i:** $ 122,100; **HDI rank:** 6; **Date of Independence:** 23rd January, 1719. **Government Type:** Hereditary Constitutional Monarchy; **Head of State:** Prince Hans Adam II; **PM:** Klaus Tschutscher.

History: Liechtenstein is a small state on the upper Rhine, between Austria and Switzerland. It measures 24 km from north to south and 9 km from east to west.

Foreign workers comprise a third of the population: Many international corporations have headquarters in Liechtenstein.

The country has remained neutral and undamaged in all European wars since

1868, when the army was abolished. In 1984, male voters granted women the right to vote.
Economy: The economy is mainly industrial. Cattle-rearing is highly developed. The country's farming population has gone down from 70% to 2% in about 60 years. Chief industries are machines and tools, textiles, foodstuffs, leather-ware, chemicals, furniture and ceramics.

101. Lithuania

(Republic of Lithuania) Lietuvos Respublika

Capital: Vilnius (Vilna); **Other Large Cities:** Kaunas, Klaipeda; **Currency:** Litas; **Area:** 65,200 sq.km; **Population:** 3,249,400; **La-****nguages:** Lithuanian; **Religions:** Roman Catholic -79%, Russian Orthodox-4.1%, Protestant-1.9%; **Literacy:** 99.7%; **Life Expectancy:** 73; **p.c.i:** $ 16,997; **HDI rank:** 44; **Date of Independence:** 11ᵗʰ March, 1990.

Government Type: Parliamentary Democracy; **President:** Dalia Grybauskaite; **PM:** Andrius Kubilius.

History: In March 1990, Lithuania formally declared its independence but USSR defeated it by cutting off supplies and by other manoeuvres. It is bordered by Latvia, Belarus, Poland and Russia.

Russia withdrew its last soldier from Lithuania on Aug. 31, 1993.

Economy: Agriculture: Grain, potatoes,

sugar-beet, vegetables, meat, milk and eggs. Natural resources: Forests cover 1,554,000 hectares, 70% of which consist of conifers, especially pines. Peat reserves total 4,000 m.cu. metres. Industry: Heavy engineering, ship-building, building material industries, electronic goods, chemicals, paper, leather, sugar and garments.

Mission in India: Hon. Consulate of the Republic of Lithuania, Mohan House, Zamrudpur Community Centre, Kailash Colony Extn., New Delhi-110 048. Tel: 26433135; Fax:26460191.

102. Luxembourg

(Grand Duchy of Luxembourg)
Grand-Duche de Luxembourg

Capital: Luxembourg; **Other Large Cities:** Petange, Sanem; **Currency:** Euro; **Area:** 2586 sq. km.; **Population:** 502,100; **Lang-**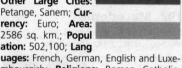**uages:** French, German, English and Luxembourgish; **Religions:** Roman Catholic-87%, Protestants, Jews and Muslims-13%; **Literacy:** 99%; **Life Expectancy:** 78.7; **p.c.i:** $ 80,304; **HDI rank:** 24; **Date of Independence:** 1839.

Government Type: Constitutional Monarchy; **Head of State:** Grand Duke Henri; **Head of Govt.:** Jean-Claude Juncker.

History: Luxembourg is a small state lying in between Gemany, Belgium and France. It is a Grand Duchy.

Economy: Iron deposits form the basis of

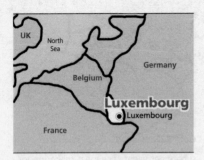

a big steel industry, which accounts for 70 per cent of the country's exports. Other industries: Chemicals, beer, tires, tobacco, metal products, cement. Agriculture occupies only 10 per cent of the population. Chief crops: Corn, wine and dairy products.

Mission in India: Embassy of the Grand Duchy of Luxembourg, 730, Gadaipur Road, Branch Post Office Gadaipur, New Delhi-110030. Tel: 26801954. Fax: 26801971.

E-mail: paulsteinmetz@internet.lu

Indian Mission in Luxembourg: Honorary Consulate General of India, "Cabinet d'Avocats" Jim Penning, 31, Grand-Rue, B.P. 282, L-2012, Luxembourg. Tel: 00-352-473886; Fax: 00-352-222584.

103. Macedonia

(Former Yugoslav Republic of Macedonia) Republika Makedonija

Capital: Skopje; Other Large Cities: Bitola, Tetovo; **Currency:** Denar; **Area:** 25,713 sq. km.; **Population:** 2,052,722; **Langua-** ges: Macedonian; **Religions:** Macedonian Orthodox 64.7%, other Christian-0.37%, Muslim-33.3%, others-1.63%; **Literacy:** 97%; **Life Expectancy:** 74.2; **p.c.i:** $ 9,350; **HDI rank:** 71; **Date of Independence:** 8th September, 1991.

Government Type: Parliamentary Democ-

racy; **President:** Georgi Ivanov; **PM:** Nikola Gruevski.

Ethnic breakdown: Macedonians- 65%; Albanians-22%; others (including Gypsies) - 13%. A third of the population is believed to be Muslim and the rest Orthodox Christians.

History: Former Yugoslavia's poorest republic, Macedonia is land-locked and is bounded by Bulgaria, Greece, Albania and Yugoslavia. On September 8, 1991 it voted to declare independence but EC and US refused to give recognition owing to Greek objections to its use of the name Macedonia. Greeks say Macedonia's name implies territorial claims on the northern Greek province of Macedonia. Macedonia has adamantly opposed a name change. Claims to the historical Macedonian territory have long been a source of contention with Bulgaria and Greece.

Macedonia became the 181st member of the UN on April 8, 1993 under the temporary name 'the former Yugoslav republic of Macedonia'. Yugoslavia and Macedonia established diplomatic ties in April, 1996.

Economy: Agricultural products: Wheat, maize, cotton, timber, livestock. Industry: Electricity, lignite, steel, cement.

Skopje, the capital of Macedonia, is the birth place of Mother Teresa

Mission in India: Embassy of the republic of Macedonia, K 80A, Hauz Khas Enclave, New Delhi-110016. Tel: 4614 2601/03; Fax; 4614 2604.

E-mail:embassy.macedonia@gmail.com

| The Green Line | The "Green Line" is the name of the border in Nicosia between the Greek and Turkish communities. It was so called because the line was drawn on the map with a green pencil (1963). |

104. Madagascar

(Democratic Republic of Madagascar)
Repoblika Demokratika Malagasy

Capital: Antananarivo; **Other Large Cities:** Toamasina, Mahajanga; **Currency:** Ariary; **Area:** 587,341 sq.km; **Population:**
20,146,000; **Languages:** Malagasy and French; **Religions:** indigenous beliefs-52%, Christian-41% and Muslim-7%; **Literacy:** 70.7%; **Life Expectancy:** 59.4; **p.c.i:** $ 910; **HDI rank:** 135; **Date of Independence:** 26ᵗʰ June, 1960.
Government Type: Republic; **President:** Andry Rajoelina; **PM:** Albert Camille Vital.
History: Madagascar, the world's fourth-largest island, lies in the Indian Ocean, off the south-east coast of Africa. It was discovered in 1500 by the Portuguese Diego Diaz; became a French colony in 1896, and an Overseas Territory in 1946. In 1958, it was proclaimed the autonomous Malagasy Republic within the French Community.

Madagascar is in many ways an Earth apart. Some 90% of the island's plants and and about 70% of its animals are endemic, meaning that they are found only in Madagascar.

Economy: Rice is the staple food and coffee the chief export (45%). Cassava, fruits, tobacco, cloves and vanilla are also cultivated. Large herds of cattle are raised. Mineral deposits include graphite, mica, nickel and copper. Industry: Food processing, textiles.

Indian Mission in Madagascar: Embassy of India, 4, Lalana Rajaonson Emile, Tsaralalanaa, Post Box No. 1787, Antananarivo, Madagascar. Tel: 00-261-20-2223334. 2227156; Fax: 00-261-20-2233790.
E-mail: hoc.aanarivo@mea.gov.in, indembmd@blueline.mg

105. Malawi

(Republic of Malawi)

Capital: Lilongwe; **Other Large Cities:** Blantyre, Mzuzu; **Currency:** Kwacha; **Area:** 118,784 sq.km; **Population:** 15,692,000;
Languages: English, Chichewa, Lomwe, Yao; **Religions:** Christian-79.9%, Muslim-12.8%, other-3% none-4.3%; **Literacy:** 71.8%; **Life Expectancy:** 48.3; **p.c.i:** $ 908; **HDI rank:** 153; **Date of Independence:** 6ᵗʰ July, 1964.
Government Type: Republic; **Head of State & Govt.(President):** Bingu wa Mutharika.
History: Malawi, formerly the British protectorate Nyasaland, (until 1907 British Central Africa) became independent in 1964 and a republic in 1966.
Economy: Poor in resources, Malawi's agriculture is still at subsistence level. Maize is the main food crop. The chief cash crops are tea, tobacco, sugar and cotton. Industry: Textiles, sugar and cement.

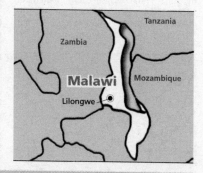

| The Eighth Continent | Madagascar's flora and fauna are so different from anywhere else on Earth that it is often referred to as the eighth continent. |

Mission in India: High Commission of the Republic of Malawi, F-63,Poorvi Marg, Vasant Vihar, New Delhi-110 057. Tel: 011-4607 8800.Fax:011-46078810.

E-mail:malawiindia@airtelmail.in

106. Malaysia

Capital: Kuala Lumpur; **Other Large Cities:** Pinang, Ipoh; **Currency:** Ringgit; **Area:** 330,434 sq.km; **Population:** 27,565,821; **Languages:** Malay, English, Chinese, Ta-mil; **Religions:** Muslim- 60.4%, Buddhist- 19.2%, Christian- 9.1%, Hindu- 6.3% Confusionism Taoism, other traditional Chinese religious 2.6%, other or unknown- 1.5%, none -0.8%; **Literacy:** 91.9%; **Life Expectancy:** 74.2; **p.c.i:** $ 14,603; **HDI rank:** 57; **Date of Independence:** 31st August, 1957.

Government Type: Constitutional Monarchy; **Supreme Head of State:** Paramount Ruler Sultan Mizan Zainal Abidin; **PM:** Mohamed Najib bin Abdul Razak.

Malaysia, at the southern end of the Malay Peninsula in south-east Asia, is a federation of 13 states comprising Johor, Kedah, Kelantan, Melakaa, Negeri Sembilan, Pahang, Perak, Perlis, Pulau Pinang, Sabah, Sarawak, Selangor and Terengganu.

History: In 1948, Malaysia negotiated independence from UK under the leadership of Tunku Abdul Rahman,who became the first Prime Minister. On September 16,1963, Singapore, Sarawak and Sabah joined the Federation to form Malaysia. But on August 9,1965, Singapore withdrew

from that Federation and became an independent republic.

Economy: Malaysia is one of the world's largest producers of rubber, tin and palm oil. It is also the world's leading exporter of pepper and timber. Other crops are rice, coconut, vegetables, pineapples, coffee, tea, cocoa, etc.

Iron ore, gold, ilmenite and bauxite are the major mineral resources. The petroleum industry in Malaysia is becoming significantly important to the economy of the nation. Leading industries are food products, tobacco, wood products, electrical goods, textiles, chemical products, construction goods, non-metallic products, transport equipment and the processing of agricultural products from estates (eg. rubber, palm oil).

Mission in India: High Commissionof Malaysia, 50-M, Satya Marg, Chanakyapuri, New Delhi - 110021. Tel: 26111291-93 & 26111297; Fax: 91-11-26881538.

E-mail: maldelhi@kln.gov.my

Indian Mission in Malaysia: High Commission of India, No.2, Jalan Taman Duta, Off Jalan Duta, 50480 Kuala Lumpur, (or) P.O. Box No. 10059 G.P.O., 50704, Kuala Lumpur. Tel: 00-603-20931015, 20933504; Fax: 20925826; E-mail: hco@indianhighcommission.com.my, admn@indianhighcommission.com.my

107. Maldives

(Republic of the Maldives)
Divedhi Raajjeyge Jumburiya

Capital: Male; **Currency:** Rufiyaa; **Area:** 298 sq.km; **Population:** 317,280; **Languages:** Divehi (Sinhalese dialect); **Religions:** Sunny Muslim; **Literacy:** 97%; **Life Expectancy:** 68.5; **p.c.i:** $ 5,483; **HDI rank:** 107; **Date of Independence:** 26th July, 1965.

Government Type: Republic; **Head of State & Govt (President):** Mohamed "Anni" Nasheed.

| Emerald Isle of the Caribbean | The Caribbean island of Montserrat is known as the Emerald Isle of the Caribbean. This is because a number of Irish colonists settled on the island. |

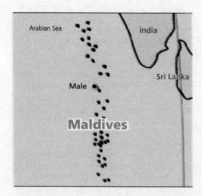

are fishing, tourism, shipping, reedware, lacquer-work, coconut processing and garment manufacturing. Tourism accounts for 28% of GDP and more than 60% of foreign exchange receipts.

Mission in India: High Commission of Maldives, B-2, Anand Niketan, New Delhi-110021; Tel: 41435701-08; Fax:41435709; E-mail:admin@maldiveshighcom.co.in

Indian Mission in Maldives: High Commission of India, Athireege Aage, Ameeru Ahmed Magu, Henveiru, Male, Republic of Maldives. Tel: 00-960-323014/16; Fax: 00-960-324778.

E-mail: hcmale@hicomindia.com.my

The Republic of Maldives lying about 675 km south-west of Sri Lanka, consists of more than 1,200 small coral islands (199 inhabited), grouped in 19 atolls, in the Indian Ocean.

History: The Maldives was long a sultanate, first under Dutch and then under British protection. President Maumoon Abdul Gayoom dominated the islands' political scene for 30 years, elected to six successive terms by single-party referendums. Following riots in Male in August 2004, the president and his government pledged to embark upon democratic reforms including a more representative political system and expanded political freedoms. Progress was sluggish, however, and many promised reforms were slow to be realized. Nonetheless, political parties were legalized in 2005. In June 2008, a constituent assembly - termed the "Special Majlis" - finalized a new constitution, which was ratified by the president in August. The first-ever presidential elections under a multi-candidate, multi-party system were held in October 2008. Gayoom was defeated in a runoff poll by Mohamed Nasheed, a political activist who had been jailed several years earlier by the former regime.

Economy: The islands are covered with coconut palms and yield millet, cassava, yams, melons and other tropical fruit as well as coconut produce. The main industries

108. Mali

(Republic of Mali) Republique due Mali

Capital: Bamako;**Other Large Cities:** Segou, Mopti; **Currency:** Franc CFA; **Area:** 1,240,192 sq. km; **Population:** 14,517,176; **Languages:** French (official), Bambara and other African languages; **Religions:** Muslim-90%, indigenous beliefs-9%, Christian-1%; **Literacy:** 26.2%; **Life Expectancy:** 54.5; **p.c.i:** $1,206; **HDI rank:**160; **Date of Independence:** 22nd September, 1960.

Government Type: Republic; **President:** Amadou Toumani Toure; **PM:** Modibo Sidibe.

History: Mali was part of the great Mali Empire, until the 15th century. In 1904, it

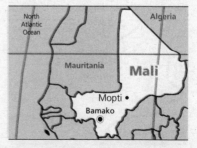

Volcanic Eruptions	No other country in Europe has as many volcanoes as Italy. This is because the Italian peninsula stands on a fault line. Three major volcanoes (Etna, Stromboli, and Vesuvius) have erupted in the last hundred years.

became a French colony named French Sudan and in 1946 part of the French Union. In June 1960 it became independent and was named the Sudanese Republic. The Sudanese Republic federated with Senegal in the Mali Federation that year. Senegal then withdrew from this and the Sudanese Republic changed its name to the Republic of Mali on Sept. 22, 1960. **Economy:** Only about 20 per cent of the land is cultivable. The main crops are rice, millet, groundnuts and cotton. Livestock-raising is important and the processing of hides and skins remains the chief industry. There is extensive river-fishing and good export trade in dried and smoked fish.

109. Malta
(Republika Ta' Malta)

Capital: Valletta; **Other Large Cities:** Birkirkara, Harum and Sliemma; **Currency:** Euro; **Area:** 316 sq. km; **Population:** 416,333; **Languages:** Maltese and English; **Religions:** Roman Catholic-98%; **Literacy:** 92.4%; **Life Expectancy:** 79.4; **p.c.i:** $ 24,081; **HDI rank:** 33; **Date of Independence:** 21st September, 1964.
Government Type: Republic; **President:** George Abela; **PM:** Lawrence Gonzi.
History: Malta is an island in the central Mediterranean Sea, 95 km from Sicily and about 290 km from the African coast. This state also includes the adjoining islands of

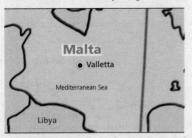

Gozo and Comino. Malta became independent in 1964 and a republic in 1974. Malta joined the European Union on May 1, 2004.
Economy: The rocky country has no natural resources. Textiles, footwear, rubber products and plastics are exported. Ship repair and ship building are major economic activities. Agricultural products include wheat, barley, citrus, onions, potatoes and tomatoes. Tourism, however, remains the island's major industry.
Mission in India: High Commission of Malta, n-60, Panchsheel Park, New Delhi-110 017. Tel: 2649 4961-5; Fax: 2649 4966.
E-mail: maltahighcommission.newdelhi@gov.mt
Indian Mission in Malta: High Commission of India, Regional Road, St. Julianas, SGN 02, Malta. Tel: 00-356-344302/03; Fax: 00-356-344259.

110. Marshall Islands
(Republic of the Marshall Islands)

Capital: Dalap-Uliga-Darrit (on Majuro atoll); **Currency:** US Dollar; **Area:** 181 sq.km; **Population:** 54,305; **Lang-** **uages:** Marshallese, English, other indigenous languages and Japanese; **Religions:** Christian (Mostly Protestant); **Literacy:** 93.7%; **Life Expectancy:** 71.19; **p.c.i:** $ 2,500; **Date of Independence:** 21st October, 1986.
Government Type: Republic; **President:** Jurelang Zedkaia.
History: The Republic of Marshall Islands consists of two island/atoll chains, in the Pacific Ocean, the Ratak (sunrise) Chain and the Ralik (sunset) Chain, totalling 31 atolls. Each atoll is a cluster of several small islands circling a lagoon. Kwajalein is the largest of the islets, which number about a hundred. The capital Majuro is about 3200 kms south-west of Honolulu. About 92% of the population are Marshallese, a Micronesian people.

Easter Island Easter Island was named by Admiral Roggeveen, a Dutch explorer, who came upon the island on Easter Sunday. It is famous for giant stone statues that were carved from the rock of an extinct volcano and then dragged across the island and set up on platforms.

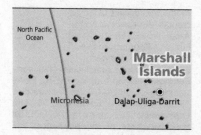

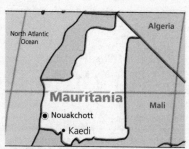

Marshall Islands was a Trusteeship territory of the United States until Oct. 1986. The Islands became a full U.N. member state in Sept., 1991. The USA controls defence policy and provides financial support. Kwajalein, one of the main atolls in the western chain, is a U.S. missile-testing range and air field.

Economy: Agriculture and tourism are mainstays. Crops: Coconuts, tomatoes, melons and bread fruit. Minerals: Phosphate deposits are mined on Ailinglaplap atoll.

111. Mauritania

(Islamic Republic of Mauritania)
Republique Islamique de Mauritanie

Capital: Nouakchott; **Other Large Cities:** Nouadhibou, Kaedi; **Currency:** Ouguiya; **Area:** 1,030,700 sq. km; **Population:** 3,366,000; **Languages:** Arabic, French and Hassanya Arabic, Wolof, Pulaar, and Soninke; **Religions:** Muslim-100%; **Literacy:** 55.8%; **Life Expectancy:** 64.2; **p.c.i:** $ 2,099; **HDI rank:** 136 **Date of Independence:** 28th November, 1960.

Government Type: Islamic Republic; **President:** Mohamed Ould Abdelaziz.

History: The Islamic Republic of Mauritania is on the Atlantic coast of the West African bulge.

This former French overseas territory became autonomous in 1958 and fully independent on Nov. 28, 1960. Opposition par-

ties were legalised and a new constitution approved in 1991.

Mauritania signed a peace treaty with the Polisario Front in 1980, and renounced sovereignty over its share of Wesern Sahara.

Economy: As much as 47% of the total area of the country is desert. The population is traditionally nomadic, rearing cattle and sheep. Main crops: dates, grain. Fishing is important. Deposits of iron and copper are being exploited. Oil prospecting is going on. Industry: Fish processing and iron mining.Mauritania has extensive deposits of iron ore, which account for nearly 40% of total exports.

112. Mauritius

Capital: Port Louis; **Other Large Cities:** Curepipe, Quatre Bornes; **Currency:** Mauritius Rupee; **Area:** 2040 sq.km; **Population:** 1,280,925; **Languages:** English, French, Creole and Hindustani; **Religions:** Hindu-48%, Roman Catholic 23.6%, Muslim-16.6%, other Christian 8.6%, unspecified-0.3% none-0.4%; **Literacy:** 87.4%; **Life Expectancy:** 72.8; **p.c.i:** $ 13,214; **HDI rank:** 72; **Date of Independence:** 12th March, 1968.

Government Type: Parliamentary Democracy; **President:** Anerood Jugnauth; **PM:** Navichandra Ramgoolam.

History: Mauritius, a volcanic island nearly surrounded by coral reefs, lies about

Dodo's Original Home The flightless dodo bird was endemic to the island nation of Mauritius. It was hunted to extinction within 50 years after the Dutch settled the uninhabited island in 1638.

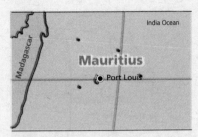

800 km east of Madagascar in the Indian Ocean. Settled by the Dutch in 1638. The French who took over in 1721, brought African slaves. The British who ruled from 1810 to 1968 brought Indian workers for the sugar plantations. The Indian majority in Mauritius are descendants of these workers. Ethnic groups: Indo-Mauritian 68%, Creole 27%.

Formally severed its association with the British crown and became a republic in 1992.

About 37,000 people live in Rodrigues, a small dependency.

Economy: Sugarcane is the predominant crop. The main secondary crops are tea, tobacco and potatoes. Tourism is a highly developed industry. (500,000 tourists a year). Other industries: rum, textiles, processing of sugar and tea. It is one of world's leading exporters of woollen knitwear.

Mission in India: Mauritius High Commission, EP-41 Jesus & Mary Marg, Chanakyapuri, New Delhi 110021 Tel: 2410 2161-63; Fax:2410 2194.

E-mail: mhcnd@bol.net.in

Indian Mission in Mauritius: High Commission of India, 6th Floor, Life Insurance Corporation of India Building, President John Kemmedy Street P.O.Box No. 162, Port Louis, Mauritius. Tel: 00-230-2083775/6; Fax: 00-230-2086859.

E-mail: coined@intnet.mu

113. Mexico

(United Mexican States)
Estados Unidos Mexicanos
Capital: Mexico City; **Other Large Cities:**

Monterrey, Puebla; **Currency:** Mexican Peso; **Area:** 1,972,547 sq. km; **Population:** 112,336,538; **Languages:** Spanish, Amerindian languages; **Religions:** Roman Catholic-76.5%, Protestant-6.3%, others- 0.3%, unspecified 13.8%, none- 3.1%; **Literacy:** 92.8%; **Life Expectancy:** 76.2; **p.c.i:** $ 14,266; **HDI rank:** 56; **Date of Independence:** 24th September, 1821.

Government Type: Federal Republic; **President & PM:** Felipe de Jesus Calderon Hinojosa.

History: The site of advanced Amerindian civilizations, Mexico came underSpanish rule for three centuries before achieving independence early in the 19th century.

Mexico is the only Latin American country not to have a military coup in the postwar period.

Economy: The important agricultural products are maize, rice, wheat, sugar, coffee and cotton. Sea fishing is also important as an occupation. it is the world's leading producer of silver, sulphur and fluorite. Other minerals include coal, zinc, lead, manganese, bauxite and uranium. Main industries: Steel, chemicals, electric goods, textiles, rubber, tourism.

Mission in India: Embassy of Mexico, C-8, Anand Niketan, New Delhi-110 021. Tel: 24117180-83; Fax: 91-11-24117193.

E-mail:embamexindia@airtelmail.in

Indian Mission in Mexico: Embassy of India, Avenida Musset 325, Colonia Polanco,

Just Two Speakers	The language of Ayapaneco has been spoken in Mexico for centuries. It has survived the Spanish conquest, seen off wars, revolutions and floods. But now, it's at risk of extinction. There are just two people left who can speak it fluently.

C.P. 11550, Mexico D.F. Tel: 00-52-55-55 311050; Fax: 00-52-55-5254 2349.

E-mail:com_eoimex@prodigy.net.mx, cons_eoimex@prodigy.net.mx

114. Micronesia

(Federated States of Micronesia)

Capital: Palikir; Other Large Cities: Weno, Tofol; **Currency:** US dollar; **Area:** 702 sq. km.; **Population:** 102,624; **Languages:** English and local languages; **Religions:** Roman Catholic-50%, Protestant-47%; **Literacy:** 89%; **Life Expectancy:** 70.94; **p.c.i:** $ 2,200; **HDI rank:** 103; **Date of Independence:** 3rd November, 1986. **Government Type:** Constitutional Government; **President:**Emanuel Mori.

History: The Federated States of Micronesia (FSM), formerly known as Caroline Islands, extends across the 1,800 mile-long Caroline Island archipelago in the Western Pacific. The 4 states of the FSM are Pohnpei, Kosrae, Truk and Yap. Each state consists of several islands, except for Kosrae, a single island. The islands, 607 in all, vary geologically from high, mountainous islands to low, coral atolls.

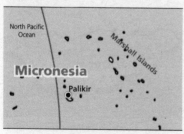

The FSM, which came into being on May 10, 1979 was a Trusteeship Territory of the United States. In November 1986 USA entered into a Compact of Free Association with it. Became a full UN member state on Sept. 17, 1991. The USA controls defence and provides financial support.

Economy: Crops: Tropical fruits, vegetables, etc. Industry: Tourism and fishing.

Mission In India: Embassy of the Federated State of Micronesia stationed at Tokyo.

115. Moldova

(Republic of Moldova)
Republica Moldav-eneasca

Capital: Chisinau (formerly Kishinev); **Other Large Cities:** Tiraspol, Beltsy; **Currency:** Leu; **Area:**33,700sq.km.; **Population:**3,563,800; **Languages:** Romanian, Ukrainian; **Religions:** Eastern Orthodox 98%, Jewish 1.5%, Babtist and other-0.5%; **Literacy:** 99.1%; **Life Expectancy:** 68.9; **p.c.i:** $ 2,959; **HDI rank:** 99; **Date of Independence:** 27th August, 1991.

Government Type: Republic; **President:** Marian Lupu; **PM:** Vladimir Filat.

History: Moldova (Moldavia until 1990) has Ukraine and Romania as neighbours. The region was taken from Romania in 1940; the people speak Romanian. In a referendum in March, 1994, Moldovans voted to remain independent, and against any union with Romania. Moldova is a fertile black earth plain. It contained about one-fourth of the former USSR's vineyards.

In May, '97, leaders of Moldova and a break-away region Transdniestria (which approved a separatist constitution in 1995) signed an agreement to keep Moldova a single state.

Economy: Agriculture: Grain, sugar-beet, vegetables, fruits, grapes. Industry: Wine-

| Bribery in Mexico | On May 10th 2011, Transparency International, an anti-corruption outfit, published a survey of 15,000 Mexican homes on bribery. Overall, Transparency reckons Mexicans paid 32 billion pesos ($2.5 billion) of bribes in 2010. |

making, tobacco, canning, wood-working, textiles, metallurgy, dairy, TV, fridge, washing machines.

116. Monaco
(Principality of Monaco)

Capital: Monaco; **Other Large Cities:** Monte-Carlo; **Currency:** Euro; **Area:** 1.95 sq.km; **Population:** 33,000; **Languages:** French, Monegasque and Italian; **Religions:** Roman Catholic-90%; **Literacy:** 99%; **Life Expectancy:** 80.09; **p.c.i:** $ 30,000; **Date of Independence**: 1419
Government Type: Constitutional Monarchy; **Head of State:** Prince Albert II; **Head of Govt:** Michel Roger.
History: Monaco is a sovereign principality on France's south-eastern Mediterranean coast. Of the resident population, 40% are French, 17% Italian and 5% British. Monaco is a member of the U.N.

Economy: Tourism, gambling, and tobacco monopoly are its main sources of income. There are a number of light industries, such as chemicals, plastics and precision instruments.
Mission in India: Hon. Consulate General of Monaco, DLF Centre, 9th Floor, Sansad Marg, New Delhi-110 001.Tel: 5150 2149; Fax: 5150 2153.E-mail: kpsindia@aol.com

117. Mongolia
(Mongolian Republic) Mongol Uls

Capital: Ulan Bator; **Other Large Cities:** Darhan, Erdenet; **Currency:** Tugrik; **Area:** 1,565,000 sq.km; **Population:** 2,798,100; **Languages:** Mongolian; **Religions:** Buddhist Lamaist 50%, Shamanist and Christian -6%, Muslim-4%, none 40%; **Literacy:** 97.3%;**Life Expectancy:** 66.8; **p.c.i:** $ 3,727; **HDI rank:** 100; **Date of Independence:** 11th July, 1921.
Government Type: Parliamentary; **President:** Tsakhia Elbegdorj; **PM:** Sukhbaatar Batbold.
History: The great Mongol warrior Genghis Khan (1162-1227) founded the Mongol world empire. It became an independent state in 1921. Political opposition was legalised in 1990. In July, Communists won the first free elections to the legislature. The constitution of 1992 abolished the 'People's Democracy', introduced democratic institutions and a market economy and guaranteed freedom of speech. The second free election in 1996 resulted in the defeat of the Communist Party which had ruled Mongolia for over 70 years.

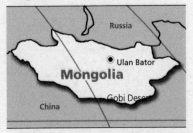

Economy: Livestock-raising is the principal occupation and comprises horses, oxen, sheep, goats and camels. The herdsmen are organised in collectives. State farms practise large-scale agriculture (crops: grains). Minerals include coal, flourspar, tungsten, tin and copper. Industry: Food processing, textiles, chemicals and cement.

Mission in India: Embassy of Mongolia, 34, Archbishop Makarios Marg, New Delhi-110003. Tel: 2463 1728, 2461 7989; Fax: 91-11-24633240. E-mail: mongemb@vsnl.net

Web: box@airtelmail.in

Indian Mission in Mongolia: Embassy of India, Zaluuchuudyn Urgun Chuluu 10, C.P.O. Box No. 691, Ulaanbaatar –14190, Mongolia. Tel: 00-976-11-329522/24/28; Fax: 00-976-11-329532.

E-mail: info@indianembassy.mn, consular@indianembassy.mn

118. Montenegro

Capital: Podgorica (administrative capital); Cetinje (capital city); **Other Large Cities:** Ulcinj, Tivat, Kolasin; **Currency:** Euro; **Area:** 14,026 sq. km; **Population:** 641,966; **Languages:** Serbian (Ijekavian dialect - official); **Religions:** Orthodox-74.2%, Muslim-17.7%, Catholic-3.5%; Literacy: 97%; **Life Expectancy:** 74.5; **p.c.i:** $ 10,432; **HDI rank:** 49; **Date of Independence:** 3rd June 2006.

Government Type: Republic; **President:** Filip Vujanovic; **PM:** Igor Luksic.

History: Montenegro became part of Serbia in 1918 and Yugoslavia in 1929.The people of Montenegro gained greater autonomy when the name Yugoslavia was discarded in favour of a democratic and federal country named Serbia and Montenegro. On May 21, 2006, 66.6 per cent of Montenegro

voted to secede from Serbia and become independent.

Economy: The economy of Montenegro is based on agriculture and animal husbandry. Important crops include cereals, tobacco, vegetables, grapes, figs and olives. The main industries are lumber milling, salt processing and tobacco processing.

119. Morocco

(Kingdom of Morocco) al-Mamlaka al-Maghrebia

Capital: Rabat; **Other Large Cities:** Fez, Marrakech; **Currency:** Dirham; **Area:** 458,730 sq.km (excluding Western Saharan territory); **Population:**32,108,000; **Languages:** Arabic, Berber; **Religions:** Muslim-98.7%, Christian- 1.1%, Jewish-0.2%; **Literacy:** 55.6%; **Life Expectancy:** 71.2; **p.c.i:** $ 4,773; **HDI rank:** 114; **Date of Independence:** 2nd March, 1956.

Government Type: Constitutional Monarchy; **Head of State:** King Mohammed VI; **PM:** Abbas El Fassi.

History: In AD 788, about a century after the Arab subjucation of North Africa, Morocco was ruled by successive Moorish dynasties.In the 6th century,the Sa'adi monarchy, particularly under Ahmad Al-Mansur, repelled foreign invaders and inaugurated a golden age. In 1860, Spain occupied northern Morocco and ushered in a half century of trade rivalry among European powers that saw Morocco's sovereignty steadily erode; in 1912, the French imposed a protectorate over the country. A prolonged independence struggle with France ended successfully in 1956.

Economy: Morocco produces cereals, including barley, wheat, corn and fruits. Vineyards are abundant and dates form a regular crop. Livestock raising is important and fishing is well-developed. About 500,000 Moroccans rely on fishing as their occupation. The most important mineral extracted is phosphate, of which Morocco remains a world supplier.

Language of Music The language of music is Italian. The word "scale" comes from scala, meaning "step." And adante, allegro, presto, and vivace are just a few of the many Italian musical notations.

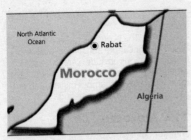

North Atlantic Ocean

● Rabat

Morocco

Algéria

Other minerals are iron ore, coal, lead and manganese. Industry: Carpets, clothing, leather goods, mining, sugar, metallurgy, chemicals and tourism.

Mission in India: Embassy of the Kingdom of Morocco, 33 Archbishop Makarios Marg, New Delhi-110003. Tel: 24636920/21 & 24636924 (Visa); Fax: 24636925.

E-mail: embassyofmorocco@rediffmail.com

Web: www.moroccoembindia.com

Indian Mission in Morocco: Embassy of India, 13, Charia Michlifen, Agdal, Rabat, Morocco. Tel: 00-212-3-7671339, 7675974/5; Fax: 00-212-3-7671269.

E-mail: india@maghrebnet.net.ma

120. Mozambique

(Republic of Mozambique)
Republica de Mocambique

Capital: Maputo; **Other Large Cities:** Beira, Nampula; **Area:** 783,030 sq.km; **Population:** 22,416,881; **Languages:** Portuguese and Bantu; **Religions:** Catholic-23.8%, Zionist Christian-17.5%, Muslim-17.8%, other-17.8%, none-23.1%; **Literacy:** 44.4%; **Life Expectancy:** 41.18; **p.c.i:** $ 982; **HDI rank:** 165; **Date of Independence:** 25th June, 1975.

Government Type: Republic; **President:** Armando Guebuza; **PM:** Luisa Diogo.

History: Mozambique was a Portuguese colony fo 470 years before achieving independence in 1975. The ruling Frelimo (Front for the Liberation of Mozambique) party formally abandoned Marxism in 1989. A new constitution in 1990 provided for multipary elec-tions and a free market economy. A UN-negotiated peace agreement between FRELIMO and rebel Mozambique National Resistance (RENAMO) forces ended the fighting in 1992. In December 2004, Mozambique underwent a delicate transition as Joaquim Chissano stepped down after 18 years in office.

Zambia

Mozambique

● Nampula

Zimbabwe   ● Beira

Mozambique Channel

Madagascar

Botswana

South Africa   ● Maputo

Economy: The major cash crops are cashewnuts, sugar, cotton and sisal. Maize, bananas, rice, groundnuts, vegetables and coconuts are also grown. Considerable mineral resources exist although only coal, diamonds and bauxite are now exploited. Mozambique has two-thirds of the world's known reserves of tantalite and is the second largest producer of beryl. Industry: Steel, cement, engineering, textiles and petroleum products.

Missions in India: High Commission of the Republic of Mozambique, B-3/24, Vasant Vihar, New Delhi - 110057. Tel: 26156663/4; Fax: 26156665;

E-mail: hcmozind@hclinfinet.com

Indian Mission in Mozambique: High Commission of India, Avineda Kenneth Kaunda No. 167, P.O. Box No. 4751, Maputo, Mozambique. Tel: 00-258-1-492437, 490717; Fax: 00-258-1-492364.

E-mail: hicomind@tvcabo.co.mz

Spanish in Africa	Equatorial Guinea is Africa's only Spanish-speaking country. Spanish is also the official language of the government, commerce, and schools.

121. Myanmar

(Union of Myanmar) Pyeidaungzu Myanma Naingangandaw

Capital: Seat of government moving to Naypyidaw, also known as Pyinmana, from Rangoon (Yangon); **Other Large Cities:** Mandalay, Bassein; **Currency:** Kyat; **Area:** 676,553 sq.km; **Population:** 50,496,000; **Languages:** Burmese, Karen, Shan; **Religions:** Buddhist-89%, Christian-4% (Baptist-3%, Roman Catholic-1%), Muslim-4%, animist-1%, others-2%; **Literacy:** 89.9%; **Life Expectancy:** 62.1; **p.c.i:** $ 1,246; **HDI rank:** 132; **Date of Independence:** 4th January, 1948.

Government Type: Military Regime; **President:** Thein Sein; **PM:** Thein Sein.

History: Britain conquered Burma over a period of 62 years (1824-1886) and incorporated it into its British empire.Burma was administered as a province of India until 1937 when it became a separate, self-governing colony; independence from the Commonwealth was attained in 1948.Gen. Ne Win dominated the government from 1962 to 1988, first as a military ruler, then as self-appointed president, and later as political kingpin.The Armed Forces set up a State Law and Order Restoration council (SLORC).

In June 1990, in the first free elections in 30 years, the National League for Democracy won by a big majority but the army was reluctant to hand over power. Aung San Suu Kyi, the leading opposition leader was kept under house arrest for almost 15 of the 21 years from 20th July 1989 until her release on 13 November 2010. The ruling junta has been promising a new Constitution for many years now but nothing concrete has emerged.

Economy: Known as the "rice bowl of the Far East", Myanmar also grows sugarcane, peanuts, and beans. The chief minerals are petroleum, lead, tin, zinc, tungsten, copper, antimony, silver and gems. The rubies, sapphires and jade found in Myanmar are especially famous. Teakwood is exported.

Mission in India: Embassy of the Union of Myanmar, 3/50F, Nyaya Marg, Chanakyapuri, New Delhi-110021. Tel: 2467 8822,2467 8823; Telefax: 2467 8824

E-mail: myandelhi@gmail.com

Indian Mission in Myanmar: Embassy of India, No. 545-547, Merchant Street, Post Box No. 751, Yangon, Myanmar. Tel:00-95-1-391219, 243972, 388412, 222619; Fax: 00-95-1-254086.

E-mail: ambassador@indiaembassy.net. mm

122. Namibia

Capital: Windhoek; **Currency:** Namibian dollar; **Area:** 826,700 sq.km; **Population:** 2,212,000; **Languages:** English, Afrikaans, German, several indigenous languages; **Religions:** Christian-80-90% (Lutheran50% at least), Indigenous beliefs-10-20%; **Literacy:** 88%; **Life Expectancy:** 52.9; **p.c.i:** $ 6,945; **HDI rank:** 105; **Date of Independence:** 21st March, 1990.

Government Type: Republic; **President:** Hifikepunye Pohamba; **PM:** Nahas Angula.

History: South Africa occupied the German colony of South-West Africa during World War I and administered it as a mandate until

---

Africa's Elephants

The African elephant population has increased fom a low of 500,000 in the 1980s to more than 600,000 today. Elephants in southern Africa are increasing by 4% a year.

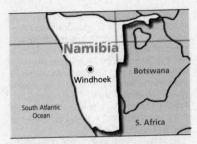

10,000; **Languages:** English and Nauruan; **Religions:** Christian (two-thirds Protestant, one-third Roman Catholic); **Life Expectancy:** 64.2; **p.c.i:** $ 5,000; **Date of Independence:** 31st January, 1968.

Government Type: Republic; **Head of State & Govt (President):** Marcus Stephen.

History: Nauru, a small coral island in the central Pacific, just 42 km. south of the equator is world's smallest republic. It has an 18–member Parliament, elected on a 3-yearly basis.

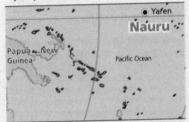

after World War II, when it annexed the territory. In 1966 the Marxist South West Africa People's Organisation (SWAPO) guerrilla group launched a war of independence for the area that was soon named Namibi, but it was not until 1988 that South Africa agreed to its administration in accordance with a UN peace plan for the entire region. Namibia has been governed by SWAPO ever since its independence in 1990.

Economy: Diamonds are Namibia's most valuable economic asset followed by copper, uranium, zinc, lead, germanium and manganese. Stock-breeding is important; cattle, sheep and goats abound. Fishing is a supplementary source of food and income. Food crops include corn, millet and sorghum. Industry: Canning, textiles, leather, dairy.

Mission in India: High Commission of the Republic of Namibia, B-8/9, Vasant Vihar, New Delhi-110057; Tel: 2614 0389/0890/4772; Fax: 26146120/26155482;

E-mail: nhcdelhi@del2.vsnl.net.in

Consulate: Mumbai: Tel: 6665 7272,6665 8282; Fax:66658028,

E-mail:syamalgupta@tata.com

Indian Mission in Namibia: High Commission of India, 97, Nelson Mandela House, P.O. Box 1209, Windhoek, 9000, Namibia. Tel: 00-264-61-226037, 228433; Fax: 00-264-61-237320.

E-mail:hciadmn@mweb.com.na

Nauru was annexed by Germany in 1888. Nauru was occupied by Australian forces in World War I and subsequently became a League of Nations mandate. After the Second World War- and a brutal occupation by Japan- Nauru became a UN trust territory. It joined UN in 1999.

Economy: About four-fifths of Nauru is phosphate-bearing rock, which accounts for 98% of its exports. It is estimated that the phosphate deposits will be exhausted by 2008.

Mission in India: Honorary Consulate General of Nauru, S-327, Greater Kailash -1, New Delhi-110048. Tel: 26414744/26215780; Fax: 262157780.

E-mail: kartarbhalla@hotmail.com

123. Nauru

(Republic of Nauru) Naoero

Capital: Yaren district; **Currency:** Australian dollar; **Area:** 21.1 sq.km; **Population:**

124. Nepal

(Federal Democratic Republic of Nepal) Sanghiya Loktantrik Ganatantra Nepal

Capital: Kathmandu; **Other Large Cities:**

Rhinos in Nepal The latest census of the indian one-horned rhinoceros shows there are 534 of the beasts in Nepal, a rise of almost a quarter since 2008. In 1975 only 600 were left in the world.

Biratnagar, Lalitpur; **Currency:** Nepaleses Rupee; **Area:** 147,181 sq.km.; **Population:** 28,584,975; **Languages:** Nepali, Maithir, Bhojpuri etc.; **Religions:** Hindu-80.6%, Buddhist-10.7%, Muslim-4.2%, Kirant-3.6%,

others-0.9%. **Literacy:** 56.5%; **Life Expectancy:** 63.8; **p.c.i:** $ 1,250; **HDI rank:** 138; **Date of Independence:** 1768.
Government Type: Federal Democratic Republic; **President:** Ram Baran Yadav; **PM:** Jhala Nath Khanal.
History: From 1846 to 1951 Nepal was virtually ruled by the Rana family, a member of which always held the office of prime minister, the succession being determined by special rules. The last Rana prime minister resigned in Nov. 1951. The 15 feudal chieftainships were integrated into the kingdom on 10 April 1961.

Following pro-democracy demonstrations on 16 April 1990 King Birendra dismissed the government and proclaimed the abolition of the panchayat system of nominated councils. Reforms in 1990 established a multiparty democracy within the framework of a constitutional monarchy.

In 2001, the crown prince massacred ten members of the royal family, including the king and queen, and then took his own life. Following the November 2006 peace accord between the government and the Maoists, an interim constitution was promulgated

and the Maoists were allowed to enter parliament in mid-January 2007.

Nepal was formerly the world's only constitutionally declared Hindu state, but following the movement for democracy in early 2006 and the breaking of King Gyanendra's power, the Nepali Parliament amended the constitution to make Nepal a secular state.
Economy: Agriculture is the mainstay of the economy. Principal exports are food grains, jute, timber, oilseeds, ghee (clarified butter), potatoes, medicinal herbs, skins and cattle. Tourism is the second largest industry.
Mission in India: Embassy of Nepal, Barakhamba Road, New Delhi - 110001. Tel. 23329969, 23329218; Fax: 23326857, 23329647.

E-mail: nepembassydelhi@airtelmail.in
Indian Mission in Nepal: Embassy of India, Post Box 292, 336 Kapurdhara Marg, Kathmandu, Nepal. Tel: 00-977-1-4410900; Fax: 00-977-1-4428279; E-mail: hoc@eoiktm. org, amb@eoiktm.org, dcm@eoiktm.org

125. The Netherlands

(Kingdom of the Netherlands)
Koninkrijk der Nederlanden

Capital: Amsterdam (Seat of Govt: The Hague); **Other Large Cities:** Rotter dam, Ulrecht; **Currency:** Euro; **Area:** 41,160

sq.km; **Population:** 16,659,300; **Languages:** Dutch; **Religions:** Roman Catholic-30%, Dutch Reformed-11%, Calvinist-6%, other Protestant- 3%, Muslim-5.8%, others-2.2%, none-42%; **Literacy:** 99%; **Life Expectancy:** 79.8; **p.c.i:** $ 40,777; **HDI rank:** 7; **Date of Independence:** 1579.
Government Type: Constitutional Monarchy; **Head of State:** Queen Beatrix Wilhelmina Armgard; **PM:** Mark Rutte.
History: The Dutch United Provinces declared their independence from Spain in 1579. During the 17th century, they became a leading seafaring and commercial power, with

Man on the Moon	Planting a man on the surface of moon was a costly game for the United States. The Apollo project cost about $150 billion in 2010 dollars, five times as much as the manhattan project and 18 times the cost of digging the Panama Canal.

settlements and colonies around the world. After a 20-year French occupation, a Kingdom of the Netherlands was formed in 1815. In 1830 Belgium seceded and formed a separate kindom.The Netherlands remained neutral in World War 1, but suffered invasion and occupation by Germany in World War II.

Economy: Agriculture has been mechanised and developed. Crops: Grains, potatoes, sugarbeets, fruits, flowers. Foodstuffs form the largest industrial sector. Dairy products account for one-quarter of exports. Other major industries include chemicals, metallurgy, machinery, ßelectrical goods and tourism. Netherlands is one of the world's 10 leading exporting countries. Amsterdam is famous as a world centre for diamonds, precious metals and art treasures. Rotterdam, along the Rhine, handles the most cargo of any ocean port in the world.

Mission in India: Royal Netherlands Embassy, 6/50 F, Shantipath, Chanakyapuri, New Delhi-110021. Tel: 2419 7600; Fax: 91-11-2419 7713 (Consular/Visa)

E-mail: nde@minbuza.nl; Web: hollandinindia.org

Indian Mission in Netherlands: Embassy of India, Buitenrustweg -2, 2517 KD, The Hague, Netherlands. Tel: 00-31-70-3469771; Fax: 00-31-70-3617072.

E-mail: fscultur@bart.nl

Dutch territories

Aruba The island (**Area:** 193 sq.km., **Population:** 107,000) which lies in the southern Caribbean, formed part of the Dutch West Indies from 1828 and part of the Netherland Antilles from 1845. Achieved internal self-government in 1954. Aruba was constitutionally separated from the Netherlands Antilles from Jan.1, 1986, and full independence was promised after a 10-year period. But an agreement of 1990 deleted references to eventual independence. Capital: Oranjestad. PM: Nelson O. Oduber.

Curacao (**Area:** 444 sq.km., **Population:** 142,180); **Capital:** Willemstad
Governor General: Frits Goedgedrag; **PM:** Gerrit Schotte.

Originally settled by Arawak Indians, Curacao was seized by the Dutch in 1634 along with the neighboring island of Bonaire. Once the center of the Caribbean slave trade, Curacao was hard hit by the abolition of slavery in 1863. Its prosperity (and that of neighboring Aruba) was restored in the early 20th century with the construction of the Isla Refineria to service the newly discovered Venezuelan oil fields. In 1954, Curacao and several other Dutch Caribbean possessions were reorganized as the Netherlands Antilles, part of the Kingdom of the Netherlands. In referenda in 2005 and 2009, the citizens of Curacao voted to become a self-governing country within the Kingdom of the Netherlands. The change in status became effective in October of 2010 with the dissolution of the Netherlands Antilles.

Sint Maarten (**Area:** 34 sq.km., **Population:** 37,429) ; **Capital:** Philipsburg
Governor General: Eugene Holiday; **PM:** Sarah Wescott-Williams.

Although sighted by Christopher Columbus in 1493 and claimed for Spain, it was the Dutch who occupied the island in 1631 and set about exploiting its salt deposits. The Spanish retook the island in 1633, but continued to be harassed by the Dutch. The Spanish finally relinquished the island of Saint Martin to the French and Dutch, who divided it amongst themselves in 1648. The establishment of cotton, tobacco, and sugar plantations dramatically expanded slavery on the island in the 18th and 19th centu-

Mussolini's Secret Mission	In the 1930s and 40s, Italian fascist Benito Mussolini tried to eliminate foreign words from Italian. In soccer, "goal" became "meta" and Donald Duck became "Paperino." Mickey Mouse became "Topolino" and Goofy became "Pippo."

ries; the practice was not abolished in the Dutch half until 1863. The island's economy declined until 1939 when it became a free port; the tourism industry was dramatically expanded beginning in the 1950s. In 1954, Sint Maarten and several other Dutch Caribbean possessions became part of the Kingdom of the Netherlands as the Netherlands Antilles. In a 2000 referendum, the citizens of Sint Maarten voted to become a self-governing country within the Kingdom of the Netherlands. The change in status became effective in October of 2010 with the dissolution of the Netherlands Antilles.

126. New Zealand

Capital: Wellington; **Other Large Cities:** Auckland, Christchurch, Hamilton; **Currency:** New Zealand Dollar; **Area:** 269,057 sq.km (excluding dependencies); **Population:** 4,406,100; **Languages:** English and Maori dialect; **Religions:** Anglican-14.9%, Presbyterian-10.9%, Roman Catholic-12.4%, Methodist-2.9%, Baptist-1.3%, Pentecostal-1.7%, other Christian- 9.4%, other-3.3%, Unspecified-17.2%, none-26%; **Literacy:** 99%; **Life Expectancy:** 80.2; **p.c.i:** $ 27,460; **HDI rank:** 3; **Date of Independence:** 26th September, 1907.

Government Type: Parliamentary Democracy; **Head of State:** Queen Elizabeth II; **Gov.Gen:** Anand Satyanand; **PM:** John Key.

History: The Polynesian Maori reached New Zealand in about A.D.800.In 1840, their chieftains entered into a compact with Britain, the Treaty of Waitangi, in which they ceded sovereignty to Queen Victoria while retaining territorial rights. In the same year, the British began the first organised colonial settlement. A series of land wars between 1843 and 1872 ended with the defeat of the indigenous population. The British colony of New Zealand became an independent dominion in 1907 and supported the UK militarily in both World Wars.

Economy: The major crops are wheat, maize, oats and barley. Minerals include coal, oil and gold. Primary industries are dairying, meat and wool. Pulp and paper industry is highly developed. Iron, steel, aluminium, textiles, transport equipment are other industries.

Mission in India: High Commission for New Zealand, Sir Edmund Hillary Marg, Chanakyapuri, New Delhi-110 021. Tel: 2688 3170; Fax: 26883165,
E-mail:nzhc@ndf.vsnl.net.in

Indian Mission in New Zealand: High Commission of India, Level 9,180 Molesworth Street,Thorndon,Wellington-6015, New Zealand. Tel: 00-64-4-4736390; Fax: 00-64-4-4990665.
E-mail: hoc.wellington@mea.gov.in

Overseas Territories

The Cook islands and Niue are self-governing territories overseas and Ross Dependency and Tokelau are territories overseas coming within New Zealand's jurisdiction.

The Cook Islands: (241 sq.km.) were placed under New Zealand administration in 1901 and they achieved self-governing status in association with New Zealand in 1965; **Population:** 23,400.

Niue (259 sq.km.), formerly administered as part of Cook Islands, achieved self-governing status in association with New Zealand in 1974. Niue is the largest uplifted coral island in the world. **Population:** 1,500.

The Ross Dependency: (414,400 sq.km.), an Antarctic region, was placed under New Zealand administration in 1923.

Vote for Women	New Zealand was the first country in the world (in 1893) to extend the franchise to women for national elections.

Tokelau: (10 sq.km.) was placed under New Zealand administration in 1925. Population: 1,200.

127. Nicaragua

(Republic of Nicaragua)
Republica de Nicaragua

Capital: Managua; **Other Large Cities:** Leon, Granada; **Currency:** Cordoba; **Area:** 130,000 sq.km; **Population:** 5,743,000; **Languages:** Spanish and English; **Religions:** Roman Catholic-72.9%, Evangelical 15.1%, Maravian 1.5%, Episcopal 0.1%, other 1.9%, none 8.5%; **Literacy:** 78%; **Life Expectancy:** 72.9; **p.c.i:** $ 2,969; **HDI rank:** 115; **Date of Independence:** 15th September, 1821.
Government Type: Republic; **Head of State & Govt.:** Daniel Ortega Saavedra.
History: Nicaragua is the largest but most sparsely populated of the Central American nations. The Somoza dynasty ruled Nicaragua from 1933 to 1979.Violent opposition to governmental manipulation and corruption spread to all classes by 1978 and resulted in a short-lived civil war that brought the Marxist Sandinista guerrillas to power in 1979.

Sandinista National Liberation Front emerged as the leading political force in the election held in 1984. Nicaraguan aid to leftist rebels in El Salvadore caused the US to sponsor anti-Sandinista Contra guerrilas through muvh of the 1980s.Free elections in 1990, 1996 and 2001, saw the Sandinistas defeated, but voting in 2006 announced the

return of former president Daniel Ortega.
Economy: Agriculture is the principal source of national income. The most important agricultural products are cotton, coffee, sugar-cane, rice, bananas, maize and fruit. Chief industries are food processing, chemicals, matches, leather, beer and plastic goods. Gold, copper, silver, lead and zinc are found.
Mission in India: Embassy of Nicaragua Stationed at Panama.

Hon. Consulate, 43-A, Prithviraj Road, New Delhi-110011. Tel: 4694469; Telefax: 3221173.

E-mail: vcb@dabur.com

128. Niger

(Republic of Niger) Republique du Niger

Capital: Niamey; **Oth-er Large Cities:** Zinder, Maradi; **Currency:** Franc CFA; **Area:** 1,267,000 sq.km; **Population:**15,203,822; **Languages:** French, Hausa and Djerma; **Religions:**Muslim-80%, remainder indigenous beliefs and Christian; **Literacy:** 28.7%; **Life Expectancy:** 52.6 **p.c.i:** $ 720; **HDI rank:** 167; **Date of Independence:** 3rd August, 1960.

Government Type: Republic; **President:** Salou Djibo; **PM:** Mahamadou Danda.
History: The Republic of Niger lies in the heart of West Africa. Formerly part of French West Africa, Niger became indepndent from France in 1960 and experienced single-party and military rule until 1991, when Gen.Ali Saibou was forced by public pressure to allow multi-party elections, which resulted in a democratic government in 1993.Political infighting brought the government to a standstill and in 1996 led to a coup by Col.Ibrahim Bare. In 1999 Bare was killed in a coup by military officers who promply restored democracy rule and held elections that brought Mamadou Tandja to power in Decemberof that year.tandja was reelected in 2004.

Nigeria's Business Capital Lagos is Nigeria's business capital. If Lagos were a country, its GDP of $43 billion would make the city-state the fifth- biggest economy in sub-Saharan Africa.

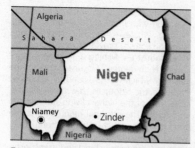

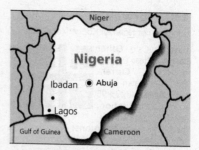

Economy: Niger is an agricultural country with very limited resources. The principal crops are millet, peanuts and cotton. Cattle-breeding is the next most important occupation of the people. Minerals: uranium, coal, iron.

Mission in India: Embassy of Niger Stationed at Moscow.

129. Nigeria
(Federal Republic of Nigeria)

Capital: Abuja; **Other Large Cities:** Lagos, Ibadan; **Currency:** Naira; **Area:** 923,768 sq.km; **Population:** 158,259,000; **Languages:** English, Hausa, Ibo and Yoruba; **Religions:** Muslim-50%, Christian-40%, indigenous beliefs-10%; **Literacy:** 72%; **Life Expectancy:** 46.9; **p.c.i:** $ 2,398; **HDI rank:** 142; **Date of Independence:** 1st October, 1960.

Government Type: Federal Republic; **Head of State & Govt (President):** Goodluck Jonathan.

The Federation of Nigeria on the south coast of West Africa is black Africa's most populous nation. It is a country of 250 tribal groups.

History: Nigeria became an independent state in 1960 and a republic within the Commonwealth in Oct. 1963. Following nearly 16 years of military rule, a new constitution was adopted in 1999, and a peaceful transition to civilian government was completed. Nigeria is currently experiencing its longest period of civilian rule since independence. General elections in April 2007 were considered significantly flawed by Nigerian and international observers but they marked the first civilian-to-civilian transfer of power in the country's history.

Economy: The chief agricultural products are cocoa, palm oil, palm kernels, grains, fish, cotton, rubber, peanuts and skins. Tin, lead, columbite, coal and iron ore are the chief minerals. Timber, hides and skins, cocoa and palm products are major export items. Industry is diversified:- beer, cement, textiles, cigarettes, assembly of vehicles, soap, canned food and aluminium products being the main items.

Nigeria is one of the world's leading suppliers of oil, but the people are among the poorest in Africa.

Mission in India: High Commission of the Federal Republic of Nigeria, Plot No.EP 4, Chandragupta Marg, Chanakyapuri, New Delhi-110021. Tel: 2412 2142, 2412 2143;

E-mail: nhcnder@.vsnl.com; Web: www.nigeriadelhi.com

Indian Mission in Nigeria: High Commission of India, 8-A, Walter Carrington Crescent, PMB. 80128, Victoria Island, Lagos, Nigeria. Tel: 00-234-1-7912442 [Direct], 2627680, 2615905, 2615078. Fax: 00-870-782670639.

E-mail: cons.lagos@mea.gov.in, fs1@hcilagos.org

| Nigeria's Unofficial Anthem | "International Thief Thief" is Nigeria's unofficial anthem. Its author, Fela Kuti, the late father of the Afrobeat genre, sang in 1980, *To become of high position here / Him go bribe some thousand naira bread / To become one useless chief.* |

130. Norway

(Kingdom of Norway) Kongeriket Norge

Capital: Oslo; **Other Large Cities:** Bergen, Trondheim; **Currency:** Norwegian Krone; **Area:** 323,895 sq.km; **Population:** 4,932,900; **Languages:** Norwegian; **Religions:** Church of Norway-85.7%, Pentecostal-1%, Roman Catholic-1%, other Christian-2.4%, Muslim-1.8%, Other- 8.1%; **Literacy:** 99%; **Life Expectancy:** 80.2; **p.c.i:** $ 52,238; **HDI rank:** 1; **Date of Independence:** 7th June, 1905. **Government Type:** Constitutional Monarchy; **Head of State:** King Harald V; **PM:** Jens Stoltenberg.

History: The adoption of Christianity by King Olav Tryggvanson in 994 almost put an end to two centuries of Viking raids into Europe. Conversion of the Norwegian kingdom occured over next several decades. In 397, Norway was absorbed into a union with Denmark that lasted more than four centuries. In 1814, Norwegians resisted the cession of their country to Sweden and adopted a new constitution. Sweden then invaded Norway but agreed to let Norway keep its constitution in return for accepting the union under a Swedish king. Rising nationalism throughout the 19th century led to a 1905 referendum granting Norway independence.

Economy: The important agricultural products are barley, oats, rye, potatoes, fruits and dairy products. Fishing is a major occupation with immense quantities of cod, herring, whale, tuna, seal, mackerel and salmon. Forests provide raw material for many industries. Mining is an important industry. High degree of industrialisation, the base for which was provided by abundant hydroelectric resources, has given Norwegians one of the highest living standards in the world. The principal manufactures are food products, machinery and metal work, wood, paper and pulp, aluminium, electrochemical products, ships and transportation equipment.

Dependencies of Norway: Svalbard (62,700 sq.km), Jan Mayen (380 sq.km.), Bouvet Island (60 sq.km.), Peter I Island (249 sq.km.), and Queen Maud Land.

Mission in India: Royal Norwegian Embassy, Shantipath, Chanakyapuri, New Delhi-110 021. Tel: 4177 9200; Fax: 4168 0145.

E-mail: emb.newdelhi@mfa.no

Indian Mission in Norway: Embassy of India, Niels Juels Gate 30, 0244 Oslo 2, Norway. Tel: 00-47-24115910; Fax: 00-968-24698291.

E-mail:mailto:indiamct@omantel.net. omm, hom@indemb-oman.org

131. Oman

(Sultanate of Oman) Saltanat' Uman

Capital: Muscat; **Currency:** Omani Rial; **Area:** 300,000 sq. km; **Population:** 2,694,094; **Languages:** Arabic; **Religions:** Ibadhi Muslim-75%, Sunni Muslim, Shi'a Muslim, Hindu; **Literacy:** 81.4%; **Life Expectancy:** 75.6; **p.c.i:** $26,197; **Date of Independence:** 1650.

Government Type: Monarchy; **Head of State & Govt:** Sultan Qabus Bin Said.

History: The Sultanate of Oman, formerly Muscat & Oman, occupies the south-eastern part of the Arabian Peninsula. In the late 18th century, newly established Sultanate in Muscat signed the first in a series of friendship treaties with Britain. Over time,

White Nights	During the last days of June, a phenomenon known as the "White Nights" can be seen in parts of Russia. It is a time when night remains bright as the sun does not sink below the horizon.

Oman's dependence on British political and military advisers increased, but it never became a British colony. In 1970, Qabus Bin Said al-Said overthrew the restrictive rule of his father; he has ruled as Sultan ever since.

Economy: Oil is the major source of income. It forms 95% of the exports. Where there is water, the land is very fertile. The Batina coastal plain is famous for its dates, fruits and grains. Major industries are petroleum drilling, fishing and construction.

Mission in India: Embassy of the Sultanate of Oman, EP 10&11, Chandragupta Marg, Chanakyapuri, New Delhi-110 021. Tel: 26885622, 26885623; Fax: 26885621

E-mail: omandelhi@yahoo.com

Indian Mission in Oman: Embassy of India, Diplomatic Area, Jami'at Al-Dowal Al-Arabia Street, Diplomatic Quarters, Al Khuwair, P.O. Box No. 1727, Postal Code: 112, Ruwi, Muscat, Sultanate of Oman. Tel: 00-968-24684500; Fax:00-968-24698291.E-mailto:indiamct@omantel.net.omm, hom@indemb-oman.org

132. Pakistan

(Islamic Republic of Pakistan)
Islam-i Jamhuriya-e Pakistan

Capital: Islamabad;
Other Large Cities: Karachi, Lahore, Peshawar; **Currency:** Pakistani Rupee; **Area:** 796,095 sq.km; **Population:** 175,646,000; **Languages:** Urdu

(Official), Punjabi, Sindhi, Pushtu, Baluchi, Brahui, English; **Religions:** Muslim-97% (Sunni-77%, Shi'a-20%), Christian, Hindu and others-3%; **Literacy:** 54.2%; **Life Expectancy:** 65.5; **p.c.i:** $ 2,789; **HDI rank:** 125; **Date of Independence:** 14th August, 1947.

Government Type: Federal Republic; **President:** Asif Ali Zardari; **PM:** Syed Yousuf Raza Gilani.

History: The Muslim state that emerged from partition of British India on 14 August 1947 included an eastern wing comprising mainly the eastern half of Bengal province and parts of Assam.

For nine years Pakistan remained a dominion. It was proclaimed an Islamic republic on 23 March 1956. A federal parliamentary system functioned until Field-Marshal Muhammad Ayub Khan seized power in a coup in October 1958. Ayub proclaimed a presidential system in the constitution of 1962 and ruled until March 1969, when he was deposed by Gen. Yahya Khan.

In the first free elections in December 1970, Zulfikar Ali Bhutto's Pakistan People's Party dominated the west, while Sheikh Mujibur Rahman's Awami League swept the board in the east, winning 160 of the 162 seats.

East Pakistan proclaimed sovereignty and formed the People's Republic of Bangladesh on 26 March 1971. Civil war followed after Yahya, supported by Bhutto, ordered troops to arrest Mujib and put

down the Bengali uprising. The east-west war ended in December 1971. Yahya handed over power to Bhutto, who ruled until July 1977, before being overthrown after an opposition campaign against alleged rigging in general elections. Gen. Zia-ul-Haq took over —initially to hold elections and transfer power to a civilian regime. But elections were twice postponed and Bhutto was tried for the murder of a political opponent and executed.

Gen. Zia was killed in a plane crash on August 17, 1988 and Senate Chairman Ghulam Ishaq Khan took over as Acting President. The country was placed under emergency rule.

In the general election held on November 16, 1988 the Pakistan Peoples' Party (PPP) led by Benazir Bhutto won the largest number of seats (92). Benazir assumed office as the PM on December 9. Ghulam Ishaq Khan was elected President on December 12.

Benazir was dismissed in Aug. '90 and Nawaz Sharif of Islami Jamhoori Ittehed took over as Pakistan's 11th Prime Minister on November 5. Sharif was dismissed in 1993. The Supreme Court annulled the dismissal leading to a constitutional impasse. Moeen Qureshi took over as caretaker Prime Minister in July. PPP returned to power in Oct. '93 and Ms. Bhutto took over as PM once again. In Apr. '96, Imran Khan launched a new party 'Movement for Social Justice'. In Nov., Ms. Bhutto was dismissed as PM, the National Assembly dissolved, and M.M. Khalid appointed caretaker PM. On Feb. 17, 1997, Nawaz Sharif was sworn in as Pakistan's 13th PM.

Tensions between the military and PM Sharif ended in a coup by army chief Gen. Pervez Musharraf on Oct.12, 1999. Nawaz Sharif was later exiled to Saudi Arabia. He was convicted and sentenced to 25-year-long life sentence on charges of hijacking and terrorism.

Gen. Musharraf pledged a return to civilian rule, but in June 2001 appointed himself president.In Oct. 2002, Pakistan held its first elections since 1997, with Musharaff's party gaining a plurality.Musharaff survived a Dec. 2003 assassintion attempt and then agreed to step down as army chief and to remain as president until 2007 eletions.But those elections were not scheduled and his popularity continued to wane dramatically, leading to the possibility of an alliance with Benazir Bhutto who returned from exile in Oct. 2007 to run for office. She was assassinated in December and her husband was later elected after Musharaff resigned.

Osama bin Laden was killed in a firefight with US Navy Seals in Abbottabad, near Islamabad on May 2, 2011.

Kashmir: Pakistan controls the northern and western portions of Kashmir, an area of about 84,160 sq km with a population of about 2.8 m. in 1985. The Pak-occupied Kashmir has its own Assembly, its own Council, High Court and Supreme Court. There is a Parliamentary form of Government with a Prime Minister as the executive head and the President as the constitutional head. The seat of government is Muzaffarabad.

The Pakistan Government is directly responsible for Gilgit and Baltistan (the north).

Economy: Agriculture (including forestry and fishing) is the mainstay of Pakistan's economy, employing about 50% of the working population. The main crops are wheat, cotton, maize, sugar-cane and rice, while the Quetta and Kalat divisions (Baluchistan) are known for their fruits and dates.

Manufacturing (refined sugar, vegetable products,jute textiles,soda ash,sulphuric acid, caustic soda, chip board and paper board, bicycles, cotton cloth, cotton yarn, cement and steel) contributes about 20% to GNP. Main exports are cotton cloth, cotton yarns, rice, leather, carpets and tapestries.

Mission in India: High Commission for Pakistan,2/50-G,Shantipath,Chanakyapuri, New Delhi - 110021. Tel. 26110601-02/05, 24676004, 24678467, 24100905; Telefax : 26872339.

| The Legend of William Tell | The legend of William Tell was based on Swiss defiance of the Holy Roman Empire in the 13th century; an overture was written by Wagner about the story. Disney produced an animated film about William Tell. |

E-mail: pakhcnd@gmail.com
Indian Mission in Pakistan: High Commission of India, G-5, Diplomatic Enclave, Islamabad, Pakistan. Tel: 00-92-51-2206950 to 54; Fax: 00-92-51-2823386. E-mail:hoc.islamabad@mea.gov.in

133. Palau
(Republic of Palau or Belau)

Capital: Melekeok;
Currency: US dollar;
Area: 1,632 sq.km;
Population: 21000;
Languages: Palauan and English and others; **Religions:** Christian, Modekngei religion (one-third of the population observes this religion, which is indigenous to Palau); **Literacy:** 92%; **Life Expectancy:** 71.22; **p.c.i:** $ 8,100; **Date of Independence:** 1ˢᵗ October, 1994.

Government Type: Constitutional Government in free association with the U.S.; **Head of State & Govt (President):** Johnson Toribiong.

History: An archipelago in the Western Pacific, Palau consists of 26 islands and over 300 islets In 1914 Japan occupied the islands, which became part of the UN Trust Territory of the Pacific Islands created in 1947, and administered by the USA. Proclaimed an autonomous republic in 1981, a freely associated state in 1992, and an independent republic on Oct.1, 1994. A self-governing state, Palau became the 185th UN member on 15 Dec. 1994. A new capital is being built in eastern Babelthuap.

Economy: Chief crops: Coconuts, cassava, sweet potatoes. Natural resources: Fisheries, mainly tuna. Tourism is a major industry. About 40,000 visitors a year. About 6000 Paluans live abroad.

134. Panama
(Republic of Panama) Republica de Panama

Capital: Panama City;
Other Large Cities: San Miguelito, David; **Currency:** Balboa; **Area:** 77,082 sq.km; **Population:** 3,405,813; **Languages:** Spanish, English; **Religions:** Roman Catholic-85%, Protestant-15%; **Literacy:** 93.4%; **Life Expectancy:** 75.5; **p.c.i:** $ 12,397; **HDI rank:** 54; **Date of Independence:** 3ʳᵈ November, 1903.

Government Type: Constitutional Democracy; **President :** Ricardo Martinelli.

History: Panama, the southern-most of the Central American nations, is a narrow strip of territory at the southern end of the isthmus separating North and South America. Panama declared its independence from Colombia on Nov. 3, 1903.

In 1979, Panama assumed sovereignty over what was previosuly known as the Panama Canal Zone and now called the Canal Area.

Control over the 81.6-km waterway Panama Canal, linking the Atlantic and the Pacific oceans, had long been a bone of contention between the US and Panama.

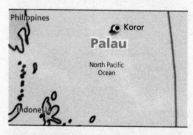

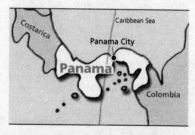

First to Use the Word "Vitamine" — Casimir Funk is known for his work on the discovery of vitamins and was the first to use the word "vitamine". Casimir Funk (1884-1967) was born in Warsaw and migrated to the USA in 1920.

On Jan.1.2000. Panama took full control of the Canal, 85 years after the strategic waterway was opened.

Economy: The soil is extremely fertile but nearly one-half of the land is uncultivated. The chief crops are bananas, coffee, pineapple, cocoa and cereals. Shrimp fishing is important. There are excellent timber resources, notably mahogany. Industry: Oil refining, sugar, food processing, international banking.

Mission in India: Embassy of Panama, 3-D,Palam Marg,Vasant Vihar, New Delhi-110 057. Tel: 2614 8268, 2614 8260; Fax: 2614 8261. E-mail: panaind@bol.net.in

Indian Mission in Panama: Embassy of India, No.10325, Avenida Federico Boyd Y Calle 51, Bella Vista, Post Box No.8400, Panama 7, Republic of Panama. Tel: 00-507-2642416, 2643043, 2648780; Fax: 00-507-2642855.

E-mail: indempan@c-com.net.pa

135. Papua New Guinea

Independent State of
Papua New Guinea

Capital: Port Moresby; **Other Large Cities:** Lae, Madang, Wawek; **Currency:** Kina; **Area:** 462,840 sq.km; **Population:** 6,888,000; **Languages:** English, Melanesian and Papuan languages; **Religions:** Roman Catholic-22%, Lutheran-16%, Presbyterian/ Methodist/ London Missionary Society-8%, Anglican- 5%, Evangelical Alliance-4%, Seventh Day Adventist-1%, Other Protestant-10%, indigenous beliefs-34%; **Literacy:** 57.3%; **Life Expectancy:** 57.8; **p.c.i:** $ 2,302; **HDI rank:** 137; **Date of Independence:** 16th September, 1975. **Government Type:** Constitutional Parliamentary Democracy; **Gov. Gen:** Sir Paulis Matane; **PM:** Sir Michael Somare.

Papua New Guinea comprises the eastern section of the island of New Guinea (the western half belongs to Indonesia) and

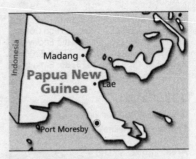

adjacent islands. New Guinea is the second largest island in the world.

History: It is a region of lofty mountains and swampy plains. The surroun-ding islands are largely of volcanic or coral origin. The population consists of dark-skinned Melanesians, who live mostly along the coasts and woolly-haired Papuans who inhabit the interior. There are more than 800 tribes, many of whom live in almost complete isolation with mutually unintelligible languages.

Economy: Agriculture occupies the majority of the population, most of whom are subsistence farmers. Main food crops: Sago, yams, taro, manioc, and sweet potatoes. Cash crops include coconuts, cocoa, coffee and rubber. The country has large deposits of copper, gold, silver and oil. Nevertheless, Papua New Guinea remains a poor country, still receiving aid from Australia. The massive mining royalties, estimated at $ 2 billion, also support economy. Industries: Food processing, beverages, tobacco, timber products.

Mission in India: High Commission of Papua New Guinea stationed at Kuala Lumpur.

Indian Mission in Papua New Guinea: High Commission of India, Lot 20, Section 8, Unit 2,Tanatana Street, Boroko,PO Box No. 86, Waigani, NCD,

Port Moresby, Papua New Guinea. Tel: 00-675-3254757; Fax: 00-6753253138.

E-mail:hcipom@datec.net.pg

| Watergate Scandal | Carl Bernstein and Bob Woodward were the *Washington Post* reporters who investigated the Watergate break-ins. President Nixon ordered a cover-up of the affair and eventually had to resign. |

136. Paraguay

(Republic of Paraguay)
Republica del Paraguay

Capital: Asuncion;
Other Large Cities:
San Horenzo, Encarnacion; **Currency:** Guarani; **Area:** 406,752
sq km; **Population:** 6,460,000; **Languages:** Spanish, Guarani; **Religions:** Roman
Catholic-89.6%, Protestant-6.2% other
Christian 1.1%, other or unspecified 1.9%,
none 1.1%; **Literacy:** 94.6%; **Life Expectancy:** 71.8; **p.c.i:** $ 4,915; **HDI rank:** 96;
Date of Independence: 14th May, 1811.
Government Type: Constitutional Republic; **Head of State & Govt (President):**
Fernando Armindo Lugo Mendez.

History: Paraguay is one of the two landlocked countries of South America surrounded by Bolivia, Brazil and Argentina.
The Paraguay river is navigable for some
3000 km. and steamers come upto Asuncion which is the chief port of the state.
This makes up for lack of coastline or sea
harbours. In the disastrous War of the Triple
Alliance (1865-70)-between Paraguay and
Argentina, Brazil and Uruguay-Paraguay lost
two-thirds of all adult males and much of its
territory. It stagnated economically for the
next half century. In the Chaco War of 1932-
35, large, economically important areas
were won from Bolivia. The 35-year military
dictatorship of Alfredo Stroessner was overthrown in 1989.

Economy: Main crops are maize, cotton,
beans, tobacco and citrus fruits. The timber resources of the state are enormous.
The chief exports are beef and other food
products, quebracho (hard wood), hides
and skins, cotton fibre and soya. Industries:
Food processing, wood products, textiles,
cement.

Indian Mission in Paraguay: Honorary Consulate General of India, Avda, Eusebio Ayale
3663,Km.4, Asuncion, Paraguay. Tel: 00-595-
21-660111; Fax: 00-595-21-660115.

137. Peru

(Republic of Peru) Republica del Peru

Capital: Lima; **Other
Large Cities:** Arequi-pa, Callao; **Currency:** Nuevo Sol;
Area: 1,281,215 sq.
km; **Population:**
29,461,933; **Languages:** Spanish, Quechua, Aymara; **Religions:** Roman Catholic-80
.9%,Evangelical 12.5%, other 3.3%, unspecified or none 2.9%; **Literacy:** 89.6%;
Life Expectancy: 71.4; **Currency:** New Sol
($1=3.158); **p.c.i:** $ 9,281; **HDI rank:** 63;
Date of Independence: 28th July, 1821.
Government Type: Republic; **President:**
Ollanta Humala

History: Ancient Peru was the seat
of several prominent Andean civilistions,
most notably that of the Incas whose
empire was captured by the Spanish
conquistadors in 1533. Peruvian independence was declared in 1821, and remaining
Spanish forces defeated in 1824. After a
dozen years of military rule, Peru returned
to democratic leadership in 1980, but experienced economic problems and the
growth of a violent insurgency. President Alberto Fujimori's election in 1990 ushered in
a decade that saw a dramatic turnaround
in the economy and significant progress in
curtailing guerrilla activity. Popular dissatisfaction with his authoritarian way of governance led to his ouster in 2000. A caretaker
government oversaw new elections in the
spring of 2001, which ushered in Alejandro
Toledo as the new head of government-
Peru's first democraticlly elected president

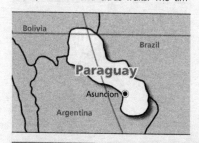

| Fishing in Peru | Thanks to the Humboldt current, Peru's inshore waters are home to one of the world's greatest fisheries. Its key-stone is the fast-growing anchoveta. For decades anchovetas have been ground into fishmeal, of which Peru is now the world's top producer. |

of Native American ethnicity.

Economy: The leading agricultural products are cotton, wool, sugar, coffee, rice, beans and potatoes. Corn which is native to Peru is the staple food of the Indians, who also cultivate alfalfa. Fishing industry is well developed and Peru is the world's most important producer of fishmeal. The country, rich in minerals, is one of the leading producers of silver. The chief exports are cotton, fish products, petroleum, copper and iron ore.

Mission in India: Embassy of the Republic of Peru, 14 Poorvi Marg, GF, Vasant Vihar, New Delhi-110 057. Tel: 26141154, 26152294; Fax: 26141155.

E-mail: consul@embaperuindia.com
Web: www.embaperuindia.com

Indian Mission in Peru: Embassy of India, 3006, Magdalena del Mar, Lima, 17, Peru. Tel: 00-51-1-4602289, 2616006, 4610371; Fax: 00-51-1-4610374.

E-mail: hoc@indembassy.org.pe
Website:commercial@indembassy.org.pe

138. The Philippines

(Republic of the Philippines)
Republika ng Pilipinas

Capital: Manila; **Other Large Cities:** Quezon City, Davao; **Currency:** Peso; **Area:** 299,404 sq.km; **Pop-** ulation: 94,013,200; **Languages:** Filipino, English and Spanish; **Religions:** Roman Catholic-80.9%, Evangelical-2.8%, Iglesia ni Kristo-2.3%, Aglipayan-2%, other Christian-4.5%, Muslim-5%, other-1.8%, unspecified-.6%, none-0.1%; **Literacy:** 93.4%; **Life Expectancy:** 71.7; **p.c.i:** $ 3,725; **HDI rank:** 97; **Date of Independence:** 12th June, 1898.

Government Type: Republic; **President :** Benigno "Noynoy" Aquino.

An archipelago of about 7100 islands, the Republic of the Philippines lies in the western Pacific Ocean, over 800 km. off the southeast coast of Asia. Just 11 islands constitute 94 per cent of the total land area. The principal islands are Luzon in the north and Mindanao in the south.

History: The Philippine islands, discovered by Magellan in 1521, were conquered by Spain in 1565. The islands, named for King Philip II of Spain, were ceded to USA in 1898. Became completely independent in 1946.

Economy: Main agricultural crops are rice, maize, sugar, tobacco, coconut, pineapple and bananas. Manufacturing is a major source of economic development. Industries include textiles, rubber products, oil refinery, pharmaceuticals, chemicals, electronics assembly, furniture, cigarettes, paper, metal, glassware and food products. The Philippines is rich in natural resources and has iron, silver, gold, chromite, manganese and copper deposits in commercial

| Coffee House | In 1683 the Polish King, saved Vienna from a Turkish siege. When the Turks left, a large amount of coffee was found in the Turkish supplies. This find led to the first coffee house in Vienna. |

quantity. It has also marble quarries, forests and extensive fishing grounds.

Philippines is the only predominantly Christian country in Asia. Philippines has the highest birthrate in Asia and the population is expected to double within three decades.

Mission in India: Embassy of the Philippines, 50-N, Nyaya Marg, Chanakyapuri, New Delhi-110 021. Tel: (91-11) 24101120, 26889091; Fax: 26876401.

E-mail: newdelhipe@bol.net.in

Consulate: Mumbai: Tel:22024792, Fax: 22814103; Kolkata: Tel: 22808353, Fax: 22808354; Chennai: Tel:2354063, Fax: 2352062

Indian Mission in Philippines: Embassy of India, 2190 Paraiso Street, Dasmarinas Village, Makati, Metro Manila, Philippines, Tel: 00-63-2-8430101/02; Fax: 00-63-2-8158151.

E-mail: admin@embindia.org.ph

139. Poland

(Republic of Poland)
Rzeczpospolita Polska

Capital: Warsaw; **Other Large Cities :** Lodz, Krakow; **Currency:** Zloty; **Area:** 312,677 sq.km; **Population:** 38,092,000; **Languages:** Polish; **Religi-ons:** Roman Catholic-89.8%, Eastern Orthodox-1.3%, Protestant-0.3%, other- 0.3% and unspecified-8.3%; **Literacy:** 99.3%; **Life Expectancy:** 75.6; **p.c.i:** $ 18,837; **HDI rank:** 41;

Date of Independence: 11th November, 1918.

Government Type: Republic; **Acting President:** Bronislaw Komorowski; **PM:** Donald Tusk.

History: A republic of upper central Europe, Poland's history goes back to the tenth century A.D. Partitioned in the 18th century, it became independent in 1918. The Nazi invasion of Poland in 1939 initiated World War II. The country was liberated again in 1944.

It was the birthplace of the former Soviet bloc's first officially recognised independent mass political movement when strikes at the Gdansk shipyard in August 1980 led to agreement with the authorities on the establishment of the Solidarity trade union. Solidarity movement led by Nobel Prize winner Lech Walesa played an important part in bringing down the communist dictatorship in 1989. The communist party was dissolved in 1990. Poland joined the European Union on May 1, 2004.

Economy: About 62% of the population are urban; 32% of the population are engaged in agriculture. Chief crops are rye, wheat, oats, potatoes, sugar beets, tobacco and flax. The country has vast resources of mineral wealth, particularly coal, besides iron, lignite, natural gas, lead, zinc and sulphur. Textiles, chemicals and metallurgy are old, established industries. New industries include automobiles, tractors, heavy machinery, ship-building and aircraft manufacturing. Main exports are ships, coal, steel and clothing. Wide ranging measures to convert the economy into a market oriented system were introduced in 1989.

Mission in India: Embassy of the Republic of Poland, 50-M Shantipath, Chanakyapuri, New Delhi-110021. Tel: 41496900 (Ambassador's Office: 41496901); Fax: 26871914(Embassy)/ 26872033(Commercial Section)

E-mail: polemb@airtelbroadband.in

Consulate General of the Republic of Poland in Mumbai: Manavi Apartments, 2nd Flr., 36, B.G. Kher Marg, Malabar Hill,

---

Schindler's List

During the Second World War Oskar Schindler ran a factory that saved the lives of over a thousand of his Jewish workers. Schindler drew up a list of his staff and persuaded the Nazis that they were essential workers.

Mumbai-400 006; Ph: (91 22) 23633863
  E-mail: poland@vsnl.com
Indian Mission in Poland: Embassy of India, Ul.Rejtana 15 (Flats 2 to 7) Mokotow, 02-516 Warasaw, Poland. Tel: 00-48-22-8495800, 8496257; Fax: -00-48-22-8496705. E-mail:pol@indem.it.pl, goi@indem.it.pl

140. Portugal

(Republic of Portugal) Republica Portuguesa

Capital: Lisbon; **Other Large Cities:** Opporto, Amadora; **Currency:** Euro; **Area:** 92,072 sq.km; **Population:** 10,636,888; **Languages:** Portuguese; **Religions:** Roman Catholic 84.5%, other Christian 2.2%, other 0.3% unknown 9%, none 3.9%; **Literacy:** 94.9%; **Life Expectancy:** 78.1; **p.c.i:** $ 23,113; **HDI rank:** 40; **Date of Independence:** 1143.
Government Type: Republic; **President:** Anibal Cavaco Silva; **PM:** Jose Socrates.

Portugal is a small rectangular territory in the southwest corner of the Iberian Peninsula.
History: After enjoying status as a world power during the 15th and 16th centuries, Portugal lost much of its wealth and status with the destruction of Lisbon in a 1755 earthquake, occupation during the Napoleonic Wars, and the independence in 1822 of Brazil as a colony. A revolution in 1910 deposed the monarchy; for most of the next six decades, totalitarian governments ran the country. In 1974, a left-wing military coup resulted in broad democratic reforms.

Portugal's history has had a lasting impact on the culture of the country with Moorish and Oriental influences in architecture and the arts. Traditional folk dance and music, particularly the melancholy fado, remain vibrant.
Economy: Nineteen per cent of the country is forest, where pine, oak, chestnut and cork grow in abundance. Winegrapes, olives, grains and potatoes are the principal agricultural products. The major minerals are coal, copper, kaolin, wolframite, lithium and titanium. Textiles, chemicals, paper, footwear and glassware are the principal manufactures. The main exports are wine, canned sardines, tuna, anchovies, resins and cork. Portugal is one of the leading producers of cork.
Mission in India: Embassy of Portugal, 8, Olof Palme Marg, Vasant Vihar, New Delhi-110 057. Tel: 26142215; Fax:26152837
  E-mail:emportin@ndf.vsnl.net.in
  Web: www.embportindia.com
Indian Mission in Portugal: Embassy of India, Rua Pero da Covilha, No.16, 1400 Lisbon, Portugal. Tel: 00-351-21-3041090; Fax: 00-351-21-3016576.
  E-mail:consular@indembassy-lisbon.org, & cons.lisbon@mea.gov.in

Overseas Territories

Azores Islands
Area: 2248.sq.km; **Population:** 238,000; In the Atlantic; Partial autonomy was offered in 1976.

The Madeira Islands
Area: 795 sq.km.; **Population:** 437,312; Off the North East coast of Africa. Autonomous Region since 1976.

141. Qatar

(State of Qatar) Dawletal-Qater

Capital: Doha; **Currency:** Qatari Rial; **Area:** 11,437 sq.km; **Population:** 1,696,563;

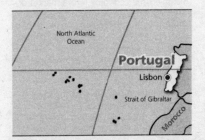

Languages: Arabic, English; **Religions:** Muslim-77.5%, Chrisitian 8.5%, others 14%; **Literacy:** 93.1%; **Life Expectancy:** 75.6; **p.c.i:** $ 88,232; **HDI rank:** 38; **Date of Independence:** 3rd September, 1971.

Government Type: Emirate; **Head of State & (The Amir):** Sheikh Hamad bin Khalifah al Thani. **PM:** Hamad bin Jasim bin Jabir al-Thani

Qatar is a 160 km. long tongue of land jutting into the Persian (Arabian) Gulf. It is surrounded almost on three sides by the Persian Gulf. Saudi Arabia lies to the south.

History: Ruled by the al-Thani family since the mid-1800s, Qatar transformed itself from a poor British protectorate into an an independent state with significant oil and natural gas revenues.During the late 1980s and early 1990s, the economy was crippled by a continuous siphoning off of petroleum by the amir, who had ruled the country since 1972. His son, the current Amir Hamad bin Khlifa al-Thani, overthrew him in a bloodless coup in 1995.

Economy: The oil industry provides over 90% of the national income but employs only less than 5% of the population. Qatar's Dukhan field has been exploited since 1980, but most attention is now focused on the North field, which is the world's largest gas field not associated with oil. Agriculture: Cereals, fruits, vegetables, dates. Industries: fertilisers, steel, petrochemicals, cement.

Mission in India: Embassy of the State of Qatar, EP-31A, Chandragupta Marg, Chanakyapuri, New Delhi-110021. Tel: 26117988, 26118486 (Ambassador's Office); Fax: 26886080.

Indian Mission in Qatar: Embassy of India, P.O. Box 2788, Al-Hilal Area, Doha, Qatar. Tel: 00-974-4255777; Fax:00-974-4670448.

E-mail:indembdh@qatar.net.qa

142. Romania

Capital: Bucharest; **Other Large Cities:** Brasov, Timisoara; **Currency:** Leu; **Area:** 237,500 sq km; **Population:** 21,466,174; **Languages:** Romanian, Hungarian, German; **Religions:** Eastern Orthodox-86.8%, Protestant-7.5%, Roman Catholic-4.7%, other and unspecified 0.9%, none 0.1%; **Literacy:** 97.6%; **Life Expectancy:** 72.5; **p.c.i:** $ 11,766; **HDI rank:** 50; **Date of Independence:** 9th May, 1877.

Government Type: Republic; **President:** Traian Basescue; **PM:** Emil Boc.

History: The largest of the Balkan countries, Romania has dramatic mountain scenery and a coastline on the Black Sea.

The principalities of Wallachia and Moldavia secured their autonomy in 1856. They were under the suzerainty of the Turkish Ottoman Empire for centuries. The principalities united in 1859 and a few years later adopted the new name of Romani. The post-war Soviet occupation led to the formation of a Communist "people's republic" in 1947 and the abdication of the king. In 1965, Romania became a socialist republic. It ended Communist dictatorship in 1989 by shooting long-time president Nicolae Ceausescu. National Salvation Front took over power in 1990. Romania's King Micheal returned home in Feb., 1997, 50 years after Communists banished him.

Economy: Industry dominates Romanian economy. Heavy industries are predomina-

ted by drilling rigs for oil, equipment for oil refineries, petrochemical industry, cement, thermo and hydro electric power, diesel and electric locomotives of high capacity, engineering and consumer goods, etc. Many state-owned companies were privatised in 1996.

Chief crops: grains, potatoes, vegetables, sunflower. Forests cover over a quarter of the country.

Mission in India: Embassy of Romania, A-47, Vasant Marg, Vasant Vihar, New Delhi-110057. Tel: 26140447, 26140700; Fax: 26140611.

E-mail:embrom@airtelbroadband.in; emrond_ ecofromania@airtelbroadband.in

Indian Mission in Romania: Embassy of India,183, Mihai Eminescu Street, Sector-2, Bucharest-020078, Romania. Tel: 00-40-21-2115451, 6190236, 2302767; Fax: 00-40-21-2110614 .

E-mail:office@embassyofindia.ro

143. Russia

(Russian Federaion) Rossiyskaya Federa-tsiya

Capital: Moscow; **Other Large Cities:** St.Petersburg, Samara; **Currency:** Rouble; **Area:** 17,075,000 sq.km; **Population:** 142,905,200;

Languages: Russian, Ukra-inian, Belarussian, Uzbek, Armenian, Azerbaijani, Georgian, and others; **Religions:** Russian Orthodox-15.20%, Muslim-10-15%, other Christian-2%; **Literacy:** 99.5%; **Life Expectancy:** 65.5; **p.c.i:** $

15,807; **HDI rank:** 65; **Date of independence:** 24th August, 1991

Government Type: Federation; **President:** Dmitriy Medvedev; **PM:** Vladimir Putin.

Russia, the largest country in the world in area, stretches across the continents of Asia and Europe. It extends for over 9600 km. from the Baltic Sea to the Pacific Ocean and for 4800 km. from north to south.

History: Russia, anindependent country since 1991, is 75% of the total area of the former Soviet Union and has 50% of its total population. About 70% of USSR's total industrial and agricultural output came from Russia.

Russia has now taken the place of the former Soviet Union in international fora. Russia adopted the name 'Russian Federation'.

On December 8, 1991, Russia, Belarus and Ukraine concluded an agreement establishing a Commonwealth of Independent States (CIS) with its headquarters in Minsk. The member states are the three founders and nine subsequent adherents: Armenia, Azerbaijan, Moldavia, and the Central Asian republics of Kazakhstan, Kirghizia, Tajikistan, Turkmeni-stan and Uzbekistan and Georgia.

The Russian Federation consists of 21 Republics, 6 Territories, 49 Provinces, 10 Autonomous Areas, 2 Cities of federal status (Moscow & St.Petersburg) and the Jewish Autonomous Region (Birobijan).

In 1993, a drive to privatise thousands of large and medium-sized state-owned enterprises was launched. President Yeltsin narrowly survived an impeachment vote by

Faberge Eggs

Carl Faberge, the famous goldsmith, designed a number of Easter Eggs for the Russian royal family. The Faberge eggs are made in the style of genuine Easter eggs, but using precious metals and gemstones rather than more mundane materials.

the Congress of Deputies in March. In Oct., Yeltsin ordered the army to attack and seize the parliament building, where anti-Yeltsin legislators had barricaded themselves. About 140 people were killed in the fighting. In Feb. '94, parliament amnestied those arrested after the occupation of the parliament building.

In July '94, Russia joined NATO's partnership for peace plan of military cooperation with former communist states. In May, '96, presidents of Russia, Belarus, Kazakhstan and Kyrgyzstan signed a treaty to boost closer links among them.

Chechen separatists have been a major problem since the winter of 1994-'95 when Russian troops were sent in to crush Chechnya's secessionist leadership. In August, '96, the war ended with an agreement between the government and the separatists to defer the decision on whether Chechenya should be independent until Dec. 31, 2001.Fighting resumed and Russia suffered heavy losses.

In Apr. '97, the presidents of Russia, Kazakhstan, Kyrgyzstan, Tajikistan and China signed a demilitarisation accord providing for considerable troop reductions along their 7000 km. common border.

Economy: Grain, cotton, potatoes, sugar beets, sunflower, are the main agricultural products. Natural resources include iron ore, oil, gold, platinum, copper, zinc, lead and tin. Russia also has the world's largest reserves of timber. Russia's gold industry is world's second largest. Steel mills, huge dams, oil and gas industries and electric rail roads have transformed parts of Siberia. The Russian fishing fleet, operating from the Arctic waters to the Pacific, is one of the biggest in the world.

Mission in India: Embassy of the Russian Federation, Shantipath, Chanakyapuri, New Delhi - 110 021. Tel: 26873800, 26873802; Fax: (9111)26876823.

E-mail:indrusem@del2.vsnl.net.in (Embassy); indconru@del2.vsnl.net.in (Consular Deptt.); Web: www.india.mid.ru

Consulate: Consulalte General of the Russian Federation in Mumbai: 42, Nepean Sea Road, "Palm Beach", Mumbai-400 006; Ph: 022-2363-36-27, 2-363-36,28, 2-368-14-31; E-mail: consul@mtnl.ne.in

Consulate: Consulate General of the Russian Federation in Chennai, 14, Santhome High Road, Chennai-600 004, Tel: 091-044-498-2320/498-2330, E-mail: madrasrus @vsnl.net

Indian Mission in Russian Federation: Embassy of India, 6-8 Ulitsa Vorontsovo Polye (Obukha), Moscow (Russia). Tel: 00-7-495-7837535; Fax: 00-7495-9163632; E-mail:ndambru@com2com.ru, dcmmos@telsycom.ru, chocmos@com2com.ru

144. Rwanda

(Republic of Rwanda)
Republica y'u Rwanda

Capital: Kigali; **Other Large Cities:** Ruhengeri, Butare; **Currency:** Rwandan Franc;
Area:26,338sqkm;**Population:**10,412,820; **Languages:** French, Kinyarwanda and Swahili; **Religions:** Roman Catholic-56.5%, Protestant-26%, Adventist-11.1%, Muslim-4.6%,indigenousbeliefs-0.1%,none-1.7%; **Literacy:** 64.9%; **Life Expectancy:** 46.2; **p.c.i:** $ 1,202; **HDI rank:** 152; **Date of Independence:** 1st July, 1962.

Government Type: Republic; **President:** Major Gen. Paul Kagame.**PM:** Bernard Makuza.

History: Formerly part of the Belgian Trusteeship of Ruanda - Urundi in east-central

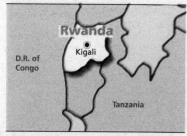

Africa, the Republic of Rwanda became independent on July 1, 1962. One of the most densely populated countries of Africa, it is known as "the nation of a thousand hills" because of its mountainous nature.

Rwanda presents a dismal scene of ethnic fighting. For centuries, the Tutsi dominated the Hutus (90% of the population). A civil war of 1959 put an end to Tutsi power. Many Tutsi went into exile. In 1963, Tutsi exiles invaded but it resulted in a large scale massacre of Tutsi. After a coup attempt by Tutsi exiles in 1990, a multi-party democracy was established. Ethnic strife resumed and a peace accord between the goverment and the Tutsi rebels was signed in August, 1993. Thousands had died and the war had led to one of world's biggest movements of refugees. President Juvenal Habyarimana, along with the Burundi President, died in a suspicious plane crash in April, 1994. Ethnic violence broke out and 50,000 died in massacres. Hutu refugees in Western Rwanda crossed into Zaire as Tutsi rebels held 2/3 of the country. In July, the Tutsi-dominated Rwandan Patriotic Front named a Hutu, the new President. About one million Hutu refugees flooded back to Rwanda from Tanzania and Zaire in Nov. '96. Paul Kagame (sworn in Apr.2000) is the first Tutsi president of Rwanda.

Economy: The economy is agricultural and remains mainly at the subsistence level. Coffee, cotton, sorghum, cassava and sweet potatoes are the principal crops. Minerals include tin ore, tungsten, tantalite, gold and beryl. Industry is undeveloped. Food manufacturing is the chief industrial activity. Livestock raising is widespread and hides and skins are exported.

Mission in India: Embassy of the Republic of Rwanda, 41, Paschimi Marg, Vasant Vihar, New Delhi - 110 057. Tel: 4166 1604; Fax: 4166 1605.

E-mail: rwandaembassy@yahoo.com and ambadelhi@minaffet.gov.rw

Indian Mission in Rwanda: Honorary Consulate General of India, M/S Sulfo Rwanda Industries, Rue de Lac Ihema, B.P. 90, Kigali, Rwanda. Tel:00-250-74556; Fax: 00-250-74290.

145. Samoa (formerly Western Samoa)

(Independent State of Samoa)
Malotuto'ata-sio Samoa i Sisifo

Capital: Apia; **Currency:** Tala; **Area:** 2835 sq km; **Population:** 187,032; **Languages:** Samoan and English; **Religions:** Christian-99.7%; **Literacy:** 98.7%; **Life Expectancy:** 71.5; **p.c.i:** $ 5,731; **Date of Independence:** 1st January, 1962.

Government Type: Parliamentary Democracy; **Head of State:** Tuiatua Tupua Tamasese Efi. **PM:** Sailele Malielegaoi Tuila'epa

History: Samoa in South Pcific consists of the two large islands of Savaii and Upolu, the small islands of Manono and Apolima and several uninhabited islets lying off the coast. The International Dateline passes very near Samoa. Eastern Samoa (American Samoa) with its capital at Fagotogo remains a dependency of the USA. (Area: 197 sq.km.).

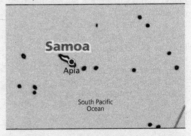

A former German protectorate, Samoa was administered by New Zealand from 1920 to 1961. Became fully independent on Jan.1, 1962. Has close links with New Zealand, on which it is dependent for military and economic assistance.

Economy: The economy is mainly agricultural. The chief products are fish, copra, bananas, taro, sweet potatoes, bark cloth and mats.

146. San Marino
(Most Serene Republic of San Marino)

Capital: San Marino; **Other Large Cities:** Seravalle, Borgo Maggiore; **Currency:** Euro; **Area:** 61 sq km; **Population:** 31,887; **Languages:** Italian; **Religions:** Roman Catholic; **Literacy:** 96%; **Life Expectancy:** 81.97; **p.c.i:** $ 41,900; **Date of Independence:** 3rd September, 301 A.D.

Government Type: Republic

Captains-Regent: Two co-regents appointed every six months from the Great and General Council of 60 members elected every 5 years.

History: The Republic of San Marino is a landlocked state in central Italy, 20 km. from the Adriatic.

It claims to be the oldest state in Europe, having been founded in A.D. 301, and the oldest republic in the world. A communist-led coalition ruled 1947-'57, a similar coalition ruled 1978-'86. San Marino has had a treaty of friendship with Italy since 1862.

A person born in San Marino remains a citizen and can vote no matter where he lives. Women were granted the vote in 1959.

Economy: The principal products are wheat, wine and olives. Industries include textiles, ceramics, cement, paper, postage stamps, leather and woollen goods. Tourism is the major source of revenue.

Mission in India: Honorary Consulate General of the Republic of San Marino, 15, Aurangzeb Road, New Delhi-110011. Tel: 23015850. Fax:23019677.

E-mail: bhaims @ndb.vsnl.net.in

147. Sao Tome & Principe
(Democratic Republic of Sao Tome and Principe)

Capital: Sao Tome; **Currency:** Dobra; **Area:** 964 sq km; **Population:** 165,000; **Languages:** Portuguese, native dialects like Fang; **Religions:** Catholic-70.3%, Evangelical-3.4%, New Apostolic-2%, Adventist-1.8%, other-3.1%, none-19.4%; **Literacy:** 87.9%; **Life Expectancy:** 65.5; **p.c.i:** $ 1,879; **HDI rank:** 127; **Date of Independence:** 12th July, 1975.

Government Type: Republic; **President:** Fradique De Menezes; **PM:** Joachim Rafael Branco.

History: These two islands, with a few other nearby islets, lie in the Gulf of Guinea, about 200 km. from Gabon. Situated north of the equator, these islands have hot steaming weather in the summer, but plenty of rainfall. Forests cover 60% of the land area. The largest of the islands is Sao Tome, on which stands Sao Tome, the capital and chief port.

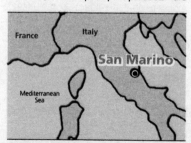

World's Oldest Republic San Marino is the world's oldest republic (A.D. 301), has fewer than 32,000 citizens, and holds the world's oldest continuous constitution. Its citizens are called the Sammarinese.

These islands were under the Portuguese until 1975 when they became independent.

Economy: Today, the country's economy is geared almost exclusively to the production of agricultural export commodities, especially cocoa (78% of exports) and coconut products. Fishing is an important activity. Sao Tome has to import most of its food. There is virtually no manufacturing industry except soap, soft drinks etc.

148. Saudi Arabia

(Kingdom of Saudi Arabia)
al-Mamlaka al 'Araiya as-Sa'udiya

Capital: Riyadh(Royal) and Jeddah (Administrative); **Other Large Cities:** Mecca, Damman, Medina; **Currency:** Rial; **Area:** 2,250,070 sq km; **Population:** 27,136,977; **Languages:** Arabic; **Religions:** Muslim-100%; **Literacy:** 85%; **Life Expectancy:** 72.8; **p.c.i:** $ 23,742; **HDI rank:** 55; **Date of Independence:** 23rd September, 1932 **Government Type:** Monarchy; **Head of State & Govt:** Abdallah bin Abd al-Aziz Al Saud.

History: Saudi Arabia, named after the ruling dynasty of Sa'ud, occupies nearly fourth-fifths of the Arabian Peninsula.

In the province of Hejaz are Medina and Mecca (the religious capital), the holy cities of Islam. The mosque of the Prophet in Medina enshrines the tomb of Mohammed, who died in the city in 632. More than 600,000 Muslims from about 60 nations pilgrimage to Mecca, the Prophet's birthplace, every year. Of the total population, 6 m. are foreigners.

The Saudi king, whose official title is custodian of the Two Holy Mosques (at Mecca and Medina), rules as absolute monarch. His heir and deputy, the crown prince, is selected from among the Sa'ud family by its leading members in consultation with the ulama, or supreme religious council. The king governs according to Islamic law, choosing a council of ministers, many of whom are Sa'uds.

Economy: Saudi Arabia has the largest reserves of petroleum in the world (25% of the proved reserves), ranks as the largest exporter of petroleum, and plays a leading role in OPEC. The petroleum sector accounts for roughly 75% of budget revenues, 45% of GDP, and 90% of export earnings. Chief agricultural products are dates, wheat, barley, fruit, hides and wool. Industry: Petrochemicals, fertilisers, steel, gas, plastics. New industrial cities are being built at Jubail and Yanbu on the Gulf.

Mission in India: Royal Embassy of Saudi Arabia, 2, Paschimi Marg, Vasant Vihar, New Delhi-110 057. Tel: 2614 4102, 26144073, 26144083, 26144093. Fax: 26144244, 26144201. E-mail: in-emb@mofa.gov.sa

Indian Mission in Saudi Arabia: Embassy of India, B-1, Diplomatic Quarter, P.B.No. 94387, Riyadh-11693, Saudi Arabia. Tel:00-966-1-4884144/ 4691/4692, 4834252/254, 4884189, 4884697, 4881982; Fax: 00-966-1-4884750.

E-mail:amb.riyadh@mea.gov.in, hoc.riyadh@mea.gov.in

149. Senegal

(Republic of Senegal)

Capital: Dakar; **Other Large Cities:** Thies, Kaolack, St. Louis; **Area:** 196,162 sq km; **Population:** 12,861,000; **Languages:**

| Largest University for Women | The world's largest women-only university is the Princess Nora bint Abdulrahman University in Saudi Arabia. It has the capacity for 50,000 students. |

French, Wolof and other native tongues; **Religions:** Muslim-94%, indigenous beliefs-1%, Christian-5% (Mostly Roman Catholic); **Literacy:** 41.9%; **Life Expectancy:** 63.1; **p.c.i:** $ 1,814; **HDI rank:** 144; **Date of Independence:** 4th April, 1960.

Government Type: Republic; **President:** Abdoulaye Wade; **PM:** Soulayemane Ndene Ndiaye.

Senegal lies on the West African bulge. Dakar, the capital, is the westernmost point in Africa.

History: Formerly a French colony, Senegal became a self-governing republic in 1960. Senegal was a one party state from 1966 to 1974, when a pluralist system was re-established. French political and economic influence is strong. In 1981, Senegal signed an agreement with the Gambia for a confederation of the two states under the name Senegambia. The confederation, established on Feb. 1, 1982, was dissolved on Sept. 21, 1989.

Economy: Agriculture and livestock-rearing are the chief occupations. Crops: Peanuts, millet, rice. There are large deposits of iron ore and phosphate. Industry: Food processing, chemicals, textiles and fishing. A long drought brought famine in 1972-73 and in 1978.

Abdoulaye Wade became President in March, 2000, succeeding Abdou Diouf.

Mission in India: Embassy of the Republic of Senegal, C-6/11, Vasant Vihar, New Delhi-110057. Tel:26147687. Fax:24142422.

Indian Mission in Senegal: Embassy of India, 5, Avenue Carde, First Floor, BP 398, Dakar, Senegal. Tel: 00-221-338495875; Fax: 00-221-338223585.

E-mail:indiacom@orange.sn

150. Serbia

Capital: Belgrade; **Other Large Cities:** Titograd, Novisad; **Currency:** Serbian dinar; **Area:** 77,474 sq. km.;
Population: 7,306,677; **Languages:** Serbo-Croatian (official) 95%, Albanian 5%; **Religions:** Serbian Orthodox, Muslim, Roman Catholic, Protestant; **Literacy:** 96.4%; **Life Expectancy:** 74; **p.c.i:** $ 10,808; **HDI rank:** 60; **Date of Independence:** 27th April 1992.

Government Type: Republic;**President:** Boris Tadic. **PM:** Mirko Cvetkovic

History: The Kingdom of Serbs, Croats, and Slovenes was formed in 1918; its name was changed to Yugoslavia in 1929. Occupation by Nazi Germany in 1941 was resisted by various paramilitary bands that fought themselves as the invaders. The group headed by Marshal Tito took full control upon German expulsion in 1945.

In the 1990s, Yugoslavia began to unravel itself along ethnic lines. Slovenia, Croatia and the former Yugoslav Republic of Macedonia all declared their independence in 1991; Bosnia and Herzegovina in 1992. In April 1992 Serbia and Montenegro announced the formation of a new Yugoslav Federation and invited Serbs in Croatia and Bosnia-Herzegovina to join. The United Nations imposed economic sanctions on Serbia when Serbian Military and financial aid poured into the Bosnian Serb campaign of "ethnic cleansing". In 1995 Milosevic signed the Dayton peace accord, which ended the Bosnian War. In 1996 local elections, the Serbian Socialist Party was defeated in many areas. In 1997 Milosevic was forced to acknowledge the

poll results after massive demonstrations in Belgrade. He later resigned the presidency of Serbia in order to become president of Yugoslavia. In 1998 fighting erupted in Kosovo between Albanian nationalists and Serbian forces. In 1999, following the forced expulsion of Albanians from Kosovo, Nato launched an airwar against Serbia and Montenegro to prevent a humanitarian crisis. Federal elections in the fall of 2000, brought about the ouster of Milosevic and installed Vojislav Kostunica as president. In 2002, the Serbian and Montenegran components of Yugoslavia began negotiation to forge a closer relationship. These talks became a reality in February 2003 when lawmakers restructured the country into a loose federation of two republics called Serbia and Montenegro.

The constitutional charter of Serbia and Montenegro included a provision that allowed either republic to hold a referendum after three years that would allow for their independence from the state union. In the spring of 2006, Montenegro took advantage of the provision to undertake a successful independence vote enabling it to secede on 3rd June. Two days later, Serbia declared that it was the successor state to the union of Serbia and Montenegro.

Mission in India: Embassy of the Republic of Serbia, 3/50 G Niti Marg, Chanakyapuri, New Delhi-110 021. Tel: 26873661 /26872073; Fax: 26885535.
E-mail:office@embassyofserbiadelhi.net.in

Indian Mission in Serbia & Monten-egro: Embassy of India, Ljutice Bogdana 8,11040 Belgrade. Tel: +381-11-266-1029, 266-1034, 2664-127; Fax: +381-11-367-4209. Email: hoc.mahe@mea.gov.in

151. Seychelles
(Republic of Seychelles)

Capital: Victoria; **Currency:** Seychellois Rupee; **Area:** 308 sq km; **Population:** 86,525; **Languages:** Creole, English and French; **Religions:** Roman Catholic-82.3%, Anglican-6.4%, Seventh Day Adventist-1.1%, other Christian-3.4%, Hindu-2.1%, Muslim-1.1%, other non-Christian-1.5%, unspecified-1.5%, none-0.6%; **Literacy:** 91.8%; **Life Expectancy:** 73.02; **p.c.i:** $ 24,837; **Date of Independence:** 29th June, 1976.
Government Type: Republic; **President & PM:** James Michel.
History: Situated in western Indian Ocean, over 1100 km. off NE of Madagascar, Seychelles is a group of about 115 lovely islands. Half the islands are coral-line and the other half granitic. The principal island is Mahe on which the capital Victoria is situated. Praslin and La Digue are two other islands. Seychelles was entirely uninhabited

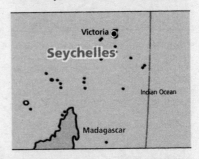

when the French established settlements there in 1768. It was ruled as part of Mauritius from 1814. Britain seized the group of islands in 1794. In 1903, it became a separate colony. Independence was declared on June 29, 1976, and Seychelles became a one - party state in 1979. In June, 1993, a new constitution provided for a multi-party state.

The population of Seychelles is of mixed origin, a unique blend of European, African, Indian and Chinese races.

Economy: Agriculture and fishing are major occupations. Chief crops: Coconuts, cinnamon, tea, vanilla and patchouli. Industry: Food processing and fishing. Tourism is a major contributor to gross domestic product.

Mission in India: Embassy of Seychelles Stationed at Kuala Lumpur.

Honorary Consulate of Seychelles, Qutab Ambience (at Qutab Minar), H-5/12, Mehrauli Rd, New Delhi-110 030. Tel:41666123; Fax: 41666126.

E-mail: sbm@bharti.in

Indian Mission in Seychelles: High Commission of India, Le Chantier, Post Box No. 488, Victoria, Mahe, Seychelles. Tel: 00-248-610301-04; Fax: 00-248-610308.

E-mail:hoc.mahe@mea.gov.in

152. Sierra Leone

(Republic of Sierra Leone)

Capital: Freetown; **Currency:** Leone; **Area:** 71,740 sq km; **Population:** 5,836,000; **Languages:** English and tribal; **Religions:** Muslim-60%, indigenous beliefs-30%, Christian-10%; **Literacy:** 38.1%; **Life Expectancy:** 42.6; **p.c.i.:** $ 803; **HDI rank:** 158; **Date of Independence:** 27th April, 1961. **Government Type:** Constitutional Democracy; **Head of State & Govt:** Ernest Bai Koroma.

History: Sierra Leone (meaning mountain of the lion) was the name originally given to this area by Portuguese sailors mainly on account of the thunder-storms around its coastal peaks. It lies on the West African bulge, between Guinea and Liberia.

Formerly under British rule, Sierra Leone became independent in 1961 and a republic in 1971.

A military coup in May '97 overthrew the government of President Ahmad Tejan Kabbah. In March, '98, the junta headed by Lt. Col. Johnny Paul Koroma was ousted by Nigeria - led troops acting in the name of ECOWAS, and President Kabbah was reinstated. In July, a UN military observer mission was authorized by the Security Council. The 70-member team was to help West African peacekeepers to demobilise remnants of the former ruling junta.

The country, after nearly nine years of civil war, lies in ruins today. Nearly 10% of the population have fled to neighbouring countries. In UNDP's list of 174 countries (1999), Sierra Leone was the last. The country lost hundreds of lives in rebellion in May, 2000.

Economy: The economy is based on agriculture and mining. Main crops: Cocoa, coffee, palm kernels, rice, ginger. Minerals: Diamonds, gold and bauxite. Industry: Light engineering.

Mission in India: Embassy of Sierra Leone Stationed at Tehran.

Indian Mission in Sierra Leone: Honorary Consulate General of India, Post Box No. 26, 5, Rawdon Street, Freetown, Sierra Leone. Tel: 00-232-22-22452; Fax: 00-232-22-226343.

Mount Rushmore	Between 1927 and 1941, Gutzon Borglum sculpted busts of Presidents George Washington, Thomas Jefferson, Theodore Roosevelt and Abraham Lincoln on Mount Rushmore.

153. Singapore
(Republic of Singapore)

Capital: Singapore city; **Currency:** Singapore dollar; **Area:** 616.3 sq km; **Population:** 5,076,700; **Languages:** Malay, Chinese, Tamil and English; **Religions:** Buddhist (Chinese), Muslim (Malays), Christian, Hindu, Sikh, Taoist, Confucianist; **Literacy:** 94.4%; **Life Expectancy:** 80; **p.c.i.:** $ 57,238; **HDI rank:** 27; **Date of Independence:** 9th August, 1965.

Government Type: Parliamentary Republic; **President:** S.R. Nathan, **PM:** Lee Hsien Loong.

Singapore is one of the smallest, most density populated and most prosperous countries in the world. Most of the population live on Singapore island; the rest inhabit 54 neighbouring islets.

History: Modern Singapore was founded in 1819 by Sir Thomas Stamford Raffles of the British East India Company, and later became a British crown colony. It was incorporated into the Federation of Malaysia in 1963, but two years later left the federation to become an independent Republic. The population of Singapore is composite. The Chinese comprise 77%, Malays 15% and Indians 6%. Lee Kuan Yew was PM for 31 years (1959-90). S.R. Nathan, a Singaporean of Indian ethnicity was elected unopposed as the country's sixth president in Aug. '99.

Economy: The country is an entrepot for

Malaysia and other southeast Asian states. It is one of the world's largest ports. The chief exports are rubber and tin. Industries include tin smelting, rubber, lumber ship-building, textiles and oil refining, (Singapore is the largest oil refining centre in Asia) machinery, chemical products, food, tourism (7.52 m. tourists in 2001) and banking. Standards in health, education and housing are high. Only about 1.7% of the total area is used for farming. Most food is imported.

On January 1, 1996, Singapore was graduated to the status of a 'developed country' by the Organisation for Economic Cooperation and Development (OECD). In May '97, the four Asian 'tigers' (Singapore, Hong Kong, Taiwan and S.Korea) were added to the industrialised countries by IMF.

Mission in India: Singapore High Commission, E-6, Chandragupta Marg, Chanakyapuri, New Delhi-110 021. Tel: 46000800, 46016420, 46000915; Fax: 46016413.

E-mail:singhc_del@sgmfa.gov.sg; Web: www.mfa.gov.sg/newdelhi

Consulate: Consulate General of the Singapore in Mumbai: 101, 10th Floor, Maker Chambers IV, 222, Jammnalal Bajaj Road, Nariman Point, Mumbai-400 021; Ph: 001-91 (22) 22043205, 001-91 (22) 22043209

E-mail: MFA_Mumbai@mga.gov.sg

Indian Mission in Singapore: High Commission of India, India House, 31 Grange Road, Singapore - 239702. Tel: 00-65-67376777; Fax: 00-65-67326909.

E-mail: indiahc@pacific.net.sg

Website:http://www.embassyofindia.com

154. Slovakia
(Slovensko)

Capital: Bratislava; **Other Large Cities:** Banska, Bystrica, Zilina; **Currency:** Euro; **Area:** 49,036 Sq. km; **Population:** 5,435,273; **Languages:** Slovak, Magyar; **Religions:** Roman Catholic-68.9%, Protestant-10.8%,

Obsession with Cleanliness

Singapore is a very clean city: there are high fines for litter, laws forbidding smoking in public places and eating on the underground and similar laws against jay walking.

Greek Catholic -4.1%, other or unspecified-3.2%, none-13%; **Literacy:** 99%; **Life Expectancy:** 74.7; **p.c.i:** $ 22,267; **HDI rank:** 31; **Date of Independence:** 1st January, 1993.
Government Type: Parlimentary Democracy; **President:** Ivan Gasparovic; **PM:** Iveta Radicova.
History: The Czechoslovak federal republic was dissolved on Dec. 31, 1992, and the two new republics of Czech and Slovakia were born on Jan. 1, 1993. (See Czech Republic for details).

In the former Czechoslavakia, Slovakia was less industrialised than the Czech land.
Economy: Wheat, barley, potatoes, vegetables, fruits, sugarbeet are the main agricultural products. In 1993, agriculture produced 20% of GDP.

Industry: Metallurgy, engineering, chemical, textile, glass. Main exports are chemicals, plastics, tractors and electronics items. Minerals: Coal, magnesite, metallic ore.

The Danube is the most important river. The underground ice and icicle caves are great tourist attractions, one of the largest being the Demanovska Cave of Freedom.
Mission in India: Embassy of the Slovak Republic, 50-M, Niti Marg, Chanakyapuri, New Delhi-110021. Tel: 24101015, 26111075; Fax: 26877941.

E-mail:emb.delhi@mzv.sk

Indian Mission in Slovak Republic: Embassy of India, Dunajska 4, (7th Floor),811 08 Bratislava,Slovak Republic. Tel: 00-421-2-5296 2915; Fax: 00-421-2-5296 2921. E-mail:eindia@slovanet.sk

155. Slovenia
(Republic of Slovenia)

Capital: Ljubljana; **Other Large Cities:** Maribor, Celje, Kranj; **Currency:** Euro; **Area:** 20,251 sq.km; **Population:** 2,046,920; **Languages:** Slovenian; **Religions:** Catholic-57.8%, Orthodox-2.3%, other Christian-0.9%, Muslim-2.4%, unaffiliated-3.5%, other or unspecified-23%, none-10.1%; **Literacy:** 99.7%; **Life Expectancy:** 77.9; **p.c.i.:** $ 27,899; **HDI rank:** 29; **Date of Independence:** 25th June, 1991.
Government Type: Parliamentary Republic; **President:** Danilo Turk; **PM:** Borut Pahor.

Ethnic breakdown: Slovenes - 91%. others- 9%.
History: The Slovenes settled in their current territory in 6th to 8th centuries but fell under German domination in the 9th century. After 1848, the struggle for unification began. In 1918, Yugoslavia was established, and the majority of the Slovenes entered the new state, which became the Kingdom of the Serbs, Croats and Slovenes. Slovenia, the most affluent Yugoslav republic, declared independence on June 25, 1991. In Feb. 1992, EC granted recognition and in May, it was admitted to the UN. It is Croatia's main ally. Slovenia joined the European Union on May 1, 2004.
Economy: Wheat, potatoes, maize, timber, livestock are the agricultural products. Industry: Steel, textiles, electricity, motor vehicles, sulphuric acid, bauxite.
Mission in India: Embassy of the Republic

Double-Landlocked Countries	There are only two countries surrounded entirely by other land-locked countries. The first is Uzbekistan, surrounded by Kyrgyzstan, Kazakhstan, Turkmenistan, Tajikstan, and Afghanistan; the second is Liechtenstein, which is surrounded by Switzerland and Austria.

of Slovenia, 46, Poorvi Marg, Vasant Vihar, New Delhi-110 057. Tel: 41662891, 41662893; Fax: 41662895.

E-mail:vnd@gov.si

156. Solomon Islands

Capital: Honiara; **Area:** 29,758 sq. km.; **Population:**530,669; **Languages:** English, Pidgin English, local languages; **Religions:** Church of Melanesia-32.8%, Roman Catholic-19%, South Seas Evangelical-17%, Seventh-Day Adventist-11.2%, United Church-10.3%, Christian Fellowhip Church-2.4%, other Christian-4.4%, other-2.4%, unspecified-0.3%, none-0.2%; **Literacy:** 76.6%; **Life Expectancy:** 63.6; **p.c.i.:** $ 2,974; **HDI rank:** 123; **Date of Independence:** 7th July, 1978

Government Type: Parliamentary Democracy; **Gov. Gen.:** Frank Kabui; **PM:** Danny Philip.

History: The Solomon Islands are in the South West Pacific and lie to the east of Papua New Guinea. The population is predominantly Melanesian.

Economy: Copra is the main cash crop and rice the chief food crop. Other crops: Bananas, yams. Industry: Fish canning, rice milling, food, tobacco. Fish is a vital element in food and an export item.

157. Somalia

(Somalia Democratic Republic)

Capital: Mogadishu; **Other Large Cities:** Hargeisa, Baidoa, Burao; **Currency:** Somali shilling; **Area:** 637,657 sq km; **Population:** 9,359,000; **Languages:** Somali,

Arabic, English, Italian; **Religions:** Sunni Muslim; **Literacy:** 37.8%; **Life Expectancy:** 48.2; **p.c.i:** $ 600; **Date of Independence:** 1st July, 1960.

Government Type: In transition; **President:** Sheikh Sharif Sheikh Ahmed; **PM:** Mohamed Abdullahi Mohamed Farmajo.

History: Comprising a former British protectorate and an Italian colony, Somalia was formed in 1960 when the two territories merged. Since then its development has been slow. Relations with neighbours have been soured by its territorial claims on Somali-inhabited areas of Ethiopia, Kenya and Djibouti.

Somalia has been without an effective central government since President Siad Barre was overthrown in 1991 by opposing clans. They failed to agree on a replacement and plunged the country into lawlessness and clan warfare.

The long-standing absence of authority in the country has led to Somali pirates becoming a major threat to international shipping in the area, and has prompted Nato to take the lead in an anti-piracy operation.

After the collapse of the Siad Barre regime in 1991, the north-west part of Somalia unilaterally declared itself the in-

Horn of Africa

The area in East Africa where the continent juts into the Arabian Sea is called the horn of Africa. It comprises Somalia, Ethiopia, Eritrea and Djibouti.

dependent Republic of Somaliland. The territory, whose independence is not recognised by international bodies, has enjoyed relative stability.

Economy: Sugarcane, bananas, sorghum, maize are the main crops.

Mission in India: Embassy of the Republic of Somalia, A-7,Defence Colony, New Delhi - 110024. Tel: 24619559, 24617453. Telex : 31-65010 ESDR IN

158. South Africa

(Republic of South Africa)

Capital: Pretoria (administrative); Cape Town (legislative); Bloemfontein (judicial); **Other Large Cities:** Durban, Johannesburg; **Currency:** Rand; **Area:** 1,223,201 sq km; **Population:** 49,991,300; **Languages:** Afrikaans, English and 9 other languages; **Religions:** Zion Christian-11.%, Pentecostal/Charismatic-8.2%, Catholic-7.1%, Methodist-6.8%, Dutch Reformed-6.7%, Anglican-3.8%, other Christian-36%, Islam-1.5%, other-2.3%, unspecified-1.4%, none-15.1%; **Literacy:** 88%; **Life Expectancy:** 49.3; **p.c.i:**$ 10,505; **HDI rank:** 110; **Date of Independence:** 31st May, 1910. **Government Type:** Republic; **Head of State & Govt (President):** Jacob Zuma.

History: Formerly known as the Union of South Africa (formed in 1910), it became a republic after leaving the Commonwealth in May 1961.

The country adopted a policy of Apartheid, the separate development of racial groups. The year 1990 witnessed softening of the Whites' attitude towards the 26 million agitating blacks. The government lifted the ban on African National Congress, the primary black group fighting to end white minority rule, and its leader 71-year-old Nelson Mandela was released from prison after 27 years of confinement.

On May 8, 1996, South Africa's Constitutional Assembly adopted a post-apartheid constitution.

Economy: South Africa is the richest African country.The major agricultural products are cotton, wheat, maize, tobacco, sugarcane, citrus fruits and dairy products. With vast mineral resources, South Africa is the biggest gold and diamond producing country in the world and one of the biggest producers of uranium. About 47 per cent of the world's total production of gold is from South Africa. Other minerals include coal, copper, tin, manganese, iron, lead and chrome. Manufacturing industries include heavy engineering, chemicals, textiles, steel, plastic and food processing.

Mission in India: High Commission of the Republic of South Africa, B 18, Vasant Marg, Vasant Vihar, New Delhi-110 057, Tel: 2614 9411-19; Fax: 2614 3605.

E-mail:immigration_section@gmail.com (Visa).

Website:www.dfa.gov.za

Indian Mission in South Africa: High Commission of India, 852, Schoeman Street, Arcadia-0083, Pretoria, South Africa. Tel: 00-27-12-3425392; Fax: 00-27-12-3425310. E-mail:polinf@hicomind.co.za

159. Spain

(Espana)

Capital: Madrid; **Other Large Cities:** Barcelona, Valecia, Seville; **Currency:** Euro; **Area:** 504,750 sq km; **Population:** 46,152,925; **Languages:** Spanish, Catalan,

Dangerously Dominant	Under the 1996 constitution, all 11 of South Africa's official languages " must enjoy parity of esteem and be treated equitably". In practice English, the mother tongue of just 8% of the people, increasingly dominates all the others.

Basque, Galician; **Religions:** Roman Catholic-94%, others-6%; **Literacy:** 97.9%; **Life Expectancy:** 80.9; **p.c.i.:** $ 29,651; **HDI rank:** 20; **Date of Independence:** 1492.

Government Type: Parliamentary Monarchy; **Head of State:** King Juan Carlos I. **PM:** Jose Luis Rodriguez Zapatero.

History: With the discovery of America for Spain by Columbus in 1492, Spain became a great colonial empire. After the defeat of the Spanish Armada by England in 1588, Spain shrunk into a minor continental power. In 1939, it passed under the dictatorship of Gen. Franco. On Franco's death in 1975, Spain became a constitutional monarchy. In 1981, there was an unsuccessful coup attempt. The Socialist Workers' Party won four consecutive general elections from 1982 to '93. In 1996, a coalition of conservative and regional parties came to power. Spain is one of the 25 members of the European Union.

In 1980, Catalonia and the Basque country were given autonomy. Basque extremists have continued their campaign for independence. The moderate nationalist Basque party, PNV emerged triumphant in May, 2001 elections in Basque province. Basque voters made it clear that they neither favour ETA's terror campaign nor approve of Govt's no-dialogue stand.

From Velazquez in the seventeenth century, through Goya straddling the eighteenth and nineteenth, to Picasso in the twentieth, Spain has the proudest of traditions in art.

Flamenco music and dance are widely admired around the world while Cervantes' novel Don Quixote is one of the most popular ever written.

Economy: Main crops are cereals, grapes, olives, vegetables and fruits. Industries include chemicals, machine tools, automobiles, ship-building, steel, textiles and processed foods, paper, cement.

Mission in India: Embassy of Spain, 12, Prithviraj Road, New Delhi-110011. Tel: 4129 3000; Fax:4129 3020.

E-mail:embspain@vsnl.com

Consulate: Mumbai: Tel: 22874797, Fax : 22043625; Calcutta: Tel:(033)2469 283, Fax: (033)2469 1283; Chennai: Tel: (044) 2812 8800, Fax: (044)2811 7411.

Indian Mission in Spain: Embassy of India, Avendia Pio XII 30-32, 28016, Madrid, Spain. Tel: 00-34-913098870 ; Fax: 00-34-91-3451112 (Embassy).

E-mail:amb@embassyindia.es

Website:www.embassyindia.es

160. Sri Lanka

(Democratic Socialist Republic of Sri Lanka)
Sri Lanka Prajathanthrika Samajavadi Janarajaya

Capital: Colombo; **Other Large Cities:** Kandy, Jaffna, Galle; **Currency:** Sri Lankan Rupee; **Area:** 65,610 sq.km.; **Population:** 20,410,000; **Languages:** Sinhala, Tamil & English; **Religions:** Buddhist-69.1%, Muslim-7.6%; Hindu-7.1%, Christian-6.2%, Unspecified-10% **Literacy:** 90.8%; **Life Expectancy:** 72.4; **p.c.i:** $ 5,103; **HDI rank:** 91; **Date of Independence:** 4th February, 1948.

Government Type: Republic; **President:** Mahinda Rajapakse; **PM:** Dissanayake Mudiyanselage Jayaratne.

Sri Lanka is an island in the Indian Ocean about 80 km east of the southern tip of India.

History: The country became independent on 4 February 1948 and on 22 May the Republic of Sri Lanka was created.

| Tomb of Saint James | One of the twelve apostles, Saint James, is said to be buried at Compostela in North West Spain. His tomb became the most important destination for Christian pilgrims apart from Rome and Jerusalem. He is Spain's patron saint. |

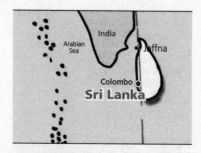

Prime Minister W.R.D. Bandaranaike was assassinated in 1959.His widow, Sirimavo Bandaranaike, leader of the Freedom Party, was elected as his successor.In 1962 her government exprppriated the property of foreign oil companies. The conservative United National Party won a majority in Parliament in 1965 and agreed to pay compensation for the expropriated assets. In May 1970 Mrs. Bandaranaike was again elected prime minister. Leftists secured the nationalisation of foreign plantations in the mid-1970s.Mrs. Bandaranaike's party was ousted by the UNP in1977.Constitutional reform in 1978 aimed at increasing stability by establishing a presidential form of government. But stability has long eluded Sri Lanka because of the long struggle between Tamils and the Sinhalese.

The growth of a more assertive Sinhala nationalism after independence fanned the flames of ethnic division until civil war erupted in the 1980s between Tamils pressing for self-rule and the government.

Most of the fighting took place in the north. But the conflict also penetrated the heart of Sri Lankan society with Tamil Tiger rebels carrying out devastating suicide bombings in Colombo in the 1990s.

A ceasefire and a political agreement reached between the government and rebels in late 2002 raised hopes for a lasting settlement. But Norwegian-brokered peace talks stalled and monitors reported open violations of the truce by the government and Tamil Tiger rebels.

Escalating violence between the two sides in 2006 killed hundreds of people and raised fears of a return to all-out war. In January 2008, the government said it was withdrawing from the 2002 ceasefire agreement. The ceasefire expired a fortnight later.

Following a renewal of fighting, a large-scale government offensive succeeded in breaking the long stalemate, and in January 2009 troops captured the northern town of Kilinochchi, held for ten years by the Tigers as their administrative headquarters.

Thereafter, the army steadily pushed the Tamil Tigers into an ever shrinking area of the north-east, before finally overrunning the last rebel-held position in May and prompting the government to declare the Tamil Tigers defeated.

International concern was raised about the fate of the estimated 70,000 to 200,000 civilians thought to have been caught up in the conflict zone.

Economy: Sri Lanka's predominantly rural population is concentrated in the west, south and south-west regions, where rubber, tea and coconuts are grown. About one-half of the working population are engaged in agriculture, forestry and fishing, and only agriculture provides 21% of the gross domestic product (GDP). Of the total area of 6,561,000 hectares, about 2m. hectares are under cultivation. Agriculture engages about 45% of the labour force. The main crops are paddy, rubber, tea and coconuts.

Mission in India: High Commission for the Democratic Socialist Republic of Sri Lanka, 27-Kautilya Marg, Chanakyapuri, New Delhi - 110021. Tel. 23010201-03; Fax:23793604.

E-mail:lankacomnd@bol.net.in

Deputy High Commission of the Democratic Socialist Republic of Sri Lanka, 196, T.T.K. Road, Alwarpet, Chennai- 600 018. Tel. 4987896, 4987612; Fax: 4987894.

India: Mumbai

E-mail:sldehico@md3.vsnl.net.in

Consulate: Consulate General of the Democratic Socialist Republic of Sri Lanka, "Sri Lanka House", 34 Homi Mody Street,

| Princess as Captive | The Indian princess Pocahontas was a friend to the colonists of Jamestown in Virginia at a time when they were finding life difficult. During a period when she was held captive, to exchange for English prisoners, Pocahontas met and married the colonist John Rolfe. |

Mumbai - 400 023, India. Tel: 2045861, 204803; Fax: 2876132

E-mail: slcon@bom5.vsnl.net.in

Indian Mission in Sri Lanka: High Commission of India, 36-38, Galle Road, P.O.Box No. 882, Colombo 3, Sri Lanka. Tel: 00-94-11-2327587, 2422788, 2421605 Fax: 00-94-11-2446403, 2448166.

E-mail: cons.colombo@mea.gov.in

161. St. Kitts-Nevis

(Federation of St. Kitts and Nevis)

Capital: Basseterre; **Currency:** East Caribbean Dollar; **Area:** 269 sq km; **Population:** 52,000; **Languages:** English and Patois; **Religions:** Anglican, Other Protestant, Roman Catholic; **Literacy:** 97.8%; **Life Expectancy:** 73.2; **p.c.i.:** $ 12,976; **Date of Independence:** 19th September, 1983.

Government Type: Parliamentary Democracy; **Gov. Gen.:** Cuthbert M. Sebastian. **PM:** Dr. Denzil Douglas.

History: St. Christopher (Kitts)-Nevis are two islands in East Caribbean separated by a narrow channel 3.2 km wide. The islands were given the status of an Associate State of the U.K. in 1967 and became independent on Sept. 19, 1983. At that time Anguilla was part of St. Kitts-Nevis. The Anguillans revolted against this arrangement and Anguilla was separated. Nevis has the right of secession.

In August, '98, the 62% of people of Nevis (population: 9000) voted in favour of leaving the federation, but failed to reach the two-thirds majority needed for secession. The population is mostly black.

Economy: The economy is agricultural, cotton and sugar being the principal crops. Industries: Sugar, construction, clothing, tourism.

162. St. Lucia

Capital: Castries; **Currency:** East Caribbean Dollar; **Area:** 616 sq km; **Population:** 166,526; **Languages:** English and French patois; **Literacy:** 80%; **Religions:** Roman Catholic-67.5%, Seventh Day Adventist-8.5%, Pentecostal-5.7%, Anglican-2%, Evangelical-2%, other Christian-5.1%, Rastafarian-2.1%, other-1.1%, unspecified-1.5%, none 4.5%; **Literacy:** 94.8%; **Life Expectancy:** 73.7; **p.c.i.:** $ 10,227; **Date of Independence:** 22nd February, 1979.

Government Type: Parliamentary Democracy; **Gov. Gen.:** Calliopa P. Louisy; **PM:** Stephenson King.

History: St. Lucia, in Eastern Caribbean, is the second largest island in the Windward group. Volcanic in origin. St. Lucia was ceded to Britain by France in 1814. Self-government was granted in 1967. It became independent on Feb. 22, 1979. There is a 17-seat House of Assembly.

Economy: The economy is agricultural, coconut, bananas and cocoa being the main crops. Manufactures include soap, plastics, garments and beer.

163. St. Vincent & The Grenadines

Capital: Kingstown; **Currency:** East Caribbean Dollar; **Area:** 388 sq km; **Population:** 109,000; **Languages:** English and

French Patois: **Religions:** Anglican-47%, Methodist-28%, Roman Catholic-13%, Hindu, Seventh-Day Adventist, Other Protestant; **Literacy:** 88.1%; **Life Expectancy:** 71.6; **p.c.i.:** $ 10,261; **Date of Independence:** 27th October, 1979.

Government Type: Parliamentary Democracy; **Gov. Gen:** Sir Fredrick Nathaniel Ballantyne; **PM:** Ralph E Gonsalves.

History: One of the Windward islands, west of Barbados, St. Vincent became a British Associated State in 1969 and achieved independence on Oct. 27, 1979.

St. Vincent (345 sq.km.), chief island of the chain, is dominated by the volcano La Soufriere. (It erupted in 1979). The Grenadines is a chain of islets with a total area of 43 sq.km.

The population is of mixed origin: European-Negro and Carib-Indian.

Economy: Bananas, arrowroot, copra, sea island cotton and spices are the main products. Industry: Food-processing, electronic equipment assembly, garments, tourism.

164. Sudan

(Republic of the Sudan)
Jumhuriyat as-Sudan

Capital: Khartoum; **Other Large Cities:** Omdurman, Port Sudan; **Currency:** Sudanese pound; **Area:**

1,886,068 sq km; **Population:** 43,192,000; **Languages:** Arabic, English, Dinka, Nubian etc.; **Religions:** Sunni Muslim-70% (in the north), indigenous beliefs-25%, Christian-5% (mostly in the south and in Khartoum); **Literacy:** 60.9%; **Life Expectancy:** 58.6; **p.c.i.:** 2,466; **HDI rank:** 154; **Date of Independence:** 1st January, 1956.

Government Type: Government of National Unity (GNU); **Head of State and Govt (President):** Lt. Gen. Omar Hassan al-Bashir.

History: The Sudan, the largest African country, is a republic in north east Africa. The White Nile flows through the middle of the country and joins the Blue Nile at

Khartoum.

The 12 northern provinces are predominatly Arab-Muslim, and the 3 southern provinces are populated largely by Christians and animists.

The Sudanese People's Liberation Army (SPLA) (the mainstream rebel group which has been fighting for 16 years to free mainly Christian and animist south Sudan from domination by Islamic, Arabised north) maintains guerilla activities in the south. 1.5m. people have been dead from violence and famine.

In Apr. '97, Sudan's Islamic government and four southern rebel groups signed a peace treaty to end the civil war, by which a referendum is to be held after four years for Southerners to decide whether to secede or remain in Sudan. Famine and starvation were reported to be the worst in 1998. UN World Food Programme were flying in food as SPLA called a unilateral ceasefire in their fight with the north. Peace talks in Addis Ababa failed in August.

Economy: The main agricultural crop sorghum is the country's staple food and cotton is the most important cash crop and main export. Other products include gum arabic (world's principal producer), sugarcane, sesame, peanuts, dates, hides and skins, chillies, beans and corn. Forests cover about one-fifth of the land area, and most productive woodland is state-owned. Sudan's mineral wealth includes copper, gold, iron and oil. Industry: Textiles, food processing.

Mission in India: Embassy of the Republic

of Sudan, Plot No.3, Shantipath, Chanaky-apuri, New Delhi-110021. Tel: 26873785, 26873185; Fax: 26883758.

E-mail:embsudin@yahoo.co.in

Indian Mission in Sudan:Embassy of India, P.O. Box 707, 61- Africa Road, Khartoum-II, Sudan. Tel:00-249-1-83574001 / 2/ 3/ 4; Fax: 00-249-1-83574050.

E-mail:cons.khartoum@mea.gov.in, consular@indembsdn.com

165. Suriname

(Republic of Suriname)

Capital: Paramaribo; **Currency:**Surinamese dollar; **Area:** 163,820 sq km; **Population:** 524,000; **Languages:** Dutch, English, Hindi, Sranantongo (Surinamese) and Javanese; **Religions:** Hindu-27.4%, Muslim-19.6%, Roman Catholic-22.8%, Protestant-25.2% (predominantly Moravian), indigenous beliefs-5%; **Literacy:** 90.4%; **Life Expectancy:** 70.2; **p.c.i.:** $ 8,955; **HDI rank:** 94; **Date of Independence:** 25th November, 1975.

Government Type: Constitutional Democracy; **President:** Desire Bouterse; **Vice President :** Robert Ameerali

History: Suriname, formerly Dutch Guyana, lies on the north east coast of South America. It became independent in 1975.

A Military Council came to power in 1982. In 1987 civilian rule was restored. Political turmoil continued, with its adverse effects on the economy.

A boundary dispute between Suriname and Guyana flared in June, 2000.

Ethnic groups: Creole 35%; Indian 33%; Javanese 16% Bushnegroes (Blacks) 10%; Amerindian 3%.

Economy: The economy is very dependent on exports and imports. Much of the land is given to rice cultivation, managed by Hindustanis. The country is rich in bauxite. Bauxite, alumina and aluminium constitute nearly 80% of the exports. Industry: Aluminium, processed foods, lumber.

Mission in India: Embassy of the Republic of Suriname, C-15, Malcha Marg, Chanaky-apuri, New Delhi-110 021; Tel: 26888435, 26888454; Fax: 26888450.

E-mail:embsurnd123@rediffmail.com

Indian Mission in Suriname: Embassy of India, Dr. Sophie Redmondstraat, No. 221, P.O. Box 1329, Paramaribo, Suriname. Tel: 00-597-498344, 498018; Fax: 00-597-491106.

E-mail:India@sr.net

166. Swaziland

(Kingdom of Swaziland) Umbuso weSwatini

Capital: Mbabane; **Other Large Cities:**Loba-mba, Manzini; **Currency:** Lilangeni; **Area:** 17,363 sq km; **Population:** 1,202,000; **Languages:** English and Swazi; **Religions:** Zionist (a combination of Christianity and indigenous ancestral worship) -40%, Roman Catholic-20%, Muslim-10%.; **Literacy:** 79.6%; **Life Expectancy:** 39.6; **Currency:** Lilangeni (pl.-emalangeni) ($1=7.034); **p.c.i.:** $5,884; **HDI rank:** 121; **Date of Independence:** 6th September, 1968.

Government Type: Monarchy; **Head of State:** King Mswati III. **PM:** Barnabas Sibu-siso Dlamini.

Swaziland is surrounded almost entirely by South Africa. Mozambique to the east is its only other neighbour.

History: Swaziland, formerly a British protectorate, attained independence on Sept.

| Lowest Life Expectancy | Residents of Swaziland have the lowest documented life expectancy in the world at 39.6 years, 40 per cent below the world average of 67.2 . |

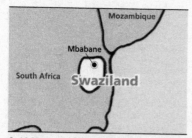

6, 1968. In 1973, the king assumed full powers. Political parties were banned in 1978. The 1990s saw moves towards a multiparty system.

The royal house of Swaziland is one of Africa's last ruling dynasties. The population is homogenous, of Nguni descent.

Economy: Sugar is the principal item in the economy, with citrus fruits, cotton, rice and maize, coming next. But the main wealth of the Swazis is cattle. There are considerable mineral reserves, especially, asbestos, iron and coal. Industry: Wood pulp, cotton ginning and meat processing.

Mission in India: Embassy of Swaziland Stationed at Kuala Lumpur.

167. Sweden

(Kingdom of Sweden) Konungariket Sverige.

Capital: Stockholm; **Other Large Cities:** Goteborg, Malmo, Uppsala; **Currency:** Krona; **Area:** 449,793 sq km; **Population:** 9,418,732; **Languages:** Swedish; **Religions:** Lutheran-87%, Roman Catholic, Orthodox, Baptist, Muslim, Jewish, Buddhist; **Literacy:** 99%; **Life Expectancy:** 80.9; **p.c.i.:** $ 37,775; **HDI rank:** 9; **Date of Independence:** 6th June, 1523. **Government Type:** Constitutional Monarchy; **Head of State:** King Carl XVI Gustaf. **PM:** Fredrik Reinfeldt.

History: Sweden which occupies the eastern part of the Scandinavian peninsula, is the largest of the Nordic countries and in terms of area, the fourth largest country in Europe. Mountains cover 25% of the country. A constitutional monarchy since 1434, Sweden is the world's first widely comprehensive welfare state. Stockholm is known as "Beauty on the Sea".

Economy: Sweden has rich natural supplies of coniferous forest, water power, iron ore and uranium.

Highly industrialised, Sweden today exports 40% of its industrial production. Major industries: Steel, machinery, instruments, autos, ship building and paper. Main crops: Grains, potatoes, sugar beets and dairy products. Forests (half the country) yield 16% of exports.

Sweden entered the EU on Jan. 1, 1995 but decided against joining NATO.

In 2000, Sweden voted in favour of adopting euro as its currency.

Mission in India: Embassy of Sweden, Nyaya Marg, Chanakyapuri, New Delhi-110 021. Tel: 4419 7100; Fax: 2688 5401.

E-mail:ambassaden.new-delhi@foreign. ministry.se; Web:www.swedenabroad.se/ newdelhi

Indian Mission in Sweden: Embassy of India, Adolf Fredriks Kyrkogata 12, Box 1340, 111 83 Stockholm, Sweden. Tel: 00-468-107008; Fax: 00-468-248505.

E-mail:information@indianembassy. se

168. Switzerland

(Swiss Confederation)

Capital: Berne; **Other Large Cities:** Zurich,

Land of Innovation	Sweden is the country that first offered the perfected zipper, the marine propeller, the fridge, the heart pace maker and even created your computer mouse. Not to forget the much-loved discount furniture retailer IKEA and fashion from H&M.

Basel, Geneva, Lausanne;
Currency: Swiss Franc;
Area: 41,293 sq.km.;
Population: 7,782,900;
Languages: German, French, Italian and Romansch; **Religions:** Roman Catholic-41.8%, Protestant-35.3%, orthodox-1.8%, other Christian-0.4%, Muslim-4.3%, other-1%, unspecified-4.3%, none-11.1%; **Literacy:** 99%; **Life Expectancy:** 81.7; **p.c.i.:** $ 41,765; **HDI rank:** 13; **Date of Independence:** 1st August, 1291.

Government Type: Federal Republic;
President: Micheline Calmy-Rey

History: Since 1291, Switzerland (called Helvetia in ancient times) has remained a compl-etely independent country, and has not been involved in a foreign war since 1515. The president is elected to a nonrenewable one-year term. It is a multi-lingual state with most people speaking more than one language. It has 1.24 million foreign residents. In a referendum in 1986, the electorate voted against joining the UN. In 1971, women were given the vote in federal elections and the right to hold federal office. Switzerland joined (June '97) NATO's security cooperation pact called the Patnership for Peace.

Economy: Crops include grains, potatoes, sugar beets, vegetables, fruits and wine.

Swiss-made watches and clocks are famous the world over. Precision tools and machines form another specialised industry. Fabrics and lace are part of Switzerland's image. Other industries: Steel, textiles, food-stuffs (cheese, chocolate), chemicals, drugs, banking. Minerals: Salt. The availability of electric power in every cottage has fostered growth of all kinds of small industries throughout Switzerland

Switzerland is a leading world banking centre and the seat of many UN and other international agencies. The nation's strict bank-secrecy rules have been eased since 1990. Geneva was the headquarters of the League of Nations.

Mission in India: Nyaya Marg, Chanakyapuri, New Delhi-110 021. Tel: 26878372, 26878534; Fax: 2687 3093.

E-mail: vertretung@ndh.rep.admin.ch
Consulate: Mumbai: 102, Maker Chambers's IV, 10th Floor, 222, Jamna Lal Bajaj Marg, Nariman Point, Mumbai-400 021, Tel: +91 22-22884563-5/22831738, E-mail: vertretung@mum.rep.admin.ch
Indian Mission in Switzerland: Embassy of India, Kirchenfeldtrasse 28, Postfach 406, CH-3005, Berne-6, Switzerland. Tel: 00-41-31-3511110; Fax: 00-41-31-3511557.

E-mail:india@indembassybern.ch

169. Syria

(Syrian Arab Republic)

Capital: Damascus;
Other Large Cities: Aleppo, Homs, Hama;
Currency: Syrian Pound; **Area:** 185,180 sq.km.; **Population:** 20,996,000; **Languages:** Arabic, Kurdish, Armenian; **Religions:** Sunni Muslim-74%. Alawite, Druze, and other Muslim sects-16%, Christian (various sects)-10%, Jewish; **Literacy:** 83.1%; **Life Expectancy:** 74.1; **p.c.i:** $ 5,108; **HDI rank:** 111; **Date of Independence:** 17th April, 1946.

Government Type: Republic (under an authoritarian regime); **President:**Basher al Azad. **PM:** Muhammad Naji al-Otari.

The Syrian Arab Republic in West Asia lies at the eastern end of the Mediterranean Sea. The Orontes and Euphrates riv-

---

Spat Over Spratly — The Spratly Islands, a group of over 100 small, uninhabited islands or reefs in the middle of the South China Sea, are claimed, in whole or in part, by five different countries.

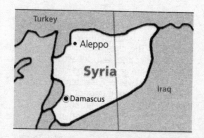

ers pass through Syria. The chief seaport is Latakia.

History: Syria, the seat of an ancient civilization, became a fully independent sovereign republic in 1946.

Syria joined with Egypt in 1958 in the United Arab Republic but seceded in 1961. Principal towns are Damascus, Aleppo and Homs.

Syria has been involved in the Arab-Israeli conflict since 1948. Syria's negotiations with Israel haven't made much headway.

Economy: Agriculture and cattle-breeding comprise the major occupations of the people. The chief crops are cotton, wheat, tobacco and olives. Minerals: Oil, phosphate, gypsum. Industries include oils, soap, textiles, leather, tobacco, sugar and glassware.

Mission in India: Embassy of Syrian Arab Republic, D-5/8, Vasant Marg, Vasant Vihar, New Delhi - 110057. Tel: 26140233; Telefax: 26143107.

Indian Mission in Syria: Embassy of India, 3455, Sharkassiyeh,

Ibn Al Haitham Street, Abu Rumaneh, PO Box. 685, Damascus. Tel: 00-963-11-3347351, 3347352; Fax: 00-963-11-3347912.

E-mail:hoc.damascus@mea.gov.in

170. Tajikistan

(Republic of Tajikistan)

Capital: Dushanbe;
Other Large Cities: Khudzand, Kulyab;
Cu-rrency: Somoni;
Area: 143,100 sq.

km.; **Population:** 7,075,000; **Languages:** Tadzhik, Russian; **Religions:** Sunni Muslim-85%, Shi'a Muslim-5%; **Literacy:** 99.6%; **Life Expectancy:** 66.7; **p.c.i:** $ 1,907; **HDI rank:** 112; **Date of Independence:** 9th September, 1991.

Government Type: Republic; **President:** Imamali Rakhmonov; **PM:** Akil Akilov.

History: A former Soviet republic that became independent in 1991, Tajikistan is bordered by Uzbekistan, Kirghizia, China and Afghanistan.

In Nov. '92, Parliament voted to abolish presidency and instal a parliamentary republic. A pro-communist regime came in Jan. '93. In Nov. '94, a constitution establishing a presidential system was approved. Muslim rebels continued to fight the regime.

In June '97, government and opposition leaders signed a peace treaty ending five years of bloody civil war. In August, fighting was reported among pro-government warlords. Russia supported President Rakhmonov.

Economy: Farming, horticulture and cattle breeding are the main occupations. Products: Grain, potatoes, vegetable, fruit, grapes, meat, milk, eggs, wool, cotton. Natural resources: Brown coal, lead, zinc, oil, uranium, radium, arsenic.Industry: Mining, engineering, food, textile, clothing, silk, bricks, ferroconcrete, knitwear, footwear.

Mission in India: Embassy of the Republic of Tajikistan,E-12/6,Vasant Vihar, New Delhi-110 057. Tel: 26154282,4601 2099; Fax: 26154282.

Indian Mission in Tajikistan: Embassy of India, 45, Bukhoro Street (Formerly Sveridenko

Museum of Comparative Zoology
Harvard's Museum of Comparative Zoology was founded in 1860 by the Swiss scientist Louis Agassiz, who is known as The Father of Glaciology from his theories about glaciers and Ice Ages.

Street), Dushanbe, Tajikistan. Tel: 00-992-372-217172,211803; Fax: 00-992-372-510045. Email: hoc.dushanbe@mea.gov.in

171. Tanzania
(United Republic of Tanzania)

Capital: Dodoma; **Other Large Cities:** Dar es Salaam, Mwanza; **Currency:** tanzanian Shilling; **Area:** 945,087 sq.km.; **Population:** 43,187,823; **Languages:** Kiswahili and English; **Religions:** Mainland–Christian-30%, Muslim-35%, indigenous beliefs-35%, Zanzibar–99% Muslim; **Literacy:** 72.3%; **Life Expectancy:** 52.5; **p.c.i:** $ 1,497; **HDI rank:** 148; **Date of Independence:** 26th April, 1964

Government Type: Republic; **President:** Jakaya Kikwete.

History: The United Republic of Tanganyika and Zanzibar was constituted on April 26, 1964 (named Tanzania on Oct. 29), when the Republic of Tanganyika in East Africa and the island Republic of Zanzibar ('the Isle of Cloves'), off the coast of Tanganyika, joined into a single nation.

President Julius K. Nyerere dominated Tanzanian politics until he resigned in 1985. In 1967, the government set on a socialist course, and nationalised banks and many industries. The country firmly abandoned socialist policies and switched over to a market-based system more than 14 years ago. Privatisation

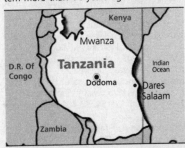

of the economy was undertaken in the 1990s. The process of economic recovery, however, has been painfully slow.

Economy: The chief cash crops are sisal, sugarcane, cotton, tea, tobacco and coffee. Cloves are grown on the islands, chiefly in Pemba. Livestock is extensively raised. Diamonds are an important export. Other minerals include gold, tin and salt. Industry: Food processing and clothing.

Three of Africa's best-known lakes-Victoria, Tanganyika and Nyasa–and Mount Kilimanjaro – the highest in Africa – are in Tanzania.

Mission in India: High Commission for the United Republic of Tanzania, EP-15C, Diplomatic Enclave, Chaanakyapuri, New Delhi-110 021; Tel: 2412 2864; Fax: 2412 2862.

E-mail: tanzrep@del2.vsnl.net.in

Indian Mission in Tanzania: High Commission of India, 82, Kinondoni Road, Kinondoni, P.O. Box No. 2684, Dares Salaam, Tanzania. Tel: 00-255-22-2669040/1/2, 669049; Fax: 00-255-22-2669043, 2669050.

E-mail: hci@hcindiatz.org

172. Thailand
(Kingdom of Thailand) Muang Thai or Prathet Thai

Capital: Bangkok; **Other Large Cities:** Songkhla, Chiang Mai; **Currency:** Baht; **Area:** 513,115 sq.km.; **Population:** 67,070,000; **Languages:** Thai, Lao, Chinese, English and Malay; **Religions:** Buddhist-94.6%, Muslim-4.6%, Christian-0.7%, others-0.1%; **Literacy:** 94.1%; **Life Expectancy:** 70.6; **p.c.i:** $ 8,643; **HDI rank:** 92; **Date of Independence:** 1238.

Government Type: Constitutional Monarchy; **Head of State:** King Bhumibol Adulyadej Abldet; **PM:** Yingluck Shinawatra.

Thailand, formerly known as Siam, is a southeast Asian country.

History: An ancient autocracy, it became a constitutional monarchy in 1932. In 1948,

the country assumed its present name Thailand. The military took over the govenment in a bloody 1974 coup. In 1988, there was a democratic election but again military came to power in 1991.

In September 2006, the military once again stepped into politics, carrying out a bloodless coup against Prime Minister Thaksin Shinawatra while he was at the UN General Assembly.

An interim prime minister was appointed a month later.

By the end of 2007, the military junta had drafted a new constitution and held general elections, marking the beginning of the transition back to civilian rule. In the elections held on July 3, 2011, Yinluck Shinawatra, the sister of exiled former PM, Thaksin Shinawatra, led Thailand's main opposition party to a landslide victory.

Economy: Thailand is world's biggest rice exporter. Coconuts, tobacco, cotton and teak are the other items of agricultural exports. Industry: Cement, processed food, textiles, wood, tin, jewelry. Minerals include tin, manganese, tungsten, antimony, lignite and lead. Since 1982 tourism has been Thailand's largest revenue earer.

Mission in India: Royal Thai Embassy, 56-N, Nyaya Marg, Chanakyapuri, New Delhi-110 021. Tel: 26118103; Fax: 26872029.

E-mail:thaidel@mfa.go.th

Indian Mission in Thailand: Embassy of India, 46, Soi 23 (Prasanmitr) Sukhumvit Road, Bangkok-10110, Thailand. Tel: 00-66-2-2580300 to 5; Fax: 00-66-2-2584627, 2621740.

E-mail:indiaemb@mozart.inet.co.th

173. Togo

(Republic of Togo) Republique Togolaise

Capital: Lome; **Currency:**FrancCFA; **Area:** 56,785 sq.km.; **Population:** 6,780,000; **Languages:** French (official) and tribal languages; **Religions:** indigenous beliefs-51%, Christian-29%, Muslim-20%; **Literacy:** 53.2%; **Life Expectancy:** 58.4; **p.c.i:** $847; **HDI rank:** 139; **Date of Independence:** 27th April, 1960.

Government Type: Republic; **President:** Faure Gnassingbe; **PM:**Gilbert Houngbo.

History: The Republic of Togo, formerly Togoland, lies on the west coast of Africa forming a narrow strip stretching from the Gulf of Guinea north to Burkina Faso. Gained independence on Apr. 27, 1960. The first multi-party elections were held in 1994. In '98, President Eyadema was re-elected.

Economy: The principal products are coffee, cocoa, cotton, palm kernels, kapok and groundnuts. Togo's considerable natural resources are still largely undeveloped. Phosphates, now being mined in increasing quantities, form the country's principal export. Industry: Textiles, shoes, handicrafts, agricultural processing.

Mission in India: Honorary Consulate of the Republic of Togo, T & T Motors Ltd., 212, Okhla Industrial Estate, Phase III, New Delhi-110 020; Tel: 26821005-06; Fax:6821013.

E-mail: tnttalwar@vsnl.net and tandt @ ndf. vsnl.net.in

| **World's First National Park** | Six hundred and forty thousand years ago, a massive volcanic eruption took place in present-day Yellowstone Park (Wyoming). The caldera is seventy kilometres long and thirty kilometres wide. Yellowstone became the world's first National Park in 1872. |

174. Tonga

(Kingdom of Tonga)
Puleanga Fakaktui O Tonga

Capital: Nuku'alofa;
Currency: Paanga;
Area: 748 sq.km.;
Population: 104,000;
Languages: English
and Tongan; **Religions:** Christian; **Literacy:** 99.2%; **Life Expectancy:** 73.3; **p.c.i:** $ 7,134; **HDI rank:** 85; **Date of Independence:** 4th June, 1970.
Government Type: Constitutional Monarchy; **Head of State:** King George Tupou V.
PM: Feleti Sevele.
History: Tonga (also called Friendly Islands) consists of 169 islands and islets in the south western Pacific Ocean. The Tropic of Capricorn and the International Dateline cross each other very near Tonga.

First visited by the Dutch in early 17th century, Tonga became a British protectorate in 1900 and independent on June 4, 1970. The island country was admitted to the United Nations in Sept. 1999.

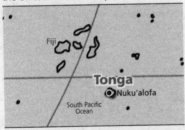

Economy: Tonga is an agricultural country. Crops: coconuts, bananas, vanilla, coffee, ginger. Copra and bananas exported. Industry: Tourism, coconut products, fishing.

175. Trinidad and Tobago

(Republic of Trinidad and Tobago)

Capital: Port-of-Spain; **Other Large Cities:** San Fernando, Arima; **Currency:** Trinidad and Tobago dollar; **Area:** 5128 sq.km.; **Population:** 1,317,714; **Languages:** English; **Religions:** Roman Catholic-26%, Hindu-22.5%, Anglican-7.8%, Baptist-7.2%, Pentecostal-6.8%, other Christian-5.8%, Muslim-5.8%, Seventh Day Adventist-4%, others-10.8%; **Literacy:** 98.7%; **Life Expectancy:** 69.8; **p.c.i:** $ 20,137; **HDI rank:** 59; **Date of Independence:** 31st August, 1962.
Government Type: Parliamentary Democracy; **President:** George Maxwell Richards; **PM:** Kamla Persad-Bissessar.

Trinidad and Tobago are the southernmost islands of the Caribbean archipelago.
History: Formerly a British Colony, it achieved independence in 1962 and became a republic in 1976.

Ethnic profile: African descent 40.8%, Indians 40.7%, mixed races 16.3%, European, Chinese and others 2.2%.
Economy: There are large reserves of petroleum and natural gas. Trinidad and Tobago has the most diversified and industrialised economy in the English- speaking Caribbean. Industries include oil processing, manufactured goods, fertilisers, rum, cement and tourism. Chief crops are sugarcane, citrus fruit, cocoa, coffee and bananas.
Mission in India: High Commission for the Republic of Trinidad and Tobago, B-3/26, Vasant Vihar, New Delhi - 1100057. Tel: 4600 7500; Fax: 4600 7505.

E-mail:admin@hctt.org
Indian Mission in Trinidad and Tobago: High Commission of India, No.6, Victoria

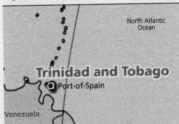

Avenue, Post Box No. 530, Port of Spain, Trinidad and Tobago, West Indies. Tel: 00-1-868-6277480, 6277481; Fax: 00-94-1-868-6276985.

E-mail: hcipos@tstt.net.tt

176. Tunisia

(Republic of Tunisia)
Al Jumhuriyah al Tunisiyah

Capital: Tunis; **Other Large Cities:** Sfax, Sousse; **Currency:** Tunisian dinar; **Area:** 164,150 sq.km.; **Population:** 10,549,100; **Languages:** Arabic (official) and French; **Religions:** Muslim-98%, Christian-1%, Jewish and others-1%; **Literacy:** 77.7%; **Life Expectancy:** 73.9; **p.c.i:** $ 9,488; **HDI rank:** 81; **Date of Independence:** 20th March, 1956.

Government Type: Republic; **President:** Fouad M'bazaa. **PM:** Beji Caid Essebsi.

History: A republic in North Africa, lying on the Mediterranean coast and formerly a French protectorate, Tunisia became autonomous in 1956 and assumed republican status in 1957.

Economy: Crops: wheat, barley, oats, dates, olives, citrus fruits, almonds, figs, vegetables and alfa grass. Minerals: phosphates, iron, lead and zinc. Industry: Oil production, textiles, leather, fertilisers, construction materials, food processing. The principal exports are olive oil, wine, phosphates and grains.

Mission in India: Embassy of the Republic of Tunisia, A-42, Vasant Vihar, New Delhi - 110 057. Tel: 2614 5346, 2614 5349; Fax: 26145301.

E-mail:tunisiaembssy@airtelbroadband.in

Indian Mission in Tunisia: Embassy of India, 4, Place Didon, Notre Dame, Tunis 1002. Tel: 00-216-1-787819; Fax: 00-216-71-787819, 790968, 78182. E-mail:com.tunis@mea.gov.in

177. Turkey

(Republic of Turkey)

Capital: Ankara; **Other Large Cities:** Istanbul, Izmir, Adana, Bursa; **Currency:** Turkish lira; **Area:** 779,452 sq.km.; **Population:** 73,722,988; **Langu-ages:** Turkish, Kurdish, Arabic; **Religions:** Muslim-99.8% (mostly Sunni), other-0.2% (mostly Christians and Jews); **Literacy:** 88.7%; **Life Expectancy:** 71.8; **p.c.i:** $ 13,392; **HDI rank:** 83; **Date of Independence:** 29th October, 1923

Government Type: Republican Parliamentary Democracy; **President:** Abdullah Gul, **PM:** Recep Tayyip Erdogan.

History: Asiatic Turkey, that is, Anatolia, was the seat of one of the earliest civilizations known. Istanbul, the largest city, was first known as Byzantium and then as Constantinople. The Ottoman Turks conquered Consantinople in 1453 and founded a Turkish Empire. The modern secular republic was established in the 1920s by nationalist leader Kemal Ataturk.

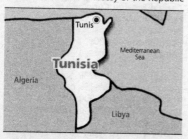

Biggest Producer of Gold

For the first time in over 100 years, in 2008, China became the world's biggest producer of gold. South Africa held the title of the world's biggest gold producer for about a century.

Economy: The chief agricultural products are tobacco, wheat, cotton, olive oil and sugar. Turkey is the world's second largest producer of sultana raisins. Sheep and cattle abound in the plateau of Anatolia and provide mohair for which Turkey is famous. Minerals: iron ore, copper, chromium, bauxite and coal. Industry: Iron, steel, machinery, petroleum, metal products, cars, processed foods.

Mission in India: Embassy of the Republic of Turkey, N-50, Nyaya Marg, Chanakyapuri, New Delhi-110021. Tel:26889053. Fax: 26881409.

E-mail: tbd@vsnl.net

Indian Mission in Turkey: Embassy of India, 77, Cinnah Caddesi, Cankaya, 06680-Ankara, Turkey. Tel: 00-90-312-4382195; Fax:00-90-312-4403429.

E-mail:chancery@indembassy.org.tr

178. Turkmenistan

(Republic of Turkmenistan)
Turkmeno-stan Respublikasy

Capital: Ashkhabad (Poltoratsk); **Other Large Cities:** Chardzhou, Mary; **Currency:** Manat; **Area:** 488,100 sq.km.; **Population:** 5,177,000; **Languages:** Turkmen, Russian; **Religions:** Muslim-89%, Eastern Orthodox-9%, unknown-2%; **Literacy:** 99.5%; **Life Expectancy:** 63.2; **p.c.i:** $ 6,597; **HDI rank:** 87; **Date of Independence:** 27th October, 1991.

Government Type: Presidential Republic; **President & PM:** Gurbanguly Berdimuhammedov.

A former Soviet republic, Turkmenistan is bounded by the Caspian sea on the west. Its neighbours are Uzbekistan, Iran and Afghanistan. The Kara Kum desert occupies 80% of the area.

History: The region became part of Russian Turkestan in 1881 and a republic of the USSR in 1925.

In Oct. 1991, Turkmenistan adopted a

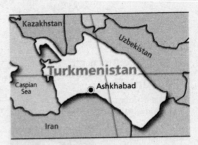

declaration of independence, and became a member of the CIS in Dec.

Economy: Maize, grapes, fruit and vegetables, cotton (key foreign exchange earner), wool, fur are the main agricultural products. Natural resources: Ozocerite, oil, coal, sulphur, salt magnesium. Extensive oil and gas reserves give Turkmenistan an edge over other former Soviet republics. Industry: Food, textile, chemical, cement, agricultural implements, ferroconcrete, footwear, knitwear.

Mission in India: Embassy of Turkmenistan, C-11,West End Colony, New Delhi -110021; Tel: 2411 6527; Fax: 2411 6526.

E-mail:turkmen@airtelmail.in

Indian Mission in Turkmenistan: Embassy of India, Emperyal's International Business Centre,Y, Emre, 1, Mir 2/1, P.O. Box No. 80, Ashgabat, Turkmenistan. Tel: 00-99-312-456152, 456153; Fax: 00-99-312-452434, 456156.

E-mail:indembadm@online.tm

179. Tuvalu

Capital: Funafuti;**Currency:** Australian dollar; **Area:** 26 sq.km.; **Population:** 10,000; **Languages:** Tuvaluan, English; **Religions:** Church of Tuvalu (Congregationalist)-97%, Seventh-Day Adventist-1.4%, Baha'i-1%, others-0.6%; **Literacy:** 74%; **Life Expectancy:** 69.29; **p.c.i:** $ 1,600; **Date of Independence:** 1st October, 1978.

Government Type: Parliamentary De-

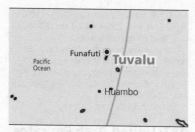

mocracy; **Gov. Gen.:** Iakoba Taeia; **PM:** Willie Telavi.

History: Formerly known as the Ellice Islands, Tuvalu is a scattered group of nine small atolls in the Western Pacific Ocean and one of the world's smallest independent nations. It separated from the British Gilbert and Ellice Islands colony in 1975 under the name Tuvalu. Full independence was granted on October 1, 1978.

Economy: The poor quality of the soil permits subsistence farming of coconuts only. Most of the foreign exchange is earned through the sale of postage stamps and coins, copra and from remittances by Tuvaluans abroad.

Tuvalu was admitted to the UN as its 189th member in Sept., 2000.

180. Uganda

(Republic of Uganda)

Capital: Kampala; **Other Large Cities:** Jinja, Mbale, Masaka, Entebbe; **Currency:** Ugandan shilling; **Area:** 241,139 sq.km.; **Population:** 31,800,000; **Languages:** English, Luganda and Swahili; **Religions:** Roman Catholic-41.9%, Protestant-42%, Muslim-12.1%, other 3.1%, none 0.9%; **Literacy:** 73.6%; **Life Expectancy:** 51.5; **p.c.i:** $ 1,245; **HDI rank:** 143; **Date of Independence:** 9th October, 1962.

Government Type: Republic; **President:** Yoweri Museveni. **PM:** Apollo Nsibambi.

History: Uganda is an equatorial state in East Africa. Formerly a British protectorate, Uganda became independent in 1962 and a republic in 1963. A military coup led by Lt. Gen. Tito Okello ousted Milton Obote's govt. in 1985. Milton Obote had himself come to power after ousting dictator Idi Amin in 1979. In 1972, nearly all of Uganda's 45,000 Asians were expelled.

Economy: The economy is agricultural. Main products are coffee (Africa's biggest producer) and cotton. Industry: Tea, sugar, tobacco, textiles, beer and cement. Minerals: Copper, cobalt. Uganda's economy has become the fastest growing in Africa.

Mission in India: Uganda High Commission, D-5/4, Vasant Vihar, New Delhi-110 057; Tel: 26145602, 26145817; Fax: 26144405.

E-mail:ughcom@ndb.vsnl.net.in

Indian Mission in Uganda: High Commission of India, Plot 11, Kyandonda Road, Nakasero, P.O. Box 7040, Kampala, Uganda. Tel: 00-256-41-4257368, Fax: 00-256-41-4254943.

E-mail:hci@hicomindkampala.org, consular@hicomindkampala.org

181. The Ukraine

(Ukrayina)

Capital: Kiev; **Other Large Cities:** Kharkiv, Donetske, Odessa, Lviv; **Currency:** Hryvnia; **Area:** 603,700 sq.km.; **Population:**

First Arab to Travel in Space	In 1985 Saudi Prince Sultan Ibn Salman travelled aboard the space shuttle Discovery becoming the first Arab and first Muslim to travel in space.

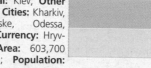

45,778,500; **Languages:** Ukrainian, Russian; **Religions:** Ukrainian Orthodox, Moscow Patriarchate, Kiev Patriarchate, Autocephalous Orthodox, Ukrainian Catholic (Uniate), Protestant, Jewish; **Literacy:** 99.7%; **Life Expectancy:** 67.9; **p.c.i:** $ 6,665; **HDI rank:** 69; **Date of Independence:** 24th August, 1991.
Government Type: Republic; **President:** Viktor Yanukovych; **PM:** Mykola Azarov.
History: The Ukraine in south-west former USSR became independent in 1991. Ukraine was one of the founder members of the CIS.

It is the most densely populated of the former Soviet republics. The second richest former Soviet republic, Ukraine contains some of the richest land in former USSR. It is considered the Soviet wheat belt.

In June, '95, Russia and Ukraine reached agreement on the disputed Black Sea fleet at Sevastopol. In June, 1996, Ukraine became a nuclear weapon-free nation with the transfer of the last of its warheads to Russia. A new constitution legalising private property and establishing Ukrainian as the sole offi-cial language was approved in the same month.
Economy: Wheat, sugarbeet, sunflower, cotton, flax, tobacco, soya, fruit and vegetables, meat and milk are the main agricultural products. Natural resources: Coal, iron ore, manganese, oil, salt and chemicals. Industry: Ferrous metallurgical, chemical, machinery, paper, television, consumer goods and food industries.
Mission in India: Embassy of Ukraine,

No.E-1/8, Vasant Vihar, NewDelhi-110 057; Tel: 26146041, 26146042, Fax: 26146043
E-mail:embassy@bol.net
Web: www. ukraineembassyindia.com
Indian Mission in Ukraine: Embassy of India, 4, Terokhina Street, Padol District, Kyiv-01901, Ukraine. Tel: 00-380-44-4686219; Fax: 00-380-44-4686619.
E-mail:india@public.ua.net

182. United Arab Emirates
Ittihad al-Imarat al-Arabiyah

Capital: Abu Dhabi; **Other Large Cities:** Dubai, Sharjah, Ras al-Khaimah; **Currency:** Dirham; **Area:** 82,880

sq.km.; **Population:** 8,264,070; **Languages:** Arabic; **Religions:** Muslim-96% (Shi'a-16%), Christian, Hindu and others-4%; **Literacy:** 90%; **Life Expectancy:** 78.7; **p.c.i:** $ 36,973; **HDI rank:** 32; **Date of Independence:** 2nd December, 1971.
Government Type: Federation of Emirates; **President:** Sheikh Khalifa bin Zayid Al Nuhayyan; **Vice President and PM:** Muhammed bin Rashid al-Maktum.
History: The United Arab Emirates consist of seven autonomous emirates in the Persian Gulf–Abu Dhabi, Dubai, Sharjah, Umm-al-Qaiwain, Ajman, Fujairah and Ras-al-Khaimah. These were formerly referred to as the 'Trucial States'. Most of the land is barren and sandy. Rainfall is limited and erratic. One-tenth of the population are nomads.

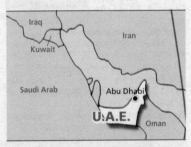

Abu Dhabi, which is the capital of the Union, is the largest of the Emirates in area. Dubai is the main port of the Union and now has the largest harbour in West Asia. Dubai, the commercial hub of the Middle East, is now transforming itself into a manufacturing location and also a cultural, sports, leisure, and shopping centre.

Economy: Both Abu Dabi and Dubai have steadily been diversifying away from oil into such areas of refining and petrochemicals. Dubai has the world's largest single-site aluminium smelter and has a major duty-free zone at Jebel. Tourism is another useful source of income. Dubai's port, airport, and glittering array of hotels, restaurants and shops draw people from all over the region.

Only a tiny proportion of the land area is suitable for agriculture. Crops include dates and alfalfa, along with other fruit varieties and cereals. Besides oil and gas industries, aluminium smelling, trade and financial services are also important.

Mission in India: Embassy of the UAE, EP-12, Chandergupta Marg, Chanakyapuri, New Delhi-110 021. Tel: 24670830, 24670945; Telefax: 26873272.

E-mail:uae_embassy_nd@yahoo.co.in

Indian Mission in UAE: Embassy of India, Plot No.10, Sector W-59/02, Diplomatic Area, Off-Airport Road, P.O.Box No.4090, Abu Dhabi (UAE). Tel: 00-971-2-4492700; Fax: 00-971-2-4444685 .

E-mail:indiauae@emirates.net.ae

183. United Kingdom

United Kingdom of Great Britain and Northern Ireland

Capital: London; **Other Large Cities:** Manchester, Birmingham, Glasgow, Leeds, Liverpool; **Currency:** Pound; **Area:** 244,108 sq km; **Population:** 62,041,708; **Languages:** English, Welsh, Scottish and Gaelic; **Religions:** Christian (Anglican, Roman Catholic, Presbyterian,

Methodist)-71.6%, Muslim -2.7%, Hindu -1%, unspecified or none-23.1%, **Literacy:** 99%; **Life Expectancy:** 79.4; **p.c.i:** $ 35,053; **HDI rank:** 26; **Date of Independence:** 1284.

Government Type: Constitutional Monarchy; **Head of State:** Queen Elizabeth II, **PM:** David Cameron.

History: The UnitedKingdom (UK) constitutes the greater part of the British Isles. Great Britain is the largest of the islands forming the United Kingdom. It comprises England, Scotland, and Wales. The next largest is Ireland, comprising Northern Ireland, which is part of the UK, and the Irish Republic. Western Scotland is fringed by the large island chains known the inner and Outer Hebrides, and to the north of the Scottish mainland are the Orkney and Shetland islands. All these, along with the Isle of Wight, Anglesey and the Isles of Scilly, have administrative ties with the Mainland, but the Isle of Man in the Irish Sea and the Channel Islands between Great Britain and France are largely self-governing, and are not part of the UK. The UK is one of the 25 member states of the European Union (UN).

The United Kingdom's system of government is known as constitutional monarchy, though its constitution is not contained in any one document; instead it has evolved over many years. Ministers of the Crown govern in the name of the Sovereign, who is both head of state and head of the government. Actual power is vested in parlia-

'UK' or 'Britain'?	The full title of this country is 'the United Kingdom of Great Britain and Northern Ireland': Great Britain is made up of England, Scotland and Wales .The United Kingdom (UK) is made up of England, Scotland, Wales and Northern Ireland.

ment which is the supreme legislative body in Great Britain. The parliament consits of two houses -the House of Lords and the House of Commons.

Economy: Britain is one of the world's leading industrial and exporting countries. Chief industries are iron and steel, engineering, chemicals, electronics, motor vehicles, metals, machinery, ship building, aircraft, textiles, cloth, other consumer goods and banking. Metals and metal using industries contribute more than 50% of the exports. Britain's coal mines yield about 128 million tons annually. Although Britain's agriculture and trawler - fishing are highly mechanised, half of the country's food supplies and most of its raw materials are imported. Chief crops: Grains, sugar, fruits, vegetables.

England: Population: 49m. A large overseas empire was established. United with Wales (1536), with Scotland (1707) and with Ireland (1801; partition in 1921) to form United Kingdom.

Wales: The principality of Wales in Western Britain has a population of 2,899,000. Cardiff is the capital. English and Welsh are spoken.

Scotland: Scotland occupies the northern 37% of the main British island, and the Herbrides, Orkney, Shetland, and smaller islands. Population: 5,111,000. Edinburgh is the capital.

Northern Ireland is situated in the northeast of Ireland and forms part of the United Kingdom. It comprises six Ulster counties of Antrim, Down, Armagh, Fermanagh, Londonderry and Tyrone. The rest of the island forms the Republic of Ireland. Northern Ireland has been rocked by bloody agitation for union with Catholic Irish Republic. 1985 saw an Anglo-Irish agreement which for the first time gave Dublin a say in the running of the province. Population: 1,610,000 and Capital: Belfast.

Agriculture is the main occupation in Northern Ireland. Cattle, sheep, hogs, eggs, poultry, potatoes and milk are the important products. Linen, ropes, twines,

rayon, clothing, tobacco, aircraft and shipping form the main branches of industry.

Mission in India: High Commission for Britain, Shantipath, Chanakyapuri, New Delhi-110021. Tel: 0091-11-2419210, 26872161; Fax:0091-11-26870060.

E-mail:postmaster.nedel@fco.gov.uk; Web: www.ukinindia.com

Consulate: Mumbai: British Deputy High Commission, Maker Chambers IV, Second Floor, 222 Jamnalal Bajaj Road, Mumbai-400021,Tel: (91-22)56502222

Kolkata: British Deputy High Commission, 1A Ho. Chi Minh Sarani, Kolkata-700 071, Tel: (91-33) 22885172/22885173-76, E-mail: kolkata@fco.gov.uk

Chennai: British Deputy High Commission, 20, Anderson Road, Chennai-600 006, Tel: (91-44) 52192151

Indian Mission in United Kingdom: High Commission of India, India House, Aldwych, London WC2B 4NA, United Kingdom. Tel: 00-44-207-8368484, 3796242 (After Office); Fax: 00-44-207-8364331.

E-mail:hoc.london@mea.gov.in, fs.hoc@hcilondon.in

Britain's Dependent Territories

Anguilla, Bermuda, British Antarctic Territory, British Virgin Islands, Cayman Islands, Falkland Islands, Gibraltar, Montserrat, Pitcairn, Ducie, Henderson and Oeno, St. Helena and St.Helena Dependencies (Ascension and Tristan da Cunha), South Georgia and the South Sandwich Islands and Turks and Caicos Islands.

Isle of Man and the Channel Islands are direct dependencies of the Crown with their own legislative and taxation systems.

Isle of Man: It is in the Irish sea. **Area:** 572 sq.km. **Population:** 80,000. **Capital:** Douglas.

The Channel Islands: Off the North-West coast of France are Jersey, Guernsey and the dependencies of Guernsey. **Area:** 194 sq.km. **Population:** 152,241.

Anguilla: Formerly Part of St.Kitts-Nevis-Anguilla, it became de facto a separate dependency of Britain in 1969; new consti-

---

Seven Pillars of Wisdom

Colonel T.E. Lawrence, a British soldier, known as Lawrence of Arabia, helped the Arabs to defeat the Turks in the 1914-1918 war. His account of the campaign is written in his book, the *Seven Pillars of Wisdom*.

tution in 1982. **Area:** 155 sq.km. **Population:** 15,236; **Capital:** The Valley.

Bermuda: Bermuda is a group of some 300 small coral islands in the Western North-Atlantic. In a referendum in Aug. '95, Bermudans rejected independence. **Area:** 53.3 sq.km; **Population:** 64,566; **Capital:** Hamilton. **PM:** Ewart Brown. Population is 60% black. Persons of British or Portuguese stock form the rest.

The chief crops are vegetables, flowers, (Easter lilies specially), bananas and citrus fruits. Tourism is the main source of revenue.

Montserrat: Capital: Plymouth; **Currency:** Euro; **Area:** 102 sq.km; **Population:** 6,000; **Languages:** English and Patois; **Literacy:** 97%; **Religions:** Christianity; **p.c.i:** $3127 (1985) **Gov:** Peter A. Waterworth; **Chief Minister:** Lowell Lewis.

From 1871 to 1956, it formed part of the federal colony of the Leeward Islands. The island, a British Associate State with full internal autonomy, adopted a constitution in 1960.

184. United States of America

United States of America

Capital: Washington D.C.; **Other Large Cities:** New York, Los Angeles, Chicago, Houston, Philadelphia, San Diego, Detroit, Dallas, Boston, Miami, Atlanta, Pittsburg, San Francisco; **Currency:** Dollar; **Area:** 9,826,630 sq.km.; **Population:** 311,097,000; **Languages:** English; **Religions:** Protestant-52%, Roman Catholic-24%, Mormon-2%, Jewish-1%, Muslim-1%, other-10%, none-10%; **Literacy:** 99%; **Life Expectancy:** 78.2; **p.c.i:** $ 47,123; **HDI rank:** 4; **Date of Independence:** 4th July, 1776.

Government Type: Federal Republic; **President:** Barack H. Obama

History: The USA is a federal republic composed of a federal district (Washington, D.C.) and 50 states, of which all except one - Hawaii islands - are in mainland America.

The United States of America, which covers the central part of North America, grew out of the British colonies that were established in North America in the first half of the 17th century. The Declaration of Independence of the 13 states of which the American Union then consisted was adopted by Congress on July 4, 1776.

The victory of the Allies in WW-I made USA a world power. The end of the WW-II saw the emergence of USA as one of the superpowers. With the break-up of USSR in 1991, it has now become the only superpower.

The US contains a highly diverse population, the product of numerous and sustained waves of immigration. Ethnic and racial diversity - the "melting pot" - is celebrated as a core element of the American ideology.

The 1964 Civil Rights Act outlawed racial and other discrimination, but race continues to be a live issue.

The election of Barack Obama as the country's first African-American president in November 2008 marked a defining moment in the country's chequered history of race relations.

The Union originally comprised 13 states, to which 7 were added subsequently. Thirty other states, which were formerly territories, were also admitted into the Union as full states, thus making up 50 states in all, apart from the District of Columbia. The following table gives the existing states of the Union with their postal abbreviations, capitals, area and population.

States of the Union

Name	Capital	Area (sq km)	Population (2010)
Alabama (AL)*	Montgomery	133916	4,779,736
Alaska (AK)	Juneau	1530700	710,231
Arizona (AZ)	Phoenix	295260	6,392,017
Arkansas (AR)	Little Rock	137754	2,915,918
California (CA)	Sacramento	411049	37,253,956
Colorado (CO)	Denver	269596	5,029,196
Connecticut (CT)	Hartford	12997	3,574,097
Delaware (DE)	Dover	5294	900,877
District of Columbia (DC)	Washington D.C	179	601,723
Florida (FL)	Tallahassee	151940	18,801,310
Georgia (GA)	Atlanta	152577	9,687,653
Hawaii (HI)	Honolulu	16760	1,360,301
Idaho (ID)	Boise	216431	1,567,582
Illinois (IL)	Springfield	145934	12,830,632
Indiana (IN)	Indianapolis	93719	6,483,802
Iowa (IA)	Des-Moines	145752	3,046,355
Kansas (KS)	Topeka	213097	2,853,118
Kentucky (KY)	Frankfort	104659	4,339,367
Louisiana (LA)	Baton Rouge	123678	4,533,372
Maine (ME)	Augusta	86156	1,328,361
Maryland (MD)	Annapolis	27091	5,773,552
Massachusetts (MA)	Boston	21456	6,547,629
Michigan (MI)	Lansing	151585	9,883,640
Minnesota (MN)	St. Paul	218601	5,303,925
Mississippi (MS)	Jackson	123515	2,967,297
Missouri (MO)	Jefferson city	180515	5,988,927
Montana (MT)	Helena	380849	989,415
Nebraska (NE)	Lincoln	200349	1,826,341
Nevada (NV)	Carson City	286353	2,700,551
New Hampshire (NH)	Concord	24033	1,316,470
New Jersey (NJ)	Treton	20168	8,791,894
New Mexico (NM)	Santa Fe	314923	2,059,179
New York (NY)	Albany	127190	19,378,102
North Carolina (NC)	Raleigh	136413	9,535,483
North Dakota (ND)	Bismarck	183118	672,591
Ohio (OH)	Columbus	107045	11,536,504
Oklahoma (OK)	Oklahoma City	181186	3,751,351
Oregon (OR)	Salem	251419	3,831,074
Pennsylvania (PA)	Harrisburg	117348	12,702,379
Rhode Island (RI)	Providence	3139	1,052,567
South Carolina (SC)	Columbia	80583	4,625,364
South Dakota (SD)	Pierre	199730	672,591
Tennessee (TN)	Nashville	109153	6,346,105
Texas (TX)	Austin	691030	25,145,561
Utah (UT)	Salt Lake City	219888	2,763,885
Vermont (VT)	Montpelier	24900	625,741
Virginia (VA)	Richmond	105587	8,001,024
Washington (WA)	Olympia	176480	6,724,540
West Virginia (WV)	Charleston	62758	1,852,994
Wisconsin (WI)	Madison	145436	5,686,986
Wyoming (WY)	Cheyenne	253325	563,626

*Postal two-letter (both capitals) abbreviations for U.S. states were introduced with the ZIP Code in 1963. These are fast replacing the older abbreviations.

Economy: Agriculture: Main crops are maize, wheat, soyabeans, barley, oats, rice, sugar, potatoes, cotton, tobacco and dairy products. Industries: Iron and steel, food and kindred products, chemicals, metal products, electronic equipment, machinery, transportation equipment, paper, petroleum products, fertilisers, plastics. Minerals: Coal, copper, lead, phosphates, uranium, zinc, gold, silver, iron, molybdenum, oil. Exports: Machinery, chemicals, motor vehicles, aircraft, military equipment, grains, cereals.

Mission in India: Embassy of the USA, American Embassy, Chanakyapuri, New Delhi-110021. Tel: 24198000; Fax: 24190017; Foreign Commercial Service and Library of Congress- 24, Kasturba Gandhi Marg, New Delhi-110 001; Tel: 011-2347-2000.

E-mail: nivnd@state.gov

Consulate: Calcutta: 5/1, Ho Chi Minh Sarani, Calcutta-700 071, West Bengal, Tel: 91 33 39842400 Email: Consular Calcutta@ state.gov; Mumbai: Lincoln House, 78, Bhulabhai Desai Road, Mumbai-400 026, Tel: (22) 2363-3611 Email: mumbai.usconsulte.gov; Chennai: Gemini circle, 220, Anna Salai, Chennai-600 006, Tel : 28574000; Email: chennai.usconsulate.gov

Indian Mission in United States of America: Embassy of India, 2107, Massachu-

---

High-speed Rail Network

China's high-speed rail network is probably the world's most ambitious public-works project, a 21st century equivalent of America's interstate highway system. In 2008 China had only 649km of high-speed railway. It now has nearly 8,400 km.

setts Ave, NW, Washington DC 20008. Tel: 00-1-202-9397000; Fax: 00-1-202-2654351.

E-mail:indembwash@indiagov.org

Outlying Territories

Puerto Rico: (Commonwealth of Puerto Rico); **Capital:** San Juan; **Area:** 13,790 sq.km; **Population:** 3,725,789; **Languages:** Spanish and English; **Religions:** Christianity; **p.c.i:** $17,800
Governor: Luis Fortuno.

The island of Puerto Rico lies 80 km east of Hispaniola (Haiti and Dominican Republics) in the outer Caribbean. In 1952, it ceased to be a colonial possession and became a free Commonwealth. It has close ties with U.S. People have U.S. citizenship with no voting rights.

From a purely agricultural country, Puerto Rico (formerly Porto Rico) is fast changing to an industrial economy and is the wealthiest Caribbean island. "The Poor house of the Caribbean" was changed to an area with one of the highest standards of living in Latin America, thanks to the famous "Operation Bootstrap" begun in the late 40s.

In a referendum in November, 1993, Puerto Ricans said no to total merger with USA.

The main crops are sugar, tobacco and coffee. Industries include textiles, clothing, cigars, alcohol, chemicals and household appliances. Tourism is an important source of revenue.

Guam: Area: 541 sq.km.; **Population:** 180,000; **Capital:** Agana.
Commonwealth of the N.Mariana Is: Area: 477 sq.km.; **Population:** 88,000; **Capital:** Saipan.
American Samoa: Area: 199 sq.km. **Population:** 65,628; **Capital:** Pago Pago.
Other Pacific territories: Johnston Atoll (Two small islands 1150 km. southwest of Hawaii. **Population:** 1200; **Midway Islands** (Two small islands at the western end of the Hawaiian chain. **Population:** 453 (1980), **Wake Island** (Three small islands

3700 k.m. **west of Hawaii. Population:** 302(1980).
Virgin Islands of the United States: Area: 342 sq.km. **Population:** 108,210; Capital: Charlotta Amalie.

185. Uruguay

(Oriental Republic of Uruguay)
Republica Oriental del Uruguay.

Capital: Montevideo; **Other Large Cities:** Salto, Rivera; **Currency:** Uruguayan Peso; **Area:** 176,215 sq.km.; **Population:** 3,356,584; **Languages:** Spanish; **Religions:** Roman Catholic-66%, Protestant-2%, Jewish-1%, non-Professing or others-31%; **Literacy:** 97.9%; **Life Expectancy:** 76.4; **p.c.i:** $ 14,342; **HDI rank:** 52; **Date of Independence:** 25th August, 1825
Government Type: Constitutional Republic; **Head of State & Govt (President):** Jose "Pepe" Mujica Cordano.

The smallest republic in South America, Uruguay lies in southern S. America, on the Atlantic Ocean.
History: Formerly a part of the Spanish Viceroyalty of Rio de la Plata and subsequently a province of Brazil, Uruguay became independent on Aug. 25, 1825. After a military coup of 1976, civilian government was restored in 1985.
Economy: Livestock-raising is Uruguay's prinicipal occupation and takes up 60 per cent of its total land area. The chief products are meat, wool, hides, corn, wheat, citrus fruit, rice, tobacco, oats and linseed.

| First Operas | The world's first operas were composed in Italy at the end of the sixteenth century. Opera reached the height of popularity in the nineteenth century, when the works of Gioacchino Rossini, Giacomo Puccini, and Giuseppe Verdi became hugely popular. |

Important industries are vinery, meatpacking, textiles, cement and oil products.

Socialist measures were adopted as far back as 1911. The welfare programmes earned Uruguay a reputation as the Switzerland of Latin America.

Mission in India: Embassy of Uruguay, A-16/2, Vasant Vihar, New Delhi-110057, Tel: 26151991, 26151992; Fax: 2614 4306.

E-mail:uruind@del3.vsnl.net.in

186. Uzbekistan

Ozbekiston Republikasy

Capital: Tashkent; **Other Large Cities:** Samarkhand, Namangan; **Currency:** Som; **Area:**447,400sq.km.; **Population:** 27,794,000; **Languages:** Uzbek, Russian; **Religions:** Muslim-88% (mostly Sunnis), Eastern Orthodox-9%, others-3%; **Literacy:** 96.9%; **Life Expectancy:** 67.2; **p.c.i.:** $ 3,022; **HDI rank:** 102; **Date of Independence:** 1st September, 1991.

Government Type: Republic; **President:** Islam A. Karimov; **PM:** Shavkat Mirziyayev. **History:** A former Soviet republic that became independent in 1991, Uzbekistan is bordered by Kazakhstan, Kyrgyzstan, Tajikistan, Afghanistan and Turkmenistan. **Economy:** Agriculture: Uzbekistan has an excellent record in agriculture. Intensive farming, based on artificial irrigation is practised. It is the chief cotton-growing area in former Soviet Union and the third in the world. It produced 65% of the total cotton, 50% of the total rice and 60% of the total lucerne grown in the former union. Crops: cotton, lucerne, grain, potatoes, vegetables, grapes, fruit and berries. Natural resources: Oil, coal, copper, ozocerite, building materials. Industry: Agricultural machinery, cement, textiles, paper, ferroconcrete.

The Roman alphabet (in use 1929-40) was re-introduced in 1994.

Mission in India: Embassy of the Republic of Uzbekistan, EP-40, Radhakrishnan Marg, Chanakyapuri, New Delhi-110021, Tel: 24670774, 24670775, 24105640; Fax: 24670773. E-mail:info@uzbekembassy.in

Indian Mission in Uzbekistan: Embassy of India, 15-16, Kara-Bulak, (Vakhshskaya) Street, Mirzo Ulugbek District, Uzbekistan. Tel: 00-998-71-1400983/97/98; Fax: 00-998-71-1400999/87.

E-mail: indhoc@buzton.com, indiaemb@buzton.com, consind@buzton.com

187. Vanuatu

(Republic of Vanuatu)
Ripablik Blong Vanuatu

Capital: Vila; **Currency:** Vatu; **Area:** 14,760 sq km; **Population:** 246,000; **Languages:** English, French and Bislama; **Religions:** Presbyterian-31.4%, Anglican-13.4%, Roman Catholic- 13.1%, indigenous beliefs-5.6%, Seventh-Day Adventist-10.8%, other Christian-13.8%, others-9.6%; **Literacy:** 78.1%; **Life Expectancy:** 70; **p.c.i:** $4,807; **Date of Independence:** 30th July, 1980.

Government Type: Parliamentary Republic; **President:** Iolu Johnson Abil; **PM:** Sato Kilman.

History: The Anglo-French condominium of the New Hebrides became independent under the name Vanuatu on July 30, 1980. It is a double chain of 13 large and 80 small islands in South West Pacific. The largest island is the Espiritu Santo. Originally a haunt of European pirates, they came under the control of

[Map showing Uzbekistan with labels: Aral Sea, Kazakhstan, Uzbekistan, Tashkent, Smarkhand, Turkmenistan, Tajikistan]

| Fashion's Capital | Italy is among the world's leaders of the fashion industry. In the 1950s, Italian designers such as Nino Cerruti and Valentino led the world in creating stylish fashions. Additionally, Armani, Versace, Gucci, and Prada have become internationally recognized. |

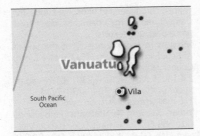

France and Britain in 1906. The population is overwhelmingly Melanesian.

Economy: The major cash crops are copra, coffee and cocoa. Vanuate is a popular tourist destination in the South Pacific.

Industry: Fish-freezing, meat canneries, tourism. Manganese has been mined since 1961 and exported to Japan.

188. Venezuela

(Bolivarian Republic of Venezuela)
Republica Bolivariana de Venezuela

Capital: Caracas; **Other Large Cities:** Maracaibo, Valencia; **Currency:** Bolivar; **Area:** 912,050 sq. km.; **Population:** 29,168,000; **Languages:** Spanish; **Religions:** Nominally Roman Catholic-96%, Protestant-2%, others-2%; **Literacy:** 95.2%; **Life Expectancy:** 73.7; **p.c.i:** $ 11,889; **HDI rank:** 75; **Date of Independence:** 5th July, 1811. **Government Type:** Federal Republic; **Head of State & Govt. (President):** Hugo Chavez.

History: Venezuela (Little Venice) on the Caribbean coast is the northernmost state of South America. Sighted by Columbus in 1498, it was formerly a Spanish colony. Venezuela became independent in 1811 and a republic in 1830. Military strongmen ruled Venezuela for most of the 20th century. Since 1959, it has had democratically elected governments. Venezuela is the richest and most urbanised Latin American nation.

Economy: Venezuela, a member of the OPEC, is one of the world's leading producers of oil and the largest oil exporter outside the Middle East. Venezuela is rich in diamonds and ranks 8th in world production. Other minerals are iron, steel, aluminium, copper, tin and manganese. Agricultural products include coffee, cocoa, bananas, maize, rice and sugar.

Mission in India: Embassy of Venezuela, N-114, Panchshila Park, New Delhi-110 017. Tel: 26496535, 26496783; Fax: 26491686.
E-mail:embavene@del2.vsnl.net.in

Indian Mission in Venezuela: Embassy of India, Quinta Tagore, No.12, Avenoda San Carlos, La Floresta, Apartado de Correo 61585, Chacao 1060, Caracas, Venezuela. Tel: 00-58-212-2857887; Fax: 00-58-212-5865131.
E-mail:admin1.caracas@mea.gov.in
Website: http://www.embindia.org

189. Vietnam

(Socialist Republic of Vietnam)
Cong Hoa Xa Hoi Chu Nghia Viet Nam

Capital: Hanoi; **Other Large Cities:** Ho Chi Minh City, Haip-Hong, Hue; **Currency:** Dong; **Area:** 329,566 sq. km; **Population:** 86,930,000; **Languages:** Vietnamese, French, English, Chinese; **Religions:** Buddhist, Hoa Hao, Cao Dai, Christian (predominantly Roman Catholic, Some Protestant), indigenous beliefs, Muslim; **Literacy:** 90.3%; **Life Expectancy:** 74.2; **p.c.i:** $ 3,123; **HDI**

Dollarisation and Goldisation	Vietnam is home to a large stock of dollars, many of them remittances by migrant workers, and a sizable stock of gold. Vietnam's banks offer dollar deposits and in Ho Chi Minh City, a bank has even installed an ATM that dispenses gold bars.

rank: 113; **Date of Independence:** 2nd September, 1945.

Government Type: Communist State; **President:** Nguyen Minh Triet; **PM:** Nguyen Tan Dung

History: The Socialist Republic of Vietnam (comprising former North and South Vietnam) is a mountainous country in south east Asia. Running almost its entire length, is a mountain chain–the Annamite Chain. On one side of the mountain chain is the fertile Red River delta in the north and on the other side is the Mekong delta in the south. The two deltas form the rice bowl of the country.

Vietnam War was fought mainly in South Vietnam from 1954 between US backed government forces and Viet Cong. guerrillas supported by North Vietnam and Soviet armaments. US support of south began in 1961 and intensified from 1964. War formally concluded in 1973 but guerrilla activities continued in South. South Vietnam fell to communist forces in 1975 and gradual political reintegration followed. The unification of North and South Vietnam into the socialist Republic of Vietnam took place formally on July 2,1976. The Northern capital, flag, anthem, emblem and currency were applied to the new state.

After 3 million died defending their country, women outnumber men three to one in Vietnam.

Economy: The country is primarily agricultural. Rice is the dominant crop and an export item. Other crops are rubber, sugarcane, coffee, maize and tea. Minerals include coal, tin, copper, chromium and phosphate. Industry: Cement, metallurgy, chemicals, paper, food processing and textiles.

Mission in India: Embassy of the Socialist Republic of Vietnam, 17, Kautilya Marg, Chanakyapuri, New Delhi-110021. Tel: 23018059 (Visa Section), 23019818 (Ambassa-dor's Office); Fax: 91-11-23017714.
E-mail:sqvnindia@yahoo.com

Indian Mission in Vietnam: Embassy of India, 58-60, Tran Hung Dao, Hanoi, Vietnam. Tel: 00-84-4-38244989; Fax: 00-84-4-38244998.
E-mail:india@netnam.org.vn

190. Yemen

(Republic of Yemen)
Al Jumhuriyah al Yamaniyah

Capital: Sana'a; **Currency:** Rial; **Capital** (Commercial and winter): Aden; **Area:** 531,000 sq km; **Population:** 22,492,035;

Languages: Arabic; **Religions:** Muslim including Shaf'i (Sunni) and Zaiydi (Shi'a), small numbers of Jew, Chistian, and Hindu; **Literacy:** 58.9%; **Life Expectancy:** 62.7; **p.c.i:** $ 2,595; **HDI rank:** 133; **Date of Independence:** 22nd May, 1990.

Government Type: Republic; **President:** Col. Ali Abdullah Saleh **PM:** Ali Muhammad Mujawwar.

History: North and South Yemen merged in May 1990 into a United Republic of Yemen in the south west of the Arabian peninsula. North Yemen was established in 1962 while South Yemen (formerly Aden and the Protectorate of South Arabia) became independent in 1967.

Centuries ago Yemen was a rich land of exotic spices, frankincense and myrrh. The legendary Queen of Sheba ruled the kingdom then known as Happy Yemen. South Yemen became the Arab world's only Marxist nation after independence.

In 1994, regional clan-based rivalries led to full-scale civil war. On May 5, S.Yemen

Victoria Falls — In November 1855 Dr David Livingstone, the Scottish explorer and missionary, saw the Victoria Falls for the first time. Livingstone named the Falls after the British queen, Victoria.

Zambia, a landlocked republic in south central Africa, takes its name from the River Zambezi, one of its biggest rivers. Originally known as Northern Rhodesia, it is separated from Zimbabwe by the Zambezi river. Kariba Dam, one of the biggest man-made dams in the world, is on the Zambezi river where it makes the border between Zambia and Zimbabwe.

declared itself an independent state, breaking away from united Yemen. The 2-month war ended on July 7, when Aden, fell to the northern forces. Losses caused by the conflict is estimated at $3 b.

Economy: The main agricultural products are coffee, dates, herbs, fruits, wheat, millet and maize. Cotton, coffee, hides and skins are exported. Industries: Food processing, mining and petroleum refining.

Mission in India: Embassy of the Republic of Yemen, D-2/5, Vasant Vihar, New Delhi-110 057, Tel: 42705723; Fax: 42705725

E-mail: yemenemb.india@gmail.com

Indian Mission in Yemen: Embassy of India, Building No. 12, Djibouti Street,Off Hadda Street,Sana'a,Republic of Yemen. Tel: 00-967-1-441251, 441252; Fax: 00-967-1-441257.

E-mail:indiaemb@y.net.ye

191. Zambia

(Republic of Zambia)

Capital: Lusaka; **Other Large Cities:** Kitwe, Chingola; **Currency:** Kwacha; **Area:** 752,620 sq km; **Population:** 13,046,508;

Languages: Bantu and English; **Religions:** Christian-50-75%, Muslim and Hindu-24-49%, indigenous beliefs-1%; **Literacy:** 70.6%; **Life Expectancy:** 42.4; **p.c.i:** $ 1,625; **HDI rank:** 150; **Date of Independence:** 24th October, 1964.

Government Type: Republic; **President:** Rupiah Banda.

History: Zambia, under the administration of the South Africa Company from 1889 to 1924, became independent republic within the Commonwealth republic in 1964. In the 1980s, decline in copper prices hurt the economy. June 1990 witnessed severe violence caused by food riots. One-party rule came to an end with October 1991 elections.

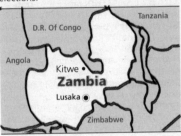

Over 500,000 children had been orphaned by the AIDS epidemic by the late 1990s.

Economy: Maize, tobacco, millet, cassava, groundnuts, cotton and sugar are produced. The country is rich in minerals including copper, zinc, cobalt, lead, uranium and manganese. Although copper mining dominates Zambia's economy, the country made a major shift to agricultural production, as a result of the crippling fluctuations of copper prices in the world market.

Mission in India: High Commission of the Republic of Zambia, E-86, Paschimi Marg,Vasant Vihar, New Delhi-110 057. Tel: 26145883, 26145764; Fax:26145764.

E-mail:zambiand@sify.com

Indian Mission in Zambia: High Commission of India, 1, Pandit Nehru Road, P.O. Box

| City of Petra | Johann Ludwig Burckhardt, the Swiss explorer, discovered the city of Petra in Jordan and the famous temple at Abu Simbel in Egypt. |

32111, Lusaka, Zambia. Tel:00-260-211-253159/60; Fax: 00-260-1-254118.
E-mail:cons.lusaka@mea.gov.in

192. Zimbabwe

(Republic of Zimbabwe)

Capital: Harare; **Other Large Cities:** Bulawayo, Gweru; **Currency:** Zimbabwe Dollar; **Area:** 390,272 sq km; **Population:** 12,644,000; **Languages:** English, Shona and Ndebela; **Religions:** Syncretic (partly Christian, partly indigenous beliefs)-50%, Christian-25%, indigenous beliefs-24%, Muslim and others-1%; **Literacy:** 91.2%; **Life Expectancy:** 43.5; **p.c.i:** $ 395; **HDI rank:** 169; **Date of Independence:** 18th April, 1980
Government Type: Parliamentary Democracy; **President:** Robert G.Mugabe. **PM:** Morgan Tsvangirai
History: Zimbabwe (formerly Southern Rhodesia) achieved independence after a bitter struggle agai-nst the white minority government in power.

A referendum rejected the new draft constitution in early 2000. In April, the constitution was amended to give the Govt. the right to seize white-owned farms without compensation. Mugabe, armed with the new law, went ahead with his plans to confiscate 804 farms belonging to Whites, to be redistributed to ordinary Zimbabweans. In June, 2000 election, Mugabe's party scored a narrow win.
Economy: Zimbabwe is rich in minerals notably copper, nickel, gold, asbestos, chrome and coal. Its platinum deposits are the world's largest. Industries include food processing, metals, textiles, furniture and engineering. Maize, groundnuts, cotton and tobacco are the chief crops, tobacco being the most important one.

Zimbabwe is home to the Victoria Falls, one of the natural wonders of the world, the stone enclosures of Great Zimbabwe - remnants of a past empire - and to herds of elephant and other game roaming vast stretches of wilderness
Mission in India: High Commission of the Republic of Zimbabwe, E-12/7, Vasant Vihar, New Delhi-110057, Tel: 26140430, 26140431; Fax:26154316.

E-mail:zimdelhi@vsnl.net
Indian Mission in Zimbabwe: High Commission of India, No. 12, Natal Road, Belgravia, Post Box 4620, Harare, Zimbabwe.
Tel: 00-263-4-795955; Fax: 00-263-4-795958.
E-mail:mailto:hci@samara.co.zw, hoc@embindia.org.zw

193. South Sudan

Capital: Juba; **Other Large Cities:** Kaohsiung, Taichung; **Currency:** South Sudanese Pound; **Area:** 619,745 sq.km.; **Population:** 8,260,490; **Languages:** Arabic, English, Juba Arabic, Nuer, Zande, Bari, Shilluk; **Religions:** Christian, Islam; **Literacy:** 27%.
President: Salva Kiir Mayardit.

South Sudan is a landlocked country in East Africa. It is bordered by Sudan to the north, Ethiopia to the east, Uganda and Kenya to the southeast, Democratic Republic of the Congo to the southwest; and the Central African Republic to the west. South Sudan includes the vast swamp region of the Sudd formed by the White Nile, locally called the Bahr al Jebel.

A referendum on independence for South Sudan was held in January 2011, with 98.83% of the electorate opting for secession. The President of Sudan, Omar al-Bashir, accepted the results and issued a Republican Decree confirming the outcome of the referendum.South Sudan became an independent country on 9 July 2011.Upon independence, the country was named Republic of South Sudan.
Economy: Industry and infrastructure are severely underdeveloped and poverty is wide-

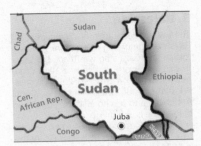

spread. Subsistence agriculture provides a living for the vast majority of the population. South Sudan has little infrastructure - just 60 km of paved roads. Electricity is produced mostly by costly diesel generators and running water is scarce. South Sudan depends largely on imports of goods, services, and capital from the north. Despite these disadvantages, South Sudan does have abundant natural resources.

South Sudan produces nearly three-fourths of the former Sudan's total oil output of nearly a half million barrels per day. The government of South Sudan derives nearly 98% of its budget revenues from oil. It also holds one of the richest agricultural areas in Africa in the White Nile valley, which has very fertile soils and more-than-adequate water supplies. Currently the region supports 10-20 million head of cattle.

South Sudan also contains large wildlife herds, which could be exploited in the future to attract eco-tourists. And the White Nile has sufficient flow to generate large quantities of hydroelectricity. Long term problems include alleviating poverty, maintaining macroeconomic stability, improving tax collection and financial management.

Non-UN Members

1. Turkish Cyprus

Turkish Republic of Northern Cyprus

Capital: Nicosia; **Currency:** Euro; **Area:** 3355 sq.km; **Population:** 264,172 (2006 census); **Languages:** Turkish.
President: Mehmet Ali Talat; **PM:** Ferdi Sabit Soyer.

The Turkish - controlled area of Northern Cyprus unilaterally declared independence in 1983. It has been named 'Turkish Republic of Northern Cyprus.' The Republic is not internationally recognised although it does have trade relation with some countries. There is a 50-strong Legislative Assembly.

2. Kosovo

(Republic of Kosovo)

Capital: Pristina; **Other large Cities:** Prizren, Pec; **Currency:** Euro; **Area:** 10,857sq km; **Population:** 2,126,708;
Languages: Albanian, Serbian, Bosniak, Turkish, Roma; **Religions:** Muslim, Serbian Orthodox, Roman Catholic; **Literacy:** 94%; **Life Expectancy:** 64; **p.c.i.:** $1,800; **Date of Independence:** 17th February, 2008; **Government Type:** Republic; **Head of State:** Fatmir Sejdiu; **Head of Government:** Hashim Thaci.
History: Kosovo, an impoverished territory with a population of mainly ethnic

Visas to the US   Almost 5% of Jamaica's population of 2.7m applies for an American visa each year; around half are successful.

Albanians,unilaterally declared independence from Serbia in February 2008.The territory immediately won recognition from the United States and major European Union countries. But Serbia, with the help of Russia, has vowed to block Kosovo from getting a United Nations seat.In a grounbreaking ruling on July 22, 2010 , the International Court of Justice (ICJ) said that Kosovo's unilateral declaration of independence from Serbia in Februay 2008 did not violate international law.

Serbia's defeat at the battle of Kosovo in 1389 ushered in centuries of rule under the Muslim Ottoman empire. Serbia regained control of Kosovo in 1913, and the province was incorporated into the Yugoslav federation. Serbs and ethnic Albanians vied for control in the region throughout the 20th century.

Economy: Kosova's people are the poorest in Europe. Remittances from the diaspora account for about 30% of GDP. Economic growth is largely driven by the private sector -mosly small-scale retail businesses. Minerals and metals -including lignite, lead, zinc, nickel, chrome, aluminium, magnesium, and a wide variety of construction materials - form the backbone of the industry. Unemployment -at more than 40% of the population - is a severe problem that encourages outward migration.

3. Palestine

The historic declaration of an independent Palestine comprising West Bank of river Jordan and Gaza strip was made by Yassar Arafat, leader of Palestine Liberation Organisation (PLO) on Nov.15,1988 in Algiers. Palestine's headquarters were in Tunis until Arafat came to Jericho in 1994. Population of Palestine is 3.5 m.

PLO was founded in 1964 to express the nationalist aspirations of Palestinian Arabs. In 1974, the UN granted it permanent observer status and in 1976, PLO became a regular member of the Arab League.

About 80 nations including India immediately recognised the new nation, which was born out of struggle extending over forty years.

However, in Israel, the government of the right-wing Likud Bloc and the left-leaning Labour Party with Yitzhak Shamir as Prime Minister still refused to recognise PLO as the legitimate representative of the Palestinian people.

In the 47-year old Arab-Israeli conflict, the demand of Palestinians had been an independent homeland in the West Bank (preferred Palestinian term, Northern District) and Gaza with capital in Jerusalem.

The Oslo Accords of the early 1990s between the Palestine Liberation Organisation and Israel led to the creation of the Palestinian Authority. This was an interim organisation created to administer a limited form of Palestinian self-governance in the territories for a period of five years during which final-status negotiations would take place. The Palestinian Authority carried civil responsibility in some rural areas, as well as security responsibility in the major cities of the West Bank and Gaza Strip. Although the five-year interim period expired in 1999, the final status agreement has yet to be concluded despite attempts such as the 2000 Camp David Summit, the Taba Summit, and the unofficial Geneva Accords.

In 2005, Israeli forces withdrew from the Gaza Strip, ceding full effective internal control of the territory to the Palestinian

Born Abroad — Over 26% of Australia's 22m population were born abroad, compared with 21% in Canada, 14% in America and 10% in Britain.

Authority. Former Palestinian Prime Minister Mahmoud Abbas, the candidate of the Fatah faction, won the January 2005 poll to replace the late Palestinian leader Yasser Arafat. The surprise victory of the militant Islamic movement Hamas in parliamentary polls in January 2006 led to heightened tension between the Palestinian factions. In February 2007, Hamas and Fatah agreed to form a government of national unity.

However, in June 2007 Hamas took control of the Gaza Strip, seriously challenging the concept of a coalition, which Abbas subsequently dissolved. Thus, the Gaza Strip and the West Bank, are divided into a Hamas leadership in the Gaza Strip and a Fatah civil leadership in the autonomous areas of the West Bank. Each sees itself as the administrator of all Palestinian territories and does not acknowledge the other one as the official government of the territories. The Palestinian territories have therefore de facto split into two entities.

Mission in India: Embassy of the State of Palestine, D-1/27 Vasant Vihar, New Delhi - 110057. Tel: 26142859, 26146605; Telefax: 26142942.

E-mail: embassy@ palestineindia.com

Indian Mission in Palestine: Representative office of India, 182-49, Shurta Street, Al Remal, P.O. Box. 1065, Gaza City, State of Palestine. Tel: 00-972-87-2825423, 2838199; Fax: 00-972-87-2825433.

E-mail: roi_gaza@trendline.co.in

4. Sahrawi Arab Demo. Rep. (S.A.D.R.)

Capital: El-Alaiun; **Currency:** Euro; **Area:** 266,000 sq.km; **Population:** 382,617; **Languages:** Arabic; **Religions:** Islam.

President: Mohammed Abdel Aziz; **PM:** Mohamm-ed Lamine.

History: The Saharawi Arab Democratic Republic set up by the Polisario Front, a liberation movement in Western Sahara, is a territory that came under Morocco's control after Spain withdrew. Algeria supported the Polisario-led struggle for independence. India accorded recognition to the new gov-

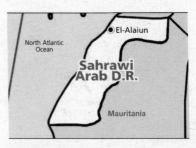

ernment on Oct. 1, 1985.

The UN will conduct a referendum in Western Sahara on whether the territory should become independent or remain part of Morocco.

Economy: Western Sahara has rich phosphate deposits. Most of the land is desert.

5. Taiwan

(Republic of China) Chung-hua Min-kuo

Capital: Taipei; **Other Large Cities:** Kaohsiung, Taichung; **Currency:** Euro; **Area:** 35,981 sq.km.; **Population:** 23,164,457; **Languages:** Mandarin Chinese, Taiwan, Hakka dialects; **Religions:** Buddhist, Confucian and Taoist-93%, Christian-5%; **Literacy:** 96.1%; **Life Expectancy:** 77.96; **p.c.i:** $ 34,743.

Government Type: Democracy; **President:** Ma Ying-jeou. **PM:** Wu Den-yih.

Taiwan, off southeast coast of China, includes the island of Taiwan, two off-shore islands Quemoy and Matsu, and the nearby islets of the Pescadores chain.

History: Originally Taiwan and adjoining areas were Chinese territory. In 1950, Chiang Kai Shek made Taiwan the headquarters of the Nationalist Republic of China. Although Taiwan still claims to be the legal government of China it lost its membership in the UN and its permanent seat in the Security Council to Communist China in 1971. In 1987, martial law was lifted after 38 years and in 1991, the 43-year period of emer-

The Lion Monument The 800 Swiss Guards of the King of France were all killed on August 10th 1792 during the French revolution protecting the King against French Sans Cullotes (the lower classes). A memorial was carved in stone in Luzern as a tribute - the Lion Monument.

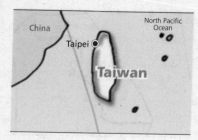

gency rule ended. In May, '96 Lee Teng-Hui stormed to a resounding victory in the island's first direct presidential election.

According to an official source, Taipei wants to be reunited with China, but not at present. Taiwan is interested in joining international organisations. In Aug. '99, China accused Taiwanese President Lee Teng-Hui of taking a 'dangerous' step towards splitting the country. Teng-Hui said 'One China' was possible but only under a democratic union with China's mainland. China threatened to invade Taiwan if the President's statehood call was made the official stand.

Economy: Taiwan has one of the world's strongest economies and is among the 10 leading capital exporters. Taiwan has foreign exchange reserves worth over $175b.

The main agricultural products are rice, tea, sugar, sweet potatoes, bananas, jute and turmeric. Camphor secured from forests is a government monopoly. Industries comprise iron works, glass, soap, textiles, clothing, electronics, chemicals, plastics and processed foods. Coal, marble, petroleum and natural gas are the principal minerals. Taiwan has made big progress in agriculture and industry and the living standards have gone high, as a result of land reform, government planning, free universal education and U.S. aid and investment.

6. Vatican City

(The Holy See) Sato della Cittadel Vaticano
Capital: Vatican City; **Area:** 0.4 sq. km.; **Po-**

pulation: 800; **Languages:** Latin and Italian; (All languages accepted); **Religions:** Roman Catholic; Literacy: 100%.; **Date of Independence:** 11th February, 1929.
Government Type: Ecclesiastical; **Supre-me Pontiff:** Pope Benedict XVI (Cardinal Joseph Ratzinger). **Secretary of State:** Cardinal Tarcisio Bertone.

The Vatican is the smallest independent state in the world and the residence of the spiritual leadership of the Roman Catholic church.Its territory is completely surrounded by the Italian capital Rome, while priests

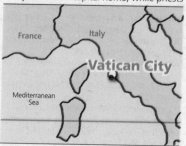

and nuns of many nationalities make up much of the resident population.

Vatican City, the City of the Pope, includes St. Peter's Cathedral, Vatican Palace and Museum, the Vatican Gardens and neighbouring buildings. Vatican has its own railway station (for freight only), postal system, police, coins and radio.Radio Vaticana broadcasts an extensive service in 34 languages.

The city state is governed by a commission appointed by the Pope, who has full legal, executive and judicial powers. The reason for its existence is to provide an extra-territorial, independent base for the Holy See, the government of the Roman Catholic Church.

Country that Locks its Gates

Vatican City is the only nation in the world that can lock its own gates at night. It has its own phone company, radio, T.V. stations, money, and stamps. It even has its own army, the historic Swiss Guard.

The United Nations

International Organisation which is the hope and conscience of the world.

The United Nations (UN), which emerged in 1945 from the devastation of global conflict, aims to "save succeeding generations from the scourge of war".

Its mission is to maintain international peace and security and to promote friendly relations between countries.

The UN Charter upholds human rights and proposes that states should work together to overcome social, economic, humanitarian and cultural challenges.

Background

The UN's predecessor, the League of Nations, was established after the 1914-18 World War.

It aimed to prevent another global conflict, but it failed to halt the slide towards war in the 1930s and was disbanded in 1946.

Civil war in Liberia prompted the UN's biggest troop deployment .

Much of the league's structure and many of its aims were adopted by its successor.

In 1944 the US, Britain, the Soviet Union and China met in Washington and agreed on a blueprint for a proposed world organisation.

The blueprint formed the basis of talks in 1945 between representatives from 50 countries. Under the terms of the resulting charter the UN came into being on 24 October 1945. United Nations Day is celebrated on 24 Oct. each year.

The United Nations is the hope and con science of the world, more especially of the smaller nations among its 192 members.

New Member States are admitted by the General Assembly on the recommendation of the Security Council. Tuvalu was admitted in Sept, 2000 as the 189th member. East Timor was admitted as a member of the UN in September, 2002. Switzerland joined the world organisation in the same month. Montenegro became a UN member on 28 June, 2006.

In 1971 Communist China was admitted as the representative of all China. Red China thus became a permanent member of the Security Council. Taiwan lost its primary membership of the UN. Vatican is a permanent observer.

Official languages of the UN are: Arabic, Chinese, English, French, Russian and Spanish.

Flag of the UN: On the flag is the UN emblem in white centred on a light blue ground.

The UN has a post office originating its own stamps. Some 63,450 people work in the UN system.

The Secretary General Kofi Annan and the UN were jointly given the Nobel Prize for Peace in 2001.

United Nations

League of Nations	The first world organization of countries was the League of Nations, founded after the World War I (back then it was called the Great War or the War to End All Wars). The aim of the League of Nations was to prevent the repeat of the war.

Headquarters: First Avenue, UN Plaza, New York City, N.Y. 10017, USA.

Principal Organs of the UN are: General Assembly, Secretariat, Security Council, Trusteeship Council, Economic and Social Council and International Court of Justice.

General Assembly

The Assembly consists of the representatives of all the member states. Each state has one vote, but may send 5 representatives. The General Assembly meets at least once in a year. It elects its own President and Vice Presidents every year.

Security Council

Security Council consists of 15 members, each of which has one vote. There are five permanent and 10 non-permanent members elected for a 2-year term by a two-thirds majority of the General Assembly. The permanent members have the power to veto any move. Retiring members are not eligible for immediate re-election.

The Presidency of the Security Council is held for one month in rotation by the member states in the English alphabetical order of their names.

Permanent Members: China, France, Russia, UK, USA. Non-permanent Members: Austria, Japan, Mexico, Turkey, Uganda (until Dec. 31, 2010), Bosnia Hercegovina, Brazil, Gabon, Lebanon, Nigeria until Dec.31,2011).

The expansion of the Security Council to include 'new powers' such as India, Germany and Japan as permanent members has been suggested by various fora.

Economic and Social Council

ECOSOC was established under the United Nations Charter as the principal organ to coordinate economic, social, and related work of the 14 UN specialized agencies, functional commissions and five regional commissions. The Council also receives reports from 11 UN funds and programmes. The Economic and Social Council (ECOSOC) serves as the central forum for discussing international economic and social issues, and for formulating policy recommendations addressed to Member States and the United Nations system.

Trusteeship Council

The Charter provides for an international trusteeship system to safeguard the interests of the inhabitants of territories which are not yet fully self-governing and which may be placed thereunder by individual trusteeship agreements. These are called trust territories.

All of the original 11 trust territories have become independent or joined independent countries.

Members: China, France, Russia, UK, USA.

International Court

The International Court of Justice was created by an international treaty, the Statute of the Court, which forms an integral part of the United Nations Charter. All members of the United Nations are ipso facto parties to the Statute of the Court. There are 15 judges. Headquarters : The Peace Palace,

Signing of the UN Charter

On October 24, 1945, the United Nations officially came into existence when its Charter was ratified by the five permanent members of the Security Council and a majority of other 46 member countries.

2517 KJ The Hague, Netherlands.

The 15 judges are elected for 9-year terms by the General Assembly and the Security Council. Retiring judges are eligible for re-election. The court remains permanently in session, except during judicial vacations. All questions are decided by majority.

Website: http://www.icj-cij.org

President : Hisashi Owada (Japan)

Registrar: Philippe Couvreur (Belgium)

The Court has its seat at The Hague, but may sit elsewhere whenever it considers this desirable. The expenses of the Court are borne by the UN.

Languages: French and English.

The Secretariat

The Secretariat is composed of the Secretary-General, who is the chief administrative officer of the organisation and an international staff appointed by him under regulations established by the General Assembly. However, the Secretary General, the High Commissioner for Refugees and the Managing Director of the Fund are appointed by the General Assembly. HQ : United Nations Plaza, New York, NY 10017, USA.

Ban Ki-moon

Website: http://www.un.org

Secretary-General: The current Secretary-General is Ban Ki-moon of South Korea. He became Secretary-General on 1 January 2007, and his first term will expire on 31 December 2011.

Dr. Asha-Rose Migiro of Tanzania took office as Deputy Secretary-General of the United Nations on 1 February 2007. She is the third Deputy Secretary-General to be appointed since the post was established in 1997.

In addition to the 18 independent specialised agencies, there are some 14 major United Nations programmes and funds devoted to achieving economic and social progress in the developing countries.

United Nations Development Programme

United Nations Development Programme (UNDP), is the world's largest agency for multilateral, technical and pre-investment co-operation. It is the funding source for most of the technical assistance provided by the United Nations system.

HQ: New York

Administrator : Helen Clark (New Zealand)

United Nations Children's Fund

United Nations Children's Fund (UNICEF), established in 1946 as United Nations International Children's Emergency Fund to deliver post-war relief to children, now concentrates its assistance on development activities aimed at improving the quality of life for children and mothers in developing countries.

HQ: New York

Executive Director:Anthony Lake (USA)

The UN Fund for Population Activities

The UN Fund for Population Activities (UNFPA), established in 1969, carries out programmes in over 130 countries and territories. The Fund's aims are to build up capacity to respond to needs in populaton and family planning.

Executive Director: Dr. Babatunde Osotimehin (Nigeria).

UN Environment Programme (UNEP)

Established in 1972, it works to encourage sustainable development through sound environmental practices.

Executive Director: Achim Steiner (Germany).

Relief Agencies

Among the organisations involved in relief activities are the Office of the UN Disaster

Origin of the Name	The name "United Nations" was proposed by US President Franklin Delano Roosevelt to Winston Churchill back in 1942. Churchill was in Washington, D.C. then - in fact, he was sitting in a bathtub when FDR was wheeled into the bathroom and proposed the name.

Relief Co-ordinator (UNDRO), the Office of the UN High Commissioner for Refugees (UNHCR) and the UN Relief and Works Agency for Palestine Refugees in the Near East (UNRWA).

Commissioner-General: Filippo Grandi.

United Nations High Commissioner for Refugees

United Nations High Commissioner for Refugees (UNHCR) was established by the UN General Assembly with effect from 1 Jan. 1951.

For its work on behalf of refugees around the world, UNHCR was awarded the Nobel Peace Prize in 1955 and again in 1981.

HQ : Palais de Nations, 1211, Geneva 10, Switzerland.

High Commissioner: Antonio Guterres (Portugal)

High Commissioner for Human Rights

The post was established in 1993. The Commission has 53 members.

High Commissioner : Navanethem Pillay (South Africa)

Specialised Agencies

International Atomic Energy Agency

International Atomic Energy Agency (IAEA), came into existence on 29 July 1957. Member States: 145.

HQ : Vienna International Centre, P.O. Box 100, A-1400 Vienna, Austria.

Director-General: Yukiya Amano (Japan).

Website: http://www.iaea.or.at/worldatom

United Nations Industrial Development Organisation

United Nations Industrial Development Organisation (UNIDO), provides developing and underdeveloped countries with advice on all aspects of industrial policy. Converted into a specialised agency of UN in 1985.

HQ: Vienna International Centre, P.O.Box 300, A-1400 Vienna, Austria.

Director-General: Kandeh Yumkella (Sierra Leone)

Website: http://www.unido.org

Food and Agriculture Organisation (FAO)

The UN Conference on Food and Agriculture in May 1943, at Hot Springs, Virginia, set up an Interim Commission in Washington in July 1943 to plan the FAO, which came into being on 16th October 1945. Sponsors the World Food Programme.

HQ: Viale delle Terme di Caracalla, 00100 Rome, Italy.

Director-General: Jacques Diouf (Senegal)

Website: http://www.fao.org

United Nations Educational, Scientific and Cultural Organisation (UNESCO)

A Conference for the establishment of an Educational, Scientific and Cultural Organisation of the United Nations was convened by the Government of the UK in association with the Government of France, and met in London, 1 to 16 Nov. 1945. UNESCO came into being on 4 Nov. 1946.

HQ : UNESCO House, 7 Place de Fontenoy, 75352 Paris 07SP, France.

Director General: Irina Bokova (Bulgaria).

Website: http://www.unesco.org

World Health Organisation (WHO)

An International Conference, convened by the UN Economic and Social Council, to consider a single health organisation resulted in the adoption on 22 July 1946 of the constitution of the WHO.

HQ : Avenue Appia 20, CH-1211 Geneva 27, Switzerland

Director-General: Dr. Margaret Chan(China)

Website: http://www.who.int

International Development Association (IDA)

A lending agency which came into existence on 24 Sept., 1960. Administered by

Rockefeller's Gift The land of the United Nations Headquarters in New York City was purchased from real estate mogul William Zeckendorf with money donated by John D. Rockefeller, Jr.

the World Bank, IDA is open to all members of the Bank.

International Finance Corporation

International Finance Corporation (IFC) is an affiliate of the World Bank. Established in July 1956.

HQ: 1850 ISt., NW, Washington, D.C., 20433, USA. Website:http://www.ifc.org

Executive Vice President & CEO: Lars H. Thunell (Sweden)

International Civil Aviation Organisation

International Civil Aviation Organisation (ICAO) formed in Nov–Dec. 1944.

HQ: 999, University Street, Montreal, PQ, Canada H3C 5H7.

Secretary-General: Raymond Benjamin (France)

Website: http://www.icao.org

Universal Postal Union

Universal Postal Union (UPU) was established on 1 July, 1875, when the Universal Postal Convention adopted by the Postal Congress of Berne on 9 Oct. 1874 came into force.

HQ: Weltpoststrasse 4, 3000 Berne 15, Switzerland.

Director-General: Edouard Dayan (France)

Website: http://www.upu.int

International Telecommunication Union(ITU)

The International Telegraph Union, founded in Paris in 1865, and the International Radiotelegraph Union, founded in Berlin in 1906, were merged by the Madrid Convention of 1932 to form the ITU.

HQ: Place des Nations, CH-1211 Geneva-20, Switzerland.

Secretary-General: Dr. Hamadoun Toure (Turkey)

Website: http://www.itu.int

International Labour Organisation

International Labour Organsation (ILO) established in 1919 as an autonomous part of the League of Nations, is an intergovernmental agency with a tripartite structure, in which representatives of governments, employers and workers participate. In 1969 the organisation won the Nobel Peace Prize. Has 183 members.

HQ: International Labour Office, CH-1211, Geneva 22, Switzerland.

Director-General: Juan Somavia (Chile).

Website: http://www.ilo.org

World Meteorological Organisation (WMO)

Conference of Directors of the International Meteorological Organisation (set up in 1873), meeting in Washington in 1947, adopted a convention creating the WMO.

HQ: Case Postale 2300, CH-1211 Geneva-2, Switzerland.

Secretary-General:Alexander Bedritsky (Russia)

The International Maritime Organisation

The International Maritime Organisation (IMO) was established as a specialised agency of the UN by the UN Maritime Conference at Geneva in Feb./Mar. 1948.

HQ: 4 Albert Embankment, London SEI 7SR, UK. Website: http://www.imo.org

Secretary-General: Efthimios Mitro-poulos (Greece)

World Intellectual Property Organisation (WIPO)

The Convention establishing WIPO was signed at Stockholm in 1967 by 51 countries, and came into force in April 1970. In Dec. 1974 WIPO became a specialised agency of the UN.

HQ: 34, Chemin des Colombettes, 1211 Geneva 20, Switzerland.

Website:http://www.wipo.int

Director-General: Francis Gurry (Australia).

Secretary-General to Die in Office

Dag Hammarskjöld was killed in a mysterious plane crash. He is the only UN Secretary-General to die in office and the only person ever to be awarded the Nobel Peace Prize posthumously.

International Fund for Agricultural Development (IFAD)

The agency began its operations in Dec 1977.

HQ: 107 Via del Serafico, Rome 00142, Italy.

President:Kanayo F. Nwanze(Nigeria).

Website: http://www.ifad.org

International Organisations

African Union

The African Union is a union consisting of 53 African states. The only all-African state not in the AU is Morocco. Established on 9 July 2002, the AU was formed as a successor to the Organisation of African Unity (OAU). The most important decisions of the AU are made by the Assembly of the African Union, a semi-annual meeting of the heads of state and government of its member states.

HQ:POB 3243, Addis Ababa, Ethiopia.

Official languages: Arabic, English French, Portuguese , Spanish, Swahili and any African language.

Chairman: Teodoro Obiang Nguema Mbasogo(Equatorial Guinea)

The Arab League

The League of Arab States, or Arab League, is a voluntary association of countries whose peoples are mainly Arabic speaking. It was formally instituted on March 22, 1945.

The League considers itself a regional organisation within the framework of the UN at which its Secretary-General is an observer.

Member countries (21): Algeria, Bahrain, Comoros, Djibouti, Egypt, Iraq, Jordan, Kuwait, Lebanon, Mauritania, Morocco, Oman, Palestine L.O., Qatar, Saudi Arabia, Somalia, Sudan, Syria, Tunisia, UAE, and Republic of Yemen.

HQ : Al Tahrir Square, Cairo, Egypt.

The Secretariat has its seat in Cairo.

Secretary General: Nabil el-Araby(Egypt).

Asia-Pacific Economic Co-operation

Members (21): Australia, Brunei, Canada, Chile, China, Hong Kong, Indonesia, Japan, Malaysia, Mexico, New Zealand, Papua New Guinea, Peru, Philippines, Russia, Singapore, South Korea, Taiwan, Thailand, the U.S. and Vietnam.

The Asia-Pacific Economic Co-operation (APEC) was founded in 1989 to further co-operation on trade and investment between nations of the region and the rest of the world. Headquarters: Singapore.

Website: www.apec.org.

The Asian Development Bank

The Asian Development Bank (ADB) is a regional development bank established on 22 August 1966 to facilitate economic developmentof countries in Asia. It has 67 member countries–48 regional and 19 non-regional members.

In June 1974, ADB launched the Asian Development Fund (ADF) with a view to providing concessional credits to needy members.

HQ: 6 ADB Avenue, Mandaluyong, Metro Manila, Philippines.

President: Haruhiko Kuroda (Japan).

Website: http://www.adb.org

The Association of South East Asian Nations

Members (10): Brunei Darussalam, Cambodia, Indonesia, Laos, Malaysia, Myanmar, Philippines, Singapore, Thailand, Vietnam.

Newest Member | **The newest member of the United Nations is South Sudan, which became the 193rd member on July 14, 2011. Besides member states, there is one non-member observer state, the Holy See in Vatican City.**

The Association of South East Asian Nations (ASEAN) is a regional organisation formed by the governments of Indonesia, Malaysia, the Philippines, Singapore and Thailand through the Bangkok Declaration which was signed by the Foreign Ministers of ASEAN countries on 8th Aug., 1967. Its aim is to accelerate economic progress and maintain the economic stability of South East Asia. Members in addition to the above five: Brunei, Cambodia, Laos, Myanmar, Vietnam.

HQ: POB 2072, Jakarta 12110, Indonesia.

Secretary-General: Surin Pitsuwan (Thailand)

Website: http://www.asean.or.id

Caribbean Community and Common Market (CARICOM)

Members: Antigua and Barbuda, Bahamas, Barbados, Belize, Dominica, Grenada, Guyana, Haiti, Jamaica, Montserrat, Saint Kitts and Nevis, Saint Lucia, Saint Vincent and the Grenadines, Suriname, and Trinidad and Tobago. Associate members in 2007 were Anguilla, Bermuda, British Virgin Islands, Cayman Islands, and Turks and Caicos Islands.

Established in 1973. Its aim is to increase co-operation in economics, health, education, culture, science and technology and tax administration, as well as the coordination of foreign policy.

HQ: Bank of Guyana Building, PO Box 10827, Georgetown (Guyana).

Secretary-General: Edwin W. Carrington (Trinidad and Tobago)

Website:http://www.caricom.org

Commonwealth of Independent States

Commonwealth of Independent States (CIS) is an organization formed in 1991 whose participating countries are former Soviet Republics, formed during the breakup of the Soviet Union.

It has 10 full members and one participating member Ukraine. Full members are Armenia, Azerbaijan, Belarus, Kazakhstan, Kyrgyzstan, Moldova, Russia, Tajikistan, Turkmenistan, Uzbekistan.

HQ:220000 Minsk, Kirava 17, Belarus

Website: http://www.cis.minsk.by

Executive Secretary: Sergei Lebedev.

The Commonwealth

Formerly known as the British Commonwealth of Nations, the Commonwealth is a loose associaton of former British colonies, dependencies and other territories - and Mozambique, which has no historical ties to Britain.

The Commonwealth has no constitution or charter, but the heads of government of its member states hold Commonwealth Heads of Government Meetings(CHOGM) every two year to discuss issues of common interest.

Founded: 1931; Members: 53 states

HQ (Secretariat): Marlborough House, Pall Mall, London. SW1Y 5HX,UK.

Secretary-General: Kamalesh Sharma (India).

Website:http://www.thecommonwealth.org

East African Community

East african Community came into force on on July 1st 2010. The member states of Burundi, Kenya,Rwanda, Tanzania and Uganda hope their common market will promote freer movement of labour, money and services,and maybe eventually the adoption of a common currency. But observers are not expecting thecountries' lucrative customs posts to be dismantled.

European Union known as the European Community

Members (27): Austria, Belgium, Bulgaria, Cyprus, Czech Republic, Denmark, Estonia, Finland, France, Germany, Greece, Hungary, Ireland, Italy, Latvia, Lithuania, Luxembourg, Malta, Poland, Portugal, Romania, Slovakia, Slovenia, Spain, Swe-den,

The Netherlands, United Kingdom.

The European Union (EU) is a sui generis political body, made up of 27 member states.

European Union was known as the European Community (EC) until 1994. The name covers 3 organisations with common membership: the European Economic Community (Common Market), European Coal and Steel Community, and European Atomic Energic Community (Euratom). The European Union covers a large part of the continent of Europe. Between 1973 and 2007 there have been six waves of enlargement bringing the current membership up to 27. The founding members of the community were Belgium, Netherlands and Luxembourg (who already co-operated as Benelux countries), France, Italy and West Germany. In 1973 the communities enlarged to include Denmark, Ireland and the United Kingdom. Greece, Spain and Portugal joined in the 1980s. In 2004, its membership increased from 15 to 25. The ten new countries which joined the EU in 2004 are: Cyprus, the Czech Republic, Estonia, Hungary, Latvia, Lithuania, Malta, Poland, Slovakia and Slovenia. Bulgaria and Romania joined in 2007. Expansion is almost certain to continue. There are five official Candidate countries, Croatia, Iceland, Macedonia, Montenegro and Turkey. Albania, Bosnia and Herzegovina and Serbia are officially recognised as potential candidates.

The euro is the currency of 17 European Union countries: Belgium, Estonia, Germany, Greece, Spain, France, Ireland, Italy, Luxembourg, the Netherlands, Austria, Portugal, Slovenia, Finland, Cyprus, Malta and Slovakia.

HQ: 200 rue de la Loi/Wetstraat, B-1049 Brussels, Belgium

President, European Commission: Jose Manuel Barroso.

Sec. Gen.: Catherine Day

Website: http://www.europa.eu.int

European Economic Area

European Economic Area (EEA) came into existence from Jan. 1, 1994 as a preliminary step of a proposed merger of European Free Trade Area and EC over the coming decade.

European Space Research Organisation

European Space Research Organisation (ESRO) was formally established in 1964 to promote collaboration among European States in space research and technology exclusively for peaceful purposes. The members are Belgium, Denmark, France, West Germany, Italy, the Netherlands, Spain, Sweden, Switzerland and UK. Austria, Ireland and Norway participate as observers.

HQ: Paris.

French Community

French Community offers to the French overseas territories, which manifest their will to adhere to it, new institutions based on the common idea of liberty, equality and fraternity and conceived with a view to their democratic evolution.

Independent members of the Community are: French Republic, Central African Republic, Republic of Congo, Gabon, Senegal, Chad, Madagascar, & Djibouti.

Group of Eight

With no headquarters, budget or permanent staff, the Group of Eight is an informal but exclusive body whose members set out to tackle global challenges through discussion and action. The G8 comprises seven of the world's leading industrialised nations, and Russia.

- Founded: 1975, Rambouillet, France
- Original Members: France, Germany, Italy, Japan, UK, US.
- Later Members: Canada (joined at 1976 summit, San Juan, Puerto Rico), Russia (joined at 1998 summit, Birmingham, UK)

| Diplomatic Missions | Belgium has the 2nd highest concentration of diplomatic missions after Washington, D.C. |

G-20

The G-20 (more formally, the Group of Twenty Finance Ministers and Central Bank Governors) is a group of finance ministers and central bank governors from 20 economies: 19 of the world's largest national economies, plus the European Union (EU). Collectively, the G-20 economies comprise 85% of global gross national product, 80% of world trade (including EU intra trade) and two-thirds of the world population.

The G-20 operates without a permanent secretariat or staff. The chair rotates annually among the members and is selected from a different regional grouping of countries.

There are 20 members of the G-20. These include the finance ministers and central bank governors of 19 countries:Argentina, Australia, Brazil, Canada, China, France, Germany, India, Indonesia, Italy, Japan, Mexico, Russia, Saudi Arabia, South Africa, South Korea,Turkey, United Kingdom, United States. The 20th member is the European Union, which is represented by the rotating Council presidency and the European Central Bank.

Gulf Co-operation Council (GCC)

Members (6): Saudi Arabia, Kuwait, the United Arab Emirates, Oman, Qatar and Bahrain The Gulf Co-operation council, or GCC, is a loose political and economic alliance made up of six Gulf states. It aims to boost economic cooperation between members and, through collective security, to guard against any threat from neighbouring states and from islamic terrorism.

The GCC was formed in May 1981 against the backdrop of the Islamic revolution in Iran and the Iraq-Iran war. Its members share similar political systems and a common social and cultural outlook. They are autocratic monarchies or sheikhdoms, with limited or non-existent political participation.

On May 10, 2011, a request by Jordan to join the GCC was formally being considered and Morocco was invited to join the council.

HQ: Riyad (Saudi Arabia).

Sec. Gen: Abdullatif bin Rashid Al-Zayani (Bahrain)

The International Air Transport Association

The International Air Transport Association (IATA) was founded in 1945 to promote safe, regular and economical air transport and to provide a forum for collaboration. Members are international and domestic airlines.

Main offices: IATA Centre, Route de l' Aeroport 33, PO Box 416,CH-1215 Geneva, Switzerland; 800 Place Victoria, PO Box 113, Montreal, Quebec, Canada H4Z 1M1; 77 Robinson Road, #05-00 SIA Building, Singapore 068896.

Director-General: Giovanni Bisignani

Website: http://www.iata.org

International Bank for Reconstruction and Development (IBRD)

Conceived at the Bretton Woods Conference, July 1944, the 'World Bank' began operations in June 1946. The World Bank is a vital source of financial and technical assistance to developing countries around the world. The World Bank is made up of two unique development institutions owned by 185 memeber countries - The International Bank for Reconstruction and Development (IBRD) and the International Development Association (IDA).

HQ: 1818 H. St. NW, Washington, D.C., 20433, USA

President: Robert B. Zoellick

Website: http://www.worldbank.org

International Monetary Fund (IMF)

The International Monetary Fund was established on 27 Dec. 1945 as an independent international organisation and began operations on 1 March 1947. The IMF aims

| The Golden Road to Samarkand | *The Golden Road to Samarkand* **is a poem by James Elroy Flecker: We travel not for trafficking alone: By hotter winds our fiery hearts are fanned: For lust of knowing what should not be known, We make the Golden Journey to Samarkand.** |

to preserve economic stability and to tackle-or ideally prevent - financial crises. Over time, its focus has switched to the developing world. HQ : 700 19th St. NW, Washington, D.C, 20431, USA. Offices in Paris and Geneva.

Christine Lagarde

Managing Director: Christine Lagarde (France)

Website: http://www.imf.org

INTERPOL

Interpol is the world's largest international police organisation, with 188 member countries. Created in 1923, it facilitates cross-border police co-operation, and supports and assists all orga-nisations, authorities and services whose mission is to prevent or combat international crime.

HQ: Quai Charles de Gaulle, 69006 Lyon, France.

Secretary-General: Ronald K. Noble

Website: http://www.interpol.int

Mercosur

Mercosur is South America's leading trading bloc. Known as the Common Market of the South, it aims to bring about the free movement of goods, capital, services and people among its member states.

North Atlantic Treaty Organisation (NATO)

Members (28): Albania,Belgium, Bulgaria, Canada,croatia,Czech Republic, Denmark, Estonia, France, Germany, Greece, Hungary, Iceland, Italy, Latvia, Lithuania, Luxembourg, Netherlands, Norway, Poland, Portugal, Romania, Slovakia, Slovenia, Spain, Turkey, United Kingdom, United States.

Formed in 1949 to counter the threat of post-war communist expansion as the Soviet Union sought to extend its influence in Europe, Nato is the world's most powerful regional defence alliance.

The original twelve members of NATO in 1949 were the United States, the United Kingdom, Canada, France, Denmark, Iceland, Italy, Norway, Portugal, Belgium, Netherlands and Luxembourg. The organisation expanded to include Greece and Turkey in 1952 and West Germany in 1955. However, then, as now, the alliance was militarily dominated by the United States.

The Czech Republic, Hungary and Poland became the first former Warsaw pact countries to gain Nato membership in 1999. The next historic step came in 2004 when Estonia, Latvia and Lithuania, republics of the USSR until its collapse in 1991, along with Slovenia, Slovakia, Bulgaria and Romania were welcomed as Nato members at a ceremony in Washington.

Bosnia, Montenegro and Serbia have joined Nato's partnership for peace programme - a first step towards membership.

HQ : NATO, 1110 Brussels, Belgium.

Secretary-General: Anders Fogh Rasmussen (Denmark)

Website:http://www.nato.int

Organisation of American States (OAS)

The Organization of American states or OAS, aims to fosterdemocracy, security, human rights and economic integration among its members. The Charter of the OAS was adopted in April 1948, at Bogota. There are 34 members.

HQ: 17th Street and Constitution Avenue, NW, Washighton, D.C., 20006, USA.

Website: http://www.oas.org

Secretary-General: Jose Miguel Insulza (Chile)

Organisation of Arab Petroleum Exporting Countries (OAPEC)

The organisation has 11 members including Egypt which was readmitted in 1989. Other members: Algeria, Bahrain, Egypt, Qatar, Libya, Iraq, Kuwait, UAE, Syria, Saudi Arabia, Tunisia.

Truly One World

As recently as 1890, almost no country required its nationals to have appropriate documents to travel abroad, and only a few countries (such as Persia, Romania, Russia, and Serbia) required foreigners to have passports to cross their borders.

Secretary-General: Abbas Ali Naqi (Kuwait)

Website: http://www.oapecorg.org

Organisation for Economic Co-operation and Development

Members(34): Australia, Austria, Belgium, Canada, Chile, Czech Republic, Denmark, Estonia, Finland, France, Germany, Greece, Hungary, Iceland, Ireland, Israel, Italy, Japan, Luxembourg, Mexico, Netherlands, New Zealand, Norway, Poland, Portugal, Slovakia, Slovenia, South Korea, Spain, Sweden, Switzerland, Turkey, UK, and the U.S.

Organisation for Economic Co-operation and Development (OECD) was formed in 1961 to replace the Organisation for European Economic Co-operation (OEEC) which was started immediately after the WWII for the reconstruction of war-ravaged European states. The OECD also collects and disseminates economic and environmental information.

HQ : 2, rue Andre Pascal, 75775 Paris Cedex 16, France.

Secretary General: Jose Angel Gurria (Mexico) (Canada)

Website: http://www.oecd.org

Organisation of Islamic Cooperation (OIC)

The Organisation was established in 1969. It has 57 members including Palestine.

The supreme body meets every third year. It aims to promote Islamic solidarity and co-operation.

Address: PO Box 5925, Jeddah, Saudi Arabia

Secretary General: Ekmeleddin Ihsanoglu (Turkey)

Website: http://www.oic-un.org

Organisation of Petroleum Exporting Countries (OPEC)

Members (12): Algeria, Angola, Ecuador, Iran, Iraq, Kuwait, Libya, Nigeria, Qatar, Saudi Arabia, United Arab Emirates and Venezuela.

Opec, the Organisation of Petroleum Exporting Countries created in Sept., 1960, attempts to set world oil prices by controlling oil production. It also pursues members' interests in trade and development deal-ings with industrialised oil-consuming nations.

HQ: Obere Donaustrasse 93, A-1020 Vienna, Austria.

Website: http://www.opec.org

Secretary-General: Abdalla Salem El-Badri(Libya)

Non-Aligned Movement

The Non-Aligned Movement (NAM) is made up of 118 developing countries and aims to represent the political, economic and cultural interests of the developing world. The principles of non-alignment were defined in the Bandung (Indonesia) Declaration of 1955 and reiterated in the Brioni (Yugoslavia) Declaration of 1956 by Jawaharlal Nehru, Josip Broz Tito, and Gamel Abdil Nasser. The first Non-aligned Conference was held at Belgrade in 1961 in which 25 countries participated. The basic thrust of the movement is in favour of peace, disarmament, development, independence, eradication of poverty and illiteracy.

Chair: Egypt.

South Asian Association for Regional Co-operation

South Asian Association for Regional Co-operation (SAARC), comprises India, Maldives, Pakistan, Bangladesh, Sri Lanka, Bhutan, Nepal and Afghanistan.. It was launched following the Dacca Summit in early December 1985.

HQ: POBOX: 4222, Kathmandu, Nepal.

Secretary-General: Fathimath Dhiyana Saeed(Maldives)

The Shanghai Cooperation Organisation (SCO)

The Shanghai Cooperaton Organisation (SCO) is an intergovernmental organisation which was founded on June 14, 2001

| Founding of the EEC | The Belgian politician, Paul Henri Spaak helped found the EEC and was Chairman of the group that signed the Treaty of Rome in 1957. |

by the leaders of China, Russia, Kazakhstan, Kyrgyzstan, Tajikistan and Uzbekistan. Except for Uzbekistan the other countries had been members of the Shanghai Five; after the inclusion of Uzbekistan in 2001, the members renamed the organisation.

The main goals of the SCO are strengthening mutual confidence and good-neighbourly relations among the member countries; promoting their effective cooperation in politics, trade and economy, science and technology, culture as well as education, energy, transportation, tourism, environmental protection and other fields; making joint efforts to maintain and ensure peace, security and stability in the region; to move towards the establishment of a new, democratic, just and rational political and economic international order.

Secretary General: Muratbek Sansyzbayevich Imanaliyev (Kyrgyzstan)

World Trade Organisation

The World Trade Organisation (WTO) is an international body whose purpose is to promote free trade by persuading countries to abolish import tariffs and other barriers. As such, it has become closely associated with globalisation.

Based in Geneva, the WTO was set up in 1995, replacing another international organisation known as the General Agreement on Tariffs and Trade (GATT). The WTO has a much broader scope than GATT regulated trade in merchandise goods, the WTO also covers trade in services, such as telecommunications and banking and other issues such as intellectual property rights.

Membership of the WTO now stands at 153 countries. China formally joined the body in December 2001 after a 15-year battle. HQ : Centre William Rappard, 154 rue de Lausanne, CH-1211 Geneva 21, Switzerland.

Website: http://www.wto.int

Director General: Pascal Lamy (France)

Non-governmental Organisations

Amnesty International

A world-wide human rights organisation, established on May 28, 1961 with a newspaper appeal by the British lawyer Peter Berenson. Now it has more than 3 million supporters, members and activists in more than 150 countries and territories who campaign to end grave charges of human rights. It won the Nobel Prize for Peace in 1977.

International Secretariat: 99-119 Rosebery Avenue, London, EC1R 3RE, UK

Secretary General: Salil Shetty (India)

Website: http://www.amnesty.org

Red Cross

International Society for relief of suffering in time of war or disaster. International Committee of Red Cross was founded (1863) on advocacy of J.H. Dunant (1828-1910). Delegates from 14 countries adopted Geneva Convention (1864), providing for neutrality of personnel treating wounded etc. Over 100 national Red Cross societies now exist. Awarded Nobel Peace Prize (1917, 1944, 1963).

HQ: 19 avenue de la Paix, CH-1202 Geneva, Switzerland

President: Jakob Kellenberger

Website: http://www.icrc.org

Scouts and Guides

Scouting is a worldwide organised movement for young people started by an Englishman, Lieutenant General Sir Robert S.S. Baden-Powell (1857-1941) in 1907. He gave boys out-door skills which he had illustrated well in his book explaining scouting, tracking and map-making skills. The movement's goals include encouraging good character, loyalty to God and country, service to other people and physical and mental fitness. "Be Prepared" is the slogan. The World Scouts Bureau is in Geneva, Switzerland.

A similar movement for girls – the Girl Guide Movement – was founded by Baden-Powell and his sister Agnes in 1910.

| Execution of a Nurse | Edith Cavell, the famous British nurse, was executed in Brussels during the First World War for helping Allied soldiers to escape to the Netherlands. |

World Languages

There are thousands of languages in the world, but most of them have few speakers compared with the major tongues. Some experts predict that between 50 and 90 percent of the world's languages will become extinct this century. Languages need at least 100,000 speakers to survive.

Rank	Language	Speakers (Millions)
1.	Chinese	1,213
	Chinese, Gan	20.6
	Chinese, Hakka	30.0
	Chinese, Huizhou	4.6
	Chinese, Jinyu	45.0
	Chinese Mandarin	845
	Chinese, Min Bei	10.3
	Chinese, Min Dong	9.1
	Chinese, Min Nan	47.3
	Chinese, Min Zhong	3.1
	Chinese, Wu	77.2
	Chinese, Xiang	36.0
	Chinese Yue	55.5
2.	Spanish	329
3.	English	328
4.	Arabic	21
5.	Hindi	182
6.	Bengali	181
7.	Portuguese	178
8.	Russian	144
9.	Japanese	122
10.	German, Standard	90.3
11.	Javanese	84.6
12.	Lahnda	78.3
	Punjabi, Western	62.6
	Seraiki	13.8
13.	Telugu	69.8
14.	Vietnamese	68.6
15.	Marathi	68.1
16.	French	67.8
17.	Korean	66.3
18.	Tamil	65.7
19.	Italian	61.7

Rank	Language	Speakers (Millions)
20.	Urdu	60.6
21.	Turkish	50.8
22.	Gujarati	46.5
23.	Polish	40.0
24.	Malay	39.1
	Malay	10.3
25.	Bhojpuri	38.5
26.	Awadhi	38.3
27.	Ukrainian	37.0
28.	Malayalam	35.9
29.	Kannada	35.3
30.	Maithili	34.7
31.	Sunda	34.0
32.	Burmese	32.3
33.	Oriya	31.7
34.	Persian	31.4
35.	Marwari	31.1
36.	Punjabi (Eastern)	28.2
37.	Filipino	25.0
38.	Hausa	25.0
39.	Tagalog	23.9
40.	Romanian	23.4
41.	Indonesian	23.2
42.	Dutch	21.7
43.	Sindhi	21.4
44.	Thai	20.4
45.	Pushto	20.3
46.	Uzbek	20.3
47.	Rajasthani	20.0
48.	Yoruba	19.4
49.	Azerbaijani	19.1
50.	Igbo	18.0

Source: Ethnologue: Languages of the World

Highest Number of Languages	**Papua New Guinea has the highest number of spoken languages in the world. There are 830 indigenous languages spoken in this country. The official language is Tok Pisin, or New Guinea Pidgin, and is the most widely spoken language after English.**

Top 30 Countries by Number of Living Languages

Rank	Country	No. of Languages	Rank	Country	No. of Languages
1.	Papua New Guinea	830	16.	Sudan	134
2.	Indonesia	722	17.	Chad	133
3.	Nigeria	521	18.	Tanzania	129
4.	India	445	19.	Nepal	127
5.	United States	364	20.	Myanmar	116
6.	Mexico	297	21.	Vanuatu	114
7.	China	296	22.	Vietnam	108
8.	Cameroon	279	23.	Côte d'Ivoire	93
9.	Democratic Republic of the Congo	217	23.	Peru	93
10.	Australia	207	25.	Laos	89
11.	Brazil	193	26.	Ethiopia	88
12.	Philippines	181	27.	Thailand	85
13.	Canada	169	28.	Ghana	84
14.	Malaysia	145	29.	Colombia	83
15.	Russian Federation	135	30.	Central African Republic	82

World Religions

Religions evolved as a set of beliefs concerning the cause, nature and purpose of the universe and grew as an organised system of beliefs that bound people to become a close-knit society.

Religion	World Population
1. Christianity	2.1 billion
2. Islam	1.3 billion
3. Secular / Nonreligious/Agnostic/Atheist	1.1 billion
4. Hinduism	900 million
5. Chinese traditional Religions	394 million
6. Buddhism	376 million
7. primal-indigenous	300 million
8. African Traditional & Diasporic	100 million
9. Sikhism	23 million
10. Juche	19 million
11. Spiritism	15 million
12. Judaism	14 million
13. Bahai	7 million
14. Jainism	4. 2 million
15. Shinto	4 million
16. Cao Dai	4 million
17. Zoroastrianism	2.6 million
18. Tenrikyo	2 million
19. Neo-Paganism	1 million
20. Unitarian-Universalism	800,000
21. Rastafarianism	600,000
22. Scientology	500,000

Guardian of the Geneva Conventions — **The International Committee of the Red Cross, or ICRC, is the guardian of the Geneva Conventions - the system of humanitarian safeguards that sets out the way in which wars may be fought.**

Civil Services: a Gateway to Distinction

B.S. Warrier
Expert in Education and Careers

Civil Services help you reach positions of authority and prestige. The glamour attached to these jobs is palpable. It is a route that thousands of youngsters would like to take. The salient features of the new CSAT are discussed here.

"Civil Services", to many youngsters, is synonymous with the office of the District Collector. This is so, perhaps for the reason that the Collector happens to be the most visible face of the Services, wielding powers on various matters touching our everyday life. The District Collector is indeed a crucial cogwheel in the administrative machine of the government, and often considered as the most empowered office in the country. But it is only an office held by a member of the IAS for a few years during the first half of his service. There are many other services which one can enter through the competitive skills proved in the Civil Services Examination (CSE) held annually by the Union Public Service Commission. However, the popular misnomer "IAS Examination" persists.

Structure of the Civil Services Examination

The emergence of the CSAT (Civil Services Aptitude Test) is the significant change that has come in recent times in CSE. This has taken effect from CSE 2011. The winds of change in the structure of CSE emanated from the 2001 report of the Civil Services Review Committee headed by Dr Y K Alagh.

CSE comprises two successive stages: The CSAT with objective multiple choice questions, with four answers against each question.

A Main Examination with nine descriptive written papers. An interview / personality test is also considered as part of the Main Examination.

For the sake of convenience in discussion, we will divide the whole process into three parts - CSAT, Main, and Interview.

CSAT replaces the 'Preliminary Examination'

Although the 'Preliminary Examination' stands replaced by 'CSAT' in popular parlance, UPSC still retains the old name for

Among the Most Reputed The Indian Institute of Science (IISc), Bangalore has been included in the list of the world's 100 most reputed universities released by the *Times Higher Education* (THE). It is the only Indian institution to figure in the list.

the first stage. The objective of CSAT is to ensure right selection of candidates for the Main Examination, keeping aptitude as a prime criterion. It is only a screening test, in the sense that the marks scored in this will not be counted for the final ranking. However, we should not forget that a person who fails in this cannot appear the Main Examination.

There are two papers of 200 marks each. The duration of each paper is two hours. The questions are set in English and Hindi. However, the passage for English Language Comprehension will have no Hindi translation.

There will be penalty in the form of negative marks for wrong answers. For each wrong answer, one-third of the marks assigned to the question will be deducted. However, there is no penalty for not answering a question.

do not require subject specialisation
General Science.

> CSAT would test the aptitude and suitability of the candidate for the civil services, rather than his capacity for memorising facts in a subject.

CSAT Syllabus:

Paper 1

Current events of national and international importance.

History of India and Indian National Movement.

Indian and World Geography - Physical, Social, Economic Geography of India and the World.

Indian Polity and Governance - Constitution, Political System, Panchayati Raj, Public Policy, Rights Issues, etc.

Economic and Social Development - Sustainable Development, Poverty, Inclusion, Demographics, Social Sector initiatives, etc.

General issues on Environmental Ecology, Bio-diversity and Climate Change - that

Paper 2

Comprehension

Interpersonal skills including communication skills

Logical reasoning and analytical ability

Decision-making and problem solving

General mental ability

Basic numeracy (numbers and their relations, orders of magnitude, etc.) (Class X level), Data interpretation(charts, graphs, tables, data sufficiency etc. - Class X level)

English Language Comprehension skills (Class X level)

A quick look at this syllabus tells that it is radically different from the syllabus of the Preliminary examination that existed till 2010. There were two objective papers - a compulsory General Studies paper with 150 marks and an Optional Subject paper with 300 marks. A candidate could choose his optional subject from a list of 23 subjects. There was a feeling that candidates choosing different optional subjects were not offered a level playing field. It would be more equitable if all the candidates were asked to face two common papers of a general nature, not focusing on any specific academic subject, at the preliminary stage. This led to the emergence of CSAT.

CSAT would test the aptitude and suitability of the candidate for the civil services, rather than his capacity for memorising facts in a subject. In the old Preliminary examination, the optional subject had double

Enrolment Plunges	Enrolment in primary classes in the country has dropped since 2007. In two years, the fall is 2.6 mn.. The biggest setback was witnessed in U.P.

What are the Services?

The UPSC notification for the Civil Services Examination 2011 offers selection to the 24 services noted below.

(i)   Indian Administrative Service.
(ii)   Indian Foreign Service.
(iii)   Indian Police Service.
(iv)   Indian P & T Accounts & Finance Service, Group 'A'.
(v)   Indian Audit and Accounts Service, Group 'A'.
(vi)   Indian Revenue Service (Customs and Central Excise), Group 'A'.
(vii)   Indian Defence Accounts Service, Group 'A'.
(viii) Indian Revenue Service (I.T.), Group 'A'.
(ix)   Indian Ordnance Factories Service, Group 'A' (Assistant Works Manager, Administration).
(x)   Indian Postal Service, Group 'A'.
(xi)   Indian Civil Accounts Service, Group 'A'.
(xii)   Indian Railway Traffic Service, Group 'A'.
(xiii) Indian Railway Accounts Service, Group 'A'.
(xiv)   Indian Railway Personnel Service, Group 'A'.
(xv)   Post of Assistant Security Commissioner in Railway Protection Force, Group 'A'
(xvi)   Indian Defence Estates Service, Group 'A'.
(xvii) Indian Information Service (Junior Grade), Group 'A'.
(xviii) Indian Trade Service, Group 'A' (Gr. III).
(xix)   Indian Corporate Law Service, Group "A".
(xx)   Armed Forces Headquarters Civil Service, Group 'B' (Section Officer's Grade).
(xxi)   Delhi, Andaman & Nicobar Islands, Lakshadweep, Daman & Diu and Dadra & Nagar Haveli Civil Service, Group 'B'.
(xxii) Delhi, Andaman & Nicobar Islands, Lakshadweep, Daman & Diu and Dadra & Nagar Haveli Police Service, Group 'B'.
(xxiii) Pondicherry Civil Service, Group 'B'.
(xxiv) Pondicherry Police Service, Group 'B'.

There may be slight changes in the number of services from year to year. The number of vacancies would also differ. The examination will be held in 45 centres distributed in various parts of the country.

the weight of the general studies making it more advantageous to those who have passed the master's degree, though the entry qualification is only graduation. The new pattern is fair to all. The first paper of CSAT focuses on general studies and the second on general aptitude. CSAT evaluates these attributes of all the candidates with total fairness. In the absence of any subject paper, cramming subject contents cannot push up our score.

The introduction of CSAT has generated a lot of unfounded anxiety. This is only a manifestation of the basic human nature that takes any change with an air of suspicion. We should face CSAT with confidence and a positive frame of mind. It is our attitude that decides our success of failure. "If you think you can do a thing or think you can't do a thing, you're right", said Henry Ford. CSAT is after all a recruitment examination which aims at ranking the applicants; it does not try to pass or fail the candidates or award any class or distinction to them.

General Studies, that has a significant role in the Mains as well, now gets more importance in the first stage. CSAT measures our cognitive abilities, aptitude, and logical approach much more than the piec-

Experience Prevents Severe Errors It's true - older people make more errors, but they don't make severe errors, because of their experience. A German research says older employees are more productive than their young colleagues.

es of information stored in our memory.

Special Strategies For CSAT

The syllabus of CSAT gives an indication of how we should proceed for effective preparation. The first paper poses no problem, since it almost follows the line of the first paper (General Studies) in the old Preliminary Examination. Mastering current affairs through systematic and regular reading of quality newspapers, watching good TV news channels, and studying in depth the subjects such as history, geography, and economic development as mentioned in the syllabus will put us in the right track for the preparation for Paper I. Answering question papers in the General Studies paper of the previous Preliminary Examinations will sharpen our test skills. We should watch recent trends in national economy as well as the economic development of our country.

Look at the emphasis on areas such as logical reasoning, analytical ability, decision-making, problem solving, and general mental ability in Paper II. These are not topics that were very seriously considered till now. But we have to drill using questions that test the skills in these areas. Let us make a brief analysis of the topics that may make a bit of confusion in the mind of some of the candidates. This would evolve a productive strategy for facing CSAT.

Comprehension Vs English Language Comprehension: Comprehension entails grasping the idea given in a statement or passage. We may have to analyse statements, separate the wheat from the chaff, get at the core of the message, appreciate the implications, identify discrepancies, arrive at inferences, and draw conclusions. Identifying and locating a required piece of information quickly from a large mass of data demands fine skill in comprehension. To test this skill, a long passage would be given and a few objective questions based on the passage posed. There would be only subtle differences among the options given as answers. We have to strike at the right option quickly.

English Language Comprehension skills (Class X level) form a different kettle of fish. The objective of this segment is to check and confirm our ability to deal with matter presented in English. We have to be familiar with common expressions and usage. A high degree of proficiency is not expected, as 'Class X level' clearly indicates. The test would involve only simple passages and

> Communication, team work, etiquette, leadership, prioritising, and appreciation of differing cultural values are essential ingredients of success in interpersonal involvement.

questions based on it. However, careful reading is essential for grasping ideas with precision.

Interpersonal skills: A good civil servant should necessarily be an adept in interpersonal skills. He should know the nuances of fine communication. These are best tested though an interview or group discussion. However, the CSAT format attempts to cover this through a paper and pencil test. Questions on communication skills may involve vocabulary, expressions, and usage. There can be questions that test our attitudes on listening, understatement, facial expression, posture, body language, tone, patience, humility, humour, or other aspects of successful interpersonal skills.

Timing

CSE generally follows the following schedule.

Notification inviting applications	: December / January
CSAT	: May / June
Results of CSAT	: July / August
Main Examination	: October / November
Interview/ Personality test	: April / May

There may be more than four lakh applicants at the initial stage. Nearly half of them would actually appear for CSAT. The number of serious candidates may be half of them. Still, the competition is tough. The number of candidates to be admitted to the Main Examination will be about 12 to 13 times the total number of vacancies in the various Services. The number of candidates to be summoned for the interview will be around twice the number of vacancies. Only 920 candidates were recommended for appointment

Aligarh Muslim University

Communication, team work, etiquette, leadership, prioritising, and appreciation of differing cultural values are essential ingredients of success in interpersonal involvement. After all, words form only one of the codes for communication.

Logical reasoning and analytical ability: This is not a fresh area. Several recruitment tests including that for the selection of bank officers have been using questions on reasoning. There is a wide variety of questions that measure diverse aspects of reasoning. We should be able to identify fallacious reasoning given in some of the answers in multiple choice questions. Cause and effect, assumptions, deduction, sequencing, and prioritising are some of the aspects in reasoning. We may have to question some of the assumptions or statements during the process of analysis.

Questions may be based on statements, tables, or diagrams.

Decision-making and problem solving: Resolution of administrative stalemates would call for skills in identifying causes that may not be obvious. An administrator will have to take quick decisions, which should be right decisions as well. The implications of our decisions should be visualised before jumping into them. In the examination, we may have to analyse real-life situations involving differing interest groups or people. Problems may have to be studied from the standpoints of law, rules, precedence, practice, conventions, ethics, and pragmatism. Wrong assumptions may lead us to wrong decisions. The questions would assess how we approach a complex situation, analyse it, and examine possible ways for resolution keeping acceptable norms of ethical values.

Decisions will have to be taken based on given circumstances and conditions. This is sometimes known as a 'caselet', which is a small case study. We should know patterns of individual and group behaviour and principles of conflict management. Further, we may have to argue within ourselves to discover the truth in a murky caselet.

General mental ability: This was part of the syllabus of the General Studies paper in the old Preliminary Examination. So we should have no difficulty in finding models of questions in this area. There are established patterns of questions based on coding, relationships, diagrams, directions, sequences, etc. The more you practise using sample questions, the better will be your performance in this type of assessment.

Basic numeracy and data interpretation: Numeracy implies the ability to understand and work with numbers. This part need not be a hard nut to crack for any serious candidate, since the syllabus unequivocally states that only Class X level is expected. We may however also be prepared to meet something slightly higher as well. Those who have not studied mathematics beyond Class X will have to brush up their school arithmetic and solve some trial problems so as to be at home with numerical work. In the examination, we may have to handle quantitative data and simple statistical tables. Numbers may have to be

> Data interpretation may involve selecting and extracting data from a body of information provided as narration, tabular statements, charts, pie diagrams, Venn diagrams, etc.

studied and interpretations made for arriving at conclusions to be used for further action. Paper II of General Studies in the Main Examination has questions of this nature. The types of questions to be expected would be more or less the same as those we find in the 'quantitative aptitude' segment in popular competitive tests. Fractions, HCF, LCM, percentages, interest on capital, ratios, square roots, averages, profit and loss, work and time, time and distance, and pipes filling tanks are some of the usual areas. Data interpretation may involve selecting and extracting data from a body of information provided as

University and Higher Education

There were 18 Universities and 500 Colleges at the time of Independence. In 2009 there were 504 universitites and university level institutions of which there were 243 State Universities, 53 private universities, 40 Central Universities , 130 Deemed Universities, 33 institutions of national importance established under Acts of Parliament. and five institutions established under various state legislations.

narration, tabular statements, charts, pie diagrams, Venn diagrams, etc. The data so selected may have to be checked for their sufficiency, and analysed and interpreted for using in necessary applications.

CSAT – Facing Objective Questions
We may not be quite familiar with answering question papers exclusively with objective questions. The style has to be different from that for facing conventional descrip-

Planning

Proper planning and execution are essential for success in any endeavour of significance. Preparation for the CSE is no exception. The test is highly competitive. We have to face the cream of our educated youth in the contest and prove our superiority and suitability for civil service, through our performance.

In the General Studies paper, questions on anything under the sun could be asked. None can master everything. With its far too vast content, General Studies demands us to concentrate on the more probable areas from the point of view of the examination. Question papers of the previous examinations are our sole guide in the matter. Of course, there can be changes in the trend; but we have to anchor on something to go ahead.

The question styles in CSAT and the Mains are totally different. When we go for any competition, we have to make preparation to suit its specific style. Training for a 10,000 metres run is different from training for a 100 metres sprint. Our preparation for CSAT should be in a style that suits the objective questions, and that for the Main should be in tune with essay-writing.

tive papers in a University examination. There are two objective papers in CSAT. What are the special features of these papers?

The questions are of the multiple-choice objective type. There is a stem and four answers, only one of which is correct. We have to choose the correct answer. If however, we feel that certain answers are partly right, we should choose the most correct answer.

We need not bring forth the answer from our memory; but we have to use our discrimination in selecting the right answer from four options.

All questions are compulsory.

All questions, irrespective of their difficulty levels, carry equal marks.

There is a penalty for wrong answers. For each wrong answer, one-third (0.33) of the marks assigned to that question will be deducted as penalty. If we give more than one answer to a question, it will be considered a wrong answer even if one of the answers happens to be correct. This will cause a deduction of 1/3 of the marks for the question. There is no point in going for guesswork and invoking negative marks.

If no answer is given to a question, there is no penalty. So it would be prudent to leave a question unanswered if we are not quite sure of the correctness of an answer.

Even the best candidate may not be able to answer all the questions correctly in the allotted time; nor is it necessary for reaching the Main.

A Time Test

The objective papers are in general a time test; much more than a knowledge test.

For many candidates the examination may prove to be a question of nerves, since they take it as a life and death struggle. The performance of those who lack in confidence may not reflect their knowledge and full capability because of their tension.

St. Xaviers College, Mumbai

So we should focus on nothing but the questions and answers, and not allow our mind to wander away during the test.

The distinctive characteristics of objective tests point to the need for systematic drilling that simulates the environment in the examination hall. We may have to increase our speed through constant practice using questions of the previous examinations or with those of comparable standard.

During rehearsals as well as the actual examination, we should follow certain styles to get the best results. We should not waste time by reading all the questions from the beginning to the end of the paper. This exercise is of no use, since there is

> We had better read the questions one by one from the beginning, and move forward answering the easy ones and skipping the tougher variety.

no 'choice' in the questions. We had better read the questions one by one from the beginning, and move forward answering the easy ones and skipping the tougher variety.

More and More Rehearsals

Self training is essential for maintaining equanimity for logical thinking in an atmosphere charged with tension caused by time constraint. How can we get such training? One method is to sit under closed doors, free from all distractions, and answer the questions of previous examinations, keeping time using a watch. In other words, we fully simulate the atmosphere in the examination hall. With every such drill, we should record the number of questions we answer in a fixed duration such as thirty minutes. We will find that as we play more and more rehearsals, we gain speed in answering. We should fine-tune ourselves to the style.

It is impossible for anyone to prepare for tests solely based on the declared syllabus. The content of the syllabus would invariably be vague. Only questions from the previous examinations can offer reliable guidance in the matter.

It is true that we would aspire to answer all the questions correctly in the given time. So it is likely that we would wait at a question to find its answer, even if we do not have a ready answer. This results in loss of time. The clock does not wait for anyone. So whenever we come across a difficult question, we should skip it without a second thought. We may get time for a second round to try our hand at the questions that were skipped in the first round. Not a moment should be wasted in the examination hall. All our movements should be rehearsed well repeatedly and things should proceed strictly according to our screenplay. We have to make our preparation an enjoyable experience. We should not consider them as difficult tasks that can never be done satisfactorily by us. It is the will that helps us to overcome difficulties. ■

Defence Studies in Universities	A committee of defence experts has suggested setting up a Council of National Security Research and Studies, corresponding with CSIR, to promote defence and strategies in the country.

Tackling the Main Examination

This is the crucial stage. The eligibility gained through CSAT for appearing in the Main Examination is valid only for the concerned year; it cannot be carried forward to another year in the future. The ranking and selection for the personality test depends on our performance in the main examination. The number of candidates to be admitted to the Main Examination will be about twelve to thirteen times the number of vacancies to be filled in the year in the various services.

The main examination is intended to assess the overall intellectual traits and depth of understanding of candidates, rather than the range of their information and memory. The scope of the syllabus for the optional subject papers for the examination is broadly of the honours degree level, which is higher than the bachelor's degree but lower than the master's degree. In the case of Engineering and Law, the questions would be at the bachelor's level.

Structure of Main Examination

The written examination consists of nine papers, each of three hours. All the questions are of the conventional essay type. The question papers other than language papers will be set both in English and Hindi.

Paper I Indian language: We can select it from the Languages included in the eighth schedule of the Constitution. Matriculation standard. Qualifying nature; the marks scored will not be counted for ranking.

Paper II English: Matriculation standard. Qualifying nature; the marks scored will not be counted for ranking.

Paper III Essay: 200 x 1 = 200 marks
Papers IV & V General Studies 300 x 2 = 600 marks

Papers V, VII, VIII, & IX 2 subjects (2 papers each) 300 x 4 = 1200 marks

Total marks of seven papers= 2000 marks

Interview (personality test) = 300 marks

Grand total marks for ranking = 2300 marks

Optional subjects in the Main Examination: Two optional subjects can be chosen from 25 subjects, and the literature of one of the 30 specified languages. The subjects we choose need not be from what we have studied in the college.

- Agriculture
- Animal Husbandry & Veterinary Science
- Anthropology
- Botany
- Chemistry
- Civil Engineering
- Commerce and Accountancy
- Economics
- Electrical Engineering
- Geography
- Geology
- History
- Law
- Management
- Mathematics
- Mechanical Engineering
- Medical Science

University Grants Commission

The University Grants Commission (UGC), which came into existence on 28 December 1953, became a statutory organisation by an Act of Parliament in 1956.

- Philosophy
- Physics
- Political Science and International Relations
- Psychology
- Public Administration
- Sociology
- Statistics
- Zoology

Literature of one of the following languages: Arabic, Assamese, Bodo, Bengali, Chinese, Dogri, English, French, German, Gujarati, Hindi, Kannada, Kashmiri, Konkani, Maithili, Malayalam, Manipuri, Marathi, Nepali, Oriya, Pali, Persian, Punjabi, Russian, Sanskrit, Santali, Sindhi, Tamil, Telugu, and Urdu.

Combinations not Allowed: The following combinations of subjects will not be allowed, since there are areas of overlap in the syllabi.

(a) Political Science & International Relations and Public Administration

(b) Commerce & Accountancy and Management

(c) Anthropology and Sociology

(d) Mathematics and Statistics

(e) Agriculture and Animal Husbandry & Veterinary Science

(f) Management and Public Administration;

(g) Of the Engineering subjects, viz., Civil Engineering, Electrical Engineering and Mechanical Engineering—not more than one subject.

(h) Animal Husbandry & Veterinary Science and Medical Science

We can answer the questions in papers III to IX in English or in any language listed in the eighth schedule of the Constitution. While doing so, we may give the English version of technical terms within brackets. But, if we misuse this rule, a deduction will be made from our total marks. The first two papers, Indian Language and English, should however be answered in the respective languages. In the question papers, SI units will be used, wherever required.

Indraprastha College, New Delhi

Economy of Words

Marks will not be allotted for mere superficial knowledge. Credit will be given for orderly, effective, and exact expression combined with due economy of words in all subjects of the examination. UPSC may fix qualifying marks in any or all the subjects of the examination. If our handwriting is not legible, a deduction may be made from our total marks.

We will be allowed the use of Scientific (Non-Programmable type) calculators in the essay type examinations. We cannot interchange calculators with other candidates in the examination hall. Calculators are not allowed in CSAT. Please note that these regulations give a hint on the style of preparation you make for the examination.

Choice of Optional Subjects

Choosing the optional subjects involves a crucial decision. There is no rule that we should select a subject that we studied in the college. We have the freedom to select any subject listed in the menu. But there are certain points one should keep in mind, for the sake of ensuring convenience in preparation.

We may normally select our subject of specialisation in the college as one of the optional subjects. But this is not a hard and fast rule.

Students of science or technology often choose subjects such as Public Administration, Sociology, History, Geography and

Political Science & International Relations. However, it is not advisable for students of humanities to select science or technology. So also, students of biological and physical sciences attempting unfamiliar subjects may find it to their detriment.

We should select subjects in which we have a passion or at least a natural interest. Our aptitude is important.
The quantum of the subject content
Availability of reference material.

We should select subjects which we feel would give us the best scores. We have to remember that we cannot get any unfair advantage by going for science subjects.

Guidance from Experts

Guidance from experts in the field may be gainfully sought for the crucial decision of selecting the optional subjects. There are special advantages for certain subjects. Take for example Public Administration. Some of the topics that come under this have to be mastered for answering questions in General Studies. So, selecting Public Administration as an optional subject has an advantage. Again, there are certain common areas in Sociology and Public Administration. So also, Economics and Public Administration have common areas of contents.

Once the optional subjects are chosen after careful consideration of all related aspects, be firm in the decision. Try to get as much knowledge as possible in the subjects, with the type of possible questions in mind. Many candidates often vacillate and change the decisions on optional subjects midstream with the result that they waste a good lot of precious time in preparation. This situation hatters their confidence.

In the main, the optional subjects have a total of 1200 marks out of the total 2000 marks. This indicates the weight of the optional subjects in CSE.

Two significant factors that determine the quality of performance in CSE. are
Good general knowledge
Proficiency in English language

Sustained Effort

These two cannot be developed overnight. It requires sustained effort stretched over a long period. So it is advisable that students aspiring focus on these two right from the time they are in the high school classes.

Elements of classical general knowledge such as countries / capitals / currencies / language, inventions, books and authors, largest / tallest / longest can be learnt gradually over a period of several years. Current affairs can be mastered only during the last few months before the examination. This is a general statement. However, there are several successful candidates who have spent only 15 to 18 months of intensive studies for the examination. It is not the duration alone that counts, but learning styles and time management. If we start concentrating on CSE by the time we are in the degree classes, this long-range preparation would be effective and relatively easy. In any case, Intensive preparation with the examination in mind has to be for nearly 15 months.

There is an interval between CSAT and the announcement of its result. This period can be gainfully utilised for further preparation. The gap should not be taken as rest period.

CSAT covers current events of national and international importance, general science, history of India and Indian national movement, Indian and world geography, Indian polity and governance, constitution, Panchayati Raj, etc. Questions on economic geography of India, planning, budgeting, developmental schemes, electoral reforms, amendments of the constitution, national level committees and commissions are common. Updating information from time to time is important for this paper.

We should undergo some self-training in answering the mental ability questions so as to familiarise ourselves with the types of questions and to develop speed in answering.

Certain Special aspects of the Main Examination

The General Studies paper in the main covers history of modern India and Indian culture (including principal features of literature, arts and architecture), geography of India, Indian polity, current national issues and topics of social relevance, India and the world, Indian economy, planning, public health, human resource management, constitution of India, International affairs and institutions, law enforcement, internal security, developments in the field of science and technology, environmental issues, communications and space, statistical analysis, graphs and diagrams.

We should not go for too many textbooks or journals. Limit their number, but ensure their quality. Remember, we would be racing against time. We should study one or two standard textbooks in our optional subjects. The school textbooks prescribed by NCERT for standards 10, 11, and 12 provide basic facts on many subjects in a simple form. The previous question papers should guide us in limiting the boundaries of our study areas.

Our descriptive answers should reveal analytical skills. News and views in the media should not be taken hook, line, and sinker. We should exercise our judgement and skills in evaluation, for sifting the wheat from the chaff. Facts and po-

litical statements should be intelligently distinguished. Make the habit of reading at least one English language daily of quality. The reading should not be casual. We should focus on names of places and people of significance, dates, numbers, important developments in the national and international scenes, and major sporting events. Editorials and leader page articles in dailies, one or two newsmagazines, one good competition journal, news and good discussions on radio / TV, etc. will help us in forming clear views and drawing inferences. It is a good idea to engage ourselves in serious discussions on burning issues, with knowledgeable friends.

Writing Essays

As part of the preparation, we should write a few essays simulating the conditions in the examination hall, using a watch to check our writing speed. Even if we know the answers well, we may not be able to transfer the knowledge to the answer book effectively within the prescribed time limit. Remedial steps should be taken in such cases. Time management is vital during the several months of preparation, as well as in the examination hall. Let us not leave anything to chance. Rehearsals will ensure our ability to perform well in the main papers, thereby boosting our self-confidence.

Whenever we read something seriously as part of the preparation, we should note down the main points as also fine expressions and significant quotes. We should not waste time by reading the same essay

| Romanians and Bulgarians | The European Foundation for the Improvement of Living and Working Conditions reported three years ago that Britons were among the hardest working people in Europe. Only Romanians and Bulgarians put in longer hours. |

Facing an Interview

Enter the interview room gracefully. Greet the Board. Take your seat when asked to do so. Remember, there is no second chance to make a first impression.

Speak with clarity. Never be vague. Use simple language.

Avoid stereotypes such as "You know". "I think", "Basically", "sort of", and "like". If you feel that you made some error during the interview, do not brood over it. Think of the next answer you have to give. Be confident of your success.

again and again. Study it once with full concentration. When we learn an essay, it is essential that we note down the main points, and if necessary make a mnemonic so that we can present all the points in the right sequence without missing any point. Remember that VIBGYOR reminds us not only the seven colours of the solar spectrum, but the colours in the order of their wavelengths. Before starting to write an essay, we can conveniently note down the points in the right sequence and then proceed to expand them appropriately and provide introductory and concluding paragraphs, as required.

Strategies for the interview

The interview is an important component of the selection exercise. What are the strategies that would help us to secure the highest possible marks in this significant segment, which carries 300 marks out of the total of 2300 marks for the final ranking?

The interview is a comprehensive personality test and not an abominable cross-examination. We will be interviewed by a Board which will have before it a record of our career. We will be asked questions on matters of general interest. The Board comprises competent and unbiased observers, who are familiar with the nature and working of the civil services, and the possible demands on officers in the services. The prime objective of the interview is to check and confirm our suitability for a career in public service.

It is not a test either of our specialised or general knowledge which has already been evaluated through written papers. The Board would examine our ability and skill to analyse facts in the crucible of our mind, draw inferences, arrive at logical conclusions, and articulate them with clarity and precision. We are expected to have taken an intelligent interest not only in our special subjects of academic study, but also in the events which are happening around us both within and outside our own state or country. We should be familiar with modern currents of thought and with new discoveries which should rouse the curiosity of well-educated youth. The interview may not be totally in a conventional Question – Answer mode. It would be in the form of a natural, but directed and purposive conversation which is intended to reveal our mental qualities.

UPSC mentions thus: "Some of the qualities to be judged are mental alertness, critical powers of assimilation, clear and logical exposition, balance of judgement, variety and depth of interest, ability for social cohesion and leadership, intellectual and moral integrity."

An Afternoon Off

The French spend an average of just 37.7 hours a week at work. This gives them an entire afternoon off.

Even though we have performed well in the written part of the examination, and there is no minimum score officially set down for the interview, our performance in the interview may tilt the balance one way or the other. So it is essential that we give our finest possible performance at this decisive stage.

We should follow the general principles for success in any interview, as also specific strategies in tune with the demands of the personality test in CSE. It is a good idea to attend a few mock interviews held by experts to identify our weaknesses and eliminate them. Further, this would enhance our confidence in facing the real interview. The slogan "I will win" should ring in our ears at every stage of preparation and performance.

Nature of interview questions

A natural question that emerges in us is, "What would be the nature of the interview questions?" Well, it is anybody's guess. The questions would depend on the first impression created by you in the mind of the Board, your background, and the mood of the members. Indeed, there are areas which you could focus during the preparation. Some of the possibilities are indicated below.

Meaning of your name.

Questions on your village / town / city / State / college

Detailed questions on your hobby

Why did you choose Mathematics / History / Electrical Engineering / .. as your subject of specialisation?

After your degree in engineering, you are opting for the Civil Services. Why? Does it not amount to wasting your hard work in technical studies? (We may avoid pleas like "opportunity for dedicated service to the nation" while answering questions of this genre.)

If you are a professional like an engineer or a surgeon, you may asked how you would use your specialised skills you have gained through hard work.

Questions based on situations, like how you would face flood havoc in the District under your control.

Your preferences among the different services

Latest developments in the national / international scene. Hot topics of the day.

Personal Effectiveness

Personal Effectiveness is a matter of concern for individuals who desire to function successfully and organizations which want to recruit manpower. Each human has a uniqueness by which he imprints his signature on individuals as well as events, as a mark of his individuality. The personality of an individual expresses itself and the resultant personal effectiveness decides the quality of that personality. The impact of situational, circumstantial and environmental influences on personal effectiveness is the deciding factor when it comes to human success.

Beyond personal effectiveness, an individual carries leader effectiveness with him. It is the quality of an individual to lead others by influencing them. This influence is very highly dependent on the personal effectiveness of the individual. All humans relate not only to the rest of the humans but also to the natural resources around. If it is just the utilization of natural resources that contributes to the leader effectiveness of the individual on one side, it is an individual's relations with others, which create an impact on them, that decide the leader effectiveness on the other. Leader effectiveness is a complement to personal effectiveness. Each individual has a personality which projects both personal effectiveness and leader effectiveness.

Higher Education in India - Opportunities Galore

The advent of private institutions has revolutionized higher education in India infusing global practices and offering world class ambience and coaching. With myriad advancements in curriculum, quality of faculty, methodology of imparting learning, resource materials and so on, these institutions are impelling a hesitant nation to make significant strides in the area of original research and development.

The result is that the young brains working fervently to invent and innovate are making a positive impact on the standard of living in our society.

Scholarships

There are countless opportunities for students to choose from any course or any discipline in India. Many institutions offer quality education on par with world universities. These institutions are not only affordable but many of them also give scholarships or fee concessions to poorer students. Besides, banks are offering loans to the tune of 4 to 12 lakh rupees without collateral as students of these institutions are assured of lucrative jobs. This year there more than 3 lakh jobs only in the software industry and TCS will be recruiting 60,000 candidates.

A healthy new trend is that students are out of the confines of classrooms and are introduced to the real world i.e. training in the industry and in many cases students are offered quality jobs in the same organisation where they interned.

Institutions that promote innovation and creativity such as the Sai Ram Engineering College, Chennai render a great service to society. The prodigies of the institution are credited with the invention of the PDS (Public Distribution System) vendor machine that is expected to do away with corruption in the system and the biometric voter cards and a host of other things of great value.

JNU New Delhi

Several colleges and institutions have an industry-institute cell which gives students exposure to current industry practices and helps teaching faculty to get sensitised to the latest practices.

Institutions like Alpha College of Engineering in Chennai use advanced technology to impart digital-oriented learning such as 3D visual representation and technology interface.

The curriculum is designed by industrial experts and the guest faculty comes from the industry. They have a tie-up with CTS and students get absorbed into jobs as soon as they pass out of college.

Students are also given opportunities and exposure to non-exam related learning such as projects, internships etc. to hone their talents. Indian students have proved that even with a graduate degree they are able to do amazingly well in international competitions for higher education.

Private institutions have also introduced a host of unconventional subjects for the undergraduate and postgraduate studies that offer great scope for unconventional jobs. New subjects such as petroleum and biochemical engineering, aeronautical engineering, space technology, marine engineering, logistics, mechatronics, nanotechnology and robotics have caught the fancy of youngsters bold enough to tread new territories. Rajiv Gandhi College of Engineering. Chennai is the first to introduce biomedical engineering (B.E) and petroleum engineering (B.Tech) with technical support from ONGC and Aban Offshore Ltd. There is a great demand for these courses for which practical training is offered by ONGC and Aban Singapore who are also major recruits of students who pass out.

Healthcare Industry

The remarkable development in healthcare industry today is the advent of the most exciting courses in the field of medical and paramedical sciences. Allied health services will not only infuse greater professionalism but will also lead to job explosion in the country. The MMM College of Health Services is an educational unit of the Madras Medical Mission offering graduate and postgraduate programmes in allied health services /paramedical courses. Year round Work-Integrated Learning Programmes (WILP) in all sectors of healthcare industry ensures students' industry worthiness and all-round excellence.

Research has reached a new momentum in India.. Velts University attaches great importance to research. Research gives students hands-on exposure to developing technologies like mechanisation of agriculture, food storage technology and software for advanced special machines. Solar and nuclear related research needs a lot of focus as India is facing a huge shortage of power.

The renaissance in education scenario in India is largely brought about by private educational institutions. We must further revamp systems to match international standards and continuously adapt to changes so that we don't lag behind global universities. Private institutional par-

National Law Universities in India

If you want quality legal education, you can think of national law universities, which aim at excellence in higher legal studies and research. They maintain fine academic ambience.

1. National Law School of India University, Bangalore
2. NALSAR University of Law, Hyderabad
3. National Law Institute University, Bhopal
4. National University of Juridical Sciences, Kolkata
5. National Law University, Jodhpur
6. Hidayatullah National Law University, Raipur
7. Gujarat National Law University, Gandhinagar
8. National Law University, Lucknow
9. National University of Law, Patiala
10. National Law University, Patna
11. National University of Advanced Legal Studies, Kochi.

Selection of candidates for admission to the Bachelor's degree programme is through an all India entrance examination, known as CLAT (Common Law Admission Test). There is a separate CLAT for LLM.

ticipation in education is only 12 per cent in India compared to 27 per cent in most countries and as high as 50 to 60 per cent in advanced countries. Government should allow complete autonomy to private institutions so that the momentum gained in higher education and research does not take a back seat.

As for the aspiring students, the ambience is right to enhance your skills and knowledge. There is a basketful of new era courses, world class ones at that, and plethora of job opportunities right on your doorsteps. Grab the chance with both hands; make hay while the sun shines There has never been a more conducive atmosphere.

(Based on 'The Week', May 2011)

Career in the Armed Forces as Officers

The armed forces protect the country from external threats, assist the police during internal disturbances and also provide help during natural calamities. There is much national pride and honour in serving in the defence forces.

The armed forces consist of Indian Army, Indian Air Force (IAF) and Indian Navy. The supreme commander of the armed forces is the President of India. Work in the armed forces is diverse and includes areas such as medicine, electronics, law, education, logistics, accounts, meteorology etc. Remuneration and benefits for those serving in the armed forces are very attractive including super–annuation benefits and post retirement opportunities.

Role of Army, Navy and Air Force

The Indian Army is the force that is trained to fight on land. It is one of the most powerful and strong forces protecting the geographical boundaries of India from illegal activities.

The IAF handles the air defence of the country. It performs both offensive and defensive roles. It is divided into three branches – Flying branch, technical branch and Ground Duties branch. It has a full-fledged meteorological section conducting research on the weather conditions. Other branches include Administration, Education and Accounts. The IAF is the fourth largest air force in the world.

The Indian Navy is the force that defends the vast coastline of the country. It also protects the country's offshore oil and gas installations, coastal shipping and fishing rights. The Indian Navy is the seventh largest naval force in the world and has tri-dimensional capabilities. The main branch-

Army Chief General J. J. Singh 2005-'07

es of the Navy are Executive, Marine Engineering, Electrical Engineering and Education.

Apart from academic excellence, one should also have leadership qualities, motivating spirit, determination, intelligence, control . of nerves, and physical stamina to qualify for a career in the armed forces. A number of qualities like courage, confidence, dedication, determination, enthusiasm, initiative, co-operative attitude, social adjustment, positive approach, analytical mind etc. are also required to become a good officer.

Entry / Eligibility

One has three options to enter into the armed forces.

NDA/Naval Academy Examination

The first option is to appear for the competitive examination being held by the Union Public Service Commission (UPSC) for the three wings of the National Defence Academy (NDA) at Pune and the Naval Academy at Ezhimala. Admission to the training courses is made on the basis of a written examination conducted by the UPSC followed by intelligence and personality test conducted by a Services Selection Board (SSB).

Candidates selected are given training both academic and physical for three years at the NDA. Those passing out of the NDA are awarded degree from JNU, Delhi. Army cadets are then sent to Indian Military Academy (IMA). Air Force cadets to the Airforce Academy, Hyderabad or BFTS (Basic Fighter Training School, Allahabad, and Naval cadets to the cadets Training ship for further training.

National Defence College

Combined Defence Services Examination (CDSE)

The CDSE is another option for candidates who want to enter into the armed forces. The CDSE allows entry into the Indian Military Academy, DehraDun or Naval Academy, Ezhimalai or the Air Force Station, Begumjet, Hyderabad, or Officers Training Academy, Chennai. Candidates in the age group of 19-23 years are eligible.

Candidates selected undergo training for 18 months at the IMA. After completion, they are awarded Permanent Commission. Those selected for training to OTA undergo training for nine months. On successful completion, they are granted short service commission.

Candidates selected for the Air Force Academy will undergo training for 75 weeks and on completion of training pass out in the rank of Flying officer.

Candidates selected to the Naval Academy undergo training in naval ships and establishment, after which they will be appointed in the executive branch of the Navy.

Services Selection Board

The third option is through the Services Selection Board (SSB) interview. The SSB conducts interviews for graduate and post graduate courses.

Selection Procedure in the Army

The selection procedure is simple. A written exam is followed by the SSB interview and medical test.

Selection to the Air Force

The candidates are to appear for an admission test called "Air Force Common Admission Test (AFCAT). Candidates who are shortlisted on the basis of the AFCAT will be called for further testing at one of the Air Force Selection Boards (AFSBs) at Dehradun, Mysore or Varanasi.

Candidates recommended by the AFSBs and declared medically fit will be detailed for training in the order of all India Merit test depending on the number of vacancies available in various branches / sub-branches.

Selection to the Navy

Candidates will be given calls for interviews based on their performance in Degree courses. Candidates recommended by the SSBs and declared medically fit will be detailed for training in order of All India Merit depending on the number of vacancies.

Selection Procedure at the SSB

Usually the test at the SSB lasts for five days. The job of the SSBs is to select people who possess requisite officer like qualities which would enable them to perform their duties efficiently as officers of the Armed Forces in war as well as peace. Their aim is to fit the right-man in the right job.

Each Service Selection Board consists of Interviewing Officer, Group Testing Officers and Psychologists. Successful candidates are sent for medical examinations.

Commission in the Armed Forces

On completion of training candidates will be commissioned in appropriate ranks by the President of India.

More Paid Annual Leave | **Working time in most west European countries is said to be decreasing because of improved employment conditons. Most fixed jobs now come with a relatively higher amount of paid annual leave than before.**

There are different types of commissions in the Armed Forces as under:

a) Cadet Entry - Permanent Commission as Army, Navy and Air Force

I) Regular Cadet Entry

ii) Graduate Entry

iii) NCC Special Entry

b) Direct Entry - Permanent Commission

c) Short Service Commission

d) Commission for Serving Armed Forces Personnel

Permanent Commissioned officers are to serve at least 20 years to become eligible for pension.

The initial tenure for short service commissioned officers is 10 years. An extension of four years may be granted subject to intelligence, service requirement and availability of vacancies.

Women in the Armed Forces

Women are also equally qualified as men to serve as commissioned officer. They are granted short service Commission.

Promotions

Promotion up to the rank of Lt. Commander is on timescale and ranks above that will be granted on selection grade. Promising officers have good chances of higher promotions.

The Armed forces offer excellent career and an exciting and extraordinary life to young men and women. A life where adventure, honour, glory are part of the day's work. where you are one among a million, and one in a million. A life where you go on to become the biggest asset of the nation.

To know more about career in the defence services see the following websites.

Army - www.joinindianarmy.nic.in

Air Force - www. careerairforce.nic.in

Navy - www.nawsenabharti.nic.in

Contributed by
Group Captain **Dr. U. Punnose** (Retd.)

Rank Structure and Pay scale of Officers

Ranks

Army	Air Force	Navy	Pay Bond/Scale	Grade Pay	Military Service Pay
Lieutenant	Flying Officer	Sub-Lieutenant	PB-3/ 15600-39100	5400	6000
Captain	Flight-Lieutenant	Lieutenant	"	6100	6000
Major	Squadron Leader	Lt. Commander	"	6600	"
Lt. Col	Wing Commander	Commander	PB-4/ 37400-67000	8000	"
Colonel	Group Captain	Captain	"	8700	"
Brigadier	Air Commodore	Commodore	"	8900	"
Major General	Air Vice Marshal	Rear Admiral	"	10,000	NIL
Lt. General	Air Marshal	Vice-Admiral	67000 -79000		
General	Air Chief Marshal	Admiral	80000 (fixed)		NIL
COAS/Field Marshal			90000		

A Fourth R

British Centre for Social Justice says employers find fault with British workers for poor work attitude and ethic. Their report calls for a fourth 'R', responsibility, to be added to the three R s: reading, writing and arithmetic.

Common Bank Test For Bank Officer Recruitment

Banks offer attractive jobs in the officer cadre and in the clerical cadre. Recruitment to the banks in our country rose to high levels consequent on nationalisation and the emergence of a large number of branches of the public sector banks. Banking Service Recruitment Boards were set up for catering to the need of fair recruitment. Candidates could gain eligibility for appointment to vacancies in different banks by sitting in a common examination held by BSRBs. Later on, a period of consolidation set in, and recruitment slowed down. For reasons of economy, the BSRBs were wound up in 2001.

Thereafter, aspirants had to appear in the separate selection tests held by different banks, leading to their hardship. In order to end the hassles in selection, a system of common written examination has been introduced with effect from June 2011 for the recruitment of Probationary Officers / Management Trainees. The following banks come under the scheme.

Allahabad Bank
Andhra Bank
Bank of Baroda
Bank of India
Bank of Maharashtra
Canara Bank
Central Bank of India
Corporation Bank
Dena Bank
Indian Bank
Indian Overseas Bank
Oriental Bank of Commerce
Punjab & Sind Bank
Punjab National Bank
Syndicate Bank
UCO Bank
Union Bank of India

JAM & JEST Entrance tests of a different genre

JAM: Joint Admission Test for M Sc Common entrance test for selection to M Sc- PhD and other Post - B Sc programs at IITs

JEST: Joint Entrance Screening Test Common qualifying test for admissions to Ph D, or Integrated M Sc - PhD, or Integrated M Tech – Ph D programs in Physics or Theoretical Computer Science at premier Indian research institutions. All selected candidates will receive Research Fellowships.

United Bank of India
Vijaya Bank

Though 19 public sector banks have joined the scheme, the State Bank of India group that has the largest number of employees will continue its own recruitment process. There may be changes in policies.

The common test will be held under the auspices of IBPS (Institute of Banking Personnel Selection, Mumbai, Web: HYPERLINK "http://www.ibps.in/"www.ibps.in). Three or four such common entrance examinations would be conducted every year at various centres distributed throughout the country.

The Banking sector in India is poised for a high trajectory growth with prospects for a bright career to several thousands of new entrants. It is estimated that more than seven lakh vacancies would arise in the next five years. According to the figures

It is the Attitude	**Studies show that British employers prefer foreign or immigrant workers to Britons because of their attitude to work.**

Indian Institute of Science

If you have a passion for a research career The Indian Institute of Science, Bangalore, the premier institution in science research for over a century, has now opened its portals to undergraduates. Those who have passed the 12th Standard with Physics, Chemistry, and Mathematics can register for a four-year Bachelor of Science (BS) Programme, designed to provide a deep interdisciplinary experience. Six major disciplines are offered: Biology, Chemistry, Environmental Science, Materials, Mathematics, and Physics. The program serves as a launching pad for research and doctoral studies in cutting-edge areas in science and technology. It develops a research mind in the student right from the undergraduate level. Selection of candidates is based on the following national examinations: KVPY / IIT-JEE / AIEEE / AIPMT.

of the Reserve Bank of India, there were 9, 44, 620 employees in all the scheduled commercial banks by the end of December 2010. Out of these, 4.7 lakh were officers and 3.19 lakh were in the clerical cadre. There will be a large number of retirement vacancies in 2012-'13. Further, a number of new branches would be opened during the period. A golden period ahead for those who aspire to find placement in the banking sector.

University graduates in the age group of 20 - 30 years can appear in the common test for the selection of officers in 19 banks. The structure of the test is indicated below.

The above tests, except the Test of English Language and the Descriptive Paper on English Composition, will be printed bilingually, in English and Hindi. The descriptive paper will be valued only if the candidate secures the minimum qualifying marks in each objective test.

The score card given by IBPS has a validity of one year. As and when each individual bank needs recruitment, it would issue a notification. Only those who have a valid score card can apply for selection. The bank concerned may prescribe a minimum score as cut off. It may conduct a group discussion, interview, or adopt other appropriate mechanism for final selection.

The system of common written test would be extended to recruitment for the clerical cadre.

BSW

S No.	Name of Test (Objective)	Questions	Marks	Duration
1	Reasoning	50	50	Composite Time of 150 minutes
2	English Language	50	5	
3	Quantitative Aptitude	50	50	
4	General Awareness (with special reference to Banking Industry)	50	50	
5	Computer Knowledge Descriptive Paper on English Composition (Essay, Précis, Letter Writing, etc.)	50 25	150 60 Minutes	
	Total		250	250

Going the Extra Mile in Crisis

Indian workers are willing to go the 'extra mile' in crisis situations, says an Indian industrialist. A commentator remarks that under the raj the British revelled in lecturing the 'lazy' natives on work ethic.

The International English Language Testing System (IELTS)

Nirmala Krishnaswamy

With the demand for personnel in various fields ever on the increase in the US and in many other countries, there are vast opportunities available for Indians. IELTS is an exam recognized by universities and employers in a large number of countries

Getting through the International English Language Testing System (IELTS) with a reasonably good band rating is a requisite for entry into many countries, either for pursuing a course of higher learning or even to take up a job.

The exam has two version academic and general training. The academic version is for those who have gained admission into an English speaking university or college. The general training version (GT), on the other hand, is for students who are looking at training programme options, or, if having done a course in Australia, for instance, and having been employed there for a while, are now looking to apply for a permanent residence status in that country. However, merely getting the required 'band' (grade) does not guarantee either a job or a PR status.

There are four parts to the IELTS: listening, reading, writing and speaking, and the exam is conducted in this order. While the listening and speaking modules are the same for both the versions, the writing and reading modules have some differences.

Listening

The listening test is in four sections with ten questions for each. The topics covered in the first two sections are about social life while the third and the fourth sections deal with education or training sessions.

Hindu College New Delhi

The listening section takes up 40 minutes when candidates listen either to recorded talks given by an individual or to a conversation between two or three people. These recordings are played only once.

Reading

The next part is the reading test. This section tests the candidate's ability in comprehending three passages which cover a wide variety of topics. This could include newspaper articles, extracts from books or opinions expressed in magazine articles. Time is of the essence. Candidates have to answer 40 questions in one hour.

The third and the fourth sections of the IELTS deal with writing and speaking. Both these depend on how well the candidate is able to generate the mechanics of the language on his own.

Writing

The writing test has two tasks. For those opting for the academic stream, the first task requires the candidates to interpret a chart or a diagram / graph, or write about a process which is pictorially represented in the question paper. Where possible, comparisons have to be made commenting on

> The IELTS band scores (one to nine) are used by universities and colleges to judge the competence level of the student, to see, whether instructions can easily be followed by them.

the general trend that a graph / chart indicates. The question may even call for a description of an object or an event. In the second part of the writing task the candidates are given a current topic of a general nature and they have to discuss the problem and give their opinions or offer solutions. Of the 60 minutes allotted for this task, candidates are advised to spend 20 minutes on task one and 40 minutes on task two.

In the general version of the writing task, task one is letter-writing, either friendly or semi-official. Three basic points are given and these have to be covered in the letter. Task two consists of writing an essay of

a minimum of 250 words on a topic of a general nature with their personal opinion made on the topic.

Speaking

The Speaking Test takes between 11 and 14 minutes. The speaking module has three parts. In the first of these, a warming up session, the examiner and the candidate introduce themselves. In the second part, the candidate responds to questions asked on one or two specific topics. These are structured questions. In the final part, the candidate has to talk in a sustained manner for one to two minutes on a given topic for which 60 seconds are given as preparation time. Following this on one-on-one discussion takes place between the examiner and the candidate for about four to five minutes.

The listening, reading and writing sections of the exam are held in a single session, whereas the speaking alone is held separately, either before or after the scheduled exam date.

The IELTS band scores (one to nine) are used by universities and colleges to judge the competence level of the student, to see, whether lectures / instructions given to them can easily be followed by them.

Are they able to understand English in most situations?

The band scores for each of the four parts of the exam are given in the form of a document. It also indicates the final average score. A 9-band score indicates exceptional ability in the communicative level of the English Language. The acceptance score varies and depends on the university or college where the candidate is seeking / has sought admission.

The IELTS exam is conducted both by the British Council (B.C.) and the IDP (International Development Programme). The exams are held four times a month.

Their offices are established in all major cities of India. Either of the offices may be contacted for more information and also for registration for taking up the exam. ■

China's Civil Service Exam	China abolished the civil service exam in 1905. For 2000 years, the exam was the chief source of social mobility and imperial stability in China.

National Skill Development Council

To begin with, let us look at some sobering facts:

Out of the estimated 30 crores children between the age of 6 and 16, only 10% will pass school education.

Of the 130 lakhs who join the labour force annually for the first time, 45% are illiterate and only 25% have primary school education.

Of the total workforce less than 10% are in the organized sector; those who are employed in the unorganized sector are victims of low wage / salary rates, inadequate or non-existent non-wage/salary benefits like PF or medical benefits and poor job security

Current training capacity in the country for skill development programmes is estimated at less than 45 lakhs; the incremental shortfall of skilled persons in 21 key sectors of the economy is estimated at 2440 lakhs by 2022.

Today, high unemployment rates co-exist with skill shortages due to the mismatch between employment opportunities and skillsets of workers

Government of India's very ambitious, game-changing initiatives aimed at meeting the huge skill deficit should be appreciated in the context of the awesome challenges that lie ahead. In fact, strengthening the links between education and employable skills and jobs is one of the greatest tasks facing the country.

The formation of the National Skill Development Council in 2008 under the Chairmanship of the Prime Minister was the first step in confronting the issues of skilling millions of people. In 2009 the National Skill Development Corporation (NSDC) was set up as the operating wing of the Council. In 2010, Dr.S.Ramadorai, former CEO of Tata Consultancy Services,

was appointed as the Advisor to the PM on skill development.

Public-Private Partnership

NSDC is a first-of-its-kind public-private partnership promoted as a not-for-profit company with GoI holding 49% and the industry holding the remaining portion of the equity capital of the company. The Chairman of the Corporation is the Chairman of the Murugappa Group; the other directors include the nominees of FICCI, ASSOCHAM, CII and other industry associations and Government Secretaries.

NSDC is mandated to skill 1500 lakhs people by the end of 2022, about 30% of the overall target of skilling or up-skilling 500 lakhs people by 2022, by helping promote skill development centers across the country jointly with private groups.

Meeting such targets would pre-suppose the expansion of the capacity of training programmes by 150 lakhs per annum during the 11th Plan period alone.

NSDC has estimated likely storage of 2400-2500 lakhs skilled people in 21 high growth industries like automobile, electronic hardware, textiles and garments, leather and leather goods, gems and jewellery, ITES and BPO, tourism, healthcare and construction.

The World Owes You Nothing | **Mark Twain said: Don't go around saying the world owes you a living. The world owes you nothing. It was here first.**

NSDC's highly innovative game plan will completely rewrite the skill development programme currently being followed in the country:

NSDC shall forge partnerships with Central / State / Local government entities, civil society institutions and all potential skill providers.

Modular courses

The focus will be on modular courses, open architecture and short-term, especially in the context of fast changing skills in the labour market.

Validation of qualifications for ensuring that qualifications reflect market needs; validation of training processes; quality assured assessment of learners; accreditation of training providers and training institutions; government financing linked to placement ratios and outcomes; using candidates as financing vehicles (scholarships, skill vouchers, outcome-based reimbursement etc.) rather than institutions to create choice; publishing rating and outcome information on training institutions; effective assessment and credible certification; exploring private use of public infrastructure like school facilities (after school hours) so that funds can be used more for activities than for buildings and other hard assets; and restructuring Employment Exchanges as career guidance centers to channelize candidates into jobs, apprenticeships and training are some of the innovations being planned.

NSDC has already approved several major projects in skill development, close to 30 projects promoted by leading private entities with funding support (loan and equity) from the Corporation amounting to about Rs.700 crores. These projects are likely to create more than 400 lakhs skilled workforce for the next 10 years.

By 2026, 65% of India's population will be in the working age group of 15-64. This is the 'demographic dividend' we have been taking about. According to Boston Consulting Group, by 2020 the world will have a shortage of 470 lakhs working people whereas India will have a surplus of 560 lakhs people to meet the global deficit. No other country in the world will have such a potential resource base and, therefore, no other country has such high stakes in skill development as India.

More importantly, skill development initiatives support employment generation, inclusive economic growth and social development processes

The Graduate Record Examination (GRE) - a new format

The GRE (Graduate Record Examination) score has all along been a requirement for admission into MS programmes not only in the US but also in many of the other English-speaking countries. Starting from August 2011, the score will be valid equally for admission into MBA programmes in a few of the universities in the US, such as MIT, Stanford, Wharton and Yale.

Therefore, the GRE format is slated to undergo the necessary changes as so that it has several features common to the other two exams, now valid for admission into any of the Business Schools, viz GMAT and CAT.

The major change will be in the area of verbal ability. Earlier, bare vocabulary was tested, where there was no context provided. Now a lot of the vocabulary will be contextualised. Consequently, there will be no

CEED – A Passport to Technical Design Studies

Common Entrance Examination for Design (CEED) for admission to the following post-graduate programs in Indian Institute of Science or IITs.

Master of Design programs at
IISc Bangalore: M Des in Product Design and Engineering

IIT Bombay: M Des in Industrial Design / Visual Communication / Animation / Interaction Design / Mobility and Vehicle Design.

IIT Delhi: M Des in Industrial Design

IIT Guwahati: M Des

IIT Kanpur: M Des in Industrial Design

Eligibility: Should have any one of the following:

Bachelor's degree in Engineering/Architecture / Design/ Interior Design Professional Diploma in Design from NID or CEPT 4-year Bachelor of Fine Arts after 12th Standard G.D. Art (5-year programme after 10th) with one year professional experience Master's degree in Arts / Science / Computer Applications.

---

antonyms and analogies section; instead, there will be greater weightage given to a candidate's reading and comprehension skills. More emphasis will be placed on reading comprehension and answering of questions based on the passages.

The changes in the verbal section will see the verbal part divided into two sections, each with 20 questions. The new format will be more user friendly, analysts say. There will be more freedom in tackling the given material, even enabling the candidate to scroll up and down, edit, skip and correct. This would allow a candidate to move within a section. They can even "highlight a sentence in a passage to answer a question."

The GRE, which is conducted by the Educational Testing Services (ETS), will even provide the candidate with an on-screen calculator.

Quantitative Aptitude

The quantitative aptitude section has two parts with 20 questions each. This section once again, lends itself to the same amount of flexibility as has been indicated above.

In the new format there will be a combination of the numeric entry type of questions as well as multiple type of questions.

Earlier, the scoring system was based on a total marks of 1600 (800 + 800); now it will be based on a total of 340 (170+170). The band variation will now be from 130 to 170. However, the analytical writing score continues to be the same; ie. based on the 0-6 score level with increments of 0.5.

The GRE score will be valid for five years. There is no change here. The huge advantage would appear to be the fact that the candidate can take time to decide either on an MS programme or opt for a course in a B-school.

Test Centres

The test centres in India for the new format are Thiruvananthapuram, Chennai, Bangalore and Hyderabad in the South Mumbai and Ahmedabad in the West, Allahabad and Kolkata in the East and Gurgaon in the North. The test timings are 9 am - 1 pm, 1 pm to 5 pm and 5 pm to 9 pm. That is, there will be three shifts. There is also a paper-based GRE test, to be held for the first time in India. It will be a replica of the computer-based test. Bangalore, Mumbai, New Delhi, BITS-Pilani and BIT-MESRA, Ranchi are the centres providing this facility and the scheduled date for this exam is 11th November, 2011.

For more information, candidates can get in touch with the local USIS office.

2.3 m. for BFSI Sector

According to the NSDC, banking, financial service and insurance (BFSI) sector alone has the potential to recruit over 2.3 m. individuals in the coming decade. Public sector banks alone plan to hire more than 200,000 employees up to 2012.

Education in India: A Chronological Chart

1792 – Sanskrit College at Banaras

1800 – Fort Williams College at Kolkota

1817 January 20 - Raja Rammohan Roy established the Hindu College, in Kolkota (renamed Presidency College in 1855)

1821 – Poona Sanskrit College

1824 - Sanskrit College at Kolkota

1826 – Governor of Madras established two schools in each collectorate and one school in each Tahsil

1834 - Basel Mission at Mangalore.

1835 February 02 – Macaulay's minute, in which he anticipated 'a class of persons, Indian in blood and colour, but English in taste, in opinions, in morals, and in intellect.'

1835 – Calcutta Medical College , the first Medical College in India (also in Asia)

1844 – Lord Harding established 101 'vernacular' schools in Bengal

1847 - Roorkee Engineering College, the first Engineering college in India

1854 - 'Wood's Despatch' - survey and suggestions for reforms; creation of Department of Public Instruction in each province.

1857 – Establishment of universities at Kolkota, Mumbai, and Chennai (Calcutta, Bombay and Madras)

1882 - Hunter Commission on education (responsibility of mass education shifted from Government to local boards / private sector; grant-in-aid system)

1882 – Punjab University

1887 – Allahabad University

1904 – Five Universities, 191 affiliated colleges, 23,000 students; 5498 secondary schools with 5. 6 lakhs students, 98, 538 primary schools with 33 lakhs students; special / industrial / technical / art / training schools.

1948 – Radhakrishnan Commission for university education – suggested 10 + 2 structure, three languages, scholarships & research.

1950 - Free and compulsory education enshrined as one of the Directive Principles of State Policy in the Constitution of the Indian Republic.

1951 - First Indian Institute of Technology (IIT) established at Kharagpur

1952 – Mudaliar Commission on secondary education

1956 - University Grants Commission (UGC) established by Act of Parliament

1961 - Dr. Sampurananand Committee on Emotional Integration

1964 – Kothari Commission on education at all stages.

1976 – Education changed from State list to Concurrent list in the Constitution.

1986 – New National Policy of Education

1988 - All India Council of Technical Education (AICTE) with statutory status; National Literacy Mission launched

1989 - Mahila Samakhya Scheme: a concrete programme for the education and empowerment of woman in rural areas

1993 - National Council of Teacher Education (NCTE)

2001 - Launch of Sarva Shiksha Abhiyan (SSA)

2002 - Constitution amended to make free and compulsory education, a Fundamental Right

2004 - EDUSAT, a satellite dedicated to education, launched

Scaling the Corporate Ladder – the Soft-skilled Way

Dr. Sebastian Narively, Pala

Can you interact positively with others? Do you impress people into your communication skills? Development of soft skills is crucial to a successful career.

"Nearly 25% time to cover the syllabus should be spent on professional skill development to improve employability."
– Dr. A.P.J. Abdul Kalam

There is no denying the fact that the requirements for professional success change rapidly and constantly. Till recently, subject knowledge and technical expertise were the cardinal criteria for employability. Soft skills were virtually sidetracked or even relegated to the back space. But times have changed, and people are now alive to the crucial importance of communication skills, corporate etiquette and leadership skills in facing a job interview or group discussion confidently. The oft-ignored soft skills have emerged, of late, as a decisive tool that could make or break one's career prospects.

It is axiomatic that notwithstanding their knowledge in academic subjects, a majority of students are deficient in soft skills that advance their profession and enhance performance. Owing to budgetary constraints, most companies are currently shying away from training fresh recruits. Hence the centrality of the acquisition of soft skills.

'Soft skills' is a sociological term related to a person's attributes like emotional intelligence, social graces, communication and cognition. These competencies complement hard skills which are the occupational requirements of a job. Also referred to as interpersonal skills or people skills, they encompass proficiencies like communication skills, professionalism, social etiquette, negotiation skills, problem solving, personal effectiveness, audience awareness, strategic thinking, team building, salesmanship, tactfulness, urbanity and adjustability. Other professional skills such as personal awareness, information management, familiarity with the pertinent terminology and grasp of the global business scene also come under the same rubric. The expression, thus, covers all the behavioural facets of individual character that determine his productive social interaction.

Flying Licence	Sylla (later Lady Dinshaw Petit) was the first woman in India to get a flying licence in India. She was J.R.D. Tata's elder sister. Her younger sister Mrs. Rodabeh Sawhney got the licence after her.

Soft skills can be broadly defined as the ability to communicate effectively in both written and oral forms, as well as the flair to interact with others positively. The ability to communicate includes speaking knowledgeably, listening attentively, reading intelligently and writing succinctly. As Anthony Robins puts it, "The way we communicate with others and ourselves ultimately determines the quality of our lives."

A well-groomed Personality

Attributes like punctuality, goal management, team skills and listening skills are regarded as the hallmark of a well-groomed personality. The list also includes body language, interpersonal skills stress management and voice modulation. Today's knowledge-based economy demands of its employees qualities that enhance organizational and leadership skills leading up to productive team results.

> If a job seeker fails to demonstrate strong inherent values like self-discipline, motivation and reliability, all his ambition is likely to come to naught.

It is to be stressed contextually that in today's competitive corporate world, if a job seeker fails to demonstrate strong inherent values like self-discipline, motivation and reliability, all his ambition is likely to come to naught. It is incontestable that a higher IQ or technical talents alone won't fill the bill.

'Employability' is the oft-chanted mantra in the corporate universe of our time. Employability skills refer to the basic skills that are indispensable to the effective performance of a task. They are indeed rated higher than job-specific accomplishments. Surveys by FICCI and NASSCOM indicate that only in the neighbourhood of 25%

of graduates are employable. Therefore, it is imperative that only adequate employability skills can bridge the wide chasm between the campus and the corporate.

Effectiveness in crisis management, team work and self-motivation also heaves one up the corporate ladder. By crisis management is meant managing a critical situation in a workplace. When diverse problems confront you, weigh them up, analyse them, and arrive at amicable solutions.

Sharing Information

Team work is what stimulates organizations to succeed in business. Information has to be shared, advice taken, feedback implemented and rapport with everyone developed. Be humorous and honestly frank. Greeting others by name, pumping hands and magic words like 'thank you', 'sorry' and 'please' can work wonders.

Motivation is the driving force in life. Self-motivated people accept responsibility for their actions and develop a positive and professionally constructive mindset. It is neither leadership nor lure of lucre that should impel you. Motivation shall indeed be a philosophy of your life. "Trust in God and have faith in thyself", says the Mahabharata.

Technical skills or 'hard skills' can be acquired from conferences, workshops, books or periodicals. But soft skills can be internalized only through keen observation and practice. Students should begin specialized training in soft skills at least when they go half way through their schooling. They should strive to refine their finesse in communication, business correspondence, presentation, team building, leadership, interviews, time management and stress management, continually and strenuously. Areas to be included in this scheme of training comprise skills related to, career excellence skills, professional thinking skills, analytical mindset and business acumen. Fortified with these accomplishments the youth of today can address every professional challenge with poise and elan. ∎

Growth in Higher Education	In 1947, India had only 18 universities, 500 colleges, 230,000 students and less than 24,000 teachers. By 2004, this grew to 345 universities, 16,000 colleges, 95 lakh students and 4.35 lakh teachers.

Courses to Watch

Animation

Animation is the art of making images that appear to come to life on screen. It features in all kinds of media, from feature films to commercials, pop videos, computer games and websites

Animation is all about team work. Apart from the animator, a host of professionals work to complete animation projects. These include – writers, storyboard artists, and character designers. In 3D projects, there are modelers, riggers, and lighting/texturing artists. Software programmers are employed to work with the software, customize applications, etc. You get an idea about the scope.

Now let's look at the job profile of an animator. An animator is expected to build models, create story boards, and finally execute parts of the project in collaboration with other team members.

An animator should: be creative and artistic • have drawing skills (and sculpting skills for stop frame animation using clay) • have excellent IT skills • be patient and able to concentrate for long periods • be interested in art and design.

Courses

Both diploma and degree courses are available across colleges in India. But, postgraduate degree courses in animation and cartoon are rare. The Industrial Design Centers in Mumbai and Guwahati offer post-graduate degree courses.

The graduate and post-graduate programmes in disciplines such as Fine Arts, Applied Art, Commercial Art, Graphic Design, Animation Design, Visual Communication, Design etc. give training in Animation art.

Eligibility

For applying for a diploma course in animation, one has to pass the 12th standard examination from any recognized board with a minimum of 45 per cent marks. For the bachelor's degree programme the same eligibility criterion is applicable, while for the PG program one must have a bachelor's degree.Though minimum qualification is +2, creativity and artistic affinity are desirable.

Admission

Admission is on the basis of the marks secured in the qualifying examination. Some institutes conduct entrance test for examining aptitude of the student.

Types of Animation: • 2D drawn animation • 2D computer animation • stop frame or stop motion animation • 3D computer generated (CG) animation.

Job Prospects

Animators have a variety of employment options – ranging from working for ad agencies and video game producers to working in the live-action movie industry. Special effects demand the skills of animators to create realistic sequences for live action films. Self employment and freelance options are also available.

Graduates in 2001	According to Census 2001, graduates in India were 37,670,147. Of these, 25,666,044 had graduate degrees other than technical degree. Graduates in Medicine were 768,964.

Architecture

Architecture is an evergreen career. As long as buildings are built, civil engineering and architecture will be in demand. Architects are typically expected to design buildings and also have an insight into civil engineering and town planning and regulations.

Landscape Architecture

This is a specialized field. Landscape architecture is the design of outdoor and public spaces. A landscape architect needs to be proficient in urban planning and design, site planning, environmental restoration, parks and recreation planning, visual resource management, and green infrastructure planning and provision. Landscape architecture's objective is to achieve urban living which is environmentally safe, aesthetically beautiful and helps in stress-free living.

Mega projects such as highways, mass transit systems, airports, ports and larges-cale land redevelopment projects would require the services of expert landscape architects.

Courses

Architecture can be pursued at graduation levels: Bachelor of Architecture (B.Arch) and then follow it up with a Masters (M.Arch).

Eligibility

B.Arch: 10+2 (senior secondary, Class XII) or equivalent referred to as the qualifying examination from a recognized Board/University with a minimum of 50 per cent marks in science subjects (physics, chemistry and mathematics). Besides this, the candidate must qualify an entrance examination. The duration of the course is five years.

M.Arch: B.Arch and the duration will be three semesters.

At the masters level, specialisation is offered in landscape architecture, architectural conservation, urban design, building engineering & management, environment planning, housing, transport planning, regional planning, town and country planning, indstrial design, etc.

Admission

Admission to B. Arch in various colleges is through entrance examinations held at state and national levels.

Government & Private Colleges: The CBSE conducts the national examination - All India Engineering Entrance Examination (AIEEE) - for entry into B. Arch and B. Planning in government and private institutes.

IITs: Entrance to architecture programmes at the Indian Institutes of Technology (IIT's) is through the national level Joint Entrance Examination (JEE).

States Colleges: Different states also hold separate entrance exams for admission to architecture and engineering colleges in the state. Some private institutes conduct entrance exams of their own also.

Generally the entrance paper consists of mathematics and a drawing test. The drawing exam is conducted by the National Institute of Advanced Studies and Architecture in association with the Council of Architecture (COA).

Computer-aided Design in Architecture

Computers have entered the offices of architects. Familiarity with CAD is now a must for architects. Although it has not been included formally in the syllabus of many universities, the present generation of architects cannot afford to ignore CAD. Many private institutes offer training in programmes such as AutoCAD and 3D Max.

| Literacy Rates | Literacy rates in British India were 3.2% in 1881, 7.2% in 1931, and 12.2% in 1947. This marked an increase to 52.21% in 1991 and 65.38% in 2001. |

Job Prospects

With rapid urbanization, there is a huge demand for skilled architects. A large number of construction firms, consultancies, municipal bodies, town planning agencies, landscaping consultancies, corporation offices, government departments are looking for talent. Another area where jobs are possible is renovation of old historical monuments. Architects with entrepreneurial drive will look for self employment.

Paramedical Services

Paramedical courses offer specialised training in areas such as - X-ray technology, medical laboratory technology, physiotherapy, occupational therapy, opthalmic technology, audiology and speech therapy, prosthetic and orthotic engineering and clinical child development.

Types of Courses
  Medical laboratory sciences
  Radiological technology and imaging,
  Radiotherapy technology,
  Audiology and speech therapy
  Physiotherapy
  Operation theatre assistance
  X-ray technology and radiology involves the use of X-rays, high frequency sound waves etc. to scan the body's entrails.
  Medical laboratory technology is concerned with the collection, sampling, test-

The Council of Architecture

The Council of Architecture (COA), a Government organization, regulates the education and practice of the profession in India besides maintaining the register of architects. To practice as an 'Architect' one must have registered himself with the COA. For registration, a candidate must possess the requisite qualification as per the Architects Act,. He or she must have undergone the education in accordance with the Council of Architecture (Minimum Standards of Architectural Education) Regulations, 1983.

The registration also entitles a person to use the title and style of Architect. The title and style of architect can also be used by a firm of architects, of which all partners are registered with COA. Limited Companies, Private/Public Companies, societies and other juridical persons are not entitled to use the title and style of architect nor are they entitled to practice the profession of architecture.

There are 135 institutions which impart architectural education in India leading to recognized qualifications. The standards of education being imparted in these institutions (constituent colleges/departments of universities, deemed universities, affiliated colleges/schools, IITs, NITs and autonomous institutions) is governed by Council of Architecture (Minimum Standards of Architectural Education) Regulations, 1983, which set forth the requirement of eligibility for admission, course duration, standards of staff & accommodation, course content, examination etc.

Sarva Siksha Abhiyan
The SSA focuses on compulsory education of children in the 6-14 age group. It has components such as Education Guarantee Scheme and Alternative / Innovative Education Scheme for those in remote areas and for dropouts.

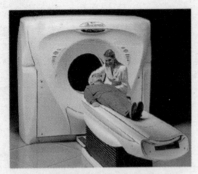

ing, reporting and documentation of laboratory investigations.

Physiotherapy covers the use of exercises, related equipment, electrotherapy, magneto therapy, massage etc. to rebuild damaged muscles, ligaments & bones.

Occupational therapy trains in the rehabilitation of physically and mentally impaired persons.

Optometry or opthalmic technology specialises in the treatment of disorders related to the eye.

Prosthetic or orthotic engineering involves the replacement of missing parts of the body with artificial structures.

Audiology and speech therapy is concerned with correcting speech defects.

Clinical child development is concerned with nutrition and treatment of growth defects in children.

New Courses: Some new courses include ophthalmology (technical course), ICU assistant, cardiac laboratory technology, lung care laboratory course, dental technology course and neuro-physiology laboratory course.

Alert: 'Though there is an increased demand for paramedical staff for teaching and working in private or corporate hospitals and private laboratories, there is an exclusive autonomous regulatory body for paramedical education in India which could regulate the training institutes so that there is uniformity to meet with world class standards in training of paramedic staff.

Courses
The courses available for paramedical sciences varies from diploma in particular field of 2 years duration, Bachelors degree course of 3 or 4 years duration, Masters degree course of 2 or 3 years as well as Ph.D. Although eligibility criteria is almost same for all the paramedical courses but it varies slightly according to particular courses and disciplines.

Eligibility
The minimum qualification for getting admission to any paramedical course is plus two (10+2) or equivalent examination with physics, chemistry, biology and English. At least 50 per cent of marks should be secured in each of these subjects. Minimum age limit is 17 years.

Admission
Some institutes conduct entrance tests, while others consider the marks secured in the qualifying examination.

Work with the Disabled
The Rehabilitation Council of India conducts job oriented courses in special education for persons who wish to work with the disabled. In India there are six centres providing 10 month diploma courses. Number of seats in each centre is 20. Qualification - + 2 or equivalent. Fees-Nil. A monthly stipend of Rs. 600/- is provided to the selected candidates. Admission begins in November.

Job Market
Experts in this field can find suitable employment in hospitals, nursing homes, psychiatric clinics, rehabilitation centres, polyclinics and diagnostic clinics. Paramedical services are also required in the R & D wing of pharmaceutical companies and institutional laboratories.

Fashion and Design
Behind everything you see and use there is a designer at work. There are interior designers at work when it comes to living and

work spaces and graphic designers when it comes to media and entertainment products like newspapers, movies, etc. Design, therefore, is a very vast field.

Choosing a Field
Categories of design. Here is a list of options:

Product Design: Designing user-friendly products.

Furniture Design: Creating not only new designs, but also experimenting with new materials to increase user comfort.

Ceramic Design: Ceramic products are widely used in lifestyle products (artistic products), tableware (dinner sets, etc), and sanitaryware (washbasins, etc).

Textile Design: This is different from fashion design. In textile design, experts create new kinds of woven and non-woven textiles with unique characteristics like "crease-resistant" varieties.

Apparel and Accessory Design: Popularly known as fashion design, here designers create clothes and accessories for fashion-conscious consumers.

Communication Design: Using design in entertainment, media and advertising industries (special effects, layout and design, animation, film and photography, etc.)

Exhibition Design: Design connected with events (cultural events), showcasing works (museums and art galleries), trade fairs, marketing events, etc.

Courses
Depending on the areas of interest, one can from the following:

Duration
BFA: 4-5 years. Diploma course: 2-3 years. Masters course (after completing BFA): 2 years.

Eligibility
BFA Course: 10+2
Masters Course: BFA
Diploma courses: 10th standard/equivalent.
Besides this academic qualification, the individual should have a creative bent of mind and an eye for detail.

Admission
To enrol for courses in Fine Arts, an entrance examination is to test the candidates' aesthetic skills. The test generally consists of (1) Study from life-face of a human model to be drawn in pencil and (2) a water colour painting on a specified theme.

Other Courses
National Institute of Design offers both UG & PG Programmes — Graduate Diploma Programme in Design (GDPD) of four years' duration for students after 10+2, or equivalent like AISSCE/ IB/ ICSE, and the Post-Graduate Diploma Programme in Design (PGDPD) of 2 to 2 ½ years duration for graduates; particularly from architecture, technology, engineering, fine and applied arts, information technology, computer science, etc. The specializations under GDPD are: Industrial Design, Communication Design and Textile and Apparel Design.

National Institute of Fashion Technology offers, among others, a course in Fashion Design. Other courses include, Leather Design, Accessory Design, Textile Design, and Knitwear Design. NIFT also offers a course in Fashion Communication. The eligibility is 10+2 from a recognized Board of Education and admission is through an entrance examination that tests an aspirant's general ability (GAT) and creative ability (CAT) and material handling (Situation Test).

Institute of Apparel Management (IAM)

Air and IQ | Pollution can affect your IQ. Living in neighbourhoods with heavy traffic pollution can lower children's IQ, a Harvard study says. The effect is as bad as in the case of kids whose mothers smoked 10 cigarettes a day while pregnant.

offers bachelor's programme in Fashion and Lifestyle Design (four years) and another one in Fashion and Textile Merchandising (three years)

Footwear Design & Development Institute offers degree and diploma courses in footwear design and development.

Apparel Training and Design Centre offers one/two-year diploma courses in fashion design and apparel manufacturing and six-months Core Certificate courses in apparel pattern making, industrial sewing machine operations, etc.

List of Institutes
NIFT: The Premier Fashion Institute
National Institute of Fashion Technology is the premier Institute of Design, Management and Technology. The Institute provides a common platform for fashion education, research and training.

The Institute has a network of 12 professionally managed domestic centres at New Delhi, Bangalore, Chennai, Gandhinagar, Hyderabad, Kolkata, Mumbai, Raebareli, Bhopal, Kannur, Patna and Shillong. NIFT has further spread its wings globally with the opening of an international centre at Mauritius.

NID: The Premier Design Institute
National Institute of Design offers professional education programmes at Undergraduate and Post Graduate level in 17 diverse design domains.

The overall structure of NID's programme is a combination of theory, skills, design projects, and field experiences supported by cutting edge design studios, skill & innovation labs and the Knowledge Management Centre.

National Institute of Design, Paldi, Ahmedabad 380 007

Institute of Apparel Management (IAM)
IAM has been very instrumental to train Designers, Design Professionals, Design Managers, Designer Merchandisers, Quality Professionals etc. with a broad base knowledge of applied Management skills, competencies & understanding the dynamics of Apparel business in Glocal context.

Job Prospects
Campus placements offer jobs to students studying in premier institutions. Otherwise, a large number of top companies in garments, fashion accessories, leather goods, media outlets, advertising, and other sectors recruit students with appropriate qualifications.

Travel and Tourism
The nature of travel and tourism sector is developing both in scope and direction as new activities such as cultural tourism, adventure tourism and eco tourism are capturing the imagination of new age tourists.

Courses
A number of courses – from certificate and diploma to graduate and post-graduate – are being offered by various institutions.

The courses can be classified into following categories:

Airline Customer Service (Ticketing and Marketing)

Cargo Marketing (Cargo Sales and Marketing

Overall Tourism Management (Comprehensive Tourism Management)

The common courses are:
Post Graduate Diploma
PG Diploma in Management (Tourism & Travel)
PG Diploma course in Tourism Studies
Bachelors Degree

ICAR | **Indian Council of Agricultural Research concentrates on human resource development in the field of agricultural sciences by setting up agricultural universities.**

Bachelor of Tourism Administration

Bachelor of Tourism Studies

Bachelor of Tourism Management

Masters Degree

Master of Tourism Administration

MBA (Tourism and Hospitality Management)

M.A. (Tourism Management)

Master of Tourism Management

Eligibility

Graduates in any discipline with 50 per cent marks are eligible for admission.

Tourism courses cover the following: historical and cultural background of India, basic management principles, computer fundamentals and principles of accounting, communication skills, hotel management and international tourism and world geography. Other subjects include, Airline ticketing, Tourism marketing, Tour Operation, Management and Event Management.

Courses offered by the International Air Transport Association (IATA)

The International Air Transport Association (IATA) is offering courses in India to serve the aviation and travel related training needs in the South Asia region.

Twelve courses have been scheduled in 2009, with the inaugural course – Professional Skills for Dangerous Goods Regulations (DGR) Instructors – commencing on 23 February. Other courses planned for 2009 include air cargo management, airline emergency planning and response management, and security management systems.

The IATA Training and Development Institute (ITDI) currently offers a continuously expanding portfolio of over 400 courses and a wide range of diplomas in the fields of Airlines, Airports, Civil Aviation, Air Navigation Services; Cargo, Safety and Security, as well as Management and Training Skills for every level - from entry level to senior managers. ITDI delivers training at more than 200 locations worldwide to over 31,000 students annually from around the world

The Indian Institute of Tourism and Travel Management (IITTM)

The Indian Institute of Tourism and Travel Management (IITTM), Gwalior – 474 011 (www.iittm.org), is a Government of India organisation under the Ministry of Tourism. It is a premier institute.

IITTM offers a post graduate diploma in management (tourism and travel) at Gwalior and Bhubaneswar and post graduate diploma in management (tourism and leisure) in New Delhi. These programmes are equivalent to MBA degrees of the universities.

The minimum eligibility for admission is a three-year Bachelors degree (10+2+3 pattern) in any discipline with 50 per cent marks (45 percent for candidates belonging to the Scheduled Castes and Scheduled Tribes categories and differently-abled candidates).

Selection is through the IITTM aptitude test, group discussion and personal interview. Students having valid scores in Indian Institutes of Management Common Admission Test (CAT), XLRI Admission Test (XAT), Management Aptitude Test (MAT) or AIMS Test for Management Admissions (ATMA) are exempted from the aptitude test conducted by the IITTM.

Duration of the programme is two years. The institute has a track record of 100 per cent placement.

Getting a certification from IATA-UFTAA (International Air Transport Association and Universal Federation of Travel Agents Association), Geneva, is an excellent qualification to get jobs in the industry. This home study programme which requires about 200 hours of study is open to anyone after Class XII. Details are available at www.iata. org/atdi/travel_tourism.

Switch off the TV during Dinner

Experts advise us to turn off the TV during meals. Mindless TV watching produces mindless eating, says Toronto nutritionist Harvey Anderson.

Group Discussions: Dos and Don'ts

Group discussion has become an integral part of the selection procedure for job recruitment, and admission to quality academic progrmmes. The strategy for success involves many do's and don'ts. Here are a few vital points to be borne in mind at the time of preparation.

- Gather full details of controversial topics of public interest by following daily news, editorial comments and articles written by experts in news magazines.
- Maintain a personal diary of events.
- Develop language skills including basic grammar, pronunciation, and effective expressions.
- Use simple yet forceful language; don't go for bombast.
- Arrange your facts logically.
- Don't take extreme positions
- Meet opposition with a smile
- Be broad-minded in your approach.
- Don't be unduly emotional during discussions.
- Discuss and not dispute.
- If you present an argument, give facts to support it.
- Be impartial. Keep a balanced view.
- Don't insult a person or a group.
- Appreciate good views expressed by others.
- Be a good listener.
- Don't try to monopolise the time given for the group.
- Speak patiently and convincingly.
- Use appropriate and relevant quotations or proverbs to establish your point.
- Encourage a silent or shy member to speak.
- Don't use provocative language or gestures.
- Don't hit on the table to prove a point.
- Look at the members by turn.

- Don't block others.
- Don't retort strongly if someone attacks you.
- Continue to be pleasant; a smile helps a lot.
- Light humour is OK; don't be a clown.
- Check your body language.
- If someone asks your views, take it as an opportunity to speak. Don't shy away from it.
- Show willingness for co-operation and teamwork.
- Be polite; show no sign of arrogance or superiority.
- Don't talk too fast sacrificing clarity; don't be dragging either.
- Don't shout or whisper; speak normally.
- Avoid mannerisms such as "you see", "I mean", "Sort of" and "Ya Ya".
- Give priority to group interest and not self-interest.
- Never give an impression that you are confused.
- Use expressions such as "As you put it rightly" and "We should appreciate the views of".
- When you want to differ, use phrases such as "Let us look at this from a different angle".
- Don't just repeat the view given by another participant.
- Don't give crude or uncivilised views or unpalatable expressions.
- Illustrate your views by examples.
- Don't get disheartened if one of your views is not being carried.
- Don't blow your trumpets.
- If you get an opportunity to open the discussion or to conclude, do it well.
- Be punctual
- Dress neatly
- Be confident of success.

| Hair Style and Success | *Fortune* says most of the successful CEOs, part their hair to the left. The list includes Warren Buffett and Indra K Nooyi. |

Part 11

India

Pages 485 - 694

Manorama
Yearbook

INDIA

States and Union Territories

The Country

The country lies between 8°4′ and 37°6′ north of the Equator and is surrounded by the Bay of Bengal in the east, the Arabian Sea in the west and the Indian Ocean to the south.

India is the seventh largest country in the world.

The country shares its political borders with Pakistan and Afghanistan on the west and Bangladesh and Burma on the east. The northern boundary is made up of China, Nepal and Bhutan.

Physical Regions

The mainland, in geographical terms is broadly divided into a) the great mountains, b) the river the plains, c) the desert and d) the peninsula.

Mountain Ranges

The mountains extend for more than 2400 km. They are seven.

1. the Himalayas,
2. the Patkai and other ranges bordering India in the north and north east,
3. the Vindhyas, which separate the Indo-Gangetic plain from the Deccan Plateau,
4. the Satpura
5. the Aravalli
6. the Sahyadri, which covers the eastern fringe of the West Coast plains and
7. the Eastern Ghats, irregularly scattered on the East Coast and forming the boundary of the East Coast plains.

Watersheds

There are main three watersheds.

1. Himalayan range with its Karakoram branch in the north,
2. Vindhyan and Satpura ranges in Central India, and
3. Western Ghats(Sahyadri)on the west coast.

Important Mountain Peaks:

Height in metre above mean sea level:

1) K2*		8,611
2) Kanchenjunga		8,598
3) Nanga Parbat		8,126
4) Gasher Brum*		8,068
5) Broad Peak*		8,047
6) Disteghil Sar*		7,885
7) Masher Brum E		7,821
8) Nanda Devi		7,817
9) Masher Brum W*		7,806
10) Rakaposhi*		7,788
11) Kamet		7,756
12) Saser Kangri		7,672

in Pak-occupied territory

Rivers and the Plains

The main rivers of the Himalayan group are the Indus, the Ganga and the Brahmaputra. These rivers are both snow-fed and rain-fed and have therefore continuous flow throughout the year. Himalayan rivers discharge about 70% of their inflow into the sea. This includes about 5% from central Indian rivers. They join the Ganga and drain into the Bay of Bengal.

The plains of Ganga and Indus run for about 2400km with a width ranging from 240 to 320km. They are formed in the river basins of Ganga-Yamuna, Brahmaputra, Indus, Godavari, Kaveri, etc.

Height of Western Ghats	The Western Ghats have a general altitude of 900-1100m but occassionally rise upto 1600m or even more.

Desert

The desert region is located in the western and north western part of the country. It can be divided into two parts: the great desert and the little desert. The great desert extends from the edge of the Rann of Kuchch beyond the Luni river northward. The whole

Sand Dunes, Rajasthan

of Rajasthan-Sind Frontier runs through this. The little desert extends from the Luni between Jaisalmer and Jodhpur up to northern wastes (dry and rocky land).

Peninsula

The Peninsula is marked by elevated landmass with height ranging from 460 to 1220m. The Deccan and the Southern part surrounded by water on three sides make the peninsula. It is flanked by Eastern Ghats on the east and Western Ghat on the west. Between the Ghats and the Sea lies the narrow coastal belt.

Climate

Traditionally, seasons in India are divided into six-Vasanta (Mar-Apr), Grishma (May-Jun), Varsha (Jul-Aug), Sharada (Sept-Oct), Hemanta (Nov-Dec) and Shishira (Jan-Feb). In broad terms, India experiences 3 main seasons, such as (a) Winter - Dec to March, (b) Summer - Apr to May and (c) Monsoon - South West Jun to Sept, and NE (retreating SW monsoon) - Oct to Nov. Between the two main seasons are Spring and Autumn.

India receives 86% of the rain during SW monsoon. NE monsoon is a very restricted one - experienced in Tamil Nadu, Kerala and sometimes AP and Karnataka.

Natural Vegetation

India has six types of forests. (a) Evergreen (Tropical Forests) - is found in areas with 200cm to 300cm rainfall; av. annual temp. 20°C to 27°C; av. annual humidity >80% (b) Deciduous (Monsoon Forests) - found in places with lesser rainfall between 150 to 200 cm; mean annual temp between 24°C and 28°C; humidity 75% (c) Dry Forest - are found where rainfall is scanty between 75 to 100 cm; mean annual temp 23°C to 29°C; humidity 50 to 60% (d) Hill Forests are common in South India and Himalayas (e)Tidal Forests (Mangrove) are found in the coastal submerged plains of Ganges (Sundarbans), Mahanadi, Godavari and Kerala and (f) Grasslands (hilly-Himalaya and Deccan hills above 100m, lowland- as in Punjab, Haryana, UP, Bihar, NW Assam and riverine grasslands- found along rivers).

Available data place India in the tenth position in the world and fourth in Asia in plant diversity. From about 70 per cent geographical

Silent Valley, Kerala

area surveyed so far, 47,000 species of plants have been described by the Botanical Survey of India (BSI), Kolkata.

Agriculture

India has two crop seasons.
(a) Kharif: Rice Jowar, Bajra, Ragi, Maize, Cotton, Jute. Sowing -Jun/Jul, Harvest - Sep/Oct
(b) Rabi : Wheat, Barley, Peas, Rapeseed, Mustard, Gram. Sowing - Oct/Dec, Harvest - Apr/May.

Race for Heritage City Status

Delhi is applying to UNESCO that it be recognised as a Heritage City. Ahmedabad is also in the race. India's campaign to get Western Ghats declared a UNESCO World Heritage Site received a setback when the UN committee postponed the decision to 2012.

The National Insignia

National Emblem

The state emblem of India is an adaptation from the Sarnath Lion, capital of Asoka the Emperor as preserved in the Sarnath Museum. The Government adopted the emblem on 26th January, 1950, the day when India became a Republic. In the original of Sarnath Capital, there are four lions, standing back to back, mounted on an abacus with a frieze carrying sculpture in high relief of an elephant, a galloping horse, a bull and a lion separated by intervening wheels

National Emblem

(chakras) over a bell-shaped lotus. Carved out of a single block of polished sandstone, the Capital is crowned by the Wheel of the Law (Dharma Chakra).

In the state emblem adopted by the Government only three lions are visible, the fourth being hidden from view. The wheel appears in relief in the centre of the abacus with a bull on the right and a horse on the left and the outlines of the other wheels on the extreme right and left. The bell-shaped lotus has been omitted. The words, Satyameva Jayate from the Mundaka Upanishad meaning "Truth alone triumphs", are inscribed below the abacus in Devanagari script.

The National Flag

The National Flag is a horizontal tri-colour of deep saffron (Kesari) (representing 'courage and sacrifice') at the top, white ('peace and truth') in the middle and dark green ('faith and chivalry') at the bottom in equal proportion. The ratio of the width of the flag to its length is two to three. In the centre of white band is a wheel, in navy blue. Its design is that of the wheel (Chakra) which appears on the abacus of the Sarnath Lion Capital of Asoka. Its diameter approximates the width of the white band. It has 24 spokes.

The design of the National Flag was adopted by the Constituent Assembly of India on 22nd July, 1947. Its use and display are regulated by a code. The Flag Code of India, 2002, took effect from 26 January 2002 and superseded the 'Flag Code-Indias' as it existed. As per the provisions of the Flag Code of India, 2002, there are no restriction on the display of the National Flag by members of general public, private organisations, educational institutions, etc., except to the extent provided in the Emblems and Names (Prevention of Improper Use) Act, 1950 and the Prevention of Insults to National Honour Act, 1971 and any other law enacted on the subject

National Anthem

Rabindranath Tagore's song Jana-gana-mana was adopted by the Constituent Assembly as the National Anthem of India on 24th Jan. 1950 and gave Vande Mataram-the national song equal honour. It was first sung on 27 Dec. 1911 at the Calcutta session of the INC. The first stanza (out of 5 stanzas) of the song forms the National Anthem.Playing time of the full version of the national anthem is approximately 52 seconds. A shorter version consisting of the first and last lines of the stanza takes 20 seconds to play and it is played only on certain occasions.

Noise Pollution	The average noise level in Chennai is more than 129 decibels. The permissible limit fixed by WHO is 85 dB.

Jana-gana-mana-adhinayaka jaya he
Bharata-bhagya-vidhata.
Punjaba-Sindhu-Gujarata-Maratha-
Dravida-Utkala-Banga
Vindhya-Himachala-Yamuna-Ganga
Uchchala-Jaladhi-taranga
Tava Subha name jage,
Tava subha asisa mange,
Gahe tava jaya-gatha,
Jana-gana-mangala-dayaka, jaya he
Bharata-bhagya-vidhata.
Jaya he, jaya he, jaya he,
Jaya jaya jaya, jaya he.

The following is Tagore's English rendering of the stanza:

Thou art the ruler of the minds of all people,
Dispenser of India's destiny.
Thy name rouses the hearts of the Punjab,
Sind, Gujarat and Maratha,
Of the Dravid and Orissa and Bengal.
It echoes in the hills of the Vindhyas and Himalayas, mingles in the music of the Jamuna and the Ganges and is chanted by the waves of the Indian Sea.
They pray for the blessings and sing thy praise.
The saving of all people waits in thy hand,
Thou dispenser of Indias destiny, Victory, victory, victory to thee.

National Song

The song Vande Mataram composed by Bankim-chandra Chatterji has an equal status with Jana-gana-mana.The first political occasion when it was sung was the 1896 session of the INC.

Vande Mataram,
Sujalam, suphalam, malayaja shitalam,
Shasyashyamalam, Mataram!
Shubhrajyothsna pulakitayaminim,
Phullakusumita drumadala shobhinim,
Suhasinim sumadhura bhashinim, Sukadam varadam, Mataram!

English translation of the stanza rendered by Sri Aurobindo (in Sri Aurobindo Birth Centenary Library Popular Edition 1972,vol. 8), is

I bow to thee, Mother,
richly-watered, richly-fruited,
cool with the winds of the south,
dark with the crops of the harvests,
The Mother !
Her nights rejoicing in the glory of the moonlight,
Her lands clothed beautifully with her trees in flowering bloom, sweet of laughter, sweet speech,
The Mother, giver of boons, giver of bliss.

National Calendar

At the time of independence, the Govt. of India followed the Gregorian calendar based on the Christian era.

The National Government adopted the recommendation of the Calendar Reform Committee that the Saka era be adopted as the basis of the National Calendar. The Saka year has the normal 365 days and begins with Chaitra as its first month. The days of the Saka calendar have a permanent correspondence with the dates of the Gregorian Calendar, Chaitra 1 falling on March 22 in a normal year and on March 21 in a Leap Year. The National Calendar commenced on Chaitra 1 Saka, 1879 corresponding to March 22, 1957 A.D.

The months of the National Calendar, with their days and the dates of the Gregorian Calendar corresponding to the first day of the Saka month are given below:

Saka	Gregorian
1 Chaitra 30/31 days	March 22/21
1 Vaishaka 31	April 21
1 Jyaistha 31	May 22
1 Asadha 31	June 22
1 Sravana 31	July 23
1 Bhadra 31	Aug. 23

Hindi at UN	On October 4, 1977, India's External Affairs Minister A.B.Vajpayee addressed the UN General Assembly in Hindi, the first ever address in this language.

1 Asvina 30	Sept. 23
1 Kartika 30	Oct. 23
1 Margasira 30	Nov. 22
1 Pausa 30	Dec. 22
1 Magha 30	Jan. 21
1 Phalguna 30	Feb. 20

National Flower

Lotus (Nelumbo Nucipera Gaertn) is the National Flower of India. It is a sacred flower

Lotus - National Flower

and occupies a unique position in the art and mythology of ancient India and has been an auspicious symbol of Indian culture since time immemorial. India is rich in flora. Currently available data place India in the tenth position in the world and fourth in Asia in plant diversity. From about 70 per cent geographical area surveyed so far, 47,000 species of plants have been described by the Botanical Survey of India (BSI).

National Animal

The combination of grace, strength, agility and enormous power has earned the tiger,

Tiger - National Animal

Panthera tigris, its pride of place as the national animal of India. Out of eight species known, the Royal Bengal Tiger, is rare. To check the dwindling population of tigers in India, 'Project Tiger' was launched in April 1973. So far, 27 tiger reserves have been established in the country under this project, covering an area of 37,761 sq km.

National River

The Ganga or Ganges is the longest river of India flowing over 2,510 kms of mountains, valleys and plains. It originates in the snowfields of the Gangotri Glacier in the Himalayas as the Bhagirathi River. It is later joined by other rivers such as the Alaknanda, Yamuna, Son, Gumti, Kosi and Ghagra. The Ganga river basin is one of the most fertile

Ganga - National River

and densely populated areas of the world and covers an area of 1,000,000 sq. kms. The Ganga is revered by Hindus as the most sacred river on earth.

National Tree

Indian fig tree, Ficus bengalensis, whose branches root themselves like new trees over a large area. The roots then give rise to

3 Teachers for 3 Students

Pudusery in Kerala's Palakkad district has an aided upper primary school with three teachers and three students. In early 2000, there were over 500 students and 21 teachers. Litigations, dismal facilities and division fall are responsible for the present plight.

Banyan Tree - National Tree

more trunks and branches. Because of this characteristic and its longevity, this tree is considered immortal and is an integral part of the myths and legends of India. Even today, the banyan tree is the focal point of village life and the village council meets under the shade of this tree.

National Fruit

Mangifera indica, the mango tree is one of the most important and widely cultivated fruit trees of the tropical world. Its juicy

Mango - National Fruit

fruit is a rich source of Vitamins A, C and D. In India there are over 100 varieties of mangoes, in different sizes, shapes and colours. Mangoes have been cultivated in India from time immemorial.

National Bird

The Indian peacock, Pavo cristatus, the national bird of India, is a colourful bird, with beautiful velvet feathers and a slender neck.

The male of the species is more colourful than the female, with a glistening blue breast and neck and a spectacular bronze-green tail of around 200 elongated feathers. The

Peacock - National Bird

female is brownish and slightly smaller than the male and lacks the tail. The dance of the male fanning out the tail and preening its feathers is a gorgeous sight.

National Sports

Hockey - National Game

Hockey is India's national game. India won the first Olympic hockey gold in 1928, in Amsterdam, beating The Netherlands 3-0.

Indian Standard Time (IST)

India has only one standard time. India is 5.5 hours ahead of GMT/UTC, 4.5 hours behind Australian Eastern Standard Time and 10.5 hours ahead of America! Eastern Standard Time.

| Congress Sessions in Madras | The Indian National Congress was 125 years on Dec.28, 2010. Madras, where the seeds of the Congress were sown, played host to eight Congress sessions. The Congress last met in Madras in 1955. |

History of India in Brief

BC

Before 10,000 BC Paleolithic Ages characterised by use of tools like hand axe, cleavers, found in Soan (now in Pak) Belan Valley (in Mirzapur, UP); stone tools like scrappers, borers, blades, burins, etc., made with flakes found in Soan, Narmada and Tungabhadra rivers and Andhra, Maharashtra, Bhopal, and Chotanagpur Plateau.

Before 6000 BC Mesolithic tools found in Chotanagpur, Vindhyas, Birbhanpur in West Bengal, Tirunelvelly in Tamil Nadu, Belan in MP, Bagor, Telure, Langhnejgunj, and Sarai Nahar Rai.

3000 - 2600 BC - Harappa Civilisation
1200 - 500 BC - Vedic Era
550 BC - Birth of Mahavira
563 BC-483- Sidhartha Gautama, the Buddha
483 BC First Buddhist Council held at Sattaparni (Rajgriha)
383 BC Second Buddhist Council at Vaishali.
336-323 Alexander the Great's conquest of Asia

Alexander the Great's conquest

327 BC - The Conquests of Alexander The Great
323 BC - Alexander The Great, dies
322 BC - Rise of the Mauryas, Chandragupta
303 BC Chandragupta Maurya defeated Seleukos Nikator and the trans-Indus region transfered to the Mauryas.
298 BC - Bindusara coronated
272 BC - Ashoka's Reign
180 BC - Fall of the Mauryas & Rise of the Sungas
30 BC - Rise of the Satvahana Dynasty

AD

40 The Sakas or Scythians in power in the Indus Valley and Western India.
50 - The Kushans and Kanishkas
52 Parthian King Gondopharnes in NW India. St.Thomas begins preaching Christ in India.
78 Saka Era begins.
98-117 Kanishka, the Kushan King.
320 Chandragupta I establishes the Gupta dynasty-Gupta Era begins.
360 Samudra Gupta conquers the whole of northern India and much of the Deccan.

Coins depicting Samudra Gupta's battle

380-413 Chandragupta II comes to power (Chandragupta Vikramaditya) - The Golden Age of the Guptas-Literary Renaissance-Kalidasa and other poets.
415 - Accession of Kumara Gupta I

Women in Panchayats

Out of the elected representatives of panchayats numbering 28.18 lakh, 36.87 per cent are women.

467 - Skanda Gupta assumes power

606 Accession of Harsha Vardhana.

609 Rise of the Chalukyas.

622 Era of the Hejira begins.

711 Invasion of Sind by Muhammad-bin-Qasim (Kassim).

753 Rise of the Rashtrakuta Empire.

892 Rise of the Eastern Chalukyas.

985 The Chola Dynasty-Rajaraja reigns

1026 Ransack of Somnath by Mahmud of Ghazni (mounted 17 plundering expedition into North India between 1000-1027AD).

1191 Prithvi Raj Chauhan, King of Delhi, routs Muhammad Ghori - the First Battle of Tarain.

1192 Muhammad Ghori defeats Prithvi Raj - Second Battle of Tarain.

1206 Qutbuddin Aibak establishes in Delhi the Slave dynasty (1206-1290: Kings - Qutub -ud-din Aibak, Shamas-ud-din Iltutmish, Rukn-ud-din, Razia Sultana, Bahram Shah, Massud Shah, Nasir-ud-din Mohammed, Balban, Kaiqubad).

1221 India threatened by Mongol invasion under Genghis Khan.

1232 Foundation of the Qutub Minar

Qutub Minar

1236-1239 Razia Sultana, daughter of Iltutmish- the first and the only Muslim lady to rule Delhi.

1266 - Balban made King after King Nasir-ud-din's death.

1290 Jalaludin Firuz Khalji establishes in Delhi the Khalji dynasty (1290-1320: Kings - Jalal-ud-din Firoz Khalji, Ala-ud-din Khalji, Kafur, Mubarak Khan, Khusrau Khan).

1298 Marco Polo visits India.

1320 Ghiyasuddin Tughluk in Delhi founds the Tughluk dynasty (1320-1414: Kings - Ghiyas-ud-din Tughlaq, Muhammad-bin-Tughlaq, Firoz Shah Tughlaq, Nasir-ud-din Tughlaq).

1325 - Accession of Muhammad-bin-Tughluk

1333 Ibn Batutah arrives in India.

1336 Founding of Vijayanagar (Deccan).

1347 Rise of the Bahmani dynasty (Deccan).

1398 Timur invades India.

1414-1451 The Sayyid Dynasty (Kings - Khizr Khan, Mubarak Shah, Muhammad Shah, Alam Shah)

1451 The Lodi dynasty (1451-1526) - Bahlul Lodi ascends the throne of Delhi. (Kings- Bahlul Lodhi, Sikander Lodhi, Ibrahim Lodhi)

1469 The birth of Guru Nanak Dev.

Guru Nanak

1489 Adil Shah dynasty at Bijapur.

1490 Nizam Shahi dynasty at Ahmadnagar.

1498 First voyage of Vasco da Gama via Cape of Good Hope and arrives at Calicut on May 27th.

1504 Babur establishes rule in Kabul, later became the first Mughal ruler.

1510 Vasco da Gama was succeeded by Captain General Alfonso de Albuqquerque (a Portuguese), who captured Goa-Albuquerque becomes the Governor.

1526 First Battle of Panipat- Babur defeats the Lodis- establishes of the Mughal dynasty.

1530 Humayun succeeds Babur. (1526-1530 - Reign of Babur)

1539 Death of Guru Nanak Dev; Sher Shah Suri defeats Humayun and becomes emperor of Delhi.

1553 The Jesuits of Goa publishes the first book in India.

1555 Humayun recovers the Delhi throne from Aslam Shah, successor of Sher Shah.

1556 Death of Humayun; Accession of Jalal-ud-din Akbar. Second Battle of Panipat - Akbar defeats Hemu.

1564 Akbar abolishes 'Jiziya' or poll tax on Hindus.

1565 Battle of Talikota-An alliance of Muslim rulers in Deccan defeats and destroys Vijayanagar Empire.

1568 Fall of Chittorgarh

1571 Foundation of Fatehpur Sikri by Akbar.

1576 Battle of Haldighati; Akbar defeats Rana Pratap Singh of Mewar.

1577 Akbar troops invade Khandesh (completes his conquests in 1597)

1582 Akbar proclaims Din Ilahi or Divine Faith-an attempt at synthesising Hinduism and Islam.

1595 The first fleet of the Dutch reached India

1597 Akbar completes his conquests. Death of Rana Pratap.

1600 English East India Company constituted through a charter, signed by Queen Elizabeth I.

Coins brought-out by East-India Co.

1602 Dutch East India Company formed

1604 Compilation of "Adi Granth" the Holy Book of Sikhs.

1605 Death of Akbar and the accession of Jehangir; Dutch established their first factory in Masulipatanam

1606 Martyrdom of Guru Arjan Dev.

1608 Captain Hawkins visit to Jehangir's court to secure trading rights for the British, failed.

1609 The Dutch open a factory at Pulicat.

1613 Sir Thomas Roe's visit yielded permission to set up their factory in Surat. Gradually trading centres were extended Bombay, Calcutta and Madras.

1616 East India Company of Denmark reached Indian coasts

1619 Jehangir granted permision to the Dutch to trade in his territories

1620 Capture of Kangra Fort; Danish traders settled in Tranqubar in Tamil Nadu and Serampore in Bengal (1676)

1627 Death of Jehangir; Accession of Shah Jehan; Birth of Shivaji Bhonsle.

1628 Shah Jehan proclaimed Emperor

1631 Death of Shah Jehan's wife Mumtaz Mahal-The building of the Taj Mahal.

1636 Aurangzeb appointed Viceroy of Deccan

1639 Fort St. George built in Madras by the English.

1646 Shivaji captures Torna

1658 Aurangzeb becomes Emperor of Delhi.

1664 Shivaji assumes royal title; Compagine des Indes Orientales (The French East India Co.) established trading centres near Madras and Chandernagore on Hoogly.

Shivaji's replica

1666 Birth of Guru Gobind Singh; Death of Shah Jahan

1675 Martyrdom of Guru Tegh Bahadur.

1684 East India Co. set up a primary press in Bombay.

1689 Execution of Sambhaji

1699 Guru Gobind Singh creates 'Khalsa'.

1707 Death of Aurangzeb.

1708 Guru Gobind Singh dies.

1720 Accession of Baji Rao Peshwa at Poona.

1738 Malwa ceded to Marathas

1739 Nadir Shah of Persia conquers Delhi: lose Kabul.

1742 Marathas invade Bengal; Dupleix, French Governor of Pondicherry.

1746 The First Carnatic War (First Anglo-French war) - The French and British companies clashed at Carnatic and the French capture Madras.

1748 First Anglo-French war ended with the treaty of Aix La Chappelle, in Europe.

1750 War of the Deccan; Death of Nasir Jang; 1750-04 Second Anglo-French War (unofficial).

1754- Mughal king Ahmad Shah deposed; Dupleix returns to France and General Godeheu signed the Treaty of Pondicherry with the British.

1756 Alivardi Khan, Nawab of Bengal dies; Siraj-ud-daulah succeeds after capturing Calcutta; Ahmad Shah Abdali in Delhi Jun. 20. Black-Hole Tragedy - where of the 146 English prisoners held by Mughals in a small chamber, 123 prisoners died of suffocation (figures disputed).

1757 Jun. 23. Battle of Plassey: The British defeat Siraj-ud-daulah through a conspiracy with Mir Jafar. Mir Jafar made Nawab of Bengal. (-60 Clive's first Governship).

1758 (-63) Third Anglo-French War; Marathas occupy the Punjab.

1760 Battle of Wandiwash-The

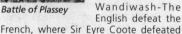

Battle of Plassey

English defeat the French, where Sir Eyre Coote defeated Count Lally, sealing the fate of the French in India..

1761 Third Battle of Panipat; Ahmed Shah Abdali, the ruler of Afghanistan defeats the Marathas; Maratha imperialism checked;

Third Battle of Panipat

Hyder Ali usurps power in Mysore (rules till '82); Fall of Pondicherry.

1764 Oct. 23. Battle of Buxar- the English defeat Mir Kasim who instigated war with the help of Nawab Shuja-ud-daula of Awadh and Shah Alam II (Mughal).

1765 The English get Diwani Rights in Bengal, Bihar and Orissa; Clive, Governor in Bengal for the second time.

1766 The English secure Northern Circars in the Carnatic.

1767-69 First Mysore war-the British suffered a humiliating peace with Hyder Ali of Mysore.

1769- The French East India Co. dissolved.

1772 Warren Hastings appointed Governor of Bengal; Return of Shah Alam to Delhi.

1773 The Regulating Act passed by the British Parliament to curb the company trader's unrestrained commercial activities and better territorial control.

1774 Warren Hastings becomes the first Governor-General of India. Calcutta made the administrative headquarters of the Company.

1775-82 First Anglo-Maratha war: The Treaty of Salbai ended the war.

1780 Birth: Maharaja Ranjit Singh; James August Hickey started a weekly paper called Bengal Gazette (also called Calcutta General Advertiser).

1780-84 The Second Mysore War. The

English defeat Hyder Ali. Tipu Sultan succeeds Hyder Ali.

1784 Pitt's India Act passed; Calcutta Gazette published; Foundation of Asiatic Society of Bengal with the help of William Jones.

1785 The Bengal Journal published.

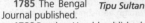

Tipu Sultan

1788 Bombay Herald published; Blinding of Shah Alam.

1790-92 Third Mysore War between the English and Tipu-Treaty of Seringapatam.

1791 Sanskrit College in Benaras opened by Jonathan Duncan.

1796 Marquess of Wellesley Governor General.

1799 Fourth Mysore War-The English defeat Tipu; Death of Tipu-Partition of Mysore; William Carey at Serampore.

1800 Fort Williams College at Calcutta started by Lord Wellesley; Death of Nana Fadnavis.

1801 The English annex the Carnatic and part of Oudh.

1802 Treaty of Bessein with Peshwa Baji Rao which helped in flushing out Holkar from Poona.

1803-5 Second Anglo-Maratha War. British under Sir Arthur Wellesley inflict a crushing defeat on the Marathas; Occupation of Delhi by Lord Lake.

1806 The Vellore Mutiny.

1809 First Treaty of Amritsar- between Ranjit Singh and East India Company regarding rights over Satluj area; The Second Treaty of Aamritsar helped English restrict Russian advance through Punjab by annexing Khyber valley and defeating Afghan ruler Dost Muhammad.

1813 Charter Act renewed for free-trade.

1815-30 Activities of Ram Mohan Roy and the Serampore missionaries alongside William Carey.

1816 Hindu College, Calcutta founded

1817-19 Mill's History of India published; Marathas finally crushed.

1818-19 Sikh conquest of Multan and Kashmir.

1823 The Licensing Regulations (Adams Regulation) directed against vernacular newspapers.

1828 Lord William Bentinck becomes Governor General; Suppression of Thugs (1837).

1829 Brahmo Samaj founded; Era of social reforms-Prohibition of Sati.

Prohibition of Sati

1831 Rise of the Sikhs under Ranjit Singh.

1835 English, made the court language.

1837-38 Famine in North India.

1838 Tripartite Treaty.

1839 Maharaja Ranjit Singh dies. First Afghan War begins.

1845-46 First Anglo-Sikh War: Sikhs defeated and Treaty of Lahore signed resulting in reducing Sikh army's size below the British.

1848 Lord Dalhousie Governor General.

1848-49 Second Anglo-Sikh War-Sikhs defeated (1848). The British annexed Punjab into British Empire.

1853 First Indian Railway - Bombay to Thane; Annexation of Nagpur, Renewal of the Charter Act; Telegraph, started from Calcutta to Agra.

1854 Rise of Jute industry.

1857 Universities of Calcutta, Bombay and Madras set up; First War of Indian Independence (The Mutiny).

1858 British Crown takes over the Indian Government-Queen Victoria's Proclamation.

1859 Indigo disputes in Bengal.

1861 Indian Councils Act, Indian High Courts Act and Indian Penal Code passed; Famine in North-West India.

1865 Famine in Orissa.

1867 The (Newspaper) Registration Act

1868 Railway opened from Ambala to Delhi.

1875 Aligarh College founded by S. Ahmad Khan; Swami Dayananda Saraswati forms Arya Samaj in Bombay; Sree Narayana Guru sets up a Shiva temple and monastery at Aruvipuram in Kerala.

1876 The Queen becomes Empress of India; Famine in South India.

1877 Delhi Durbar-the Queen of England proclaimed Empress of India.

1878-80 Second Afghan War.

1879 Vernacular Press Act; Duties on Cotton abolished

1881 Factory Act-Rendition of Mysore-Mysore State restored to its original ruler.

1882 Punjab University set up.

1885 Indian National Congress founded - first meeting.

1886 Shri Ram Krishna Paramhansa dies.

1887 Allahabad University established.

1892 Indian Council Act to regulate Indian administration.

1893 Vivekananda participates in the World Parliament of Religions in Chicago.

1896-1900 Plague and Famine; Prince KS Ranjisinhji of Jamnagar became the first batsman in Cricket to score over 3000 runs in one season.

Vivekananda

1897 The Ramkrishna Mission founded by Swami Vivekananda

1899 Lord Curzon becomes Governor General and Viceroy.

1900 The North-West Frontier Province created; Lumiere Brothers, on 7 July, just six months after cinema's invention in France, brought it into India.

1901 Feb. 12 The Viceroy, Lord Curzon creates the North-West Frontier province between Afghanistan and Punjab; India's love for films started in Mumbai on 1 Oct. with the screening of the silent film, Life of Christ.

1902 Jul. 4. Swami Vivekananda dies; The first foreign film show - Aladin and the Wonderful Lamp.

1903 Jan. 1. A Durbar held in Delhi to announce King Edward VII, Emperor of India; 26. Gandhiji begins legal practice in South Africa.

1904 Indian Universities Act enacted in the viceroyalty of Lord Curzon; passed ancient monument protection Act and subsequently establishment of Archeological Survey of India; Dec. 26. The first Delhi-Bombay car race takes place.

1905 First Partition of Bengal; Aug. 7. INC declare boycott of British goods as a protest against the partition.

1906 Formation of the All India Muslim League; INC Calcutta Session for the first time uses 'Swaraj.' Servants of India Society founded by G.K. Gokhale.

1907 Jan. 22. Opposed to the new laws on race, Gandhiji begins the civil disobedience movement in South Africa; May 7. Electric tram-car starts service in Bombay; Oct. 4. Riots in Calcutta; Dec. 27. INC Surat Session ends with recriminations and violence; Tata Iron and Steel Company founded; First electric train started in Bombay.

1908 Jan. 30. MK Gandhi released from South African prison; Oct. 2. Khudiram Bose hanged; The Newspaper Press Act.

1909 Gandhiji writes Hind Swaraj; Minto-Morley Reforms Bill or Indian Councils Act passed.

1910 The Indian

Gandhiji

Press Act passed; Feb. 23 Chinese Army occupies Lhasa, forces Dalai Lama to flee to India; Aug. 22. Mother Teresa born in Albania as Agnes Ganxha Bojaxhiu.

1911 Jun. 22. King George V declared Emperor of India; Dec. 2. The first ever British King and Queen, King George V and Queen Mary arrive in Bombay, holds Durbar in Delhi; Partition of Bengal annulled to create the Presidency of Bengal; The first all-India Cricket team sails to England under the captaincy of Bhupinder Singh, the Maharaja of Patiala.

1912 Apr. 1. India's Imperial capital officially, shifted from Calcutta to Delhi; Apr. 18. The first Indian film by RG Torney, 'Pundalik', released; Rabindranath Tagore publishes Gitanjali; Orissa and Bihar separates.

1913 May 3. 'Raja Harishchandra,' India's first feature film, made by Dadasaheb Phalke released; Nov. 6. Gandhiji arrested in Johannesburg; 25. Jailing of Gandhiji causes riots in Natal; Dec. 1. Nobel Prize (Literature) for the first Asian for 'Gitanjali' by Rabindranath Tagore.

Tagore

1914 The First World War begins

1915 Jan. 9. Gandhiji returns to India from South Africa; Feb. 19. GK Gokhale dies; Mar 6. Gandhiji meets Rabindranath Tagore for the first time; Jun. 20. First Women's University established in Pune; Defence of India Act; Dec. Home Rule League - a movement started by Bal Gangadhar Tilak.

1916 Lucknow Pact signed between INC and Muslim League; Home Rule League similar to that of Tilak started by Annie Besant.

1917 Annie Besant becomes President of Indian National Congress; Kaira Satyagraha in Gujarat; Mar. The first feature film of Bengal was JF Madan's Satyavadi Raja Harishchandra; Apr. 10. Champaran Satyagraha in Bihar.

1918 World War ends.

1919 Mar. 1. Gandhiji introduces 'satyagraha'; Rowlatt Act intended to perpetuate

Passing of Rowlatt (Act) Bill

the extraordinary powers provokes countrywide protests; Apr. 13. The massacre at Jalianwala Bagh, Amritsar (Punjab) killed 500 and injured 1500 people by Gen. Reginald Dyer's soldiers; Ali brothers and Maulana Abul Kalam Azad start the Khilafat movement (for restoring the Turkish Khalifate) with Gandhiji's support. Montague-Chelmsford Reforms offer limited provincial autonomy to Indians; India becomes the member of the League of Nations.

1920 Aug. 1. 'Lokmanya' Bal Gangadhar Tilak, the revolutionary who said 'Swaraj is my birthright,' dies; Sept. 10. INC okays Gandhiji's nonviolent non-cooperation movement against the British government; Bonfire of British clothes to show popular dissatisfaction with the reforms.

1921 Jan. 9. The Duke of Connaught opens the new Indian Central Legislature in Delhi; Excavation under the supervision of Dayaram Sahani unfolds Harappa civilisation at he bank of river Ravi in the Larkana and Montgomery districts of Pakistan; Moplah or Mapilla (Muslim) rebellion in Malabar (Kerala) where the leader Ali Musaliar and 37 others were sentenced to death; Nov. Riots in Bombay as Gandhiji burns foreign cloths coinciding with the visit of the Prince of Wales - INC boycotts Prince's visit. Film-

MEA's First Woman Spokesperson	The first woman spokesperson of the Ministry of External Affairs was Nirupama Rao, now India's Ambassador to the US.

maker V. Shantaram made his first screen appearance in a film titled Surekha Haran; Dec. 23. Vishwa Bharati University established.

1922 Dr. RD Banerjee and his team excavates Mohenjodaro (in Sindhi means the mound of death); Civil Disobedience

Gandhiji addressing people during Civil Disobedience movement

Movement; Congress makes Gandhiji sole leader of Bardoli satyagraha; Outburst of violence at Chauri Chaura led to suspension of Civil Disobedience Movement by INC; Mar 10. Gandhiji arrested for the first time in India; 18. Gandhiji, on charges of sedition, sentenced to 6-years 'simple imprisonment.' In South India, the film industry took off with the screening of the first film Bhisma Pratigya. Swarajya Party started by C.R.Das and Motilal Nehru.

1923 Swarajists propose to enter the councils and wreck the government from within. Khilafat movement fizzles out as Kemal Pasha declares Turkey a secular state. Apr. 8. Plague in India; 'Indian Party,' started by Madan Mohan Malviya. Sep. 18. The INC agrees to launch the civil disobedience campaign; Gandhiji starts his 21 day fast in despair at Hindu-Muslim riots. The first radio programme was broadcast by the Radio Club of Bombay.

1924 Feb. 24 Gandhiji released from prison; Aug. 21. Gandhiji elected President of INC in Belgaum; 25000 die due to plague; Sept. 18 Gandhiji starts 21 day hunger strike; Director and actor Homi Master's thriller film Kala Naag, shifted the focus

from mythological films to modern themes. Indian Communist Party formed in Kanpur.

1925 Death of C.R.Das; KB Hedgewar establishes Rashtriya Swayam Sevak Sangh (RSS) in Nagpur; EV Ramaswamy Naicker "Periyar" launches Self-respect Movement. The first electric train ran on Feb. 3 between Bombay VT and Kurla.

1926 May 2. Women allowed to stand for election to public office in India.

1927 Indian Navy Act; Simon Commission appointed; Jan. 8. The first scheduled London-Delhi flight arrives; Muslim League splits. Broadcasting Services set up with 2 private transmission from Bombay and Calcutta.

1928 Feb. 3. Simon Commission comes to India - boycott by all parties; 28. Scientist CV Raman discovers the 'Raman Effect; All Parties' Conference - Muslim leaders leave the Conference; Aug. 15. Motilal Nehru report demands constitutional framework of a free India; Dec. 17. Lala Lajpat Rai dies; 20. India wins gold medal in hockey in Amsterdam Olympics.

1929 Feb. 10. JRD Tata becomes the first

Indian to get a pilot's license; Jawaharlal Nehru elected President of INC; Lord Irwin, Viceroy of India, promises Dominion Status for India; Nov. 5 The longest electric railway opens from Bombay to Poona for 116 miles; On the midnight of Dec. 31,

JRD Tata

At Lahore session, Pandit Jawaharlal Nehru, as President of the Congress, demands Swaraj and hoists the National Flag.

1930 Jan. 1. Gandhiji begins Civil Disobedience Movement; 26. Observed as Independence Day all over India; Mar. Gandhiji agrees to discontinue civil disobedience if Lord Irwin released political prisoners who had not been guilty of violence; Mar. 12. Gandhiji begins Dandi march; Apr. 6. Gandhiji defies salt-tax

Salt March

law at Dandi (salt satyagraha); Repression let loose by the government; Nov. 12. First Round Table Conference in London; Jun. 23. Simon Commission recommends a federal India and separation from Burma; Dec. 10. Nobel Prize in Physics (Raman effect) awarded to Sir C. V. Raman. India forms Indian Broadcasting Service.

1931 Mar. 4-5 Gandhi-Irwin Pact signed; Mar 14. Ardeshir Irani's Alam Ara projected at Bombay's Majestic Cinema; Sep.7 Gandhiji attends the Second Round Table conference.

1932 Jan. 4. Gandhiji arrested and INC outlawed; Jun. 25. Indian cricketers begins their first Test Match at Lords against Douglas Jardine's team. 28. India lose their first Test Match; Oct. 15. Air India's Bombay-Karachi service inaugurated; India wins gold medal for hockey in Los Angeles Olympic. Nov. 17. Third Round Table Conference.

1933 White Paper on Indian reforms.

1934 Nov. 19. The INC wins almost half the seats in elections to the Indian legislative assembly; Congress Socialist Party formed under the patronage of Acharya Narendra Dev; Civil Disobedience Movement called off; Bihar earthquake.

1935 Government of India Act passed. Gandhiji publishes Wardha Scheme of Basic Education in 'The Harijan.'

1936 Death of King George V; Accession of George VI; India wins the Berlin Olympic hockey gold medal. All India Radio formed.

1937 The Indian constitution comes into being under Government of India Act; Inauguration of Provincial Autonomy; British India divided into 11 provinces Congress ministries formed in a majority of the provinces; India and Burma separated as per the Govt. of India Act.

1939 Beginning of World War-II; Political deadlock in India as Congress ministries resign; Subash Chandra Bose starts Forward Block.

1941 Subash Chandra Bose escapes from India.

1942 Mar 22. Cripps Mission arrives in India to find out a formula for Indian independence; Both Congress and Muslim League refuse Sir Stafford Cripps' offer. Aug.

Gandhiji with Stafford Cripps

8. Congress adopts Quit India Resolution. Gandhiji gives call for 'Do or Die'; Aug. 9. Netaji Subhas Chandra Bose forms the Indian National Army in Malaya with the help of the Japanese. 'August Kranti movement,' mass social upheaval as senior Congress leaders arrested and Congress declared an illegal body;

1943 Bengal famine; Lord Wavell Viceroy and Governor General of India. Oct. 1. Netaji Subhas Chandra Bose inaugurates the Azad Hind Sarkar (Government of Free India) in Singapore.

1944 - Gandhi-Jinnah talks break down on Pakistan issue.

1945 The Indian National Army under Bose surrenders to the British after collapse of Japan. Dec. 31. Indian National Army personnel tried for treason in Red Fort, India; Shimla Conference.

PDS — **The Public Distribution System (PDS) in India operates through a network of more than 4.99 lakh Fair Price Shops. It is the largest distributional network of its kind in the world providing food safety net to more than 400 mn.people.**

1946 Jan. 12. Demonetisation of currency notes of the value of Rs. 500 and above; Demonstrations against the trial of the INA men; Feb. 18. 1100 naval ratings of signal school of HMIS Talwar in Bombay went on strike against racial discrimination; 19. Cabinet Mission comprising three ministers of the British cabinet-Lord Patrick Lawrence, Sir Stafford Cripps and AV Alexander, arrives in India; Cabinet Mission announces its plan for an interim government and a constituent assembly.- Congress accepts it. The interim government is formed by inducting only Congress nominees . The Muslim League takes umbrage and starts direct action. Viceroy persuades the Muslim League to come in; September: Sporadic violence in Bombay. 320 people were killed; Dec. 9. Constituent Assembly's first meeting; But the League declines to join the Constituent Assembly unless the demand for a separate state-Pakistan, is conceded.

1947 - Jan. 6. All India Congress Committee accepts partition of India by a majority vote of 99 in favour and 52 against the resolution; Jan. 18. The great popular singer Kundan Lal Saigal dies in Jalandhar; Feb. 20. The British Prime Minister Clement Attlee announces in the House of Commons about the British intention to transfer power into reasonable Indian hands by a date not later than June 1948; 20. Lord Mountbatten becomes the last Viceroy of India replacing Wavell, even as Britain prepares to transfer its power over India; Aug. 15. India and Pakistan gain Dominion Status and a wave of violence and killing triggered by Partition of Punjab and Bengal; May 29 The Indian Standards Institution is established; June 2. Lord Mountbatten declares the British decision on partition on June 3 (known as June 3rd Plan); Indian

Jawaharlal Nehru

leaders accept decision of Lord Mountbatten on partition; Jul. 15. Indian Independence Bill passed by British Parliament's House of Commons passed the bill and the House of Lords passed it the next day. Aug. 14. India is divided and Pakistan is created with full independence; The assets of the world's largest empire which had been integrated in countless ways for more than a century divided. As son as the new borders were made known, about 1 crore Hindus, Muslims and Sikhs fled from their homes on one side of the newly demarcated borders to what they believed to be their 'shelter.' About 10 lakh people were slaughtered in communal massacres; Aug. 15. India's declared independent of British rule with New Delhi as capital; Jawaharlal Nehru is sworn in as the first Prime Minister by Lord Mountbatten (the last Governor General of India); All the 562 states except Kashmir, Hyderabad and Junagarh incorporated in to the new federal union; Aug.-Sept. Punjab massacres; 27. Press Trust of India founded; Oct. 22. Invasion of Kashmir by Pakistani tribesmen with the abetment of Pakistan Government; Accession of Kashmir to India.

1948 Jan. The Films Division constituted. 30. Gandhiji is assassinated in Birla House prayer meeting in New Delhi through revolver shots by Nathuram Vinayak Godse; Mar 8. Air India International is established for overseas services; Jun. 8. Air India's first international flight, 'Malabar Prince,' takes of from Bombay to London; 21. C. Rajagopalachari becomes the first and only Governor General of India; 22. Britain's

Sir Mountbatten

king relinquishes his title 'Emperor of India.' Aug. 13. UN. Truce Line in Kashmir agreed; Sept. 17. Rebellion crushed in Kingdom of Hyderabad; Nov. 23. The National Cadet Corps is first organised for the student community; wins London Olympic hockey gold. Indian Atomic Commission created.

1949 Jan. 1. India and Pakistan agree truce in war over Kashmir; Feb. 1. Press Trust of India started functioning. Apr. 27. Republic of India created; Nov. 26. Constitution of India adopted by the Constituent Assembly.

1950 Jan. 26. India becomes a Sovereign Democratic Republic as Constitution of India comes into force with universal adult franchise; Dr. Rajendra Prasad becomes the first President of India; Feb. 28. National Planning Commission formed; Mar. 1. Population figures announced; Apr. 8. Nehru and Ali Khan sign the

B.R. Ambedkar

Indo-Pakistan Pact which relieved mounting pressure; Oct. 7. Missionaries of Charity founded by Mother Teresa in Calcutta; Dec. 15. Sardar Vallabhbhai Patel dies.

1951 Feb. 28. Kashmir issue taken-up in UN Security Council; Mar 4-11. First Asian Games in New Delhi; Jul. 9. First 5-year Plan (1951-56) announced. Most of its funds spent on rebuilding war- shattered railroads, irrigation schemes and canals. Oct.

Rajendra Prasad

21. Dr. Shyam Prasad Mukherjee forms Jan Sangh.

1952 Jan. 24. India's first International Film festival opens in Bombay; The first National General Election in India (Oct. 1951 - Feb. '52); Dr. Rajendra Prasad elected Rashtrapati (Head of State); India wins Helsinki Olympic hockey gold. Panchayati Raj - pilot scheme commenced. The Cinematograph Act of 1918 Indianised. The Central Board of Film Certification set up to certify films for public exhibition in India.

1953 Tenzing Norgay and Sir Edmund Hillary climb Mt. Everest; Excavation under the supervision of A. Ghosh and B. Lal uncovers Kalibangan (meaning black bangle), one of the Harappan settlements, on the bank of Ghaggar river in Hanumangarh district in Rajasthan. UGC established.

1954 Jul. 8. World's longest canal Bhakra-Nangal opened in Punjab. This multi-purpose river valley project is the largest irrigation system of its kind in Asia; 21. Agreement to bring peace to Indo-China. Sahitya Akademy, the Indian academy of letters established.

1955 Panch Sheel agreement (outlining Nehru's foreign policy of mutual respect for territorial integrity, benefit and co-existence) between China and India; Jun. 1. India's Untouchability (Offence) Act comes into force; Jul. 1. The office of the Registrar of Newspapers for India (RNI) came into existence; Avadi session of the Indian National Congress adopts a socialistic pattern of society for India; Hindu Marriage Act passed.

1956 Life Insurance nationalised; States Reorganisation Act; India wins Melbourne Olympic hockey gold. Hindu Succession Act passed. Jul. 1. The Office of the Registrar of Newspapers for India came into existence. Aug. 4. Asia's first atomic reactor, Apsara, goes critical in Trombay; Nov. 1. Indian states re-organised on linguistic basis. All India Institute of Medical Sciences set up in Delhi. BR Ambedkar embraces Buddhism along with 2 lakh followers in Nagpur.

1957 BARC opens in Trombay. Second National General Election. AIR renamed as Akashvani.

1958 Metric system of weights and measures introduced. Nationwide Panchayati Raj launched. Sept. 27. Mihir Sen, first Indian to cross English Channel. Supreme Court of India built.

Filming an Execution

Andrew DeYoung of the US, condemned to death for the murder of his parents and sister, was executed in July on camera. The execution was by a 3-drug lethal injection, using the anesthetic pentobarbital, which is also used to euthanise animals.

1959 Swatantra Party formed. Sept. 15. For the first time, a 30 minute television programme started transmiting educational and developmental programmes. Dec. 19. United News of India (UNI) incorporated

Dalai Lama

under Companies Act-1956. Dalai Lama get political asylum in India.

1960 Bombay bifurcated into Maharashtra and Gujarat states. The Indus Water Treaty. Union of Kashmir with India. At Christian Medical College, Vellore, Dr. N Gopinath and Dr. RH Betts perform the firs successful open heart surgery on a 12-year old child.

1961 Mar 4. India's first aircraft carrier, INS Vikrant, commissioned; 21. United News of India started functioning. Dec. 18. India occupies the Portuguese enclaves of Goa, Daman and Diu. Portuguese-India ceded by constitutional amendment, into the Indian Union in 1962.

1962 Third general election in India; Sept. 19. Sino-Indian War - China attacks India on the northern border and advances virtually unopposed toward the plains of Assam; Oct. 10. Fighting between People's Liberation Army of China and Indian Army; Nov. 12. Winter halts Chinese advance into India. 20. Ceasefire declared.

1963 Feb. 28. Rajendra Prasad dies.

1964 Feb. National Film Archive of India established; May 27. Jawaharlal Nehru, PM and architect of modern India, dies; Lal Bahadur Shastri becomes India's second PM; Communist Party of India splits; India wins Tokyo Olympic hockey gold. India's

first indegenous computer, ISIJU developed by Indian Statistical Institute and Jadavpur University, Calcutta.

1965 Commencement of regular television service as part of AIR began in Delhi. Apr. 9. Indo-Pakistan war in the Rann of Kutchh; 20. First Indian team led by MS Kohli ascends the Everest; Aug. 15. Indian forces crosses the ceasefire line and launched attack on Pak. administered Kashmir; Sept. 6. India crosses International Border on the western front marking official beginning of the war; 22. UN Security Council unanimously passed a resolution calling unconditional cease-fire from both nations; Sept. 1. Pakistan attacks India in Akhnoor sector of Kashmir.

1966 Tashkent Agreement reached; Jan. 11. Lal Bahadur Shastri dies at Tashkent, USSR, during the South Asia Peace Conference after inking the Agreement (meant to restore normalcy and peace between India and Pakistan); Jan. 19. Indira Gandhi elected leader of the Congress Party to succeed the late PM L.B. Shastri; Oct. 30. Mihir Sen crosses Panama Canal; Nov. 1. Dr. Homi Bhabha dies in a plane accident; The states of Haryana and Punjab comes into existence.

Lal Bahadur Shastri

1967 Fourth general election. Dr. Zakir Hussain elected President.

1968 May 29. Dara Singh becomes world wrestling champion; Oct. 16 Dr. Hargovind Khurana shares the Nobel Prize for Medicine and Physiology.

1969 May 3. Zakir Hussein dies; Jul. 19. 14 leading banks nationalised with a view to diversify and enlarge the scope of banking operations; Aug. 20. V.V. Giri elected President. Congress splits - Indira Gandhi forms her own Congress.

1970 Apr. 2. Former Indian rulers' privy

purses abolished; Nov. 21. Dr. C.V. Raman dies.

1971 Feb. 8. Indira Gandhi becomes PM; Mar 27. PM Indira Gandhi expresses full support to the Bangladeshi struggle for freedom; Dec. 3. Pakistan attacks Indian airfields in the west; Indian army joins hands with 'Mukhti Bahini' of Bangladesh

Indira Gandhi

to form 'Mitro Bahini' (Allied Forces) and overturns East Pakistan by taking 93,000 POWs in a quick campaign; Dec. 16. War ends when Pakistani army in Bangladesh surrenders to the Indian Commander, Lt. Gen. Aurora; 18. PM Indira Gandhi receives Bharat Ratna, the highest civilian award.

1972 Apr. 21. Pakistan leaves Comonwealth; Jul. 2. Shimla Agreement (on Kashmir), signed between India and Pakistan by Indira Gandhi and ZA Bhuto; Dec. 25. C. Rajagopalachari, the only Indian Governor General, dies.

1973 India's first Field Marshal named-Manekshaw.

1974 May 18. India's first atomic device, code-named 'Smiling Buddha,' exploded at Pokhran in Rajasthan; Aug. 20. Fakhruddin Ali Ahmed elected President; BD. Jatti Vice-President.

1975 Jan. 1. Bombay High - oil located; Apr. 17. Dr. S. Radhakrishnan, former President, dies; 19. Indian satellite Aryabhatta' launched; Jun. 12. Indira Gandhi's election set aside; 25-National emergency declared and censorship introduced.

1976 Mar 23. Indo-Sri Lanka boundary pact signed; Jun. 11. Indo-Soviet Moscow Declaration of Friendship and Co-operation signed by Indira Gandhi and President Brezhnev; Sept. 15. Doordarshan established.

1977 Jan. 18. The President dissolves Lok Sabha; Feb. 1. President Fakhrudin Ali Ahmed dies; March 16—20. Sixth General Election; 21 Emergency officially withdrawn;

22. Janata and its allies gain absolute majority in Lok Sabha; Indira Gandhi resigns; 24. Morarji Desai, a non-Congress leader becomes PM; Jul. 21. Sanjiva Reddi elected (unopposed) President of India; Sept. 15. Doordarshan established.

1978 Jan. 1. Air India's first Jumbo Jet, Emperor Ashoka, falls into the Arabian Sea killing 213 passengers and crew; Nov. Indira Gandhi re-elected to the Lok Sabha as a member of the newly formed Congress (I) party; Dec. 19. The Lok Sabha expels Indira Gandhi, from the House and sentences her to imprisonment for a term lasting until its prorogation.

1979 Jul. 15. Morarji Desai resigns in order to avoid facing a no-confidence motion

Morarji Desai

in the Lok Sabha; 17. Charan Singh is PM heading Janata (S)-Congress coalition; Oct. 8. Jayaprkash Narayan dies; 17. Mother Teresa wins Nobel Peace Prize.

1980 Jan. 14. Mrs. Gandhi's new Ministry at Centre, sworn in; 30. Mother Teresa awarded Bharat Ratna; India wins Moscow Olympic hockey gold.

1981 Jun. 24. APPLE, India's satellite launched; Sept. 29. Khalistan activists hijack Indian Airlines Boeing 737 to Lahore, Pakistan; Oct. 1. Activists of the Dal Khalsa who masterminded the hijacking of Indian Airlines plane arrested.

1982 Jan. 14. Indian team of 21 members land on Antarctica; Apr. 10. INSAT 1A launched from Cape Canaveral, USA; Jul. 25. Zail Singh sworn in President; Nov. 15 Acharya Vinoba Bhave dies; 30. World Premier of Richard Attenborough's film, Gandhi, in New Delhi.

1983 Mar 3. Seventh Non-Aligned Movement's summit in New Delhi; Apr. 12. Richard Attenborough's "Gandhi" wins 8 Oscars; Oct. 19. Prof. Subramanyam Chandrashekhar of India shares Nobel Prize for Physics with Prof. William Fowler, USA; Nov. 23. Comonwealth Summit in New Delhi; Bhanu Athaiya is the first Indian to win an Oscar for costume design (Gandhi) shared with John Melo.

1984 Operation Meghdoot seized greater portion of Siachen Glacier from Pak. occupation; Apr. 4 Rakesh Sharma becomes India's first spaceman; May 23. Miss Bachendri Pal becomes the first Indian woman and 4th in the world to conquer Mount Everest;

Rakesh Sharma

Jun. 5. Operation Blue Star; Oct. 31. Indira Gandhi assassinated by her bodyguards; Rajiv Gandhi sworn in PM; Dec. 3. In Bhopal, 2,500 persons die in Union Carbide gas leak tragedy; PT Usha becomes the first Indian woman to appear in an Olympic final; GAIL India established.

1985 Jan. 10. Ravi Shastri scores 6 sixes of Tilak Raja in Bombay; Feb. 1. Azharuddin hits a century in each of his first three tests; Jun. 23. Air India 747, Kanishka, crashes off the coast of Ireland killing 329 people on board; Sept. Indira Gandhi National Open University (IGNOU) established, in order to promote distance education system and open universities.

1986 Feb. 1. Pope John Paul II arrives in New Delhi; Mar 16. Notorious criminal, Charles Shobraj, escapes Tihar Jail with six criminals after drugging the guards; May 6. The Muslim (divorce protection) Bill passed, entitling a divorced woman a reasonable provision; Jul. 15. India's Sandhya Agarwal sets world record by scoring 190 runs in the third test Match against England; Aug. 7. The first wholly Indian test-tube baby born at the REM hospital, Bombay; Gen. AS Vaidya, the chief of Army Staff during Operation Blue Star, shot dead; Nov. 17. SAARC SUMMIT in Bangalore. Shah Bano,

a Muslim divorcee and Mary Roy, a Keralite Christian respectively win alimony and inheritance cases in Supreme Court.

1987 March 7. Sunil Gavaskar becomes the first batsman to make 10,000 runs; May 12. INS Virat (originally Harmiz) commissioned in Indian Navy, 30. Goa becomes the 25th state of India; Sept. 3. Viswanathan Anand, 17, becomes India's first Grand Master and the World's youngest.

1988 Feb. 25. Prithvi, the first tactical surface-to-surface short range ballistic missile, test-fired; Mar. 17. IRS-IA, India's first remote-sensing satellite, launched; Oct. 23. The Power Grid Corporation of India established.

1989 Jan. 19. Indian national flag hoisted in South Pole; May 22. Agni, the first surface-to-surface intermediate range ballistic missile, test-fired; Jun. 5.

Prithvi Missile

TRISHUL, the first surface-to-air short range missile, test-fired; Nov. 10. Foundation stone laid for the Ram Janambhoomi temple at Ayodhya; Dec. 2. VP Singh, JD leader, sworn in as India's seventh PM.

1990 Jan. 22. FIR registered in Bofors kickbacks case; Aug. 7. GOI accepts Mandal Commission recommendations; 14. AKASH, the first surface-to-air medium range missile, test-fired; Sept. 25. LK Advani starts his rathayatra; Nov. 7. VP Singh tenders resignation; 10. S. Chandrasekhar sworn in as PM.

1991 Jan. 17. About 1.25 lakh Indian expatriates from Kuwait begin to return to India as a result of Gulf War (against Iraq); Mar. 6. Chandrasekhar resigns as PM; May 21. Former Prime Minister Rajiv Gandhi killed by a suicide bomber in Sriperumbudur; Jun.

21. A 54-member Narasimha Rao ministry sworn in; Dec. 15. Satyajit Ray awarded Special Oscar. India's first indigenous supercomputer built by CDAC Lab. in Pune.

1992 Jan. 29. India and Israel to establish full diplomatic relations; Oscar for lifetime achievement awarded to Satyajit Ray; Apr. 28. Sensex fell 570 points (12.77%); May 5. 'Prithvi' launched; Jul. 10. INSAT 2A shot into space; 25. Dr. Shankar Dayal Sharma sworn in as ninth President of India; Nov. 27. 19 year old Sachin Tendulkar scores one thousand test runs; Dec. 6. The domes of Babri Masjid Ayodhya demolished by fanatics.

1993 Feb. 12. Kapil Dev crosses 400 wickets and 5000 runs in test cricket; 26. Allan Border beats Gavaskar's record of the highest test runs of 10,122; Sep. 30. Quake kills thousands in Latur around Osmanabad.

1994 May 21 Sushmita Sen is Miss Universe. Nov. 19. Aishwarya Rai selected Miss World.

1995 Apr. 10 Morarji Desai dies.

A.B. Vajpayee

1996 May 16. A.B. Vajpayee is PM, until May 28; June 1. H.D. Deve Gowda's 21-member Central cabinet sworn in.

1997 Jan. 31. INS Vikrant decommissioned from Indian Navy, April 21. IK. Gujral sworn in PM; July 25. K.R. Narayanan sworn in President of India; Sept. 5. Mother Teresa, 87, dies. Nov. 28. IK Gujral resigns as PM. Manjula Padmanabhan receives Onassis Award for The Bitter Harvest.

1998 March 14. Sonia Gandhi takes over as Cong. (I) president; 19. A.B. Vajpayee takes over as PM; May 11. India conducts Operation Shakti, code-name for Pokhran-II nuclear tests, by detonating fission devices; Oct. 14. Amartya Sen wins the Nobel Prize for Economics; Nov. 19. National Security Council to give policy direction and safeguard India's security. Arundhati Roy wins the 1997 Booker Prize for 'The God of Small Things.'

1999 Feb. 20. PM Vajpayee arrives in Pakistan by Delhi-Lahore bus; Lahore Declaration signed to provide a peaceful and bilateral solution to the Kashmir issue; May 26. Oceansat-1 (IRS-P4) launched by PSLV-C2; June-July: Intense fighting in Kargil due to infiltration of Pak-soldiers (called Operation Badr) inside Line of Control (the de facto border between the two nations); July 26. India declares Kargil as completely free of Pak. intruders; Sep. 5. Lok Sabha election begins; Oct. 10. 13th Lok Sabha constituted; 13. Vajpayee Govt. sworn-in; 19. Devastating cyclone hits Orissa and A.P.

2000 Mar 19. US President Clinton visits India; Jul. 31. Matinee idol Rajkumar abducted by Veerappan; Sep. 14. Bill Gates in Delhi; 19. Karnam Malleswari wins a bronze at Sydney Olympics; Oct. 30. Azharuddin and four others named by CBI in cricket match fixing; Nov.1. Chhattisgarh, the 26th state is born; 15. Jharkhand, the 28th State is born; Matinee idol Rajkumar released by bandit Veerapan; Dec. 24. Viswanathan Anand becomes world chess champion.

Viswanathan Anand

2001 Jan. 21. India and Bangladesh starts train service after 21 years; Feb. 9. 14th Census of India begins; Mar 1. India clocked 1027015247 people, to become the world's second most populous nation after China; Apr. 4. Bismillah Khan awarded Bharat Ratna; 18. GSAT-1 launched by GSLV-D1 from Sriharikota; May 27. Koodiyattam receives UNESCO approval; Jul. 15-16 The Agra Summit between Pak. President Parvez Musharraf and Prime Minister Atal Behari Vajpayee; Oct. 22. PSLV-C3 successfully launched. Dec. 13. Suicide squad attacks parliament in New Delhi, killing several police. The 5 gunmen die in the assault.

World's 68th bank

India's largest bank, State Bank of India, is 68th among the world's largest banks. In March, 2010 it had 13,039 branches and 200,299 employees.

2002 Jan. 15. Cabinet allows every Indian citizen to hoist the flag anytime; Feb. 7. INSAT-3C put in geosychronous orbit; Mar 26. POTO Bill passed; Apr. 20. Sachin Tendulkar equals Sir Donald Bradman's record of 29 centuries; Jul. 25. APJ Abdul Kalam becomes 12th President; Aug. 19. Bhairon Singh Shekhawat sworn in as 12th Vice-President; Sept. 12. METSAT (KALPANA-1) put in orbit.

2003 Feb. 12. 'BrahMos,' super sonic anti-ship cruise missile test-fired off the Orissa coast; May 4. Indian Light Combat

Tejas - Light Combat Aircraft

Aircraft rechristened 'Tejas'; Aug. 1. LCA makes maiden flight.

2004 May 20. Manmohan Singh appointed Prime Minister by the President of India; Aug. 17. Major RS Rathore wins Olympic silver medal for Double Trap firing; Sept. 20. EDUSAT launched; Dec. 23. Former PM Narasimha Rao dies.

2005 Feb. 12. Sania Mirza becomes the first ever India woman to win a WTA event; Aug. 2. National Knowledge Commission launched; 8. Nanavati Commission report tabled in the Parliament; Oct. 12. The Right to Inforamtion Act comes into effect except in J&K; Nov. 9. Former President KR Narayanan dies.

2006 Jul. 31. Parliament (Prevention of Disqualification) Amendment Bill passed; Aug. 10. Vinda Karandikar, Marathi writer, conferred 39th Jnanpith Award; Sept. 9. Kanshi Ram, BSP founder, dies; Shabana Azmi receives Gandhi International Peace Prize; Nov. 20. President of China Ho-Jintao visits India; Dec. 15. Prevention of Child Mar-

riage Bill-2004, passed in Rajya Sabha.

2007 Apr. 12. 14th SAARC Summit at New Delhi; Agni-III, successfully test fired; 18. 'Saras,' prototype of India's first commercial civilian aircraft made its maiden flight; Jet Airways acquires Air Sahara; .

2008 Jan. 1 India Pak exchange list of nuclear installations; Feb 9 Baba Amte, 94, dies at Anandvan, Warora, Maharashtra; Apr 10. Supreme Court upholds 27% OBC quota in Central higher education institutions; Jun 27. Field Marshal Sam Manekshaw, 94, dies in Ootty; Jul. 22. UPA Govt. of Manmohan Singh wins the trust vote in Lok Sabha by 19 votes; 25. Bangalore city rocked by 9-serial blasts in 24 hours killing 2 people; 26. Ahmedabad stunned by 12 explosions in 45 minutes, killing about 50 people; Aug 11. Abhinav Bindra wins a gold medal at Beijing Olympics in 10m air rifle category; 20. Sushil Kumar win a bronze medal for 66 kg wrestling in Beijing Olympics; 22. Vijender wins India's first Olympic medal (bronze) in boxing, in Beijing; 25. Swami Lakshmananda shot dead by Maoist extremists in Orissa sparks widespread communal violence against Christian institutions and communities; Sep 6. India enters the nuclear club as NSG lifts a 34-year old trade embargo; Oct 7. Tata decides to relocate Nano car plant in Singur- West Bengal to Sanand

Chandrayaan I

in Gujarat; 22. Chandrayaan-1, India's first moon mission launched successfully form Sriharikota; Nov. 12. Chandrayaan-1reaches the final lunar orbit of 100 km above the moon; 14. Chandrayaan-1's Moon impact Probe lands on the Moon; 26. Pak terrorists

Taj Hotel when bombed by militants

strikes Mumbai from sea; 29. Operation Cyclone, the war on terror ends after 60 hours of battle killing 183 people; Dec. 18. Paliament approves setting up National Investigating Agency; 31. New anti-terror law comes into effect.

2009 Jan 1 – National Investigation Agency (NIA) Bill and the Unlawful Activities (Prevention) Amendment (UAPA) Bill, the new anti-terror regime came into force with President Pratibha Patil giving her assent; Five persons were killed and about 50 injured in serial bomb blasts in Guwahati, Assam; Indian Government constitutes a separate pay commission in a move to redress the grievances of Indian Armed Forces personnel over anomalies in pay structures. Jan 2 – Indian Government in tandem with the Reserve Bank of India (RBI) announces the second Stimulus Package aimed at reversing the economic slowdown; Kapil Dev, Sunil Gavaskar and Bishan Singh Bedi figure among the 55 players in the ICC's inaugural Hall of Fame list. Jan 5 – Indian Government summons Pakistan High Commissioner Shahid Malik to hand over evidence about Pakistans involvement in the Mumbai terror attacks Feb 13 - A passenger train derails in Bhubaneswar, Orissa, killing at least 15 people and injuring 150 others. Feb 23 – India approves a £1.7-billion plan to launch its first astronauts into outer space by 2015. Feb 25 – Former Indian Communications Minister Sukhram is jailed for three years for corruption. Mar 24 – Sixteen militants and eight Indian Army soldiers are killed in

Jammu and Kashmir's Kupwara District. Apr 1 – No additional charges on withdrawing money from an ATM of a different bank. Apr 16 – The Naxalite movement kills 17 people as India's general election begins. Apr 20 – India's Space Research Organization launches its RISAT-2 reconnaissance satellite May 19 – Manmohan Singh of the National Congress is reelected as Prime Minister of India. May 25 - Cyclone Aila ravages the east coast killing at least 149 and hundreds left homeless as torrential rains led to flooding. June 3 – Indian Member of Parliament Meira Kumar becomes the first female Speaker of the House of the People. June 4 – Two hundred thousand people attend the funeral of Dera Sach

Meira Kumar

Khand leader Sant Ramanand Dass in Jalandhar, Punjab. June 17 – Indian Prime Minister Manmohan Singh meets with Pakistani President Asif Ali Zardari. June 20 – Indian troops enter Lalgarh, a Maoist stronghold in West Bengal, claiming a partial victory. July 2 – A 148-year old colonial law banning homosexual intercourse in India is overturned by the High Court in New Delhi. July 5 – At least eight people die in blasts at two explosives factories in Madhya Pradesh July 12 – Five people are killed and

Lalgarh Maoist violence

| **Helpline for Investors** | SEBI plans to start a nationwide toll-free helpline to resolve investors' grievances and educate them about markets. It will also launch awareness campaigns through newspapers, radio and TV channels. |

INS Arihant

several injured in India after a bridge being constructed for the Delhi Metro collapses. July 20 – Ajmal Kasab, the only surviving gunman in the 2008 Mumbai attacks, pleads guilty in an Indian court, ending months of denials July 20 – India and the United States sign a defence pact. July 26 – India launches its first nuclear submarine, the INS Arihant. Aug 6 – An Indian court sentences to death three people for carrying out bombings that killed more than 50 people in Mumbai in 2003. Aug 11 – A 7.5 magnitude earthquake occurs in the Andaman Islands of India. Aug 24 – At least 200 children are killed and around 900 hospitalised by Japanese encephalitis in Uttar Pradesh, India. Sep 1 – An outbreak of diarrhoea in Orissa, India, kills at least 26 people and hospitalises 237. Sep 2 – A Bell 430 helicopter crashes during a flight in southern India. Fatalities included Y. S. Rajasekhara Reddy, the CM of the Indian state of Andhra Pradesh. Sep 14 – Chandrayaan-1, India's first unmanned

lunar probe, discovers large amounts of water on the Moon. Sep 30 – 2009 Thekkady boat disaster: the double-decker passenger boat Jalakanyaka capsized in Lake Thekkady, killing A total of 45 passengers. Nov 24 – Prime Minister Manmohan Singh had the first official state visit to the White House during the administration of U.S. President Barack Obama. Discussions included matters on trade and nuclear power. Dec 10 – India announces it is to create a new state, Telangana, out of Andhra Pradesh. Dec 13 – India successfully test fires its nuclear-capable "Dhanush" missile off the Orissa coast.

2010 Jan 2- SENSEX is 25.12-The office of CJI brought under RTI by the Delhi High Court.17- Jyoti Basu, veteran Marxist leader and former West Bengal CH passes away at 95. Feb. 7- Agni III launched successfully. 10. Dr. KN Raj is no more.12-Bomb explosion in German Bakery, popular with tourists in Pune, Maharashtra, kills 16 people, sparking security fears. Mar 2- Chandra-yaan's sensors find traces of water on the other side of the moon.9- Rajya Sabha passes Women's Reservation Bill. 23- Maruthi's 1 Millionth vehicle rolls out. April 1- Census 2011 begins. 6- 74 CPRF men killed by Maoists in Chhattisgarh's Dantewada district.12-Shoaib Malik and Sania Mirza gets married in Hyderabad; PM Manmohan Singh meets Barak Obama in Washington before nuclear summit. 29- India commissions its first stealth warship INS Shivalik. May 03- The lone surviving gunman of the 2008 Mumbai attacks, Ajmal Amir Qasab, is convicted of murder, waging war on India and possessing explosives. 05- Supreme Court declares Narco Analysis unconstitutional.18 - Laila cyclone strikes south India.

June 02- Nano car rolls out of Sanand. 03- India unveils anti-swine flu vaccine. 07- A court in Bhopal sentences eight Indians to two years each in jail for "death by negligence" over the 1984 Union Carbide gas plant leak.

Tata's Nano

Y.S.R. Reddy dies in a plane crash

Thousands died in this, the world's worst industrial accident. **27**- PM Manmohan Singh and Prez Obama meets at G-20 summit at Toranto. **July 15**- The symbol for Indian Rupee unveiled- was designed by D.Uday Kumar. **27**- SY Quraishi, the new CEC; British PM David Cameron visits India.**29**- President's rule in Jharkhand. **31**-Jnanpith Award 2006 goes to Ravindra Kelkar, Konkani writer. **Aug. 1**- Chief Editor, KM Mathew, 93, Malayala Manorama, passes away.**08**-Tejaswini Sawant becomes the first Indian women shooter to win a gold medal at the World Championship. **17**- Mammen Mathew becomes the new Chief Editor of Malayala Manorama.**30**- Parliament adopts nuclear liability bill. **Sep. 27** ONV Kurup and Akhlaq Khan Shahrayar wins Jnanpith Award for 2007 and 2008 respectively. **30**- Allahabad High Court rules that disputed holy site of Ayodhya should be divided between Hindus and Muslims; the destruction of a mosque on the site by Hindu extremists in 1992 led to rioting in which about 2,000 people died. **12** Aug. :The Indian cabinet has approved India's first caste-based census since 1931, to be held between June-Sep. 2011 after the full census has been held. The Cabinet hopes the move will help target aid and funding to those currently under-supported with regard to benefits and employment rights. **20** Aug. The Indian foreign ministry has offered $5 million to Pakistan to assist flood victims of the worst monsoon flooding in that country in generations. **30** Aug. Police have shot dead an eleven year old boy who was throwing stones during a street protest in Indian-administered Kashmir in the southern town of Anantnag. The protest took place despite a government imposed curfew. **20 Sep.** Kashmir separatist leaders,

Tejaswini Sawant

LOGO   MASCOT

XIX Commonwealth Games, New Delhi

Syed Ali Shah Geelani and Mirwaiz Umar Farooq, meet Indian MPs 'peace delegation' on a fact-finding mission. Both have long criticised the Indian government's policy in Kashmir. They are thought to be behind the anti-government protests in Indian-administered Kashmir. **Oct 03**- XIX Commonwealth Games in New Delhi inaugurated - Participants: 71 countries and 6000 athletes (619-Indian contingent). **5** Oct. Former Pakistan leader Pervez Musharraf admits in a German magazine article that Pakistani security forces trained militant groups fighting in Indian-administered Kashmir in the 1990s. Musharraf told Der Spiegel magazine that the Pakistan government turned a blind eye to force India into peace talks. **12** Oct. India wins two year seat on UN Security Council India has won a two-year term on the UN Security Council. **14**-Commonwealth Games concludes with Australia leading the medal tally with 177(74 G, 55 S, 48 B), followed by India with101 medals (38G, 27S, 36B) and England came third with 37 gold.59 silver and 46 bronze. **19** Oct. The general secretary of the All Parties Hurriyat Conference, Masrat Alam, is arrested in Srinagar. Police have been looking for him because he is believed to be responsible for the recent 'Quit Kashmir' protests against Indian rule in the Kashmir valley. **21** Oct. The Indian government has established a welfare programme for pregnant women

---

Air Pollution Kills 2 mn.	**Air pollution is responsible for around 2 mn. premature deaths worldwide every year, says WHO, which describes it as a major environmental risk to health.**

Dmitry Medvedev and Manmohan Singh

and breast-feeding mothers. The women will be given 12,000 rupees ($270) over a six month period and will get regular health checks and necessary vaccinations. **2 Nov.** Environmental ministry puts brakes on building of the largest dam in South Asia over concerns that the reservoir the dam will make 200,000 people homeless in Andhra Pradesh and that costs will spiral above the professed $2 billion budget. 8 Nov. President Barack Obama supports India's aspiration to become a permanent memner of the UN Security Council. During his three day state visit to India, Obama describes India as a strategic partner of the US and pledges to increase trade between the two countries to $10 billion. **9** Nov. Ashok Chavan, India's chief minister of the western state of Maharashtra, resigns from the ruling Congress Party over his role in a scam that cheated war widows out of free housing. Suresh Kalmadi, who organised the Commonwealth Games, also steps down. **15** Nov. A report by the Indian Comptroller and Auditor-General has accused former telecoms minister Andimuthu Raja of massive phone corruption totalling £22 billion. Raja is alleged to have under-sold mobile phone network licences in 2008 for a fraction of their true value. This is suspected to be India's biggest case of official corruption. **24** Nov. Nitish Kumar, Bihar State's chief minister, has won a landslide election in the northern Bihar state, which has a population of more than 80 million people. Kumar's Janata Dal (United) party-led alliance won at least 200 out of 243 seats in the Bihar assembly. **3 Dec.** India's third richest man, Azim

Premji has donated £1.27 billion to a children's charity that provides education for underprivileged children in rural areas. **6** Dec. Prime Minister Manmohan Singh has signed a deal to buy two nuclear reactors from France, as a result of a four-day official visit by President Nicolas Sarkozy. The deals are worth an estimated $20 billion. **16** Dec. India and China sign a bilateral deal to increase trade between the two countries to £66 billion by 2015, on the second day of Chinese Prime Minister Wen Jiabao's three day official **21** Dec. Russian President Dmitry Medvedev has ended a two day state visit to India by signing business, defence and nuclear trade agreements worth billions of dollars. **25** Dec. An Indian space rocket carrying the country's largest

Dr Binayak Sen

communications satellite into orbit explodes soon after launch from the Sriharikota space centre in Andhra Pradesh state. **26** Dec. Dr Binayak Sen, acclaimed human rights activist and a pioneer of medical work amongst tribal peoples, has been convicted of helping Maoist guerrillas fighting in the Chhattisgarh region. He was convicted of sedition and conspiracy against the State after allegedly being caught passing messages to the Naxalites. **28** Dec. The Indian government has deployed thousands of troops after warnings that Lashkar-e-Taiba, the Pakistan-based militant group, is planning further attacks over the New Year.

| There is Danger in Cereal Boxes | Breakfast cereal manufacturers are to stop using recycled cardboard in packaging after a study showed that they could pose a cancer risk. |

Provisional Figures

Population: 2011 Census

India is one of the very few countries in the world, which has a proud history of holding census after every ten years. The Indian Census has a very long history behind it. The earliest literature 'Rig Veda' reveals that some kind of population count was maintained during 800-600 BC. Kautilya's Arthasastra, written around 321-296 BC, laid stress on census taking as a measure of state policy for purpose of taxation.

During the regime of Mughal king Akbar the Great, the administrative report 'Ain-e-Akbari' included comprehensive data pertaining to population, industry, wealth and many other characteristics. In ancient Rome, too, census was conducted for purpose of taxation. The history of Indian Census can be divided in two parts i.e. Pre-Independence era and Post Independence era.

The first complete census of an Indian city was conducted in 1830 by Henry Walter in Dacca. In this Census the statistics of population with sex and broad age groups and also the houses with their amenities were collected.

After 1941 Census India got its independence in 1947. The Bhore Committee

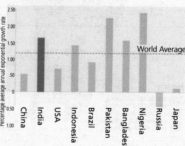

constituted for making plans for post war development in the field of health made a comprehensive review of the field of population and recommended that a Registrar General of Vital and Population Statistics at the centre be appointed and at provincial level, a Superintendent may be appointed with a view to improving the quality of population statistics. The first census of Independent India was conducted in 1951, which was the seventh census in its continuous series. The enumeration period of this census was from 9th to 28th, February 1951.

The number of questions canvassed during Population Enumeration in Censuses of 1951 and 2011 are: 1951 Census 14 Questions and 2011 Census 29 Questions.

10 Most Populated Nations

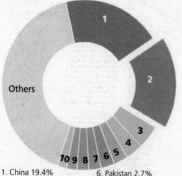

1. China 19.4%
2. India 17.5%
3. USA 4.5%
4. Indonesia 3.4%
5. Brazil 2.8%
6. Pakistan 2.7%
7. Bangladesh 2.4%
8. Nigeria 2.3 %
9. Russia 2.0%
10. Japan 1.9%

Population growth rate, Selected Countries: 2000-2010

World Average

China India USA Indonesia Brazil Pakistan Bangladesh Nigeria Russia Japan

Figures At A Glance

No. of States/UT 35 / 35*
No. of Districts 593 / 640*
No. of Sub-Districts 5,463 / 5,924*
No. of Towns 5,161 / 7,935*
No. of Villages 638,588 / 640,867*

*(2001 / 2011)

Population

	Total	Rural	Urban
Persons	1210,193,422	833,087,662	377,105,760
Male	623,724,248	427,917,052	195,807,196
Female	586,469,174	405,170,610	181,298,564

Decadal Pop. Growth 2001-2011 (Percentage)

	Total	Rural	Urban
Persons	17.64	12.18	31.80
Male	17.19	12.12	30.06
Female	18.12	12.25	33.73

Literates

	Total	Rural	Urban
Persons	778,454,120	493,020,878	285,433,242
Male	444,203,762	288,047,480	156,156,282
Female	334,250,358	204,973,398	129,276,960

Sex Ratio

	Total	Rural	Urban
Persons	940	947	926

Sex Ratio (0-6 yrs)

	Total	Rural	Urban
Persons	914	919	902

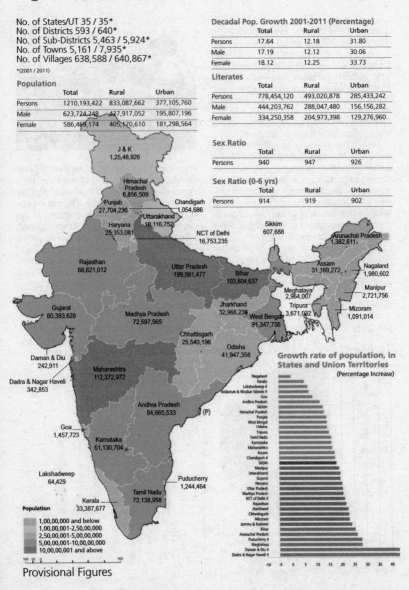

J & K
1,25,48,926

Himachal Pradesh
6,856,509

Punjab
27,704,236

Chandigarh
1,054,686

Uttarakhand
10,116,752

Haryana
25,353,081

NCT of Delhi
16,753,235

Sikkim
607,688

Arunachal Pradesh
1,382,611

Rajasthan
68,621,012

Uttar Pradesh
199,581,477

Bihar
103,804,637

Assam
31,169,272

Nagaland
1,980,602

Meghalaya
2,964,007

Manipur
2,721,756

Gujarat
60,383,628

Madhya Pradesh
72,597,565

Jharkhand
32,966,238

West Bengal
91,347,736

Tripura
3,671,032

Mizoram
1,091,014

Chhattisgarh
25,540,196

Odisha
41,947,358

Daman & Diu
242,911

Dadra & Nagar Haveli
342,853

Maharashtra
112,372,972

Growth rate of population, in States and Union Territories
(Percentage Increase)

Andhra Pradesh
84,665,533 (P)

Goa
1,457,723

Karnataka
61,130,704

Lakshadweep
64,429

Puducherry
1,244,464

Kerala
33,387,677

Tamil Nadu
72,138,958

Population
- 1,00,00,000 and below
- 1,00,00,001-2,50,00,000
- 2,50,00,001-5,00,00,000
- 5,00,00,001-10,00,00,000
- 10,00,00,001 and above

Provisional Figures

Distribution of population, sex ratio, density and decadal growth rate of population : 2011

India/State/UT #	Total population	Males	Females	Sex ratio	Density (Per sq.km)	Dec. gro. rate
INDIA	1,210,193,422	623,724,248	586,469,174	940	382	17.64
A & Nr Islands	379,944	202,330	177,614	878	46	6.68
Andhra Pradesh	84,665,533	42,509,881	42,155,652	992	308	11.10
Arunachal Pradesh	1,382,611	720,232	662,379	920	17	25.92
Assam	31,169,272	15,954,927	15,214,345	954	397	16.93
Bihar	103,804,637	54,185,347	49,619,290	916	1,102	25.07
Chandigarh #	1,054,686	580,282	474,404	818	9,252	17.10
Chhattisgarh	25,540,196	12,827,915	12,712,281	991	189	22.59
Dadra & Nagar Haveli #	342,853	193,178	149,675	775	698	55.50
Daman & Diu #	242,911	150,100	92,811	618	2,169	53.54
Goa	1,457,723	740,711	717,012	968	394	8.17
Gujarat	60,383,628	31,482,282	28,901,346	918	308	19.17
Haryana	25,353,081	13,505,130	11,847,951	877	573	19.90
Himachal Pradesh	6,856,509	3,473,892	3,382,617	974	123	12.81
Jammu & Kashmir	12,548,926	6,665,561	5,883,365	883	124	23.71
Jharkhand	32,966,238	16,931,688	16,034,550	947	414	22.34
Karnataka	61,130,704	31,057,742	30,072,962	968	319	15.67
Kerala	33,387,677	16,021,290	17,366,387	1,084	859	4.86
Lakshadweep #	64,429	33,106	31,323	946	2,013	6.23
Madhya Pradesh	72,597,565	37,612,920	34,984,645	930	236	20.30
Maharashtra	112,372,972	58,361,397	54,011,575	925	365	15.99
Manipur	2,721,756	1,369,764	1,351,992	987	122	18.65
Meghalaya	2,964,007	1,492,668	1,471,339	986	132	27.82
Mizoram	1,091,014	552,339	538,675	975	52	22.78
Nagaland	1,980,602	1,025,707	954,895	931	119	-0.47
NCT of Delhi #	16,753,235	8,976,410	7,776,825	866	11,297	20.96
Odisha	41,947,358	21,201,678	20,745,680	978	269	13.97
Puducherry #	1,244,464	610,485	633,979	1,038	2,598	27.72
Punjab	27,704,236	14,634,819	13,069,417	893	550	13.73
Rajasthan	68,621,012	35,620,086	33,000,926	926	201	21.44
Sikkim	607,688	321,661	286,027	889	86	12.36
Tamil Nadu	72,138,958	36,158,871	35,980,087	995	555	15.60
Tripura	3,671,032	1,871,867	1,799,165	961	350	14.75
Uttar Pradesh	199,581,477	104,596,415	94,985,062	908	828	20.09
Uttarakhand	10,116,752	5,154,178	4,962,574	963	189	19.17
West Bengal	91,347,736	46,927,389	44,420,347	947	1,029	13.93

Provisional Figures

Literates and literacy rates by sex : 2011

	*Persons	Males	Females	**Persons	Males	Females
INDIA	**778.4**	**444.2**	**334.2**	74.04%	82.14%	65.46%
A & N Is.	**293.7**	**164.2**	**129.4**	86.27%	90.11%	81.84%
Andhra Pradesh	51.4	28.7	22,.7	67.66%	75.56%	59.74%
Arunachal Pradesh	789.9	454.5	335.4	66.95%	73.69%	59.57%
Assam	19.5	10.7	8.7	73.18%	78.81%	67.27%
Bihar	54.4	32.7	21.7	63.82%	73.39%	53.33%
Chandigarh #	809.6	468.2	341.4	86.43%	90.54%	81.38%
Chhattisgarh	15.6	8.9	6.6	71.04%	81.45%	60.59%
Dadra & Nagar Haveli #	228.8	144.9	83.1	77.65%	86.46%	65.93%
Daman & Diu #	188.9	124.9	64.0	87.07%	91.48%	79.59%
Goa	1.1	0.6	0.5	87.40%	92.81%	81.84%
Gujarat	41.9	23.9	17.9	79.31%	87.23%	70.73%
Haryana	16.9	9.9	6.9	76.64%	85.38%	66.77%
Himachal Pradesh	5.1	2.8	2.3	83.78%	90.83%	76.60%
Jammu & Kashmir	7.2	4.3	2.8	68.74%	78.26%	58.01%
Jharkhand	18.7	11.1	7.6	67.63%	78.45%	56.21%
Karnataka	41.0	22.8	18.2	75.60%	82.85%	68.13%
Kerala	28.2	13.7	14.5	93.91%	96.02%	91.98%
Lakshadweep #	52.9	28.2	24.6	92.28%	96.11%	88.25%
Madhya Pradesh	43.8	25.8	17.9	70.63%	80.53%	60.02%
Maharashtra	82.5	46.3	36.2	82.91%	89.82%	75.48%
Manipur	1.9	1.2	0.8	79.85%	86.49%	73.17%
Meghalaya	1.8	0.9	0.9	75.48%	77.17%	73.78%
Mizoram	847.6	438.9	408.6	91.58%	93.72%	89.40%
Nagaland	1,357.6	731.8	625.8	80.11%	83.29%	76.69%
NCT of Delhi #	12.7	7.2	5.5	86.34%	91.03%	80.93%
Orissa	27.1	15.3	11.8	73.45%	82.40%	64.36%
Puducherry #	966.6	502.6	464.0	86.55%	92.12%	81.22%
Punjab	18.9	10.6	8.3 76.	68%	81.48%	71.34%
Rajasthan	38.9	24.2	14.7	67.06%	80.51%	52.66%
Sikkim	449.3	253.3	195.0	82.20%	87.29%	76.43%
Tamil Nadu	52.4	28.3	24.1	80.33%	86.81%	73.86%
Tripura	2.8	1.5	1.3	87.75%	92.18%	83.15%
Uttar Pradesh	118.4	70.5	47.9	69.72%	79.24%	59.26%
Uttarakhand	6.9	3.8	3.1	79.63%	88.33%	70.70%
West Bengal	62.6	34.5	28.1	77.08%	82.67%	71.16%

Union Territory #; *No. of Literates; **Literacy rate (%)

Provisional Figures

Population Growth Patterns

The growth of India's population since Aryan migration to Gangetic plains, followed a pattern similar to those observed in this area. At a closer look, the growth rates of 8 States refered to in administrative parlance as the Empowered Action Group (EAG) States, namely, Rajasthan, UP, Uttarakhand, MP, Chhattisgarh and Odisha is compared with the rest of the States and UT. The EAG group, from 1951 till 2011, have hosted between 43 to 46% of India's population.

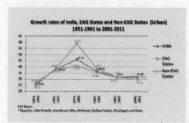

Growth rates of India, EAG States and Non-EAG States (Urban) 1951-1961 to 2001-2011

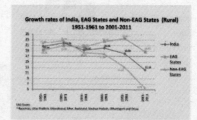

Growth rates of India, EAG States and Non-EAG States (Rural) 1951-1961 to 2001-2011

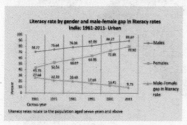

Literacy rate by gender and male-female gap in literacy rates India: 1961-2011- Urban

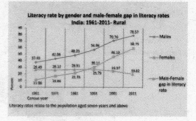

Literacy rate by gender and male-female gap in literacy rates India: 1961-2011- Rural

Growth of population, GDP and foodgrain production: 1950-2011

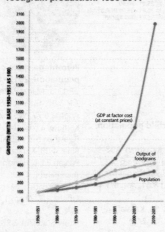

Population in Millions: 1901-2011

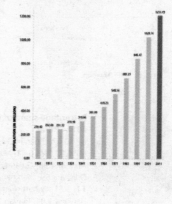

Provisional Figures

Rural-Urban Population Distribution

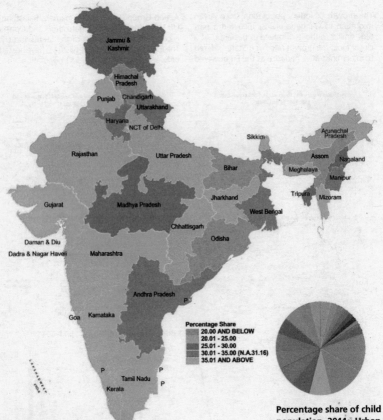

Percentage Share
- 20.00 AND BELOW
- 20.01 - 25.00
- 25.01 - 30.00
- 30.01 - 35.00 (N.A.31.16)
- 35.01 AND ABOVE

P - Puducherry

Percentage share of child population, 2011 - Rural
UP 20.62, Bihar 14.37, Rajasthan 7.08, MP 6.92, WB 6.41, Maharashtra 6.33 Andhra 4.98, Gujarat 3.98, Karnataka 3.7 Odisha 3.69, Jharkhand 3.61, Asom 3.47 T N 3.11, Chhattisgarh 2.44 Haryana 1.91, Punjab 1.59, Kerala 1.49 J&K 1.36, Other States /UT 2.97

Percentage share of child population, 2011 - Urban
UP 13.3, Maharashtra 13.11 T N 7.87, Gujarat 6.84 Andhra 6.77, WB 6.26 Karnataka 6.08, MP 5.86 Rajasthan 5.3, N Delhi 4.65 Bihar 4.08, Kerala 3.82 Punjab 2.61, Haryana 2.56 Jharkhand 2.4, Chhattisgarh 1.74 Odisha 1.7, Asom 1.04 J&K 1 Other States/Ut 2.98

Provisional Figures

Towards Normalizing Indo-Pak Relations

G. Parthasarathy
Former Indian High Commissioner to Pakistan & Australia

The world is watching the moves in Asia where India and Pakistan are the major players. India's efforts at peace between the two have been thwarted by the ISI and the military establishment in Pakistan.

While there is broad consensus across the political spectrum in India on the need to normalize India-Pakistan relations, such a consensus does not exist in Pakistan. Moreover, within Pakistan, relations with India are determined primarily

Pak President Pervez Musharraf with Indian Prime Minister A B Vajpayee at Agra Summit, 15.07.2001

by the military establishment, of which the ISI is an integral part. While the army's approach towards India has invariably been marked by "compulsive hostility", the period November 2003 to July 2008 was one where the military ruler, President General Pervez Musharraf evidently realized that normalization of relations with India was imperative if Pakistan was to recover economically, or face challenges posed by the entry of American forces into Afghanistan or for the ouster of the ISI–backed Taliban Regime there.

Composite Dialogue Process

India and Pakistan agreed in November 2003 to a ceasefire along the Line of Control in Jammu and Kashmir. This ceasefire has remarkably been sustained ever since. Then on January 4, 2004, India and Pakistan agreed to resume the stalled *Composite Dialogue Process* consequent to a categorical assurance from President Musharraf to then Prime Minister Atal Bihari Vajpayee, that he would not allow "territory under Pakistan's control" to be used for terrorism against India. The resumption of the *Composite Dialogue Process* led to some progress in resolving the issue of demarcating the boundary in the Sir Creek area, though differences on resolving differences on the Siachen Glacier Region still remain. The period prior to 2007 also saw significant progress in furthering people–to–people contact be-

Post-Partition Scenes

The Name Pakistan	Rahmat Ali Chaudhuri, an Indian Muslim graduate in Cambridge, read out a note in 1933 proposing division of India in London. There in the name of the Muslim majority state was proposed as Pakistan.

tween the two countries, with the opening of new rail and road links, most importantly the Khokhrapar-Munnabao rail link across the Sind-Rajasthan border. Trade and economic ties, however, showed little progress with Pakistan continuing to deny "Most Favoured Nation" treatment to Indian exports and remaining opposed to normal business, industrial and investment collaborations, even in the private sector.

A Framework to Resolve Kashmir Issue

Backdoor discussions on Jammu and Kashmir were conducted with substantial measure of secrecy. There have been indications from reports in the media and in comments by President Musharraf and Pakistan's former Foreign Minister Mr. Khurshid Kasuri that there was agreement on a Kashmir settlement. Well informed American writers like Steve Coll and Bruce Reidel have confirmed that by February 2007, not only had agreement been reached on a frame-

> Complementing the dialogue between the two Governments, were measures to promote dialogue and cooperation across the Line of Control (LOC) in Jammu and Kashmir.

work to resolve the Kashmir issue, but also that General Musharraf had informed his Senior Military colleagues about it. While the exact contours of the framework then discussed are not known publicly, reports in the media confirm that it involved the Line of Control becoming a de facto International Border, with provisions for free travel and trade across it. There was reportedly agreement on harmonizing the nature of "self-governance" on both sides of the Line of Control. Responding to General Musharraf's proposal for "demilitarization," India reportedly indi-

Indian Prime Minister Indira Gandhi with Pakistan President Z A Bhutto before their Summit talks in Simla, 28.06.1972

cated its readiness to reduce and redeploy forces in Jammu and Kashmir on a reciprocal basis, once it is reassured that there is an irrevocable end to infiltration across the Line of Control. There also appears to have been understanding on the need for mechanisms and institutions to promote cooperation across the Line of Control, in areas like trade, travel, tourism, education, health, environment and water resources.

Cooperation Across the LoC

Complementing the dialogue between the two Governments, were measures to promote dialogue and cooperation across the Line of Control (LOC) in Jammu and Kashmir. A series of measures to promote travel, trade and dialogue across the LOC were agreed upon. For the first time after five decades, people in Jammu and Kashmir were given facilities to travel across the LOC to meet friends and relatives. In the Kashmir valley, a bus service has been instituted between Srinagar and Muzaffarabad and in the Jammu Region, between Poonch and Rawalkot. In addition, five crossing points have been opened to enable people to meet friends and relatives across the LOC. Trade across the LOC has been permitted for the first time, with goods carried by trucks on the Srinagar-Muzaffarabad road. There are also proposals under discussion

Control of Kashmir	Pakistan controls the northern and western portions of Kashmir, an area of about 84,160 sq.km. The Pak-occupied Kashmir has its own Assembly, Council, High Court and Supreme Court.

Benazir Bhutto

to establish bus links between Jammu and Sialkot in the Jammu Region and between Kargil and Skardu linking the valley of Kashmir with the Northern Areas, under Pakistan's control. While the goods presently traded are restricted to locally produced products, this trade can be vastly expanded as and when India and Pakistan move towards the stated goal of SAARC countries to establish a South Asian Economic Union. There are, however, misgivings and grievances in Jammu and Kashmir that despite the openings for trade and travel, the procedures for such cross–LOC links have been made too cumbersome and restrictive. Moreover, there are numerous complaints from people, who find permission to travel either delayed or effectively denied. These shortcomings and misgivings are to be addressed in the Composite Dialogue Process.

Musharraf's Internal Problems

Progress in strengthening India-Pakistan relations received a setback after President Musharraf faced a series of internal problems that seriously eroded his standing and powers domestically. On March 9, 2007, he unceremoniously sacked the country's Chief Justice Iftikhar Mohammed Chaudhury, sparking off a countrywide agitation by lawyers that forced him to impose draconian measures to deal with the agitation. He was, at the same time, under pressure from the Americans to permit the return of Benazir Bhutto to the country, to participate in free and fair elections. Facing pressures, President Musharraf was forced to permit former Prime Minister Nawaz Sharif, whom he had jailed and exiled, to return to the country. In the meantime, radical militants took control of the *Lal Masjid* in the

heart of the capital Islamabad. When the militants sought to impose Sharia Law and practices in the capital, external pressures, including from China, compelled President Musharraf to order a military crackdown against the militants occupying the Masjid.

Between July 3 and July 11, 2007, elite commandos of the Pakistan army mounted a siege and then an attack on the Masjid premises. According to reports from Pakistan, roughly 300 to 500 women students in the Madrassa adjacent to the Masjid perished in the army action. These women students were predominantly Pashtuns, from the tribal areas of the Northwest Frontier Province (NWFP, now renamed as *Pakhtunkhwa*). This action evoked prompt reprisals from the Tehriq–e *Taliban e Pakistan* (TTP), a group of radical Pashtun tribesmen, who were supporting the Afghan Taliban in enforcing Sharia Law across the NWFP and seeking to seize control of the scenic Swat Valley located near

Delhi - Lahore Bus

the Islamabad. In the meantime, Benazir Bhutto was assassinated in Rawalpindi and the elections subsequently held produced a PPP–led Government, headed by her husband Asif Ali Zardari. Under pressure from all directions, Musharraf relinquished the Post of Chief of Army Staff to General Ashfaq Parvez Kayani and was compelled to make way for Asif Zardari as President, before heading into exile.

General Kayani

General Kayani's assumption of office as

Islamic Republic	Pakistan, which remained a dominion for nine years, was proclaimed an Islamic republic on March 23, 1956.

Army Chief has been accompanied by a reversion to the earlier military policy of compulsive hostility towards India. Despite indications by President Zardari that he favoured reconciliation, improved trade and economic ties and support for the framework on Jammu and Kashmir finalized between India and Pakistan in 2007, General Kayani prevailed in rejecting President Zardari's friendly approach to relations with India. Internally, the army assumed a higher profile, when following attacks by the (TTP) across Punjab and the NWFP and even of the Army's GHQ in Rawalpindi, the army mounted operations using heavy firepower and air support on TTP strongholds in the tribal areas of the NWFP. This standoff still continues, with the Army being placed in

Wagah border Daily Retreat ceremony

> The Afghan Intelligence Services confirmed that the attack had been executed by militants from across the border with Pakistan and that the attack was undertaken with high–level ISI involvement.

the embarrassing position of attacking pro-Taliban Pashtun militants that it had nurtured earlier, while continuing to extend support to the Afghan Taliban led by Mullah Omar and his military Commander Sirajuddin Haqqani to fight American forces and the Karzai Government in Afghanistan.

Attack on Embassy

The manifestations of renewed hostility towards India became evident, when militants attacked the Indian Embassy in Kabul on July 7, 2008. Around 58 people died in the attack, including the Embassy's Military Attaché Brigadier Ravi Datt Mehta and Counselor (Information) Venkateshwar Rao. Within days, the Afghan Intelligence

Services confirmed that the attack had been executed by militants from across the border with Pakistan and that the attack was undertaken with high–level ISI involvement. Rejecting Pakistani denials, President Bush sent an envoy to Islamabad to present evidence his Administration had of high–level Pakistani involvement on the attack in the Indian Embassy. India's reaction to this terrorist outrage was strangely muted. Just over four months later, on November 26, ten terrorists of the *Lashkar e Taiba* mounted a seaborne terrorist attack on Mumbai, holding virtually the entire city to ransom for almost four days. About 167 people lost their lives, including nationals of the US, UK and Israel. Wireless intercepts clearly showed that the handlers of the terrorists were issuing orders from Pakistan. Here again, apart from speaking to Prime Minister Gilani, the Indian Government's reaction was muted, without even a single meaningful action being taken to convey India's outrage to Pakistan, like even the recall of India's High Commissioner from Islamabad. More seriously, evidence emerged of serious failures by the Police, Intelligence Services and Coastguard to act on intelligence inputs warning of a seaborne attack.

At a loss to think through a suitable diplomatic response which would make Indian outrage at the terrorist attack evident, all

| Shimla Agreement | The Shimla Agreement was signed by Indian Prime Minister Indira Gandhi and Zulfikar Ali Bhutto of Pakistan on July 2, 1972. |

that the Government of India did was an announcement that it would suspend the Composite Dialogue process with Pakistan. Even here, the Government gave every indication that it was itching for resumption of dialogue, even though it was clear that Pakistan had no intention of acting against the masterminds, including LeT leader Hafiz Mohammed Saeed. It also soon became known from American reports that Lashkar Commander Zakiur Rehman Lakhvi, who had been arrested for his involvement in the Mumbai attack, was actually continuing to coordinate *Lashkar–e–Taiba* operations from his jail cell, and among the visitors he had received in jail was ISI Chief Lieutenant General Ahmed Shuja Pasha.

SAARC Summit, Thimpu

Despite the absence of any serious action by the Pakistan Government against the perpetrators of the 26/11 terrorist outrage, the Government of India decided to head into summit level negotiations with Pakistan during the Nonaligned Summit in Sharm el Sheikh in Egypt. Strangely, this Summit meeting took place with virtually no preparatory meetings between the two sides. Not surprisingly, the Sharm el Sheikh Summit, like the Agra Summit in July 2001, was a diplomatic disaster for India. Disregarding clear indications that with General Kayani at the helm, Pakistan was stepping up terrorist activities in both India and Afghanistan and ignoring the fact that the Composite Dialogue with Pakistan was resumed in 2004 only after a categorical assurance from General Musharraf that he would not allow territory under Pakistan's control to be used for terrorism against India, major policy changes were effected, to the detriment of India's interest at the Sharm el Sheikh Summit on July 16, 2009. The Joint Statement issued by Dr. Manmohan Singh and Prime Minister Gilani stated:- "Dialogue is the only way forward. Action on terrorism should not be linked to the Composite Dialogue Process and these should not be bracketed". Pakistan was, in effect, told by India's Prime Minister that he would happily continue the Compos-ite Dialogue Process even if Pakistan took no action against the perpetrators of the 26/1 terrorist outrage and the ISI continued its terrorist attacks against India and Indian interests in Afghanistan. Worse still, the Joint Statement gave credence to Pakistan's unfounded allegations that India was backing separatist and terrorist elements in Pakistan's Baluchistan Province.

Furore in Parliament

The Sharm el Sheikh Joint Statement resulted in furore in Parliament and widespread public and media criticism in India. By virtually letting Pakistan off the hook in its continuing support for terrorism, the feeling across the country was that the Government had seriously let down, if not betrayed, all those who had suffered in the 26/11 attack. But, it was evident that having entered into dialogue, would be counter–productive not to proceed on the road with Pakistan. External Affairs Minister S.M. Krishna visited Pakistan on July 14-15, 2010. It was, however, evident that despite proclamations of friendship, no progress was achieved on getting Pakistan to act against those responsible for the Mumbai carnage, even though Mr. Krishna provided his Pakistani counterpart with details of what India had learnt from the interrogation of David Coleman Headley in Chicago. Headley had given Indian investigators details of his own involvement and that of his friend, Canadian national

Tahawur Hussain Rana, with LeT leaders and ISI officials, in planning the Mumbai terrorist attack. Moreover, the concluding joint press conference on July 15 addressed by Mr. Krishna and his Pakistani counterpart Mr. Mohammed Shafi Qureishi clearly brought out the chasm between India and Pakistan in the dialogue process.

Cricket Diplomacy

Determined to carry forward the dialogue process, Prime Ministers Manmohan Singh and Gilani met at the sidelines of the SAARC Summit in Thimpu, Bhutan in February 2011. While India's Foreign Secretary Nirupama Rao spoke of a new "Thimpu Spirit" guiding the diplomatic exchanges, what emerges is that while the Government of India refuses to acknowledge that it has re–entered and resumed the "Composite Dialogue Process", the reality is that it has done so, knowing fully well that there is no reason to believe that Pakistan has any intention of bringing to book

> It is against this background, that Prime Minister Manmohan Singh gave "Cricket Diplomacy" a try by inviting Prime Minister Gilani to the India-Pakistan World Cup semifinal in Mohali.

those resorting to terrorism against India. It is against this background, that Prime Minister Manmohan Singh gave "Cricket Diplomacy" a try by inviting Prime Minister Gilani to the India-Pakistan World Cup semifinal in Mohali. It is, however, clear that in the absence of political will and a conducive political climate, difficult issues are not going to be resolved, even as the dialogue process continues with ritualistic Secretary Level meetings.

Pak PM Gilani with Indian PM Manmohan Singh at the World Cup, Mohali

Osama Killed in Pakistan

In the meantime, the spectacular American military action that killed Osama bin Laden in a house in the Cantonment city of Abbotabad, located just next to the Pakistan Military Academy, where the most wanted terrorist had been residing since 2011, has reinforced the view internationally that the Afghanistan-Pakistan region remains the epicentre of global terrorism. It has focused world attention on the links between the Pakistan military establishment and radical Islamic elements in Pakistan and Afghanistan, which are challenging the writ of the Afghan Government and continuing to pose the threat of terrorist violence against India. Moreover, Pakistan itself now faces terrorist threats from groups like the TTP and the *Jaish e Mohammed*, which were for years armed and trained by the ISI. There is even global concern at the possibility of Pakistani nuclear weapons being taken over by radical Islamic forces. All this has not, however, chastened the Pakistan military, which has sought to divert public attention, by fostering anti-American sentiments and raising concerns about the alleged "Indian threat" to the country's security. Conducting a meaningful and productive dialogue with Pakistan in such an environment, is going to remain a major diplomatic challenge for India. ∎

Benazir Bhutto | Benazir Bhutto was assassinated in Rawalpindi on Dec. 27, 2007. Her son 19-year-old Bilawal was named chairman of PPP.

Timeline: India-Pakistan Relations

1947: India gains independence from Britain. Muslim-majority areas are partitioned to form Pakistan, triggering bloody riots and large scale migration of people.

1947-48: Pakistan attacks India in Kashmir.

1965: Pakistan attacks India again in Kashmir and also in the Rann of Kutch.

1971: Bangladesh war.

1972: Prime Ministers Indira Gandhi and Zulfikar Ali Bhutto sign Shimla Agreement.

1974: India carries out its first nuclear test.

1998: Second nuclear test by India followed by Pakistan carrying out its own nuclear tests.

1999 February: Prime Minister Atal Behari Vajpayee visits Lahore.

1999: Pakistan attacks India in Kargil in Jammu and Kashmir.

Kargil Jawans Remembered

2001 July: President Pervez Musharraf visits Agra and holds talks with Prime Minister Vajpayee.

2001 December: India's parliament is attacked by Pakistan-based Kashmiri terrorists. Tension leads heavy troop deployment on both sides of the border.

2004: India and Pakistan launch formal peace process.

2008 July: Deadly bomb attack on Indan embassy in Kabul. India blames Pakistan's ISI.

2009 February: Pakistan admits for the first time that the Mumbai attack was launched and partly planned from inside Pakistan.

2009 June: Prime Minister Manmohan Singh President Asif Ali Zardari on the sidelines of the Shanghai Cooperation Organisation summit in Russia.

2009 July: Prime Ministers Manmohan Singh and Yusuf

Manmohan Singh and Azif Ali Zardari

Raza Gilani meet on the sidelines of the Non-Aligned Movements, summit in Egypt.

2010 February: India offers new talks with Pakistan at the top diplomatic level.

2010 July: India's External Affairs Minister S.M. Krishna visits Islamabad to hold talks with his Pak counterpart Shah Mohammed Qureishi.

2011 July: Pakistan Foreign Minister Hina Rabbani Khar visits New Delhi for talks with Krishna.

S M Krishna with Hina Rabbani

States of India

India, for administrative purposes, is divided into the national capital territory of Delhi, 28 states, and 6 centrally administered union territories.

States: Andhra Pradesh, Arunachal Pradesh, Assam, Bihar, Chhattisgarh, Goa, Gujarat, Haryana, Himachal Pradesh, Jammu & Kashmir, Jharkhand, Karnataka, Kerala, Madhya Pradesh, Maharashtra, Manipur, Meghalaya, Mizoram, Nagaland, Orissa, Punjab, Rajasthan, Sikkim, Tamil Nadu, Tripura, Uttarakhand, Uttar Pradesh, West Bengal.

Union Territories: Andaman and Nicobar Islands, Chandigarh, Dadra & Nagar Haveli, Daman & Diu, Lakshadweep, Puducherry.

National capital territory: Delhi

Population share of States and Union Territories, India: 2011

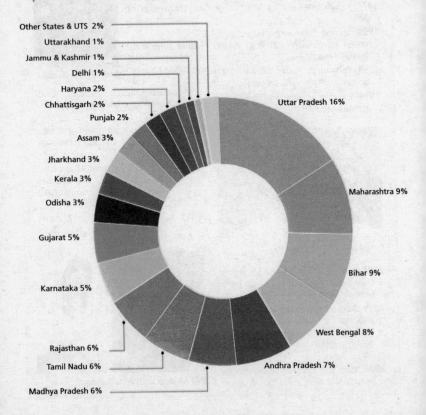

Other States & UTS 2%
Uttarakhand 1%
Jammu & Kashmir 1%
Delhi 1%
Haryana 2%
Chhattisgarh 2%
Punjab 2%
Assam 3%
Jharkhand 3%
Kerala 3%
Odisha 3%
Gujarat 5%
Karnataka 5%
Rajasthan 6%
Tamil Nadu 6%
Madhya Pradesh 6%
Andhra Pradesh 7%
West Bengal 8%
Bihar 9%
Maharashtra 9%
Uttar Pradesh 16%

Top 10 Populous States of India

Rank State/UT	Population in 2011
1. Uttar Pradesh	19,95,81,477
2. Maharashtra	11,23,72,972
3. Bihar	10,38,04,637
4. West Bengal	09,13,47,736
5. Andhra Pradesh	08,46,65,533
6. Tamil Nadu	07,21,38,958
7. Madhya Pradesh	07,25,97,565
8. Rajasthan	06,86,21,012
9. Karnataka	06,11,30,704
10. Gujarat	06,03,83,628
** NCT of Delhi	1,67,53,235

UTs

1. Puducherry	12,44,464
2. Chandigarh	10,54,686
3. Andaman and Nicobar Islands	3,79,944
4. Dadra and Nagar Haveli	3,42,853
5. Daman and Diu	2,42,911

States of India - areawise

Rank State/UT Size	(Area in Sq. km.)
1. Rajasthan	342,236
2. Madhya Pradesh	308,144
3. Maharashtra	307,713
4. Andhra Pradesh	275,068
5. Uttar Pradesh	238,566
6. Jammu and Kashmir	222,236
7. Gujarat	196,024
8. Karnataka	191,791
9. Odisha	155,707
10. Chhattisgarh	135,194

UTs

1. Andaman and Nicobar Islands	8,249
2. Delhi	1,483
3. Puducherry	492
4. Dadra and Nagar Haveli	491
5. Chandigarh	144

• The top five populous States in India are: Uttar Pradesh (199.6 million), Maharashtra (112.4 million), Bihar (103.8 million), West Bengal (91.3 million) and Andhra Pradesh (84.7 million).

Cities/Urban Agglomerations with over a million people (2001)

**	Urban Agglomerations /City	Population
01	Greater Mumbai	16,368,084
02	Kolkata	13,216,546
03	Delhi	12,791,458
04	Chennai	6,424,624
05	Bangalore	5,686,844
06	Hyderabad	5,533,640
07	Ahmedabad	4,519,278
08	Pune	3,755,525
09	Surat	2,811,466
10	Kanpur	2,690,486
11	Jaipur*	2,324,319
12	Lucknow	2,266,933
13	Nagpur	2,122,965
14	Patna	1,707,429
15	Indore	1,639,044
16	Vadodara	1,492,398
17	Bhopal	1,454,830
18	Coimbatore	1,446,034
19	Ludhiana*	1,395,053
20	Kochi	1,355,406
21	Visakhapatnam	1,329,472
22	Agra	1,321,410
23	Varanasi	1,211,749
24	Madurai	1,194,665
25	Meerut	1,167,399
26	Nashik	1,152,048
27	Jabalpur	1,117,200
28	Jamshedpur	1,101,804
29	Asansol	1,090,171
30	Dhanbad	1,064,357
31	Faridabad*	1,054,981
32	Allahabad	1,049,579
33	Amritsar	1,011,327
34	Vijayawada	1,011,152
35	Rajkot	1,002,160
	Total	107,881,836

* Municipal Corporation **Rank in 2001
Source: Census of India, 2001

• Fifteen States and Union Territories have grown by less that 1.5% per annum during 2001 - 2011, while the number of such States and Union Territories, were only four during the previous decade.

Beginning of States & UTs

The period between 1947 and 1950 witnessed the consolidation of the former princely states into new provinces, usually governed by a Rajpramukh, (Governor) appointed by the Governor-General of India. In 1950, the Indian constitution took effect, the office of the Governor-General was abolished, and India created several different categories of states.

Between 26 Jan 1950 and 1 Nov 1956 there were four types of divisions: Part A states (under a governor), Part B states (under a rajpramukh), Part C states (under a chief commissioner), and one Part D territory; from 1956 there were only states (former Part A and B states) and union territories (former Part C states and Part D territory). Gaps in the lists of chief ministers usually signify periods of "president's rule."

Part A states, which were the former provinces, were ruled by an elected governor and state legislature. The Part A states (nine) were Assam, West Bengal, Bihar, Bombay, Madhya Pradesh (formerly Central Provinces and Berar), Madras, Orissa, Punjab, Uttarakhand, and Uttar Pradesh (formerly United Provinces).

The **Part B states** (eight) were former princely states or groups of princely states, governed by a Rajpramukh. They were Hyderabad, Saurashtra, Mysore, Travancore-Cochin, Madhya Bharat, Vindhya Pradesh, Patiala and East Punjab States Union (PEPSU), and Rajasthan.

The **Part C states** (ten) included both former princely states and provinces. They were governed by a chief commissioner. The Part C states included Delhi, Kutch, Himachal Pradesh, Bilaspur, Coorg, Bhopal, Manipur, Ajmer, and Tripura. J&K had special status until 1957. The Andaman and Nicobar Islands was a territory, ruled by a governor appointed by the Indian president.

The **French enclaves** of Pondicherry, Yanam, Karaikal, and Mahe, were administered by India after 1954, formally becoming a Union Territory in 1962. Dadra and Nagar Haveli was occupied by India in 1954, and Goa, Daman, and Diu in 1961, and they subsequently became UTs.

In 1953, the Telugu-speaking portion

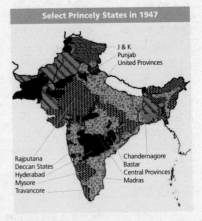

Select Princely States in 1947

J & K
Punjab
United Provinces

Rajputana
Deccan States
Hyderabad
Mysore
Travancore

Chandernagore
Bastar
Central Provinces
Madras

of Madras state voted to become the new state of Andhra Pradesh, the first of India's linguistic states.

In 1956, when the States Reorganisation Act took effect, the distinction between part A, B, and C states was gone, and instead state boundaries were drawn along linguistic lines. The new states, mostly the former Part A states, were Assam, West Bengal, Bihar, Maharashtra, Gujarat, Kerala, MP, Madras, Mysore, Orissa, Punjab, Rajasthan, and UP. Delhi, Himachal Pradesh, Manipur, Tripura, Pondicherry, the Andaman and Nicobar Islands, and the Laccadive, Minicoy, and Amandivi Islands became Union Territories. The remainder of the states were merged into the new states or UTs.

Several new states and UTs were created out of existing states since 1956. Haryana was created in 1966 out of Punjab. The UTs of Arunachal Pradesh, Meghalaya, Mizoram, and Nagaland were created out of Assam. In 2000, 3 new states were created; Jharkhand was created out of Bihar, Chhattisgarh out of MP, and Uttarakhand out of UP. The Kingdom of Sikkim was annexed to India as a state in 1975. In addition, several Union Territories have become states, namely Goa, Arunachal Pradesh, Meghalaya, Mizoram and Nagaland.

NOTE: Under Population, inside Literacy, letter t denote %age for total, m-% of male and f-% of female.

Rank of States (categorywise)

Rank	Population	Area	Density	Literacy	SC	ST
1	UP	Rajasthan	Delhi	Kerala	UP	MP
2	Maharashtra	MP	Chandigarh	Lakshadweep	WB	Maharashtra
3	Bihar	Maharashtra	Puducherry	Mizoram	Bihar	Orissa
4	WB	AP	Daman & Diu	Tripura	AP	Gujarat
5	AP	UP	Lakshadweep	Goa	TN	Rajasthan
6	MP	J&K	Bihar	Daman & Diu	Maharashtra	Jharkhand
7	TN	Gujarat	WB	Puducherry	Rajasthan	Chhattisgarh
8	Rajasthan	Karnataka	Kerala	Chandigarh	MP	AP
9	Karnataka	Odisha	UP	Delhi	Karnataka	WB
10	Gujarat	Chhattisgarh	D&NH	A&N Is	Punjab	Karnataka
11	Odisha	Tamil Nadu	Haryana	HP	Odisha	Asom
12	Kerala	Bihar	TN	Maharashtra	Haryana	Meghalaya
13	Jharkhand	West Bengal	Punjab	Sikkim	Gujarat	Nagaland
14	Asom	Arunachal	Jharkhand	TN	Jharkhand	J&K
15	Punjab	Jharkhand	Asom	Nagaland	Kerala	Tripura
16	Chhattisgarh	Asom	Goa	Manipur	Chhattisgarh	Mizoram
17	Haryana	HP	Maharashtra	Uttarakhand	Delhi	Bihar
18	Delhi	Uttaranchal	Tripura	Gujarat	Asom	Manipur
19	J&K	Punjab	Karnataka	D&NH	Uttarakhand	Arunachal
20	Uttarakhand	Haryana	Gujarat	WB	HP	TN
21	HP	Kerala	AP	Punjab	J&K	Kerala
22	Tripura	Meghalaya	Odisha	Haryana	Tripura	Uttaranchal
23	Meghalaya	Manipur	MP	Karnataka	Chandigarh	HP
24	Manipur	Mizoram	Rajasthan	Meghalaya	Puducherry	D&NH
25	Nagaland	Nagaland	Uttarakhand	Odisha	Manipur	Sikkim
26	Goa	Tripura	Chhattisgarh	Asom	Sikkim	UP
27	Arunachal	A&N Is.	Meghalaya	Chhattisgarh	Goa	Lakshadweep
28	Puducherry	Sikkim	J&K	MP	Meghalaya	A&N Is.
29	Chandigarh	Goa	HP	UP	Arunachal	Daman & Diu
30	Mizoram	Delhi	Manipur	J&K	Daman & Diu	Goa
31	Sikkim	Puducherry	Nagaland	AP	D&NH	Punjab
32	A&N Is.	D&NH	Sikkim	Jharkhand	Nagaland	Chandigarh
33	D&NH	Chandigarh	Mizoram	Rajasthan	Mizoram	Haryana
34	Daman&Diu	Daman&Diu	A&N Is	Arunachal	Lakshadweep	Delhi
35	Lakshadweep	Lakshadweep	Arunachal	Bihar	A&N Is.	Puducherry

SC & ST figures are from 2001 Census. Area, Density, Literacy - 2011.

The First Mughal Garden The first Mughal garden in India was laid out by Babur. It was called **Aram Bagh (now Ram Bagh)**

Ready Reckoner: States

State/UTS	Capital	% N.Pop	Governors	Chief Ministers
Andhra Pradesh	Hyderabad	7.0	E.S.L. Narasimhan	Kiran Kumar Reddy
Arunachal Pradesh	Itanagar	0.11	Chief Gen. (Rtd) Joginder J. Singh	Jarbom Gamin
Asom	Dispur	2.58	Janaki Ballabh Patanaik	Tarun Kumar Gogoi
Bihar	Patna	8.58	Devanand Konwar	Nitish Kumar
Chhattisgarh	Raipur	2.11	Shekhar Dutt	Dr. Raman Singh
Goa	Panaji	0.12	Dr. Shivinder Singh Sidhu	Digambar Kamat
Gujarat	Gandhinagar	4.99	Dr. Kamla Beniwal	Narendra Modi
Haryana	Chandigarh	2.09	Jagannath Pahadia	Bhupinder Singh Hooda
Himachal Pradesh	Shimla	0.57	Smt. Urmila Singh	Prof. Prem Kumar Dhumal
Jammu & Kashmir	Srinagar (Summer) Jammu (Winter)	1.04	N.N. Vohra	Omar Abdullah
Jharkhand	Ranchi	2.72	M.O.H. Farook Maricar	Arjun Munda
Karnataka	Bangalore	5.05	Hans Raj Bhardwaj	Sadanand Gowda
Kerala	Thiruvananthapuram	2.76	Hans Raj Bhardwaj (Additional)	Oommen Chandy
Madhya Pradesh	Bhopal	6.00	Rameshwar Thakur	Shivraj Singh Chouhan
Maharashtra	Mumbai	9.29	K. Shankarnarayan	Prithviraj Chavan
Manipur	Imphal	0.22	Gurbachan Jagat	Okram Ibobi Singh
Meghalaya	Shillong	0.24	Ranjit Shekhar Mooshahary	Dr. Mukul Sangma
Mizoram	Aizawal	0.09	Lt. Gen. (Retd.) M.M. Lakhera	PU Lalthanhawla
Nagaland	Kohima	0.16	Nikhil Kumar	Neiphiu Rio
Odisha	Bhubaneswar	3.47	Murlidhar C. Bhandare	Navin Patnaik
Punjab	Chandigarh	2.29	Shivraj Patil	Prakash Singh Badal
Rajasthan	Jaipur	5.67	Shivraj Patil	Ashok Gehlot
Sikkim	Gangtok	0.05	Balmiki Prasad Singh	Pawan Chamling
Tamil Nadu	Chennai	5.96	Surjit Singh Barnala	J. Jayalalithaa
Tripura	Agartala	0.30	Dr. D.Y. Patil	Manik Sarkar
Uttar Pradesh	Lucknow	16.49	B.L. Joshi	Kumari Mayawati
Uttarakhand	Dehradun	0.84	Smt. Margaret Alva	Ramesh Pokhriyal
West Bengal	Kolkata	7.55	M.K. Narayanan	Mamata Banerjee

National Capital Territory

Capital Territory	Capital		Lt. Governor	Chief Minister
Delhi	Delhi	1.35	Tejender Khanna	Smt. Sheila Dikshit

Union Territories

State/UTS	Capital		Lt. Governors/Administrator	Chief Minister
Andaman & Nicobar	Port Blair	0.03	Lt. Gen. (Retd.) Bhopinder Singh	-
Chandigarh	Chandigarh	0.09	Shivraj Patil	-
Dadra & N.Haveli	Silvassa	0.03	Narendra Kumar (Administrator)	-
Daman & Diu	Daman	0.02	Narendra Kumar (Administrator)	-
Lakshadweep	Kavaratti	0.01	Amar Nath	-
Puducherry	Puducherry	0.10	Thiru Iqbal Singh	N. Rangaswamy

Status: as in July-Aug. 2011   *Note:* Kindly check the Stop Press for the updates.

Party Position - Rajya Sabha

As on : Wednesday, August 10, 2011

Sl	Party	Strength
1	Indian National Congress (INC)	71
2	Bharatiya Janata Party (BJP)	51
3	Bahujan Samaj Party (BSP)	18
4	Communist Party of India (Marxist) (CPI(M))	15
5	Dravida Munnetra Kazagham (DMK)	7
6	Janta Dal (United) (JD(U))	7
7	Nationalist Congress Party (NCP)	7
8	Biju Janata Dal (BJD)	6
9	All India Anna Dravida Munnetra Kazagham (AIADMK)	5
10	Communist Party of India (CPI)	5
11	Samajwadi Party (SP)	5
12	Rashtriya Janata Dal (RJD)	4
13	Shiv Sena (SS)	4
14	Telugu Desam Party (TDP)	4
15	All India Trinamool Congress (AITC)	3
16	Shiromani Akali Dal (SAD)	3
17	Asom Gana Parishad (AGP)	2
18	J&K National Conference (J&KNC)	2
19	Lok Janasakti Party (LJP)	2
20	All India Forward Block (AIFB)	1
21	Bodoland People's Front (BPF)	1
22	Indian National Lok Dal (INLD)	1
23	Mizo National Front (MNF)	1
24	Nagaland People's Front (NPF)	1
25	Rashtriya Lok Dal (RLD)	1
26	Revolutionary Socialist Party (RSP)	1
27	Sikkim Democratic Front (SDF)	1
28	Nominated (NOM)	8
29	Independent & Others (IND)	6

Party Position - Lok Sabha

As on : Wednesday, August 10, 2011

Total Members **545**
Vacant Constituencies **1** *(Hisar - Haryana)*
Nominated Member **2**

Sl	Name of Party	Members	Leader
1	Indian National Congress (INC)	208	Pranab Mukherjee
2	Bharatiya Janata Party (BJP)	115	Sushma Swaraj
3	Samajwadi Party (SP)	22	Mulayam Singh Yadav
4	Bahujan Samaj Party (BSP)	21	Dara Singh Chauhan
5	Janata Dal (United) (JD(U))	20	Ram Sundar Das
6	All India Trinamool Congress (AITC)	19	Km. Mamata Banerjee
7	Dravida Munnetra Kazhagam (DMK)	18	R.Baalu
8	Communist Party of India (Marxist) (CPI(M))	16	Basudeb Acharia
9	Biju Janata Dal (BJD)	14	Arjun Charan Sethi
10	Shiv Sena (SS)	11	Anant G. Geete
11	All India Anna Dravida Munnetra Kazhagam (AIADMK)	9	M. Thambidurai
12	Nationalist Congress Party (NCP)	9	Sharad Pawar
13	Telugu Desam Party (TDP)	6	Nama Nageswara Rao
16	Rashtriya Lok Dal (RLD)	5	
15	Communist Party of India (CPI)	4	Gurudas Dasgupta

Note: All the figures are as per the date of declaration of election results

16	Rashtriya Janata Dal (RJD)	4	Lalu Prasad
17	Shiromani Akali Dal (SAD)	4	Dr. Rattan Singh Ajnala
18	Jammu and Kashmir National Conference (J&KNC)	3	
19	Janata Dal (Secular) (JD(S))	3	
20	All India Forward Bloc (AIFB)	2	Narahari Mahato
21	Jharkhand Mukti Morcha (JMM)	2	
22	Jharkhand Vikas Morcha (Prajatantrik) (JVM (P))	2	Babu Lal Marandi
23	Muslim League Kerala State Committee (MLKSC)	2	E. Ahamed
24	Revolutionary Socialist Party (RSP)	2	
25	Telangana Rashtra Samithi (TRS)	2	K. Chandrasekhar Rao
26	All India Majlis-E-Ittehadul Muslimeen (AIMIM)	1	Asaduddin Owaisi
27	All India United Democratic Front (AIUDF)	1	Badruddin Ajmal
28	Asom Gana Parishad (AGP)	1	Joseph Toppo
29	Bahujan Vikas Aaghadi (BVA)	1	Jadhav Baliram Sukur
30	Bodoland Peoples Front (BPF)	1	Sansuma Khunggur Bwiswmuthiary
31	Kerala Congress (M) (KC(M))	1	Jose K. Mani
32	Marumalarchi Dravida Munnetra Kazhagam (MDMK)	1	Ganeshamurthi A.
33	Nagaland Peoples Front (NPF)	1	C.M. Chang
34	Sikkim Democratic Front (SDF)	1	Prem Das Rai
35	Swabhimani Paksha (SWP)	1	Raju Shetti
36	Viduthalai Chiruthaigal Katchi (VCK)	1	Thirumaavalavan Thol
37	Yuvajana Sramika Tythu Congress Party (YSRCONG)	1	Y.S. Jagan Mohan Reddy
38	Independent (Ind.)	9	Dinesh Yadav

State Assemblies : Party Positions

Andhra Pradesh (2009)
Total Seats: 294
INC 156
TDP 92
PRP 18
TRS 10
AIMIM 7
CPI 4
BJP 2
CPM 1
LSP 1
Ind 3

Arunachal Pradesh (2009)
Total seats: 60
Congress 42
NCP 5
Trinamool Congress 5
BJP 3
Others 5

Asom (2011)
Total Seats: 126
INC 78
AIUDF 18
BPF 12
AGP 10
BJP 5
Others 3

Bihar (2010)
Total Seats : 243
JD(U) 115
BJP 91
RJD 19
LJP 6
INC 4
CPI 1
JMM 1
Ind 6

Chhattisgarh (2008)
Total seats: 90
BJP 50

(INC 38
BSP 2

Goa (2007)
Total seats : 40
Congress 16
NCP 3
MGP 2
Ind 2
BJP 14
SGF 2
United Goans 1

Gujarat (2007)
Total Seats: 182
BJP 117
INC 59
NCP 3
Janata Dal (U) 1
Ind 2

Haryana (2009)
Total Seats: 90
Congress 40

INLD 31
SAD (B) 1
Janhit Congress 6
BJP 4
BSP 1
Ind 7

Himachal Pradesh (2007)
Total seats: 68
BJP 41
INC 23
BSP 1
Ind 3

Jammu & Kashmir (2008)
Total Seats: 87
Jammu Kashmir National
 Conference 28
Jammu Kashmir
 PDP 21

INC	7
BJP	11
Panthers Party	3
CPM	1
DPN	1
PDF	1
Ind	4

Jharkhand (2009)
Total Seats : 81

INC	14
JVM (P)	11
BJP	18
JDU	2
JMM	18
RJD	5
AJSU	5
JPE	1
JJM	1
RKP	1
CPI (ML)(L)	1
JBSP	1
MCC	1
Ind	2

Karnataka (2008)
Total seats: 224

BJP	110
INC	80
Janata Dal (S)	28
Ind	6

Kerala (2011)
Total Seats : 140

UDF	72
Indian National Congress	38
Muslim League	20
Kerala Congress (M)	9
Socialist Janata (Democratic)	2
Kerala Congress (B)	1
Kerala Congress (Jacob)	1
RSP (Baby John)	1
LDF	**68**
CPM	47*
CPI	13
Janata Dal (S)	4
RSP	2
NCP	2
* Including Ind.	

Madhya Pradesh (2008)
Total Seats: 230

BJP	143
INC	70

BSP	7
Bharatiya Jan Shakti	6
SP	1
Ind	3

Maharashtra (2009)
Total Seats: 288

Congress	82
NCP	62
BJP	46
Shiv Sena	44
MNS	13
CPM	1
SP	4
PWP	4
Others	32

Manipur (2007)
Total Seats: 60

INC	30
NCP	5
MPP	5
RJD	3
NPP	3
CPI	4
Ind	10

Meghalaya (2008)
Total seats: 60

INC	25
NCP	15
UDP	11
HSPDP	2
BJP	1
KHNAM	1
Ind	5

Mizoram (2008)
Total Seats: 40

Congress	32
Mizo National Front	3
Zoram Nationalist Party	2
Mizoram Peoples Conference	2
MDF	1

Nagaland (2008)
Total Seats : 60

NPF	26
INC	23
BJP	2
NCP	2
Ind	7

Odisha (2009)
Total Seats: 147

BJD	103
INC	27
BJP	6
NCP	4
CPI	1
Ind	6

Punjab (2007)
Total Seats: 117

SAD (Badal)	49
BJP	19
INC	44
Ind	5

Rajasthan (2008)
Total Seats: 200

Indian National Congress	96
BJP	78
BSP	6
CPM	3
SP	1
JDU	1
LSP	1
Ind	14

Sikkim (2009)
Total Seats: 32

SDF	32

Tamil Nadu (2011)
Total Seats : 234

AIADMK Front	**203**
AIADMK	150
DMDK	28
CPM	10
CPI	9
MMK	2
Puthiya Tamizhakam	2
SMK	1
Forward Bloc	1
DMK Front	**31**
DMK	23
INC	5
PMK	3

Tripura (2008)
Total seats: 60

CPM	46
RSP	2
CPI	1
INC	10
INPT	1

UTTARAKHAND (2007)
Total Seats: 70

BJP	34
INC	22
BSP	8
UKD	3
Ind	3

Uttar Pradesh (2007)
Total Seats: 403

BJP	51
BSP	206
INC	22
JDU	1
RLD	10
SP	97
ABLTC	1
BJSH	1
RPD	2
RSBP	1
UPUDF	1
JM	1
Ind	9

West Bengal (2011)
Total Seats : 294

AITC	184
INC	42
SUCI	1
CPM	40
CPI	2
Forward Bloc	11
RSP	7
SP	1
Others	6

Delhi (2008)
Total seats : 70

INC	42
BJP	24
BSP	2
Lok Janshakti Party	1
Ind	1

Puduchery (2011)
Total Seats: 30

AIADMK Front	**20**
AINRC	15
AIADMK	5
Congress Front	**9**
INC	7
DMK	2
Others	1

1. Andhra Pradesh

Governor: E.S.L. Narsimhan
CM: Kiran Kumar Reddy - (INC)
Date of Formation: 1 Oct. 1953 Andhra Part A state created from part of Madras; 1 Nov. 1956 Andhra Pradesh State formed.
Area: 2,75,069 sq. km.
Capital: Hyderabad.
Neighbouring States/UT: Maharashtra, Chhattisgarh, Odisha, Karnataka, Tamil Nadu, Sea: Bay of Bengal.
Population: 84,665,533 **Male:** 42,509,881 **Female:** 42,155,652 **Sex-ratio:** 992 **Density:** 308, **Decadal growth:** 11.10%, **Literacy:** 51,438,510 (t 67.66%, m 75.56% f 59.74%).

No. of Districts: 23

Kiran Kumar Reddy

District	Area (sq km)	Population (2011)	Head-quarters
Rayalaseema Region			
Anantapur	19,130	4083315	Anantapur
Chittoor	15,152	4170468	Chittoor
Y.S.R. (Cuddapah)	15,359	2884524	Cuddapah
Kurnool	17,658	4046601	Kurnool
Andhra Region			
E. Godavari	10,807	5151549	Kakinada
Guntur	11,391	4889230	Guntur
Krishna	8,734	4529009	Machilipatnam
Sri Potti Sriramulu Nellore	13,076	2966082	Nellore
Prakasam	17,626	3392764	Ongole
Srikakulam	5,837	2699471	Srikakulam
Visakhapatnam	11,161	4288113	V. Patnam
Vizianagaram	6,539	2342868	Vizianagaram
W. Godavari	7,742	3934782	Eluru
Telangana Region			
Adilabad	16,128	2737738	Adilabad
Hyderabad	217	4010238	Hyderabad
Karimnagar	11,823	3811738	Karimnagar
Khammam	16,029	2798214	Khammam
Mahaboob nagar	18,432	4042191	Mahaboob nagar
Medak	9,699	3031877	Sangareddy
Nalgonda	14,240	3483648	Nalgonda
Nizamabad	7,956	2552073	Nizamabad
Ranga Reddy	7,493	5296396	Hyderabad
Warrangal	12,846	3522644	Warrangal

Villages: 26,613; **Towns:** 210
Legislative Bodies: State Legislature - Bicameral Assembly Seats: 294 (excluding nomination) (Reserved: SC-39, ST-15); Legislative Council: 90; Parliament: Lok Sabha Seats: 42 (Gen 32+SC 7+ST 3); Rajya Sabha Seats: 18.
Main Political Parties: Indian National Congress, Telugu Desam Party, Telengana Rashtra Samithi, Communist Party of India (Marxist), Communist Party of India, All India Majlis-E-Ittehadul Muslimeen, Bharatiya Janata Party, Bahujan Samaj Party, Samajwadi Party.
Seat of High Court: Hyderabad [Kurnool was the first capital of the Andhra state with the high court established at Guntur].
Chief Languages: Telugu and Urdu.
Major Religions: Hinduism, Islam, Christianity.
Main Towns/Cities: Hyderabad, Secunderabad, Guntur, Kurnool, Karimnagar, Visakhapatnam, Vijayawada, Kadapa, Kakinada, Nalgonda, Ramagundam, Khammam, Machilipatnam, Anantapur, Adilabad, Warrangal, Nellore, Rajahmundry, Srikakulam, Tirupati, Vizianagaram.
Geography: (a) Rivers: Godavari, Krishna, Chitravati, Papagni, Musi, Pranhita, Wainganga, Banda, Tungabhadra. (b) Mountains: (Mt. Range- Eastern Ghat), Nalamala Hills, Satmala Hills, Erramala Hills, Horsley Hills, Palikonda Range, Velikonda Range; (c)

Museum of Statistics

India's first national museum of statistics is coming up in Hyderabad. It will showcase the history of statistics, early applications and its emergence for solving problems in all areas of human endeavour. The Rs. 6 crore facility is laid out on the Hyderabad University campus.

Plateau: Telengana, Golconda, Rayalasima, Srisailam, Nalgonda, Warrangal, Khammam; (d) Lake: Pulicat, Kolleru, Nagarjuna Sagar, Nizam Sagar (e) Forest: 63000 sq. km (23%) Coastline: 974 km. Staple Food: Rice.

Economy: Andhra is called the Rice Bowl of India. Agriculture - occupation of 62% people. (a) Agricultural Products: Rice [77% of foodgrain production], jowar, bajra, maize, ragi, small millets, pulses, castor, tobacco, cotton, and sugarcane. Other products are cashew, eucalyptus oil, etc. (b) Minerals: Chrysolite asbestos, barytes, copper ore, manganese, mica, coal and limestone; (c) Industries: machine tools, synthetic drugs, pharmaceuticals, heavy electrical machinery, fertilizers, cement, electronic equipment, watches, chemicals, asbestos, glass, etc.

IT: AP is one of the leading states in India. The govt. is extending IT to tier II cities like Warangal, Tirupath, Kakinada, Vishakhapatanam, Vijaywada, Guntur & Kadapa.

Power: 13,472.33 MW (in Jun 09; Installed capacity) Revenue from sale: Rs.13,945cr.

Transport & Communications: (a) Road Length: National highways in A.P. are 4,472 km., and State highways cover 10,519 km. The total R&B roads: 69,051 km (b) Railway Length: Railway routes cover 5,107 km; (c) Main Railway Stations: Hyderabad, Secunderabad, Guntakal, Warangal, Renigunta, Vijayawada, Visakhapatnam; (d) Airports: Shamshabad (Intl.), Tirupati, and Visakhapatnam; (e) Ports: It handled 26.88 m tones of cargo (2009-10) - the 2nd largest cargo handling state in India. 1 major- Visakhapatnam; 13 non-major: Kakinada, Machilipatnam...

Religious Places: Tirupati in Chittoor district is famous for Venkateswara temple - situated on the hilltop Tirumalai; the temple of Sriramachandra, Bhadrachalam; the Mallikarjunaswami temple, Srisailam; the Ahobala temple, Srikurmam temple and the Simhachalam temple are other famous temples. Prashanthi Nilayam at Puttaputhi, is the abode of Sri Satya Sai Baba. Lepakshi, Mahastupa (Amaravati), Mecca Masjid, the largest mosque in south India, are the other attractions.

Culture: (a) Dances: Kuchipudi; (b) Festivals: Samkranti - Jan (Harvest festival); Visakha- Jan; Shivratri - Feb/Mar; Ugadi - Mar (Telugu New Year); Mahakali Yatra and Mrigasira- Jun/Jul; State Formation Day - 1 Nov. Industrial Exhibition - Jan/Feb.

2. Arunachal Pradesh

Governor: Chief Gen. (Rtd) Joginder Jaswal Singh.

CM: Jarbom Gamlin - (INC)

Date of Formation: 20 Feb 1987 State; 20 Jan 1972 Union territory created from part of Assam. Till 1972, it was known as North East Frontier Agency (NEFA).

Area: 83,743 sq. km.

Capital: Itanagar.

Neighbouring States: Assam, Nagaland.
Countries: Bhutan, Myanmar, China.

Population: 1,382,611 **Males:** 720,232 **Females:** 662,379 **Literacy:** 789,943 **Males:** 454,532 **Females:** 335,411 (t66.95%, m73.69%, f59.57%); **Sex ratio** 920; **Density:** 17 **Decadal growth:** 25.92%.

No. of Districts: 16

District	Area (sq km)	Population (2011)	Head-quarters
1.Changlang	4,662	147951	Changlang
2.UpperDibang Valley	13,029	7948	Anini
3.East Kameng	4,134	78413	Seppa
4.East Siang	4,005	99019	Pasighat
5.Lohit	--	145538	Tezu
6.Lower Subansiri	10,135	82839	Ziro

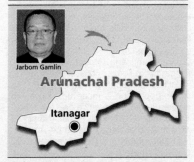

Jarbom Gamlin

Arunachal Pradesh

Itanagar

7.Papum-Pare	2,875	176385	Yupia
8.Tawang	2,172	49950	Tawang
9.Tirap	2,362	111997	Khonsa
10.Upper Siang	6,188	112272	Yingkiong
11.Upper Subansiri	7,032	83205	Daporijo
12.West Kameng	7,422	87013	Bomdila
13.West Siang	8,325	112272	Along
14. Anjaw		21089	
15. Lower Dibang Valley		53986	
16. Kurung Kumey		89717	

Villages: 3,863; **Towns:** 17.

Legislative Bodies: State Legislature - Unicameral: Assembly Seats: 60 (59 reserved for ST); Parliament: Lok Sabha Seats: 2; Rajya Sabha Seats: 1.

Main Political Parties: Indian National Congress, Bharatya Janata Party, Nationalist Congress Party, Arunachal Congress...

Seat of High Court: Guwahati.

Chief Languages: Arunachal Pradesh houses over 50 distinct dialects, mostly of the Sino-Tibetan language family. Monpa, Miji, Aka, Sherdukpen, Nyishi, Apatani, Tagin, Hill Miri, Adi, Digaru Mismi, Idu-Mishmi, Khamti, Miju-Mishmi, Nocte, Tangsa, Wancho.

Major Religions: Buddhism, Hinduism, Christianity.

Main Towns: Seppa, Itanagar, Seppa, Daporijo, Along, Pasighat, Tezu, Naharlagun, Khonsa, Yingkiong, Anini, Walong, Tawang, Bomdila, Ziro.

Geography: (a) Rivers: Siang (name of Brahmaputra), its tributaries - Lohit, Subansiri, Dibang, Kameg, Dikrong River (famous for water sports). (b) Mountains: Greater Himalaya, Lesser Himalaya, Assam Shiwalik: Dafla Hills, Miri Hills, Mishmi Hills, Abor Hills Peaks: Shallum-4336, Ddaphabum-4578; (c) Pass Bum La, Tse La, Tunga, Yonggyap, Diphu, Kumjawng, Hpungan, Chaukan, Pangasau (d) Forest: 60% of the state (e) Wildlife: Namdapha NP, Monling NP. The state's population is made up of over 26 different tribes and many more sub-tribes.

Economy: (a) Minerals: Coal (Namchik-Namphuk coal fields), dolomite, marble, lead, zinc, graphite; (b) Industries: sawmills, plywood (these two trades however have been stopped by law), rice mills, fruit preservation units and handloom handicrafts; (c) Agricultural Products: Among the crops grown here are rice, maize, millet, wheat, pulses, sugarcane, ginger and oilseeds. Arunachal is also ideal for horticulture and fruit orchards. [Agriculture is the primary driver of the economy. Jhum or shifting cultivation, is widely practised among the tribal groups] Cash crop like potatoes and horticulture crops like apple, oranges and pineapples are getting good promotion.

Transport & Communications: (a) Main Railway Stations: Bhalukpong; (b) Airports: Itanagar, Daparjio, Ziro, Along, Tezu, Pashigat.

Shopping: Handicrafts, jackets, bags, Sherdukpan shawls are very popular.

Culture: (a) Dances: Popir, Aji Lama, Hiiri Khaning, Cham, War dance; (b) Festivals: Mopin, Solung, Lossar, Booriboot, Sherdukpens, Dree, Si-Donyi, Reh, Nyokum, Chalo-loku.

3. Asom

Governor: Janaki Ballabh Patanaik

CM: Tarun Kumar Gogoi - (INC)

Date of Formation: 26 Jan 1950 The arrival of Ahoms in 1228AD and their reign for 6 centuries was the turning point in Asom history. Asoma (Sanskrit) means unparalleled.

Area: 78,438 sq km.

Capital: Dispur.

Neighbouring States: Meghalaya, Arunachal Pradesh, Nagaland, Manipur, Tripura,

Tarun Kumar Gogoi

Mizoram, West Bengal. Bhutan, Bangladesh. **Population:** 31,169,272 **Males:** 15,954,927 **Females:**15,214,345 **Sex-ratio:** 954, **Density:** 397, **Decadal growth:**16.93%. **Literacy:** 19,507,017 (t73.18% m78.81% f67.27%).

No. of Districts: 27

District	Area (sq km)	Population in lakhs(2011)	Head- quarters
Barpeta	3,245	1693190	Barpeta
Bongaigaon	2,510	732639	Bongaigaon
Cachar	3,786	1736319	Silchar
Darrang	3,481	908090	Mangaldoi
Dhemaji	3,217	688077	Dhemaji
Dhubri	2,838	1948632	Dhubri
Dibrugarh	3,381	1327748	Dibrugarh
Goalpara	1,824	1008959	Goalpara
Golaghat	3,502	1058674	Golaghat
Hailakandi	1,327	659260	Hailakandi
Jorhat	2,851	1091295	Jorhat
Kamrup	4,345	1517202	Guwahati
Karbi Anglog	10,434	965280	Diphu
Karimganj	1,809	1217002	Karimganj
Kokrajhar	3,129	886999	Kokrajhar
Lakhimpur	2,277	1040644	N.Lakhimpur
Morigaon	1,704	957853	Morigaon
Dima Hasao	4,888	213529	-
Nagaon	3,831	2826006	Nagaon
Nalbari	2,257	769919	Nalbari
Sibsagar	2,668	1150253	Sibsagar
Sonitpur	5,324	1925975	Tezpur
Tinsukia	3,790	1316948	Tinsukia
Baksa		953773	Baksa
Chirang		481818	Chirang
Udalguri		832769	Udalguri
Kamrup Metropolitan		1260419	

Villages: 25,124; **Towns:** 125
Legislative Bodies: State Legislature Unicameral: Assembly Seats: 126; Parliament: Lok Sabha Seats: 14 (11+1+2); Rajya Sabha Seats: 7
Main Political Parties: INC, AGP, BJP, NCP, Trinamool Congress, Samata Party, Samajwadi Party,
Seat of High Court: Guwahati.
Chief Languages: Assamese, Bengali, Bodo, Mishing, Karbi, Ramling. It is mainly a combination of Indo-European and Indo-Mongolian or Tibeto-Burmese languages.
Major Religions: Hinduism, Islam, Buddhism.
Main Towns: Guwahati, Dispur, Tezpur, Silchar, Jorhat, Dibrugarh, Sibsagar, Karimganj, Tinsukia, Diphu, Dhemaj, Nagaon, Marigaon, Barpeta, Goalpara, Dhuburi, Bongaigaon, Nalbari, Dhubri, North Lakhimpur.
Geography: It is a meeting point of Mongoloids and Caucasoids.(a) Rivers: Brahmaputra, Manas, Subansiri, Sonai; (b) Mountains: Mikir Hills, Rengma Hills, Barail Range. (c) Wildlife: Kaziranga National Park-Golaghat (famous for rhinos and elephants), Manas NP-Barpeta, Nameri National Park-Sonitpur, Pobitora WS- Morigaon, Dibru Ssaikhow NP-Tinsukia, Laokhowa WS-Nagaon, Pobha WS-N. Lakhimpur, Orang WS-Sonitpur.
Economy: (a) Minerals: Oil and natural gas, coal, limestone; (b) Industries: Agro-industries, refinery, cottage, handicraft, silk; (c) Agricultural Products: Rice, jute, tea, cotton, oilseeds, sugarcane, potato, orange, pineapple.
Transport & Communications: (a) Road Length: 37,515 km; NH - 2754 km (b) Railway Length: 2,284.28 km.; (c) Main Railway Stations: New Bangaigaon, Maligaon, Dispur, Rangia, Lumding, Jorhat; (d) Airports: LG Bordoloi Airport -Guwahati, Salonibari-Tezpur, Mohanbari-Dibrugarh, Kumbhrigram-Silchar, Rawriah-Jorhat, N. Lakhimpur and Silonibari- N. Lakhimpur.
Temples: Kamakhya temple (Nilachal hills), Umananda mandir (Peacock Is.), Navagraha mandir (Chitrachal hill).
Shopping: Sualkuchi (famous for muga silk, endi and pat). Handicrafts: bamboo articles, cane, brass and metal crafts. Assam is famous for varities of silk, bangles, clay dolls, pottery, woodworks, mattresses, etc.
Culture: (a) Dances: Rongali Bihu, Bohag Bihu, Magh Bihu, Kongali; (b) Festivals: Baisakhi.

Child Labour There are 215 mn. child labourers worldwide, of which 115 mn. work in hazardous occupations, says ILO report for 2010. According to NGO estimates, there are 6 cr. child labourers in India, i.e, 6 percent of the population.

4. Bihar

Governor: Devanand Konwar
CM: Nitish Kumar - (JD-U)
Date of Formation: 15 Aug., 1947 Province; 26 Jan. 1950 state (until 1956 : part (A).
Area: 94,163 sq km.
Capital: Patna.
Neighbouring States: Jharkhand, UP, West Bengal. Country: Nepal.
Population: 103,804,637 **Males:** 54,185,347 **Females:** 49,619,290 **Sex-ratio:** 916 **Density:**1,102 **Decadal growth:** 25.07%. **Literacy:** 54,390,254 (t63.82% m73.39% f53.33%).

No. of Districts: 38

District	Area (sq km)	Population (2011)	Head-quarters
Araria	2,830	2806200	Araria
Arwal	637	699563	Arwal
Aurangabad	3,389	2511243	Aurangabad
Banka	3,020	2029339	Banka
Begusarai	1,918	2954367	Begusarai
Bhagalpur	2,569	3032226	Bhagalpur
Bhojpur	2,395	2720155	Arrah(Ar(a)
Buxar	1,703	1707643	Buxar
Darbhanga	2,279	3921971	Darbhanga
Gaya	4,976	4379383	Gaya
Gopalganj	2,033	2558037	Gopalganj
Jehanabad	932	1124176	Jhanabad
Jamui	3,098	1756078	Jamui
Kaimur(Bhabhua)	3,362	1626900	Bhabhua
Katihar	3,057	3068149	Katihar
Khagaria	1,486	1657599	Khagaria
Kishanganj	1,884	1690948	Kishanganj
Lakhisarai	1,228	1000717	Lakhisarai
Munger	1,419	1359054	Munger
Madhepura	1,788	1994618	Madhepura
Madhubani	3,501	4476044	Madhubani
Muzaffarpur	1,419	4778610	Muzaffarpur
Nalanda	2,355	2872523	Biharsharif
Nawada	2,494	2216653	Nawada
Paschimi Champaran	5,228	3922780	Bettiah
Patna	3,202	5772804	Patna
Purbi Champaran	3,968	5082868	Motihari
Purnia	3,229	3273127	Purnia
Rohtas	3,851	2962593	Sasaram
Saharsa	1,687	1897102	Saharsa
Samastipur	2,904	4254782	Samastipur
Saran	2,641	3943098	Chhapra
Sheikhpura	689	634927	Sheikhpura
Sheohar	349	656916	Sheohar
Sitamarhi	2,294	3419622	Sitamarhi
Siwan	2,219	3318176	Siwan
Supaul	2,425	2228397	Supaul
Vaishali	2036	3495249	Hajipur

Nitish Kumar

Villages: 39,015; **Towns:** 130.
Legislative Bodies: State Legislature-Bicameral: Assembly Seats: 243, Legis. Council: 95; Parliament: Lok Sabha Seats: 40 (34+6+0); Rajya Sabha Seats: 16
Main Political Parties: Bharatiya Janata Party, Rashtrya Janata Dal, INC, NCP, CPI, BSP, CPI(M), Janata Dal (United), Samajwaadi Party, Lok Jan Shakti Party...
Seat of High Court: Patna
Chief Languages: Hindi, Urdu, Angika, Bhojpuri, Magadhi, Maithili.
Major Religions: Hinduism, Islam, Buddhism, Christianity.
Main Towns: Patna, Gaya, Biharsharif, Bhagalpur, Purnia, Muzaffarpur, Bettah, Motihari, Siwan, Munger, Bhagalpur, Araria, Arrah, Chhapra, Sasaram, Buxar, Darbhanga, Raxaul.
Geography: (a) Rivers: Ganga, Gandak, Burhi Gandak, Son, Saryu (Ghaghara), Kosi, Kamla, Panar, Saura, Lakhandai, Keul, Ghuari, Pun-pun; (b) Mountains: Bapabar Hills, Mandargiri Hills, Kharagpur, Rajgir, Mirzapur, Kaimur Plateau, Nawada Up-

land; (c) Plains North Bihar Plains, South Bihar Plains, Saran, Lower Son, Bettiah, Motihari, Sitamarhi, Madhubani, Saharsa, Aaria, Dharampur, Katihar, Bhagalpur (d) Valmiki Nat. Park. Forest : 7.1%.

Economy: (a) Minerals: Ilmenite, Kaolin, Limestone, Mica, fuller's earth; (b) Industries: cotton spinning mills, sugar mills, jute mills and leather industries; (c) Agricultural Products: rice, wheat, maize and pulses, cash crops like sugarcane, oilseeds, tobacco, jute and potato.

Transport & Communications: (a) Road Length: 46107 km (in 2001), NH-3734 km, SH-3989 km; (b) Main Railway Stations: Patna, Gaya, Muzaffarpur, Samastipur, Barauni, Katihar, Chapra, Siwan; (d) Airport: Patna.

Culture: (a) Dances: Seraikella; (b) Festivals: Chhath, tribal -Sarhul, Karam.

Korba	5,769	1206563	Korba
Koriya	5,978	659039	Baikunthpur
Mahasamund	4,963	1032275	Mahasamund
Narayanpur	6,640	140206	Narayanpur
Raigarh	6,528	1493627	Raigarh
Raipur	13,445	4062160	Raipur
Rajnandgaon	8,023	1537520	Rajnandgaon
Sarguja	16,034	2361329	Ambikapur

*New districts: Sukma, Kodgaon, Gariaband, Baloudabazar, Baaloud, Bemetara, Mungeli, Surajpur, Balrampur

5. Chhattisgarh

Governor: Shekhar Dutt.
CM: Dr. Raman Singh - (BJP)
Date of Formation: 1 Nov. 2000 State
Area: 1,36,034 sq km.
Capital: Raipur.
Neighbouring States: MP, Odisha, Andhra Pradesh, Maharashtra, UP, Jharkhand.
Population:25,540,196 **Males:**12,827,915
Females: 12,712,281 **Sex-ratio:** 991
Density: 189 **Decadal growth:** 22.59%.
Literacy: 15,598,314 (t71.04% m81.45%, f60.59%.

No. of Districts: 27*

District	Area (sq km)	Population (2001)	Head-quarters
Bastar	10,376	1411644	Jagdalpur
Bijapur	6,555	255180	Bijapur
Bilaspur	8,569	2662077	Bilaspur
Dantewada,D.Bastar	9,055	532791	Dantewada
Dhamatari	4,081	799199	Dhamtari
Durg	8,702	3343079	Durg
Janjgir Champa	4,467	1620632	Janjgir
Jashpur	6,457	852043	Jashpur
Kabeerdham	3,958	822239	Kabirdham
Kanker, U. Bastar	6,434	748593	Kanker

Dr. Raman Singh
Chhattisgarh

Raipur ⊙

Villages: 19,744; **Towns:** 97.
Legislative Bodies: State Legislature- Unicameral: Assembly Seats: 90; Parliament: Lok Sabha Seats:11(6+1+4); Rajya Sabha Seats: 5.
Main Political Parties: BJP, INC, BSP, NCP.
Seat of High Court: Bilaspur.
Chief Languages: Chhattisgarhi, Hindi
Major Religions: Hinduism.
Main Towns: Raipur, Bilaspur, Baikunthpur, Jashpur, Champa, Raigarh, Jagdalpur, Korba, Mahasamund, Ambikapur, Raj Nandgaon, Durg, Bhilai.

Secret Service Fund

A 'Secret Service Fund' has been instituted by National Highway Authority of India, aimed at rewarding whistle blowers providing information regarding corruption and irregularities. This is in line with the practice of doling out rewards to information in the police department.

Geography: (a) Rivers: Mahanadi, Indravati, Pairi, Hasdo, Son, Sabari; (b) Mountains: Maikala Range, Ramgarh Hills (c) National Park: Indravati NP-Dantewadi, Sanjay NP in Sarguja-Koriya Dist, Kangerghati NP-Kanker. Cultivation: in 35% land area. Irrigation: 13.28 lakh hectares.

Sanctuaries: Udanti, Pamed, Samarsot, Sitanadi, Achanakmar, Badalkhole, Gomardhs, Bbhoram Deo.

Economy: (a) Minerals: Copper, Coal, Iron, Limestone, Manganese and a diamond reserve; (b) Industries: most industries are mineral based like BALCO or Bhilai Steel plant, or forest based; (c) Agricultural Products: Tendu leaves, chironji, harhar, baheda, mahu flowers and sal seeds - predominently forest products. 80 % people are occupied in agriculture.

Transport & Communications: (a) Road Length: 34,930 km NH -2,225 km; SH-3, 213.5 km (b) Railway Length 1,053km; (c) Main Railway Stations: Raipur, Bilaspur, Durg, Korba, Raigarh, and Rajnandgaon); (d) Airports: Raipur, (Airstrips: Bilaspur, Bhilai, Jagdalpur, Ambikapur, Korba, Jashpurnagar and Rajnandgaon).

Tourism: Important attracrtions: Champaran, the birthplace of the Saint Vallabhacharya, with a temple named after him; National parks (3), wildlife sancturies (11); a major destination for eco-tourism.

Culture: (a) Festivals: Pola, Nawakhai, Dussehara, Diawali, Holi, Govardha Puja.

6. Goa

Governor: Dr. S.S. Sidhu

CM: Digambar Kamat - (INC)

Date of Formation: 30 May, 1987

Area: 3,702 sq.km

Capital: Panaji

Neighbouring States: Karnataka, Maharashtra. Sea: Arabian Sea

Population: 1,457,723 Males: 740,711 Females: 717,012 Sex-ratio: 968 Density: 394 Decadal growth: 8.17%. Literacy: 1,152,117 (t 87.40%, m92.81%, f81.84%).

Digambar Kamat

Panaji

Goa

No. of Districts: 2

District	Area (sq km)	Population (2011)	Head-quarters
North Goa	1,736	817761	Panaji
South Goa	1,966	639962	Margao

Villages: 359; Towns: 44

Legislative Bodies: State Legislature-Unicameral: Assembly Seats: 40; Parliament: Lok Sabha Seats: 2, Rajya Sabha: 1.

Main Political Parties: BJP, INC, United Gomantwadi Democratic Party, NCP, Maharashtrabadi Gomantak Party.

Seat of High Court: Bombay.

A bench of Bombay High court is at Panaji. District Court is in South Goa.

Chief Languages: Konkani and Marathi

Major Religions: Hinduism and Christianity.

Main Towns: Panaji, Margao, Vasco, Mapusa, Ponda, Vagator

Geography: (a) Rivers: Mandovi, Zuari, Terekhol, Chapora and Betul; (b) Mountains: Western Ghats; (c) Lake: Mayem; (d) Caves Khandepur, Arvalem. (e) Wildlife: Dr. Salim Ali Bird Sanctuary, the Bondla Wildlife Sanctuary, Cotigoa Wildlife Sanctuary,

Infant Mortality Rate

Melghat in Amravati district is infamous for its poor IMR and child mortality rate: Of the 6951 live births that took place in 2010-11, 335 infants died within a year, according to government figures. This tribal belt of Maharashtra recorded an IMR of 48 in 2010-11.

Molem National Park, Bhagwan Mahavir Wildlife Sanctuary, the Mormugao harbour. (f) Beaches : Bogmalo (water sports), Calangute, Colva, Mandrem, Morjim, Anjuna, Baga, Candolim, Sinquerim, Majorda, Benaulim, Varca, Agonda and Vagator.(g) Waterfalls: The Aravelam waterfalls-adjacent to it is Rudreshwara temple and interesting rock-cut caves, the Mayem lake, the Du-dsagar waterfalls-little downward is the Devil's Canyon suitable for trekkers and hikers. Forest: 1424 sq km. Irrigation: 43000 hectares.

Economy: Paddy is the main agricultural crop, followed by ragi, cashew and coconut. The state has a rich forest cover of more than 1,424 sq.km. Fishing sustains a work force of 40,000 people. (a) Minerals: Iron ore, manganese, ferro-manganese, bauxite, silica sand; (b) Industries: Mining industries, small scale industries like breweries, fruit canning, fish canning, stoves, automobile batteries, printing press, computer peripherals, zip fastner, etc.; (c) Agricultural Products: rice, pulses, ragi, groundnut, maize, jowar, bajra, sugarcane, coconut, cashewnut, arecanut, pineapple, mango, banana.

Transport & Communications: (a) Road Length: National highway-224 km, state highways-232 km, district roads-815 km.; (b) Railway Length: Goa is linked with Mumbai, Mangalore and Thiruvananthapuram through the Konkan railway; (c) Main Railway Stations: Margoa, Canacona, Balli, Verna, Karmali,Thivim, Pernem; (d) Airports: Dabolim International (29km from Panaji); (e) Chief Port: Mormugao, Dona Paula, Panaji.

Fort: Tiracol - built by Marathas in 1745, Cabo da Ramajuts into the sea, Cabonow governor's house, Reis Magos-named after Biblical Magi Kings who is believed to have owned this place and the Aguada Fort-built by Portuguese between 1609-1612 - now used as central prison.

Cuisine: Sweets: Bebinca, Dodol, Sanna, Delicacies: Bangra, pork vindaloo, sorpotel, acuti, chourisso.

Culture: (a) Dances: Fugdi, Dhalo (folk); Dekni, Kumbi, Bandhap (women); Mando (love - east-west mix), Ghode Mondi (Ranes victory over Portuguese), Goff & Hanpet Sword (during Shigmo), Dhangar (Navratri), Kala and Dashavtari; (b) Festivals: Carnival, Shigmotsav (Feb/Mar), Sabado Gordo (Feb), Beach Bonanza (Apr), Konkani Drama Fest (Nov/Dec).

7. Gujarat

Governor: Dr. Kamla Beniwal
CM: Narendra Modi - (BJP)
Date of Formation: 1 May 1960
Area: 196,024 sq km
Capital: Gandhinagar
Neighbouring States/UT: Rajasthan, Maharashtra, MP, Daman-Diu, Dadra Nagar Haveli. Country:Pakistan. Sea:Arabian Sea.
Population: 60,383,628 **Males:** 31,482,282 **Females:**28,901,346 **Sex-ratio:** 918 **Density:** 308 **Decadal growth:** 19.17%. **Literacy:** 41,948,677 (t79.31% m87.23%, f70.73%.

Narendra Modi

No. of Districts: 26

District	Area (sq km)	Population (2011)	Headquarters
Ahmedabad	8,087	7208200	Ahmedabad
Amreli	7,397	1513614	Amreli

Book on Gandhi Banned	Gujarat government has banned the controversial book "Great Soul: Mahatma Gandhi and His Struggle with India" by Pulitzer-winning author Joseph Lelyveld.

Anand	2,941	2090276	Anand
Banas Kantha	10,757	3116045	Palanpur
Bharuch	6,527	1550822	Bharuch
Bhavnagar	9,981	2877961	Bhavnagar
Dohad	3,646	2126558	Dahod
Dangs	1,764	226769	Ahwa
Gandhinagar	2,163	1387478	Gandhinagar
Jamnagar	14,125	2159130	Jamnagar
Junagadh	8,846	2742291	Junagadh
Kheda	4,219	2298934	Nadiad
Kuchchh	45,652	2090313	Bhuj
Mahesana	4,384	2027727	Mehsana
Narmada	2,755	590379	Rajpipla
Navsari	2,209	1330711	Navsari
Panch Mahals	5,220	2388267	Godhara
Patan	5,730	1342746	Patan
Porbandar	2,298	586062	Porbandar
Rajkot	11,203	3799770	Rajkot
Sabar Kantha	7,390	2427346	Himatnagar
Surat	7,657	6079231	Surat
Surendranagar	10,489	1755873	Surendranagar
Vadodara	7,549	4157568	Vadodara
Valsad	3,035	1703068	Valsad
Tapi		806489	-

Villages: 18,066; **Towns:** 242
Legislative Bodies: State Legislature-Unicameral: Assembly Seats: 182; Parliament: Lok Sabha Seats: 26 (20+2+4); Rajya Sabha Seats: 11
Main Political Parties: BJP, INC, JD...
Seat of High Court: Ahmedabad
Chief Language: Gujarati
Major Religions: Hinduism, Islam
Main Towns: Ahmedabad, Vadodara, Bhavnagar, Bhuj, Surat, Jamnagar, Kandla, Mehsana, Porbandar, Rajkot.
Geography: (a) Rivers: Sabarmati, Mahi, Narmada, and Tapti. Smaller rivers like Banas, Saraswati and Damanganga; (b) Mountains: Gir Range, Barda Hills, Girnar Hills. (c) National Parks: Gir NP-asiatic lions, Pirotan Marine National Park-known for corals and fish, Wild Ass Sanctuary-Rann of Kutchch, Nal Sarovar Bird Sanctuary, Ratanlal & Jessore Sloth Bear Sanctuary-Gujarat-MP border, Velavadhar NP, Vansda NP.(d) Beaches: Porbandar, Chorwad, Beyt Dwaraka, Somnath and Veraval, Mandvi near Delvada. Irrigation: 64.88 lakh hectares.
Economy: (a) Minerals: petroleum oil, natural gas; (b) Industries: Textiles, inorganic chemicals (caustic soda, soda ash), petrochemicals, drugs, oil refinery, pharmaceuticals, cement, electronic and electrical goods, machine tools, sugar, oil, etc.; (c) Agricultural Products: Bajra, jowar, maize, rice, wheat, tobacco, cotton, groundnut, isabgol, sugarcane, mangoes, bananas. Installed capacity of power: 8763 MW in 2005.
Transport & Communications: (a) Road Length: 74038km.; (b) Main Railway Stations: Ahmedabad, Vadodara, Bharuch, Valsad, Navsar, Surat, Dahod, Nadiad, Bhavnagar, Bhuj, Jamnagar, Rajkot, Mehsana, Himatnagar, Palanpur; (c) Airports: Ahmedabad International, Vadodara, Bhavnagar, Bhuj, Surat, Jamnagar, Rajkot; (d) Port: Kandla.
Shrines: Modhera Sun temple-Mehsana, Hatheesing Jain Temple, Bhadreshwar-Jain pilgrimage, Shamlaji -famous Vaishnava temple, Jama Masjid, Rani Rupmati mosque, Akshardham temple-made of sandstone, Parsees Fire temple-Udwada.
Historic Places: Patan-remains of Solanki dynasty, Lothal and Dholavira-remains of Harrappan civilisation, Adlaj Vav (world's most famous elaborated well)-Gandhinagar, Rani ki Vav-built by Udayamati (queen of Bhimdeva 1 between 1022 and 1063, Uperkot Fort - built by Yadavas.
Shopping: Patola saris, bead-embroidered ghagras, cholis,torans,tondris, chakla, zari, chandrawas, Namdas-felt embroidered with wool, block printed textiles, clay painting,hand painted fabrics.
Culture: (a) Dances: Garba (Lasya Nrity(a) and, Dandia Ras (Ras Leela, folk), Tippani (women labourers); (b) Festivals: Janmastami, - Dwarka and Dakor, Mahavir Jayanti-Palitana, International Kite Festival- Jan, Makar Sankranti, Navratri-Sep/Oct, Tarnetar fair (Aug-Sept), Madhavrai fair - Porbandar (Mar-April), Ambaji fair- Banaskanta dist, Shamalji fair, Dangi durbar- March, etc.

8. Haryana

Governor: Jagannath Pahadia
CM: Bhupinder Singh Hooda - (INC)
Date of Formation: 1 Nov 1966 State created from part of Punjab
Area: 44,212 sq km
Capital: Chandigarh
Neighbouring States: Punjab, Himachal Pradesh, Uttaranchal, Uttar Pradesh, Delhi, Rajasthan, Chandigarh (UT).
Population:25,353,081 **Males:**13,505,130 **Females:** 11,847,951 **Sex-ratio:** 877 **Density:** 573 **Decadal growth:**19.90%. **Literacy:** 16,904,324 (t76.64% m85.38%, f66.77%.

No. of Districts: 21

Bhupinder Singh
Hooda

District	Area (sq km)	Population (2011)	Head-quarters
Ambala	1,574	1136784	Ambala
Bhiwani	4,778	1629109	Bhiwani
Faridabad	2,151	1798954	Faridabad
Fatehabad	2,538	941522	Fatehabad
Gurgaon	2,714	1514085	Gurgaon
Hissar	3,983	1742815	Hissar
Jhajjar	1,834	956907	Jhajjar
Jind	2,702	1332042	Jind
Kaithal	2,317	1072861	Kaithal
Karnal	2,520	1506323	Karnal
Kurukshetra	1,530	964231	Kurukshetra
Mahendragarh	1,899	921680	Narnaul
Panchkula	898	558890	Panchkula
Panipat	1,268	1202811	Panipat
Rewari	1,594	896129	Rewari
Rohtak	1,745	1058683	Rohtak
Sirsa	4,277	1295114	Sirsa
Sonipat	2,122	1480080	Sonipat
Yamunanagar	1,768	1214162	Yamunanagar
Mewat	1859	1089406	Nuh
Palwal	-	1040493	Palwal

Villages: 6,764; **Towns:** 106

Legislative Bodies: State Legislature-Unicameral : Asembly Seats: 90; Parliament: Lok Sabha Seats:10 (8+2+0); Rajya Sabha Seats: 5.

Main Political Parties: INC, Indian National Lok Dal, BJP, BSP, NCP.

Seat of High Court: Chandigarh.

Chief Languages: Hindi, Punjabi.

Major Religions: Hinduism, Islam, Christianity.

Main Towns: Karnal, Rohtak, Panipat, Hisar, Yamunanagar, Kaithal, Gurgaon, Faridabad, Sirsa, Rewari, Bhiwani, Narnaul, Kurukshetra, Mahendragarh, Sonepat.

Geography: (a) Rivers: Ghaggar, Yamuna; (b) Mountains: Lower Shiwalik Range, Rewari Upland, Delhi Range (c) Lakes: Sirajkhand, Badkhal, Chakarvaty. (d) National Park: Sultanpur Bird Sanctuary. It is the first state in India to achieve 100% rural electrification.

Economy: (a)Minerals: Limestone, slate, dolomite, china clay, graphite and quartz; (b) Industries: cement, sugar, paper, cotton, textiles, glassware, brassware, cycles, tractors (largest production in the country), motorcycles, timepieces, automobile tyres and tubes, sanitaryware, television sets, steel tubes, hand tools, cotton yarn, refrigerators, vanaspati, ghee and canvas shoes; (c) Agricultural Products: Rice, wheat, maize, bajra, cotton, sugarcane, barley, potato, and pulses. 75% people are occupied in agriculture. Installed capacity of power: 4,033MW in Mar 2006.

Transport & Communications: (a) Road Length: 34,772 km; (b) Main Railway Sta-

The Sacred City Mathura	Mathura on the west bank of the Yamuna is one of the most sacred cities of Hinduism dating back to 600 B.C. Ptolemy mentioned the town. When the Chinese traveller Hiuen Tsang visited it in 634A.D., it was an important Buddhist centre with several monasteries.

tions: Kalka, Ambala, Panipat, Kurukshetra and Rohtak, Jind, Jakhal. Hissar (Jagadhari - railway workshop). (d) Airports: Pinjore, Karnal, Hissar, Bhiwani, Narnaul.

Culture: (a) Festivals: Holi, Teej, Diwali, Ggugga Pir, Sanjhi, Karva Chauth- for women; Surajkund -famous for popular crafts mela-held in February, Janmashtami Fair-Bhiwani, Masani Fair-Gurgaon; (b) Crafts: Moorah making, khes, druggets, Punja durries.

9. Himachal Pradesh

Prem Kumar Dhumal

Himachal Pradesh

Shimla

Governor: Smt. Urmila Singh
CM: Prem Kumar Dhumal - (BJP)
Date of Formation: 15 Apr. 1948 Statehood
Area: 55,673 sq km
Capital: Shimla
Neighbouring States: J&K, Punjab, Haryana, Uttarakhand. **Country:** China.
Population: 6,856,509 **Males:** 3,473,892 **Females:** 3,382,617 **Sex-ratio:** 974 **Density:** 123 **Decadal growth:** 12.81%. Population is divided into five major groups: the Gaddis, Kinners, Gujjars, Pangawals, and Lahaulis. **Literacy:** 5,104,506 (t83.78%, m90.83%, f76.60%).

No. of Districts: 12

District	Area (sq km)	Population (2011)	Headquarters
Bilaspur	1,167	382056	Bilaspur
Chamba	6,528	518844	Chamba
Hamirpur	1,118	454293	Hamirpur
Kangra	5,739	1507223	Dharamsala
Kinnaur	6,401	84298	Reckong Peo
Kullu	5,503	437474	Kullu
Lahaul & Spiti	13,835	31528	Keylong
Mandi	3,950	999518	Mandi
Shimla	5,131	813384	Shimla
Sirmaur	2,825	530164	Nahan
Solan	1,936	576670	Solan
Una	1,540	521057	Una

Villages: 17,495; **Towns:** 57
Legislative Bodies: State Legislature-Unicameral: Assembly Seats: 68; Parliament: Lok Sabha Seats: 4 (3+1+0); Rajya Sabha Seats: 3

Main Political Parties: INC, BJP, Himachal Vikas Congress, Lok Jan Shakti Party, Loktantrik Morcha Himachal Pradesh.
Seat of High Court: Shimla
Chief Languages: Pahari, Hindi, Punjabi, Kinnauri.
Major Religions: Hinduism, Buddhism, Islam, Sikh.
Main Towns: Shimla, Mandi, Dharmashala, Kullu, Manali, Bilaspur, Chamba, Keylong, Solan, Kangra, Dalhousie
Geography: (a) Rivers: Ravi, Beas, Chenab, Satluj, Yamuna; (b) Mountains: Greater Himalaya, Nag Tibba Range; (c) Lake/ Valley: Kangra Valley, Mahasu Valley, Rampur Valley, Spiti Valley, Lahul Valley, Baspa Valley, Govind Sagar; (d) Pass: Rohtang.(e) Parks and Valleys: Kufri-Himalayan Nature Park, Sangla, (f) Lake: Renuka, Rewalsar - Mandi. Irrigation: 5.83 lakh hectares.
Economy: (a) Minerals: Rock salt, slate, gypsum, limestone, barytes, dolomite, pyrites; (b) Industries: IT, Bio-technology, brewery, fruit processing, cement, electronics; (c) Agricultural Products: wheat, maize, rice, barley, vegetable, potato, ginger, soyabean, oilseed, pulses. Fruits: apple, pear, peach, plum, apricot, mango, litchi, guava, strawberry. 71% people are occupied in agriculture.
Transport & Communications: (a) Road Length: 30264 km. NH-1235 kms.; (b) Main Railway Stations: The only broad

Largest Solar Project

Maharashtra has cleared the proposal by the state power generation company MAHAGENCO to set up a 150MW solar energy project in Dhule district.

gauge railway station is Una; two narrow gauge lines (Pathankot to Joginder-nagar and Kalka to Shimla); (c) Airports: Bhuntar (Kullu Valley), Jubbarhatti (Shimla) and Gaggal (Kangra). Airstrip: Banikhet (being built).

Shrines: Mata Chintpurni Shri, Baba Barabhag Singh Gurudwara- Una and Baba Balak Nath. Lakshmi Devi-Manimahesh, Paonta Sahib Gurudwara, Jwalamukhi, Jakhu Hanuman temple-Shimla, Bhimkali temple- Sarahan, Bajreshwari Devi temple-Kangra.

Shopping: Pashmina shawls are very famous, rugs, namdas, gudma, are some of the native attractions. McLeod Ganj- Tibetan textiles, Dalhousie- Kulu shawls and Tibetan handicrafts, Lakkar Bazar,

Culture: (a) Dances: Nati; (b) Festivals: Dussehra of Kulu - begins on Vijay Dashmi; Shivratri of Mand (Feb/Mar); Minjar Fest in Chamba; Lavi Fair at Rampur; Renuka Fair (Aug/Sep); Lohri or Maghi, Lahual and Phulech-festival of flowers (c) Crafts: Pashmina and woollen shawls, namdas, gudma, thobis (floor covering made of goat hair), pullas (straw shoes).

10. Jammu & Kashmir

Governor: N.N. Vohra
CM: Omar Abdullah - (J&K Nat. Conf.)
Date of Formation: 26 Oct 1947

Omar Abdullah

Jammu & Kashmir

● Srinagar

Area: 2,22,236 sq km
Capital: Srinagar (Summer) Jammu (Winter)
Neighbouring States: Himachal Pradesh, Punjab. Countries - Pakistan, Afghanistan, China.
Population: 12,548,926 **Males:** 6,665,561 **Females:** 5,883,365 **Sex-ratio:** 883 Density: 124, **Decadal growth:** 23.71%. **Literacy:** 7,245,053 (t68.74%, m78.26%, f58.01%).

No. of Districts: 22

District	Area (sq km)	Population (2011)	Head-quarters
Anantnag	2,917	1070144	Anantnag
Badgam	1,371	735753	Badgam
Bandipore	398	385099	
Baramula	4,190	1015503	Baramula
Doda	4,500	409576	Doda
Ganderbal	1,945	297003	
Jammu	3,097	1526406	Jammu
Kargil	14,036	143388	Kargil
Kathua	2,440	615711	Kathua
Kishtwar	7,737	231037	
Kulgam	1,097	422786	
Kupwara	2,379	875564	Kupwara
Leh	45,100	147104	Leh
Poonch	1,674	476820	Poonch
Pulwama	1,090	570060	Pulwama
Rajouri	2,630	619266	Rajauri
Ramban	1138	283313	
Reasi	1517	314714	
Samba	910	318611	
Shupiyan	612,87	265960	
Srinagar	294	1269751	Srinagar
Udhampur	2380	555357	Udhampur

Villages: 6,417; **Towns:** 75
Legislative Bodies: State Legislature-Bicameral: Assembly: 87 (originally 100 but parts of it are illegally under POK); Legislative Council: 36. Parliament-Lok Sabha Seats: 6; Rajya Sabha Seats: 4
Main Political Parties: Jammu and Kashmir National Conference; INC, People's Democratic Party, J&K National Panthers Party, CPI-M, J&K Awami League, Democratic Movement, BSP, BJP.
Seat of High Court: Srinagar and Jammu
Chief Languages: Urdu (official), Kash-

New Kashmir Bridge

A bridge over the river Ravi is to link it to Punjab and Himachal Pradesh. Foundation stone for the bridge has been laid.

miri, Dogri, Pahari, Dalti, Ladakhi, Purig, Punjabi, Gurji, Dadri.

Major Religions: Islam, Hinduism, Buddhism

Main Towns: Srinagar, Jammu, Leh, Anantnag, Baramula, Pulwama, Punch, Doda, Udhampur, Gilgit, Punch

Geography: Location (degrees): 32.15 & 37.05 N–72.35&83.20E (a) Rivers: Chenab, Jhelum, Zanskar, Indus, Suru, Nubra and Shyok; (b) Mountains: (divided into 4 regions) Khandi Belt -Greater Himalayas, Great Karakoram, Trans-Himalaya; Siwalik range- Zaskar range, Kunlun; Kashmir Valley -Pirpanjal range; Tibetan tract- Ladakh range; (c) Lakes Wular, Achar, Dal, Pangong, Moriri, and Kar. (Mountain Lakes-Satsar, Vishansar, Kishansar, Gadsar, Gangabal); (d) Pass Zoji La pass; (e) Range Pir Panjal, Great Himalaya, Zanskar, Ladakh. Ladakh is also called 'Little Tibet' and sometimes 'the last Shangri La.' This region is marked by Buddhist monastries (gompas), and forts. Hemis Gompa- Leh offers some tough mountain treks to Zanskar valley-Pangong Lake-Tso Moriri Lake. The highest point there is at Zoji La pass.

Economy: (a) Minerals: Mica, fire clay, limestone, kaolin, bauxite; (b) Industries: Handicrafts, carpet, wood carving, shawl-making; (c) Agricultural Products: Paddy, maize, wheat, gram, bajra, jowar, barley, fruits like apple, and walnuts.80% people depend on agriculture.

Transport & Communications: (a) Road Length:18809 km.; (b) Main Railway Stations: Jammu, Udhampur. The railway line will be extended to Srinagar and Baramulla (c) Airports: Sheikh-ul-Alam International-Srinagar, Jammu, Leh and Kargil.

Shopping: Kashida embroidery, sonzi -fine needle work, and chikindozi-hookwork-jalakdozi-rafookari-Pashmina and kani shawls, silver jewellery, etc.

Culture: (a) Dances: Ruf (women-romance and heroic), Kud (Dogra men), Hemis Gumpa; (b) Festivals: Assuj, Lohri, Sinh Sankranti, Bahu Mela in Jammu, Mela Losar, Mela Pat; Id-ul-fitr, Id-ul-Zzuha, Id Milad-un-Nabi,

Meraj Alam in Kashmir, Muharram, Hemis in Ladakh.

11. Jharkhand

Governor: M.O.H. Farook Maricar

CM: Arjun Munda - (BJP)

Date of Formation: 15 Nov 2000 (State created from part of Bihar)

Area: 79,714 sq km

Capital: Ranchi

Neighbouring States: Bihar, UP, Chhattisgarh, Odisha, West Bengal.

Population:32,966,238**Males:**16,931,688

Arjun Munda

Females: 16,034,550 **Sex-ratio:** 947 **Density:** 414 22.34. **Literacy:**18,753,660 (t67.63%, m78.45%, f56.21%.

No. of Districts: 24

District	Area (sq km)	Population (2011)	Head-quarters
Bokaro	2,861	2061918	Bokaro
Chatra	3,706	1042304	Chatra
Deoghar	2,479	1491879	Deoghar
Dhanbad	2,075	2682662	Dhanbad
Dumka	3,716	1321096	Dhumka
Garhwa	4,044	1322387	Garhwa
Giridih	4,887	2445203	Giridih
Godda	2,110	1311382	Godda
Gumla	5,321	1025656	Gumla
Hazaribagh	4,519	1734005	Hazaribagh
Kodarma	1,311	717169	Kodarma
Lohardaga	1,491	461738	Lohardaga
Pakur	1,806	899200	Pakaur
Palamau	4,015	1936319	Daltonganj
Paschimi Singhbhum	5,290	1501619	Chabasa

Man-Elephant Conflicts

As many as 116 people lost their lives in man-elephant conflicts in Asom during 1997-2010. Villagers were trampled to death by elephants migrating to Sonitpur distict.

Purbi Singhbhum	3,553	2291032	Jamshedpur
Ranchi	4,963	2912022	Ranchi
Sahibganj	1,706	1150038	Sahibganj
Latehar	3,660	725673	Latehar
Jamtara	1,802	5,44,856	Jamtara
Saraikela Kharsawan	2,725	1063458	Seraikela
Simdega	3756	599813	Simdega
Ramgarh	1211	949159	Ramgarh
Khunti	2611	530299	Khunti

Villages: 29,354; **Towns:** 152

Legislative Bodies: State Legislature-Unicameral : Assembly Seats: 81; Parliament: Lok Sabha Seats: 14 (8+1+5); Rajya Sabha Seats: 6

Main Political Parties: BJP, INC, NCP, JMM, RJD, JD- United, All India Forward Block, CPI-ML, Jharkhand Students Union, Jharkhand Party...

Seat of High Court: Ranchi

Chief Languages: Hindi, Urdu, Kurmati, Santhali, Ho, Kuruk, Bengali.

Major Religions: Hinduism, Islam, Buddhism

Main Towns: Bokaro, Jamshedpur, Ranchi, Dhanbad, Daltonganj, Singhbhum, Deogarh, Dumka, Hazaribagh, Chaibasa, Gumla, Garwa, Giridih

Geography: (a) Rivers: Sankh, South Koel, Damodar, Subarnarekha, Barakat; (b) Mountains: Chotanagpur Plateau, Hazaribagh Plateau, Rajmahal Hills, Parasnath (1366m); (c) Reservoir: Tilaiya, Konar, Govind Bballabh Pant Sagar (d) National Park: Palamau NP, Hazaribagh NP. Cultivation: 18lakh hectares. Irrigation: 8% of land area. Forest: 18423 sq km.

Economy: Jharkhand's economy is sustained by mining and heavy industry. It is India's second most important source of coal, mining 26 per cent of the total. In minerals, Jharkhand is probably India's richest state. Jharkhand has rich reserves of iron ore and coal and several industries. The two major steel plants of India are located in Jharkhand: at Jamshedpur and Bokaro. (a) Minerals: iron ore and coal; (b) Industries: Steel, mining, heavy industries.

Transport & Communications: (a) Road Length: 4,311km, including 1,500 km NH and 2,711km SH; (b) Main Railway Stations: Ranchi, Bokaro, Dhanbad, Jamshedpur, Muri, Deogarh; (c) Airports: Ranchi, Jamshedpur.

Tourism: Attractions include Deoghar, home to a complex of 22 temples, Parasnath, the highest hill and the chariot-shaped Sun temple.

Culture: (a) Dances: Chhau; (b) Festivals: Chhath, Diwali, Id, Buddha Purnima, Durga Puja. Tribal Festivals: Sarhul, Bandna, SSohraj and Dasai.

12. Karnataka

Governor: Hans Raj Bhardwaj

CM: Sadananda Gowda - (BJP)

Date of Formation: 15 Aug 1947 Mysore state (1950-56: part (B); 1 Nov 1973 Renamed Karnataka

Area: 1,91,791 sq km

Capital: Bengaluru

Neighbouring States: Kerala, Goa, Maharashtra, AP, Tamil Nadu. Sea: Arabian Sea.

Population: 61,130,704 **Males:** 31,057,742 **Females:** 30,072,962 **Sex-ratio:** 968 **Density:** 319 **Decadal growth:** 15.67%. **Literacy:** 41,029,323 (t75.60%, m82.85%, f68.13%.

Sadananda Gowda

Karnataka

Bangaluru

No. of Districts: 30

District	Area (sq km)	Population (2011)	Head-quarters
Baglkot	6,575	1890826	Bagalkot
Bengaluru	2,190	9588910	Bengaluru
Bengaluru Rural	5,815	987257	Bengaluru
Belgaum	13,415	4778439	Belgaum
Bellary	8,450	2532383	Bellary
Bidar	5,448	1700018	Bidar
Bijapur	10,494	2175102	Bijapur
Chamarajanagar	5,101	1020962	Ch.nagar
Chikmagalur	7,201	1137753	Chikmagalur
Chitradurga	8,440	1660378	Chitradurga
Dakshina Kannada	4,560	2083625	Mangalore
Davanagere	5,924	1946905	Davanagere
Dharwad	4,260	1846993	Dharwad
Gadag	4,656	1065235	Gadag
Gulbarga	16,224	2564892	Gulbarga
Hassan	6,814	1776221	Hassan
Haveri	4,823	1598506	Haveri
Kodagu	4,102	554762	Madikeri
Kolar	8,223	1540231	Kolar
Koppal	7,189	1391292	Koppal
Mandya	4,961	1808680	Mandya
Mysore	6,854	2994744	Mysore
Raichur	6,827	1924773	Raichur
Shimoga	8,477	1755512	Shimoga
Tumkur	10,597	2681449	Tumkur
Udupi	3,880	1177908	Udupi
Uttara Kannada	10,291	1436847	Karwar
Ramanagara	-	1082739	Ramanagata
Chikkabellapura		1254377	Chikkabellapura
Yadgir		1172985	

Villages: 27,481; **Towns:** 270
Legislative Bodies: State Legislature-Bicameral: Assembly Seats 224, Legislative Council- 75; Parliament: Lok Sabha Seats: 28 (21+5+2); Rajya Sabha Seats: 12
Main Political Parties: BJP, INC, JD (S), JD (U), CPI-M, Kannada Nadu Paksha, Kannada Chaluvali Vatal Paksha
Seat of High Court: Bengaluru
Chief Languages: Kannada
Major Religions: Hindu, Islam, Christianity
Main Towns: Bengaluru, Bidar, Gulbarga, Bijapur, Belgaum, Dharwad, Hubli, Raichur, Bellary, Shimoga, Mangalore, Madikeri, Mysore, Kolar, Tumkur, Hassan, Davanagere. Udupi.

Geography: Location (degrees): 11.31 & 18.14 N–74.12&78.10. (a) Rivers: Krishna, Tungabhadra, Cauvery, Kabini; (b) Mountains: Western Ghats, Chitradurga Hills, Mysore Plateau, Biligiri Rangan Hills, Nandi Hills, Gokak Hills, Badami Hills. (c) National Park: Bandipur Wildlife Sanctuary

Economy: (a) Minerals: Gold silver, iron ore, copper, chromite, magnesite, corundum, garnet, limestone; (b) Industries: Aircraft, electronics, software,telecom equipment, alloy steel, machine tools, watches, porcelain, automobiles, etc.; (c) Agricultural Products: Rice, jowar,bajra, ragi, maize, groundnut, sunflower, mulberry, coconut, Potato, grapes, watermelon, etc. 46% people are are engaged in agriculture and allied activities. Horticulture: 15.81 lakh hectares. Installed capacity of power: 5836MW. Rural electrification: 100%. Software exports: 35 % of India's exports.
Transport & Communications: (a) Road Length: 2,15,849 km; NH-3967 km; SH-9590 km(b) Railway Length: 3172km. The Konkan Railway, the new rail link between Mumbai and Mangalore was dedicated to the nation on May 1,1998; (c) Main Railway: Stations Bengaluru, Mysore, Tumkur, Hosur, Hassan, Mandya, Bellary, Hubli, Bijapur, Gulbarga, Belgaum, Dharwad; (d) Airports: Bengaluru-Devanahalli, Belgaum, Mangalore, Hubli; (e) Port: New Mangalore port is the main all-weather seaport.

Adventure Sports: Ramanagaram-rock climbing-50 km from Bengaluru, Honnemardu on Sharavathy-coracle rafting, canoeing and wind surfing, Cauvery Fishing Camp-82 km from Mysore for anglers, Kudremukh and Kemmangundi -trekking.

Culture: Festivals: Mysore Dussera, Karaga, Ugadi (Kannada New Year), Diwali, Kar Hunnive, Navaratri, Yellu Amavasya, Ramzan.

13. Kerala

Governor: Hans Raj Bhardwaj (Additional)
CM: Oommen Chandy - (UDF)
Date of Formation: 1st Nov. 1956

Kerala Assembly has 35 Crorepatis

About one-fourth of the 140 newly elected Kerala Assembly members are crorepatis. 35 members have assets exceeding Rs.1 cr. Of the 35, 30 belong to the United Democratic Front.

Area: 38,863 sq km
Capital: Thiruvananthapuram
Neighbouring States/UTs: Tamil Nadu, Karnataka, and Lakshdweep Is.
Population: 33,387,677 **Males:** 16,021,290, **Females:** 17,366,387 **Sex-ratio:** 1,084 **Density:** 859 Decadal growth: 4.86%. **Literacy:** 28,234,227 **Males:** 13,755,888 **females:** 14,478,339 93.91 **Density:** 96.02 **Decadal growth:** 91.98%.
No. of Districts: 14

Oommen Chandy

Kerala

Thiruvananthapuram

District	Area (sq km)	Population (2011)	Head-quarters
Alappuzha	1,414	2121943	Alappuzha
Ernakulam	3068	3279860	Kochi
Idukki	4,358	1107453	Painavu
Kannur	2,966	2525637	Kannur
Kasargode	1,992	1302600	Kasargode
Kollam	2,491	2629703	Kollam
Kottayam	2,208	1979384	Kottayam
Kozhikode	2,344	3089543	Kozhikode
Malappuram	3,550	4110956	Malappuram
Palakkad	4,480	2810892	Palakkad
Pathanamthitta	2,637	1195537	Pathanamthitta
Thiruvan-anthapuram	2,192	3307284	Thiruvan-anthapuram
Thrissur	3,032	3110327	Thrissur
Wayanad	2,131	816558	Kalpetta

Villages: 1,364; **Towns:** 159
Legislative Bodies: State Legislature-Unicameral: Assembly Seats: 140 (excluding nomination); Parliament: Lok Sabha Seats: 20 (18+2+0); Rajya Sabha Seats: 9.
Main Political Parties: INC, CPI-M, Muslim League Kerala State Committee, Kerala Congress (M), CPI, JD(S), Revolutionary Socialist Party of Kerala, Kerala Congress, Kerala Congress (B), Kerala Congress (J), Democratic Indira Congress, NCP, CMP
Seat of High Court: Kochi.
Chief Languages: Malayalam
Major Religions: Hinduism, Islam, Christianity.
Main Towns: Thiruvananthapuram, Kochi, Kozhikode, Trissur, Kannur, Kottayam, Kollam, Allapuzha, Palakkad, Malappuram, Pathanamthitta.
Geography: (a) Rivers (km): Periyar-244, Bharatapuzha, also called Nila-209; Pamba -176, Chaliyar-169, Kadaundi & Chalakkudy-130, Achenkovil-128, Kalada, Muvatupuzha -121; (Total 44 rivers - out of which 41 are west flowing and 3 eastward - Pambar, Bhawani and Kabani) (b) Mountains: Anamala (8841 ft, the Highest), Karinkulam (8455ft), Mukutti (8330ft), Devimala (8273 ft) Highest Peak- Anamudi 2695 msl. (c) Lakes(sq km): Vembanad - 205, Kayamakulam - 51, Ashtamudi - 50, Anjuthengu - 20. Fresh water lake (sq km)- Shastamcota- 3.7, Vellayni, and Pookat (d) Beaches: Kovalam, Varkala, Vizhinjam, Shankumukham - Trivandrum, Muzhapilangad and Payyambalam-Kannur, Kappad-Kozhikode. (e) Hill Stations: Munnar, Nelliyampathy. (f) Backwaters: Alapuzha, Kollam, Veli, Kochi, Kumarakom-Kottayam. (g) Wildlife: Eravikulam National Park- known for Nilgiri Tahr, Periyar National Park, Parambikulam National Park, Silent Valley, Peppara National Park. (h) Waterfalls: Athirapally, Vazhachal, Palaruvi.
Economy: (a) Minerals: Ilmenite, Rutile, Kaolin, Limestone; (b) Industries: Coir and cashew are 2 large industries. Handloom and bamboo-based industries are well-developed. Kerala accounts for about 1/3

Gold from Nepal King	The King of Nepal presented 25,000 gold coins to the Maharaja of Travancore a century ago. The coins were brought on elephants from Kathmandu. Half the gold was used for making the Vishnu idol in the Thiruvananthapuram Sree Padmanabha Swamy temple.

of India's marine exports. Software development and export is picking up; (c) Agricultural Products: The state has developed commercial agriculture more than food crops. Consequently, the state is short of foodgrains. Kerala accounts for 91% of India's rubber, 70% of coconut, 60% of tapioca and almost 100% of lemon grass oil. Kerala is the single largest producer of a number of other crops like banana and ginger, besides tea and coffee in abundance.50% people engaged in agriculture.

Main Irrigation Projects: Malampuzha, Chalakkudy, Peechi, Pamba, Periyar, Chittoorpuzha, Kuttiyadi, Neyyar, Chimmini

Main Power Projects: Idukki Hy., Pallivasal Hy., Chenkulam Hy, Peringalkut Hy., Neriyamangalam Hy., Paniyar Hy., Sabarigiri Hy., Sholayar Hy. Brahmapuram Diesel, Kanjikode Wind farm, Kozhikode Diesel, Kayamakulam Thermal Power plant.

Transport & Communications: (a) Road Length: 1.61 lakh km; (b) Railway Length: 1,148km; (c) Main Railway Stations: Thiruvananthapuram, Kollam, Chenganur, Thiruvalla, Kottayam, Alappuzha, Ernakulam, Trissur, Palakkad, Kozhikode, Kannur, Kasargod; (d) Airports: Thiruvananthapuram, Nedumbassery (Kochi-India's first private airport, was opened in June, '99), and Karipur. Port: Kochi. (e) Inland waterways: 1687 kms.

Education: The first fully literate municipal town (Kottayam-1989), and district (Ernakulam-1990) in India are in Kerala. In 1991, Kerala became the first fully literate state in India with literacy among adults: 89.9%.

Culture: (a) Dances: Kathakali, Mohiniattam, Theyyam, Thullal, Margamkalli, Oppana; (b) Festivals: Onam, Vishu, Ramzan, Christmas, Aluva Shivratri.

Famous Shrines: Jewish Synagogue (Mattancherry, Kochi)-St Francis Church - Kochi, Padmanabhaswamy temple -Trivandrum, Ayyappa temple-Sabarimala, Guruvayoor (Lord Krishna shrine)-Dwarka of the south, Attukal temple- Trivandrum, Methala mosque, Malik Dinar Mosque, St Thomas Memorial Church-Kodungalloor, St Thomas Church- Malayatoor, Mannarasala temple-Harippad, Parimala Church, and Kalady (the birthplace of Sri Sankaracharya.

14. Madhya Pradesh

Governor: Rameshwar Thakur
CM: Shivraj Singh Chouhan - (BJP)

Date of Formation: 1 Nov. 1956
Area: 3,08,000 sq km
Capital: Bhopal
Neighbouring States: Maharashtra, Gujarat, Rajasthan, UP, Chhattisgarh
Population:72,597,565**Males:**37,612,920
Females: 34,984,645 **Sex-ratio:** 930 **Density:** 236 **Decadal growth:** 20.30%. **Literacy:** 43,827,193 (t70.63%, m80.53%, f60.02%.

No. of Districts: 50

District	Area (sq km)	Population (2011)	Head- quarters
Ashoknagar	4674	844979	Ashoknagar
Alirajpur	-	728677	Alirajpur
Anuppur	3746	749521	Anuppur
Balaghat	9,229	1701156	Balaghat
Barwani	(5,432)	1385659	Barwani
Betul	10,043	1575247	Betul
Bhind	4,459	1703562	Bhind
Bhopal	2,772	2368145	Bhopal
Burhanpur	2,473	756993	Burhanpur
Chhatarpur	8,687	1762857	Chhatarpur
Chhindwara	11,815	2090306	Chhindwara
Damoh	7,306	1263703	Damoh
Datia	2,038	786375	Datia
Dewas	7,020	1563107	Dewas
Dhar	8,153	2184672	Dhar
Dindori	7,427	704218	Dindori
Guna	11,065	1240938	Guna
Gwalior	5,214	2030543	Gwalior
Harda	(3,339)	570302	Harda
Hoshangabad	10,037	1240975	Hoshangabad
Indore	3,898	3272335	Indore
Jabalpur	10,160	2460714	Jabalpur
Jhabua	6,782	1024091	Jhabua
Katni	(4,947)	1291684	Katni
Khandwa(E.Nimar)	10,779	1309443	Khandwa
Khargone (W.Nimar)	13,450	1872413	Khargone

Mandla	13,269	1053522	Mandla
Mandsaur	9,791	1339832	Mandsaur
Morena	11,594	1965137	Morena
Narsimhapur	5,133	1092141	Narsimhapur
Neemuch	4,267	825958	Neemuch
Panna	7,135	1016028	Panna
Raisen	8,446	1331699	Raisen
Rajgarh	6,154	1546541	Rajgarh
Ratlam	4,861	1454483	Ratlam
Rewa	6,134	2363744	Rewa
Sagar	10,252	2378295	Sagar
Satna	7,502	2228619	Satna
Sehore	6,578	1311008	Sehore
Seoni	8,758	1378876	Seoni
Shahdol	14,028	1064989	Shahdol
Shajapur	6,196	1512353	Shajapur
Sheopur	(6,585)	687952	Sheopur
Shivpuri	10,278	1725818	Shivpuri
Sidhi	10,256	1126515	Sidhi
Singrauli	-	1178132	Singrauli
Tikamgarh	5,048	1444920	Tikamgarh
Ujjain	6,091	1986597	Ujjain
Umaria	(4,026)	643579	Umaria
Vidisha	2,742	1458212	Vidisha

Shivraj Singh Chouhan

Villages: 52,117; **Towns:** 394

Legislative Bodies: State Legislature-Unicameral: Assembly Seats: 230 (excluding nomination); Parliament: Lok Sabha Seats: 29 (19+4+6); Rajya Sabha: 11.

Main Political Parties: BJP, INC, Samajwadi Party, BSP, CPI-M, NCP, JD-U.

Seat of High Court: Jabalpur and benches at Gwalior and Indore

Chief Languages: Hindi

Major Religions: Hinduism, Islam, Buddhism

Main Towns: Indore, Bhopal, Gwalior, Sagar, Rewa, Jabalpur, Ujjain, Bhind, Ratlam, Balaghat, Betul, Seoni, Shajapur, Sagar, Guna, Itarsi, Shivpuri, Morena, Guna, Chindwara, Katni, Mandla, Umaria, Shahdol, Vidhisha.

Geography: (a) Rivers: Narmada, Chambal, Sindh, Betwa, Ken, Son, Tapi; (b) Mountains: Vindhya Range, Satpura Range, Malwa Plateau, Kaimur Hills, Maikala Range, Mahadeo Hills. (c) National Park / Sanctuary: Kanha, Bandhavgarh, Madhav, Karera Bird Sanctuary (Great Indian Bustard), Indravati tiger reserve; Dhuandhar Fall (Bhedaghat) and Marble rock - Jabalpur; Irrigation: 6.19million hectares

Economy: (a) Minerals: diamond, dolomite, limestone, bauxite, iron-ore, copper, coal, lead, tin, rock phosphate, traditional handicraft and handloom; (b) Industries: Heavy electricals, Govt. Mint, Security Paper mill, sugar mills, refractories, textile machinery, steel casting, electronics, automobiles, optical fibre, newsprint, rerolling, industrial gases, synthetics, drugs, engineering tools, chemical fertilisers, solvent extraction; (c) Agricultural Products: Jowar, wheat, rice, gram, oilseeds, pulses, soyabean, cotton, sugarcane. 75% of people are engaged in agriculture.

Transport & Communications: (a) Road Length: 73311 km. NH 4280 km, SH 8729 km; (b) Main Railway Stations: Bhopal, Bina, Gwalior, Indore, Itarsi, Jabalpur, Katani, Ratlam and Ujjain; (c) Airports: Bhopal, Gwalior, Indore, Khajuraho

Famous Temple towns: Khajuraho, Maheshwar, Omkareshwar, Ujjain, Chitrakoot, Orchha, Amarkantak, Bhojpur, Udaypur.

Archaeological Sites: Bhimbetka, Satna, Sanchi stupas (Buddhist), Vidisha, Mandsaur.

Culture: (a) Dances: Gaur - bison hunt dance; (b) Festivals: Tan Sen Music Festival-Gwalior; Ustad Allauddin Festival -Maihar;

Rs. 100 Crore Scheme for Cancer

Government has launched a Rs. 100 crore programme for treatment of cancer patients in 100 districts. Bhatinda and Hoshiarpur districts of Punjab have more cancer cases - with a prevalence of 775 cases and Hoshiarpur 46.47 cases per lakh of population. Cause: tobacco.

Kalidas Samaroh- Ujjain; Festival of Dances- Khajuraho.

Bhagoriya - Jhabua(tribal), Holi, Sravan Somvar, Diwali, Id, Dussehra, Shivratri - Khaju-raho, Bhojpur, Pachmarhi, Ujjain; Ramnavami - Chitrakoot, Orcha, Malwa, Pachmarhi.

15. Maharashtra

Governor: K. Sankaranarayanan
CM: Prithviraj Chavan - (INC)
Date of Formation: The state of Bombay was bifurcated into Maharashtra and Gujarat on May 1,1960, Maharashtra retaining the old capital Bombay.
Area: 3,07,713 sq km
Capital: Mumbai
Neighbouring States: Gujarat, Madhya Pradesh, Andhra Pradesh, Karnataka, Goa, Dadra and Nagar Haveli, Chhattisgarh. Sea: Arabian Sea.
Population: 112,372,972 **Males:** 58,361,397 **Females:** 54,011,575 **Sex-ratio:** 925 **Density:** 365 **Decadal growth:** 15.99%. **Literacy:** 82,512,225 (t82.91%, m89.82%, f75.48%).

No. of Districts: 35

District	Area (sq km)	Population (2011)	Head-quarters
Ahmednagar	17,034	4543083	Ahmednagar
Akola	5,431	1818617	Akola
Amaravati	12,235	2887826	Amaravati
Aurangabad	10,106	3695928	Aurangabad
Beed	10,692	2585962	Beed
Bhandara	3,890	1198810	Bhandara
Buldana	9,680	2588039	Buldana
Chandrapur	11,417	2194262	Chandrapur
Dhule	8,061	2048781	Dhule
Gadchiroli	14,477	1071795	Gadchiroli
Gondiya	5,430	1322331	Gondiya
Hingoli	4,526	1178973	Hingoli
Jalgaon	11,757	4224442	Jalgaon
Jalna	7,715	1958483	Jalna
Kolhapur	7,692	3874015	Kolhapur
Latur	7,166	2455543	Latur
Mumbai City	157	3145966	Mumbai City
Mumbai (Sub.)	446	9332481	Mumbai(Sub.)
Nagpur	9,810	4653171	Nagpur
Nanded	10,545	3356566	Nanded
Nandurbar	5,035	1646177	Nandurbar
Nashik	15,539	6109052	Nashik
Osmanabad	7,550	1660311	Osmanabad
Parbhani	6,511	1835982	Parbhani
Pune	15,637	9426959	Pune
Raigad	7,162	2635394	Alibag
Ratnagiri	8,196	1612672	Ratnagiri
Sangli	8,577	2820575	Sangli
Satara	10,475	3003922	Satara
Sindhudurg	5,222	848868	Oras
Solapur	(14,886)	4315527	Solapur
Thane	9,563	11054131	Thane
Wardha	6,311	1296157	Wardha
Washim	5,150	1196714	Washim
Yavatmal	13,594	2775457	Yavatmal

Villages: 41,095; **Towns:** 378

Legislative Bodies: State Legislature-Bicameral: Assembly Seats: 289 (1 nomina-

Prithviraj Chavan

tion); Legislative Council: 78; Legislative Assembly: 288; Parliament: Lok Sabha Seats: 48 (39+5+4); Rajya Sabha Seats: 19

Main Political Parties: NCP, INC, Shiv Sena, BJP, CPI-M, Jan Surajya Sharti, Peasant and Workers Party of India, Akhil Bharatiya Sena.

Seat of High Court: Mumbai (benches at Nagpur, Aurangabad and Panaji)

Chief Languages: Marathi.

Major Religions: Hinduism, Islam, Parsi, Christianity, Jainism.

Main Towns: Mumbai, Pune, Nagpur, Nashik, Nanded, Nandubar, Akola, Aurang-

50% Reservation for Women Maharashtra has approved a proposal for 50% reservation for women in local self-government bodies in the State.

abad, Ahmednagar, Beed, Gondia, Jalgaon, Jalna, Kolhapur, Kudal, Parbhani, Sholapur, Satara, Sangli, Wardha, Yavatmal

Geography: (a) Rivers: Godavari, Penganga, Manjra, Bhima, Varna, Panjhra, Wardha, Wainganga, Purna, Dudhana, Pravara, Mula, Ghod, Sina, Tirna; (b) Mountains: Ajanta Range, Harishchandra Range, Balaghat Range, Satmala Hills, Gawligarh Hills, Mahabaleshwar, Kalsunai; (c) Lakes: Beale, Tansa, Andhra, Mulshi, Koyna Reservoir. (d) National Park: Nawegaon, Pench Taroba.

Sanctuaries: Nagzira, Tousa, Yawal, Doe, Devlagaon.

Economy: (a) Minerals: Coal, Iron ore, Manganese, Chromite, Bauxite, Oil & Natural Gas; (b) Industries: Major industries are chemicals and allied products, textiles, electrical and non-electrical machinery and petroleum and allied products, pharmaceuticals, engineering goods, machine tools, steel and iron castings and plasticware. Santa Cruz Electronics Export Processing Zone (SEEPZ), is a free trade zone for cent per cent export. India's first gold refinery is at Shirpur. The development of offshore oil fields at Mumbai High and the nearby Bassein North Oil Fields have contributed greatly to the industrial development of the state; (c) Agricultural Products: Main food crops: wheat, rice, jowar, bajra and pulses. Cash crops: cotton, sugarcane, groundnut and tobacco. Alphonso mangoes, Thomson seedless grapes, Cavendish bananas and soft seeded pomegranates are the state's produce.

Transport & Communications: (a) Road Length: 2.66 lakh km. consisting of 4367 km. of national highways, 33,406 km. of state highways, 44,792 km. of major district roads, and 97,913 km of village roads; (b) Railway Length: 5,527 km. (c) Main Railway Stations: Chhatrapati Shivaji Railway Terminus (Victoria Terminus-VT) station; Bandra, Thane, Vasai, Khurd, Pune, Solapur, Satara, Jalgaon, Bhusaval, Nagpur, Kholapur, Kudal; (d) Airports: Mumbai. There are four airports under the control of International Airport Authority or Airport Authority of India (e) Port: Mumbai.

Forts: Pratapgarh, Daulatabad, Shivneri, Vijaydurg, Sindhudurg, Marnd, Janjira.

Culture: (a) Dances: Tamasha and Lavni (folk drama); (b) Festivals: Ganesh Chaturthi; (c) Craft: Paithani, Chandrakala, Pasodi, Ghongodi, Dharwadi and brocade sarees, silk-bordered dhoties, himru and bidri work, terracotta pottery, copper and zinc vessels, etc.

16. Manipur

Governor: Gurbachan Jagat
CM: Okram Ibobi Singh - (INC)
Date of Formation: 21 Jan 1972 State; State (from 1950: Part C); Union Territory 1963.
Area: 22,327 sq km
Capital: Imphal
Neighbouring States: Mizoram, Asom, Nagaland. Country: Myanmar.
Population: 2,721,756, **Males:** 1,369,764, **Females:** 1,351,992, **Sex-ratio:** 987, **Density:** 122, **Decadal growth:** 18.65%. **Literacy:** 1,891,196 (t79.85%, m86.49%, f73.17%).

No. of Districts: 9

District	Area (sq km)	Population (2011)	Head-quarters
Bishnupur	496	240363	Bishnupur
Chandel	3,313	144028	Chandel
Churachandpur	4,570	271274	Churachandpur
Imphal East	709	452661	Porompat
Imphal West	519	514683	Lamphelpat

Okram Ibobi Singh

Senapati	3,271	354972	Senapati
Tamenglong	4,391	140143	Tamenglong
Thoubal	514	420517	Thoubal
Ukhrul	4,544	183115	Ukhrul

Villages: 2,199; **Towns:** 33

Legislative Bodies: State Legislature-Unicameral: Assembly Seats: 60; Parliament: Lok Sabha Seats: 2 (1+0+1); Rajya Sabha Seats: 1

Main Political Parties: INC, Federal Party of Manipur, Manipur State Congress Party, CPI, BJP, NCP, Samata Party, Manipur People's Party, Manipur National Conference, Democratic Revolutionary Peoples Party...

Seat of High Court: A permanent bench of the Guwahati High Court, Imphal Bench (functional since 14-3-1992)

Chief Languages: Meiteilon (Manipuri).

Major Religions: Hinduism, Christianity.

Main Towns: Imphal, Thoubal, Churachandpur, Ukhrul, Bishnupur, Moirang, Moreh, Senapati, Tamenglong, Chandel.

Geography: (a) Rivers: Barak, Manipur; (b) Mountains: West Manipur Hills, Laimatol Range, Letha Range, East Manipur Hills; (d) Lake: Loktak.

Economy: (a) Minerals: Limestone; (b) Industries: Handloom weaving, cottage industries like sericulture, bamboo and cane articles, rice mills, edible oil crushing and leather goods; (c) Agricultural Products: Paddy, wheat, maize.

Transport & Communications: (a) Road Length: 12618 km; NH.#53, #39, #150; (b) Main Railway Stations: Jiribam; (d) Airports: Imphal

Culture: Manipuri dancing is one of the classical dances of India. Male dancers perform acrobatics and the graceful movements of female dancers are delightful.

(a) Dances: Manipuri; (b) Festivals: Dol jatra, Lai Haraoba, Rasa Leela, Cheiraoba, Ningol Chakouba, Imoinu Irtapa, Gaan-Nagai, Lui-Nagai-ni, Yaoshang (Holi), Mera Houchongba, Kut, Id-ul-Fitr, Christmas. (c) The favourite sport is polo and Manipur claims to have invented it. Polo is also popular in few other places in Asia.

17. Meghalaya

Governor: Ranjit Shekhar Mooshahary
CM: Dr. Mukul Sangma - (INC)
Date of Formation: 2 April 1970 State within Assam; 21 Jan 1972 Separate state
Area: 22,429 sq km
Capital: Shillong
Neighbouring States: Asom. Country: Bangladesh.
Population: 2,964,007 **Males:** 1,492,668, **Females:** 1,471,339, **Sex-ratio:** 986, **Density:** 132, **Decadal growth:** 27.82%. **Literacy:** 1,817,761 (t75.48%, m77.17%, f73.78%).

No. of Districts: 7

District	Area (sq km)	Population (2011)	Head-quarters
East Khasi Hills	2,820	824059	Shillong
West Khasi Hills	5,247	385601	Nongstoin
Jaintia Hills	3,819	392852	Jowai
Ri-Bhoi	2,376	258380	Nongpoh
South Garo Hills	1,849	142574	Baghmara
West Garo Hills	3,715	642923	Tura
East Garo Hills	2,603	317618	Williamnagar

Villages: 5,782; **Towns:** 16

Legislative Bodies: State Legislature-Unicameral : Assembly Seats: 60; Parliament: Lok Sabha Seats: 2 (0+0+2); Rajya Sabha Seats: 1.

Main Political Parties: INC, NCP, United Democratic Party, Meghalaya Democratic Party, BJP, Hill State People's Democratic

Dr. Mukul Sangma

Party, Khun, Hyneutrip National Awakening Movement.

Seat of High Court: Guwahati. A High Court Bench is located at Shillong.

Chief Languages: Garo, Khasi, and English.

Major Religions: Hinduism, Christianity

Main Towns: Shillong, Tura, Williamnagar, Nongpoh, Nongstoin, Jowai, Baghmara, Mawphlang

Geography: (a) Rivers: Simsang, Manda, Darming, Ringge, Gamol, Bugi, (Khri, Krishnai, Kapili, Sareswari, Bhogai); (b) Mountains: Garo Hills, Khasi Hills, Jaintia Hills; Nokrek Peak.

Economy: (a) Minerals: Sillimanite, Coal, limestone, dolomite, fireclay, felspar, quartz, glass sand, sandstone; (b) Industries: Cement: Industrial units are fast coming up. There is a public sector cement factory at Cherrapunjee. Meghalaya's hydro-electric and thermal power potential has been estimated at about 2500 and 1000 megawatts respectively; (c) Agricultural Products: Rice and Maize are the major food crops. Potato, tezpata, sugarcane, oilseeds, cotton, jute, mesta, arecanut besides fruits like pineapple, orange, and bananas are the important products. 'Khasi Mandarin' oranges are famous. Area under forest is 950,000 hectares.

Transport & Communications: (a) Road Length: 7,860 km of both surfaced and unsurfaced roads; (b) Railway: None; (c) Airports: Umroi, 35 km from Shillong

Culture: (a) Dances: Nongkrem at Smit village; Laho (Jaintias); (b) Festivals: Shad Suk Mynsiem - April 2nd week (Khasis); Wangala Oct-Nov (Garos); Behdiengkhlam at Jowai - July (Jaintias).

18. Mizoram

Governor: Lt. Gen. (Retd.) M.M. Lakhera
CM: Pu Lalthanhawla - (INC)

Date of Formation: 20 Feb 1987
Area: 21,081 sq km
Capital: Aizawl
Neighbouring States: Tripura, Asom, Manipur. Country: Myanmar.

Population: 1,091,014 **Males:** 552,339, **Females:** 538,675, **Sex-ratio:** 975, **Density:** 52, **Decadal growth:** 22.78%. **Literacy:** 847,592 (t91.58%, m93.72%, f89.40%).

No. of Districts: 8

District	Area (sq km)	Population (2011)	Head-quarters
Aizawl	3,576	404054	Aizawl
Champhai	3,186	125370	Champhai
Kolasib	1,283	83054	Kolasib
Lawngtlai	2,557	117444	Lawngtlai
Lunglei	4,538	154094	Lunglei
Mamit	3,026	85757	Mamit
Saiha	1,400	56366	Saiha
Serchhip	1,422	64875	Serchhip

Villages: 707; **Towns:** 22

Legislative Bodies: State Legislature-Unicameral: Assembly Seats: 40 members; Parliament: Lok Sabha Seats:1(0+0+1); Rajya Sabha Seats:1

Main Political Parties: Mizo National Front, INC, Mizoram People's Conference, Zoram Nationalist Party, Hmar People's Convention, Maraland Democratic Front.

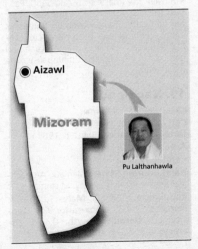

Pu Lalthanhawla

Seat of High Court: Guwahati. A bench at Aizawl.

Chief Languages: Mizo and English

Major Religions: Christianity

Main Towns: Aizawl, Mamit, Lunglei, Lawngtlai, Saiha, Champhai, Chhimtuipui, Saiha

Geography: (a) Rivers Tlawng (or the Dhaleswari), the Sonai and the Tuivawl; (b) Mountains: Mizoram is a land of hills, the highest point being the Blue Mountain (2165 metres).

Economy: (a) Industries: Handloom, rice mills, flour mills, brick making, bamboo handicrafts, sericulture, electronics; (b) Agricultural Products: Maize and paddy. Pulses, sugarcane, chilly, ginger, turmeric, potato, tobacco, vegetables, banana and pineapple are the other important crops.

Transport & Communications: (a) Road Length: 5982 km; (b) Main Railway Stations: Bairabi; (c) Airports: Aizawl, Lunglei

Culture: (a) Dances: Bamboo dances, Khantum Solokia, Kuallam, Cheraw Kan, Chheiraw and Iam. Chheihlam (recounts heroics around rice beer) and Khuallam (a dance of guests); (b) Festivals: Chapchar Kut, Mim Kut (maize fest- Aug-Sept), Pawl Kut (harvest- Dec-Jan), Christmas, Easter; (c) Crafts: Puans woven on traditional looms, thi-hi (amber bead necklace), Dar-hi (glass bead necklace), shawls, cane and bamboo work, Lunglei, Chintapai, Vakiria (headgear).

19. Nagaland

Governor: Nikhil Kumar

CM: Neiphiu Rio - (NPF)

Date of Formation: 1st Dec. 1963

Area: 16,579 sq km

Capital: Kohima

Neighbouring States: Manipur, Arunachal Pradesh, Asom. Country: Myanmar.

Population: 1,980,602, **Males:** 1,025,707, **Females:** 954,895, **Sex-ratio:** 931, **Density:** 119, **Decadal growth:** -0.47%. **Literacy:** 1,357,579 (t80.11%, m83.29%, f76.69%).

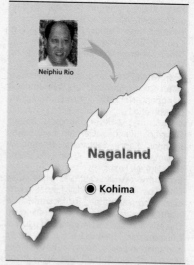

Neiphiu Rio

Nagaland

● Kohima

No. of Districts: 11

District	Area (sq km)	Population (2011)	Head-quarters
Dimapur	927	379769	Dimapur
Kohima	3,144	270063	Kohima
Phek	2,026	163294	Phek
Mokokchung	1,615	193171	Mokokchung
Mon	1,876	250671	Mon
Tuensang	4,228	196801	Tuensang
Wokha	1,628	166239	Wokha
Zunheboto	1,255	141014	Zunheboto
Kiphire		74033	Kiphire
Longleng		50593	Longleng
Peren		94954	Peren

Villages: 1,278; **Towns:** 9

Legislative Bodies: State Legislature-Unicameral: Assembly Seats: 60; Parliament: Lok Sabha Seats: 1; Rajya Sabha Seats: 1

Main Political Parties: INC, Nagaland Peoples Front, BJP, Nationalist Democratic Movement, JD-U, Samta Party.

Seat of High Court: Guwahati High Court. A bench is located at Kohima.

Chief Languages: Angami, Ao, Chang, Konyak, Lotha, Sangtam, Sema and Chakhesang

An 8-km Borehole	Scientists are planning to drill a borehole upto 8 km deep into the earth in the quake-prone Koyna region in Maharashtra in order to understand the changes that occur underground when an earthquake strikes. The project is to cost Rs. 300 crore.

Major Religions: Hinduism, Christianity
Main Towns: Kohima, Phek, Mon, Wokha, Mokokchung, Tuensang, Zunheboto
Geography: (a) Rivers: Dhansiri, Doyang, Dikhu and Jhanji; (b) Mountains: Saramati, the highest peak, is 3841 m high (c) National Park Intangki, known for the Blythe Tragopan, very colourful cock, found only at Phek.

Economy: (a) Minerals: Nagaland's mineral wealth (coal, limestone, iron, nickel, cobalt, chromium and marble) is immense, though unexplored yet; (b) Industries: Nagas make beautiful decorative materials. Nagaland has achieved remarkable progress in small and medium industries. Today the state has 30 industrial units, and over 300 small-scale industries. The Nagaland Sugar Mill at Dimapur has an installed capacity of 1,000 tonnes per day; (c) Agricultural Products: Rice, vegetable.

Transport & Communications: (a) Road Length: 9,860 km; (b) Main Railway Stations: Dimapur; (c) Airports: Dimapur

Culture: (a) Dances: Naga dance and music are intrinsic part of Naga life mostly eulogising bravery, beauty, love and generosity; (b) Festivals: Hornbill festival (1st week of Dec); Sekrenyi of Angamis (Touphema-Kohima, Feb 26-27); Monyu (Pongo-Longleng, Apr 1-3); Moatsu (Chuchuyimlang-Mokokchung, May 1-3); Tokhu Emong, Tuluni - of Semas and Christmas. Aoling festival of Konyaks, Pikhuchak festival of Lothas in Wokha; (c) Crafts: wood carving, hand woven shawl, baskets like Akhi, Akha, Chakhe-sang, Angami jewellery.

20. Odisha (Orissa)

Governor: Murlidhar C. Bhandare
CM: Navin Patnaik - (BJD)
Date of Formation: 15 Aug 1947 Province
Area: 155,707 sq km
Capital: Bhubaneswar
Neighbouring States: Andhra Pradesh, Chhattisgarh, Jharkhand, West Bengal.
Sea: Bay of Bengal.
Population: 41,947,358, **Males:** 21,201,678

Navin Patnaik

Females: 20,745,680, **Sex-ratio:** 978, **Density:** 269, **Decadal growth:** 13.97%. **Literacy:** 27,112,376 (t73.45, m82.40%, f64.36%).

No. of Districts: 30

District	Area (sq km)	Population (2011)	Head-quarters
Angul	6,375	1271703	Angul
Bolangir	6,575	1648574	Bolangir
Balasore	3,806	2317419	Balasore
Bargarh	5,837	1478833	Bargarh
Bhadrak	2,505	1506522	Bhadrak
Boudh	3,098	439917	Boudh
Cuttack	3,932	2618708	Cuttack
Deogarh	2,940	312164	Deogarh
Dhenkanal	4,452	1192948	Dhenkanal
Gajapati	4325	575880	Paralakhemundi
Ganjam	8,206	3520151	Chhatrapur
Jagatsinghpur	1,668	10,57,629	Jagatsinghpur
Jajpur	2,899	1826275	Jajpur
Jharsuguda	2,081	579499	Jharsuguda
Kalahandi	7920	1573054	Bhavanipatna
Kandhamal	8021	731952	Phulbani
Kendrapara	2,644	1439891	Kendrapara
Keonjhar	8,303	1802777	Keonjhar
Khurda	2,813	2246341	Khurda
Koraput	8,807	1376934	Koraput
Malkangiri	5791	612727	Malkangiri
Mayurbhanj	10,418	2513895	Baripada
Nabarangpur	5,291	12187626	Nabarangpur
Nayagarh	3,890	962215	Nayagarh
Nuapada	3,852	606490	Nuapada
Puri	3,479	1697983	Puri
Rayagada	7,073	961959	Rayagada

Raigad and Sivaji	Raigard (Maharashtra), the 12th century fort town, was Sivaji's headquarters during the latter part of his reign. In 1648, Sivaji regained it and made it home in 1690, but reverted to the Marathas who surrendered it to the British in 1818.

Sambalpur	6,657	1044410	Sambalpur
Subarnapur	2,337	652107	Subarnapur
Sundargarh	9,712	2080664	Sundargarh

Villages: 47,529; **Towns:** 138

Legislative Bodies: State Legislature-Unicameral: Assembly Seats: 147; Parliament: Lok Sabha Seats: 21 (13+3+5); Rajya Sabha Seats: 10

Main Political Parties: INC, Biju Janata Dal, INC, BJP, Jharkhand Mukti Morcha, Orissa Gana Parishad, CPI, CPI-M

Seat of High Court: Cuttack

Chief Languages: Odiya (Oriya)

Major Religions: Hinduism, Jainism, Islam

Main Towns: Bhubaneshwar, Cuttack, Chhatrapur, Puri, Sambalpur, Bolangir, Jharsuguda, Baragarh, Koraput, Rourkela, Balasore, Baripada, Berhampur, Bhadrak, Nabrangpur, Rayagada, Bhawanipatna, Phulbani, Dhenkanal, Kendrapara, Keonjhar, Konark, Sundargarh.

Geography: (a) Rivers: Mahanadi, Brahmani, Baitarani, Tel, Pushikulya, Sabari; (b) Mountains: Garhjat Hills, Mahendra Giri; (d) Lake/Reservoir: Hirakud, Balimela, Chilka (The biggest and the most famous lake in Odisha is the Chilka lake. It is 64 km long and 16 to 20 km wide. There are two beautiful islands in the lake namely Parikud and Malud). Hirakud Dam, the fourth largest in the world, on Mahanadi is another attraction. Chilka, the largest brackish water inland lake in Asia, stretches over an area of 1100 sq.km. (d) National Parks: The largest Lion Safari of India, and the only White Tiger Safari in the world, are located on the outskirts of Bhubaneswar.

Economy: (a) Minerals: Chromite, bauxite, dolomite, graphite, iron-ore, coal, copper, kaolin, lead, quartzite, steatite and tin; (b) Industries: The Central Sector Projects are: Steel Plant at Rourkela, SAND Complex at Chhatrapur, Heavy Water Project at Talcher, Coach Repairing Workshop at Mancheswar, Aluminium Complex at Koraput, Captive Power plant at Angul, Aluminium Smelter at Angul and Fertiliser Plant at Paradeep. Major thermal and hydel power stations are Talcher, Hirakud and Chiplima. Other power projects are Upper Indravati, Upper Kolab, Rengali and Ib. Centre has cleared a 10000 MW power project at Hirma, Odisha to be commissioned by 2008; c) Agricultural Products: 64% of the working population is dependent on agriculture. Rice, pulses, oil-seeds, jute, mesta, sugarcane (the main cash crop), coconut and turmeric are important crops. The state contributes one-tenth of the rice production in India.

Transport & Communications: (a) Road Length: 3596km NH; 29 km state express highways; 3855 km SH; (b) Railway Length 2,339 km - broad-guage and 90 km narrow-guage lines; (c) Main Railway Stations: Bhubaneshwar, Puri, Cuttack, Behrampur, Bolangir, Raurkela, Sambalpur; (d) Airports: Bhubaneshwar. (e) Ports: Paradeep (major) and Gopalpur (all-weather)

Culture: (a) Dances: Odissi, the dance form of Odisha, evolved in the shadow of the magnificent temples of the state. Dalkhai (tribal dance), Ghoomra, Ranapa and Chhadaya (folk dance); (b) Festivals: Rath Yatra (Puri), Shraban Purnima, Ashokastami, Chandan Yatra, Snana Yatra and Konark festival; (c) Handloom products of silk and tussar, silver filigree work (tarkashi), Pat chitra paintings, golden glass work.

21. Punjab

Governor: Shivraj Patil

CM: Prakash Singh Badal - (SAD)

Date of Formation: 15 Aug 1947 Province; 26 Jan 1950 State (until 1956: part (A)

Area: 50,362 sq km

Capital: Chandigarh

Neighbouring States: Jammu & Kashmir, Himachal Pradesh, Haryana, Rajasthan. Country: Pakistan.

Population: 27,704,236 **Males:** 14,634,819 **Females:** 13,069,417, **Sex-ratio:** 893, **Density:** 550, **Decadal growth:** 13.73%. **Literacy:** 18,988,611 (t76.68%, m81.48%, f71.34%).

No. of Districts: 20

District	Area (sq km)	Population (2011)	Head-quarters
Amritsar	5,075	2490891	Amritsar
Bhathinda	3,377	1388859	Bhathinda

Punjab's Agriculture	According to a report, Punjab's agricultural growth is 1.0 p.c. today, down from 2.4 p.c. in 2004-08. The overall growth is 7.8 p.c., less than the national average of 8.7 p.c. Of the state's 46 lakh families, 13 lakh live below the poverty line.

Prakash Singh Badal

Punjab

Chandigarh ◉

Faridkot	1,472	618008	Faridkot
Fatehgarh Sahib	1,180	599814	Fatehgarh Sahib
Firozepur	5,865	2026831	Firozepur
Gurdaspur	3,570	2299026	Gurdaspur
Hoshiarpur	3,310	1582793	Hoshiarpur
Jalandhar	2,658	2181753	Jalandhar
Kapurthala	1,646	817668	Kapurthala
Ludhiana	3,744	3487882	Ludhiana
Mansa	2,174	768808	Mansa
Moga	1,672	992289	Moga
Muktsar	2,596	902702	Muktsar
Patiala	3,627	1892282	Patiala
Rupnagar	2,117	683349	Rupnagar
SAS Nagar	1093	986147	Roop Nagar
SBS Nagar	1267	614362	Roop Nagar
Sangrur	5,021	1654408	Sangrur
Tarn Taran	2449	1120070	
Barnala		596294	Barnala

Villages: 12,278; **Towns:** 157
Legislative Bodies: Legislature-Unicameral: Assembly Seats: 117; Parliament: Lok Sabha Seats: 13 (9+4+0); Rajya Sabha Seats: 7
Main Political Parties: INC, Shiromani Akali Dal (Badal), BJP, CPI.
Seat of High Court: Chandigarh
Chief Languages: Punjabi
Major Religions: Sikhism, Hinduism, Christianity.
Main Towns: Amritsar, Ludhiana, Faridkot, Bathinda, Jalandhar, Patiala, Moga, Gurudaspur, Kapurthala, Pathankot, Ropar, Sangur, Taran.

Geography: (a) Rivers: Beas, Sutlej, Ravi; (b) Mountains: Katar Dhar (Shiwalik Range), Hoshiarpur Choaland, Chandigarh Choaland; (c) Plain Malwa, Sirhind, Manjha.
Economy: (a) Industries: The chief manufactures are textiles, sewing machines, sports goods, sugar, starch, fertilizers, bicycles, scientific instruments, electrical goods, machine tools and pine oil. A Science City is being set up at Jalandhar; (b) Agricultural Products: Wheat, rice, maize, bajra, jowar, barley, oilseeds, sugarcane, potato, cotton, pulses, tobacco.
Transport & Communications: (a) Road Length: 63833 km, NH-1739km, SH-1462-km; (b) Railway Length: 3726.06 km; (c) Main Railway Stations: Patiala, Jalandhar, Amritsar, Bhatinda; (d) Airports: Rajasansi international airport (Amritsar), Chandigarh, Bathinda, and Ludhiana.
Culture: (a) Dances: Bhangra, Gidda and Thumar, (b) Festivals: Gurpurab, Lohri, Dussehra, Diwali, Holi, Hola Mohalla (Anandpur Sahib), Rauza Sharif Urs (Sirhind), Baisakhi (Talwandi Saboo), Chappar Mela, Sheikh Farid Agam Purb (Faridkot), Shaheedi Jor Mela (Sirhind), Harballah Sangeet Sammelan (Jalandhar); (c) Crafts: Pulkari embroidery on bed sheets, durries, shawls, jerseys.

22. Rajasthan

Governor: Shivraj Patil
CM: Ashok Gehlot - (INC)
Date of Formation: 1 Nov 1956 Rajasthan (full statehood); 25 Mar 1948 Rajasthan Union; 18 Apr 1948 United states of Rajasthan; 30 Apr 1949 United states of Greater Rajasthan (from 1950: Part (B)
Area: 3,42,239 sq km
Capital: Jaipur
Neighbouring States: Gujarat, MP, UP, Delhi, Haryana, Punjab.Country: Pakistan.
Population: 68,621,012 **Males:** 35,620,086, **Females:** 33,000,926, **Sex-ratio:** 926 **Density:** 201, **Decadal growth:** 21.44%. **Literacy:** 38,970,500 (t67.06%, m80.51%, f52.66%).

Regional Centres for IIMC

The Ministry of Information is opening four regional centres of the Indian Institute of Mass Communication in Jammu, Aizawal, Amravati and Kottayam.

Ashok Gehlot

Jaipur ●
Rajasthan

No. of Districts: 33

District	Area (sq km)	Population (2011)	Head-quarters
Ajmer	8,481	2584913	Ajmer
Alwar	8,380	3671999	Alwar
Banswara	5,037	1798194	Banswara
Baran	6,955	1223921	Baran
Barmer	28,387	2604453	Barmer
Bharatpur	5,066	2549121	Bharatpur
Bhilwara	10,455	2410459	Bhilwara
Bikaner	27,244	2367745	Bikaner
Bundi	5,550	1113725	Bundi
Chittorgarh	10,856	1544392	Chittorgarh
Churu	16,830	2041172	Churu
Dausa	2,950	1637226	Dausa
Dholpur	3,034	1207293	Dholpur
Dungarpur	3,770	1388906	Dungarpur
Ganganagar	7,944	1969520	Ganganagar
Hanumangarh	12,690	1779650	Hanumangarh
Jaipur	11,588	6663971	Jaipur
Jaisalmer	38,401	672008	Jaisalmer
Jalore	10,640	1830151	Jalore
Jhalawar	6,219	1411327	Jhalawar
Jhunjhunu	5,928	2139658	Jhunjhunu
Jodhpur	22,850	3685681	Jodhpur
Karauli	5,014	1458459	Karauli
Kota	5,481	1950491	Kota
Nagaur	17,718	3309234	Nagaur
Pali	12,387	2038533	Pali
Partapgarh	4189	868231	Partapgarh
Rajsamand	4,768	1158283	Rajsamand
S. Madhopur	5,043	1338114	S.Madhopur
Sikar	7,732	2677737	Sikar
Sirohi	5,136	1037185	Sirohi
Tonk	7,194	1421711	Tonk
Udaipur	12,511	3067549	Udaipur

Villages: 39,753; **Towns:** 222

Legislative Bodies: State Legislature-Unicameral: Assembly Seats:200; Parliament: Lok Sabha Seats: 25 (18+4+3); Rajya Sabha Seats: 10

Main Political Parties: BJP, INC, Indian National Lok Dal, BSP, JD-U, CPI-M, Lok Jan Shakti Party, Rajasthan Samajik Nyaya Manch.

Seat of High Court: Jodhpur and a bench at Jaipur.

Chief Languages: Rajasthani, Hindi, Gujarati

Major Religions: Hinduism, Jainism, Islam

Main Towns: Jaipur, Kota, Tonk, Jodhpur, Bikaner, Ganganagar, Pali, Nagaur, Udaipur, Bhilwara, Sikar, Alwar, Sawai Madhopur, Jaisalmer, Ajmer, Chittorgarh, Jalor,

Geography: (a) Desert: Great Indian Desert (The Thar); (b) Rivers: Luni, Banas, Kali Sindh, Chambal, Indira Gandhi Nahar (Canal); (c) Mountains: Aravalli Range (Guru Shikhar Peak, 1722m), Alwar Hills, Sojat Hills, Mewar Hills, Mukandwara; (d) Lakes/Reservoirs Sambhar Salt Lake, Gudha, Rana Pratap Sagar, Gandhi Sagar, Dhebar Lake, Mandor (e) Wildlife Sariska Tiger Park-Alwar, Keoladeo Ghana National Park.

Economy: (a) Minerals: zinc concentrates, emerald, garnet, gypsum, silver ore, asbestos, felspar, mica, rock phosphate, marble and red stone; (b) Industries: Textiles, rugged and woollen goods, sugar, cement, glass, sodium, oxygen and acetylene units, pesticides, insecticides and dyes are some of the major industries. Other enterprises include the manufacture of caustic soda, calcium carbide and nylon tyre cord and copper smelting. Marble work, woollen carpets, jewelry, embroidery, articles of leather, pottery and brass embossing. Rajasthan handicrafts are famous all over the world; (c) Agricultural Products: The principal crops are jowar, bajra, maize, wheat, grams, oilseeds, cotton, sugarcane and tobacco.

A Maneater Shot
The Champawat tigress in Kumaon region took a toll of 436 human lives. It was shot by Jim Corbett in 1907.

Transport & Communications: (a) Road Length: 1,86806 km; (b) Railway Length 6228 km; (c) Main Railway Stations: Jaipur, Jodhpur, Kota, Bikaner, Sawaai Madhopur, Bharatpur; (d) Airports: Jaipur, Jodhpur

Culture: (a) Dances: Khayal (dance-music), Ghumar during Teej and Gangaur festivals, Panihari, Chari, Kachchi Ghori; (b) Festivals: Deepawali, Vijayadashami, Holi, Teej, Gangaur (Jaipur), Urs of Ajmer Sherif and Galiakot, Christmas; (c) Fairs: tribal Kumbh of Bene-shwar (Dungarpur), Ramdeora (Jaisalmer), Mahavir fair at Shri Mahavirji in Sawai Madhopur, Janbeshwari Fair (Mukam-Bikaner), Kartik Poornima and Cattle Fair (Pushkar-Ajmer) and Shyamji Fair (Sikar); (d) Craft: Bandhini (tie and dye) work, block printing, hand-knotted woollen carpets, massoria work, gharas kagzi pottery, pichwais (painting on cloth), phads (cloth scroll painting), lacquer-works.

23. Sikkim

Governor: Balmiki Prasad Singh
CM: Pawan Chamling - (SDF)
Date of Formation: 16 May 1975 State
Area: 7,096 sq km
Capital: Gangtok
Neighbouring States: West Bengal. Countries: China, Nepal, Bhutan.
Population: 607,688 **Males:** 321,661, **Females:** 286,027, **Sex-ratio:** 889, **Density:** 86, **Decadal growth:** 12.36%.
No. of Districts: 4

District	Area (sq km)	Population (2011)	Head-quarters
East	954	281293	Gangtok
North	4,226	43354	Mangan
South	750	146742	Namchi
West	1,166	136299	Gyalshing

Villages: 450; **Towns:** 9
Legislative Bodies: State Legislature-Unicameral: Assembly Seats: 32; Parliament: Lok Sabha Seats: 1; Rajya Sabha Seats: 1
Main Political Parties: Sikkim Democratic Front, INC.
Seat of High Court: Gangtok
Chief Languages: Nepali, Lepcha, Bhutia, Hindi, Limbu

Major Religions: Buddhism, Hinduism.
Main Towns: Gangtok, Namchi, Gyalshing, Mangan, Jelep La, Pemayangtse, Lachen, Yunthang, Tashiding, Rumtek
Geography: (a) Rivers: Teesta, Rangit; (b) Mountains: Kanchenjunga-the highest peak in India is situated here. (c) Khan-gchendzonga National Park is one of the highest national parks in the world and includes the world's third highest mountain (Kanchenjunga). Deorali is another National Park. The yak and the musk deer are animals found in Sikkim. There are over 4000 species of plants.
Economy: (a) Minerals: Gold, silver, copper, zinc; (b) Industries: There are units engaged in food processing, tanning, watch assembling and distilleries, breweries and flour mills; (c) Agricultural Products: The principal crops are maize, paddy, millet, wheat and barley. Orange, potatoes, apples and cardamom are also produced. Sikkim has the largest area and the highest production of large cardamom in India. Tea is grown in Sikkim. Sikkim is very rich in varieties of orchids.
Transport & Communications: (a) Road Length: 2383 km; (b) Main Railway Stations: No stations but the closest ones are Siliguri (114 km) and Jalpaiguri (125 km); (c) Airports: Gangtok.
Culture: (a) Dances: Mask dances of Bhutias, Nepalis and Lepchas are famous; (b) Festi-

Sikkim
Gangtok ●
Pawan Chamling

vals: Maghey Sankranti, Durga Puja, Chaite Dasai (Nepali), Pang Lhabsol and Losar (Bhutias), Namsoong and Tendong Hlo Rum Faat (Lepchas); (c) Crafts: Woollen carpets, with Tibetan designs, rough blankets, saris, cane and bamboo works, wood carving, handmade paper and silver works.

24. Tamil Nadu

Governor: Surjit Singh Barnala
CM: J Jayalalithaa - (AIDMK)
Date of Formation: 15 Aug 1947 Madras province; 26 Jan., 1950 State (until 1956: Part (A); 14 Jan., 1969 Renamed Tamil Nadu
Area: 1,30,058 sq km
Capital: Chennai
Neighbouring States: Kerala, Karnataka, Andhra Pradesh, Puducherry. Sea: Bay of Bengal & Indian Ocean. Country: Sri Lanka.
Population: 72,138,958 **Males:** 36,158,871, **Females:** 35,980,087, **Sex-ratio:** 995, **Density:** 555, **Decadal growth:** 15.60%. **Literacy:** 52,413,116 (t80.33%, m86.81%, f73.86%).

No. of Districts: 32

District	Area (sq km)	Population (2011)	Headquarters
Ariyalur	1,944	752481	Ariyalur
Chennai	174	4681087	Chennai
Coimbatore	7,469	3472578	Coimbatore
Cuddalore	3,706	2600880	Cuddalore
Dharmapuri	9,622	1502900	Dharmapuri
Dindigul	6,058	2161367	Dindigul
Erode	8,209	2259608	Erode
Kancheepuram	4,307	3990897	Kancheepuram
Kanyakumari	1,684	1863174	Nagercoil
Krishnagiri	5,143	1883731	Krishnagiri
Karur	2,901	1076588	Karur
Madurai	3,696	3041038	Madurai
Nagapattinam	2,417	1614069	Nagapattinam
Namakkal	3,404	1721179	Namakkal
Nilgiris	2,549	735071	(Ootty) Udagamandalam
Perambalur	1,750	564511	Perambalur
Pudukkottai	4,651	1618725	Pudukkottai
Ramanathapuram	4,175	1337560	Ramanathapuram
Salem	5,425	3480008	Salem
Sivagangai	4,143	1341250	Sivagangai
Thanjavur	3,476	2402781	Thanjavur
Theni	2,869	1243684	Theni
Thiruvannamalai	6,190	2468965	Thiruvannamalai
Thiruvarur	2,377	1268094	Thiruvarur
Tirunelveli	6,810	3072880	Tirunelveli
Tiruvallur	3,550	3725697	Tiruvallur
Trichirappalli	4,511	2713858	Trichirappalli
Thoothukudi	4,621	1738376	Thoothukudi
Vellore	6,077	3928106	Vellore
Viluppuram	7,190	3463284	Viluppuram
Virudhunagar	4,283	1943309	Virudhunagar
Tirupur	4720	2471222	Tirupur

Villages: 15,400; **Towns:** 832
Legislative Bodies: State Legislature-Unicameral: Assembly Seats: 234 (excluding nomination); Parliament: Lok Sabha Seats: 39 (32+7+0); Rajya Sabha Seats: 18
Main Political Parties: All India Dravida Munetra Kazhagam, Dravida Munetra Kazhagam, Tamil Manila Congress (Moopanar), Pattali Makkal Katchi, INC, CPI-M, CPI, BJP, MGR Anna DMK, All India Forward Bloc.
Seat of High Court: Chennai.
Chief Languages: Tamil.

Chennai

Tamil Nadu

J Jayalalithaa

Richer than the Vatican   Media reports say the value of the treasure found recently in the safe vaults of Padmanabhaswamy Temple, Thiruvananthapuram is over Rs. 1 lakh crore and it is the richest temple in the world, richer than the Vatican.

Major Religions: Hinduism, Islam, Christianity.

Main Towns: Ambattur, Chennai, Avadi, Coimbatore, Madurai, Erode, Vellore, Salem, Tanjavur, Cuddalore, Tutucorin, Tiruchirapalli, Tirunelveli, Neyveli, Udagamandalam, Nagercoil. Pudukotai, Thanjavur,

Geography: (a) Rivers: Palar, Kaveri, Vaigai, Cheyyar, Ponniyar, Meyar, Bhavani, Tamarapani, Chittar, Vellar, Noyal, Suruli, Vaipar, etc.; (b) Mountains: Along the whole length of the western part, is the range of the Western Ghats. The Palghat Gap about 25 km in width is the only marked break in the great mountain wall. To the south of this Palaghat Gap, the range is known as Anamalai (Elephant Hills).

On the east are the Palani Hills on which is situated the famous hill station Kodaikanal. In the famous Ootacamund area of the Nilgiris District, highest peak Doddabetta, 2640 metres above the sea level.

Economy: (a) Minerals: Lignite, limestone, magnesite, mica, quartz, felspar, bauxite, gypsum; (b) Industries: Cotton textile, automobiles, chemical fertiliser, paper and paper products, railway wagons and coaches, army tank, cement, iron & steel, computer peripherals and software; (c) Agricultural Products: Rice, maize, jowar, bajra, ragi, pulses, sugarcane, oilseed, cotton, chillies, coffee, tea, rubber, cardamom.

Transport & Communications: (a) Road Length: 61641 km; (b) Railway Length 3927 km; (c) Main Railway Stations: Chennai, Madurai, Tiruchirapalli, Coimbatore, Erode, Salem and Tirunelveli; (d) Airports: Meenambakam International, Chennai; Madurai, Tiruchirapalli, Coimbatore, Salem; (e) Ports: Chennai and Thoo-thukudi (Tuticorin), Cuddalore, Naga-pattinam.

Culture: (a) Dances: Bharathanatyam, Kalakshetra, Kollattam, Kummi, Kavadi, Karagams; (b) Festivals: Pongal (harvest), Jallikattu (bull fight), Chitirai-Madurai, Adipperukku (on river banks during sowing season), Mahamagam fest, Dance festival-Mamalapuram, Kanthuri festival, Karthigai festival, Navaratri festival, Music Festival.

25. Tripura

Governor: Dr. D.Y. Patil
CM: Manik Sarkar - (CPI-M)
Date of Formation: 21 January, 1972.
Area: 10,491.69 sq km
Capital: Agartala
Neighbouring States: Asom, Mizoram
Country: Bangladesh.
Population: 3,671,032, **Males:** 1,871,867, **Females:** 1,799,165, **Sex-ratio:** 961, **Density:** 350, **Decadal growth:** 14.75%. **Literacy:** 2,831,742 (t87.75 %, m92.18%, f83.15%.)

No. of Districts: 4

District	Area (sq km)	Population (2011)	Head-quarters
Dhalai	2,552	377988	Ambassa
North Tripura	2,821	693281	Kailasahar
South Tripura	2,152	875144	Udaipur
West Tripura	2,997	1724619	Agartala

Villages: 858; **Towns:** 23
Legislative Bodies: State Legislature-Unicameral: Assembly Seats: 60; Parliament: Lok Sabha Seats: 2(1+0+1); Rajya Sabha Seats: 1
Main Political Parties: CPI-M, INC, Indigenous Nationalist Party of Tripura, RSP, CPI.
Seat of High Court: Guwahati High Court Agartala bench.
Chief Languages: Bengali, Kokborak and Manipuri.
Major Religions: Hinduism, Islam, Christianity
Main Towns: Agartala, Belonia, Kumarghat, Kailashahar, Udaipur, Khowai and Kamalpur.
Geography: (a) Rivers: Gomti
Economy: (a) Minerals: Natural Gas; (b) Industries: Registered factories-1,282. Handloom weaving is the single largest industry. There are several jute factories that make gunny bags and other products for the market. It is essentially a tribal household industry. The sericulture industry is developing fast. Energy generated-337.68 m.u. Tripura is abundant in natural gas and a number of gas-based industries have sprung up. There are 809 small scale

Scout Movement Boy Scout Movement began in India in 1907. It was converted to Bharat Scouts and Guides in 1949.

Manik Sarkar

Tripura

● Agartala

Pradesh. Countries - China, Nepal.
Population:10,116,752, **Males:**5,154,178, **Females:** 4,962,574, **Sex-ratio:** 963, **Density:** 189, **Decadal growth:** 19.17%. **Literacy:** 6,997,433 (t79.63, m88.33%, f70.70%).

No. of Districts: 17*

District	Area (sq km)	Population (2011)	Head-quarters
Almora	3,139	621927	Almora
Bageshwar	1,696	259840	Bageshwar
Chamoli	7,520	391114	Gopeshwar
Champawat	2,004	259315	Champawat
Dehradun	3,088	1698560	Dehradun
Pauri Garhwal	5,329	686527	Pauri
Hardwar	2,360	1927029	Hardwar
Nainital	3,422	955128	Nainital
Pithoragarh	7,169	485993	Pithoragarh
Rudra Prayag	2,439	236857	Rudra Prayag
Tehri Garhwal	3,796	616409	New Tehri
Udhamsingh Nagar	3,055	1648367	Rudrapur
Uttarkashi	8,016	329686	Uttarkashi

*****New districts:** Yamunotri, Kotdwar, Didihat, Raniket.

Villages: 15,761; **Towns:** 86

industrial units in Tripura; (c) Agricultural Products: Rice, sugarcane, jute, mesta, potatoes, tea and rubber.

Transport & Communications: (a) Road Length: 1997 km; (b) Railway Length: 64 km; (c) Main Railway Stations: Manughat, Dharamnagar; (d) Airports: Agartala

Culture: (a) Dances: Cherolaw - Bamboo dance; (b) Festivals: Makar Sankranti at Tirtha-mukh and Unakoti, Bengali New Year, Garia Puja, Hozagiri, Mansa Mangal, Ker and Karachi Puja, Ganga Puja, Christmas, Buddha Purnima, Ashokasthami at Unakoti, Sarad festival, Rash Leela, Jhulan Jatra, Rath Jatra; (c) Crafts: Bamboo handicrafts esp. sitalpatti (mats), lasing-phee (quilt like weaving), terracotta and cane.

26. Uttarakhand

Governor: Smt. Margaret Alva
CM: Ramesh Pokhriyal - (BJP)
Date of Formation: 9 November, 2000 as Uttaranchal; renamed Uttarakhand in 2007.
Area: 53,484 sq km
Capital: (provisional): Dehra Dun
Neighbouring States: UP, Himachal

Legislative Bodies: State Legislature-Unicameral: Assembly Seats: 70; Parliament: Lok Sabha Seats:5 (4+1+0); Rajya Sabha Seats: 3; Jurisdiction of High Court: Uttaranchal.

Main Political Parties: INC, BJP, BSP, Uttarakhand Kranti Dal, NCP.

Seat of High Court: Nainital.

Chief Languages: Hindi, Garhwali, Kumaoni.

Major Religions: Hinduism, Sikhism.

Main Towns: Dehra Dun, Gairsen, Gopeshwar, Pithoragarh, Rudrapur Haridwar, Almora, Nainital, Mussoorie, Rishikesh, and Haldwari-cum-Kathgodam.

Geography: (a) Rivers: Yamuna, Bhagirathi, Ganga, Ramganga, Tons, and Kali; (b) Mountains: Shiwalik range, Great Himalaya, Garhwal Hills, Kumaon Hills; (c) Peaks: Nanda Devi -7817m, Kamet-7756m, Badrinath-7138m, Dunagiri-7066m, Bandarpunch-63020; (d) Passes: Thaga La, Tsang Chok La, Muling La, Mana Pass, Niti

First Steel Company

Tata Iron & Steel Company, the first steel company of India, was established on March 1, 1908. Production commenced in 1911.

Ramesh Pokhriyal

Mela (Almor(a), Gauchar Mela (Chamoli), Baisakhi & Maga Mela (Uttarkashi), Uttaraini Mela (Bageshwar), Vishu Mela (Jaunsar Vavar), Peerane-Kaliyar (Roorkee), Nanda Devi Raj Jat Yaatra -every 12th year, and Puranagiri Mela.

27. Uttar Pradesh

Governor: B. L. Joshi
CM: Kumari Mayawati - (BSP)
Date of Formation: 15 Aug 1947 United province; 26 Jan, 1950, Uttar Pradesh state (until 1956: Part (A)
Area: 2,40,928 sq km
Capital: Lucknow
Neighbouring States: Uttarakhand, Himachal Pradesh, Haryana, Delhi, Rajasthan, Madhya Pradesh, Chhattisgarh, Jharkhand, Bihar. Country: Nepal.
Population: 199,581,477, **Males:** 104,596,415, **Females:** 94,985,062, **Sex-ratio:** 908 **Density:** 828, **Decadal growth:** 20.09%. **Literacy:** 118,423,805, (t69.72%, m79.24%, f59.26%)

No. of Districts: 71

District	Area (sq km)	Population (2011)	Head-quarters
Agra	4,027	4380793	Agra
Aligarh	3,650	3673849	Aligarh
Allahabad	5,482	5959798	Allahabad
Ambedkar Nagar	2,350	20,26,876	Akbarpur
Azamgarh	4,054	4616509	Azamgarh
Baghpat	1,321	1302156	Baghpat
Bahraich	4,420	3478257	Bahraich
Ballia	2,981	3223642	Balia
Balrampur	3,349	2149066	Balrampur
Banda	4,460	1799541	Banda
Barabanki	4,402	3257983	Barabanki
Bareilly	4,120	4465344	Bareilly
Basti	2,688	2461056	Basti
Bijnor	4,561	3683896	Bijnore
Budaun	5,168	3712738	Budaun
Bulandshahar	4,352	3498507	Bulandshahar
Chandauli	2,541	1952713	Chandauli
Chitrakoot	3,164	990626	Chitrakoot
Deoria	2,538	3098637	Deoria
Etah	4,446	1761152	Etah

Pass, Darma Pass, Lampiya Dhura Pass, Mangsha Dhura Pass. (e) Hill Stations: Mussoorie - (Lal Tiba, Gun Hill, Kempty Falls, Lake, Surkunda Devi temple), Dehra Dun (IFRI, Sahasradhar(a), Chakrata, Nainital & Kumaon (mountaineering), Ranikhet, Bhim Tal, Naukuchia Tal, Bageshwar, and Kausani. (f) Six of the seven national parks including Corbett National Park, Rajaji National Park, Nanda Devi National Park, Valley of Flowers, Kedarnath Sanctuary are in Uttaranchal.
Economy: (a) Minerals: limestone, rock phosphate, dolomite, magnesite, copper graphite, soapstone, gypsum, etc.; (b) Industries: forest-based, handicraft; (c) Agricultural Products:
Transport & Communications: (a) Road Length: 19,543 km.; (b) Main Railway Stations: Dehra Dun, Hardwar, Roorkee, Kotdwar, Kashipur, Udhamsingh Nagar, Kathgodam, Haldwani; (c) Airport Jolly Grant (Dehra Dun). Airstrips: Pantnagar (Udham Singh Nagar), (Naini-Seni (Pithoragarh), Gauchar (Chamoli) and Chinyalisaur (Uttarkashi) - are being built).
Culture: (a) Dances: folk dances; (b) Festivals: Kumbh Mela / Ardh Kumbh Mela (Hardwar- every 12th / 6th year interval); Devidhura Mela (Chamawat), Nanda Devi

Birthplace of Lord Krishna
For Vaishnavites, Mathura is the supremely sacred city of India, being the birthplace of Krishna, the most human aspect of Vishnu.

District	Area	Population	Headquarters
Etawah	2,311	1579160	Etawah
Faizabad	2,341	20,88,928	Faizabad
Farrukhabad	2,181	1887577	Fatehgarh
Fatehpur	4,152	2632684	Fatehpur
Firozabad	2,361	2496761	Firozabad
Gautam Buddha Nagar	1,442	1674714	Gautam Buddha Nagar
Ghaziabad	1,148	4661452	Ghaziabad
Ghazipur	3,377	3622727	Ghazipur
Gonda	4,003	3431386	Gonda
Gorakhpur	3,321	4436275	Gorakhpur
Hamirpur	4,282	1104021	Hamirpur
Hardoi	5,986	4091380	Hardoi
Mahamaya Nagar	1840	1565678	Hathras
Jalaun	4,565	1670718	Orai
Jaunpur	4,038	4476072	Jaunpur
Jhansi	5,024	2000755	Jhansi
JyotibaPhuleNagar	2,249	1838771	Amroha
Kannauj	2,093	1658005	Kanauj
Kanpur (Dehat)	3,021	1795092	Akbarpur
Kanpur (City)	3,155	4572951	Kanpur
Kanshi Ram Nagar	-	1438156	Kanshi Ram Nagar
Kaushambi	1780	1596909	Kaushambi
Kushinagar	2,906	3560830	Podarauna
Kheri	7,680	4013634	Kheri
Lalitpur	5,039	1218002	Lalitpur
Lucknow	2,528	4588455	Lucknow
Maharajganj	2,952	2665292	Maharajganj
Mahoba	2884	876055	Mahoba
Mainpuri	2,760	1847194	Mainpuri
Mathura	3,340	2541894	Mathura
Mau	1,713	2205170	Mau
Meerut	2,590	3447405	Meerut
Mirzapur	4,521	2494533	Mirzapur
Moradabad	3,718	4773138	Moradabad
Muzaffarnagar	4,008	4138605	Muzaffarnagar
Auraiya	2,015	1372287	Aurraiya
Pilibhit	3,499	2037225	Pilibhit
Pratapgarh	3,717	3173752	Pratapgarh
Rae Bareilli	4,609	3404004	Rae Bareli
Rampur	2,367	2335398	Rampur
Saharanpur	3,689	3464228	Saharanpur
Sant Kabir Nagar	1,646	1714300	Khalilabad
Sant RavidasNagar	1,015	1554203	Bhadhohi
Shahjahanpur	4,575	3002376	Shahjahanpur
Shrawasti	2,458	1114615	Shrawasti
Siddharth Nagar	2,895	2553526	Navgarh
Sitapur	5,743	4474446	Sitapur
Sonbhadra	6,788	1862612	Robertsganj
Sultanpur	4,436	3790922	Sultanpur
Unnao	4,558	3110595	Unnao
Varanasi	1,535	3682194	Varanasi

Villages: 97,942; **Towns:** 704

Legislative Bodies: State Legislature-Bicameral: Assembly Seats: 403; Legislative Council - 100; Parliament: Lok Sabha Seats: 80(63+17+0); Rajya Sabha Seats: 31

Main Political Parties: Samajwadi Party, BSP, BJP, INC, Rashtriya Lok Dal, Rashtriya Kranti Party, Apna Dal, CPI-M, Akhil Bharatiya Lok Tantrik Congress, JD-U, Akhil Bharat Hindu Mahasabha, Janata Party, Lok Jan Shakti Party, National Loktantrik Party, Samajeadi Janata Party (Rashtriya).

Seat of High Court: Allahabad and a bench at Lucknow.

Chief Languages: Hindi and Urdu.

Major Religions: Hinduism, Islam.

Main Towns: Lucknow, Allahabad, Kanpur, Varanasi, Aligarh, Gorakhpur, Agra, Jhansi, Saharanpur, Etawah, Meerut, Ghaziabad, Noida, Rae Bareli, Faizabad, Sarnat, Mathura.

Geography: (a) Rivers: Ganga, Yamuna, Gomti, Ghagra, Ramganga, Betwa; (b) Mountains: Lower hills of Shiwalik range, Kaimur range; (c) Plains: Gangetic Plain, Rohilkhand Plain, Avadh Plain. (d) Wildlife:

Kumari Mayawati

Uttar Pradesh

● Lucknow

IIT to Rescue Monument

The Indian Institute of Technology, Rourkee, has been entrusted with the job of restoring Lucknow's Satkhanda and Hussainabad Clock Tower built in 1842 by King Muhamad Ali Shah, now in ruins.

eral: Assembly Seats: 70; Parliament: Lok Sabha Seats: 7(6+1+0); Rajya Sabha Seats 3.

Main Political Parties: INC, BJP, NCP, JD-Secular.

Chief Languages: Hindi, Punjabi, Urdu and English.

Major Religions: Hinduism, Islam, Sikhism, Christianity, Jainism

Main Towns: New Delhi, Delhi Cantt, Palam, Mehrauli, Shahdara, Alipur, Badaali, Nazafgarh, Narela.

Geography: Rivers: Yamuna

Economy: (a) Industries: electronics, light engineering machines, automobile parts, sport goods, bicycles, PVC goods, footwears, textiles, fertiliser, medicines, hosiery, leather goods, software, etc.; (b) Agricultural Products: wheat, bajra, jowar, gram, maize. Now fruit crops, vegetables, floriculture, dairy and poultry farming are more common.

Transport & Communications: (a) Road Length: Inter-State terminuses: Kasmere Gate, Sarai Kalen Khan and Anand Vihar; (b) Railways Delhi Metro Service is very important connecting important places within the city; (c) Main Railway Stations: Delhi Jn., New Delhi, Hazrat Nizamuddin; (d) Airports: Indira Gandhi International Airport, Domestic flight -Palam and for training Safdarjung.

National Museum: Nehru Memorial Museum, Craft Museum, National Museum of Natural History, National Museum of Modern Art, Central Cottage Industries Emporium (Janpath), States Emporia (Baba Kharak Singh Marg), Dili Haat - handicrafts.

Culture: (a) Festivals: Roshnara festival, Shalimar festival, Qutab festival, Winter Carnival, Garden Tourism & Mango festival. Besides International Industrial Exhibitions, Automobile Exhibitions, Defense Exhibitions, etc.

30. Andaman & Nicobar Is.

Lt. Governor: Lt.Gen.(Retd.)Bhopinder Singh
Date of Formation: 1 Nov , 1956- UT.

Area: 8,249 sq km
Capital: Port Blair
Neighbouring States: Sea
Population: 379,944 **Males:** 202,330, **Females:** 177,614, **Sex-ratio:** 878 **Density:** 46 **Decadal growth:** 6.68%. **Literacy:** 293,695 164,219 129,476 (t86.27%, m90.11%, f81.84%).

Until the colonisation of India, Andaman Islands were inhabited by 4 Negrito tribes viz., the Great Andamanese, Onge, Jarawa & Sentinalese and 2 Mongoloid tribes viz., Nicobarese and Shompens.

No. of Districts: 3

District	Area (sq km)	Population (2011)	Head-quarters
South Andaman	3,181	237586	Port blair
Nicobar	1,841	42,026	Car Nicobar
N & Mid.Andaman	3,227	105539	Mayanunder

Villages: 501; **Towns:** 3
Legislative Bodies: State Legislature: None;

Port Blair

Andaman & Nicobar Is.

Bhopinder Singh

Parliament: Lok Sabha Seats:1; No. of Rajya Sabha Seats None

Seat of High Court: Calcutta H.C., circuit bench at Port Blair.

Chief Languages: Local dialects, Nicobarese, Bengali, Hindi, Nicobarese, Telugu, Tamil & Malayalam

Main Towns: Shyamnagar, Nabagram, Mayabunder, Uttara, Checkpoint, Herbertahad, Bamboo Flat, Wrightmyo, Port Meadows, Wandoor.

Geography: Mountains: The islands form the peaks of several submerged mountain range that extends for almost 1000km between Myanmar and Sumatra. Saddle Peak (732 m), is the highest peak.

Economy: A total of 48,594 hectares of land is used for agriculture purposes. The principal crops are rice, coconuts and arecanut. Other crops are sugarcane, pulses, fruit and vegetables. Spices and rubber are being tried. Fisheries, tourism and ship repairing are the areas that can create jobs. There are 3 newspapers and 22 periodicals. Schools number 316 in all. The islands have a fleet of 57 ships. The installed capacity of power generation is 30,000 kw, with all revenue villages electrified; (a) Industries: There are 1421 registered small scale village units viz., fish processing factory, soft drinks, beverages, PVC conduit pipes, paints, furniture, etc., and handicraft units; (b) Agricultural Products: Rice, pulses, coconut, arecanut, coffee, sugarcane.

Transport & Communications: (a) The islands are accessible by air and sea. It is well connected to Kolkata, Chennai by air and by sea to Kolkata, Chennai and Vishakapatnam. The UT's transport system serves 9 major islands from Diglipur to Campbell Bay. Andaman Trunk Road services connects Rangat, Mayabunder and Diglipur using 3 ferry boats. There are 5 wharfs and 41 jetties linking all inhabited islands; (b) There is a network of 866 km of black-tarred roads; (c) Airports: Port Blair

Sanctuaries: Mahatma Gandhi Marine National Park, Barren Is., Narcondum Is., North Reef Is., and South Sentinel.

Islands: Havelock, Neil, Jolly Buoy, Cinque, Red Skin, Chidiya Tapu (Bird Island), Viper Island.

Beaches: Corbyn Cove, Radha Nagar, Cutbert Bay, Karmatang, Ross& Smith, Wandoor Beach.

31. Chandigarh

Administrator: Shivraj Patil
Date of Formation: UT since 1966
Area: 114 sq km
Capital: Chandigarh
Neighbouring States: Punjab, Haryana
Population: 1,054,686 **Males:** 580,282 Females: 474,404 **Sex-ratio:** 818 **Density:** 9,252 **Decadal growth:** 17.10%. **Literacy:** 809,653 468,166 341,487 (t86.43%, m90.54%, f81.38%).

No. of Districts: 1
Villages: 23; **Towns:** 1
Legislative Bodies: Parliament: Lok Sabha Seats:1; Rajya Sabha Seats: None
Seat of High Court: Punjab & Haryana (at Chandigarh)

Chandigarh

⬤ Chandigarh

Shivraj Patil

Chief Languages: Hindi, Punjabi and English

Major Religions: Sikhism, Hinduism

Main Towns: Chandigarh

Economy: (a) Industries: Hosiery, antibiotics, cycles, electrical meters, home appliances, electronic equipments. There are 15 large and medium scale industrial units in Chandigarh, out of which two are public sector undertakings. More than 3,000 units are registered under small scale sector and they offer employment to about 30,000 persons. The neighbouring States have developed industrial estates right next to the city; (b) Agricultural Products: The Territory has 1,400 hectares of cultivable land. The irrigated area is about 1,450 ha. Wheat, maize and paddy are the major crops. The forest covers 27 per cent of the area.

Transport & Communications: (a) Road Length: NH-15.275 km.; (b) Main Railway Stations: Chandigarh; (c) Airports: Chandigarh.

Tourist Destinations: Zakir Rose Garden, Rock Garden, Shanti Kunj, Lake, Museum, Art Gallery, Capital complex and National Gallery of Portraits.

Culture: Festivals: Lodhi, Baisakhi

Narendra Kumar

32. Dadra & Nagar Haveli

Administrator: Narendra Kumar

Date of Formation: 11 Aug 1961

Area: 491 sq km

Capital: Silvassa.

Neighbouring States: Gujarat, Maharashtra.

Population: 342,853 **Males:** 193,178 **Females:** 149,675 **Sex-ratio:** 775 **Density:** 698 **Decadal growth:** 55.50%. **Literacy:** 228,028 144,916 83,112 (t77.65%, m86.46%, f65.93%).

No. of Districts: 1

Villages: 70; **Towns:** 2

Legislative Bodies: State Legislature: None; Parliament: Lok Sabha Seats: 1(0+0+1); Rajya Sabha Seats: None

Seat of High Court: Mumbai

Chief Languages: Bhili, Gujarati, Bhilodi, Marathi and Hindi

Main Towns: Silvassa

Geography: Rivers: Silvasa, Khanvel

Economy: (a) Industries: Textiles, engineering, chemicals, electronics, cottage; (b) Agricultural Products: Ragi, wheat, sugarcane, paddy, pulses, mango, chiku, lichi

Transport & Communications: (a) Road Length: 635 km; (b) Main Railway Stations: Vapi is 18 km from Silvassa; (c) Airports: Nearest one is Mumbai.

Tourist Destinations: Bindrabin, Deer Park, Khanvel, Vanganga Lake and Island garden, Dadra, Vanvihar Udyan, Tribal Cultural museum.

Culture: Festivals: Diwaso, Bhawada, Kali Puja.

33. Daman & Diu

Administrator: Narendra Kumar

Date of Formation: 30 May 1987

Area: 112 sq km

Capital: Daman

Neighbouring States: Gujarat.

Population: 242,911 Males: 150,100 Females: 92,811 Sex-ratio: 618 Density: 2,169 Decadal growth: 53.54%. Literacy: 188,974 (t87.07%, m91.48%, f79.59%).

Civil Honours	Personal civil honours like Bharat Ratna, Padma Vibhushan, Padma Bhushan and Padma Shree were withdrawn in July 1977. They were reintroduced in January, 1980.

No. of Districts: 2

District	Area (sq km)	Population (2011)	Head-quarters
Daman	72	190855	Daman
Diu	40	52056	Diu

Diu

Daman

Narendra Kumar

Villages: 23; Towns: 2
Legislative Bodies: State Legislature: None
Parliament: Lok Sabha Seats: 1; Rajya Sabha Seats: None
Seat of High Court: Mumbai
Chief Languages: Gujarati, Hindi
Major Religions: Hinduism, Christianity
Main Towns: Daman, Diu
Geography: Rivers: Kalem, Bhagwan (Daman)
Economy: (a) Minerals: Salt; (b) Industries: Fishing, tourism, and distillery.
Transport & Communications: (a) Road Length: 191 - Daman, 78 - Diu; (b) Nearest Railway Stations Vapi for Daman and Delvada for Diu; (c) Airports: Daman, Diu.

34. Lakshadweep

Administrator: Amar Nath
Date of Formation: 1 Nov 1956 Laccadive, Minicoy, and Amindivi Islands union territory (separated from Madras [see Tamil Nadu]) 1 Nov 1973. Renamed Lakshadweep

Area: 32 sq km.
Capital: Kavaratti.
Neighbouring States: Kerala, Karnataka. Sea:Arabian Sea.
Population: 64,429 **Males:** 33,106 **Females:** 31,323 **Sex-ratio:** 946 **Density:** 2,013 **Decadal growth:** 6.23%. **Literacy:** 52,914 (t92.28%, m96.11%, f88.25%).
No. of Districts:1. The entire group of islands is considered one district and divided into four tahsils.
Villages: 28; **Towns:** 3
Legislative Bodies: State Legislature: None; Parliament: Lok Sabha Seats: 1; Rajya Sabha Seats: None
Seat of High Court: Kerala (located in Kochi)
Chief Languages: Jeseri (Dweep Bhash(a), Mahal and Malayalam.
Major Religions: Islam.
Major Islands: Kavaratti, Agati, Minicoy, Andrott, Kalpeni, Amini, Kadamatt, Kiltan.
Geography: Its 36 islands covering an area of 32 sq. km only 10 are inhabited. Androth, 4.8 sq. kms, is the largest inhabited island and closest to the Kerala coast. Lakshadweep with its lagoon area of about 4,200 sq. km, 20,000 sq. km of territorial waters and about seven lakh sq. km of economic zone, is one of the largest territories of our nation.
Economy: (a) Minerals: silica, corals; (b) Industries: Fishing, boat building - fishing and travel, coir; (c) Agricultural Products: Coconut, Copra, banana.

Lakshadweep

Kavaratti

Amar Nath

Transport & Communications: These islands and Kochi are linked by ship, which takes about 18 to 20 hours, and by air; (a) Airports: Agatti; (b) Port: Kavaratti, Minicoy, Agatti, Kadamatt, Kalpeni.

35. Puducherry

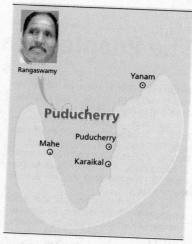

Rangaswamy

Lt. Governor: Thiru Iqbal Singh.
CM: Rangaswamy - (AI NRC)
Date of Formation: 7 Jan 1963 Pondicherry union territory
Area: 479 sq. km
Capital: Puducherry
Neighbouring States: Bay of Bengal, Tamil Nadu.
Population: 1,244,464 **Males:** 610,485 **Females:** 633,979 **Sex-ratio:** 1,038 **Density:** 2,598 **Decadal growth:** 27.72%. **Literacy:** 966,600 502,575 464,025 (t86.55%, m92.12%, f81.22%).
No. of Districts: 4

District	Area (sq km)	Population (2011)	Head-quarters
1. Karaikal	161	200314	Karaikal
2. Mahe	9	41934	Mahe
3. Puducherry	290	946600	Pondicherry
4. Yanam	20	55616	Yanam

Villages: 92; **Towns:** 6
Legislative Bodies: State Legislature: Unicameral -Seats: 30; Parliament: Lok Sabha Seats:1; Rajya Sabha Seats:1
Seat of High Court: Madras High Court.
Chief Languages: Tamil, Telugu, Malayalam, English and French.
Major Religions: Hinduism, Islam, Christianity.
Main Towns: Pondicherry, Karaikal, Yanam, Mahe.
Geography: Rivers: Gingee, Mahe
Economy: (a) Industries: Textiles, computer hardware, electronics, plastic, bicycle parts, alcoholic beverages, electrical appliances, automobile parts, soap, rice bran oil, cotton yarn, sugar, glazed tiles, etc.; (b) Agricultural

Products: Rice, pulses, coconut, arecanut, condiments etc. Groundnut, chillies are grown in Yanam.
Transport & Communications: (a) Road Length: 2,443 km.; (b) Main Railway Stations: Villupuram Jn. (nearest railway link.); (c) Air-ports: (nearest-Chennai); (d) Port:Pondicherry.
Tourist Destinations: Pondicherry possesses a rich French cultural and architectural heritage. The erstwhile French Town ensconced in 4 boulevards, a well-planned town, neatly laid roads and vibrant beaches, French War Memorial, botanical garden, Aurobindo Ashram, Bharati and Bharatidasan Memorial Museum, Govt. Museum, Govt. Square, French Institute, Statue of Joan of Arc, Auroville, lighthouse, Romain Rolland Library, Varadaraja-perumal temple, Sri Vedapureeswarar temple.
Culture: (a) Dances: Podikazhi attam; (b) Festivals: Mascarade (mask festival, Mar-Apr), Masimagam (Feb-Mar), eve of French Bastlle Day- is marked by flags and parade; (c) Crafts: Hand-printed textiles, Kalakari batik, marbling work, handmade paper, bronze work.

Ban of Entry to Old Ships Gujarat government has desided to ban entry of ships above 25 years of age at its ports. A 27 - year - old ship m.v. Rak Carrier sank off the Mumbai coast early August.

The People of India

Indian population is said to be the melting pot of various races. Few, if any, can claim to belong to any particular stock.

Races (as per classical pattern): According to Dr. B. S. Guha, the population of India is derived from 6 main ethnic groups: 1. Negrito; 2. Proto-Australoids or Austrics ; 3. Mongoloids; 4. Mediterranean or Dravidian; 5. Western Brachycephals and; 6. Nordic Aryans.

The major tribes who inhabit India are Abors-Arunachal Pradesh, Assam; Adi, Apatami-Arunachal Pradesh; Angami, Ao-Nagaland; Badagas-Tamil Nadu; Baiga-MP, Rajasthan, Gujarat; Bhils-MP, Gujarat, Rajasthan; Bhotias-UP (Garhwal and Kumaon); Bhutias-Sikkim; Birhor-Bihar; Bodos-Assam; Chenchus-AP, Orissa; Chutia-Assam; Dangs-Gujarat; Gaddis-HP; Garos-Meghalaya; Gonds-MP, Bihar, Orissa, AP; Great Andamanese-Andaman Is.; Irulas-Tamil Nadu; Jaintias-Meghalaya; Jarawas-Little Andamans; Kanis-Kerala; Kacharis, Karbi-Assam; Khampti-Arunachal Pradesh; Khasis-Meghalaya, Assam; Khonds-Orissa; Kol-MP; Kotas-Tamil Nadu; Kuki-Manipur; Lepchas or Rongpa-Sikkim; Lushais-Tripura; Meiteis-Manipur, Nagaland; Mina-Rajasthan; Miri-Arunachal Pradesh; Mishing-Assam; Murias-MP; Mikirs-Assam; Mundas-Bihar; Oarons-Bihar,Orissa; Onges-Little Andamans; Rabhas-Assam; Rengma-Nagaland; Santhals-W.Bengal, Bihar; Sema-Nagaland;

Sentinelesse-Andaman & Nicobar Is.; Shompens-Great Nicobar Is.; Tagin-Arunachal Pradesh; Todas-Tamil Nadu; Uralis-Kerala; Zeliang-Nagaland.

Scheduled Castes & Tribes: There are 13.82 crores people belonging to the Scheduled Castes in the country. This constitutes 16.48% of the country's total population. The States of UP, West Bengal, Bihar, Tamil Nadu and Andhra Pradesh account for more than 50% of the SC population, with UP and West Bengal having more than 20% of its population from the SCs. Members of the SC earn their livelihood through their own labour, either on land belonging to others or in occupations like scavenging, flaying and tanning of leather. More than 3 quarters of the SC workers are engaged in primary occu-

Religions of India

Religious group	1971		1981		1991		2001	
	Total (m.)	Per cent	Total (m.)	Per cent	Total (m.)	Per cent	Total (m.)	Per cent
Hindus	453.4	82.7	549.7	82.6	672.6	82.41	827.5	80.44
Muslims	61.4	11.2	75.6	11.4	95.2	11.67	138.2	13.42
Christians	14.3	2.6	16.2	2.4	18.9	2.32	24.1	2.33
Sikhs	10.4	1.9	13.1	2.0	16.3	1.99	19.2	1.84
Buddhists	3.9	0.7	4.7	0.7	6.3	0.77	7.9	0.68
Jains	2.6	0.5	3.2	0.5	3.4	0.41	4.2	0.38
Others	2.2	0.4	2.8	0.4	3.5	0.43	7.3	0.65
Total	548.2	100.0	665.3	100.0	816.2	100.0	1028.4	100.0

pations and the proportion of those engaged in the tertiary sector is nearly half the national average. In the field of literacy, as against the national average of 52%, the literacy rate of SCs is around 37%. Among the SC women, more than three quarters are illiterate. Moreover, the drop out rate in formal education is very high. Such factors put the community at a disadvantage.

The population of Scheduled Tribes was 6.78 crore ('91 Census) constituting 8.08% of the countr's total population. Their literacy is just 29.60%. Literacy among the women is 18.19% compared to the national average of 39.29%.

Indian Languages

India is believed to have 1652 mother tongues of which 33 are spoken by people numbering over a lakh. The officially recognised languages are 22. In fact, English is widely spoken and perhaps the link between North and South India.

Scheduled Languages: A schedule––the 8th Schedule –was added to the Constitution to indicate all regional languages statutorily recognised. The Schedule originally contained 14 languages as follows: (1) Assamese; (2) Bengali; (3) Gujarati; (4) Hindi; (5) Kannada; (6) Kashmiri; (7) Malayalam; (8) Marathi; (9) Oriya; (10) Punjabi; (11) Sanskrit; (12) Tamil; (13) Telugu; (14) Urdu.

Sindhi was added in 1962. By the 71st Amendment to the Constitution, Konkani, Manipuri and Nepali were added to the list in 1992. In 2003, four more languages, were added: Bodo, Dogri, Maithili and Santhali. (92nd Amendment)

Speakers of Indian Languages

Scheduled and Non-Scheduled languages in India are given below in descending order of speakers' strength. Figures are based on 2001 Census.

Language	Speakers
Hindi *	422,048,642
Bengali*	83,369,769
Telugu*	74,002,856
Marathi*	71,936,894
Tamil*	60,793,814
Urdu*	51,536,111
Gujarati*	46,091,617
Kannada*	37,924,011
Malayalam*	33,066,392
Oriya*	33,017,446
Punjabi*	29,102,477
Assamese*	13,168,484
Maithili*	12,179,122
Bhili/Bhilodi	9,582,957
Santali*	6,469,600
Kashmiri*	5,527,698
Nepali*	2,871,749
Gondi	2,713,790
Sindhi*	2,535,485
Konkani*	2,489,015
Dogri*	2,282,589
Khandeshi	2,075,258
Kurukh/Oraon	1,751,489
Tulu	1,722,768
Manipuri*	1,466,705
Bodo*	1,350,478
Khasi	1,128,575
Mundari	1,061,352
Ho	1,042,724
Kui	916,222
Garo	889,479

Tripuri	854,023
Lushai/Mizo	674,756
Halabi	593,443
Korku	574,481
Miri/Mishing	551,224
Munda	469,357
Karbi/Mikir	419,534
Koya	362,070
Ao	261,387
Savara	252,519
Konyak	248,109
Kharia	239,608
English	226,449
Malto	224,926
Nissi/Dafla	211,485
Adi	198,462
Thado	190,595
Lotha	170,001
Coorgi/Kodagu	166,187
Rabha	164,770
Tangkhul	142,035
Kisan	141,088
Angami	132,225
Phom	122,508
Kolami	121,855
Khond/Kondh	118,597
Dimasa	111,961
Ladakhi	104,618
Sema	103,529
Kabui	94,758
Lahnda	92,234
Yimchungre	92,144
Tibetan	85,278
Sangtam	84,273
Chakru/Chokri	83,560
Hmar	83,404
Bhotia	81,012
Bishnupuriya	77,545
Kinnauri	65,097
Paite	64,100
Chang	62,408
Zeliang	61,547
Rengma	61,345
Konda	56,262
Monpa	55,876
Kuki	52,873
Arabic/Arbi	51,728
Parji	51,216
Lepcha	50,629
Wancho	49,072
Bhumij	47,443
Koda/Kora	43,030
Khezha	40,768
Tangsa	40,086
Vaiphei	39,673
Jatapu	39,331
Halam	38,275
Khiemnungan	37,755
Maram	37,340
Limbu	37,265
Lakher	34,751
Korwa	34,586
Shina	34,390
Liangmei	34,232
Zemi	34,110
Mishmi	33,955
Nocte	32,957
Koch	31,119
Mogh	30,639
Nicobarese	28,784
Deori	27,960
Lalung	27,072
Gadaba	26,262
Pawi	24,965
Juang	23,708
Anal	23,191
Lahauli	22,646
Maring	22,326
Zou	20,857
Balti	20,053
Sherpa	18,342
Tamang	17,494
Pochury	16,744
Kom	14,673
Gangte	14,500
Rai	14,378
Sanskrit*	14,131
Persian	11,688
Chakhesang	11,417
Afghani/Kabuli/Pashto	11,083
Simte	10,225

* Scheduled language. Twenty-two languages come under this category.

Youth Power - World's Demographic Dividend

C. Sarat Chandran

The youth, with a fresh perspective and new insights, have made their presence felt today. It is a power to be reckoned with.

"The Youth can see a door where others might see a wall" -
Mark Zukerberg,
Founder of Face book.

If the second half of the 20th century saw a global movement to bring women into the centre stage of society, the first decades of 21st century are witnessing a dramatic surge in the power of young generation. Political leadership as much as corporate leadership is increasingly falling into younger and younger hands. While the empowerment of women was essentially a move to restore social justice to half of humanity, the youth movement today is more assertive in establishing its identity in a changing world.

A New Set of Values

However, the change goes beyond mere demographics. The youth brings to the world a new set of values. The young people think differently on almost every aspect of life and living. Power and politics, market and economy, family relationships, religious values, sex, gender, race and colour, in all these, the youth brings a fresh perspective and some new insights. It can be said that today's youth is the product of globalization while the earlier generation was the children of nationalism.

Youth has been in the forefront of many of the historic moments in the 21st century. From the collapse of the Berlin Wall to the revolution in Tiananmen Square in China, to the more recent anti Iraq wars, the youth has been revolting for change,

some successfully, others less so. The youth again is in the spotlight today with the recent Arab uprising that is sweeping across the whole of Middle East. Tahirir Square in Cairo has now become a symbol of youth power. A couple of thousand young Egyptians who gathered at the Square, enlarged into a mass movement of a million people and succeeded in removing the Egyptian dictator Mubarak from power.

| National Youth Day | Hindu spiritual leader and reformer Swami Vivekananda was born Narendranath Datta on Jan. 12, 1863. His birthday is celebrated as National Youth Day in India. |

Although youth movements in different regions take shape in varying circumstances and conditions, there are a number of sharply defined features that unite them into a single global phenomenon. We can identify some of these elements:

The Overpowering Influence of Technology

Today's technology is not only user friendly but even more youth friendly. The lap top has irreversibly replaced the brief case as a symbol of the young professional today. From websites to video conferences, technology is the face of business today.

Mobile phones, Internet and electronic media have together unleashed an information revolution in the world today. With over 800 million mobile phone owners, India has one of the largest concentration of cell phones among third world countries. Internet cafes are sprouting even in tier-II and tier-III cities. Television channels are becoming a powerful source for news and entertainment. The youth is leading this digital revolution.

Technology has also changed the way we do retailing, banking, educate our children, manage our health and the way we communicate with one another. Many would have noticed, telegrams have now almost disappeared as a means of communication. Emails and text messages through mobile phones have replaced them. ATMs are steadily making cheque books less common. The youth is a major beneficiary of these changes.

The Youth is Emerging as a Single Global Community

In a world divided by race, religion and language, youth is emerging as a global community. Youth across the world is evolving a lifestyle which is more global than regional. In the food they consume, in the dress they wear, in the rock music they listen to, in the sports cars and motor cycles they speed fast, in their passion for electronic gadgets, the youth, particularly the urban youth has strikingly similar tastes and preferences which cross national boundaries.

Technology has been a catalyst for this change. In a symbolic move that captured the imagination of the world, Time maga-

> Youth across the world is evolving a lifestyle which is more global than regional-in the food they consume, in the dress they wear, in the rock music they listen to.

zine nominated Mark Zukerberg, founder of face book, as the person of the year for 2010 and carried him on the cover pages of the global magazine. Facebook has brought together 500 million people and created a vibrant online community. If Facebook was a country, it would have been the third biggest nation in the world, after China and India. Face book and other social groups like Twitter have been emerging as important influences on young minds in exchanging freewheeling ideas and opinions.

| The Tiananmen Square | Chinese army troops stormed Tiananmen Square in Beijing on June 4, 1989 to crush the pro-democracy movement. Some 2600 people were killed and as many as 10,000were injured. |

Less Ideological, more Pragmatic

The New Youth has seen the collapse of communist states in the last decades of the 20th century and the crisis that capitalism faces in the first decades of the 21st century. There is thus a growing disenchantment among the younger generation with a polarized world driven by two opposing ideologies. There is a greater realization that there is no pure communism or pure capitalism anywhere in the world. Communist countries like China have moved along capitalist paths for several years now and on the other side, there are considerable government regulations even in free markets like the USA. The new youth, thus yearns for a political culture that goes beyond rigid ideological divisions.

The young are equally disillusioned with religious dogma and its sway on millions of people in the world. Religion has been a tool of exploitation in many societies and in the name of religious values; women in several countries have been denied their legitimate freedom. The young respects all religions equally and see faith in God, essentially as a personal choice to be practiced by an individual unhindered by outside interference.

New Heroes, New Icons

In the early 70s, the well known British newspaper *Guardian* in the course of a survey carried on a number of young people who have gathered at Kolkata's famed Coffee House in College Street, widely seen as a hub of leftist thinking, and asked them who their hero was and whom they idolized most. Not surprisingly their common choice was Che Guevara. Che's revolutionary spirit and the mythology around him dominated the young minds in the seventies. Forty years later, *Guardian* came to Kolkata again to talk to a number of young people in the same College Street and asked them the same question. This time the answer was different. A good number of them said they admired Bill Gates, most as a symbol of change and 21st century values.

That reply signalled a generational change. Business, money, wealth and good

living all have become respectable. The guilt complex associated with money making is disappearing from our conscience. Businessmen are the new icons of our time. Their pictures adorn the pages of popular magazines as in the case of film stars and cricket heroes.

One reason for this change of attitude is the way business has transformed itself. Money is today not just seen as a product of greed, but as a fuel for growth. Wealth created through business seems to benefit not some, but the whole of community. The inspiring stories of Bill Gates and Warren Buffett, donating a part of their wealth to the community, have helped to change the perception of the common man on busi-

The Gates Saga	Microsoft Corporation's stock began trading publicly in 1986 at $25.75. In less than a year Bill Gates became a billionaire - the journey to world's richest man had begun.

ness and businessmen. Mr. Azim Premji, the philanthropist Chairman of Wipro has announced that he will donate a part of his wealth to charity. Millionaires and billionaires are increasingly sharing their wealth with society, Corporate Social Responsibility (CSR) has become the buzz word today.

Unleashing the Entrepreneurial Talent

Phenomenal growth of the information technology industry has unleashed the entrepreneurial talent of the young population across the world. A generation of techno-entrepreneurs has emerged in the past quarter century and they are changing the landscape of business and its val-

> A generation of techno-entrepreneurs has emerged in the past quarter century and they are changing the landscape of business and its values.

ues. In Silicon valley, 60% of new entrepreneurs are less than 35 years in age. The seven founders of Infosys were in their 20s when they launched their path breaking company. Bill Gates was only 20 when he founded Microsoft in 1975.

The traditional view of business as a factory building with huge machines churning out physical products has undergone a change. Knowledge and information have become the most important raw material for business. Using that resource, business decisions are increasingly taken on computers and smart phones. Virtual office, e-commerce and online marketing all have changed the idea business in our time. Technology, knowledge and youth power, form the new triangle of global business.

Flip Side of the Youth Revolution

While the world has seen an explosion of

power, we must recognize the fact that the revolution itself has many limitations, road blocks and challenges.

Firstly, the impact of the current youth movement is largely confined to techno-savy, well educated urban youth. The revolution has side-stepped millions of young people who are denied a decent education or have dropped out of school before they reach the age of 10. A large number of girls never reach the school at all. There is thus a huge "wasted resource" which does not participate in the momentum that the youth power brings to the world. Secondly, many of the urban youth continue to be victims of drug addiction. Drug habits are spreading across campuses worldwide even in Third World countries. There is growing recognition that the world has lost many young talents due to drug addiction.

In spite of these challenges, the world has gained significantly from the current surge in youth power. India with over 500 million people below 30 years of age is the major gainer of this demographic dividend. India has today become not only the largest market in the world, but also one of the "youngest". Indian market is significantly tilted in favour of the young consumer and his lifestyle. ■

| College Dropouts | From the five richest Americans, four are college dropouts. Bill Gates, Sheldon Adelson (casino owner), Paul Allen and Larry Ellison of Oracle are in the list. Warren Buffett is not. |

The Constitution

The Constitution of India was drawn up by a Constituent Assembly (established in accordance with the Cabinet Mission Plan) initially summoned on Dec. 9, 1946, under the presidentship of Sachidananda Sinha, for undivided India. On July 1, 1947, the British parliament passed the 'Indian Independence Act', to divide the country into India and Pakistan. With the partition of India the representatives of East Bengal, West Punjab, Sind and Baluchistan, N-W Frontier Province and the Sylhet Dist. of Assam, which joined Pakistan, ceased to be members of the Constituent Assembly. On August 14, 1947, the Constituent Assembly met again as the Sovereign Constituent Assembly for the Dominion of India under the presidentship of Sachidananda Sinha. On the demise of Sinha, Dr. Rajendra Prasad became the President of the Assembly. A draft Constitution was published in February 1948. 284 out of 299 members appended their signature to the Constitution and finally adopted it on 26th Nov 1949. It came into effect on 26th Jan 1950.

Draft Constitution Drafting Committee

The work started with the presentation of the 'Objective Resolution' (the underlying ideology/philosophy) moved by Pandit Jawaharlal Nehru was adopted on Jan. 22, 1947. The committee for scrutinising the draft constitution and suggesting amendments was formed on August 29, 1947. The draft was readied by Feb. 1948. The Constituent Assembly met thrice to read the draft clause-by-clause in Nov. 1948, Oct. 1949 and Nov. 1949. After the third reading, it was signed by the President and adopted on Nov. 26, 1949. In fact, a Committee on Rules of Procedure was in place as early as Dec. 1946. Chairman: Dr. B.R. Ambedkar.

Members: Alladi Krishnaswami Ayyar, N.

Preamble of Indian Constitution

Gopalaswami Ayyangar, Dr. K.M. Munshi, Syed Md. Saadulla, B.L. Mitter (was replaced by N. Madhava Rao) and D.P. Khaitan (was replaced by T.T. Krishnamachari).

The Indian Constitution closely follows the British Parliamentary model but differs from it in one important respect that is, the Constitution is supreme, not Parliament. So the Indian courts are vested with the authority to adjudicate on the constitutionality of any law passed by Parliament.

The Constitution consists of the following: 1. The Preamble; 2. Parts I to XXII covering Articles 1 to 395; 3. Schedules 1 to 12 and 4. An Appendix. Part IX-The panchayats and Schedule XI (Article 243-G) have been incorporated under 73rd Constitution Amendment Act, 19920.

Constituent Assembly Begins	Constituent Assembly began its session on Dec. 9, 1946 in the Constitution Hall. Dr. Rajendra Prasad was elected Chairman on Dec. 11.

The Union : Executive

The Union executive consists of the President, the Vice-President and the Council of Ministers with the Prime Minister as the head to aid and advise the President.

President

The President is elected by members of an electoral college consisting of elected members of both Houses of Parliament and Legislative Assemblies of the states in accordance with the system of proportional representation by means of single transferable vote. To secure uniformity among state inter se as well as parity between the states, as a whole, and the Union, suitable weightage is given to each vote. The President must be a citizen of India, not less than 35 years of age and qualified for election as member of the Lok Sabha. His term of office is five years and he is eligible for re-election. His removal from office is to be in accordance with procedure prescribed in Article 61 of the Constitution. He may, by writing under his hand addressed to the Vice-President, resign his office.

Dr. Rajendra Prasad

Executive power of the Union is vested in the President and is exercised by him either directly or through officers subordinate to him in accordance with the Constitution. Supreme command of defence forces of the Union also vests in him. The President summons, prorogues, addresses, sends messages to Parliament and dissolves the Lok Sabha; promulgates Ordinances at any time, except when both Houses of Parliament are in session; makes recommendations for introducing financial and money bills and gives assent to bills; grants pardons, reprieves, respites or remission of punishment or suspends, remits or commutes sentences in certain cases. When there is a failure of

Pratibha Patil

the constitutional machinery in a state, he can assume to himself all or any of the functions of the government of that state. The President can proclaim emergency in the country if he is satisfied that a grave emergency exists whereby security of India or any part of its territory is threatened whether by war or external aggression or armed rebellion.

Vice-President

The Vice-President is elected by members of an electoral college consisting of members of both Houses of Parliament in accordance with the system of proportional representation by means of single transferable vote. He must be a citizen of India, not less than 35 years of age and eligible for election as a member of the Rajya Sabha. His term of office is five years and he is eligible for re-election. His removal from office is to be in accordance with procedure prescribed in Article 67 b.

Dr. S.Radhakrishnan- the first V-P

The Vice-President is ex-officio Chairman of the Rajya Sabha and acts as President when the latter is unable to discharge his functions due to absence, illness or any other cause or till the election of a new President (to be held within six months when a vacancy

Hameed Anzari

The Youngest Speaker

The 11th Lok Sabha will be remembered for electing to the office of the Speaker for the first time a member of the opposition, P.A. Sangma. He was also the first tribal, the first Christian and the youngest ever Speaker.

is caused by death, resignation or removal or otherwise of President). While so acting, he ceases to perform the function of the Chairman of the Rajya Sabha.

Prime Minister and Council of Ministers

There is a Council of Ministers, headed by the Prime Minister, to aid and advise the President in exercise of his functions. The Prime Minister is appointed by the President who also appoints other ministers on the advice of Prime Minister. The Council is collectively responsible to the Lok Sabha. It is the duty of the Prime Minister to communicate to the President all decisions of Council of Ministers relating to administration of affairs of the Union and proposals for legislation and information relating to them.

Jawaharlal Nehru

The Council of Ministers comprises Ministers who are members of Cabinet, Ministers of State (independent charge), Ministers of State and Deputy Ministers.

Dr.Manmohan Singh

Legislature

Legislature of the Union which is called Parliament, consists of President and two Houses, known as Council of States (Rajya Sabha) and House of the People (Lok Sabha). Each House has to meet within six months of its previous sitting. A joint sitting of two Houses can be held in certain cases.

Rajya Sabha

The Constitution provides that the Rajya Sabha shall consist of 12 members to be

Rajya Sabha

nominated by the President from among persons having special knowledge or practical experience in respect of such matters as literature, science, art and social service; and not more than 238 representatives of the States and of the Union Territories.

Elections to the Rajya Sabha are indirect; members representing States are elected by elected members of legislative assemblies of the States in accordance with the system of proportional representation by means of the single transferable vote, and those representing union territories are chosen in such manner as Parliament may by law prescribe. The Rajya Sabha is not subject to dissolution; one-third of its members retire every second year.

Rajya Sabha, at present, has 244 seats. Of these, 233 members represent the states and the union territories and 11 members have been nominated by the President and one seat under nomination category is vacant. The names of members of Rajya Sabha and party affiliation are given in Appendices.

Lok Sabha

The Lok Sabha is composed of representatives of people chosen by direct election on the basis of adult suffrage. The maximum strength of the House envisaged by the Constitution is now 552 (530 members to represent the States, 20 members to represent the Union Territories and not more than two members of the Anglo-Indian community to be nominated by the President, if, in his opinion, that community is not adequately represented in the House). The total elective membership

National Anthem and Song	'Jana Gana Mana...' was adopted as the National Anthem of India on January 24, 1950. 'Vande Mataram....' was adopted as the National Song with the same status.

Lok Sabha

Enactment of Laws

The Indian Parliament makes laws on matters enumerated in the Union List. State Legislatures make laws on matters enumerated in the State List. While both the Union and the States have power to legislate on matters enumerated in the Concurrent List, only Parliament has power to make laws on matters not included in the State List or the Concurrent List. In the event of repugnancy, laws made by Parliament shall prevail over laws made by State Legislatures, to the extent of the repugnancy. The State law shall be void unless it has received the assent of the President, and in such case, shall prevail in that State.

of the Lok Sabha is distributed among the states in such a way that the ratio between the number of seats allotted to each State and the population of the state is, as far as practicable, the same for all states. The Lok Sabha at present consists of 545 members. Of these, 530 members are directly elected from the states and 13 from union territories while two are nominated by the President to represent the Anglo-Indian community. This includes one vacant seat of Banka Constitutency of Bihar and the seat of MP Smt. Meira Kumar who has become Speaker of Lok Sabha and two nominated members of Anglo-Indian community. It means after excluding the vacant seat and the seat of the Speaker, there are at present 543 seats of the House. Following the Constitution's 84th Amendment Act, 2001 the total number of existing seats as allocated to various states in the Lok Sabha on the basis of the 1971 census shall remain unaltered till the first census to be taken after the year 2026.

Law, Courts and the Constitution

India's law and jurisprudence stretches back to centuries. India's commitment to law is created in the Constitution which constituted India into a Sovereign Democratic Republic, containing a federal system with Parliamentary form of Government in the Union and the States, an independent judiciary, guaranteed Fundamental Rights and Directive Principles of State Policy containing objectives which though not enforceable by law are fundamental to the governance of the nation.

Judiciary

One of the unique features of the Indian Constitution is that, notwithstanding the adoption of a federal system and existence of Central Acts and State Acts in their respective spheres, it has generally provided for a single integrated system of Courts to administer both Union and State laws. At the apex of the entire judicial system, exists the Supreme Court of India below which are the High Courts in each State or group of States. Below the High Courts lies a hierarchy of Subordinate Courts. Panchayat Courts also function in some States under various names like Nyaya Panchayat, Panchayat Adalat, Gram Kachheri, etc. to decide civil and criminal disputes of petty and local nature. Different State laws provide for different kinds of jurisdiction of courts. Each State is divided into judicial districts presided over by a District and Sessions Judge, which is the principal civil court of original jurisdiction and can try all offences including those punishable with death. The Sessions Judge is the highest judicial authority in a district. Below him, there are Courts of civil jurisdiction, headed by judicial officials known in different States as Munsifs, Sub-Judges, Civil Judges and the like. Similarly, the criminal judiciary comprises the Chief Judicial Magistrates and Judicial Magistrates of First and Second Class.

First Coins

Following the Independence of India, the currency system continued with the British series of coins till the establishment of the Indian Republic. The first coins of independent India were introduced on Aug. 15, 1950.

Constitution of Supreme Court

On the 28th of January, 1950, two days after India became a Sovereign Democratic Republic, the Supreme Court came into being.

The Supreme Court of India comprises the Chief Justice and not more than 25 other Judges appointed by the President of India. Supreme Court Judges retire upon attaining the age of 65 years. In order to be appointed as a Judge of the Supreme Court, a person must be a citizen of India and must have been, for at least five years, a Judge of a High Court or of two or more such Courts in succession, or an Advocate of a High Court or of two or more such Courts in succession for at least 10 years, or he must be, in the opinion of the President, a distinguished jurist. Provisions exist for the appointment of a Judge of a High Court as an Ad-hoc Judge of the Supreme Court and for retired Judges of the Supreme Court or High Courts to sit and act as Judges of that Court.

The Constitution seeks to ensure the independence of Supreme Court Judges in various ways. A Judge of the Supreme Court cannot be removed from office except by an order of the President passed after an address in each House of Parliament supported by a majority of the total membership of that House and by a majority of not less than two-thirds of members present and voting, and presented to the President in the same Session for such removal on the ground of proved misbehaviour or incapacity. A person who has been a Judge of the Supreme Court is debarred from practising in any court of law or before any other authority in India.

The proceedings of the Supreme Court are conducted in English only. Supreme Court Rules, 1966 are framed under Article 145 of the Constitution to regulate the practice and procedure of the Supreme Court.

Supreme Court Registry

The Registry of the Supreme Court is headed by the Registrar General who is assisted in his work by three Registrars, four Additional Registrars, twelve Joint Registrars, etc. Article 146 of the Constitution deals with the ap-

Supreme Court

pointments of officers and servants of the Supreme Court Registry.

Attorney General

The Attorney General for India is appointed by the President of India under Article 76 of the Constitution and holds office during the pleasure of the President. He must be a person qualified to be appointed as a Judge of the Supreme Court. It is the duty of the Attorney General for India to give advice to the Government of India upon such legal matters and to perform such other duties of legal character as may be referred or assigned to him by the President. In the performance of his duties, he has the right of audience in all Courts in India as well as the right to take part in the proceedings of Parliament without the right to vote. In the discharge of his functions, the Attorney General is assisted by a Solicitor General and four Additional Solicitors General.

Supreme Court Advocates

There are three categories of Advocates who are entitled to practise law before the Supreme Court of India:-

(i) Senior Advocates: They are Advocates who are designated as Senior Advocates by the Supreme Court of India or by any High Court. A Senior Advocate is not entitled to appear without an Advocate-on-Record in the Supreme Court or without a junior in any other court or tribunal in India. He is also not entitled to accept instructions to draw

---

An Elitist House — The First Lok Sabha (1952-57) was constituted on April 17, 1952. Its first sitting was held on May 13. The House was highly elitist. Most members came from urban background. Lawyers constituted the single largest professional group. 37 % of members were graduates.

Gram Nyayalaya

The Gram Nyayalayas Act passed in January 2009 proposes to set up a Magistrate's court at the Mandal level. There shall be 5000 new courts instituted across the country, that the Central Govt.shall spend approximately 1400 crores for this purpose. The same press release added that the setting up of the Gram Nyayalaya is part of drawing a larger road map for judicial reforms.

pleadings or affidavits, advise on evidence or do any drafting work of an analogous kind in any court or tribunal in India or undertake conveyancing work of any kind whatsoever but this prohibition shall not extend to settling any such matter as aforesaid in consultation with a junior.

(ii) Advocates-On-Record: Only these Advocates are entitled to file any matter or document before the Supreme Court. They can also file an appearance or act for a party in the Supreme Court.

(iii) Other Advocates: These are Advocates whose names are entered on the roll of any State Bar Council maintained under the Advocates Act, 1961 and they can appear and argue any matter on behalf of a party in the Supreme Court but they are not entitled to file any document or matter before the Court.

Jurisdiction of the Supreme Court

The Supreme Court has original, appellate and advisory jurisdiction. Its exclusive original jurisdiction extends to any dispute between the Government of India and one or more States or between the Government of India and any State or States on one side and one or more States on the other or between two or more States, if and insofar as the dispute involves any question (whether of law or of fact) on which the existence or extent of a legal right depends. In addition, Article 32 of the Constitution gives an extensive original jurisdiction to the Supreme Court in regard to enforcement of Fundamental Rights. It is empowered to issue directions, orders or writs, including writs in the nature of habeas corpus, mandamus, prohibition, quo warranto and certiorari to enforce them. The Supreme Court has been conferred with power to direct transfer of any civil or criminal case from one State High Court to another State High Court or from a Court subordinate to another State High Court. The Supreme Court, if satisfied that cases involving the same or substantially the same questions of law are pending before it and one or more High Courts or before two or more High Courts and that such questions are substantial questions of general importance, may withdraw a case or cases pending before the High Court or High Courts and dispose of all such cases itself. Under the Arbitration and Conciliation Act, 1996, International Commercial Arbitration can also be initiated in the Supreme Court.

The appellate jurisdiction of the Supreme Court can be invoked by a certificate granted by the High Court concerned under Article 132(1), 133(1) or 134 of the Constitution in respect of any judgement, decree or final order of a High Court in both civil and criminal cases, involving substantial questions of law as to the interpretation of the Constitution.

The Supreme Court has special advisory jurisdiction in matters which may specifically be referred to it by the President of India under Article 143 of the Constitution.

Under Articles 129 and 142 of the Constitution the Supreme Court has been vested with power to punish for contempt of Court including the power to punish for contempt of itself. The Court may take action (a) Suo motu, or (b) on a petition made by Attorney General, or Solicitor General, or (c) on a petition made by any person, and in the case of a criminal contempt with the consent in writing of the Attorney General or the Solicitor General.

Under Order XL of the Supreme Court

British Declaration British Prime Minister Clement Attlee announced in the House of Commons on Feb. 20, 1947 that the British would leave India by a date not later than June, 1948.

Rules the Supreme Court may review its judgment or order but no application for review is to be entertained in a civil proceeding except on the grounds mentioned in Order XLVII, Rule 1 of the Code of Civil Procedure and in a criminal proceeding except on the ground of an error apparent on the face of the record.

Public Interest Litigation

Although the proceedings in the Supreme Court arise out of the judgments or orders made by the Subordinate Courts including the High Courts, but of late the Supreme Court has started entertaining matters in which interest of the public at large is involved and the Court can be moved by any individual or group of persons either by filing a Writ Petition at the Filing Counter of the Court or by addressing a letter to the Hon'ble Chief Justice of India highlighting the question of public importance for invoking this jurisdiction. Such concept is popularly known as 'Public Interest Litigation' and several matters of public importance have become landmark cases. This concept is unique to the Supreme Court of India only and perhaps no other Court in the world has been exercising this extraordinary jurisdiction. A Writ Petition filed at the Filing Counter is dealt with like any other Writ Petition and processed as such. In case of a letter addressed to the Hon'ble Chief Justice of India the same is dealt with in accordance with the guidelines framed for the purpose.

Provision of Legal Aid

If a person belongs to the poor section of the society having an annual income of less than Rs. 18,000/- or belongs to Scheduled Caste or Scheduled Tribe, a victim of natural calamity, is a woman or a child or a mentally ill or otherwise disabled person or an industrial workman, or is in custody including custody in protective home, he/she is entitled to get free legal aid from the Supreme Court Legal Aid Committee. The aid so granted by the Committee includes cost of preparation of the matter and all applications connected

E-Court

E.-courts is one of the mission-mode projects of e-governance under the Nationftl e-Governance Plan. Under the project, comprehensive computerisation and Information and Communication Technologies (ICT) enablement of 12,000 courts in 2,100 court complexes is scheduled to be completed by March 2012 and the balance by March 2014. India's first District level E-Court has been inaugurated on 8th February 2010 at District East, Karkardooma Courts by Chief Justice of High Court of Delhi.

therewith, in addition to providing an Advocate for preparing and arguing the case. Any person desirous of availing legal service through the Committee has to make an application to the Secretary and hand over all necessary documents concerning his case to it. The Committee after ascertaining the eligibility of the person provides necessary legal aid to him/her.

Persons belonging to middle income group i.e. with income above Rs. 18,000/- but under Rs. 1,20,000/- per annum are eligible to get legal aid from the Supreme Court Middle Income Group Society, on nominal payments.

Amicus Curiae

If a petition is received from the jail or in any other criminal matter if the accused is unrepresented then an Advocate is appointed as amicus curiae by the Court to defend and argue the case of the accused. In civil matters also the Court can appoint an Advocate as amicus curiae if it thinks it necessary in case of an unrepresented party; the Court can also appoint amicus curiae in any matter of general public importance or in which the interest of the public at large is involved.

High Courts

The High Court stands at the head of a

The National Emblem	The National Emblem adopted on Jan. 26, 1950, is the replica of the Lion Capital of Ashoka's pillar at Sarnath. The original Lion Capital is 210 cm in height, and is now in Sarnath Museum.

not within those territories.

Each High Court has powers of superintendence over all Courts within its jurisdiction. It can call for returns from such Courts, make and issue general rules and prescribe forms to regulate their practice and proceedings and determine the manner and form in which book entries and accounts shall be kept. The following Table (*Ann.A) gives the seat and territorial jurisdiction of the High Courts.

Advocate General

There is an Advocate General for each State, appointed by the Governor. He must be a person qualified to be appointed as a Judge of High Court. His duty is to give advice to State Governments upon such legal matters and to perform such other duties of legal character, as may be referred or assigned to him by the Governor. The Advocate General has the right to speak and take part in the proceedings of the State Legislature without the right to vote.

State's judicial administration. There are 18 High Courts in the country, three having jurisdiction over more than one State. Among the Union Territories Delhi alone has a High Court of its own. Other six Union Territories come under the jurisdiction of different State High Courts. Each High Court comprises of a Chief Justice and such other Judges as the President may, from time to time, appoint. The Chief Justice of a High Court is appointed by the President in consultation with the Chief Justice of India and the Governor of the State. The procedure for appointing Judges is the same except that the Chief Justice of the High Court concerned is also consulted. They hold office until the age of 62 years and are removable in the same manner as a Judge of the Supreme Court. To be eligible for appointment as a Judge one must be a citizen of India and have held a judicial office in India for ten years or must have practised as an Adovcate of a High Court or two or more such Courts in succession for a similar period.

Each High Court has power to issue to any person within its jurisdiction directions, orders, or writs including writs which are in the nature of habeas corpus, mandamus, prohibition, quo warranto and certiorari for enforcement of Fundamental Rights and for any other purpose. This power may also be exercised by any High Court exercising jurisdiction in relation to territories within which the cause of action, wholly or in part, arises for exercise of such power, notwithstanding that the seat of such Government or authority or residence of such person is

Lok Adalats

Lok Adalats which are voluntary agencies are monitored by the State Legal Aid and Advice Boards. They have proved to be a successful alternative forum for resolving of disputes through the conciliatory method.

The Legal Services Authorities Act, 1987 provides statutory status to the legal aid movement and it also provides for setting up of Legal Services Authorities at the Central, State and District levels. These authorities will have their own funds. Further, Lok Adalats which are at present informal agencies will acquire statutory status. Every award of Lok Adalats shall be deemed to be a decree of a civil court or order of a Tribunal and shall be final and binding on the parties to the dispute. It also provides that in respect of cases decided at a Lok Adalat, the court fee paid by the parties will be refunded.

Amendments to the Indian Constitution

After the enactment of the Constitution of India on 26 November 1949, there have been

95 amendments made. A number of Bills are introduced before Lok Sabha and Rajya Sabha for further improving the Constitution. Parliament has been bestowed with the constituent power, using which changes in the Indian Constitution can be made. However, the basic structure of the Indian Constitution cannot be changed under any circumstances.

Provision for Amendment

Part XX of the Constitution of India deals with the Amendment of the Constitution. The Article 368 specifies the power of Parliament to amend the constitution and the procedure of it. It is also mentioned in the Article that there will be no limitation on the constituent power of the Parliament for amending it by adding, removing or improving the provisions made in it.

Procedure of Amendments

The method of an amendment to the constitution is considered to be a highly complicated procedure. Amendment can be made by various methods, which have been modelled based on the South African Constitution.

Methods of Amendment

I. *Method of Simple majority:* Applies to matters related to citizenship, abolishing or creating second chambers in the states, provisions relating to Scheduled Castes and Scheduled Tribes, etc.

II. *In this, the following conditions should be fulfilled*: Both the houses *must pass the proposal by a majority of the total membership.* By a 2/3 majority of the members present. After this, the amendment *bill must also be ratified by not less than half of state legislatures.* Applies to matters relating to election of President and Vice-President, executive powers of union and states, subjects relating to the division of legislative powers between Centre and States, matters relating to Supreme Court and High Court, representation of States in Parliament, amendment of article 368

Seats of High Courts and Jurisdiction

Allahabad: Uttar Pradesh, (Bench at Lucknow)
Hyderabad: Andhra Pradesh
Bombay: Maharashtra, Goa, Dadra and Nagar Haveli and Daman and Diu, (Benches at Nagpur, Panaji and Aurangabad)
Kolkata: Paschimbanga, (Circuit Bench at Port Blair)
Delhi : Delhi
Guwahati: Asom, Manipur, Meghalaya, Nagaland, Tripura, Mizoram and Arunachal Pradesh (Benches at Kohima, Aizwal & Imphal. Circuit Bench at Agartala & Shillong)
Ahmedabad : Gujarat
Shimla: Himachal Pradesh
Srinagar&Jammu: Jammu & Kashmir
Bangalore: Karnataka
Ernakulam: Kerala & Lakshadweep
Jabalpur: Madhya Pradesh (Benches at Gwalior and Indore)
Madras: Tamil Nadu & Puducherry
Cuttack: Odisha
Patna: Bihar (Bench at Ranchi)
Chandigarh: Punjab, Haryana & Chandigarh
Jodhpur: Rajasthan (Bench at Jaipur)
Gangtok: Sikkim

---

itself, etc.

III. *This method consists of first two conditions of the II method.* In this, there is no need of ratification by the States.

List of Important Amendments

1st Amendment (1951): Added Ninth Schedule. This amendment provided several new grounds of restrictions to the right to freedom of speech and expression and the right to practise any profession or to carry on any trade or business as contained in Article 19 of the Constitution.

7th Amendment (1956): Re-organisation of States (14 States , 6 U.Ts)

First Law Minister — Dr. B.R. Ambedkar, the prime architect of the constitution of India, was independent India's first Union Law Minister.

Independent Departments of Central Government

• Department of Space • Department of Atomic Energy • Ministries of Central Government Apex/Independent Offices • Comptroller and Auditor General of India • Union Public Service Commission • Central Bureau of Investigation • Office of the Principal Scientific Adviser • National Commission for Scheduled Tribes • National Commission for Backward Classes • Central Information Commission • Telecom Regulatory Authority of India • Election Commission of India • National Human Rights Commission • National Commission for Scheduled Castes • Planning Commission • National Commission for Minorities • National Commission on Population • Central Vigilance Commission • National Commission for Women

9th Amendment (1961): Gave effect to the transfer of certain territories to Pakistan in pursuance of the agreement between Governments of India and Pakistan.

10th Amendment (1961): Incorporated Dadra & Nagar Haveli as a U.T.

12th Amendment (1962): Incorporated Goa, Daman & Diu as a U.T.

13th Amendment (1962): Created Nagaland as a State.

14th Amendment (1962): Inclusion of Pondicherry in the First Schedule.

18th Amendment (1966): Reorganized Punjab into Punjab, Haryana and the UT of Chandigarh.

21st Amendment (1967): Included Sindhi as the 15th Regional Language.

22nd Amendment (1969): Created Meghalaya as a Sub-State within Assam.

24th Amendment (1971): This amendment was passed in the context of a situation that emerged with the verdict in Golaknath's

case by Supreme Court. Accordingly, this Act amended Article 13 and Article 36B to remove all doubts regarding the power of Parliament to amend the Constitution including the Fundamental Rights.

25th Amendment (1971): This amendment further amended Article 31 in the wake of the Banks Nationalization case.

27th Amendment (1971): Established Manipur and Tripura as States and Mizoram and Arunachal Pradesh as UTs.

31st Amendment (1973): The total strength of Lok Sabha was increased from 525 to 545 (on the basis of Census 1971)

36th Amendment (1975): Established Sikkim as a State.

38th Amendment (1975): It seeks to make a declaration of Emergency non-judiciable and places beyond the jurisdiction of Courts, the Ordinances and Proclamation of Emergency issued by the President and Governors.

39th Amendment (1975): Placed beyond judicial scrutiny, the election of President, Prime Minister and Chairman to either House of Parliament.

42nd Amendment (1976): The working of the Preamble is changed from "Sovereign Democratic Republic" to read as: Sovereign Secular Democratic Republic". The life of the Lok Sabha and all State Assemblies is extended from 5 to 6 years. It lays down 10 Fundamental Duties for all Citizens, existing 12 principles of state policy have been expanded and given precedence over Fundamental Rights.

44th Amendment (1978): Deletion of Right to Property from the Fundamental Rights. Limiting the declaration of Emergency only to cases of Armed Rebellion. The restoration of life of Lok Sabha and State Assemblies to 5 years

52nd Amendment (1985) Added Tenth Schedule which contains provisions as to disqualification on ground of defection.

53rd Amendment (1986): Granted statehood to the UT of Mizoram.

55th Amendment (1986)': Granted statehood to the UT of Arunachal Pradesh.

Soumitra Sen Case — When Rajya Sabha wanted Justice Soumitra Sen removed for corruption, it was the second time a judge had been arraigned in parliament for impropriety of the charges against him.

56th Amendment (1987): Goa was made a state.

61st Amendment (1989):Reduced the voting age from 21 to 18 years.

71st Amendment (1992): Konkani, Manipuri and Nepali were included in the Eighth Schedule.

72nd Amendment (1992): Panchayati Raj Bill passed. Constitution of Panchayats at Village and other levels. Direct elections to all seats in Panchayats and reservation of seats for the SCs and STs and fixing of tenure of 5 years for Panchayats.

73rd Amendment (1992): Nagarpalika bill passed. Constitution of three type of municipalities. Reservation of seats for SC, ST and women.

74th Amendment (1993): A new Part IX-A relating to the Municipalities has been incorporated in the Constitution of three types of Municipalities, i.e., Nagar panchayats for areas in transition from a rural area to urban area, Municipal Corporations for larger urban areas.

80th Amendment (2000): Deals with an alternative scheme for sharing taxes between the Union and the States.

81st Amendment (2000): Provides that the unfilled vacancies of a year reserved for SC/ST kept for being filled up in a year as per Article 16, shall be considered separately for filling vacancies in the succeeding year and the previous list will not be considered for filling the 50% quota of the respective year.

82nd Amendment (2000): Provides that

A Day for the Voters

The 25th of January every year, will be observed as the "National Voters' Day", throughout the country, starting from this year. It is the Election Commission's foundation day. In this launch year, the day coincides with the conclusion of the Diamond Jubilee celebrations of the Commission. The Election Commission of India (ECI) was set up on 25th January, 1950 while the Constitution came into force a day after, i.e 26th January, 1950.

The Election Commission's objective behind National Voters' Day is to increase enrolment of voters, especially the newly eligible ones, by using this occasion so as to make universal adult suffrage a complete reality and thereby enhance the quality of Indian democracy. The day will also be utilized to spread awareness among voters regarding effective participation in the electoral process.

Election Process
During the last 60 years, the Election Commission of India has conducted 15 General Elections to the Lok Sabha (House of the People) and 326 general elections to State Legislative Assemblies, thus facilitating peaceful, orderly and democratic transfer of power.

Quality and Scale of its Operations
In 1962, the voting process moved from the balloting system to marking system and then, from 2004 onwards, to the present system based on Electronic Voting Machines. Multi-member constituencies have given way to single member constituencies. Printed electoral rolls have now been substituted by computerized photo-electoral rolls. The Elector's Photo Identity Cards (EPICs), by now a cherished possession of all citizens, were issued to over 582 million voters in time for General Election 2009. Elections to the 15th Lok Sabha held in April-May 2009 have been described as the biggest management event in the world. It involved 714 million voters, 835,000 polling stations, 1.2 million Electronic Voting Machines and 11 million polling personnel.

Ministers Turn Students

When Kerala's Council of Ministers met at IIMK for a workshop, they had to follow the rules in line with the campus. Mobile phones had to be switched off. A call would cost the fine of Rs. 1000, ministers were told.

Right to Free Education

The Right of Children to Free and Compulsory Education
Act 2009, of the
Parliament received the assent
of the President
on 26 Aug 2009.
This Act provides
for free and compulsory education
to all children of

the age of six to fourteen years till the completion of elementary education. This Act disallows any school or person from collecting any capitation fee and subjecting the child or student to any kind of screening procedure. The punishment for collecting capitation fee could be as high as ten times the capitation amount charged and Rs 25,000 for the first contravention of screening test and Rs 50,000 for each subsequent contraventions.

nothing in Article 355 shall prevent the state from making any provisions in favour of the members of SC/ST in Arunachal Pradesh where the whole population is tribal.

84th Amendment (2001): The Act amended Article 82 and 170(3) to read just the territorial constituencies in the States, without altering the number of seats allotted to each State in House of People and Assemblies, including the SC and ST constituencies 1991.

85th Amendment (2001): Amended Article 16(4A) to provide for consequential seniority in promotion by virtue of rule of reservation for the Government servants belonging to the Scheduled Castes and the Scheduled Tribes.

86th Amendment (2002): Provides for (i) insertion of a new article 21A that the State shall provide free and compulsory education to all children of the age of six to fourteen years in such manner as the State may, by law, determine.

87th Amendment (2003): This Article provides that in Article 81 of the Constitution, in clause (3), in the provision, in clause (ii), for the figures "1991", the figures "2001" shall be substituted.

88th Amendment (2003): This Article provides for the insertion of a new Article 268A which states that taxes on services shall be levied by the Government of India and such tax shall be collected and appropriated by the Govt. of India and the States in the manner provided in clause (2).

89th Amendment (2003): This Article provides for the amendment of Article 338 and insertion of a new article 338A which provides that there shall be a National commission for ST.

90th Amendment (2003): This Amendment provided that for elections to the Legislative Assembly of the State of Assam, the representation of the Scheduled Tribes and non-Scheduled Tribes in the constituencies including in the Bodoland Territorial Areas District, so notified, and existing prior to the constitution of the Bodoland Territorial Areas District, shall be maintained.

91st Amendment (2003): This Article provides that the total number of Ministers, including the Prime Minster, in the Council of Ministers shall not exceed fifteen per cent of the total number of members of the House of the people.

92nd Amendment (2003): This Article provides for the inclusion of four new languages, viz. Bodo, Dogri, Maithili, and Santhali in the Eighth Schedule of the Constitution.

93rd Amendment (2005): In this Amendment, a provision has been inserted that the State (i.e., parliament or other legislatures) can make laws for the advancement of the SC, ST or the OBCs of citizens in matters of admission to educational institutions, including private unaided institutions.

94th Amendment (2006): This article provides that in article 164 of the Constitution in clause (1), in the provisio, for the word "Bihar", the words "Chhattisgarh" and "Jharkhand" shall be substituted.

Learning Chinese & HIndi

Learning of Chinese and Hindi is on the upsurge. Hindi is being taught in nine universities in China. India is introducing Chinese language in CBSE syllabus. Students are learning the two languages to cash in on the booming bilateral trade.

Flora

India is rich in flora. Available data place India in the tenth position in the world and fourth in Asia in plant diversity. From about 70% geographical area surveyed so far, over 46,000 species of plants have been described by the Botanical Survey of India (BSI), Kolkata. The vascular flora, which forms the conspicuous vegetation cover, comprises 15,000 species.

With a wide range of climatic conditions from the torrid to the arctic, India has a rich and varied vegetation, which only a few countries of comparable size possess. India can be divided into eight distinct-floristic-regions, namely, the western Himalayas, the eastern Himalayas, Asom, the Indus plain, the Ganga plain, the Deccan, Malabar and the Andamans.

The Western Himalayan region extends from Kashmir to Kumaon. This temperate zone is rich in forests of chir, pine, other conifers and broad-leaved temperate trees. Higher up, forests of deodar, blue pine, spruce and silver fir occur. The alpine zone extends from the upper limit of the temperate zone of about 4,750 metres or even higher. The characteristic trees of this zone are high-level silver fir, silver birch and junipers. The eastern Himalayan region extends from Sikkim eastwards and embraces Darjeeling, Kurseong and the adjacent tract. The temperate zone has forests of oaks, laurels, maples, rhododendrons, alder and birch. Many conifers, junipers and dwarf willows also grow here. The Asom region comprises the Brahamaputra and the Surma valleys with evergreen forests, occasional thick clumps of bamboos and tall grasses. The Indus plain region comprises the plains of Punjab, western Rajasthan and northern Gujarat. It is dry, hot and supports natural vegetation. The Ganga plain region covers the area which is alluvial plain and is under cultivation for wheat, sugarcane and rice. Only small areas support forests of widely differing types. The Deccan region comprises the entire table land of the Indian Peninsula and supports vegetation of various kinds from scrub jungles to mixed deciduous forests. The Malabar region (as part of Western Ghats) covers the excessively humid belt of mountain country parallel to the west coast of the Peninsula. It has 5000 vascular plants, of which 30% are endemic to the Ghats. Besides being rich in forest vegetation, this region produces important commercial crops, such as coconut, betelnut, pepper, coffee, tea, rubber and cashewnut. The Andaman region abounds in evergreen, mangrove, beach and alluvial forests. The Himalayan region extending from Kashmir to Arunachal Pradesh through Sikkim, Meghalaya and Nagaland and the Deccan Peninsula is rich in endemic flora, with a large number of plants which are not found elsewhere.

Ethno-botany

Ethno-botanical study deals with the utilisation of plants and plant products by ethnic races. A scientific study of such plants has been made by BSI. A number of ethno-botanical explorations have been conducted in different tribal area. More than 800 plant species of ethno-botanical interest have been collected and identified at different centres. About 1,336 plant species are considered vulnerable and endangered. BSI's inventory of endangered plants is titled Red Data Book.

Forests

According to State of Forests Report 2005, the total forest cover of the country as per 2005 assessment is 6,77,088 km² and this constitutes 20.60% of the total geographic area of the country. Of this, 54,569 km² (1.66%) is very dense forest, 3,32,647 km² (10.12%) is moderately dense forest, while 2,89,872 km² (8.82%) is open forest cover. The scrub accounts for 38,475 km² (1.17%).

While computing the percentage of forest cover of the country, the total geographic area of 2,287,263 km² is taken. A closer analysis of this reveals that a sizeable part of the country's area lies in high altitude mountainous region under permanent snow / glaciers, steep slopes and rocks which are not available for free planting due to climatic and physical reasons.

The State/UTwise forest cover in the country shows that Madhya Pradesh with 76,013 km² has the largest area under forest cover, followed by Arunachal Pradesh (67,777 km²), Chhattisgarh (55,863 km²). Considering the proportion of geographic area under forest cover, Mizoram has the maximum percentage of 88.63% followed by Nagaland (82.75%), Arunachal Pradesh (80.93%) and Andaman & Nicobar Islands (80.36%). Andhra Pradesh has the largest area under scrub (9,862 km²).

Tree Cover Tree cover estimate comprises

Black Buck

Kaziranga National Park

tree patches outside the recorded forest cover. The total tree cover of India has been estimated to be 91,663 km², which constitutes 2.79% of the country's geographic area. The tree cover for each physiographic zone has been estimated. It is observed that the tree cover is the maximum in East Deccan (11,293 km²), followed by Northern Plains (10,747 km²) and West Coast (8,307km²). However, West Coast has maximum percentage of tree cover (6.85%) with respect to geographic area followed by Western Ghats (5.37%) and East Coast (4.84%). Eastern Himalayas has the lowest tree cover of 255 km² as the area is full of forest.

Forest: Major Types

1. Moist Tropical Forests
(i) Tropical Wet Evergreen Forests (ii) Tropical Semi-Evergreen Forests (iii) Tropical Moist Deciduous Forests (iv) Tidal Forests

2. Dry Tropical Forests
(v) Tropical Dry Deciduous Forests (vii) Tropical Dry Evergreen

3. Montane Sub-Tropical Forests
(viii) Sub-Tropical Moist (pint';) (ix) Sub-Tropical Dry Evergreen Forests, (x) Sub-Tropical Wet Hill Forests

4. Montane Temperate Forests
(xi) Wet Temperate Forests (xii) Himalayan Moist Temperate Forests (xiii) Himalayan Dry Temperate Forests (xiv) Alpine Forests

Biogeographic Region India has been

divided into 10 biogeographic zones and these zones together consist of 25 biogeographic provinces. The aim is to designate one representative site as Biosphere Reserve in each bio-geographic province for long term conservation.

Parks and Sanctuaries The Protected Area network in India includes 99 National Parks and 513 Wildlife Sanctuaries, 41 Conservation Reserves and four Community Reserves. Realizing the gigantic task of managing our protected areas, the National Wildlife Action Plan (2002-2016) was adopted in 2002, emphasizing the people's participation and their support for wildlife conservation.

Coral Reefs The four major coral reefs areas identified for intensive conservation and management are: • Gulf of Mannar • Gulf of Kachchh • Lakshadweep and • Andaman and Nicobar Islands.

Mangrove The latest assessment shows that mangrove cover in India is 4,445 km², which is 0.14% of the country's total geographic area. The very dense mangrove comprises 1,147 km² (25.8% of mangrove cover), moderately dense mangrove is 1,629 (36.6%) while open mangrove covers an area of 1,669 km² (37.6%).

Animal Welfare The Animal Welfare Division is entrusted with the implementation of the provisions of the Prevention of Cruelty to Animals Act, 1960 (59 of 1960). The mandate of the Animal Welfare Division is to prevent the infliction of unnecessary pain or suffering on animals. The Wildlife Crime Control Bureau has been constituted through amendment of the Wildlife (Protection) Act, 1972 in 2008. The powers and functions of the bureau have been defined under Section 38z of the Act.

Project Tiger The centrally sponsored scheme 'Project Tiger' was launched in April, 1973 with the objective "to ensure maintenance of the viable population of tigers in India for scientific, economic, aesthetic, cultural and ecological values, and to preserve for all times, areas of biological importance as a national heritage for

Project Elephant

the benefit, education and enjoyment of the people". According to a refined methodology for estimating tiger population, an estimated land of 93,697 km² has been observed as tiger habitat. The estimated number of tigers is 1411 (with an upper limit 1657 & lower limit 1165).

Project Elephant Project Elephant was launched in February, 1992 to assist States having free ranging populations of wild elephants to ensure long term survival of identified viable populations of elephants in their natural habitats. The Project is being implemented in States, viz Andhra Pradesh, Arunachal Pradesh, Assam, Jharkhand, Karnataka, Kerala, Meghalaya, Nagaland, Orissa, Tamilnadu, Uttarakhand, Uttar Pradesh and West Bengal.

Agro-ecological regions (AERs)

1. Western Himalayas cold arid ecoregion, 2. Western plain, Kachchh and part of Kathiawar peninsula, 3. Deccan plateau, hot arid ecoregion, 4. Northern plain and central highlands including Aravallis, hot semi-arid ecoregion, 5. Central (Malwa) highlands, Gujarat plains and Kathiawar peninsula, 6. Deccan plateau, hot semi-arid ecoregion, 7. Deccan (Telangana) plateau and Eastern Ghats, 8. Eastern Ghats, Tamil Nadu uplands and Deccan (Karnataka) plateau, 9. Northern plain, hot sub-humid (dry) ecoregion, 10. Central Highlands (Malwa, Bundelkhand and Eastern Satpura), hot sub-humid ecoregion, 11. Eastern plateau (Chhattisgarh), hot subhumid ecoregion, 12. Eastern (Chhotanagpur) plateau and Eastern Ghats, 13 Eastern plain, hot subhumid (moist) ecoregion, 14. Western Himalayas.

Low Carbon Economy The National Environmental Appraisal and Monitoring Authority (NEAMA) will change the process of giving environment clearance to projects. It will focus on creating a low carbon economy.

Biosphere Reserves

Biosphere Reserves are areas of terrestrial and coastal ecosystems which are internationally recognized within the framework of UNESCO's Man and Biosphere (MAB) programme. These Reserves are required to meet a minimal set of criteria and adhere to a minimal set of conditions before being admitted to the World Network of Biosphere Reserves designated by UNESCO. These Reserves are rich in biological and cultural diversity and encompass unique features of exceptionally pristine nature. The goal is to facilitate conservation of representative landscapes and their immense biological diversity and cultural heritage, foster economic and human development which is culturally and ecologically sustainable and to provide support for research, monitoring education and information exchange. The scheme is a pioneering effort at pursuing the increasingly difficult yet urgent task of conserving ecological diversity under mounting pressures. India has been divided into ten Biogeographic zones and these zones together consist of twenty-five bio-geographic provinces. The aim is to designate one representative site as Biosphere Reserve in each bio-geographic province for long term conservation.

Mangrove forest

• The programme was initiated in 1986 and till date 16 sites have been designated as Biosphere Reserve (BR) in different parts of the country.

• Sixteen Biosphere Reserves have been designated in India. They are - 1. Nilgiri (Tamil Nadu, Kerala and Karnataka); 2. Nanda Devi (Uttarakhand); 3. Nokrek (Meghalaya); 4. Manas (Assam); 5. Dibru-Saikhowa (Assam); 6. Sundarban (West Bengal); 7. Gulf of Mannar (Tamil Nadu); 8. Great Nicobar (Andaman & Nicobar Islands); 9. Similipal (Orissa); 10. Dehang-Debang (Arunachal Pradesh); 11. Khangchendzonga (Sikkim); 12. Pachmarhi (Madhya Pradesh); 13. Achanakmar-Amarkantak (Chhattisgarh and Madhya Pradesh);14. Agasthyamalai (Tamil Nadu and Kerala); 15. Katchchh (Gujarat) and 16. Cold Desert (Himachal Pradesh).

• The Biosphere Reserve core continue to be protected under the Wildlife (Protection) Act, 1972, Indian Forest Act, 1927 and Forest Conservation Act, 1980. However, separate Regulation within the framework of existing Environment (Protection) Act, 1986 is being firmed up to regulate activities within Buffer Zone of the Biosphere Reserves.

Biodiversity Conservation

Biodiversity is the variability among living organisms and ecological complexes oi which they are part, including diversity within and between species and ecosystems. Biodiversity has direct consumptive value in food, agriculture, medicine and industry. A scheme on biodiversity conservation was initiated earlier to ensure coordination among various agencies dealing with the issues related to conservation ofbiodiversitv and to review, monitor and evolve adequate policy instruments for the same.

• The Convention on Biological Diversity (CBD), one of the key agreements adopted during the Earth Summit held in Rio de Janeiro in 1992, is the first comprehensive global agreement which addresses all aspects

Cyclone Tracking — Rs. 1500 crore has been approved by the Centre for a national cyclone risk mitigation project for coastal states. The first phase of the project will be implemented in the next five years and will be listed from A.P. and Orissa to start with.

relating to biodiversity. The CBD, which has near universal membership with 190 countries as its Parties, sets out commitments for maintaining the world's ecological underpinnil,1gs, while pursuing economic development. The Convention, while reaffirming sovereign rights of nations over their biological resources, establishes three main goals: the conserva tion of biological diversity, the sustainable use of its components, and the fair and equitable sharing of the benefits from the useoi genetic resources. India is a party to the CBD.

• India hosted two meetings for the CBD in 2009 i.e. an Expert Meeting on Traditional Knowledge in Hyderabad from 16-19 June 2009 and an Asia Pacific Regional Workshop on Protected Areas in Dehradun on 12-15 October 2009.

• In pursuance to the CBD, India had enacted the Biological Diversity Act in 2002. The Biological Rules were notified in 2004. The Act addresses access to biological resources and associted traditional knowledge to ensure equitable sharing of benefits arising out of their use to the country and its people. India is one of the first few countries to have enacted such a legislation. The Act is to be implemented through a three-tired institutional structure: National Biodiversity. Authority; State Biodiversity Authority and Biodiversity management committees.

Fauna

The Zoological Survey of India (ZSI), with its headquarters in Kolkata and 16 regional stations is responsible for surveying the faunal resources of India. Possessing a tremendous diversity of climate and physical conditions, India has great variety of fauna numbering over 90,000 species. Of these, protista number 2,577, mollusca 5,072, anthropoda 69,903, amphibia 240, mammalia 397, reptilia 460, members of protochordata 119, pisces 2,546, aves 1,232 and other invertebrates 8,329.

The mammals include the majestic elephant, the gaur or Indian bison-the largest of existing bovines, the great Indian rhinoceros, the gigantic wild sheep of the Himalayas, the swamp deer, the thamin spotted deer, nilgai, the four-horned antelope, the Indian antelope or black-buck - the only representatives of these genera. Among the cats, the tiger and lion are the most magnificent of all; other splendid creatures such as the clouded leopard, the snow leopard, the marbled cat, etc., are also found. Many other species of mammals are remarkable for their beauty, colouring, grace and uniqueness. Several birds, like pheasants, geese, ducks, myanahs, parakeets, pigeons, cranes, hornbills and sunbirds inhabit forests and wetlands.

Amongst the crocodiles and gharia/s, the salt water crocodile is found along the east-

Jungle Fowl

ern coast and in the Andaman and Nicobar Islands. A project for breeding crocodiles which started in 1974, has been instrumental in saving the crocodile from extinction.

The great Himalayan range has a very interesting variety of fauna that includes the wild sheep and goats, markhor, ibex, shrew and tapir. The panda and the snow leopard are found in the upper reaches of the mountains.

Depletion of forest cover due to expansion of agriculture, habitat destruction, over-exploitation, pollution, introduction of toxic imbalance in community structure, epidemics, floods, droughts and cyclones, contribute to the loss of flora and fauna.

* As per information available upto January 2007 on the ZSI Website.

Wildlife Sanctuaries

National parks and sanctuaries are administered at the state level and are promoted by them as a tourist attraction, which earns them sufficient revenue to keep the sanctuaries running.

Most of the sanctuaries provide well are at least optimum accommodation and other facilities but they had to be booked in advance. Some parks even provide modern guest houses. Usually van and jeep rides and also boat trips are arranged to give the visitors a good view of the animals in their natural habitats. Watchtowers and hides are also available.

Some of the notable parks and sanctuaries are listed below.

Dachigam Wildlife Sanctuary This sanctuary has a scenic valley and a meandering river. Wildlife here includes rare Kashmiri stags, black bears, and musk deers. In recent years the wildlife here have been vastly endangered. It is 22 km by road from Srinagar.

Corbett National Park This park in Uttar Pradesh is famous for its tigers. Other wild lives include cheetahs, deer, elephants, leopards, and sloth bears. The park has good scenery with sal and hardwood trees. There are numerous watch towers and daytime photography is allowed.

Sunderbans Wildlife Sanctuary This reserve in West Bengal is to the southeast of the city of Calcutta. It contains the mangrove forests of the Gangetic delta. It is an important haven for tigers but it also includes fishing cats and a wide variety of birds. It is accessible by a boat ride only.

Manas Wildlife Sanctuary

This area bordering Bhutan is formed by the rivers Manas, Hakua and Beki Rivers and is situated in Assam state. The wildlife includes tigers, buffaloes, elephants, samb-hars, swamp deers and langurs. The bodo rebels of Assam have recently used it and consequently most of its infrastructure has been destroyed.

Kaziranga National Park This park in Assam is famous for its one-horned Rhinos which are almost extinct now but for a few. The park is full of tall grasses and swampy areas. The rhinos can be spotted around the swampy areas, bathing. Egrets and other birds are also accommodated here.

Ranthambore National Park Ranthambore or Sawai Madhopur in Rajsthan is smaller in size when compared to most of the parks in India. It is famous for its lake tigers but nowadays the number has dwindled thanks to large-scale poaching in these areas. It is located on the Mumbai- Delhi rail-line and is 160 kms by road from Jaipur.

Keoladeo Ghana Bird Sanctuary This is the best-known bird sanctuary in India, situated in Rajasthan. It is also called Bharatpur Bird Sanctuary and features a large number of migrating birds from Siberia and China, which include herons, storks, cranes and geese. It also houses deers and other wildlife.

Sasan Gir National Park This Oasis in the deserts of Gujarat is famous for the Asiatic lions, which number around 250. They can be

| Tiger Density | Kaziranga National Park in Asom, a world heritage site, has 32.64 tigers per 100 sq. km. It is better than in Kanha in M.P. and Corbett National Park in Uttarakhand. |

Bison

spotted around the lakes and other watering holes. It also includes crocodiles.

Kanha National Park This is one of the spectacular and most exciting parks for wildlife in India and is in Madhya Pradesh. Originally it was conceived to protect the swamp deers also called Barasinghas but now it also includes tigers, chitals, blackbucks, langurs and leopards.

Periyar Wildlife Sanctuary This is a large and scenic park in Kerala state built around an artificial lake. It is famous for its large elephant population. Others include the wild dogs, Nilgiri Langurs, otters, tortoise, and hornbills.

Vedanthangal Bird Sanctuary This is situated around 35kms to the south of Chengalpattu in Tamilnadu and is home for a large variety of birds. Cormorants, egrets, herons, storks, ibises, pelicans, grebes and hornbills breed here from October to March. At the peak season of December to January more than 30, 000 birds can be spotted.

Calimere Wildlife Sanctuary This one also known as Koddikarai is situated in Tamilnadu, around 90 kms from Tanjore. This is a wetland area jutting out of the Palk Strait that separates India and Sri Lanka. It is famous for flocks of migratory birds mainly flamingoes. Black bucks, spotted deers and wild pigs are found here.

Mudanthurai Tiger Sanctuary This is located in Tamilnadu along its border with Kerala. It mainly consists of tigers but also has chitals, sambhars and lion tailed macaques. But it is extremely difficult to spot the tigers.

Anamalai Wildlife Sanctuary This is along the slopes of the western ghat mountains in the border between Tamilnadu and Kerala. It is also known as Indira Gandhi Wildlife Sanctuary. It has an area of around 1000 sq Km and houses elephants, gaurs, tigers, panthers, deers, boars, porcupines and wild cats. In its heart lies the Parambiculam Dam, which is of good scenic beauty.

Minorities in India

The Constitution of India uses the word 'minority' or its plural form in some Articles – 29 to 30 and 350A to 350 B. Article 29 has the word "minorities" in its marginal heading but speaks of "any sections of citizens.... having a distinct language, script or culture." This may be a whole community generally seen as a minority or a group within a majority community. Article 30 speaks specifically of two categories of minorities – religious and linguistic. The remaining two Articles– 350A and 350B relate to linguistic minorities only. In common parlance, the expression "minority" means a group comprising less than half of the population and differing from others, especially the predominant section, in race, religion, traditions and culture, language, etc.

A special Sub-Committee on the Protection of Minority Rights appointed by the United Nations Human Rights Commission in 1946 defined the 'minority' as those "non-dominant groups in a population which possess a wish to preserve stable ethnic, religious and linguistic traditions or characteristics markedly different from those of the rest of population." As regards religious minorities at the national level in India, all those who profess a religion other than Hindu are considered minorities since over 80 % population of the country professes Hindu religion. At the national level, Muslims are the largest minority. Other minorities are much smaller in size. Next to the Muslims are the Christians (2.34 %) and Sikhs (1.9 %); while all the other religious groups are still smaller. As regards linguistic minorities, there is no majority at the national level.

Green Revolution

India was at the verge of mass famine in the beginning of 1960s because of its rapidly growing population. Norman Borlaug was invited to India and the Ford Foundation and Indian government collaborated to import wheat seed. Punjab was declared the test ground for the the new crops by the Indian government because of its reliable water supply and a history of agricultural success. Borlaug and the Ford Foundation then implemented research there and they developed a new variety of rice, IR8 - a semi-dwarf rice variety developed by the International Rice Research Institute (IRRI), that produced more grain per plant when grown with irrigation and fertilizers. India, thus, began its own Green Revolution program of plant breeding, irrigation development, and financing of agrochemicals. In the 1960s, rice yields in India were about two tons per hectare; by the mid-1990s, they had risen to six tons per hectare. In the 1970s, rice cost about $550 a ton; in 2001, it cost under $200 a ton.

During the 1980s the growth in area in rice was marginal at 0.41% but growth in production and yield was above 3%. From 2001-01 to 2009-10 the situation changed with growth in area turning negative and in production and yield standing at 1.59 and 1.61% respectively.In 2009-10, India produced about 90 million tonnes of rice. India shipped nearly 4.5 million tons in 2006. Since 2007 export of non-basmati rice is prohibitted. Export of Basmati rice is permitted at a cost of US $900 per ton (Rs. 41000/ton.)

At present, India is one of the world's leading rice producers and IR8 rice usage spread throughout Asia in the decades following the rice's development in India.

Plant Technologies

The crops developed during the Green

IR8 revolutionised agriculture

Revolution were high yield varieties - meaning they were domesticated plants bred specifically to respond to fertilizers and produce an increased amount of grain per acre planted.

The terms often used with these plants that make them successful are harvest index, photosynthate allocation, and insensitivity to day length. The harvest index refers to the above ground weight of the plant. During the Green Revolution, plants that had the largest seeds were selected to create the most production possible. After selectively breeding these plants, they evolved to all have the characteristic of larger seeds. These larger seeds then created more grain yield and a heavier above ground weight.

This larger above ground weight then led to an increased photosynthate allocation. By maximizing the seed or food portion of the plant, it was able to use photosynthesis more efficiently because the energy produced during this process went directly to the food portion of the plant.

Finally, by selectively breeding plants that were not sensitive to day length, researchers like Borlaug were able to double a crop's production because the plants were not limited to certain areas of the globe based solely on the amount of light available to them.

| Cooking Rice for a PM | Marcus Samuelsson cooked at President Obama's first state dinner, which was for the Indian PM, in 2009. He was nervous about making Basmati rice for the PM. Every Indian knows the taste. He did it and the PM loved it. |

Health Indicators

AIDS: There were 156 districts in category A, 39 districts in B, 296 in C and 118 in D category in 2006. HIV prevalance rate is 0.36% and the total number is less than 3 million.

Cancer: There are 7-9 lakh cases occurring every year and 0.4 million deaths every year. There are about 2.5million cases in the country.

Filariasis : The disease is endemic in 250 districts in 20 states and UTs. The population of about 600 million is at risk of lymphatic filariasis. The global target year for its elemination is 2020.

Kala-Azar: It is caused by a protozoan parasite Leishmania donovani and spread by sandfly. It is endemic in 52 districts(31 in Bihar, 4 in Jharkhand, 11 in West Bengal and 6 in UP). The annual incidence in 2009 was 20,478 and 70 deaths (upto Oct.).

Chikungunya: It is a debilitating non-fatal viral illness caused by Chikungunya virus. Its outbreak results in large number of cases. In 2009, till Nov. 66,281 cases were registered. The deaths were not directly associated with it.

Dengue: It is a viral disease, transmitted by Aedes Aegypti mosquito. It breeds in stagnant water. Some infections result in Dengue Haemorrhagic Fever (DHF) and in its severe form, Dengue Shock Syndrome (DSS), can threaten patient's life. The case of fatality was 0.59% in 2009.

Japanese Encephalitis: It is a zoonotic disease which is transmitted by vector mosquito belonging to Culex vishnui group. The transmission cycle is maintained in the nature by animal reservoirs JE virus like pigs and water birds. Man is the dead-end ogf the host. It is not contagious through human contact. In 2009, up to Nov., 4,090 cases and 650 deaths were reported.

Malaria : There are 9 major species of mosquitoes, transmitting malaria in India.

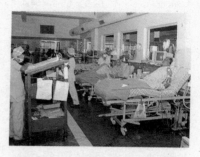

There are an estimated 75 million cases in India and 0.8M deaths annually.

Leprosy: By March 2009, the prevalence rate(PR) declined to 8.72/10,000 population. Annual new case detection rate is 11.19 per 100,000 population. 3763 new grade -II disability cases were detected.

Tuberculosis: India accounts for 1/5th of the global TB incidence - nearly 1.8M new cases and of which 0.8M are infectious. Two persons die every 3 minutes of TB.

1. Infant Mortality Rate: National Status (NS): 58 for the country with a low of 12 for Kerala and a high of 79 for Madhya Pradesh

2. Maternal Mortality Rate: NS: 301 for the country with a low of 110 for Kerala and a high of 517 for UP and Uttarakhand in the 2001-03 period.

3. Child Morbidity NS: 32% children had fever, 21% had diarrhea, 17% had persistent cough, 11% suffered from extreme weakness, 5% had skin rashes, 2% had eye infections during the two weeks preceding the survey. 50% children had one of the above problems.

Source: Sample Registration System, 2004; National Sample Survey 60th Round 2004; DLHS and Facility Survey coordinated by IIPS 2003; National Family Health Survey 2005-06; FOCUS Survey 2004; India 2010.

India Presides	When India assumed presidency of the UN Security Council for the month of August, 2011, it was the first time that it did so after Dec. 1992. India is a temporary member of the Security Council.

Selected Indicators of Human Development for Major States

Sl. No.	Major State	Life expectancy at birth ('02-'06)			Infant Mortality Rate (per 1000 live births)			Birth rate (per 1000)	Death rate (per 1000)
		Male	Female	Total	Male	Female	Total	(2008)	(2008)
1	Andhra	62.9	65.5	64.4	51	54	52	18.4	7.5
2	Assam	58.6	59.3	58.9	62	65	64	23.9	8.6
3	Bihar	62.2	60.4	61.6	53	58	56	28.9	7.3
4	Gujarat	62.9	65.2	64.1	49	51	50	22.6	6.9
5	Haryana	65.9	66.3	66.2	51	57	54	23.0	6.9
6	Karnataka	63.6	67.1	65.3	44	46	45	19.8	7.4
7	Kerala	71.4	76.3	74	10	13	12	14.6	6.6
8	MP	58.1	57.9	58	68	72	70	28.0	8.6
9	Maharashtra	66.0	68.4	67.2	33	33	33	17.9	6.6
10	Orissa	59.5	59.6	59.6	68	70	69	21.4	9
11	Punjab	68.4	70.4	69.4	39	43	41	17.3	7.2
12	Rajasthan	61.5	62.3	62	60	65	63	27.5	6.8
13	Tamil Nadu	65.0	67.4	66.2	30	33	31	16.0	7.4
14	Uttar Pradesh	60.3	59.5	60	64	70	67	29.1	8.4
15	West Bengal	64.1	65.8	64.9	34	37	35	17.5	6.2
	India	62.6	64.2	63.5	52	55	53	22.8	7.4

Source : Sample Registration System, Office of the Registrar General, India, Ministry of Home Affairs.
* Data relating to Bihar, M.P. and U.P. includes Jharkhand, Chattisgarh, and Uttarakhand respectively.

Dams

In 1947, there were less than 300 large dams in India. By the year 2000 the number had increased to over 4000, more than half of them built between 1971 and 1989. India ranks third in the world in dam building, after US and China. While some of these dams were built primarily for flood control, water supply, and hydroelectric power generation, the primary purpose of most Indian dams (96%) remains irrigation. In fact, large dam construction has been the main form of investment in irrigation undertaken by the Indian government. But, starting in the 1980s, public investment in large dams in India has been the subject of a controversy—like the Sardar Sarovar Project—centering on the balance between the social, environmental, and economic costs and their benefits. There are about 34,798 large dams in the world, out of which 83 % are embank-

Bhakra Nangal Dam

ment dams. In India, the total number of large dams are 1,554.

Categories: VH – Very High Large Dam (Large dams being of 100 meters height or above) **HH** - High Height Large Dam (Large dams being of 30 meters height or above, but less than 100 meters height) **MH** - Medium Height Large Dam (large dams being of 15 meters height or above, but less than 30 meters height) **LH** - Low Height large Dam (Large dams being of 10 meters height or above, but less than 15 meters height)

State-Wise Infant Mortality Rate

Sl. No.	States/UTs	1961			2007			2008		
		Male	Female	Person	Male	Female	Person	Male	Female	Person
1	Kerala	55	48	52	14	10	13	10	13	12
2	Puducherry	77	68	73	31	22	25	22	27	25
3	Mizoram	73	65	69	27	16	23	37	38	37
4	Manipur	31	33	32	13	9	12	13	15	14
5	A & N Is.	78	66	77	38	23	34	29	32	31
6	Lakshadweep	124	88	118	25	23	24	29	34	31
7	Chandigarh	53	53	53	25	28	27	27	29	28
8	Goa	60	56	57	11	13	13	10	11	10
9	Arunachal	141	111	126	41	15	37	30	34	32
10	J & K	78	78	78	53	38	51	48	51	49
11	Maharashtra	96	89	92	41	24	34	33	33	33
12	Tripura	106	116	111	40	32	39	34	35	34
13	Delhi	66	70	67	41	35	36	34	37	35
14	Meghalaya	81	76	79	57	46	56	58	58	58
15	Sikkim	105	87	96	36	20	34	34	32	33
16	Tamil Nadu	89	82	86	38	31	35	30	33	31
17	West Bengal	103	57	95	39	29	37	34	37	35
18	Punjab	74	79	77	47	35	43	39	43	41
19	Karnataka	87	74	81	52	35	47	44	46	45
20	D & N Haveli	102	93	98	38	18	34	33	35	34
21	Gujarat	81	84	84	60	36	52	49	51	50
22	Himachal	101	89	92	49	25	47	43	45	44
23	Andhra	100	82	91	60	37	54	51	54	52
24	Bihar	95	94	94	59	44	58	53	58	56
25	Haryana	87	119	94	60	44	55	51	57	54
26	Assam	na	na	na	68	41	66	62	65	64
27	Rajasthan	114	114	114	72	40	65	60	65	63
28	Uttar Pradesh	131	128	130	72	51	69	64	70	67
29	MP	158	140	150	77	50	72	68	72	70
30	Odisha	119	111	115	73	52	71	68	70	69
31	Nagaland	76	58	68	18	29	21	23	29	26
32	Daman & Diu	60	56	57	29	23	27	26	37	31
33	Chhatisgarh	a	a	a	61	49	59	57	58	57
34	Jharkhand	a	a	a	51	31	48	45	48	46
35	Uttarakhand	a	a	a	52	25	48	44	45	44

Source : Sample Registration System, Office of the Registrar General, India, Ministry of Home Affairs.
a : Created in 2001.
Note : For 2008, Infant mortality rates for smaller States and UTs are based upon the three year period 2006-08.

Surrogacy in India

The studies in the human reproductive sciences have advanced so much that it is possible for couples and others to have biologically their own children who otherwise cannot for a number of reasons. This has given rise to surrogacy. Surrogacy is a method of assisted reproduction through-surrogate mothers. More common form is IVF/Gestational surrogacy in which the surrogate child biologically belongs completely to the social parents. The other type is gestational surrogacy where the surrogate child is genetically related to the male parent and the surrogate mother.

India is an important destination for surrogacy and its Assisted Reproductive Technology (ART). It has taken an industrial proportion worth a 25-billion rupee business annually. It is often described as "a gold pot". The phenomenal rise in surrogacy in India has been due to its low cost factor, and social acceptance. Besides, surrogacy is a preferred option because of the complicated adoption procedures.

Foreign nationals including NRIs are seeking surrogacy for both medical and personal reasons. It has contributed to the rise of the Indian surrogacy industry predominantly because of it being at least ten times cheaper than in their respective countries. No statistics exist on the number of foreign couples coming to India to have a child.

In India surrogacy began with the delivery of its first surrogate baby on June 23rd, 1994, but it took eight more years to draw world attention to it when an Indian woman in 2004 delivered a surrogate child for her daughter in the U.K.

Today there are an estimated 200,000 clinics across the country offering artificial insemination, IVF and surrogacy or Assisted Reproductive Technology (ART).

Presently, because there is no law governing surrogacy in India, eventually the activity including renting a womb (commercial surrogacy) would be considered legitimate. In the absence of any law the Indian Council of Medical Research (ICMR) in 2005 issued guidelines for accreditation, supervision and regulation of ART clinics in India. But the ICMR guidelines are often violated and reportedly there are rampant exploitation of surrogate mothers including cases of extortion.

The government of India has set-up an expert committee to draft a legislation known as Assisted Reproductive Technology (Regulation) Bill, 2010 for legalizing surrogacy. It defines a 'couple' as two persons living together and having a sexual relationship and as such, following Delhi High Court's verdict on homosexuality, gives gays besides the singles the legal right to have surrogate babies. It also stipulates the age of surrogate mother to be within 21-35 years and limits her deliveries to five including her own children. The surrogate mother will have to enter into a legally enforceable surrogacy agreement as per the proposed legislation.

According to many legal experts, the draft Bill will end the present confusion and help regulate the functioning of the IVF centers and ART clinics.

Under the proposed law, foreign couples including NRIs seeking surrogacy in India will have to submit certificates that their country recognizes surrogacy as legal and also that the surrogate child after birth would get their country's citizenship. The Law Commission of India in its 228th Report on "Need for legislation to regulate assisted reproductive technology clinics as well as rights and obligations of parties to a surrogacy," has by and large supported surrogacy in India.

There are worries too as to what impact it will have on the society in terms of commercialization. Poor illiterate Indian women with the lure of money could be forced into repeated surrogate pregnancies risking their lives. There are also ethical and moral issues as well as the human dignity involved besides questions about the rights of surrogate mother. As such the draft legislation on surrogacy needs to be debated in detail in social, legal and political circles as well as by the civil society before it is approved by law.

Energy Scenario

India has an estimated sedimentary area of 3.14 million sq. km, comprising 26 sedimentary basins. Prior to the adoption of the New Exploration Licensing Policy (NELP), only 11% of India's sedimentary basin was under exploration. Since operationalization of the NELP in 1999, the Government of India has awarded 47.3 % of it for exploration. So far 87 oil and gas discoveries have been made by private/joint venture (JV) companies in 26 blocks and more than 640 MMT of oil-equivalent hydrocarbon reserves have been added. As on 1 October 2010, investment made by Indian and foreign companies was of the order of US $ 14.8 billion, of which, US $ 7.5 billion was in hydrocarbon exploration and US$ 7.3 billion in development of discoveries

Rural Electrification
Under the RGGVY, 87,791 villages have been electrified and connections released to 135.31 lakh below poverty line(BPL) households up to 30 November 2010. Under the Tenth Five Year Plan, 235 projects covering 68,763 villages and 83.10 lakh BPL connections were sanctioned at a cost of ` 9,732.90 crore. In Phase I of the Eleventh Plan period, 338 projects have been sanctioned for implementation at a cost of ` 16,620.61 crore for electrification of 49,736 villages and release of connections to 163.34 lakh BPL households. Till 30 November 2010, 333 projects have been awarded and franchisees are in place in 1,10,567 villages in 16 States.

Koodankulam Nuclear Power Station

Oil and gas production
Efficient and reliable energy supplies are a precondition for accelerated growth of the Indian economy. While the energy needs of the country, especially oil and gas, are going to increase at a rapid rate in the coming decades, the indigenous energy resources are limited. Oil and gas constitute around 45 per cent of total energy consumption. At the same time, the dependence on imports of petroleum and petroleum products continues to be around 80 per cent of total oil consumption in the country.

National Grid
An integrated power transmission grid helps even out supply-demand mismatches. The existing inter-regional transmission capacity of about 22,400 MW connects the northern, western, eastern, and north-eastern regions in synchronous mode operating at the same frequency and the southern region in asynchronous mode. This has enabled inter-regional energy exchanges of about

Power Generation by Utilities (Billion KWh)

Category	2008-09	2009-10	April-December		Growth (%)
			2009-10	2010-11	
Power Generation	723.8	771.551	571.573	597.290	4.50
Hydroelectric*	113.0	106.680	83.360	90.145	8.14
Thermal	590.0	640.876	469.694	483.932	3.03
Nuclear	14.8	18.636	13.408	17.849	33.12

Note: *Excludes generation from hydro stations up to 25 MW.   Source: Ministry of Power

Wind Power

38,000 million units in financial year 2010-11 (till November 2010), thus contributing to greater utilization of generation capacity and an improved power supply position. Proposals are under way to have synchronous integration of the southern region with the rest.

Alternative Sources

Green Power: The CERC has amended the Terms and Conditions for Tariff Determination from Renewable Energy Sources Regulations 2010 for increasing the visibility of the generic tariff determined for solar photo voltaic (PV) and solar thermal projects. The Renewable Energy Certificate (REC) framework is expected to give a push to renewable energy capacity addition in the country. The REC is a market-based instrument to promote renewable energy, facilitate renewable purchase obligations (RPOs) by maximizing the benefits of renewable generation while reducing costs.

Shale Gas: Shale gas is being explored as an important new source of energy in the country. India has several shale formations which seem to hold shale gas. The shale gas formations are spread over several sedimentary basins such as Cambay, Gondwana, and KG on land and Cauvery river.

Coal Bed Methane (CBM): CBM is found embedded in coal seams. The CBM policy has provided a level playing field for exploration and commercial exploitation of CBM by national and international companies since the 2000. Total CBM resources in 26 blocks awarded so far are estimated at 1374 BCM. In the fourth round, the Government of India has awarded 7 CBM blocks in the States of Assam, Chhattisgarh, Jharkhand, Madhya Pradesh, Odisha, and Tamil Nadu and signed 33 contracts. Commercial production of CBM in India has now become a reality with current CBM gas production at about one lakh cu.m per day. The CBM gas produced in the country is being utilized by nearby industries in and around Raniganj block in West Bengal.

Underground Coal Gassification (UCG): The Oil and Natural Gas Commission (ONGC) has entered into an Agreement of Collaboration (AOC-MOU) with the National Mining Research Centre-Skochinsky Institute of Mining (NMRC-SIM) in Russia. In the selected Vastan mine block, seismic survey was carried out and 18 boreholes drilled for detailed UCG site characterization. Based on geological, hydrological, and geo-mechanical data analysis, Vastan in Gujarat and Hodu Sindri in Rajasthan have been found suitable for UCG stations. Pilot production of UCG at Vastan by the ONGC is expected to commence by the end of the Eleventh Five Year Plan period.

Gas Hydrate: Gas hydrate is at research and development (R&D) stage world over. A cooperation programme between the Directorate General of Hydrocarbons (DGH) and U S Geological Survey (USGS), USA for exchange of scientific knowledge and technical personnel in the field of gas hydrate and research energy is in progress. An MOU was recently signed in the area of marine gas hydrate research and technology development between the Leibniz Institute of Marine Sciences, Germany, and DGH for research on methane production from gas hydrate by carbon dioxide sequestration.

Small Hybrid System is gaining prominence among the available renewable micro-generation technology due to non-availablity of continuous power supply in both urban and rural areas and inaccessible hilly areas.

Wind Energy: Wind power has emerged as a key factor in India's quest for energy as fossil-fuel based power generation has failed to keep pace with growing energy requirements of a surging economy. Turbine with100kW capacity are called small wind turbines and those above 225kW are large wind turbines. India has an installed capacity of 1.07 MW. Tamil Nadu continues to be the state with the highest wind pwere capacity of 43% in the national aggregate. Tamil Nadu-5502.9MW, Rajasthan-1333.4MW, Gujarat-2005.3MW, Maharashtra-2201 MW.

Defence

India's national security objectives have evolved against a backdrop of India's core values namely, democracy, secularism and peaceful co-existence and the national goal of social and economic development. India's security concerns are moulded by a dynamic global security environment and the perception that South Asia region is of particular global security interest. The continuing presence of terrorist and fundamentalist forces in its neighbourhood and within has prompted India to maintain a high level of alert and preparedness to face any challenge to its security.

India's Nuclear Policy

India's nuclear weapons capability is meant only for self-defence and seeks only to ensure that India's security, independence and integrity are not threatened in the future. India is not interested in a nuclear arms race. This is the rationale behind the two pillars of India's nuclear policy – credible minimum deterrence and no-first use. But India holds the option to respond with punitive retaliation should deterrence fail.

India's Strategic Nuclear Command was formally established in 2003, with an Air Force officer, Air Marshal Asthana, as the Commander-in-Chief. The joint services SNC is the custodian of all of India's nuclear weapons, missiles and assets. It is also responsible for executing all aspects of India's nuclear policy. However, the civil leadership, in the form of the CCS (Cabinet Committee on Security) is the only body authorized to order a nuclear strike against another offending strike."

India possesses nuclear weapons and maintains short- and intermediate-range ballistic missiles, nuclear-capable aircraft, surface ships, and submarines.

India is not a signatory to either the Nu-

1. *Chief of Army Staff: Gen. VK Singh*
2. *Chief of Air Staff: Air Chief Marshal NAK Browne*
3. *Chief of Naval Staff: Adm. Nirmal Verma*
4. *Chief of Integrated*
   Defence Staff: Vice Adm. Shekhar Sinha

clear Non-Proliferation Treaty (NPT) or the Comprehensive Test Ban Treaty (CTBT), but did accede to the Partial Test Ban Treaty in October 1963. India is a member of the International Atomic Energy Agency (IAEA), and four of its 17 nuclear reactors are subject to IAEA safeguards.

The Integrated Space Cell is the nodal agency within the Government of India which oversees the security of its space based military and civilian hardware systems and is jointly operated by all the three services.

The Army

The Indian Army's HQ is located in New Delhi and functions under the Chief of Army Staff (COAS), who is responsible

Nuclear Systems	Indian Strategic Nuclear Command controls its land-based nuclear warheads, while the Navy controls the ship and submarine based missiles and the Air Force the air based warheads.

AWACS Phalcon

for the command, control and administration as a whole. The Army is divided into six operational commands (field armies) and one training command.

Regional Commands and HQ: (i) Central Command - Lucknow; (ii) Eastern Command - Kolkata; (iii) Northern Command - Udhampur; (iv) Western Command - Chandimandir; (v) Southern Command - Pune. Army Training Command at Shimla (for the purpose of laying down the training policy for the Army). Personnel in Army: 980,000 active troops. Army Reserves: 300,000 first line troops (within five years of full time service).

Air Force

The Indian Air Force was officially established on 8 October 1932. Its first flight took place on 01 April 1933.

Operational commands They are: Western Air Command, South-Western Air Command, Central Air Command, Eastern Air Command and Southern Air Command. In addition, there are two functional commands–Maintenance Command and Training Command. The Air Force Headquarters is in New Delhi.

Navy

The Navy is responsible for defence and security of India's maritime interests and assets, both in times of war and peace. Our offshore assets within the Exclusive

Research and Analysis Wing

Research and Analysis Wing (RAW) is India's external intelligence agency. It was formed in September 1968. Its primary function is collection of external intelligence, counter-terrorism and covert operations. In addition, it is responsible for obtaining and analyzing information about foreign governments, corporations, and persons, in order to advise Indian foreign policy-makers.

Economic Zone (EEZ) of 2.02 million sq. kms, oil and natural gas, fisheries and deep sea interests, major and minor harbours and the overall seaward security of 7,517 km long coastline and island territories are other vital aspects of our maritime dimension and Navy's responsibilities. The Chief of the Naval Staff at the Naval Headquarters, New Delhi.

Regional Commands. Their headquarters are: (i) Eastern Naval Command, Visakhapatnam (ii) Western Naval Command, Mumbai; and (iii) Southern Naval Command, Kochi.

Coast Guard

The Coast Guard came into being on 1 February 1977 and was constituted as an independent Armed Force of the Union of India with the enactment of CG Act 1978 on 18 August 1978 with its motto as `VAYAM RAKSHAMAH (meaning `We Protect'). The Charter of Duties includes: (a) Safety and protection of offshore installations and maritime environment; (b) Assisting Customs in anti-smuggling operations.

NIA

National Investigation Agency (NIA) is the Central Counter Terrorism Law Enforcement Agency in India. NIA was born through the enactment of NIA Act on 31-12-2008. NIA deals with militancy and insurgency and Left-wing extremism, various forms of terrorist attacks and bomb blasts, infiltration from across the borders, complex inter-State and international linkages, other activities like the smuggling of arms and drugs, pushing in of fake Indian currency, etc.

Commissioned Ranks

Army	Navy	Air Force
General	Admiral	Air Chief Marshal
Lieutenant General	Vice-Admiral	Air Marshal
Major General	Rear Admiral	Air Vice-Marshal
Brigadier	Commodore	Air Commodore
Colonel	Captain	Group Captain
Lieutenant Colonel	Commander	Wmg Commander
Major	Lieutenant Commander	Squadron Leader
Captain	Lieutenant	Flight Lieutenant
Lieutenant	Sub-Lieutenant	Flying Officer

Explosives, Rockets and Missiles

Grenade 36mmHand Grenade - Multi Mode Grenade ShivalikHand grenade RPG-7Rocket propelled grenade (40mm) BEL Battlefield Surveillance Radar-Short Range (BFSR-SR)

Armoured recovery vehicle-Vijayanta ARV, WZT-2/3, VT-72B ARV

Mine protected and mine clearing vehicles: Hydremma

Combat vehicles like Arjun MBT Mk1; T-90S "Bhishma"/T-90M, Aditya; Bomb disposal robot - DRDO Daksh; Armoured personnel carrier-Casspir

Artillery Howitzer like Haubits FH77/B, M-46, D-30, M-46; Self-propelled artillery like Indian Field Gun, Light Field Gun; Multiple rocket launcher like Smerch 9K58 MBRL, Pinaka MBRL;

Missile systems - Anti-tank guided missile like Nag, MILAN, Spike (missile), Lahat

Ballistic and cruise missiles like Brahmos-300 km range; Short-range ballistic missile like Prithvi-I, II, III -150/ 250/ 350 km range; Medium-range ballistic missile - Agni-I 700 –800 km range; Intermediate-range ballistic missile - Agni-II 2000 – 3500 km range; ICBM - Agni-III 3500 – 5000 km range

Air defence missiles and Systems- Anti-ballistic missile - Prithvi Air Defense (PAD), Advanced Air Defence (AAD); Strategic Surface-to-air missile- S300-PMU-2, SA-5 Gammon; Surface-to-air missile -Akash, SA-6

Prahaar SS Missile

Gainful, SA-8 Gecko, SA-13 Gopher; Anti-aircraft artillery -Bofors L/70, ZSU-23-2; Self-propelled anti-aircraft weapon - Tunguska M1, ZSU-23-4M 'Shilka'

Aircraft: Light Combat Helicopter: HAL Dhruv, Sukhoi 30.

Aircraft Carriers: Viraat Destro-yers: 1.Delhi class 2. Rajput class Frigates: 1. Godavari class, 2. Talwar class, 3. Brahmaputra class 4. Giri class. Corvettes: 1. Khukri class, 2. Kora class, 3. Veer class, 4. Abhay Class

Minesweepers: 1. Pondicherry/Karwar Class 2. Mahe Class

Landing Ships: 1. Magar Class (LST), 2. Kumbhir Class (LST(M)), 3. LCU. Missile Boats: Chamak Class

Seaward Defence Forces: 1. Tarasa Class FAC(G), 2. Seaward Defence Boats, 3 FACs, 4. Water Jet FACs

Pinaka missiles

Special Security Forces

National Security Guard is India's premier counter-terrorism force, created by the Cabinet Secretariat under the National Security Guard Act of 1985. The NSG operates under the Ministry of Home Affairs and is headed by the Director General of the Indian Police Service (IPS). The NSG members are also known as Black Cats because of the black nomex cover alls and balaclavas (assault helmets) they wear. The NSG's roles include protecting VIPs, conducting anti-sabotage checks, rescuing hostages, neutralizing terrorist threats to vital installations, engaging terrorists and responding to hijacking and piracy.

Special Protection Group

The Special Protection Group, with about 3000 personnel, is used for the protection of VVIPs such as the Prime Minister and his/her immediate family members. The force was created in 1985 following the assassination of former Prime Minister Indira Gandhi. Today, the SPG is one of the elite agencies of its kind in Asia. Recruits include police and the NSG commandos who are trained like the US Secret Service. The officer cadre is mainly IPS Officers from various state/central cadres.

Rapid Action Force

It is a specialised wing of the Indian CRPF. It was formed in October 1992, to deal with riots and related unrest, with 10 of its battalions. The battalions are numbered 100 to 110.

Border Security Force

Established on December I, 1965, BSF is responsible for guarding India's land borders during peacetime and preventing trans-border crimes. It is a central paramilitary force operating under the Union Ministry of Home Affairs.

Central Reserve Police Force

Functioning under the aegis of Ministry of Home Affairs, the CRPF's primary role lies in assisting the State/Union Territories in police operations to maintain law and order and contain insurgency. It came into existence as the Crown Representative's Police on July 27, 1939. After Indian Independence, it became the Central Reserve Police Force on enactment of the CRPF Act on December 28, 1949. The role of CRPF in the General Elections has been very significant and vital.

Indo-Tibetan Border Police

It is a paramilitary force conceived on 24-10-1962 for security along the Indo-Tibetan Border. The ITBP is trained in mountaineering, disaster management, and nuclear, biological and chemical disasters. ITBP have been deployed in UN peacekeeping missions.

Central Industrial Security Force

Established in its present form on June 15, 1983. Its headquarter is in New Delhi. The CISF provides security cover to industrial units located all over India like atomic power plants, space installations, defence units, mints, oil fields and refineries, major ports etc.

| Salwa Judum | Salwa Judum means purification hunt in Bastar's tribal dialect. It started as a spontaneous uprising against Naxals in 2005. The Supreme Court has pronounced Chhattisgarh governments' Salwa Judum movement to fight against Maoist violence as illegal. |

Window to the Poles

India has successfully launched 30 scientific expeditions to Antarctica and 5 expeditions each to Arctic and Southern Ocean till now. It is all done by National Centre for Antarctic and Ocean Research (NCAOR), which is the nodal agency responsible for research programs in the Polar regions (Arctic, Antarctic and southern Ocean). It is the only institute in the country that has the capability to archive & process ice cores from Polar Regions. In the year 2010-11, NCAOR accomplished the first ever Indian expedition to South Pole. Apart From Maitri in Antarctica, India now has a research Base – Himadri – in Arctic. The first phase of the construction of new research base in eastern Antarctica, Bharati, is complete and station is likely to be commissioned in 2012-13.

The Research programmes include Ice Core Studies, Remote Sensing, Polar Lake Studies, Climate Change Studies, Southern Ocean Processes, Exclusive Economic zone Survey, Legal continental Shelf Mapping, Environmental Impact Assessment and Microbial Biodiversity & Biogeochemistry.

New Initiatives

Second phase of construction of India's Third Permanent Research Station Bharati at

Indian Flag at South Pole

Larsemann Hills is likely to be completed by 2012-13 Season. First phase comprising site preparation, transportation of construction machinery, erection of fuel farm, laying of pipe lines for drinking and waste water, fuel supply, helipad, piling for main station was completed as per schedule this year.

Geotraces & Biogeochemistry Studies

In all three Poles (Arctic, Antarctic and Himalaya) will result in better understanding of Ocean processes, global climate, biogeochemical cycles and marine productivity that is critical for society to respond effectively to the challenges of climate change, sea level rise, ocean acidification, and for the sustainable use of marine resources. They will be carried out during 12th Five Year Plan. GEOTRACES is an international programme which aims to improve the understanding of biogeochemical cycles and large-scale distribution of trace elements and their isotopes in the marine environment. Scientists from approximately 30 nations have been involved in the programme, which is designed to study all major ocean basins over the next decade.

Cryosphere Program

NCAOR will initiate multidisciplinary glaciologi-

Bharati at Larsemann Hills

| Utoya | Norwegian island northwest of Oslo, where 69 people were killed during a youth camp, by Andres Behring Brevik on the killer, described the attacks 'an attempt at purging Europe of Muslims'. |

Arctic Research

During the 29th Antarctica expedition concluded in March 2009, the studies accomplished din Larsemann Hills area for setting up the Third Station in Antarctica. India has a strong presence in Antarctica for the past 27 years. Expedition to Arctic: India already has a strong presence in the Antarctica for the past 27 years. However, despite the scientific and logistics expertise gained by the country over the years in Antarctica, a wide gap exists in our knowledge of the Arctic, hindering a much-needed bi-hemispherical approach to polar sciences. The Arctic Ocean and the surrounding regions are one of the most important areas that not only

Dakshin Gangotri

from two Antarctic stations in near future as also in Arctic.

India is in the process of claiming Legal Continental Shelf and the second partial submission for an additional area of 0.6 million square km is already under way for submission. India already made its first partial submission for an extended continental shelf of approx. 0.6 million square km in May 2009.

NCAOR is now is a position to provide logistic and scientific support to scientists interested in pursuing high end research in highly inaccessible regions of Antarctica beyond the reach of helicopters. This is a possibility now for South Pole Expedition & Beyond due to establishing the rout across the mountains in interiors of Antarctica since their trips in this continent. Gains accrued from the First Every Scientific Expedition to farthest end of Earth – South Pole will be consolidated for future landing at the polar plateau for deep ice core drilling.

Southern Ocean Expeditions will be launched to understand complex ocean fronts, biological diversity and biogeochemical processes in the oceans south of 33 degree latitudes in southern hemisphere. The expedition is open to all Indian universities, national organizations and research institutions.

Scientists staying in Antarctica for longer duration will be able to keep track of scientific publications from across the world as connectivity with Antarctica will be strengthened. Data transfer and voice transmission between Antarctica and India will improve by increasing band width. This would enhance the data transfer capabilities and update the scientists.

cal studies on snow, ice, and permafrost in Arctic, Antarctica as also in selected glaciers in Himalaya to fill the gaps information especially in the field of snow-ice chemistry, dating of the ice cores and palaeoclimate studies. The study will generate long term data essential for coming to a conclusion on health of glaciers and thereby the impacts of climate change.

Marine Geophysics Program

It will unravel the bed rock geological features in Andaman Nicobar area, post tsunami tectonic changes, evolution of Indian Ocean, geophysical anomalies in Indian Ocean region etc.

Ice Breaker Vessel

To facilitate the Indian researchers with better equipments who are engaged in the studies in polar regions an Ice Breaker Vessel will be acquired. This is required to enhance their data collecting capabilities. So long, India was hiring cargo vessels for taking its scientists to Antarctica because of which no meaningful data could be acquired en route to Antarctica. Acquiring our own vessel has also been made necessary because India would be operating

Antarctica It is the world's last great wilderness. It is so hostile and remote that it has no permanent residents. Surrounded by the Southern Ocean, Antarctica covers nearly 9% of the Earth's land, and is the fifth largest continent. It is also the least polluted of all the continents.

Bhuvan

Bhuvan is an interactive versatile visualization system that allows users to navigate the entire globe, scanning satellite imagery with overlays of natural resource information, roads, geographic features, and numerous other location-specific data points. Users can add their own points of interest and share them with others, chart routes, plot areas, calculate distances, and overlay separate images onto the application. Bhuvan connects to the Internet, making online resources available in connection with particular places. Bhuvan is also a geoportal of ISRO showcasing Indian imaging capabilities in multi-sensor, multi-platform and multi-temporal domain. This earth

browser allows discovering virtual earth in 3D space with specific emphasis on Indian region besides an unbroken 360 degree view of the physical space, in interactive video for easy learning, and allows interactive 3D modeling and guided tours.

Direct to Home

DTH (Direct To Home) is the transmission mode by which satellite TV programming can be received at home. Currently there are six main DTH providers in India, namely Dish TV, TataSky, Big TV, Airtel Digital, Sun Direct and Videocon D2H. Direct To Home (DTH) is an alternative to Cable TV. Cable TV outages, breakdowns and in most cases their services are not dependable. Since DTH signals come directly from the broadcast satellite to the consumer's dish, it can even reach remote places. With the widespread implementation of Conditional Access System (CAS) throughout India, DTH is a good alternative.

When choosing a DTH provider, one has to consider various factors like picture quality, transmission during rough weather, suitability of the plans / packages, package pricing, and other value added services. The DTH service quality depends on the signal strength, so it is always better to check for excellent reception in one's own area.

DTH services offer MPEG4 quality or DVD quality or MPEG4 with DVB-S2 (Digital Video Broadcasting) digital transmission. It has provision for HD quality, enhanced interactive services and access to the Internet. Airtel and Videocon offer MPEG4 with DVB-S2. Almost each DTH provider has special packs. Many providers provide a Mega Package (₹ 330 for 193 channels) or Childs Pack (₹ 165 for 190 channels) or Economy Pack (₹ 220 for 155 channels).

DTH provides Movie On Demand, accessed through the service interface or DTH website or SMS. Check for the availability of the latest movies in Pay Per View (Movie on Demand) when making a decision. Most providers give Interactive services to interact with the TV. Some DTH providers give matrimonial or job services while others like Airtel allows setting up widgets that give information and news snippets, weather, stock updates and breaking news.

ANTRIX | **ISRO's unit that co-operates with other space agencies with respect to catering to satellite launch needs. It provides training in space field to personnel from other countries. ISRO's hardware and services available commercially through Antrix Corporation.**

Space Initiatives

Human Space Flight

India's developments in key elements of human space flight are progressing as in habitable crew module, environmental and life support systems and crew escape and recovery. It is now well recognised that a robust and reliable human rated space transportation system is what is required for this venture. PSLV and GSLV Mk-III will be initially used to conduct unmanned test flights to qualify various sub-systems.

The Beginnings

In June 1972, the Government of India set up Space Commission and Department of Space (DOS). Indian Space Research Organisation (ISRO) under DOS executes space programme through its establishments located in different places in India. The objective of India's space programme are development of satellites, launch vehicles, sounding rockets and associated ground systems.

Major milestones

Experimental phase included Satellite Instructional Television Experiment (SITE), Satellite Telcommunication Experiment (STEP), remote sensing application projects, satellites like Aryabhata, Bhaskara, Rohini and APPLE and launch vehicles, SLV-3 and ASLV.

Present operational space systems include Indian National Satellite (INSAT) for telecommunication, television broadcasting, meteorology and disaster warning and Indian Remote Sensing Satellite (IRS) for resources monitoring and management.

Polar Satellite Launch Vehicle (PSLV) and Geosynchronous Satellite Launch Vehicle

Aryabhata

(GSLV) are intended for launching various class of satellites.

Space Science activities include SROSS and IRS-P3 satellites, participation in international science campaigns and ground systems like MST Radar.

Chandrayaan-1, India's first spacecraft mission beyond Earth's orbit is aimed to further expand our knowledge about Earth's only natural satellite - the moon.

Launch infrastructure

The Satish Dhawan Space Centre (SDSC) SHAR, Sriharikota Island is on the East Coast of India. The newly built second launch pad at SDSC SHAR as a redundancy to the existing launch pad, was commissioned on 5 May 2005.

Satellites

Satellites, Launched, dates and purpose Aryabhata/ 19.04.1975/ First Indian satellite. Provided technological experience in building and operating a satellite system. Launch: Russian launch vehicle Intercosmos. Bhaskara-I/ 07.06.1979/ First experimental remote sensing satellite. Carried TV and microwave cameras. Launch: Intercosmos.

Indian National Satellite System

INSAT, a joint venture of Department of Space (DOS), Department of Telecommunications, India Meteorological Department, All India Radio and Doordarshan, became operational in 1983 with commissioning

Launch Vehicles

India has Polar Satellite Launch Vehicle (PSLV) and Geosynchronous Satellite Launch Vehicle(GSLV) to launch satellites.

PSLV The four-stage PSLV is capable of launching upto 1,600 kg satellites into a 620 km polar orbit. It has provision to launch payloads from 100 kg micro-satellites or mini

or small satellites in different combinations. It can also launch one-ton class payloads into Geosynchronous Transfer Orbit (GTO).

GSLV was commissioned on 8 May 2003. It is capable of launching 2,000 kg class satellites into Geosynchronous Transfer Orbit (GTO) at 200 to 36,000 km.

of INSAT-1B. INSAT space segment consists of 21 satellites out of which 11 are in service. It is one of the largest domestic communication satellite systems in the Asia-Pacific region providing about 175 transponders in the C, Extended C and Ku-bands. It serves telecommunications, television broadcasting, weather forecasting, disaster warning and search and rescue fields.

INSAT-1A/ 10.04.1982/ First operational multi-purpose communication and mete-orology satellite procured form USA.

Remote Sensing Satellites
IRS system is India's largest constellation of Remote Sensing Satellites. It can photograph a variety of spatial resolutions starting from 360 metres and highest resolution being 2.5 metres and several spectral bands. • IRS-1A the first ever IRS launched on March 17, 1988 by Vostok (USSR) (the first ever mission – completed).

Satellite Launches: 2008-2011

Satellite	Launch Date	Launch Vehicle	Type of Satellite
GSAT-12	15.07.2011	PSLV-C17	Geo-Stationary Satellite
GSAT-8	21.05.2011	Ariane-5 VA-202	Geo-Stationary Satellite
RESOURCESAT-2	20.04.2011	PSLV-C16	Earth Observation Satellite
YOUTHSAT	20.04.2011	PSLV-C16	Experimental / Small Satellite
GSAT-5P	25.12.2010	GSLV-F06	Geo-Stationary Satellite
STUDSAT	12.07.2010	PSLV-C15	Experimental / Small Satellite
CARTOSAT-2B	12.07.2010	PSLV-C15	Earth Observation Satellite
GSAT-4	15.04.2010	GSLV-D3	Geo-Stationary Satellite
Oceansat-2	23.09.2009	PSLV-C14	Earth Observation Satellite
ANUSAT	20.04.2009	PSLV-C12	Experimental / Small Satellite
RISAT-2	20.04.2009	PSLV-C12	Earth Observation Satellite
Chandrayaan-1	22.10.2008	PSLV-C11	Space Mission
CARTOSAT - 2A	28.04.2008	PSLV-C9	Earth Observation Satellite
IMS-1	28.04.2008	PSLV-C9	Earth Observation Satellite
INSAT-4B	12.03.2007	Ariane-5ECA	Geo-Stationary Satellite
CARTOSAT - 2	10.01.2007	PSLV-C7	Earth Observation Satellite
SRE - 1	10.01.2007	PSLV-C7	Experimental / Small Satellite
INSAT-4CR	02.09.2007	GSLV-F04	Geo-Stationary Satellite
INSAT-4C	10.07.2006	GSLV-F02	Geo-Stationary Satellite
INSAT-4A	22.12.2005	Ariane-5GS	Geo-Stationary Satellite
HAMSAT	05.05.2005	PSLV-C6	Experimental / Small Satellite
CARTOSAT-1	05.05.2005	PSLV-C6	Earth Observation Satellite
EDUSAT (GSAT-3)	20.09.2004	GSLV-F01	Geo-Stationary Satellite
Resourcesat-1(IRS-P6)	17.10.2003	PSLV-C5	Earth Observation Satellite
INSAT-3A	10.04.2003	Ariane-5G	Geo-Stationary Satellite
INSAT-3E	28.09.2003	Ariane-5G	Geo-Stationary Satellite
GSAT-2	08.05.2003	GSLV-D2	Geo-Stationary Satellite
KALPANA-1(METSAT)	12.09.2002	PSLV-C4	Geo-Stationary Satellite
INSAT-3C	24.01.2002	Ariane-42L H10-3	Geo-Stationary Satellite
Technology Experiment Satellite (TES)	22.10.2001	PSLV-C3	Earth Observation Satellite
GSAT-1	18.04.2001	GSLV-D1	Geo-Stationary Satellite
INSAT-3B	22.03.2000	Ariane-5G	Geo-Stationary Satellite

Space Reuseable Launch Vehicle

India is seriously pursuing its dream for Reusable Launch Vehicle (RLV), that can go to space, deploy the payload and return to earth safely in a condition that can be refurbished, charged with propellants and sent on the next mission, repeatedly like the present day operational aircraft.

Resusable Launch Vehicle model

The launch vehicle is a complex and expensive piece of hardware by virtue of the exotic materials and cutting edge technology used in building it. The potential cost savings is in not having to spend on a new launch vehicle hardware for repeated routine transfer of men and material to space. The first phase of RLV-TD envisages re-entry and landing of the booster stage configured as a winged lifting body to facilitate aircraft like return to the spaceport after each mission.

A scale model of this craft weighs 1.5-tonne, 6.5m long with a wing span of 3.6m which will be boosted atop a 89 Solid Rocket (PSLV strap-on motor). The mission would take it up to 70 km altitude and allow it to return back to earth on an unpowered trajectory to characterise the hypersonic aerodynamics and re-entry/recovery trajectory control required for soft landing.

The realisation of proto models is progressing and the test matrix and facilities to carry out the ground tests have been finalised.

Air Breathing Propulsion

The application of air-breathing propulsion for space launch vehicles has been an attractive possibility much investigated world over. The advantage of not having to carry the oxidiser but to draw it from ambient atmosphere through which the vehicle flies during the ascent phase promises potential reduction in the vehicle size and lift-off weight as well as cost. When air-breathing propulsion is employed to a launch vehicle, a combination of seamlessly merging propulsion modes namely, the air augmented rocket mode, ramjet mode. scramjet mode and finally pure rocket mode is the preferred sequence during the ascent phase.

Cutting Edge Technology

The scramjet mode with supersonic combustion is a difficult technology and ISRO has already demonstrated 'supersonic combustion in ground tests. The flight demonstration of the scramjet mode of propulsion is planned by integrating the propulsive modules to the sustainer stage of a two stage advanced technology vehicle (ATV). The ATV-DOI flight to characterise this new vehicle along with Dual Mode Ram Jet (DMRJ) modules attached as appendages on to sustainer base shroud was successfully accomplished, implementing a real time decision (RTD) strategy for sustainer ignition timing to ensure that the Air-breathing propulsion modules can be tested in the specified Mach number/dynamic pressure window for a period of 5 to 7 sec. The overall flight outcome is quite satisfactory and the next flight will carry live and functional DMRJ modules which will be ignited and operated in flight and their net thrust will be derived from the body acceleration change.

This difficult technology has to be mastered through several well planned steps before it can be harnessed to the 'on-going operational programmes.

Mineral Resources in India

India produces as many as 86 minerals which include 4 fuel, 10 metalic, 46 non-metalic, 3 atomic minerals and 23 minor minerals (including building and ot materials). The total value of country's mineral production in 2008-09 is estimated be about ₹ 115981 crores, an increased of about 7% over the previous year. Of this, fuel minerals constituted ₹ 73063 crores (63%), metalic minerals ₹ 29189 crores (25%) and non-metalic minerals including minor minerals about ₹ 13728 crores (12%).

The classification of most of the mineral resources are based on 01. 04. 2005 United Nations Frame work Classification (UNFC) consisting of a three dimensional system with the 3 axes:
* Economic Viability
* Feasibility Assessment and
* Geological Assessment

Gold

The Principal Minerals

Bauxite
The total resources of bauxite in the country are placed at about 3,290 million tonnes. These resources are found in Odisha, Andhra Pradesh, Gujarat, Chhattisgarh, Madhya Pradesh, Jharkhand and Maharashtra. Major deposits are concentrated in the East Coast Bauxite deposits of Odisha and Andhra Pradesh.

Chromite
The total resources of Chromite is estimated at 213 million tonnes. In India 95% of these resources are located in Odisha, mostly in the Sukinda valley in Cuttack and Jai districts and the remaining 5% resources are distributed in Manipur and Karnataka and meagre quantities in the states of Jharkhand, Maharashtra, Tamil Nadu and Andhra Pradesh.

Copper
The total resources of copper ore are placed at 1.39 billion tonnes with a metal content of 11,418 thousand tonnes. Rajasthan is credited with the largest resource of copper ore at 668.5 million tonnes followed by Madhya Pradesh and Jharkhand. Copper resources are also established in Andhra Pradesh, Gujarat, Haryana, Kamataka, Maharashtra, Meghalaya, Odisha, Sikkim, Tamil Nadu, Uttarakhand and West Bengal.

Gold
There are three important gold fields in the country, namely, Kolar Gold Field -Kolar district and Hutti Gold Field - Raichur district (both in Kamataka) and Ramgiri Gold Field in Anantpur district (Andhra Pradesh). The total resources of gold ore (primary) in the country were estimated at 390.29 million tonnes with a metal content of 490.81 tonnes. The resources include placer-type gold ore in Kerala estimated at 26.12 million tonnes. Largest resources of gold ore (primary) are located in Bihar followed by Karanataka, Rajasthan, West Bangal, Andhra Pradesh, Madhya Pradesh, etc. While in terms of metal content, Karnataka remained on the top followed by Rajasthan, West Bengal,

Protecting the Ecozone | Western Ghat Ecology Expert Panel (WGEEP) is considering capping mining as the only way to protect the fragile and sensitive ecozone along the Western Ghats. The bad effects are felt in Maharashtra, Goa, Karnataka nd Kerala.

Quartz

Bihar and Andhra Pradesh.

Iron Ore

Haematite and Magnetite are the most important iron ores in India. About 60% haematite ore deposits are found in the Eastern sector and about 87% magnetite deposits occur in Southern sector, specially in Kamataka. The total resources of Iron ore are placed at 25,249 million tonnes. These resources are distributed mainly in Odisha. Jharkhand, Chhattisgarh, Kamataka and Goa. The resources of very high grade ore are limited and are restricted mainly in Bailadila sector of Chhattisgarh and to a lesser extent in Bellary-Hospet area of Kamataka and Barajamda sector in Jharkhand and Orissa. Iron ore (magnetite) resources are placed at 10,619 million tonnes. The magnetite resources are mainly found in Karnataka (74 %) and Andhra Pradesh (14%). Other deposits are located in Goa, Rajasthan, Tamil Nadu, Kerala, Asom, Jharkhand, Nagaland, Meghalaya, Bihar, Maharashtra and Odisha.

Lead-Zinc

Lead-Zinc resources are located in Rajasthan, Bihar, Maharashtra, Madhya Pradesh, Andhra Pradesh, Gujarat, Uttarakhand, West Bengal, Odisha, Sikkim, Tamil Nadu and Meghalaya. The total resources of lead and zinc ores are estimated at 522.58 million tonnes with a metal content of 7207 thousand tonnes of lead metal and 24260 thousand tonnes of zinc metal.

Manganese

The total resources of manganese are placed at 379 million tonnes. Out of these, 138 million tonnes are categorized as reserves and the balance 240 million tonnes in the remaining resources. Main deposits fall in Odisha, followed by Karnataka, Madhya Pradesh, Maharashtra, Goa and Andhra Pradesh. Minor occurrences of manganese are in Rajasthan, Gujarat, Jharkhand and West Bengal.

Nickel

The total resources of Nickel ore have been estimated at 189 million tonnes. About 92% resources, i.e. 174.48 million tonnes are in Odisha and remaining 8% are distributed in Jharkhand, Nagaland and Kamataka.

Tungsten

The total resources of tungsten ore have been estimated at 87.39 million tonnes with a with content of 142094 tonnes. All these resources are placed under 'Remaining Resources' category. The main deposits are Degana in Nagaur district, Rajasthan. It also occurs in Kamataka, Andhra Pradesh, Maharashtra, Haryana, West Bengal, Uttarakhand and West Bengal.

Barytes

The total resources of barytes in India are placed at 74 million tonnes. The Mangampet deposit in Cuddapah district (Andhra Pradesh) is the single largest barytes deposit in the world. Andhra Pradesh alone accounted for more than 94% country's resources. Minor occurrences of barytes are located in Rajasthan, West Bengal, Madhya Pradesh, Tamil Nadu, Himachal Pradesh, Maharashtra, Jharkhand, Uttarakhand, Kamataka and Haryana.

Diamond

Diamond deposits occur in three types of geological settings such as kimberlite pipes, conglomerate beds and alluvial

Almandyn

Lunar Exploration Chandrayaan II mission by ISRO will explore the possibilities on the moon surface. The Moon Impact Throbe (MIT) in Chandrayaan-1 had discovered the presence of Molecular-18, proof of water vapour on the surface of the Moon.

gravels. The main diamond bearing areas in India are Panna belt in Madhya Pradesh, Munimadugu-Banganapalie conglomerate in Kurnool district, Wajrakarur kimberlite pipe in Anantapur district, the gravels of Krishna river basin in Andhra Pradesh and dimendiferous kimberlite in Raipur, Bastar and Raigarh districts in Chhattisgarh. Reserves have been estimated in Panna belt, Madhya Pradesh, Krishna Gravels in Andhra Pradesh and in Raipur district, 'Chhattisgarh. The total resources are placed at around 4582 thousand carats.

Dolomite

Total resources of dolomite are placed at 7533 million tonnes, out of which Reserves are 985 million tonnes and the balance i.e. 6548 million tonnes are in the 'Remaining Resources'. Dolomite occurrences are widespread in almost all parts of the country. Distribution: Madhya Pradesh, Andhra Pradesh, Chhattisgarh, Odisha, Karnataka, Gujarat, Rajasthan and Maharashtra.

Fireclay

Fireclay occurs as a bedded deposit, mostly associated with coal measures Gondwana and Tertiary periods. Important deposits are associated with Jharia and Raniganj coalfields in Jharkhand and West Bengal, Korba coalfield in Chhattisgarh and Neyveli Lignite field in Tamil Nadu. Notable occurrences of fireclay not associated with coal measures are known in the state of Gujarat, Jabalpur region of Madhya Pradesh and Belpahar-Sundergarh areas of Odisha. The total resources of fireclay are about 705 million tonnes in India. The reserves are substantial but resources of high grade (non-plastic) fireclay containing more than 37% alumina are limited.

Fluorspar

The total resources of fluorite were estimated al 20.16 million tonnes. Out of these, 9.21 million tonnes were placed under 'Reserves' category and the remaining 10.95 million tonnes under Remaining Resources' category. Major deposits of Fluorspar are

Dolomite

located in Gujarat, Rajasthan, Chhattisgarh and Maharashtra.

Gypsum

The total resources of mineral Gypsum are estimated at 1,237 million tonnes. The main occurrences; of gypsum are located in Rajasthan, Jammu and Kashmir, Gujarat and Tamil Nadu. Rajasthan alone accounts for more than 80% country resource. Minor occurrences of gypsum are in Andhra Pradesh, Himachal Pradesh, Karnataka, Madhya Pradesh and Uttarakhand.

Graphite

The total resources of graphite in the country are p laced at about 168.77 million tonnes. Out of total resources, Arunachal Pradesh accounts 43% followed by J&K (37%), Jharkhand (6%). Tamil Nadu (5%) and Odishaa (3%). However, in term of reserves, Tamil Nadu has major share of about 37%.

Ilmenite

The resources of Ilmenite are 461.37 million tonnes as per Department of Atomic Energy. Ilmenite occurs mainly in beach sand deposits right from Ratnagiri (Maharashtra) to coast in Kerala, Tamil Nadu and Odisha. The mineral is also found in Andhra Pradesh, Bihar and West Bengal.

Kaolin

India possesses fairly large resources of china clay. The total resources are about 2596 million tonnes out of which, 222 million tonnes are placed in reserves category. The occurrences of china clay are distributed in Kerala, West Bengal, Rajasthan, Odisha,

Karnataka, Jharkhand, Gujarat Meghalaya, Andhra Pradesh and Tamil Nadu.

Limestone

The total resources of limestone of all categories and grades are estimated at 175345 million tonnes. Of which 12,715 million tonnes under 'Reserves' category and 162,630 million tonnes are under 'Remaining reources' category. Karnataka is the leading state followed by Andhra Pradesh, Gujarat, Rajasthan, Meghalaya, Chhattisgarh, Madhya Pradesh, Odisha, Maharashtra and Uttarakhand.

Mica

Important mica bearing pegmatite ore occurs in Andhra Pradesh, Jharkhand, Maharashtra, Bihar and Rajasthan. The total resources of mica in the country are estimated at 393,855 tonnes, out of which only 68570 nes are placed under 'Reserves' category. 'Remaining resources' are placed at 325,285 tonnes. Rajasthan accounts for about 51% resources, followed by Andhra Pradesh, Maharashtra and Bihar.

Magnesite

The total resources of magnesite are about 338 million tonnes, of which reserves and remaining resources are 76 million tonnes and 262 million tonnes, respectively. Substantial quantities of resources are established Uttarkhand (68%) followed by Rajasthan (16%) and Tamil Nadu (13%). Andhra Pradesh, Himachal Pradesh, J&K, Karnataka and Kerala contribute for the balance.

Kyanite And Sillimanite

The total resources of kyanite and sillimanite are 103 million tonnes and 74 million tonnes, respectively. Kyanite deposits are located in Maharashtra, Karnataka, Jharkhand, Rajasthan, Andhra Pradesh, Kerala, Tamil Nadu and West Bengal. Sillimanite

Fealdspar

resources are found mainly in Odisha, Tamil Nadu, Uttar Pradesh, Kerala, Andhra Pradesh, Asom and West Bengal with minor occurrences in Jharkhand, Karnataka, Madhya Pradesh, Maharashtra, Meghalaya and Rajasthan.

Phosphate Minerals

Deposits of phosphorites are located in Madhya Pradesh, Rajasthan, Uttarakhand, Jharkhand, Uttar Pradesh and Gujarat. Besides, apatite deposits of commercial portance are reported from Jharkhand, West

Soap Stone

Bengal, Andhra Pradesh, Tamil Nadu and Rajasthan. The total resources of apatite are estimated at 26.86 million tonnes. Out of the total resources, the bulk 61% are located in West Bengal. The total resource of rock phosphate are placed at 305 million tonnes. Bulk of reserves are located in Rajasthan and Madhya Pradesh.

Other Minerals

Other minerals occurring in significant quantities in India are **bentonite** (Rajasthan, Gujarat, Tamil Nadu, Jharkhand and Jammu and Kashmir), **calcite** (Andhra Pradesh, Rajasthan, Madhya Pradesh, Tamil Nadu, Haryana, Karnataka, Uttar Pradesh and Gujarat), **fuller's earth** (Rajasthan, Andhra Pradesh, Arunachal Pradesh, Asom, Madhya Pradesh and Karnataka), **garnet** (Tamil Nadu, Odisha Andhra Pradesh, Rajasthan and Kerala), **pyrites** (Bihar, Rajasthan, Karnataka, Himachal Pradesh, West Bengal and Andhra Pradesh), **steatite** (Rajasthan, Uttarakhand, Kerala, Maharashtra, Andhra Pradesh and Madhya Pradesh), **wollastonite** (Rajasthan Gujarat), **zircon** (beach sand of Kerala, Tamil Nadu, Andhra Pradesh and Odisha and **quartz and silica** minerals are widespread and occur in nearly all states. **Granite** is mainly mined in Tamil Nadu, Karnataka, Andhra Pradesh and Rajasthan; **marble** in Rajasthan, Gujarat and Madhya Pradesh; **slate** in Madhya Pradesh and Andhra Pradesh **sandstone** in Rajasthan.

A Cybersecurity Agreement

Jennifer McIntyre
Consul General of the United States of America, Chennai

The MOU shows a commitment by both nations to advance global security and thwart online terrorism, by fighting cyber crime and its various forms, including malware, worm and virus attacks.

The United States and India took another step toward enhancing their relationship in 2011, agreeing to closer cooperation and timely exchangeof information on cyber security.Almost exactly two years to the day from the launch of the U.S.-India Strategic Dialogue, the world's oldest and largest democracies ratified a Memorandum of Understanding (MOU) on cybersecurity. The historic agreement was signed in New Delhi on July 19 while U.S. Secretary of State Hillary Clinton was in India's capital for the second annual meeting of the U.S.-India Strategic Dialogue. The pact, signed by Jane Holl Lute, Deputy Secretary of the U.S. Department of Homeland Security (DHS) and R. Chandrashekhar, Secretary of the India Department of Information Technology, sets forth a plan for the two countries' Computer Emergency Response Teams (CERT-IN and US-CERT) to exchange information with dispatch and best practices on cyber attacks and cybersecurity policies. The MOU shows a commitment by both nations to advance global security and thwart online terrorism, by fighting cyber crime and its various forms, including malware, worm and virus attacks.

Strategic Dialogue

A statement about the agreement reads: "Through this arrangement, the respective governments and broader cybersecurity communities in both the United States and India will have the ability to coordinate with their counterparts on a broad range of technical and operational cyber issues." The agreement was finalized during cyber consultations held by the two countries' National Security Councils on July 18. The decision to craft the agreement was made by the co-chairs of the Indo-U.S. Information, Communication and Technology Working Group Ambassador Phillip Verveer and, then, Department of Information Technology Secretary Shashi Kant Sharma during the December 2010 meeting in New Delhi. Further details were discussed in May 2011 when U.S. Secretary of Homeland Security Janet Napolitano traveled to India. Napolitano and Indian Minister of Home Affairs P. Chidambaram launched the U.S.-India Homeland Security Dialogue (HSD). The HSD marked the first expansive discussions of homeland security issues conducted by the two countries. Much the way virtual technology – and the potential for undermining it – is moving at lightning speed, negotiations to create the non-binding agreement wrapped up quickly at a June meeting of the Indo-U.S. Information, Communication and Technology Working Group in Washington, D.C.

Cybersecurity is a key element of the Strategic Dialogue, which also includes cooperation on a variety of other issues, including education, science, trade, and health. Secretary of State Clinton and India External Affairs Minister S.M. Krishna launched the U.S.-India Strategic Dialogue on July 20, 2009 to formalize relations between the two countries. U.S. President Barack Obama has described the friendly nature of the relationship as "the defining partnership of the 21st Century." Clinton continued that theme with a policy speech in Chennai on July 20, 2011 which she gave under the banner: "India and the United States: A Vision for the 21st Century." "I am very pleased to report to you that our work together is producing real results," Clinton told a full house at the Anna Centenary Library that day. "We have worked together for the important task of preventing cyber attacks on our respective infrastructures." ∎

Crime in India

Crime is not gender specific. Both men and women have moral codes and both are equal. Men have more testosterone and are typically more aggressive which might make them more prone to committing crimes, but women are more likely to be psychotic. Crimes are crimes. Violent crimes are bad because it ruin lives, ruin harmony in the society and instill fear. The crime rate defined as the 'number of crimes' per 1,00,000 population is universally taken as a realistic indicator since it balances the effect of growth in population.

The Criminal Procedure Code (Cr.P.C.) divides all the crimes into two categories: (i) Cognizable - Sec.2(c) CrPC and (ii) Non-cognizable - Sec.2(l) CrPC.

Cognizable Crimes

A cognizable offence or case is defined as the one which an officer in-charge of a police station may investigate without the order of a magistrate and affect arrest without warrant. The police has a direct responsibility to take immediate action on the receipt of a complaint or of credible information in such crimes, visit the scene of the crime, investigate the facts, apprehend the offender and arraign him before a court of law having jurisdiction over the matter. Cognizable crimes are broadly categorised as those falling either under the 'Indian Penal Code (IPC)' or

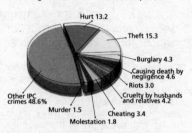

Percentage Distribution of IPC Crimes, 2009

Hurt 13.2
Theft 15.3
Burglary 4.3
Causing death by negligence 4.6
Riots 3.0
Other IPC crimes 48.6%
Cruelty by husbands and relatives 4.2
Murder 1.5
Cheating 3.4
Molestation 1.8

under the 'Special and Local Laws (SLL)'.

Non-Cognizable Offence

Non-Cognizable crimes are defined as those which can not be investigated by police without the order of a competent magistrate. Police does not initiate investigation in non-cognizable crimes except with magisterial permission. First schedule of the Cr.P.C. gives the classification of the offences of the IPC into cognizable & non-cognizable categories. The various crimes that are being registered and investigated by different law enforcement agencies are broadly grouped under the following categories for Statistical Information System.

Cognizable crimes

As many as 66,75,217 cognizable crimes were reported in the country during 2009

Crimes under the Indian Penal Code (IPC)

i) Crimes Against Body: Murder, Its attempt, Culpable Homicide not amounting to Murder, Kidnapping & Abduction, Hurt, Causing Death by Negligence.
ii) Crimes Against Property: Dacoity, its preparation & assembly, Robbery, Burglary, Theft.
iii) Crimes Against Public Order: Riots, Arson.
iv) Economic Crimes: Criminal Breach of Trust, Cheating, Counterfeiting.

v) Crimes Against Women: Rape, Dowry Death, Cruelty by Husband and Relatives, Molestation, Sexual Harassment and Importation of Girls.
vi) Crimes Against Children: Child Rape, Kidnapping & Abduction of Children, Procuration of minor girls, Selling/Buying of girls for Prostitution, Abetment to Suicide, Exposure and Abandonment, Infanticide, Foeticide.
vii) Other IPC crimes.

Percentage Distribution of SLL Crimes, 2009

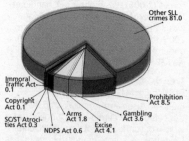

Other SLL crimes 81.0
Immoral Traffic Act 0.1
Copyright Act 0.1
SC/ST Atrocities Act 0.3
NDPS Act 0.6
Arms Act 1.8
Excise Act 4.1
Gambling Act 3.6
Prohibition Act 8.5

Road Accidental Deaths	
(by type of vehicles for all India- 2009)	
Truck/Lorry	24968
Bus	12683
Tempo/Van	7328
Jeep	9820
Car	11682
3-wheeler	6616
2-Wheeler	26219
Bicycles	3267
Pedestrians	11109
Total	**1,26,896**

comprising 21.21 lakh cases under the IPC and 45.53 lakh cases under the SLL. The ratio of IPC to SLL crimes varied from 1:1.76 in 2005 to 1:2.15 in 2009. In terms of percentage, 68.2% of total cases (IPC + SLL) during 2009 were accounted for by Special Acts & Local Laws and the rest of the cases (31.8%) by the Indian Penal Code. The rate of total crimes (IPC + SLL) was 570.8 in 2009 showing an increase of 25.23% over 2005 and an increase of 10.83% over 2008.

Crime Incidence (IPC + SLL) (Incidence: 66,75,217) Total incidence of crime gives an absolute picture of the crime situation in the country or the State. Comparative figures over a period of time indicate an increase or decrease in the incidence of crime requiring appropriate crime control efforts by the State police.

The IPC crimes reported a higher growth rate of 20.2% as compared to the fast pace of population growth of 18.5% in the decade. The crime rate in respect of IPC crimes has decreased marginally from 181.5 in 2008 to 181.4 in 2009 and that for SLL crimes has increased by 16.8% from 333.4 in 2008 to 389.4 in 2009.

Trends: Crimes Against Body

These comprise murder and its attempt, culpable homicide not amounting to murder, kidnapping & abduction, hurt and causing death by negligence as defined in the beginning of the chapter. A total of 4,76,943 crimes were reported under this head in the country accounting for 22.5% of the total IPC crimes during the year 2009. Crimes Against Body showed an

Crimes under the Special and Local Laws (SLL)

i) Relating to Arms
ii) Relating to Narcotic Drugs & Psychotropic Substances
iii) Relating to Gambling
iv) Relating to Excise
v) Relating to Prohibition
vi) Relating to Explosives & Explosive Substances
vii) Relating to Immoral Traffic
viii) Relating to Railways
ix) Relating to Registration of Foreigners
x) Relating to Protection of Civil Rights
xi) Relating to Indian Passport
xii) Relating to Essential Commodities
xiii) Relating to Terrorist & Disruptive Activities
xiv) Relating to Antiquities & Art Treasures
xv) Relating to Dowry Prohibition
xvi) Relating to Child Marriage Restraint
xvii) Relating to Indecent Representation of Women
xiii) Relating to Copyright
xix) Relating to Sati
xx) Relating to SC/ST (Atrocities)
xxi) Relating to Forest
xxii) Other crimes (not specified above) under Special and Local Laws including Cyber Laws under Information Technology

Crime Against Children - Statewise distribution, 2009 / 2008

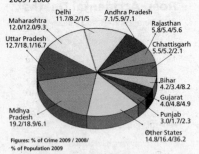

Delhi 11.7/8.2/1/5
Andhra Pradesh 7.1/5.9/7.1
Maharashtra 12.0/12.0/9.3
Uttar Pradesh 12.7/18.1/16.7
Rajasthan 5.8/5.4/5.6
Chhattisgarh 5.5/5.2/2.1
Bihar 4.2/3.4/8.2
Gujarat 4.0/4.8/4.9
Punjab 3.0/1.7/2.3
Mdhya Pradesh 19.2/18.9/6.1
Other States 14.8/16.4/36.2

Figures: % of Crime 2009 / 2008/
% of Population 2009

increase of 0.9% during 2009 over 2008. The share of these crimes to total IPC crimes was highest in Andhra Pradesh at 35.6% compared to National average of 22.5%. The rate of crimes against body was also second highest in Andhra Pradesh (77.2 per lakh population) after UT of Puducherry (111.1) compared to National rate of 40.8.

Trends: Crimes Against Property

These comprise Dacoity, its preparation & assembly, robbery, burglary and theft. A total of 4,46,110 such crimes were reported during 2009 as compared to 4,38,772 crimes during 2008 showing an increase of 1.7%. The share of these crimes to total IPC crimes at the National level was 21.0% during the year.

The share of these crimes (56.4%) to total IPC crimes (2,006) was highest in Chandigarh. The share of such crimes in the country was around 21% in each of the year from 2005 to 2009. The average rate of crime under this head in the country during 2009 was 38.1.

Trends: Crimes Against Public Order

Riots and Arson are the major components of this category of crimes against public order which constitute 3.4% of the total IPC crimes. Incidence of crimes under this head has decreased by 4.8% from 75,267 in 2008 to 71,678 in 2009. The rate of such crimes has marginally decreased from 6.5 in 2008 to 6.1 in 2009. The rate of such crime was highest in Lakshadweep at 64.8 as compared to National average of 6.1.

Crimes comprising Criminal Breach of Trust, Cheating and Counterfeiting, showed an increase of 6.9% in 2009 as there were 91,979 reported crimes as compared to 86,057 in 2008. The rate of such crimes varied from 6.3 to 7.9 during 2005 to 2009. These crimes have accounted for 4.3% of the total IPC crimes. Rajasthan and Punjab reported the highest share of 9.6% each of these crimes to its IPC component which has also reported the highest crime rate of 24.1 as compared to National average of 7.9.

Crime Against Sceduled Castes

% Crime for 2009 / 2008 / % of Popn 2009

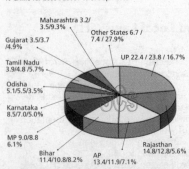

Maharashtra 3.2/ 3.5/9.3%
Other States 6.7 / 7.4 / 27.9%
Gujarat 3.5/3.7 /4.9%
UP 22.4 / 23.8 / 16.7%
Tamil Nadu 3.9/4.8 /5.7%
Odisha 5.1/5.5/3.5%
Karnataka 8.5/7.0/5.0%
MP 9.0/8.8 6.1%
Bihar 11.4/10.8/8.2%
AP 13.4/11.9/7.1%
Rajasthan 14.8/12.8/5.6%

Crime Against Sceduled Tribe

% Crime for 2009 / 2008 / % of Popn 2009

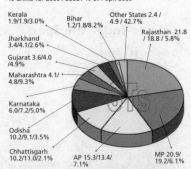

Kerala 1.9/1.9/3.0%
Bihar 1.2/1.8/8.2%
Other States 2.4 / 4.9 / 42.7%
Jharkhand 3.4/4.1/2.6%
Rajasthan 21.8 / 18.8 / 5.8%
Gujarat 3.6/4.0 /4.9%
Maharashtra 4.1/ 4.8/9.3%
Karnataka 6.0/7.2/5.0%
Odisha 10.2/9.1/3.5%
Chhattisgarh 10.2/11.0/2.1%
AP 15.3/13.4/ 7.1%
MP 20.9/ 19.2/6.1%

Newborn Deaths

Newborn deaths account for 41 p.c. of child deaths, according to a study reported in PLoS Medicine. The number of newborn deaths in India - over 9 lakh a year - is the highest in the world. Nigeria, Pakistan, China and DR of Congo also report high child death percentages.

Prisons in India

Ministry of Home Affairs is responsible for Prison administration •Prison population total (including pre-trial detainees /remand prisoners): 376,396 at 31.12.2007 (National Crime Records Bureau) • Prison population rate (per 100,000 of national population): 32 based on an estimated national population of 1,160.9 million at end of 2007 (from United Nations figures) • Pre-trial detainees / remand prisoners (percentage of prison population): 66.6% (31.12.2007) • Female prisoners (percentage of prison population): 4.1% (31.12.2007)•Juveniles/minors/young prisoners incl.definition(% of prison population): 0.1%(31.12.2007-under18)•Foreign prisoners (percentage of prison population): 1.3% (31.12.2007) • Number of establishments / institutions: 1,276 *(31.12.2007 - comprising 113 central jails, 309 district jails, 769 sub jails, 16 women's jails, 28 open jails, 25 special jails, 10 Borstal schools and 6 other jails)* •Official capacity of prison system: 277,304 (31.12.2007)

•Occupancy level (based on official capacity): 135.7% (31.12.2007)

Recent Prison Population Trend:

Year	Prison pop. total	Prison pop. rate
2001	313,635	(30)
2007	376,396	(32)

According to the Home Ministry, prisons are overcrowded by more than 135%, mainly due to inmates on remand. Many of India's nearly 1,300 jails are thought to contain at least double the number of prisoners they were originally built to house. There are 250,000 undertrials. Seven out of every ten persons in jail are in this situation. In some jails as high as 300%. Inmates sleep in shifts.

High Security Jails: Tihar Jail, New Delhi; Cellular Jail, Andaman Islands; Alipore Jail, Kolkata; Vellore Central Prison, Vellore; Arthur Road Jail, Mumbai; Chanchalguda Central Jail, Chanchalguda; Hyderabad Jail, Hyderabad; Raipur Prison, Raipur.

Tihar Jail

Started in 1958, it was a maximum security prison run by the State of Punjab. In 1966 control was transferred to the National Capital Territory of Delhi.The prison status is open type and has a capacity for 6250 prisoners. Beginning in 1984 additional facilities were constructed, and it became the Tihar Prison. After a number of prison reforms,its name has been changed to Tihar Ashram. The Integrated Counseling and Testing Centre reports that around 6% to 8% of the 11,800 Tihar inmates are HIV positive, which is considerably much higher than the general population HIV rate in India Inmates include Charles Sobraj (international serial killer); Ripun Bora, (former education minister of the Asom, the main accused in the Daniel Topno murder case); 2G spectrum scamsters — A. Raja, M. K. Kanimozhi, Vinod

Goenka, Shahid Balwa and Sanjay Chandra; 2010 Commonwealth Games scamster - Suresh Kalmadi (former president of Indian Olympic Association, arrested for alleged corruption). Notable inmates include Anna Hazare, Arvind Kejriwal (Indian social activists fighting for Jan-Lokpal Bill).

Communications

India has the largest postal network in the world. Lord Clive in 1766 started the postal system, which was further developed by Warren Hastings by establishing the Calcutta G.P.O. under a Postmaster General in the year 1774. In the other Presidencies of Madras and Bombay, the General Post Offices came into existence in 1786 and 1793 respectively. The Act of 1837 first regulated the Post Office on a uniform basis to unite the post office organisation throughout the three Presidencies into one all-India Service. The Post Office Act of 1854 reformed the entire fabric of the postal system, and the Post Office of India was placed on the present administrative footing on 1st October 1854. The statute presently governing the postal services in the country is the Indian Post Office Act, 1898.

Besides providing postal communication facilities, the post office network has also provided facilities for remittance of funds, banking and insurance services from the latter half of the 19 th century.

Postal Network

At the time of Independence there were 23,344 post offices throughout the country. Of these 19,184 post offices were in the rural areas and 4,160 in the urban areas. As on 31 March 2009 the country has 1,55,035 post offices, of which, 1,39,144 are in rural areas and 15,871 in urban areas. On an average in India, a post office serves an area of 21.21sq km, and a population of 7175. Post Offices are opened subject to satisfaction of norms regarding population, income and distance stipulated by the Department.There is an element of subsidy for opening post offices in rural areas, which is to the extent of 85% of the cost in hilly, desert and inaccessible areas, and 67% of the cost in normal rural areas.

The postal network consists of four categories of post offices, viz, Head Post Offices, Sub-Post Offices, Extra Departmental Sub-Post Offices and Extra Departmental Branch Post Offices. All categories of Post Offices retail similar postal services, while delivery function is restricted to specified offices. In terms of management control, accounts are consolidated progressively from Branch Post Offices to Sub-Post Offices and finally in Head Post Offices.

The post offices currently offer financial services like savings bank, postal life insurance, pension payments and money transfer services. Its total corpus stood at ₹ 5,82, 832.9 crore as on March 31, 2011.

The Department of Posts' revenue grew 11 per cent to ₹ 6,954.09 crore in 2010-2011 from ₹ 6,266.70 crore in 2009-2010. However, negative growth rate in some circles pushed its deficit to ₹ 6,625 crore in the financial year 2011, almost equal to the annual revenue of the department. There is a proposal to convert over 1.5 lakh post offices across the nation into full-fledged banks.

The Department has about 2.10 lakh departmental employees and about 2.73 lakhs Gramin Dak Sevaks. Their training needs are met through a well-developed training infrastructure.

| A Sacred Tree | The banyan is considered a sacred tree in India. It is a long evergreen which can reach a height of 26 m. Its huge horizontal branches grow aerial roots which hang down. These branches eventually act as supporting struts. |

Postal code

Postal Index Number (PIN) is a 6 digit code. There are nine PIN zones in India, including eight regional zones and one functional zone. The first digit indicates one of the regions, the first 2 digits together indicate sub region or one of the postal circles. The first 3 digits together indicate a sorting/revenue district. The last 3 digits refer to the delivery post office.

Postcode Areas in India

First 2/3 Digits of PIN Postal Circle

11	Delhi
12 and 13	Haryana
14 to 15	Punjab
16	Chandigarh
17	Himachal Pradesh
18 to 19	Jammu & Kashmir
20 to 28	Uttar Pradesh/Uttrakhand
30 to 34	Rajasthan
36 to 39	Gujarat
40	Goa
40 to 44	Maharastra
45 to 48	Madhya Pradesh
49	Chattisgarh
50 to 53	Andhra Pradesh
56 to 59	Karnataka
60 to 64	Tamil Nadu
67 to 69	Kerala
682	Lakshadweep (Islands)
70 to 74	West Bengal
744	Andaman & Nicobar Islands
75 to 77	Orissa
78	Assam
79	Arunachal Pradesh
793, 794, 783123	Meghalaya
795	Manipur
796	Mizoram
799	Tripura
80 to 85	Bihar and Jharkhand

Hundred Years of Airmail

India Post celebrated the centenary of the World's official airmail flight on February 18. It was in 1911, on the same day a flight carried 6,500 letters from Allahabad to Naini. To commemorate the occasion a set of four stamps on aero philately was issued at Allahabad on February 12, 2011. The historic flight was also re-enacted, courtesy Indian Air Force. Post is said to be the treasure house of history but even the way it was carried and delivered, makes an interesting piece of history.

The glory came accidentally in an interesting unfolding of events. The idea of the World's First Official air mail was born out of a fund raising request to an invitee to the Allahabad exhibition in 1910 to demonstrate aero planes. The mail flight flew on February 18, 1911, two days earlier than planned. Thousands of Indian citizens witnessed French Pilot Henry Pequet's take off. At least one million Indians were in Allahabad at that time to observe the religious festival of Purna Kumbh held only once in 12 years.

Henri Pequet flying the Humber biplane took off around 5.00 PM from the aviation ground, circled around twice and then flew across the river Yamuna to Naini Junction creating history by carrying approximately 6500 letters and cards on the first official airmail flight. Among these letters of many eminent people was one from Pt. Motilal Nehru to his son Jawaharlal Nehru. In contrast to his departure from Allahabad, Pequet descended to be greeted by only a postal employee. He handed over the mail bag and returned to Allahabad. The entire trip lasted around 30 minutes. The mail was then transported further by surface to their destination all over the world. After Allahabad the Windham team proceeded to Bombay for another appearance before departing for home. Windham used his experience in India for organizing the well known Hendon to Windsor (U.K.) and return flight for the coronation, Aerial Post of September 1911. Windham was Knighted in 1923, and made a freeman of the city of London in 1933.

Transport

Roads

India has one of the largest road networks in the world, aggregating to about 3.62 million kilometres at present. The country's road network consists of National Highways, State Highways, major / other district roads and village/rural roads. Though the National Highways, which is the responsibility of the Central Government, has about 70,934 km length and comprises only 2 per cent of the total length of roads, it carries over 40 per cent of the total traffic across the length and breadth of the country.

National Highways, State Highways, major / other district roads and village/rural roads

National Highways/Expressways	70,934 KM
State Highways	1,33,000 KM
Major and other District Roads	34,17,000 KM
Rural Roads	26,50,000 KM

The National Highways have further been classified depending upon the carriageway width of the Highway. Generally, a lane has a width of 3.75 m in case of single lane and 3.5 m per lane in case of multilane National Highways. The break-up of National Highways in terms of width is as under:

The Break-up of National Highways in terms of width

Single Lane	28%
Double/Intermediate Lanes	53.5%
Four Lane/Six Lane/Eight Lane	18.5%

About 60 per cent of freight and 87.4 per cent passenger traffic is carried by the roads. The number of vehicles has been growing growing at an average pace of around 10 per cent per annum (2001-2002 to 2005-2006). The share of road traffic in total traffic has grown from 13.8 per cent of freight traffic 15.4 per cent of passenger traffic in 1950-51 to an estimated 60 per cent of freight traffic and 87.4 per cent of passenger traffic by the end of 2005-06.

Railways

The Railways in India provide the principal mode of transportation for freight and passengers. It brings together people from the farthest corners of the country and makes possible the conduct of business, sightseeing, pilgrimage and education. The Indian Railways have been a great integrating force during the last more than 155 years. It has bound the economic life of the country and helped in accelerating the development of industry and agriculture. From a very modest beginning in 1853, when the first train steamed off from Mumbai to Thane, a distance of 34 kilometres Indian Railways have grown into a vast network of 7,030 stations spread over a route length of 64,015 kilometres, with a fleet of 8,592 locomotives, 49,110 passenger service vehicles, 5,985 other coaching vehicles and 2,11,763 wagons as on 31st March, 2009.

Private Funded Metro — India's first fully privately funded metro project to be operational by Jan. 2013 is Gurgaon's rapid metro. Trains on the corridor will have coaches made of aluminium with air-conditioning to cope with temperature above 50°C.

Guage	Route Km	Running Track Km	Total Track Km
Broad Guage (1.676 mm)	52,808	75,228	27,95,965
Metre Gauge (1.000 mm)	8,473	8,973	10,656
Narrow Guage (762 mm and 610 mm)	2,734	2,736	3,043
Total	64,015	86,937	1,13,115

The growth of Indian Railways in the 150 years of its existence is thus phenomenal. It has played a vital role in the economic, industrial and social development of the country. The network runs multi-gauge operations extending over 64,015 route kilometres.

The gauge-wise route and track lengths of the system as on 31st March, 2008 are as under:

About 29 per cent of the route kilometre, 41 per cent of running track kilometer and 42 per cent of total track kilometre is

electrified. The network is divided into 16 Zones. Divisions are the basic operating units. The 16 zones and their respective headquarters are given below:

The rolling stock fleet of Indian Railways in services as on 31st March 2008 comprised 44 steam, 4,843 diesel and 3,443 electric locomotives. Currently, the Railways are in the process of inducting new designs of fuel-efficient locomotives of higher horse power, high-speed coaches and modern bogies for freight traffic. Modern signalling like panel inter-locking, route relay inter-locking, centralized traffic control, automatic signalling and multi-aspect colour light signalling are being progressively introduced. The Indian Railways have made impressive progress regarding indigenous production of rolling stock and variety of other equipment over the years and is now self-sufficient in most of the items.

Railways Network Zones and Headquarters

Zonal Railways	Headquarters
Central Railway	Mumbai CST
Northern Railway	New Delhi
North Eastern Railway	Gorakhpur
North-East Frontier Railway	Maligaon (Guwahati)
Southern Railway	Chennai
South Central Railway	Secunderabad
South Eastern Railway	Kolkata
Western Railway	Church Gate, Mumbai
East Central Railway	Hajipur
East Coast Railway	Bhubaneswar
North Central Railway	Allahabad
North Western Railway	Jaipur
South East Central Railway	Bilaspur
South Western Railway	Hubli
West Central Railway	Jabalpur

Ports

The coastline of India is dotted with 12 major ports and about 200 Non-major Ports. The major ports are under the purview of the central government while the

Delhi-Patna in Five Hours — A British firm Mott Macdonald is to conduct a pre-feasibility study of the 993 - km - long Delhi-Patna route. The proposed high speed train will cover Delhi-Patna in five hours, as against the 12 hours taken by Delhi-Patna Rajdhani.

Shipping

Shipping plays an important role in the transport sector of India's economy. About 95 per cent of the country's trade by volume (68 per cent in terms of value) is moved by sea. India has the largest merchant shipping fleet among the developing countries and ranks 16th amongst the countries with the largest cargo carrying fleet with 10.11 million GT as on 31.08.2010 and the average of the fleet being 18.03 years. Indian maritime sector facilitates not only transportation of national and international cargo but also provides a variety of other services such as cargo handling services, shipbuilding and ship repairing, freight forwarding, lighthouse facilities and training of marine personnel, etc.

India's shipping policy aims at the promotion of national shipping to increase self-reliance in the country's overseas trade and protection of stakeholders' interest in EXIM trade.

at the end of the 10th Plan (i.e. as on 31st March, 2007) thereby achieving the capacity addition 160.80 MTPA. In all the years of 10th Five Year Plan the capacity at the major ports exceeded the traffic handled. The non-major ports handled traffic of 185.54 MT in 2006-07 and had a capacity of 228 MTPA at the end of 2006-07.

The total traffic handled at the Major Ports has increased from 313.55 MT at the beginning of the 10th Five Year Plan to 519.67 MT in 2007-08 out of which the container traffic was 73.48 MT. The container traffic in the major ports has increased from 61.98 MT in 2005-06 to 78.87 MT is 2007-08.

In order to improve efficiency, productivity and quality of services as well as to bring in competitiveness in port services, the port sector has been thrown open to private sector participation. The Major Port Trust Act, 1963, permits private sector participation in major ports, Foreign Direct Investment (FDI) up to 100% under the automatic route is permitted for construction and maintenance of ports and harbours. Private sector participation has been allowed in a variety of ports services which includes construction and operation of terminals/berths, warehousing/storage facility, dry docking and ship repair facilities.

Non-major ports come under the jurisdiction of the respective state governments. The 12 major ports (including the port of Ennore which is a corporate port set up under the Indian Companies Act, 1956) are evenly spread out on the Eastern and Western coast. The ports of Kolkata, Paradip, Visakhapatnam. Chennai, Ennore and Tuticorin are on the Eastern coast of India while the ports of Cochin, New Mangalore, Mormugao, Mumbai, Jawaharlal Nehru at Jhavasheva and Kandla are on the Western Coast.

The capacity of major ports has increased from 20 million tonnes per annum (MTPA) in 1951 to 504.75 MTPA as on 31st March, 2007. At the beginning of the 10th Plan, the capacity of the major ports was 343.95 MTPA which has increased to 504.75 MTPA

Till date 17 private sector projects involving an investment of ₹ 4927 crores have been operationalised which involves capacity addition of 99.30 MTPA. Eight projects are under various stages of evaluation and implementation which involves an investment of ₹ 5181 crores and capacity addition of 75.40 MTPA.

A Low-Cost Car

Government of India set up a committee headed by L.K. Jha in 1959 to look into the possibility of making a low-cost car for ₹ 5000 -7000. Proposals included models such as Baby Hindustan, Baby Fiat, DKW, Renault, and Standard.

Civil Aviation

Civil aviation in India is in the limelight as this year, 2011, marks its centenary celebrations in India.

Civil aviation is one of two major categories of flying, which covers all forms of non-military aviation. It includes both private and commercial aviation. Most countries in the world are members of the Montreal-based International Civil Aviation Organization (ICAO), which is a specialized agency of the United Nations, and work together to establish common standards and recommended practices. India ratified the Convention on International Civil Aviation (the Chicago Convention) on March 1, 1947. The Ministry of Civil Aviation (MoCA), Government of India, is responsible for civil aviation in India and ensuring India's compliance with the Chicago Convention. The MoCA establishes the overall aviation policy for civil aviation in India. The Directorate General of Civil Aviation (DGCA) is the overall safety regulator.

Civil aviation in India is in the limelight as this year, 2011, marks its centenary celebrations in India. On February 18, 1911, the first commercial plane flew in India between Allahabad and Naini with a consignment of mails. It has been a huge leap since then and its growth has ensured that India is now the ninth largest civil aviation market in the world. Centenary celebrations have been organized all over India across the period 2011-2012.

According to the Ministry of Civil Aviation, the first commercial flight was between Allahabad and Naini over a distance of six miles. Its pilot, Henri Piquet, had a consignment of 6,500 pieces of mail in his Humber biplane. In addition to heralding the beginning of civil aviation in India, it is also considered to be the world's first airmail service.

The next year, in December 1912, Indian State Air Services in collaboration with the U.K.-based Imperial Airways introduced its London-Karachi- Delhi flight, the first international flight to and from India. In 1915, Tata Sons Ltd. started regular air mail services between Karachi and Madras. On January 24, 1920, the Royal Air Force started regular airmail services between Karachi and Bombay.

The building of civil airports began in 1924. Constructions began in Calcutta at Dum Dum, in Allahabad at Bamrauli and in Bombay at Gilbert Hill.

In April 1927, a department of Civil Aviation was set up to look after issues on civil aviation matters. The Aero Club of India was formed.

In February 1929, the legendary J.R.D. Tata was awarded the first pilot license

Too Few Cars	Automobile output in India doubled in the 50s. From 14,602 units in 1950 it rose to 26,800 units in 1985, still reflecting a tiny sector.

by Federation Aeronautique International on behalf of the Aero Club of India and Burma.

In 1931, Lt. Col. Shelmerdine was appointed the first Director General of Civil Aviation to look after civil aviation regulatory issues.

1932 saw Tata Sons Limited forming Tata Airlines. It launched air mail services on the Karachi, Ahmedabad, Bombay, Bellary, Madras routes on October 15. (J.R.D. Tata, the father of civil aviation in India and founder of Air India, took off from Karachi, in a single-engined aircraft on a flight to Bombay via Ahmedabad.) The same year, 1932, also saw Urmila K. Parikh become the first Indian woman to be granted a pilot's license.

The years 1933 and 1934 were busy with a number of operators such as Indian Trans Continental Airways, Madras Air Taxi Services and Indian National Airways starting operations.

The Indian Aircraft Act was promulgated in 1934 and formulated in 1937.

Hindustan Aeronautics Limited (HAL) was started by Walchand Hirachand in association with the then Mysore Government in 1940 at Bangalore.

India's first aircraft, the Harlow trainer was made ready for a test flight in July 1941.

In 1946, Tata Airlines changed its name to Air India.

In 1948, Air India signed an agreement with the Government to operate international services under the name Air India International Ltd. On June 8, it started its international services with a weekly flight between Bombay and London via Cairo and Geneva. Prem Mathur became the first woman commercial pilot and started flying for Deccan Airways, a venture between the Nizam of Hyderabad and the Tatas. She obtained her commercial pilot's license in 1947.

In March 1953, Parliament passed the Air Corporations Act. Indian Airlines and Air India International were set up after na-

tionalisation of the airline industry. Eight domestic airlines were merged.

Civil helicopter services were introduced in 1953.

In 1956, Indian Airlines inducted its first woman pilot, Ms. Durba Banerjee.

India entered the jet age in 1960 with the introduction of the Boeing 707 into Air India. India was also linked with the U.S.

In 1972, the International Airports Authority of India (IAAI) was constituted.

In 1984, Squadron Leader Rakesh Sharma of Indian Air Force became the first Indian cosmonaut and the 138th man in space spending eight days in space abroad Salyut 7.

In 1985, Indian Airlines achieved a landmark when it operated its first all women crew flight on the Calcutta-Silchar route.

Pawan Hans Helicopters Limited (PHHL)

and the Indira Gandhi Rashtriya Uran Academy (IGRUA) in Fursatganj, Rai Bareli in Uttar Pradesh to train pilots were set up in 1985.

After an Air India flight was lost in a terrorist act over the Atlantic Ocean in 1985, it led to changes and the

Women in Aviation

Bureau of Civil Aviation Security was established in 1987.

The National Airports Authority was constituted in 1986.

The period 1990-91 saw the entry of private airlines after the de-regulation of the civil aviation sector. They were given permission to operate charter and non-scheduled services under the 'air taxi' Scheme. East West Airlines became the first national level private airline to operate in the country after almost 37 years.

1990 was a landmark year for Indian civil aviation and Air India when the airline entered the Guinness Book of World Records for the largest evacuation effort by a single civilian airline when it flew over 1,11,000 people from Amman to Mumbai in 59 days operating 488 flights just before the Gulf War began.

After the Air Corporation Act was repealed in 1994, the private airlines were permitted to operate scheduled services. Soon, Jet Airways, Air Sahara, Modiluft, Damania Airways, NEPC Airlines and East West Airlines commenced domestic operations.

In 1995, these six private airlines accounted for more than 10% of domestic traffic and 42 (international) airlines operated air services to, from, and through India.

Rakesh Sharma

The year 1995 saw the formation of the Airport Authority of India (AAI), the result of a merger between the International Airport Authority of India and the National Airports Authority.

In 1998 the late Kalpana Chawla became the first Indian-born woman to fly to space as part of a NASA team. The first private airport also came up in Cochin (Kochi), Kerala.

The year 2003 saw a landmark year when 'low cost carriers' started their services. The first among them was Air Deccan. Later SpiceJet, Indigo, MDLR Airways and Paramount Airways came into existence.

In 2004, the government of India approved private airports at Hyderabad and Bangalore.

In December 2004, airlines with a minimum of five years of continuous operations and a minimum fleet size of 20 aircraft, were permitted to operate scheduled services to international destinations.

In 2005, Kingfisher Airlines began operations. Air India, Indian Airlines, Jet Airways and Air Sahara to began international services.

In 2006 the Government granted its approval for the restructuring and modernization of the Mumbai and Delhi Airports through public-private partnership.

The year 2007 saw the regional airlines policy being announced where licenses were given for airline operations within a particular region. A Greenfield Airports Policy was announced in 2008. (A greenfield airport means a new airport

Kalpana Chawla

which is built from scratch in a new location because the existing airport is unable to meet the projected requirements of traffic. The term 'greenfield' originates from software engineering, meaning a project which lacks any constraints imposed by prior work. Those projects which are modi-

Indians Lead European Companies	Rakesh Kapoor was named CEO of Reckitt Benckiser. Nestle appointed Nandu Nandkishore as its executive president for Asia, Oceania, Africa and Middle East.

AIR India Express

Air India Express is a low-cost airline subsidiary of Air India. The airline was established in May 2004, after a long demand from Malayalee expatriates in the Middle East, seeking for a low cost budget airline. It operates services mainly to the Middle East and Southeast Asia. The airline belongs to Air India Charters Limited, a wholly-owned subsidiary of Air India Limited, which was formed in order to facilitate the seamless merger of Air India and Indian. Today Air India Express operates nearly 100 flights per week, mainly from southern states of Tamilnadu and Kerala.

fied or upgraded from existing facilities are called 'brownfield projects'.)

Parliament passed the Airports Economic Regulatory Authority(AERA) Bill, in order to regulate the economic aspects of airports. It was set up in 2009.

The brand new integrated terminal T-3 was inaugurated at New Delhi's Indira Gandhi International Airport in July 2010. In December 2010, Pawan Hans started its sea plane service Jal Hans. (It is based in Andaman and Nicobar Islands, India. The project was launched on December 30, 2010 by the former Civil Aviation Minister, Praful Patel, at Juhu in Mumbai. The airline is jointly owned by Pawan Hans and the Andaman and Nicobar Administration. The airline expects to expand to Lakshadweep Islands, the backwaters in Kerala, Gujarat, the Sundarbans in West Bengal and Puri in Orissa.)

India is the ninth largest aviation market in the world with 82 operational airports, 735 aircraft, 12 operational scheduled airlines and 121 non-scheduled operators. The number of air passengers in India is expected to cross 50 million this year. It also saw the private and low cost airlines challenging the national carrier in terms of passenger carriage.

The three major airlines Air India, Jet Airways and Kingfisher Airlines are also expected to join the three major and global airline alliances Oneworld, SkyTeam and Star Alliance.

Air India is on track to receive its first Boeing 787 aircraft, labelled to be a very fuel efficient aircraft built with advanced composite technology. As part of its plans to celebrate the centenary of civil aviation, the Government has decided to work towards the setting up of the Rajiv Gandhi National Museum for Civil Aviation at Safdarjung airport, New Delhi; the establishment of a National University of Aviation and the involvement of all flying clubs in the celebrations.

Though the outlook for India's private airlines is said to be optimistic, with likely combined profits in the region of $350-400 million in the fiscal year beginning April 1, 2011, the same is not true for state-owned

Air India, which is likely to post a loss of $1-1.25 billion, according to the consulting firm Centre for Asia Pacific Aviation (CAPA). It says that Indian airlines carriers are likely to place orders for 200 new aircraft this fiscal, with a list price of $11-12 billion. Unfortunately, this year was marred by scandal with the discovery of some pilots forging marksheets and documents in order to obtain a flying license. It has led to calls for a complete overhaul and review of the system. ■

Abroad for a Degree   **More than 1.5 lakh students leave India every year for a college degree.**

Microfinance in India

The poor find it very difficult to access credit in our country. Most banks and other financial institutions often turn a deaf ear to their requests for credit. The poor, like the rest of society, need financial products and services to build assets, stabilize consumption and protect themselves against risks. Microfinance serves as the last resort to the low-income population excluded from the traditional financial services system and seeks to fill this gap and alleviate poverty. Microfinance loans serve the low-income population in multiple ways by: (1)providing working capital to build businesses; (2) infusing credit to smooth cash flows and mitigate irregularity in accessing food, clothing, shelter, or education; and (3) cushioning the economic impact of shocks such as illness, theft, or natural disasters. Moreover, by providing an alternative to the loans offered by the local moneylender priced at 60% to 100% annual interest, microfinance prevents the borrower from remaining trapped in a debt trap which exacerbates poverty.

Microfinance in India started in the early 1980s with small efforts at forming informal self-help groups (SHG) to provide access to much-needed savings and credit services. From this small beginning, the microfinance sector has grown significantly in the past decades. National bodies like the Small Industries Development Bank of India (SIDBI) and the National Bank for Agriculture and Rural Development (NABARD) are devoting significant time and financial resources to microfinance. This points to the growing importance of the sector. The strength of the microfinance organizations (MFOs) in India is in the diversity of approaches and forms that have evolved over time. In addition to the home-grown models of SHGs and mutually aided cooperative societies

(MACS), the country has learned from other microfinance experiments across the world, particularly those in Bangladesh, Indonesia, Thailand, and Bolivia, in terms of delivery of microfinancial services.

As of March 2009, the MFIs in India reported a client base of 22.6 million with an outstanding portfolio of more than $2 billion. Over the past five years, the sector has delivered a CAGR of 86% in the number of borrowers and 96% in portfolio outstanding. In the 12 months from March 2008 to March 2009, the microfinance industry experienced a 59% growth in its client base from 14.2 million to 22.6 million and 52% growth in its portfolio outstanding which increased from $1.5 billion to $2.3 billion. This reflects a 14% increase in the absolute growth in portfolio outstanding and 33% increase in the absolute growth in the number of borrowers from 2008 to 2009.

These numbers demonstrate the fundamental strength of the industry and the potential it still has to expand. As the industry matures, it is also nearing an inflexion point and is considering more sophisticated growth strategies through diversifying product offerings, client targeting and creative financial and nonfinancial solutions, which will allow the sector to grow at a continuous pace while preserving its solid performance and abiding by its social mission.

70% in Poverty	**Seventy per cent of 1.3 billion people living in poverty around the world are female.** *(Source: UN)*

District Planning in India

Jacob Easow
Senior Town Planner, Department of Town and Country Planning, Government of Kerala.

Decentralized planning has made considerable headway in India. Governments are now working on formulating district plans in line with the strategy laid out.

Decentralized planning found expression for the first time in the First Year Plan (1951-56), when it suggested the establishment of District Development Council for co-ordinating the development activities of different agencies of the district level. During the Second Five Year Plan the Balwantrai Mehta Study Team was appointed to evaluate the plan projects under the Community Development Programme. The recommendations of the committee led to the genesis of Panchayati Raj Institutions.

Constitutional Amendment, 1992

It was the Third Five Year Plan which emphasized the need for a balanced regional development and as a first step prepared the regional development plans for five resource regions namely Damodar Valley, Dandakaranya, Rihand, Bhakhra Nangal and Rajasthan Canal. This planning attempt was as the recommendation of the Housing and Regional Planning Panel (1955) of the Planning Commission.

In the Fourth Plan concrete steps were taken by the Planning Commission to decentralize the Planning System. The Commission advised the states to adopt district as the unit of planning below the State level and put emphasis on the integration of the plans of local self government bodies, Panchayati Raj Institutions, cooperative organizations and government departments'.

The idea of district planning got further fillip in the recommendations of the Sarkaria Commission (1983).

The most important event in the history of district planning in India was the promulgation of 74th Constitutional Amendment Act in 1992 conferring constitutional status to District Planning Committee for the preparation of 'a draft development plan for the district as a whole'. Developed a viable methodology of decentralized participatory planning as a part of Ninth Five Year Plan popularly known as 'Janakeeyasoothranam'. In order to implement these guidelines, later in 2008, the Planning Commission published a Manual for Integrated District Planning.

The concepts of the micro level (district/regional) planning in India vary with time and profession. In the beginning there were mainly two streams in micro level planning, one originated from decentralized planning concept and the other from regional planning concept. The former was propagated by economists and administrators, the lat-

---

ter by town planners and geographers. Both these concepts have grown with time to redress the problems of Five Year Plans, viz. lack of decision making process closer to the people and community participation in the first while regional disparities and backwardness in the second.

Under decentralization stream, efforts were made in successive Five Year Plans to initiate decentralization at the district level and block level and to promote the establishment of three tier Panchayat Raj Institutions namely Panchayats at village, block and district levels. District planning has become the most important link in the whole system of decentralized planning because this is the culminating point of de-centralized planning process. On the other hand, under the regional planning stream, delineation of the operational area of plan-ning i.e. the planning region for which all regional studies could be undertaken and developments envisaged.

> The idea of district plan-ning got further fillip in the recommendations of the Sarkaria Commission.

Working Group on District Planning (1984) of the Planning Commission moved one step ahead and found that the states are at different stages of progress towards decentralized planning. It has, therefore, advocated a gradual, step by step, ap-proach towards the final goal, ie district planning with the concept of integrated area planning or in other words compre-hensive district planning.

Scope of District Planning

Article 243 ZD(1) of the Constitution lays down that "There shall be constituted in every state at the district level a District Planning Committee to consolidate the plans prepared by the Panchayats and the Municipalities in the district and to prepare a draft development plan for the district as

a whole". Second Administrative Reforms Commission (ARC) interprets the above article of the Constitution as follows. "A development plan for the whole district, for example, has to take into consideration both rural and urban areas. A district plan is something more than the two sets of separate plans - one consisting of micro-plans for rural areas and the other com-prising plans for individual towns. As one moves from the micro-levels to the meso- and macro-levels, perspectives and priori-ties of plans change. The Constitution rec-ognises this and accordingly prescribes that the district plan, as distinguished from the individual Panchayat and Municipal plans, should have regard to 'matters of common interest between the Panchayats and the Municipalities'. This, in other words, means that the development needs of the rural and urban areas should be dealt with in an integrated manner and, therefore, the district plan, which is a plan for a large area consisting of villages and towns, should take into account such factors as 'spatial planning', sharing of 'physical and natural resources', integrated development of in-frastructure' and 'environmental conserva-tion' [Article 243ZD (3)]. All these are im-portant, because the relationship between villages and towns is complementary. One needs the other. Many functions that the towns perform as seats of industry, trade and business and as providers of various services, including higher education, spe-cialized health care services, communica-tions etc have an impact on the develop-ment and welfare of rural people. Similarly,

Sex Ratios in India & China	Wealthy urbanites in Asia want sons. They have skewed the sex ratio from a natural 105 boys for every 100 girls at birth to 112 in India and 121 in China.

the orderly growth of the urban centre is dependent on the kind of organic linkage it establishes with its rural hinterland."

Thus the scope for a district planning as envisaged in the Constitution is:

Should be prepared through participatory process ensuring consultation of all stake holders.

To be successful in ensuing integrated planning for all the rural and urban areas in the district.

Assess the physical and natural resources of the district and give proposals for their sharing.

Have an integrated approach in the development of infrastructure. Address Environmental Conservation.

Include financial investment plans.

To be planned in a spatial platform.

Search of Methodological Paradigms.

Several reports, studies and models are available on District Planning.

Formulation of a District Plan

'Report of the Working Group on District Planning' (Government of India, Planning Commission, 1984) popularly known as Hanumantha Rao Committee Report on District Planning may be considered by many as the bible for district planning. The Working Group (WG) Report recommended following steps in sequence, for the formulation of district plans.

Formulation of major objectives of the district plan.

Compilation of data for district planning

Bringing out the profile of the district in relation to the basic objectives.

Formulating the main strategy and thrust area of district planning.

Assessment of resources for allocation to various programmes and projects.

Statements of physical and financial components of the district plan.

Relationships and links betweens the district plan and regional and state development plans.

The 'Guidelines for Preparation of District Plans in the Eleventh Five Year Plan' issued by the Planning Commission stresses that the 'district plan process' should be an integral part of the process of preparation of state's Eleventh Five Year Plan and annual plan 2007-08. In continuation to the Guidelines, the Planning Commission issued a "Manual for Integrated District Planning" (2008) aiming to make district planning an intrinsic part of the Eleventh Plan itself. The guidelines envisage preparation of a vision document for the district by the District Planning Committee in consultation with the local government institutions.

The Integrated District Development Plan entails all features of the constitutionally mandated draft development plan for a district. Preparation of such a plan will surely need decisions and commitment at various levels due to the multiplicity of agencies involved and the vast spectrum of aspects to be addressed. In a vast country like India having 640 districts in its different geographical, developmental and political regions, district planning will no doubt be a simple task. Hence a strategy of step by step approach leading to District Plan is to be adopted and thus need to trace a road map for this. ∎

Education

The Right of children to Free and Compulsory Education Act came into force on April 1, 2010. This is a historic day for the people of India as from this day the right to education has been accorded the same legal status as the right to life as provided by Article 21A of the Indian Constitution. Every child in the age group of 6-14 years will be provided 8 years of elementary education in an age appropriate classroom in the vicinity of his/her neighbourhood.

Any cost that prevents a child from accessing school will be borne by the State which shall have the responsibility of enrolling the child as well as ensuring attendance and completion of 8 years of schooling. No child shall be denied admission for want of documents; no child shall be turned away if the admission cycle in the school is over and no child shall be asked to take an admission test. Children with disabilities will also be educated in the mainstream schools.

All private schools shall be required to enroll children from weaker sections and disadvantaged communities in their incoming class to the extent of 25% of their enrolment, by simple random selection. No seats in this quota can be left vacant. These children will be treated on par with all the other children in the school and subsidized by the State at the rate of average per learner costs in the government schools (unless the per learner costs in the private school are lower).

All schools will have to prescribe to norms and standards laid out in the Act and no school that does not fulfill these standards within 3 years will be allowed to function. All private schools will have to apply for recognition, failing which they will be penalized to the tune of ₹ 1 lakh and if they still continue to function will be liable to pay ₹ 10,000 per day as fine. Norms and standards of teacher qualification and training are also being laid down by an Academic Authority. Teachers in all schools will have to subscribe to these norms within 5 years.

The National Commission for Protection of Child Rights (NCPCR) has been mandated to monitor the implementation of this historic Right. A special Division within NCPCR will undertake this huge and important task in the coming months and years. NCPCR welcomes the formal notification of this Act and looks forward to playing an active role in ensuring its successful implementation.

A comprehensive programme called Sarva Shiksha Abhiyan (SSA) was launched in November 2000 in partnership with the States. The programme aims at improving the performance of the school system through a community-owned approach and to impart quality elementary education to all children in the age group of 6-14 by 2010. The achievements of the SSA are opening of 3,02,872 schools, construction of 2,42,608 school buildings, construction of 10,77,729 additional classrooms, 1,92,486 drinking water facilities, construction of 3,19,607 toilets, supply of

IIT & Medical Entrance Exams	The IIT Entrance Examination is taken by 8.5 lakh students every year. CBSE All India Engineering Entrance Exam is taken by 7.7 lakh. All India Pre-Medical Test is taken by over 2 lakh students.

free textbooks to approximately 10 crore children and in-service training for 35 lakh teachers.

There were 7.52 lakh primary schools and 2.62 lakh upper primary schools in 2003-04. During 2001-02 and 2002-03 the growth rate of enrolment for girls at the elementary level was higher than that of boys. Participation of girls at all levels of school education has improved appreciably over the years, but vast disparities amongst the States in Gross Enrolment Ratio (GER) at primary/upper primary level persist with States in the North-East performing better than others.

The dropout rate at elementary level has declined from 78.3 in 1960-61 to 52.32 per cent in 2003-04. The number of out-of-school children has reduced steadily since 2002-03. This number came down to 1.35 crore in November 2005. States and UTs have reported that by March 2006 this number has further reduced to 95 lakh only.

The Pupil Teacher Ratio (PTR) at the primary level has remained more or less constant at 43:1 during 2001-02. At the upper primary level, it was 34:1.

Secondary Education

The Secondary Education sector prepares students in the age group of 14-18 years for entry into higher education as well as for the world of work. The number of secondary schools in India increased from 7,416 in 1950-51 to 1,68,900 in 2006-07. Total enrolment in secondary and higher secondary schools has increased correspondingly from 1.5 million in 1950-51 to 39.44 million in 2006-07.

Technical Education

Technical Education plays a vital role in human resource development of the country by creating skilled manpower, enhancing industrial productivity and improving the quality of life. Technical Education covers courses and programmes in engineering,

List of University Level Educational Institutions (as on 31.12.2010)

No.	Institutional Category	No. of Institutions
1.	Central Universities	42
2.	Institutions Deemed to be Universities	130
3.	State Universities	261
4.	Private Universities	73
5.	Institutions of National Importance	33
6.	Institutions Established under State Legislature Acts	5
	Total Number of Institutions	544
7.	Number of Colleges	31,324
	recognized under Section 2(f) of the UGC Act 1956	7,678 (24.5%)
	recognized under Section 12 (B) of the UGC Act 1956 V	6,257 (20.0%)
8.	Women's Colleges	3,432
9.	Enrollment (at the beginning of academic year 2010-11 in the formal system	146.25 lakh
	* in University Departments	19.19 lakh (13.1 %)
	* in Affliated Colleges	127.06 lakh (86.9%)
	* women enrolment	60.80 lakh (41.6%)
	* women enrolment in Professional Courses	18.45%
10.	* Faculty Strength in Universities (at the beginning of the academic tear 2010-11)	6.99 lakh
	* in universities	1.0 lakh (14%)
	* in colleges	5.99 lakh (86%)

technology, management, architecture, town planning, pharmacy and applied arts & crafts, hotel management and catering technology.

The technical education system in the country can be broadly classified into three categories - Central Government funded Institutions, State Government / state-funded Institutions & Self-financed Institutions. In 2010-11 there were 81 centrally funded Institutions in the country.

The 81 centrally funded Institutes of Technical & Science Education are as follows:

Centrally Funded Institutions	Number of Institutions
Indian Institutes of Technology (IITs)	15
Indian Institutes of Management (IIMs)	13
Indian Institutes of Science (IISc)	1
Indian Institutes of Science Education & Research (IISERs)	5
National Institutes of Technology (NITs)	30
Indian Institutes of Information Technology (IITs)	4
National Institutes of Technical Teachers Training & Research (NITTTRs)	4
Others	9
School of Planning & Architecture (SPAs)-3, Indian School of Mines (ISM), North-East Regional Institute of Science & Technology (NER-IST), National Institute of Industrial Engineering (NITIE), National Institute of Foundry & Forge Technology (NIFFT), Sant Longowal Institute of Engineering & Technology (SLIET), Central Institute of Technology (CIT)	
Total	81

University & Higher Education

There has been an impressive growth in the area of university and higher education. Accreditation of all Universities and Colleges has been made mandatory.

At present, there are 544 university-level institutions in India (including 42 Central Universities, 261 State Universities, five Institutions established under State Legislature Act, 130 Deemed Universities and 33 Institutes of national importance). There are nearly 31,324 colleges including 3,432 women's colleges in the country.

Ther are 15 Indian Institutes of Technology.The older ones are at Kharagpur, Bombay, Madras, Kanpur, Delhi, Guwahati and Roorkee. Six new Indian Institutes of Technology (IITs), one each in Bihar (Patna), Andhra Pradesh (Hyderabad), Rajasthan (Jodhpur), Orissa (Bhubaneswar), Gujarat (Gandhinagar) and Punjab (Ropar) have been set up during 2008-2009.

Two more IITs have been established in 2009– Himachal Pradesh (Mandi) and Madhya Pradesh (Indore).

The Indian Institutes of Management (IIMs) were set up with the objective of providing management education and to assist the industry through research and consulting services. The IIMs award only diplomas, and not degrees. There are 13 IIMs in India. The IIMs are at Calcutta (West Bengal), Ahmedabad (Gujarat), Bangalore (Karnataka), Lucknow (Uttar Pradesh), Kozhikode (Kerala), Indore (Madhya Pradesh), Shillong (Meghalaya), Ranchi (Jharkhand), Rohtak (Haryana), Raipur (Chhattisgarh), Tiruchirappalli (Tamil Nadu), Udaipur (Rajasthan) and Kashipur (Uttarakhand).

Adult Education

The National Literacy Mission was launched on May 5, 1988 as a Technology Mission to impart functional literacy to non-literates in the country in the age group of 15-35 years in a time-bound manner. The National Education Policy-1986 as modified in 1992, also has recognized the National Literacy Mission as one of the three instruments to eradicate illiteracy from the country, the other two being Universalisation of Elementary Education and Non-formal Education.

The Mission objective is to attain a sustainable threshold literacy rate of 75 percent by 2007. The Total Literacy Campaign (TLC) has been the principal strategy of National Literacy Mission for eradication of illiteracy in the target age-group.

Indian Writing in English

Khyrunnisa A

Ever since Bankim Chandra Chatterjee's work *Rajmohan's Wife appeared* in book form in 1864, Indian Writing in English has been watched with great interest in the English-speaking world.

Indian Writing in English (IWE), earlier referred to as Indo Anglian Writing, refers to the works of those Indian writers whose literary output is in the English language and who have earned recognition as fine writers of English literature.

For the last 30 years or so, a wealth of exciting Indian writers of English have appeared on the scene and held the unriveted and envious attention of the rest of the world. While the economic recession led to a slump in the demand for new books in the foreign market, India remained amazingly unaffected and showed no signs of downing its shutters on the printing of books. The trend continues. Foreign publishing houses too have identified India as the happening country as far as publication is concerned.

Sarojini Naidu

NRI Writers

NRI writers have mushroomed overnight leading to acrimonious debates about the authenticity of their writing. A divide already exists between the regional language writers and the writers of IWE. Regional language writers attack the IWE writers who they claim are once removed from reality. Their argument is that IWE writers portray their characters as speaking a language that they do not use in real life and thereby lose out on authenticity. Now it is the turn of the native IWE writer to criticize the NRI or the diasporic IWE writer who is accused of being twice removed from reality by writing about India from abroad

and therefore 'exoticising' the country and its people. Much can be said on all sides, but it must not be forgotten that Indian authors writing in English, whether native or NRI, have conquered the literary world by winning prestigious awards, capturing media attention and most important, by helping the publishing industry get a new lease of life.

Raja Ram Mohan Roy

The beginnings of IWE can be traced to the nineteenth century, to the time of Raja Ram Mohan Roy (1774-1833), the enlightened social reformer who emphasized the importance of education in English if India wished to be a leading nation of the world. To Sake Dean Mahomet, an Indian traveller and entrepreneur, goes the credit of writing *Travels of Dean Mahomet* (1794), the first book in English by an Indian author.

The century also produced outstanding poets like Henry Derozio, (1809-1831), Michael Madhusudan Dutt (1824-1873), and Toru Dutt (1856-1877) who wrote poetry in English and French. Both Derozio and Toru Dutt showed great promise and tragically died very young. Toru Dutt's poem, *Our Casuarina Tree*, is believed to be autobiographical. Sarojini Naidu, Tagore's contemporary and an active figure in politics, left her mark in literature too by writing romantic poetry that earned her the sobriquet 'The Nightingale of India'. Her brother Harindranath Chattopadhyay was another renowned poet. Sri Aurobindo (1872-1950), mystic, philosopher and poet, wrote his highly rated epic *Savitri: A Legend and a Symbol* (1950-51), one of the longest poems in IWE.

The outstanding names in later IWE poetry are Nissim Ezekiel, Dom Moraes, A.K Ramanujan, Kamala Das and Vikram Seth.

Other famous names include Jayanta Mahapatra, Gieve Patel, Keki Daruwalla, Eunice De Souza, P.Lal, R.Parthasarathy, Kersi Katrak, Sujata Bhatt, Hoshang Merchant, Smita Agarwal, Ranjit Hoskote, Arundhathi Subramaniam and Sudeep Sen.

Dom Moraes

First Nobel Prize

Bankim Chandra Chatterjee's work, *Rajmohan's Wife* (serialized in 1834 but published in book form posthumously in 1864), is acknowledged to be the first Indian novel in English. Rabindranath Tagore (1861-1941), the pride of India, is the outstanding literary figure of this age. He was awarded the Nobel Prize for Literature in 1913 and remains the only Indian to have won the coveted award for Literature.

Dhan Gopal Mukherji (1890-1936), was one of the first popular Indian writers in English and won the Newbery Medal in the US for his *Gay Neck, the Story of a Pigeon* (1927). An important contribution to IWE was made by P.Lal (1929-2010), a poet, essayist, translator and publisher, who established 'Writers Workshop', a press for Indian English writing, in 1958.

The 1930s saw the emergence of the formidable trio of novelists, Raja Rao, R.K Narayan and Mulk Raj Anand who went on to gain international fame and prestige. The novels of Raja Rao (1908-2006) with their rural settings won praise for the Indianness of their themes and his *Kanthapura* (1938) wooed the West with its unique story telling methods. His later works like the semi autobiographical *The Serpent and the Rope* (1960) and *Cat and Shakespeare* (1965) established his credentials as one of India's finest stylists. R.K Narayan (1906-2001) was introduced to the western world by Graham Greene

who found great talent in his first novel *Swami and Friends* (1935) and helped him find a publisher. R.K Narayan created a fictional town, Malgudi, as the locale for most of his novels and his simple style and realistic narration won him many admirers. *The Bachelor of Arts* (1937), *The Guide* (1958), *The Man-eater of Malgudi* (1961) and *Grandmother's Tale* (1992) are some of his famous novels. The realistic novels of Mulk Raj Anand (1905-2004) like *The Untouchable* (1935) and *Coolie* (1936) reflect the harsh social divides that are the bane of India.

G.V Desani (1909-2000) is another important IWE writer whose cult novel *All About H. Hatterr* (1948) about an Anglo-Malay man in search for enlightenment took the world by storm and was compared to James Joyce's *Ulysses*.

The spirit of an independent India that was struggling to establish an identity of its own was captured by later novelists like Manohar Malgaonkar in his *Distant Drum* and *The Devil's Wind*, Kamala Markhandaya in *Some Inner Fury*, Anita Desai in *Clear Light of Day* and Nayantara Sahgal in *From Fear Set Free*.

Booker of Bookers

The Grand Old Man of IWE, Khushwant Singh, born in 1915, attracted notice with his 1956 novel, *Train to Pakistan* about the violent aftermath of partition and has held public attention since. His prodigious output includes short stories, novels, plays and nonfiction. *The Sunset Club* (2010) is his latest literary offering.

The entry of Salman Rushdie into the literary scene marked the beginning of a new era in IWE. His path breaking novel *Midnight's Children* (1981) became a book for the Booker, winning the Booker Prize in 1981, Booker of Bookers in 1992 and the Best of the Bookers in 2008. Rushdie used an innovative hybrid language in which English mingled easily with Indian terms to represent the complexities of India. His style has been described as magic realism

Gitanjali wins Nobel
Rabindranath Tagore was awarded the Nobel Prize for his *Gitanjali* on November 13, 1913. The message reached Calcutta on November 15.

and his latest novel is *Luka and the Fire of Life* (2010).

Booker Prizes

Rusdie triggered off a Booker Prize rush and since then three Indians have won the Booker – Arundhati Roy for *The God of Small Things* (1997), Kiran Desai for *The Inheritance of Loss* (2006) and Aravind Adiga for *The White Tiger* (2008).

Shashi Deshpande

Jhumpa Lahiri, the Indian American writer won the Pulitzer Prize for Fiction in 2000 for *Interpreter of Maladies* (1999) and V.S Naipaul, the Trinidadian-British writer of Indian descent won the Nobel Prize for Literature in 2001.

A host of names jostle for attention in the Indian literary pantheon. Shashi Tharoor's *The Great Indian Novel* (1989) is a satirical take on the Mahabharata. Vikram Seth's *A Suitable Boy* (1993) at 1474 pages is one of the longest novels. Anita Desai, Shashi Deshpande, Ruskin Bond, Ruth Prawer Jhabvala, Ved Mehta, Manoj Das, Gita Mehta, Bharati Mukherjee, Namita Gokale, Manju Kapur, Allan Sealy, Arun Joshi, Vikram Chandra, Chitra Banerjee Diwakaruni, Rohinton Mistry, Upamanyu Chatterjee, Raj Kamal Jha, Amit Chaudhuri, Gita Hariharan, Tarun Tejpal, Kiran Nagarkar, Manjula Padmanabhan, Ashok Banker, David Davidar, Hari Kunzru, Kalpana Swaminathan, Pinky Virani, Vikas Swaroop, Namita Devidayal, Shobha De, Jaishree Misra, Anita Nair and Anurag Mathur are some of the names that have made their mark in IWE.

Amitav Ghosh has just come out with his *River of Smoke*, the second in a planned trilogy, the first being *The Sea of Poppies* (2008). Chetan Bhagat, named by Time Magazine as one of the 100 Most Influential People of the World, deserves special mention for the phenomenal success of his four popular novels. Exciting new names that have entered the fray recently include Manu Joseph (*Serious Men*), Tishani Doshi (*The Pleasure Seekers*) and Anjali Joseph

whose *Saraswati Park* recently won two global awards.

In the field of drama, IWE may not have created the ripples it did in fiction and poetry but it has creditable exponents. Krishna Mohan Banerjee's *The Persecuted* (1831) is considered the first Indian English play though Michael Madhusudan Dutt's *Is This Called Civilization?* (1871) is believed to be the play that gave direction to Indian English drama. Major IWE playwrights of the pre independence era include Tagore, Sri Aurobindo, Harindranath Chattopadhyay, A S P Ayyar, T.P Kailasam, Bharati Sarabhai, and J.M Lobo Prabhu. The names of Asif Currimbhoy, Pratap Sharma, Gurucharan Das, G.V.Desani, Lakhan Deb and Pritish Nandy rank high among the playwrights of the post independence era.

Two promising contemporary dramatists who have already made their presence felt are Mahesh Dattani (*Final Solutions, Dance Like a Man, Tara*) the first playwright in English to be awarded the Sahitya Akademi Award and Manjula Padmanabhan whose play Harvest reaped her the rich harvest of the Onassis Prize in 1997.

Important nonfiction IWE of early 20th century includes Jawaharlal Nehru's *Glimpses of World History*, a collection of letters written by Nehru to his daughter from various prisons in British India between 1930- 33, *The Discovery of India* (1946) and Dr S. Radhakrishnan's *Eastern Religion and Western Thought* (1939). The works of Nirad C Chaudhuri (1897-1999) gained great acclaim and include *The Autobiography of an Unknown Indian* (1951), *A Passage to England* (1959) and *The Continent of Circe* (1965). Following the tradition of Nirad Chaudhuri by using fine prose to explore and describe contemporary Indian reality is a group of very competent nonfiction writers. They include Pankaj Mishra, Arundhati Roy, Ramachandra Guha, Mukul Kesavan and Sudhir Kakar.

Indian Writing in English has never had it so good with such a wealth of talent, so many authors on best seller lists, and so much critical acclaim coming its way. The future looks very promising for Indian writers in English. ∎

Media

The origin of newspapers in India dates back to the eighteenth century. India's first newspaper Hicky's *Bengal Gazette* or the *Calcutta General Advertiser* was published in English in Calcutta by James Augustus Hicky on 29 Jan, 1780. Hickey's Bengal Gazette was the first English language newspaper, and indeed the first printed newspaper, to be published in the Indian sub-continent.

Other newspapers such as *The India Gazette, The Calcutta Gazette, The Madras Courier, The Bombay Herald* etc. soon followed. These newspapers carried news of the areas under the British rule. The Times of India was founded in 1838 as The Bombay Times and Journal of Commerce

by Bennett, Coleman and Company. The Times group publishes *The Economic Times* (launched in 1961), *Navbharat Times* (Hindi language), and the *Maharashtra Times* (Marathi language).

The first newspaper in an Indian language was the *Samachar Darpan* in Bengali that was followed by *Bengal Gazette*, in Bengal and *Bombay Samachar*, in Mumbai. Later on in 1854, the first Hindi newspaper *Samachar Sudha Varshan*, was established. The circulation of *Samachar Sudha* brought a breakthrough in the Indian media industry. After this newspaper became widely popular amongst Indians, many more newspapers had been released in almost all Indian languages.

Today, India has a very vibrant print and electronic media. The total number of registered newspapers/periodicals was 73,146 as on 31 March 2009. The print media comprises 8,475 dailies, 383 tri/bi-weeklies, 24,544 weeklies, 9,458 fortnightlies, 22,124 monthlies, 4,864 quarterlies, 653 annuals and 2,645 publications of other periodicity.

Top Dailies in India

Rank	Publication	Language	Circulation
1.	The Times of India	English	38,77,533
2.	Dainik Jagran	Hindi	27,95,965
3.	Dainik Bhaskar	Hindi	20,95,241
4.	Malayala Manorama	Malayalam	19,03,331
5.	Lokmat	Marathi	17,50,303
6.	Hindustan	Hindi	16,99,489
7.	Eenadu	Telugu	16,70,750
8.	The Hindu	English	15,15,158
7.	Daily Sakal	Marathi	15,01,033
8.	Rajasthan Patrika	Hindi	14,68,455
Weeklies			
1.	Malayala Manorama	Malayalam	5,82,180
2.	The Week	English	2,04,429
3.	Balarama	Malayalam	1,92,550
4.	Kungumam	Tamil	1,33,458
5.	Kalikkudukka	Malayalam	1,30,631
Fortnightlies & Monthlies			
1.	Vanitha	Malayalam	6,31,373
2.	Meri Saheli	Hindi	3,26,415
3.	Grehlakshmi	Hindi	3,00,226
4.	Grihalakshmi	Malayalam	2,27,159
5.	Mathrubhumi Arogya Masika	Malayalam	2,04,128

Audit Bureau of Circulations, July-Dec.2010

Registrar of Newspapers for India

The Office of the Registrar of Newspapers for India (RNI) came into existence on 1 July 1956, on the recommendation of the First Press Commission in 1953 and by amending the Press and Registration of Books Act, 1867. The Registrar of Newspapers for India commonly known as Press Registrar is required, inter alia to submit an Annual Report to the

All India Radio Thiruvananthapuram

Government of the status of newspapers before 31 December every year.

Press Information Bureau

The Press Information Bureau (PIB) is the nodal agency of the Central Government to disseminate information to the print and electronic media on government policies, programme initiatives and achievements. The Bureau disseminates information through Press Releases, Press Notes, Feature Articles, Backgrounders, Press Briefings Photographs, Press Conferences, Interviews, Database available on Bureau's website, Press tours, etc.

News Agencies
Press Trust of India

India's largest news agency, Press Trust of India (PTI), is a non-profit sharing cooperative owned by the country's newspapers with a mandate to provide efficient and unbiased news to all subscribers. Founded on 27 August, 1947, PTI began functioning from 1 February, 1949.

The PTI offers its news services in English and Hindi languages. Bhasha is the Hindi language news service of the agency. PTI subscribers include 500 newspapers in India and scores abroad. All major TV/radio channels in India and several abroad, including BBC in London, receive PTI service.

Besides the news and photo services, the other services of the agency include mailer packages of Feature, Science service, Economic service and Data India and screen-based services as News-scan and Stockscan. A television wing, PTI-TV, does features and undertakes corporate documentaries on assignment basis.

United News of India

United News of India (UNI) was incorporated under the Companies Act, 1956 on 19 December, 1959 and started functioning effective from 21 March, 1961.

UNI's innovative spirit was evident when it became the first news agency in India to launch a full-fledged Hindi wire service `UNIVARTA' in 1982 and a Photo Service and a Graphics Service in the same decade. In the early 90s, it launched the first-ever wire service in URDU.

Press Council of India

The Press Council of India has been established under an Act of Parliament for the purpose of preserving the freedom of the press and of maintaining and improving the standards of newspapers and news agencies in India. The Chairman of the council is by convention, a retired judge of the Supreme Court of India. The Council has 28 members—20 forms the newspaper world, five are Members of Parliament (three nominated by the speaker of the Lok Sabha and two by the Chairman of the Rajya Sabha and of the remaining three, one each is nominated by the Sahitya Akademi, the Bar Council of India and the University Grants Commission.

Prasar Bharati

Prasar Bharati is India's largest public broadcaster. It is an autonomous body set up by an Act of Parliament and comprises Doordarshan television network and All India Radio which were earlier media units of the Ministry of Information and Broadcasting, Government of India.

Prasar Bharati was established on November 23, 1997 following a demand that the government owned broadcasters in India should be given autonomy like those in many other countries. The Parliament of India passed an Act to grant this autonomy in 1990, but it was not enacted until September 15, 1997.

Radio Broadcasting

Radio broadcasting began in India in the early 1920s. The first programme was broadcast in 1923 by the Radio Club of Bombay. This was followed by the setting up of a Broadcasting Service in 1927 on an experimental basis in Bombay and Calcutta. The government took over the transmitters and began operating them under the name

Indian Broadcasting Service. It was changed to All India Radio in 1936.

All India Radio is now one of the largest broadcast networks in the world. At the time of independence there were six radio stations and 18 transmitting which covered just 11% of the population and 2.5% area of the country. As of December 2009, the network comprises 233 stations and 375 transmitters which provide radio coverage to 99.16% of population and reach 91.82% area of the country.

The turning point for the industry came with the phase-II privatization reforms when the Government rationalized the licensing fee by fixing it at 4 per cent of the gross revenue. This, for the first time, made the business model viable for the companies. Consequently, many large corporate houses entered the private FM business. From 21 operationalized private FM stations before the phase-II licensing, the number of stations shot out to 251 including 21 channels of phase-I.

Government had introduced FM phase I Policy in 1999. This met with limited success and resulted in large scale defaults and court cases. Out of 108 channels put for auction only 21 channels could be operationalised. Due to limited success of FM Radio Phase I, FM Phase II Policy was notified in 2005 after considering recommendations of Dr. Amit Mitra Committee and TRAI. Phase II policy was widely accepted. Growth in the future is likely to go through continued increase in the number of radio stations after Phase III licensing, further liberalization of regulations as well as better ability of the radio stations to sell advertisement space.

In FM Phase II — the latest round of the long-delayed opening up of private FM in India — some 338 frequencies were offered of which about 237 were sold.The government may go for rebidding of unsold frequencies quite soon. In Phase III of FM licensing, smaller towns and cities will be opened up for FM radio.

Television

Television transmission began in India from a makeshift studio in the Akashvani Bhawan in New Delhi on 15th September 1959. A 500 watt transmitter carried the signal within a radius of 25 km. around Delhi. However, a regular service with a news bulletin became

Channel OB Vans

a reality only in 1965.

After seven years, the second television centre commenced service in Bombay. By 1975 TV service was available in Kolkata, Chennai, Srinagar, Amritsar and Lucknow. Colour transmission was introduced during the Asian Games held in New Delhi in 1982.

Television has come a long way since its humble beginnings in 1959. As of 2010, over 500 TV Satellite television channels are broadcast in India. This includes channels from the state-owned Doordarshan, News Corporation owned STAR TV, Sony-owned Sony Entertainment Television, Sun Network and Zee TV. Direct to Home service is provided by Airtel Digital TV, BIG TV owned by Reliance, DD Direct Plus, DishTV, Sun Direct DTH, Tata Sky and Videocon. DishTV was the first one to come up in Indian market, others came only years later.

As per the TAM Annual Universe Update - 2010, India now has over 134 million households (out of 223 million) with television sets, of which over 103 million have access to cable TV or satellite TV, including 20 million households which are DTH subscribers.

Parliament Channels

A landmark in the history of telecasting of parliamentary proceedings was reached on 14 December 2004 when two separate dedicated satellite channels for telecasting live the entire proceedings of Rajya Sabha and Lok Sabha were launched. The entire proceedings of the two Houses of Parliament are since being telecast live through separate dedicated satellite channels by Doordarshan.

Media Entrepreneurship

Sree Sreenivasan
Professor and Dean, Columbia Graduate School of Journalism

The role of digital media in branding products has assumed greater significance in the days of social networking.

When talking of digital media and so-cial media, it is important to see how global the story has become. Statistics show there are 750 million users globally on Facebook today. Of them, around 250 million users log into the social network-ing site everyday. A user spends around 23 minutes a day on an average on Fa-cebook. Around 30 billion pieces of con-tent are shared every month on the site. So advertising on these sites can have enormous marketing and connection op-portunities, and that is crucial for business. Likewise, the YouTube is the world's sec-ond largest search engine after Google. More than 48 hours of video is uploaded every minute on YouTube. Twitter and Linkedin are less dramatic, with 200 mil-lion and 100 million users respectively. It is important however, to be a sceptic and an evangelist where technology is concerned. One has to be an early tester of technology and a late adopter. To de-cide if a new piece of technology makes sense, you have to test it out first. Have you used it, understood it? Are you ready for that technology in your life? When there was trouble in Egypt early this year, the first thing the Egyptian gov-ernment did to suppress public dissent against authority was to shut down the Internet service in the country. That is an indicator of how digital media has invad-ed and become an important part of our lives – whether you are a dictator trying to stay in power, or young people trying

to change the world, or whether you are trying to sell an idea, service or product. Digital media allows targeted marketing – a level of advertising where targeting the product can get so detailed like never be-fore. From a marketing angle this means a lot and can reap huge benefits. Today in-dustries are changing, and using the digital media to market and connect. The social media help to make connections with your audience that are deeper and more loyal. Branding is an important part of market-ing strategies these days, and utilising the digital media in branding your prod-uct is crucial. What is the role they will play in the marketing of products? The captains of industries should assess each social network from the point of view of their product and its impact on users. The drivers of digital marketing are: local, social, mobile and video. Those in business who wish to advertise their products online will have to arrive at the right mix of these drivers for their product.

Film About Facebook	**The Social Network is a 2010 drama film about the founding of the social networking website Facebook and the resulting lawsuits. The film was directed by David Fincher and features a cast including Jesse Eisenberg, Andrew Garfield, Justin Timberlake and Armie Hammer.**

The scarcest resource of the 21st century is human attention, said Les Hinton, the publisher of the Wall Street Journal. Businesses, companies, brands, leaders and organisations who know how to deliver of that attention are going to be the ones to stay in business. Everybody else will die. While marketing your product you don't need 100% attention of your potential customers. If you manage to get a sliver of their attention you will be successful in reaching out. And the digital media is one more strategic place to do that. Take the idea of social transformation (eg. drive against corruption) in the social media. The ability of people to galvanise important subjects like this is going to increase with the evolution of the digital media. Connecting at the right time with the right audience on the social networking sites can only amplify what you do well and what you do badly. So if the product is

> One has to be an early tester of technology and a late adopter.

anti-corruption or transparency, it can happen if people genuinely want it to happen. What about ethics in business? Can the social media help focus attention on the problems in business? While it cannot solve all problems, social media can be a great start to this end. We can expose to the world through advertising what are the safety threats in a product or service and how to protect against it. As you expand the number of people you are touching with technology, you increase your market. But there is the likelihood of running into problems as well. Problems do not mean you should shy away from using technology. For example, 90% of the world's emails are spam. But the golden 10% makes our world function miraculously. So the watchword is to be 'careful' in the use of technology. There is a dichotomy in the use of these social tools. While you may want to use these tools to get to as many people as possible in business, as a person you may not want that extent of invasion in your personal domain. We have to learn to walk this tightrope gingerly. Technology should not govern our lives such that it takes control, spoils person-to-person contact in real (not virtual) terms, or stunts creativity. As people we need to exercise our own controls – so that this is not the only thing, but among one of the things we do. In the US, it is not just the young, even the decision makers are using social media tools – going to where the audiences are. There can be no denying that social media are engaging and useful experiences – a window to our world tomorrow. Nitin Nohria, dean of the Harvard Business School, who has been pushing the values of ethics and transparency in business puts it succinctly. He said people are angry with corporate houses and CEOs because they are claiming value without creating value. No one will mind a business head claiming value if they are creating value for their shareholders, for society, for people at large. That should be the mantra for successful business: Claim value after creating value. ∎

Based on the talk on July 8, as part of Asian School of Business' Leadership Lecture Series.

Time Spent Online   **Social networking now accounts for 22% of all time spent online in the US.**

Music and Dance

Music is one of the oldest and finest forms of human expression. Music can be divided into Western classical, Hindustani classical, Carnatic classical, Folk, Jazz, Pop, Fusion, etc. The main schools of classical music, Hindustani and the Carnatic, continue to survive through oral tradition being passed on by teachers to disciples. This has led to the existence of family traditions called gharanas and sampradayas.

A new form of Hindustani music known as Khayal emerged during the 13th & 14th centuries. This style gave an entirely new dimension to Hindustani classical music tradition. Amir Khusro is considered the proponent of this style. Thyagaraja, Muthuswami Deekshithar and Shyama Shastri are popularly known as the trinity of Carnatic music.

The pivotal concept of Indian music (Carnatic and Hindustani) is Raga (melody). Ragas are made of different combinations of sapta (seven) swaras: Sa Sadjam; Ri Rishabam; Ga Gaandhaaram; Ma Madhyamam; Pa Panchamam; Dha Dhaivadam; Ni Nishadam.

In Western classical, piano one octave consists of twelve notes whereas in Indian music the same octave contains 22 (srutis) notes. The twenty two srutis are called Siddha, Prabhavati, Kantha, Suprabha, Shikha, Diptimati, Ugra, Hladi, Nirviri, Dira, Sarphara, Kshanti, Hridayonmulini, Visarini, Prasuna, Vibhuti, Malini, Chapala, Vala, Sarvaratna, Sitantaj and Vikalini.

Swara is generally defined as a note whereas sruti constitutes the macrotonal intervals between two swaras. The nuances of these can be best understood in prayoga (practice) rather than theory.

Taala is defined as rhythm. But in vocal music or instrumental music taala plays a

Chembai Vaidyanatha Bhagavatar

creative and organic part in bringing out the essence and elevating the musical expressions to new dimensions. The major taalas are Aadi Taala, a cycle of eight maathras (beats), Chautal or Eaka Taal consisting of twelve maathras mostly played on the Pakhawaj, Jhaptal consisting of ten maathras, Roopak taala of seven maathras, and Teen Tala of sixteen maathras.

Violin is a widely accepted musical instrument of foreign origin which has an unavoidable presence in Indian classical music.

Famous Musicians

Ariyakudi Ramanuja Iyengar (1890-1967) • Maharajapuram Viswantha Iyer (1896-1970) • Papanasam Sivan (1890-1973) • Mysore Vasudevachariar (1865-1961) • Madurai Mani Iyer (1912-1968) • M.D. Ramathan (1923-1984) • Chembai Vaidyanatha Bhagavatar (1896-1974) • Pt. Vishnu Digambar Paluskar (1872-1931) • Ustad Faiyaz Khan (1886-1956) • Pt. Omkarnath Thakur (1897-1967) • Ustad Bade Gulam Ali Khan (1903-1968) • Pt. Malliakarjun Mansur (1910-1992) • Kumar Gandharva (1924-1992).

Chair for India at Edinburgh
A chair of Contemporary Indian Studies, to be held by an Indian academic, is to be created at the University of Edinburgh in collaboration with the Indian Council for Cultural Relations.

Famous Instrumentalists

Sarod: Ali Akbar Khan, Allauddin Khan, Amjad Ali Khan, Buddhadev Desgupta, Bahadur Khan, Sharan Rani, Zarin S. Sharma

Tabla: Alla Rakha Khan, Kishan Maharaj, Nikhil Ghosh, Zakir Hussain

Violin: Baluswamy Dikshitar, Gajanan Rao Joshi, Lalgudi G. Jayaraman, M.S. Gopala-krishnan, Mysore T. Chowdiah, T.N. Krishnan

Shehnai: Bismillah Khan

Sitar: Nikhil Banerjee, Ravi Shankar, Vilayat Khan, Hara Shankar Bhattacharya

Flute: Hari Prasad Chaurasia, Pannalal Ghose, T.R. Mahalingam

Veena: K.R. Kumaraswamy Iyer, Doraiswamy Iyengar.

Dances

Dance in India has an unbroken tradition of over 2000 years. Two main divisions of its forms are classical and folk. Classical dance forms are based on ancient dance discipline and have rigid rules of presentation. Important among them are Bharatanatyam, Kathakali, Kathak, Manipuri, Kuchipudi and Odissi.

Folk dances of India vary according to the region and have no specific grammar. They fit in with the scheme of festivals in each region.

India's contemporary classical dances trace their origin far back in Indian history. Dance like any other aspect of Indian culture and tradition has developed over thousands of years. It is a very influential art form, for sculptures and pieces of literature from the past all depict some form of dance. Classical Indian dances today trace their roots to a book called the Natyasastra which forms the basis of all the performing arts today.

Bharatanatyam

Bharatanatyam originated in Tamilnadu and was earlier known as Daasiyattam. This dance form has been handed down through the centuries by dance teachers (or gurus) called nattuwanars and the temple dancers, called devadasis. In the sacred environment of the temple these familes developed and propagated their heritage. The training traditionally took around

Bharatanatyam

seven years under the direction of the nattuwanar who were scholars and persons of great learning.

Famous Dancers: Bala Saraswati, C.V. Chandrasekhar, Leela Samson, Mrinalini Sarabhai, Padma Subramanyam, Rukmini Devi, Sanyukta Panigrahi, Sonal Mansingh, Yamini Krishnamurthi

Kathak

Kathak means 'to tell a story'. This north Indian dance form is inextricably bound with classical Hindustani music, and the rhythmic agility of the feet is accompanied by the table or pakhawaj. Traditionally the stories were of Radha and Krishna, in the Natwari style (as it was then called) but the Moghul invasion of North India had a serious impact on the dance. The dance was taken to Muslim courts and thus it became more

Kathak

entertaining and less religious in content. More emphasis was laid on nritta, the pure dance aspect and less on abhinaya (expression and emotion).

Famous Dancers: Bharati Gupta, Birju Maharaj, Damayanti Joshi, Durga Das, Gopi Krishna, Kumudini Lakhia, Sambhu Maharaj, Sitara Devi

Kuchipudi

Kuchipudi derives its name from the village Kuchipudy (Kuchelapuram) in Andhra Pradesh from where it originated .The dance drama that still exists today and can most closely be associated with the Sanskrit theatrical tradition is Kuchipudi which is also known as Bhagavata Mela Natakam. The actors sing and dance, and the style is a blend of folk and classical. Arguably this is why this technique has greater freedom and fluidity than other dance styles.

Famous Dancers: Josyula Seetharamaiah, Vempathi Chinna Sathyam

Manipuri

This dance style was originally called jogai which means circular movement. In ancient texts it has been compared to the movement of the planets around the sun.

It is said that when Krishna, Radha and the gopis danced the Ras Leela, Shiva made sure that no one disturbed the beauty of the dancing. Parvati, the consort of Lord Shiva also wished to see this dance, so to please her he chose the beautiful area of Manipur and re-enacted the Ras Leela. Hundreds of centuries later, in the 11th century, during the reign of Raja Loyamba, prince Khamba of the Khomal dynasty and Princess Thaibi of the Mairang dynasty re-enacted the dance and it became known as Lai-Haraoba, the most ancient dance of Manipur.

Famous Dancers: Guru Bipin Sinha, Jhaveri Sisters, Nayana Jhaveri, Nirmala Mehta, Savita Mehta

Mohiniyattam

The theme of Mohiniyattam dance is love and devotion to god. Vishnu or Krishna is most often the hero. The spectators can feel His invisible presence when the heroine or her maid details dreams and ambitions through circular movements, delicate footsteps and subtle expressions. Through slow and medium tempos, the dancer is able to find adequate space for improvisations and suggestive bhavas or emotions.

The basic dance steps are the Adavus which are of four kinds: Taganam, Jaganam, Dhaganam and Sammisram. These names are derived from the nomenclature called vaittari.

The Mohiniyattam dancer maintains realistic make-up and adorns a simple costume, in comparison to costumes of other dances, such as Kathakali. The dancer is attired in a beautiful white with gold border Kasavu saree of Kerala, with the distinctive white jasmin flowers around a French bun at the side of her head.

Famous Dancers: Kalamandalam Kshemavati, Kanak Rele, Kalamandalam Satyabhama, Bharati Sivaji, Sunanda Nair

Odissi

Odissi, the dance form from Orissa, is supposed to be the oldest surviving classical dance form from India.Odissi is based on the popular devotion to Lord Krishna and the verses of the Sanskrit play Geet Govinda are used to depict the love and devotion to God. The Odissi dancers use their head, bust and torso in soft flowing movements to express specific moods and emotions.

The form is curvaceous, concentrating on the tribhang or the division of the body into three parts, head, bust and torso; the mudras and the expressions are similar to those of Bharatnatyam. Odissi performanc-

Odissi

es are replete with lores of the eighth incarnation of Vishnu, Lord Krishna. It is a soft, lyrical classical dance which depicts the ambience of Orissa and the philosophy of its most popular deity, Lord Jagannath, whose temple is in Puri. On the temple walls of Bhubaneshwar, Puri and Konark the dance sculptures of Odissi are clearly visible.

Famous Dancers: Debaprasad Das, Dhirendra Nath Pattnaik, Indrani Rahman, Kelucharan Mahapatra, Priyambada Mohanty, Sonal Mansingh.

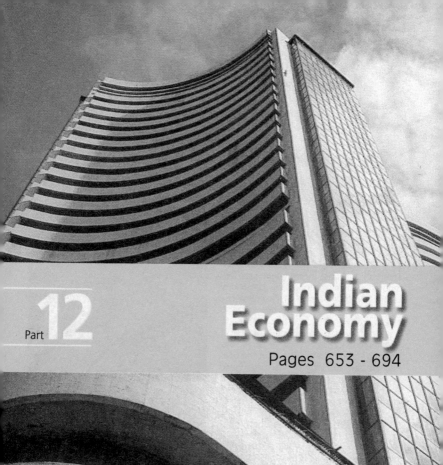

Part **12**

Indian
Economy

Pages 653 - 694

20 Years of Economic Reforms

Dr V K Vijayakumar
Investment Strategist, Geojit BNP Paribas

Economic reforms have changed India in the past 20 years. Liberalization, privatization and globalization form the new mantra of development.

In 1991 India faced her worst economic crisis of the post independent era. Deteriorating macroeconomic conditions culminated in a Balance of Payments crisis. In June 2011 India's foreign exchange reserves declined to less than $1 billion – just sufficient for two weeks of import requirements. Fiscal Deficit at 9 % and Current Account Deficit at 4 % of the GDP had crossed all limits of macroeconomic prudence. Credit rating agencies Standard & Poor and Moody's downgraded India's credit rating to speculative grade, triggering a flight of capital from the country. India came close to defaulting on her international commitments. The government had to sell gold and the RBI was forced to pledge part of its gold reserves with the Bank of England to raise the much needed foreign exchange. Finally, the government approached the IMF which granted two loans of $1.03 billion and $789 million under two different schemes.

In June 1991 a new government under the leadership of Prime Minister Narasimha Rao assumed office. Rao chose a technocrat with proven academic and administrative credentials- Manmohan Singh- as his finance minister and he initiated far reaching economic reforms whose consequences on the economy in the years that followed have been truly profound. Manmohan Singh began by devaluing

the Rupee by 9 % and 11% respectively on July 1st and 3rd. This was followed by trade liberalization that helped improve India's credit rating. On July 24th Manmohan Singh presented his epoch making budget which initiated the process of dismantling the 'License Raj' which had stifled the initiative and enterprise of Indians for long. From 1991 onwards reforms became a continuous process encompassing almost all sectors of the economy.

The salient features of the reforms are summarised as under:

Industrial Reforms

Delicensing: the number of industries that required licenses was reduced

The number of industries reserved for the public sector was reduced to six.

All others were opened to the private sector.

Three Historic Dates	In May 1846, Britain voted to repeal the Corn Laws. In Dec. 1978, China's Communist Party approved the opening up of its economy. In July 1991, liberalisation was launched in India by Finance Minister Manmohan Singh.

Automatic approval for foreign investment up to 51 percent

Removal of MRTP restrictions on investment

Public sector units were given more autonomy

Disinvestment of a part of government securities in many PSUs initiated

Capital Market Reforms

Abolition of CCI (Controller of Capital Issues) and free pricing of IPOs

SEBI (Securities Exchange Board of India) empowered

Mutual funds opened to the private/foreign sector

Indian companies allowed to raise capital abroad through GDR/ADR issues

Foreign Portfolio Investment (FPI) by FIIs allowed

Investment norms for NRIs and OCBs(Overseas Corporate Bodies) liberalised

NSE (National Stock Exchange) set up.

Online trading and dematerialization of securities initiated

Rolling settlement and derivatives trading (Options and Futures) allowed

Trade Reforms

Trade liberalised: quantitative restrictions on imports removed.

Since 1992 imports are regulated through a negative list which has been reduced in successive budgets.

EPZ (Export Processing Zone) scheme and 100% EOU schemes introduced to provide for duty free enclaves.

Rupee made convertible on the trade account and later on the current account

FERA (Foreign Exchange Regulation Act) replaced by FEMA (Foreign Exchange Management Act)

Infrastructure Reforms

Basic telecom services opened to private sector

Foreign equity participation allowed in telecom joint ventures

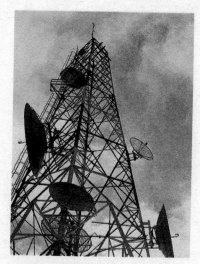

TRAI (Telecom Regulatory Authority of India) set up.

National Highway Act amended to levy fee on national highways

Road sector declared an industry to facilitate borrowing on easy terms

Private investment in road projects liberalised

A National Integrated Highway Project merging the Golden Quadrilateral connecting Delhi, Mumbai, Chennai and Calcutta with the East-West (Silchar to Saurashtra) and North-South (Kashmir to Kanyakumari) corridors launched.

Financial Sector Reforms

Banking sector

Narasimham Committee recommendations on banking reforms implemented:

New Generation Banks allowed in the private sector

Bank branch licensing liberalised

Statutory Liquidity Ratio (38.5 % in 1991) and Cash Reserve Ratio (10 % in 1991) reduced. Presently (2011) SLR and CRR stand at 24% and 6% respectively.

The Leading Gold Buyer	Gold purchases in India accounted for 32 p.c. of the global total in 2010, says the World Gold Council. Indian householders hold the largest stock of gold in the world at 18,000 tonnes.

Number of administered interest rates on bank advances reduced from 20 in 1989-90 to 2 by 1994-95

Interest rates on loans above Rs 2 lakhs completely deregulated

Nationalised banks allowed to access the capital market for debt and equity

Weak public sector banks recapitalised to the extent of Rs 11100 crores

Prudential norms for capital adequacy, income recognition, asset classification and provisioning for NPAs introduced

Insurance Sector

Malhotra Committee recommendations on insurance reforms implemented:

IRDA (Insurance Regulatory Development Authority) Act passed in 1999 facilitating private/foreign investment in life and general insurance.

Foreign equity stake up to 26% allowed in domestic insurance companies.

Taxation Reforms

Direct and Indirect taxes rationalised

Maximum marginal rate of personal income tax (56% in 1990) and corporate tax (51.75% in 1990) reduced in successive budgets to touch 30 % by early 2000s.

Peak customs duty (300% in 1990) reduced in successive budgets. Presently, excluding a small list consisting of liquor, used cars etc, the peak customs duty stands at 10 %.

Switch over from a system where excise duties were specific and numerous to a simple system where duties are small in number and imposed on advalorem basis.

VAT (Value Added Tax) in lieu of sales tax introduced at the state level

New Direct Taxes Code (DTC) and GST (Goods and Services Tax) subsuming VAT, excise and octroi expected by 2012

Service tax introduced

Impact of Reforms

The sweeping reforms initiated since 1991 led to profound economic consequences. Major consequences are summarised below:

Transition from a 'seller's market' to a 'buyer's market'

The pre-liberalization era was characterised by the dominance of sellers. Pre-empting of licenses by profiteering businessmen and restrictive provisions like MRTP Act ensured chronic shortages. In the 1970s the waiting period for a Bajaj Chetek scooter was 8 years. Customers used to pay Rs 8600 under OYT and wait for 3 years to get a telephone connection. This sellers market is now history. Liberalization and competition have ensured easy availability of quality products.

Transition from a command economy to a market economy

The pre-liberalization economic strategy based on comprehensive planning, leadership role for the public sector, import substitution and government intervention produced a command economy. This command economy has been replaced, since liberalization, by a market economy responding to impulses from the market.

Transition from a semi-closed economy to an open economy

The pre-liberalization Indian economy was characterised by restrictions on trade and severe curbs on foreign investment. Peak import duty was 300 % in 1990. With such absurd levels of protection, there was no pressure on domestic producers to perform. Liberalization of trade and investment and rationalization of duties slowly transformed the Indian economy from a semi-closed economy to an open economy.

Gold for a Loan to India — **Reserve Bank of India was forced to airlift 47 tonnes of gold to the Bank of England as a collateral for a loan in 1991.**

Trade - GDP ratio expanded from 15% in 1991 to 35% in 2010.

Transition from a low growth economy to a high growth economy

The annual average growth rate in India during 1950-80 was a dismal 3.5% - the so called 'Hindu Growth Rate.' Introduction of initial dose of reforms in the 1980s saw the Indian economy moving up to a growth rate of 5.6%. In the 1990s the growth rate picked up momentum exceeding 6 %. During 2000-2010 India became the second fastest growing economy in the world with an average growth rate of 7.3 %.The average growth rate during 2005-2011climbed to 8.4%. During 1950-80, per capita income increased only by 1.2 % annually- doubling only once in 70 years. Now per capita income is increasing at 7 % annually- doubling every 10 years. It is this spurt in per capita income that is driving India's robust domestic consumption driven growth.

Higher growth has generated millions of jobs and reduced poverty. Poverty ratio declined from 36 % in 1994 to 27.5 % by 2005. 10 million jobs (2 million direct jobs and 8 million indirect jobs) were generated in IT/ITES industry alone.

Emergence of globally competitive enterprises

In many areas like IT/ITES, petroleum refining, metals, telecom, auto-ancillaries, pharmaceuticals etc Indian companies emerged strong and globally competitive. Presently, there are 40 Indian MNCs with an annual turnover exceeding $1 billion.

Many Indian companies have successfully acquired foreign MNCs - Tata Steel (Corus), Tata Motors (Jaguar Land Rover) Bharti (Zaine) to name just three - enhancing India's standing in the global corporate arena. India's IT/ITES exports shot up from $100million in 1990-91 to $59 billion in 2010-11.

Massive Spurt in Social Sector Spending

A major benefit of the high growth was the spurt in tax- GDP ratio from 8% in 1991 to 11.5% by 2008. This tax buoyancy enabled the government to undertake ambitious social sector projects like MGNREGS, Bharath Nirman etc. The annual outlay for MGNREGS in 2010-11 (Rs 39500 crores) was higher than the total tax revenue of the central government in 1990-91. The ambitious food security program planned to be implemented from 2012 would entail huge expenditure. For sustaining such ambitious social sector programs it is very important that India should target for a higher growth rate, say above 9 % and sustain it for a long time.

The Challenges Going Forward

India's spectacular economic performance since liberalization is, indeed, a great achievement. India was one of the few economies of the world which did not experience recession during the Great Recession of 2009. However, it is important that some deficiencies of this growth be recognised and addressed. A major deficiency of India's spectacular growth is that the growth has not been 'inclusive'. Large number of poor, marginalised, vulnerable sections of the society has been left out of the growth process. This deficiency has to be addressed and growth has to be made inclusive.

Another major deficiency is the infrastructure deficit which is becoming a major constraint on sustainable high growth. Land acquisition, environmental clearances and speedy execution of infrastructure projects brooks no delay. If India can address these challenges and move forward with determination, she is destined to become an economic super power of the 21st century.

Agriculture

The agriculture sector is the backbone of Indian economy as it accounts for about 58 per cent of employment in the country (as per 2001 census). In terms of composition, out of a total share of 14.6 per cent of the GDP in 2009-10 for agriculture and allied sectors, agriculture alone accounted for 12.3 per cent followed by forestry and logging at 1.5 per cent and fisheries at 0.8 per cent.

The growth of agriculture and allied sectors is a critical factor in the overall performance of the Indian economy. As per the 2010-11 advance estimates released by the Central Statistics Office (CSO) on 07.02.2011, the agriculture and allied sector accounted for 14.2 per cent of the gross domestic product (GDP), at constant 2004-05 prices. During the period 2004-05 to 2007-08, the GDP for agriculture and allied sectors had increased from ₹ 5, 65,426 crore to ₹ 6,55,080 crore, at constant 2004-05 prices; thereafter it stagnated at this level for two years (2008-09 to 2009-10. In 2009-10, it accounted for 14.6 per cent of the GDP compared to 15.7 per cent in 2008-09 and 19.0 per cent in 2004-05. Its share in GDP has thus declined rapidly in the recent past. This is explained by the fact that whereas overall GDP has grown by an average of 8.62 per cent during 2004-05 to 2010-11, agricultural sector GDP has increased by only 3.46 per cent during the same period.

Performance During 2007-2012

During the first three years of the current Five Year Plan, the agriculture sector (including allied activities) recorded an average growth of 2.03 per cent against the Plan target of 4 per cent per annum. In the first year, 2007-08, of the current Plan the agriculture sector had achieved an impressive growth of 5.8 per cent. However, this high growth could not be maintained in the following two years and agriculture-sector growth fell into the negative zone of - 0.1 per cent in 2008-09, although this was a

year of a record 234.47 million tonnes food production. The decline in growth of agricultural GDP was primarily due to the fall in the production of agricultural crops such as oilseeds, cotton, jute and mesta, and sugarcane. In 2009-10, despite experiencing the worst south-west monsoon since 1972 and subsequent significant fall in kharif foodgrain production, the growth marginally recovered to 0.4 per cent primarily due to a good rabi crop.

Crop Production

For four consecutive years from 2005-06 to 2008-09, foodgrains production registered a rising trend and touched a record level of 234.47 million tonnes in 2008-09. The production of foodgrains declined to 218.11 million tonnes during 2009-10 (final estimates) due to the long spells of drought in various parts of the country in 2009. The productivity of almost all the crops suffered considerably, which led to decline in their production in 2009. As per the second advance estimates released by Ministry of Agriculture on 9.2.2011, production of foodgrains during 2010- 11 is estimated at 232.07 million tonnes compared to 218.11 million tonnes during 2009-10. This is only marginally below the record production of 234.47 million tonnes of foodgrains in 2008-09. The country is likely to achieve record production of wheat (81.47 million tonnes), pulses (16.51 million tonnes) and cotton (33.93 million bales of 170 kg. each) this year. This high level of production has been achieved despite crop damage due to drought in Bihar, Jharkhand, Orissa and West Bengal and the effects of cyclones, unseasonal and heavy rains, and cold wave and frost conditions in several parts of the country.

Rice and wheat: During the 1980s the growth in area in rice was marginal at 0.41 per cent but growth in production and yield was above 3 per cent. From 2000-01 to 2009-10 the situation changed with growth in area turning negative and in production and yield standing at 1.59 per cent and 1.61 per cent respectively. In wheat too, during the 1980s the growth in area was marginal at 0.46 per cent but in production and yield was above 3 per cent. During 2000-01 to 2009-10 the growth in area in wheat was 1.21 per cent and in production and yield was 1.89 per cent and 0.68 per cent respectively. This suggests that in these two crops the yield levels have plateaued and there is need for renewed research to boost production and

productivity. Given the constraints in area expansion, there is no other alternative. Both public and private-sector investment in research and development (R&D) needs to be encouraged.

Coarse Cereals: In coarse cereals the situation is totally different. Since there was no technological breakthrough in these crops, the growth rate in area of total coarse cereals, in both the periods (1980-81 to 1989-90 and 2000-01 to 2009- 10) was negative reflecting either shift to other crops or relatively dry area remaining fallow. In all the major coarse cereals there was negative growth in area during both the periods except for maize, which recorded a growth rate of 2.98 per cent in the 2000- 01 to 2009-10 period. However, growth in production and yield for coarse grains which was 0.40 per cent and 1.62 per cent respectively in the 1980s improved significantly to 2.46 per cent and 3.97 per cent respectively in the 2000-01 to 2009-10 period. This increase is primarily driven by maize and bajra.

Spicewise Area & Production (Area in hectares, Production In Tonnes)

	2006 - 07		2007 - 08		2008 - 09	
	Area	Prodn.	Area	Prodn.	Area	Prodn.
Pepper	236177	50000	196297	50000	181074	46745
Cardamom (Small)	73228	11235	69280	9470	71170	10999
Cardamom (Large)	30039	4303	30039	4920	27034	4300
Chilli	809437	1325273	836684	1371250	801070	1353796
Ginger	129014	721539	120056	710476	138479	795028
Turmeric	183917	856464	175947	826030	194358	892213
Coriander	361767	287647	458473	286377	507935	416663
Cumin	409033	176511	477936	264860	527132	283000
Fennel	61128	92260	84479	131652	74149	114277
Fenugreek	44984	55780	54965	67645	103097	95833
Garlic	169612	833157	219814	1088800	194274	1009116
Vanilla	5129	233	4734	182	4477	169
Clove	1941	742	1902	716	2172	1002
Nutmeg	13709	11564	14921	11217	16400	11362
Cinnamon	530	27	530	27	186	37
Tamarind	58624	190073	55682	188278	54222	193873
Dill seed	11083	9679	15912	18465	8620	11522
Ajwan	31657	15850	19590	11196	20776	16299
Saffron	2928	4.85	3000	5	3000	9
Celery	1799	2350	3158	4239	4117	5329
Tejpat	6140	15961	6646	17277	6646	17277
Grand Total	2649075	4664210	2850044.59	5063082.03	2940388	5278851
Grand Total (in Mln Tonnes)		4.66		5.06		5.28

Source: Spices Board, Ministry of Commerce and Industry

Plantation Crops

Plantation crops in India are considered to be the main segment of the horticulture crops. They are the mainstay of agrarian economies in many States and Union Territories (UTs) of the country. They play an important role in the agricultural and industrial development of the country as a whole. They contribute a significant amount to the national exchequer and the country's exports by way of excise and export earnings. They also provide direct and indirect employment to a large number of people in the country, and thus try to supplement the poverty alleviation programmes, especially in the rural sector.

Major Crops

Plantation crops constitute a large group of crops. The major plantation crops include coconut, arecanut, oil palm, cashew, tea, coffee and rubber; and the minor plantation crops include cocoa. India is the largest producer and consumer of cashew nuts. India also occupies the number one position in arecanut production.

Tea and coffee are the main and oldest industries in the country, which provide ample employment opportunities to the people at large and hold immense potential for export. India is one of the largest tea producers in the world. Coffee is the second largest traded commodity in the world and is an extremely important foreign exchange earner. The coffee industry of India is one of the largest producers of coffee in the world.

India is the third largest producer of coconut and leads 90 coconut-producing countries of the world. The area for coconut plantation in India has been mainly distributed over 18 States and 3 UTs, under different agro-climatic conditions. Wide range of coconut products, edible and non-edible, are available for both domestic and export market. India is a premier manufacturer of coir which is a coconut product. Tender coconut water concentrate is another product, apart from soft drinks, which is manufactured and marketed successfully.

What Ails Plantation Sector?

But, in India, plantation crops have been continuously facing the problem of lack of investment and depressed yields, and are in great need of modernisation. Their total coverage is comparatively less and they are mostly confined to small holdings. The Government of India has identified some prominent crops as high-value crops of great economic importance and is taking all possible steps and initiatives to commercialize the sector. Tea, coffee, rubber and coconut industries are providing great business opportunities to the investors worldwide.

India is also the largest producer and consumer of cashew nuts. It is estimated that total production of cashew is around 0.57 million tonnes from an area of 0.24 million hectares. The cultivation of vanilla in India started in 1990s and was confined mostly to Karnataka and Kerala and to a lesser extent in Tamil Nadu, Northeast region, Lakshadweep and the Andaman

40 mn.
Indians Go
Hungry

In India, 40 mn. people go hungry every day. The country is 67th in a ranking of 122 most malnourished countries.

and Nicobar Islands. India's production of vanilla was about 169 metric tonnes from about 4,477 hectare in 2008-09. Coconut is grown in an area of 1.93 million ha. with a production of 12,148 million nuts and productivity of 6285 nuts per ha. India occupies number one position in arecanut production. Out of these, about 65 plants have large and consistent demand in world trade. As a result, horticulture is not only an integral part of food and nutritional security, but also an essential ingredient of economic security.

Rubber is a major plantation crop. The total production of rubber in 2010-11 was 861,950 metric tonnes and the area under cultivation was 712,000 hectares. The yield in 2010-11 was 18.07 kg/ ha. as against 17.75 kg/ha. in 2009-10.The number of growers is 1.16 million and the average holding area per grower is only 0.53 ha.

Contribution to Economy

Plantation Crops play an important role in the economy of india. The value of the plantation commodities in 2009-10 is estimated at ₹ 25,443 crore, nearly 2.53 per cent of India's total agricultural GDP, while export realisation is estimated at ₹ 5,645 crore accounting for nearly 7.9 per cent of the total agricultural and allied products exports.

India has been considered as a treasure house of valuable medicinal and aromatic plant species. The Government of India have identified and documented over 9,500 plant species considering their importance in the pharmaceutical industry.

Animal Husbandry

Animal Husbandry and Dairy Development plays a prominent role in the rural economy in supplementing the income of rural households, particularly the landless and small and marginal farmers. It also provides subsidiary occupation in semiurban areas and more so for people living in hilly, tribal and drought-prone areas where crop output may not sustain the family. According to estimates of the Central Statistical Organization (CSO), the value of output from livestock and fisheries sectors together at current prices was about ₹ 2,82,779 crores during 2007-08 (₹ 2,40,601 crores for livestock sector and ₹ 42,178 crores for fisheries) which is about 30 per cent of value of output of ₹ 9,36,597 crores from

total of Agriculture, Animal Husbandry & Fisheries sector. The contribution of these sectors to the total GDP during 2007-08 was 5.21%. India is endowed with the

India's economy has almost quadrupled in size since 1991. It has been growing by about 7% a year on average over the past two decades and by over 9% from 2005 to 2007.

Livestock Population in India by Species
(In Million Numbers)

Species	1951	1961	1972	1982	1992	2003
Cattle	155.3	175.6	178.3	192.5	204.6	185.2
Adult Female Cattle	54.4	51.0	53.4	59.2	64.4	64.5
Buffalo	43.4	51.2	57.4	69.8	84.2	97.9
Adult Female Buffalo	21.0	24.3	28.6	32.5	43.8	51.0
Total Bovines	198.7	226.8	235.7	262.2	288.8	283.1
Sheep	39.1	40.2	40.0	48.8	50.8	61.5
Goat	47.2	60.9	67.5	95.3	115.3	124.4
Horses and Ponies	1.5	1.3	1.1	0.9	0.8	0.8
Camels	0.6	0.9	1.1	1.1	1.0	0.6
Pigs	4.4	5.2	6.9	10.1	12.8	13.5
Mules	0.1	0.1	0.1	0.1	0.2	0.2
Donkeys	1.3	1.1	1.0	1.0	1.0	0.7
Yak	NC	0.0	0.0	0.1	0.1	0.1
Mithun	NA	NA	NA	NA	0.2	0.3
Total Livestock	292.9	336.5	353.2	419.6	470.9	485.0
Poultry *	73.5	114.2	138.5	207.7	307.1	489.0
Dogs	NC	NC	NC	18.5	21.8	29.0

NC : Not Collected; NA: Not Available   * Includes chicken, ducks, turkey & other birds
Source : Livestock Census 2003

largest livestock population in the world. It accounts for 57 per cent of the world's buffalo population and 14 per cent of the cattle population. According to Livestock Census (2003), the country has about 18.5 crore cattle and 9.8 crore buffaloes.

Contribution Of Livestock Sector To Food Basket

The contribution of livestock sector to the food basket in the form of milk, eggs and meat has been immense in fulfilling the animal protein requirement of ever-growing human population. The present availability of human protein in an Indian diet is 10gm per person per day, as against a world average of 25 gm. However, keeping in view the growing population, the animal protein availability has to increase at least two fold, for maintaining the nutritional level of growing children and nursing mothers in India.

Milk Production: During past five-year plans, several measures were initiated by the Government to increase the productivity of livestock, which has resulted in significant increase in the milk production to the level of 104.9 million tonnes in the year 2007- 08. India continues to be the largest producer of milk in the world.

Egg-Production: The egg production in the country has reached 53.5 billion numbers in 2007-08.

Wool Production: The wool production in the country reached 44.0 million kg during 2007-08.

Other Livestock Products: Livestock sector not only provides essential protein and nutritious human diet through milk, eggs, meat etc., but also plays an important role in utilization of non-edible agricultural by-products. Livestock also provides raw material by–products such as hides and skins, blood, bone, fat etc.

6th Economic Census

The government is planning to conduct the Sixth Economic Census in collaboration with states and union territories. Establishments in economic activities in both organised and unorganised sectors will be covered by the census.

Inclusive Growth

There is, these days, a widespread perception that the fruits of economic growth are simply passing too many people by. This general feeling of exclusion has led to the framing of policies and the initiation of measures by the government. The theme of the Eleventh Five Year Plan (2007-12) is 'towards faster and more inclusive growth'. This clearly reflects the need for striking a sustainable balance between growth and inclusion.

Inclusive growth, as the literal meaning of the two words, refers to the pace and pattern of economic growth. In this context, it is useful to distinguish between direct income redistribution or shared growth and inclusive growth. While the focus of direct income redistribution is reducing the disparities between the rich and the poor in the 'short period', the inclusive growth approach takes a 'long–term; perspective with its focus on productive employment.

Four attributes of inclusive growth can be identified.

1. Opportunity:- There is opportunity when more and more varied ways are opened up for people to earn a living and increase their income over a period of time.

2. Capability:- There is capability when means are provided to the people to create or enhance their capabilities to exploit available opportunities.

3. Access: There is access when means are provided to bring opportunities and capabilities together.

4.Security:- There is security when means are provided to protect the people against a temporary or permanent loss of livelihood.

Inclusive growth can be defined as a process in which economic growth, measured by a sustainable increase in Gross Domestic Product (GDP), contributes to an enlargement of the scale and scope of all four attributes.

The opportunity dimension relates to the question of whether the growth process gives a large (and increasing) number of people legitimate opportunities to earn incomes. The capability dimension relates to education and skill creation. Access refers to the ability of the system to bring together opportunities and capabilities. In other words, it is the ability of the system to avoid 'skill mismatch' and 'geographical mismatch'. Access can be enhanced by the ease with which people can move from location to location in search of jobs. The concept of security implies that in a dynamic and evolving economy, the benefits of growth can be derived by providing a reasonable safety net to the people as they go through temporary ups and downs.

India initiated economic reforms in a big way in 1991. It is now being realised that the reform process has only widened disparities between the rich and the poor. Poverty has been reduced to a modest figure of 0.74% for the period 1993-94 and 2004-05. Unemployment has risen from about 6% in 1993-94 to 7.32% in 1999-2000 and to 9% in 2004. Besides, the reforms have sharpened the rural-urban divide as well as the regional divide between the fast growing states and the slow growing states.

In this context, the question arises as to whether the Eleventh Five Year Plan really addresses the concerns of inclusive growth. The Approach document to the Eleventh Five Year Plan has fixed a target of stepping up overall GDP growth during the plan period to an average rate of 8.5%. This will be achieved by boosting growth of agriculture to about 4% and that of industry to 9.9% and services to 9.4%. This implies that the success of the Eleventh Five Year Plan hinges on achieving the growth target of agriculture. This is especially so because agriculture is now accounting for 22% of the GDP, but is supporting 60% of the labor force. Inclusive growth will become a reality in India only if there is a rapid decline in poverty along with a sharp decline in unemployment during the Eleventh Plan.

Corporate Sector

India has a very vibrant corporate sector which is one of the major driving forces of its economic growth.

From major multinational corporations to small and medium enterprises and ranging across a wide diversity of sectors, including manufacturing, construction, telecom and services, corporate sector has played a significant role in the economic development of the country. This growth and development of corporate sector was enabled by the liberal reforms introduced in the country from time to time.

The Corporate Sector, apart from creating wealth for the nation, plays a significant role in the national economy by providing investment and employment opportunities to millions of our people in India. There were about 30,000 registered companies at work in 1957, i.e. initial year of 2nd five year plan and this number has increased to about 8.73 lakh registered companies at work at the end of December, 2010.

The corporate sector consists mainly of non-government companies which form 99% of the total sector whereas government owned companies are a negligible 1%.

The companies are of three types - companies limited by guarantee, companies limited by shares and unlimited companies; with companies limited by shares forming the major chunk of the corporate sector (98%).

The corporate sector in India is dominated by small and medium sized companies as they constitute 92% of the sector. These companies have authorized capital of less than one crore rupees. The remaining 8% companies have authorized capital of more than one crore rupees. Only 1% companies have authorized capital of more than ₹ 25 crores.

The industrial sectors having major con-

centration of Indian companies are the manufacturing sector, finance, insurance, real estate & business activities, wholesale & retail consists of 31% of total companies followed by finance, insurance, real estate & business activities which together form 30% of the Indian Corporate sector. The industrial sector with the activities of wholesale & retail trade, hotel & restaurants forms 16% whereas construction forms 8% of the corporate sector.

The three largest states constituting 54% of the corporate sector are Maharashtra, Delhi and West Bengal.The top fifteen states having largest concentration of Indian companies are Maharashtra, Delhi and West Bengal, Tamil Nadu, Andhra Pradesh, Gujrat, Karnataka, Uttar Pradesh, Rajasthan, Kerala, Punjab, Madhya Pradesh, Bihar, Haryana and Chandigarh in that order. These states constitute 96% of the sector.

Statutory Reforms

The Ministry has been working on wide ranging reforms in the statutory frameworkmrelating to the corporate sector. Some of the major initiatives taken in this direction are as under :

I. Comprehensive revision of the Companies Act, 1956: In today's globalized

No. of Companies Limited by Shares at work as on 31st December, 2010

S.No.	State/UT	Public No.	Private No.	Total No.
1	Andhra Pradesh	6,488	56,971	63,459
2.	Asom	716	5,630	6,346
3.	Bihar	1,211	8,868	10,079
4.	Chhatisgarh	379	3,901	4,280
5.	Gujarat	5,921	44,956	50,877
6.	Haryana	1,060	10,223	11,283
7.	Himachal Pradesh	318	2,474	2,792
8.	J & K	246	2,295	2,541
9.	Jharkhand	310	4,377	4,687
10.	Karnataka	3,089	42,669	45,758
11.	Kerala	1,474	18,114	19,588
12.	Madhya Pradesh	1,429	12,966	14,395
13.	Maharashtra	15,895	1,67,159	1,83,054
14.	Manipur	43	151	194
15.	Meghalaya	131	545	676
16.	Mizoram	10	49	59
17.	Nagaland	24	234	258
18.	Odisha	930	8,135	9,065
19.	Punjab	2,211	14,376	16,587
20.	Rajasthan	1,801	25,706	27,507
21.	Tamil Nadu	7,149	62,892	70,041
22.	Tripura	29	157	186
23.	Uttar Pradesh	4,191	24,407	28,598
24.	Uttaranchal	255	1,975	2,230
25.	West Bengal	8,939	97,019	1,05,958
26.	A & N Islands	4	144	148
27.	Arunachal Pradesh	26	282	308
28.	Chandigarh	1,174	6,368	7,542
29.	D & N Haveli	62	227	289
30.	Daman & Diu	50	169	219
31.	Delhi	16,006	1,60,891	1,76,897
32.	Goa	251	5,135	5,386
33.	Lakshadweep	0	11	11
34.	Puducherry	104	1,338	1,442
	Total	**81,926**	**7,90,814**	**8,72,740**

environment, India's corporate sector is expanding its operations rapidly beyond India's border. To achieve levels of management and governance that inspire investor confidence internationally, legal and regulatory framework for corporate sector is being developed to provide a business friendly structure for entrepreneurs without compromising on the need for protection of investors and other stakeholders. The exercise was started with the preparation of the Concept Paper and its dissemination on the website of the Ministry to seek public comment, followed by constitution of an Expert Group headed by Dr J J Irani and consisting of representatives from corporate, industry bodies and professionals. Based on the inputs received from various segments, a draft Companies Bill prepared in consultation with the Ministry of Law & Justice will be introduced in the Parliament after requisite approvals.

Liberalization

Liberalization refers to the process by which government controls, usually in the areas of social or economic policies are relaxed or even removed. Most often, the term is used to refer to economic liberalization, particularly trade liberalization and capital market liberalization. In the post-independence period, India resorted to socialistic pattern of devlopment . The policies framed by the government tended towards protectionism, import substitution, industrialization under state monitoring, a large public sector and centralized economic planning. Between the period 1950 and 1990, elaborate licences, quotas, permits and regulations and a set of labyrinthine bureaucratic procedures were required to set up business in India. This is commonly referred to as the License Raj. The Indian currency was inconvertible and pegged to a basket of major currencies. High tariffs and import licensing prevented foreign goods from reaching the domestic market in the required quantities. The central planning machinery allocated resources in the economy and the market mechanism had a relatively passive role to play. The State decided what to produce how much to produce, and at what prices, leaving little or no space for the private sector. Under these circumstances the annual growth rate of Indian economy stagnated around 3.5% from 1950s to 1980s, while per capita income growth rate averaged 1.3%. This, along with the age-old customs and religious superstitions that prevailed in India that time, prompted the economist, Raj Krishna to refer to India's economic growth rate as the 'Hindu Rate of Growth'.

By the end of 1990, India ran into serious balance of payment crisis. The government was on the verge of default, Foreign Exchange (FOREX) reserves were precariously low due to increasing import payments and the RBI refused to grant credit to the government. The government sought IMF bailout for which 67 tons of gold was transferred to London as collateral. Indian

Rupee was devalued to tide over the Balance of Payments crisis. The then Finance Minister, Dr. Manmohan Singh took vigorous steps to modernise Indian economy and initiated economic reforms in a way to free the economy from the fetters of 40 years of state control and licensing. Controls were dismantled, tariffs, duties and taxes progressively lowered, privatization and de-nationalization were initiated, Foreign Direct Investment (FDI) was encouraged, and globalization was slowly but surely embraced. The License-Permit-Quota (LPQ) era had ended and the new age of Liberalization-Privatization-Globalization (LPG) had been ushered in.

The economic reforms initiated since 1991 were translated into significant gains for the economy. Forex reserves that stood at $42 billion in 2000-01 increased to nearly $152 billion at the end of 2005-06. In 2007, India recorded its highest GDP growth rate of 9%. With this India became the second fastest growing economy in the world, next only to China. For the year 2010, India was ranked 124th among 179 countries in the Index of Economic Freedom World Ranking, an improvement from the preceding year. In Purchasing Power Parity (PPP) terms, India is the world's fourth largest economy behind only the US, China and Japan.

India is going ahead with the liberalization initiatives started in 1991 but the pace has somewhat slackened. One plausible reason for this slackening pace might be the financial crisis that gripped the US and other major free market economies recently. However, if India is to catch up with China, it has to speed up the reforms.

Privatization

Peter F. Drucker, the renowned management expert, was the first to use the concept of privatization. The term privatization, when used in a narrow sense, is the process of transferring ownership of a business or enterprise from the public sector (the state or government) to the private sector (business that operate for private profit) or private non-profit organizations. In a broader sense, it connotes besides private ownership, the induction of private management and control in the public sector enterprises. Barbara Lee and John Nellis define privatization in the following words: "Privatization is the general process of involving the private sector in the ownership or operation of a state–owned enterprise. Thus the term refers to private purchase of all, or part of a company. It covers 'contracting out' and the privatization of management - through management contracts, leases or franchise arrangements." Thus, privatization covers ownership measures, organizational measures and operational measures. Ownership measures are intended to transfer ownership of public enterprises, fully or partially to the private sector. Such measures include total denationalization, joint ventures liquidation and management buy-outs. Organizational measures such as a holding company structure, leasing, restructuring etc. are intended to limit state control in public enterprises. Operational measures are intended to improve efficiency and productivity by infusing the spirit of enterprise and commercialisation in public enterprises. The measures include grant of autonomy in decision making, provision of incentive to the employees etc.

Privatization is often thought of as the transfer of ownership of public enterprises to private hands. However, the real signifi-

cance of privatization comes only with the induction of private managerial control in public enterprises. Sometimes voucher privatization is resorted to whereby shares of ownership in public enterprises are distributed to all citizens, usually at low prices. In some contexts, even 'taken privatization' in the sense of 'disinvestment' has also been referred to as a measure of privatization.

Proponents of privatization believe that market forces can deliver goods and services more efficiently than governments due to free market competition. This will eventually lead to lower prices, better quality of products, greater choices, less corruption and redtape and less wastages. The basic rationale for privatization is that in public enterprises there are few incentives to ensure that these enterprises are well run. In state monopolies and public utility services there is no competition from the private sector without which efficiency cannot be evaluated. Another argument for privatization is that managers of privately–owned enterprises are accountable to the shareholders and customers and can thrive only when their needs are met. Managers of publicly owned companies, on the other hand, are more accountable to the general community and political 'stakeholders', which is likely to undermine their capac-

Third Largest Economy	At the current rate of growth, India will be the third largest economy in the world by 2025, Prime Minister Manmohan Singh said in August, 2011.

ity to serve the needs of their customers. Loss-making public sector enterprises are sometimes 'bailed out" by the government to prevent employees from being laid-off, when it may be more economical to shut them down. Poorly managed private companies, on the other hand, could go bankrupt, have their managements replaced or be simply taken over by more efficient competitors.

Opponents of privatization argue that democratically elected governments are accountable to the people who elected them to power and, therefore have an incentive to maximize efficiency in public enterprises. They also believe that public goods and services are best left in the hands of government. There is a positive externality when the government provides these goods and services to the society at large. Market is inherently guided by self-interest and profit and therefore players in the market are committed to charging the maximum price. This is not compatible with the social welfare motive of the government whose aim is to provide public goods and services (like basic education, health case, defence etc.) at affordable prices.

Multinational corporations often resort to retrenchment and laying-off workers as part of their cost-cutting measures. Thinkers like Noam Chomsky believe that "putting profit before people" is not a socially compatible strategy.

This eighties witnessed a wave of privatization sweeping the whole world. Privatization gained momentum under the leadership of Margaret Thatcher in the U.K. and Ronald Reagan in the U.S. In India, too, privatization became a buzz word along with liberalization and globalization, especially since 1991. However, attempts at privatization in our country have been half-hearted. This is due to various reasons such as the resistance of trade unions, lack of determination on the part of political parties to take a frontal position against public sector etc. Besides, unlike the U.S and west European countries, India lacks a sound social security system to support' people who cannot survive the vicissitudes of free market. In spite of all this, more and more areas have been opened up to the private sector and the public sector has been relegated to strategic areas like infrastructure and defence.

Globalization

The concept of globalization means different things to different people. To the pro-globalizers it reflects images of prosperity, abundance and a general rise in the incomes and standards of living of people around the world. The *New York Times* columnist Thomas L. Friedman celebrated its virtues. To the anti-globalizers and hard-core leftists, globalization is a much detested term meaning the expansion of imperialist capitalism throughout the world. Groups as diverse eco–feminists,

deconstructionists, etc. tend to hold the latter view. The French sociologist, Pierri Bourdieu proclaimed its vices, its vulnerability. Economists Jagdish Bhagwati defines globalization in the following words: "Economic globalization constitutes integration of national economies into the international economy through trade, direct foreign investment (through corporations and multinationals), short-term capital flows, international flows of workers and humanity generally, and flows of technology."

The origin of globalization can perhaps be traced to the Doctrine of Comparative Cost Advantage propounded by the classical economists like David Ricardo. The theory extols the virtues of free trade and international specialization which fetch gains for all trading partners. Thus, if country A can produce cars cheaply and country B computers, they specialize in their respective areas of strength and then exchange their surpluses with each other, which will mean more cars and computers in both countries. More recently, the term globalization has come to be used in a wider context, including cultural globalization.

The pro-globalizers argue that the process of globalization would promote Foreign Direct Investment (FDI) in the less-developed countries (LDCs) which, in turn, would step up employment opportunities in these countries. The poor countries, they point out, would also benefit from the use of the technology of the advanced countries. Other professed merits of globalization include export-led growth for the LDCs and diffusion of knowledge, reduction in the costs of transport and communication and tariffs.

On the flip side, globalization is said to exclude from its purview, a vast majority of people living on the fringes of society. Critics point out that the free flow of capital and technology would widen the disparity in incomes and wealth and aggravate the problem of poverty and unemployment in the less developed countries. Free trade, they reason, does not necessarily mean fair trade, as is evidenced by the experience of the poor countries. Goods exported by the poor countries are typically agricultural (whose prices are relatively volatile) and those exported by the rich countries are predominantly industrial (which fetch relatively higer prices). It follows, therefore, that when trade is opened up, the rich countries would stand to gain.

Globalization is believed by many to be one of the major causes of environment pollution and ecological degradation. Mindless consumerism and self-aggrandizement which are part of the globalization agenda would eventually lead to the progressive degradation of the environment. The problem of e-waste is a case in point.

Globalization is said to lead to cultural homogenization, in which local and ethnic cultures are destroyed through the homogenizing effects of the western media. The ubiquitous western brands like Coca Cola, McDonalds and KFC bear testimony to this fact. American symbols like Jeans, Hollywood movies and pop stars are adored by young people around the world and the western lifestyle is emulated by them.

Prof. Jagdish Bhagwati, a staunch supporter of globalization, believes that the problem is not globalization itself, but the way it is managed, globalization needs to be supplemented by the safety net measures of the govt. The solution does not lie in trickle-down growth economics, but a direct and frontal attack on poverty and unemployment. A more inclusive pattern of growth needs to be followed. Basic amenities like food, housing, education and healthcare must be provided to the vulnerable and needy people. Concentration of wealth in the hands of international conglomerates must be effectively checked. The issue is not whether we should go for globalization or not, but how the fruits of globalization are distributed. Only a fair distribution of the gains from globalization would make it meaningful.

385mn. BPL Indians	There are about 385 mn. Indians below the poverty line. i.e. 32 p.c. of the 1.21 bn. people. In 2004, there were 370 mn. Indians bpl, which was 37% of total population of one billion. Thus, poverty has increased in absolute terms, says the Planning Commission.

Indian Agriculture at the Crossroads

S. Bala Ravi
Advisor and Former Assistant Director General, ICAR
M.S. Swaminathan Research Foundation, Chennai

What is ailing Indian agriculture? Why are young men not attracted to farming?

The share of agriculture to India's GDP was 46.3% in 1950, and it declined to 16% in 2008. However, agriculture continues to be the principal sector supporting the livelihood of about 600 million rural population. Such dependence of the largest number of people on agriculture and its relatively low GDP are the primary causes for many of the ills plaguing the current crisis in Indian agriculture.

High rate of farmer suicides and reluctance of farmers to stay in farming are two major problems today. According to one estimate the number of farmers who committed suicide between 1995 and 2010 had reached 2,56,949. For many, agriculture had ceased to be a worthwhile profession. The National Sample Survey Organisation (NSSO) report stated that about 40% of farm households preferred to leave agriculture, if only they had an alternative. Another sign of deepening crisis is reluctance of youth, to enter agriculture. Equally disturbing is the trend in the rapid fragmentation of farm holdings rendering their cost-risk-return structure more unfavourable. Number of farm holdings is increasing at annual growth rate of 1.84% with their average size shrinking. Thus farming as an important livelihood option of many is becoming increasingly unviable. Those who stay put are getting pushed into debt trap

and below poverty line. And more recently the rising demand on fertile agricultural land for non-agricultural use are drawing farmers into conflicts with other sectoral interests and adding more pressure on the dwindling strength of agriculture for serving its strategic national role.

Global Position

India is the second largest producer of agricultural products and it also has second largest arable land. India occupies top global position in the production of milk and pulses and the second position in the production of rice, wheat, cereal grains, sugarcane, fruits and vegetables, tea, egg and culture fishery. India and China are in a see-saw game for top position for the total irrigated area. Indian agriculture during the five decades since the 1960s has set several milestones in production and productivity of major food crops, some of the

| Greatest Living Industry | Lord Curzon, the then Viceroy of India, while inaugurating IARI at Pusa, Bihar, in 1905 , referred to farming as India's greatest living industry. |

commercial, horticultural and plantation crops, livestock and fishery, particularly the inland fishery. These remarkable achievements were made with a right combination of appropriate technology, right policy and institutional support and above all the enthusiasm of farmers. Despite these, it is an irony that the very farmers who played a key role for the historic transformation of Indian agriculture are now left behind in poverty, underdevelopment and indebtedness in the resurgent India.

A *Ship-to-Mouth* Nation

In 1950, India with 360 million people produced 40 million tonnes of cereal grains. She could not feed her people without regular food imports. As the young India did not have hard currency to pay for the food imports, she went on pleading to certain countries for food aid to prevent mass starvation. The United States of America offered assistance to help Indian agriculture and to provide food aid under its Public Law 480. The assistance continued up to the late 1960s. The world media sarcastically branded India with many humiliating epithets; "the begging bowl", "country of starving millions" and "ship-to-mouth nation". This period of dependence on food aid was a period of extreme national distress and disgrace. Indian agriculture under 'Green Revolution' made a historic transformation from "ship-to-mouth" years to a period of self sufficiency in food production. This had been lauded as one of the two outstanding achievements during the 50 years of Indian independence, the other being the remarkable rise in the average life expectancy.

Another dimension to the dependence on food aid is its use as a political tool to make inroads into the national sovereignty and independent policies of the receiver country to the extent of subservience. Therefore, India's agricultural transformation in the 1960's and 1970's had a profound impact not only on the national food security and its ability to export certain amount of food grains, but also on other unrelated domains of national polity, which contributed to restoration of national pride and sovereignty. A highly populated country like India needs to avoid high dependence on others for food supply in the interest of its sovereignty and freedom to choose its own domestic and foreign policies.

> These achievements were made with a right combination of appropriate technology, right policy and institutional support and the enthusiasm of farmers.

Reasons for the Setback

The restoration of national pride and esteem achieved by the food sufficiency has no economic equivalent. But, the image of the national agricultural sector seems to have suffered setbacks in many ways since the 1990s under economic liberalization. The following factors seem to be responsible for the current setback: (1) the race for rapid economic growth has ignored the inherent nature of slow growth of agriculture; (2) the historic weakness of agricultural sector, in influencing national policies and investment priorities; (3) propagation of a prominent economic thought that food can always be imported by an economically strong India and therefore prior-

Rural Population	In 1901, percentage of rural population to total population was as high as 89.2. By 1951, the percentage fell to 82.7. In 1991, percentage of rural population was 74.3 and it reached 72.22 in 2001.

agriculture and industry and the strength of these sectors in influencing government policies. The loan issued to agriculture in 2007-08 was Rs. 194,953 crores, while the same made available to the industry in 2007 was more than three times. In the case of subsidies, the total subsidies given to agriculture during 2007-08 were Rs 87708 crores, while the same extended to the industry was many times higher.

Many have ventured into commercial agriculture from marginal farming. Suicides have been higher in regions where high investment commercial agriculture has higher risks.

Economic Growth vs Domestic Food Production: The food grain production of India in 2010-11 is estimated to be about 240 million tonnes. Even with such production, food import at small level will become essential to substitute export of high value food items and to regulate domestic supply and prices. Now the government is to legislate and implement the food security bill to entitle a section of citizens to receive certain quota of food grains at subsidized prices. India has ceased to be a regular food importing country since the 1970s. Most of the imports made since then were to substitute the food grain exported.

ity on investment and subsidy should be to faster growing sectors of economy rather than to agriculture; (4) increased cost of production; (5) longstanding neglect in reforming agricultural market to ensure a fair deal to farmers; (6) archaic and anti-farmer land policies allowing diversion of prime farm lands for non-agricultural activities;

> Now the government is to legislate and implement the food security bill to entitle a section of citizens to receive certain quota of foodgrains at subsidized prices.

(7) poor coping capacity of farmers in the free market system.

Economic Growth and Agriculture: The liberalisation of the economy had certainly re-invigorated the national economic growth. In 1990-91, the share of services, industry and agriculture to the GDP was 44.5 %, 19.4 % and 26.5 %, respectively, while in 2008-09 these shares shifted respectively to 59.1 %, 18.6 % and 16.1 %. The liberalised economic growth excluded a large section of population that depended on agriculture and to that extent enlarged the economic inequity. This inequity is deepening the crisis in Indian agriculture.

Marginalization of Agriculture

Marginalization of agriculture is evident from a comparison of public investment in

Need for a Strong Agricultural System

By 2020, India is poised to overtake China in population. Ten percent reduction in India's food production, which is a normal event during unfavourable agricultural years, may force India to import food grains. But,

Nearly 80% of the land holdings in India are below two hectares in size. Unlike in industrialised countries where only 2-4% of the population depend upon farming, agriculture is the backbone of the livelihood security system for 2/3 of India's population.

Size of Holdings

the global agricultural productivity growth is declining and this may force constraints in coming years on availability of tradable food produces. All these underscore the huge tactical importance of ensuring domestic food production to meet substantive level of demand. This cannot be achieved without continuous strengthening of the national agricultural system. Promotion of all other sectors of economy, which offer higher growth rate, will not be sustainable without a strong national agricultural system. "If agriculture goes wrong in India, nothing else will have a chance to go right", says Prof. M.S. Swaminathan, the renowned agricultural scientist. Rural India carries largest burden of below poverty line population, who heavily depend on agriculture for livelihood. This includes about 233 million people or almost 60 % of the rural labour force who depended on agriculture. Vast majority of them are unskilled. The rate of employment for every million rupees investment in industry and services sectors is far lower than that in agriculture. Therefore, larger investment in agriculture and skill development in related sectors such as value chain and agri-business are the only option for immediate alleviation of rural poverty.

Farm Fragmentation and Economic Viability of Farming: One of the reasons is the rapid fragmentation of farm holding.

The size of majority of farm holdings is decreasing to below the economic threshold. In 1960, India had 48 million holdings with an average size of 2.7 hectares and this leapfrogged to 120 million holdings in 2000-01 with an average size of 1.33 hectares. Currently 95% of the 120 million holdings have only 4 ha and below and they share 65 % of the total operational area. Such rapid fragmentation is disabling farmers from accessing technologies, credit and other paid services. The average monthly income from these holdings is a meagre ₹ 2115, comprising 46 % from crop husbandry, 39 % from wages, 4 % from animal husbandry and 11 % from non-farm sources. Given the average family size of five, it means a per capita daily income of ₹ 14.1. This is below the poverty line defined by the Planning Commission. It is predicted that by 2050 the per capita grain land availability will be 0.06 hectares.

Decreasing Income from Farming: Increasing cost of production and lack of commensurate produce price have been important aspects behind the decreasing farm income. Food crops occupy 63% of gross cropped area. There is a perceptible decline in national rice area and this decline is very drastic in regions having high cost of production.

Lack of fair market in home and away: Unlike industrial producers, farmers have no control over any of the components, except their own labour, influencing production and market. Apart from farming being heavily subject to the vagaries of weather, particularly in the 60% rain-fed area, farmers are at the receiving end for the supply, quality and prices of inputs such as seeds, fertilizers, other agrochemicals, labour wages, water, electricity. Indian agriculture,

Comparative Crop Productivity (Kg / hectare)

Crop	USA	China	India
Maize	8900	4900	2100
Paddy	7500	6000	3000
Soybeans	2250	1740	1050
Seed Cotton	2060	3500	750
Tomato	6250	2400	1430

until the recent past, was served largely by the public research and extension system which provided technology either free or at low price. The post-liberalisation period witnessed decline of the public research and extension system in quality of service and rise of private sector research and input services. While many of the state Agricultural Universities are starving for funds, more are being created. The funding on national agricultural R&D is stuck at 0.6% of agricultural GDP, while this share in developed countries is 2 to 3%. The far less organised farming community of India is no match to the politically influential and economically powerful private interests in getting a fair deal. The budget crunch to the state agricultural departments stands on the way of strengthening the technology transfer service, which has virtually paralysed in many states. The culture of

> India has emerged as a net exporter, although she is a marginal player with a share close to 1% of the world trade in agriculture.

bureaucracy and insulation from farming realities are making agricultural departments irrelevant.

Agricultural Trade: Trade in farm produces has always been in private hands. The extent of market exploitation being meted out to them is shocking. Whether the harvest is good or bad, farmers are always the victims of a vicious market. No institutional support reaches them, whether the produce is perishable or not.

Diversion of Agricultural Land: India has the seventh largest land area and second largest area in arable land. Unlike other countries with larger land area, India is naturally gifted by having higher share of its land (62%) suitable for agriculture. India also has the largest irrigated area under ag-

riculture. However, the current per capita land availability in India (0.13 ha) is one of the lowest and this poorly compares with 75-fold higher per capita land area available in many developed countries. India hardly has any more arable land to bring under agriculture. Under this scenario, diversion of agricultural land, particularly the prime land, for non-agricultural uses such as special economic zones, real estate business, town building and land degrading mining will hasten the shrinkage of per capita food production area.

Free Trade in Agriculture and Indian Farmers: A decade of WTO negotiations started from Doha Round on Agreement on Agriculture (AoA) for dismantling of huge subsidies being allowed to agriculture in developed countries, market access to agricultural and non-agricultural products (NAMA), removal of non-tariff trade barriers and review of Trade-Related aspects of Intellectual Property rights (TRIPs) have reached nowhere. In the meantime status quo has been continuing to the net disadvantage of developing countries. When India removed quantitative restrictions in 2001, about 300 plus agricultural commodities were identified as 'sensitive' for monitoring and regulating their imports. While India's total export and imports have increased under the WTO regime, the balance sheet of foreign trade shows a steady and rapidly rising deficit. India has emerged as a net exporter, although she is a marginal player with a share close to 1 % of the world trade in agriculture.

India's increased growth rate in agricul-

| ICAR Set Up | The Indian Council of Agricultural Research was established in 1929 on the basis of a recommendation of the Royal Commission on Agriculture headed by Lord Linlithgow. |

tural exports started in 1986, well before the economic liberalisation. However, since 1990-91, the value of agricultural imports increased 31-fold, while the same for agricultural exports was only 14-fold. Import-export ratio, in value terms, of agricultural products in 1990-91 was 1:5 and this dwindled to almost 1:2 in 2008-09. Major importing items are vegetable oils (palm oil and soybean oil), raw cashew nut, cotton, and pulses. The major source of import in value terms is ASEAN. This has been the reason for India go for a FTA with ASEAN and also for negotiating another FTA with EU. The FTA with ASEAN is unfavourably viewed by producers of plantation crops such as coconut, pepper, coffee and certain spices. This takes to the issue of preparing national agriculture to the emerging global trade regime and to withstand competition under FTAs and regional trade agreements (RTAs) like SAFTA with appropriate policies, capacity building and non-tariff based interventions. Imposition of high tariff line had been the main national strategy in the past for safeguarding domestic agriculture from external competitions. India is facing huge pressure at WTO for substantial reduction of the tariff lines of many agricultural commodities and this appears largely inevitable. However, there are no anticipatory measures on policy formulations, institutional arrangements and capacity building to farmers to mitigate the setback agriculture may face under the emerging trade order.

Growth at a Snail's Pace

Indian agriculture during last two decades has been growing at a snail's pace, while farmers have been facing unprecedented distress on multiple counts. Distress is due to yield and price instability, decreased income, mounting indebtedness, increasing cost of living and erratic weather. This in different regions of the country, particularly the rain-fed regions, has been making tragic manifestations in the suicides of thousands of farmers. According to the government of India there are at least 33 districts experiencing high distress among farmers. Indian agriculture in the present state cannot modestly cope with the free trade regime and climate change. A populous country like India cannot depend on huge food import. National food sufficiency has strong bearing on sovereignty and independent domestic and foreign policies. The Northern heartlands of Indian food production (Punjab, Haryana and Western Uttar Pradesh), had slumped in productivity fatigue since a decade. The productivity fatigue is rather widespread and sustainable growth ahead of population growth has become a major challenge. Equally challenging is that all additional food demand of future from growing population and rising living standard will have to come only from productivity growth. Another concern is the decreasing area under food crops, while the projected cereal grain demand by 2020 is 296 million tonnes. The economic policies and investment in agriculture are far inadequate to meet the current and emerging challenges. ■

| Livelihood for 600 mn. | Agriculture, comprising crop and animal husbandry, fisheries, forestry and agro-forestry and agro-processing is the largest private sector industry in India, providing livelihood opportunities for over 600 mn. men and women. |

Five Year Plans

Soon after gaining independence, India was beset by a host of economic and political problems. The political situation in the country was not very stable due to the partition of the nation and the influx of refugees. On top of this were severe food shortage and mounting inflation. The Indian administrators under the leadership of Prime Minister Jawaharlal Nehru took a major decision - one which was to leave its legacy for the next 40 odd years - to take the country along the path of social-istic pattern of economic development and centralised planning. Indeed, the Soviet model of Gos Plan provided inspiration to the Indian leaders.

First Five –Year Plan (1951-'56)

The First Five –Year Plan was launched on 8th December, 1951. The Plan emphasized, as its primary objectives, the rehabilitation of refugees, rapid agricultural develop-ment and the control of inflation. The to-tal planned budget of ₹ 206.8 billion was allocated to seven broad areas: irriga-tion and energy (27.2%), agriculture and community development (17.4%), trans-port and communication (24%), industry (8.4%), social services (26.64%), land re-habilitation (4.1%) and for other sectors and services (2.5%). The target growth rate was 2.1% and the realized growth rate was 3.6%.

Second Five–Year Plan (1956-61)

The Second Five–Year Plan was conceived in the background of economic stability. Inflation had been contained and agricul-tural targets fixed in the First Plan had been achieved. The basic thrust in the Second Five Year Plan was in favour of basic and heavy industries, such as iron and steel, heavy chemicals heavy engineering and machine building industry. The basic philosophy of the Second Plan was to give a 'big push' to the economy. The total amount allocated under the Plan was ₹ 4800 crore. The tar-get growth rate was 4.5%. However, the actual growth rate was only 4.27%.

Third Five –Year Plan (1961-66)

The Third Five–Year Plan set as its goals, the establishment of a self-reliant and self-generating economy. The experience of the Third Plan had shown unequivocally that agriculture was the mainstay of Indian economy and neglecting agriculture would be perilous for the economy. Hence, top pri-ority was assigned to agriculture. Emphasis was also placed on basic industries. How-ever, the brief Sino-Indian war in 1962 and the Indo-Pak war in 1965 shifted the focus from development to defence. The target growth rate of GDP was 5.6% whereas the actual growth rate was only 2%.

Fourth Five–Year Plan (1969-74)

The original draft outline of the Fourth Five Year Plan prepared in 1966 had to be abandoned in the wake of two years of drought, devaluation of the rupee and the stagflation. Instead three Annual Plans (1966-'69) euphemistically referred to as "Plan Holiday" were implemented. The fourth Plan (1969-74) set two principal ob-

| Satellite Phone | **The first satellite-based telephone communication network ITINET was commissioned on March 9, 1986 at Manakpur in U.P. by Indian Telephone Industries.** |

jectives namely "growth with stability" and "progressive achievement of self-reliance". The targeted rate of growth was 5.5% and the actual rate was 3.3%.

Fifth Five–Year Plan (1974-'79)

The Fifth Five–Year Plan was introduced at a time when the Indian economy was reeling under a hyper inflation due to hike in oil prices and the failure of the government to take over the wholesale trade in wheat. The final draft of the Plan set two objectives, viz., removal of poverty and the attainment of self-reliance through promotion of higher rate of growth, better distribution of income and an increase in the domestic rate of saving. The Fifth Plan was terminated by the newly elected Janatha Government in March 1978. The targeted growth rate was 4.4% and the actual growth rate was 4.8%.

Sixth Five–Year Plan (1980-'85)

There were two Sixth Plans. The Janatha Sixth Plan (1978-83) focused on the enlargement of employment potential in agriculture and allied activities, encouragement to small scale industries producing consumer goods for mass consumption and the raising of incomes of the lowest income groups through a minimum needs programme.

The new Sixth Five Year Plan ((1980-85) introduced by the Congress government rejected the Janatha Plan and reintroduced the Nehruvian model of growth by aiming at a direct attack on the problem of poverty by creating conditions of an expanding economy. The targeted growth rate was 5.2% whereas the actual growth rate was 5.66%.

Seventh Five–Year Plan (1985-'90)

The Seventh Five–Year Plan was introduced in April 1985. During the Sixth Five Year Plan the country had enjoyed a reasonable rate of growth of foodgrains production, generation of employment opportunities and the increase in productivity. The Plan had a long-term objective of achieving self-sustaining growth by the year 2000. The

targeted growth rate was 5%, while the actual growth rate was 6%.

Eighth Five–Year Plan (1992-'97)

During the period 1989-91, India witnessed political instability and so between 1990 and '92 there were only annual plans. Finally, the Eighth Five Year Plan (1992-'97) was finalized at a time when the country was going through a serious balance of payments crisis, rising debt burden, widening budget deficit, mounting inflation and recession in industry. The Narasimha Rao government initiated the process of fiscal reforms and economic reforms with a view to reviving a near bankrupt nation. This period marked the beginning of privatization and liberalization in India. The major objectives of the Eighth Plan were modernization of industry, controlling of population growth, poverty reduction, employment generation, strengthening of infrastructure, tourism management, human resource development etc. Energy was given priority with 26.6% of the total outlay. An annual average growth rate of 6.78% against the target of 5.6% was achieved.

Ninth Five–Year Plan (1997-2002)

The focus of the Ninth Five–Year Plan was on "growth with Social Justice and Equality". The Plan assigned priority to agriculture and rural development with a view to generating adequate gainful employment and eradication of poverty. It also aimed to stabilize the prices in order to accelerate the growth rate of the economy and to ensure food and nutritional security. The

Black Money : **According to Central Board of Direct Taxes (CBDT), black money worth Rs. 30,000 crore has been seized in the past two years.**

targeted rate of growth was 7% per annum but the actual growth rate came to only 5.35%.

Tenth Five–Year Plan (2002-2007)

The Tenth Five–Year Plan was conceived in the backdrop of a vibrant and fast growing economy in the post-liberalization period. The main objective was to attain 8% growth rate of GDP per annum. In addition to the targeted growth rate, the Plan had the following targets:-

* Reduction of poverty ratio by 5 percentage points by 2007 and by 15 percentage points by 2012.

* Gainful employment to the addition to the labour force over the Tenth Plan period.

* Universal access to primary education by 2007

* Reduction in the decadal rate of population growth between 2001 and 2011 to 16.2%

* Increase in literacy to 75% by 2007

* Reduction in infant mortality ratio (IMR) to 45 per 1000 live births by 2007.

* All villages to have access to potable drinking water by 2012.

The Tenth Five Year Plan which set out to achieve 8% growth rate had to satisfy with an actual growth rate of around 7%. Besides, the performance of the agricultural sector was not very encouraging. Regional inequalities had only increased and unemployment rate shot up. On the whole, the Tenth Five Year Plan did not met the objective of promoting growth with social justice.

The Eleventh Five–Year Plan (2007-2012)

The Eleventh Plan visualizes "faster and more inclusive growth" as its basic objective. In order to realize this objective it is imperative to reduce poverty, to bridge the divide between the rich and the poor, and to extend basic amenities like health, education, clean drinking water, sanitation etc. to larger sections of the population. Simultaneously, we must strive to achieve rapid growth in order to raise the standards of living of the people.

The monitorable socio-economic targets of the 11th Plan are as follows: To accelerate growth rate of GDP from 8% to 10% and then maintain it at 10% in order to double per capita income by 2016-17; to increase agricultural growth rate to 4% per year to ensure a broader spread of benefits, to create 70 million new work opportunities; to reduce educated unemployment to below 5%; to raise real wage rate of unskilled workers by 20% and to reduce the headcount ratio of consumption poverty by 10 percentage points. Some important targets in the fields of education, health and infrastructure are as follows: Increase the literacy rate for persons of age 7 years or more to 85%; reduce Infant Mortality Rate (IMR) to 28 and Maternal Mortality Rate (MMR) to 1 per 1000 live births; provide clean drinking water for all by 2009 and ensure that there are no slip-backs at the end of the 11th plan; reduce malnutrition among children of age group 0-3 to half its present level; ensure electricity connection to all villages and BPL households by 2009 and round-the clock power by the end of the Plan.

With the 11th Five–Year Plan in its 4th year, the economic growth of the country has not reached the targeted level and has fallen short of the objective of inclusive growth. It is, therefore, important to step up economic growth to realize the basic goal of the Eleventh Plan.

A Private Sector Phone	Indore became the first city in India to have a private sector-run telephone provided by AirTel.

Economy of India
Key Indicators

Data Categories and Components	Units	2005-06	2006-07	2007-08	2008-09	2009-10	2010-11
1 GDP and Related Indicators							
GDP (current market prices)	₹ crore	3692485	4293672	4986426	5582623[PE]	6550271[QE]	7877947[AE]
Growth Rate	%	13.9	16.3	16.1	12.0	17.3	20.3
GDP (factor cost 2004-05 prices)	₹ crore	3254216	3566011	3898958	4162509[PE]	4493743[QE]	4879232[AE]
Growth Rate	%	9.5	9.6	9.3	6.8	8.0	8.6
Savings Rate	% of GDP	33.5	34.6	36.9	32.2	33.7	na
Capital Formation (rate)	% of GDP	34.7	35.7	38.1	34.5	36.5	na
Per Cap. Net National Income (factor cost at current prices)	₹	27123	31198	35820	40605	46492	54527
2 Production							
Foodgrains	Mn tonnes	208.6	217.3	230.8	234.5	218.1[a]	232.1[b]
Index of Industrial Production[c] (growth)	Per cent	8.0	11.9	8.7	3.2	10.5	na
Electricity Generation (growth)	Per cent	5.2	7.2	6.4	2.8	6.0	na
3 Prices							
Inflation (WPI) (52-week average)	% change	4.3	6.5	4.8	8.0	3.6	9.4[d]
Inflation CPI (IW) (average)	% change	4.4	6.7	6.2	9.1	12.4	11.0[d]
4 External Sector							
Export Growth (US$)	%change	23.4	22.6	29.0	13.6	-3.5	29.5[e]
Import Growth (US$)	%change	33.8	24.5	35.5	20.7	-5.0	19.0[e]
Current Account Balance (CAB)/GDP	Per cent	-1.2	-1.0	-1.3	-2.3	-2.8	na
Foreign Exchange Reserves	US$ Bn.	151.6	199.2	309.7	252.0	279.1	297.3[f]
Average Exchange Rate	₹/ US$	44.27	45.25	40.26	45.99	47.42	45.68[g]
5 Money and Credit							
Broad Money (M3) (annual)	% change	16.9	21.7	21.4	19.3	16.8	16.5[h]
Scheduled Commercial Bank Credit (growth)	% change	30.8	28.1	22.3	17.5	16.9	24.4[h]
6 Fiscal Indicators (Centre)							
Gross Fiscal Deficit	% of GDP	4.0	3.3	2.5	6.0	6.3[i]	4.8
Revenue Deficit	% of GDP	2.5	1.9	1.1	4.5	5.1[i]	3.5
Primary Deficit	% of GDP	0.4	-0.2	-0.9	2.6	3.1[i]	1.7
7. Population	Million	1106	1122	1138	1154	1170	1186
		(2005)	(2006)	(2007)	(2008)	(2009)	(2010)

AE GDP figures for 2010-11 are advance estimates; PE Provisional Estimates QE Quick Estimates
na not yet available / released for 2009-10.

a. Final estimates.

b. Second advance estimates.

c. The annual growth rates have been recompiled from 2005-06 onwards since the indices have been recompiled from April 04 onwards using new series of WPI for the IIP items reported in value terms.

d. Average Apr. - Dec. 2010.

e. Apr. - Dec. 2010.

f. as of December 31, 2010.

g. Average exchange rate for 2010-11 (Apr.-Dec. 2010).

h. Provisional.

i. fiscal indicators for 2009-10 are based on the provisional actuals for 2009-10.

Source: Economic Survey 2010-11

Indian Industry - An Overview

India has been successful in achieving autonomy in producing different basic and capital products since independence The productivity of the major Indian industries incorporates aircraft, vessels, automobiles, steam engines, heavy electrical equipment, construction machinery, chemicals, precision equipments, communication instrument, power generation and transmission tools and computers.

From independence to 1980: During this period there was restrictive growth of private sector and government's permission was required to set up any private enterprise in India. Despite this the GDP grew at the rate of 1.4% per annum from 1940-1970. Other factors such as poverty and famine lowered India's economic growth rate during this period and with the presence of very few top producers of major industrial goods the absorption of domestic productivity was greater, which led to monopolistic pricing. India during this phase lagged behind in terms of economic growth as the rest of world grew and flourished through overseas trade.

1980 to mid-1990s: The post 1980 period w itnessed economic growth which received further impetus with liberalization in mid-1991. The nation witnessed a historic upsurge in per capita GNP. In 1994-95 the industrial output-growth registered 8.4% growth and the exports rose by 27%. This resulted in a 10% drop in inflation in the mid-1990s

1990s to 2000s: Since the start of its liberalization policy, India has opened several public sector enterprises. The exports saw a 17% rise in 1994 and 28% in 1995-96. Over 90% of India's imports are backed by export revenues. At present the current account deficit is quite manageable and foreign-exchange reserves are showing a

healthy trend. The food stocks have witnessed an all-time increase of 37m tonnes.

The Index of industrial production (IIP) registered a growth rate of 10.4% in 2009-10 against a growth rate of 2.6% in 2008-09.

The private sector, which was neglected by previous governments, contributes two-thirds of India's GDP. The shift of the state's responsibility from a chief investor to a catalyst of private enterprise has paved the way to a new accord on liberalization.

Experts believe that the contribution of India to the world GDP is estimated to increase from 6% to 11% by the year 2025, while the contribution of the U.S. to world GDP is presumed to decline from 21% to 18%. This indicates the emergence of India as the third biggest global economy after U.S. and China. The evaluation is support-

Bank Credit Growth

Credit from banks in India reached Rs. 40.76 lakh crore in April 2011. This was a 22 p.c. growth of credit from Rs. 33.37 lakh crore in April, 2010. Growth of credit meant an upsurge in industrial activity.

ed by the overall development in all the sectors in India, of which the key sector is the industry sector.

Major industries in India

Automobile Industry: One of the major industrial sectors in India is the automobile sector. Subsequent to liberalization, the automobile sector has been aptly described as the sunrise sector of the Indian economy as this sector has witnessed tremendous growth.

Automobile Industry was delicensed in July 1991 with the announcement of the New Industrial Policy. The passenger car industry was delicensed in 1993. No industrial licence is required for setting up any unit for manufacture of automobiles except in some special cases. The norms for Foreign Investment and import of technology have also been progressively liberalized over the years for manufacture of vehicles including passenger cars in order to make this sector globally competitive. At present 100% Foreign Direct Investment (FDI) is permissible under automatic route in this sector including passenger car segment. The import of technology/technological upgradation on the royalty payment of 5% without any duration limit and lump sum payment of US$ 2 million is also allowed under automatic route in this sector. With the gradual liberalization of the automobile sector since 1991, the number of manufacturing facilities in India has grown progressively.

According to data released by Society of Indian Automobile Manufacturers (SIAM), the total number of vehicles including passenger cars, commercial vehicles, two wheelers and three wheelers produced in 2009-10 was 14,049,830, as compared to 11,172,275 produced in 2008-09.

Surge in automobile industry since the nineties has led to robust growth of the auto component sector in the country. During the year 2008-09,the turnover and export for auto component industry was recorded at US $ 15.85 billion and US $ 3.11 billion respectively.

Cement Industry: Cement is one of the most technologically advanced industries in the country. During the industry's humble beginning in 1914, it has grown from a meagre one lakh tonnes to a mammoth 262.91 million tonnes. As on 1st April 2008, there were 159 large cement plants in the country. India is the second largest producer of cement with a production capacity of 262.91 million tonnes as on June 30, 2010, next only to China.

Chemical Industry: Indian Chemical industry generates around 70,000 commercial goods ranging from plastic to toiletries and pesticides to beauty products. It has an estimated size of $35 billion, which is equivalent to about 3% of India's GDP. The total investment in indian chemical sector is approximately $60 billion and total employment generated is about 1 million. The Indian chemical sector accounts for 13-14% of total exports and 8-9% of total imports of the country.

Construction: The construction industry in India is an important indicator of development as it creates investment opportunities across various related sectors. The construction industry has contributed an estimated

₹ 3,84,282 crore (at constant prices) to national GDP in 2010-11 (a share of around 8 per cent). The industry is fragmented, with a handful of major companies involved in construction activities across all segments; medium sized companies specializing in

niche activities; and small and medium contractors who actually work on subcontract basis and carry out the work in the field. The sector is labour–intensive and, including indirect jobs, provides employment to more than 35 million people.

Fertilizers : Foodgrain production is closely related to fertilizer consumption. India being a highly populated country, ensuring food security is the prime agenda of the government. Food security primarily depends on fertizer security. Consumption of fertilizer nutrients increased from 78 lakh tonnes in 1965-66 to 24.91 million tonnes in 2008-09. Correspondingly , foodgrains production rose from 72.35 million tonnes to 234.47 million tonnes during the same period.

India is meeting 85 per cent of its urea requirement through indigenous production but is largely import dependent for meeting the phosphorus and potassium (P&K) fertilizer requirements either as finished fertilizers or raw materials. The entire requirement of potash, about 90 per cent of phosphatic, and about 20 per cent of urea is met through imports.

In addition to urea, 21 grades of P & K fertilizers, namely di-ammonium phosphate (DAP), muriate of potash (MOP), mono-ammonium phosphate (MAP), triple super phosphate (TSP), ammonium sulphate (AS), single super phosphate (SSP), and 15 grades of NPK complex fertilizers are pro-

vided to farmers at subsidized rates, which are much below the actual cost. Farmers pay only 25 to 40 per cent of the actual cost and the rest is borne by the Government in the form of a subsidy that is reimbursed to the manufacturers/importers.

The domestic production of urea in the year 2009-10 was 211.12 lakh MT, as compared to 199.20 lakh MT in 2008-09. The production of DAP increased sharply in 2009-10 and was at 42.46 lakh MT as compared to 29.93 lakh MT in 2008-09. The estimated production of urea in 2010-11 is projected at 215.37 lakh MT and that of DAP and complexes at 39.58 lakh MT and 91.66 lakh MT respectively.

Food Processing Industry: Indian food processing industry is widely recognized as a 'sunrise industry' having huge potential for uplifting agricultural economy, creation of large scale processed food manufacturing and food chain facilities, and the resultant generation of employment and export earnings. The industry is estimated to be worth around US$ 67 billion and employing about 13 million people directly and about 35 million people indirectly. The food processing sector in India is geared to meet the international standards. Food Safety and Standards Authority of India has the mandate to set standards and also to harmonise the same with International Standards consistent with food hygiene and food safety requirement and to the conditions of India's food industry.

Two nodal agencies, Agricultural & Processed food products Export Development Authority (APEDA) and Marine Products Export Development Authority (MPEDA), were formed for promoting exports from India. MPEDA is responsible for overseeing all fish and fishery product exports; APEDA, on the other hand, holds responsibility for the exports of other processed food products.

IT and ITeS: India has gained a brand identity as a knowledge economy due to its IT and ITeS sector. The IT-ITeS industry has four major components: IT services, business process outsourcing (BPO), engineering services and R&D, and software products. The growth in the services sector in India has been led by the IT-ITeS sector which has become a growth engine for the economy, contributing substantially to increases in the GDP, employment, and exports. This sector has improved its contribution to India's GDP from 4.1 per cent in 2004-05 to 6.1 per cent in 2009-10 and an estimated 6.4 per cent in2010-11. The industry has also helped expand tertiary education significantly. The top seven States that account for about 90 per cent of this sector's exports have started six to seven times more colleges than other States.

The Indian IT-ITeS industry has registered robust growth since 2004-05. According to NASSCOM, the year 2010-11 is characterized by broad-based growth across mature and emerging verticals. The overall Indian IT-ITeS revenue has grown to US $ 63.7 billion in 2009-10 and an estimated US $ 76.1 billion in 2010-11, translating into a CAGR of 22.5 per cent from 2004-05 to 2010-11. The industry grew by an estimated 19.5 percent in 2010-11 compared to the moderate growth of 6.2 per cent in 2009-10. Exports dominate the IT-ITeS industry, and constitute about 77 per cent of total industry revenue. Total IT-ITeS exports have grown from US$ 17.7 billion in 2004-05 to US $ 49.7 billion in 2009-10 and an estimated US $ 58.9 billion in 2010-11 registering a CAGR of 22.2 per cent from 2004-05 to 2010-11.

Though the IT-ITeS sector is export–driven, the domestic market is also significant with a revenue growth of US $ 14 billion in

2009-10 and an estimated revenue of US $ 17.2 billion in 2010-11. The IT and BPO industry (excluding hardware) witnessed a quick rebound in growth and has been estimated to have grown by 19.5 per cent, aggregating revenues of US$ 76.1 billion in 2010-11 with exports at US$ 58.9 billion accounting for a major portion.

This sector has also led to employment generation. Direct employment in the IT services and BPO/ITeS segment was 2.3 million in 2009-10 and is estimated to reach nearly 2.5 million by the end of financial year 2010-11. Indirect employment of over 8.3 million job opportunities is also expected to be generated due to the growth of this sector in 2010-11. These jobs have been generated in diverse fields such as commercial and residential real estate, retail, hospitality, transportation, and security.

India continues to be the dominant player in the global outsourcing sector. However, its future will depend on how the challenges related to its continued competitiveness are tackled. These include increasing competition, rising costs, tal-

IT-ITeS Revenue and Exports (US $ billion)

Year	2009-10	2010-11 (Estimated)	Growth Rate in 2010-11 (%)	CAGR (2005-06 to 2010-11) (%)
Total IT-BPO Services Revenue	63.7	76.1	19.5	22.5
Exports	49.7	58.9	18.5	22.2
Domestic, of which	14.0	17.2	22.8	23.7
(i) IT Services	8.9	10.9	22.5	20.8
(ii) ITeS-BPO	2.2	2.8	27.3	29.3
(iii) Software Products	2.9	3.5	20.7	30.7

Source : Nasscom.

ent shortfall, infrastructure constraints, increasing risk perception, protectionism in key markets, and deteriorating business environment.

The Government has been supporting the IT and ITeS sector in many ways. This was continued in the 2010-11 Budget with policies like Government expenditure for improving IT infrastructure and delivery mechanism, reduction in surcharge from 10 per cent to 7.5 per cent for IT companies and governments.

E-Governance Plan. There are some issues in the IT-ITeS sector which need attention. These include shifting from low-end services to highend services like programming in the light of competition in BPO from other countries and policies in some developed countries like UK to employ locals; addressing data protection issues as half of offshore work does not come to India; concluding totalization agreements with target countries to resolve the social security benefits issue as is being done now; and increasing the coverage and depth of IT and ITeS services in the domestic sector.

Electronics Hardware Manufacturing: The production of electronics is estimated to grow by 13 per cent to reach ₹109,940 crore in 2009-10 as compared to ₹ 97,260 crore in 2008-09. Electronics hardware exports are estimated to be ₹ 31,250 crore in 2009-10 as compared to ₹ 31,230 crore in 2008-09. The cumulative export figure in electronics during 2010-11 (April to July) is estimated at US $ 1.36 billion (₹ 6259 crore) whereas during the same period in the previous year, exports of electronics amounted to US $ 1.92 billion (₹ 9339 crore).

Mining Industry: The GDP contribution of the mining industry varies from 2.2% to 2/5% only but going by the GDP of the total industrial sector it contributes around 10% to 11%. Even mining done on small scale contributes 6% to the entire cost of mineral production. Indian Mining Industry

provides job opportunities to around 0.7 million individuals.

Oil and Natural Gas: The Indian oil and gas sector is one of the six core industries in India and has very significant forward linkages with the entire economy. India has been growing at a decent rate annually and is committed to accelerate the growth momentum in the years to come. This would translate into India's energy needs growing many times in the years to come. Hence, there is an emphasized need for wider and more intensive exploration for new finds, more efficient and effective recovery, a more rational and optimally balanced global price regime - as against the rather wide upward fluctuations of recent times, and a spirit of equitable common benefit in global energy cooperation.

Oil and Natural Gas Corporation Limited (ONGC) and Oil India Ltd. (OIL), the two National Oil Companies (NOCs) and private and joint-venture companies are engaged in the exploration and production (E&P) of oil and natural gas in the country. During the year 2008-09, crude oil production has been 33.51 million metric tonnes (MMT) with natural gas at 32.85 billion cubic metre (BCM). Natural gas production in 2009-10 is targeted to be about 52.116 BCM.

During the financial year 2008-09, imports of crude oil was 128.16 MMT valued at US$ 73.97 billion. Imports of crude oil

Indians on
Rs. 115
a Day

The per capita income of the average Indian is around Rs. 42,000, or Rs. 115 a day.

during 2007-08 was 121.67 MMT valued at US$ 58.98 billion. This marked an increase of 5.33 per cent during 2008-09 in quantity terms and increased by 25.37 per cent in value terms.

During the financial year 2008-09, exports of petroleum products in quantity terms is 36.93 MMT valued at US$ 25.41 billion marking an increase of 6.02 per cent in value terms compared to 2007-08.

Pharmaceutical Industry: India's pharmaceutical industry is now the third largest in the world in terms of volume and stands 14th in terms of value. According to data published by the Department of Pharmaceuticals, Ministry of Chemicals and Fertilizers, the total turnover of India's pharmaceuticals industry between September 2008 and September 2009 was US$ 21.04 billion. Of this the domestic market was worth US$ 12.26 billion. Sale of all types of medicines in the country is expected to reach around US$ 19.22 billion by 2012.

Export of pharmaceutical products from India increased from US$ 6.23 billion in 2006-07 to US$ 5.92 billion in 2007-08 and to US$ 8.7 billion in 2008-09 - a combined annual growth rate (CAGR) of 21.25 per cent.

According to a report by PricewaterhouseCoopers (PwC) in April 2010, India will join the league of top 10 global pharmaceuticals markets in terms of sales by 2020 with the total value reaching US$ 50 billion.

The Indian pharmaceutical industry is a major player in the $80 billion global generics market.

Steel Industry: India ranked as the fourth largest producer of crude steel in the world during January–November 2010, after China, Japan, and the USA as per the World Steel Association. This was a slip in rank from its number three position in 2009. The country has also been the largest sponge iron producer in the world since 2002. Domestic crude steel production grew at a compounded annual growth rate of 8.4 per cent during 2005-06 to 2009-10. The increase in production rode on the back of capacity expansion, mainly in private-sector plants, as also higher utilization rates. The Steel Ministry has targeted 124 million tonnes a year domestic steel production capacity by 2012-13.

The Indian steel industry has diversified its product mix to include sophisticated value-added steel used in the automotive sector, heavy machinery, and physical infrastructure. It, however, suffers from the high ash content of locally available metallurgical coal and a marked dependence on imported coal. The issues regarding raw material security (e.g. getting iron ore mining lease), infrastructure (affecting logistics and transport), and uncertainties in land acquisition have emerged as bottlenecks to greenfield expansion. During April- November 2010-11, consumption, imports, and exports of finished steel recorded growth rates of 9.8 per cent, 11.1 per cent, and 13.8 per cent respectively.

Textile Industry: Traditionally, after agriculture, the only industry that has generated huge employment for both skilled and unskilled labour is textiles. The textile industry continues to be the second largest employment generating sector in India. It offers direct employment to over 35 million people in the country.

According to the Ministry of Textiles, the sector contributes about 14% to industrial production, 4% to the country's gross domestic product (GDP) and 17% to the country's export earnings.

Highest ORA | **Indian Bank claims it has emerged with the highest ROA (return on assets) at 1.53 per cent for 2010-11. Return on assets is a key efficiency parameter which shows the quality of assets vis-a-vis return thereon.**

The share of textiles in total exports was 11.04% during April-July 2010, as per the Ministry of Textiles.It is estimated that India would increase its textile and apparel share in the world trade to 8% from the current level of 4.5% and reach US$ 80 billion by 2020. In the last 10 years, the textile industry has attracted foreign direct investment (FDI) worth US$ 861.47 million.During 2009-10, Indian textiles industry was pegged at US$ 55 billion, 64% of which services domestic demand.

Telecom: The telecom sector has grown from a level of 22.8 million telephone subscribers in1999 to 54.6 million in 2003, and further to 764.77 million at the end of November 2010. Wireless telephone connections have contributed to this growth as the number of wireless connections rose from 3.57 million in March 2001 to 729.58 million by the end of November 2010. Teledensity, which was 2.32 per cent, increased to 64.34 per cent in November 2010. However, there is a wide gap between rural tele-density (30.18 per cent in November 2010) and urban tele-density (143.95 per cent in November 2010).

The Internet, which is another growing mode of communication, is a worldwide system of computer networks. Broadband is often called 'highspeed' Internet, because it usually has a high rate of data transmission. Broadband subscribers grew from 0.18 million in 2Q05 to 10.71 million as at the end of November 2010. Introduction of BWA (Broadband Wireless Access) services will enhance the penetration as

well as growth of broadband subscribers. Wi-Max has also been making headway in penetration of wireless broadband connectivity across all sectors.

The Indian telecom services industry grew almost 15 percent to post revenues of ₹ 166,168 crore in 2010-11, up from the previous fiscal's ₹ 144,600 crore.Telecom services, revenue includes revenue from cellular, fixed line, broadband and VSAT services.

The cellular or mobile services market, the largest among all the communication services offered in the country, saw revenues rise 16.6 percent to cross the ₹100,000 crore revenue milestone, according to a survey conducted by leading telecom industry journal Voice & Data.

At end of the financial year 2010-11, revenues from this segment had grown to ₹102,230 crore from ₹ 87,680 crore a year before.

Fixed lines and revenues, the only significant means of telecommunications until the mid 1990s, continued to decline both in terms of number of connections and revenues. It grossed earnings of ₹ 11,602 crore, a decline of 15.6 percent year-on-year.

Broadband services saw revenues grow 22.4 percent to ₹ 6,846 crore, but the industry as a whole failed to achieve the government's target of 20 million broadband connections by 2010, ending with just 11.87 million subscribers for the fiscal ended on March 31.

Travel and Tourism: Travel and Tourism is now the biggest service industry in India. In 2007-08, the contribution of tourism to the country's GDP, and to total jobs (direct and indirect) in the country was estimated at 5.92 per cent, and 9.24 per cent respectively. In absolute numbers, the total number of tourism jobs in the country increased from 38.6 million in 2002-03 to 49.8 million in 2007-08. According to the UN World Tourism Organization, tourism provides 6 per cent to 7 per cent of the world's total jobs directly and millions more

10 Mn. Workers a Year

The labour force increases by 10 mn. or more as 25 mn. Indians enter the world every year.

indirectly through the multiplier effect in this sector. Tourism also plays an important role in the country's foreign exchange earnings, as its share in India's export of services accounted for 13 per cent of the total export of services in 2009-10.

In 2009, India registered 563 million domestic tourism visits, which represents a rise of over 15 per cent over the previous year. According to the World Travel and Tourism Council, india will be a tourism hotspot from 2009-18, with the highest 10-year growth potential globally.

Travel and Tourism Competitiveness Report of 2009 from the World Economic Forum, has ranked India as 11th in the Asia Pacific region and 62nd overall on the list of the world's most attractive destinations.

Infrastructure Development holds the key to India's sustained growth in the tourism sector. Therefore, the Ministry of Tourism has been making efforts to develop quality tourism infrastructure at tourist destinations and circuits. The Ministry of Tourism has sanctioned 94 projects for an amount of ₹ 394.85 crores for infrastructure augmentation including rural tourism projects in the year 2009-10 (up to November 09).

The Ministry has launched a scheme for development of nationally and internationally important destinations and circuits through mega projects. To date 29 mega projects have already been identified and of these 21 projects have been sanctioned.

Foreign tourist arrivals in India during the month of May 2010 were 345,000, an increase of 15.5 per cent over May 2009. Foreign tourist arrivals during January-May 2010 were 2.263 million, an increase of 11.3 per cent over the corresponding pe-

riod last year. Foreign exchange earnings during May 2010 were US$ 951 million, an increase of 42.2 per cent over May 2009. Foreign exchange earnings during January-May 2010 were US$ 5,822 million, an increase of 38.3 per cent over the corresponding period last year, according to data released by the Ministry of Tourism.

The hotels and restaurants sector is an important sub-component of the tourism sector. Availability of good quality and affordable hotel rooms plays an important role in boosting the growth of tourism in the country. Presently there are 1593 classified hotels with a capacity of 95,087 rooms in the country. The hotels sector comprises various forms of accommodation, namely star category hotels, heritage category hotels, timeshare resorts, apartment hotels, guest houses, and bed and breakfast establishments.

Share of the hotels and restaurant sector in the overall economy.

The CAGR in the GDP contributed by the hotels and restaurants sector was 8.5 per cent in 2004–05 to 2009–10. There was, however, negative growth (-3.41 per cent) in 2008–09 over the year 2007– 08, which was due to the adverse global economic conditions in this year, while in 2009-10, the sector registered a growth of 2.2 per cent. Several studies have identified the demand-supply gap in hotel rooms in India; some of them have estimated a gap of 150,000 hotel rooms, of which 100,000 rooms are in the budget segment. Since the construction of hotels is primarily a private-sector activity and is capital intensive with a long gestation period, the Government is making efforts to stimulate investments in this sector and speed up the approval process.

Medical Tourism: The market size of the Indian medical tourism sector is likely to more than double to ₹ 10,800 crore by 2015 from ₹ 4,500 crore at present. The inflow of medical tourists in India is also likely to cross 32 lakhs by 2015 from the current level of 8.5 lakhs. Top-notch healthcare sectors like cardiology, joint replacement, orthopaedic surgery, transplants and urology at a low price are certain key factors making India a favoured destination in terms of medical tourism.

Banking

Banking in India has its origin as early as the Vedic period. It is believed that the transition from money lending to banking must have occurred even before Manu, the great Hindu Jurist, who has devoted a section of his work to deposits and advances and laid down rules relating to rates of interest. During the Mogul period, the indigenous bankers played a very important role in lending money and financing foreign trade and commerce. During the days of the East India Company, it was the turn of the agency houses to carry on the banking business. The General Bank of India was the first Joint stock bank to be established in the year 1786. The others which followed were the Bank of Hindustan and the Bengal Bank. The Bank of Hindustan is reported to have continued till 1906 while the other two failed in the meantime. In the first half of the 19th century the East India Company established three banks; the Bank of Bengal in 1809, the Bank of Bombay in 1840 and the Bank of Madras in 1843. These three banks also known as Presidency Banks, were Independent units and functioned well. These three banks were amalgamated in 1920 and a new bank, the Imperial Bank of India was established on 27th January 1921. With the passing of the State Bank of India Act in 1955 the undertaking of the Imperial Bank of India was taken over by the newly constituted State Bank of India. The Reserve Bank which is the Central Bank was created in 1935 by passing the Reserve Bank of India Act 1934. In the wake of the Swadeshi Movement, a number of banks with Indian Management were established in the country namely, Punjab National Bank Ltd., Bank of India Ltd., Canara Bank Ltd., Indian Bank Ltd., The Bank of Baroda Ltd., The Central Bank of India

Ltd. On July 19, 1969, 14 major banks of the country were nationalised and on 15th April 1980 six more commercial private sector banks were also taken over by the government. Today the commercial banking system in India may be classified into

Public Sector Banks

a. State Bank of India and it associate banks called the State Bank group
b. 20 nationalised banks
c. Regional rural banks mainly sponsored by public sector banks

Private Sector Banks

a. Old generation private banks
b. New generation private banks
c. Foreign banks in India
d. Scheduled co-operative banks
e. Non-scheduled banks

Co-operative Sector

The Co-operative banking sector has been developed in the country to supplement the village money lender. The co-operative banking sector in India is divided into 4 components.
1. State Co-operative Banks
2. Central Co-operative Banks

| Goodbye to Cheques | Germany has greatly reduced the use of cheques. Quoting the bank a/c number is the way now. In UK, cheques have been in play for over 300 years but there are plans to give them up by 2018. |

3. Primary Agriculture Credit Societies
4. Land Development Banks
5. Urban Co-operative Banks
6. Primary Agricultural Development Banks
7. Primary Land Development Banks
8. State Land Development Banks

Development Banks

1. Industrial Finance Corporation of India (IFCI)
2. Industrial Development Bank of India (IDBI)
3. Industrial Credit and Investment Corporation of India (ICICI)
4. Industrial Investment Bank of India (IIBI)
5. Small Industries Development Bank of India
6. SCICI Ltd.
7. National Bank for Agriculture and Rural Development (NABARD)
8. Export Import Bank of India
9. National Housing Bank.

Currently, overall, banking in India is considered as fairly mature in terms of supply, product range and reach–even though reach in rural India still remains a challenge for the private sector and foreign banks. Even in terms of quality of assets and capital adequacy, Indian banks are considered to have clean, strong and transparent balance sheets-as compared to other banks in comparable economies in its region. The Reserve Bank of India is an autonomous body, with minimal pressure from the government. The stated policy of the Bank on the Indian Rupee is to manage volatility without any stated exchange rate–and this has mostly been true.

With the growth in the Indian economy expected to be strong for quite some time-especially in its services sector, the demand for banking services-especially retail banking, mortgages and investment services are expected to be strong. M&As, takeovers, asset sales and much more action (as it is unravelling in China) will happen on this front in India.

Bank penetration in India is woefully inadequate on all fronts. Branch penetration, deposit and credit activity are much lower than the benchmarks. Manipur has the lowest branch penetration with one branch covering 33,000 people, while Nagaland and Bihar come second and third at 26,000 and 25,000 people per branch

respectively.

When it comes to deposit and credit accounts with banks, the difference between rural and urban areas is stark. There are 978 deposit accounts for every thousand people in urban areas, while in rural areas, this is just 245. When it comes to accessing credit, there are 42 accounts per 1,000 people in rural India whereas urban areas average 161 accounts per 1,000 people.

Total outstanding deposits of scheduled commercial banks as of August 27, 2010 was ₹ 46,70,237.91 crore, according to RBI data. There has been an increase of 14.44 per cent on a year-on-year basis, in bank deposits. The outstanding bank credit was reported to be at ₹ 33,51,396 crore as of August 27, 2010. Bank credit had increased by 19.81 per cent on a year-on-year basis.

Reserve Bank Of India

The Reserve Bank of India (RBI) was established under the Reserve Bank of India Act, 1934 on 1 April 1935 and nationalised on 1 January 1949. The Bank is the sole authority for issue of currency in India other than one-rupee coins and subsidiary coins. As the agent of the Central Government, the Reserve Bank undertakes distribution of one-rupee coin as well as small coins issued by the Government. The Bank acts as banker to the Central Government, and state governments by virtue of agreements entered into with them. The Reserve Bank also handles the borrowing programme of the Central and State Governments. It formulates and administers monetary policy with a view to ensuring price stability while promoting higher production in the real sector through proper deployment of credit. The RBI plays an important role in maintaining orderly conditions in the foreign exchange market and acts as an agent of the Government in respect of India's membership of International Monetary Fund.

Mutual Fund Industry

The formation of Unit Trust of India in 1963, at the initiative of the Government of India and Reserve Bank of India, marked the evolution of the mutual fund industry in India. The history of mutual funds in India can be broadly divided into four distinct phases

First Phase – 1964-87

Unit Trust of India (UTI) was established on 1963 by an Act of Parliament. It was set up by the Reserve Bank of India and functioned under the regulatory and administrative control of the Reserve Bank of India. In 1978 UTI was de-linked from the RBI and

the Industrial Development Bank of India (IDBI) took over the regulatory and administrative control in place of RBI. The first scheme launched by UTI was Unit Scheme 1964. At the end of 1988 UTI had ₹ 6,700 crores of assets under management.

Second Phase – 1987-1993 (Entry of Public Sector Funds)

1987 marked the entry of non- UTI, public sector mutual funds set up by public sector banks and Life Insurance Corporation of India (LIC) and General Insurance Corporation of India (GIC). SBI Mutual Fund was the first non- UTI Mutual Fund established in June 1987 followed by Canbank Mutual Fund (Dec 87), Punjab National Bank Mutual Fund (Aug 89), Indian Bank Mutual Fund (Nov 89), Bank of India (Jun 90), Bank of Baroda Mutual Fund (Oct 92). LIC established its mutual fund in June 1989 while GIC set up its mutual fund in December 1990.

At the end of 1993, the mutual fund industry had assets under management of ' 47,004 crores.

Third Phase – 1993-2003 (Entry of Private Sector Funds)

With the entry of private sector funds in 1993, a new era started in the Indian mutual fund industry, giving the Indian investors a wider choice of fund families. Also, 1993 was the year in which the first Mutual Fund Regulations came into being, under which all mutual funds, except UTI were to be registered and governed.

The erstwhile Kothari Pioneer (now merged with Franklin Templeton) was the first private sector mutual fund registered in July 1993.

The 1993 SEBI (Mutual Fund) Regulations were substituted by a more comprehensive and revised Mutual Fund Regulations in 1996. The industry now functions under the SEBI (Mutual Fund) Regulations 1996.

The number of mutual fund houses went on increasing, with many foreign mutual funds setting up funds in India and also the industry has witnessed several mergers and acquisitions. As at the end of January 2003, there were 33 mutual funds with total assets of ₹ 1,21,805 crores. The Unit Trust of India with ₹ 44,541 crores of assets under management was way ahead of other mutual funds.

Fourth Phase – since February 2003

In February 2003, following the repeal of the Unit Trust of India Act 1963 UTI was bifurcated into two separate entities. One is the Specified Undertaking of the Unit Trust of India with assets under management of ₹ 29,835 crore as at the end of January 2003, representing broadly, the assets of US 64 scheme, assured return and certain other schemes. The Specified Undertaking of Unit Trust of India, functioning under an administrator and under the rules framed by the Government of India and does not come under the purview of the Mutual Fund Regulations.

The second is the UTI Mutual Fund, sponsored by SBI, PNB, BOB and LIC. It is registered with SEBI and functions under the Mutual Fund Regulations. With the bifurcation of the erstwhile UTI which had in March 2000 more than ₹ 76,000 crores of assets under management and with the setting up of a UTI Mutual Fund, conforming to the SEBI Mutual Fund Regulations, and with recent mergers taking place among different private sector funds, the mutual fund industry has entered its current phase of consolidation and growth.

The total assets under management of the mutual fund industry stood at ₹ 7.27 lakh crore as on July 2011.

Insurance

In India, insurance has a deep-rooted history. The year 1818 saw the advent of life insurance business in India with the establishment of the Oriental Life Insurance Company in Calcutta. This Company however failed in 1834. In 1829, the Madras Equitable had begun transacting life insurance business in the Madras Presidency. The year 1870 saw the enactment of the British Insurance Act and in the last three decades of the nineteenth century, the Bombay Mutual (1871), Oriental (1874) and Empire of India (1897) were started in the Bombay Residency. This era, however, was dominated by foreign insurance offices which

Houses are vulnerable. You don't have to be.

UNITED INDIA INSURANCE CO. LTD.
Registered & Head Office: 24, Whites Road, Chennai-600 014.

did good business in India, namely Albert Life Assurance, Royal Insurance, Liverpool and London Globe Insurance and the Indian offices were up for hard competition from the foreign companies.

In 1914, the Government of India started publishing returns of Insurance Companies in India. The Indian Life Assurance Companies Act, 1912 was the first statutory measure to regulate life business. In 1928, the Indian Insurance Companies Act was enacted to enable the Government to collect statistical information about both life and non-life business transacted in India by Indian and foreign insurers including provident insurance societies. In 1938, with a view to protecting the interest of the Insurance public, the earlier legislation was consolidated and amended by the Insurance Act, 1938 with comprehensive provisions for effective control over the activities of insurers.

The Insurance Amendment Act of 1950 abolished Principal Agencies. However, there were a large number of insurance companies and the level of competition was high. There were also allegation of unfair trade practices. The Government of India, therefore, decided to nationalize insurance business.

An ordinance was issued on 19th January, 1956 nationalising the Life Insurance sector and Life Insurance Corporation came into existence in the same year. The LIC absorbed 154 Indian, 16 non-Indian insurers as also 75 provident societies - 245 Indian and foreign insurers in all. The LIC had monopoly till the late 90s when the Insurance sector was reopened to the private sector.

General Insurance in India has its roots in the establishment of Triton Insurance Company Ltd., in the year 1850 in Calcutta by the British. In 1907, the Indian Mercantile Insurance Ltd., was set up. This was the first company to transact all classes of general insurance business.

The year 1957 saw the formation of the General Insurance Council, a wing of the Insurance Association of India. The General Insurance Council framed a code of conduct for ensuring fair conduct and sound business practices.

In 1968, the Insurance Act was amended to regulate investments and set minimum solvency margins. The Tariff Advisory Committee was also set up then.

In 1972 with the passing of the General Insurance Business (Nationalisation) Act, general insurance business was nationalized with effect from 1st January, 1973. 107 insurers were amalgamated and grouped into four companies, namely National Insurance Co. Ltd., the New India Assurance Co. Ltd., the Oriental Insurance Co. Ltd and the United India Insurance Co. Ltd. The General Insurance Corporation of India was incorporated as a company in 1971 and it commenced business on January 1st 1973.

This millennium has seen insurance come a full circle in a journey extending to nearly 200 years. The process of re-opening of the sector had begun in the early 1990s and the last decade and more has seen it being opened up substantially. In 1993, the Government set up a committee under the chairmanship of RN Malhotra, former Governor of RBI, to propose recommendations for reforms in the insurance sector. The objective was to complement the reforms initiated in the financial sector. The committee submitted its report in 1994 wherein, among other things, it recommended that the private sector be permitted to enter the insurance industry. They stated the foreign companies be allowed to enter by floating Indian companies, preferably a joint venture with India partners.

Following the recommendations of the Malhotra Committee report, in 1999, the Insurance Regulatory and Development Authority (IRDA) was constituted as an autonomous body to regulate and develop the insurance industry. The IRDA was incorporated as a statutory body in April, 2000. The key objectives of the IRDA include promotion of competition so as to enhance customer satisfaction through increased consumer choice and lower premiums, while ensuring the financial security of the insurance market.

The insurance sector was opened for private participation with the enactment of the Insurance Regulatory and Development Authority Act 1999. While permitting foreign participation in ventures set up by the private sector, the Government restricted participation of the foreign joint venture partner through the FDI route to 26 per cent of the paid-up equity of the insurance company.

Since the opening up of the sector, the number of participants has gone up from six insurers (including LIC of India, four public-sector general insurers, and the General Insurance Corporation as national reinsurer) in the year 2000 to 48 insurers operating in the life, non-life, and reinsurance segments (including specialized insurers, namely the Export Credit Guarantee Corporation [ECGC] and Agricultural Insurance Company [AIC]). Three of the general insurance companies, namely Star Health and Alliance Insurance Company, Apollo DKV, and Max Bupa Health Insurance Company Ltd., function as stand alone health insurance companies.

Of the 22 insurance companies that have set up operations in the life segment post opening up of the sector, 20 are in joint ventures with foreign partners. Of the 18 (including stand alone health insurance companies) insurers who have commenced operations in the non-life segment, 16 are in collaboration with foreign partners. The three stand alone health insurance companies have been set up in collaboration with foreign joint venture partners. Thus, as on date, 36 insurance companies in the private sector are operating in the country in collaboration with established foreign insurance companies from across the globe.

The post-liberalization period has witnessed tremendous growth in the insurance industry, more so in the life segment. In 2009-10, even after the outcome on account of the financial meltdown, the life insurance segment saw an upward trend. The first-year premium, which is a measure of new business secured, underwritten by the life insurers during 2009-10 was ₹ 1,09,894.02 crores as compared to ₹ 87,331.09 crores in 2008-09, registering a growth of 25.84 per cent. In terms of linked and non-linked business during the year 2009–10, 54.53 per cent of the first-year premium was underwritten in the linked segment while the remaining 45.47 per cent was in the non-linked segment as against 51.13 and 48.87 respectively in the previous year.

Non-life insurance

Non-life insurers in India (excluding specialized institutions like the Export Credit Guarantee Corporation and Agriculture Insurance Corporation and the stand-alone health insurance companies) underwrote premiums of ₹ 34,620 crores in 2009-10, as against ₹ 30,352 crores in 2008-09.

Insurance Penetration

Insurance penetration is defined as the ratio of premium underwritten in a given year to the GDP. Insurance penetration in the year 2000 when the sector was opened up to the private sector was 2.32 (life 1.77 and non-life 0.55) and it has increased to 5.39 in 2009 (life 4.73 and non-life 0.66).

The increase in levels of insurance penetration has to be assessed against the average growth of over 8 per cent in the GDP in the last five years.

Securities Market

The Indian Securities Market dates back to the 18th century when the securities of the East India Company were traded in Mumbai and Kolkata. However, the orderly growth of the capital market began with the setting up of the Stock Exchange, Mumbai, in July 1875 and Ahmedabad Stock Exchange in 1894 and 22 other exchanges in various cities over the years.

As on 31 December 2010, Indian benchmark indices, the BSE Sensex and Nifty, increased by 17.0 per cent and 17.9 per cent respectively over the closing value of 2009-10. Nifty Junior and BSE 500 also increased by 17.8 per cent and 15.1 per cent respectively over their values in the previous financial year.

In the capital market segment, the total turnover of the BSE stood at ₹ 8,93,839 crores and of the NSE at ₹ 27,87,862 crore as on 31 December 2010 as compared to ₹ 13,78,809 crores and ₹ 41,38,024 crore respectively in 2009-10.

Renren, the Chinese Facebook

Renren, sometimes called the Chinese Facebook, is China's biggest social networking site. It raised $743 mn. in its IPO in New York in May, 2011. It was the latest in a string of share offerings by Chinese technology companies.

Foreign Direct Investment in India

The World Investment Report, 2011 (WIR) issued by the United Nations Conference on Trade and Development (Unctad) shows that in 2010, when the emerging economies had recovered from the economic downturn, FDI inflows into India were below pre-crisis levels by as much as 42%. Even in the first four months of the calendar 2011 the pick-up in FDI inflows has been slow—they have been almost 9% below the levels recorded in the corresponding period last year.

But while the government of India is engaged in formulating the policies that would be helpful in reversing the recent trends of FDI inflows, WIR provides useful insights on the mode of operations of the enterprises that are the source of this form of capital, the transnational corporations (TNCs).

India slipped 10 positions on the list of countries attracting the highest foreign direct investment (FDI) and fell to 14th position in the 2010 list. India ranked fourth on the list of top 10 recipients and sources of FDI inflows in developing Asia in 2009 and 2010 behind China and Singapore. FDI in India declined to $25 billion as against $36 billion last year, according to a UN survey.

The list is headed by U.S. with $228 billion, second comes China with $106 billion. The U.S tops the list of countries with overseas fund inflows at $228 billion, followed by the Chinese mainland, which attracted inflows of $106 billion, and Hong Kong at $69 billion. Belgium was the fourth largest FDI inflow destination at $62 billion.

According to the UNCTAD's annual investment survey, World Investment Report 2011, the FDI to South Asia declined to $32 billion, reflecting a 31 per cent slide in inflows to India and a 14 percent drop

in flows to Pakistan. In contrast to this, inflows to Bangladesh increased by nearly 30 percent to $913 million.

As a result of a number of major global acquisitions by Indian companies in the period between 2007 and 2011, India is the fifth largest source of funds (FDI outflow) in developing Asia. Among the major buyouts that figured in the UN report was Tata Steel's acquisition of UK based Corus group worth $11.8 billion and Hindalco Industries's acquisition of U.S. firm Novelis worth $5.8 billion. Tata Motors also acquired UK-based Jaguar Cars for $2.3 billion, Essar Steel Holdings bought Canada's Algoma Steel for $1.6 billion and United Spirits acquired Whyte & Mackay of UK for $1.17 billion.

The report also said that global FDI investment inflows rose 5 percent to $1.24 trillion in 2010. However, it added that FDI flows at the end of the year were over 15 per cent below their pre-crisis average and nearly 37 percent below their peak in 2007.

Road Networks | **India's road networks are 3,316,452 km., as against China's 1,930,544 km. and USA's 6,465,799 km.**

Part 13

General Knowledge

Pages 695 - 972

Who is Who

Politics

Abdullah, Sheikh (1906-'82): Indian political leader and founder of National Conference. Chief Minister of Jammu & Kashmir.

Abu Bakr (573-634): Muslim leader, first caliph, chosen successor to Mohammed.

Acheson, Dean (Gooderham) (1893-1971): American lawyer and statesman, Secretary of State. Promoted Marshall Plan and helped to establish NATO.

Adams, Gerry (b.1948): President of Irish Republican Army's political wing Sinn-Fein.

Adulyadej, Bhumibol (b. 1927): King of Thailand since 1946. World's longest ruling monarch.

Advani, Lal Kishinchand (b.1927): BJP's Parliamentary Party chairman. India's Deputy Prime Minister from 2002 to 2004. Minister for Information, Mar. '77- July '79. Home Minister, 1998-2002. Bharatiya Janata Party President until 1998, and again in 2005.

L.K. Advani

Ahmed, Fakruddin Ali (1905-'77): Freedom fighter. Union Minister from 1966. Fifth President of Indian Republic (1974-77).

Akbar, Jalal-ud-din Mohammed (1542-1605): Mughal emperor of India, (1556-1605) known as Akbar the Great. He extended the imperial power over much of India. Promoted commerce and learning,

showed a receptive interest in Hinduism and Christianity.

Alexander The Great (356-323 B.C.): Greek conqueror, educated by Aristotle; king of Macedonia; conquered south-west Asia and Egypt; founded Alexandria; penetrated India; died at Babylon.

Alfred The Great (849-899): King of Wessex who became a national figure of Britain.

Ali, Aruna Asaf (1909-96): Indian freedom fighter; Mayor of Delhi, 1958. A devoted socialist, radical in her views. Bharat Ratna, '97.

Allende, Salvador (1909-73): Chilean statesman; elected President (1970), becoming the first Marxist head of government in S. America.

Ambedkar, Bhimrao Ramji (Dr.) (1891-1956): Indian jurist, social worker, politician, writer, educationist. Emancipator of the 'untouchables' and crusader for social justice. Drafted the Indian constitution. Minister in Nehru's cabinet. Bharat Ratna in 1990.

Amin, Idi (1925-2003): President of Uganda (1971-79). One of modern Africa's harshest dictators. Overthrown.

Amrit Kaur, Rajkumari (1887-1964): Indian freedom fighter. Health Minister in the Nehru Cabinet.

C.N. Annadurai

Annadurai, C.N. (1909-'69): Most popular Chief Minister (1967) of Tamil Nadu, and eminent writer in Tamil. Formed Dravida Munnetra Kazhakam.

Fearless Nadia Mary Evans Nadia was an Indian film actress (1909-1996) who was famous as 'Fearless Nadia.'

Anne, Queen (1665-1714): Queen of Great Britain and Ireland. (1702-1714).

Ansari, Mohammad Hamid (b.1937-): Vice President of India since August, 2007. Scholar-diplomat-writer. Formerly Chairman of National Commission for Minorities, Ambassador, V-C of AMU.

Antonius Marcus (Mark Antony) (c. 83-30 B.C.): Roman politician and general; triumvir. Fell in love with Cleopatra; committed suicide.

Arafat, Yasser (1929-2004): (Mohammed Abdel-Raouf Arafat al-Oudwa al -Husseini) Palestinian President until death. Leader of PLO from 1968; Shared Nobel Peace Prize, '94.

Asoka (3rd C. B.C.): Emperor of India. After victory in the Battle of Kalinga (261 B.C.), he renounced war and embraced Buddhism.

Yasser Arafat

Ataturk, Kemal (Mustafa Kemal Ataturk) (1881-1938): Builder of modern Turkey, fine soldier, President of the Turkish Republic.

Attila The Hun (406-53): Barbarian leader who helped to bring about the fall of the Roman Empire.

Attlee, Clement Richard (1883-1967): Labour Prime Minister of Britain, 1945-51. His Government granted independence to India.

Augustus, Caius Octavianus (63 B.C.-A.D. 14): First Roman emperor.

Aurangazeb (1618-1707): Mughal emperor of India; Empire reached its fullest extent, but he estranged Hindus and Sikhs.

Azad, Abul Kalam (1888-1958): Indian freedom-fighter, staunch nationalist; first Education Minister of free India. Bharat Ratna, 1992. India Wins Freedom.

Azad, Chandra Sekhar (1906-'31): Indian revolutionary; involved in Non-Cooperation Movement, the Assembly bomb incident, Delhi conspiracy, Lahore conspiracy.

Azana, Manuel (1880-1940): PM of Spain from 1931 to '33 and President from 1936 to '39. Spanish Civil War sent him into exile.

Babar, Zahirud–din Mohammed (1483-1530):** Founder of the Mughal dynasty which ruled northern India for nearly three centuries.

Bahadur Shah II (1775-1862): The last king of Mughal empire. Took part in the 1857 war of Independence in exile.

Bandaranaike, Solomon (1899-1959): PM of Ceylon from 1956 until assassination. Widow Sirimavo (1916–2000)became world's first woman PM, 1960. In 1994, daughter Chandrika Kumaratunga became President and Sirimavo PM of Sri Lanka.

Bannerjee, Surendranath (1848-1952): One of the first Indians to qualify the ICS examination. Held the presidentship of Indian National Congress twice.

Bannerjee, Womesh Chandra (1844-1906): First President of Indian National Congress, Migrated to England in 1902.

Barbie, Klaus (b.1913-91): Nazi leader, 'the Butcher of Lyon'. Held responsible for the death of some 4,000 and deportation of 7,500.

Basu, Jyoti (1914-2010): Veteran communist leader. CM of West Bengal for a record five consecutive terms until Nov. 2000.

Begin, Menachem (1913-'92): Israeli Prime Minister, 1977-'83. Made

Jyoti Basu

peace with Egypt (1979). Nobel Peace Prize, 1978.

Ben Gurion, David (1886-1973): The first Prime Minister of Israel, 1948-63.

Benes, Eduard (1884-1948): Czech statesman, President from 1935 to '38.

Bhutto, Zulfikar Ali (1928-'79): Prime Minister of Pakistan who was ousted (1977) by Gen. Zia-ul Haq whose government executed him. His daughter **Benazir Bhutto (b.1953-2007)** be-

came Prime Minister, 1988- the first woman to head a modern Islamic state. Ousted in 1990.

Bimbisara (c.544 - 493 BC): Ruler of the kingdom of Magadha, which he expanded. Built

Benazir Bhutto

city Rajagriha. Patron to Mahavira and the Buddha.

Bismarck, Otto Von (1815-'98): German statesman, chief architect of the German empire, known as 'the man of blood and iron'.

Boleyn, Anne (1507-'36): Queen of Henry VIII of Britain and mother of Queen Elizabeth I. Beheaded.

Bolivar, Simon (1783-1830): South American revolutionist, called the Liberator. He founded Grand Colombia (now Venezuela, Colombia, Panama, Ecuador).

Bolkiah, Hassanal (b. 1946): Sultan of Brunei. One of the richest men in the world.

Bonfield, Margaret Grace (1873-1953): Labour politician and trade unionist. First British woman to hold cabinet office-minister of labour, 1923-31.

Bordoloi, Gopinath (1890-1950): One of the makers of modern Assam. Educationist. CM of Assam twice before Independence. Bharat Ratna, 1999.

Bose, Netaji Subhas Chandra (1897-

1945): One of the leaders of India's freedom struggle. Formed the Indian National Army in 1943 to fight the British with the help of Japan. Reportedly killed in an air crash, though there are some who don't agree.

Subhas Chandra Bose

Botham, Ian Terence (b. 1955): English cricketer and coach, a great all-rounder with 14 test centuries (5200 runs) and 373 test wickets. First player to score a century and take 10 wickets in a test (1979).

Bourguiba, Habib (1903-2000): First President of Tunisia (1957-87). Proclaimed president for life in 1975. A coup overthrew him.

Brandt, Willy (1913-'92): First Social Democratic chancellor of the Federal Republic of Germany, 1969-74. Nobel Prize, 1971.

Brezhnev, Leonid (1906-'82): Soviet President (1977); succeeded Khrushchev as First Secretary of the Communist Party, (1964-82).

Bruce, Robert (1274-1329): Scottish national leader. King in 1306; defeated Edward II of England in 1314.

Brundtland, Gro Harlem (b.1939): Norway's first woman PM. She was PM in '81, '86, & '90. Active environmental-

ist. Former Director General, WHO.

Brutus, Marcus Junius (85-42 B.C.): Roman senator famed as a conspirator against Julius Caesar.

Burke, Edmund (1729-'97): British parliamentarian, po-

Brundtland

Fullbright Scholarships — The international exchange programme for scholars known as Fullbright scholarship was initiated by American senator James William Fullbright in 1955.

litical philosopher; and orator.

Bush, George Herbert Walker (b. 1924): American President, 1988-'92. Son George W. Bush (b.1946) 43rd U S President 2001- 09.

Caesar, Julius (c. 101-44 B.C.): A great Roman general. Invaded Britain (55 B.C.), defeated Pompey whom he pursued to Egypt, where he established Cleopatra as queen. At Rome he became dictator, and his reforms include the Julian calendar. Murdered.

Cama, Bhikaji (1861-1936): Born in Bombay, she moved to Europe where she met Dadabhai Naoroji and other revolutionaries. Her home in Paris served as headquarters for Indian rebels against British rule. Imprisoned for revolutionary activities, she returned to India in 1935.

Carter, James Earl (b. 1924): American Democratic President 1977-'81.

Castro, Fidel (b. 1927): Cuban revolutionary and political leader. In 1959 overthrew a police state. In power for the longest period. Convalescing after a surgery in 2006, Castro handed over power to brother Raul on July 31, 2006.

Catherine de Medicis (1519-89): Of France; Queen consort of Henry II, regent of France.

Catherine II (The Great) (1729–'96): Tsarina of Russia, a monarch of the Enlightenment.

Chamberlain, Neville (1869-1940): English statesman, Prime Minister 1937-40.

Chanakya (also known as Kautilya) **(4th century B.C):** Author of Artha Shastra, an authentic book on statecraft. Prime Minister to Chandragupta Maurya.

Chandrasekhar (1927- 2007): Indian politician, parliamentarian, socialist. President, Socialist Janata Party from 1977. Prime Minister, Nov. '90 to June '91.

Charlemagne (724-814): (Charles the Great). King of the Franks and Lombards, he founded a new Roman Empire comprising Gaul, Italy, and large parts of

Prince Charles

Spain and Germany; crowned Emperor.

Charles (Philip Arthur George) (b. 1948): Prince of Wales, eldest son of Qn. Elizabeth II; married Diana Spencer ('81) divorced ('96), she died in 1997. Charles married Camilla Parker Bowles in 2005.

Charles I (1600-'49): King of England, Scotland and Ireland, 1625. Attempted to rule without parliament; Beheaded.

Chernenko, Konstantian Ustinovich (1911-'85): Soviet politician. Succeeded Andropov as General Secretary of the Communist Party.

Chiang Kai–Shek (1887-1975): Chinese general. After Sun Yat-sen's death (1925), as commander of the Kuomintang army, he attempted to unite China; in 1949 retired to Formosa (Taiwan) after the victory of the Communists.

Churchill, Sir Winston (1874-1965): British statesman, soldier and author. Prime Minister and Minister of Defence 1940-45; Prime Minister, 1951-55. Nobel Prize for Literature.

Cicero, Marcus Tullis (106-43 B.C.): Roman orator, statesman, executed by Antony.

Winston Churchill

Clemenceau, Georges (1841-1929): French statesman who was premier twice. Led the French delegation at the Versailles peace conference.

Cleopatra (69-30 B.C.): Egyptian queen. Became joint ruler, with brother Ptolemy XII, at age of 17; was wife of Julius Caesar and later mistress of Mark Antony.

Dame Jean Iris Murdoch

Dame Jean Iris Murdoch was a British novelist and philosopher who was born in 1919 and died in 1999.

Committed suicide.

Clinton, William Jefferson (b. 1946): 42nd U.S. President (Jan. '93). Re-elected Nov. '96. Wife Hillary Clinton is US Secretar of State.

Constantine I (285-337): Roman emperor who founded the Christian empire. Known as Constantine the Great. Rebuilt Byzantium as his capital and renamed it Constantinople.

Cornwallis, Lord (1738-1805): Governor General of India, 1786. Laid the foundation of the Indian Civil Service.

Cromwell, Oliver (1599-1658): English soldier, statesman and leader of the Puritan revolution.

Cuellar, Javier Perez De (b.1920): Peruvian diplomat. UN Sec.General, 1982-91.

Curson, George Nathaniel (1859-1925): British statesman. Viceroy of India (1899-1905). Foreign Secretary (1919-24).

Dalai Lama (b. 1935): (Tenzing Gyatso) Spiritual leader of Tibet. Fled to India after Tibetan uprising, and established Govt-in-exile at Dharamsala in Himachal Pradesh, India (1959). Nobel Peace Prize (1989).

Dange, Shripat Amrit (1899-1994): Leader of Communist Party of India, parliamentarian.

Darius I (548-486 B.C.): Persian king and founder of Persepolis.

Desai, Bhulabhai (1877-1946): Indian national leader who defended Bardoli peasants before Broomfield committee. Founded Swadeshi Sabha to boycott foreign goods.

Desai, Mahadev (1892-1942): Freedom fighter. He was personal secretary to Mahatma Gandhi. Edited Independent and Navjivan.

Desai, Morarji Ranchodji (1896-1995): Indian politician who was Prime Minister from Mar. '77 to July '79. Staunch Gandhian. Chief Minister of Bombay (1952-'56). Union Minister, 1956-63. Deputy P.M. & Finance Minister,1967-69.

Bharat Ratna.

Descartes, Rene (1596-1650): French mathematician, pioneer of modern philiosophy.

Deve Gowda, Hardanahalli Doddegowda (b. 1933): Janata Dal leader. India's PM June,'96 to Apr. '97. Formerly CM of Karnataka.

Diana, Princess of Wales (1961-'97):

Princess Diana

Born Diana Spencer, married Prince Charles of Britain (1981), separated (1992), divorced (1996). Mother of Prince William and Prince Henry. Killed in a car crash.

Disraeli, Benjamin (1804-'81): British statesman and novelist. Prime Minister, 1868 and 1874-'80.

Dulles, John Foster (1888-1959): US Secretary of State 1953-9, opposed negotiation with Russia.

Dupleix, Joseph Francois (1697-1763): French Governor in India.

Duvalier, Francois ('Papa Doc') (1907-'71): Dictator of Haiti (1957-'71). Used personal police force (Tonton Macoutes).

Eisenhower, Gen. Dwight (1890-1969): American general and statesman. He was C-in-C, Allied Forces, N. Africa 1942-3, and in the European theatre of operations, 1943-5; Republican President, 1953-61.

Elizabeth II (b. 1926): Queen of Gt. Britain and N. Ireland; ascended the throne, 1952.

Elizabeth II

Fawkes, Guy (1570-1606): English conspirator. Involved in

Gunpowder Plot (Nov.5, 1605) to blow up Houses of Parl. Executed.

Fazal, Abul (1561-1602): Prime Minister of Akbar the Great. Scholar, Wrote Ain-i-Akbari and Akbarnama.

Ford, Gerald R (1913-2006): American Republican President, 1974-77.

Frederick II (the Great) (1712-'86): King of Prussia for 46 years. Able ruler and great scholar.

Gaddafi, Muammar al (b. 1942): Libyan leader and military dictator; took power in a coup in 1969 and became President in 1977. Ousted by rebels in August, 2011.

Gaddafi

Galbraith, John Kenneth (1908-2006): American economist, diplomat and writer. Ambassador to India, 1961-3. The Affluent Society; The Great Crash, 1929

Gandhi, Indira (1917-'84): Daughter of Nehru. India's first woman prime minister (1966-'77, 1980-'84). Assassinated. Her son, Rajiv Gandhi was PM, '84-'89. Bharat Ratna, 1971.

Gandhi, Mohandas Karamchand (Mahatma) (1869-1948): Father of the Indian nation, and one of the greatest personalities of the 20th century. From 1893 to 1914 he lived in South Africa opposing discrimination against Indians. In 1915, returned to India, dominated the Congress party. Without weapons or armies, he led India to independence. Lived an austere life, devoted to truth, non-violence and worked for Hindu-Muslim unity. Assassinated. The Story of My Experiments with Truth.

Gandhi, Rajiv (1944-'91): Grandson of Jawaharlal Nehru; a commercial pilot turned politician; Indian Prime Minister from 1984 to 1989. Assassinated. Bharat Ratna, 1991. Son of Rajiv Gandhi is Congress General Secretary and M.P.

Gandhi, Sonia (b. 1946): Congress President, Chairperson, UPA. Italian by birth, naturalised in India. Wife of former Indian PM Rajiv Gandhi, widowed on his assassination. Meteoric rise from primary membership to presidentship of Congress Party in just two years. Elected to Lok Sabha in 1999, 2004, 2006 and 2009. The Party's surprise victory in 2004 made her Leader of Congress - led United Progressive Alliance, but Ms Gandhi declined to become PM.

Garibaldi, Giuseppe (1807-'82): Italian general and patriot, who, with Mazzini and Cavour, created a united Italy.

Gaulle, Charles de (1890-1970): French general and statesman; first president of the Fifth Republic, 1958-69.

Genghis Khan (1162-1227): Mongol conqueror who overran the greater part of Asia and founded the Mongol world empire.

Ghali, Boutros-Boutros (b. 1922): Egyptian politician. The first African UN Secretary General 1992-'96.

Giri, Varahagiri Venkata (1894-1980): Third Vice-President and fourth President of India. Veteran trade unionist. Bharat Ratna, '75.

Gladstone, William Ewart (1809-'98): British Liberal statesman. Prime Minister four times between 1868 and 1894.

V.V. Giri

Gokhale, Gopal Krishna (1866-1915): Indian statesman whom Gandhi regarded as his political guru. Founded Servants of India Society (1905).

Gorbachev, Mikhail (b. 1931): Soviet leader largely responsible for the political transformation in Eastern Europe in '89. Policy of 'glasnost' and 'perestroika'. The

Indian Parachuter	Squadron-Leader Sanjay Thapar of the IAF became the first Indian to parachute down to the geometric North Pole and unfurl an Indian flag on April 21, 1996.

Soviet Union broke up and Gorbachev resigned ('91). Nobel Prize for Peace, '90.

Gorbachev

Guevara, Ernesto 'Che' (1928-'67): Latin American revolutionary who took part in the Cuban guerrilla war and became a minister in Cuba 1959-65.

Gujral, Inder Kumar (b. 1919): Prime Minister of India from Apr. 21, 1997 to Nov. 97 and caretaker PM until Mar. 98. Formerly in Union Cabinet from '67 to '76 and '89-'90, Minister of External Affairs and Ambassador to USSR.

Haile Selassie I (1891-1975): Emperor of Ethiopia, 1930-74. Deposed in 1974.

Hammarskjold, Dag (1905-'61): Swedish diplomat. Secretary-General of the United Nations, 1953-61. Killed in an air crash. Nobel Peace Prize, 1961.

Hannibal (247-182 B.C.): Carthagini-an general who fought two wars against Rome. Regarded as the greatest general of antiquity.

Havel, Vaclav (b.1936): Dramatist who became President of Czechoslovakia (1989) and President of the Czech Republic. The Garden Party. Gandhi Peace Prize.

Vaclav Havel

Heath, Edward (1916-2005): British Prime Minister, 1970-74.

Hedgewar, Keshavrao Baliram (1889-1940): Founder of Rashtriya Swayamsevak Sangh.

Hidayatullah, Mohammed (1905-'92): Jurist who was Chief Justice and later Vice-President of India, 1979-84.

Hirohito (1901-89): 124th Emperor of Japan, (1926). Renounced his legendary divinity in 1946.

Hitler, Adolf (1889-1945): Austrian-born German dictator. Reich Chancellor in 1933 and Fuhrer in 1934; All his opponents were persecuted and murdered.

Adolf Hitler

Ho Chi Minh (1890-1969): Vietnamese revolutionary leader and the first President of North Vietnam (1954-69).

Honeker, Erich (1913-'94): The stolid Marxist who ruled East Germany for 18 yrs. until people's uprising swept him aside in Oct. 89.

Hume, Allan Octavian (1829-1912): Born in London, worked in India. Founded Indian National Congress in 1885.

Hussain, Dr. Zakir (1897-1969): Second Vice-President and third President of India ('67-'69). Nationalist, educationist. Bharat Ratna.

Inonu, Ismet (1884-1973): Turkish leader, president ('38-'50), PM thrice between 1923 and '65.

Ivan the Terrible (1530-'84): Crowned as the first Tsar of Russia in 1547; an autocratic ruler.

Jatti, Basappa Danappa. (1912-2002): Vice President of India, 1974-'79. Formerly Chief Minister of Mysore and Governor of Orissa.

Jayalalithaa, Jayaram (b. 1948): Indian film actress-turned-politician, AIADMK chief and Tamil Nadu CM (91-96, 2002-'06, 2011-).

Jefferson, Thomas (1743–1826): Third American president (1801-9), author of

The Declaration of Independence.

Jinnah, Mohammed Ali (1876–1948): Pakistani statesman, who became president of the Muslim League. First Governor-General of Dominion of Pakistan, 1947.

Johnson, Lyndon Baines (1908-'73): President of the United States, 1963-'69.

Kamaraj, Kumaraswami (1903-'75): Leader of the Indian national movement; President, Indian National Congress 1963; earlier Chief Minister, Tamil Nadu (1954-'63). Bharat Ratna.

Kanishka (1st or 2nd century C.E.): The greatest ruler of the Kushan dynasty, with his capital at Purushapura or Peshwar. Patronised Buddhism.

Karat, Prakash (b. 1948): General Secretary of CPI (M) elected 2005. Wife Brinda Karat, first woman Politburo member.

Kasavubu, Joseph (1917-69): First President of Independent Congo, ousted by Joseph Mobutu in 1965.

Prakash Karat

Kaunda, Kenneth (b. 1924): Architect of the independence of Zambia and its first president (1964-'91). Freed in June '98 after five months under house arrest on coup plot charges.

Kennedy, John Fitzgerald (1917-'63): 35th U.S. President (1961-3). Youngest to be elected. A man of vision and courage. Assassinated. Profiles in Courage.

Kenyatta, Jomo (1894-1978): A tall African leader who was the first President of independent Kenya.

Khalji, Alauddin (1255-1316): Delhi ruler who came to power by murdering his aged father-in-law. Able and ruthless, gained vast treasure by conquests.

Khan, Khan Abdul Gaffar (1890-1988): The 'Frontier Gandhi' worked among the Pathans of North West Frontier Province. Built the Khudai Khidmatgar (Servants of God) movement; opposed partition of India. Bharat Ratna, 1987.

Khan, Liaquat Ali (1895-1951): Leader of the Muslim League (1946) and first premier of Pakistan (1947). Assassinated.

Khan, Mohammed Ayub (1907-'74): Military leader; President of Pakistan, 1958-69.

Khrushchev, Nikita Sergeyevich (1894-1971): The Russian statesman who became the leader of the Soviet Union soon after the death of Stalin. First Secretary 1953-64; PM, 1958-64.

Kissinger, Henry (b. 1923): American foreign policy expert, Secretary of State (1973-6). Known for his 'shuttle diplomacy'. Shared Nobel peace prize (1973).

Kohl, Helmut (b. 1930): First Chancellor of united Germany in 1990. Chancellor of West Germany from 1982-'90. Influenced European affairs for two decades.

Kosygin, Alexei Niklayevich (1904-'80): Chairman of the Council of Ministers of the USSR (PM) after Khrushchev ('64).

Kripalani, Acharya, J.B. (1882-1982): Freedom fighter, parliamentarian, close associate of Mahatma Gandhi, President of INC 1946. Started Kisan Mazdoor Party and Praja Socialist Party. Wife **Sucheta** (1908-'74): freedom fighter and first woman Chief Minister of independent India (U.P.), 1963-'67.

Krishan Kant (1927-2002): Vice-President of India (1997-2002). Gandhian and freedom fighter. Rajya Sabha, '66-'77. Lok Sabha, '77. Governor, A.P. for 7 years.

Kruger, Paul (1825-1904): South African statesman. Secured indepen-

Krishan Kant

dence of Transvaal, of which he was president four times. Resisted spread of British influence.

Kublai Khan (1216-'94): The first Mongol emperor of China. Extended Mongol empire by conquest and lived in unparalleled splendour.

Laden, Osama bin (1957-2011): Saudi Arabian millionaire was 'most wanted' in several terrorist attacks, and prime suspect in the destruction of WTC, New York. Caught and killed by American forces.

Lakshmibai, Rani of Jhansi (1835-'58): Queen of Jhansi, a brave warrior who took active part in the first war of Indian independence.

Osama bin Laden

Lebrun, Albert (1871-1950): A mining engineer who became the last President of France's Third Republic.

Lenin (Vladimir Ilyich Ulyanov) (1870-1924): Russian revolutionary leader and statesman who liberated the country from the Tsars (1917). Then headed the Soviet government until his death.

Lie, Trygve (1896-1968): Norwegian politician who became the first U.N. Secretary General. ('46-53).

Lincoln, Abraham (1809-'65): Sixteenth president of USA (1861). Formed Republican party in 1856 to oppose slavery. Assassinated.

Lloyd-George, David (1863-1945): British statesman, PM 1916-'22.

Louis XIV (1638-1715): King of France. Longest reign (72 years). A despotic ruler, dominated the Europe of his day. His exhausting wars weakened France.

Lumumba, Patrice (1925-'61): Congolese politician. Premier at Independence. Civil war resulted in his murder.

MacArthur, Douglas (1880-1964): US general, army chief of staff. In WWII, he received Japan's surrender in Sept. 1945. Allied Commander of the postwar occupation of Japan.

Macbride, Sean (1904-88): Irish statesman, Chief of Staff of IRA, founder of Irish Republican Party, external affairs minister, first chairman of Amnesty International (1961-75). Nobel Peace Prize, 1974.

Machel, Samora (1933-86): Mozambique politician, first President, died in air crash. His widow Graca married Nelson Mandela.

Machiavelli, Niccolo (1469-1527): Italian writer and diplomat. Name associated (erroneously?) with immorality and despotism in politics. The Prince.

Makarios III (1913-'77): Archbishop, head of the Greek Orthodox church and Cypriot national leader. President of Cyprus, 1960.

Malaviya, Madan Mohan (1861-1946): Indian patriot, national leader and social reformer. Founder of Hindu Mahasabha (1906) and Banaras Hindu University (1916).

Malcom X (1925-'65): Born Malcom Little, also known as El Hajj Malik El-Shabass. US black militant leader who preached black people must create a separate society by violence, if necessary. Assassinated.

Mandela, Nelson Rolihlala (b. 1918): First black President of South Africa (May '94). Imprisoned for about 27 years (1964-1990) for fighting apartheid. Under his leadership, South Africa became a non-racist democracy. Bharat Ratna, 1990. Nobel Prize, '93. Long Walk to Freedom.

Nelson Mandela

No History, Only Biography

Who said, "There is properly no history, only biography"?

Ralph Waldo Emerson, American Philosopher

Manin, Daniele (1804-57): Italian patriot who was imprisoned for opposing Austrian rule of his town Venice. After the Revolution (1848) he became President of the new Venetian Republic.

Mao Zedong (1893-1976): Architect of the Chinese Revolution and founder of the People's Republic of China. Experiments include 'Communes', the 'Great Leap For-ward' and the 'Cultural Revolution' (65-69). Writings have influenced revolutionary thinking.

Marie Antoinette (1755-'93): Queen of France, wife of Louis XVI; accused of treason, beheaded in the French Revolution.

Marshall, George Catlett (1880-1959): U.S. Secretary of State (1939-'45). Known for the Marshall Aid plan for European reconstruction. Nobel prize for peace (1953).

Marti, Jose (1853-95): Cuban leader of the independence struggle; poet.

Marx, Karl (1818-'83): Great German socialist thinker. With friend Engels, wrote the Communist Manifesto (1848). Founder of modern international communism. Das Kapital.

Karl Marx

Masani, Minoo (1906-'98): Politician. Founded Swatantra Party.

Matternich, Klemens Wenzel Napomum Lothar (1773-1859): Austrian statesman. As Foreign Minister, helped form the Quadruple Alliance which defeated Napoleon.

Mavalankar, Ganesh Vasudeo (1888-1956): First Lok Sabha Speaker, who had played active role in India's Non-cooperation and Civil Disobedience movements.

Mazarin, Jules (1602-61): French cardinal and statesman, born in Italy. Chief minister under Anne of Austria.

Mazzini, Giuseppe (1805-'72): Italian patriot; dominated movement for nationalism.

Mboya, Tom (1930-69): Kenyan political leader. General Secretary of KANU, minister under Jomo Kenyatta. Assassinated

Meera Behn (1892-1982): British disciple of Gandhiji. Real name Madeline Slade. Padma Vibhushan.

Mehta, Pherozeshah (1845-1915): One of the founders of the Indian National Congress, a pioneer of 'Swadeshi'.

Meir, Mrs. Golda (1898-1978): First woman to be Israeli Prime Minister, 1969-1974.

Menon, Vengalil Krishnan Krishna (1896-1974): Defence Minister and Minister without Portfolio in Nehru Cabinet. Orator and writer, distinguished himself with incandescent eloquence at the U.N. on Kashmir issue, 1955.

Merkel, Angela (b.1954): The first woman to become Chancellor of Germany. Topped the Forbes list of 100 most powerful women in the world 2009.

Angela Merkel

Mitterrand, Francois (1916-'96): French socialist politician, fourth president of the Fifth Republic, 1981. Re-elected, 1988.

Mohamad, Dr. Mahathir bin (b. 1925): Prime Minister of Malaysia from 1981 to 2003.

Molotov, Vyacheslav Mikhailovich (1890-1986): Russian revolutionary leader and Soviet statesman. Commissar for foreign affairs.

More, Sir Thomas (1478-1535): English statesman, author and martyr; Lord Chancellor. On his refusal to recognise Henry VIII as head of the church, he was executed. His Utopia describes an ideal state.

Mountbatten of Burma (Louis Mount-

Tanzania's Nyerere | The first President of Tanzania was Julius Nyerere. Tanzania was formed in 1964 by the union of Tanganyika and Zanzibar.

batten) (1900-'79): British admiral and statesman, great-grandson of Queen Victoria. In WW II, chief of combined operations in 1942. Last Viceroy of India and first Governor-General of the dominion. Assassinated.

Mugabe, Robert Gabriel (b. 1924): First Prime Minister of independent Zimbabwe, 1980; now President.

Mussolini, Benito (1883-1945): Fascist dictator of Italy, 1922-43. In 1940 he entered the war on the side of Hitler. Defeat in North Africa and the invasion of Sicily caused the collapse of his government. Killed by partisans.

Mugabe

Nader, Ralph (b.1934): American lawyer and consumer protectionist. Candidate in 2000 and 2004 Presidential elections.

Nagy, Imre (1896-1958): Communist Prime Minister of Hungary, assassinated after the 1956 uprising was crushed by Soviet Union.

Namboodiripad, Elamkulam Manac-kal Sankaran (1909-'98): Indian politician, writer, General Secretary of Communist Party of India (Marxist) until 1992, Chief Minister, (of Asia's first elected Communist government) Kerala-1957-'59, '67-'69.

Nanda, Gulzari Lal (1898-1998): Gandhian, India's acting Prime Minister twice and veteran labour leader. One of the chief authors of India's planned economy. Bharat Ratna, 1997.

Naoroji, Dadabhai (1825-1917): Pioneer of Indian nationalism. First Indian to become member of British Parliament (1862). Congress President thrice. 'Grand Old Man of India'.

Napoleon I (Bonaparte) (1769-1821): French emperor and general. Brilliant victories over Austrians and Russians. The Allies forced him to abdicate. In 1815, defeated at Waterloo and exiled to St. Helena.

Narain, Jayaprakash (1902-'79): Sarvodaya leader of India, known popularly as Loknayak. Social reformer with socialistic zeal; author. Instrumental in the formation of the Janata Party. Bharat Ratna.

Narayanan, Kocheril Raman (1921-2005): President, from 1997-2002. Vice President, 1992-'97. Joined the foreign service after graduating from London School of Economics. Diplomat (was ambassador to China, USA, etc.), M P, educationist (V.C., Jawaharlal Nehru University), Union Minister (Planning, External Affairs, Science and Technology).

K.R. Narayanan

Nassar, Gamal Abdel (1918-'70): Egyptian statesman and leader of the Arab world. Deposed General Neguib (1954). President, 1956. Nationalised the Suez Canal (1956). One of the founders of NAM.

Nehru, Pandit Jawaharlal (1889-1964): First Prime Minister (1947-1964) and architect of modern India. Close associate of Mahatma Gandhi. Ardent democrat, internationalist, advocate of scientific method and modern technology. One of the founders of NAM. Daughter Indira Gandhi and grandson Rajiv Gandhi became PMs. Bharat Ratna. Glimpses of World History, Discovery of India.

Nero, Claudius Caesar (A.D. 37-68): Roman emperor. Weak and licentious; persecuted Christians. The fire of Rome during his reign. Committed suicide.

Nicholas II (1868-1918): Last emperor

Grace Kelly's Death	Princess Grace of Monaco, formerly actress Grace Kelly, met with a road accident on Sept.13, 1982. She died the next day, at the age of 52, of injuries sustained from the car crash.

and Tsar of Russia. When revolution broke out in 1917 he and his family were shot dead.

Nixon, Richard Milhous (1913-'94): Republican President of the U.S., 1969-74. A process of reconciliation with China begun. The Watergate conspiracy led to his resignation, 1974.

Nkrumah, Kwame (1909-'72): First premier of Ghana, 1957 and first President of the republic, 1960. Overthrown in 1966.

Nyerere, Julius (1922-'99): Former Tanzanian President and popular African leader. Chairman, South Commission.

Obama, Barack (b. 1961): US President since Jan., 2009. First African-American to occupy the White House. Kenyan father, white mother. Formerly Professor of law. Brilliant orator, author.

Barack Obama

Ojukwu, Odumegwu (b. 1933): Head of the secessionist state of Biafra (1967-70), which was part of Nigeria. After the conflict, he fled the country but returned later.

Otto I (The Great) (912-973): King of Germany and Holy Roman Emperor.

Pandit, Vijayalakshmi (1900-'90): Sister of Jawaharlal Nehru; First woman in India to become Minister (U.P., 1937); India's High Commissioner to UK (1956-'62); Ambassador to the U.S. and USSR. First woman President of UN General Assembly (1954). Governor, Maharashtra (1962-'64).

Pant, Gobind Ballabh (1887-1961): Freedom fighter; Chief Minister, U.P. and Home Minister in Nehru cabinet. Bharat Ratna.

Patel, Sardar Vallabhbhai (1875-1950): The "Iron-Man of India". Leading freedom fighter. Worked closely with Mahatma Gandhi. Key role in the integration of India's princely states with the Union. Deputy Prime Minister in Nehru government. Bharat Ratna.

Pathak, Gopal Swarup (1886-1982): Vice-President of India, 1969-1974.

Patil, Pratibha Devisingh (b. 1934): President of India since July 25, 2007. The first Indian woman to hold the post of Head of State. Formerly Governor of Rajasthan (2004-07), Cabinet Minister, Maharashtra. Began political career in 1962. Social worker and advocate.

Pearson, Lester Bowles (1897-1972): Canadian statesman, PM (1963-'68). Nobel Peace Prize, 1957.

Peron, Juan Domingo (1895-1974): President and dictator of Argentina. Deposed by army (1955), went into exile, returned (1973), re-elected president. Third wife Maria Isabel succeeded him as President.

Pitt, William (1759-1806): ('the Younger Pitt') English statesman; the youngest Prime Minister (at 24), 1783.

Pol Pot (1928-'98): Notorious leader of the dreaded Khmer Rouge (Cambodia) accused of genocide and held responsible for massacre of 1.5 to 2 m. people during his regime of 1975-'79. Also known as Saloth Sar.

Pompidou, Georges (1911-'74): French PM and President, after de Gaulle ('69).

Powell, Colin L (b. 1937): Former US Secretary of State. General who served for three decades in the army. My American Journey.

Colin Powell

Prasad, Dr. Rajendra (1884-1963): States-man and Gandhian. First President of the Republic of In-

---

Padukone is World Champion

Prakash Padukone became the World Champion in the first World Open Badminton Tournament in London in 1979. He beat Norten Frost Hansen of Denmark.

708

dia, 1950-'62. Bharat Ratna.

Quisling, Vidkun (1887-1945): Norwegian politician who helped the enemy during German invasion of Norway. Seized as a traitor and shot. The word 'quisling' means 'traitor'.

Radhakrishnan, Dr. Sarvepalli (1888-1975): The second President (1962-7) and first Vice-President ('52-'62) of India. Scholar, philosopher, writer and statesman. Formerly a professor at Oxford, and Chairman of UNESCO. Bharat Ratna, Templeton award. The Hindu View of Life, Indian Philosophy.

S. Radhakrishnan

Rahman, Sheikh Mujibur (1920–'75): Father of the new nation of Bangladesh, and its first President and Prime Minister. Killed in a coup on Aug. 15, 1975. His daughter Sheikh Hasina became PM in 1996.

Rahman, Ziaur (1937–1981): Former President of Bangladesh; rose to power in 1975, through a coup; assassinated. His wife, Begum Khaleda Zia, later became PM.

Rai, Lala Lajpat (1865-1928): Indian patriot and prominent freedom fighter, known as the 'Lion of the Punjab' (Punjab Kesri).

Rajagopalachari, Chakravarti (1878-1972): The first and last Indian Governor-General of India (1948-'50). Rajaji. CM, Madras; Union Minister, Home Minister in Nehru's cabinet, and Governor, West Bengal. Founded Swatantra Party. Bharat Ratna, 1954.

Ramachandran, Marathur Gopala (1917-'87): Film star-turned politician of India, Chief Minister of Tamil Nadu. Bharat Ratna, 1988.

Rao, Pamulaparti Venkata Narasimha (1921-2004): Prime Minister of India, 1991-'96. Formerly, Chief Minister (Andhra Pradesh) 1971-'73. Union Minister (External Affairs, Defence, Human Resources) 1980 onwards.

Rasputin, Grigori (1871-1916): Russian courtier and religious figure. At the court of Nicholas II, he exerted influence over the Tsarina. Murdered by a group of nobles.

Reagan, Ronald (1911-2004): U.S. President, 1981-'88; former T.V. and film star, 1937-'66. Governor of California, 1967-'74.

Ronald Reagan

Reddy, Neelam Sanjiva (1913–'96): President of India, 1977-1982, before which he was Chief Minister (A.P.), Union Minister, and Speaker, Lok Sabha. Freedom fighter.

Rhee, Syngman (1875-1965): Ardent Korean nationalist and first President of S. Korea. Rule noted for repression and corruption.

Rhodes, Cecil John (1853-1902): British statesman and empire builder. At 35, one of world's richest men. Prime Minister, Cape Colony. Developed Rhodesia, which was named after him. Scholarships in his name.

Robespierre, Maximilien (1758-'94): French revolutionary; controversial, guillotined.

Roosevelt, Franklin Delano (1882-1945): American statesman. U. S. President in 1933 till his death. The only man ever elected to four terms. Wife Eleanor was a public figure and a political personality .

Roosevelt, Theodore (1858-1919): American President. Popular because of

| Gaddafi and Finger Bowl | According to a university dissertation by former Libyan foreign minister Moussa Koussa, Muammmar Gaddafi, was so 'unworldly' that he drank water from a finger bowl during a state occassion, as he did not know what it was for. |

T. Roosevelt

his exploits in the Spanish-American war. Nobel prize.

Roy, Bidhan Chandra Dr. (1882-1962): Chief Minister of West Bengal (India), 1948-62; prominent physician. Bharat Ratna, 1961.

Roy, Manabendra Nath (1887-1954): Real name, Narendranath Bhattacharya. Communist. Organised the Radical Democratic Party and Indian Federation of Labour and founded Mexican Communist Party.

Sadat, Anwar El (1919-'81): Egyptian soldier and politician. President, 1970-'81. Known for Camp David peace treaty. Assassinated. Nobel Peace Prize.

Serpa, Kazi Lhendup Dorjee Khang (1904-2007): The first Chief Minister of Sikkim who was instrumental in the merger of Sikkim with the Indian Union. Padma Vibhushan, Sikkim Ratna.

Shaftesburg, Anthony (1621-83): English statesman. Founded the Whig Party in 1673. Exiled, 1682.

Sharma, Dr. Shankar Dayal (1919-1999): President of India, 1992-97. Scholar, freedom fighter. Was Chief Minister of M.P., Congress President, Union Cabinet Minister, Governor and Vice-President.

Shastri, Lal Bahadur (1904-'66): Indian politician who succeeded Nehru as India's second Prime Minister (June 1964-Jan. 1966). Earlier, Cabinet Minister. A simple and selfless Gandhian. Died at Tashkent. Bharat Ratna.

Shivaji (1627-1680): The great Maratha leader who fought Mughal emperor Aurangzeb and established a Hindu state in the Deccan. Crowned king in 1674. Great general and wise ruler.

Singh, Bhagat (1907-'31): Indian patriot and revolutionary, hanged by British government for participation in the Lahore conspiracy.

Singh, Charan (1902-'87): Prime Minister of India July 1979-Jan. 1980. Deputy Prime Minister during Janata regime.

Singh, Dr. Manmohan (b.1932): Indian statesman and economist. Prime Minister since May 22, 2004. Second term as PM began in May, 09.The bureaucrat-turned-politician was formerly Finance Secretary, RBI Governor and UGC Chairman. As Finance Minister,1991-96, introduced the pro-reform and liberalisation programme.

Singh, Viswanath Pratap (b. 1931-2008): Prime Minister of India, Dec. 1989 Nov. 1990. Crusader for social justice. Earlier, Union Minister. Janata Dal leader, and a painter.

Singh, Zail (1916-'94): President of India, 1982-87. A veteran freedom fighter; was minister (State and Central) and Chief Minister (Punjab).

V.P. Singh

Stalin, Joseph (1879-1953): Soviet statesman who for nearly 30 years was leader of the Russian people. General Secretary of CEC of USSR, 1924-41. He modernised agriculture on socialist lines by ruthless means and introduced the famous Five Year Plans in 1929.

Subramaniam, C (1910-2000): Freedom fighter, known for his contribution to India's Green Revolution. Held posts of Union Minister, interim President of INA and Governor of Maharashtra (1990). Bharat Ratna, 1998.

Sun Yat-Sen (1867-1925): Chinese nationalist leader and statesman. He played a leading role in the revolutionary movement that overthrew monarchy in China in 1911. First President of the Republic of China.

Asha a Stalwart

Asha Bhosle is now the owner of about 10 restaurants - in Dubai, Abu Dhabi, Kuwait, Bahrain, Doha, Muscat and London. Two more are planned, one in Manchester and one in Egypt. She is also making her acting debut with 'Maae', at age 78.

Suu Kyi, Aung San (b.1945): Myanmar's champion of democracy, opposition leader detained by the military junta. Spent over 13 years under house arrest. Nobel Prize.

Aung San Suu Kyi

Tandon, Purshottam Das (1882-1962): Prominent figure in the Indian freedom movement, Bharat Ratna 1961.

Thackeray, Balasaheb (b. 1926): Shiv Sena supremo who began his career as a cartoonist at the age of 18.

Thatcher, Margaret Hilda (b. 1925): British Prime Minister 1979-90; first woman head of govt. in modern Europe. Third successive election victory, June 1987. On Jan.3, 1988 longest serving PM since Asquith. Described as 'The Iron Lady'.

Thiers, Adolphe (1797-1877): French historian who was premier and foreign minister. Authored the 10-volume History of the French Revolution and 20-volume History of the Consulate and the Empire.

Tilak, Bal Gangadhar (Lokmanya) (1856-1920): Indian patriot and statesman. "Swaraj is my birthright", the revolutionary said. In Burma, as exile for 6 years. The British called him the 'Father of Indian unrest'. Gitarahasyam.

Tipu, Sultan (c. 1750-'99): Indian prince, sultan of Mysore. French-backed wars against British. Defeated by Cornwallis. Killed when British stormed Seringapatam.

Tito (Josip Broz) (1892-1980): The Father of 'Modern Yugoslavia', Tito liberated his country from the Axis invaders. The exponent of 'national communism', he was the first communist Prime Minister (1945) and President, 1953. Co-founder of Non-Aligned Movement

Trotsky, Leon (1879-1940): Russian revolutionary; Supported the Mensheviks against Lenin's Bolsheviks. Expelled from party. Assassinated.

Trudeau, Pierre (1919-2000): Prime Minister of Canada-1968-79, 1980-84.

Truman, Harry S. (1884-1972): U.S. President, 1945-53. Took the decision to drop the first atom bomb.

Tunku, Abdul Rehman (1903-1990): Malaysian politician, first PM of the independent country of Malaya (1963-70). The 'father of Malaysian independence'.

Vajpayee, Atal Bihari (b. 1924): Prime Minister of India from 1998 to 2004. Brilliant parliamentarian, orator, poet and journalist. Freedom fighter and social worker. Leader of Opposition in Lok Sabha (1993). Headed BJP-led minority coalition govt. from May 16 to 28, 1996. Minister of External Affairs 1977-'79.

A.B. Vajpayee

Venkataraman, R. (1910-2009): President of India, 1987-92. Vice-President, 1984-87. Was Union Minister (Defence, Finance) before.

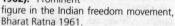
R. Venkataraman

Victor Emmanuel II (1820-'78): First king of Italy.

Victoria (1819-1901): Queen of Britain and Empress of India. The monarch with the longest reign in British history (64 years).

Waldheim, Kurt (1918-2007): Austrian diplomat, President of Austria, 1986.

A Galaxy of Lawyers Vladimir Lenin, the first Premier of the Soviet Union, used to be a lawyer. Nelson Mandela of South Africa, Jawaharlal Nehru of India, novelist Sir Walter Scott and British PM Clement Attlee were lawyers too.

Lech Walesa

Secretary-General of the United Nations, 1972-81.

Walesa, Lech (b. 1943): Polish trade union leader who became the country's President (1990). An electrician at the Lenin Shipyard in Gdansk in 1970, ten years later he led the strikers as leader of 'Solidarity'. Nobel Peace Prize.

Washington, George (1732-'99): First U.S. President, 1789-'97.

Wilhelmina (1880-1962): Queen of the Netherlands from 1890 until she abdicated in favour of her daughter Juliana in 1948.

Wilson, Sir Harold (1916-'95): British states-man, PM 1964-'66, 1966-7'0, 1974-'76.

Wilson, Woodrow (1856-1924): U.S. President, 1913-'21

Windsor, Duke of (Formerly Edward VIII) (1894-1972): English monarch who abdicated to marry the American divorcee Wallis Simpson.

Wolsey, Cardinal Thomas (1475-1530): Cardinal and Lord Chancellor of England. In virtual control of all state business, his ambitions led to his doom. Failing to get King Henry VIII a divorce from Catherine of Aragon, he was charged with high treason.

Xerxes (c.519-465 B.C): King of Persia, 485 to 465 B.C.; a great commander; assassinated.

Xiaoping, Deng (1904-'97): Chinese politican rehabilitated in 1977. The country's senior leader until death.

Yeltsin, Boris (1931-2007): President of Russia (1991-99). The first leader of Russia ever to be chosen by popular vote. Presided over the dissolution of the Soviet Union.

Yew, Lee Kuan (b.1923): Singaporean statesman. Became the first PM of Singapore in 1959 and held the post for 31 years. Dominated the affairs of the region for three decades.

Zedong, Mao (1893-1976): Architect of the Chinese Revolution and founder of the People's Republic of China. Experiments: 'Communes', the 'great leap forward' and the 'cultural revolution'.

Mao Zedong

Zhou En–lai (1898-1976): Chinese revolutionary statesman. Formed close partnership with Mao Zedong. Prime Minister of the new China in 1949.

Literature

Abul Fazal (1551-1602): Persian scholar and writer, patronised by Akbar.

Achebe, Chinua (b.1930): Nigerian novelist. Arrow of God.

Acton, John (1834-1902): British historian who authored the adage "power tends to corrupt and absolute power corrupts absolutely".

Aeschylus (524-456 B.C.): Greek dramatic poet, founder of Greek tragic drama.

Aesop (6th cent. B.C.): Semi- historical, semi-legendary fabulist, originally a slave.

Akilan (or Akilandam, P.V.) (1922-'88): Noted Tamil author. Jnanpith award.

Anand, Dr. Mulk Raj (1905-2004): Indian author, novelist, critic who wrote in English. Padma Bhushan; Untouchable, Coolie.

Anderson, Hans Christian (1805-75): Danish fairy-tale writer, novelist, playwright and poet.

New Singapore FM

An Indian-origin lawyer K. Shanmugam is Singapore's new Foreign Affairs Minister.

Arnold, Mathew (1822-'88): English poet and critic. The Scholar Gypsy.

Ashapurna Devi (1909-'95): Bengali writer. First woman Jnanpith award winner. Prathama Pratishruti, Subarnolata, Bokul Katha.

Asturias, Miguel Angel (1899-1974): Guatemalan writer and diplomat. Men of Maize, novel. Nobel Prize, 1967.

Auden, Wystan Hugh (1907-'73): Poet, b. in England, a naturalised American. Professor of poetry at Oxford.

Austen, Jane (1775-1817): British novelist. Emma, Pride and Prejudice.

Balzac, Honore de (1799-1850): French novelist. La Comedie Humaine.

Banabhatta (7th c.): Indian Sanskrit scholar and poet. Kadambari, Harsh Charit.

Becket, Samuel (1906-'89): Irish playwright and novelist. Nobel Prize, 1969.

Bharat Muni (5th c.): Sanskrit writer. Natya Shastra.

Bharati, Subramanya (1881-1921): Indian poet, patriot and philosopher. His impact on Tamil literature is great. Title 'Bhavati' conferred by the Raja of Ettayapuram, Tamil Nadu.

Bhasa (5th c.): Sanskrit playwright. Swapna Yaugandharayana, Charudatta.

Bhavabhuti (8th c.): A great Sanskrit dramatist. Malatimadhava.

Blake, William (1757-1827): English poet, philosopher, artist. Songs of Innocence.

Bond, Ruskin (b.1934   ): Author of many English books for Indian children.

Boswell, James (1740-'95): Scottish author of the celebrated biography, The Life of Samuel Johnson.

Boyd, William (b. 1952): British novelist. The New Confessions.

Bronte, Charlotte (1816-'55): One of the three Bronte sisters, forceful novelist, author of Jane Eyre. Her sister Emily (1818-'48) wrote Wuthering Heights; and another sister Anne (1820-'49) wrote Agnes Grey.

Brooke, Rupert (1887-1915): English poet. Fought in WW I. The Soldier, Clouds, The Dead.

Brown, Dan (b. 1964): American author of best selling novel The Da Vinci Code (2003) with 36 million copies in print.

Dan Brown

Browning, Robert (1812-'89): English poet of the Victorian Era, famous for his dramatic monologues. Wife Elizabeth Barrett Browning (1806-'61) was poet too.

Buck, Pearl S. (1892-1973): American author. Nobel Prize (1938), Pulitzer Prize, (1932). The Good Earth.

Bunin, Ivan (1870-1953): The first Russian to win the Nobel Prize for literature in 1933, after a long rivalry with Maxim Gorky.

Burns, Robert (1759-'96): Scotland's unofficial national poet.

Butler, Samuel (1835-1902): English scholar, novelist. The Way of All Flesh.

Byron, George Gordon (1788-1824): English romantic poet. At 20, he published Hours of Idleness; Childe Harold's Pilgrimage (1812).

Camus, Albert (1913-'60): French novelist, dramatist; native of Algeria. The Price of Justice, and L' Etranger. Nobel prize, 1957.

Carlyle, Thomas (1795-1881): Scottish author. Heroes and Hero Worship.

Carnegie, Dale (1888-1955): American writer famous for self improvement manuals.

Albert Camus

Cartland, Barbara (1902-2000): American best selling author, who wrote 723 books. 1b. copies sold in 36 languages.

Cervantes, Saavedra Miguel de (1547-1616): Spanish novelist and dramatist. Don Quixote.

Chandler, Raymond Thornton (1888–1959): American detective story writer. Created cynical private detective Philip Marlowe.

Chatterji, Bankim Chandra (1838-'94): Poet, novelist and a great patriot of India (Bengal). Vande Mataram (Anand Math).

Chaucer, Geoffrey (1340-1400): English poet. The Canterbury Tales.

Chaudhuri, Nirad C. (1897-1999): Indian writer, and social critic, wrote in English and lived in England. Autobiography of an Unknown Indian, A Passage to England.

Chekhov, Anton (1860-1904): Russian dramatist and short story writer. Uncle Vanya.

Chesterton, Gilbert Keith (1874-1936): English essayist, novelist and poet.

Christie, Agatha (1890-1976): English writer of detective fiction. Her two detectives are Miss Marple and Hercule Poirot. Play Mousetrap has run in London for over four decades.

G.K. Chesterton

Coleridge, Samuel Taylor (1772-1834): English poet, critic and philosopher.

Colette (1873-1954): French novelist whose early works were published under her first husband's pseudonym, Willy.

Collins, Wilkie (1824-'89): British novelist, who collaborated with Charles Dickens. The Woman in White, The Moonstone.

Conrad, Joseph (1857-1924): British novelist and short story writer born in Poland. Was a ship's officer before. Heart of Darkness, Nostromo, The Secret Agent.

Dante Alighieri (1265-1321): Italian poet. The Divine Comedy.

Daudet, Alphonse (1840-1897): French short-story writer and novelist whose first novel was written at age 14. Monday Tales, The Nabob.

De Quincey, Thomas (1785-1859): English essayist and critic.

Defoe, Daniel (1660-1731): English political writer; also author of Robinson Crusoe.

Dickens, Charles (1812-'70): Popular English novelist of the 19th cent. David Copperfield, Pickwick Papers, Oliver Twist.

Charles Dickens

Dickinson, Emily (1830-'86): American poet. Published almost nothing in her lifetime.

Donne, John (1572 -1631): One of the great Metaphysical poets. He was chaplain to King James of England, and later Dean of St. Paul's.

Dostoevsky, Feodor Mikhailovich (1821 -'81): Russian novelist. Sent to hard labour in Siberia for revolutionary activity. Crime and Punishment, The Idiot, The Possessed.

Doyle, Sir Arthur Conan (1859-1930): British writer of detective stories. Creator of detective Sherlock Holmes and Dr Watson.

Dryden, John (1631-1700): Poet laureate and dramatist. The Indian Emperor, Heroic Stanzas, All for Love.

Dumas, Alexandre (1802-'70): French romantic novelist. The Three Musketeers.

Eckermann, Johann Peter (1792-1854): German writer who was an assistant to

Mother of Two Creates History Anusha Jamsenpa, 32, from Arunachal Pradesh, made history by climbing Mt. Everest twice in 10 days - May 12 and May 22. She is the first woman mountaineer in the world to achieve the feat twice in the same season. She is mother of two children.

Goethe. Conversations with Goethe.

Eco, Umberto (b. 1932): Italian novelist who authored the historical thriller The name of the Rose, and the novel Foucault's Pendulum. Also wrote A Theory of Semiotics.

Umberto Eco

Ehrenburg, Liya Grigoryevich (1891-1967): Russian writer whose novel The Thaw gave the name to post-Stalin relaxation.

Eliot, George (1819-'80): Pen-name of English woman novelist Mary Anne (later Marion) Evans. Middlemarch.

Eliot, Thomas Stearns (1888-1965): English Poet and critic, born in U.S. The Waste Land, Murder in the Cathedral. Nobel Prize.

Euripides (480-406 B.C.): The greatest of the Greek dramatists, who wrote about 80 plays. Trojan Woman, Alcestis, Medea.

Falk, Lee (1912-'99): Creator of the popular cartoon characters Mandrake the Magician and the Phantom.

Farah, Nuruddin (b. 1945): Somali novelist, and a major writer of Africa.

Faulkner, William (1897-1962): American novelist, whose series of novels (The Sound and the Fury, etc.) depict the American South. Nobel prize, 1949.

Fielding, Henry (1707-'54): English author known for Tom Jones (1749).

Fitzgerald, Edward (1809-'83): English poet and translator. Translated The Rubaiyat of Omar Khayyam (1859).

Flaubert, Gustave (1821-80): French novelist, leading exponent of French realism. Madame Bovary.

Forster, Edward Morgan (1879-1970): Novelist, shortstory writer and essayist. Author of A Passage to India.

Forsyth, Fredrick (b. 1938): British journalist and author of best-sellers like Day of the Jackal, The Odessa File and The Dogs of War.

Frank, Anne (1929-c.1945): Jewish girl who fled Germany with family to escape Nazi persecution, and author of The Diary of a Young Girl.

Frost, Robert (1874-1963): American poet well-known for his poem Stopping by Woods on a Snowy Evening.

Anne Frank

Galsworthy, John (1867-1933): English novelist and dramatist. The Forsyte Saga. Nobel prize, 1932.

Gargi, Balwant (1916-2003): Punjabi writer who wrote popular plays. Sahitya Akademi Award for Rang Manch; Nangi Dhup was autobiographical.

Geisel, Theodor Seuss (pen name: Dr. Seuss) (1904-'91): Writer of nearly 50 books of rhymes and doodles, including The Cat in the Hat.

Ghalib, Mirza Asadullah Khan (1796-1868): Renowned Urdu poet. Diwan-e-Ghalib.

Gibran, Kahlil (1883-1931): Lebanese-born US writer and artist. He has written in Arabic and English.Hispoetry translated into more than 20 languages and his paintings exhibited across the world.

Gide, Andre (1869-1951): French writer of short novels. The Counterfeiters.

Goethe, Johann Wolfgang von (1749-1832): German poet and thinker. Faust.

Golding, Sir William (1911-'93): English novelist. First novel The Lord of the Flies. Booker Prize, Nobel Prize.

Goldsmith, Oliver (1728-'74): Irish poet, dramatist and novelist. The Vicar of Wakefield.

Obama's Irish Roots — US President Obama, visiting Ireland in May, 2011, explored his Irish roots. He made a brief visit to a village that was home to his great-great-great grand father.

Gorky, Maxim (1868-1936): Russian writer. Mother.

Greene, Graham (1904-'91): English novelist and journalist. The Power and the Glory.

Grass, Gunter Wilhelm (b. 1927): German novelist, poet and playwright. The Tin Drum, Dog Years, The Call of the Toad. Nobel Prize. Revealed in Aug. '06 that he had served in Nazi elite force Waffen-SS.

Gunter Grass

Gupta, Maithili Saran (1886-1964): A national poet of India, and one of the makers of modern Hindi literature. Bharat Bharati. Padma Vibhushan.

Hardy, Thomas (1840-1928): English novelist and poet, sometimes called the 'last of the Victorians'. Far from the Madding Crowd.

Harris, Joel Chandler (1848-1908): American author of the Uncle Remus stories.

Hauptmann, Gerhant (1862-1946): German writer whose play Vor Sonnenaufgamg marked the birth of German naturalist drama. Nobel Prize 1912.

Hazarika, Dr. Bhupendra Kumar (b. 1926): Renowned film-maker and composer of lyrics and music. Phalke Award, '93.

Hemingway, Ernest (1898-1961): Eminent American novelist of new technique and wide influence. The Sun Also Rises, The Old Man and the Sea. Nobel Prize, 1954.

Henry, O. (real name William Sydney Porter) (1862–1910): Master story-teller. The Gift of the Magi.

Homer (c. 700 B.C.): Epic poet. He is supposed to have been a Greek. The Iliad, The Odyssey.

Hugo, Victor (1802-'85): French poet, dramatist, and novelist. Lucrece , Les Miserables.

Huxley, Aldous (1894-1963): English novelist. Grandson of T. H. Huxley (1825-95, biologist-educator, ardent evolutionist), brother of Julian Huxley (1887-1975, biologist and writer, first D-G of UNESCO), and grandnephew of Mathew Arnold. Brave New World.

Ibsen, Henrik Johan (1828-1906): Norwegian playwright and poet. 'the father of modern drama'. Ghosts, A Doll's House.

Jalloun, Taher Ben (b. 1945): Morocco's best known writer. Writes in French.

Jayadeva (12th c.): Famous Sanskrit poet. Gita Govinda.

Jonson, Ben (c. 1573-1637): English dramatist and poet who ranks with Shakespeare. The Alchemist.

Johnson, Dr. Samuel (1709-'84): English lexicographer, critic and literary figure. Dictionary was publised in 1755. Rasselas.

Kadare, Ismail (b.1934): Exiled Albanian writer. Essays, poems and works of fiction. Translated into more than 40 languages.

Kafka, Franz (1883-1924): Czech-born German novelist. The Trial, The Castle.

Ismail Kadare

Kalidasa (c. A.D. 400): India's greatest poet, dramatist and chief figure in classic Sanskrit literature, known as Indian Shakespeare. Abhigyana Shakuntalam, Kumarasambhava, Meghadoot, Raghuvamsa etc.

Karanth, Shivarama (1902-1997): A literary giant; novels, plays, travelogues, essays, general science encyclopedia. Chomana Dudi.

Karnad, Girish Raghunath (b.1938): Noted Indian playwright, actor and director.

Chairman, Sangeet Natak Akademi, (1988-93). Director, Nehru Centre, London. Jnanpith. Padma Shri, Padma Bhushan.

Kawabata Yasunari (1899-1972): Japanese novelist, one of he Neo-Impressionists: Works

Girish Karnad

(Snow Country, The Sound of the Mountain) are characterized by melancholy and loneliness. Committed suicide. Nobel Prize, 1968.

Keneally, Thomas Michael (b. 1935): Australian writer. His novel Schindler's Ark won 1982 Booker Prize. It was made into a prize winning film by Steven Spielberg - Schindler's List.

Kipling, Rudyard (1865-1936): British writer born in Bombay. Kim, Jungle Books. Nobel prize.

Krishnamurthy, Kalki (1899-1954): Tamil novelist, short story writer and music critic.

Kundera, Milan (b. 1929): Czech novelist. The Unbearable Lightness of Being.

La Fontaine, Jean De (1621-'95): French poet of the Fables and author of stories in verse.

Lahiri, Jhumpa (b.1967): Writer of Indian origin. Won Pulitzer Prize (2000) for 'The Interpreter of Maladies: Stories of Bengal, Boston and Beyond'.

Le Carre, John pen-name of David John Moore Corn-well (b. 1931): English writer of thrillers,

Jhumpa Lahiri

who had been a diplomat. The Spy Who Came In From The Cold.

Lee, Harper (b.1926): Pulitzer Prize winning author of To Kill a Mockingbird. Enigmatic, reclusive never published another book.

London, Jack (1876-1916): American writer known for short stories and adventure tales. Call of the Wild.

Longfellow, Henry Wadsworth (1807-'82): American poet. The Golden Legend, Hiawatha.

Macaulay, Thomas Babington (1800-'59): English historian, poet and Indian civil servant. Reformed the Indian education system. History of England.

Marlowe, Christopher (1564-'93): English dramatist and precursor of Shakespeare. Dr. Faustus, Tamburlaine.

Marquez, Gabriel Garcia (b.1928): Colombian writer and poet. Nobel Prize, 1982. One Hundred Years of Solitude.

Martin du Gard, Roger (1881-1958): French novelist known for his 8-novel series Les Thibault dealing with family life in early 20th century. Nobel Prize, 1937.

Marquez

Maupassant, Guy De (1850-'93): French author, one of the masters of the short story. La Parure (The Necklace).

Mehta, Ved (b. 1934): Indian author and journalist. Settled in New York. Blind at age 3. Writer for the New Yorker. Portrait of India, Face to Face, Walking the Indian Streets.

Menon, Vallathol Narayana (1878-1958): Indian (Malayalam) poet, patriot. Founder of Kerala Kala Mandalam. Badhiravilapam.

Milne, Alan Alexander (1882-1956): English humorist and poet whose work

The Golden Triangle | **The Golden Triangle was probably named after the gold once traded for opium. Th area once provided at least half of the world's opium supply. Burma alone produced 1800 metric tons in 1993.**

for children is still widely read.

Milton, John (1608-'74): English poet. After he went blind he wrote Paradise Lost, one of world's greatest epics. Paradise Regained.

Moliere (Jean Baptiste Poquelin), (1622-'73): French playwright and actor. Tartuffe.

Morris, Jan (b.1926): England-born Welsh travel writer and historian. 40 books and countless essays. Venice, Pax Britannica trilogy, Hav, Trieste and the Meaning of Nowhere.

Morrison, Toni (b.1931): Black US novelist. Won the Pulitzer and Nobel Prizes and the PEN/Borders Literary Service Award. Beloved, Paradise.

Nabokov, Vladimir (1899-1977): Russian-American novelist, poet and an authority on butterflies. Lolita.

Toni Morrison

Naipaul, Vidiadhur Surajprasad (b. 1932): British writer, born in Trinidad of Indian descent. Nobel prize, 2001. Miguel Street, A House for Mr. Biswas, A Bend in the River, A Way in the World.

Nair, Madath Thekkepat Vasudevan (b. 1934): Well-known Malayalam novelist; Jnanpith award, 1995. Nalukettu.

V.S. Naipaul

Narayan, Rashipuram Krishnaswami (1906-2001): Indian writer in English. Padma Bhushan. The Guide, Swami and Friends, Malgudi Days.

Omar Khayyam (c. 1050-1123): Persian poet and astronomer. His Rubaiyat, translated into English by Edward Fitzgerald.

Orwell, George (Eric Arthur Blair) (1903-50): English satirist, born in India. Animal Farm.

Parker, Dorothy (1893-1967): American writer, known for her wit. Enough Rope and Death and Taxes are poetry volumes. Laments for the Living and After Such Pleasures are short story collections.

Pasternak, Boris (1890-1960): Russian writer and poet. In 1958 awarded Nobel Prize **but declined the offer. Dr. Zhivago.**

Pillai, Thakazhi, Sivasankara (1915-'99): Indian writer (Malayalam) Gyanpith award. Chemmeen, Kayar.

Pinter, Harold (1930-2008): British dramatist, actor and director. Plays known for their elusive dialogue and atmosphere of menace. The Caretaker, The Homecoming,Moonlighting. Nobel Prize, 2005.

Poe, Edgar Allan (1809-'49): American poet and story writer. The Raven, To Helen.

Harold Pinter

Pope, Alexander (1688-1744): English poet, The Rape of the Lock, The Dunciad.

Premchand, Munshi (1880-1936): Hindi writer whose real name was Dhanpat Rai. A pioneer of modern social fiction. Godan, Sevasadan, Rangamanch, Ghaban, Nirmala.

Priestley, John Boynton (1894-1984): English novelist, essayist, critic and playwright. The Good Companions, Angel Pavement.

Pritam, Amrita (1919-2005): Indian poetess and novelist. Gyanpith award. Kagaz ke Kanwaz.

Proust, Marcel (1871-1922): French novelist whose masterpiece was the 12- volume Remembrance of Things Past.

The Bhutan Queen

Jetsun Pema, the future queen of Bhutan, was a student of Lawrence School Sanawar in Himachal Pradesh. She passed class XII in 2008, having studied English, history, geography, economics and painting. She was a good athlete and basketball player.

Quasimodo, Salvatore (1901-'68): Italian poet associated with hermeticism. Nobel Prize.

Rao, Raja (1908-2006): Novelist, famous for his contributions to Indian English literature. Kanthapura, Serpent and The Rope. Padma Bhushan.

Rolland, Romain (1866-1944): French novelist and dramatist. Jean-Christophe, a ten-volume novel. Wrote biographies of Mahatma Gandhi and Vivekananda.

Rowling, J.K (b.1965): British author of the internationally famous series of children's fantasy stories concerning the exploits of the boy wizard Harry Potter. 400 mn. copies of her books sold. Fortune at $798mn.

J.K. Rowling

Roy, Arundhati (b. 1960): The first Indian author to win Booker Prize (The God of Small Things), Environmentalist. In Forbes list of world's 30 most inspiring women, 2010.

Rushdie, Salman (b. 1946): Indian born British writer. His controversial book Satanic Verses made Iran's spiritual leader Ayatollah Khomeini sentence him to death. Booker Prize. Midnight's Children, The Moor's Last Sigh.

Salman Rushdie

Ruskin, John (1819-1900): English author, social reformer and art critic. Modern Painters (5 volumes), Unto This Last.

Ryunosuke, Akutagawa (1892–1927): Japanese writer, dealt with madness and macabre social contradictions. Committed suicide. Akutagawa Prize is Japan's top literary award.

Saki, (pseudonym of Hector Huge Munro) (1870-1916): British satirist and humorist. The Unbearable Bassington, Reginald.

Sappho (c. 612-c.580 B.C.): The greatest female lyric poet of ancient Greece.

Saramago, Jose (1924-2010): Portuguese novelist. Baltasar and Blimunda. Nobel Prize, 1998.

Sartre, Jean-Paul (1905-'80): French dramatist, essayist, novelist and leader of the philosophical movement, existentialism. Being and Nothingness, The Roads to Freedom, The Flies. Nobel Prize (1964) but he declined it.

Jose Saramago

Scott, Sir Walter (1771-1832): Scottish novelist and poet. Ivanhoe, Kenilworth.

Shakespeare, William (1564-1616): Greatest dramatist and poet of England. Unbeatable in mastery of language, understanding of character and dramatic perception.37 plays, 154 sonnets, two poems. Romeo and Juliet, Julius Caesar, Hamlet, Othello, Macbeth, The Tempest.

Shaw, George Bernard (1856- 1950): Irish dramatist and the greatest critic of his age. Conquered England by his wit. Nobel Prize. Man and Superman, Saint Joan, Pygmalion.

Shelley, Percy Bysshe (1792-1822): English Romantic poet, renowned for his daring views; a passionate advocate of freedom. Prometheus Unbound, Ode to the West Wind, The Skylark.

Sholokhov, Mikhail (1905-'84): The foremost Russian realistic novelist. And Quiet Flows the Don. Nobel prize, 1965.

Singh, Khushwant (b. 1915): Jour-

Oxford Chair for Sanjaya Lall

A visiting professorship in memory of Sanjaya Lall, one of India's pioneering development economists, has been launched at Oxford University.

nalist and writer, was editor of Illustrated Weekly, National Herald, Hindustan Times, etc. Member, Parliament. History of the Sikhs, Train to Pakistan, End of India. Padma Bhushan and Padma Vibhushan.

Snow, Charles Percy (1905-'80): British writer and scientist, author of the essay The Two Cultures and the Scientific Revolution.

Solzhenitsyn, Alexander (1918-2008): Russian novelist, expelled from Soviet Union in 1974, returned home, in '94. Nobel Prize, 1970. Cancer Ward, The First Circle.

Solzhenitsyn

Sophocles (495-406 B.C.): Athenian dramatic poet, ranking with Aeschylus and Euripides. Oedipus Tyrannus, Electra.

Soyinka, Wole (b. 1934): Nigerian dramatist. First black African to get Nobel Prize for literature (1986). The Intrepreters, Death and the King's Horseman.

Wole Soyinka

Spender, Stephen (1909-'95): English poet, critic, essayist.

Spenser, Edmund (1552-'99): English poet, ranking with Shakespeare and Milton. He is called 'the poet's poet'. The Faerie Queene.

Stevenson, Robert Louis (1850-'94): Scottish author. Treasure Island, Kidnapped, Dr. Jekyll and Mr. Hyde.

Subramaniam, Ka Na (1912-'88): Renowned Tamil poet and critic. Oru Nal, Poi Thevu.

Surrey, Henry Howard, Earl of (1517-47): English poet. Wrote sonnets and introduced blank verse into English poetry. Accused of treason, he was executed.

Swift, Jonathan (1667-1745): English satirist. Gulliver's Travels.

Jonathan Swift

Tagore, Rabindranath (1861-1941): Indian poet and philosopher who introduced Indian culture to the West and vice versa. Founded Shantiniketan which later became Viswabharati University. Wrote national anthems of both India and Bangladesh. Sonar Tari, Chaitali, Kalpana, Chitrangada, Gitanjali. Nobel Prize 1913-first Asian to get it.

Tendulkar, Vijay (1928-2008): Marathi playwright. Sangeet Natak Academy Award, Kalidas Samman, Padma Bhushan. Kanyadaan.

Tennyson, Alfred (1809-'92): English poet-laureate. The Princess, In Memoriam.

Thackeray, Balasaheb (b. 1926-): Shiv Sena supremo who began his career as a cartoonist at the age of 18.

Thiruvalluvar (c. 1st century): The greatest ever Tamil poet. Thirukural.

Tolstoy, Leo (1828-1910): Russian novelist and writer on ethics and religion. War and Peace, Anna Karenina, Resurrection.

Tulsi Das (1532-1623): Indian poet whose Hindi masterpiece Ram-Charit-Manas (the Ramayana) is venerated by Hindus as the Bible is in the West.

Twain, Mark (pseudonym of Samuel Langhorne Clemens) (1835-1910): Ame-rica's leading humorist who used his wit to comment on social, political and moral problems. Tom Sawyer, Huckleberry Finn.

Vatsyayan, Sachidananda Hiranand (Agyeya) (1911-'87): Hindi writer, journalist. Gyanpith award, '78 (Kitni Navom Me Kitni Bar).

Vatsyayana (5th Century A.D.): Sanskrit writer who wrote the famous Kamasutra ('Art of Sex').

Verne, Jules (1825-1905): French writer of science fiction. Around the World in Eighty Days, Journey to the Centre of the Earth.

Vicente, Gil (1465-1536): Portuguese playwright,regarded as the founder of Portuguese drama. The Forge of Love, The Pilgrimage of the Aggrieved.

Vijayan, O.V. (1930-2005): Political cartoonist and writer in Malayalam. Khasakinte Ithihasam. Padma Bhushan.

Virgil (Publius Vergillius Maro) (70-19 B.C.): Roman epic poet. The Aeneid.

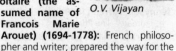

O.V. Vijayan

Voltaire (the assumed name of Francois Marie Arouet) (1694-1778): French philosopher and writer; prepared the way for the French Revolution. Candide.

Walcott, Derek (b.1930): West Indian poet and dramatist. Omeros. Nobel (1992).

Wallace, Edgar (1875-1932): English novelist and playwright; wrote detective thrillers. The Four Just Men, The Ringer.

Wells, Herbert George (1866-1946): English author. The Time Machine, Kipps, The Outline of History, The Shape of Things to come.

White, Patrick Victor Martin Sale (1912-90): Novelist, the first Australian to win a Nobel Prize for literature (1973). The Tree of Man, The Eye of the Storm.

Whitman, Walt (1819-'92): American poet. Leaves of Grass, Drum Taps. Known for his elegies to Abraham Lincoln, ("O Captain! My Captain!").

Wiesel, Elie (b. 1928): Romanian-US novelist. Works reflect his experiences as a survivor of the Holocaust. Nobel Peace Prize, 1986. Night, A Beggar in Jerusalem, The Forgotten.

Wilde, Oscar (1854-1900): Irish author and dramatist, remembered for his flamboyant style and caustic wit. A Woman of No Importance, The Picture of Dorian Gray, The Importance of Being Earnest.

Wodehouse, Pelham Grenvile (1881-1975): English comic novelist; creator of the immortal butler, Jeeves.

Woolf, Virginia (1882-1941): English writer who developed the stream-of-consciousness technique. To the Lighthouse, Mrs. Dalloway, The Waves, Orlando.

Virginia Woolf

Wordsworth, William (1770-1850): English Romantic poet, interpreter of nature in her many moods. Poet Laureate, 1843. The Prelude, Sonnets.

Wouke, Herman (b.1915): US novelist. The Caine Mutiny. Pulitzer prize.

Yeats, William Butler (1865-1939): Irish lyric poet and playwright. The Hour Glass, Deidre, The Second Coming.

Zacharia, Paul (b. 1945): Malayalam short story writer, novelist and essayist. Zachariyayude Kathakal. Sahitya Akademi award winner.

Zacharia

Zola, Emile (1840-1902): French novelist. L'Assommoir, Nana, Germinal.

Arts

Anand, Dev (b. 1923): Evergreen Indian film star, with the longest period as hero. Romancing with Life (autobiography) Phalke Award.

Dev Anand

Anderson, Marian (1897-1993): American contralto, who pioneered acceptance of black singers in concert and opera worlds.

Antonioni, Michelangelo (b.1912-2007): Italian avant-garde motion-picture director and screenwriter, whose films are known for their haunting images of human isolation. Oscar, 1995. L'Avventura, Blow Up.

Armstrong, Louis 'Satchmo' (1900-71): American jazz trumpeter, and singer, a popular entertainer of 20th century

Ashcroft, Peggy (1907-1991): One of the greatest actresses of British stage. Remembered for her role in the film A Passage to India (Oscar) and the TV series The Jewel in the Crown.

Attenborough, Sir Richard (b. 1923): British actor-director whose Gandhi (1983) won 8 Oscars.

Azmi, Shabana (b. 1950): Indian film actress who won the national award five times. Social activist, former Rajya Sabha member. Ankur, Arth, Khandhar, Paar, Godmother.

Shabana Azmi

Bach, Johann Sebastian (1685-

1750): Prolific German baroque composer.

Bachchan, Amitabh (b.1942): India's most popular film star ever. Over 100 movies. M.P. for a short while. Zanjeer, Sholay, Diwar, Black. National award for Best Actor, 2005. Son of poet Harivansh Rai Bachchan (1907-2003), known for his work Madhushala and autobiography in 4 volumes Kya Bhoolun, Kya Yad Karoon. Amitabh's son Abhishek, leading film star.

Bala Saraswati, T. (b.1918-1984): Foremost exponent of the Bharatanatyam style of dance.

Bartok, Bela (1881-1945): Hungarian composer and pianist.

Beatles, The (Paul Mc Cartney, John Lennon (1940-80), George Harrison (1943-2001), Ringo Starr): English vocal and instrumental rock 'n'roll quartet whose highly original and melodic songs held the attention of youth all over the world in the 60s.

Beethoven, Ludwig Van (1770-1827): German musician and composer. His symphonies, 9 in number, rank as the greatest ever written.

Belafonte, Harry (b.1927): American entertainer, civil rights leader.

Benegal, Shyam (b.1934): Indian film director. Akrosh, Mandi, Bharat Ek Khoj. Phalke award. Padma Shri, Padma Bhushan.

Berry, Halle (b. 1968): US film actress. First black actress to win Oscar for best actress. Monster's Ball.

Bertolucci, Bernardo (b. 1940): Italian film director. The Last Emperor won 9 Oscars in 1987.

Bloch, Ernest (1880-1959): Swiss-born

Halle Berry

US composer, famous for his chamber music. Israel Symphony (1916).

Borodin, Alexander Porfirevich (1833-87): One of the 'Russian Five' group of composers.

Borromini, Francesco (1599-1667): Italian architect. One of the three masters of Roman Baroque, the other two being Bermini and Pietro da Cortona.

Bosch, Hieronymus (1450-1516): Flemish painter. The Garden of Earthly Delights, The Temptation of St. Anthony.

Bose, Nandalal (1883-1966): Father of Modern Painting in India. Padma Bhushan.

Brahms, Johannes (1833-97): German composer, who moved to Vienna. Orchestral works: four symphonies, two piano concertos and a concerto for violin.

Brando, Marlon (1924-2004): Outstanding American stage and film actor. On the Waterfront, The Godfather.

Capra, Frank (1897- 1991): American moviemaker, a trendsetter who grabbed many firsts in film techniques.

Cezanne, Paul (1839-1906): French post-impressionist painter.

Chan, Jackie (b.1954): Movie star from Hong Kong. Made 40 films since '76, when he was touted as the new Bruce Lee.

Chaplin, Charles Spencer (Charlie) (1889-1977): Film star comedian, first international screen star, with more than 50 years' achievement. Born in London, he went to the United States in 1916. The Kid, The Gold Rush, Limelight, The Tramp.

Charlie Chaplin

Chattopadhyay, Kamaladevi (1903-'88): The high priestess of Indian culture, arts, theatre and literature. Magsaysay award, 1966.

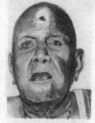

Chembai

Chembai Vaidyanatha Bhagavathar (1889-1974): Great (Carnatic) musician of India.

Chevalier, Maurice (1888–1972): French film actor, singer who became an international filmstar. Love Me Tonight, Gigi.

Chopin, Fre'de'ric Francois (1810-'49): Polish pianist, composer; 'the poet of the piano'.

Choudhary, Sarbari Roy (b. 1933): Indian sculptor. Works include portraits and abstract bronzes.

Connery, Sean (b.1930): Scottish actor who won acclaim as screen's secret agent James Bond. Awards: BAFTA, Golden Globe & Academy.

Correggio (1494-1534): Italian painter of the Renaissance era. Adoration of the Shepherds.

Crow, Russell (b.1965): Oscar (Gladiator, 2000) winning actor, born in New Zealand, raised in Australia; wife Danielle Spencer.

Cruise, Tom (b.1962): Actor. No. 1 in Forbes 2006 list of world's 100 most powerful stars. Annual earnings $67m.

Russel Crow

Culkin, Macaulay (b.1981): Child star of the 1990 film Home Alone.

Davis, Bette (1908-'89): Originally Ruth Elizabeth Davis. American film actress.

De Mille, Cecil (1881-1959): American film producer-director. Grand old man of Hollywood. The Ten Commandments.

De Sica, Vittorio (1901-'74): Italian film

director and actor. Shoeshine, Bicycle Thieves.

Deshpande, Purushottam Lakshman (1919-2000): Veteran Marathi writer and performer known as Pu La.

Dietrich, Marlene (1901-'93): Actress and singer, native of Berlin who flourished in the USA. Blue Angel.

Disney, Walter Elias ('Walt') (1901-'66): American film cartoonist famous for animated cartoons. Creator of characters Mickey Mouse (1928) and Donald Duck (1936).

Dix, Otto (1891-1969): German painter and engraver. Jailed in 1939 for an alleged plot to kill Hitler. Post-war themes included religion.

Donatello (1386-1466): Florentine sculptor, a pioneer of the Renaissance style, born Donato di Niccola di Betto Bardi. Famous for the marble sculptures of St. Mark and St. George.

Duncan, Isadora (1877-1927): American expressive dancer who united free movement with serious music; one of the founders of modern dance.

Dutt, Nargis (1929-'81): The greatest film actress of her time. Paired in several immortal films with Raj Kapoor. Married actor Sunil Dutt, who later became a Union Minister until death in 2005. Best actress award. Padmashri. Nominated to Rajya Sabha. Son Sanjay Dutt, a leading Hindi film actor.

Dylan, Bob (b.1941):): US singer and composer, born Robert Allen Zimmerman. Blood on the Tracks. Pulitzer

Bob Dylan

Ellington, Edward Kennedy ('Duke') (1899-1974): American pianist, composer.

Fellini, Federico (1920-'93): Great Italian film maker. Five-time Academy Award winner. La Strada (1954), La Dolce Vita (1959), 8 1/2 (1963).

Fonda, Henry (1905-'82): US actor who became a Hollywood star. Won Academy Award in '82 for On Golden Pond. Daughter Jane and son Peter joined films.

Gainsborough, Thomas (1727-88): British portrait and landscape painter. Viscount Kilmorey, Blue Boy, The Watering Place.

Gaitonde, V.S. (1924-2001): India's celebrated abstract painter.

Ganesan, Sivaji (1927-2001): Legendary actor; over 300 Tamil films in five decades. Dada Saheb Phalke Award, 1996.

Garbo, Greta (1905-'90): Swedish film actress of poetical quality. Ninotchka.

Gaugin, (Eugene Henri) Paul (1848-1903): French painter. Sought the simplicity of primitive life in Tahiti. The Yellow Christ.

Sivaji Ganesan

George, Boy (real name: George O'Dowd) (b.1962): The gender bender pop idol of the 1980s.

Giacometti, Alberto (1901-66): Swiss painter and sculptor.

Gielgud, Sir John (b.1904-2000): One of the century's great classical actors and the finest speaker of Shakespearean verse in the history of theatre. Acted even at 90.

Gish, Lillian (1896-1993): American silent film actress whose career spanned 8 decades. Sister Dorothy Gish (1898-1968), also actress.

Goldberg, Whoopie (b.1956): Actress-comedienne. The Colour Purple.

Gopalakrishnan, Adoor (b. 1941): Outstanding Indian script writer and film director. Four times winner of National

Deenabandhu Charles Freer Andrews, a Christian missionary from Britain, made India his spiritual home. He was a good friend of Mahatma Gandhi who called him 'Charlie'. Andrews stood for the poor and oppressed and was known as 'Deenbandhu'.

Award for Best Director. Phalke Award 2004, Padma Vibhushan. Swayamvaram, Mathilukal, Kathapurushan, Nizhal Kuthu.

Gopi, Kalamandalam (b. 1937): Kathakali maestro. Kalidas Samman, 2011. Padma Shri.

Graham, Martha (1893-1991): American dancer, teacher and choreographer of more than 140 works.

Grant, Cary (1904-86): American film star born in Britain as Archibald Leach. Girl Friday, North by Northwest.

Herge (Georges Remi) (1907-83): World famous author of Tintin cartoon series.

Hitchcock, Alfred (1899-1980): British-American film director, 'the master of suspense'. Vertigo, Psycho, The Birds.

Holbein, Hans (1465-1524): German painter. Called 'the Elder'. His son portrait painter Hans Holbein (1497-1543) is called 'the Younger'.

Husain, Maqbool Fida (1915-2011): Leading Indian artist popularly known as 'MF'. Member, Rajya Sabha, '86. Padma Bhushan, Padma Vibhushan. Became an honorary citizen of Qatar in 2010, died in London.

Ilaiyaraja (b. 1943): Superstar of Indian film music. Music director of over 900 films. Padma Bhushan.

Iqbal, Muhammad (1877-1938): The greatest 20th century Indian poet to write in Urdu. The Secrets of the Self, The Song of Eternity. Author of the famous line 'Sare jahan se acha yeh hindustan hamara'.

Ilaiyaraja

Iyer, Semmangudi Srinivasa (1907-2003): Great musician (Carnatic) of India. Padma Vibhushan.

Jackson, Michael Joe (1958-2009):

Popular black American singer and entertainer who grew into a legend. Thriller (global sales: 47 m), Dangerous, History.

Jagger, Mick (b.1944): Lead singer of The Rolling Stones, rock group. British.

Jooss, Kurt (1901-79): Dancer and choreographer of Germany, whose dance dramas combined modern dance with ballet techniques.

Joshi, Pandit Bhimsen Gururaj (1922-2010): Internationally acclaimed Hindustani vocalist, who led the renaissance of Indian classical music. Bharat Ratna, 08.

Kamalahasan (b. 1954): India's top film actor who won three national awards and 15 Filmfare awards in 37 years. Appu Raja, Sadma.

Kapoor, Raj (1924-'88): Indian film actor, director, producer; one

Kamalahasan

of the greatest entertainers the country has produced. Barsaat, Awara, Shri 420, Sangam.

Kapoor, Shekhar (b. 1946): Indian film director. Bandit Queen, Elizabeth.

Kazan, Elia (1909-2003): US film director, born in Turkey. A Streetcar Named Desire, On the Waterfront.

Kelly, Grace (1929-'82): American film actress who married Monaco's Prince Rainier III and left acting.

Elia Kazan

Khan, Bismillah (1916-2006): Shehnai maestro from Varanasi, India. Bharat Ratna, 2001.

Khan, Ustad Allauddin (1862-1972) of Malhar: One of the all-time greats of the century in the Hindustani music tradition.

Khusro, Amir (1253-1325): The Persian poet of Delhi who is believed to be the father of Sahatara (Sitar). Saw 11 Badshahs and served under 7 sultans.

Kingsley, Ben (b. 1944): London-based actor who played the role of Gandhi in Attenborough's film, Gandhi. Oscar .

Kumar, Ashok (1911-2002): India's longest serving film star. Debut in 1936. Achhut Kanya, Kismet, Ashirwad. Phalke Award.

Ben Kingsley

Kumar, Dilip (b.1922): Top matinee idol of India. *Andaz, Devdas, Mughal E Azam, Deedar*. Phalke award. Lifetime achievement award, 09. Wife actress Saira Banu.

Kurosawa, Akira (1910-'98): Japan's greatest filmmaker , creator of such classics as Rashomon and The Seven.

Laxman, Rasipuram Krishnaswami (b.1927): Outstanding Indian cartoonist. Magsaysay award, 1984. Brother to writer R.K. Narayan.

Leigh, Vivien (1913-'67): British actress who won Oscar in 1940 for Gone With The Wind portraying Scarlett O'Hara.

Leonardo da Vinci (1452-1519): A great genius, one of the master artists of the high Renaissance. Italian. Man of science who was painter, architect, philosopher, poet, composer, sculptor, athlete, mathematician, inventor, and anatomist. Last Supper and Mona Lisa.

Liszt, Franz (1811-'86): Hungarian-French composer. Debut at age 11. Transcendental Etudes, Paganini Etudes, A Faust Symphony.

Lloyd Webber, Andrew (b. 1948): British composer. Rock opera Jesus Christ Superstar. Cats, the longest running musical ever in London and New York.

Lopez, Jennifer (b. 1970): American singer and actress of Peurto Rican parentage. Highest-paid Latina actress in Hollywood history. Her debut album 'On the 6' was a major hit with the infectious single "If you had my love".

Loren, Sophia (b. 1934): Italian actress, two Oscars. Two Women, Millionairess.

Madonna (Madonna Louise Veronica Ciccone) (b. 1958): World's number one female pop star with over 80 m. albums sold

Sophia Loren

and more consecutive top hit singles than the Beatles; a self-made icon. Italian American. Japan Gold International Artist of the year on March, 2009.

Mahapatra, Kelucharan (1926-2004): Exponent of Odissi dance. Trained and produced two generations of world-class dancers. Padma Bhushan.

Maharaj, Pandit Birju (b.1938): Eminent Kathak dancer. Padma Vibhushan in 1986.

Mahmood, Talat (1924-1998): Celebrated ghazal and playback singer. Lata Mangeshkar award 1995.

Manessier, Alfred (1912-'93): One of France's greatest abstract artists; also a master of tapestry and stained glass.

Mangeshkar, Lata (b. 1929): Melody queen of India. Most prolific playback singer active for half a century. Phalke award, Rajiv Gandhi Sadbhavana Award, Bharat Ratna (2001).

Lata Mangeshkar

Mansingh, Sonal (b.1944): Started Centre for Indian Classical Dances

(1977). First woman to learn Chhau dance. Padma Bhushan.

Marceau, Marcel (1923-2007): The Picasso of the mime. Bip, his celebrated mime creation.

Sonal Mansingh

Martin, Ricky (b. 1971): Latino pop singer, a member of Menudo, the Puerto Rican boy band. Grammy award.

Mayer, Louis Burt (1885-1957): Film executive of note in USA in the thirties and forties. Founded a film production company in 1912. Vice President of Metro-Goldwyn-Mayer.

Mehmood, Talat (1924-'98): Ghazal singer par excellence. Once Dilip Kumar's voice.

Mehndi, Daler (b. 1968): Popular Punjabi pop singer.

Daler Mehndi

Mehta, Zubin (b. 1936): Indian-born musician and conductor of world-famous Israel Philharmonic Orchestra and the 130-member New York Philharmonic Orchestra.

Menuhin, Yehudi (1916-'99): World-famous violinist. New York of Russian Jewish parentage. First appeared as soloist at age 7.

Mercouri, Melina (1924-'94): Greek actress and activist. Became an instant international star ('60) in Never On Sunday.

Michelangelo (1475-1564): Italian painter, sculptor, architect and poet. Painted the ceiling of the Sistine Chapel (a surface of about 6,000 square feet), Last Judgement, Pieta.

Mitra, Sombhu (1915-'97): A peerless stage actor with great influence on Indian theatre scene.

Modigliani, Amedeo (1884-1920): Italian painter and sculptor.

Monroe, Marilyn (1926-'62): (real name: Norma Jean Mortenson (later) Baker). American film star and charming sex symbol of her times. The Seven Year Itch, The Misfits.

Mozart, Wolfgang Amadeus (1756-'91): Austrian composer. One of world's great musical geniuses. Began his career at four and toured Europe at six. Three of the greatest operas in musical history are his Marriage of Figaro, Don Giovanni and The Magic Flute.

Naidu, Sarojini (1879-1949): Indian poetess of English language, known as the 'Nightingale of India'. Took part in freedom struggle. First woman Governor of an Indian state (U.P.). *Golden Threshold, Bird of Time, Broken Wing*.

Nair, Mira: (b. 1957): Indian film director. Salaam Bombay, Mississippi Masala, Monsoon Wedding (Golden Lion, Venice 2001).

Olivier, Laurence (1907-'89): British actor and director, especially in Shakesperean roles.

Mira Nair

Pasolini, Pier Paolo (1922-'75): Italian film maker, poet, novelist and critic.

Pavarotti, Luciano (1935-2007): Italian singer, considered the greatest tenor of his times. Retired from staged opera in 2004.

Picasso, Pablo Ruiz (1881-1973): Spanish painter, sculptor and ceramicist. Described as the century's most prolific and versatile artist. One of the originators of Cubism. Guernica.

Poitier, Sidney (b. 1927): US film ac-

Z. A. Bhutto | Former Pakistan Prime Minister Zulfikar Ali Bhutto was hanged at Rawalpindi in 1979. His daughter Benazir was premier in 1988.

tor. First black actor to win Oscar for best actor. Lilies of the Field, Good-bye Mr.Chips.

Pollock, Paul Jackson (1912-56): American painter famous for his 'drip painting' technique.

Pookutty, Resool (b.1971): Indian film sound engineer, sound editor and mixer. Won Academy award for Sound Mixing for *Slumdog Millionaire. Sabdatharapadham* (autobiography).

Presley, Elvis (1935-'77): US popular singer, whose fusion of Black rhythm and blues and white country styles created modern pop music. He is the most successful recording artist in history with hits like Hound Dog, Don't be cruel, and Suspicious Minds. He also acted in numerous films.

Priyadarshan (b.1957): Indian film director and screenwriter. Successful with his Bollywood remakes of popular Malayalam movies. His Kanchivaram won National Award, 2008 for the best feature film.

Rafi, Mohammed **(1926-'80):** India's top playback singer. More than 20,000 songs.

A.R. Rahman

Rahman, A.R. (b. 1967): India's leading film music director. Winner of two Oscars, 2009. Also Golden Globe and BAFTA award. His album 'Vandemataram', a bestseller. Roja, Bombay.

Aishwarya Rai

Rai, Aishwarya (b. 1974): Indian beauty queen who was crowned Miss World at Sun City, Johannesburg in 1994. A brilliant Bollywood star, the first Indian actress to be on Cannes jury. Married to Amitabh Bachchan's son Abhishek Bachchan. Padma Shri.

Raphael, Saint (1438-1520): Italian painter and architect. Associated with the rebuilding of St. Peter's.

Ray, Satyajit (1921-'92): The greatest Indian film director. Won special Oscar award and Bharat Ratna in 1992. His films are notable for their realistic portrayal of everyday life. Pather Panchali, Aparajita, Charulata.

Reeve, Christopher (1942-2004): Actor best known for the' Superman' movies. A horseback riding accident in 1995 left him paralysed. Still Me.

Rembrandt, Harmenszoon (1606-'69): Dutch painter and etcher, one of the undisputed giants of Western art.

Richard, Cliff (b. 1940): British pop star, born in India as Harry Rodger Webb. Living Doll (1959), Congratulations (1969). 115 songs.

Rimbaud, Jean Nicolas (1854-'91): French poet. Prepared the way for symbolism. At 18 completed his memoirs. Une Saison en Enfer.

Roberts, Julia (b.1967): Academy award-winning American actress. Oscar for Best Actress for playing the title role in the movie Erin Brockovich.

Robeson, Paul (1898-1976): Black American singer and actor especially remembered for his singing of Negro spirituals.

Julia Roberts

Rooney, Mickey (b.1920): US film actor who often teamed with Judy Garland. A Midsummer Night's Dream, The Human Comedy.

Rousseau, Henri (1844-1910): French primitive painter. A collector of tolls

(Hence also known as Le Douanier, meaning 'the customs official') who retired at 41 to take up painting.

Rubinstein, Arthur (1887-1982): US pianist, born in Poland. Began public performance at age 11.

Rublyov, Andrey (1370-1430): Russian artist, iconographer who retired to monastic life. Also known as Rublev.

Sanyal, B.C. (1901-2003): Eminent Indian painter, President of Lalit Kala Akademy. Padma Bhushan.

Sen, Mrinal (b. 1923): Famous Indian film director. Bhuvan Shome, Kharz.

Shah, Nazeeruddin (b.1950): Indian film actor and director. One of India's best actors. Nishant, Aakrosh, Sparsh, Mirch Masala, Masoom, Monsoon Wedding. Acted as Gandhi in Hey Ram and in the play Mahatma Vs.Gandhi, as Mirza Ghalib (TV series), as Shivaji in Bharat Ek Khoj.Padma Bhushan.

Mrinal Sen

Shankar (1902-'89) (Sankara Pillai): Indian cartoonist. Known for 'Shankar's Weekly', the International Children's Art Competition and the International Dolls Museum, all founded by him.

Shankar, Ravi (b. 1920): Internationally known Indian sitar maestro. Bharat Ratna. My Music, My Life. Three Grammy awards.

Shyamalan, Manoj Night (b. 1970): Acclaimed Indian-born Hollywood film director. The Sixth Sense, Unbreakable.

Sinatra, Frank (1915-'98): (Francis Albert) American singer, film actor. Singing idol of bobbysoxers in 1940s. 100 albums, 58 feature films. Oscar (From Here To Eternity) and Grammy lifetime achievement awards.

Spears, Britney (b.1981): Hugely successful American pop singer. Her albums... Baby One More Time (1999) and Oops!... I Did It Again (2000) were huge hits. Sold 60 m. albums.

Spielberg, Steven (b. 1947): One of world's most successful film directors. Jaws (1975); E.T.– the Extra Terrestrial (1983), Jurassic Park (1993), Minority Report (2002)– the last has broken all box-office records. Schindler's List won him Oscar for best director (1994) and 6 other awards.

Steven Spielberg

Srinivas, Uppalapu (b. 1970): Mandolin player of India who began playing it at the age of six. The youngest to receive the title "Asthana Vidwan" ('90). Padma Shri.

Stallone, Sylvester (b. 1946): One of Hollywood's highest-paid actors. Rocky, Cliffhanger.

Stradivari, Antonia (1644-1739): Most well-known Italian maker of musical instruments. Developed the 'long Strad' style of violins. Some of his violins still survive.

Streep, Meryl (b. 1949): A first-rank American film actress. Oscar and Bette Davis Life Achievement award. Kramer Vs Kramer, Sophie's Choice.

Stroheim, Erich von (1885–1957): Austrian director, writer and actor. Greed.

Subbulakshmi, Madurai Shanmugavadivu (1916-2004): Famous Carnatic singer of India. Magsaysay award,

M.S. Subbulakshmi

1974. Gave a special recital of devotional songs for the silver jubilee celebrations of UN in 1970. Bharat Ratna, 1998-first musician to receive the honour.

Subramaniam, Padma (1943): Indian dancer of Bharata Natyam. variety of classical dance, musician, composer, choreographer, author. Sangeet Natak Akademi Award, Padma Bhushan, Kalidas Samman.

Padma Subramaniam

Tansen (c. 1492-1589): Original name Ramatanu Pande. Symbolises the best in Hindustani music. Name Tansen conferred by Akbar when he joined the Mughal court.

Taylor, Elizabeth (b. 1932): English-born American film actress. Married Richard Burton twice. Cat on a Hot Tin Roof, Who's Afraid of Virginia Woolf?

Temple, Shirley (b.1928): American film actress, and politician. The world's leading child film star in the thirties.

Titian (Tiziano Vecelli): (c. 1487-1576): Venetian painter. Sacred and Profane Love.

Shirley Temple

Travolta, John (b.1954): US film actor. He starred in the wildly successful Saturday Night Fever.

Turner, Joseph (1775-1851): English painter. The Fighting Temeraire.

Ustinov, Sir Peter (1921-2004): British actor, director and raconteur. Oscar award. Dear Me.

Van Gogh, Vincent (1853-'90): Distinguished Dutch painter - the first of the great modern Expressionist painters. Committed suicide.

Van Gogh

Varma, Raja Ravi (1848-1906): One of the greatest early Indian artists, from the royal family of Kilimanoor, Kerala.

Velazquez, Diego (1599-1660): Spanish painter, influenced by Titian. Court painter to Philip IV. One of the greatest painters in history.

Vicky (Victor Weisz) (1913-'66): German-born British cartoonist.

Wagner, Richard (1813-'83): German composer, who made revolutionary changes in the structure of opera.

Wells, (George) Orson (1915-'85): American film actor, writer, director, producer, Citzen Kane (1941), The Third Man (1949).

West, Mae (1892-1980): American vaudeville artist and film actress.

Wonder, Stevie (b. 1950): American singer. A precocious child, despite being blind from birth. First album at age 12. Talking Book, Hotter than July.

Yesudas Kattassery Joseph (1940): Leading playback singer, composer, music director. Recorded about 50,000 songs in about 17 languages during a career spanning five decades. Fondly called Gana Gandharvan. National Award for Best Male Playback Singer seven times, State award over 30 times. Padma Shri, Padma Bhushan.

K.J. Yesudas

Gagarin Dies, A Town is Born

Yuri Gagrin, the first man in space, was killed on March 27, 1968 not in a space flight but in an aeroplane crash. After his death, the town of Gzhatsk was renamed Gagarin.

Science & Technology

Adler, Alfred (1870–1937): Viennese psychologist who introduced inferiority complex.

Aiken, Howard H. (1900-'73): U.S. mathematician, credited with designing forerunner of digital computer.

Alberuni (c.970-1039): Astronomer, mathematician, philosopher and author. Studied Indian civilization and languages and wrote about India. Alberuni's India.

Ampere, Andre Marie (1775-1836): French physicist after whom the unit of electric current is named.

Amundsen, Roald (1872-1928): Norwegian explorer, first to reach South Pole (1911).

Angstrom, Anders Jonas (1814-74): Swedish physicist who founded the science of spectroscopy. The angstrom unit of measurement is named after him.

Archer, Thomas (1668-1743): British architect. Practitioner of Baroque style.

Archimedes (287-212 B.C.): Greek mathematician and engineer. Known for Archimedes Principle. Invented Archimedean screw.

Armstrong, Neil (b. 1930): American astronaut, the first man to set foot on the moon, (Apollo XI mission) 21 July 1969.

Neil Armstrong

Aryabhatta (476-520): Indian mathematician and astronomer. India's first satellite was named after him.

Asimov, Isaac (1920-92): US biochemist and writer of non-fiction. Born in Russia. Foundation Trilogy, The Edge of Tomorrow, Inside the Atom, The Stars in their Courses.

Babbage, Charles (1792-1871): English mathematician. His primitive 'calculating machines' were the precursors of the modern computer.

Bacon, Roger (c.1214-92): English philosopher and scientist, called 'Doctor Mirabilis'. First European to describe the process for making gunpowder.

Bahuguna, Sundarlal (b.1927): Environmentalist. Known for the Chipko movement and fight against the building of the Tehri Dam. Padma Vibhushan, 2009.

Bahuguna

Baker, Laurie (1917-2007): British-born Indian architect who has pioneered innovative low-cost, environment-friendly housing.

Barnard, Christiaan Neethling (1922-2001): South African surgeon who performed the first human heart transplant operation.

Baskerville, John (1706-'75): British typographer who is known for the widely used Baskerville typeface.

Bell, Alexander Graham (1847-1922): Scottish-born inventor of the telephone.

Bessemer, Sir Henry (1813-'98): British metallurgist who invented the process of converting cast iron direct into steel.

Bhabha, Homi J. (1909-'66): The Indian scientist who was mainly responsible for creating the Bhabha Atomic Research Centre. Described as the father of Indian nuclear science.

Homi Bhabha

Bhaskara I (7th c. AD): Indian astronomer who

A Spaceman Dies of Cancer — The first American space explorer to die of natural causes was John L Swigert. He had survived the ill-fated Apollo 13 mission in 1970. He died of cancer on Dec. 27, 1982.

was a contemporary of Brahmagupta.

Bhaskaracharya II (1114-c.1185): Great Indian mathematician and astronomer, who was the first to use the decimal system in a written work,invented the + and - convention, and used letters to represent unknown quantities as in modern algebra. Sidhanta Shiromani.

Bhatia, Sabeer (b. 1968): Indian-born co-founder of Hotmail. He sold Hotmail to Microsoft for US$400 million.

Bhatnagar, Shanti Swarup (1894-1955): Indian scientist who created a chain of national laboratories. Director of CSIR, Secretary to AEC, Chairman of UGC. Science awards after his name.

Bohr, Niels (1885 -1962): Danish physicist. Nobel Prize, for work on atomic structure.

Boole, George (1815-'64): English mathematician best known for his invention of Boolean algebra.

Borlaug, Norman Ernest (1914-2009): American wheat scientist responsible for the 'green revolution'. Nobel Peace Prize, 1970.

Bose, Jagadish Chandra (1858-1937): Doyen of Indian science. Did original work in electricity.

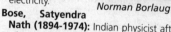

Norman Borlaug

Bose, Satyendra Nath (1894-1974): Indian physicist after whom an elementary particle, the boson is named.

Bragg, Sir William Lawrence (1890-1971): English physicist born in Australia. With his father Sir William Henry Bragg (1862-1942), won Nobel Prize for Physics (1915).

Brahmagupta (598-680): The Indian mathematician who was the first to treat zero as a number. Brahma Siddhanta.

Carver, George Washington (1864-

1943): American agricultural chemist.

Celsius, Anders (1701-'44): Swedish inventor, astronomer. Devised (1742) Celcius or centigrade temperature scale.

Cernan, Eugene Andrew (b. 1934): US astronaut; been to space 3 timesl 'The last man on the moon'.

Chandrasekhar, Subrahmanyan (1910-'95): Born at Lahore, an American citizen; nephew of Nobel laureate C. V. Raman. Won the Nobel prize for physics in 1983.

Chawla, Kalpana (1961-2003): The first Indian American space woman. Travelled aboard space shuttle Columbia in Nov. '97. Died on her second space mission aboard Colombia.

Kalpana Chawla

Cherenkov, Pavel Alekseyich (1904-1990): Soviet physicist. Discovered Cherenkov effect. Shared Nobel Prize (1958).

Chichester, Sir Francis (1901–'72): English yachtsman, aviator, sailed around world single-handed in Gipsy Moth IV, (1966-'67).

Chidambaram, Rajagopala (b. 1936): Chief scientific advisor to Govt. of India, led the Pokhran nuclear test team (1998).

Cockerell, Christopher (1910-1999): English inventor of the hovercraft.

Colins, Lt. Col. Eileen (b.1956): The first female to take over the controls of a NASA spaceship.

Columbus, Christopher (c.1451-1506): Italian explorer known as the discoverer of the Americas.

Eileen Colins

| A Moon-walker's End | The first moonwalker to die was James B. Irwin, who died on Aug. 8, 1991 as a result of a heart attack. |

In 1492 discovered the Bahamas, Cuba, and other West Indian Islands.

Copernicus, Nicolas (1473-1543): Polish astronomer; considered founder of modern astronomy. Put forward the novel theory that the planets, including the Earth, revolve round the sun.

Correa, Charles (b.1930): India's eminent architect, educated at Michigan and MIT.

Crookes, Sir William (1832-1919): British chemist and physicist. Inventor of radiometer and Crooke's tube. Discovered thallium.

Curie, Marie Sklodowska (1867-1934): Scientist, (b. Poland) who jointly with husband Pierre Curie discovered radium for which they shared the Nobel Prize for physics (1903). She won Nobel Prize again for chemistry (1911).

Cushing, Harvey (1869-1939): American surgeon whose pioneering techniques for brain surgery improved neuro-surgery tremendously. Cushing's syndrome, named after him.

Daimler, Gottlieb (1834-1900): German engineer, inventor. He improved internal combustion engine, furthering car industry.

Dam, Henrik (1895-1976): Danish biochemist who discovered vitamin K. Nobel Prize.

Darwin, Charles Robert (1809-'82): English naturalist who argued that the evolution of present-day morphology had been built up by the gradual and opportunistic mechanism of natural selection. On the Origin of Species.

Charles Darwin

Davy, Sir Humphry (1778–1829): British chemist and inventor of the Davy miner's safety lamp.

Dhawan, Satish (1920-2002): Scientist, Director of IIS, Bangalore, Chairman of ISRO. Padma Vibhushan 1981.

Diesel, Rudolf (1858-1913): German engineer, inventor of an internal combustion engine which he patented in 1893.

Du Pont, Eleuth–Ere Irenee (1772-1834): American chemicals manufacturer, b. France.

Dunlop, John Boyd (1840-1921): Scottish veterinary surgeon. Patented (1888) Dunlop version of pneumatic tyre.

Eastman, George (1854-1932): American inventor; manufacturer of photographic equipment.

Eckert, John Presper (1919-'95): Co-inventor of the computer. Developed world's first electronic digital computer with John W. Mauchly.

Edison, Thomas Alva (1847-1931): American inventor who held more than 1300 U.S. and foreign patents for his inventions: the phonograph, the incandescent lamp, etc.

Edison

Ehrlich, Paul (1854-1915): German scientist, one of the pioneers of bacteriology.

Eiffel, Alexandro Gustave (1832-1923): French engineer, remembered for Eiffel Tower, Paris and Panama Canal locks

Einstein, Albert (1879-1955): Mathematical physicist whose theory of relativity superseded Newton's theory of gravitation. His work led on to the making of the nuclear bomb. Nobel Prize, 1921.

Einthoven, Willem (1860-1927): Dutch physiologist. Invented the electrocardiogram. Nobel Prize.

Ellis, Havelock (1859-1939): English psychologist and writer. Studies in the Psychology of Sex (7 vols; 1898-1928).

Ellsworth, Lincoln (1880-1951): Ameri-

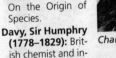

Spaceflight Experience: **In spaceflight experience, the USA and Russia are the leaders. They are followed by France, Germany, Canada, Japan, Bulgaria, Belgium, Afghanistan and China.**

can engineer, the first to fly over Antarctica (1935).

Empedocles (c. 490-430 B.C.): Greek philosopher who held that all matter was composed of four ingredients - fire, air, water and earth. Only 500 lines from two of his poems remain in his writing

Fahrenheit, Gabriel Daniel (1686-1736): German physicist who introduced the mercury thermometer and fixed thermometric standards.

Fallopio, Gabriele (1523-'62): Italian anatomist, discovered Fallopian tubes, leading from ovaries to the uterus, in which fertilisation takes place.

Faraday, Michael (1791-1867): English physicist who founded the science of electro-magnetism.

Fermi, Enrico (1901-'54): Pioneering scientist who discovered over 400 radio isotopes. Element number 100 is named Fermium after him.

Fleming, Sir Alexander (1881-1955): British bacteriologist and discoverer of penicillin (1928). Nobel Prize (1945).

Ford, Henry (1863-1947): Pioneer (American) motor car manufacturer and industrialist. Founder of Ford Motor Company and Ford Foundation.

Franklin, Benjamin (1706-'90): American statesman, and scientist. Invented the lightning conductor.

Freud, Sigmund (1856-1939): Austrian psychiatrist and founder of psychoanalysis. The Interpretation of Dreams.

Gagarin, Yuri (1934-'68): Soviet cosmonaut, the first man to orbit the earth in spacecraft Vostok I in 1961.

Yuri Gagarin

Galileo Galilei (1564-1642): Italian scientist and astronomer who laid the foundations of modern science. The first man to see the satellites of Jupiter.

Gamow, George (1904-68): Russian-born US nuclear physicist. With Ralph Alpher and Hans Bethe, he developed the Big Bang theory. Gamow-Teller theory of beta decay is known after him and Edward Teller.

Gates, Bill (b. 1956): World's second richest private individual. Co-founder of Microsoft Corp.; he revolutionised the computer industry. Philanthropist who has made record donations. In 2006 announced decision to focus on charity work.

Bill Gates

Goodyear, Charles (1800-'60): American inventor who discovered the art of vulcanising rubber.

Guttenberg, Johann (1400-'68): German inventor who invented printing with movable types cast in moulds.

Haffkine, Waldemar (1860-1930): First Director of Plague Research Laboratory, Bombay later renamed The Haffkine Institute.

Hahn, Otto (1879-1968): German chemist, chief discoverer of nuclear fission, on which the atom bomb is based. Nobel prize, 1944.

Haldane, J.B.S. (1892-1964): British biochemist and geneticist. He emigrated to India in 1957.

Harvey, William (1578-1657): English physician who discovered the mechanics of the circulation of blood, 1616.

Hawking, Stephen (b. 1942): British astrophysicist, widely regarded as the greatest physicist since Einstein. Victim of a degenerative nerve disease. He can communicate only through a computer,

---

Michelle Yeoh Deported

Former Bond girl Michelle Yeoh, who plays Myanmars' pro-democracy leader Aung San Suu Kyi, has been deported from the country.

attached to his motorized wheelchair. A Brief History of Time, Black Holes and Baby Universes.

Hensen, Victor (1835-1924): The German physiologist who first used the name plankton to describe the organisms that live suspended in the sea.

Heyerdahl, Thor (1914- 2002): Norwegian scientist and adventurer, best known for his voyage aboard the Kon-Tiki raft.

Hillary, Edmund (1919-2008): New Zealand explorer, the first to climb Mount Everest in 1953.

Edmund Hillary

Hipparchus (2nd cent.BC): Greek astronomer. Founder of systematic astronomy.

Hippocrates of Cos (c. 430 B.C.): Greek physician, called the Father of Medicine.

Hodgkin, Dorothy (1910-94): Nobel Prize winner (Chemistry) who founded Pugwash Conference on nuclear weapons. Determined the structure of penicillin, insulin and Vitamin B12.

Hofmann, Albert (1906-2008): Swiss chemist who discovered the now-banned hallucinogenic drug LSD.

Hollows, Fred (1929-93): Australian doctor whose work improved the eyesight of millions of people.

Huygens, Christiaan (1629-'95): Dutch mathematician. Invented pendulum clock.

Jenner, Edward (1749–1823): English country practitioner who invented vaccination.

Joliot-Curie, Jean Frederic (1900-'58) and his wife Irene (1896-1956): French scientists who discovered artificial radioactivity. Nobel prize winners, 1935.

Joule, James Prescott (1818-'89): British physicist. Gave his name to the unit measuring energy.

Jung, Carl Gustav (1875-1961): Swiss psychologist, one of the founders of analytical psychology. Worked with Freud.

Jussieu, Bernard de (1699-c.1777): French botanist who devised the system of plant classification based on natural affinities.

Kalam, Dr. Abdul Avul Pakir Jainu-labdeen (b.1931): President of India from 2002 to 2007. Former Scientific Adviser to Defence Minister. The man behind India's missile programme. Known for his dedication to science, commitment to professional excellence and simplicity of lifestyle. Bharat Ratna, 1998.

Kalashnikov, Mikhael (b. 1919): Russian; creator of the famous Kalashnikov rifle (1946).

Kepler, Johannes (1571-1630): German astronomer and mystic.

Khorana, Har Gobind (b. 1922): Born in India, a naturalized citizen of USA. Synthesized the first wholly artificial gene. Shared Nobel prize, 1968.

Khosla, Vinod (b. 1955): Co-founder of Sun Microsystems. One of world's most influential venture capitalists. General Partner at venture capital firm Kleiner Perkins Caufield & Byers.

Khorana

Kilby, Jack S (1924-2005): Inventor of the integrated circuit (commonly called the microchip) that gave rise to the information age. Nobel Prize in Physics.

Koch, Robert (1843-1910): German physician and bacteriologist who discovered the bacillus of tuberculosis. Nobel prize, 1905.

Krupp, Alfred (1812-'87): German armaments magnate.

Le Corbusier (1887-1965): Pseudonym

Dewey's Theory of Teaching

John Dewey, the author of *Democracy and Education*, rejected old-fashioned, autocratic teaching methods in favour of curricula that fostered independent thinking and problem solving.

of architect Charles Edouard Jeanneret. Born in Switzerland, became a French citizen in 1930. Architect of Chandigarh (India).

Leakey, Louis Seymour Bazett (1903-'72): Kenyan-born British archaeologist and anthropologist, and Mary Doughlas Leakey (b. 1913), English archaeologist. Made several important discoveries about men's origins in East Africa. Son Richard Leakey (b. 1944).

Lesseps, Ferdinand (1805-'94): French engineer who built the Suez Canal in 1869.

Lorenz, Konrad (1903-1989): Zoologist from Austria, co-founder of modern ethology. Authored On Aggression. Shared Noble Prize, 1973.

Lores, Bonney (1898-1994): Pioneering aviatrix (of Australia) who in 1933 became the first woman to make the solo trip from Australia to England, flying without a radio.

Lovelock, James (b.1919): Creator of the field of Geophysics, responsible for much of our environmental consciousness.

Lutyens, Sir Edwin (1869-1944): English architect; City plan of New Delhi, viceroy's house, British Embassy in Washington and Roman Catholic cathedral of Liverpool.

Macadam, John Loudon (1756-1836): Scottish inventor of the 'macadamising' system of road repair.

Magellan, Ferdinand (c.1480-1521): Portuguese navigator, and commander of the first expedition (1519) to circumnavigate the globe.

Marconi, Guglielmo (1874-1937): Italian inventor who developed the use of radio waves as a means of communication. Nobel Prize.

Marggraf, Andreas Sigismund (1709-82): German chemist. His discovery of beet sugar led to the development of the sugar industry.

Mashelkar, Dr. R.A (b. 1943): Former Director General of CSIR. Elected Fellow of the Royal Society in 1998. Padma Bhushan.

Maxim, Hiram Stevens (1840-1916): American who invented the Maxim machine gun.

Maxwell, James Clerk (1831-'79): British physicist, whose work revolutionised fundamental physics. First scientific paper at 15.

Mazumdar Shaw, Kiran (b.1953): Entrepreneur who has become 'India's biotech queen'. M.D. of Biocon, one of world's leading biotechnology companies. Padma Bhushan, 2005.

Mazumdar

Mendel, Gregor Johann (1822-'84): Austrian botanist who discovered the basic laws of heredity.

Minkowski, Hermann (1864-1909): German mathematician who propounded the idea of a four-dimesional space. Minkowski space combined the three dimensions of physical space with that of time.

Monod, Jacques (1910-'76): French biochemist who, with Francis Jacob, proposed the existence of messenger RNA. Nobel Prize 1965 shared with Jacob and Andre Lwoff.

Morita, Akio (1921-99): Electronic pioneer; Co-founder of Sony Corp.

Morse, Samuel (1791-1872): American artist and inventor; invented telegraphy and the dot-and-dash code that bears his name.

Murdoch, Colin (1929-2008): Inventor of the disposable syringe, the tranqulliser gun, the childproof bottle cap and the silent burglar alarm. Accused of fraud in 2002 election.

Napier, John (1550-1617): Scottish

Dr. Mukherjee Wins Pulitzer

Dr. Siddhartha Mukherjee, 41, assistant professor of medicine at Columbia University and cancer physician at University Medical Centre is the fourth writer of Indian origin to win the Pulitzer Prize. His work: *The Emperor of All Maladies: A Biography of Cancer.*

mathematician and clergyman. Invented logarithms and the modern notation of fractions.

Narlikar, Dr. Jayant V. (b. 1938): Indian astronomer. Research into 'black holes'. Worked with Prof. Fred Hoyle in Cambridge. Bhatnagar Award, Kalinga Award (1996). Padma Bhushan and Padma Vibhushan.

Newton, Sir Isaac (1642-1727): English scientist, known for his work on the composition of white light, calculus and the theory of gravitation. Principia Mathematica

Nostradamus or Michel De Notre Dame (1503-66): *Isaac Newton* French astrologer and physician, known for his prophecies.

Oort, Jan (1900-'92): Dutch astronomer. Proposed the existence of the Oort Cloud, a vast collection of ice chunks far beyond Pluto.

Osborne, Adam (1939-2003): Computer technologist. He produced the first portable computer.

Pachauri, Dr. Rajendra K (b. 1940): Economist and environmental scientist, Chairman of the Intergovernmental Panel on Climate Change (IPCC) which won the Nobel Prize in 2007. Head of TERI since 1981. Padma Bhushan.

Pasteur, Louis (1822-'95): French chemist, founder of microbiology. His investigations led to the science of immunology.

Pauling, Linus Carl (1901-'94): American scientist who won Nobel Prize for Chemistry (1954) and for Peace (1962). Known for his opposition to nuclear tests.

Paz, Octavio (1914-'98): Mexican poet. Nobel Prize, 1990. Ambassador to India,1962-68. Labyrinth of Solitude, Sun Stone.

Pickering, William (1909-2004): American space programmer who guided NASA's moon missions.

Pitroda, Satyanarayan Gangaram (b. 1942): Technocrat. Popularly known as Sam Pitroda. The man behind India's telecom revolution in 1980s. Chairman of World Tel (an agency for ITU). Chairman of National Knowledge Commission. Padma Bhushan

Sam Pitroda

Planck, Max (1858-1947): German physicist who originated the quantum theory. His theory was applied by Einstein, Bohr and others. Nobel 1918.

Premji, Azim Hasham (b.1945): Chairman, Wipro, an IT giant. Richest Indian in the world for several years, third richest person in the world, 2000. Sixth among 10 richest Tech Titans, in Forbes list, 2006. Founded a university.

Pythagoras (c. 582-500 B.C.): Greek philosopher and mathematician. He saw in numbers the key to the understanding of the universe.

Raman, Dr. Chandrasekhara Venkata (1888-1970): Indian physicist whose research on the diffusion of light (discovery of "Raman effect") a phenomenon of scattered light rays earned him Nobel Prize, 1930. Founded Indian Institute of Science, Bangalore. Lenin Peace Prize, Bharat Ratna.

Ramanujan, Srinivasa (1887-1920): One of the greatest mathematicians India has ever produced.

Ramanna, Dr. Raja (1926-2004): Indian nuclear physicist; He was Di-

Raja Ramanna

rector, Bhabha Atomic Research Centre, Secretary, Atomic Energy Dept., Chairman, Atomic Energy Commission (1984) and Union Minister.

Richter, Dr. Charles F. (1900-'85): American inventor of Richter scale, which gauges the energy released by an earthquake as measured by ground motion recorded on a seismograph.

Roentgen, Wilhelm Konrad von (1845-1923): German scientist who discovered X-rays (1895). Nobel prize, 1901.

Ross, Ronald (1857-1932): British physician and bacteriologist who discovered the malaria parasite. Born in India. Nobel prize, 1902.

Row, Yellam Pragada Subba (1896-1948): Indian scientist (in US, 1920-1940's) who, along with Fiske, discovered creatine phosphate (1926), worked on the isolation and synthesis of folic acid.

Roy, Prafulla Chandra (1861-1944): Great scientist and father of modern Indian chemical industry. The History of Hindu Chemistry.

Saha, Meghnad (1893-1956): Indian scientist who first attempted to develop a consistent theory of spectral sequence of the stars from the point of view of atomic theory.

Sakharov, Andrei (1921-'89): Soviet nuclear physicist, human rights activist. Nobel prize.

Salk, Jonas (1915-'95): US microbiologist who developed the first successful vaccine against polio.

Sarabhai, Dr. Vikram (1919-'71): Indian nuclear scientist who was Chairman of the Atomic Energy Commission. Helped set up the Thumba rocket station.

Savitskaya, Svetlana (b. 1949): Soviet cosmonaut; the first woman to walk in space; the only woman to have made two space flights.

Sharma, Rakesh (b. 1954): The first Indian cosmonaut to go into space, aboard

Soyuz-T 11 for a rendezvous with Salyut-7 (1984).

Stephenson, George (1781-1848): English engineer; inventor of locomotive en**gine**.

Rakesh Sharma

Sudarsan, Prof. Ennackal Chandy George (b. 1931): Indian physicist famous for his particle theory on 'tacheons', faster than light. Advanced the theory of V-A (left handed) current, one of the four fundamental forces of nature. Worked in Rochester. Padma Vibhushan, 2007. Dirac Prize 2010.

Sullivan, Louis (1856-1924): American architect; pioneered steel-frame construction; coined dictum 'Form Follows Function'.

Swaminathan, Mankombu Sambasivan (b. 1925): Internationally known agricultural scientist of India. Was member, Planning Commission; Director General of IRRI, Manila. Heads M.S. Swaminathan Research Foundation. Presently Chairman, Commission for Farmers. Padmashri, Padmabhushan, Padmavibhushan, Magsaysay Award, World Food Prize.

Swedenborg, Emanuel (1688-1772): Swedish scientist, mystic, philosopher and theologian. Heavenly Arcana.

Tatum, Edward Lawrie (1909-'75): American biochemist.

Tereshkova

Tereshkova, Valentina (b. 1937): soviet cosmonaut who in 1963 became the first woman to make a space flight, aboard Vostok-VI.

Tim Berners-Lee, Sir Tomothy John (b. 1955): The inventor of the World Wide Web. Named

Napoleon's Hiccups	**Napoleon tried to kill himself in 1814. The vial of the poison he used was two years old and it merely gave him a violent attack of hiccups, which made him vomit and that saved his life.**

by Time magazine as one of the top 20 thinkers of the 20th century. Knighted in 2003.

Venkatraman, Ramakrishnan (b.1952): Structural biologist who shared the 2009 Nobel Prize in Chemistry for studies of the structure and function of the ribosome. Born in Tamil Nadu, US citizen, residence UK. Padma Vibhushan.

Vespucci, Amerigo (1454-1512): Italian explorer, after whom America is named. Explored Venezuela.

Wadia, Ardaseer Cursetjee (1808-'77): Mechanical and marine engineer, the first Indian Fellow of the Royal Society, London, at the age of 33.

Walton, Ernest (1904-'95): Irish scientist, who along with John Cockcroft, split the atom artificially for the first time, thus ushering in the nuclear age in 1932. Shared Nobel Prize.

Watt, James (1736-1819): Scottish engineer and inventor after whom the watt as a unit of power is named.

Whitney, Eli (1765-1825): American manufacturer, invented cotton gin.

James Watt

Wilkinson, John (1728-1808): British industrialist who found many applications for iron. Known as 'the great Stafforeshire ironmaster'.

Woulfe, Peter (1727-1803): British chemist after whom glass laboratory bottle with two or more necks is known.

Wright, Orville (1871-1948) and his brother Wilbur (1867-1912): American inventors and pioneers in aviation. The two brothers were the first men to design and fly a powered, man-carrying airplane.

Young, Thomas (1773-1829): English physicist who uncovered some of the mysteries of light and colour. He spoke nine languages, including Latin, by the age of 16.

Zeppelin, Ferdinand (1838-1917): German inventor who built the first rigid frame motor-driven airship (1900); subsequent models named after him.

Zworykin, Vladimir (1889-1982): Russian inventor of the iconoscope, first electronic-scanning television camera.

Sports

Agassi, Andre (b.1970): American tennis star. Wimbledon (92), US Open (94, 99), Australian Open (95, 2000, 2001, 2003), French Open (99).

Ali, Muhammed (Originally Cassius Marcellus Clay) (b. 1942): American pugilist famous for his unorthodox style and colourful personality. First boxer to win the heavy-weight title three times.

Andre Agassi

Amritraj, Vijay (b. 1953): India's Captain to Davis Cup from 1982. Only player to win Hall of Fame Tennis thrice. Actor in Hollywood movies and TV serials.

Anand, Visvanathan (b. 1969): Grandmaster. World No. 1 in speed chess. Youngest Asian to win International Master's title. World Champion 2000-2002 (FIDE), 2007-present (undisputed). No.1 on the July 2008 FIDE ratings list. Won 6th Chess Oscar, 2009. World chess champion 2010.

Honouring Aish	Aishwarya Rai Bachchan has been named officer Dan Ordre Des Arts Et Des Lettre by the French government. Previous recipients of this award of distinction include Shah Rukh Khan and Nandida Das.

Ao, Talimeren Dr. (1916-'98): First captain of independent India's Olympic football team.

Azharudin, Mohammed (b. 1963): Indian cricketer, former Captain. Made a world record of 9079 runs in one-day internationals in June '99. Accused of involvement in match-fixing scam. In May 2009, he was elected to the Indian Parliament.

Bannister, Sir Roger (b.1929): British athlete and doctor who became the first man to run a mile in four minutes in 1954.

Batistuta, Gabriel (b.1969): Former Argentine international footballer. Retired 2005.

Becker, Boris (b. 1967): German tennis player. Youngest Wimbledon champion, 1985, 1986, 1989. Retired in 1997.

Boris Becker

Beckham, David (b.1975): British football player with a huge fan following. His marriage to Victoria Adams, otherwise known as Posh Spice, has made them both targets for the tabloid press.

Bedi, Bishen Singh (b. 1946): Indian cricketer. Captain for 33 tests.

Baichung Bhutia

Bhutia, Baichung (b.1976): Indian footballer from Sikkim. At 15, highest goal-getter in the Subroto Mukherjee tournament in Delhi. Arjuna Award, Padma Shri.

Bindra, Abhinav (b. 1983): Shooter from Chandigarh, won gold in 2008 Beijing Olympics. Padma Bhushan.

Bolt, Usain (b. 1986): Jamaican sprinter who holds the world records for 100 metres, 200 metres and 4x100 metres relay. First man to win all three events at a single Olympics since Carl Lewis in 1984. In August 2009 in Berlin, Bolt broke two world records to win his first World Championship gold medals

Border, Allan (b. 1955): Former Australian cricket captain who holds the world record of 156 Test matches. 11,174 test runs.

Allan Border

Borg, Bjorn (b. 1956): Swedish tennis player. Greatest player of all time. Fifth consecutive Wimbledon in 1980.

Botvinnik, Mikhail (1911-'95): Russian electrical engineer who used his scientific training to hold the world chess title three times (1948-57, 58-60, 61-63).

Bradman, Sir Donald (1908–2001): Australian cricket legend. Captain, 1936-48. 6996 runs in 52 games (average 99.94) including 29 centuries and a highest score of 334.

Bubka, Sergei (b.1964): World's best pole vaulter from Ukraine. In '94, at 6.14m. World title six times.

Chand, Dhyan (1906-'79): Hockey wizard. Olympic gold in Amsterdam 1928, Los Angeles 1932, Berlin 1936. Padmabhushan.

Kim Clijsters

Clijsters, Kim (b.1983): Belgian World No.2 tennis star. Second US Open title 2009. First mother since

Kuppuswamy Scale

Kuppuswamy scale proposed by Kuppuswamy in 1974 is widely used to measure the socio-economic status of an individual in the urban community. It is based on education, occupation and income.

1980 to win a Grand Slam.

Cronje, Hansie (1970-2002): Former S. African cricket captain who died in a plane crash. Involved in 'match-fixing' scandal.

Davis, Dwight F. (1879-1945): American who donated the tennis trophy, Davis Cup. He played for the US team in the opening contest.

Deodhar D.B.(1892-1993): The Grand Old Man of Indian Cricket, after whom Deodhar Trophy is named.

Evert, Chris (b. 1954): of USA. One of the all-time greats in tennis. Won 20 championships from 1974 to 1986, and 157 tournament titles.

Chris Evert

Federer, Roger (b.1981-): Switzerland, Tennis champion at 24. World No.3. Won fourth successive Wimbeldon in 2006. 16 Grand Slam single titles, 55 career titles. Gold medal in 2008 Olympics.

Fischer, Bobby (1943-2008): World Chess Champion, 1972-75.

Gavaskar, Sunil (b. 1949): Indian cricketer who scored 1000 runs in Tests in a calendar year thrice; scored 34 centuries in Tests (world record).

Nawang Gombu

Gombu, Nawang (b. 1936): Mountaineer who climbed Everest twice. Padma Shri, Padma Bhushan.

Grace, William Gilbert (1848-1915): Cricketer who captained England 13 times. Scored over 54,000 runs includ-

ing 126 centuries. Over 2800 wickets.

Graf, Steffi (b. 1969): German tennis legend. The third woman in tennis history to win all four major world tournaments - the Australian Open, French Open, Wimbledon

Steffi Graf

and the US Open - in a single calendar year (1988). She also won the Olympic gold medal that year. Won 22 Grand Slam titles and 107 WTA titles. Retired Aug. 99. Wife of Andre Agassi.

Greene, Maurice (b.1974): First sprinter ever to win both 100 and 200 m. at world championships. Announced his retirement.

Hendry, Stephen (b. 1970): The greatest snooker player of all time. World Champion seven times.

Isinbayeva, Yelena (b. 1982): The undisputed queen of women's pole vault, the first female, from Russia, to cover five metres. Olympic Gold, 2004, 2008.

Johnson, Michael (b.1967): The first man to complete the 200-400 m. double at a major international championship. Retired US spinter.

Jones, Wilson (1922-2003): Twelve-time national amateur billiards champion of India; winner of three world titles. Arjuna, Dronacharya, Padma Shri.

Michael Jordan

Jordan, Michael (b. 1963): US basketball player. He played for the Chicago Bulls (1984-93, 1995-). He announced his retirement in 1999.

Kapil Dev (Nikhanj, Kapil Dev) (b. 1959): Indian cricket all-rounder, former captain and national team coach. World record of claiming 100 wickets in the shortest time. Achieved the unique double of 4000 runs and 400 wickets, the first ever player to do so. Set world record of 432 wickets in test matches in Feb.1994.

Karpov, Anatoly (b. 1951): Soviet chess champion, 1975-85; the highest-rated player in chess history.

Karthikeyan, Narain (b. 1977): First Indian to drive a Formula One car. Formula Asia Champion, 1996.

Kasparov, Garry (b. 1963): Russian chess grandmaster. Highest-rated player in chess history, theyoungest-ever world champion in 1985.

Garry Kasparov

King, Billie Jean (b. 1943): American tennis player. Wimbledon champion 5 times between 1966 and 1973; US champion 4 times. 20 titles between 1961 and 1979.

Kramnik, Vladimir (b. 1975): Of Russia. World Chess Champion.

Lendl, Ivan (b. 1960): Tennis player, born in Czechoslovakia. Former world No.1.

Lewis, Carl (b. 1961): American winner of 8 Olympic gold medals and former 100 m. world record holder. In 1984 he won four Olympic gold medals.

Malleswari, Karnam (b. 1976): Indian weight-lifter. First Indian woman to win an Olympic medal (bronze, Syd-

Carl Lewis

ney). Rajiv Gandhi Khel Ratna Award. Arjuna, Padma Shri.

Mani, Ehsan (b. 1945): Pakistani, the third President of ICC.

Maradona, Diego (b. 1961): Argentinian football star. Famous for the 'hand of God' goal against England in 1986. Banned for 15 months for drug problems. Head coach of the Argentina national football team.

Mauresmo, Amelie (b.1979): First French woman in 81 years to win Wimbledon singles title, beating Belgium's Justine Henin-Hardenne in July, 2006.

McEnroe, John (b. 1959): U.S. tennis genius, youngest to win seven grand slam singles, 9 grand slam

Mauresmo

men's doubles titles and one grand slam mixed doubles title.

Mirza, Sania (b. 1986): India's highest ranked female tennis player and first Indian woman to enter the third round of a Grand Slam tournament (Australian Open 2005). Reached US Open third round, 2007. Arjuna Award, Padma Shri. Won mixed doubles in 2009 with Mahesh Bhupathi.

Moore, Bobby (1941-'93): Soccer legend, he captained England to its World Cup triumph in 1966. Played 1000 league games.

Muralitharan, Muttiah (b. 1972): Sri Lankan cricketer. The greatest spinner in the history of the game. In 133 matches he has 800 wickets at an average of 22.72.

Muralitharan

Nadal, Rafael (b.1986): Spanish professional ten-

First Woman
FM

Hina Rabbabi Khar, 34, is Pakistan's first woman foreign minister. She is also the youngest to hold the post.

nis player, currently Rank 1. Eight Grand slam singles titles, 2008 Olympic Gold, ATP World Tour Masters 1000 tournaments. 'The King of Clay'.

Navratilova, Martina (b. 1956): One of the all time greats in tennis. U.S. citizen born in Czechoslovakia. Wimbledon 9 times, US Open 4 times. 167 singles and 162 doubles titles.

Navratilova

Nehwal, Saina (b.1990): World No.2 badminton player. The first Indian woman to become Badminton Grand Prix champion and also the first Indian woman shuttler to win a Super Series tournament. Rajiv Khel RatnaAward, 2010.

Olajuwon, Hakeem (b. 1963): US basketball player, born in Nigeria. Held the record for blocked shots. Nickname: 'The Dream'.

Owens, John Cleveland ('Jesse') (1913-80): American athlete. First man to win 4 track and field gold medals (100 m, 200 m, long jump, 4x100 m relay) in single Olympics (1936).

Paes, Leander (b. 1974): Indian winner of Wimbledon junior men's singles title, Davis Cup Captain, 1990. In '96, won a bronze medal at Atlanta Olympics. Six-time Grand Slam doubles title winner. US Mixed Doubles 2008, French Open and US Open Men's Doubles 2009, Wimbledon mixed Doubles, 2010.

Bachendri Pal

Pal, Bachendri (b. 1956): The first Indian woman and

the fifth woman in the world to scale Mount Everest (1984).

Pele (Edson Arantes Do Nascimento) (b. 1940): Brazilian soccer player. A world star at 17. Played in all four World Cup championship tournaments from 1958 to 1970. The first player ever to play on three world championship teams. Scored 1281 goals in 1363 games.

Pele

Phelps, Michael (b. 1985): American swimmer who has won 14 career Olympic gold medals, the most by an Olympian. Phelps also holds the record for the most gold medals won at single Olympics, eight golds at Beijing.

Ronaldo (Ronaldo Luiz Nazario D lima) (b.1977): Brazilian footballer, considered the next Pele. Top scorer in 2002 World Cup.

Ruth, Babe (1895-1948): US baseball player whose real name was George Herman. Known by the nickname 'Sultan of Swat'.

Saha, Arati (1933-'94): Indian swimmer, the first woman from Asia to cross the English Channel.

Sampras, Pete (b. 1971): American tennis star. Six Wimbledon men's singles titles. First player since Boris Becker in 1989 to win Wimbledon and the US Open in the same year (1993). Retired, 2003,

Pete Sampras

Schumacher, Michael (b. 1967):

Swadhinata Sammanona	Bangladesh President Zillur Rahman handed over the country's highest award Swadhinata Sammanona to Sonia Gandhi, who received it on behalf of Indira Gandhi, who won the award posthumously.

German 7-time Formula One world champion. The first to win French Grand Prix eight times. Retired in 2006.

Virender Sehwag

Sehwag, Virender (b. 1979): Cricketer. The first Indian to hit a triple century in Tests. His 309 at Multan is India's highest Individual score.

Seles, Monica (b. 1973): of Yugoslavia. At 17, the youngest world champion of women's tennis. Twenty titles before the age of 18. Stabbed mid-match in Hamburg in 1993, stayed away from tennis for two years. Retired 2008.

Monica Seles

Sen, Mihir (1930-'97): First Indian to swim the English Channel. World record in long distance swimming.

Senna, Ayrton (1960-'94): Race driver of Brazil, one of only 7 drivers to win the world championship three times. Killed in a crash during the San Marino Grand prix.

Sethi, Geet (b. 1962): This unseeded player from India became the king of the world billiards championship in 1985. The youngest ever to wear the crown in his maiden appearance. Rajiv Khel Ratna and Padma Shri.

Shackleton, Ernest Henry (1874-1922): Antarctic explorer from Ireland. His expedition was within 155 km of the South Pole in 1909.

Sharapova, Maria (b. 1987): Russian golden girl of tennis. Wimbledon 2004, US Open 2006, Aus. Open 2008. Highest paid female athlete.

Singh, Paramjit (b. 1973): Indian sprinter who broke Milka Singh's 38-year old national 400 m. record in 1998.

Sobers, Gary (b. 1936): West Indian cricketer, an excellent all-rounder.

Spassky, Boris Vasilyevich (b.1937): World chess champion (1969-'72), from Russia

Tendulkar, Sachin (b. 1973): Indian cricketer, former Captain. At 16 played his first Test in Karachi. The youngest (at 19) to score 1000 runs in test cricket. The first batsman to score 10,000 runs in one-day cricket. India's highest scorer in One Dayers. His 48 centuries in One-Day and 51 in Tests is a world record. Arjuna Award. Rajiv Gandhi Khel Ratna Award, '98, Padma Vibhushan.

Tenzing, Norgay (1914-'86): With Edmund Hillary, he was the first to climb the Everest in 1953.

Thorpe, Ian (b.1982): Australian swimmer. A record six titles at 9th FINA world swimming championships at Fukuoka.

Tyson, Mike (b. 1967): Youngest man to win the world heavy weight championship. Retired from competitive boxing in 2005.

Mike Tyson

Usha, P.T. (b. 1964): The first Indian woman (and the fifth Indian) to reach the final of an Olympic event by winning her 400 m hurdles semi-final. Missed a bronze by 1/100 of a second. Created new Asian Games records in all events she participated in X Asian Games, Seoul. 101 international medals. Known as Payyoli Express, Sprint Queen, and Golden Girl. Runs a sport academy.

Vaidyanathan, Nirupama (b. 1977):

First Indian woman to win a round in a Grand Slam tournament (Australian Open, Jan. 98).

Williams, Venus (b. 1980) and Serena (b. 1981): Most successful tennis-playing sisters (USA). In 1999 won both French and US open doubles titles. Venus, holder of 19 Grand Slam titles, beat beat Serena to win US Open 2001, and won Wimbledon in 2005. Serena Williams has 23

Venus Williams

Grand Slam titles to her credit. She has also won more Grand Slam titles than any other active female player.

Wilson, Shiny (b. 1965): Athlete, represented India in more than in 75 competitions, including four Olympic Games. First Indian woman athlete to enter semi-finals in Olympics. Arjuna Award, Padma Shri.

Woods, Tiger (b.1975): Golfer, youngest ever to win the sport's career Grand Slam (all 4 majors), at age 24, when he won the British Open, 2000. Won 14 professional major golf championships.

Yadav, Santosh (b. 1969): An Indo-Tibetan Border Police officer, the only woman in the world to have climbed the Everest twice ('92. '93).

Santosh Yadav

Zidane, Zinedine (b.1972): One of the greatest footballers of his generation. French Captain. With a transfer fee of $66 m. in 2001, most expensive football player in history. In 2006 World Cup, he won the Golden Ball. Retired in 2006.

Miscellaneous

Adiseshaiah, Malcom (1910-'94): Indian educationist and economist who was the Vice-Chancellor of Madras University and Deputy D-G of UNESCO. Padma Bhushan.

Aga Khan IV (b. 1936): Spiritual head of 20 million Shia Ismaili Muslims in the world.

Ali, Salim (1896-1987): Indian ornithologist, known as "The Birdman of India". Fall of a Sparrow.

Ambani, Dhirubhai (Dhirajlal Hirachand) (1932 - 2002): Indian industrialist. Reliance Industries that he set up is India's largest private sector company. Sons Mukesh and Anil have now split into two business groups.

Amte, Murlidhar Devidas (Baba Amte) (1914-2008): Indian social activist, best known for his work among leprosy patients. Awards: Magsaysay, Templeton, Padma Vibhushan.

Andrews, Charles Freer: (1871-1940): Englishman who adopted India

Baba Amte

as his home, and worked with Gandhi. Known as 'Deenabandhu'.

Annan, Kofi (b.1938): Ghanaian-born UN Secretary General, 1997-2007. Nobel Prize, 2001.

Antony, St. (c. 251-356): Father of Christian monasticism and founder of religious community life.

Aquinas, Thomas St. (c. 1225-'74): Italian theologian and scholastic philosopher.

Aristotle (384-322 B.C.): Greek teacher and philosopher, pupil of Plato, tutor to the young prince Alexander of Macedon.

Sufferings of Patients | Charles Darwin was so disgusted by the sufferings of the patients that he discontinued his medical studies at Edinburgh in 1827. In 1846 US dental surgeon William Morton successfully demonstrated the anaesthetic effects of ether.

Arundale, George Sydney (1878-1945): An Englishman who adopted India as his home. Advocate of national education and the Swadeshi movement. Married Rukmini Devi.

Aurobindo, Sri (Aurobindo Ghosh) (1872-1950): Indian philosopher, a revolutionary in his early days. Set up an Ashram in Pondichery. Retired into seclusion in 1926.

Ayyankali (1863-1941): Leader of Harijans, in Kerala. Mahatma Gandhi called him 'pulayaraja'. Great organiser.

Ayyar, Alladi Krishnaswami, Sir (1883-1953): Scholar and brilliant lawyer of Tamil Nadu.

Bacon, Francis (1561-1626): English philosopher and essayist. Novum Organum.

Ayyankali

Baden Powell, Robert (1857-1941): Founder of Boy Scouts (1908). His sister Agnes founded Girl Guides (1910).

Bajaj, Jamnalal (1886-1942): Mahatma Gandhi's associate, founded Satyagraha Ashram at Wardha; Gifted Segaon village to Gandhi who named it Sevagram.

Bancroft, George (1800-1891): American historian who wrote the 10-volume History of the United States.

Bandopadhyay, Padmavathy (b. 1944): The first woman Air Marshal of Indian Air Force. Received AVSM and VSM.

Batuta, Ibn (1304-1378): Traveller from North Africa wh æfixo spent eight years in India. His travelogue is a source for the political history of the Khalji and Tuglaq dynasties of the Delhi sultanate.

Becket, Thomas (1118-'70): Saint and martyr. Archbishop of Canterbury who made the position of the church his first care and, came into conflict with King Henry II. Murdered in Canterbury Cathedral. Murder in the Cathedral.

Bedi, Kiran (b. 1949): First woman Indian Police Service officer (1972). A former Asian Games women's tennis champion. Magsaysay award, 1995. UN medal for outstanding service, 2004.

Benedict XVI (b. 1927): The Pope, head of the Roman Catholic Church since April 2005. Formerly Josef Ratzinger, the German archbishop. Scceeded John Paul II.

Bentham, Jeremy (1748-1832): British philosopher who developed the theory of utilitarianism.

Besant, Annie (1847-1933): An Irish woman, staunch supporter of Indian independence movement. Social worker, educationist and reformer. Set up Home Rule League. President of INC, 1917. Established Theosophical Society of India.

Bhagwan Dass, Dr. (1869-1958): Vedic scholar, Indian freedom fighter. Bharat Ratna.

Bhagwati, Prof. Jagdish (b. 1934): India-born U.S. Professor of Economics at Columbia University.

Bhatt, Ela (b.1933): Emancipator of women in the self-employed sector. Founded SEWA. Magsaysay award,1977.

Bhave, Vinoba (1895-1982): Disciple of Gandhi who led the Bhoodan movement. Bharat Ratna 1983, first Magsaysay award.

Booth, William (1829-1912): English religious leader, founder of the salvation Army.

Bose, Amar Gopal (b.1929): American-born Indian professor of electrical engineering at MIT. In 1964, he founded the Bose Corporation, which specializes in designing and producing high quality sound systems.

Braille, Louis (1809-'52): French educationist who, as a (blind) teacher of the blind, devised the touch system of reading and writing for the blind.

Brown, John (1800-'59): Hero of the song

First Bond Girl Linda Christian who died in July, 2011 is the first Bond girl. She starred in the 1954 TV adaptation of 'Casino Royale'.

'John Brown's Body'. An anti-slavery crusader who tried to start a slave revolt, was caught, and hanged.

Bunyan, John (1628-'88): A popular preacher and religious thinker. The Pilgrim's Progress.

Byrd, Richard Evelyn (1888-1957): American explorer. The first to fly over both North and South poles.

Cabot, John (1425/50-c. 1500): Italian explorer. Discovered Newfoundland and Nova Scotia. Son Sebastian Cabot (1476-1557) made voyages to the New World.

Cabral, Pedro Alvarez (c.1467-c. 1520): Portuguese navigator, discovered Brazil.

Calvin, John (1509-'64): French Protestant reformer and theologian.

Cardin, Pierre (b.1922): Internationally known Master designer. The haute couture czar with licencees in 125 countries.

Cariappa, Field Marshal. K.M (1900-'93): First Indian C-in-C of Indian Army, 1949-'53.

Cartier-Besson, Henri (1908-2004): One of the master photographers of 20th century.

Cave, Edward (1691–1754): English publisher. Founded The Gentleman's Magazine.

Cariappa

Caxton, William (1422-'91): the first English printer and publisher.

Noam Chomsky

Chakravarty, Nikhil (1913-'98): Indian journalist, first Chairman of Prasar Bharati Board.

Chomsky, Noam (b. 1928): American scholar, commentator on global politics and one of world's most distinguished linguists.

Comenius, John Amos (1592-1670): Czech religious leader and educational reformer who wrote The Visible World in Pictures.

Comte, Auguste (1798-1857): French philosopher. Founder of Positivism.

Confucius or K'ung Fu–Tse (c. 551-478 B.C.): Chinese philosopher, founder of the system of cosmology, politics, and ethics known as Confucianism.

Cook, Captain James (1728-'79): English navigator. Discovered the Sandwich Is. (Hawaiian).

Cook, Thomas (1908-'82): British Baptist priest turned tour operator, established Thomas Cook. Father of modern tourism.

Damien, Father Joseph (1840-'89): Originally Joseph de Veuster. Belgian Catholic missionary. Worked until his death from leprosy in leper colony on Molokai, Hawaii.

Demosthenes (384-322 B.C.): Greek orator who roused the Athenians to resist the growing power of Philip of Macedon.

Desai, Lord Meghnad (b. 1940): Professor of Economics at London School of Economics. British peer.

Dewey, Melvil (1851-1931): American library pioneer, originator of Dewey decimal system of book classification.

Dior, Christian (1905-'57): French fashion designer.

Donahue, Phil (b.1936): The man who virtually invented the single topic TV talk.

Drake, Sir Francis (c. 1540-'96): English seaman; in 1577-'80 he sailed round the world in the "Golden Hind".

Drucker, Peter F. (1909-2005): Management expert and author of international fame.

Peter Drucker

Sheep in Sheep's Clothing

'A sheep in sheep's clothing'. This is attributed to Winston Churchill on Clement Attlee.

Dunant, Jean Henri (1828-1910): Swiss philanthropist. Promoted the establishment of the International Red Cross (1863). Shared the first Nobel Prize (1901).

Durant, Will (1885-1981): American historian. The Story of Civlisation, The Story of Philosophy.

Emeneau, Prof. Murray Branson (1904-2005): Western indologist.

Engels, Friedrich (1820-'95): German socialist, lifelong friend of Karl Marx, with whom he wrote the Communist Manifesto.

Erasmus, Desiderius (1466-1536): The greatest humanist and scholar of Dutch Renaissance. Praise of Folly.

Flinders, Mathew (1774-1814): English explorer who charted large parts of the land he named Australia. Flinders River, Flinders Island named after him.

Francis of Assisi, St. (1181/2-1226): Founder of the Franciscan Order.

Fry, Elizabeth (1780-1845): English prison reformer, philanthropist.

Gallup, George Horrace (1901-'84): Renowned American statistician who studied public opinion through questions put to a representative group - 'Gallup poll'.

Gama, Vasco da (1460-1524): Portuguese navigator, discoverer of the sea route from western Europe to India.

Vasco da Gama

Gautama, Siddhartha (Buddha, The Enlightened) (c. 563-c. 483 B.C.): Founder of Buddhism. The Indian prince who renounced luxury and became an ascetic.

Getty, Jean Paul (1892-1976): American. Founded oil empire.

Ghosh, Tushar Kanti (1899-1994): Prominent Indian journalist, one of world's longest-serving editors.

Ghoshal, Sumantra (1949-2004): Management guru who was professor at London Business School. Founder director of Indian Business School, Hyderabad.

Gibbon, Edward (1737-'94): English historian who wrote Decline and Fall of the Roman Empire.

Goebbels, Paul Joseph (1897-1945): Nazi propaganda minister; orator.

Graham, Billy (b. 1918): Most celebrated U.S. evangelist of the 1960's and 1970's.

Graham, Katharine (1917-2001): Influential American newspaper proprietor, who as publisher of The Washington Post presided over the decision to go public with the Pentagon papers and Watergate. Pulitzer for her memoirs Personal History.

Herman Gundert

Gregory XIII (1502-'85): Pope (1572-'85) who introduced the Gregorian calendar.

Gundert, Dr. Herman (1814-'93): A linguist of Germany who lived in India, where he learnt 18 local languages and compiled a Malayalam dictionary.

Harris, Paul (1868-1947): American who founded Rotary International in 1905.

Hazare, Anna (b. 1937) : Indian crusader against corruption. A leading figure in the civil movement for the drafting committee for Lokpal Bill.

Hayek, Friedrich August Von (1899-1998): British economist. Taught at Lon-

Anna Hazare

don, Chicago and Freiburg - Nobel Prize for Economics, 1974.

Hayek

Hearst, William Randolph (1863-1951): A dominant figure in American journalism; built vast publishing empire.

Hegel, Georg Wilhelm Friedrich (1770-1831): German idealist philosopher: the dialectic method of reasoning. The Science of Logic.

Heraclitus (554-483 BC): Greek philosopher. His sayings: 'All things change'; 'You cannot step into the same water twice'.

Herodotus (c. 485-425 B.C.): Greek historian, 'the father of history'.

Hill, Sir Rowland (1795-1879): Originator of the penny postal system.

Hiuen-Tsang (7th c.): Buddhist pilgrim from China who visited India, 629 to 644 A.D.

Hobbes, Thomas (1588-1679): English philosopher who wrote Leviathan.

Hope, Bob (orig. Leslie Townes Hope) (1903-2003): Great American entertainer. Has 54 honorary doctorates.

Houdini, Harry (1874-1926): Pseudonym of Erich Weiss. American escapologist.

Hughes, Howard (1905-'76): US industrialist, financier, movie maker.

Hume, David (1711-76): Scottish philospher and historian.

Iacocca, Lee (b. 1924): American management wizard of Italian origin. Headed Ford Motor Company, and later Chrysler Corporation.

Jackson, Rev. Jesse (b. 1941): American civil rights leader.

Joan of Arc, St. (Jeanne D'Arc) (1412-'31): French patriot and national heroine called the Maid of Orleans; of peasant parentage, she believed herself called to save France from English domination. Captured by the English, she was burned as a heretic, but canonised in 1920.

John Paul II (1920-2005): The first non-Italian Pope in 455 years and the first Polish Pope (1978). Formerly Cardinal Karol Wojtyla.

John Paul II

Jones, Sir William (1746-'94): British indologist. Mastered 28 languages.

Juran, Dr. Joseph (1905-2008): American industrial engineer, thinker in quality management.

Kane, Pandurang Vaman (1880-1972): Indian indologist, orientalist, social reformer. History of Dharmasastra. Bharat Ratna, 1963.

Kant, Immanuel (1724-1804): German philosopher. Critique of Pure Reason.

Kao, Rameshwar Nath (1918-2002): Founder of Research and Analysis Wing (RAW), India's external intelligent agency, and its chief 1969-77.

Karve, Dhondo Keshav (1858-1962): Indian social worker who championed the causes of widow marriage and women's education. Bharat Ratna.

Kelappan, Kizhariyoor (1890-1971): Sarvodaya leader and social reformer, Kerala.

Kelkar, Vijay Lakshman (b.1942): Economist, Chairman of 13th Finance Commission. Chairman of Direct Taxes Committee known as Kelkar Committee. Padma Bhushan.

Keller, Helen (1880 -1968): American author and educator of the blind. Deaf and blind when 19 months old. Inspiration to millions of blind and deaf people all over the world. The Story of My Life.

Kesavan, Bellari Shamanna (1909-

Thatcher and Falklands — British PM Margaret Thatcher won popularity by standing up to Argentina in the 1983 Falkland Islands war.

2000): Founding father of the National Library (Kolkata), introduced Indian National Bibliography; first director of Indian National Scientific Documentation Centre (INSDOC). History of Indian Printing.

Kevorkian, Dr. Jack (1928-2011): Pathologist, known as Dr. Death for assisting in suicide of terminally ill patients in pain. Prosecuted.

Keynes, John Maynard (1883-1946): The most influential British economist of early 20th century. The General Theory of Employment, Interest and Money.

Khusro, A.M. (1925-2003): Indian agricultural economist who was Chairman of the 11th Finance Commission.

Kierkegaard, Soren Aabye (1813-'55): Danish philosopher, regarded as the founder of existentialism.

Kim Woo Choong (b. 1936): The South Korean tycoon who built the Daewoo Group into a global empire ($ 67 billion in annual sales). It crashed and he fled the country, accused of fraud and smuggling, to return home in 2005.

King, Larry (b. 1933): American TV host. Popular 'Larry King Live' show, CNN's most watched programme since 1985. King has announced the end of the show.

King, Martin Luther, Jr. (1929-'68): Black

Martin Luther King

American clergyman, a non-violent civil rights leader and Negro integration leader; Nobel Peace Prize. Assassinated. Why We Can't Wait.

Kitchener General Lord Horation Hubert (1850-1916): C-in-C of Indian Army, 1902-07.

Kitchlew, Saifuddin (1888-1963): Associate of Mahatma Gandhi, founder President of the All India Peace Council. Stalin Peace Prize.

Kotnis, Dr. Dwarkanath (1910-'42): The legendary Indian doctor who became the hero of the Indian medical mission to war-torn China in 1938.

Krishnamurthy, Jiddu (1895-1986): Indian philosopher of international reputation. At 20, he headed a new sect 'The Order of the Star of the East'. The Songs of Life.

Kurien, Dr. Verghese (b. 1921): 'Father of India's white revolution', a synonym for co-operative milk sector. The brain behind Operation Flood. Chairman, NDDB until 1998. World Food Prize ('89), Magsaysay award ('63), Padmavibhushan.

Verghese Kurien

Lao Tsze (c. 600 B.C.): Chinese philosopher who founded Taosim.

Laski, Harold Joseph (1893-1950): British political scientist, influential Fabian. Taught at London School of Economics.

Lippmann, Walter (1889-1974): American journalist of influence. His column was carried world-wide.

Livingstone, David (1813-'73): Scottish missionary and explorer in Africa. He discovered the course of the Zambezi, the Victoria Falls and Lake Nyasa (now Lake Malawi).

Locke, John (1632-1704): English philosopher. An Essay Concerning Human Understanding.

Loreton, Erhard (b. 1959): The Swiss mountaineer who is the third man to have climbed world's 14 highest peaks.

Loyola, St. Ignatius of (1491-1556): Spanish founder of the Society of Jesuits, a missionary order.

Luther, Martin (1483-1546): German religious reformer who began the Protestant Reformation.

Mandela at his Birthplace	**Nelson Mandela's family has confirmed that he is to remain at his birthplace, his rural home in the Eastern Cape indefinitely.**

Luxemburg, Rosa (1871-1919): Polish born German revolutionary and socialist theorist.

Lynch, Peter (b. 1944): America's leading money manager, financial consultant. One Upon Wall Street, Beating The Street.

Madhavacharya (1238–1317): Exponent of Dwaita philosophy; wrote commentaries on Gita, interpreted Upanishads in a new way.

Mahalanobis, Prasanta Chandra (1893-1972): Economist and statistician, who contributed to laying the foundation of India's statistical system and economic planning.

Mahavira, Vardhmana (6th cent. B.C.): Indian. Founder of Jainism, which teaches the sacredness of all life.

Mahesh Yogi, Maharishi (1917-2008): Immensely rich Indian Yoga expert. Transcendental Meditation movement in 1959. Founded the Maharishi University of Management.

Malinowski, Bronislaw (1884-1942): of Poland. Father of social anthropology.

Malthus, Thomas Robert (1766-1834): British economist who contended that population increases faster than the means of subsistence and that its growth could only be checked by moral restraint or by disease and war.

Manekshaw, Field Marshal S.H.F.J. (1914-2008): India's first Field Marshal. War hero who masterminded the victory over Pakistan in 1971. Padma Vibhushan.

Manekshaw

Manohar, Sujata Vasant (b. 1934): India's second woman judge of Supreme Court. (The first-Fathima Beevi).

Mappillai, K. C. Mammen (1873-1953): Eminent journalist, social worker and community leader , Kerala. He was influenced and inspired by his uncle Kandathil Varghese Mappillai, a renowned litterateur, who in 1888 founded Malayala Manorama, India's first language daily to sell over 1.8 million copies.

Mata Hari (1876-1917): (Margarethe Geertruida Zelle) Dutch spy. A dancer in Paris with many lovers, she became a German spy and was shot for treason.

Mathai, Dr. John (1886-1959): Economist, administrator and educationist. Union Finance Minister, V-C of Bombay and Kerala Universities. Padma Vibhushan.

Mathew, Kandathil Mammen (1917-2010): Son of veteran journalist and entrepreneur K.C. Mammen Mappilai. The doyen of Indian media, Patriarch of Malayala Manorama group until 2010. Managing Editor (1954-1973), Chief Editor (1973-2010). Founder – Chief Editor of *The Week*.

K.M. Mathew

Under his captaincy, the group grew into 48 publications, most of them best sellers nationally in their categories. The daily grew from a single edition and 30,000 copies to 17 editions and 1.8 million copies. A courageous innovator, he introduced 'MM News Channel', the TV news network, 'Radio Mango' the first private FM Radio station in Kerala and the Online division. Modernisation was his trademark. He organised social campaigns like rainwater harvesting, free open heart surgery for poor children and rebuilding of earthquake-hit villages of Maharashtra.

He practised journalism with a human touch. His generosity, humility and affection touched the lives of millions. Was chairman of PTI, INS and ABC. B.D. Goenka Award, Padma Bhushan. Books:

| A Cricketer's Mother | The Indian cricketer Rahul Dravid's mother has won the Vikram Samman of Vikram University for her contribution in the field of paintings. |

Annamma, Eighth Ring (autobiography). His son Mammen Mathew is the present Chief Editor and Managing Director of *Malayala Manorama*.

Menchu, Rigoberta (b. 1959): Guatemalan Indian leader and human rights campaigner. Nobel Peace Prize, 1992.

Menon, Kumara Padmanabha Sivasankara (1898-1982): Indian diplomat and author. Foreign Secretary whose son K.P.S. Menon Jr. also held the same post later. The Flying Troika.

Merrill, Charles (1885-1956): American investment banker, who co-founded Merrill Lynch & Co.

Mill, John Stuart (1806-'73): English philosopher and economist. On Liberty.

Mittal, Lakshmi (b. 1950): Billionaire steelmaker. Chairman of Arcelor-Mittal Co. The richest man in Europe and 5th richest in the world. Son Aditya Mittal is its CFO. Lakshmi Mittal built up his empire from a single steel mill on Indonesian rice fields in 1976.

Lakshmi Mittal

Mohammed, Prophet (570-632): Mohammed is believed by Muslims to be the Last Messenger of God to mankind. The Quran, the Sacred Book of Islam, is believed to be the Word of God, revealed to Mohammed in stages over 23 years. Received the first revelation and the command to preach at the age of 40; taught that there is only one God. Forced to migrate from Mecca to Medina in 622, the year of the Hegira. He returned to Mecca, where the Kaaba is regarded as the holiest shrine in Islam and the focal point of the Haj pilgrimage.

Montessori, Maria (1870-1952): Italian educationist, who developed an educational system based on giving children freedom in a specially prepared environment.

Moon, Dr. Sun Myung (b.1920): Evangelist born in Korea, founder of the Unification Church, which he shifted to USA; has a multimillion dollar business empire.

Moraes, Frank (1907-'74): Eminent Indian journalist. Editor, Indian Express, Times of India. His son Dom Moraes (1938-2004), poet.

Mueller, Prof. Max (1823-1900): German indologist and linguist. Taught Sanskrit at Oxford University, 1848. India-What Can It Teach Us, The Science of Lanugage.

Murdoch, Rupert (b. 1931): US publisher and entrepreneur born in Australia. His company, News Corp., owns Fox Broadcasting Company and several British national papers, including The Times and The Sun. He also owns 20th Century Fox, Harper Collins (UK publishers), and the satellite broadcasting company DirecTV. His media empire was engulfed by a phone hacking scandal in July 2011.

Rupert Murdoch

Murthy, N.R. Narayana (b.1946): Co-founder, (1981), CEO of India's IT leader Infosys Technologies. Small-town boy who rose to be a billionaire and a pioneer of 21st century Indian industry. Retired in 2006; Chief Mentor and non-executive Chairman until 2011. Now Chairman emerities. World's 8th most admired CEO in 2006.

Nagarjuna (1st century): Philosopher, scientist and a great figure of Court of Kanishka.

Nanak, Guru (1469-1538): Indian guru, who tried to put an end to religious strife,

---

The Spy — **David Cornwell was better known as John Le Carre. He was an English writer of spy novels. He is known for his *The Spy Who Came in from the Cold.***

teaching that 'God is one, whether he be Allah or Rama'. His followers are the Sikhs.

Narayana Guru, Sri (1855-1928): One

Sri Narayana Guru

of the most illustrious social reformers and religious leaders, born in Kerala, India. Thinker and mystic who tried to improve the lot of backward classes. Spread the message of equality of men, irrespective of religion. Sri Narayana Dharma Paripalana Sangam formed in 1903

Narendra Dev, Acharya (1889-1956): Indian scholar, socialist leader and educationist. A leader of the Congress Socialist Party (1934) and V C of Lucknow university and B.H.U.

Nelson, Horatio (1758-1805): Foremost admiral in the history of England. Destroyed the French fleet at Trafalgar (1805), but lost his life.

Newman, John Henry Cardinal (1801-'90): Outstanding religious thinker and essayist of 19th century; author of Lead Kindly Light.

Nietzsche, Friedrich (1844-1900): German philosopher and poet, known for his concept of the overman or superman. Thus Spake Zarathustra.

Nightingale, Florence (1820-1910): English nurse and founder of modern

Sister Nivedita

nursing. During the Crimean war, she organised a nursing service. Known as 'The Lady with the Lamp'.

Nivedita, Sister (1867-1911): Irish woman (Margaret Elizabeth Nobel)

who became disciple of Swami Vivekananda and was in India for 12 years.

Nobel, Alfred Bernhard (1833-'96): Swedish inventor and philanthropist. Discovered dynamite. Bequeathed a fund for annual prizes now known as Nobel Prizes.

Nooyi, Indra (b.1955): CEO,of Pepsi Co. Born in Chennai. World's fifth most powerful woman, in Forbes poll, 2007. Fortune magazine's Most Powerful Woman in Business, 2006. Named CEO of the Year (2009).

Oberoi, Mohan Singh (1900-2002): India's famous hotelier. From humble beginning rose to own international chain of hotels.

Ogilvy, David (1912-'99): Doyen of the advertising world, founder of the international ad agency, Ogilvy & Mather.

Onassis, Aristotle (1906-'75): Greek billionaire and shipping magnate. Married Jacqueline, widow of former US president Kennedy.

Packer, Kerry (1937-2005): Australian media mogul believed to have been the richest person in Australia.

Palkhivala, Nani (1920-2002): Eminent Indian jurist. Ambassador to USA, 1977-79. Padma Vibhushan, 1998.

Panikkar, Sardar K. M. (1894-1963): Scholar, historian, diplomat. Minister in Patiala, Bikaner. Ambassador to China, Egypt and France. Member, States Reorganisation Commission. V-C, Kashmir & Mysore Universities.

K.M. Panikkar

Parks, Rosa (1913- 2005): US black civil rights activist. Made news by refusing to give her seat on a public bus to a white man. This incident resulted in boycott of

They Also Serve 'They also serve who only stand and wait' is the closing words of John Milton's work *On His Blindness*.

the bus system and strengthened civil rights movement.

Patel, Dr. Indraprasad Gordhanbhai (1924-2005): Indian economist. Principal of Baroda College at age 25. Served in IMF; Governor, RBI; Director, London School of Economics (1984-1990).

Patkar, Medha (b. 1956): Indian social activist, environmentalist; firebrand leader of Save Narmada movement. Right Livelihood Award.

Paul, Lord Swraj (b. 1931): Britain-based Indian industrialist. Member, House of Lords; VC of Wolverhampton University. Padma Bushan, 1983. In Dec. '08, he was appointed deputy speaker of House of Lords in UK.

Medha Patkar

Peale, Rev. Norman Vincent (1898-1993): American religious leader, who preached positive thinking for more than half a century.

Pepys, Samuel (1633–1703): British naval administrator, known for his Diary, written from Jan. 1, 1660 to May 31, 1669.

Phule, Mahatma Jotirao Govindrao (1827-'90): Social reformer of India who worked for the downtrodden, women's education, social justice and against child marriage. Wife Sovitribai (1831-'97) was harbinger of women's liberation, pioneer in women's education.

Pitman, Sir Isaac (1813-'97): English inventor of a system of phonographic shorthand.

Plato (427-347 B.C.): Greek philosopher and educator; pupil of Socrates, teacher of Aristotle. Dialogues, which includes the Republic, the longest and most celebrated work.

Polo, Marco (C. 1256-1323): The most famous European traveller in the Far East, China, India.

Post, Emily (1873-1960): Writer and arbiter of American manners. Emily Post's Etiquette.

Raj, Dr. Kakkadan Nandanth (1924-2010): Indian economist and Professor, former V C of Delhi University, Director of Delhi School of Economics. Co-founder, Centre for Development Studies, Thiruvananthapuram.Padma Vibhushan.

Rajneesh (Chandra Mohan Jain) (1931-'90): Charismatic godman of India, also known as Osho. Set up ashram at Pune, and 'Rajneeshpuram' on 64,000 acres in Oregon, USA. Turned controversial.

Rajneesh

Raleigh, Sir Walter (1552-1618): adventurer and writer. In 1584 began the colonisation of Virginia. He was executed.

Ramakrishna Paramhansa, Sri (1836-'86): Religious leader of India who taught that God-realisation is the only goal of life. Chief disciple was Swami Vivekananda. Ramakrishna Mission after his name.

Ranganathan, S.R. (1892–1972): Originator of the Colon Classification. Known as the Father of Indian Library Science.

Ravi Shankar, Sri Sri (b. 1956) : Modern day spiritual icon and founder of Art of Living. Has a big following in India and abroad.

Reuter, Paul Julius (1816-'99): German pioneer of telegraphic press service, who organised Reuter's international news agency.

Sri Sri Ravishankar

Ricardo, David (1772-1823): English political economist. Principles of Political Economy and Taxation.

Robinson, Sir Edward Austin Gossage (1903-'93): Economist, Professor Emeritus at University of Cambridge, and abiding friend of India. Wife Joan Robinson, economist.

Rockefeller, John Davidson (1839-1937): American philanthropist and founder of the Rockefeller business empire; Founded Rockefeller University and Foundation.

Roddick, Anita (1943-2007): Founded Children on the Edge, a charitable organisation.

Rousseau, Jean–Jacques (1712-'78): French political philosopher whose views did much to stimulate the movement leading to the French Revolution. Emile, Le Contrat Social.

Roy, Prannoy (b. 1946): India's leading psephologist and TV commentator. President of NDTV.

Roy, Raja Rammohan (1774-1833): Indian social reformer and scholar. Worked for the abolition of 'sati', child marriage and

Prannoy Roy

'Purdah'. Founder of Brahmo Samaj.

Russell, Bertrand (1872-1970): English philosopher, mathematician and essayist. The Principles of Mathematics, The Scientific Outlook, The Conquest of Happiness, The Autobiogrpahy, History of Western Philosophy. Nobel Prize.

Sankaracharya (788-820): (Adi Sankara) Scholar and philosopher from India, who revived the Hindu religion; founder of Advaitic philosophy; established 'mutts' all over India.

Saraswati, Dayanand (1824-'83): Hindu social reformer. Founded Arya Samaj school and fought for removal of social evils.

Sastry, V.S. Sriniwasa (1869-1946): Associated with Servants of India Society; promoted education and worked for women's legal status.

Schwarzenegger, Arnold (b.1947): Austrian-born Hollywood action hero (Termi-

nator, Predator and Total Recall). Took to Republican politics, Governor of California until January 2011.

Schweitzer, Albert (1875-1965): German medical missionary, humanitarian, musician and philosopher. Found-

Schwarzenegger

ed at Lambarene in Africa a hospital to fight leprosy and sleeping sickness and worked there for over 50 years. Nobel Peace Prize, 1952.

Sen, Amartya Kumar (b. 1933): Indian economist, the Lamont Professor of Philosophy and Economics at Harvard University, Master of Trinity College, Cambridge. Nobel Prize (1998), Bharat Ratna.

Seshan, Tirunellay Narayana Iyer (b. 1932): India's Chief Election Commissioner 1990-'96. Defence Secretary (1988) and Cabinet Secretary (1989). Magsaysay award.

Sethi, Dr. P.K (1927-2008): Noted Indian orthopaedic surgeon and inventor of the 'Jaipur Foot'.

T.N. Seshan

Magsaysay Award, 1981.

Shiva, Vandana (b. 1952): Economist, environmentalist and physicist. Leads campaigns on biopiracy and biosafety. Right Livelihood award, 1993.

Shourie, Arun (b. 1943): Outstanding Indian journalist. Former Union Cabinet

---

The Mind, Not the Eyes   Swami Chinmayananda said, 'The eye sees all, but the mind shows us what we want to see.'

Minister. Magsaysay award.

Smith, Adam (1723-'90): Scottish economist, known as the 'Father of Economics'. Wealth of Nations.

Socrates (470-399 B.C.): Greek philosopher, Plato's master. Charged with impiety and with corrupting the young, found guilty, died by drinking hemlock.

Solon (c. 638-558 B.C.): Athenian lawgiver; one of the Seven Wise Men of Greece.

Sorcar, Pratul Chandra (1913-71): Famous magician India has ever seen. He was popular all over the world in 1950 & 60s. Sons magician PC Sorcar Jr and director Manick Sorcar.

Spock, Benjamin (1903-'98): Author of The Common Sense Book of Baby and Child Care (1945) which influenced parents worldwide.

Sreedharan, Elattuvalapil (b. 1932): The Metro Man of India. Managing director of Delhi Metro. Formerly MD of Konkan Railway (completed in 7 years). Padma Shri (2001), Times of India's Man of the Year (2002), Knight of Legion of Honour (France). Padma Vibhushan 2008.

Swami, Chattambi (1853-1924): (Srividyadhiraja Kunjan Pillai, later Sribalabhatarakeswaran). Indian visionary and social reformer. Held close association with Sri Narayana Guru.

E. Sreedharan

Tamerlane (Timur the Lame) (1336-1405): A great warrior of Central Asia; ruler of Samarkand.

Tata, Jahangirji Ratanji Dadabhai (b. 1904-'93): Top Indian industrialist and organiser known for his vision and dynamism. He was the first Indian pilot to get a license. Chairman of Air India. Bharat Ratna. Tata, Ratan Naval (b. 1937): industrialist, business tycoon currently Chairman of Tata Group, great grandson of Jamshedji Tata. Padma Vibhushan.

JRD Tata

Teresa, Mother (1910-'97): Roman Catholic nun, born to Albanian parents in Yugoslavia, and baptized Agnes Gonxha Bejaxhui. Came to India as a teacher at Calcutta. Founded "Missionaries of Charity", devoted to working for destitutes. Citizen of India, 1962. Set up about 570 homes for the poor, spread in about 125 countries. Nobel Peace Prize, Magsaysay award, Templeton Award, Bharat Ratna.

Thant, Sithu U. (1909-'74): Burmese diplomat; U.N. Secretary-General, 1962-1972.

Tharoor, Shashi (b. 1956): Minister of State for External Affairs, 2009-2010. UN Under Secretary General for Communication and Public Information, 2002-07. Selected in 2006 as India's candidate for the post of UN Secretary-General. Writer. Authored The Great Indian Novel, India: from Midnight to Millennium.

U. Thant

Thomas, St. : One of the 12 disciples of Christ who came to India in A.D. 52 and founded seven churches in Kerala.

Thoreau, Henry David (1817-'62): American essayist, naturalist and iconoclast, who rebelled against society and lived for a time in a solitary hut. Walden, Civil Disobedience.

Toynbee, Arnold Joseph (1889-1975): English historian and reformer. A Study

---

The Car with Number 'O'

The first automobile imported India was a French-made De Dion Bouten. It was imported by the Maharaja of Patiala in 1892. The car had the licence plate number 'O'.

of History (1934-54) in 10 volumes. His uncle Arnold Toynbee who died in 1883 was a reformer (and historian) who worked among the poor.

Trevelyan, George Macaulay (1876-1962): English historian. History of England.

Turner III, Ted (Robert Edward) (b. 1938): The man whose vision created CNN (Cable News Network) Married Jane Fonda.

Tussaud, Madame (1761-1850): Swiss wax modeller. Opened a museum in London containing life-size models of famous people, which is still a major tourist attraction.

Tutu, Desmond (b. 1931): South African clergyman who advocated nonviolent resistance to apartheid. First black Anglican bishop of Johannesburg. Nobel peace prize.

Vidyasagar, Ishwar Chandra (1820-1891): Great Indian scholar and reformer. Fought for widow remarriage, higher education for women, and against child marriage.

Visvesarayya, Mokshagundam (1861-1962): Engineer, educationist and statesman. Was Dewan of Mysore. Bharat Ratna.

Vivekananda, Swami (1863-1902): A saint philosopher who made India's greatness known to the world. Disciple of Ramakrishna Paramahamsa, saint (1836-86) who worked for the uplift of Hindu society. Established Sri Rama krishna Mission.

Swami Vivekananda

Walton, Sam (1918 -'92): One of the world's leading departmental-store-retail business magnates. Owner of Wal-Mart

stores chain.

Webster, Noah (1758-1843): American lexicographer.

Whitefield, George (1714-70): Founder of the Calvinistic Methodist Church in England.

Willard, Van Orman Quine (1908-2000): American philosopher and logician. Two Dogmas of Empiricism,The Time of My Life.

Winfrey, Oprah (b.1954): American TV talkshow host. First woman to top the Forbes magazine list of entertainment millionaires.

Oprah Winfrey

Wright, Frank Lloyd (1869-1959): American architect who gained fame for building the Imperial Hotel in Tokyo that withstood the 1923 earthquake.

Yashpal, Prof. (b. 1926): Scientist, UGC Chairman, missionary of scientific thinking. His TV show 'Turning point' was very popular.

Yunus, Mohammed (b. 1940): Bangladesh's micro-credit leader. Among the 30 all time top entrepreneurs identified by 'Business Week'. Nobel Prize. He stepped down from Grameen Bank in 2011.

Mohammed Yunus

Zoroaster (Zarathustra) (6th cent B.C.): Persian founder of the Parsee religion. He was a monotheist, and saw the world as a struggle between good and evil.

Zwingli, Ulrich (1484-1531): Swiss religious (Protestant) reformer.

| August for Augustus | Augustus Caesar persuaded the senate to change the name of the sixth month of the old Roman year, known as Sixtilis, to Augustus in his honour. |

Quiz Show, 2012

A General Knowledge Test

V. George Mathew

1. The 193rd member of the UN
2. The southern-most Arabic speaking town in the world
3. Value of book advances secured by Wikileaks founder Julian Assange
4. What did white-nose syndrome kill in the US in 2009?
5. What is called 'brain bucket'?
6. In assisted dying, the life – ending medication is administered by the patient himself/ a doctor / a nurse.
7. A great year is equal to about .....years.
8. Who was behind the change of name from Narendra Dutt to Vivekananda?
9. The book that won 'Booker of the Booker' award:
10. The oldest national song in the world is that of
11. World Day against the Death Penalty
12. Britain abolished death penalty in
13. Who among these wrote a biography of Mahatma Gandhi: Romain Rolland / M.L. King / Jose Saramago
14. What did Henry Cavendish discover?
15. Vietnam's national flower
16. The first Indian to win Gandhi Peace Prize
17. The tennis player whose career ended with a horseback-riding accident.
18. Head of the world's largest army in size.
19. Goatee is (camel / small goat / a beard)
20. India's first individual owner of an ATM
21. Who has an Indian son-in-law: Kofi Annan, Ban Ki Moon, Nelson Mandela, Aung San Suu Kyi
22. Vijay Nambiar is adviser to
23. Al Gore's award winning documentary
24. Salary of the Supreme Court Chief Justice
25. India's chief import item
26. In what is lithium kept?
27. The common element in all acids
28. RBI's first Indian Governor
29. Bronze is the alloy of .... and ....
30. Who was known by the nickname Sultan of Swat?
31. The first Chinese citizen to win a Nobel Prize
32. Biographee is the .... of a biography
33. Bugatti is part of the .... group
34. Ovaries are (two, three, four, six)
35. Burma was administratively part of .... until 1937.
36. Highest paid actor in Asia
37. Macrobiotics is the study of prolonging
38. Gum-shoe is slang for a (detective / dealer in rubber / close friend)

ANSWERS

1. South Sudan; 2. Juba; 3. $1.3 m; 4. bats; 5. a motor cycle helmet; 6. the patient; 7. 25,800; 8. Sri Ramakrishna Paramahamsa; 9. Salman Rushdie's *Midnight's Children*; 10. Japan; 11. Oct. 10; 12. 1965; 13. Romain Rolland; 14. Hydrogen; 15. Lotus; 16. Baba Amte; 17. Maureen Connolly; 18. Hu Jintao; 19. beard; 20. Rajesh Jethpuria of Bhopal; 21. Ban Ki Moon; 22. Ban Ki-Moon; 23. An Inconvenient Truth; 24. Rs. 1,00,000; 25. Petroleum products; 26. wax; 27. hydrogen; 28. C D Deshmukh; 29. tin and copper; 30. Babe Ruth; 31. Liu Xiaabo; 32. subject; 33. Volkswagen; 34. two; 35. India; 36. Jackie Chan (*Rush Hour, The Karate Kid*); 37. life; 38. detective.

Good Explanations

Quantum physicist at Oxford David Dentsch says science is successful because it provides good explanations. Explanations hold a special status as fundamental descriptions of the world.

The Star Spangled Banner

The US national anthem 'The Star Spangled Banner' was written in 1814 by Francis Scott Key, an American lawyer, on the British ship HMS Minden.

39. Puerperium: the period during and just after
40. Ptomaine poisoning was the early term for
41. Bugatti claims its Veyron can touch a top speed of
42. *The Bell Jar* is a novel written by American poet
43. The Charter 77 movement is related to ....
44. The first film personality to be nominated to the Rajya Sabha
45. 'Temple Trees' is associated with a) Tibet b) Meghalaya c) Sri Lanka d) Cambodia
46. The University that has decided on having an Indian dress at convocation
47. The minister who removed his robe in Bhopal to prove his point in favour of an Indian dress at convocation.
48. What was special about Lt. Gen. Pankaj Joshi, the first Chief of Integrated Defence Staff?
49. The number of passengers the Navi Mumbai International Airport is expected to handle by 2030
50. The poet-professor who was Government of India's Hindi Officer
51. Who is a screenior citizen?
52. Who among these is an author and an FRCS surgeon (Kavery Nambisan / Anita Nair / Arundhati Roy.
53. Jimmy Wales is founder of
54. Kavery Nambisan started writing initially in
55. Which word means relating to the sense of touch': sensitive, haptic, toothsome, sensuous

56. What is SHU, in the context of chilli peppers?
57. Who shot King Faisal of Saudi Arabia to death in 1975?
58. Founder and Executive Chairman of World Economic Forum
59. The Irish folkrock legend who co-founded Band Aid to raise money for famine relief in Africa in 1984
60. The first recipient of Gandhi Peace Prize
61. Fullbright programme was created by .... in 1946.
62. Clarence House is the official residence of
63. SEWA's membership
64. How old was the Duchess of Cornwall when she became Prince Charle's second wife in 2005?
65. Who said necessity is the mother of invention?
66. Who said doubt is the father of invention.
67. The only Sikh ruler of Punjab
68. How many paintings did Vincent Van Gogh sell in his life?
69. The first in the world to legislate assisted dying in 1997.
70. MENA countries
71. "Investing in women is one of the most powerful ways to fight poverty" Whose words?
72. The only Communist country in Europe in 2009
73. India's largest beer guzzling state.
74. Arnold Schwarzenegger's bike in 'Terminator'
75. Chogal was the last monarch of
76. Research In Motion manufactures
77. 'Toonie' is, a tonne, a coin, a bird, a girl
78. World's biggest orchestra
79. Money Order commission for Rs. 5000
80. Lusophone is 'speaking what as the main language'?
81. What is common to Milton Friedman, Amartya Sen and Paul Krugman?
82. The four C's on which a diamond's price is based:

A Million Descendants Rats multipy so quickly that in 18 months two rats could have over a million descendants.

83. Bush 41, Bush 43 What do these mean?
84. The country's largest employer of disabled people
85. The male goat is a ram or billy, the female a .... or ....
86. The unit of measurement for radio frequency exposure is called
87. The country that imports the most rice in Asia
88. Complete this for Tintin: "billions of billions blue........."
89. A vegivore has a special fondness for
90. Complete this Tamil triumvirate: Sivaji Ganesan, MGR and ....
91. In the Hindi version of Tintin, what is Natkhat and what is Santu & Bantu?
92. European Commission's statistical arm
93. The first Latin American country to legalize same sex marriage
94. Billionaires in 2000 were 306. In 2010, they were
95. All-time top grossing film. It was produced in 2010
96. More than 1 in 100 adults are behind bars in (US / China)
97. Who rated M.S. Dhoni as the most entertaining and exciting cricketer in the world?
98. World's largest tyre maker
99. Godthab is the Danish name for
100. The highest tiger density in the world is in:
101. Who said that economists know the price of everything and the value of nothing?
102. The TAPI gas pipeline will terminate in India at
103. The deepest port in India.
104. What did Prof. Nouriel Roubini of New York University predict: a. WWI / b. WWII / c. Internet / d. the global meltdown
105. The ornithologist who was associated with the formation of a major political party in India
106. Who among these was not a Union Minister: M.G.K. Menon, S. L. Rao, Arun Shourie, Shatrughan Sinha?

107. Tintin created by Herge 80 years ago has been translated into 59 languages from the original
108. The Malegam Committee looked into the activities of

ANSWERS

39. childbirth; **40.** food poisoning; **41.** 407 kmph; **42.** Sylvia Plath; **43.** Czechoslovakia; **44.** Prithviraj Kapur; **45.** c; **46.** Ambedkar University, Lucknow; **47.** Jairam Ramesh; **48.** lost both his legs in 1967 in a mine blast at Sikkim; **49.** 60 m.; **50.** Harivansh-rai Bachchan; **51.** Senior citizen spending time in front of a screen – tv or computer; **52.** Kavery Nambisan; **53.** Wikipedia; **54.** Kannada; **55.** haptic; **56.** Scoville heat units, which indicate measure of chemical compound capsaichin; **57.** Prince Museid, a nephew with a history of mental illness; **58.** Klaus Schwab; **59.** Bob Geldoff; **60.** Julius Nyerere; **61.** Senator J. William Full-bright; **62.** Prince of Wales; **63.** over 1.2 mn.; **64.** 57; **65.** Plato; **66.** Galileo; **67.** Ranjit Singh; **68.** only one; **69.** The State of Oregon, US; **70.** Middle East and North African countries; **71.** Hillary Clinton; **72.** Moldova; **73.** Andhra Pradesh; **74.** the Fatboy; **75.** Sikkim, then an independent Himalayan Kingdom; **76.** BlackBerry; **77.** a coin; **78.** Leipzig Gewandhaus Orchestra; **79.** Rs. 250; **80.** Portuguese; **81.** Winners of Nobel for Economics; **82.** carat, clarity, colour and cut; **83.** 41st President Bush and 43rd President Bush; **84.** Titan Industries; **85.** a doe or nanny; **86.** specific absorption rate or SAR; **87.** Bangladesh; **88.** blistering barnacles; **89.** vegetables; **90.** Gemini Ganesan; **91.** Snowy; Thomson & Thompson; **92.** Eurostat; **93.** Argentina; **94.** 1011; **95.** Cameron's *Avatar*, $2.8 billion.; **96.** US; **97.** Pervez Musharraf, former Pakistan President; **98.** Michelin Group; **99.** Nuuk, capital of Greenland; **100.** Kaziranga National Park in Assam; **101.** Oscar Wilde; **102.** Fazilka in Punjab; **103.** Gangavaram; **104.** d; **105.** A.O. Hume; **106.** S L Rao; **107.** French; **108.** micro finance institutions.

Urine Can't Reduce Pain — The widespread belief that urine lessens the pain of jellyfish stings is misplaced, says British Red Cross. Seawater or vinegar is more effective, it says.

Five Minutes with the Voter

Winston Churchill said, the best argument against democracy is a five-minute conversation with the average voter.

109. UP's first woman chief secretary
110. Agricultural scientist Yuan Longping of China is known as the father of
111. Whom did A P J Abdul Kalam beat to become the President of India?
112. Panchumarthi Anuradha was the country's youngest Mayor, in 2000. Which was her Corporation?
113. Which bird is also called the 'owl parrot'?
114. Average daily income of Tirupathi temple
115. The largest power generating company in India:
116. Germany's busiest airport
117. 'Rai' means paradise in this country. Aish is a popular actor there. Name the country.
118. World's largest producer of metals.
119. Which is 'the gentleman's game'?
120. Identify 'The Farmer Suicide belt'
121. The popular name of the forty-two-line-Bible
122. Gyanpith Award prize money
123. First literary work to win Gyanpith award.
124. What is known as Asian Nobel
125. Age of Dr. K N Raj when he wrote the preface to First Five Year Plan.
126. What replaced 'pint' in British pubs in Jan. 2011?
127. Talking of Nobel Prizes, who has been called the Missing Laureate?
128. In 'Hobson's choice', Hobson was a man who hired out horses. His first name?
129. Foolscap is a size of paper that measures 81/2 by .... inches.
130. The term in botany meaning living together for mutual benefit

131. The American Governor whose parents are Sikh immigrants
132. Transport Ministry's target of road building in km per day
133. Number of jails in India
134. Whom did Nikki Haley, 38, replace in Jan. 2011 as the youngest current governor of the US?
135. The first Chinese to reach the final of a Grand Slam (at the Australian Open)
136. 'Survival International' is a London-based organisation which campaigns for the rights of
137. Why was Belgium's Kim Clijsters known as 'Aussie Kim'?
138. Which former President's personal wealth was estimated to top £20 bn. in 2011?
139. A 13th Zodiac sign suggested by US astronomer Parke Kunkle in 2011
140. 'Masra' is the Arabic word for a
141. Age at which Rupert Murdoch bought his first newspaper.
142. The online newspaper for the Apple iPad launched in New York in Feb. 2011
143. The world's largest coal-miner
144. How is Ian Fleming remembered in Boscobel, Jamaica?
145. The number of domestic pigs buried alive in South Korea after the outbreak of foot-and-mouth disease in 2011?
146. The actor who flew an F-series plane (an F15) in 'Top Gun'
147. Fredrik Cotting's sequel to 'A Catcher in the Rye'
148. Most airports in India are named after (places, festivals, leaders).
149. India's 'new wave' cinema is associated with whose 1969 low-budget film named what?
150. The country that has 12 seas on its territory.
151. A half sister is your sister only through one
152. The country called 'The Country of Gorillas'
153. The name of island St. Christopher was later shortened to
154. The Incas lived in the region now known as

155. The country whose flag is hoisted up-side-down when the country is at war
156. What is COIN in military jargon?
157. Men who have won all the four civil honours:
158. Weevil is a (bat/ hyena/ beetle/cobra)
159. Half Nelson is a term in a. naval war-fare b. a South African dance c. wres-tling d. Italian cooking
160. The country where the sun rises over the Pacific Ocean and then sets over the Atlantic
161. The country with the highest number of banks per capita
162. The Olympic star Johnny Weissmuller became the most famous Macbeth / Tarzan / Napoleon / Oliver Twist
163. The two countries that own the world's largest dam
164. The first US President to institute an income tax
165. 'The King's Speech' is the dramatisa-tion of the true-life relationship be-tween King .... and his speech therapist.
166. The word 'sahara' means (a. great b. controversial c. God's creation d. des-ert)
167. What was unique about the fruit flies aboard the USV2 rocket in 1947?
168. You love the environment. What are the three Rs?
169. The .... Indian citizen was born in 2000. Give the missing ordinal number
170. USP is one of the two regional univer-sities in the world. Expand USP.
171. What was described in 1914 as "the greatest liberty Man has ever taken with nature"
172. The country where Romuva was the religion before the people were con-verted to Christianity
173. The first Polish Pope
174. The couple responsible for the discov-ery of artificial radioactivity
175. The third oldest civilization after Mes-opotamia and Egypt.
176. Jhelum and Chenab are the major riv-ers in which Indian State

177. Indian Roller is a (flag/bird/bull/spider)
178. Which of these is spoken by most people: Russian, Japanese, German?
179. Anita and Arabella are a. monkeys sent to space in 1951 b. Clinton's cats c. Putin's dogs d. garden spiders taken into space in 1973

ANSWERS

109. Neera Yadav; **110.** hybrid rice; **111.** Lakshmi Sehgal; **112.** Vijayawada; **113.** kakapo; **114.** Rs. 1.5 cr.; **115.** NTPC, a Maharatna enterprise; **116.** Frankfurt; **117.** Russia; **118.** China; **119.** cricket; **120.** Maharashtra, Karnataka, A.P., M.P. and Chhattisgarh; **121.** Gutenberg Bible; **122.** Rs. 7 lakh; Originally 2 lakh. **123.** Odak-kuzhal; **124.** Magsaysay Award; **125.** 26; **126.** schooner; **127.** Mahatma Gandhi; **128.** Tobias; **129.** 13 1/2; **130.** Symbiosis; **131.** Namrata Nikki Randhawa Haley; **132.** 20; **133.**1356; **134.** Bobby Jindal; **135.** Li Na; **136.** indigenous peoples; **137.** since her engagement to Australian star Lleyton Hewitt; **138.** Hosni Mubarak; **139.** Ophi-uchus, the serpent holder; **140.** goat farm; **141.** 22; **142.** *The Daily*; **143.** Coal India Ltd., turnover Rs. 52,000 cr. in 2009-10; **144.** There is a international airport there in his name; **145.** 1.4 mn.; **146.** Tom Cruise; **147.** *Coming Through the Rye*; **148.** leaders; **149.** Mrinal Sen, *Bhuvan Shome*; **150.** Russia, **151.** parent; **152.** Rwanda; **153.** St. Kitts; **154.** Peru; **155.** The Philippines; **156.** counterinsurgency; **157.** Satyajit Ray, Bhimsen Joshi, Bismillah Khan; **158.** beetle; **159.** c; **160.** Panama; **161.** Luxembourg; **162.** Tarzan; **163.** Brazil and Paraguay; **164.** Abraham Lincoln; **165.** George VI; **166.** d; **167.** the first animals to be sent to space; **168.** Reduce, Re-use, Recycle; **169.** billionth; **170.** University of the South Pacific; **171.** the Panama Canal; **172.** Lithuania; **173.** John Paul II; **174.** Jean Frederic Joliot Curie and Irene; **175.** Indus Valley; **176.** J&K; **177.** bird; **178.** Russian. **179.** d.

And Women Created... It is interesting that bullet proof vests, fire escapes, windshield wipers and laser printers were all invented by women.

First Nobel

The first American to win the Nobel Peace Prize was Theodore Roosevelt (1906), the 26th American President.

180. Mythology: The Sicilian shepherd punished with blindness for infidelity in love.
181. He is considered infallible. He won the Nobel Prize in 1989. Who is it?
182. Locarno is a holiday resort in
183. The treaty that established the European Union
184. The Croatian who designed the first hydroelectric power plant at Niagara Falls
185. Who won Bharat Ratna on his 100th birthday?
186. One in five black people in the world is (American/ Nigerian/ Indian/ South African)
187. The average pencil holds enough graphite to write how many words?
188. The largest island sea
189. The number of princes in Saudi Arabia's royal clan
190. Who was known as Malik Abdul Aziz while in jail?
191. The country that had six different national anthems since WWII
192. The first words recorded
193. What is Gay Plague?
194. Where was the first PM of Israel Ben Gurion born?
195. Dar-el-Bedia is the Arabic name of
196. Eleven out of the 12 men to have walked on the moon were (a. left handed/ b. in the Bay Scouts/ c. vegetarian/ d. coloured)
197. The English title of Jana Gana Mana, given by Tagore who composed it
198. Salil Shetty is Secretary-General of
199. Which of these countries have women as Governor-General: a. UK and Australia b. Australia and Canada, c. Canada and New Zealand
200. Which of these is a capital?: Bermuda, Nuuk, Chicago, Mombasa
201. The country that has the world's first beer museum
202. Which statement is true?
 a. Oman is the capital of Muscat
 b. Mombasa is in Uganda.
 c. Eritrea was formerly part of Ethiopia.
 d. Pretoria is the legislative capital of South Africa.
203. Pranab Mukherjee's 'very senior citizens' are those above
204. The official song of 2011 Cricket World Cup is trilingual and is composed by the musician trio of
205. Johann II's 70-year-old reign is the second longest in European royal history. He was Prince of
206. The strongest bone in the human body
207. What is Phi Beta Kappa?
208. A surfer stands on a surfboard to ride on the wave. A body boarder lies on
209. The plural of 'pharynx'
210. People under 18 are not allowed to see these movies because they contain sex and /or violence
211. The full name of painter Rembrandt
212. What did Van Gogh send a cousin with whom he was in love, after a violent quarrel with Paul Gaugin?
213. Germany was the first country to have a regular television service, named 'Fernseh', which meant
214. What did Dr. James Naismith invent?
215. The football coach who ended his coaching career at the age of 91 and lived to 102.
216. The Muslim lunar calendar.
217. 'The Ancient Mariner' was planned jointly by .... and Coleridge. The former soon separated himself from the undertaking. Coleridge finished the poem in 1798.
218. The Japanese firm that developed the first all-transistor portable television in 1960.

Recharge the Battery in Minutes

Researchers at the University of Illinois led by Paul Barun have suceeded in building prototype batteries that can be recharged fully in two minutes.

219. Ben Jonson who became England's first .... was a former London bricklayer.
220. The Gaugin oil painting painted in Tahiti in 1892 and sold at Sotheby's in London in 1980 for £380,000.
221. The first Roman emperor to be baptized
222. Mickey Rooney's real name
223. The Governor-General who outlawed the practice of 'sati'
224. The English word to·describe a huge machine that crushed all in its path
225. At the base of what is the sonnet 'The New Colossus' inscribed?
226. One fathom is how many feet?
227. What per cent of people are totally covered by health insurance in India?
228. Who produces more tobacco products than any other country?
229. In the 1980s, what was known as 'the financial factory'?
230. The founder of Saudi Arabia
231. 'Meluhha' is associated with a. Eurphrates and Tigris b. Greece and Rome c. David and Goliath d. Mohenjodaro and Harappa
232. Wife of Ravana
233. 'Call me Ishmael' is the first words of which classic?
234. Who said: "My idea of an agreeable person is a person who agrees with me".
235. The education channel jointly owned by Doordarshan and IGNOU
236. Personal civil honours in India were withdrawn by Government of India in 1977 and reintroduced in January, ...
237. 'Bhasha' is the Hindi language news service of
238. What is MARCOS?
239. King George V changed the name of the royal house from the German Saxe-Coburg-Gotha to
240. The selling method which attracts buyers through advertisements for low-priced products who are then made to buy expensive items

241. The founder of Oslo, capital of Norway
242. INS Prahar is world's
243. The President who dissolved the Lok Sabha on Sept. 22, 1979
244. Who said: Politics are not my concern... They impressed me as a dog's life without a dog's decencies
245. Kushinagar is where Buddha attained Parinirvana after his death. Where is It?

ANSWERS

180. Daphnis; 181. The 14th Dalai Lama; 182. Switzerland; 183. Maastricht Treaty; 184. Nikola Tesla; 185. D.K. Karve; 186. Nigerian; 187. 45,000; 188. Caspian Sea; 189. about 7000; 190. Mike Tyson; 191. Romania; 192. Mary had a little lamb; 193. AIDS; 194. Poland; 195. Casablanca; 196. in the Boy Scouts; 197. Morning Song of Indian; 198. Amnesty International; 199. b; 200. Nuuk. 201. Czech Republic; 202. c; 203. 80; 204. Shankar, Ehsaan and Loy; 205. Liechtenstein; 206. Shin bone; 207. A society for university students in the US who are very successful in studies; 208. his stomach on a bodyboard; 209. pharynges; 210. X-rated; 211. Rembrandt van Rijn; 212. his own right ear; 213.'far-seeing'; 214. basketball; 215. Amos Alonzo Stagg; 216. Hijri; 217. Wordsworth; 218.Sony; 219. poet laureate; 220. *The Guitar Player*; 221. Constantine; 222. Joe Yule; 223. Lord William Bentinck, 1829; 224. Juggernaut; 225. Statue of Liberty in New York; 226. six; 227. less than 0.1 percent; 228. China; 229. The Man from U.N.C.L.E. -United Network Command for Law and enforcement, a popular TV show; 230. Abdel Aziz ibn Saud; 231. d; 232. Mandodari; 233. *Moby Dick*; 234.Benjamin Disraeli; 235. Gyan Darshan; 236. 1980; 237. PTI; 238. Marine Commandos; 239. Windsor; 240. bait-and-switch; 241. King Christian IV; 242. fastest missileship; 243. N. Sanjiva Reddy; 244. Rudyard Kipling.; 245. U.P.

Guernica

The first major bombing of a civilian population occurred at the Basque town of Guernica raided by German planes in 1937 during the Spanish Civil War. Pablo Picasso's famous mural painting "Guernica" highlighted this destruction.

Most Expensive Engagement Ring

Reese Witherspoon's 4-carat Ashoka cut diamond is the world's most expensive engagement ring. The ring cost her fiance, Jim Toth, $1.5 m.

246. A homilist delivers a
247. The beer called 'Pils' was originally made in which country?
248. The active underwater volcano in the Solomon Islands
249. The largest raspberry producer in the world
250. Emma Jane Harfield is a character in which Agatha Christie novel?
251. The country where Pierre E. Trudeau was PM
252. Mao Tse-tung's name in the officially approved Pinyin spelling
253. The Beveridge Report in Britain, 1942 urges social insurance from 'the cradle to ....'
254. Which country has the highest rate of twin births?
255. The number of seas on Russian territory
256. The largest landlocked Asian country
257. Hindu mythology. When did Kaliyuga start?
258. The national flag of Pakistan was designed by
259. Who was known as Supermac?
260. Who had the nickname 'the Bulldozer': Winston Churchill / Bill Clinton / Jacques Chirac?
261. Which of these Presidents was a Democrat: Theodore Roosevelt / Herbert Hoover/ F.D. Roosevelt / Eisenhower?
262. John Hinkley Jr. shot from close range. Who was the victim?
263. With which country is liberator Artigas associated:Panama/ Uruguay/ Ecudaor?
264. Of which two countries was Christian X king?
265. Who founded Rotary International?
266. The break in the business of British House of Commons created to give the Speaker a chance to eat something
267. Which politician is known as 'The Knight'?
268. The 13 stripes on the US flag stand for
269. A cougar is a big .cat as well as the name of a ....
270. What is Ameslan?
271. Who presented a carnation to all mothers present at the memorial service for her mother and started the Mother's Day?
272. Thomas Alva Edison's companies, holding about 1300 patents, were consolidated as
273. What does Kiki Joachin remind us of?
274. Naturism is another word for (nature study / nudism / nationality)
275. An Asian country whose name can mean 'shiny black enamel'
276. The name given to the groove between one's nose and lips
277. The patent for what was given to Remington company in 1873?
278. Which of these are noble metals: silver, gold, platinum, palladium.
279. The pulse (slows down/ increases / remains the same) as age advances.
280. The 24-hour period between midnight and the next midnight is .... day.
281. Which word means 'uninteresting'? jaunty, scant, jejune, hortative
282. Long time (not seen/ no seen/ no see) means 'we haven't met for a long time'
283. The plural of 'child' in Middle English was
284. The only temperature that is the same in both Fahrenheit and Celsius.
285. What is gazpacho in Spain?
286. Phosphorus is (found / not found) free in nature.

287. The circular disc with a horizontal line drawn through its centre, marked upon the side of a ship is known as
288. The war that ended with the Treaty of Portsmouth, 1905
289. Greek legend: Who carried off Helen, wife of Menelaus?
290. Park Chung-hee was President of which country?
291. Insectivorous plants eat
292. Miraya Moscoso was President of
293. This Asian country had no PM from 1958 to 1973
294. Car index for Sweden is 'S'. Which country has SF as the index?
295. The substance stored in liver and muscles
296. Caledonian' is connected with: a. Canada b. Scotland c. California
297. The Nobel Peace Prize of 1944 (a. wasn't announced b. went to Amnesty International c. was given to Cordell Hull d. went to International Committee of the Red Cross
298. When he became the de facto ruler of China, how old was Deng Xiaoping?
299. Whose favourite horse was named Incitatus?
300. What is MV as used before the name of a ship?
301. Franklin D. Roosevelt's middle name
302. The shooter who was crowned Champion of Champion at Tughlakabad, Delhi in January?
303. Myxomatosis is an infectious disease of (peacocks/ pigeons/ rabbits/ cats)
304. After the *Titanic* struck the iceberg, in how many hours did it sink?
305. The British medical researcher who perfected *in vitro* fertilization of the human egg
306. Roger Bannister was the first man to run the mile under
307. The capital of East Timor
308. The first woman press photographer of India
309. While living in Chandni Chowk, who made crude bombs during Quit India Movement?

310. The first Chinese player to win a Grand Slam title
311. The murderer in Dostoyevsky's *Crime and Punishment*
312. The hamburger chain that Ray Kroc founded?
313. In MGNREGS, 'NRE' stands for
314. Inchon is a seaport in a. Bangladesh b. Japan c. Malta d. South Korea
315. The stadium where the 34th National Games was opened is named after

ANSWERS

246. sermon; **247.** Czech Republic; **248.** Kavachi; **249.** Serbia; **250.** Murder on the Blue Train; **251.** Canada; **252.** Mao Zedong; **253.** 'the grave'; **254.** Nigeria; **255.** 12; **256.** Kazakhstan; **257.** 3102 B.C.; **258.** Muhammad Ali Jinnah; **259.** Harold Macmillan, UK; **260.** Jacques Chirac; **261.** F.D. Roosevelt; **262.** Ronald Reagan; **263.** Uruguay; **264.** Denmark and Iceland; **265.** Paul Harris; **266.** Speaker's Chop; **267.** Silvio Berlusconi; **268.** Original States; **269.** car; **270.** American Slang Language; **271.** Anna Marie Jarvis; **272.** General Electric Company; **273.** the Haiti earthquake. He was buried beneath the ruins of his apartment building for 8 days; **274.** nudism; **275.** Japan. **276.** filtrum; **277.** typewriter; **278.** all; **279.** slows down; **280.** mean solar; **281.** jejune; **282.** no see; **283.** childer; **284.** ¯40°; **285.** a cold tomato-based vegetable soup; **286.** not found; **287.** Plimsoll line; **288.** Russo-Japanese War; **289.** Paris; **290.** Republic of Korea; **291.**insects; **292.** Panama; **293.** Pakistan; **294.** Finland; **295.** Glycogen; **296.** Scotland; **297.** d; **298.** 72; **299.** Emperor Caligula; **300.**motor vessel; **301.** Delano; **302.** Anjali Bhagwat; **303.** rabbits; **304.** in less than 3 hours; **305.** Patrick Steptoe.; **306.** four minutes; **307.** Dili; **308.** Homai Vyarawalla; **309.** L.C. Jain; **310.** Li Na; **311.** Raskolnikov; **312.** McDonald's; **313.** National Rural Employment; **314.** d; **315.** Birsa Munda.

The Oldest Human Beings

Mountana's Walter Breuning, the world's oldest man (and the second oldest person) died on April 14, 2011. Days later, the new oldest man turned 114. He lives in Japan.

Father & Son as Presidents

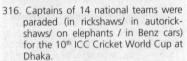

Bush Jr.

John Quincy Adams, the 6th US President, was the son of John Adams, the 2nd President. George W Bush, the 43rd president, was son of George Bush Sr, the 41st President.

316. Captains of 14 national teams were paraded (in rickshaws/ in autorickshaws/ on elephants / in Benz cars) for the 10th ICC Cricket World Cup at Dhaka.
317. The members of the Second Triumvirate (*Julius Caesar*)
318. The term used to describe a group of British writers of the 1950s, whose works express bitterness of the lower classes towards the upper classes
319. What is common to 'James Bond', 'Harry Potter' and 'Star Trek'?
320. The film on Lee Harvy Oswald, convicted of the crime of shooting President J.F. Kennedy, on the afternoon of Nov. 22, 1963
321. Blean is the scientific measure of
322. What did mountaineer Edmund Hillary bury at the top of Mt. Everest?
323. The filmstar who said 'Frankly, my dear, I don't give a damn' in an immortal film
324. Which is correct: nook and look, nook and corner, nook and cranny?
325. A north wind blows (to/from) the north.
326. A beret (a. is not a hat b. has no brim c. is a small giant d. is a kind of tortoise)
327. 'The real thing is coming' was the first advertisement of what in 1983 India?
328. The Argentines called islands 'Islas Malvinas' . We know the islands as
329. Who said, "I am extraordinarily patient, provided I get my own way in the end?
330. Part of the secret of success in life is to eat what you like and let the food fight it out inside." Whose words?
331. The language in which the Buddha preached
332. Who said, 'Being Prime Minister is the easiest job in the world. Everyone else has an instrument to play. You just stand there and conduct.'
333. Dickens' *Oliver Twist* has another name. What?
334. Cherries grow on a cherry / berry.
335. Dewlap is a. formation of dew b. dew point c. loose fold of skin under one's chin d. a growth on the forehead
336. The picaresque novels of the 18th century had .... as heroes
337. 'Easter' is a Christian festival a. in March-April b. immediately after Christmas c. July-August d. none of these
338. Which word is spelt incorrectly: ecstatic, ecstasy, ecstacy, ecstasies
339. Bill Sikes' mistress in *Oliver Twist*
340. 'Newspeak' and 'Doublethink' are coinages in which novel?
341. The American university named after a British Governor of Madras
342. An 'easel' is used by a (musician/ artist /pugilist)
343. P.B. Shelly said, 'there is no real wealth but the .... of man (love/ labour/ hands/ brain)
344. Novelist Graham Greene was educated at Berkhamsted School where .... was headmaster. a. R.K. Narayan b. his father c. William Wordsworth d. J.B.S. Haldane
345. The author of 'The Infernal Marriage', a light-hearted tale published in 1834
346. The shortest of Shakespeare's tragedies
347. Government statistics put the number of small scale protests China suffers a year at
348. The word that means 'a half': moeity, semidome, semester, semblance
349. Which river did Hernando de Soto discover?
350. Sardar Patel's daughter who served as his secretary and nurse

351. Shih Huang Ti was the first emperor of
352. Expand 'GIP' Railway
353. Dr. Binayak Sen took his MBBS and M.D. in pediatrics from
354. The first planned city in Palestinian history will, when completed, be a modern 40,000-person metropolis in the West Bank called
355. Rawabi means .... in Arabic. It is the largest construction project in the Palestinian territories.
356. Who wrote *Why England Slept*
357. The first high priest of the Jews: Moses/ David/ Aaron
358. Who became President for Life at the age of 19?
359. In Britain who sits on the woolsack, a large seat stuffed with wool?
360. Author of the best seller 'The Joy of Living'
361. iL2L is a non-profit organisation in Washington D C. What does the name mean?
362. The president of an African country who never revealed his age
363. Asia's first woman railway engine driver
364. At what age did Fidel Castro become the Head of State?
365. 'Best Boy' in film industry is assistant to the gaffer (the chief lighting technician) What is a female assistant called?
366. Who is widely regarded as Pakistan's wealthiest man?
367. The only Indian astronomer to become President of International Astronomical Union
368. How old was Anna Paquin when she won the Oscar for the best supporting actress for *The Piano*?
369. The Tyeb Mehta painting auctioned for Rs. 8 crore by Christies
370. Who created the famous painting *Wish dream*?
371. A deep adult male singing voice, lower than tenor and higher than bass.
372. The French film actress whose husband from 1952 to 1957 was the director of her first major film
373. *Ben Hur* (1925) was banned in China in 1930 for containing 'propaganda of
374. A bride's outfit of clothes, beginning with 't'
375. In falconry, the female is a falcon. What about the male?
376. Who wanted to be an artist but had to work as a housepainter? Mussolini / Homer / Hitler
377. In film classifiction, what is 'PG'?

ANSWERS

316. in rickshaws; **317.** Octavius, Antony and Lepidus; **318.** Angry Young Men; **319.** Successful film series; **320.** *Cry of Battle*; **321.** luminosity; **322.** a crucifix; **323.** Clark Gable; **324.** nook and cranny; **325.** from; **326.** b; **327.** Coca-Cola; **328.** Falkland Islands; **329.** Margaret Thatcher; **330.** Mark Twain; **331.** Pali; **332.** British PM James Callaghan; **333.** *The Parish Boy's Progress*; **334.** cherry; **335.** c; **336.** rogues and villains; **337.** a; **338.** ecstacy; **339.** Nancy; **340.** George Orwell's *Nineteen Eighty Four*; **341.** Yale; **342.** artist; **343.** labour; **344.** b; **345.** Benjamin Disraeli; **346.** Macbeth; **347.** 80,000; **348.** moeity; **349.** the Mississippi; **350.** Maniben Patel; **351.** China; **352.** Great Indian Peninsular; **353.** C.M.C. College, Vellore; **354.** Rawabi; **355.** hills; **356.** J.F. Kennedy; **357.** Aaron; **358.** Jean Claude 'Baby' Doc Duvalier of Haiti; **359.** The Lord Chancellor, Speaker of the House of Lords; **360.** Miugyur Rinpoche; **361.** I Live To Lead; **362.** Dr. Hastings Kamuzu Banda of Malawi; **363.** Surekha Yadav; **364.** 32; **365.** Best Boy; **366.** Mian Muhammad Mansha; **367.** M.K. Vainu Bappu; **368.** 12; **369.** *Falling Bird*; **370.** Arpita Singh; **371.** baritone; **372.** Brigitte Bardot, Film: *And God Created Woman*, 1956; **373.** superstitious beliefs, namely Christianity; **374.** trousseau; **375.** tiercel; **376.** Hitler; **377.** Parental Guidance – All ages are admitted but parents are advised that certain scenes may be unsuitable for small children.

No Woman President

No woman has been the US President so far. All Presidents had been white till Barack Obama came to power. Most presidents were protestants, until John F. Kennedy was elected in 1960.

The Last Czar

Nicholas II was the last czar. He, his wife Alexandra and their children were reportedly shot dead by Bolsheviks in a grimy cellar in July 1918.

378. The virus named after a region of former Zaire. It causes an acute infection in humans

379. The electronics engineer, who with John W. Mauchly built the first electronic computer in 1946 known as ENIAC.

380. The two Muslim festivals known loosely as Id

381. The British cricketer who scored 61237 runs and 197 centuries. 98 of the centuries were made after he was 40.

382. Histology is the story of (history/tissues/acting)

383. 'parry' and 'lunge' are terms related to (scrabble/ fencing /psychology)

384. James Cameron who declared 'I am the King of the World' in his acceptance speech (for best director - *Titanic*, 1997) was mimicking

385. Before 1997, 'TIFF' (Toronto Film Festival) was

386. Shakespeare's 'Swan Song'

387. They cannot spend more than Rs. 13 on a wedding. Name this community.

388. Shah Bano's divorced husband

389. What made the aircraft Enola Gay known?

390. The first actress to appear on a postage stamp

391. One ton of computer scrap contains more gold than 17 tons of .... ore.

392. 'Taoiseach' is the Prime Minister of

393. The second President of Pakistan

394. The longest elevated expressway in India is 11.6 km long and named after

395. What per cent of Canadian population are immigrants?

396. The mineral from which common salt comes

397. Bioluminescence is the production of light by

398. President of which country lives in Merdeka Palace?

399. The Indian who awarded medals at Moscow Olympics?

400. Absolute zero' is equal to .... degrees Celsius, the lowest possible temperature

401. Who paid £ 954,104 for David O Selznick's Oscar for *Gone with the Wind*?

402. The film in which the first screen kiss was performed

403. The country where the cabinet in 1996 had 22 ministers, of whom 11 were women

404. The President of which country was 'accidentally' shot by, his chief of intelligence services in 1979?

405. Imran Khan captained Pakistan to success in the 1991 Cricket World Cup. Seats his Justice Party won in the 1997 elections

406. A boodler (a. pays bribes b. takes bribes c. intimidates officials

407. 24 Sussex Drive is the Canadian equivalent of London's

408. 'Piscatorial' is the adjective of (fishing / picture/ archery)

409. First woman to take a seat in the House of Commons

410. Vanilla's birthplace

411. Asia's largest cinnamon estate is in

412. India's per capita income

413. The number of children in India aged between 10 and 19

414. The world's most famous civil engineer of all times

415. The world's most southerly continent

416. A cutaneous disease affects (blood/ kidney / the skin/ hair)

417. The first ever casualty in a space mission

418. India's longest railway tunnel

419. *The Last Temptation of Christ*, a 1988 film, was based on a novel by

Animals Domesticated

In the last 4000 years, no new animals have been domesticated. Cats and dogs are kept for pleasure, cattle, chickens and pigs for food, sheep and silkworms for clothing and camels, donkeys and horses for transportation and labour.

420. 'Piddle' is (urine/ riddle / toilet / axis)
421. Walter Hunt is remembered for the invention of
422. The oldest synagogue in the Commonwealth is situated at
423. The Indian prime minister who was not a member of the Congress party at any stage
424. How long is the Konkan railway line?
425. The world's biggest free-standing rock
426. The first Indian to become prime minister after having been the opposition leader in Lok Sabha
427. Who founded the magazine 'Arya: A Philosophical Review'?
428. 'Anthariksh Bhawan' is the headquarters of
429. The chief exporter of cumin
430. 'Alto' is (an opera/ a song / a voice / an instrument).
431. 'Junk bond' is another name for a
432. The driest of the six inhabited continents
433. How many of the Group of 77 developing nations are in Asia?
434. A broodmare is a female
435. How many nations gathered in Athens in 1896 to revive the Olympics?
436. The world's busiest port
437. What spice is known as devil's dung
438. The first Pope to come to India
439. Portion of the circumference of a circle
440. The University that introduced correspondence courses in India first
441. The Mughal emperor who was in power at age 14?
442. These countries, which experienced rapid economic growth in the 1970s and 1980s, were called 'little tigers'
443. What is common to *Gandhi, Men in Black* and *Spider-Man*?
444. Three films that won the Academy Awards for best picture, best director, best actor, best actress and best screenplay
445. Alexia is the inability to read, and agraphia is the inability to .... caused

by damage to the angular gyrus.
446. Elizabeth Taylor's middle name
447. India's largest consumer goods company
448. The multi-media campaign 'Swabhimaan' is aimed at informing, educating and motivating people to
449. What was turned into Nehru Memorial Museum?

ANSWERS

378. Ebola virus; **379.** John Presper Eckert, Jr.; **380.** Id-ul-Adha and Id-ul-Fitr; **381.** Sir John Berry Hobbs; **382.** tissues. **383.** fencing; **384.** Leonardo Di Caprio's line from the film; **385.** Festival of Festivals; **386.** *The Tempest;* **387.** Namdhari Sikhs; **388.** Mohammed Ahmed; **389.** It dropped atomic bomb on Hiroshima, 6-8-1945; **390.** Grace Kelly; **391.** gold; **392.** Ireland; **393.** Ayub Khan; **394.** P.V. Narasimha Rao; **395.** 19%; **396.** Halite; **397.** living things; **398.** Indonesia; **399.** Ashwini Kumar; **400.** -273.15; **401.** Michael Jackson; **402.** The Kiss; **403.** Sweden; **404.** South Korea; **405.** None; **406.** b; **407.** No. 10 Downing Street; **409.** Nancy Astor; **410.** Mexico; **411.** Kannur, Kerala; **412.** Rs.46,492; **413.** 24.3 cr.; **414.** Alexander Gustav Eiffel; **415.** Antarctica; **416.** the skin; **417.** Vladimir Komarov; **418.** Karbude, 6.5 km.; **419.** Nikos Kazantzakis; **420.** urine; **421.** the safety pin; **422.** Mattancherry, Kerala; **423.** A.B. Vajpayee. **424.** 760 km; **425.** Uluru in Australia; **426.** A. B. Vajpayee; **427.** Aurobindo Ghose; **428.** ISRO; **429.** Iran; **430.** a voice; **431.** high-yielding bond; **432.** Australia; **433.** 37; **434.** horse used for breeding ; **435.** 14; **436.** Singapore; **437.** Asafoetida; **438.** Paul VI; **439.** arc; **440.** Delhi; **441.** Akbar the Great; **442.** South Korea, Taiwan, Singapore, Hong Kong; **443.** Columbia Pictures' recent box office successes; **444.** *It Happened One Night, One Flew Over the Cuckoo's Nest,* and *The Silence of the Lambs;* **445.** write; **446.** Rosemond; **447.** Hindustan Unilever; **448.** open bank accounts; **449.** Teen Murti House.

Natural Disaster No.1

A provisional estimate put the cost of the economic damage from Japan's recent earthquake at $235 bn., which would make it the most expensive natural disaster in history.

Police-Population Ratio

Police-popula-tion ratio in Mumbai is 1:300. The number of constables is 18,666 and police vehicles 3055.

450. Beatrix Wilhelmina Armgard has been the queen of which country since 1980?

451. The capital city that replaced the old capital when it was hit by a hurricane. The answer begins with 'B'.

452. An airport designed for STOL aircraft.

453. The 7-letter word that begins with 'n' and means a narrow passage between two bodies of water

454. Jeanne Calment of France who lived to be 122 credited her long life to, among other things, a diet rich in

455. Marriage between persons of different religions or races is called

456. Who named China 'Cathay'

457. The country with the world's largest postal network

458. Interest rate in banks' savings accounts

459. The Prime Minister who presided over the transformation of an empire to a Commonwealth

460. The three-letter word which can precede 'black' to make it a deep shiny black

461. Passchendaele 1917 was one of the great conflicts of WWI or WWII?

462. Who named his German shepherd 'Che', after the Argentina revolutionary?

463. A word meaning a student and a part of the body. It begins with P.

464. Albert Einstein was working as a .... when he published his theory of relativity

465. 'Kristallnacht' launched by Hitler in 1938 may be translated as

466. The historical significance of November 11, 1918.

467. A scientist doing research is a .... The word begins with 'b'.

468. The most dangerous country in the world, according to Pervez Musharraf, in March 2011. Cuba/ India/ Pakistan/ Afghanistan.

469. The 14th point in 'The Fourteen Points' proposed by Woodrow Wilson dealt with

470. Lasalgaon is Asia's biggest

471. The economist who wrote "Fault Lines"

472. The first motor bike was developed in 1885. It was named 'Reitwagen' in German. It means

473. Number of foreigners enrolled in Chinese universities this year.

474. Kosovo declared independence from .... in 2008.

475. A Nobel laureate who was premier of France 11 times

476. The country known as 'Africa's Last Eden'

477. Father of Pakistan's bomb

478. The Iranian filmmaker banned from film making for 20 years

479. Tahrir square in Cairo made news in January. What does 'tahrir' mean?

480. Where was the first light house constructed?

481. International Mother Language Day falls on

482. The first jurist to state that it is better that the guilty escape than the innocent be punished

483. What is FMD?

484. There are 200 .... in a carat

485. To which state did Anant Pai of *Amar Chitra Katha* fame belong?

486. Japan relies on its nuclear plants to provide what per cent of its energy needs?

487. The only country in the world with cases of urban polio

488. 'Friends of Grameen', a Paris-based organisation to promote micro credit is headed by this former President of

Ireland

489. The most populous Commonwealth country

490. The Earth's twin

491. In which state is the Bhakra Dam?

492. Antrix Corporation Ltd. is the commercial wing of the

493. Lara Dutta's husband

494. The city that Maharashtra wants designated as the national tiger capital

495. Female literacy in India in 1951

496. The first Indian to reach North Pole and South Pole

497. The D-shaped Ocean

498. Who was known as the Saint of Paunar

499. The first Asian country to hold general elections

500. The organisation which has its headquarters in Belur

501. The Indian President who was re-elected

502. Which district is the smaller of the two - Bilaspur in Himachal Pradesh or Bilaspur in Chhattisgarh?

503. Chhattisgarh and Karnataka have a district each of the same name. Which district?

504. The first British muslim woman to represent UK at Miss Universe contest

505. Neville Maxwell's famous book on Indo-China relations

506. Total number of fours in 2011 World Cup

507. Which branch of Indian armed forces has most women in percentage?

508. The first batsman to score five centuries in the World Cup

509. The number of Indian tax payers above 80

510. Which Indian state has 697 engineering colleges, with 183,169 seats - the highest for any state?

511. The Hong-Kong born daughter of a British charity worker is one of the highest grossing Bollywood stars

512. Nepal's first President R.B. Yadav is a former

513. Wikipedia was Jimmy Wales' second attempt at creating a free encyclopedia for everyone. The first was a failure. What was it called?

514. The computer scare at the turn of the millennium

515. ICC is based in (London /Abu Dhabi / Dubai)

516. Indian ambassador to Russia

517. How old was Divya Prakash Pandey when she was awarded a degree in the craft and design course from IGNOU in March, 2011?

ANSWERS

450. The Netherlands; 451. Belmopan; 452. stolport; 453. narrows; 454. olive oil; 455. mixed marriage; 456. Marco Polo; 457. India; 458. 4 p.c.; 459. Harold Macmillan; 460. jet.; 461. WWI; 462. Former Pak President Pervez Musharraf; 463. pupil; 464. patent clerk; 465. the night of broken glass; 466. WWI was declared over; 467. boffin; 468. Afghanistan; 469. the establishment of the League of Nations; 470. onion market; 471. Raghuram Rajan; 472. Riding Car; 473. 265,090; 474. Serbia; 475. Aristide Briand; 476. Gabon; 477. A.Q. Khan; 478. Jafer Panahi; 479. liberation; 480. at Port of Alexandria built by Ptolemy II of Egypt in 3rd BC; 481. Feb 21; 482. Sir John Fortescue; 483. foot-and-mouth disease', a devastating livestock disease; 484. milligrams; 485. Karnataka; 486. 30; 487. Angola; 488. Mary Robinson; 489. India; 490. Venus; 491. Himachal Pradesh; 492. ISRO; 493. Mahesh Bhupati; 494. Nagpur; 495. 8.86%; 496. Ajesh Bajaj; 497. The Arctic; 498. Vinoba Bhave; 499. India; 500. Ramakrishna Mission; 501. Rajendra Prasad; 502. The one in Himachal; 503. Bijapur; 504. Shanna Bhukhari; 505. *India's China War*; 506. 1901; 507. Air Force; 508. Sachin; 509. 5000; 510. Andhra Pradesh; 511. Katrina Kaif; 512. physician; 513. Nupedia; 514. Y2K; 515. Dubai; 516. Ajai Malhotra; 517. 61/2 years.

When the Cockpit Caught Fire

In Jan., 1967, Virgil Grisson, Edward White and Roger Chaffee died during a practice countdown for Apollo I when the cockpit caught fire. The Apollo programme was delayed for 18 months.

The Papal Call to Space

The 12 astronauts circling the Earth received a blessing from the Pope Benedict XVI in May, 2011. It was the first ever papal call to space.

518. South Africans whose family originally came from the Netherlands

519. What is common to these names: Africa, America, Antarctica. They begin with the same letter. Anything more?

520. How many miles above the earth is the International Space Station?

521. Swa-rig-pa is Tibetan

522. Warfalla is the largest tribe in which country?

523. What is carried in a body bag?

524. A hendecagon has how many sides?

525. Mizoram's Serchhip district made news as the district with the

526. The 200th man to walk in space

527. Name given to a repetitive strain injury, resulting from widespread use of a hand-held device

528. Agastya Sen is the lead character of Upamanyu Chatterjee's first novel
....

529. The first woman cadet of AFMC to receive three top honours: Sword of Honour, Presidents Gold Medal and the Kalinga trophy

530. $10,000 invested in Berkshire Hathaway in 1991 was worth how much in March 2011?

531. The first Indian state to announce free dole for the unemployed

532. The average net worth of India's billionaires

533. No. of India's billionaires (55 / 155 / 555/ 1555)

534. The god of fire in Roman mythology

535. The famous novel that was completed in 1777 under the title 'First Impressions'

536. In Greek legend, the king of Cyprus who fell in love with an ivory statue he had carved

537. Its ears are about one fourth of its body size. Which animal, part of the dog family, are we talking about?

538. Both male and female African elephants have tusks. True or False

539. One-hump camels

540. A political party of India has the initials of the name of a former CM in its name. Name the party.

541. The world's highest restaurant

542. Language into which some matter is being translated.

543. Harry Wesley who held about 460 patents is the chemist who is best known for his invention of

544. The United States' largest civilian employer

545. The European country with the largest Muslim population

546. Which War is also known as Saltpeter War?

547. SBI accounts form nearly (a quarter / two thirds / a half) of the banking business in India.

548. Expand IAC, in relation to Anna Hazare's anti-corruption movement

549. The worst natural calamity that a rich Asian nation has suffered in many years

550. The Prakash Jha film about an enthusiastic sports teacher

551. What is known as The War Between the States'?

552. What does a fabulist do ?

553. The statement in the US constitution that protects freedom of speech and religion

554. What is Yakuza? The Japanese ....

555. Saltpeter is a (military general / mineral/ town in Chile /mountain)

556. The mid-80s TV series that gave us characters who played cricket

557. The 2008 Chinese Olympic stadium was known as

558. The first Indian to win the Merlin Award

559. Cisse Mariam Kaidama is the first fe-

male prime minister of

560. Whose last book was about earth-worms?

561. What are these: Xstrata's Brunswick in Canada and Minmetals Resource's Century in Australia?

562. Complete the lines of Edgan Allan Poe: "To the glory that was Greece And the .... that was Rome"

563. A key that will open several different locks

564. Find the one that doesn't belong to the group: moccasins, loafer, mule, shindies, sneakers.

565. Chelsea's billionaire owner

566. Who created the first exclusively Afri-kaner government in South Africa?

567. The American President who twice married Rachel Donelson, a wealthy divorcee.

568. How many siblings did the first British Prime Minister Robert Walpole have?

569. Who among these was a research chemist: Ian Smith / Tony Blair / Wil-liam Hague / Margaret Thatcher?

570. The other name of the State of the Vatican City?

571. The only US president to share the na-tion's birthday

572. Which expression is correct: spice and span, spick and kick, clean and span, spick and span ?

573. Which belongs to the group known as 'giant planets': Mars, Venus, Mercury, Saturn?

574. A bursar in a college is a (pillar/ trea-surer/ hall / lecture)

575. Angina pectoris is sudden pain in

576. Graham Greene's first novel

577. Sawbones is slang for (a surgeon / coffins / bonemeal)

578. What is common to Jacques Kallis, Shane Warne, Andrew Flintoff, Muttiah Muralitharan and Sachin Tendulkar?

579. 'Veep' is informal usage for

580. The prefaces to his plays were pub-lished separately. Who is this Nobel winning playwright?

581. The curriculum of IIM-A is modelled

according to that of

582. The British poet who died of blood poisoning on a hospital ship

583. The word candidate comes from the Roman 'candidatus' which means ...., as someone would have been if they were seeking office.

584. The English footballer who moved to Newcastle in 1996 for a world record transfer fee of £15 mn.

ANSWERS

518. Boers; 519. They end with the same letter; 520. 220; 521. medicine; 522. Lib-ya; 523. a dead body; 524. 11; 525. high-est literacy rate, 98.76 p.c.; 526. Col. Alvin Drew; 527. a Blackberry thumb; 528. *Eng-lish, August*; 529. Shikha Awasthi; 530. $188,903, a return of 16%; 531. Goa; 532. $4.5 bn; 533. 55; 534. Vulcan; 535. *Pride and Prejudice;* 536.Pygmalion; 537. The fennec; 538. True; 539. Drom-edary camels; 540. AINRC of Puducherry, NR = N. Rangaswamy; 541. Atmosphere, 1350' in the sky, on the 122nd floor of Burj Khalifa, Dubai; 542. target language; 543. Super Glue; 544. Walmart; 545. France; 546. The War of the Pacific; 547. a quar-ter; 548. India Against Corruption; 549. The March 11, 2011 quake and tsunami in Japan; 550. 'Hip Hip Hurray'; 551. Ameri-can Civil War; 552. tell stories; 553. The First Amendment; 554. mafia; 555. min-eral; 556. Bodyline; 557. the Bird's Nest; 558. P.C. Sorcar Jr.; 559. Mali; 560. Charles Darwin; 561. Zinc mines; 562. grandeur; 563. skeleton key; 564. shindies; 565. Ro-man Abramovich; 566. D.F. Malan, PM, 1948-54; 567. Andrew Jackson; 568. 16; 569. Margaret Thatcher; 570. The Holy See; 571. Calvin Coolidge; 572. spick and span; 573. Saturn; 574. treasurer; 575. the chest; 576. *The Man Within*; 577. a surgeon; 578. Wisden Cricketers; 579. vice president; 580. George Bernard Shaw; 581. Harvard Business School; 582. Rupert Brooke; 583. 'clothed in white'; 584. Alan Shearer.

Battle of the Sexes

Billie-Jean King, the US tennis player defeated the 55-year-old former men's champion Bobby Riggs in the famous 'battle of the sexes'.

Kindergarten

Friedrich Froebel of Germany coined the term kindergarten, a school for children aged five.

585. World's top two handset makers
586. What is known as the Bible of Cricket?
587. Mikado was a title used for
588. In a buyer's market (a. the supply is small b. the conditions are favourable to the seller c. prices are high d. prices are low)
589. Kamban's Ramayana is written in?
590. In Psychoanalysis, a fantasy in which a person thinks he is the child of parents of a higher social class.
591. 'oodles' denotes (little / very little / zero / a great amount)
592. The number of miles a tyre will run before it wears out is called
593. Bernard Shaw's play *Pygmalion* was turned into the musical
594. What is the 'Beautiful Game'?
595. The earliest full-length Western
596. Who is the fifth most translated writer in the world.
597. The winner of which prize is awarded a case of Bollinger champagne?
598. The South-East Asian country with the highest percentage of obese citizens
599. J. Thomas & Company is the world's oldest auctioneer in what commodity?
600. Dwarfs are small stars - the brightest are (blue /red) dwarfs.
601. What has long been known as the 'dogstar'?
602. What is Indy500?
603. Which of these is a crop: days/ dates / months / years?
604. Zanzibar was separated from (Tanzania / Oman / Muscat) in 1856
605. To which country was Oman's city-state Gwadar ceded in 1958?
606. Both indoor volleyball and beach volleyball are played at the Olympics. True or False?
607. A maiden aunt is an aunt who has not
608. Extra pay for doing work that is dangerous.
609. World's largest foods company.
610. Barack Obama defeated Senator John McCain of .... who was making his second bid for the presidency.
611. Who created a foundation to award a a$1.6 mn. prize for 'progress in religion'?
612. Whose play of the same name mad the expression ' the fifth column' popular?
613. The period Mahatma Gandhi's 'The Story of My Experiments with Truth? dealt with
614. Born in Allahabad, grew up in Sudan, lived in Delhi, Hyderabad, England. Now in New York. Her motherland: Kerala. Name this poet.
615. *Keeping the Faith: Memoirs of a Parliamentarian* is written by
616. The author of 'The Armies of the Night' and 'The Executioner's Song', both Pulitzer prize winners
617. Who in Buckingham Palace shared his birthday with an Indian Prime Minister?
618. Cotton price is quoted for a 'candy'. How much is a 'candy'?
619. Britain's first stamp without the Queen's portrait came out on what occasion?
620. Jacqueline Kennedy's maiden name
621. What did Satya Sai Baba mean by 'my previous body'?
622. The only foreign country Satya Sai Baba visited
623. 'estival' relates to (a. festivals b. east c. digestion d. summer)
624. Which is equal to Rs. 45000 cr.?
a. $45 bn. b. £15,000 bn c. $10 bn. d. $1000 bn.
625. SAIC is China's largest

Women's Tennis Association

Tennis legend Billie-Jean King was cofounder and first president of the Women's Tennis Association. In 1974, she founded the famous World Team Tennis, with her husband Larry King.

626. The Anglo-Iranian Oil Company is now known as
627. 'Best-ball' refers to a type of team competition in golf. What is 'better-ball'?
628. The full name of English lexicographer Fowler
629. The name 'Akashvani' for All India Radio was suggested by
630. Which is true K.L. Saigal a. recorded 185 songs b. never acted c. acted only in 'Devdas'
631. The author of 'The Emperor of All Maladies: A Biography of Cancer'
632. Queenbury Rules apply to which sport?
633. Prince Charles set a record on Apr. 20, 2011. How?
634. The former body builder who became a film star and then a Governor
635. The Norwegian writer in the latest Cannes Film Festival jury
636. The country that set the record as the one with the longest time without government, in Apr. 2011
637. The oral pill aimed at preventing HIV infection in African women, the trial of which has now been halted
638. Who got the title of Prince of Wales just a month after his birth?
639. The Mecca of Indian cricket
640. A girl who broadcasts live pictures of herself over the World Wide Web
641. The Pope who was 'a skiing cardinal'
642. Who designed the Padma Awards?
643. The first foreign country to issue a Gandhi stamp
644. 1 mn. yen is how many US dollars?
645. 'Timbuktu', meaning a place very far away, comes from the name of a town in
646. Grand Slam titles won by Martina Navratilova
647. What is OWN? The person's name is in it.
648. The boy who never grew up. Who authored the Peter Pan story?
649. Which of these is a disease: sprout / gout / gourd / grout?
650. The minimum you need in a private Swiss bank account
651. The Anna Hazare movement against corruption which spearheaded the Lok Pal Bill agitation.
652. To type copy so as to leave two full spaces between lines
653. Where is India's geophysical observatory for studying earthquake precursors located?

ANSWERS

585. Nokia and Samsung; 586. Wisden; 587. the emperor of Japan; 588. d; 589. d; 589. Tamil; 590. family romance; 591. a great amount; 592. mileage; 593. *My Fair Lady*; 594. football; 595. *The Great Train Robbery*; 596. Enid Blyton; 597. The Wodehouse Prize; 598. Malaysia; 599. tea; 600. blue; 601. sirius; 602. Indianapolis 500, the automobile race; 603. dates; 604. Oman; 605. Pakistan; 606. True; 607. married; 608. danger money; 609. Nestle; 610. Arizona; 611. John Templeton; 612. Ernest Hemingway; 613. 1869-1921; 614. Meena Alexander; 615. Somnath Chatterjee; 616. Norman Mailer; 617. Prince Charles, Nov. 14, with Jawaharlal Nehru; 618. 356 kg; 619. Mahatma Gandhi's 100th birth anniversary; 620. Jacqueline Lee Bouvier; 621. Shirdi Baba; 622. Uganda; 623. d; 624. c; 625. domestic carmaker; 626. British Petroleum; 627. The same as best-ball; 628. Henry Watson Fowler; 629. Rabindranath Tagore; 630. a; 631. Siddhartha Mukherjee; 632. Boxing; 633. By becoming the longest-waiting heir apparent in British history - 59 years, 2 months, 14 days; 634. Arnold Schwarzenegger; 635. Linn Ullmann; 636. Belgium; 637. PrEP- pre-exposure prophylaxis; 638. King Edward VII; 639. Eden Gardens; 640. camgirl; 641. John Paul II, 642.Nandalal Bose, 643. USA; 644. 12,000; 645. Mali; 646. 59; 647. Oprah Winfrey Network; 648. J. M. Barrie; 649. gout; 650. a million dollars; 651. IAC. India Against Corruption; 652. to triple-space; 653. Atop an isolated hill in Ghuttu in Uttarakhand.

Gaypride Parade | On June 26, 2011, the world's largest gay pride parade was held in Sao Paulo, Brazil. Organizers put the attendance at 4 million.

Two Doctors for 100,000 People

In Jharkhand and Chhattisgarh there are only two doctors for 100,000 people. The Indian average is 6 doctors for every 10,000 people, and the global average 15.

654. What is common to Deepak Obhrai, Devinder Shory, Tina Oppal and Neena Grewal?

655. What does a personnel carrier carry?

656. The first Indian company to list on an American bourse

657. The Jnanpith award winner who authored 'Prathama Pratishuthi'

658. Ravana was a skilled player of which musical instrument?

659. In a restaurant, who helps customers to choose wines?

660. Which of these is a bird: crush, thrush, rabble, merino

661. India's oldest credit information bureau

662. A dog that helps find birds that have been shot

663. The last stop on a bus route

664. The sugar (pot/ jar / bowl / cup) in the tea set was missing.

665. Advances offered at a lower rate of interest for the first few years, after which rates are re-set higher

666. The countries covered by the acronym PIGS

667. An open space in a forest. Begin with 'c'.

668. Who were the first to use tanks?

669. What prize did Wole Soyinka win in 1986?

670. An atomic bomb or a hydrogen bomb

671. A five time Mr. Universe and seven-time Mr. Olympia

672. This 71-year-old politician was an Assembly member at age 27 and Chief Minister at 38?

673. Mint Street' stands for (RBI/ Planning Commission/ Udyog Bhavan / PMO)

674. Brigadier Sawar Bhawani Singh, the last titular Maharaja of Jaipur, was the High Commissioner to .... from 1994 to 1997

675. The International Space Station (ISS) is a collaboration between

676. How long did the fire of AD 64 that destroyed Rome last

677. The company that Herman J Hollerith started in 1860 eventually became what?

678. The Great Hunger in Ireland, 1845-48, is also known as

679. The world's second most populous Muslim country

680. The host city for the 2014 Winter Olympics

681. Which of these was a nickname of this Argentinian physician?
a. Che b. Guevara c. Ernesto

682. Bond wrote 'A Bear Called Paddington' in 1958. What was the writer's first name?

683. They were called 'landships'. Sometimes they were referred to as water-carriers? What are we talking about?

684. Who was the 'Wizard of Menlo Park'?

685. Whitcomb L. Judson's 1893 invention?

686. All the competitors (male only) in ancient Olympic Games were a. farmers b. foreigners c. naked d. soldiers

687. Who invented the safety razor?

688. Jawaharlal Nehru's constituency in the 1952 elections

689. The first communications satellite, launched by the US in 1958

690. The world's largest amphibian

691. Because it carries its eggs around on its back until they are ready to hatch, this toad is called

692. Who won Best Actor Oscar posthumously?

693. The march that lasted 370 days

694. Who was Achmed Sukarno?

No Drugs, Yes Death

Swaziland is short of AIDS drugs. In July 2011, the hospitals were to run out of anti retroviral drugs in two months. It was feared that this would cause the death of 60,000 people.

695. Cliff Richard was born in (London / Bombay / New York / Lucknow)

696. When was the tank first used in battle?

697. The title "Who's' Afraid of Virginia Woolf' is an adaptation of the nursery rhyme

698. The play 'Who's Afraid of Virgina Woolf' was once performed as "Who's afraid of Franz Kafka". Where?

699. The mountain system that runs from the Arctic to the Caspian Sea

700. Actor Ashok Kumar's two famous brothers

701. Kaziranga Reserve Forest was declared a game sanctuary in 1916 to save

702. Karnataka's second largest city

703. The world-famous university on river Isis

704. How old was Daniel Defoe when he wrote 'Robinson Crusoe'?

705. The hedonistic philosophy: 'eat, drink and ...., for tomorrow we may die.'

706. The main compound used in 'smelling salt'

707. Who were the men and women that accompanied Noah and his wife in the Noah's Ark?

708. *Matters of Discretion* is the autobiography of which former Indian Prime Minister?

709. How did Bin Laden's father die?

710. A small round boat: coracle / oracle / cornetto/ cornice.

711. Canada has (2, 4, 6, 8) time zones.

712. A hatter (hates all / is hated by all / sells hats / scores three goals in one game).

713. Tier-6 centres, according to RBI definition, have a population below

714. How old is the 'I have a Dream' speech?

715. The first country to elect an animal rights party to parliament

716. Who is said to have described compound interest as the eighth wonder of the world?

717. In Spanish, it is MILA. What is it?

718. Who started the PEN World Voices Festival?

719. Where did Osama bin Laden graduate in civil engineering?

720. The number that perfectly divides 333,666 and 999 (23, 27, 37, 43)

721. In a reverse-charge phone call, the payment is made by the person who .... the call.

722. In 2008, who did 100 m. in 9.72 seconds?

ANSWERS

654. Sitting Indo-Canadian MPs; **655.** soldiers; **656.** Infosys Technologies; **657.** Ashapurna Devi; **658.** the Veena; **659.** wine waiter; **660.**thrush; **661.** CIBIL; **662.** gun dog; **663.** terminus; **664.** bowl; **665.** teaser loans; **666.** Portugal, Iceland, Greece, Spain; **667.** clearing; **668.** the British; **669.** Nobel for Literature; **670.** a nuclear-bomb; **671.** Arnold Schwarzenegger; **672.** Sharad Pawar; **673.** RBI; **674.**Brunei; **675.** the US, Russia, Canada, Japan and ten European countries; **676.** 6 days; **677.** IBM; **678.** Potato Famine; **679.** Pakistan; **680.** Sochi; **681.** a; **682.** Michael; **683.** Tanks; **684.** Thomas Alva Edison; **685.** Zip fastener; **686.** c; **687.** King Camp Gillette; **688.** Phulpur; **689.** Score; **690.** the giant salamander. Grows to 5 ft.; **691.** the midwife toad; **692.** Peter Finch; **693.** The Long March, 1934; **694.** First President of Indonesia; **695.** Lucknow; **696.** 1916; **697.** "Who's afraid of the big bad wolf?"; **698.** Prague; **699.** Ural; **700.** Kishore Kumar, Anoop Kumar; **701.** the Indian greater one-horned rhino; **702.** Mysore; **703.** Oxford; **704.** 60 years; **705.** be merry; **706.** ammonium carbonate; **707.** Their three sons and their wives; **708.** I.K. Gujral; **709.** in a plane crash; **710.** coracle; **711.** 6; **712.** sells hats; **713.** 5000 people; **714.** 49 years; **715.** the Netherlands; **716.** Albert Einstein; **717.** Integrated Latin American Market, uniting Chile, Colombia and Peru; **718.** Salman Rushdie; **719.** King Abdul Aziz University; **720.** 37; **721.** receives; **722.**Usain Bolt.

A New High-Speed Train

A new Beijing-to-Shanghai high-speed train opened to the public officially on July 1. Top speed of the train is 305 km per hour.

Emmy Award

It is an annual award for outstanding achievement in US television. Its name is taken from the nickname 'immy' for the image orthicon, a television camera tube.

723. There was a long queue at the .... Complete the sentence. The first letter of the four-letter word is 't' and the last 'l'.

724. A polysemous word has more than one

725. The word that refers to the comparison of relative sizes of different parts of animals.

726. The man who rose from a government servant in the AG's office to a leading film personality

727. In the Sai Baba legend, what is the significance of Mandya in Karnataka?

728. It didn't matter whether a cat was black or white so long as it caught mice. Whose words?

729. The first Indian winner of Pulitzer

730. Where is Asia's largest tulip garden?

731. A male bee that doesn't work

732. Who donated $108 mn. to Sai Baba's trust?

733. Pony up' means a . purchase b. keep a horse c. pay d. on horseback.

734. The metal gauge that measures the length and width of one's feet

735. Cargill is a global .... conglomerate.

736. (Rural / Urban) areas account for about 70 p.c. of India's annual gold consumption.

737. The last sale price of a Stradivarius violin put on for auction to benefit earthquake victims

738. The money that belonged to Libya's Gaddafi and former rulers of Egypt ad Tunisia, and was frozen in Swiss bank accounts.

739. The biggest metropolis in the Western Hemisphere

740. The river that flows through four capitals in Europe.

741. The first woman from North-east to climb the Everest

742. Number of foreigners residing in China

743. The country with the largest cattle, buffalo and goat population.

744. Age of consent is the age at which the law allows people.

745. An animal that has been killed by a car on the road is a

746. Robben Island is where Nelson Mandela spent much of his 27 years of incarceration. 'Robben' is Dutch for

747. White-collar crime is crime relating to the

748. The medical condition of being a dwarf

749. The city that accounts for about 65 p.c. shoes supplied in India

750. Who is Dallas Wiens?

751. Zugspitze is Germany's

752. 'Footy' is informal word for

753. Take away 4 of its 5 letters. The pronunciation of this world remains the same.

754. What is 'Halakhah?

755. British anthropologist L.B. Leakey was born in

756. Projected population of Tokyo in 2020

757. Pedal pushers are: a. a kind of bicycle b. a toy train c. apparel d. migrants

758. Osama bin Laden's last wife was from (Afghanistan / Pakistan)

759. Peg leg: a. a lame person b. treatment of the feet c. seller of illegal drugs d. artificial leg.

760. President Obama was sworn in to office on whose personal copy of the Bible?

761. What on a barrister represents the two tablets on which Moses was given the Ten Commandments?

762. Who described the British parliament as the 'Mother of Parliaments?

Two Cousins

Were the two Roosevelts who were US Presidents related? Theodore and Franklin were distant cousins.

763. The Jewish Sabbath is on Saturday, as was the (Romans'/Greeks')
764. Sikhs were (present/absent) at the Parliament of World Religions in Chicago in 1893.
765. Okapi's scientific name Okapia johnstoni is given in honour of
766. Host to the first Youth Olympics
767. Who wrote *All Round View*?
768. How old was Pele when he scored his first World Cup goal?
769. The National Institute of Naturopathy is in
770. The Beatle whose records were burned because he claimed that the Beatles' popularity matched that of Jesus Christ.
771. History's most expensive painting, according to Guinness World Records
772. Angkor was the capital of which kings?
773. What in Finland is known as 'Eduskunta'?
774. There are four Inns of Court in London. The term 'inn' derives from what?
775. A juror in Britain is aged between .... and 70.
776. (Zinc/Copper/Iron) helps the skin repair itself.
777. Liberal Party of Britain is now called
778. The country whose parliament met six metres under water
779. The first Indian to be elected President of WAN-IFRA
780. The year Ram Mohan Roy landed in England
781. The first Marathi newspaper
782. Darjeeling was obtained by the East India Company from the King of ....
783. Kapoor Singh, an advisor to Maharaja of Patiala, coined the word .... referring to an independent Sikh state.
784. The first Indian airport to acquire the status of international airport after independence.
785. The second Howrah bridge was officially named .... in Oct, 1992
786. How old was Sushmita Sen when crowned Miss Universe?
787. Clocks all over India were set to Indian Standard Time in year
788. Who died on Feb. 22, 1944 in Aga Khan palace at Pune?
789. Manikarnika was the original name of

ANSWERS

723. till; 724. meaning; 725. zoometry; 726. K. Balachander; 727. it is the village in which Sai Baba said his successor or Prema Sai would be born some years after his death; 728. Deng Xiaoping; 729. Gobind Behari Lal; 730. Jammu; 731. drone; 732. the American Isaac Tigrett, co-founder of the Hard Rock Cafe; 733. c; 734. Brannock Device; 735. agribusiness; 736. Rural; 737. $10mn.; 738. $960 mn.; 739. Mexico City; 740. The Danube. Cities are: Vienna, Bratislava, Budapest & Belgrade; 741. Tine Mena; 742. 593,832 in May 2011; 743. India; 744. to agree to have sex; 745. roadkill; 746. 'seal'; 747. professional occupations; 748. dwarfism; 749. Agra; 750. first full face transplant recipient; 751. highest mountain; 752. football; 753. queue; 754. Jewish law; 755. Kenya; 756. 37 mn; 757. c; 758. Pakistan; 759. d; 760. Abraham Lincoln; 761. a double-tabbed linen band that is used as a collar; 762. John Bright; 763. Romans'; 764. absent; 765. Sir Harry Johnston; 766. Singapore; 767. Imran Khan; 768. 17 yrs, 7 months, 23 days; 769. Pune; 770. John Lennon; 771. Garcon a la Pipe; 772. The Khmer; 773. the parliament; 774. the accommodate where barristers lived; 775. 18; 776. zinc; 777. the Liberal Democrats; 778. The Maldives; 779. Jacob Mathew; 780. 1831; 781. Bombay Darpan; 782. Sikkim; 783. Khalistan; 784. Thiruvananthapuram; 785. Vidyasagar Setu; 786. 18; 787. 1965; 788. Kasturba Gandhi; 789. Rani Lakshmi of Jhansi.

| The Water-Babies | Charles Kingsley's popular children's book *The Water-Babies* was inspired by his acceptance of Darwin's theory of evolution. |

Star Clusters

French astronomer Charles Messier was the first to compile a systematic catalogue of nebulae and star clusters.

790. The world's longest-serving democratically elected Communist government was where and how long?
791. The CM who came to power for the third consecutive time in May, 2011?
792. The average lifespan of a cow
793. Which war saw Gandhiji joining a voluntary ambulance unit?
794. The weight of INS Shivalik, the first indigenously built stealth warship
795. The surname of Harsha, the first test tube baby of India
796. Kathryn Bigelow's Oscar winning Iraq war classic
797. Who among these was blind: Swami Dayananda Saraswati, Swami Virjananda, Ram Mohan Roy?
798. Ochterlony Movement (later known as Shahid Minar, in Calcutta, was built to the memory of the hero of which campaign?
799. Mythology: Shiva's bow
800. The Nobel laureate of Indian origin born in Lahore
801. A President who had been his country's Ambassador to China and USA
802. India's first Deputy PM
803. The physicist who spoke nine languages including Latin by the age of 16
804. 'Serendipity' is a word coined by
805. The name given to Nazi Germany's invasion of Russia on June 22,1941
806. The American counterpart to Penguin titles
807. Why is Library of Congress in Washington, founded in 1800, named so?
808. Few pigs are found in Islamic countries. True or False?
809. Camel-hair brushes are made from the hair from tails of which animal?
810. A two-word phrase meaning 'all the oceans of the world'.
811. India's annual budget
812. The number of children Gandhiji had
813. The life expectancy of a blue whale
814. The number of wings on a housefly
815. The number of petals on a buttercup
816. The number of arms on a squid
817. Which weighs more: a bird's skeleton or its feathers?
818. Number of universities is around 1000, each with 25,000 -30,000 students. The country?
819. No. of Indians in the university system
820. Abbotabad, near Islamabad where bin Laden was killed, is named after
821. The PhDs produced by China in a year
822. The first native state to issue its own postage stamp
823. Chairperson of the National Commission for Women
824. Darfur in Sudan is the size of this European country.
825. The country with the second-largest number of patents
826. How much was celebrity couple David and Victoria Beckham worth in May 2011?
827. The first American astronaut to be honoured, all by himself, on a stamp
828. Number of Indians below 30
829. Copyright expires how many years after an author's death?
830. This Japanese religion has no founder, text, or god?
831. This country has one lawyer per 390 citizens
832. Peel P50 is the world's smallest
833. Population of Rome in 133 BC
834. The Commonwealth of Australia, including the island of Tasmania, is nearly as large as (Africa / Europe / India)
835. During emergency, the Governor can act regardless of the advice of his ministers but must act according to the directions of the
836. The largest presidential suite is the Villa Salaambo attached to Hasdrubal

Thakssa Hotel, covering 16,597 sq.ft. Where is it?

837. The time during which the earth makes a complete revolution on its axis in respect of the fixed stars

838. Wheat, gram, maize, mustard. Which is not a Rabi crop?

839. What post did Kurt Waldheim assume in 1972?

840. The 3911-metre long bridge linking Honshu and Shikoku. It is the longest suspension bridge

841. The archipelago that became the 185th UN member

842. The prize for which US song writer Burt Bachavach was selected in 2001

843. USA's highest civilian honour

844. Magsaysay Award winner Aruna Roy is from which state?

845. The last known WWI combat veteran

846. A meeting to discuss an urgent situation is a council

847. The Asian member of G-8

848. Which region is referred to as MENA?

849. The so-called Unabomber who waged a parcel-bomb campaign in the US

850. Mt. Everest is 332 higher than the technically difficult Mount

851. The record set by policewoman Sushma and husband Vikas

852. How long is the Giro d'Italia bike race?

853. A shoo-in (a. is expected to win easily b. has lost an election c. has just joined a race)

854. Willard Boyle is the Nobel laureate who invented

855. What does 'Libreville' (capital of Gabon) mean?

856. The city that was capital of Hungary for over two centuries. Today it is the capital of another country.

857. USA's southern-most town

858. The constellation that covers 3.16% of the whole sky

859. Eritrea's capital that was formerly an Ethiopian city

860. Whose remains (he died in 1904) were removed to Jerusalem after the creation of the Jewish State and entombed on a hill west of the city

861. The celebrity who drowned in his swimming pool after a drug overdose in 1969?

ANSWERS

790. West Bengal, 35 years; **791.** Tarun Gogoi, Assam; **792.** 22 years; **793.** Anglo-Boer War in South Africa; **794.** 6000 tonnes; **795.** Chawda; **796.** *The Hurt Locker*; **797.** Swami Virijananda; **798.** Nepal Campaign; **799.** Pinaka; **800.** Subrahmanyan Chandrasekhar; **801.** K. R. Narayanan; **802.** Sardar Vallabhbhai Patel; **803.** Thomas Young; **804.** Horace Walpole; **805.** Operation Barbarossa; **806.** Pocket Books; **807.** Originally founded to make books available to Members of Congress; **808.** True; **809.** squirrels; **810.** seven seas; **811.** Rs. 12 lakh crore; **812.** four; **813.** 90 years; **814.** 4, or two pairs; **815.** 5; **816.** 10; **817.** feathers; **818.** China; **819.** 13 m.; **820.** Major James Abbott, the colonial officer of the Bengal Artillery, administrator of the town; **821.** 50,000, the highest in the world; **822.** Kathiawar of Saurashtra; **823.** Yasmeen Abrar; **824.** France; **825.** China; **826.** £165 mn.; **827.** Alan Shepard; **828.** 650 m.; **829.** 70; **830.** Shinto; **831.** USA; **832.** street-legal car; **833.**1100,000; **834.** Europe; **835.** President; **836.** In Tunisia; **837.** Sidereal Day; **838.** Maize; **839.** UN Secretary General; **840.** Akashi Kaiyo Bridge; **841.** Palau; **842.** Polar Music Prize; **843.** Presidential Medal of Freedom; **844.** Rajasthan; **845.** Claude Choules; **846.** of war; **847.** Japan; **848.** Middle East and South Africa; **849.** Theodore Kaczynski; **850.** Lhotse; **851.** first Indian couple to climb together to the top of Everest; **852.** 3523 km; **853.** a; **854.** the digital eye; **855.** free town; **856.** Bratislava; **857.** Hawaii; **858.** Hydra- the Sea Serpent; **859.** Asmara; **860.** Theodore Herzel, founder of modern Zionism; **861.** Brian Jones of Rolling Stones.

A Claim of 3000 Patents

There is a Japanese inventor who claims to hold a world record of 3000 patents. He is the inventor of the floppy disk in 1950 – Yoshiro Nakamats. His claim, however, has been refuted.

Crime Rate

Crime rate is defined as crime per 100,000 of population.

862. The Chief Minister of this State died in 1965 when his plane was shot down at the border
863. Where did Annie Besant die?
864. Georgetown, Guyana's capital, was renamed in 1812 in honour of
865. Representation in US Senate is fixed at how many senators per state?
866. Which country's parliament is officially known as 'Majlis-e-Shoora'?
867. Who are known as 'parliamentari'?
868. The British merchant who was governor of Madras
869. The first Asian to become the Dean of Harvard Business School
870. First woman CM of Tamil Nadu
871. Who is referred to as India's 'missile woman'?
872. First Indian PM to win a seat from outside UP
873. Where in London was the Mahatma Gandhi statue installed in 1968?
874. This two-letter word can mean 'die'
875. The Bretton Woods duo
876. The Asian country that had no currency or roads until the 1960s.
877. Founder of the NGO globally known as Barefoot College with its hq. in a poor Rajasthan village
878. Actor Aamir Khan is reported to have a knack for solving the Rubik's cube in around how many seconds / minutes?
879. It has been the practice to have (an American/ a European /an Australian / an Arab) as the Managing Director of IMF
880. He discontinued his engineering studies at Stanford, USA and took over family business at age 21
881. The state minister who met with his

death in 2011, 7 days after he was sworn in
882. What do people do on Arbor Day?
883. The only woman in the Kerala cabinet is adept at which sport?
884. The chief minister who donates from earnings from auction of his / her paintings
885. Hair that is not chemically treated is called
886. A diet that a bride relies on to lose weight before the wedding day
887. Can dimples be created? (Yes / No)
888. What is common to Sushma Swaraj and Mamata Banerjee?
889. The woman described by *New York Times* as 'India's Mother of Invention'
890. The party that Solomon Bandaranaike founded
891. 29 Afro-Asian nations met here in 1955 for an important conference
892. HUGO was formed in 1988 in Washington D.C. What is HUGO?
893. Fleming is similar to
894. Sir Patrick Geddes, Scottish sociologist and a pioneer of the concept of town planning coined a term meaning area of large urban communities
895. The famous comic strip that was first published in a newspaper in 1950
896. The fur trader who founded a famous university in Montreal
897. Rock musician who organised Live Aid for famine affected areas
898. The principal patron saint of Italy
899. The man who drew 'Flash Gordon' comics
900. The number of elephants in India
901. The number of tuskers in India
902. When is the Halley's comet expected to reappear?
903. Who was known as DSK?
904. 'Rose Bowl' is the newsletter of
905. Expand SRCC
906. Who ordered Pakistan's first nuclear test at Chagal in 1998?
907. A hundred years ago, Hiram Bingham discovered
908. United's young team, England's champions, are known as the Busby Bees,

after their manager

909. Kahuta is Pakistan's main

910. What is 7RCR? It is an important New Delhi address.

911. The meaning of 'Laissez-faire', the mid-19th c. economic doctrine.

912. Women's salaries in France are a. the same as men's b. 20% less than men's c. 10% more than men's

913. Benjamin Hall reminds us of a. Big Ben b. Benjamin Netanyahu c. Benjamin Bailey d. White House

914. Hoofed mammals that walk on their toes are

915. MC Mary Kom won her 5th world boxing champion title where?

916. Lion Mound is a) where Emperor Haile Selassie died b) the site of the battle of Waterloo c) where Napoleon spent his last days d) where David Livingstone was born

917. Which of these is written on the Palestinian passport?
a. The Palestinian State b. The State of Palestine c. The Govt. of Palestine d. The Palestinian Authority

918. Sir Elton John's civil partner David Furnish is a filmmaker / a doctor/ a singer/ a sculptor

919. Hashim Adul Halim was Speaker of West Bengal for how long?

920. For every four students admitted in the IITs in 2011, one is from (which state?)

921. The term 'duck' (a zero score by a batsman) is a shortening of

922. Expand K.D. in law:

923. The Italian biologist Marceilo Malpighi gave his name to the deeper layers of the

924. How long did Pablo Picasso's career last?

925. The acid found in unripe fruit, especially apples

926. Whose government did Chile's Pinochet overthrow in 1973?

927. The centre of the Californian gold rush. The name begins with 'Mother'

928. The Spanish town that holds the annual tomato festival on the last Wednesday of August

929. At what age did Gandhiji first go to England?

930. Richter scale is named after (a person. a town, a country, a wind)

931. The Indian philosopher SN Dasgupta's famous work

932. Major Gen. J. P. Candeth was Military Governor of

933. Where did the last King of Burma, Thibaw, die?

ANSWERS

862. Gujarat; **863.** In Madras; **864.** George III, **865.** two; **866.** Pakistan; **867.** members of Italian parliament; **868.** Thomas Pitt; **869.** Dr. Nitin Nohria; **870.** Janaki Ramachandran; **871.** Tessy Thomas; **872.** Morarji Desai; **873.** Tavistock Square; **874.** go; **875.** IBRD and IMF; **876.** Bhutan; **877.** Sanjit Bunker Roy; **878.** 28 seconds; **879.** a European; **880.** Azim Premji; **881.** Tamil Nadu's Mariam Pitchai; **882.** plant trees; **883.** archery; **884.** Mamata Banerjee; **885.** virgin hair; **886.** briet; **887.** Yes; **888.** First woman CMs of Delhi and W. Bengal, respectively; **889.** Kiran Mazumdar-Shaw; **890.** Sri Lankan Freedom Party; **891.** Bandung; **892.** Human Genome Organisation; **893.** Dutch; **894.** conurbation; **895.** Peanuts; **896.** James McGill; **897.** Bob Geldof; **898.** St. Francis of Assisi; **899.** Alexander G. Raymond; **900.** 25,800; **901.** 1200; **902.** In 2061, 3; **903.** Dominique Strauss Kahn, former IMF head; **904.** Doon School Old Boys Society; **905.** Shri Ram College of Commerce; **906.** Nawaz Sharif, PM; **907.** Machu Picchu; **908.** Matt Busby; **909.** nuclear facility; **910.** 7 Race Course Road; **911.** Leave alone to do; **912.** b; **913.** a; **914.** ungulates; **915.** Haiku, China; **916.** b; **917.**d; **918.** a film-maker; **919.** 29 years; **920.** Andhra Pradesh; **921.** duck's egg; **922.** Known Depredator; **923.** skin; **924.** 75 years; **925.** malic acid; **926.** Allende; **927.** Mother Lode; **928.** Bunol; **929.** 18 years; **930.** a person; **931.** *History of Indian Philosophy*; **932.** Goa; **933.** Ratnagiri Fort in India.

| St. Kitts | Columbus' patron saint was St. Christopher. Saint Kitts, the island, was named after the St. Christopher. The name later shortened to St. Kitts. |

Dracula

Bram Stoker's Dracula is inspired by a Romanian count Vlad Dracul. His castle the Bran Castle is an important tourist site in Romania.

934. The world's tallest (8') statue of a cartoon character

935. Full name of Soviet statesman Brezhnev

936. In 1967 Greece saw the regime of the Greek (Marshals / Colonels / Majors / Captains)

937. William Styron's "*The Confessions of Nat Turner*" was based on the 1831 .... in Virginia.

938. "Le Redoutable" was France's first

939. What was discovered by Hewish and Bell, UK in 1967?

940. The film based on the real-life story of two American criminals in the early 1930s.

941. Hong Kong returned to Chinese sovereignty in the year

942. The two novelists who shook hands after 15 years, in May 2011 - a triumph of the Hay Festival

943. Lionel Messi, Xavi and Andres Iniesta, the three of world's finest footballers, are graduates of

944. The man responsible for stepping up wheat production in a big way in Latin American countries is this Indian who has spent 39 years there.

945. The world's highest battlefield

946. Filling government jobs with one's own loyalists is known as the

947. The first Indian woman to enter a Grand Slam doubles final

948. Baba Ramdev's original name

949. A spiv lives by his

950. The 1973 B R Ishra film *Charitra*'s hero, (a cricketer), and heroine

951. The world's fastest passenger trains are operated by

952. Travel time between Beijing and Shanghai will be cut by the high-speed railway by how much?

953. Spondylitis is the inflammation of the

954. The Chancellor of the University of Wolverhampton

955. What did Stephen Hawking's daughter Lucy co-author with her father?

956. Uddham Singh was hanged in 1940 for killing Punjab Lt. Governor

957. The Indian currency note has value inscribed in how many languages?

958. An incandescent lamp has a life of 1,000 hours while a fluorescent lamp lasts .... hours.

959. The official language of Nagaland

960. Maginot Line is border between

961. Who founded the Indian Statistical Institute at Kolkata?

962. The writer who withdrew from all social contacts at age 23 and lived a life at Amherst

963. What does Capek's play 'R.U.R.' mean?

964. Where is the hill station Pachmarhi?

965. Amole Gupta's 'Stanley Ka Dabba' starred his .... Partho in the lead.

966. The two disciples who were with Gandhiji when he breathed his last

967. The writer who gave us Uncle Tom

968. 20/20 vision is: a) watching cricket b) a t.v. set c) poor visibility d) the ability to see perfectly

969. The Treaty of Versailles was named for

970. The first studio owned and run by Charlie Chaplin, Douglas Fairbanks, Mary Pickford and D.N. Griffith in 1919

971. What made the Uruguayan government proclaim a national holiday in July 1930?

972. The world's youngest religion

973. The famous Indo-Anglian writer trained as an anthropologist at Oxford

974. The Japanese puppet state established in Manchuria in 1932

975. A teeny-bopper is a) girl who watches

TV all the time b) a boy who dislikes girls c) a 10-13 year-old girl, fond of pop music d) a girl who doesn't play any games

976. More than 50 Sikh shrines in India are named after (flowers / trees / birds / animals)

977. The youngest freedom fighter to fast unto death

978. What is known as Yarlung Tsangpo in China?

979. Electromagnetic field is measured in

980. The man who redrew the map of India along linguistic lines

981. The Bank of Sweden established the additional Nobel Prize for economic sciences in 1968. What was the occasion?

982. The Presidential address to the Lok Sabha was telecast for the first time when .... was the President.

983. The first black writer to try to live by his writings

984. Indian cricket's first couple

985. The only country where there is an official ban on women driving

986. The original name given by Batholomew Dias, the Portuguese explorer, to Cape of Good Hope?

987. Remittances from NRIs to India annually

988. How many people in India pay income tax?

989. The queen who had the nickname 'Bloody Mary'

990. Gandhiji's last confinement was in the

991. Birla House, where Gandhiji was shot dead, is now known as

992. Ruth Perry of Liberia was Africa's first

993. The country where Kirundi is spoken

994. The year Coca Cola was banned in India

995. The youngest tennis millionaire

996. Devan Nair was elected the President in 1981. In which country was this person of Indian-origin President?

997. The full title of the Booker-winning book *Paddy Clarke*.

998. If you stand facing the rising sun, North is to your (right/left)

999. The fastest 100 m. race until then was of Levoy Burrell. The time recorded

1000. The first movie shown on an aircraft

ANSWERS

934. R.K. Laxman's *The Common Man*; **935.** Leonid Ilich Brezhnev; **936.** Colonels; **937.** slave rebellion; **938.** nuclear-powered submarine; **939.** the first pulsar; **940.** Bonnie and Clyde; **941.** 1997; **942.** Paul Theroux and V.S. Naipaul; **943.** La Masia, Barcelona's youth academy; **944.** Dr. Mohan Kohli; **945.** Siachin glacier; **946.** spoils system; **947.** Sania Mirza; **948.** Ramkrishna Yadav; **949.** wits; **950.** Salim Durrani and Parveen Babi; **951.** China; **952.** half (from 10 hours to 4 hours 48 mins); **953.** vertebrae; **954.** Lord Swarj Paul; **955.** *George's Secret Key to the Universe*; **956.** Sir Michael O. Dyer; **957.** 17; **958.** 5000; **959.** English; **960.** France and Germany; **961.** P.C. Mahalanobis; **962.** Emily Dickinson; **963.** Rossum's Universal Robots; **964.** In M.P.; **965.** son; **966.** Manu and Abha; **967.** Harriet Beecher Stowe; **968.** d; **969.** the French palace where it was signed; **970.** United Artists; **971.** It won the 1st World Cup soccer; **972.** sikhism; **973.** Amitav Ghosh; **974.** Monchukuo; **975.** c; **976.** trees; **977.** Jatin Das, 25; **978.** The Brahmaputra; **979.** milligauss; **980.** Potti Sriramulu; **981.** 300th anniversary of the Bank; **982.** R. Venkataraman; **983.** Paul Laurence Dunbar; **984.** M.S. Dhoni and Sakshi; **985.** Saudi Arabia; **986.** Cape of Storms; **987.** $60 bn.; **988.** 31 mn; **989.** Mary I, Queen of England; **990.** Aga Khan Palace, Pune; **991.** Gandhi Sadan; **992.** female head of state; **993.** Burundi; **994.** 1977; **995.** Martina Hingis; **996.** Singapore; **997.** *Paddy Clarke Ha Ha Ha*; **998.** left; **999.** 9.9 sec.; **1000.** *The Lost World*, 1925.

3000 Suicides a Year

According to the World Health Organization, 3000 people committed suicide every day in the world.

Aadhaar: World's Most Complex Data Management System

G.Vijaya Raghavan & V.S.M. Nair
Venture Management Associates

Aadhaar is the most complex data management system the world has ever known. A 12-digit unique number is to be issued to all residents - a number that will mean a lot. When fully operational, the system will cover 1200 million people.

For getting a sense of the theme of this article one has to get one's head around a 12-digit number, the smallest being ten thousand crores. In fact, a greater appreciation of the unimaginably complex computations underlying the Aadhaar initiative

Aadhaar Launched

could be had when we attempt to imagine the process involved in ensuring that the unique 12-digit number the UID (the Unique Identification Number) project will generate for the 600 millionth person is indeed unique. The process involves comparing:

✦ 59 crores 99 lakhs 99 thousand 9 hundred ninety nine photographs

✦ 119 crores 99 lakhs 99 thousand 9 hundred ninety eight irises

✦ 1299 crores 99 lakhs 99 thousand 9 hundred ninety fingerprints

Imagine, again, a Government initiative attracting exceptionally fine Indian minds from within and outside the country:

✦ The initiative is being led by one of the smartest technocrats of the country

✦ The head of the technical centre of the project has had over 20 years of exposure to technology, most of which in Silicon Valley.

✦ Financial inclusion and mobile strategy are being looked after by a seasoned professional with engineering degrees from Mysore, Paris and Washington who nurtured India's first highly successful mobile payment service provider

✦ An IIT topper, who is on loan (sabbatical) from McKinsey, handles process operations

✦ An entrepreneur-turned-social activist who spent 40 years in the US, is helping to form partnerships with NGOs around the country

✦ HR operations are overseen by a graduate from IIM (A) with over 10 years of ex-

Social Security in USA	In USA, three types of Social Security Numbers and Cards are issued: US-born or foreign-born US citizens (age 12 or older), non-citizens who are admitted to the country on temporary basis with the permission to work from the Department of Homeland Security and those who are admitted to the country but not permitted to take up any employment.

perience, on loan from an MNC

✦ An accomplished professional who is on sabbatical from Intel is in charge of the hardware platform.

✦ A post-graduate in Law with several years of experience with a leading consultancy firm in Brussels handles communications

✦ A professional with PhD from the University of California and 12 years of experience with Texas Instruments looks after Biometrics.

✦ The designer who created the world's thinnest watch for Titan has designed a portable kit that houses a laptop, cameras and iris and fingerprint scanners

Many of them joined the programme as volunteers, some are on sabbatical and others took massive pay cuts. What excites these professionals most is the thought that they are part of a small team which power a profoundly transformational initia-

> The audacity of the goal it has set for itself is so staggering that the project is a once- in- a- lifetime opportunity

tive. The audacity of the goal it has set for itself is so staggering that the project is a once- in- a- lifetime opportunity.

The mind-boggling numbers presented earlier relate to the project currently on for allotting UID numbers to 600 million people by 2014. No system in the world has handled anything on this scale. Even this mammoth project is only half the story; another over 600 million numbers have to be allotted to cover the entire population. When fully operational, the system will be the world's largest database of citizens.

What is *Aadhaar*?

Aadhaar (formerly called UID Numbers)

is a 12-digit unique number which the Unique Identification Authority of India (UIDAI) issues for all residents in the country. Aadhaar translates into 'Foundation' or 'Support'.

The number will be stored in a centralized database and linked to the basic demographic and biometric information of each individual. *Aadhaar* will be: easily verifiable in an online, cost-effective way; unique and robust enough to eliminate the large number of duplicate and fake identities in government and private databases; a random number generated, devoid of any classification based on caste, creed, religion or geography.

Aadhaar database has an inbuilt security and privacy component that ensures that the data from the data bank could not be accessed except on grounds like national security. The data base could only be read for authentication (whether or not Mr. X is Mr. X) which will provide only an Yes or No response.

Aadhaar is not mandatory and even people without proper identification documents can obtain it. *Aadhaar* will not replace the identification documents like Ration Card or Passport. *Aadhaar* number is an officially valid document to satisfy the Know Your Customer norms for opening bank accounts.

How to get an *Aadhaar*

The residents need to go to the nearest Enrolment Camp to register for an *Aad-*

ID Number in France — Each French person receives at birth a national identification number called Social Security Number. It is a 13 digit + a two-digit key. The rationale behind it makes it easy for individuals to remember at least the first 7 digits of it: sex (1 or 2), year (the last 2 digits), month of birth (01 to 12) and the place of birth (2 digits or 1 digit and 1 letter in metropolitan France and 3 digits for overseas)

Aadhaar: A mechanism to right the wrongs

The kind of deprivations the poor, the disadvantaged and the disfranchised millions of Indians suffer can be soul-searing. The inability to prove their identity is one of the toughest barriers in the country for the poor, illiterate or nomads in accessing their entitlements: benefits or subsidies or services. What is worse, different service providers often have different requirements in the documents they demand.

A sizeable proportion of the poor (more than 35% of the population - over 400 million - belongs to BPL), the illiterate and the nomads are currently outside the system. India has about 75 million homeless, 75 million tribals and another 100 million who are on the move, migrating from one place to another in search of livelihood. Most of these people have no birth certificate, no address, no SSLC certificate, no Ration Card, no Voters ID Card, no Drivers License, no PAN Card, nothing to prove that they exist – legally!

Just imagine the costs and extreme inconvenience that such people have to bear to get some document to establish their identity.

Another morbidly dispiriting phenomenon is the widespread corruption corroding the nation's vital systems. Leakages based on identity are a common feature of all Government-sponsored schemes.

It is assessed that for every Rs.4 spent on the Public Distribution System (which supplies food grains at subsidized prices) only Re.1 reaches the poor. Bogus ration cards (in the name of non-existing families) and Shadow cards (availing benefits in the name of rightfully entitled families without their knowledge) represent a major source of leakage.

There is rampant practice of inflating enrolment figures at the school level leading to significant leakages from mid-day meals, books, scholarships, school uniforms, bicycles.....

Ministry of petroleum loses about Rs.1200 crores per year in subsidies on LPG cylinders registered under duplicate or ghost identities. The total cost of kerosene leaked from PDS for adulterating diesel could well be lot more.

There is, therefore, nothing more important than a government initiative which can take on these two sets of challenges head – on. The value of a mechanism that uniquely identifies a person and ensures instant identity verification is immeasurable at the individual level as well as at the societal level.

haar number. They need to carry specific documents, if available, to establish their identity.

The enrolment form collects the following information: own name; name of mother, father, husband, guardian (name of mother, father or guardian is mandatory for children below 5 years of age); date of birth; gender; residential address; phone no. & e-mail id, if applicable; whether or not wanting to open *Aadhaar*-enabled bank a/c or to link existing bank a/c to *Aadhaar* number (in which case the a/c number and the bank branch)

| Identifying Citizens in Finland | In Finland, the personal identity code is used for identifying the citizen in government and civilian systems. It uses the format DDMMYYCZZZQ where DDMMYY is the date of birth, C is the century identification sign (+ for the 19th century, - for the 20th century and A for the 21st), ZZZ is the personal identification number. |

Nandan Nilekani

Date of birth is optional for those who do not remember it or do not have any proof; an approximate age is to be specified.

Those residents without any identification documents, should be introduced by any authorised person including one who already has an *Aadhaar* number.

Upon registering for an *Aadhaar* number, residents will go through a biometric scanning of ten fingerprints and iris. They will then be photographed.

There will be an attempt to back the process by reliable and verifiable identity checks including residential address.

The data collected will be sent to the Central Identity Data Repository (CIDR) where the biometrics are checked for duplicates. Once it has been verified, an Aadhaar number will be issued. The entire process can take 20-30 days.

Children below 15 would be given an *Aadhaar* number based on the Aadhaar number of their parents. Since their biometric details change as they grow, they

would have to re-register their biometric details and renew the *Aadhaar* number once again when they turn 15.

The UIDAI's Ecosystem

UIDAI is based on a partnership model. UID-AI will partner with such entities as Central and State departments, banks, insurance companies and private sector agencies and will leverage their existing infrastructure.

UIDAI's ecosystem comprises Registrars & Enrolling Agencies, IT process consultants, IT hardware &software vendors, Biometric Devices vendors, Systems Integrators & IT Service providers, communication service providers, training agencies and logistics facilitators.

UIDAI is the regulatory authority managing a CIDR which will issue *Aadhaar* numbers, update resident information and authenticate the identity of residents as required.

> The first *Aadhaar* number (7824 7431 7884) was allotted to a lady who lives in a tribal village in Maharashtra in September 2010.

Registrars are an entity authorized / recognized by the UIDAI for the purpose of enroling the individuals for *Aadhaar* numbers. Typically, Registrars are government departments, PSUs, banks and insurance companies.

UIDAI has empanelled a number of Enrolment Agencies which can be engaged by the Registrars for the purpose of enroling the residents for *Aadhaar*.

Some of the leading IT firms like TCS, IBM, Wipro, HCL, Accenture and Mindtree have already been undertaking specific as-

ID Card in China	An ID Card is mandatory for all citizens over 16 years old. The number has 18 digits and is in the format RRRRRRYYYYMMDDSSSC. R......R is a standard code for the political division where the holder is born, YYYYMMDD is the birth date of the holder and SSS is a sequential code for distinguishing people with identical birth dates and birth places.

UK's Experience

There is no nation in the world which has completely documented every citizen as they are and not as they claim to be. Many countries which launched similar programmes had to abandon them subsequently. UK (with a fraction of India's population) spent £250 million and 8 years on its National ID Card Scheme but discontinued it citing high cost, impracticability and ungovernable breaches of privacy.

signments for the programme.

The status of the project

UIDAI was constituted in January 2009. Mr. Nandan M Nilekani (who co-founded Infosys and was its Co-chairman) joined as the Chairman of the Authority in July 2009.

The first *Aadhaar* number (7824 7431 7884) was allotted to a lady who lives in a tribal village in Maharashtra in September 2010. The one millionth *Aadhaar* number was allotted in January 2011 to a resident in North Tripura.

It took 6 weeks to cross the first one lakh enrolments; it took the same time to complete the remaining of the ten lakhs enrolments. As on March 2011, 2 million *Aadhaar* numbers were issued.

During the months of November and December 2010, close to 80 homeless daily workers in Delhi were issued *Aadhaar* numbers and bank accounts were opened for them. They can sleep peacefully now without the fear of whatever savings as they have being stolen from under their pillow!!

Benefits of *Aadhaar*

The direct and indirect benefits of *Aadhaar* are indeed immense.

Once for all, *Aadhaar* will dispense with the need for multiple documentary proof (thereby bringing down the transaction costs for those who can least afford such costs); will check corruption by stemming leakages from the government remittances by eliminating fraud and duplicate identities and ghost beneficiaries; will help welfare programmes reach intended beneficiaries; can serve as the basis for e-governance services; education and health sectors will benefit substantially in terms of efficiency and outcomes when Aadhaar is incorporated into the process.

Aadhaar would be a foundation for the effective enforcement of individual rights – to employment, education, food etc. *Aadhaar* will help integrate the services catering to the underprivileged like PDS, NREGA Payment, Old Age / Widow and Handicapped Pension Schemes, State Stipend Scheme and Mid-day Meal Scheme.

Aadhaar will lead to the discovery of a number of innovative and exemplary us-

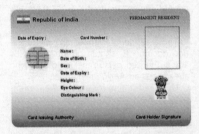

ages to ensure more transparent, efficient and effective governance at all levels of the government.

Besides the above direct benefits for the poor and the deprived, the potential commercial opportunities this initiative throws up are estimated at about Rs.90,000 crores during the first 5 years and Rs.45,000 crores annually thereafter (These are, of course, order of magnitude projections).

By 2014, the government intends to open the UIDAI database to companies which can deploy applications suitable for Citizens Identity Management. This process

| Aadhar Numbers for LPG Connections | **Applicants for new domestic LPG cooking gas connections can now produce the letters of allotment of Aadhaar numbers as proof of identity and proof of address.** |

would give birth to hundreds of start-ups for developing citizen-centric applications.

Even if only a share of this potential is realized, *Aadhaar* project will be one of the largest, not only in terms of scale but also in revenue potential.

Other than software and hardware providers who will provide systems and services to implement the project, telecom operators and banks will be big beneficiaries. Telcos stand to gain 60 million new subscribers, Rs.20,250 crores in mobile payments and Rs.9,000 crores in ARPU (Average Revenue Per User) and handset sales. Banks can gain several million new accounts.

A major market opportunity will be available for the manufacturers of biometric devices

Direct and indirect employment generated by the project will naturally be equally awesome.

> *Aadhaar* will check corruption by stemming leakages from the government remittances by eliminating fraud and duplicate identities and ghost beneficiaries.

The Challenges UIDAI Confronts

That a project of this scale and complexity will face seemingly insurmountable obstacles is indisputable. There are Cassandras, Doubting Thomases, detractors and, of course, those who are genuinely concerned about critical issues.

There are those who believe that the initiative is illegal, unconstitutional and an assault on the privacy of people and that the data collected will be used for purposes other than what is proposed. These are indeed baseless allegations.

Many suspect that, given India's infra-structural deficits, weak administrative mechanisms, vast and inaccessible geographical features and the massive population, the country will find it extremely difficult to pull it off as envisaged or within the timeline set. These reservations cannot be ignored.

Due to the benefits the *Aadhaar* number delivers, the programme is conceived to be demand-driven and, hence, voluntary in nature; if one doesn't want it, one doesn't have to enrol. In such a context, the assumption that we can capture the demographic and biometric data of the entire population is somewhat optimistic.

The fuzziness of biometrics can pose problems when used as ID, requiring re-enrolments. The size of biometric elements like fingerprints and faces change significantly through the years. Visual disabilities, diabetic retinopathy, blindness etc. affect iris images. Fingers of the working poor get dirty, cut, bruised, hardenedcalloused limiting the process of getting a clear print.

The equipment used may not be entirely reliable:

Human error is a constant threat; the over-worked enumerator/ agent may by

The First Census	The first population census in India was organised by Lord Mayo in 1871. The figure 206 million was a near estimate.

mistake register biometrics of one against another; people may misrepresent themselves for a variety of reasons; the State may misrepresent because of lack of proper documents.

When a false positive arises (two persons having the same biometric parameters), while CIDR's authenticating a new entry, it has to be investigated by a team and not machines. When thousands such occur, the possibility of which cannot be ruled out when dealing with millions of entries, such investigations and re-enrolments can be a drag on the administration.

When fully operational, the system would be the world's largest biometric – centric citizen database. For instance, the compressed fingerprint (ten fingers) images of the entire population will require 6 petabytes of space. There are other biometric components to be accounted for.

> We have more than an even chance of conquering one of the toughest tasks the nation took on since independence

Each new entry has to be validated against the existing entries to eliminate the possibility of duplication. This would mean, when fully operational, comparing each new applicant against, say, +1000 mn. entries in the database.

Creating, maintaining and updating such a gargantuan database of exceptional speed surely calls for efforts that have never been attempted anywhere

Facilitating financial inclusion is perceived to be one of the most desirable outcomes of widespread acceptance of *Aadhaar*. But then, extreme poverty, illiteracy and lack of awareness and trust, corruption and inadequate willingness among the banks are limiting the scope for financial inclusion. Providing an unique identity number alone may not achieve the mission

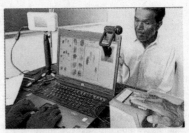

of financial inclusion without addressing the systemic issues.

At several levels of the government, politics is geared towards leaking benefits to the ineligible. The routine leakage of rations meant for Below the Poverty Line (BPL) families is a case in point. Any clean, fool-proof and transparent administrative mechanism can be anathema to those who have been enjoying the ill-gotten benefits for so long. Such people are unlikely to be ardent advocates promoting *Aadhaar*.

What's the takeaway?

There are going to be glitches, millions of them. There will be setbacks; targets will be missed and timelines overshot. But then, what UIDAI is attempting is an incredibly relevant and rewarding exercise. This is the proposition at the heart of this essay.

Even if we achieve only 50% what we set out to, the direct and indirect benefits the country earns will be significantly more than the cost we incur. That a group of extremely dedicated professionals is driving the project provides the guarantee that we have more than an even chance of conquering one of the toughest tasks the nation took on since independence.

In the final reckoning, *Aadhaar's* power to help fight the plague of endemic corruption in the country and cut corruption's systemic roots, thereby enabling inclusive growth and social equity, will represent its greatest contribution. Almost always corruption of every kind hurts the poor and the powerless more than the rich and the powerful. ∎

---

1 mn. Enrolments a Day

The UIDAI targets 1 million enrolments a day from October, 2011, according to Chairman Nandan Nilekani. By June, 9.5 m. enrolments had been completed.

50 Great Hollywood Classics

Prof. Joseph Mathew Palai

Fifty Classics that entertained the world and enriched man's life ever since Hollywood emerged as the Film Hub.

Here is a selection of 50 great films from Hollywood, the land of Cinema. These films belong to various genres like Epic, Drama, Musical, Horror, Romance, Comedy, War, Western, Mystery / Thriller, Action / Adventure, Science Fiction and Fantasy. The films are listed chronologically.

1. *It happened One Night*

(1934)   105 min
Director : Frank Capra **Cast :** Clark Gable, Claudette Colbert, Walter Connolly, Alan Hale, Roscoe Karns, Jameson Thomas, Arthur Hoyt, Charles C. Wilson.

One of the greatest romantic comedies in film history, this film is about a runaway heiress and a wandering journalist who form a lasting relationship in their journey across the country together. This screwball comedy was an unexpected box office hit winning the top five Academy Awards: Best Picture, Director, Actor, Actress and Screenplay.

2. *Snow White and the Seven Dwarfs* (1937)   83 min

Director : David Hand

Based on the well–known fairy tale by Brothers Grimm, this milestone in Animation history was Walt Disney's first full length feature. It is an extraordinary well crafted film with each cartoon character vividly drawn and given a distinct personality. The seven dwarfs Bashful, Doc, Dopey, Grumpy, Happy, Sleepy ad Sneezy are endearing and wonderful. The wicked queen is the epitome of cold, dark beauty. And snow white is a charmer. This delightful, colourfilm is a treat for the whole family. Even the songs of the film have become very popular and famous. The film received a Special Academy award consisting of one regular sized statuette and seven dwarf statuettes.

It happened one night

3. *The Wizard of Oz* (1939)101min

Director : Victor Fleming **Cast :** Judy Garland, Frank Morgan, Bert Lahr, Ray Bolger, Jack Haley, Margaret Hamilton, Billie Burke, Pat Walshe

Based on the Wonderful Wizard of Oz, the turn of the century children's novel by L. Frank Baum, this evergreen classic is one of the great film fairy tales. Dorothy Gale and her house are caught in a tornado and blown to the land of Oz. The house lands on, and kills, a wicked witch whose sister soon arrives to seek revenge. Dorothy escapes from there with the aid of three friends. Filled with extravagant sets, costumes, memorable song and dance routines Dorothy's adventures in Oz are pure delight. Winner of Two Oscar awards; Best Song and Best Score.

4. *Stage Coach* (1939)　96 min

Director : John Ford **Cast :** John Wayne, Claire Trevor, Andy Devine, John Carradine, George Bancroft, Louise Platt, Berton Churchill, Thomas Mitchell, Donald Meek, Tim Holt.

Nine people are making a coach trip through dangerous Indian territory: an outlaw under arrest called the Ringo Kid, a marshal accompanying him, along with an exiled prostitute, a banker, an alcoholic doctor, a sheriff, a pregnant woman, a gambler and the driver. Enroute, love and hate develop among them, a baby is born and there are deaths during an attack by Apaches at the climax. Stage coach is a

Stage Coach

landmark in the history of the Western. It raised the genre to artistic status, bringing about a revival, stamped John Ford as one of the great Hollywood directors. Won Two Academy Awards: Best Supporting Actor and Best Score.

5. *Gone with the Wind*

(1939)　　　　　　　　238 min

Director: Victor Fleming, George Cukor **Cast:** Clark Gable, Vivien Leigh, Leslie Howard, Olivia de Havilland, Thomas Mitchell, Barbara O'Neil, Hattie Mc Daniel, George Reeve, Evelyn Keyes.

Gone with the Wind

Adapted from Margaret Michell's best selling novel of the American South during the years of the Civil war and Reconstruction, Gone with the Wind was a monumental piece of Hollywood film–making in every conceivable respect. Costing $ 4.25 million (roughly equivalent to $ 50 million today), the film won ten Oscars. This film can be properly considered as the prototype of the Hollywood 'block buster'. The film received Ten Oscar Awards.

6. *The Great Dictator*

(1940)　　　　　　　124 min

Director: Charles Chaplin **Cast:** Charles Chaplin, Jack Oakie, Grace Hayle, Paulette Goddard, Billy Gilbert, Henry Daniel, Reginald Gardiner.

The first talkie film of Chaplin in which he plays two characters, a Jewish barber and Adenoid Hynkel, Dictator of Tomania,

| First Actor to Earn $ 1m. | It was for Cleopatra (1960) that Elizabeth Taylor was paid $1mn. She was the first actor to earn a $1 mn. on a film. She won Oscars for Butterfield 8 (1960) and Who's Afraid of Virginia Woolf (1966). |

This is a satire on Adolf Hitler and the Nazis. The film marks last time Chaplin used the little tramp characterization. The film was banned by the Nazis in all occupied territories. It is reported that Hitler was sufficiently intrigued to have a print brought in through Portugal. The film was Chaplain's greatest financial success.

7. *Citizen Kane* (1941)   119 min
Director: Orson Welles **Cast:** Orson Welles, Joseph Cotton, Ray Collins, Agnes Moorehead, Everett Sloane, Paul Stewart, Ruth Warrick, Dorothy Comingore, Erskine Sanford, William Alland, Harry Shannon

Citizen Kane

The rise to power of an American newspaper tycoon Charles Foster Kane, told in a series of flashblacks through interviews with people who were close to him in his life time. Closely based on the career of Newspaper magnate William Randolph Hearst, this remarkable movie is regarded as one of the greatest films ever made. The film's radically innovative use of sound and deep focus photography also reserve its place in history. Nominated for nine Academy awards, it finally managed to win only One, Best original Screenplay (Herman Mankiewiz and Welles).

8. *Casablanca* (1942)   102 min
Director: Michael Curtiz **Cast:** Humphrey Bogart, Ingrid Bergman, Claude Rains, Paul Henreid, Peter Lorre, Dooley Wilson, Joy Page, Conrad Veidt.

Casablanca

The story of Casablanca is based on an unproduced play entitled 'Everybody comes to Ricks' by Murray Burnett and Joan Alison. Critically acclaimed, bittersweet, popular, much–loved world war II flavoured, nostalgic story of intrigue and love that teamed Bogart and Bergman as ill-fated lovers. A rock solid example of Hollywood studio craftsmanship Winner of Three Oscars : Best picture, Director and Screenplay.

9. *The Best years of Our Lives* (1946)   172 min
Director: William Wyler **Cast:** FredricMarch, MyrnaLoy, Dana Andrews, Harold Russel, Virginia Mayo, Teresa Wright, Cathy O'Donnel, Ray Collins

A landmark classic about three World War II veterans (Al, Homer and Fred) attempting readjustment to peace time life and discovering that they have fallen behind. The most memorable film about the aftermath of World War II. Winner of Seven Academy awards including Best Picture, Director, Actor, Screenplay and Editing.

10. *All About Eve* (1950)   138min
Director: Joseph L. Mankiewicz **Cast:** Bette Davis, Anne Baxter, George Sanders, Hugh Marlowe, Thelma Ritter, Barbara Bates, Eddie Fisher, Marilyn Monroe, Celeste Holm, Gary Merrill

This film is a brilliant expose of the backstage life of Broadway. The cynical and witty screenplay features full–blooded charac-

Film on Ramabai	The sacrifices of Ramabai, wife of Dalit icon B.R. Ambedkar will be chronicled in a telefilm Yug Stri Mata Ramabai, "The film will be directed by Ashok Kambil and Rajesh Anshane.

All About Eve

about soldiers and the women in their lives is set in Hawaii at the time prior to Pearl Harbour, Shot in documentary style this film is an unflattering look at military life tackling issues like adultery, injustice, corruption and murder. The film received 13 nominations and won eight Academy awards. (Best Picture, Director, Supporting Actor, Supporting Actress, Screenplay, Cinematography, Sound Recording and Editing)

13. *On The Waterfront*
(1954)   108 min

Director: Elia Kazan **Cast:** Marlon Brando, Karl Malden, Rod Steiger, Lee J. Cobb, Eva Marie Saint, Rudy Bond, Pat Henning, James Westerfieled, Arthur Keegan, Don Blackman, John F Hamilton.

ters. The film was based on a short story and radioplay 'The wisdom of Eve' by Mary Orr. The film was nominated for fourteen Academy awards, however it managed to win only six. Best Picture, Director, Supporting Actor, Screenplay Sound Recording and Costume Design.

11. *An American in Paris*
(1951)   113 min

Director: Vincente Minnelli **Cast:** Gene Kelly, Lesile Caron, Oscar Levant, Nina Foch, Georges Guetary

This delightful Hollywood fantasy with its romantic vision of Paris was shot entirely on the MGM studio set. With lavish sets and costumes and a superlative cast, an American in Paris is a superb movie entertainment. One of the celebrated musicals of 1950s, this film got eight Academy award nominations and won six.

12. *From Here to Eternity*
(1953)   118 min

Director: Fred Zinnemann **Cast:** Burt Lancaster, Montgomery Clift, Deborah Kerr, Frank Sinatra, Ernest Borgnine, Jack Warden, Tim Ryan, John Dennis, Arthur Keegan, Philip Ober, Donna Reed.

Based on James Joness novel, this movie

The film was most visibly inspired by "Crime on the Water front", a series of newspaper articles by Malcolm Johnson exposing racketeering in the New York/ New Jersey dockyards. Marlon Brando is superb as Terry Malloy who tries to overthrow a corrupt union and succeeds. The

On the Waterfront

film received a phenomenal twelve Oscar nominations and finally won eight including Best Picture, Director, Actor, Supporting Actress, Screenplay, Cinematography, Art Direction and Editing.

14. *The Ten Commandments*
(1956)   220 min

Director: Cecil B. De Mille **Cast:** Charlton

First Dubbing The first Indian feature film to be dubbed was *Harischandra* (1944). It was dubbed from Kannada to Tamil.

The Ten Commandments

Heston, Yul Brynner, Ann Baxter, Debra Paget, Nina Foch, Judith Anderson, Vincent Price, John Carradine, Edward G. Robinson, John Derek, Martha Scott, Yvonne De Carlo

Shot in wide screen technicolor, this spectacular film set the standard by which many epics, biblical or otherwise, would be measured. De Mille pulled out all the stops in terms of special effects–the images of Moses turning his staff into a snake and the Nile into blood were unprecedented visual innovations at the time and the parting of the Red Sea remains one of Hollywood's most treasured 'Miracles' of special effects. The film won Academy awards for Best Effects /Special Effects (John P. Fulton).

15. *Gigi* (1958)　　　119min
Director: Vincente Minnelli **Cast:** Leslie Caron, Maurice Chevalier, Louis Jordan, Eva Gabor, Jacques Bergerac, John Abbott, Isabel Jeans

Based on Colette's short story and winner of nine Academy awards, Gigi is truly a musical classic. Shot entirely in Pairs, this film concerns a young girl raised to be a courtesan who gains the heart of a bored Parisian.

16. *Ben Hur* (1959)　　212 min
Director: William Wyler **Cast:** Charlton

Heston, Jack Hawkins, Stephen Boyd, Haya Harareet, Hugh Griffith, Martha Scott, Cathy O' Donnel., Sam Jaffe, George Relph, Terence Longdon, Frank Thring, Finlay Currie.

This spectacular 15 million dollar epic set in the Roman empire's province of Judea, starred Charlton Heston as Jewish prince Judah Ben–Hur whose childhood friendship with the Roman tribune Messala turns to enmity when Messala destroys Ben-Hur family. Sentenced to the gallows Ben-Hur rescues a Roman admiral during a sea battle and is adopted by him. Making his way back to Jerusalem Ben-hur defeats Messala in a climactic chariot race and rescues his mother and sister who have become lepers. They are cured by Christ at the moment of crucifixion.

The film set a record at the Oscars Nominated for twelve awards, it walked away with eleven; Best Picture, Actor, Supporting

Ben Hur

Actor, Director, Colour Photography, Best colour art direction/set direction, Sound, Score, Editing, Costume Design and Special effects.

17. *Psycho* (1960)　　109 min
Director: Alfred Hitchcock **Cast:** Anthony Perkins, Vera Miles, John Gavin, Martin Balsam, Janet Leigh, John McIntire, Simon Oakland, Vaughn Taylor, Frank Albertson, Patricia Hitchcock.

Psycho is regarded as the 'mother' of all modern horror suspense films which inspired plenty of future screen 'slashers' The murder of Marion Crane (Janet Leigh)

| First Movie Camera | The first practical motion-picture camera was invented by a French scientist Etienne Jules Mary in 1882. In 1893 Mary patented a film projector. |

Psycho

in the shower of Room One in Bates Motel is one of the most shocking and famous scenes in the history of films. Anthony Perkin's haunting portrayal of Norman Bates is one of the cinema's most chilling performances. The film was nominated for 4 Academy awards but failed to win any.

18. *West Side Story* (1961) 151 min

Director: Robert Wise, Jerome Robbins **Cast:** Natalie Wood, Richard Beymer, Rita Moreno, Russ Tamblyn Ned Glass, George Chakiris, Simon Oakland, William Bramley, Bert Michaels, David Winters.

A musical updating of Shakespeare's Romeo and Juliet. The pair trot the slums of New York with Tony and Maria trying to find peace and love despite the gang wars between the immigrant Puerto Ricans and the native New Yorkers going an around them. The film won Ten Oscar awards from eleven nominations.

19. *The Great Escape*
(1963) 172 min
Director: John Sturges **Cast :** Steeve McQueen, James Garner, Richard Attenborough, Charles Bronson, James Coburn, Donald Pleasence, David McCallum, Gordon Jackson, Jud Taylor, Nigel stock.

A terrific war film boasting an all-star cast from Director John Sturges, this film remains as entertaining, moving and thrilling now as when it was first released. Nearly every scene is a classic, as the American and British prisoners of war plot to escape from their camp using three tunnels they have dug named Tom, Dick and Harry.

20. *My Fair Lady* (1964) 170 min
Director : George Cukor **Cast:** Audrey Hepburn, Rex Harrison, Stanley Holloway, Gladys Cooper, Jeremy Brett, Wilfrid Hyde-white, Theodore Bikel

The film version of Bernard Shaws 'Pygmalion' written in 1913. The story concerns an arrogant linguist Professor Henry Higgins betting his friend Colonel Pickering that he can transform cockney flower girl Eliza Doolittle into a lady. After six months Higgins wins the best, but Eliza feels betrayed. She decides to leave him, but finds it is not easy. Winner of eight academy

My fair Lady

awards-Best Picture, Director, Actor, Colour Photography, Color Art Direction/Set direction, Sound, Score, Color Costume Design.

21. *The Sound of Music*
(1965) 174 min
Director: Robert Wise **Cast:** Julie Andrews, Christopher Plummer, Eleanor Parker, Peggy Wood, Anna Lee, Debbie Turner, Kym Karath, Angela Cartwright, Duane Chase, Heather Menzies, Nicholas Hammond, Richard Haydn.

'The sound of Music' was an adaptation of a Richard Rodgers and Oscar Hammer-

---

The Most Seen Movie

When Gone With The Wind was premiered in Atlanta in 1939, the city proclaimed a holiday and the producer and stars Vivien Leigh and Olivia de Havilland paraded down boulevards lined with excited fans. The film became the 'most-seen' movie in history.

The Sound of Music

stein Broadway hit based on the true story of the Von Trapp family singers and their heroic escape from Nazi-occupied Austria.

Maria is a free spirited novice at a convent who is hired by Baron Capt. George von Trapp, an ex-naval officer to be the governess to his seven children. She becomes friends with the children and opens them to the joy of music, winning the heart of their father whom she marries later. When the Nazi invasion of Austria threatens their happiness they plot a dramatic escape.

The musical was nominated for ten Academy awards, and came away with Five major wins : Best Picture, Director, Score, Sound and Editing.

22. *Midnight Cowboy*

(1969)   113 min
Director: John Schlesinger **Cast:** Jon Voight, Dustin Hoffman, Sylvia Miles, Ruth White, John McGiver, C Brenda Vaccaro, Jennifer Salt, Barnard Hughes.

In this tremendous film about the struggle for existence in the urban nightmare of New York's 42nd street area, Jon Voight and Dustin Hoffmann deliver brilliant performances. Voight plays Joe Buck an aspiring male prostitute from Texas who heads to New York for making money by living as a stud. Hoffmann plays Rasto Rizzo, a slimy con artist suffering from tuberculosis. They depend on each other for their existence. Winner of Three Academy awards.

23. *Patton*   (1970)   170 min
Director: Franklin J. Schaffner **Cast:** George

C. Scott, KarlMaldon, Stephen Young, Michael Strong, Cary Loftin, Frank Latimore, Patrick J. Zurica, James Edwards, Bill Hickman, Kar/Michael Vogler

The war time career of one of the most controversial American commanders of World War II, General George S. Patton who forfeited command of the 7th army in Sicily after he had struck a soldier suffering form battle fatigue. George C. Scott gives the performance of his career as the tireless warrior. Winner of Seven Oscar awards.

24. *The Godfather* (1972) 175 min
Director: Francis Ford Coppola **Cast:** Marlon Brando, Al Pacino, James Caan, Robert Duvall, John Cazale, Richard L. Castellano,

The Godfather

Talia Shire, Diane Keaton, Sterling Haydon, John Marley, Richard Conte.

The gangster film of the contemporary cinema, a massive saga of honour, loyalty and brutal murder as the Corelone family of New York fights to keep its ascendancy over rival Mafia type families. Based on Mario Puzo's best Selling novel, The film received ten nominations and won three Oscars.

25. *Cabaret*   (1972)   113 min
Director : Bob Fosse **Cast :** Liza Minnelli, Michael York, Marisa Berenson, Fritz Wepper, Joel Grey, Helen Vita, Elisabeth Neumann – Viertel.

'Cabaret' was the only truly great musical made in the 1970s, chronicling the adventures of an American singer in Berlin, in the days immediately preceding World War II. Winner of Eight Academy Awards.

26. *The Exorcist* (1973) 122 min

Director: William Friedkin **Cast:** Linda Blair, Ellen Burstyn, Max von Sydow, Lee J. Cobb, Jason Miller, Kitty Winn, Barton Heyman, Peter Masterson, Jack Mac Gowran.

The Exorcist

The first major block buster in horror movie history, this film has exerted a powerful influence on the subsequent development of the genre.

Fourteen year-old Regan Teresa Mac Neil is suddenly prone to fits and bizarre behaviour. After exhausting all the options of science and medicine, Regan's mother Chris turns to young priest Father Karras. Convinced that the girl is possessed by the devil, they call in a mysterious exorcist named Father Lankester Merrin. Their foe is no ordinary devil. Both the girl and the priest suffer numerous horrors during the struggle. It is based on William Peter Blatty's best-selling horror novel. Winner of two Oscar awards, Best adapted screenplay and Best sound.

27. *One Flew over The Cuckoo's Nest* (1975) 133 min

Director: Milos Forman **Cast:** Jack Nicholson, Louise Fletcher, Danny De Vito, William Red field, Peter Brocco, Michael Berryman, Dean R. Brooks, Alonzo Brown, William Duell, Nathan George, Ken Kenny, Josip Elic.

Patrick McMurphy is a drifter who pretends to be mentally ill in order to get out of work duty at prison. He is sent to a mental ward ruled by the tyrannical nurse Mildred Ratched who regiments the lives of the patients without helping them. Mc Murphy who sees the absurdity of the situation becomes the patients' symbol of non conformity and rebellion.

Winner of Five major Academy awards- Best Picture, Director, Actor, Actress and Screenplay.

28. *Jaws* (1975) 124 min

Director: Steven Spielberg **Cast:** Roy Scheider, Robert Shaw, Richard Dreyfuss, Lorraine Gary, Murray Hamilton, Jeffrey Kramer, Jonathan Filley, Peter Benchley, Jay Mello, Carl Gottileb, Chris Rebello.

Based on the best-selling novel by Peter Benchley, this adventure classic is set at an East Coast resort town, Amity Island which is being terrorized by a great white shark. A trio of shark hunters team up to hunt down the rogue. One of the highest gross-

Jaws

ing films of all time. The film won yhree Academy awards.

29. *Rocky* (1976) 119 min

Director: John G. Avildsen **Cast:** Sylvester Stallone, Talia Shire, Burt Young, Bill Baldwin, Joe Spinell, Carl Weathers, Burgess Meredith.

The story centres on Rocky Balboa, a boxer beyond his prime. He falls in love with Adrian, the sister of his friend Paulie, and then works to earn the respect of his trainer Mickey. On the receiving end of a publicity stunt, he eventually gets a chance to unseat Apollo Creed, the heavyweight boxing champion of the world. Shot with gritty realism, Rocky introduced a new kind of Cinematic hero. The film won three Oscars, Best Picture, Director and Editing. The film had four sequels – Rocky II (1979), Rocky) III (1982) and Rocky IV (1985) all directed by Sylvester Stallone and Rocky V (1990) directed by John G. Avildsen.

30. *Annie Hall* (1977)   93 min
Director: Woody Allen **Cast:** Woody Allen, Diane Keaton, Tony Roberts, Shelley Duvall, Carol Kane, Paul Simon, Janet Margolin, Christopher Walken.

WOODY ALLEN
DIANE KEATON
TONY ROBERTS
CAROL KANE
PAUL SIMON
SHELLEY DUVALL
JANET MARGOLIN
COLLEEN DEWHURST

Annie Hall

An autobiographical urban comedy by Woody Allen following the up and down relationship between a neurotic night club comedian Alvy Singer and a young mid western singer Annie Hall, who meet, fall in love, quarrel and finally break up. Winner of Four Academy awards.

31. *Star Wars* (1977)   121 min
Director: George Lucas **Cast:** Harrison Ford, Mark Hamill, Peter Cushing. Carrie Fischer, Anthony Daniels, Alec Guinness, Kenny Baker, Peter Mayhew.

One of the most inventive and entertaining films ever made, Star Wars knits together fragments of science and mythology into a tale everyone can relate to. A big budget block buster with astounding special effects. The film was nominated for ten Academy awards and won Seven.

32. *The Deer Hunter*
(1978)   183 min
Director: Michael Cimino **Cast:** Robert De Niro, John Savage, Christopher Walken, John Cazale, Meryl Streep, Shirley Stoler, Amy Wright, Mady Kaplan, Richard Kuss, George Dzundza

A Huge Sprawling movie about the effects of the Vietnam War on three young Pennsylvanian steelworkers when they leave their home town for a tour of duty at the front. Only the strongest of the three survives; the others are crushed physically and mentally by the war and torture at the hands, of the Viet Cong. Winner of Five Academy awards.

33. *Kramer Vs Kramer*
(1979)   105 min
Director: Robert Benton **Cast:** Dustin Hoffman, Meryl Streep, Justin Henry, Jane Alexander, Howard Duff, George Coe, Bill Moor, Jo Beth Williams, Carol Nadell, Jess Osuna, Ellen Parker, Shelby Brammer

Kramer Vs Kramer is a moving account of the aftermath of divorce and a memorable exploration of parenthood. Advertising executive Ted Kramer and his wife Joana have a Seven year old son Billy. One day Joana leaves her husband and son .Ted and Billy have learned to live with each other.

Kramer Vs Kramer

What is Dolly?   The dolly is a small truck that rolls along tracks and carries the camera filming a scene. It may also carry part of the camera crew. The dolly grip moves this equipment.

Joana returns and demands Billy's sole custody.

The film is based on the 1977 novel by Avery Corman. The film received nine Oscar nominations and won Five. (Best Picture, Director, Actor, Best Supporting Actress and Best adapted Screenplay.

34. *Apocalypse Now*
(1979)   153 min

Director : Francis Ford Coppola **Cast:** Marlon Brando, Robert Duvall, Martin Sheen, Dennis Hopper, Frederic Forrest, Albert Hall, Harrison Ford, Scott Glenn, Sam Bottoms,

The most realistic account of the physical and psychological horrors of the Vietnam War. Inspired by Joseph Conrad's 1902 novella 'Heart of Darkness', the film is about an army captain who is ordered to hunt down a deranged American officer operating in Cambodia with an army of guerilla tribesmen. Undeniably brilliant, this film is also claustrophobic and terrifying. It won two Academy awards for Best Cinematography and Best Sound. It also won the Palm D' Or at the Cannes Festival.

35. *E.T. The Extra Terrestrial*
(1982)   115 min

Director: Steven Spielberg **Cast:** Henry Thomas, Dee Wallace-Stone, Peter Coyote, Drew Barrymore, C. Thomas Howell, Richard Swingler, Sean Fyre, K.C Martel, Robert Barton

A Science fiction adventure for the whole family, this was Spielberg's homage

ET The Extra Terrestrial

to childhood. On a special mission to Earth, an alien spacecraft mistakenly leaves a crew member behind. Elliott, a lonely boy living with his single mother, chances upon the stranded alien and hides him in his home. The alien, a toddler sized creature, who Elliott starts to call E.T. forms a bond with the boy. Elliott introduces him to earth customs such as how to communicate, drink beer, eat candy, and dress up in his little sister Gerties's clothes. But a few government scientists are out to get hold of ET, and Elliott must help him get back to his planet fast. The film won Four Oscar awards out of nine nominations.

36. *Amadeus* (1984)   160 min

Director: Milos Forman **Cast:** F. Murray Abraham, Tom Hulce, Simon Callow, Charles Kay, Kenny Baker, Jeffrey Jones, Elizabeth Berridge, Roy Dotrice, Christine Ebersole, Martin Cavina

Amadeus

One of the most entertaining movies to emerge from Hollywood in the 1980's, Amadeus has beautiful music, colorful costumes, a terrific script based on the original stage play, super acting performances and a stirring and exciting story. Tom Hulce starred as the immortal Wolfgang Amadeus Mozart and F.Murray Abraham as his embittered rival, court composer Antonio Salieri. The film received eleven nominations and won eight Academy awards.

37. *Rain Man* (1988)   133 min

Director: Barry Levinson **Cast:** Dustin Hoffman, Tom Cruise, Valeria Golino, Gerald R.

2012 Films in 1939   **Worldwide 2012 feature films were released in 1939, 438 of them produced in the US. It was a year of brilliant films - *Gone With The Wind* winning the Oscar.**

Molen, Jack Murdock, Ralph Seymour, Lucinda Jenney, Bonnie Hunt, Beth Grant

Dustin Hoffman gives the performance of his career as the autistic older brother Raymond Babbit of Tom cruise who plays a thoughtless, self–centered hustler Charlie Babbitt with room in his life only for money, Greed propels him to take a cross country road trip with Raymond, who inherited the bulk of Dad's vast estate Won Four Academy awards for Best Picture, Director, Actor and Original Screenplay.

38. *Dances With Wolves*

(1990)   183 min

Director: Kevin Costner **Cast:** Kevin Costner, Graham Greene, Mary McDonnell, Michael Spears, Rodney A. Grant, Charles Rocket, Jimmy Herman, Robert Pastorelli, Tantoo Cardinal

Dances With Wolves

It is a breathtakingly well–made film about a white man lieutenant John J. Dunbar who comes into contact with a peaceful Indian tribe and adopts their way of life. He also falls in love with a white girl raised by the tribe . It is both a stirring drama and a touching romance. Winner of Seven Oscar awards.

39. *The Silence Of the Lambs*

(1991)   118 min

Director: Jonathan Demme **Cast:** Anthony Hopkins, Jodie Foster, Scott Glenn, Ted Levine, Frankie Faison, Kasi Lemmons, Brooke Smith

In this shock–filled movie, an FBI trainee Clarice Starling is assigned by her superior to interview Dr. Hannibal Lecter an impris-

The Silence of the Lambs

oned, cannibalistic psychopath in the hopes of getting his help in capturing a crazed serial killer named Buffalo Bill. Superb performances by Hopkins and Foster. Based on Thomas Harris's 1988 best selling novel of the same name, the film won five Academy awards namely Best Picture, Director, Actor, Actress and Adapted Screenplay

40. *Schindler's List* (1993) 197 min

Director: Steven Spielberg **Cast:** Liam Neeson, Ben Kingsley, Ralph Fiennes, Caroline Goodall, Jonathan Sagall, Andrzej Seweryn

The story of Oscar Schindler's struggle to save the lives of thousand Polish Jews during the Third Reich's implementation of Hitler's final solution. In this masterpiece of film craft, Spielberg tells an incredible story about hope and dignity in the midst of a monstrous tragedy. The entire film is shot in black and white, except for its opening and closing scenes and two other brief shots(The little girl in a red coat and candles burning with orange flame). The

Schindler's List

Battleship Potemkin	Sergei Einstein made a film for the Soviet government to mark the 20th anniversary of the failed 1905 revolution 'Battleship Potemkin'. Charlie Chaplin called it 'the best film ever made'.

film won seven Academy awards, including Best Picture, Director, Cinematography, Adapted Screenplay, Original Score, Editing and Art Direction.

41. *Jurassic Park* (1993) 127 min
Director: Steven Spielberg **Cast:** Jeff Goldblum, Sam Neill, Laura Dern, Richard Attenborough, Bod Peck, Samuel L. Jackson, Joseph Mazzello, Ariana Richards, Martin Ferrero, B.D. Wong, Wayne Knight

Jurassic Park

In this adaptation from the novel by Michael Crichton, dinosaurs are genetically recreated to populate the ultimate theme park and a special few are allowed a sneak preview. Awe and wonder soon turns to terror as the creatures break out of their confines and go on a rampage. Winner of Three Academy Awards.

42. *Forrest Gump* (1994) 142 min
Director: Robert Zemeckis **Cast:** Tom Hanks, Sally Field, Robbin Wright Penn, Re-

Forrest Gump

becca Williams, John Randall, George Kelly, Garry Sinise, Bob Penny, Sam Anderson.

A brisk trot through events in American history from the 1950s until the 1980s as seen through the eye of one man, Forrest Gump succeeds as both epic and character study. The film received thirteen Academy nominations and won six. Based on the novel by Winston Groom. The feel–good movie boasts a magnificent performance by Tom Hanks and remarkable special effects.

43. *The English Patient*
(1996) 160 min
Director : Anthony Minghella **Cast:** Ralph Fiennes, Juliette Binoche, Willem Dafoe, Colin Firth, Julian Wadham, Keistin Scott Thomas, Naveen Andrews

The film is an adaptation of Michael Ondaatjes' Booker prize–winning novel. A severely burned and disfigured pilot is found in the wreckage of his biplane in North Africa near the end of Word War II. Apparently amnesiac, unidentified but presumed to be English, he is dying and in the care of French- Canadian nurse Hanna. Taking refuge in a devastated Italian monastery, the mystery patient revealed as Hungarian Count Laszlo Almasy- recall his past gradually between 1930s and 1945, in Tuscany, Cairo and the Sahara Desert. The film won Nine Oscar awards including Best Picture, Director, Actress in a Supporting Role, Cinematography, Sound, Art Direction, Original Score, Costume design and Editing

44. *Titanic* (1997) 194 min
Director: James Cameron **Cast:** Leonardo Di Caprio, Kate Winslet, Kathy Bates, Billy Zane, Billy Paxton, Gloria Stuart, Jonathan Hyde, David Warner, Danny Nucci, Victor Garber, France Fisher

A treasure hunter looking for diamonds in the wreck of the Titanic, discovers in a safe the nude picture of a young woman. After it is shown on television, Rose Dawson aged 101, comes forward and reveals

Chaplin's Body Charlie Chaplin's body was stolen from its grave in 1978 and held for a 60,000 francs ransom by a Pole and a Bulgarian who said they needed the money to start a garage business.

Titanic

that she is the person in the portrait and tells her story. She was travelling with her mother and her wealthy fiancé, whom she desperately didn't want to marry. She was about to throw herself over the rails when she was stopped by Jack, a young man. They fell in love and spent every moment together until the iceberg broke the ship apart. Even then, they were determined to stay together.

The movie cost about $200,000 million. It won fourteen academy nominations and received eleven Oscars an all–time record.

45. *The Matrix* (1999)   136 min
Director: Andy Wachowski, Larry Wachowski **Cast:** Keanu Reeves, Laurence Fishburne, Carrie-Ann Moss, Hugo Weaving, Gloria Foster, Matt Doran, Belinda Mc Clory, Paul Goddard, Robert Taylor, David Aston, Marc Gray

A Sci–fi block buster that manages to effectively fuse pop philosophical themes with skillfully choreographed action sequences and state of the art special effects. A computer hacker, Anderson, discovers mankind is actually held captive by alien machines who feed us an artificial, computer–created perception of reality while draining the electrical current produced by our brains. Winner of four Oscar awards.

46. *Gladiator* (2000)   155 min
Director : Ridley Scott **Cast :** Russel Crowe, Joaquin Phoenix, Connie Nielson, Oliver Reed, Richard Harris, Derek Jacobi

AD 180. General Maximus Decimus Meridius is named 'Keeper of Rome' by the dying Emperor Marcus Aurelius after successfully vanquishing the Barbarian hordes. But the Emperor's son Commodus has other ideas. Following a foiled execution, Maximus flees to his Spanish home to discover his wife and son have been murdered. Enslaved and trained as a gladiator, Maximus is one of a troupe of warriors called to Rome for the gladiatorial games where he

Gladiator

is soon involved in plots to overthrow the emperor. Won Six Academy awards.

47. *Chicago* (2002)   113 min
Director: Rob Marshall **Cast:** Renee Zellweger, Catherine Zeta Jones, Richard Gere, Lucy Liu, Dominic West, Christine Baranski, John C. Reilly, Taye Diggs, Queen Latifah.

The film 'Chicago' takes a famed Broadway musical and gives it a fresh cinematic treatment. Chicago works well for the 21st century audience, as the dialogue and action are slotted in between the musical numbers rather than the classic formula.

Chicago received thirteen nominations and won six, Best Picture, Supporting Actress, Film Editing, Sound, Art Direction/Set Decoration and Costume.

48. *The Lord of the Rings;*
   The Return of the King
   (2003)   201 min
Director : Peter Jackson **Cast :** Sean Astin, Cate Blanchett, Billy Boyd, Liv Taylor,

| The Lumiere Brothers | The first commercial showing of a film was in the basement of the Grand-Cafe in Paris on Dec. 28, 1895. The films were made by the brothers Louis and Auguste Lumiere. Each reel of film lasted a minute. |

Elijah Wood, John Noble, Andy Serkis, Ian McKellen, Orlando Bloom, Dominic Monagham, Viggo Mortensen, David Wenham, Miranda Otto.

Based on the epic fantasy by J.R.R. Tolkien, 'The Return of the King' marks the end of the journey that began with 'The fellowship of the ring' It tells the concluding story of the hobbits Frodo and Sam, who must make a perilous journey across dangerous enemy lands in order to cast the One Ring, which is the source of all evil. The three films of the trilogy: The Lord of the Rings: The Fellowship of the Ring (2001), The Lord of the Rings: The Two Towers (2002) and The Lord of the Rings : The Return of the King (2003) were all filmed simultaneously.

The Lord of the Rings;
The Return of the King

The Return of the King was nominated for eleven Oscars and won all the eleven, an all time record like Ben-Hur and Titanic.

49. *The Hurt Locker*
(2008) 131min
Director: Kathryn Bigelow **Cast:** Jeremy Renner, Anthony Mackie, Ralph Fiennes, David Morse, Sam Red Ford, Guy Pearce, Evangeline Lilly, Christian Camargo, Nabil Koni, Barrie Rice, Brian Geraghty, Sam Spruell.

The Hurt Locker

Set during the Iraq war, The Hurtlocker Skillfully pulls us into the chaos of an elite U.S. bomb deactivation unit by concentrating on authenticity and character. Through a series of escalating set pieces and minute dollops of personal information, Bigelow presents not the nature of war, but rather the nature of the warrior. The film's director Kathryn Bigelow made history as the first female director ever to win an Oscar. Hurt locker won Academy awards for Best Picture, Director, Screenplay, Editing, Sound Editing.

50. *Avatar* (2009) 162 min
Director: James Cameron **Cast:** Sigourney Weaver, Sam Worthington, Zoe Saldana, Stephen Lang, Joel Moore, Giovanni Ribsi, Michelle Rodriguez, Laz Alonso

The culmination of a master film maker's career, Avatar marks a decades worth of work and hundreds of millions of dollars of investment. This box office record breaker

Avatar

has won Oscar awards for Best Cinematography, Art Direction and Visual Effects. ∎

World Cinema: Milestones

A chronology of the world cinema from 1824 when the phenomenon of Persistence of Vision was first discussed by two British scientists. The 100th anniversary of Hollywood adds significance to this list.

1824 British physicist Peter Mark Roget and Michael Faraday discuss the phenomenon of 'Persistence of Vision' which is the primary principle on which cinema is based. It states that 'the retina of the eye retains an impression for a fraction of a second after the image producing the impression has been removed'

1832 Belgian Joseph A Plateau (Phenakitoscope), Austrian Simon Stampfer (Stroboscope), English scientist Sir John Herschel and Dr. John Ayrton Paris (Thaumotrope) devise some optical toys to demonstrate the illusion of moving pictures.

1834 William George Horner creates 'Zoetrope'

1853 Franz Von Uchatius develops a 'Projecting Phenakitoscope'.

1876 Emil Reynaud comes up with an improved gadget - 'Praxinoscope'.

1877 Muybridge's experiments on animal locomotion

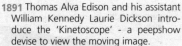

Horner

1882 Etienne Jules Marey of Beaune, France, photographs birds in flight and animals in motion with his Photographic Revolver.

1888 Appearance of Kodak roll film made it possible for E.J.Marey to devise a 'Chronophotographe', a camera capable of taking a series of photographs on a continuous strip of film.

1891 Thomas Alva Edison and his assistant William Kennedy Laurie Dickson introduce the 'Kinetoscope' - a peepshow devise to view the moving image.

1893 Edison builds his studio - Black Maria - a tar paper hut with an open roof.

1894 'Kinetoscope Parlours' - opened for public viewing on Broadway.

1895 Lumiere Brothers, Louis and Auguste in Lyon develop their 'Cinematographe'- a devise which would both photograph and project film.

1895 December 28, First public screening of silent short films by Lumiere Bros. at Salon Indian of Grand Cafe, 14, Boulevard des capucines Paris.

1896 The first public showing of a motion picture to a paying audience occurs on April 23 in New York, featuring Edison and Thomas Armat's 'Vitascope'.

• First Lumiere showing at the Watson Hotel, Bombay on July 7. By the end of the year, cinema had spread throughout Europe and America.

• Max Skladanowsky presents his 'Bioskop' - an elaborate affair using two parallel film strips and two lenses.

1898 Opening of the first film studio at New Southgate in UK. Prof. Stevenson brings first 'Bioscope' to Calcutta at the Star Theatre.

1901 First Indian actual film shot by Harischandra Sakharam Bhatvadekar (Save Dada)- "Return of Wrangler Paranjpe"

1902 George Melies shoots 'A Trip to the Moon', a screen fantasy, making the first significant use of both narrative and spe-

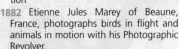

'The England Returned' **Bilet Pherat (The England Returned) was one of the first social satires of Indian cinema. It was produced by Dhiren Ganguly of Calcutta in 1921.**

Hollywood is 100 Years Old

A suburb of Los Angeles, California, which after 1912 developed into the centre of film production in the USA.

Known as the 'Dream Factory, Hollywood was originally an escape route from the controlling powers over film companies of the Eastern Trust (1909). The climate, the mountains and plains of California made Hollywood an ideal and profitable place to set up film studios. Huge studios were built in the Hollywood neighbourhood (Fox, Paramount, Warners, MGM, RKO, Universal, Columbia, United Artists Corporation). David Wark Griffith was the most influential pioneer of the cinema in the U.S. He produced films for Biograph Co. during 1908-13.

By the 1920s Hollywood was producing 90% of the American film product, and exporting massively abroad so that it was the most important film industry worldwide. By the 1930s the Hollywood studios were totally vertically integrated (controlling production, distribution and exhibition) In the same period, Hollywood was making around 600 films a year and exercised a major influence over American audience.

All changed in 1948 when a Supreme Court decision put an end to the vertical integration of the Hollywood major rival. Hollywood is presently losing its all American status and being bought up by multinational, primarily Japanese companies.

The star system is generally associated with Hollywood

cial effects in a film.

1903 Edwin S Porter shoots '*The Great Train Robbery*', the first great film spectacle.

1907 J.F. Madan opens his Elphinstone Picture Palace in Calcutta.

1908 • Formation of Motion Picture Patents Company (Dec. 8).
• National Board of Censorship founded.

1912 • Birth of Hollywood.
• Adolf Zukar launches the Paramount.
• Mack Sennett begins producing comedy shorts for the Keystone Company

1913 First Indian story film '*Raja Harischandra*' made by Dhundiraj Govind Phalke is released at Coronation Theatre, Bombay on May 3.

1915 D.W.Griffith's '*Birth of a Nation*' - famous reconstruction of the American Civil War and its aftermath.

1916 Release of Griffith's '*Intolerance*' boasting spectacular sets and spanning four epochs

Birth of a Nation - a scene

The Pioneer of Indian Cinema	The pioneer of Indian cinema was Dada Saheb Phalke who made the country's first indigenous feature film (silent) - *Raja Harishchandra*, released on May 3, 1913 at the Coronation cinema, Bombay.

1917 • The Nationalisation of Cinema in USSR.
• The Technicolour Corporation is founded in the US.
1918 • Louis Delluc starts a regular column of film criticism in Paris-Midi.
• Indian Cinematograph Act is passed.
1919 • Douglas Fairbanks forms the United Artists Company with Griffith, Chaplin and Mary Pickford.

The Cabinet of Doctor Caligari - a scene

• *'The Cabinet of Doctor Caligari'* is released, bringing the German Expressionist movement to film; Lev Kuleshov helps found the Moscow Film School, which leads to the development of montage.
1921 Charles Chaplin shoots 'The Kid'.
1922 Robert Flaherty makes 'Nanook of the North'.
1924 Erich Von Stroheim's 'Greed' is released.
1925 • Chaplin makes his 'Gold Rush'.
• In USSR, 'Battleship Potemkin' of Sergie M Eisenstein released.
1926 • Release of Vsevolod Pudovkins *'Mother'*.
• Himansu Rai's *'Light of Asia'* - an Indo German co-production creates an impact abroad.
1927 •The Sound Era begins when The Jazz Singer opens on October 6 featuring a synchronised sound track on its musical numbers.

1928 • The first all talking film *'The Lights of New York'* is released on July 6.
• Release of Carl Theodore Dreyer's 'The Passion of Joan of Arc' and Walt Disney's *'Steam boat Willie'* and Charlie Chaplin's *'The Circus'*.
1929 •The first Academy Award presentation is held on May 16 (Best film : Wings, Best Director: Frank Borzage)
• Hitchcock's 'Black Mail' the first talking film made in England establishes him as a master of thriller.
1930 • The Studio Era begins in Hollywood (1930-1945).
• Beginning of Documentary School in UK.
• Release of Joseph von Sternberg's *'Blue Angel'* (Germany).
• The Hollywood Production Code is put into use.
1931 • Charlie Chaplin's *'City Lights'* released with sound track.
• Release of Tod Browning's *'Dracula'*
• Death of the Cinema Pioneer Thomas Alva Edison.
1932 • Death of George Eastman, founder and President of Eastman Kodak.
• Venice launches International festival.
1933 • Merian C Cooper and Edgar B Schoedsack make 'King Kong'
• Darryl F. Zanuck founds 2th century.
• British Film Institute has been established.
1935 • The Television is introduced and the movies declare war.

The Informer - a poster

• Release of John Ford's first major hit *'The Informer'* and Alfred Hitchcock's *'The 39 Steps.'*
1936 • Leni Riefenstahl was commissioned by Hitler to film the Berlin Olympic Games.
1937 • Jean Renoir's *'Grand Illusion'* and Walt Disney's *'Snowwhite and*

Darsheel Vs. Shah Rukh   **Darsheel Safari was only 11 years old when he competed with Shah Rukh Khan for the best actor's crown in Filmfare Awards.**

---

the Seven Dwarfs' released.

1938 •Sergie Eisenstein's first sound film *'Alexander Nevsky'* released.

1939 • Victor Fleming's *'Gone with the Wind'* and the *'Wizard of Oz'*. John Ford's *Stage Coach*, William Wyler's *'Wuthering Heights'* released.

1940 • Oscar Award for *'Gone with the Wind'* (9 awards).

Chaplin in The Great Dictator

• Chaplin's *'The Great Dictator'*, Walt Disney's Pinocchio and Fantasia released.

1941 • Orson Welles makes *'Citizen Kane'*.

• Greta Garbo bids farewell to the screen.

1942 • Germaine Dulac, the avant-garde director and cinema theorist died on July 19 at Paris.

• Deaths of Carole Lombard & John Barrymore.

1943 • Release of Akira Kurosawa's first film *'Sugata Sanshiro'* Luchino Visconti's *'Ossessione'*, and Michael Curtiz's *Casablanca'*.

1944 • Release of Laurence Olivier's *'Henry V'*, a brilliant adaptation of Shakespeare's war play and Billy Wilder's *Double Indemnity*.

1945 • Roberto Rossellini enters neo-realist field with *'Rome, Open City'*.

• Eisenstein completes the first part of *'Ivan The Terrible'*.

• The Motion Picture Export Association of America is founded.

• Release of the *Lost Weekend*, (Billy Wilder) and *Brief Encounter* (David Lean).

1946 •Jean Cocteau's *'Beauty and Beast'* released and wins Louis Delluc Prize.

• David Lean's *'Great Expectations'* and Charles Vidor's *'Gilda'* are released.

• The International Film Festival returns to Cannes.

1947 • William Wyler's *'The Best Years of Our Lives'* walked away with seven Academy awards.

• Release of Chaplin's 'Monsieur Verdoux', Elia Kazan's 'Gentle Man's Agreement' and Eisensteins 'Ivan The Terrible' Part II are released.

• Satyajit Ray helps found the first film society in India, the Calcutta Film Society.

1948 • Release of Vittorio De Sica's *'The Bicycle Thief'*.

• Deaths of Louis Lumiere, and D.W. Griffith and Sergie Eisenstein.

• Laurence Oliver's *'Hamlet'* wins Grand prize at the Venice Festival.

1949 • Deaths of Victor Fleming and Wallace Beery.

1950 • The Studio system collapses.

• Hollywood converts to colour film.

• Release of *'All about Eve'* by Joseph Mankiewicz, *'Stromboli'* by Rossellini; *'Rashomon'* by Akira Kurosawa, *'Sunset Boulevard'* by Billy Wilder.

1951 • Release of Elia Kazan's *'A Street Car Named Desire*, Robert Wise's *'The Day the Earth Stood Still'* and Vincente Minnellis' *'An American in Paris'*.

• *'Rashomon'* wins Golden Lion prize at Venice Film Festival.

1952 • The Opening of the Indian International Film Festival marks the first festival of cinema in Asia (Bombay).

• The new projection system known as Cinerama was put on display. The tripanel panoramic picture is thrown from three projectors but looks like a single picture.

THX Sound

THX Sound was a multi speaker sound system developed by Lucasfilm and used in selected motion picture theatres to increase frequency range, audience coverage and dialogue intelligibility while decreasing low bass distortion.

- The Hollywood premiere of Arch Oboler's 3D Film *'Bwana Devil'*.
- Release of Chaplin's *'Limelight'*, Fred Zinnemann's *'High Noon'*, Stanley Donen & Gene Kelly's *'Singin' in the Rain'*.

1953 • Cinemascope becomes a popular technique for recording motion pictures when the first Cinemascope film *'The Robe'* is released.
- Release of Henry George Clouzot's *'The Wages of Fear'*, Fred Zinnemann's *'From Here To Eternity'* and William Wyler's *'Roman Holiday'*.
- Mizoguchis *'Ugetsu monogatari'* is released

1954 • Release of Elia Kazan's, *'On the Waterfront'*, Hitchcock's *'Rear Window'*, Federico Fellinis' *'La Strada'* & Kurosawa's *'Seven Samurai'*

1955 • Satyajit Ray's *'Pather Panchali'* is

A scene from Pather Panchali

released. Also Clouzot's *Diaboliques'*, Nicholas Ray's *'Rebel with a Cause'* and Delbert Mann's *'Marty'* are released
- Carl Dreyers *'Ordet'* wins Golden Lion from Venice.
- Disneyland opens its gates to public.
- The Era of Polish Cinema begins (1955-1964).

1956 • Release of *'Burmese Harp'* by Kon Ichikawa, *'Searchers'* by John Ford, *'War and Peace'* by KingVidor, *'Baby Doll'* by Elia Kazan and Roger Vadim's *'And God Created Woman'*.
- Rock 'n' Roll sensation Elvis Presley made his movie debut in *'Love Me Tender'*.

- Death of Prof. Henri Chretien who developed Hypergonar from which cinemascope is derived.
- Satyajit Ray's *'Pather Panchali'* wins 'best human document prize' at Cannes.

1957 • Release of Ingmar Bergman's *'The Seventh Seal'* and *'Wild Strawberries'*, Kurosawa's *'The Throne of Blood'*, David Lean's *'The Bridge on the River Kwai'*.
- Deaths of Erich Von Stroheim, Humphrey Bogart, Louis B Mayer, Gene Lockart and Oliver Hardy.
- Andrzej Wajda revives cinema in Poland with his *'Kanal'*.

1958 • Seven Oscar awards for David Lean's *'The Bridge on the River Kwai'*.
- Release of Andrej Wajdas *'Ashes and Diamonds'*, Bergman's *'The Magician'*, Richard Brooke's *'Cat on a Hot Tin Roof'* & Vincent Minnellis' *'Gigi'*,

1959 • *'New Wave'* begins in France.
- Truffauts' *'The 400 Blows'*, Godard's' *'Breathless'*, and Alan Resnai's *Hiroshima mon Amour'* are released.
- *'Gigi'* wins nine academy awards.
- Satyajit Ray's *'Apur Sansar'* is released.
- Deaths of Cecil B De Mille, Preston Sturges, Errol Flynn, Victor Mc Lagen, Ethel Barrymore and Lou Costello

1960 • *BenHur* wins eleven Oscar awards.
- Release of Ingmar Bergman's *'The Virgin Spring'*, Hitchcock's *'Psycho'*. Kurosawa's *'Yojimbo'*, Daniel Mann's *'Butterfield 8'*, Jack Clayton's *'Room at the Top'*, Stanley Kubrick's *'Spar-tacus'* and John Sturge's *'The Magnificent Seven'*.
- Deaths of Clark Gable, Cedric Gibbons, Mack Sennett, Victor Sjostrom, Margaret Sullivan.
- Fellini's *'La*

Elizabeth Taylor in Butterfield

What's a Hybrid Film

Hybrid film is a film that is not exclusively fictional or documentary or avant – garde but instead shares characteristics of two or all three of the major types of films. An example is Andy Warhol's 'Sleep', which can be characterized as avant-garde documentary.

Dolce Vita' wins Golden Palm at Cannes.

1961 • Golden Bear for 'La Notte' at Venice Festival.

• Vittorio De Sica's 'Two Women' displays Sophia Loren's mettle.

• Elizabeth Taylor gets Best Actress Oscar for 'Butterfield-8'.

• World premiere of 'The Misfits' directed by John Huston. starring Montgomary Clift, Marilyn Monroe and Clark Gable.

• Release of Alan Resnais' 'Last year at Marienbad'.

Marilyn Monroe

• Release of Truffaut's 'Jules et Jim', Bunuels' Viridiana' and Godard's 'A Woman is a Woman', and Robert Wise's 'Westside story.'

1962 •Release of Lean's 'Lawrence of Arabia', Yasujiro Ozu's 'An Autumn Afternoon', Robert Mulligan's 'To Kill A Mocking Bird', Kubrick's 'Lolita', J Lee Thompson's 'Cape Fear' and Kurosawa's 'Sanjuro'.

Lawrence of Arabia - a scene

• 'Westside Story' scooped ten Oscars.

• Golden Lion to Tarkovsky's 'Ivan's Childhood' and Valerio Zurlini's 'Family Diary'.

• Death of Marilyn Monroe.

• Screen debut of Sean Connery as James Bond in Dr. No.

Sean Connery

1963 • The Czech New Wave (1963-1969) begins

• Release of Fellini's 8–1/2, Kubrick's Dr. Strangelove', John Sturge's 'The Great Escape', Hitchcock's "The Birds', Ralph Nelson's 'Lilies of the Field', Bergman's 'The Silence', Joseph L.Mankiewicz's 'Cleopatra' and Visconti's 'The Leopard'.

• Deaths of Yasujiro Ozu, Jean Cocteau.

• Stanley Kramer's 'It is a Mad, Mad, Mad World' boasts a colossal comedy.

1964 • Sergio Leone makes his first Spaghetti Western 'A Fistful of Dollars'

• Release of Roman Polanski's 'Repulsion', Pasolini's 'The Gospel According to St. Mathew', George Cukor's 'My Fair Lady', 'and Joseph Losey's 'The Servant', Guy Hamilton's 'Gold finger', Antonioni's 'Red Desert'.

• Robert Stevenson's delightful musical comedy, 'Mary Poppins' released.

1965 • Release of David Lean's 'Doctor Zhivago', Milos Forman's 'A Blonde's Love', Godard's 'Alphaville', Robert Wise's 'The Sound of Music'.

Richard Lester's 'The Knack - And How to Get It' wins Grand Prix at Cannes.

George Cukor's 'My Fair Lady' wins eight Academy awards.

1966 • Release of Antonioni's 'Blow up', Bergman's 'Persona', Jiri Menzel's 'Closely Watched Trains', Polanski's 'Cul- de - Sac', Godard's 'Masculin Feminin', and Hitchcoock's 'Torn Curtain'.

• Five Oscars for 'The Sound of Music'.

One Flew Over

Ken Kesey, the American author, wrote the novel *One Flew Over the Cuckoo's Nest* (1962). He had served as an experimental subject and aide in a hospital. This experience helped in writing the book. The film came in 1975.

• Death of Walt Disney.

• Andy Warhol's *'The Chelsea Girl'* has made history as the first ever Underground film to play in a theatre.

• Former Actor Ronald Reagan is elected as Governor of California.

1967 • Release of Arthur Penn's *'Bonnie and Clyde'*, Mike Nichol's *'The Graduate'*, Norman Jewison's *'In the Heat of the Night'*, Luis Bunuel's *'Belle de jour'*, Stanley Kramer's *'Guess who's coming to Dinner'*, and Godard's *' Weekend'*. Creation of American Film Institute.

• Death of Vivien Leigh, Spencer Tracy, Anthony Mann, Ann Sheridan.

Vivien Leigh - a scene from 'Gone with the Wind'

1968 • Release of Franco Zeffirelli's *'Romeo and Juliet'*, Stanley Kubrick's *'2001: A Space Odyssey'*, Roman Polanski's' *'Rosemary's Baby'*, William Wyler's *'Funny Girl'*, and Paul Morrissey's *'Flesh'*, Humberto Solas' *'Lucia'*, Tomas Gutierrez Alea's *'Memories of Underdevelopment'*.

1969 • Release of John Schlesinger's *'Midnight Cowboy'*, Richard Attenborough's *'Oh! What a Lovely War'*, Costa Gavra's *'Z'*.

• Founding of American Zoetrope by Francis Ford Coppola and George Lukas.

• Deaths of Robert Taylor, Joseph von Sternberg

1970 • Release of Kurosowa's first colour film - *'Dodeskaden*

• Claude Chabrol's *'The Butcher'*, Robert Altman's M.A.S.H., Mike Nichol's *"Catch 22'*, David Lean's 'R*yan's Daughter'*, Arthur Penn's *'Little Big Man'* and Michael Wadleigh's documentary *'Woodstock'* and Franklin Schaffner's *Patton*.

• Motion Picture Rating Syatem is developed and replaces the maturity rating system.

1971 • Cannes Festival celebrates 25th birthday

• Release of William Friedkins' *"The French Connection"*, Norman Jewison's *'Fiddler On The Roof'*, Stanley Kubrick's, *A Clockwork Orange'* Alan J. Pakula's *'Klute'*, and Nicholas Roeg's *'Walkabout'*.

• Deaths of Harold Lloyd, Audie Murphy, Paul Lukas, Bebe Daniels, Billy Gilbert.

1972 • Release of Francis Ford Coppola's *'The Godfather'*, Bob Fosse's *'Cabaret'*. Bernando Bertolucci's *'The Last Tango in Paris* and John Boorman's *'Deliverance'*.

• Chaplin has been awarded a 'Special Oscar' for his "exceptional and invaluable contribution to the art of cinema in the 20th century".

• Deaths of Maurice Chevalier, George Sanders, Miriam Hopkins and William Dieterle.

1973 • Release of Ingmar Bergman's *'Cries and Whispers'*, Werner Herzog's *'Aguirre, The Wrath of God'*, George Lucas' *'American Graffiti'*, Franklin J. Schaffner's *'Papillon'*, William Friedkin's *The Exorcist*, and Peter Bogdanovich's *Paper Moon'*, and George Roy Hill's *'The Sting'*.

• Deaths of John Ford, Bruce Lee.

1974 • Release of Coppola's *'The God Father Part II*, Roman Polanski's *'China Town'*, Fellini's *'Amarcord'*, and Youssef Chahine's *'The Sparrow'*, Alan Resnais' *Stavisky.*

1975 • Steven Spielberg's 'Jaws' is released and begins the era of the blockbuster film.

• Release of Milos Forman's *'One Flew over the Cuckoo's Nest'*, Kubrick's,

The *Psycho* Sequence	In *Psycho*'s most sensational sequence, motel keeper Norman watches through a peephole as a young woman undresses. Minutes later she is knifed. The scene contains 70 shots in less than a minute.

'*Barry Lyndon*', Robert Altman's '*Nashville*', Peter Weir's '*Picnic at Hanging Rock*', Woody Allen's '*Love and Death*', Bergman's '*Magic Flute*', Antonioni's '*The Passenger*', Volker Schlondorff's '*The Lost Honor of Katharina Blum*', Tomas Aleas' *The Last Supper*.

• Deaths of George Stevens, Susan Haywand, Fredric March, William Wellman, Larry Parker and Pier Paolo Pasolini.

1976 • Release of John Guillermin's '*King Kong*' John G.Avildson's '*Rocky*', Polanski's '*The Tenant*', Alan J. Pakula's '*All The President's Men*' Bergmans '*Face to Face*' and Bertolucci's '*1900*'.

• Jean Renoir receives the 'Legion of Honor'

1977 • Release of George Lucas' '*Starwars*', Woody Allen's '*Annie Hall*', Pasolini's '*Salo*', Spielberg's '*Close Encounters of the Third Kind*', Luis Bunuel's '*That Obscure Object of Desire*', Claude Goretta's '*The Lacemaker*' and John Badham's '*Saturday Night Fever*'.

• Deaths of Groucho Marx, Joan Crawford, Elvis Presley, Bing Crosby, Howard Hawks, Stephen Boyd and Sir. Charles Chaplin.

1978 • Release of Michael Cimino's '*The Deer Hunter*', Louis Malle's '*Pretty Baby*', Hal Ashby's, '*Coming Home*', Bergman's '*Autumn Sonata*', Richard Donner's '*Superman*', John Carpenter's '*Halloween*',

• Deaths of Charles Boyer, Robert Shaw, and Jack L.Warner

1979 • Release of Coppola's '*Apocaypse Now*', Woody Allen's '*Manhattan*', Schlondorff's '*The Tin Drum*', Ridley Scotts' '*Alien*', Rainer Werner Fassbinder's '*The Marriage of Maria Braun*', Robert Benton's '*Kramer vs Kramer*'; Herzog's '*Nosferatu-the Vampire*', Hal Ashby's '*Being There*', Bob Fosse's '*All That Jazz*' and Polansky's '*Tess*'.

• Deaths of Jean Renoir, Mary Pickford, Nicholas Ray, John Wayne, Jean Seberg, Darryl Zanuck, and John Cromwell.

• Golden Palm for '*The Tin Drum*' and *Apocalypse Now*.

• Alfred Hitchcock receives 'Lifetime Achievement Award' from The American Film Institute.

• Several advancements in movie making, such as the Dolby system and special effects.

1980 • The Hollywood years begin, characterised by several sub-genres of films.

• Andrzej Wajda's '*The Conductor*', Martin Scorcese's '*Raging Bull*', Robert Redford's '*Ordinary People*', and Kubrick's '*The Shining*' are released.

• Kurosawa's '*Kagemusha*' and Bob Fosses's '*All That Jazz*' shares the Golden Palm from Cannes.

• Deaths of Alfred Hitchcock, Peter Sellers, Steve Mc Queen, Mae West, George Raft and Raoul Walsh.

1981 • Release of Istvan Szabo's '*Mephisto*', Warren Beatty's '*Reds*', Karel Reisz's '*The French Lieutenant's Women*', Peter Weirs '*Gallipolli*', and Spielberg's '*Raiders of the Lost Ark*' .

• 'Golden Palm' for Wajda's '*Man of Marble*'.

• Oscar (Best foreign film) for a film from USSR- '*Moscow Does Not Believe in Tears*'.

Elvis Presley

| Black Comedy | Black comedy is a style used in some narratives since World War II that shows the humorous possibilities in subjects previously considered off limits to comedy, such as warfare, murder, death, and dying. Black comedies are often also satiric. |

Chariots of Fire

• Deaths of Glauber Rocha, William Holden, Natalie Wood, Melvyn Douglas, William Wyler, Robert Montgomery.

1982 • Release of Costa- Gavras's *Missing'*, Bergmans' *Fanny and Alexander'*, Richard Attenborough's *'Gandhi'*, Sidney Lumet's, *The Verdict*; Alan J. Pakula's *Sophie's Choice*, Spielberg's *'E.T. The Extra Terrestrial'*, and Hugh Hudson's *Chariots of Fire*.

• Deaths of King Vidor, Eleaner Powell, Rainer Werner Fassbinder, Jacques Tati, Kenneth More, Henry King, John Belushi Ingrid Bergman Grace Kelly, and Lee Strasberg.

• Frank Capra honoured with American Film Institute's 'Lifetime Achievement Award'.

1983 • Release of *Danton* – Andrzej Wajada, *First Name Carmen* - Jean Luc Godaed, *Ballad of Narayama* - Shohei Imamura, *Silkwood* - Mike Nichols, *First Blood* - Ted Kotcheff, *Erendira*- Ruy Guera, *Koyanisqatsi* - (avant garde documentary)- Godfrey Reggio, *Yentl* – Barbra Streisand, *Terms of Endearment* - James L. Brooks.

• HBO begins producing feature films.

• Deaths of George Cukor, David Niven, Luis Bunuel, Gloria Swanson.

• Bhanu Athaiya wins Oscar for Costume Design.

1984 • Release of *Amadeus*- Milos For-

man, *Paris Texas*- Wim Wenders, *Yellow Earth*- Chen Kaige, *Frida*- Paul Leduc.

• PG-13 film rating begins.

• Creation of a new Production Company *'Touch stone'* by Disney.

• Deaths of Richard Burton, Francois Truffaut, Joseph Losey Janet Gaynor, James Mason.

• Satyajit Ray receives honorary Oscar.

1985 • Release of *Ran*- Akira Kurosawa, *Prizzi's Honor*- John Huston, *Witness*- Peter Weir, *Colonel Redl*- Istvan Szabo, *Vagabond*- Agnes Varda, *The Purple Rose of Cairo*- Woody Allen, *The Official Story*- Luis Puenzo, *Pale Rider*- Clint Eastwood.

• Sundance Film Festival founded by Robert Redford to promote independent films.

• First laser video disc players and video discs with digital sound.

• For the first time home movie video revenues exceed those of theatrical revenues.

• Deaths of Orson Welles, Rock Hudson, Yul Brynner, Simone Signoret, Michael Redgrave.

1986 • Release of *Platoon*- Oliver stone, *Ginger and Fred*- Fellini, *Sacrifice*- Andrei Tarkovsky, *Monalisa*- Neil Jordan, *Hannah and her Sisters*- Woody Allen, *Blue Velvet*- David Lynch, *The Color of Money*- Martin Scorcese; *The Fly*- David Cronenberg.

• Deaths of Vincent Minnelli. Cary Grant, Andrei Tarkovsky James Cagney, Otto Preminger.

1987 • Release of *The Dead*- John Huston, *Hope and Glory*- John Boorman, *The Last Emperor*- Bernado Bertolucci, *Red Sorghum*- Zhang Yimou, *Cry Freedom* – Richard Attenborough, *Wings of Desire*- Wim Wenders, *Full Metal Jacket*- Stanley Kubrick. *Surrogate Mother*- Im Kwon Taek.

• Deaths of Rita Hayworth, John Huston, Lee Marvin, Danny Kaye, Fred Astaire, Joseph E. Levine, Andy Warhol, Geraldine Page.

Sophia Loren

In *La Ciociara*, Sophia Loren was the mother of a teenage daughter in WWII-ruined Italy. The 1961 film, directed by Vittorio de Sica, is known in English as *Two Women*. It gave Sophia Loren the best role of her career.

1988 • Release of *The Last Temptation of Christ*- Martin Scorcese, *Dangerous Liaisons*- Stephen Frears, *Rain Man*- Barry Levinson, T*he Accused*- Jonathan Kaplan, *Who Framed Roger Rabbit*- Robert Zemeckis, *A Short Film About Killing*- Krzystof Kieslowski, *Mississippi Burning*- Alan Parker, *Little Vera*- Vasily Pichul.

• Prince Charles opened England's new temple of cinema- The Museum of The Moving Images (MOMI).

• Morphing first used in making parts of a feature film.

• Deaths of Trevor Howard, Joshua Logan, Hal Ashby.

'Sex, lies and Videotape'

1989 • Release of *Sex, lies, and Videotape*- Steven Soderbergh, *My Left Foot*- Jim Sheridan, *Born on The Fourth of July*- Oliver stone, *Cinema Paradiso*- Giuseppe Tornatore, *Driving Miss Daisy*- Bruce Beresford, *Women on the Verge of a Nervous Breakdown*- Pedro Almodavar.

• Canada's film industry turns 50 years.

• U.S. National Film Registry established to recognize significant American Films.

• Time, Inc. buys Warner Communications, creating world's largest entertainment group.

• Deaths of Laurence Oliver, John Cassavetes, Sergio Leone, Bette Davis, Franklin J. Schaffner.

1990 • Rapid growth of Cable Television Video once again threatens movie audi-

ence and major studios launch their own channels.

• NC-17 rating instituted. First film so rated: *Henry and June*. Release of *Dances With Wolves* – Kevin Costner, *Home Alone*- Chris Columbus, *Nikita*– Luc Besson, *Pretty Woman* – Gary Marshall. *Good Fellas*– Martin Scorcese, *Reversal of Fortune*– Barbet Schroeder.

• Deaths of Ava Gardner, Rex Harrison, Greta Garbo, Martin Ritt, Barbara Stanwyck, Paulette Goddard.

1991 • Release of *The Silence of the Lambs*- Jonathan Demme. V*an Gogh* – Maurice Pialet, *Raise the Red Lantern*- Zhang Yimou, *Life is Sweet*- Mike Leigh, *Urga*- Nikita Mikhalkov, *Robinhood: Prince of Thieves*- Kevin Reynolds. J*FK*- Oliver Stone, *The Prince of the Tides*- Barbra Streisand.

• Deaths of David Lean, Frank Capra, Lino Brocka, Yves Montand, Lee Remick, Tony Richardson.

1992 • Release of *Unforgiven*- Clint Eastwood, *Basic Instinct*- Paul Verhoeven, *The Player* – Robert Altman- Malcom X- Spike Lee, *Batman Returns*- Tim Burton, *The Divine Comedy*- Manoel de Oliveira, *Chaplin*- Attenborough; *Agantuk*- Satyajit Ray.

• Deaths of Satyajit Ray, Marlene Dietrich, Anthony Perkins.

1993 • Release of *Jurassic Park and Schindler's List*- Steven Spielberg, *Piano*-Jane Campion, *Farewell My Concubine* – Chen Kaige, *Three colors Blue* – Krzystof Kieslowski, *Sleepless in Se-*

A scene from 'Jurassic Park'

Five Cents Theater

Nickelodeon, literally, 'Five cents theater', is a small store front movie theatre popular in the United States, 1905 to 1915. It was the successor to one –person peephole machines and the forerunner of large movie theaters that were called 'movie palaces'.

attle- Nora Ephron, *Demolition Man*-
Macro Brambilla.
- Deaths of Audrey Hepburn, Lilian Gish,
Joseph L. Mankiewicz, Stewart Granger,
Federico Fellini.

1994 • IMAX 3-D films shown in the U.S.
- Kodak introduces a digital imaging system.
- Spielberg, Jeffrey Katzenberg and David Geffen form - SKG to produce theatrical films, animation, TV programmes,
and interactive media.
- Release of *Forrest Gump*- Robert
Zemeckis, *Four Weddings and a Funeral*- Mike Newell, *Ed Wood*- Tim
Burton, *The Lion King*- (Disney Animation), *Speed*- Jan De Bont, *Pulp Fiction*-
Quentin Tarantino, Red- Kieslowski,
Vanya on 42nd Street-Louis Malle,
Exotica- Atom Egoyan, *Bullets over
Broadway*- Woody Allen.

'Toy Story'

1995 • 'Toy Story' is the first feature film
made entirely with computer animation.
- Release of *Babe*- Chris Noonan, *Shanghai Triad*- Zhang Yimou, *Brave heart*-
Mel Gibson, *Apollo 13*- Ron Howard,
Leaving Las Vegas- Mike Figgis, *The
Unusual Suspects*- Bryan Singer.

1996 • Release of 'The English Patient'-
Anthony Minghella, *Crash*- David
Cronenberg, *Evita*- Alan Parker, *Secrets
& Lies* – Mike Leigh, *Mission Impossible*- Brian De Palma, *Independence
Day*- Roland Emmerich, *Fargo*- Joel
Coen, *Shine*- Scott Hicks. *Breaking the
Waves*- Lars Von Trier, *The Nutty Professor*- Tom Shadyac, *Prisoner of the

'Titanic'

Mountains- Sergei Bodrov.
- Deaths of Krzysztof Keislowski, Tomas
Gutierrez Alea, Claudette Colbert, Dean
Martin, Albert R. Broccoli.
- French Actor Gerard Depardieu has
been made Chevalier de la Legion d'
Honneur.

1997 • 'Starwars' is revised slightly and re
released to theatres and passes ET as the
highest grossing movie in history so far.
- Release of *Titanic* – James Cameron,
L.A. Confidential- Curtis Hanson, T*he
Apostle*- Robert Duvall, *The Ice Storm*-
Ang Lee, *The Taste of Cherries*- Abbas
Kiarostomi, *Men in Black*- Barry Sonnenfeld, *My Best Friends Wedding* – P.J.
Hogan.
- The 50th Anniversary of the British
Academy Awards (BAFTA).
- At the 50th Cannes Film Festival, Shonei Imamura's '*The Eel*' and Kiarostomi's
'*The Taste of Cherries*' shared the Palm
d' Or.
- Deaths of James Stewart, Fred Zinnemann, Robert Mitchum, Bo Widerberg, Toshiro Mifune.

1998 • 'Titanic' passes 'Starwars' as the
highest grossing movie in history.
- Release of *Saving Private Ryan*- Steven Spielberg, *The Truman Show*- Peter
Weir, *Leila*- Dariush Mehrjui, *Elizabeth*-
Shekhar Kapur, *Beloved*- Jonathan
Demme, *Central Station*- Walter Salles,

| Surrealism | **Surrealism is a movement in 1920s and 1930s European art, drama, literature, and film in which an attempt was made to portray or interpret the working of the subconscious mind as manifested in dreams.** |

Everest (a narrative documentary commercially successful film in IMAX history), Shakespeare in Love- John Madden.

• Deaths of Frank Sinatra, Akira Kurosawa, Alan J. Pakula.

1999 • Release of *Run Lola Run*- Tom Tykwer, *All about My Mother*- Pedro Almodovar, *The Matrix*- Larry Wachowski, and Andy Wachowski, *Notting Hill*- Roger Michell, *The Sixth sense* Manoj Night Shyamalan, *Sleeply Hollow* – Tim Burton.

• Deaths of George C. Scott, Oliver Reed, Dirk Bogarde, Stanley Kubrick, Buddy Rogers, Victor Mature, Mario Puzo.

2000 • Release of *American Beauty* – Sam Mendes, *Dancer in the Dark* – Lars von Trier, *The Circle* – Jafar Panahi, *Erin Brockovich*- Steven Soderberg, *Being John Malkovich*- Spike Jonze, *Crouching Tiger, Hidden Dragon*- Ang Lee, *Gladiator*- Ridely Scott

• Deaths of Hedy Lamarr, Alec Guiness, John Gielgud, Roger Vadim, George Montgomery, Walter Matthau, Jason Robards.

2001 • Release of *Cast Away*- Robert Zemeckis, *Moulin Rouge*- Baz Luhrman, *Lord of the Rings: The Fellowship of*

A scene from 'Lord of the Rings'

the Ring – Peter Jackson. *Harry Potter and the Philosopher's Stone*- Chris Columbus, *A Beautiful Mind*- Ron Howard.

• Deaths of Anthony Quinn, Stanley Kramer, Jack Lemmon, Pauline Kael (film critic).

2002 • ET: The Extra Terrestrial has a 20th anniversary re- release with computer generated improvements.

• Release of *Adaptation*- Spike Jonze, *Road To Perdition*- Sam Mendes, *Ocean Eleven* – Steven Soderbergh, *Monsoon Wedding*- Mira Nair, *Chicago*- Rob Marshall, *The Pianist*- Roman Polansky.

• Deaths of Billy Wilder, Rod Steiger, Dudley Moore, Richard Harris, Karel Reisz, George Roy Hill, James Coburn.

2003 • Release of *The Pirates of the Caribbean – The curse of the Black Pearl*- Gore Verbinsky, *Catch Me If you Can* – Steven Spielberg, *Finding Nemo*- Andrew Stanton, *Cold Mountain*- Anthony Minghella. *Mystic River*- Clint Eastwood; *The Matrix Revolutions*- Wachowski Brothers; *The Return*- Andrey Zvyagintesev. *Spring, Summer, Fall, Winter* - Kim Ki-duk.

• Deaths of Gregory Peck, Katherine Helpburn, Bob Hope, Elia Kazan, John Schlesinger, Charles Bronson, Leni Riefenstahl, Alan Bates.

2004 • Release of *Lost in Translation*- Sofia Coppola, *The Passion of the Christ*- Mel Gibson, *Fahrenheit-9/11*- Michael Moore, *Neverlands*- Daniel Frohman, *The Aviator*- Martin Scorcese, V*era Drake*- Mike Leigh, *Million Dollar Baby*- Clint Eastwood. *Free Zone* - Amos Gitai

• Peter Jackson's *The Lord of the Rings: The Return of the King*, wins 11 Oscar Awards.

• Deaths of Peter Ustinov, Ronald Reagan, Marlon Brando, Christopher Reeve, Howard Keel.

2005 • Release of *Turtles Can Fly*- Bahman Ghobadi, *Ray*- Taylor Hackford, *Crash*- Paul Haggis, *Brokeback Moutain*- Ang Lee, *Harry Potter and the Goblet of Fire*- Mike Newell, *War of the Worlds*- Steven Spieberg, *Capote*- Bennett Miller, *Melinda and Melinda*- Woody Allen;

| Light of Asia | In 1926, a film made Indian cinema widely known on the international level - Light of Asia (Prem Sagar) directed by Franz Osten and Himansu Rai. |

Vanity Fair -
a poster

Vanity Fair- Mira Nair. *Saraband-*Ingmar Bergman. *The Bow-* Kim Ki-duk, *The Last Moon-* Miguel Littin.

• Deaths of John Mills, Robert Wise, Virginia Mayo, Ann Bancroft, Richard Pryor, and Ismail Merchant.

2006 • Release of *Munich-*Spielberg, *Memoirs of a Geisha* – Rob Marshall, *Tsotsi-*Gavin Hood, *Syriana-*Stephen Gagha, *Half Moon-* Bahman Ghobadi, *Lights in the Dusk* – Aki Kaurismaki, *Coeurs-*Alan Resnais, *Time* – Kim Ki-duk, *I served the King of England-*Jiri Menzel, *Marie Antoinette-*Sofia Coppola, *Pan's Labyrinth-*Guillermo Del Toro, *The Depart*ed –Scorcese.

• Deaths of Shelly Winters, Gordon Parks, Moira Shearer.

• Ken Loach's *'The Wind That Shakes the Barley'* released

2007 • Release of *No country For Old Men* – Joel and Ethan Coen, *Ulzhan-*Volker Schlondorff, *A Girl Cut in Two* – Claude Chabrol, *The Song of the Sparrows* – Majid Majidi, *The Rebirth-*Kobayashi, *Breath* – Kim Ki-duk; *Buddha Collapsed out of shame* – Hanna Makmal Baff.

• Deaths of Ingmar Bergman, Michelangelo Antonioni.

2008 • Release of *Shirin-Abbas Kiarostami, Funny Games* – Michael Haneke, *Slum Dog Millionaire* - Danny Boyle, *Burn after Reading-*Joel and Ethan Coen. *The Dark Knight-*Christopher Nolan, *The Wrestler-*Darren Aronofsky, *Hurt Locker-*Kathryn Bigelow, *Avatar-*James Cameron.

• Deaths of Paul Newman, Anthony Minghella.

2009 • Release of *Broken Embraces-*Pedro Almodovar, *Dream* – Kim Ki-duk, *Vision-*

Slumdog Millionaire - a scene

Margaretha Von Trotta, *Antichrist* – Lars Von Trier, *About Elly-*Asghar Farhadi, *Re visited* – Krzysztof Zanussi, *Sweet Rush-*Andrzej Wajda, *True Noon-*Nosir Saidov. The White Ribbon – Michael Haneke, Inglourious Basterds – Quentin Tarantino.

• Slumdog Millionaire brings India Oscars: A.R. Rehman and Resul Pookutt.y

2010 • Release of *'The King's Speech'*, *'Black Swan'-*Darren Aronofsky

A scene from The King's Speech

2011 • Release of *The Tree of Life* – Terrence Malik, *Thor-*Kenneth Branagh, *Priest-*Scott Stewart, *The Beloved* – Christophe Honore, *Hanna* – Joe Wright, *Melancholia-* Lars Von Trier, *Midnight in Pairs-*Woody Allen, *Unlawful Killing* – Keith Allen, *Pirates of the Carribean: On strange Tides-* Rob Marshall.

• Deaths of Elizabeth Taylor, Michael Sarrazin

• Oscar Winner Colin Firth was honoured by Queen Elizabeth. He was made a Commander of the British Empire (CBE). ∎

Seema in 'Queens!'

Bandit Queen actor Seema Biswas is to play a transsexual in Queens! Destiny of Dance a film directed by David Atkin. Seema's role is inspired by the trials of Manvendra Singh Gohil, the first person of royal lineage in India to reveal his homosexuality.

50 World Classics

Prof P. Vijaya Kumar

World classics are literary works of eternal value. They are generally recognisesd as deserving to be the best. They set quality standards for other books. They are like jewels.

The idea of the classic took shape in 18th century France, solidified in 19th century Germany and spread around the world through education systems that imitated German or European models. A classic means one of the very best. While a variety of things can be termed classic – from civilizations and languages to designs and performances – the word is primarily used for individual works. The works could be musical compositions or poems or those of other genres. "Classic" is, however, used more often for works of imaginative literature. Being a derivative of an essentially early 19th century German idea there is a certain elitism and a suggestion of "high culture" associated with it. But, shorn of its lack of egalitarianism, it is still a useful idea and worthwhile ideal simply for its suggestion that a classic is a work of high quality and of enduring value and timeless appeal. Note: The dates indicated are those of composition or first publication. Some are conjectural. (CE stands for Common Era and BCE for Before Common Era.)

1. The Mahabharata
(BCE 500 – CE 500)

Tells the story of war between rival bands of brothers, the Pandavas and the Kauravas both of whom claim the land of Kuru. It also contains innumerable subplots, episodes and philosophical, ethical and religious digressions making it a Leviathan of an epic. The gambling contest in which Yu-

Mahabharata

dhistira loses Draupadi, the stories of Nala and Damayanthi and Krishna's sermon to Arjun – considered by many to contain the quintessence of Hinduism - are among the most well know parts. At around 100,000 couplets it is the longest poem that has ever existed and is the mother of all epics.

2. The Analects
by Confucius (6th century BCE)

The Chinese sage's sayings and some of that of his disciples are collected here in 20 short books. Many deal with life in general, good conduct and right behaviour but some are on governance and justice. In content they share much with similar material from other parts of the world but their simplicity, pithiness of expression and universal relevance mark them out as special. Sample: Asked for one word that could be adopted as a "lifelong rule of conduct" the

| TV and Books | Television encouraged Groucho Marx to read. How? Everytime someone switched on the TV, he rushed out to another room and read a book. |

Master answered. "Is not Sympathy the word? Do not do to others what you would not like yourself."

3. *The Odyssey*

by Homer (Probably 8th century BCE)

The second of the two epics attributed to Homer. While the Iliad has a martial flavour

Odyssey

the Odyssey, which narrates the story of the wanderings of Odysseus after the battle of Troy, is more on social life, domesticity and love. The early books focus on his wife Penelope and son Telemachus and the attempts of Penelope to ward of a number of suitors. Odysseus adventures in various lands are described. After ten years he returns to his native land – Ithaca – but is not recognised. He slays the suitors and is reestablished with his wife and countrymen.

4. *The Republic*

by Plato (4th century BCE)

This, the most famous of the dialogues of Plato, is in the form of a conversation between Socrates and a group of fellow Athenians. From a discussion on old age Socrates, with gentleness, intelligence and irony, directs the conversation to a sophisticated exploration of the question of jus-

Plato

tice. For this an ideal republic is described. It would have division of labour and be ruled by a set of philosopher-guardians. There would be no private property. The education of the guardians and the qualities and defects of different types of government are examined. Thoughts on immortality and reincarnation close the discussion.

5. *Oedipus Rex*

by Sophocles (5th century BCE)

Sophocles' play has for its theme the story of Oedipus who inadvertently murdered his father and married his mother. The play focusses not on these horrendous deeds but on Oedipus's discovery of these truths, until then hidden from all. A plague has devastated Thebes and the people of Thebes arrive to request Oedipus, their king, to rescue the country. Searching for the cause of the plague leads Oedipus, by degrees, to realise that a prophesy that the son of Laius, the earlier king, would murder his father has come true. Devastated, he puts out his eyes and leaves Thebes.

6. *The History*

by Herodotus (5th century BCE)

Called "the Father of History" by Cicero Herodotus, born in Asia Minor, (modern day Turkey) travelled widely as a young man collecting information on the war between the Persians and the Greeks. The first six of its nine books describe the expansion of Persia under Cyrus and his successors. The rest is about how Xerxes continued the Persians campaign and how the Greeks rallied against them. The defeat of the Greeks at Marathon is among the highlights of the book. Stating that he was only reporting what he had heard Herodotus recorded a range of matter, some historical others fantastic.

7. *The Poetics*

by Aristotle (4th century BCE)

Plato banned poets from the ideal republic. Aristotle's defence of imaginative literature takes the form of a treatise on poetry. The nature of poetry is examined. Aristotle then looks at tragedy in some detail. All art is imitation or mimesis. The medium, the manner and the subjects produce different kinds of art. Tragedy is the noblest of arts. It is in the form of an imitation of an action which is serious and complete and which results in a catharsis of the emotions of pity and fear. Much of the literary criticism of the West springs from this work.

8. *Fables of Aesop*

by Aesop **(4th century BCE)**

A set of fables of timeless appeal, first written down in the 4th century BCE; they are

Aesop's Fables

attributed to Aesop, said to have been a slave who lived two centuries earlier. Each tale is brief, describes an incident and draws a moral from it that is both wise and practical. Asses, foxes, lions, monkeys, snakes and other animals figure in most of them, always with clear human qualities. Aesop himself appears in a few as do people who clearly represent human traits. Aesop's Fables have circulated in oral culture from ancient days and have inspired later writers to retell them.

9. *The Aeneid*

by Virgil **(1st century BCE)**

Written partly to glorify the Emperor Augustus and partly to cement the greatness of Rome by hitching it to the tale of Greece, this poem is about the beginnings of the state of Rome and the role of Aeneas in founding it. Aeneas and a set of his followers flee Troy on its defeat and reach Carthage, After telling their story to Dido, the Queen of Carthage, they sail for Italy.

Here Aeneas is welcomed by Latinus who offers him his daughter Lavinia's hand. War with a rival Turnus follows in which, in single combat, Aeneas is victorious.

10. *The Sakuntala*

by Kalidasa **(4th century CE)**

A tale from mythology, and an episode in the Mahabharata, is the matter of this classic play. It opens with dialogue between a stage manager and an actress and proceeds in seven acts to show the story of Sakuntala and Dushyanta. Dushyanta's meets Sakuntala while hunting, is smitten and gets married to her. He gives her a ring and departs. Her longing for him, the curse of forgetfulness effected by Durvasa, the loss of the ring, her rejection by Dushyanta, the recovery of the ring and the subsequent recognition of his folly by Dushyanta form the matter of the play.

Sakuntala

11. *Kadambari*

by Bana (7th century CE)

The sophistication and beauty of Sanskrit poetry and drama are also available in the prose works of India's classical period. Such was the profusion of stories in ancient India it was believed that India was the motherland of all stories. Bana's Kadambari, completed by his son Bhushanabhatta, is a complicated, circular narrative that centres around the love of two romantically attached pairs - Kadambari and Chandrapida and Pundarika and Mahashveta - through many incarnations.. Multiple narrators, including a parrot, lyrical prose and romance make it a work that inspires wonder. All the rasas are delineated with skill and great charm.

12. *The Tale of Genji*

by Lady Shikubu Murasaki (CE 1001- 1015)

From the aristocratic and cultured milieu of 10th century Japan comes this breathtaking story of a Prince and his loves and losses. The storyline – for most of the book about Genji and in the last part about one of his sons – is never very clear, but great care is taken in depicting his life and thoughts as he

The Tale of Genji

negotiates the vicissitudes of life. More than the story it is the gentle, subtle and sensitive style and treatment that makes this one of the great works of world literature. Regarded by some scholars as the first novel in world literature.

13. *Thousand and One Nights*

(10th century CE?)

This absolutely magical collection of stories is redolent of much of Asia, especially the cultures of India, Persia, and Arabia. King Shahryiar, distrusting all women, orders his vizier to get him a virgin every night and has her killed in the morning. The vizier's daughter Sheharazade is the offering once. She survives by telling the king a story but not revealing the ending at dawn. She is allowed to live for a day. This continues for a 1001 nights when the King pardons her. Many wondrous tales make up the collection – among them those of Aladin, Ali Baba and Sindbad.

14. *The Travels of Marco Polo*

by Marco Polo (1298)

First called 'Il Milione' the book is a travel record of a Venetian trader from Italy to China and back and covers the period between 1271 and 1295. The book was dictated by Polo, when he was jailed, to a fellow prisoner Rusticiano. Various versions exist, but the core narrative is about Polo's journey to, sojourn at and return from the

Marco Polo

Mongol court of Kubla Khan. The descriptions of sights and people along the Silk Route and the Indian Ocean are, although fantastic and exaggerated at times, an invaluable source of information on many parts of Asia during that time.

15. *The Divine Comedy*

by Dante Alighieri (1314-21)

This is considered the greatest work of the European Middle Ages. The poem narrates how Dante is guided by Virgil and later Beatrice, his beloved, through Hell, Purgatory and finally Heaven. The descent to hell through various levels culminates at the centre of the Earth where Satan is confined. Purgatory is a mountain on the other side where the sins of those who are finally

---

47th Edition of A Novel | **Kerala Sahitya Akademi President Perumpadavam Sreedharan, 73, who started his literary life as a poet, shot to instant fame with his 1993 novel *Oru Sankeerthanam Pole*, now in its 47th edition, based on the life of Fyodor Dostoevsky.**

saved are cleansed. From its top – the Garden of Eden – the elect go up to Heaven. Dante's journey culminates with a joyous vision of the Trinity. The allegorical journey is from damnation to bliss.

16. The Decameron
by Giovanni Boccaccio (1348-53)

To escape the plague a small group of aristocrats from Florence escape to the countryside. They tell each other stories to wile away the time. A 100 tales make up the collection. A variety of stories are told over ten days; those on all but the first and last days are united thematically. The originals probably came from a number of sources, but Boccaccio turns them into small and simple tales that are essentially plot-driven. In them can be found humour, irony, elegance, surprises and beauty and, above all, a tolerant and tender concern with the affairs of this world.

17. In Praise of Folly
by Desiderius Erasmus (1511)

This satirical gem, written in Latin, during a stay by the Dutch author at the home of his English friend Sri Thomas More, is a refined,

ironic examination of human folly. The book in the form of an oration "spoken by Folly in her own person". She praises herself throughout the different sections – one on her birth and education, one on her achievements and attributes and one on her followers. Through this device Erasmus criticizes the men, manners, beliefs and practices of his time from the point of view of a Christian humanist concluding, ironically, that being wise is foolish.

In Praise of Folly

18. The Prince
by Niccolo Machiavelli (1513)

This clear, neatly organised and pithily rendered set of observations on statecraft and politics grew out of the author's experience as a Florentine statesman who served the Medicis. The acquisition and retention of power and the duties of a prince are the main concerns. Each of its 26 chapters examines, with a cool objectivity that is sometimes mistaken for cynicism, some aspect of statecraft. The final chapter "An Exhortation to Liberate Italy from the Barbarians" gives an insight into the new thinking of the time that resulted in the birth of nationalism, a force that has shaped the modern world.

19. Utopia
by Sir Thomas More (1516)

Coining a word meaning nowhere More describes an imaginary, ideal community. He set it in the New World and had a narrator Raphael Hythloday, a supposed companion of Amerigo Vespucci, describe it. Hythloday begins by demonstrating how it is impossible to be a good counsellor to a king, then talks about the founding of Utopia. He then speaks about some of the distinguishing features of Utopia – lack of private property, division of labour, a thorough egalitarianism, a democratic and paternalistic government and so on. More's

Utopia

twin purposes of criticising his society and of sketching an alternative are beautifully served.

20. *Essays*

by Michel de Montaigne (1580)

The personal essay was born out of the efforts of this cultured Frenchman. Starting with the intention of portraying himself "without sham or artifice" Montaigne went on to produce charming and witty pieces that have universal appeal. Some of the titles will indicate the starting point of his observations: Of Sorrow, Of Idleness, Of Sleep, Of Age, Of Vanity, Of Drunkenness, Of the Affection of Fathers to Their Children, Defence of Seneca and Plutarch, Of the Most Excellent Men and so on. Stoical, sceptical, epicurean, meditative and above all undogmatic and tolerant Montaigne's literary introspections enhance our knowledge and understanding.

21. *Hamlet*

by William Shakespeare (1603)

A student in Paris, Hamlet returns home on hearing that his father the King has died. On arrival, he finds that his mother, Gerturde, has married his uncle Claudius. His father's ghost tells him that he was murdered by Claudius and that he should take revenge. He feigns madness, repudiates his beloved Ophelia, kills her father by accident and outwits Claudius who tries to arrange his murder on a trip abroad. He returns and in a climatic scene kills and is

Hamlet Play scene

killed by Laertes. Gertrude and Claudius are also killed. The dark, brooding Hamlet is said to anticipate modern man.

22. *Don Quixote*

by Miguel de Cervantes (1605-1615)

Don Quixote

Don Quixote, an ordinary man from La Mancha, has his head turned after reading a number of chivalric romances, gets a lady-love and a page and goes out in search of adventure on his horse Rosinante. Quixote's vivid imagination turns windmills into giants, slaves into aristocrats and inns into castles. After a series of misadventures he is made to return home to live as a shepherd but dies shortly afterwards. Apart from providing superb entertainment, the novel is a serious examination into the nature of appearance and reality and the heart of man. Quintessentially Spanish yet universal in its appeal.

23. *King James Bible*
(1611)

Also called Authorized Version. It was published on the orders of King James of England and came to be seen, at least in the English speaking world, as a work of surpassing beauty and grandeur. Its significance, going much beyond its religious use, is enormous. Simple, elegant and clear, the Authorised Version used an earlier translation by William Tyndale and the scholarship of Myles Coverdale, among others, in translating from the original Hebrew and Greek. A good number of expressions from this version entered the common language. Its literary influence is unmatched and can be felt in English even today.

24. *Gulliver's Travels*
by Jonathan Swift (1726)

This novel combines the everyday with the fantastic and is narrated by Lamuel Gulliver, a solid, practical, middle-class Englishman. It is simultaneously a gripping story

Jonathan Swift

of adventure and a searing satire on humanity. Each of the four parts of the book describes Gulliver's visit to some strange land. Part I is about the land of the Lilliputs, men so small adults are only a few inches high. Part II describes a land of giants, Brobdingnag; Part III the flying island of Laputa; Part IV the Houyhnhnms, horses so rational and cultured that they scorn humans as ineducable and barbaric "Yahoos".

25. *The History of the Decline and Fall of the Roman Empire*
by Edward Gibbon (1776-88)

This monumental work, in seven volumes, spans 13 centuries, from the time of Marcus Aurelius (CE 180) to the **Fall of Constantinople** (1453). In grand style Gibbon chronicles the decline while explaining why the greatest and most civilized empire the world had seen till then slowly disintegrated. The establishment of Christianity, the resulting enfeeblement of Roman culture, the barbarian attacks on Rome, the crusades and the final "triumph of barbarism and religion" are his themes. His vision of history, his witty, ironic and erudite style and his diagnosis of the causes of Rome's decline were all deeply influential.

26. *Candide, or Optimism*
by Voltaire (1758)

This short, racy and delightful narrative tells the story of Candide, a naive youth of Westphalia, his beloved Cunégonde, and their guide Pangloss teacher of "meta-physico-theologo-cosmolo-nigology" who believed that we lived in the best of all possible worlds. Candide, forced out of Westphalia, travels to various places in Europe the New World and Turkey, has the most bizarre of adventures and returns to live a peaceful life, observing that the secret of happiness is that "one must cultivate one's garden". Part utopian literature, part adventure story, part philosophical criticism and part satire Candide has proved to have enduring appeal.

27. *Pride and Prejudice*
by Jane Austen (1813)

Set among the English middle classes of the 19th century the book opens thus: "It

Pride and Prejudice

is a truth universally acknowledged that a single man in possession of a fortune must be in want of a wife". It describes the trials and tribulations of the Bennets and the games people play in their quest for status and partners. With irony, subtle humour and sharp observations on society and human foibles Austen narrates the story of Elizabeth and Darcy and Jane and Bingley and three other Bennet girls. Pride, prejudice, malice and snobbery are all overcome as the deftly sketched novel closes.

28. *The Voyage of the Beagle*
by Charles Darwin (1839)

It was while on a five-year voyage as a naturalist on the HMS Beagle that Darwin had a chance to see first hand the immense variety of life different parts of the world had. He made meticulous notes and col-

The Voyage of the Beagle

lected specimens and data with zeal. In 21 chapters Darwin, methodically and in elegant prose that is a model of scientific exposition, described the sights he saw and the botanical, zoological and geological phenomena he observed. Two interesting sidelights: a description of Napoleon's house on St Helena and kind remarks on the first Indians he saw, on the island of Mauritius.

29. *The Count of Monte Cristo*
by Alexandre Dumas (1844-46)

Extravagantly conceived and dramatically narrated this colourful tale of injustice and revenge is one of the most popular of romantic tales. Edmond Dantès is unjustly imprisoned and spends 15 years in a horrible jail in Marseille. He escapes taking the place of a dead friend, Abbe Faria, in a sack that is buried at sea. He travels to Italy, gets hold of a treasure his dying friend had spoken of and spends the rest of his life taking revenge on the people who had sent him to jail and generously helping those who were kind to him.

30. *David Copperfield*
by Charles Dickens (1849-50)

Young David's idyllic life ends when his widowed mother remarries. A cruel stepfather, the harshness of boarding school, the horrors of child labour in London and other misfortunes lead to a life of some success. Happiness still eludes him until he marries a second time and embarks on a literary career. A number of finely sketched characters – like Peggotty, Barkis, Micawber, and Uriah Heep - add to the richness of the novel. Acute social observation, an unerring eye for the comic and deep compassion for the miserable inform his story telling and give this thinly veiled autobiography perennial value.

31. *Moby Dick or The Whale*
by Herman Melville (1851)

A depressive Ismael joins a whaler, the Pequod, to get over his condition. It is cap-

Moby Dick

tained by Ahab, a man with an ivory leg, the result of an encounter with a white whale, Moby Dick. Ahab, and a crew of powerfully sketched individuals go whaling, but their real purpose is to kill the whale that crippled Ahab. With monomaniacal fury and demonical purposefulness Ahab sails the oceans looking for his prey. Moby Dick is finally sighted and chased for three days. But Capt Ahab, his ship and crew fall victims to Moby Dick and Ismael alone is saved.

32. *Madame Bovary*
by Gustave Flaubert (1857)

Charles Bovary, a country doctor, has an af-

Madame Bovary

Uncle Tom   **Uncle Tom's Cabin** was first published in 1856. It was a novel about slavery, written by Harriet Beecher Stowe.

fair with a patient's daughter, Emma, and later marries her. She is quickly bored by provincial life, conditioned as she is by the romances she has read to find love and life unendingly exciting. She embarks on more than one adulterous relationship but never finds emotional fulfilment. Miserable and in debt she commits suicide. Unaware of his wife's true nature Charles sinks into depressive mourning and dies leaving their child an orphan. The novel brilliantly captures the sordidness and mediocrity of French provisional life and details the lives of those trapped in it.

33. *Les Misérables*

by Victor Hugo (1862)

From the most famous of French Romantic poets comes this epic historical novel. Set in the early decades of the 19th century this sentimental work tells the story of Jean Valjean, a simple and honest peasant who is

Victor Hugo

forced to steal to feed his hungry relatives. He is jailed and later released but his past continues to haunt him. With superhuman courage and perseverance he makes good but is often hounded by Javert, a policeman who knows about his criminal past. He escapes again and helps other victims of society until, at the close of the novel, he dies.

34. *War and Peace*

by Leo Tolstoy (1862-69)

In scale and size, range and number of characters, breadth of vision and wealth of incidents few novels can match Tolstoy's magnum opus. Set against the background of the Napoleonic wars between 1805 and 1812 it follows the fate of a host of characters many of whom are Russian aristocrats. Tolstoy's views on history, the role of fate,

and other inexplicable social forces in life shape the story more than do individual characters. Tolstoy seems to suggest that among all the tumult of history and war the simple things of life, like love and kindness, are the most significant.

35. *Alice in Wonderland*

by Lewis Carrol (1865)

A Cambridge mathematician's attempt to entertain a group of children produced this wonderful tale. Alice falls asleep and in a dream falls down a hole while following a White Rabbit. Many strange characters and adventures await her. She drinks a magic potion and, among other things, grows big and small inexplicably, nearly drowns in her tears, talks to a vanishing cat, attends a tea-party, is present at a trial and plays croquet with animals for mallets and balls.

Alice in Wonderland

Just as she accuses everyone of being just a pack of cards she wakes up. "Nonsense" has been transmuted into art.

36. *Crime and Punishment*

by Fyodor Dostoevsky (1866)

Raskolnikov, a brooding, intellectually inclined student living in St Petersburg murders a moneylender more to test out his idea that the intellectual elite are not constrained by ordinary morals than for the money he takes from her. But the consequences of his action are far from what he had anticipated. The police are after him, but what troubles him are his own thoughts about the deed and his search for meaning in life. His confession and the conduct of Sonia, a prostitute he meets, leads him to moral redemption. Psychologically thrilling and philosophically profound; often considered the best novel ever.

37. *Boule de Suif*

by Guy de Maupassant (1880)

A group of Frenchmen, trying to escape from German occupation by coach, are held up by a German officer. The group represent French society. One, crudely nick-named "Ball of Fat" is a prostitute and is shunned by the others. But she is generous and the company warm to her. The officer will release them only if she sleeps with him. She refuses but her companions slowly pressure her into doing so. The group is released, but now her use is over Boule de Suif is once again treated with disdain and callousness. Superb naturalistic narration makes it a little gem.

38. *The Adventures of Huckleberry Finn*

by Mark Twain (1884)

Huck who has come into some money at the end of The Adventures of Tom Sawyer resists all attempts to "civilize" him by the kind Widow Doug-

las. His nasty father kidnaps him but Huck escapes and sets out on a life of adventure with Jim the runaway slave, both being fugitives. While sailing along the Mississipi they meet all kinds of people and have hair raising adventures especially after

Huckleberry Finn

a couple of con-men join them. It turns out that Jim's owner had freed him before she died and that Huck's treasure is safe. He wants to resume his gypsy existence.

39. *The Golden Bough*

by J. G. Frazer (1890)

Why was it that at Nemi in Italy there was a grove sacred to Diana where one could become a priest only by slaying one's predecessor? Looking for a literary answer to this question Frazer roamed across the world in search of similar beliefs and myths and un-covered a fascinating set of beliefs and ritu-als. He describes patterns that hide among myriad customs and practices. Myth, folk-lore, witchcraft, taboos, legends and fable are examined. Ways of thinking embedded in these are unravelled and he looks to the day when men will supersede the stages of magic, religion and science.

40. *Tess of the D'Ubervilles*

by Thomas Hardy (1891)

Tess, a innocent young girl, is sent to Alec D'Uberville an imposter in the hope of establishing a fam-

ily connection. She is seduced and the baby dies. Working in a dairy for a living she falls in love with Angel Clare. They marry. Clare deserts her on learning of her past. Desperate and poor Tess has to accede to Alec who has re-entered her life. Clare returns and is willing to for-

Tess

give her. In despair Tess murders Angel, is caught and hanged. A dark vision of the fragility and impotence of goodness and the implacability of fate informs the work.

41. *Heart of Darkness*

by Joseph Conrad (1902)

Marlowe, the narrator, tells a group of fel-low sailors a strange tale. Once he had to go in search of Mr Kurtz, an ivory trader of great ability, who appeared to be lost. Captaining a ship for the first time, Marlow sailed up the Congo, away from civilization and into what seemed the heart of dark-ness. Deep in the interior, after witnessing scenes of incomprehensible barbarism, he meets Kurtz who dies uttering the words "The horror, the horror". Sobered by the experience he returns, hands over a packet

Pope Dunciad	The Dunciad, a satirical poem by Alexander Pope, was first pub-lished anonymously in 1728. The New Dunciad was published in 1742 and the complete work in 1743.

of letters to Kurtz's beloved and ponders on his unnerving experience.

42. *Metamorphosis*

by Franz Kafka (1916).

Gregor Samsa, a travelling salesman, cannot get up one morning having turned into an insect. His parents, sister and supervisor turn up to find out why he refuses to come out of his room. They are shocked and disgusted to see his transformation and seem to blame him for it. Confined to his room and alienated from his people his circumstances deteriorate until he dies and is thrown out with the waste. The family go on a picnic and the future seems bright. Realistic prose is combined with telling black humour to paint a bleak, disturbing picture of modern life.

Metamorphosis

43. *All Quiet on the Western Front*

by Eric Maria Remarque (1929).

Literature traditionally glorified war. One of the earliest and most moving novels to tell of the inhumanity, cruelty, waste and purposelessness of war is this powerful German work. It tells the story of Paul Baumer and his friends who enroll in the army and are thrust into the hellish trenches of the First World War. The horror of war reduces everyone to animals trying their best to survive. A spell of leave produces no relief; Paul's mother is dying of cancer. Paul returns to the front and after many more agonising experiences dies on the day that peace breaks out.

44. *The Outsider*

by Albert Camus (1942).

When Meursault, the young narrator of the story, receives a telegram stating that his mother is dead he appears to react unemotionally. He goes to the funeral, attends office, spends time with a girl-friend, talks to his neighbours and engages in other activities with cool detachment. He murders a man, almost by accident, but does not defend himself. The prosecutors take him to be cold-blooded and he is condemned. None see him as honest and unhypocritical. As he awaits death he reflects on his mother's death and his life and recognises and accepts "the benign indifference of the universe".

45. *Animal Farm*

by George Orwell (1945).

The animals in Manor Farm, inspired by the teachings of Old Major, overthrow their human exploiters, establish a just society, rename their home Animal Farm and adopt a philosophy called Animalism to guide them. All the animals work hard to make a success of their society. Napoleon and Snowball, both pigs, take on leadership roles but quarrel. Snowball is exiled and the principles of animalism are corrupted till all the old evils reappear, but in officially sanctioned forms.

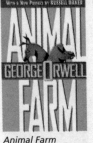

Animal Farm

The cardinal principal of animalism "All animals are equal" is modified with the addition "but some animals are more equal than others."

46. *Waiting for Godot*

by Samuel Beckett (1953).

Minimalist yet profoundly eloquent this play shows two vagabonds, Vladimir and Estragon or Didi and Gogo as they call themselves, waiting for one mysterious Godot. Who he is and when or why he will come are not known but they are sure that

---

A Farewell to Arms

A Farewell to Arms by Ernest Hemingway, published in 1929, was set mainly in war-torn Italy of 1917-18. The story focuses on Frederic Henry, an ambulance driver for the Italian army.

things will be better once that happens. Meanwhile they pass the time as best they can; in absurd conversation or watching the antics of a passing master-slave pair called Pozzo and Lucy. Every known rule of dramaturgy is broken but this searing search for meaning, cry of loneliness and celebration of fellowship touches the heart.

47. *Things Fall Apart*

by Chinua Achebe (1958).

Set in Nigeria in the 19th century this novel tells the story of Okonkwo. Okonkwo is strong, proud, resourceful, a model farmer

and a dignified and respected tribesman. Exiled from his village, for breaking a taboo, he tries to start life anew at his mother's village. Tension enters his life as a group of white missionaries try to win converts.

Chinua Achebe

Enraged at an act of sacrilege and the humiliation of his people Okonkwo kills a government emissary. He then kills himself rather than succumb to the white man. The experience of an entire culture distilled in one short, powerful book.

48. *One Hundred Years of Solitude*

by Gabriel Garcia Marquez (1967).

A rambling, magical narrative that tells the story, over a long span of time, of a small town in South America called Macondo and the most important family there – the Buendias. The fortunes of the two are interlinked. Strange

Marquez

and eccentric members of the clan play a part in the growth of the town. A civil war in the country, the setting up of a banana plantation in Macondo, a strike there and the crushing of the strikers are important events against which characters and events drift in and out. Inevitably, the town and the family collapse together.

49. *The Name of the Rose*

by Umberto Eco (1980).

It's 1327, and a learned monk Roger of Baskerville arrives at an abbey in Italy to participate in a religious conclave and to solve a murder mystery. Scholar, philosopher and a canny reader of signs he encounters a set of strong monks; several with motive and means. But he is steadfast and identifies the criminal. The crime is

linked to the library and the only copy of a book with such subversive potential that some people are willing to kill to preserve its secret existence. Theology, philosophy, history and semiotics are the unlikely components of this thrilling detective story.

Umberto Eco

50. *Midnight's Children*

by Salman Rushdie (1981).

Saleem Sinai and a thousand other children are born on the midnight of August 14 as India becomes free. Saleem tells their stories in what is a sprawling, labyrinthine and magical narrative. He can communicate telepathically with all other midnight's children. His story, inextricably linked to that of Siva, another midnight's child and one with whom he was switched at birth by a nurse, is narrated against the background of much of the 20th century and the whole of the Indian subcontinent. Loosely allegorical but rich in its allusions and suggestiveness this award winner is Rushdie's magnum opus. ∎

Creations of Falstaff	King Henry IV is a history play in two parts by Shakespeare. So popular was the magnificent creation of Falstaff in it that he had to write *The Merry Wives of Windsor* to statisfy popular demand.

Historical Places

Abbottabad (Pakistan) The town where Osama bin Laden, leader of al Qaeda terror outfit was killed by US forces on May 2, 2011.

Acropolis (Ancient Greece): The citadel of ancient Athens, which contained the Parthenon, the Erechtheum, etc.

Actium (Ancient Greece): Known for the Battle of Actium, which established the victory of Octavian over Antony and Cleopatra (31 BC).

Agadir (Morocco): Port. Town was destroyed in a major 1960 earthquake. The Portuguese named it Santa Cruz (1505-41).

Al Aqsa Mosque (Jerusalem): Islam's third holiest place, after Mecca and Medina.

Alaska (USA): Bought by USA from Russia in 1867.

Alaska

Albany (USA): Capital of N. York state. Albany Congress (1754) was the US colonial gathering of delegates at which Benjamin Franklin proposed a plan of union for the separate British colonies.

Alexandria (Egypt): City founded by Alexander the Great.

Altamira (Spain): Site of palaeolithic cave paintings and engravings.

Amethi (UP, India): VVIP constituency,

associated with the Gandhis for long. In 1977, Sanjay Gandhi contested from Amethi. Rajiv contested the seat in 1984, 1989 and 1991. Over 100 industries (BHEL, HAL, Indo-Gulf Fertilizer, LML Vespa, Malvika Steel,Samrat Bicycles etc.) have come to Amethi.

Amsterdam (The Netherlands): Capital. Major European port.

Anatolia (another name for Asia Minor): Turkey's Asian region that was part of the Ottoman Empire until Republic of Turkey came into existence.

Anchorage (USA): Alaskan city founded in 1915 as the headquarters for the building of the Alaska railway.

Angkor (Cambodia): It is the ancient Khmer capital and the temple complex.

Angkor Wat

The greatest structure is Angkor Wat. The complex was destroyed by Thai invaders.

Annapolis (USA): Capital of Maryland; the site of the signing of the peace treaty ending American Revolution. US Naval Academy here.

Antananarivo (Madagascar): Capital. Formerly Tananarive. Founded early 17th c. as a walled citadel.

Antioch (Turkey): New name is Antakya. City founded in 300 BC by Seleucus I. Antioch was 'the queen of the east'.

Antwerp (Belgium): Prominent trade

Lost and Found | Bouvet Island in the South Atlantic was discovered in 1739 but then lost. It was sought by Captain Cook and others and was rediscovered in 1808. Most remote island in the world.

centre in 15th century. Site of Europe's first stock exchange (1460). Cathedral of Norte Dame (14th century). Bombed in WWII. Diamond cutting is well developed.

Apia (Western Samoa): Capital. Vailima, the former home of R.L. Stevenson, happens to be the residence of the head of state.

Andes (S. America): Longest mountain range in the world.

Aqaba (Jordan): Seaport, captured from Turks in 1917 by T.E. Lawrence. Gulf of Aqaba had important role in Arab-Israeli wars.

Arlington (USA): Location of the Pentagon. National Cemetery built in 1864, where prominent Americans have been buried.

Arlington

Ashanti (Ghana): A kingdom of the Ashanti people annexed to the British colony of Gold Coast (Ghana) in 1901. Now a province with capital at Kumasi.

Assal (Djibouti): Lake; lowest point in Africa, 157 m. below sea level.

Astana (Kazakhstan): Capital of Kazakhstan. Its name was Akmola until 1961 and from 1994 to '98. From 1961 to 1994 it was Tselinograd. Until 1998 the name

Aswan

> ### A Shark Sanctuary
> The Bahamas has banned shark fishing. The country's 629,000 sq.km. of territorial waters has thus become a shark sanctuary. Sharks are at risk because of demand for their fins in Chinese cuisine.

was Alma Ata. Since 1998, present name.

Asti (Italy) : Town known for its sparking white wine, Asti Spumante.

Aswan (Egypt): City on the bank of the Nile. Aswan High Dam was built (1960-1970) with Soviet aid.

Atacama Desert (Chile): The most arid region in the world. Stretches about 1000 km.

Atlanta (USA): Capital of Georgia. Founded in 1837, originally called Terminus, Marthasville in 1845, and Atlanta in 1947. Headquarters of Coca Cola. Hosted 1996 summer Olympic Games.

Atlanta

Auschwitz (Poland): Notorious as Nazi Germany's largest concentration camp and extermination camp. Between 1m. and 2.5 m. people are believed to have died here.

Axum or Aksum (Ethiopia): Centre of N.Ethiopian empire, 1st-8th c. Kings converted to Christianity in 4th c. It is believed that the Arc of the Covenant was brought here from Jerusalem and placed in church of St.Mary of Zion where the emperors of Ethiopia were crowned.

Baikonour (Kazakhstan): The only cos-

San Marino's Communist Government	San Marino claims to be the oldest state in Europe and to have been founded in the 4th century. A Communist-led coalition ruled 1947-57, a similar coalition ruled 1978-86.

modrome in erstwhile USSR. Baikonour to Russia is what Cape Canaveral is to the US.

Balaklava (Russia): Known for the British base at Balaklava and the Battle of Balaklava in the early stages of the Crimean War, between Britain and Russia.

Bali (Indonesia): Mountainous island. Stronghold of Hinduism.

Balkans (SE Europe): This area consists of Greece, Albania, Croatia, Bosnia-Hercegovina, Macedonia, Serbia and Montenegro, Bulgaria, part of Romania and the European part of Turkey. Competition between European powers for control of the Balkans resulted in WWI. All States (except Greece) became communist after WWII. The 1990s saw turmoil in the region with the breakup of Yugoslavia, Bosnian civil war and Kosovo conflict.

Bandung (Indonesia):The Non-Aligned Movement had its beginning in the Bandung Conference, 1955 with 29 countries representing more than half the world attending.

Bandung

Barcelona (Spain): Country's second largest city. Venue of Olympics, 1992.

Bastille (France): A symbol of Bourbon despotism, this mediaeval fortress was stormed by a mob in 1789.

Bay of Pigs (SW coast of Cuba): Spanish name: Bahia de Cochinos. About 1500 Cuban exiles tried unsuccessfully to invade the country and overthrow Fidel Castro on Apr. 17, 1961 at this bay.

Beijing

Beijing (China). Capital. Formerly Peking. Settled since ancient times. Tiananmen Square, world's largest public square is here. Venue of 2008 Summer Olympics.

Beira (Mozambique): Chief port of Mozambique, Zimbabwe and Malawi. Founded 1891. Under Portugal until 1942.

Beirut (Lebanon): Capital. At the foot of Lebanon Mountains. It was the chief banking and cultural centre of the Middle East. Heavily damaged in civil war 1979-90.

Belgrade (E. Europe) : Formerly capital of Yugoslavia and of the kingdom of Serbia. An important commercial centre in the Balkans. Suffered under Nazi occupation ('41 - '44). Kosovo conflict hit Belgrade. Now, capital of Serbia-Montenegro.

Belitung or Billiton (Indonesia): An island in the Java sea, whose tin mines have attracted a large Chinese community.

Belmopan (Belize): Made capital of Belize in 1970, following major hurricane damage to Belize city in 1961.

Belorussia (Central Europe): Modern name Belarus. Was part of USSR, now member, CIS.

Benin Kingdom (Africa): A historic kingdom (13th-19th c.). Trade centre for ivory and slaves. Later became part of British Nigeria.

Berchtesgaden (Germany): A resort in the Bavarian Alps, the site of Hitler's fortified mountain retreat, the Beghof.

Bering Sea (Pacific Ocean): Its islands include the Pribilofs, Aleutians, Nunivak, etc. Discovered by Danish explorer Vitus

The Two Samoas	Samoa was formerly known as Western Samoa to distinguish it from American Samoa, a small US territory. It was a German colony 1899 to 1914, when New Zealand landed troops and took over.

Bering. The Bering Strait is said to have formed a land bridge by which on final inhabitants of N. America arrived from Asia.

Berlin(Germany): Capital. Founded 13th c., capital of Prussia, of German empire (1871). In 1948 Soviet-controlled East Berlin and West Berlin (controlled by US,UK, France) were born. The airlift of supplies by British and American aircraft, following WWII, after Soviet attempts to isolate the city from the West is known as Berlin Airlift. The blockade was lifted in 1949. Berlin Wall was built by East German government

Why K2?

The Everest is No.1, K2 is No.2 and Kanchenjunga No.3. In Tibetan, the Everest is known as Chomolungma. ("Goddess Mother of World") K2 (it was the second mountain in the Karakoram range counting from Kashmir end) is Chogori, and sometimes Godwin-Austen, after Lt. Henry Haversham Godwin-Austen, who first surveyed it in 1865.

Reichstag Building, Berlin

Birmingham

(1961) to seal off E.Berlin from W.Berlin to prevent illegal migration. Wall was opened in 1989.

Bermuda (West Atlantic): A British overseas territory. Old name: Somers Islands. Bermuda, the Greater Antilles and the US coast make 'Bermuda Triangle', an area where aircraft are reported to have vanished mysteriously.

Bethlehem (now under Palestine): Birthplace of Jesus Christ. The early home of King David. Annexed by Jordan in 1950. Later, was part of West Bank. Turned over to Palestine in 1995.

Biafra (Nigeria): Under Col. Ojukuvu, the Igbo people of Biafra tried to break away from Nigeria. Civil war of 1967-70.

Bikini (Pacific) Atoll in the Marshall islands. Site of US nuclear tests, and first H-bomb test (1952).

Birmingham (U.K.): Britain's second largest city, developed rapidly in the Industrial Revolution.

Bloomsbury (U.K.): Intellectuals who are known as Bloomsburry Group (early years of 20th century) met here. E.M. Forster, Virginia Woolf and J.M. Keynes were members.

Bonn (Germany): Capital of West Germany from 1949 to 1990, when the two Germanys were unified. Beethoven was born here.

Borneo (Malay Archipelago): World's third largest island. Thinly populated. Sabah and Sarawak are part of Malaysia, Brunei is independent, Kalimantan state belongs to Indonesia.

Bosnia (E.Europe): The international crisis that led to the outbreak of WWI had its roots here. Austria-Hungary annexed Bosnia and Herzegovina and trouble began. It has been in the news since 1990 as a scene of ethnic war. Now part of the country Bosnia-Herzegovina.

Boston (USA): This Atlantic seaport, capital of Massachusetts, was focus of pre-

Origin of Pall Mall London's Pall Mall, SWI was named after 'Paille maille', a French ball and mallet game once played there.

Boston

Revolution activity (Boston Massacre 1770, Boston Tea Party 1773, etc). Now an important manufacturing, financial and educational centre.

Bougainville (PNG): Volcanic island in southwest Pacific Ocean. Scene of guerrilla warfare since 1980s.

Bradford: The northern English city has been named UN's first-ever city of Film. A testimony to the city's dedication to the film and media industry. It has long-standing links to movie business, including being home to an international film festival and the National Media Museum.

Brasilia (Brazil): Capital, laid out in the shape of an aircraft. Inaugurated in 1960.

Bratislava (Slovakia): Capital. It was the capital of Hungary from 1541 to 1784. In Czechoslovakia, it was the third largest city. Bratislava is on the river Danube. An industrial city.

Bretton Woods (USA). A 1944 international conference here led to the establishment of IMF.

Brindisi (Italy): A centre of the crusades in the middle ages. A naval base.

Brisbane (Australia): Founded as a penal colony. Town (1834) named after former governor of New South Wales. The country's third largest city.

British East Africa: Former British teritories in East Africa - Uganda, Kenya, Tanganyika, Zanzibar.

British West Africa: Former name for Nigeria, Gambia, Sierra Leone, Gold Coast, Togoland, Cameroon.

Brno: The Czech industrial city where the Bren gun, a gas-operated light machine gun, was developed.

Broadway (USA): Principal theatre district located on or near the street Broadway in New York.

Brunei (Southeast Asia): Sultanate. Sultan Bolkiah was world's richest person for many years. In 16th c., Brunei ruled over the whole of Borneo and parts of the Philippines.

Brunswick (Germany): It has the oldest technical university in Germany.

Brussels (Belgium): Capital. It was capital of the Spanish Netherlands in the Middle Ages. Hq. of EU and NATO.

Budapest (Hungary): Capital created in 1873 by merging the towns of Buda and Pest, on the two sides of the Danube. It

Budapest

was one of the two capitals of the Austro-Hungarian Empire.

Bukhara (Uzbekistan): City. One of the oldest cities and trading centres of Asia. It was the centre of a powerful kingdom. Rapid growth after discovery of natural gas in the '50s.

Byblos (Ancient Phoenicia): Chief city of Phoenicia in 2nd millennium B.C., on the site of modern Jebeil. Famous for Papyrus, nicknamed biblos, from which the word 'Bible' is derived.

Caen (France): Port, tomb of William the Conqueror.

Lotuseaters' Island	Djerba is an island of SE Tunisia. It is traditionally Homer's island of the lotuseaters.

Cairo

The 7 Daughters of Robert Bruce

The Seven Sisters Road, N4 in London was originally named after the seven daughters of Robert Bruce, who planted seven elm trees on Seven Sisters Road.

Cairo (Egypt): Largest African city. Pyramids are nearby.

Calabar (Nigeria): Port, centre of the slave trade in 18th & 19th centuries.

California (USA): Most populous US state. Major towns: San Francisco, Los Angeles, San Diego, Sacramento. Centre of micro electronics industry in Silicon Valley. Disneyland.

Calvary (Jerusalem, Golgotha in Hebrew): The hill outside the city of Jerusalem where Jesus Christ was crucified.

Cambridge (UK): City on River Cam. One of world's greatest universities. First college Peterhouse founded in 1284.

Cambridge (USA): Harvard University is the oldest (1636) US college. MIT moved from Boston, 1915.

Camp David (USA): The US President's retreat in the Appalachian Mountains where the Middle East peace treaty was signed by Sadat and Begin (1978) with President Carter mediating.

Campoformido (Italy): Treaty of Campo Formio of 1979 was signed here between Austria and France, after Austria was defeated by Napoleon.

Cana (Palestine): Northeast of Nazareth. Jesus Christ is believed to have performed his first miracle here.

Canaan (Israel): Ancient Palestine before it was occupied by the Jews was 'Canaan' - referred to in the Bible as the land promised to the Israelites by God.

Canary Islands (Spain): Group of islands in the Atlantic Ocean, of volcanic formation.

Cannes (France): Venue of the most prestigious international film festival.

Canterbury (England): City in east Kent, seat of the Archbishop of the Anglican Church. Famous for the cathedral where Thomas Becket was assassinated (1170).

Canton (China): Port, commercial centre of S. China. Focus of the first Opium War. Sun Yat Sen was born here.

Canyon de Chelly (USA): National monument in Arizona , established in 1931 to protect Indian cliff dwellings dating from AD 350.

Cape Canaveral (USA): Known as Cape Kennedy, 1963-73. Launch site for US space programme.

Cape Chelyuskin (Russia): A headland in north-central Russia, the most northerly point of any continent.

Cape of Good Hope (S. Africa): Discovered by Bartolomeu Diaz in 1488. He called it the Cape of Storms.

Capernaum (Israel): Site of many biblical events, situated on the northern shore of the Sea of Galilee.

Cannes

Where is Champagne? Champagne is a region that includes more than 300 villages. It is 160 km. east of Paris. The site of the wine champagne's origin.

Cape Town Port

Cape Town (S.Africa): The oldest white settlement in S.Africa. Founded 1652. Country's legislative capital, second largest city and chief seaport. Venue of CHOGM summit of 1999.

Cape Verde (Africa): Country occupying an archipelago in the North Atlantic Ocean. Consists of 10 islands and 5 islets.

Capitol (USA): Where the US Congress meets in Washington.

Capri (Italy): Island, which was a favourite resort of Roman emperors. Today a big tourist attraction.

Cardiff (UK): Capital of Wales. Its Welsh name is Caerdydd.

Carthage (Tunisia): Ancient town founded by Phoenicians (814 BC). Destroyed in Punic Wars. It was founded again by Caesar and Octavian. Arabs destroyed it (698).

Casablanca (Morocco): The port city where Churchill and F.D. Roosevelt met for the Casablanca Conference in 1943.

Catania (Italy): In Sicily. Often damaged by eruptions of Mt.Etna.

Cayenne (French Guiana): Capital and seaport. Founded in 1643 by the French. A penal colony.

Chaco (Paraguay-Bolivia). Chaco War (1932-35) between the two countries in the disputed Northern Chaco area. Paraguay was the winner. Abundant wild life.

Champagne (France): Noted for the production of champagne wine.

Changdu: Capital of China's south-west Sichuan province that was reduced to rubble in the 7.9 magnitude earthquake of May, 2008.

Changsha (China): Historic trade centre, capital of Hunan Province.

Channel Islands (US): Island group of the British Isles in the English Channel (Jersey, Guernsey, etc).

Chechnya (Russia): A constituent republic of Russia in north Caucasus. Resistance to Russian rule by Chechnya since 19th c. Chechen rebels keep carrying out attacks.

Chicago (USA): City on the shore of Lake Michigan. Devastated by fire in 1871. Transport, industrial, shipping, cultural centre. Largest rail terminal in the world. O'Hare is one of the busiest airports. World's first skyscraper was built here in 1885-Sears Tower.

Chittagong (Bangladesh): Seaport. Country's chief port.

Cluny (France): Town where the Cluniac order of Benedictine monks was established in 910. Its Romanesque Basilica was

Cluny

world's largest church until erection of St. Peter's Basilica.

Cognac (France): Town on river Char-

It was Ethiopia's second most important city which, on the formation of the new nation Eritrea, became the capital of that country.

ente, known for the brandy of the same name produced here.

Colditz (Germany): A castle here was used as a prison camp in WWII, for Allied escapers.

Coldstream (Scotland, UK): Town known for Regiment of Coldstream Guards raised here first (1660) to restore Charles II.

Colorado

Colorado (USA): Famous for Colorado National monument (1911) which has towering monoliths and canyons.

Colosseum (Rome): Amphitheatre built in AD 70-82 for contests between gladiators and of men with animals.

Columbia (U.S.A): State capital. Burned by Gen.Sherman in 1865.

Communism Peak (Tajikistan): Mountain in central Asia, known as Mount Garmo until 1933 and Stalin Peak until 1962. It was the highest peak in the former Soviet Union. Present name: Ismail Samani Peak.

Concord (USA): The beginning of American War of Independence was marked by Battle of Concord (1775).

Constantinople (Turkey): Byzantium from 330 to 1930 Capital of Byzantine Empire, the eastern half of the Roman empire. Fell to Ottoman Turks (1453). Now, Istanbul.

Cook Strait (Pacific Ocean Channel): Separates New Zealand's North and South Islands. Visited by Captain Cook in 1770.

Special Terminal for Low-Cost Airlines

Delhi is to become the first Indian city to have an integrated domestic-cum-international terminal exclusively for low-cost carriers (LCC), like London's Stanstead.

Copperbelt (Africa): A region in central Africa, with the largest copper deposits in Africa.

Coral Sea (or Solomon Sea): It has many coral islands. Was scene of US victory over Japanese, 1942.

Cordoba (Spain): City which was the capital of Moorish Spain in 8th c. Great Mosque (990).

Corfu (Greece): Island in the Ionian Sea. British protectorate from 1815 to 1864.

Corinth (Greece): A powerful city of ancient Greece. Destroyed by Romans, 146 B.C., rebuilt by Caesar, 44 BC.

Corpus Christi (USA): A port, on Corpus Christi Bay, channel access to Gulf of Mexico.

Corsica (France): Largest island of France. Napoleon Bonaparte was born here.

Cotopaxi

Cotopaxi (Ecuador): Highest active volcano in the world.

Crete (Greece): Largest Greek island.

Dover	Town and seaport on the Strait of Dover, a leading passenger port. A naval base in WWI. Famous for the white chalk cliffs.

Settled from 6000 BC. Minoan civilization, 2000 BC.

Crimea (Ukraine): Peninsula in South Ukraine, now an autonomous republic of Ukraine. Crimean War (1853-56) fought by Britain, France and Ottoman Turks against Russia.

Curzon Line: Poland-Soviet Russia demarcation line proposed in 1919. In 1994, another line, almost identical, was accepted as Soviet-Polish border.

Daklak (Vietnam): One-third of Vietnam's coffee output comes from this province.

Darwin (Australia): Port, Allied hq in WWII. Bombed by Japan in 1942. A 1974 cyclone destroyed the city.

Davos (Switzerland): A resort, the venue of World Economic Forum.

Dayton (USA): The scene of the Peace Accord of 1995 that ended the Bosnian civil war.

Dearborn (USA): Birthplace of Henry Ford and the headquarters of Ford Motor Co.

Delphi (Greece): A village famous in ancient Greece as the sanctuary of Apollo and the seat of his oracle.

Dhaka (Bangladesh): Capital. From 1608-1704, capital of Mughal province of East Bengal, of British province of East Bengal & Assam, 1905-1912. of East Pakistan, 1947; of Bangladesh since 1971. 'The city of mosques'. Centre of world's biggest jute-growing region.

Diego Garcia (India Ocean): Island, American military airbase. Treaty was signed in 1966 by US and UK for the use of the island.

Doogton (Ohio,USA): Hometown of Wilbur and Orville Wright.

Dresden (Germany): A centre of Napoleon's military operations. The beautiful city was damaged in WWII bombing. Known for art galleries and other cultural institutions.

Dumbarton

Dumbarton Oaks (US): The first blueprints for setting up UN were formulated here in 1944.

Dumbarton (Scotland): An engineering and ship building centre.

Dunkirk (France): Seaport. Scene (in 1940) of the evacuation of over 300,000 Allied troops under fire, as France fell to Germany.

East Anglia (UK): A powerful Anglo-Saxon kingdom of 6th century. The region of east England, it has vey fertile agricultural land.

Edinburgh (UK): Capital of Scotland. Robert the Bruce was king of Scotland from 1306-29. Home to Adam Smith, David Hume, Robert Burns and Walter Scott. Home to University of Edinburgh. Famous for Edinburgh Festival of music and drama.

Elba (Italy): Island in the Tyrrhenian sea where Napoleon lived after his abdication.

Eiffel Tower (Paris): An iron tower erected for the Paris Exhibition of 1889, on

Diego Garcia

Panipat | **Panipat is the site of three great battles which mark the rise and fall of the Mughal Empire. Today an important textile town.**

Eiffel Tower

tina and Britain over the Islands in 1982.

Fatima (Portugal) : Small village where three shepherds children claimed to have seen visions of the Virgin Mary in 1917.

Finland (Northern Europe): A wealthy country. Thousands of lakes. Some think human habitation here dates back 100,000 years.

Flanders (Belgium-France): The region frequently fought over by France, Spain and Austria is divided between Belgium and France. Scene of big trench warfare in WW I.

Seine river, Paris, designed by A.G.Eiffel. World's most visited site.

Essen (Germany):On the Ruhr river, it is home to the Krupp steel works, Europe's most extensive iron and steel works. Destroyed in WW II.

Eton (UK): Seat of Britain's most famous public school, Eton College, founded in 1440.

Eureka Stockade (Australia): Scene of an armed clash in 1854 when government was forced to back down, in the face of public opinion following goldminers on whom expensive mining license was imposed.

Evian (France) : Venue of the G8 summit, June 2003.

Eyre, Lake (Australia): At 15 m.below sea level, it is the lowest point on the continent.

Falkland Islands (UK): British crown colony in S.Atlantic Ocean. To Argentina, they are 'Malvinas'. War between Argen-

Florence

Florence (Italy): Cultural, intellectual centre of Italy, the rule of the Medice family being the most glorious time. Leading centre of the Renaissance. Capital of the Kingdom of Italy, 1865-71. The School of Florence includes Leonardo da Vinci, Michaelangelo and Raphael.

Florida (USA): It forms a long peninsula with thousands of lakes and many rivers. Belonged to the Spanish. America puchased it in 1819. Everglades, Florida Keys,

Messina | **Messina is a town of NE Sicily, Italy. Now an important Italian port. University founded in 1548.**

Disney World, Miami, etc are here.

Forbidden City (China): The public museums in Beijing, were in the past imperial palaces where no commoner or foreigner could enter without special permission. The complex had some 9000 rooms.

Formosa

Formosa (Taiwan's former name, Republic of China): Island in the Pacific. The Portuguese named it Formosa ("beautiful"), then was under the Dutch, and then under the Ming dynasty of China. Chiang Kaishek fled to Taiwan. Economic growth was spectacular from the 1950s.

Freetown (Sierra Leone) Capital. Founded in 1790s as a foundation for freed slaves. From 1808 to 1874, it was capital of British West Africa.

Galliopoli (Turkey): Port on the European side of the Dardanelles; the first European city to be conquered by Ottoman Turks (1354). Famous for the Allied operation against Turks in WW I. After eight months of inconclusive fighting and deaths of 145,000 men, the Allies withdrew.

Gaul (France). Transalpine Gaul, the region that developed into the mediaeval kingdom of France.

Gauteng (S.Africa). Province, whose capital is Johannesburg. Pretoria is S. Africa's administrative capital.

Gaza Strip: Area (146 sq.mile) captured by Israel from Egypt, 1967. Mostly statelss Palestinians live there in refugee camps.

Gdansk(Poland). Formerly Danzig. Industrial port. 1980 saw labour unrest in the Lenin Shipyard, in support of 'Solidarity'. Lech Walesa, an electrician here, rose to become President of Poland.

Gedrosia (Pakistan): Historical region west of the Indus River, in what is now the Baluchistan region of Pakistan.

Genoa (Italy): The country's largest seaport. Birthplace of Columbus.

Gettysburg (USA): Famous for Abraham Lincoln's Gettysburg Address (1863) at the dedication of a war cemetery in Pennsylvania, where the Battle of Gettysburg was fought (1863) in the American Civil War.

Gettysburg

Ggantija (Malta): Ggantija Temples (built 3600-3300 BC) are a Copper Age complex on island Gozo (the 'Isle of Calypso')

Gibraltar (UK): British Crown Colony. Smallest (6.5 sq.km) colony in the world. Played important role in Allied naval operations in WW I & WW II. Gibralar Rock's height 426 m.

Gobi (Central Asia): Desert of 1,295,000 sq.km. extending across China and Mongolia.

Golan Heights (Syria-Israel) This strategically important area of Syria was oc-

Louisville

Louisville is a city in N. Kentucky. It has the annual Kentucky Derby horse race. Fort Knox (US gold bullion stores) is nearby.

cupied by Israel in 1967 and annexed in 1981.

Granada (Spain): City founded by the Moors the 8th century. Capital of the Kingdom of Granada, 1238. Tombs of Ferdinand and Isabella can be seen.

Golconda (A.P): Capital of the Qutb Shahi Sultans of 16th c. Rich in historical monuments including the Golconda Fort.

Great Rift Valley: East African Rift System, extending from Jordan to Mozambique.

Great Slave Lake (Canada): Lake named for the slave Indians, drained by the Mackenzie River.

Great Smoky Mountains (USA): Part of the Appalachian Mountains. 2025m.

Greenwich (UK): The village near London. Greenwich Mean Time , the UK stan-

Greenwich

dard time, (GMT) is based on local time of the meridian passing through Greenwich.

Hamburg (Germany): Germany's largest port and foremost industrial city. It was a member of the German Confederation as a free city in 1815. Allied bombing destroyed the city in WWI, was rebuilt. Home to the Hamburg Opera.

Harappa (Pakistan): The site of a great city of the Indus Valley civilization. Cemeteries and brick buildings of Harappa were excavated in 1920s and 1946.

Harrow (London): Site of world famous private preparatory school for boys founded 1571.

Caracas

is the capital of Venezuela , founded by the Spanish as Santiago de Leon de Caracas in the 16th century. Big growth witnessed since the oil boon of the 50s. It is the birthplace of Simon Bolivar.

Harvard (USA): Harvard University at Cambridge, Massachusetts is the earliest (1636) US college. Almamater of seven American Presidents.

Heiligendamm (Germany): Resort town which hosted G-8 summit, 2007.

Hiroshima (Japan): City destroyed on Aug.6, 1945 by the first atomic bomb dropped by USA.

Hiroshima Peace Memorial Park

Ho Chi Minh City (Vietnam): New name of Saigon. Former Capital of French Indo-China. Hq of US military operations in Vietnam War. Captured by N.Vietnamese troops and renamed.

Holstein: A region in Germany. A breed of large, black-and-white dairy cattle of this name.

Huntingdon (UK): Birthplace of Oliver Cromwell.

Ibadan (Nigeria): City founded in 1830s. Country's intellectual centre.

Ingushetia (Russia): The smallest and poorest republic of Prussia, whose history

| Hamburg | Hamburg in North Germany is on the Rivers Elbe and Alster. It is the birthplace of Mendelssohn and Brahms. It was severly bombed during WWII. |

is tied to Chechnya. A violence-plagued region.

Iona(UK): A remote island off Mull in Scotland, the site of a monastery set up in AD 563.

Islamabad (Pakistan): Capital since 1967. A new city.

Jakarta (Indonesia): Capital. Formerly Batavia. The Dutch founded it in 1619. Important centre of the Dutch East India Company.

Jakarta Port

Jerusalem (Israel): A holy city of Christians, Jews and Muslims. Capital (declared 1950, lacks international recognition). Capital of Palestine 1922-48. Divided between Israel and Jordan, 1949.

Kampala (Uganda): Capital since 1962. It is on Lake Victoria. Founded by the Brit-

Kampala

ish near Mengo, the seat of the King of Buganda.

Kampuchea (or Cambodia): Kingdom

in S-E Asia. Pol Pot's regime saw deaths of about 3 m. people (1975-8).

Kandy (Sri Lanka): City. Royal city until 1815. Important Buddhist Sinhalese culture centre. 'Temple of the Tooth' is here. known as 'City of the Five Hills'

Karachi (Pakistan): Port , largest city in the country. First capital of Pakistan (1947).

Katanga (Congo): The province (known as Shaba) attempted to secede under Moise Tshombe, 1960.

Kawasaki (Japan): Port city in Honshu.

Khasi (China): Centre of trade with CIS republics and West Africa.

Khartoum (Sudan): Sudanese capital. In 1885 the Mahdi defeated the. British here. It is the economic link between the Arab countries and African countries.

Khmer (SE Asia): An empire founded in 6th century. Its capital from 802 was Angkor Thom. The empire fell in 15th.

Kiritmati (Kiribati): Christmas Island. Largest atoll in the world. nuclear testing site in '50s. Britain annexed it.

Kisangani (Zaire): Founded as Stanleyville, renamed in 1966. A rebel government was established briefly during civil war (1960-64).

Kobe

Kobe (Japan): Japan's commercial port. Badly damaged by the 1995 earthquake. Kobe has 15 universities.

Kola Peninsula (Russia): A promontory between the Barents Sea and the White Sea. It is mostly granite, and is mined for apatitie and nephelimite.

Cro-Magnon	Cave in the Les Eyzies region in southern France, where discovery of human skeletons was made first in 1868.

Konya (Turkey): It was capital of sultanate of Konium or Rum under Seljuk Turks (11th c.).

Kosovo (Serbia): The autonomous province of the Yugoslav republic of Serbia that declared independence in 1990. Years of unrest and violence followed. Ethnic Albanians were repressed by Serbs. NATO's air strikes (1999) hit Kosovo badly.

Krakov or Cracow (Poland): Poland's third largest city. Pope John Paul II was born here.

Kremlin (Russia): The residence of tsars until 1712, political and administrative headquarters of USSR since 1918. Kremlin is a huge palatial building, the headquarters of Russian Government, along with the Duma (parliament). It is surrounded by the famous Kremlin wall with lofty towers.

Kuala Lumpur (Malaysia): Capital. Petronas Twin Towers, until recently world's tallest building are here.

Kuala Lumpur

Kurdistan (Iran): Inhabited by Kurds, who also live in Iraq, Turkey and Syria. 20 m. in number, the world's largest ethnic group without its own state.

Kuril Islands (Russia): Chain of 30 large and 26 smaller islands in Sakhalin region. In 1875 Russia gave the islands to Japan in exchange for full control of Sakhalin island. Ceded to USSR, after WWII.

New IIM

Kashipur in Uttarakhand is the site of the 12th Indian Institute of Management. With help from its mentor institute IIM, Lucknow, the Kashipur Institute has the first batch of 60 students.

La Paz (Bolivia): The highest capital in the world (3631 m.)

Lappland (Arctic region of Europe): Extends over Norway, Sweden, Finland and the Kola peninsula.

Lausanne (Switzerland): On the northern shore of Lake Geneva. Tourist resort, convention centre. International Olympic Committee hq.

Leeds (UK): This West Yorkshire city was famous in 18th c. for its textile manufacturing. Industrial, cultural centre. Leeds Music Festival, International Pianoforte Competition, etc.

Leeds

Leningrad (Russia): Founded by Peter the Great in 1703. Called St.Petersburg, it was the capital of Russia for 200 years until 1918. For some time it was known as Petrograd. Russia's second largest citiy. The Hermitage Museum is here.

Leshan (China) : World's tallest Buddha statue (71 metres) is here. It has a unique 24-hour 'electronic bodyguard'.

Lake Victoria

John Hanning Speke was a British explorer who became the first European to reach lake Victoria in East Africa. He correctly identified it as the source of the Nile.

Lhasa (Tibet): At 3684 m., it was the highest capital in the world before domination of Tibet by China.

Libreville (Gabon): Capital. The name was given in 1848 after freed slaves were settled there.

Liechtenstein (Central Europe): A small principality of 157 sq.km, with very high per capita income

Lisieux (France): A town in northern France. The shrine of Ste Therese attracts pilgrims.

Little Rock (USA): Capital of Arkansas. US Supreme Court enforced a ruling against racial discrimination in schools in 1957.

Liverpool (UK): Sixth largest city in England and the principal Atlantic port. The Beatles belonged to Liverpool.

Locarno (Switzerland): Locarno Pact of 1925, resolving the status of the Rhineland and guaranteeing French-German and Belgian-German borders.

London (UK): Capital. A major trade, financial, cultural, political centre. Buckingham Palace, Westminister Abbey, Tower

London

of London, Big Ben, Hyde Park, St.Paul's, British Museum, Downing Street, etc are landmarks.

Lord's (London,UK) Cricket ground; hq of M.C.C.

Lusatia (Germany): The home of the Sorbs, an ancient Slav people.

Maastricht (Netherlands): European Union conference of 1991 was held in this city. Maastricht Treaty was the agreement on Europe's political, economic and monetary union.

Macedon (SE Europe) : Ancient country (roughly the modern Macedonia).

Machu Picchu (Peru): Ruined Inca city, discovered in 1911. A world heritage site.

Machu Picchu

Madagascar (Indian Ocean): World's fourth largest island, settled by Indonesians in 1st c. AD.

Madrid (Spain): Capital. Highest capital city in Europe (altitude 655 m).

Malaga (Spain): Port. Ancient Malaca. Founded by Phoenicians in 12th c.B.C. Birthplace of Picasso.

Mali (Africa): A republic in West Africa. A mediaeval state which reached its peak in 14th c. Ruled by France 1881-95, territory of French Sudan until 1959.

Manchuria (China): Sparsely populated mountainous area. The last Chinese emperors were Manchus. Under Russian control for long.

Maramba (Zambia): Capital of N. Rhodesia 1911-1935. City first named 'Livingstone' after the first explorer David Livingstone.

Marrakesh (Morocco): One of Morocco's four imperial cities (founded 1062). Former capital. Islamic, commercial, tourist centre.

Masada (Israel): The desert fortress famous as the scene of a mass suicide 2,000 years ago.

Mashhad (Iran): The holy city that attracts the most number of pilgrims (over

The Eight Nuclear Powers The world's eight nuclear powers are Britain, China, France, India, Israel, Pakistan, Russia and the US. They possess more than 20,500 warheads.

20 m.) a year who come to the holy shrine of the 8th Shiite Imam.

Mount Matterhorn

Matterhorn (Switzerland): 4477 m. high mountain in the Pennine Alps on Swiss Italian border.

Medina (Saudi Arabia): Islamic holy city that contains the tomb of Prophet Mohammed.

Mekong Delta (S.E. Asia): Mekong river's lower course has 1/3 of the population of Cambodia, Laos, Thailand and Vietnam. In 1957, UN's Mekong River Development Project began.

Memphis (USA): In Tennessee. Martin Luther King Jr. was assassinated here (1968).

Mexico City (Mexico): Capital. Largest city in the world. Olympic Games (1968). About 20,000 killed in an earthquake (1985).

Mexico City

Marquesas Islands

A group of 12 volcanic islands in the South Pacific Ocean. Nuku Hiva is the largest. The second largest is Hiva Oa, where Gauguin is buried.

Mohanjo-Daro(Pakistan): A great site of the Indus valley civilization. The excavation in 1920s brought to light extensive brick-built remains.

Mombasa (Kenya): Chief port, industrial centre. It was the capital of East Africa Protectorate, 1888-1907. A British naval base in WWII.

Monaco

Monaco (France-Italy border): Independent principality, 1.95 sq.km. A luxurious resort known for Monte Carlo gambling centre, car races and beaches.

Mont Blanc (French-Italian border): Highest mountain in the Alps. There is a 12 km road tunnel connecting the two countries.

Monte Cristo(Italy): Islet in the Tyrrhenian Sea. Association with the Duma novel The Count of Monte Cristo.

Montego Bay (Jamaica): Port and tourist capital of the country. Locally called Mobay.

Monte San Giorgio (Switzerland): A pyramid-shaped, wooded mountain

Gaza Blockade	On June 14, 2011 the Gaza Strip entered its fifth year of full Israeli blockade by land, air and sea.

Guam

Guam, an unincorporated US territory, is the largest of the Mariana islands Micronesia. Now it is a major US air and naval base. In 1950 it was made a US territory.

regarded as the best fossil record of marine life.

Montserrat (UK): Territory in the Caribbean. A 1997 volcanic erruption made two-thirds of the island uninhabitable.

Montreal (Canada): Second largest French- speaking city in the world. Venue of 1976 Olympics. Trade, finance centre.

Montreux (Switzerland): The 13th century chateau de Chillon. Figures in Byron's poem Prisoner of Chillon. Annual television festival awards the Golden Rose of Montreux.

Mount Ararat (Turkey): Extinct volcanic peak. Noah's Ark is said to have come to rest here.

Mount Isa (Australia): World's largest city in area- 41, 225 sq.km.

Mount Kailas (Tibet): Also known as Mount Meru. The world's highest altitude pilgrimage ends here.

Mycenae

Mount Li (China): A life-size army of about 7500 painted terracotta figures deployed in military formation underground

was discovered here in 1974. First Chinese Emperor Qin Shihuangdi buried here.

Munich (Germany): Capital of Bavaria. Swedes occupied it in 1632 and the French in 1800. In 1920s, it was the centre of the Nazi Party. Munich Putsch (Beer hall Putsch) was an attempted coup in 1923 by Hitler to overthrow the republican government. Munich Agreement of 1938 was a pact signed by Britain, France, Italy and Germany to settle the German claims on Czechoslovakia.

Murfreesboro (USA): In Tennessee, site of a union victory over Confederate forces during Civil War (1863).

Murmansk

Murmansk (Russia): The only major ice-free port in the former USSR.

Mycenae : Mycenaen civilization was a brilliant Bronze Age culture which flourished in Greece and the Aegean in 2nd millennium.

Nagorno-Karabakh (Azerbaijan): Azerbaijan's autonomous region whose population is about 80% Armenian. Armenian claims to the area in 1988 led to riots. Fighting broke out in 1991. Ceasefire in 1994 but tension continues.

Namur (Belgium): The city's strategic position at the confluence of two rivers caused fighting over it many times. Damaged in both World Wars.

Nancy (France): Former seat of the Dukes of Lorraine. France got it in 1766.

Naples (Italy): Seaport, industrial, cultural centre. In 6th BC, it was founded by

Saving Venice

Venice is to charge a hotel tax to earn money to save the city from rising sea levels. Visitors staying in five-star hotels will see £4 added to their bills.

Naples

Greeks. Capital of the Kingdom of Naples, 1270-1860.

Nauru (Western Pacific): World's smallest republic, area 21 sq.km. Independent in 1968. Known for phosphate deposits.

Nepal (Asia): Until 2006, the only official Hindu kingdom in the world.

New York City (USA): The country's largest city. The Dutch who colonised it called it New Amsterdam (1625). In 1644, Britain captured it and named it New York after the king's brother, the Duke of York. Erie Canal opened in 1825, paving the way for rapid growth. George Washington was

Hudson River, New York City

inaugurated here as the first President. UN is located here. World Trade Centre, until Sept. 2001. Largest American port.

Niagara (USA): known for Niagara Falls on the US-Canada border

Nineveh (Assyria): Important city of Assyria in Upper Mesopotamia. In the area around the town of Asur on the Tigris, a

vast empire was built up which was at its height in 9th-8th c.BC.

Normandy (France): Seat of William I who invaded England in 1066. French recovered it in 1204. Site of the Normandy Campaign (June 6, 1944), the allied invasion of German-occupied France- the largest amphibious operation in history.

Novogorod (Russia): One of the oldest Russian cities. On a major trade route of eastern Europe, it became commercially prosperous in the Middle Ages.

Nunavat (Canada): Eskimo territory. Created in 1999 after negotiations with Inuit leaders.

Nuremberg (Germany): The trials of Nazi criminals after WWII (Nuremberg Tri-

Nuremberg

als) took place in this city, which was heavily bombed in the war.

Nyasa Lake or Malawi Lake (Africa): Africa's third largest. Known as Calendar Lake, because it is 365 miles long and 52 across at its widest point.

Oberammergau (Germany): Passion play is performed here every ten years following a vow made by the villagers when they were saved from the plague in 1633.

Odessa (Ukraine): Black Sea port. Centre of the battleship 'Potemkin' mutiny in the Revolution of 1905.

Okinawa (Japan): Island taken by USA in WW II, returned to Japan, 1972.

Oklahoma City (USA): Terrorists bombed a government office building in

Lifeline of Jaffna	Kankasanthurai port in Sri Lanka was the lifeline of Jaffna. Work has now started on a port project there, as part of rebuilding infrastructure in the North.

Cathay

Cathay is the medieval European name for China. It is derived from Khitan, the name of a Mongol people who invaded N. China in the 10th century. Russians still call China, Khitan.

1904, killing 168 people.

Olduvai Gorge (Tanzania): Rich archaeological site, where fossils and paleolithic implements were found. 'Homo habilis' was discovered by the Leakeys. Some 'Homo erectus' remains too found here.

Oxford (UK): City on the Thames. Oxford university, one of the oldest in Europe, dating from the 12th century.

Oxford

Palermo (Italy): Port, capital of Sicily. Phoenicians founded it in 8th BC.

Palembang (Indonesia). Port. It was capital of a Hindu Sumatran kingdom of 8th c.

Pamplona (Spain): The celebration, running of the bulls held here every year. 200,000 tourists arrived in 2006.

Panama (Central America): Occupies the Isthmus of Panama, the strip of land that links North and South America. USA built the Panama Canal, connecting the Atlantic and Pacific Oceans. In 1903 US got

sovereignty over the Panama Canal Zone. Political turbulence tormented Panama for long. USA interfered on several occasions.

Paris (France): Capital. Treaty of Paris (1761-3) ended Seven Years' War. Paris Peace Conference held after WWI. Hq.of UNESCO, etc. A main world tourist centre, centre of high fashion and luxury goods. Louvre, Eiffel Tower, Elysee Palace, Paris University (1170) etc.

Patmos (Greece): Island. Apostle St. John lived here for two years.

Pearl Harbour (USA): Naval base was bombed by Japan on Dec.7, 1941.This brought USA into WW II.

Pedra Furada (Brazil): Rock shelter, believed to be the earliest human settlement in the Americas.

Penang

Penang (Malaysia): First British settlement in Malaya. Capital Pinang was formerly George Town.

Pentagon (USA): A huge five-sided building in Arlington. Hq of US Defence Dept. It was world's largest office building (34 acres) when completed. On Sept.11, 2001 part of the building was destroyed by terrorists who crashed an aircraft into Pentagon.

Perak (Malaysia): One of the wealthiest states, after tin was discovered in the 1840s.

Pergamum (Asia Minor): Ancient city, was capital of the Attalids.

Persepolis (Iran): Palaces and graves of the Achaemenid rulers of Persia are here

Rembrandt's Birthplace

Leiden (Netherlands) is a centre of theology, science and art. University was founded in 1575. Birthplace of Rembrandt and Gayen.

in the mountains. Sacked byAlexander the Great (331 BC).

Peter and Paul Fortress (Russia): A stronghold founded by Peter the Great (1703) on an island. St. Petersburg sprang up around it. A museum.

Piltdown (UK): Fossilised skull fragments 'discovered' in 1912 in Piltdown, Sussex, were believed to be the earliest human remains found in Europe. 'The Piltdown Man' was a hoax, it was known 40 years later.

Pitcairn Island (S. Pacific): One of a small group of islands, UK overseas territory. Area is 4.6 sq.km. and population only 48.

Pittsburgh(USA): The British took Fort Duquesne (built by the French) and re-named it Fort Pitt (1758). Third largest US corporate hq.

Plymouth (USA): Site of the first permanent European settlement in New England founded by the pilgrims in 1620. A tourist destination.

Polish Corridor (Poland): A belt of land that separated Prussia from the rest of Germany and was granted to Pland in the Treaty of Versailles (1919). Annexed by Germany (1939), returned to Poland (1945).

Pompeii

Pompeii (Italy): Ancient city at the foot of Vesuvius, which erupted in AD 79 covering the city with ashes and pumicestone 6-7m. deep.

Potala Palace, Lhasa

Potala Palace, Lhasa Founded in 7th century. Symbol of old Tibet.

Potsdam (Germany): That is where Churchill, Truman and Stalin met for the conference in 1945

Prussia (Germany): The most powerful German state in 19th c. It disappeared when Germany was divided after 1945. Frederick William (the Great Elector)and Frederick William III, King of Prussia (1797-1840) were great personalities.

Pusan

Pusan (Korea) : Seaport. A UN supply base during Korean war.

Rhodesia (Africa): Modern states Zimbabwe and Zambia constitute the old Rhodesia named after Cecil Rhodes.

Riga (Latvia): Capital, seaport, under Germany in WWII.

Rijeka(Croatia): Croatia's largest port, was naval base of Austro Hungarian em-

| Sanya | The third BRICS summit was held in the coastal city of Sanya in the Hainan island of China in April, 2011. Leaders signed the Sanya Declaration at the summit. |

pire until 1918. Ceded to Italy in 1924 and to Yugoslavia in 1947.

Ripon (UK): Reckoned to be England's second oldest town.

Roanoke Island (USA): Off the coast of N. Carolina. Site of the first English colonies in North America.

Rome (Italy): Capital. It was the capital of the Roman empire, which extended

Rome

to continental Europe. Reached the highest point of glory in 1st and 2nd centuries. Then came the Holy Roman Empire. The seat of Papacy. Vatican City is within Rome.

Salzburg (Austria): Birthplace of Mozart.

San Francisco (USA): Californian city. Formerly Yerba Buena, renamed in 1848. Golden Gate Bridge is one of longest single-span suspension bridges. Terminus of the first transcontinental railway (1869).

San Francisco

Sao Paulo (Brazil): Founded in 1554, city in 1711. Brazilian independence was declared here in 1822 by Emperor Pedro I.

Sapporo (Japan) City, ski resort: Hokkaido University here. Site of 1972 Winter Olympics.

Sarajevo (Bosnia Herzegovina): WWI had its beginning here when in 1914 the Archduke of Fancis Ferdinand of Austria-Hungary was assassinated by a Serb. It was the focal point of civil war after 1992, with refugees coming into Sarajevo. Hosted 1984 Winter Olympics.

Saskarchewan (Canada): Prairies of this province supply two-thirds of Canada's wheat.

Serengeti (Tanzania): National Park (14,500 sq.km) on the southeast shores of Lake Victoria.

Sevastapol (Ukraine): Seaport city. In Crimean War, Anglo-French forces besieged it (Tolstoy's Sevastopol Sketches).

Shanghai (China): Largest city, seaport, industrial, cultural, educational centre.

Shanghai

Sharpeville: South African township 80km from jo' burg where 69 peaceful demonstrators protesting the Pass Laws were killed by the police, March 21, 1967. S. Africa's new constitution was inaugurated here, 1996.

Sheba (Southern Arabia): Ancient kingdom (Biblical). Covered present day Yemen. Region of great wealth in 6th & 5th c. B.C. Queen of Sheba who visited Soloman the Wise.

Cajamarca — Cajamarca is a town in Peru which was the site of Pizarro's execution of Atahualpa, the last Inca ruler.

Sheffield (UK): City famous for cutlery manufacture.

Shenyang (China): The city was known as Mukden. In 1905, the city fell to the Japanese. In the Mukden (Manchurian) Incident (1931) Japanese used an explosion on the railway as an excuse to occupy the city, and then Manchuria.

Sherwood forest (UK): The legendary 13th c. outlaw Robin Hood lived in

Sherwood

Sherwood Forest in English North Midlands.

Siberia (Russia-Kazakhstan) Land of rich minerals and extremely cold climate. For long, a place of exile for Russian criminals. Trans-Siberian Railway (1891-1905) is the longest in the world (9335 km).

Sinai (Egypt): Triangular peninsula between the Suez Cananl and the Gulf of Suez. Rich in petroleum and manganese. Has had vital role in Arab Israeli relations. Mount Sinai is important to Jews, Muslims and Christians.

Spitsbergen (Norway): The largest island in the Sualbond Svalbard archipelago of Norway.

Spratly Islands (South China Sea): Strategicelly important archipelago claimed variously by China, Malaysia, Philippines, Taiwan and Viuetnam.

Sriperumbadur (Tamil Nadu): This is where former PM Rajiv Gandhi was assasiinated on May 21, 1991. It is the birthplace of Ramanuja, the founder of the Vaishnava

---

Jodhpur

This city in Rajasthan is noted for handicraft industries. It also gave its name to a style of riding breeches that were introduced into Britain during the 19th century.

---

sect. On the Chennai-Bangalore highway, Sriperumbudur is 55 km from the Chennai port. Several automobile companies (Hyundai, Ford, Mitsubishi and BMW) have set up plants here.

St.Helena (U.K): In S.Atlantic. Island where Napoleon was exiled 1815-21.

St. Louis (USA): HQ of World Agricultural Forum. Associated with the great humorist Mark Twain. Charles Lindberg off his skeletal airplane "The Spirit of St.Louis" from there.

Strasbourg (France): Seat of the Council of Europe. EU's parliament meets here.

Stratford-upon-Avon (UK): William Shakespeare's place of birth, and death.

Stromboli (Italy): A 3038 feet high volcano from which lava flows continuously. It attracts tourists to the island.

Sumer (ancient Mesopotamia): Site of an old civilisation, dating back to 5th millennium B.C. Sumerians invented cuneiform writing, wheeled vehicles and the plough.

Tashkent (Uzbekistan): The oldest and largest city of central Asia. Peace talks beteen India and Pakistan began at Tashkent, capital of Uzbekistan on January 4, 1966. Indian PM Lal Bahadur Shastri suddenly expired here on Jan. 11.

Tasmania (Australia): An island and the smallest state of Australia, sighted by Abel Tasman in 1642. Until 1856, it was called Van Diemen's Lord.

Tehran (Iran): Capital. Became capital in 1788. Tehran conference of Roosevelt, Churchill and Stalin to coordinate Allied strategy in WWII (1943).

Brabourne Stadium

The Brabourne stadium in Mumbai was opened in 1937. Lord Brabourne after whom it was named had left Bombay by then to become Governor of Bengal.

Tel Aviv-Jaffa (Israel): Tel Aviv was originally a suburb of Jaffa. Towns separated in 1921.. When captured by Jewish forces in 1949, almost the entire Arab population fled Jaffa. Reunited Tel Aviv-Jaffa in 1950. UN recognises Tel Aviv as capital.

Tema (Ghana): Port. Africa's largest man-made harbour is here (1968).

Temple Emanu-El (New York): The world's biggest synagogue (3523 sq.m.)

Terre Adelie (Antarctica): It is the only French territory in Antarctica. It has a research station.

Texas (USA): Major agricultural region and chief oil and natural gas producer. Dallas, a major commercial and trading centre, and Houston a space centre.

The Hague (The Netherlands): Seat of the Dutch government, Hq. of International Court of Justice.

Thermophylae (Grecee): A pass in eastern Greece, the scene of Battle of Thermopylae (the Persian Wars), 480 BC-unsuccessful defence by Spartans against the Persians.

Tikal (Guatemala): Ancient Mayan city which was settled in 250 BC. Abandoned by AD 900.

Timbuktu: (Mali) A centre of Muslim learning, 1400-1600 a market for slaves and gold; presently salt is its main trading commodity.

Titicaca (Peru-Bolivia border): World's highest lake at 3810 m.

Titicaca

Truskavets (Ukraine): Resort town renowned for its life-preserving mineral springs.

One Out of Five

Only about one-fifth of the population of Qatar is Qatari. Migratory workers from other Arab countries and Asia make up the rest.

Ulan Bator (Mongolia): Capital. Centre of trade between China and Japan in 17th c. Outer Mongolia declared independence in 1921. Then Ulan Bator became capital.

Ulster (Ireland): Historical province. Northern Ireland partitioned in 1921, six counties formed Northern Ireland. Three counties became province of Ulster in the Irish Republic.

Uppsala (Sweden): City known as educational centre, with university and cathedral with tombs of king Grustavus Vasa.

Ur (Iraq) : Ancient city of Sumer. Jewish patriarch Abrahams' home.

Urumqi (China): The capital city of the Xinjiang Uyghur Autonomous Region in north western China was the scene of a bloody ethnic conflict between the Hans, the largest ethnic group in China and the Uyghurs in July 2009.

Utrecht (The Netherlands): Treaties of Utrecht (1713-14) ended the War of Spanish Succession.

Vancouver Island (Canada): The largest offshore island on the west coast of North America. Vancouver is Canada's third largest city and its chief pacific port.

Venice (Italy): City, Port. Capital of Venetia and of Venezia. Built on 118 islands, with 170 canals, 400 bridges. It was a rich medieval maritime republic founded in 5th c. Venetian Republic in 15th c. Territories lost to Turks, republic fell to Austria. Excellent centre for art and architecture (the Byzantine cathedral of St.Mark).

Versailles (France): Venue of the peace treaty signed in 1919 between Germany and Allied powers. Versailles war.

Vicksburg (USA): On the Mississippi. The site of a siege in American Civil War

| Bielsko-Biala | Bielsko-Biala is a city in southern Poland formed from the merger of Bielsko and Biala Krakowska. |

that ended in the Confederate surrender, 1863.

Victoria Peak (Hong Kong): The principal peak on Hong Kong Island, named after Queen Victoria.

Vienna (Austria): Capital. It was the seat of the Habsburgs (1278-1918) and the residence of the Holy Roman emperors (1558-1806). A cultural centre in 18th and 19th c. with associations with composers

Vienna

like Haydon, Mozart, Beethoven, Schubert and the Strauss family. Congress of Vienna, 1814-15.

Waco (USA): Headquarters of David Koresh's Branch Davidian religious cult. An FBI storming after a 51-day siege killed Koresh and 70 followers, in April 1993.

Wall Street (USA): Street in Manhattan, N.Y. City, where the New York Stock Exchange is located.

Wall Street

Warsaw (Poland): Capital. It was occupied by Germany in both World Wars. 'Warsaw Pact' is the countries that came together in response to the formation of NATO by the Western powers.

Washington D.C. (USA): Capital of USA, on the east bank of the Potomac river covering the District of Columbia.

Waterloo (Belgium): Where the Battle of Waterloo, the final defeat of Napoleon, took place in 1815.

Watergate (Hotel complex in Washington): Known for Watergate affair, the US political scandal that ended in President Nixon's resignation. The attempted burglary took place in Democratic Party hq. in Watergate building.

Watergate

West Bank: Palestinian territory west of the River Jordan. Jordan claimed it from 1949 to 1988. Israel has occupied it since 1967. Israeli troops withdrew in 1993.

Westminster Abbey (UK): The burial place of 18 monarchs. Its Poet's corner is here.

White House (USA): Official residence of US President in Washington, D.C. Designed by James Hoban in 1792. It was burnt by the British during the War of 1812 but restored subsequently. It was painted white to hide the smoke stains. Partly rebuilt in 1949-52.

Windsor Castle (UK): British royal res-

Limestone Buildings   Cotswold Hills in England is noted for its picturesque towns and villages built in the local limestones.

idence in southern England. The complex includes the burial place of 10 monarchs.

Winnipeg (Canada): The major city of the Canadian prairies, it has one of the world's largest wheat markets.

Wittenberg (Germany): Associated with the beginning of the Reformation, 1517. Martin Luther nailed his 95 theses to the doors of Schlosskirche.

Woomera Maralinga (Australia): Site of a space and rocket test centre.

Worcester (UK): Country town on river Severn which was the site of Cromwell's defeat of Charles II and the Scots in 1651.

Yale (USA): One of the oldest American universities, founded in 1701 as a college. Named in 1716 after Elihu Yale who donated his books to the college. Women's education in Yale is 134 years old.

Yalta (Ukraine): Port on the Black Sea. Crimean resort, the site of Yalta Conference (1945) attended by Roosevelt, Stalin and Churchill.

Yalta

Yekaterinburg (Russia): City that hosted the first official summit of BRIC group on May 16, 2009.

York (UK): A former Anglo-Saxon capital and a Roman military post. Second-highest office of the Church of England is Archbishop of York.

Yorktown (USA): Scene of last major campaign of American Revolution

Ypres (Belgium): Known for the battles of WWI fought around Ypres, in 1914, in 1915, in 1917. The second saw the first use of poison gas, the third ended in the Passchendaele campaign.

Chichen Itza, Yucatan

Yucatan (Mexico): Once the centre of the Mayan civilization

Yumen (Tibet): The least populous town. Three residents. The town has a township Government.

Yunnan (China): Conquered by the Mongols in 1253. Became a province of China in 1659. Plant species and wildlife are rich.

Zagreb (Croatia): Capital. It has a Gothic cathedral and a university founded in 1669.

Zanzibar (Africa): Island in the Indian Ocean, part of Tanzania. Centre for ivory and slave trade in 18th c. The Sultanate of Zanzibar was a British protectorate in 1890. Independent in 1963. Merged with Tanganyika to form Tanzania. World's largest producer of cloves.

Zaragoza

Zaragoza (Spain): Scene of resistance against the French in the Peninsular War.

Corpus Christi Corpus Christi is a town and a popular resort in Texas, USA. Its port exports cotton, petroleum and sulphur.

A Register of Records

Adventure

First woman to conquer world's 14 highest mountains - Oh Eun-sun, South Korea (2010 Aug)

First arctic balloon crossing - Jean-Louis Etienne, a French doctor and traveller, travelled 3130 km in his special balloon sailing over the Arctic Ocean and landed in the tundra of eastern Siberia five days after taking off in Norway (2010 Apr).

First Indian to circumnavigate the globe solo on a sail boat - Commander Dilip Donde, a naval officer (2009 Aug - 2010 May).

First marina in India - Kochi (2010 Apr)

First woman to win the Nobel Prize for Economics - Elinor Ostrom, USA. She shared the Prize with Oliver Williamson, USA (2009 Oct)

Venkaraman R.

First Indian to win the Nobel Prize for Chemistry- Ramakrishnan Venkatraman (2009 Oct)

First Indian woman to ski to the South Pole - Reena Kaushal. She was part of the eight-woman Commonwealth team that crossed a 900 km Antarctic ice trek to reach the South Pole to mark the 60th anniversary of the founding of the Commonwealth (2009 Dec)

First man to fly solo non stop across the Atlantic - Charles Lindbergh (1927)

First person to fly faster than the speed of sound - Charles Elwood Chuck Yeager (1947)

First man to reach the South Pole - Roald Amundsen, Norwegian explorer and team (1911)

First person to swim across the English Channel - Matthew Webb (1875)

First person to cross Antarctic Circle -James Cook (1773)

First people to sight the North Pole - Roald Amundsen and his sponsor Lincoln Ellsworth from the airship 'Norge' piloted by Umberto Nobile (1926)

First people to reach the North Pole - Lt. Col. Joseph O. Fletcher and Lt. William P.

Tenzing and Hillary

Benedict landed their plane (1952)

First successful conquest of Mount Everest -Tenzing Norgay & Sir Edmund Hillary (New Zealand) via the South-East Ridge Route (1953)

First conquest of Everest via the North Ridge - Chinese team (1960)

First American to conquer the Everest - James Whittaker (1963)

First person to conquer the Everest twice - Nawang Gombu Sherpa. Both of his ascents were via the South east ridge (1965)

First ascent of Everest without bottled oxy-

Woman to Get Artificial Heart

Mary Lund was the first woman to receive an artificial heart, Jarvik VII in 1986.

gen - Peter Habeler (Austria) and Reinhold Messner, (Italy) via the South - East Ridge (1978)

First couple to conquer the Everest together - Andrej & Marija Stremfelj, Slovenia.

Marija was also the first Slovenian woman to climb Everest (1990)

First son of a mountaineer to climb the Everest - Peter Hillary, New Zealand (1990)

First father and son to climb the Ever-

Peter Hillary

est together -Jean Noel Roche and his son Roche Bertrand aka Zebulon (1990)

First Pakistani to conquer the Everest - Nazir Sabir (2000)

First blind person to conquer the Everest - Erik Weihenmayer, USA (2001)

First nonstop solo flight around the world without refueling.- Steve Fossett flew the Virgin Atlantic Globalflyer around the world From Salina, Kansas. It covered 22,878 miles in 67 hrs (2005)

First round the world solo flight - Wiley Post (1933)

First woman to fly solo around the world - Jerrie Fredritz Mock. She made the flight in 29 days flying 22,860 miles.(1964)

First woman to fly solo across the English Channel - Harriet Quimby, from Dover, England, to Hardelot, France, in a monoplane. She was later killed in a flying accident.(1912 April 16)

First woman to climb Everest without bottled oxygen - Lydia Bradey of New Zealand (1988 Nov 14)

First woman to summit from the North (Tibet) side.- Phantog, a Tibetan woman, reached the Summit only a few days after Junko, becoming the second woman to summit Everest (1975 May 27)

First European woman to summit Everest - Wanda Rutkiewicz. She was the third

woman to summit Everest (1978)

First woman to die on Everest - Hannelore Schmatz, while descending from the Summit after becoming the 4th woman to summit Everest (1979)

First Asian woman to swim across the English Channel - Arati Saha, India (1959 Sep 29)

First woman to summit Everest - Junko Tabei of Japan via the South East Ridge (1975 May 16)

First Indian woman to summit Mount Everest - Bachendri Pal. She was the 5th woman in the world to achieve this (1984 May 23)

First woman to conquer Everest twice - Santosh Yadav, India (1993 May 10)

First woman to fly solo across the Atlantic - Amelia Earhart, from Harbor Grace, Newfoundland, to Ireland in 15 hrs. (1932 May)

First Indian woman to swim across seven seas of the world - Bula Choudhary, In-

Bula Choudhary

dia. She was the first Indian woman to cross English Channel twice.(2004)

First Indian woman to reach Antarctica - Meher Moos (1976)

First woman to set foot on North Pole - Ann Bancroft, USA (1986)

First woman to sail around the world solo in under 100 days - Ellen MacArthur, English Sailor (2001)

| Hot Air Balloon Marriage | **Vandana Sharma and Sunil Sharma were the first Indians to be married in a hot air balloon. The venue was SMS Grounds, Jaipur, Rajasthan. It happened on Dec. 31, 2006.** |

Awards & Honours

First journalist to win four pulitzer prizes - Carol Guzy, Photographer, The Washington Post (2011 Apl)

First Indian woman to win a Grammy - Tanvi Shah, For the Spanish version of the lyric "Jai Ho" of the Oscar winning film "Slum Dog Millionaire" (2010 Feb)

Tanvi Shah

First Indian to win two Grammys in a year - A.R. Rahman, for his foot-tapping number 'Jai Ho' and outstanding soundtrack for the film Slumdog Millionaire (2010 Feb)

First sportsman to be honoured with the Group Captain rank of the Indian Air Force - Sachin Tendulkar (2010 Jun)

First actor to be honoured with the Lieutenant Colonel rank of the Indian Army - Mohanlal (2009)

First Nobel Prize winner for Literature - Sully Prudhomme, France (1901)

First Nobel Prize winner for Peace -Jean Henri Dunant, Switzerland & Frederic Passy, France (1901)

First Nobel Prize winner for Economics - Ragnar Frisch, Norway & Jan Tinbergen, Netherlands (1969)

First person to win two Nobel Prizes - Marie Sklodowska Curie (first in Physics, 1903 and the second in Chemistry (1911)

First black to receive the Nobel Peace Prize - Ralph Bunche (1950)

First Indian to win Nobel Prize in Literature - Rabindranath Tagore. He was also the first Asian to get the prize (1913)

First Indian to win Booker Prize - Arundhati Roy. For 'The God of Small Things' (1997)

First Indians to win Bharat Ratna - Dr. S. Radhakrishnan, C. Rajagopalachari, and Dr. C.V. Raman (1954)

Arundhati Roy

First woman Nobel Prize winner - Marie Sklodowska Curie, Physics. She is the first to win Physics Nobel (1903)

First woman Nobel Prize winner for Chemistry - Marie Sklodowska Curie (1911)

First Mother and daughter to win Nobel prize - Marie Sklodowska Curie (1903) and daughter Irene Joliot Curie (1935)

First woman Nobel Prize winner for Peace - Baroness Bertha Sophie Felicita von Suttner (1905)

Marie Curie

First woman Nobel Prize winner for Literature - Selma Ottilia Lovisa Lagerlof (1909)

First woman from India to win a Nobel Prize - Mother Teresa, Peace Prize (1979)

First American woman to win the Nobel Prize for Peace - Jane Addams, social worker (1931)

First Black woman to win the Nobel Prize for literature - Toni Morrison (1993)

First Muslim woman to win a Nobel Prize -

Railway Engine Driver	Sukhdev Yadav set a record in 1992 when she became the first woman railway engine driver in Asia.

Shirin Ebadi (2003)

First Black woman to win a Pulitzer prize - Gwendolyn Brooks (1950)

First Woman selected as Time magazine's "Man of the Year"-Wallis Warfield Simpson (1936)

First Black woman to win an Oscar for Best Actress - Halle Berry (2002)

First woman to win the Jnanpith - Ashapurna Devi (1976)

First woman to receive Bharat Ratna - Indira Gandhi (1971)

First Indian woman to win a Pulitzer Prize - Jhumpa Lahiri (2000)

First woman Pulitzer Winner for fiction - Edith Wharton, American novelist for "The Age of Innocence" (1921)

First Black Miss America - Vanessa Williams (1983)

First Miss Universe - Armi Kuusela, Finland (1952)

First Miss World - Kerstin Kiki Haakonson, Sweden (1951)

First Indian to win the Miss Universe title - Sushmita Sen (1994)

First woman to appear on a US postage stamp - Queen Isabella of Spain (1893)

First Indian woman featured in a postal stamp - Meera Bai (1952)

First Indian to be the Miss World - Reita Faria (1966 Nov 17)

First Beauty Contest in the world - Started by Cypselus, (700 BC)

Reita Faria

First Miss America - Margaret Gorman (1921)

Business & Commerce

Firt Indian Automobile company to cross the production mark of one crore cars -

Maruti

Maruti Suzuki India Ltd (2011 Mar)

First Titanium Sponge Plant in India - Titanium Sponge Plant of the Kerala Minerals and Metals Ltd, Chavara, Kollam (2011 Feb)

India's first international container transhipment terminal - Vallarpadam Inter-

Vallarpadam Terminal

national Container Transhipment Terminal, Kochi (2011 Feb)

First private company in India to get protection from the Central Industrial Security Force (CISF) - Infosys Technologies Ltd (2009 Jul)

First bank in the world - Egibi bank founded in Babylon during the period of Nebuchadnezzar (605 - 562 BC)

First bank in India - Bank of Hindustan-- (1779)

First ATM in India- HSBC, Mumbai (1987)

First Indian bank to open a branch outside India - Bank of India, London (1946)

First Special Economic Zone (SEZ) in India - Kandla, Gujarat (1965)

First sugar factory in India - set up at Saran, Bihar (1903)

Montessori's Record	Maria Montessori is known as the founder of the Montessori system of education. She was the first woman to qualify as a doctor in Europe.

First oil well and oil refinery in India - Digboi, Borbil (1890)

First Iron and Steel factory in India - Bengal Iron Works Company, Kulti, West Bengal (1870)

First private sector Steel Plant in India - Tata Steel founded by Jamsetji Nusserwanji Tata (1907 Aug)

Hotel Taj

First Five Star hotel in India - Taj Mahal Hotel, Bombay, started by Tata (1903)

First underground bazaar in India - Palika Bazaar, New Delhi (1978)

First Tea Museum in India - Munnar, Kerala, established by the Tata Tea (2004 Mar)

First skyscraper in the world - Home Insurance Building, Chicago, Illinois. William LeBaron Jenny was the architect of this 10 storey, 138 ft., building (1885)

Education

First fisheries university in India - Kerala University of Fisheries and Ocean Studies (KUFOS) (2011 Feb)

First Indian woman Professor at Harvard University - Gita Gopinath, Economics (2010 May)

First first space university in India (and Asia)- Indian Institute of Space Science and Technology (IIST), Thiruvananthapuram (2009 Aug)

First woman head of UNESCO - Irina Bokova. She was Bulgaria's former foreign minister (2009)

First Education Minister of free India - Maulana Abul Kalam Azad (1947)

First women's university in India - Indian Womens University, Pune. now known as SNDT Women's University, Mumbai (1916)

First women's college in India - Bethune College, Calcutta (1879)

First national professor in India - C.V. Raman (1947)

First Indian professor at the Oxford University - Dr. S. Radhakrishnan (former president of India) 1936 Feb

C.V. Raman

First woman law gaduate in India - Cornelia Sorabji, Calcutta (1894)

First deaf and dumb woman to be a graduate - Helen Keller, Radcliffe College (1904)

First university in India - Calcutta University (1857)

First open university in India - Andhra Pradesh Open University. In 1991 it was renamed as (1982)

First college in India - Fort William College, Calcutta (1800)

First Engineering College in India - Roorkee Engineering College. It was renamed The Thomason College of Civil Engineering in 1854. In 1949 it was given University status, making it the first engineering university of independent India. In 2001 it was declared an Indian Institute of Technology, making it the seventh IIT of India (1847)

First educational institution for the blind in India - Sharp Memorial School, Dehradun (1887)

First Medical University in India - University of Medical Sciences, Vijayawada (1986)

Film

First woman cinematographer to win national film award - Anjali Shukla, Cam-

Anjali Shukla

erawoman of the film Kutty Srank by Shaji. N. Karun (2010 Sep)

First cinematographer to win the Dada Saheb Phalke award - V.K. Murthy, Mysore (2010 Jan)

First 70 mm animation film in India - Lava-Kusa the Warrior Twins (2010)

First Indian to win an Oscar in the technical category - Resul Pookutty, Sound Mixing (2009 Feb)

First Indian lyricist to win an Oscar - Gulzar (2009 Feb)

First Indian to win Dadasaheb Phalke Award - Devika Rani (1970)

First talkie movie in the world - "The Jazz Singer" (1927)

Gulzar

First Oscar winner for the Best Actor - Emil Jannings (1928)

First black actor to win an Oscar in a major category - Sidney Poitier, "Lilies of the Field" (1964)

First Indian Oscar winner - Bhanu Athaiya, For Best Costume Design for the film 'Gandhi' (1982)

First Indian Oscar nomination for Best Foreign Language Film - Mother India (1957)

First Oscar winner for Best Actress - Janet Gaynor, for her total work (1928)

First black actress to win an Oscar - Hattie McDaniel. (Best Supporting Actress for "Gone with the Wind" (1939)

First Actress of Indian talkies - Rani Zubeida, Alam Aara. She acted in 36 silent films (1931)

First American woman film director - Alice Guy Blache (1896)

Literature & Media

First talking newspaper in India (world) - A special issue of The Hindu issued in Mumbai to introduce the Vento, Volkswagen's premium entry level sedan car in India (2010 Sep)

First golden stamp replicas issued by the postal department - "The pride of India collection", a set of 25 classic stamp replicas struck on pure Swiss silver and layered with 24 carat gold (2010 Oct)

First SMS in the world - "Merry Christmas" sent by Neil Papworth to Richard Jarvis in UK. It was send by using an Orbitel 901 handset (1992 Dec 03)

First American novel -The Power of Sympathy by William Hill Brown (1789)

First dictionary in the world - 'Explaining Words, Analysing Characters' (Chinese) Compiled by Hsew Shen (C 100 AD)

First Thesaurus in the world - Chinese 'Literary Approximater' (C 800 BC)

First Encyclopaedia in the world-'Antiquities of Things Human and Divine' written by Roman scholar Marcus Terentius Varro (47 BC)

First daily newspaper in the world - The Daily News (Acta Diurna), Rome (1st BC)

First printed book in the world - Diamond Sutra. This Chinese book on buddhist scriptures (868 AD)

First novel in the world - Cyropaedia, historical Greek novel written in Corinth about the life of Cyrus (360 BC)

First Indian Sponsored TV serial - Hum Log (1984)

First woman photojournalist in India - Homai Vyarawalla, Bombay Chronicle (1938)

First woman editor of a newspaper - Ann Franklin, sister of Benjamin Franklin, in the "The Newport Mercury" (1762)

Homai Vyarawalla

Inventor of the first sign language alphabet for the use of the deaf - George Dalgarno, Scottish school teacher (1680)

World's first crossword - Devised by Arthur Wynne, England (1913)

World's first television service - The British Broadcasting Corporation (BBC) started from Alexandra Palace with three hours of programming a day (1936)

BBC

First Indian city to introduce the mobile phone service - Kolkata (1995 Jul)

Medicine

First direct transfusion of blood performed by Richard Lower, English physician and physiologist (1666)

First person to be executed by the guillotine - Nicolas J. Pelletier (1792)

First sex-change operation in the world - George (Christine) Jorgenson (1952)

First human heart transplant was performed by - Dr. Christian Barnard (1967)

First successful heart transplant in India - by Dr. P. Venugopal, AIIMS, New Delhi, on Devi Ram, a mechanic (1994 Aug 03)

First recipient of a permanent artificial heart - Barney Clark (1982)

First Indian Test tube baby - Harsha, at KEM hospital Mumbai. Indira Hinduja was the doctor (1986)

First to qualify as a medical doctor in Europe - Dr. Maria Montessori, University of Rome, Italy (1896)

First Indian lady doctor - Kadambani Ganguly (1886)

First woman President of the World Health Assembly of WHO - Rajkumari Amrit Kaur, India (1950)

Politics & Government

First woman Prime Minister of Mali - Cisse Mariam Kaidama Sidibe (2011 Jan)

First woman Prime Minister of Thailand - Yingluck Shinawatra (2011 Aug)

First woman to head a major US Intelligence Agency - Leticia A. Long as the director of National Geospatial Intelligence Agency (NGA) (2010 Aug)

First Indian Origin woman to become the governor of a state in the USA - Nikki Haley, South Carolina (2011 Jan)

First woman chief minister of West Bengal - Mamata Banerjee, Trinamool Congress (2011 May)

First Muslim woman Minister in the UK - Sayeeda Warsi (2010 May)

First woman Prime Minister of Australia - Julia Gillard (2010 Jun)

First woman Prime Minister of Trinidad and Tobago - Kamla Persad-Bissessar (2010 Jun)

Mamata Banerjee

First woman President of Costa Rica - Laura Chinchilla (2010 Feb)

Warship Commander	The first woman warship commander in the 500-year history of the British Royal Navy is Lt. Commander Sarah West, appointed to command HMS Portland, a frontline warship in 2012.

First woman Speaker of Lok Sabha, the Lower House of Indian Parliament - Meira Kumar (2009 Jun)

First woman Prime Minister of Croatia - Jadranka Kosor (2009 Jul)

Jadranka Kosor

First Cabinet Meeting held at the Everest base camp - Nepal's cabinet meeting (2009 Dec)

Frst woman head of a state to fly in a fighter jet - Pratibha Patil, President of India (2009 Nov)

First US President - George Washington (1789)

First US president to be inaugurated in Washington, D.C - Thomas Jefferson (1801)

First US president to die in office - William Henry Harrison. He also had the shortest term in office, 32 days (1841)

First US President to be assassinated - Abraham Lincoln (1865)

First and only US president to resign from office - Richard Nixon (1974)

First and only US President to win election to nonconsecutive terms - Grover Cleveland. He is also the first US President married inside the White House in1886 (1892)

First US President to reside in the White House - John Adams (1797)

First American Indian to become a US Senator - Charles Curtis (1907)

First openly gay U.S. Congress person - Barney Frank (1981)

First Jew to become US Secretary of State - Henry Kissinger (1973)

First Black to become US secretary of state - Colin Powell (2000)

First black Secretary General of the United Nations - Kofi Annan (1987)

First Secretary General of United Nations

-Trygve Lie, Norway (1946)

First Prime Minister of UK - Robert Walpole (1721)

First English Monarch to live in Buckingham Palace - Queen Victoria (1837)

First British Monarch to have a televised coronation - Elizabeth II (1953)

First Prime Minister of Canada - Sir John Alexander McDonald (1867)

First Tsar of Russia-Ivan IV, the Terrible (1547)

First reigning queen of England - Queen Mary I (Bloody Mary) (1553)

First Indian Prime Minister to be voted out of office - Indira Gandhi (1977)

First Non Congress government in India -Janata Party Government with Morarji Desai as the Prime Minister (1977-1979)

First Emperor of Rome - Augustus (27 BC)

First Prime Minister of Canada - Sir John A. Macdonald (1867)

Nelson Mandela

First Black President of South Africa - Nelson Mandela (1994)

First country to implement 'right to vote' for women (female suffrage) -New Zealand (1893)

First great woman in recorded history - Hatshepsut (1479 BC)

First woman ruler of India - Razia Sultana. She is the first woman ruler in South Asia (1236)

First woman minister in India - VIjayalakshmi Pandit, Uttar Pradesh (1937)

First woman foreign secretary of India - Chokila Iyer (2001)

| The Youngest Footballer | Souleymane Mamam was 13 years 310 days when he appeared in a preliminary qualifying game in 2001. He played for Togo against Zambia. |

Kanchan Bhattacharya

First woman Air marshall in India - Padma Bandopadhyay (2002)

First woman DGP in India - Kanchan Bhattacharya, Uttaranchal (2004)

First woman union minister in India Raj kumari Amrit Kaur, Cabinet Minister, Health portfolio (1947)

First Black woman in US Senate - Carol Elizabeth Moseley Braun, Illinois (1992)

First woman prime minister in the world - Sirimavo Bandaranaike, Prime Minister of Sri Lanka (1960)

First woman President in the world- Isabel Peron, Argentina (1974)

First Democratically elected woman head of state - Vigdís FinnbogadÛttir, President of Iceland (1980)

First woman Prime minister of Israel - Golda Meir. She is the first Jewish woman Prime Minister. (1964)

First woman Prime Minister of Canada - Kim Campbell (1993)

First woman Chancellor of Germany - Dr. Angela Merkel (2005)

First woman Prime minister of India - Indira Gandhi (1966)

First woman President of Chile - Michelle Bachelet (2006)

First African elected woman head of state - Ellen Johnson Sirleaf as President of Liberia (2005)

First woman to become president of UN General Assembly - Vijayalakshmi Pandit (1953)

First woman US Secretary Of State - Madeleine Albright (1996)

First Black woman to serve as US secretary of state - Condoleezza Rice (2005)

First woman to serve as US national security adviser - Condoleezza Rice (2001)

First First Lady of the US - Martha Washington (1789)

First woman MP in Britain - Viscountess (Nancy) Astor, House of Commons (1919 Nov 28)

First woman President of the Indian National Congress - Annie Besant (1917)

First woman Chief minister of a state in India - Sucheta Kripalani, Uttar Pradesh (1963 - 67)

First woman Governor of a State in India - Sarojini Naidu, United Provinces (UP) (1947- 49)

First woman Speaker of the US House of Representatives - Nancy Pelosi (2007)

First woman Deputy chairman of Indian Rajya Sabha - Violet Alva (1962 - 69)

Nancy Pelosi

First woman Prime Minister of Turkey - Tansu Ciller (1993 Jun 14)

First woman Prime minister of Britain - Margaret Thatcher (1979 May 04)

First woman ambassador in the World- Rosika Schwimmer, Hungarian ambassador to Switzerland (1918)

First Indian woman Ambassador - Vijayalaksmi Pandit, USSR (1947-49)

First live broadcast of the Inaugural ceremony of the US President on the Internet.- William J. Clinton (1997)

Science & Technology

First cloned buffalo calf in India - Samrupa (2009 Feb)

First cloned camel in the world - Injaz,

First Black Mayor	In 1983, America had her first black mayor. Harold Washington was elected the Mayor of Chicago on April 12.

Camel Reproduction Centre, Dubai (2009 Apr 08)

First Indian research station in the Arctic - 'Himadri'. It will carry out research in contemporary fields of Arctic Science with special emphasis on climate change (2008 Jul 02)

First Atom Bomb -"Little Boy" dropped over Hiroshima by the US during the second world war (1945)

Little Boy

First cloned mammal - Dolly, the lamb (1996)

First mechanical computer was conceived by - Charles Babbage (1835)

First computer programmer - Ada Byron's (Ada Lovelace). She wrote the first algorithm for the analytical engine of Charles Babbage (1842)

First working programmable automatic computer - Z3 (1941)

First programmable electronic computer - Colossus, designed by Tommy Flowers (1943)

First Compact Disc (CD) - Jointly developed by two companies, Sony and Philips (1978)

First Hard Disk - IBM's 305 RAMAC. It has a capacity of about 5 MB (1956)

First digitally operated and programmable robot - The Ultimate. It was used to liftn and stock hot pieces of metal. (1961)

First practical threshing machine for separating cereal grains from the husks - designed and built by Andrew Meikle, Scottish millwright (1785)

First sound recording - Thomas Alva Edison's phonograph was the first instrument used for recording sound (1877)

First Atom Bomb - "Little Boy" dropped over Hiroshima by the US during the second world war (1945)

Space

First artificial satellite launched into orbit - Sputnik 1, USSR (1957)

First artificial satellite by the United States - Explorer 1 (1958)

First manned space vehicle - Vostok 1, USSR (1961)

First international co-operative space flight - A US Apollo spacecraft docks with a Soviet Soyuz spacecraft while in Earth orbit. The two flight crews visited each other's spacecraft and had meals together (1975)

First US astronaut to orbit earth -John Glenn (1962)

First manned private spaceflight - 'Space ShipOne' piloted by Mike Melvill (2004)

Laika

First living creature to orbit the earth - Laika, the dog, aboard the Soviet satellite, Sputnik 2. (1957)

First man in space - Yuri Gagarin of USSR. He is the first human to orbit Earth (1961)

| Quillagua | Quillagua in Chile is the driest place on Earth. It had 5 mm of rainfall in 1964-2001. |

Rakesh Sharma

First Indian in space - Rakesh Sharma aboard Salyut 7 (1984)

First American in space - Alan B Shepherd (1961)

First human to walk on the Moon - Neil Armstrong, Apollo 11 (1969)

First human to walk in space - Alexei Arkhovich Leonov (1965)

First American to walk in space - Edward Higgins White, Jr. (1965)

First woman in space - Valentina Tereshkova, Russian cosmonaut, aboard Vostok - 6 (1963)

First American woman in space - Dr. Sally K. Ride, Space Shuttle Challenger (1983)

First black woman in space - Mae Carol Jemison, aboard the Endeavor (1992)

First Indian Woman in space - Kalpana Chawla aboard Space Shuttle Columbia flight STS - 87.She was a naturalized US citizen, and represented the US during the event (1997 Nov 19)

First woman to walk in space - Svetlana Savitskaya, while on Salyut - 7 (1984)

First American woman to walk in space - Kathryn D. Sullivan, Space Shuttle challenger mission (1984)

First woman space tourist - Anousheh Ansari. She was the first Iranian and first Muslim woman in space (2006)

First woman space shuttle pilot - Eileen Marie Collins. She piloted STS 63, which involved rendezvous between Discovery and space station Mir.(1995)

Sports

First player from Asia to win a Grand Slam singles title - Li Na (China), French Open Women's final after defeating Francesca Schiavone of Italy in two sets 6-4, 7-6 (2011 Jun)

Li Na

First Indian gold medal winner in a rowing event in Asian Games - Bajrang Lal Takhar in men's single sculls rowing event of 16th Asian Games in Guangzhou, China (2010 Nov)

First Indian to be a five-time world boxing champion - M.C. Mary Kom (2010 Sep)

Mary Kom

First cricketer to score double century in One Day Cricket - Sachin Tendulkar (2010 Feb)

First Indian woman shooter to win Gold Medal in World Shooting championship - Tejaswini Sawant (2010 Aug)

First Indian to win a Gold Medal in World Wrestling Championship. He is also the first Indian to win Olympic (2008) and World Championship medals - Sushil Kumar (2010 Sep)

First batsman to complete 30,000 runs in international cricket - Sachin Tendulkar (2009 Nov)

First woman Chess grandmaster of India - S. Vijayalakshmi (2000)

First Indian woman medal winner in Olympics - Karnam Malleswari, Bronze in weightlifting, Sydney (2000)

First Asian city to host Olympics - Tokyo, Japan (1964)

5 Presidents in 2 Weeks — **A South American country that had five presidents in two weeks in 2001: Argentina.**

First Tour de France (road bicycle race) winner - Maurice Garin (1903)

First world chess champion - Wilhelm Steinitz (1886)

First man to run a mile under 4 minutes - British athlete Sir Roger Bannister (1954)

First Indian Olympic team medal - Gold for Hockey. At Amsterdam beating the Netherlands (1928)

First Indian Olympic individual medal winner - K. D. Jadhav, Bronze in wrestling at Helsinki (1952)

First athlete disqualified at the Olympics for drug use - Hans-Gunnar Liljenwall at the Mexico summer Olympics (1968)

First Indian Cricket tournament -The Bombay Triangular which later became the Bombay Quadrangular (1912)

First Indian Cricket test match - Against England at Lord's (1932)

K.D. Jadhav

First Indian Cricket captain - CK Nayudu, for the tour of England (1932)

First Indian cricketer to score a century - Lala Amarnath, against England in South Bombay (1933)

First Indian cricketer to score a triple century - Virender Sehwag, against Pakistan at Multan (2004)

First Indian hat-trick in Test cricket - Harbhajan Singh, against Australia (2001)

First Indian Tennis Grand Slam title - Mahesh Bhupathi, partnering with Japanese Rika Hiraki, Mixed Doubles, French Open (1997)

First Indian woman to appear in an Olympic final - P.T. Usha, Los Angeles Olympics (1984)

First woman to win an Olympic Gold Medal - Charlotte Cooper, UK, Tennis singles (1900)

First American woman to win three gold medals in a single Olympics - Wilma Rudolph, Rome Olympics (1960 Sep 7)

Wilma Rudolph

First Indian woman to win a round at a Grand Slam - Nirupama Vaidyanathan beat Italian Gloria Pizzichini in the first round of the Australian Open (1998)

First Indian woman in the third round (highest so far) of a tennis Grand Slam event - Sania Mirza, Singles category of the Australian Open (2005 Jan)

First woman black tennis player to win a

Althea Gibson

singles title at Wimbledon - Althea Gibson (1957)

First Indian woman to win an individual gold medal in Asian Games - Kamaljit Sandhu, Bangkok, 400 m (1970)

First woman to win a Grand Slam - Maureen Catherine ("Little Mo") Connolly (1953)

First Indian to win an individual Olympic Gold - Abhinav Bindra (2008)

Compiled by: **V. Vijayakumar**

Highest Railway Station

The highest train station is Conder station, in Bolivia. It is at 4786 m. (15,702 feet).

English Language Section

Most Confusable Words

Nirmala Krishnaswamy

Is it ingenious / ingenuous, obsequious / obsequies, venal / venial? - words which look alike and have very small differences in spelling but have a difference in meaning, although some may be very subtle, as well as homographs (words that are spelt alike but have different pronunciation, for example: bow and bow), homonyms (words spelt alike, and may be pronounced alike but have different meanings, for example: 'can' meaning 'be able to' and 'can' meaning a container) and homophones (words pronounced alike but have a different spelling and meaning, for example: 'hoard' and 'horde') are some of the aspects of the English vocabulary which candidates appearing for various entrance exams, and job aspirants are tested on.

These can be clubbed under 'confusable words'. Some of the more common ones are discussed below .

1. abjure /adjure

Abjure is to give up or to renounce.
If the rebels want to talk peace, they must first abjure violence.
Adjure means to ask or order someone to do something. The judge adjured him to answer truthfully.

2. adapt / adopt

Adapt is a verb meaning either conform, change, adjust or modify to suit whatever the circumstance. Its noun form is adaptation.
Adopt also a verb (noun form is adoption) means accept as one's own that belongs to someone else. Adapt a play to make into a movie.
Adopt a child; the people who adopt a child become the adoptive parents.

3. adjacent / adjoining

The common perception is that these two words can be inter-changed. However, the two have distinct meanings. If two things, such as two rooms, are adjoining, they are literally joined. Adjoining rooms, therefore, may have a common wall or a door or even a passage.
If two things are adjacent, they are near each other as in adjacent angles, 'adjacent flats or a road adjacent to the one a person lives on.
The word contiguous is very close to the word *adjoining*. Contiguous states will share a common border.

4. adverse / averse

Adverse (adjective) means unfavourable or hostile or contrary.
An officer can make an adverse remark on a junior personnel; adverse comment.
Averse means opposed, loath.
Government officials ought to be averse to accepting a bribe.

5. affect / effect (verbs)

Affect means have an influence on, bring about a change in and usually has a negative connotation.
Unusual rains at this time of the year have affected the standing crops.
Effect means bring about a result, make something happen.
We easily effected the changeover from summer timings to winter timings of our classes. His affected way of speaking is supposed to impress others.

6. allusion / illusion

An *allusion* is an indirect reference: it is what is alluded to.

Cyprus & Cypress

Cyprus is a country. It is an island state in the E. Mediterranean Sea. Its Greek name is Kypros and Turkish name Kibris. Cypress is a type of evergreen tree. There is a city by name Cypress near Los Angeles.

He didn't like people making an allusion to his new hairstyle.

If someone is obese you make an allusion to it when you say: "You must find it difficult to find your size of clothes."

Illusion is a fancied vision, may be a false impression, a figment of one's imagination.

7. alternate / alternative

Alternative is when one has another choice. The word can be used in the plural when there are more than two other choices.

I'm afraid he has no other alternative; he has to go. The alternative numbers are 1, 3, 5.........

Alternate can be a verb too.

The weather alternated between being unbearably hot and unbelievably balmy.

8. altruism / egoism

Altruism describes a principle, feeling or practice of selfless consideration and concern for others.

An altruist is one who does things for others without expecting anything in return. Mother Teresa is an example of absolute altruism.

Egoism is selfish concern only for oneself, with neither consideration nor care for others - it is the 'I - me - myself-culture'. An egoist is self-centred looking after his own interests.

An egotist is also self-centred but additionally he has an all-consuming conviction that he is superior to everyone else. He constantly brags / boasts about himself. He is full of himself.

9. ambiguous / ambivalent

Ambiguous means 'open to more than one interpretation, uncertain in meaning'.

The word *'ambivalent'* is from the word 'ambivalence' coined by the psychoanalyst, Sigmund Freud. It refers to "the simultaneous presence in a person's mind of conflicting feelings towards someone or something."

Today, it has come to mean 'with mixed feelings, or involving contradictory emotions.'

10. amend /emend

Amend means 'add to a text'. Anything that is added is called an amendment.

The provisions added to the Constitution are called amendments.

Emend is a formal word that means 'make corrections or changes in a text'.

11. amiable / amicable

People and other living beings can be amiable, whereas we can reach an amicable agreement when relationships, differences among people and nations are ironed out.

12. among / amongst / between

Among and *amongst* are the same; the former being more common in the US and the latter in the UK.

The difference between *among / amongst* and *between* is that *among / amongst* is used when more than two items or individuals are being considered and *between* when two are involved. We can divide the amount between the two of us.

13. amoral / immoral

The prefix a- in English comes from the Greek a- meaning 'not, lacking in, without'. So we have words such as asymmetry, asymptomatic, amorphous.

Immoral means 'not moral' and has a negative connotation of 'possessed of bad morals' . An immoral person is one who knows what moral behaviour is but chooses to act otherwise.

Amoral means one who has not the slightest idea of what others would consider to be moral behaviour. He is a person devoid of moral sense or sensibility.

14. amuse / bemuse

Amuse means to entertain; make smile or laugh. She knew nothing of dancing and so was amused at the suggestion that she might be a skilful dancer. Bemuse means 'to confuse or bewilder'.

15. apogee / perigee

Both the words refer to points in an orbit around the earth, *apogee* being the point where the orbiting body is at its farthest from the earth, and *perigee* the point where it is closest.

16. appraise / apprise

Appraise means provide an estimate of the value of something; whereas apprise means to keep someone informed or advise

Before buying a second-hand car you will get it appraised.

You will *apprise* your boss of what happened in the office during his absence for a few days.

17. atheist / agnostic

While an *atheist* asserts that there is no God or gods, an *agnostic* neither denies nor acknowledges the presence of a God.

18. auger / augur

Though pronounced alike, the two words have distinct meanings.

An *auger* is a tool used for boring holes, either a hand-held device, rather like a gimlet, used for piercing wood.

Augur is used as a verb meaning 'to prophesy or predict.'

With the share prices of the company going up this season, it augurs well for the organisation.

19. authoritarian / authoritative

Both of these words are derived from 'authority'.

Authoritarian means 'exercising authority; dominating; bossy'.

Authoritative means 'supported, approved or validated by authority; official.'

A government or a person might be authoritarian or domineering whereas a reference book or information authoritative.

20. beside / besides

Both of these words serve as prepositions and as adverbs. The difference can best be seen in the following examples:

beside (preposition): Come and sit beside me. She was beside herself with grief.

beside (adverb): Whenever she went out, her dog went along beside

besides (preposition): Besides Bengali, he also speaks Hindi.

besides (adverb): I'm not going to the party; besides I wasn't even invited.

21. blue collar / white collar

Workers whose jobs involve physical labour are called *blue-collar* workers or jobs.

Those whose work is in an office or of a managerial nature are called *white-collar* workers or jobs.

22. callous / callus

Callous is related to being hard-hearted. Someone who is callous in his attitude is insensitive, unfeeling and emotionally unmoved.

The noun *callus* refers to a hardened patch of skin, as on the hands or feet, caused by pressure or friction.

23. canvas /canvass

The noun '*canvas*' refers to the coarse cloth that artists paint on, sails are made of and it is the same canvas from which some form of sport shoes is made.

Theist	Theism is belief in a god or gods. Belief in one god is monotheism. Polytheism, is belief in many gods. Pantheism is worship or toleration of worship of all gods of various cults. The opposite of theist is atheist.

Kangaroo

Kangaroo is a large Australian animal that moves by jumping. It has a strong tail. The female carries its young in a pocket of skin called a pouch in front of its body. A young kangaroo is a joey. The plural of kangaroo is kangaroos.

Canvass is a verb. A politician can canvass for votes ie. ask for support.

One can canvass for a particular candidate.

24. carat / karat/ caret

In British English, carat has two meanings.

a) It is a unit weight for precious stones, chiefly diamonds.

b) '*Carat*' is also used to refer to the proporrition of gold in an alloy, 24 carats signifying pure gold. *Karat* is the spelling used in US and Canada.

'*Caret*' is a symbol, written like an inverted 'v' marked at a place in written material where something has been omitted and should be inserted: The omitted word (s) is / are then written above the caret.

25. climatic / climactic

Climatic is the adjectival form of climate and it is to do with climate, weather or atmosphere. The drastic climatic changes one witnesses today is directly linked to global warming.

Climactic is the adjectival form of climax, 'a culmination, or point of greatest intensity'.

The climactic words of his speech moved the audience.

26. compliment / complement

Since these two words sound exactly alike, it is easy to get them mixed up .

Complement has the sense of 'complete or completion of something'. One way to remember this is to realise that '*com-*

plement' and '*complete*' have the same first six letters. This word also has the sense of 'set off to advantage'.

The upholstery complements The decor in the room.

Compliment has the sense of 'admire; praise; respect'.

I felt uncomfortable with too many compliments showered on me.

'With best compliments' is what we use when sending a card or a gift.

27. contemptible / contemptuous

Contemptible is fomed from 'contempt', hatred

A contemptible act is a hate-able act.

Contemptuous means hateful or full of contempt.

We can be contemptuous of others' behaviour.

28) continuous / continual

Continuous means without interruption.

Thus one can speak of continuous development of technology; of continuous breathing.

Continual means repeatedly; again and again at close intervals. One can refer to continual work stoppages or continual nagging.

29. corps / corpse / corpus

Derived from Latin, *corpus* (= a body) the word now means 'a collection or body of texts of literary works'.

A *corpus* of several hundred written and spoken texts was analysed for information on how the language works:

A 'corpus fund' is used in finance.

Corps refers to a group of people involved in a common endeavour, specially, in the army. It also refers to a group of dancers in a ballet troupe who have no solo parts.

Corpse refers to a dead body. (The dead body of an animal is a carcass)

30. council / counsel

Counsel is advice or guidance. A counsellor is one who gives advice.

Crockery, Cutlery

Crockery: Plates, pots, cups and dishes (made of baked clay)
Cutlery: Knives, forks and spoons

Council on the other hand, is a body of people assembled for some purpose or with specifically designated authority.

31. current / currant

'*Currant*' refers to small dried grapes, often used in sweet dishes or desserts. The same spelling holds good for red currant and black currant.

'*Current*', as an adjective means 'present, or now in progress' - current price of a commodity.

The noun meaning 'a flow, a movement in one direction' is used in phrases as 'the current of the river' or 'electric current'.

32. deprecate / depreciate

'Appreciate' is a common word in English and '*depreciate*' is the antonym.

Depreciate means to 'devalue' or 'minimise the value of' and is commonly used in the world of finance. The value of something depreciates as time goes by.

Deprecate means to 'disapprove of; object to'. You may treat someone in a deprecating way.

33. diagnosis / prognosis

Used mostly in the realm of medicine, *diagnosis* refers to the identification of a disease. *Prognosis*, on the other hand, deals with the prediction of the course of a disease. It would clarify the chances of a patient's future condition or even his survival. The verb form of '*diagnosis*' is 'diagnose' and that of '*prognosis*' is 'prognosticate', which strangely enough is used in general language with the meaning of 'prophesy'.

34. discover / invent

A person may *discover* something that is already there; something that has existed but is unknown. A planet or a star, a chemical element or a creature that was thought to be extinct are discovered. (A chance discovery is called 'serendipity'.)

A person invents things that never before existed. In the story of man's development the wheel, the screw, the transis-

tor and many others were all invented.

35. discreet / discrete

These two words are pronounced the same way and therefore their spellings are sometimes confused.

Discreet means 'tactful, prudent; careful in exercising judgement' and often refer to things which are meant to be kept secret, under wraps, and not any publicity given to it.

One can make discreet enquiries about a particular person. A person can be 'discreet' too. The noun form of this, word is 'discretion' and 'indiscretion'.

'Indiscretion' refers to one's lack of judgement, lacking common sense.

A good, diplomat is the soul of discretion.

Discrete means separate; distinct'.

36. disinterested / uninterested

These two words do not mean the same. '*Disinterested*' means 'without personal prejudice or bias'.

A judge ought to be disinterested if his judgement is to be fair. His decisions cannot be coloured by his personal gain or motive. '*Uninterested*' means 'not interested / bored'.

37. dispassionate / impassive / impassioned

Dispassionate' means 'claim' without passion'. A judge has to remain dispassionate so that his judgement remains just and fair.

Impassive is apathetic - revealing no emotion. 'Impassive Countenance' is a common collocation.

Impassioned is full of passion, ardent. An impassioned speech would move or influence an audience.

38. economic / economical

Economic means 'concerning or relating to economics or finance.

Economical means thrifty.

Neither word has anything to do with how much something costs. Even if something were to cost a lot, it would still be eco-

Autopsy, Biopsy	**Autopsy is the post-mortem examination of a body. It comes after one's death. Biopsy: examination of tissue or fluid removed from a living body.**

nomical if it can be shown to save money in the long run. A writer or speaker who does not waste words can be called as a writer or a speaker of an economical style. Special Economic Zones (SEZ's) are the offshore areas regarded by a nation as its exclusive domain for fishing, oil and mineral explorations / exploitations to its economic advantage.

39. egoist / egotist

Someone who practises egoism is an *egoist*. He is obsessed with himself and behaves in a selfish manner. He is caught up in trying to satisfy his own needs.

An *egotist* is equally self-centred as an egoist, but additionally, he has a strong conviction that he is superior to everyone else an spends a lot of his time singing praises of himself.

40. elegy / eulogy

An *'elegy'* is a mournful poem - it is a song of mourning. Although originally *'eulogy'* referred to an oration in praise of a dead person, today it has come to stand for any speech of praise or written tribute.

41. endemic / epidemic / pandemic

All the three words are used in talking about diseases.

An *endemic* disease is one that is associated with a particular group of people or with a particular region. For example,

Sickle cell anaemia is endemic among blacks; Tay-Sachs disease is endemic among Jews and Filariasis is endemic in the Tropics, i.e., Filariasis is prevalent among people living in the Tropics.

An *epidemic* disease is one that affects a large number of people at the same time.

It may affect a large number of people of a certain age, of a particular sex, of a certain occupation etc.

A *pandemic* disease is one that affects a high proportion of the people of a given region, country or of the world.

42. enervate / innervate

The two are opposite in meaning.

Enervate means to make weak or enfeeble. It is the opposite of 'energise'.

Innervate is to stimulate or energise.

43. etymology / entomology

These are names of subjects. *Etymology* means 'the history of a word' or the study of the history or derivation of words.

Entomology is the scientific study of insects.

44. explode / implode

Explode is to blow up from a confined area outward. Bursting of a balloon is an example of 'explode'.

Implode means blow up inward

45. flaunt /flout

Both verbs, *flaunt* means display proudly or show off.

One can flaunt his wealth by driving round in very expensive cars.

Flout, on the other hand, means 'to treat with very little respect', 'look down upon', 'scoff at'.

One can flout authority, all rules.

46. flotsam / jetsam

Words associated with seafaring, *flotsam* and *jetsam* are often used, together, much like the words part and parcel are linked. However, the two words have different meanings: *flotsam*: is The wreckage found floating in water whereas *jetsam*: is stores, equipment or other materials found aboard a vessel and which are then deliberately thrown overboard during an emergency, either to gain stability or to avoid sinking. Both flotsam and jetsam (jettisoned) can either sink or get washed ashore.

47. gourmet /gourmand

A *gourmet* refers to 'a connoisseur of fine food', also called an epicure.

In English, a gourmand is a glutton.

| Order: 2 Uses | He ordered some new furniture (verb).
He placed an order for some new furniture (noun). |

48. graceful / gracious

Graceful refers to movement, style or form. It means 'effortlessly beautiful.' It appears in phrases such as a graceful prose, a graceful leap, a graceful dancer.

Gracious refers to states of mind. It means kind, sympathetic and courteous as in 'a gracious deed'.

49. hoard /horde

An unscrupulous shopkeeper hoards grains and creates an artificial scarcity so that he can sell them at a much higher price.

Horde originally meant a vast and threatening army as it used to refer to the tribes of Turkic nomads who migrated from northeast Asia and threatened the civilizations of Asia and Europe.

Today, a horde refers to a large threatening crowd as in a horde of football hooligans. Being angry and hugely disappointed, hordes are barbarous and disorganised and are menacing because of their sheer numbers.

More generally, horde can refer to an aggressive group of animals or insects - a horde of stampeding buffalo.

50. hung / hanged

Pictures are *hung*.

People are *hanged*

We hung the pictures on the wall facing the door. They hanged him at dawn.

51. imperial / imperious / imperative

These three words, all adjectives, are closely related in origin and share certain shades of meaning.

Imperial means primarily relating to an empire or emperor - an imperial crown, an imperial decree.

Today it is also used in the sense of commanding or being majestic.

Imperial is the traditional system of weights and measures as distinct from the metric system.

Imperious has a negative connotation. It means arrogant and overbearing or

Hotel and Restaurant

People stay in *hotels*. They eat in restaurants. A person who owns a restaurant is a restaurateur. A hotelier owns or manages a hotel.

domineering or dictatorial.

Imperative, on the other hand, is related 'to expressing a command or plea'. In grammar it refers to the form of a verb expressing a command or request.

It is probably used most frequently today in the sense of 'absolutely necessary, crucial or even obligatory'.

It is *imperative* that we inform the police at once.

52. imply / infer

One infers something said or written by another, who may or may not have intended that the inference be drawn.

When a speaker or writer hints at something and does not express it in a direct outright fashion, he is implying it by indirection.

Therefore, if someone says, "I hope you won't be late." He is actually implying that the person addressed should be on time. If the person addressed is usually late in coming, he might infer that the speaker is pulling him up for his casual approach to time.

53. incredible / incredulous

Incredible means unbelievable, difficult or impossible to believe

No one believed his incredible story.

What an incredible victory it was!

Incredulous is disbelieving, doubting or sceptical

54. indict / indite

Both are pronounced the same way but mean quite different things.

Do these Words Confuse You?

reign: It happened during King George's reign.
rain: It is going to rain.
rein: It was time for him to hand over the reins of power to his son.

'To *indict*' means 'to accuse of, or to charge with a crime'. An 'indictable offence' could result in a criminal charge.

The public indicted the state government for the deteriorating law and order situation. (= held the government guilty)

Indict is followed by the preposition for, as in the example above. 'Accuse' is followed by of and 'charge' by with.

'To *indite*' means 'to put into words, compose, set down in writing' in the form of a speech or a poem.

55. inequity / iniquity

Inequity means inequality, injustice or unfairness. So we have 'an inequitable distribution of wealth'.

Iniquity means, 'wickedness, immorality, a sin or immoral act.'

56. ingenious / ingenuous

Ingenious is clever, inventive or resourceful. The ingenious device opened the locked car door.

An ingenious suggestion broke the deadlock in the negotiations.

He is so ingenious in solving practical problems.

Ingenuous means artless, gullible, naive, innocent.

Her ingenuous ways won over the audience.

57. insidious / invidious

Both the adjectives have the sense of causing harm, but they are used in different contexts.

'Insidious' means 'spreading or, working harmfully in a subtle or sheatthy way'. The word also means 'wily or treacherous': an insidious argument; insidious brainwashing by propaganda.'

'Invidious' is related to 'envious' and the word means 'likely to cause ill-will, offensive'.

58. inveigh / inveigle

Inveigh, used with the preposition 'against', means 'protest vehemently, give vent to angry censure'.

He inveighed against the incompetence of the officer-in-charge.

Inveigle means either 'to entice or win over by deceit, flattery or persuasion.

He inveigled me into joining his plot to cheat people.

59. Lama / Llama

Lama, with a single 'l', is a Buddhist monk of Tibet or Mongolia. The highest priest of the Lamas is the Dalai Lama.

'*Llama*, with a double 'l' is the South American domesticated animal which belongs to the camel family.

60. laudable / laudatory

Laudable means deserving praise, praiseworthy: a laudable attempt at solving a problem.

Laudatory means giving praise: a laudatory speech about Dhoni as a captain.

61. libel / slander

While both of these terms refer to defamatory statements made about a person, in libel the statements appear in writing, print, pictures or some other graphic medium whereas in slander the statements are oral.

The target of the *libel* or *slander* feels ridiculed and experiences a sense of shame or disgrace.

62. luxurious / luxuriant

These two words do not mean the same.

Luxurious means characterised by luxury, sumptuous living.

One who has luxurious life-style is obviously living in the lap of luxury; he enjoys everything that money can buy.

Luxuriant is used in the context of growth of vegetation. It is characterised by abundance and lushness.

63. meritorious/ meretricious

Meritorious is a laudatory adjective and means 'worthy of merit, deserving praise or a reward': a meritorious service to his country.

Meretricious means 'superficially attrac-

tive, insincere or vulgarly conspicuous':
a meretricious argument.

64. mote / moat

A *mote* is a speck, particularly a speck of
dust.

A *moat* is a ditch, typically filled with water, surrounding a castle, a fort or a
modern zoo enclosure.

65. negligent / negligible

Both the words are derived from 'to neglect'.

Negligent has the sense of neglectful. It is
being careless, lacking proper care and
attention.

A negligent teacher is probably the reason
why some children in the class get hurt
physically. It is the lack of supervision
on the part of the teacher. *Negligent*
can also mean careless in an easy-going
way. Someone can be negligent in the
way he dresses.

Negligible means capable of being neglected because it is too small or trivial.

The new machine is much more efficient
and the wastage is negligible.

66. noisome / noisy

Noisome means noxious, foul, offensive,
disgusting as an odour. It does not mean
noisy.

67. oblivious / oblivion

Oblivion, a noun, is the state of being
completely forgotten.

These models will be around for a year or
two, then fade into oblivion.

'*Oblivious*' is not being aware of something, especially what is happening
around you.

The government seems oblivious to the
likely effect of this new law that comes
into being very soon.

68. obsequious / obsequies

Obsequious' means too eager to praise or
obey someone. She has no dignity; she is
obsequious to anyone in authority.

Obsequies refer to the rites and rituals,

Goose and Mongoose

Goose is a bird like a
large duck with a long
neck. The plural of
goose is geese. Mon-
goose is a small tropi-
cal animal that kills rats
and snakes. The plural
of mongoose is mongooses.

religious in nature, connected with the
dead.

The *obsequies* will be observed on the
tenth day.

69. official / officious

Official is connected with authority or position.

It could mean 'authorised'; done with the
approval of some recognised 'authority'.

Officious, on the other hand, means inter-
fering too intrusive.

Officious is used of people.

70. orient / occident

orient refers to 'east'. It comes originally
from the Latin verb 'orire' and refers to
the place where the sun comes up, the
east.

The *occident* is the 'west'.

71. ostensible / ostentatious

ostensible means 'outwardly appearing to
be so; alleged to be so; apparent'

The ostensible purpose of the meeting was
to plan how the 'one-child per family
norm' should be popularised, but that
was hardly discussed at all.

Ostentatious often means 'attention-
seeking showing off or be pretentious'.
It suggests display of wealth. One can
arrange for an ostentatious wedding
or lead an ostentatious life of lavish
parties.

72. perceptibly / perceptively

Perceptibly, is related to perceive and

A Country of 823 Languages The country with the largest number of languages spoken is Papua New Guinea. This country has 823 languages.

means noticeably or even 'glaringly or obviously'

He is perceptibly obese, much fatter than when I saw him a couple of year ago.

Perceptively means 'in a manner which shows insight and good judgement'. It is related to the word perceptive.

She assessed the drawbacks of the plan very perceptively.

73. perspicacious / perspicuous

Both these adjectives are easy to confuse.

'*Perspicacious*' is usually used to refer to people .

A person who is perpicacious is 'actually discerning and is able to see through situations. He assesses a situation easily and quickly.

Perspicuous is usually used to refer to things, very rarely to people.

If some thing is perspicuous, it is clearly expressed, easy to understand and is lucid.

74. precede / proceed

Precede means to go before in time, order or rank. Curtain-raisers precede the showing of the main movie.

Proceed is to continue with an action after pausing for a while.

Proceed with your narration.

75. prerequisite / perquisite

Prerequisite has a prefix pre-. It means 'a requisite required beforehand' - an advance condition or necessity'.

If you want to travel abroad, a visa is a prerequisite for gaining entry to the country chosen.

A *perquisite* is a totally different word. It is an additional payment of some kind made over and above a person's wages or salary. Usually shortened to 'perks', it might be in the form of money (as a bonus, for instance), in the form of being provided with a company car, privileges at a company-owned holiday house, or any of a variety of other emoluments regarded as desirable by the employee.

76. prescribe / proscribe

A doctor can prescribe a medicine. He writes out a prescription.

A university can prescribe a textbook for study.

Proscribe goes back to the Latin root form which means 'prohibit'. It means to denounce or condemn.

77. principal / principle

Principal means 'chief or the most important'. The principal reason why I am unable to join you is that I can't afford it.

It is often used as a noun to refer to the head of a school.

A *principle* is a rule or belief of some sort which is related to behaviour or moral standards. It can also refer to some basic facts.

He stands by his principles and would never cheat. She is a woman of principles.

The screw is based on the principle of the inclined plane.

78. prophecy / prophesy

The spelling with the '-c' is the noun, the one with the '-s' is verb. (This is true of all pairs of words where a -c and an -s is involved. The former is the noun, the latter verb. For example: advice / advise, practice / practise.)

The verb form *prophesy* rhymes with 'sigh' and the noun form prophecy with 'see'.

79. raise / raze

To *raze* means to tear down, demolish, whereas raise means the opposite: to lift up.

Raze is used in the phrase 'to raze to the ground'.

Since the building was deemed to be an unauthorised construction, the authorities razed it to the ground.

80. repetitious/repetitive

Both the adjectives are related to 'repetition'.

However, '*repetitious*' has a derogatory

Plaintiff & Defendant

A *plaintiff* is a person who makes a formal complaint against another person in a court.

A *defendant* is a person accused of committing a crime.

slant to it. It means needless or tedious repetition.

'*Repetitive*' tends to be neutral, referring, for instance, to work on an assembly line.

81. restful / restive

Restful means 'of a nature, mood, or atmosphere that allows a person to relax and feel at ease';

Restive means 'nervously active; fidgety'.

Restful is seldom said of people. So, you can have a restful holiday / vacation.

Restive, on the other hand, is used almost entirely of people and animate things.

Children can be restive if they are bored with a long holiday as they have nothing much to do. A restive horse is common enough.

82. rotund / orotund

Rotund means round, plump, almost round and comes in phrases such as ' a jovial, rotund, red-faced little man'.

Orotund, derived from the Latin phrase ore rotundo literally means 'with round mouth'. If someone speaking has a clear, strong voice, then it would be described as 'orotund delivery'. Orotund, at times, has negative overtones and can be equivalent to being pompous.

83. sanguinary / sanguine

Both the words have the same root, 'sanguis' meaning 'blood'

Sanguinary means 'bloody' and is used in phrases such as: a sanguinary battle (which resulted in a lot of bloodshed). A cruel and sanguinary tyrant is bloodthirsty and will think nothing of killing people.

Sanguine originally meant blood-coloured or ruddy as in a sanguine complexion or a sanguine sunset. Today it is used in expressions such as a sanguine temperament, where sanguine means cheerful, energetic or bold.

84. sedition / treason

Treason is an attempt to overthrow the

> ## Alphabet and Letter
>
> An alphabet is not a letter.
> A letter is not an alphabet.
> An alphabet has many letters in it.
> In English the alphabet consists of 26 letters.
> A, B and C are not alphabets, they are letters.
> The word alphabet comes from *alpha* and *beta*, the first two letters of the Greek alphabet.

government of one's own country by any means, especially by betrayal to a foreign power, allegiance to an enemy of the state and giving the enemy aid and support; these are the essential characteristics of treason.

Sedition is any act against the government to which one owes allegiance. It includes inciting others to commit treasonable acts, belonging to an organisation that advocates the overthrow of the government, publishing or distributing any material that calls for a change in the existing government by illegal means. In general, it 'disturbs the tranquility of the state'.

85. sensual / sensuous

Both the adjectives refer to the enjoyment of physical sensation as both originally meant simply sensory: referring to the senses.

Sensuous is today leaning more towards the more refined sense of sensitive - enjoying or providing fine sensations. Sensuous pleasures may be derived from music, painting, sculpture – in other words, it is all to do with refined tastes.

Tobacco, alcohol and all other earthier pleasures including sexual is closer to sensual pleasures. It implies physical gratification.

The difference between the two: *sensuous* and *sensual* is subtle, but nevertheless it cannot be ignored.

Grape and Wine	Wine is made from grapes. Grape is a small fruit (green or purple) that grows in bunches on a vine, a climbing plant. Grapefruit is a large yellow citrus fruit. It has lot of a slightly sour juice.

Minister

Minister: A member of a country's cabinet or council of ministers.

A *minister* in an embassy is a representative of his country in a foreign country, below the rank of an ambassador.

A priest in a Christian church.

As a verb, to *minister* is to serve or to give help.

86. spasmodic / sporadic

The first word, *spasmodic*, is related to spasms, which describes the convulsive and involuntary muscular contractions. It's a term used in medicine, A person describing the pain he experiences in his stomach, if he has a medical problem, would describe it as spasmodic when the pain comes and goes.

Sporadic means at irregular intervals or occasional. Sporadic rains, sporadic enquiries or sporadic eruptions of a volcano are apt descriptions.

87. spurious / specious

Both these words have a shared, common meaning of 'false'. However, it is the context that decides which of the words is to be used. 'Spurious' means fake, not real or genuine spurious drugs have flooded the market. 'Specious' is 'apparently or superficially true or correct, deceptively genuine or pleasing, but at bottom false, incorrect and without merit. 'Specious argument' is a common collocation and would refer to an argument which sounds reasonable but is actually based on false premises.

88. stanch / staunch

Stanch means stop the flow of blood. It is, in fact, stop the flow of any liquid. In an injury the doctor will try and stanch a wound or the blood from a wound.

Staunch, as in a 'staunch supporter' is a loyal, steadfast or dependable supporter.

89. stimulus / stimulant

A *stimulus* usually refers to a general incentive, something that rouses the mind or spirit.

A *stimulant* is usually more concrete; such as coffee or an alcoholic beverage. This, in turn, produces temporary stimulation.

The upright politician's life was a stimulus for the youngsters to aim high in whatever they did. Taking a stimulant before going to bed may keep a person awake throughout the night.

90. timidity / temerity

The first word is related to being *timid*. A timid person is shy and retiring; he exhibits timidity.

A person who is timorous is nervously fearful, he is meek and is decidedly afraid.

'*Temerity*', on the other hand, is being rash and bold.

He had the temerity to challenge the learned professor.

91. tortuous / torturous

Tortuous is used in the sense of 'twisting', full of twists and turns. A winding road up a hill can be tortuous and so causes discomfort to many a traveller.

Torturous is related to 'torture'. It is related to being tormented and has to do with infliction of pain.

Many cancer patients refer to chemotherapy - a process of treatment of the disease - as being torturous.

92. turbid/turgid

'*Turbid*' means muddy, unclear, cloudy, as in 'turbid water'. It can be used metaphorically too. A turbid argument is a confused, unclear argument.

'T*urgid*' (pronounced /turjid/) means literally 'bloated, swollen' .

The camel's stomach was tight and turgid after it had drunk its fill.

93. venal / venial

Venal goes back to the Latin venum, 'sale' and is related to vend 'sell'; however, the

'Queue' can be abbreviated to Que or even Q. Look at the spelling of 'queueing'. It is the only word with five consecutive vowels.

modern meaning of the word is 'available for bribery, mercenary; capable of being bought' Venial is used in phrases: a venial sin, i.e. the sin is so insignificant that the person committing it can be easily forgiven.

'*Venal*', today, is associated with politicians and other public officials.

94. vertex / vortex

Vertex is the highest point of a hill or structure, or the apex of a cone or upright triangle. The word is used in different areas of knowledge.

In anatomy and zoology it is the crown of the head.

In astronomy: zenith

In geometry: the point at which two or more lines or edges intersect.

A *vortex* is a flow round an axis, or a whirl of air, water or flame. It can refer to a cyclone or whirlpool and "sometimes specifically to the core or centre of such a whirl".

95. Wait for / await

The two should not be confused in their usage. Both mean the same. Awaiting MUST NOT be followed by 'for'.

'*Awaiting* for your reply' as a last sentence in a letter is a totally wrong usage; awaiting your reply will do.

96. warp / weft

These are words used in the handloom textile industry. The warp is the set of threads or yarn stretched lengthwise between which the yarn is woven from side to side (selvage to selvage), to form the weft.

Woof and *weft* are the same.

Warp is also a verb. Typically, wood, especially plywood, can get warped if it is left exposed to the elements.

97. wreak / wreck / wrack /rack

Wreak almost always appears in the idioms 'wreak havoc' or 'wreak vengeance'. In these expressions wreak means 'inflict'.

Wreck is a common enough word (a noun

or a verb) which means destroy.

He wrecked my plans.

He was a mental wreck after the accident.

'*Wrack*' is a rare word. It means destruction and almost always appears in the collocation 'wrack and ruin'

Rack, as a verb, means shake, batter violently.

The stormy weather racked the region resulting in a lot of destruction.

Rack also has the meaning of 'suffer mental agony.' She was racked with guilt when she left home without, letting anyone know.

'Rack' in the sentence 'I racked my brain to try and remember his name', means 'made after a mental effort'.

98. whither / wither

Whither is the old-fashioned term for 'where to'.

The verb *wither* means to dry up or shrivel.

A horse's withers (with only one - h) is the point between its shoulder blades.

99. yoke / yolk

A *yoke* is the connecting crossbar, as used for a pair of oxen. Yoke also means the tight part at the neck or hips of a woman's garment, and in the phrase the 'yoke of marriage', yoke stands for 'a bond'.

Yolk, on the other hand, is the yellow centre of an egg.

100. zenith / nadir

Originally both the words were used in a technical reuse, the **zenith** being the point directly above the observer, a point on the celestial sphere and *nadir*, the point directly below. Today, metaphorically they are used to refer to the 'highest thing or goal obtainable; acme'.

Her career reached the zenith when she headed the ministry.

When he was implicated in the crime, he knew he had reached his nadir; he had no one to turn to.

Two Countries

The name of a country has a subject and a verb in it. Name the country. *Ans.* Iran.

A country whose name has four letters of which three are the first letters of the alphabet. *Ans.* Cuba

Abbreviations and Acronyms

AA: Alcoholics Anonymous

AAFI: The Amateur Athletics Federation of India

ABC: Atomic Biological and Chemical (Warfare); Audit Bureau of Circulations

AC: Ante Christum (Before Christ), Alternating Current; Ashoka Chakra; Air Conditioner.

ACR: Annual Confidential Report

AD: Anno Domini (in the year of our Lord)

ADB: Asian Development Bank

ADC: Aide-de-camp (help or assistant)

AFI: Athletics Federation of India

AFMC: Armed Forces Medical College

AFP: Agence France–Presse

AG: Accountant General; Adjutant General

AI : Artificial Intelligence; Air India

AICTE: All India Council for Technical Education

AIDS: Acquired Immune Deficiency Syndrome

AIFF: All India Football Federation

AIIMS : All India Institute of Medical Sciences

AITUC: All India Trade Union Congress

AM: Ante Meridiem (before noon); Amplitude Modulation

Amfi: Association of Mutual Funds of India

ANC: African National Congress

ANERT: Agency for Non–conventional Energy and Rural Technology

ANZUS: Australia, New Zealand US (Pacific Pact Nations)

AOC: Air Officer Commanding

APEC: Asia Pacific Economic Cooperation

APM: Administered Price Mechanism

ARPANET: Advanced Research Project Agency Network

ASAP: as soon as possible

ASEAN: Association of South East Asian Nations

ASLV: Augmented Satellite Launch Vehicle

ASSOCHAM: Associated Chamber of Commerce and Industry

ATC: Air Traffic Control

ATM: Automated Teller Machine, Adobe Type Manager

ATR: action taken report

ATS: Anti-Tetanus Serum

AU: Astronomical Units; African Union

AWACS: Airborne Warning And Control System

B2B: Busines to Business

B2C : Business to Consumer

BARC: Bhabha Atomic Research Centre

BBC : British Broadcasting Corporation

BC: Before Christ

BCG: Bacillus Calmette-Guerin (anti-TB vaccine)

BENELUX: Belgium, Nether-lands and Luxembourg

BHEL: Bharat Heavy Electri-cals Ltd

bhp: brake horsepower

BIFR: Board for Industrial and Financial Reconstruction

BIMARU: Bihar, Madhya Pradesh, Rajasthan, Uttar Pradesh

BIMSTEC: Bangladesh, India, Myanmar, Sri Lanka, Thailand Economic Cooperation

BIOS: Basic Input Output System

BIS: Bank of International Settlement; Bureau of Indian Standards

BIT: Binary Digit

Acronyms	Acronyms are pronounceable words formed from first letters or syllables of other words. e.g. AIDS, NATO. Some acronyms are words coined as abbreivations and written in lower case. e.g. radar, yuppie.

BOT: Build, Operate and Transfer
BPL: Below Poverty Line
BPO: Business Process Outsourcing
bps: bytes per second
BRO: Border Roads Organi-sation
BSE: Bombay Stock Exchange
BSF: Border Security Force
BSNL: Bharat Sanchar Nigam Limited

C2C: Consumer to Consumer
C-in-C: Commander–in–Chief
c.v.: Curriculum vitae
C/o: care of
CA: Chartered Accountant
CAD: Command Area Development; Computer Aided Design
CADA: Command Area Development Authority
CAG: Comptroller and Auditor General of India
CAGR: compounded annual growth rate
CAN : Calcium Ammonium Nitrate
Cantab: Cantabrigian (of Cambridge University)
CAS: Conditional Access System
CAT: Career Aptitude Test; Common Admission Test; Computerized Axial Tomo-graphy (also called CT); Computer Adaptive Test
CBDT: Central Board of Direct Taxes
CBFC: Central Board of Film Certification.
CBI : Central Bureau of Investigation
CBM: Confidence Building Measures
CBSE: Central Board of Secondary Education
CD: Compact disk; Certificate of deposit
CDAC: Centre for the Development of Advanced Computing
CEO: Chief Executive Officer
CERN: Conseil European pour la Researche Nucleare (European Laboratory for Nuclear Research)
cf compare / refer
CFC: Chloro Fluoro Carbon; Common Fund for Commodities
CFL: Compact Fluorescent Lamps
CFO: Chief Financial Officer
CGFNS: Commission on Graduates of Foreign Nursing Schools
CGPA: Cumulative Grade Point Average

The Title of a Dictionary

The full title of Samuel Johnson's 'A Dictionary of the English Language' (1755) was : A Dictionary of the English Language: In which the Words are Deduced from Their Originals, and Illustrated in Their Different Significations by Examples from the Best Writers. To Which Are Prefixed a History of the Language and an English Grammar.

CGS: Chief of General Staff; Centimetre, Gram, Second
CIA: Central Intelligence Agency
CID: Criminal Investigation Department
cif: cost, insurance and freight
CII: Confederation of Indian Industry
CIS: Commonwealth of Independent States
CISCE: Council for the Indian School Certificate Examinations
CITU: Centre of Indian Trade Unions
CKD: Completely Knocked Down
CMIE: Centre for Monitoring the Indian Economy
CMP: Common Minimum Programme
CNN: Cable News Network
CO: Commanding Officer
COD: cash on delivery
COFEPOSA: Conservation of Foreign Exchange and Prevention of Smuggling Act
COPRA : Consumer Protection Act
COSTFORD: Centre of Science and Technology for Rural Development
CPI/M: Communist Party of India/ Marxist
CPR: Cardio Pulmonary Resuscitation
CPWD: Central Public Works Department
CRISIL: Credit Rating Information Services of India Ltd.
CRR: Cash Reserve Ratio
CRY: Child Relief and You
CSIR: Council of Scientific and Industrial Research
CSO: Central Statistical Organisation

Women Writers | Of the 218 new plays produced in Britain in 2004, only 38 were written by women.

CT: Computerised Tomography
CTC (tea): Crushed tear curl
CTBT: Comprehensive Test Ban Treaty
CVC: Chief Vigilance Commission
CWC: Chemical Weapons Convention; Congress Working Committee
cwt: Hundredweight (112 lb)

D & C: Dilation and Curettage
D.Litt.: Doctor of Literature
D.Phil.: Doctor of Philosophy
D.Sc: Doctor of Science
DC: Direct Current; District of Columbia
DDT: Dichloro-diphenyl-trichloro-ethane
DGCI: Drug Controller General of India
DIG: Deputy Inspector General
DJIA: Dow Jones International Average
DMK: Dravida Munetra Kazhagam
DMZ: Demilitarized Zone
DNA: Deoxyribo-nucleic Acid
DPEP: District Primary Education Programme
DPT: Diphtheria, pertussis and tetanus (vaccine)
DSB: Digital Satellite Broadcasting
DSL: digital subscriber line
DSP: Digital Signal Processing
DTH: Direct- to-Home
DTP: Desktop Publishing
DTS: Digital Theatre System
DV: Deo Volente (God willing)
DVC: Damodar Valley Corporation
DVD: Digital Versatile/Video Disc
DVI: Digital Video Interactive
DVS: Desktop Video–Con-ferencing Software

E & OE: Errors and Omissions Excepted
E&Y: Earnest & Young
E-MAIL: Electronic Mailing
EAM: emergency action message
ECA: Essential Commodities Act
ECG: Electro Cardiogram
ECGC: Export credit guarantee corporation of India
ECOSOC: Economic and Social Council (UN)
ECR: Electron Cyclotron Resonance
EDI: Electronic Data Interchange
EDMS: Electronic Document Management System
EDT: Eastern Daylight Time
EEG: Electro Encephalo-gram
EEZ: Exclusive Economic Zone
EFTA: European Free Trade Association
e.g.: exempli gratia (for example)
EGP: Exterior Gateway Protocol
EIS: Executive Information System
EL: Electro–luminescent
ELINT: Electronic Intelligence
ELISA: Enzyme Linked Immuno-Sorbent Assay
EMI: Equated Monthly Instalments
ENIAC: Electronic Numerical Integrator and Calculator
ENT: Ear, Nose and Throat
EOF: end of file
EOS: Electronic Online System International
EOU: Export Oriented Unit
EPABX: Electronic Private Automatic Branch Exchange
EPG: Eminent Persons Group
EPI: Expanded Programme of Immunisation
EPIRB: Emergency Position Indicating Radio Beacon
EPNS: Electroplated Nickel Silver
EPROM: Erasable, Programmable Read Only Memory
EPS: Encapsulated Postscript
EPZ : Export Processing Zone
EQ: Emotional Quotient
ER&DC: Electronic Research and Development Center
ERM : European Exchange Rate Mechanism
ERNIE: Electronic Random Number Indicator Equipment
ESA: European Space Agency
ESCAP: Economic and Social Commission for Asia and the Pacific
ESMA: Essential Services Maintenance Act
ESP: Extra Sensory Perception
et al.: et alii (and others)
et. seq: et sequentia (& what follows)
etc.: et cetera (and so forth)
ETR: Educational Devt. Index
ETT: Embryo Transfer Technology

EURATOM: European Atomic Community
EUTELSAT: European Telecommunications Satellite
EVA: Economic Value Added
EVE: economic valuation of the environment
EVR: Electrovideo Recording

FAO: Food and Agriculture Organisation
FAQ: Fair Average Quality; Frequently Asked Question
FBI: Federal Bureau of Investigation
FBT: Fringe Benefit Tax
FBTR: Fast Breeder Test Reactor
FBW: Fly–By–Wire
FCCB: Foreign Currency Convertible Bond
FCI: Food Corporation of India; Fertilizer Corporation of India
FCNRA: Foreign Currency Non-Resident Accounts
FCRA: Foreign Contribution Regulation Act
FDI: Foreign Direct Investment
FEMA: Foreign Exchange Management Act
FICCI: Federation of Indian Chambers of Commerce and Industry
FIDE: Federation Inter-nationale d'Echecs
FIFA: International Football Federation (Federation Internationale de Football Association)
FII: Foreign Institutional Investors
FIPB: Foreign Investment Promotion Board
FIR: First Information Report
FIRE: Fully integrated robotised engine
FLC: Foreign Legal Consultant
FM: Frequency modulation
FMC: Forward Markets Commission
FMCT: Fissile Material Cut-off Treaty
fob: free on board
for: free on rail
FPO: Fruit Products Order
FRCP: Fellow of the Royal College of Physicians
FRCS: Fellow of the Royal College of Surgeons
FRS: Fellow of the Royal Society
FTII: Films and Television Institute of India
FYI: for your information

3G: Third Generation

---

33 Lakh NGOs

There are about 40,000 internationally operating NGOs across the globe. India has the highest member of nationally and locally operating NGOs. According to Union Home Ministry, India has 33 lakh NGOs, i.e. one NGO for every 400 persons.

G2B: Government-to-Business
G2C: Government-to-Citizens
G7: Group of Seven (US, UK, Germany, France, Italy, Japan and Canada) G8 includes G7 plus Russia
GATE: Graduate Aptitude Test in Engineering
GATS: General Agreement on Trade and Services
GAVI: Global Alliance for Vaccines and Immunisation
GBP: Geosphere–Biosphere Programme
G.B.E.: Grand Cross of the British Empire
G.B.H.: Grievous Bodily Harm
GCC: Gulf Co–operation Council
GCR: Grey Component Replacement
GDP: Gross Domestic Product
GDR: Global Depository Receipt
GEDIS: Gateway Electronic Data Interchange Services
GEF: Global Environment Fund
GEMS: Gateway Electronic Mail Service
GHQ: General Headquarters

Film and Television Institute of India

GI: Government Issue (American soldiers)

GIS: Geographical Information System

GMAT: Graduate Management Admission Test

GMO: Genetically Modified Organisms

GMRT: Giant Metrewave Radio Telescope

GMT: Greenwich Mean Time

GNP: Gross National Product

GOOS: Global Ocean Observing System

GOP: Grand Old Party(Republican Party)

GPA: Grade Point Average

GPS: Global Positioning System

GRE: Graduate Record Examination

GRS: Gender Reassignment Surgery (Sex Change)

GRSE: Garden Reach Shipbuilders and Engineers Ltd.

GSI: Geological Survey of India

GSLV: Geo-Synchronous Satellite Launch Vehicle

GSM: Global System for Mobile Communications

GSP: Generalised System Preference

GST: Goods and Service Tax

GUI: Graphical User Interface

GVW: Gross Vehicle Weight

HAL: Hindustan Aeronautics Limited.

HB: Hard Black (pencil)

HBV: Hepatitis–B Virus

HDML: Hyper Devices Mark-up Language

HF: High Frequency

HIV: Human Immunodeficiency Virus

HMV: His Master's Voice, Heavy Motor Vehicle

Hon: honourable, Honorary

hp: horse power

HRPT: High Resolution Picture Transmission

HSD: High Speed Diesel

HSRRSS: High Spatial Resolution Remote Sensing Satellite

HT : High Tension

HTML: Hyper Text Markup Language

HTR: High Temperature Reactor

http: Hypertext Transfer Protocol

HUDCO: Housing and Urban Development Corp.

HV: High Voltage

HVAC: Heating, Ventilating and Air Conditioning

HVNET: High Speed VSAT Network

i.e.: id est (that is)

IA: Indian Airlines

IA&AS: Indian Audit and Accounts Services

IAAI: International Airport Authority of India

IAEA: International Atomic Energy Agency

IARI: Indian Agricultural Research Institute

IAS: Indian Administrative Service

IATA: International Air Transport Association

ibid or ib. ibidem (Latin): in the same place; book or chapter

IBM: International Business Machines

IBRD: International Bank for Reconstruction and Development

IC: Indian (airlines)

ICAO: International Civil Aviation Organisation

ICAR: Indian Council of Agricultural Research

ICBM: Inter-Continental Ballistic Missile

ICCR: Indian Council for Cultural Relations

ICJ: International Court of Justice

ICMR: Indian Council of Medical Research

ICPD: International Conference on Population and Development

ICRA: Investment Information and Credit Rating Agency of India

ICRISAT: International Crops Research Institute for Semi Arid Tropics

ICSE: Indian Certificate of Secondary Education

ICT: Information & Communication Technology

ICU: Intensive Care Unit

ICWAI: Institute of Cost and Works Accountants of India

IDBI: Industrial Development Bank of India

IEEE: Institute of Electronics and Electrical Engineers

IELTS: International English Language Testing System

C.I.D, the Yard

The 'Yard' is an informal name for 'New Scotland Yard'. It is the London Metropolitan Police, especially the Criminal Investigation Department (C.I.D.).

IFS: Indian Foreign Service; Indian Forest Service

IGF: India Growth Fund

IGNOU: Indira Gandhi National Open University

IGY: International Geophysical Year

IISCO: Indian Iron and Steel Company

IISS: International Institute of Strategic Studies

IIT: Indian Institute of Technology

ILA: Indian Library Association

ILO: International Labour Organisation

IMAP: Internet Mail Access Protocol

IMF: International Monetary Fund

INA: Indian National Army

INDIPEX: Indian International Philatelic Exhibition

infra dig infra dignitatum (below status)

Inkel: Infrastructure Kerala Ltd.

I.N.R.I.: Iesus Nazarenus Rex Iudaeorum (Jesus of Nazareth, King of the Jews)

INS: Indian Newspaper Society

INSAT: Indian National Satellite

INSPIRE: Innovation in Science Pursuit for Inspired Research

INTACH: Indian National Trust for Art and Cultural Heritage

INTELSAT: International Telecommunication Satellite

INTUC: Indian National Trade Union Congress

IOC: Indian Oil Corporation

IOU: I Owe You

IP: Internet Protocol

IPC: Indian Penal Code

IPCL: Indian Petro-Chemicals Corporation Ltd

IPI: International Press Institute

IPO: Initial Public Offering

IPS: Indian Police Service; Inter Press Service

IQ: Intelligence Quotient

iq: idem quod (the same as)

IRA: Irish Republican Army

IRBM: Intermediate Range Ballistic Missile

IRC: International Red Cross

IRDP: Integrated Rural Development Programme

IRE: Indian Rare Earth Ltd.

IREDA: Indian Renewable Energy Development Agency

IRRI: International Rice Research Institute

IRS: Indian Revenue Service

ISB: Indian School of Business, Hyderabad

ISBN: International Standard Book Number

ISC: Indian School Certificate

ISDN: Integrated Services Digital Network

ISI: Indian Standards Institution, Inter Services Intelligence

ISKCON: International Society for Krishna Consciousness

ISO: International Standards Organisation

ISRO: Indian Space Research Organisation

ISSN: International Standard Serial Number

IST: Indian Standard Time

ITA: Information Technology Agreement

ITBP: Indo-Tibetan Border Police

ITes: Information Technology enabled services

ITI: Indian Telephone Industries; Industrial Training Institute

ITU: International Telecommunication Union

IUCD: Intra-Uterine Contraceptive Device

IUI: Intrauterine Insemination

IVF: In–Vitro Fertilisation

JCO: Junior Commissioned Officer

JIPMER: Jawaharlal Nehru Institute of Postgraduate Medical Education and Research

JP: Justice of Peace

JPEG: Joint Photographic Expert Group

KFC: Kentucky Fried Chicken

KG: Knight of the Garter; Kindergarten

KKK: Ku Klux Klan (U S.secret society-Anti-Negro, Anti-Jewish)

KRC: Konkan Railway Corporation

KRL: Kochi Refineries Ltd.

KYC: Know Your Customer

LASER: Light Amplification by Stimulated Emission of Radiation

BC and AD	The period beginning with the birth of Jesus Christ (conventionally in A.D.1) is referred to as Christian era. Dates in this era are marked A.D., and dates before it B.C. Christian era is also called Common Era.

National Science Day

February 28 is India's National Science Day. It is on Feb. 28, 1928 that C.V. Raman discovered the change in the wavelength of light that occurs when a light beam is reflected by molecules. The phenomenon, known as 'Raman Effect' won him the Nobel Prize for Physics in 1930

LCA: Light Combat Aircraft
LCD: Liquid Crystal Display, Least Common Denominator
LCM: Lowest Common Multiple
LDL: Low-Density Lipoprotein (Cholesterol)
LERMS: Liberalised Exchange Rate Management Scheme
LeT: Lashkar-e-Taiba
LIC: Life Insurance Corporation (of India)
LIPS: Language Independent Programme Subtitles
LIS: Land Information System
LL.B. : Bachelor of Laws
LMC: Large Megallanic Cloud
Loc.cit: Loco citato (at the place quoted)
LPG: Liquefied Petroleum Gas
LSD: Lysergic acid di–ethylamide
Lt.Col. : Lieutenant Colonel
LTTE: Liberation Tigers of Tamil Elam

M: Monsieur (Mister)
M.A.: Magisiter Artium (Master of Arts)
M.D: Doctor of Medicine
MACT: Motor Accident Claims Tribunal
MAD: Mutually Assured Destruction
MASER: Microwave Amplification by Stimulated Emission of Radiation
MBA: Master of Business Administration
MBBS: Bachelor of Medicine and Bachelor of Surgery
MCC: Marylebone Cricket Club
MCI: Medical Council of India
MDA: market development assistance
MDGs: Millennium Devlopment Goals
MICR: Magnetic ink character recognition
MIDI: Musical Instrument Digital Interface

MIFOR: Mumbai Inter-Bank Forward Offer Rate
MIN: Mutual Fund Identification No.
MIPS: Million Instructions per Second
MIRU: Million Independently targeted re-entry Vehicle
MISA: Maintenance of Internal Security Act
Misc.: Miscellaneous
MIT: Massachusetts Institute of Technology, US; Master Instruction Tape
MKS: Metre Kilogram Second (System)
MI: Military Intelligence
MLA: Member of Legislative Assembly
Mlle: Mademoiselle (Miss)
Mme: Madame (Mrs.)
MMR: Maternal Mortality Rate
MMTC: Minerals and Metals Trading Corporation
MNC: Multi-National Corporation
MODEM: modulator demodulator
MODVAT: Modified Value Added Tax
MOR: middle-of-the-Road
MOSFET: Metal Oxide Semiconductor Field Effect Transistor
MOU: Memorandum of Understanding
MP: Member of Parliament; Madhya Pradesh
mph: miles per hour
MPLAD: Member of Parliament Local Area Development
MRA: Moral Re-Armament
MRCP: Member of the Royal College of Physicians
MRTPC: Monopolies and Restrictive Trade Practices Commission
MS/MSS: Manuscript/ Manuscripts
MSCI: Morgan Stanley Capital International
MT: Metric Ton
MVC: Maha Vir Chakra

NAA: National Airports Authority
NAAC: National Assessment and Accreditation Council
NABARD: National Bank for Agriculture and Rural Development
NAC: National Advisory Council

ASA and ISO

ASA is a standard system developed by the American Standard Association to rate film speed. It was replaced by the ISO (International Standards Organization) system which uses the same scale.

NAFED: National Agricultural Co-operative Marketing Federation

NAFTA: North American Free Trade Agreement

NALCO: National Aluminium Company Ltd.

NASA: National Aeronautics and Space Administration

NASDAQ: National Association of Securities Dealers Automated Quotation

NASSCOM: National Association of Software and Service Companies

NATO: North Atlantic Treaty Organisation

NAV: Net Asset Value

NB: nota bene (note well)

NBE: National Board of Examination

NC: Network Computer

NCAER: National Council of Applied Economic Research

NCC: National Cadet Corps

NCERT: National Council of Educational Research and Training

NCI: Nursing Council of India

NCO: Non-Commissioned Officer

NDA: National Defence Academy

NDC: National Development Council

NDDB: National Dairy Development Board

NDES: New Data Encryption Standard

NEOCONS: Neo-Conservatives

NGO: Non-Government Organisation; Non-Gazett-ed Officer

NHPC: National Hydroelectric Power Corporation

NICD: National Institute of Communicable Diseases

NIMHANS: National Institute of Mental Health And Neuro Sciences

NIPER: National Institute of Pharmaceutical Education and Research

NIV: National Institute of Virology

NKC: National Knowledge Commission

NLC: Neyveli Lignite Corporation

NMDC: National Mineral Development Corporation

NMR: Nuclear Magnetic Resonance

NMS: Network Management System

NOC: No Objection Certificate

NPA: Non-performing Assets

NPC: National Productivity Council

NPCIL: Nuclear Power Corporation of India Ltd.

NPL: National Physical Laboratory; Non-performing Loans

NPT: Nuclear Non-Proliferation Treaty

NREGA: National Rural Employment Guarantee Act

NRF: National Renewal Fund

NRS: National Readership Survey

N&S: Network and Systems

NSA: National Security Advisor

NSEI: National Stock Exchange of India

NSG: Nuclear Suppliers Group

NSP: Native Signal Processing

NSUI: National Students Union of India

NSTM: Nano Science and Technology Mission

NTPC: National Thermal Power Corporation

NTSC: National Television System Commission

NTSE: National Talent Search Examination

O & M: Organisation & Methods

OAPEC: Organisation of Arab Petroleum Exporting Countries

OAS: Organisation of American States

OAU: Organisation of African Unity (now AU)

OBC: Other Backward Classes

OCD: Obsessive Compulsive Disorder

OCR: Optical Character Recognition

ODA: Overseas Development Administration

ODI: Open Data Link Interface

OECD: Organisation for Economic Co-operation and Development

OGL: Open General Licence

OIC: Organisation of Islamic Conference

OIGS: On India Government Service

OLE: Object Linking and Embedding

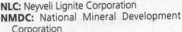

Did You Know?

ASAP = as soon as possible
AWOl = absent without leave
COLA = cost of living allowance
DNR = do not resuscitate
DOA = dead on arrival
DWI = driving while intoxicated
FYI = for your information
GIGO = garbage in, garbage out
MIA = missing in action
MVP = most valuable player
SASE = self-addressed stamped envelope
SIDS = sudden infant death syndrome
SRO = standing room only
TGIF = Thank God It's Friday
Wasp = white Anglo-Saxon Protestant
yuppie = young urban professional

ONGC: Oil and Natural Gas Corporation
OOP: Object Oriented Programme
Op. cit.: Opero citato (in the work cited)
OPCW: Organisation for the Prohibition of Chemical Weapons
OPEC: Organisation of Petroleum Exporting Countries
OPM: Operating Profit Margin
OPV: Oral Polio Vaccine
ORT: Oral Rehyderation Therapy
OSCAR: Orbiting Satellite Carrying Amateur Radio
OXFAM: Oxford Committee for Famine Relief
Oxon: Oxoniensis (of Oxford University)

PAC: Public Accounts committee
PAL: Phase Alternation Line
PAN: Permanent Account Number
PAR: Performance Appraisal Report
PAT: Profit After Tax
PAYE: pay as you earn
PC: post card; Personal Computer
p.c.: per cent
PCA: Professional Chess Association
PCM: Pulse code modulation
PDA: Preventive Detention Act, Personal Digital Assistant
PDS: Public Distribution System
PFRDA: Pension Fund Regulatory and Development Authority
PEC: Project and Equipment Corporation
PEN: (International club of) Poets, Playwrights, Essayists, Editors and Novelists
PERT: Project Evaluation and Review Technique
PETA: People for Ethical Treatment of Animals
PGM-FI: Programmed Fuel Injection
PGP: Pretty Good Privacy
Ph.D.: Doctor of Philosophy (Philosophiae Doctor)
PIB: Press Information Bureau
PIGS: Pre-implantation Genetic Screening
PII: Press Institute of India
PIL: Public Interest Litigation
PIM: Personal Information Management
PIN: Postal Index Number
Pixel: Picture element
PLAB: Professional and Linguistic Assessment Board
PM: Post Meridiem; Prime Minister
PMG: Post Master General
PNR: Passenger Name Recorder
POTA: Prevention of Terrorism Act
POW: Prisoner of War
PPP: Purchasing power parity; Point-to-point Protocol
PPPP: Public Private Panchayat Partnership
PPS: Post Post Scriptum (additional post script)
Pro-tem: Pro tempore (for the time being)
PROLOG: Programming logic
PS: Post Scriptum (written after); Private Secretary
PSB: Public Sector Bank
PSLV: Polar Satellite Launch Vehicle
PSN: Processor Serial Number
PTA: Parent-Teacher Association
PTI: Press Trust of India
PTO: Please Turn Over
PVC: Poly vinyl Chloride; Param Vir Chakra
PWD: Public Works Department; Persons with Disability
PZD: Partial Zonal Drilling

QED: Quod Erat Demonstrandum [which was to be demonstrated or proved]
QR: Quantitative restriction
QSO: Quasi-stellar object
qv: quod vide ((which see)

R&D: Research and Development

R&M: Renovation and Modernisation
RAC: Reservation Against Cancellation
RADAR: Radio Detecting and Ranging
RAM: Random Access Memory
RAPD: Random Amplified Polymorphic Deoxyribonucleic Acid
RAW: Research & Analysis Wing
RBI: Reserve Bank of India

RCC: Reinforced Cement Concrete
RD: refer to drawer
RDX: Research Department Explosive (Cyclotrim-ethylin Trinitrate)
REM: Rapid Eye Movement
RFC: Request for Comments
RH: Rainwater Harvest
RIP: Requiescat in pace (May he or she rest in peace); Raster Image Processor
RISC: Reduced instruction–set computing
RITES: Rail India Technical & Economic Services
RLO: Returned Letters Office
RMS: Railway Mail Service
RNA: Ribonucleic acid
ROM: Read Only Memory
RONW: return on net worth
RPM: Revolutions Per Minute
RSE: Renewable Source of Energy
RSS: Rashtriya Swayam Sewak Sangh
R.S.V.P./R.s.v.p.: Repondez S'il Vous Plait (Reply if you please)
RTG: Radio-isotope Thermoelectric Generator
RTI: Right to Information

SAA: South African Airways

SACLANT: Supreme Allied Commander Atlantic
SASE: Self-addressed stamped envelope
S&T: Science and Technology
SAC: Space Application Centre
SAIL: Steel Authority of India Limited
SAM: Surface to Air Missile
SAPTA: South Asian Preferential Trade Agreement
SARS: Severe Acute Respiratory Syndrome
SASER: Sound Amplification by Stimulated Emission of Radiation
SAT: Scholastic Aptitude Test
SCI: Shipping Corporation of India
SCM: Supply Chain Management
SCSI: Small Computer Systems Interface
SCUBA: Self-contained Underwater Breathing Apparatus
SDR: Special Drawing Rights
SEBI: Securities and Exchange Board of India
SENSEX: Sensitivity Index (of Share Price)
SET: Secure Electronic Transmission
SEZ: Special Economic Zone
SGPC: Siromani Gurudwara Prabandak Committee
SHAPE: Supreme Head-quarters Allied Powers, Europe
SHG: Self Help Group
SIDS: Sudden Infant Death Syndrome (Crib Death)
SIFT: Sperm Intra–Fallopian Transfer
SIM: Subscriber Identification Module
SIP: Systematic Investment Planning
SITA: Suppression of Immoral Traffic Act
SITE: Satellite Instructional Television Experiment
SLBM: Submarine Launched Ballistic Missile
SLFP: Sri Lanka Freedom Party
SLR: Statutory Liquidity Ratio; Single Lens Reflex
SLV: Satellite Launch Vehicle
SMTP: Simple Mail Transfer Protocol
SMS: Short Message Service
SNA: System Network Architecture
SOHO: Small Office Home Office
SOLAS: Safety of Life at Sea

| Centenarians of Japan | 37 out of every 1 lakh people in Japan are now 100 years old. 47,700 Japanese are over 100. Of these, 87% are women. It is a record high for the 41st consecutive year. |

SPCA: Society for Prevention of Cruelty to Animals
SPECT: Single Photon Emission Computed Tomo-graphy
SPTM: Self-Printing Ticketing Machine
STAR(TV): Satellite Television Asian Region Ltd.
START: Strategic Arms Reduction Talks
STC: State Trading Corporation
STD: Subscriber Trunk Dialling; Sexually Transmitted Diseases
STP: Software Technology Park
SUV: sports utility vehicle
SVP: Saturated Vapour Pressure
SWOT: Strengths, Weaknesses, Opportunities and Threats

T& D: Transmission & Distribution
TA: Territorial Army; Travelling Allowance
TACAMO: take charge and move over
TADA: Terrorist and Disruptive Activities (Prevention) Act
TAFE: Tractor and Farm Equipment Ltd.
TAFTA: Trans-Atlantic Free Trade Agreement
TAPS: Tarapur Atomic Power Station
TB: tuberculosis
TBSE: Technology Bureau for Small Enterprise
TCP: Transfer Call Protocol, Transmission Control Protocol
TDA: Trade Development Authority
TDMA: Time Division Multiple Access
TELCO: Tata Engineering and Locomotive Company
TEQIP: Technical Education Quality Improvement Programme
TERLS: Thumba Equatorial Rocket Launching Station
TFT: Thin-Film Transistor
TFYP: Tenth Five Year Plan
TIFAC: Technology and Information Forecasting and Assessment Council
TIFR: Tata Institute of Fundamental Research
TIPS: Technology Information Pilot System
TIPTOP: Tape input–tape output
TISCO: Tata Iron and Steel Company
TLC: Total Literacy Campaign

TMO: Telegraphic Money Order
TNT: Trinitro-toluene
TOEFL: Test of English as a Foreign Language
TPM: Total Productivity Maintenance
TQM: Total Quality Management
TRIMS: Trade Related Investment Measures
TRIPS: Trade Related Intellectual Property Rights
TSE: Test of Spoken Eng-lish
TTC: Telemetry, Tracking & Command
TTE: Travelling Ticket Examiner
TWE: Test of Written English

UAV: Unmanned Aerial Vehicle
UCI: Universal Childhood Immunisation
UCIL: Uranium Corporation of India Ltd.
UCLA: University of California Los Angeles
UCR: Under Colour Removal
UGC: University Grants Commission
UHF: Ultra High Frequency
UHNWI: Ultra-high networth individual
UIDAI: Unique Identification Authority of India
ULFA: United Liberation Front of Asom
UNCED: UN Conference on Environment & Development
UNCTAD: United Nations Conference on Trade and Development
UNEP: United Nations Environment Programme
UNESCO: United Nations Educational, Scientific and Cultural Organi-sation

CMYK

CMYK, stands for 'cyan', 'magenta' 'yellow', and 'black' - the primary colours used in four-colour printing to create full colour images, with black added for true black.

UNFPA: United nations Population Fund
UNI: United News of India
UNICEF: United Nations International Children's Emergency Fund (now, 'United Nations Children's Fund')
UNIDO: United Nations Industrial Development Organisation
UNITA: Union for the Total Independence of Angola
UNMOGIP: United Nations Military Observer Group in India and Pakistan
UNOPS: UN Office for Project Services
UNPROFOR: UN Protection Force
UNRRA: United Nations Relief and Rehabilitation Administration
UNU: United Nations University
UPA: United Progressive Alliance
UPS: Uninterrupted Power Supply
UPSC: Union Public Service Commission
USAID: United States Agency for International Development
USO: Udaipur Solar Observatory
USP: Unique selling proposition

VAT: Value Added Tax
VC: Vice-Chancellor, Victoria Cross; Venture Capital
VCR: Video Cassette Recorder
VD: Venereal Disease (see STD)
VDIS: Voluntary Disclosure of Income Scheme
VHS: Video Home System
VIP: Very Important Person
VIRUS: Vital Information Resources Under Siege
VPP: Value Payable Post
VRS: Voluntary Retirement Scheme
VSAT: Very Small Aperture Terminal
VSSC: Vikram Sarabhai Space Centre

WAN: World Association of Newspapers
WCC: World Council of Churches
WDM: World Debt Market
WEF: World Economic Forum
WGPA: Weighted Grade Point Average
WHO: World Health Organisation
WMD: Weapons of Mass Destruction
WMO: World Meteorological Organisa-tion

'Bowdlerize' from 'Bowdler'

An English editor by name Thomas Bowdler produced expurgated versions of literary works such as Shakespeare and the 'Old Testment'. Bowdlerize is a synonym for expurgate. Now it is used in a perjorative sense.

WPI: Wholesale Price Index
WTI: World Tribunal on Iraq
WTO: World Trade Orga-nisation

WWF: World Wildlife Fund, now renamed Worldwide Fund for Nature
WWW: World Wide Web

XPD: X–Ray Photoelectron Diffraction

YMCA: Young Men's Christian Association
YWCA: Young Women's Christian Association

ZIP: Zone Improvement Plan
ZOPFAN: Zone of Peace, Freedom and Neutrality

Sphairistike   **The game of lawn tennis was patented by an Englishman Major Walter Wingfield in 1944, under the name of 'Sphairistike'.**

A Democracy Under Pressure

Sachidananda Murthy
Resident Editor, *The WEEK* and *Malayala Manorama*, New Delhi

Confrontation between the various constitutional institutions has caused a weakening of the democratic system. Indian democracy will survive these challenges.

Harmonious functioning of the organs in the human body contributes to the well being of the person but when organs are at odds with each other, or some of them are dysfunctional, the person's health suffers. A similar affliction has affected Indian democracy putting the Constitutional organisations at odds with each other, even as the body politic is diagnosed with the cancer of corruption. The years 2010 and 2011 saw an alarming clash of interests among the institutions, which tore the democratic fabric to some extent. The scams which enveloped the UPA government at the centre, some governments at the state level, as well as corruption in higher judiciary, caused immense confrontations. It was not only between the executive and judiciary, plus legislature and judiciary. Parliament and some state legislatures were paralysed for long periods due to the confrontation. Adding fuel to the fire was the standoff between the executive and the Constitutional Office of the Comptroller and Auditor General of India (CAG), as well as between local Lokayukta and the governments in Karnataka and Delhi.

The Governance Crisis

The additional dimension to the governance crisis has been arrival of non-state movements on the centre stage, whether it is the maoists espousing violent overthrow of the government, or the so-called civil society activists who want to enforce their will and agenda on the executive, legislature and judiciary. Neither group is keen on achieving their goals through popular mandate by participation in elections. The crisis of India has been compounded by the cyni-

cism about the political parties and leaders domestically, and by the spiralling global economic crisis. In this pressure cooker atmosphere, the role of organisations itself is getting metamorphosed and according to purists, even getting distorted.

This is not the first such crisis where there is clash between three estates of democracy - executive, legislature and judiciary - with the additional involvement of public agitations. The period 1973-77 was a severe test for Indian democracy, as the Congress party and its highly popular prime minister Indira Gandhi assumed that it had the mandate for sweeping reforms, and that the judiciary has to adjust to the public mandate. Supersession of judges of the Supreme Court triggered a confrontation which was confounded by a judicial order by the Allahabad High Court unseating the prime minister on the charge of electoral malpractice.

Prime Minister Indira Gandhi, who also faced a virulent public agitation on corruption led by Sarvodaya leader Jayaprakash Narayan, took the unprecedented step of declaring an internal emergency suspending fundamental rights, enforcing press censorship, ordered preventive detention of lakhs of people, including opposition stalwarts. The suspension of the emergency and the 1977 Lok Sabha elections restored the democratic balance.

The late 1980s saw a similar confrontation between the government of Rajiv Gandhi, who had won the biggest mandate in Indian political history, and the opposition over the issue of corruption in high places. This was a crisis where apolitical constitutional institutions like the Election Commission and the CAG got dragged into the pit of controversy. But the crisis actually helped to establish the election commission as a truly independent body, thanks to the individual spirit of defiance of then Chief Election Commissioner T N Seshan, which was followed up by his successors by less confrontationist methods.

Coalition Politics

The root cause of the current crisis afflicting the nation, which has sent negative vibes, is the distortions in functioning of coalition governments. India has been having multi party governments as well as minority governments with outside support since 1989, when V.P. Singh formed the National Front government, with outside support from the Right and the Left. Even though P.V. Narasimha Rao led a single party government, for the first two years he had to depend on outside support. Only in 1993, he managed to "buy" up a majority through defections and merger of splinter groups, which strategy benefitted the Congress again in 2008, when Manmohan Singh lost the outside support of Left parties .Only the elections of 1999 and 2009 produced stable majority for Atal Behari Vajpayee and Manmohan Singh respectively.

Coalition politics has led to the crisis because of the erosion of the authority and accountability of the prime minister to parliament and to the nation. The regional parties like DMK, AIADMK, Shiv Sena, Nationalist Congress Party, Trinamool Congress, Janata Dal (United), Rashtriya Janata Dal have demanded and got autonomy for the portfolios allotted to them. Both the

BJP and later the Congress were happy to give such autonomy to ministers and regional satraps, for three reasons. First, they got uninterrupted support from the regional parties for the government, and secondly the Congress had full control over vital ministries like finance, defence, home, external affairs, and finally, by dealing with each regional party separately, there was no gang up of smaller parties. When UPA was formed in 2004, both Lalu Prasad and Sharad Pawar representing the smaller parties, wanted to form a small front within the UPA so that they would get better bargaining powers. They wanted to rope in DMK, whose alliance had swept the Lok Sabha elections in Tamil Nadu. But DMK President M. Karunanidhi made it clear that he would only deal with Congress and its leaders, and he would not be part of any mini front. Karunanidhi told the Congress that his party would not brook any interference in portfolios like communication and

> Coalition politics has led to the crisis because of the erosion of the authority and accountability of the prime minister to parliament and to the nation

IT, surface transport and shipping, environment and forests. Interestingly these are among the ministries which have caused the greatest crisis for Manmohan Singh.

It is to Manmohan Singh's credit that the cabinet has met most frequently and regularly in the modern era. Yet the cabinet system got debilitated due to players sitting outside the cabinet room. The independence of DMK ministers was matched by other coalition ministers, and even Congress ministers felt they were accountable to party president Sonia Gandhi rather than to the prime minister, who was her appointee. The UPA which had the distinction of bringing landmark legislation

Civil Honours	**Personal civil honours (Bharat Ratna, Padma Vibhushan, etc.) withdrawn by the Government of India in 1977 were reintroduced in 1980 after Indira Gandhi again became the PM.**

changing the lives of the *aam aadmi* than any other government in independent India's history, has not been able to bask in the glory of the initiatives because of the mega scams which hit the government one after the other. Otherwise a government which brought in a national rural employment guarantee scheme, the right to information law, a national project for urban renewal and the right to education would have been applauded. These initiatives were contributory factors for the UPA's return to power. If these were among the assets, there were too many liabilities.

The Commonwealth Games

The government's writ would still have been strong if only it could have managed the conduct of the Commonwealth Games in Delhi without a fuss or crisis. But the systemic faults of the government were again evident in the way the domestic sports administrator lobby led by Indian Olympic Association President Suresh Kalmadi hijacked the games and landed the prime minister and many other worthies in the soup. It was not Kalmadi alone, but it was the administrator caucus with members from major and regional political parties which insisted on autonomy for the Indian Olympic Association to conduct the games with a massive outlay of funds. Being an influential Congressman, Kalmadi had his own way, trampling the sports ministers and bureaucrats who came in his path. The mess, which was exemplified by a collapsed bridge just before the Games were to start, dealt a major blow to the government's ability to deliver. The Organising Committee headed by Kalmadi, as well as the union and Delhi governments were enmeshed in controversies. Though the Commonwealth Games were rescued from the mess and were declared a success, the skeletons continued to tumble out, and again

the CAG came with a damning report, indicting the central and Delhi governments. Kalmadi and associates went to jail on the charges of causing major losses to the exchequer.

2G Spectrum Licences

The CAG became the focal point of the governmental crisis, as its first report on the 2G scam pushed forth the concept of "presumptive loss" to the government due to a policy decision, rather than the actual loss suffered due to faulty implementation of policy decision. There was intense corporate rivalry over the 2G spectrum licences and as overlord of the communication ministry, DMK's A Raja threw prudence and caution to the winds, as his ministry manipulated the rules of the games to favour "the chosen few." The highest of the different estimates of the Presumptive Loss to the government, based on the revenues actually earned on the subsequent auction of 3G spectrum was ₹ 1,76,000 crores.

The CAG Report

The government protested saying the CAG report was speculative and did not understand the environment in which government took decisions, but the opposition and the Supreme Court stepped in, leading to a criminal prosecution, A Raja bowed out and was arrested. The DMK was a major beneficiary of the licences which was evident in the "friendly loan' of Rs. 200 crores to Karunanidhi family owned Kalaignar channel from a licence allottee. Raja, Karunanidhi's daughter Kanimozhi, key bureaucrats and CEOs of some telecom companies went to jail in what has been described as the biggest scam in the history of Independent India.

The CAG report on 2G spectrum losses and irregularities caused a big logjam of the parliament. Once CAG presets the report to Parliament on how the government spends its money, the report becomes the property of the Public Accounts Committee of the Parliament, which is headed by a prominent opposition leader. But the opposition BJP sprang a surprise by demanding a special parliamentary committee, and when the government resisted it, an entire session of parliament was lost due to disruptions. The confrontation put the committee system, which has worked well all these years under strain, because the PAC rejected the draft report on the 2G spectrum scam prepared by its own chairman Murli Manohar Joshi of BJP. Normally PAC reports are unanimous documents, with rare notes of dissent.

It was not just the government and parliament which were on a collision course, but the Supreme Court cracked the whip repeatedly on several sensitive issues, and the government cried foul about "judicial overreach." The confrontation between the executive and the judiciary led to several embarrassing judgements for the government, questioning of the ideological motives of a Supreme Court bench, the resignation of the solicitor general of India, and the change of the law minister.

CVC Appointment

The big blows were many. The Supreme Court repeatedly slapped the government on its knuckles. When the apex court thought that the CBI and Enforcement Directorate were not vigorous in their investigations into the 2G scam, the court decided to directly monitor the progress. A major embarrasment for the government was on the appointment of the chief vigilance commissioner, the principal fighter against corruption, who has his officials posted in every ministry, every public sector company, and other autonomous entities. The CVC has a network of officials who are supposed to check corrupt practices real time, apart from advising whether policy decisions at the highest level are irregular or prone to moneymaking. The government unwisely decided to push for a former telecom secretary who had been charged in Kerala for involvement in a corruption case involving the then chief minister. The officer P J Thomas had protested his innocence, but the case was meandering its way through courts and government departments. Secondly he had been incharge of telecom portfolio at a time when the ministry had come under the harsh glare

of publicity. But the prime minister and the home minister overruled the objections of the leader of the opposition in appointing Thomas. The Supreme Court quashed the appointment and enunciated the doctrine of "organisational integrity", and said the appointment of Thomas did not meet this highest criterion of integrity.

Two of the most confrontational decision taken by the Supreme Court, one of whose judges rather unwisely insisted "sky is the limit" for the powers of the supreme court, dealt with the menace of black money, and the appointment of special police officers in disturbed areas. The black money menace came to the fore

> The UPA government sought a review of the judgement, and it was supported by BJP.

with the income tax department insisting that a Pune based businessman was one of the biggest hawala dealers in the country, and said he had evaded taxes worth one fourth of the total annual income tax collected in the country. The Hasan Ali case also was used by yoga teacher Ramdev to launch an agitation which fizzled out. But the Supreme Court was not ready with the nuanced replies of the government and the reluctance to name Indians who had black money accounts in European tax havens. The court, exasperated by the government, ordered that a special task force headed by a retired judge, and having heads of the investigative and intelligence agencies would directly monitor the investigation and took away the powers of the finance ministry. This was a blatant example of the Supreme Court taking away executive powers, and caused much heartburn in the government, which called it as a case of judicial overreach.

Another judgement which rattled both the government and the BJP, which rules Maoist violence affected states of Chhattis-

UNSC Non-Permanent Members	In January, 2011 India joined th UN Security Council as a non-permanent member after 19 years. The other four countries were Germany, Portugal, South Africa and Columbia.

garh, Jharkhand and Madhya Pradesh, was the taking away of the right of the state goverments to appoint citizens as special police officers, and arming them to take on the gun-toting Maoists. The government insisted that this was a direct interference in the power of the governments to maintain law and order, and said the judgement by abolishing the salwa judam corps of armed tribals, would lead to heavy killings by Maoists in Chhattisgarh. The UPA government sought a review of the judgement, and it was supported by BJP.

Interestingly the institutions which are respected for their independence and integrity inside and outside the system - higher judiciary, the armed forces and the media - also faced credibility crisis. The higher judiciary was rocked by the allegations of corruption and there were two impeachment motions moved in parliament against a high court chief justice and a high court judge. The monitoring of the provident fund scam in Uttar Pradesh did not bring any credit to higher judiciary. The armed forces were rocked by a series of scandals involving land, liquor, rations and even sexual offences, and high ranking generals were punished by the system. The media, which has grown exponentially in print and electronic sectors, faced a crisis when some media organisations indulged in the paid news practice, where advertising hype masqueraded as genuine news. There were corrective steps, but the episodes showed how once respected institutions are not immune to the general rot.

Judicial Overactivism

Some state governments too felt the heat of judicial overactivism, especially the Allahabad High Court judgement quashing the compulsory acquisition of thousands of acres of land by the government in Greater Noida, on the fringes of New Delhi. Federal equations also became tense as some states complained that the centre was steadily eroding their powers in the areas of law and order (through communal violence bill, expanding powers of national investigation agency, too many central commissions for special interest groups), education (the permission for deemed universities and enforcement of English in place of mother tongue), and finance (the proposed goods and services taxation law).

Anna Hazare

As corruption became the talking point of the nation, Anna Hazare tapped into the nation's conscience with his fast demanding a tough Lokpal law to handle the cancer of corruption in the government. The drama played out in the streets and committee rooms of Delhi pitted the government against Hazare's team. And no consensus could be built. Hazare has been backed by activists who have crusaded for judicial accountability and right to information, but the political class was skeptical whether the present constitutional arrangement can deliver everything Team Anna demanded. Other civil society activists also questioned the monopolising of their space by one group, but Hazare's campaign added more to the problems of the UPA government. The corporate sector too has not escaped the fallout as the involvement of top companies, iconic chief executives and lobbying agents like Nira Radia in the telecom sector, has led to calls for greater accountability from the private sector, and there were suggestions that their activities should come under the CBI scanner. In the Karnataka mining scandal, major mining and steel companies gave donations to trusts controlled by family members of B.S. Yedyurappa, who was forced to resign following a very adverse Lokayukta report.

India faced multiple challenges even as the battle over limited resources like land, water, minerals and spectrum became intense, and there was competitive politics, and institutional confrontation. But the Indian democracy would survive these challenges and internalise the lessons of the crisis.

Corruption in India

Dr. Samuel Paul,
Former Director, IIM, Ahmedabad,
founder of Public Affairs Centre, Bangalore and a former World Bank and UN Adviser

India's corruption stories made headlines in 2011. Treating the symptoms of corruption will not eradicate the evil. Political will is the most important factor. Civil society has a vital role to play too.

2011 will be known as the "Year of Scams" in India. The housing scam in Mumbai, the Commonwealth games scam and the telecom 2G scam made media headlines for months. The fall of corrupt chief ministers, arrests of the telecom minister and his business accomplices signaled the deep inroads corruption had made in a government led by a prime minister known for his personal integrity. Public anger against corruption reached an all time high. These developments have also dented India's international image as an emerging economic power.

Delayed actions by governments to deal with scams, coupled with public dissatisfaction with the harassment and corruption citizens faced in their day to day transactions with governments and their agencies, propelled anti-corruption movements led by civil society in 2011. Anna Hazare's Lok Pal crusade became a rallying point for large numbers of people from major cities and even small towns. Government of India was forced to negotiate with these civil society activists because of the public support and media pressure behind them.

We should not conclude from this that corruption was suddenly discovered in 2011. The fact is that corruption was always in the news ever since Independence. However, in recent years, people have seen the scale and spread of corruption increasing by leaps and bounds. They have seen

successive governments' reluctance to tackle the problem in earnest. Anti-corruption laws are passed, but seldom enforced, and the guilty rarely punished. The political will to improve essential public services and make them corruption free was not in evidence. Discretion in policy decision making and the award of large contracts by ministers have led to abuse of power and corruption. The Lok Pal Bill, to set up an essential anti-corruption institution, was pending for over four decades. The tipping point was reached in 2011 as these factors converged.

Why is India Corrupt?

Why is corruption so rampant in India? There are several reasons. First, certain traditional practices of paying bribes to public officials may have created a tolerance of corruption in our society. In many government offices such as registrar's offices, it was a normal practice to pay bribes. Politi-

> **Rs. 21,069 Crore in Bribe**
>
> According to a 2005 study, common citizens of the country pay a bribe of Rs.21,069 crore while availing one or more of the eleven public services in a year.

cal parties have openly distributed cash and goods to voters during election time. Once such practices are widespread, it is difficult to root them out. Second, since many government services are monopolistic in nature (only government supplies them), it becomes easy for corrupt officials to extort money or favours from those who seek the services. Third, when decisions are made without transparency, it becomes easier for public officials to favour those who are willing to give them bribes. Fourth, when those in authority are unwilling or unable

> The key pre-requisites are a critical mass of political leaders committed to this cause and a section of business and civil society that respects the rule of law

to monitor the actions and performance of those working under them, corruption becomes a low risk activity. Fifth, political parties need large funds for fighting elections. There is little accountability and transparency in the collection and use of these funds, creating in the process enormous scope for corruption.

Corruption in the Private Sector

So far, we have talked about corruption in government, meaning the abuse of public power for private gain. But corruption in the private sector is also a serious problem and needs to be dealt with. In fact, the two are often linked. To avoid tax, many persons and businesses engage in real estate and other transactions in cash, creating unaccounted money in the process. Many firms generate black money through partially accounted purchases and sales. Businessmen need to create black money in order to make political donations or to win contracts. It encourages them to siphon off some of their funds from business, thus evading taxation, and deceiving

their shareholders. We have here a vicious circle that is difficult to break and that perpetuates corruption and abuse of power all around.

The key pre-requisites for effectively tackling corruption are a critical mass of political leaders committed to this cause and a significant section of business and civil society that respects the rule of law. While punishing the guilty is important, preventive measures can play a significant role in fighting corruption.

A complex phenomenon like corruption needs to be fought on multiple fronts. Concerted efforts by government, civil society and business are essential for success in the long run. The core components of the strategy are the adoption of major electoral reforms, effective use of existing laws that mandate governments to empower people with information, greater transparency in discretionary decision making, prompt and severe punishment of the guilty, and citizen friendly public services.

Electoral Reforms

Of these, electoral reforms, including election financing, have been widely debated, but not acted on. Those who are to lead these reforms are trapped in a political culture that resembles the corrupt 19th century politics of the West. Significant public financing of elections, limits on electoral expenditure, and its disclosure and audit are examples of preventive action that can help control corruption.

Much less attention has been given to the effective use of existing laws to work in a preventive mode. A classic case is the Right to Information Act, Section IV of which requires governments to provide a great deal of useful information to the public suo moto. When citizens are aware of their entitlements and rights, they are more likely to demand them and resist corruption. The failure to implement this section is a major reason why people are forced to seek information under RTI that in other countries are readily available to the public.

Corruption Index	The Transparency International, an NGO based in Berlin, annually publishes the grading of the countries on the basis of what is called Corruption Perception Index (CPI).

Transparency in public governance can go a long way in reducing the scope for corruption. Major policy decisions, award of contracts and licenses and discretionary decisions that benefit private parties are the contexts in which big scams emerge. To access information on these require heroic efforts. It often takes much staying power and the use of the RTI sledgehammer to crack this nut. Since these are matters of public interest, should not the information be disclosed to the public without anyone asking for it?

That discretionary decision making under the shadow of non-transparency is tailor made to breed corruption is borne out by numerous recent cases. Land acquisition and allocation by governments offer considerable scope for corruption. After acquiring land for public purposes, authorities may denotify and gift or sell parts of the land using their discretionary powers. These non-transparent transactions are a fertile source of corruption and nepotism as such information is never placed in the public domain.

Regulatory agencies also indulge in similar opaque practices. The Medical Council of India (MCI) regulates admission to medical colleges and lays down the standards for medical education. After years of corruption allegations against the MCI by medical colleges, its president was recently caught in a bribery case and imprisoned. Though standards and regulatory norms can be clear and lend themselves to be applied transparently, MCI had followed an opaque regime that did not permit its decisions to be placed in the public domain or subject to challenge by the affected parties.

The widespread public rage against corruption is to a large extent driven by what citizens experience in their day to day interactions with governments and their agencies. The answer to this problem lies in the reform of public service delivery at all levels of government. Some shrug off this phenomenon as petty corruption, while others attribute it to the failure of a few officials

and politicians. This is a big mistake as it reflects a major systemic failure of the state for which the blame should be put at the door of those at the top.

Corruption in Public Service

There are four major gaps in the public service arena that breed corruption and hence need to be rectified. First, there is a lack of information that makes it difficult for citizens to know what they should do to access services, and what they are entitled to once they gain access. Next, there is a one sided agreement a citizen must enter with the service provider. The latter will insist on the citizen paying the fee, providing the needed documents and other terms, but does not promise to deliver a predictable service or benefit. The citizen cannot hold the provider accountable for time deadlines, quality and standards of service, or penalty in case of failure. The third is the lack of grievance redress when problems arise. Government can terminate a service or penalise the citizen if he fails to comply with the rules. But Government does not provide the latter with a credible grievance redress mechanism to respond to his/her complaints. Finally, there is a reluctance on the part of public officials to listen to the voice of the people, especially the poor. Though government has control over its services and makes the rules, it seldom monitors the actual delivery of its services. Under these conditions, corruption tends to thrive. Influential citizens may make their voice heard. Some others pay bribes and get what they need from government.

Finland, The Least Corrupt	According to the 2005 Corruption Perception Index, India ranked at 88 out of the 156 countries. The least corrupt was Finland and the most corrupt country Bangladesh. China figured at rank 78.

But the vast majority of people do not get their entitlements in full.

Empowering People

What are the remedies? Empowering people with the information they need about their entitlements, rights and remedies is the first step. Government has taken some halting steps in this direction, but needs to do much more. A more balanced and transparent contract between citizens and service providers is the next step. Government has to allocate more resources and install more robust systems if this remedy is to work. Putting in place effective grievance redress mechanisms, using new technologies where appropriate, is the third requirement. Several experiments are under way in this arena. Replication of the best

> Influential citizens may make their voice heard. Some others pay bribes and get what they need from government

among these on a large scale is the obvious answer. Furthermore, all governments and their service providers must periodically gather systematic feedback from citizens on their services and programmes and use the findings to continuously improve their quality and reduce corruption.

Finally, there should be swift and severe penalties for those found guilty of corruption. Today, corruption is a low risk activity. Our judicial system is slow, and very few are caught and punished in a way that has a deterrent effect on others. A strong Lok Pal institution could make a difference. It remains to be seen whether the proposed bill will in fact live up to this expectation.

Treating the symptoms of corruption will not result in the eradication of this evil. Black money is an example of a symptom. Remedies such as an amnesty scheme to legitimize black money, or bringing back some black money from Swiss banks or other tax havens may create a sense of fear among the corrupt for some time. But if the root causes of corruption are not dealt with, new ways of creating and hiding black money will be found. Similarly, a Lok Pal may investigate corruption cases against the Prime Minister or other top public officials. This, however, is like tackling the problem after the damage has been done. What is urgently needed is the political will to implement the wider set of reforms discussed above. Prevention is better than cure.

Civil society has an important role to play in this context. It can exert pressure on the government to control corruption. It can monitor areas in which public and private sector corruption is rampant, and engage in educating citizens to resist corruption. It can present plans and reforms that can reduce the scope for corruption in the public arena. While their conduct may not have been acceptable to all, both Anna Hazare and his supporters have played this role in their recent encounters with government. Civil society movements, however, should be clear about their role in this process. They do not represent all people, nor do they have the right to insist that their proposals alone should be adopted by government. Representative institutions already exist. Civil society should strive to influence and energise these institutions of governance to fight corruption through the power and logic of their ideas. ∎

The writer is author of Corruption in India: Agenda for Action

Life without Corruption | A 1999 UNDP Report pointed out that if India's corruption level comes down to that of the Scandinavian countries, the GDP will grow by 1.5% and FDI will increase by 12.5%.

Terrorism Post-Osama

R. Prasannan
Chief of Bureau, *The Week*, New Delhi

Osama is gone more but terrorism will continue to haunt the world because the issue has several other faces.

In a major speech on Afghanistan policy at West Point on December 1, 2009, US President Barack Obama had said: "Our overarching goal [in Afghanistan] remains the same: to disrupt, dismantle, and defeat Al Qaeda in Afghanistan and Pakistan, and to prevent its capacity to threaten American and our allies in the future."

On May 2, 2011, Barack Obama announced to the world: "Good evening. Tonight, I can report to the American people and to the world that the United States has conducted an operation that killed Osama bin Laden, the leader of Al-Qaeda, and a terrorist who's responsible for the murder of thousands of innocent men, women, and children."

If the US's long-term objective was merely to "disrupt, dismantle and defeat al Qaida," that objective, at least a good part of it, was achieved on May 1. Al Qaida may have been crippled; it may - and it is a very uncertain 'may' - now disintegrate.

But terrorism will continue to haunt the world.

A Grave Misconception

Much of the euphoria expressed after the killing of Osama bin Laden has been caused by a grave misconception over which western, particularly American counter-terror strategies have been premised. That misconception was especially manifest in the West Point speech. That the goal was merely to defeat Al Qaeda and not terrorism.

This misconception is based on another wrong premise that terrorism began with Al Qaeda and bin Laden and it has to end with Al Qaeda and bin Laden. Even a Congres-

sional Research Report published soon after the killing of Osama bin laden has made this fundamental error - of identifying al Qaida as perhaps the only face of terror in the world.

This was typical of the United States' compartmental and episodal approach to the challenges faced by the world and even itself. So far, the only terrorism that the United States has confronted has been the terrorism of Al Qaeda. So the US policies seem to be conditioned by the premise that terrorism has to end with bin Laden and his Al Qaeda.

On the other hand, countries like India which have lived with terror before the arrival of bin laden or the advent of Al Qaeda realise that they will have to live with terror even after bin Laden. Even Europe should share this view. The Irish Republican Army had been terrorising the United Kingdom long before bin Laden. Baader Meinhoff had been terrorising continental Europe; Shining Path guerrillas spread terror in Peru. Nearer home and at home, we had seen Tamil Tigers sowing and reaping in Sri Lanka, Khalistani militants in Punjab, not to speak of the terror tactics used by several separatist groups in India's northeast. Even the terror that Indian has been facing in Kashmir and

The Worst Ever	The deadliest terrorist attack ever was the one on Sept. 11, 2001 when suicide terrorists hijacked four airplanes and crashed two of them into the World Trade Centre complex and one into the Pentagon building in Washington, D.C.

elsewhere contemporaneous to bin Laden's activities had little to do with him. Neither Hizbul Mujahideen nor any of the terrorist organisations that operated in Jammu and Kashmir throughout the 1990s had any original links to bin Laden or the al Qaeda network that he spawned.

Al Qaeda's Global Affiliates

American policy-making seems to be based on the premise that al-Qaeda is a kind of mother organisation which spawned or created several smaller groups that have since spread out across the world and are terrorising the so-called civilised world. This is obvious even in the Congressional report which refers to al Qaeda's 'global affiliates'. Even the term affiliates is a misnomer. The several territorially local organisations that are now waging

> Rajiv Gandhi was assassinated by a suicide terrorist several years before bin Laden came on the south Asian terror horizon

the so-called jihad are by no means affiliates of Al Qaeda. On the contrary, Al Qaida, if it exists, is a creation of several outfits joining hands or at least comparing notes with one another. Al Qaeda is the child of these outfits and not the mother.

Perhaps a hydrological analogy may be more appropriate. In the US world view, Al Qaeda is the 'main stream' of terror and the several score outfits like Lashkar-e-Tayyeba, Hizbul Mujahideen, the Haqqani network are distributaries that flow out from the main stream. So, if the main stream is dammed, the distributaries too should also dry up. The Congressional report too makes this folly: "The most common reported type of linkage between the core and global affiliates has taken the form of pledges of ideological fealty by regional affiliates to OBL [Osama bin Laden], along with mutual statements of support for shared goals. A second, more opaque link between the core and the global affiliates

are reported periodic exchanges for strategic planning between the core and affiliates and, in some cases, the exchange of financing or the deployment of technical experts to the affiliates by the core group. To the extent that the killing of OBL disrupts the organizational cohesion of the core group, these pledges and apparently limited exchanges may decline in frequency and scope."

The Child of Several Outfits

Nothing could be farther from truth. Al Qaeda (again, if it exists) is only the child of several outfits. Even if al Qaida is eliminated, as has bin Laden, the capacity of the groups to create terror and mayhem will continue. To revert to the hydrological analogy, the several score outfits are the small mountain streams that have come together to the form the main stream of Al Qaeda. These outfits are tributaries to the main stream and not its distributaries.

Opinions have been expressed in certain quarters that infusion of suicide terrorism or fidayeen terrorism was an innovation of the bin Laden brand of terror. Nothing could be farther from truth. After all, Rajiv Gandhi was assassinated by a suicide terrorist several years before bin Laden came on the south Asian terror horizon.

The international concern, or more particularly the US concern over terrorism, as former RAW chief Vikram Sood wrote in Counter-Terrorism South Asia, "is about a global jihad, but for countries like India, the threats range from left wing extremism, ethnic separatism to religious militancy." Naturally, the US counter-terrorism strategy is essentially aimed at defeating jihad or jihadis. If one could quantify the terror experience of countries, it might appear that, of the total corpus of terror that India has experienced over the decades, the jihadi terror comprises only a negligible per cent.

This is true of the western, especially European experience too. Even before the advent of jihadi terror or the arrival of Osama bin Laden on the terror horizon, European airports had been bombed, and rulers kidnapped and assassinated.

Most Failed States	India's neighbours - Pakistan, Bangladesh, Nepal and Sri Lanka among others - are featured in the list of world's most failed states released in June, 2011 by *Foreign Policy* magazine. African countries dominate the 60-nation list.

Indeed, the Congressional report does take into account the divergent views on terror. "Experts have a range of views about the killing of OBL," the report says. "Some consider his death to be a largely symbolic event, while others believe it marks a significant achievement in U.S. counter terrorism efforts. Individuals suggesting that his death lacks great significance argue that U.S. and allied actions had eroded OBL's ability to provide direction and support to Al Qaeda (AQ). For these analysts, OBL's influence declined following the U.S. invasion of Afghanistan to a point where prior to his death he was the figurehead of an ideological movement. This argument reasons that a shift of terrorist capability has occurred away from the core of AQ to affiliated organizations. Still others argue that OBL pursued a strategy of developing the AQ organization into an ideological movement thus making it more difficult to defeat. They contend that, even if OBL were no longer involved in the decision-making apparatus of AQ, his role as the inspirational leader of the organization was far more important than any operational advice he might offer. As such, his death may not negatively affect the actions of the ideological adherents of AQ and as a martyr he may attract and inspire a greater number of followers."

The study report continued: "Individuals suggesting that his death is a major turning point in U.S. counter-terrorism efforts contend that OBL remained an active participant in setting a direction for the strategy and operations of AQ and its affiliates. In addition to disrupting Al Qaeda's organizational activities some believe his death may serve as a defining moment for the post 9/11 global counterterrorism campaign as current and potential terrorists, other governments, and entities that wish to threaten U.S. interests will take note of the U.S. success in achieving a long-held security goal. The death of OBL may have near and long-term implications for AQ and U.S. security strategies and policies."

Terror Before Osama

The fact is that terror pre-existed Osama bin Laden and Al Qaeda, but the US woke up to the reality only after 9/11. Once America woke up and took up cudgels, apparently on behalf of the terrorised world, the war on terror became too narrow-focused, the

with the primary and final objective being the defeat of Al Qaeda. Terror came to be jihadi and jihadi alone, and terror mastermind bin Laden. Bin Laden was finally located and killed in the Pakistani city of Abbotabad, and soon the US announced its commitment to gradually exit Afghanistan.

That Pak-Afghan region is the hotbed of jehadi terrorism is now more or less acknowledged by the west too. As the Congressional report said, "there are hopes among some analysts that the circumstances of OBL's death will inspire soul-searching in Pakistani leaders and perhaps more robust cooperation with the United States in the future..... Some senior Members of Congress have voiced the opinion that present circumstances call for "more engagement [with Pakistan], not less." Meanwhile, in the prevailing anti-US atmosphere in Pakistan, several influential persons have demanded exit of the US from the region now that the primary target of their counter-terror war has been accomplished.

It was to be noted that while Indian leaders described the killing of Osama as "a significant step forward" and a "historic development and victorious milestone in the global war against forces of terrorism.", they also took the opportunity to focus on the new evidence that terrorists find sanctuary in Pakistan, and expressed concerns about the possibility of reprisal attacks in Kashmir. More concern was expressed about the US move to hasten out of Afghanistan. As the Congressional report noted, "India is averse to seeing a Kabul government too friendly with Islamabad in the future and has a keen interest in precluding the resurgence of Islamist extremist groups in Afghanistan, which it fears could be the case if the Pakistani military has excessive influence on the anti-Taliban campaign's endgame."

A statement from a Tehrik-e-Taliban Pakistan ("Pakistani Taliban") spokesman vowed retaliation for OBL's killing, saying, "President Zardari and the army will be our first targets, America will be our second target." Intelligence agencies reportedly have warned that Pakistan could see a steep rise in domestic terrorist attacks in the near-term, with U.S. diplomatic missions named as primary targets, along with Pakistani government and military facilities.

Interestingly, the Congressional paper takes note of the divergent views. "Although the stated goal of U.S. policy focuses on eliminating safe haven for terrorist groups, preventing reinfiltration of terrorist groups into Afghanistan is predicated on establishing durable security and capable and effective governance throughout Afghanistan. The death of OBL, and potential weakening of AQ, does not, in and of itself, accomplish these objectives." But US policy-making does not seem to be bothered by these views, as is obvious from the fact that the United States is determined to go ahead with its drawdown policy in Afghanistan.

The Remnants of Al Qaeda

The remnants of Al Qaeda are now estimated to be not more than a few hundred. But most security experts believe that the core of the insurgency remains the Taliban movement centered around Mullah Omar, now believed to be hiding in Pakistan. Reports that he has been killed have not yet been confirmed. Then there are outfits like the one led by Jalaluddin Haqqani.

Despite all the international punditry on jehadi terrorism, the fact remains that the links between several Kashmiri outfits with the mainstream Afghan terrorism has been rather tenuous. The links were essentially through the state conduits in Pakistan which actually made the groups on its west and

its east find common cause. Even after the defeat of Al Qaeda, these groups will continue to operate and spread terror either for the religious cause, the Kashmir cause or some imaginary social justice cause, as long as there is direct or indirect encouragement from the state actors in Pakistan, especially its intelligence agency ISI which believes that the long-term strategic goal of Pakistan - of weakening India - can be achieved only by waging a low-intensity war with terror as the main weapon.

Even in the US there are many who believe that the killing of Osama bin Laden might "motivate revenge or publicity seeking homegrown jihadists to attack the United States." This could be true of not only the US but also Afghanistan, Pakistan and even peripheral regions of India. Such attacks or episodes of terror could be more decentralised, though low-key, making it more difficult for investigators to trace the culprits.

That much is conceded by the Congressional report, too. "These plots and attacks reflect a global shift in terrorism toward decentralized, autonomously radicalized, violent jihadist individuals or groups who strike in their home countries. Global counterterrorism efforts have made it harder for international terrorist networks to formulate plots, place their recruits in targeted countries, and carry out violent strikes in locations far from their bases of operation. AQ and affiliated groups are moving "away from what we are used to, which are complex, ambitious, multi-layered plots."

India has been facing such attacks before and after 9/11 and before and after the death of Osama bin Laden. The attacks in Mumbai in July 2011, weeks after the killing of Osama bin laden, are a case in point. They were low-key attacks, using ordinarily available explosives and there was nothing dramatic or theatrical about them. But the fact is that they too killed people. Such attacks, being low-key and carried out by elements low down in the terror groups' hierarchy are more difficult to trace, and the culpability of the accused still more difficult to be proven in judicial courts.

In other words, terrorism will continue. It will be less theatrical than World Trade Tower bombings, but could be more widespread.

Awards & Honours

Padma Awards, 2011

Padma Vibhushan

1. Dr. (Smt.) Kapila Vatsyayan (Art – Art Administration and Promotion, Delhi); Mrs. Homai Vyarawalla (Art – Photography, Gujarat); Shri A Nageshwara Rao (Art- Cinema, Andhra Pradesh); Shri Parasaran Kesava Iyengar (Public Affairs, Delhi); Dr. Akhlaq-ur-Rehman Kidwai (Public Affairs, Delhi); Shri Vijay Kelkar (Public Affairs, Delhi); Shri Montek Singh Ahluwalia (Public Affairs, Delhi); Shri Palle Rama Rao (Science and Engineering, Andhra Pradesh);Shri Azim Premji

Vijay Kelkar

(Trade and Industry, Karnataka); Shri Brajesh Mishra (Civil Services, Madhya Pradesh); Prof. (Dr.) Ottaplakkal Neelakandan Velu Kurup (Literature and Education, Kerala); Dr. Sitakant Mahapatra (Literature and Education, Orissa); Late Shri L. C. Jain (Public Affairs, Delhi).

Sitakant Mahapara

Padma Bhushan

Shri Satyadev Dubey (Art–Theatre, Maharashtra); Shri Mohammed Zahur Khayyam Hashmi alias Khayyam (Art–Cinema– Music, Maharashtra); Shri Shashi Kapoor (Art

Waheeda Rehman

– Cinema, Maharashtra); Shri Krishen Khanna (Art – Painting, Haryana); Shri Madavur Vasudevan Nair (Art – Dance – Kathakali, Kerala); Ms. Waheeda Rehman (Art – Cinema, Maharashtra); Shri Rudrapatna Krishna Shastry Srikantan (Art – Music-Vocal, Karnataka); Ms. Arpita Singh (Art – Painting, Delhi); Dr. Sripathi Panditharadhyula Balasubrahmanyam (Art – Playback Singing, Music Direction & acting, Tamil Nadu); Shri C.V. Chandrasekhar (Art – Classical Dance-Bharatanatyam, Tamil Nadu); Shri Dwijen Mukherjee (Art, West Bengal); Smt. Rajashree Birla (Social work, Maharashtra); Mrs. Shobhana Ranade (Social work, Maharashtra); Dr. Suryanarayanan Ramachandran

Kris Gopalakrishnan

(Science and Engineering, Tamil Nadu); Shri S. (Kris) Gopalakrishnan (Trade and Industry, Karnataka); Shri Yogesh Chander Deveshwar (Trade and Industry, West Bengal); Ms. Chanda Kochhar (Trade and Industry, Maharashtra); Dr. K. Anji Reddy (Trade and Industry- Pharmacy, Andhra Pradesh); Shri Analjit Singh (Trade and Industry, Delhi); Shri Rajendra Singh Pawar (Trade and Industry, Haryana); Dr. Gunapati Venkata Krishna Reddy (Trade and Industry, Andhra Pradesh); Shri Ajai

Most Mined Countries	**Afghanistan and Iraq are the most land-mined countries, says the UN. It is estimated that these countries have 10,000,000 mines each.**

Chowdhary (Trade and Industry, Delhi); Shri Surendra Singh (Civil Services, Delhi); Shri M. N .Buch (Civil Services, Madhya Pradesh); Shri Shyam Saran (Civil Services, Delhi); Shri Thayil Jacob Sony George (Literature and Education, Karnataka); Dr. Ramdas Madhava Pai (Literature and Education, Karnataka); Shri Sankha Ghosh (Literature and Education, West Bengal); Late Shri K. Raghavan Thirumulpad (Medicine – Ayurveda, Kerala*); Late Dr. Keki Byramjee Grant (Medicine–Cardiology Maharashtra*); Late Shri Dashrath Patel (Art, Gujarat*).

Padma Shri

Ms. Neelam Mansingh Chowdhry (Art–Theatre, Chandigarh); Shri Makar Dhwaja Darogha (Art- Chhau Dance, Jharkhand); Shri Shaji Neelakantan Karun (Art – Film Direction, Kerala); Shri Girish Kasaravalli (Art – Film making,

Girish Kasaravalli

Karnataka); Ms. Tabassum Hashmi Khan alias Tabu (Art – Cinema, Maharashtra); Shri Jivya Soma Mase (Art – Warli Painting, Maharashtra); Guru (Ms.) M.K. Saroja (Art–Dance-Bharatnatyam, Tamil Nadu); Shri Jayaram Subramaniam (Art – Cinema, Tamil Nadu); Pandit Ajoy Chakraborty (Art – Music-Indian Classical Vocal, West Bengal); Smt. Mahasundari Devi (Art – Mithilia/ Madhubani Painting, Bihar); Shri Gajam Govardhana (Art – Handloom Weaving, Andhra Pradesh); Ms. Sunayana Hazarilal (Art–Dance – Kathak, Maharashtra); Shri S.R. Janakiraman (Art – Carnatic Vocal Music, Tamil Nadu); Shri Peruvanam Kuttan Marar (Art–Chenda Melam- Drum concert, Kerala);

Mahasundari Devi

Smt. Kalamandalam Kshemavathy Pavithran (Art–Dance–Mohiniattam, Kerala); Shri Dadi Dorab Pudumjee (Art–Puppetry, Delhi); Shri Khangembam Mangi Singh (Art–Traditional Music of Manipur (Pena), Manipur); Shri Prahlad Singh Tipaniya (Art – Folk Music, Madhya Pradesh); Smt. Usha Uthup (Art–Music, West Bengal); Smt. Kajol (Art–Cinema, Maharashtra); Shri Irfan Khan (Art– Cinema, Maharashtra); Shri Mamraj Agrawal (Social work, West Bengal); Shri Jockin Arputham (Social work, Maharashtra); Ms. Nomita Chandy (Social work, Karnataka); Ms. Sheela Patel (Social work, Maharashtra); Ms. Anita Reddy (Social

Usha Uthup

work, Karnataka); Shri Kanubhai Hasmukhbhai Tailor (Social work, Gujarat); Shri Anant Darshan Shankar (Public Affairs, Karnataka); Prof. M. Annamalai (Science and Engineering, Karnataka); Dr. Mahesh Haribhai Mehta (Science and Engineering-Agricultural Science, Gujarat); Shri Coimbatore Narayana Rao Raghavendran (Science and Engineering, Tamil Nadu); Dr. (Mrs.) Suman Sahai (Science and Engineering, Delhi); Prof.(Dr.) E.A. Siddiq (Science and Engineering - Agricultural Science, Andhra Pradesh); Shri Gopalan Nair Shankar (Science and Engineering - Architecture, Kerala); Shri Mecca Rafeeque Ahmed (Trade and Industry, Tamil Nadu); Shri Kailasam Raghavendra Rao (Trade and Industry, Tamil Nadu); Shri Narayan Singh Bhati (Civil Services, Andhra Pradesh); Shri P K Sen (Civil Services, Bihar); Ms. Shital Mahajan (Sports – Adventure Sports- Para Jumping, Maharashtra); Ms. Nameirakpam Kunjarani Devi (Sports – Weightlifting, Ma-

N. Kunjarani Devi

The Smallest Army

Vatican's Swiss Guards form the smallest any. In 2006 it had 110 active guards. The Guards were created in 1506. The Guardsmen are over 5'8" tall.

nipur); Shri Sushil Kumar (Sports –Wrestling, Delhi); Shri. Vangipurapu Venkata Sai Laxman (Sports–Cricket, Andhra Pradesh); Shri Gagan Narang (Sports – Shooting, Andhra Pradesh); Smt. Krishna Poonia Sports – Discus Throw Rajasthan; Shri Harbhajan Singh (Sports – Mountaineering, Punjab); Dr. Pukhraj Bafna (Medicine – Paedeatrics, Chhattisgarh); Prof. Mansoor Hasan (Medicine- Cardiology, Uttar Pradesh); Dr. Shyama Prasad Mandal (Medicine – Orthopaedics, Delhi); Prof. (Dr.) Sivapatham Vittal (Medicine – Endocrinology, Tamil Nadu); Prof. (Dr.) Madanur Ahmed Ali (Medicine

Indira Hinduja

– Gastroenterology, Tamil Nadu); Dr. Indira Hinduja (Medicine – Obstetrics and Gynaecology, Maharashtra); Dr. Jose Chacko Periappuram (Medicine – Cardio-Thoracic Surgery, Kerala); Prof. (Dr.) A. Marthanda Pillai (Medicine – Neurosurgery, Kerala); Shri Mahim Bora (Literature and Education, Assam); Prof. (Dr.) Pullella Srirama Chandrudu (Literature and Education- Sanskrit, Andhra Pradesh); Dr. Pravin Darji (Literature and Education, Gujarat); Dr. Chandra Prakash Deval (Literature and Education, Rajasthan); Shri Balraj Komal (Literature and Education, Delhi); Mrs. Rajni Kumar (Literature and Education, Delhi); Dr. Devanooru Mahadeva (Literature and Education, Karnataka); Shri Barun Mazumder (Literature and Education, West Bengal); Dr. Avvai Natarajan (Literature and Education, Tamil Nadu); Shri Bhalchandra Nemade (Literature and Education, Himachal Pradesh); Prof. Riyaz Punjabi (Literature and Education, Jammu and Kashmir); Prof. Koneru Ramakrishna Rao (Literature and Education, Andhra Pradesh); Ms. Buangi Sailo (Literature and Education, Mizoram); Prof. Devi Dutt Sharma (Literature and Education, Uttarakhand); Shri Nilamber Dev Sharma (Literature and Education, Jammu and Kashmir); Ms. Urvashi Butalia

(Literature and Education, Delhi); Ms. Ritu Menon (Literature and Education, Delhi); Prof. Krishna Kumar (Literature and Education, Delhi); Shri Deviprasad Dwivedi (Literature and Education, Uttar Pradesh); Ms. Mamang Dai (Literature

Urvashi Butalia

and Education, Arunachal Pradesh); Dr. Om Prakash Agrawal (Others – Heritage Conservation, Uttar Pradesh); Prof. Madhukar Keshav Dhavalikar (Others – Archaeology, Maharashtra); Ms. Shanti Teresa Lakra (Others-Nursing, Andaman & Nicobar); Smt. Gulshan Nanda (Others – Handicrafts promotion, Delhi); Dr. Azad Moopen (Social work, UAE*); Prof. Upendra Baxi (Public Affairs -Legal Affairs, United Kingdom*); Dr. Mani Lal Bhaumik (Science and Engineering, USA *); Dr. Subra Suresh (Science and Engineering,USA *); Prof. Karl Harrington Potter (Literature and Education, USA*); Prof. Martha Chen (Social work, USA*); Shri Satpal Khattar (Trade and Industry, Singapore*); Shri Granville Austin (Literature and Education, USA*)

Note: * indicates awardees in the category of Foreigners / NRIs/ PIOs/ Posthumous.

Films

International

BAFTA Award: Film: *The King's Speech;* **Actor:** Colin Firth; **Actress:** Natalie Portman.
83rd Oscar Academy Award Winners 2011: Actor in a Leading Role: Colin Firth, *The King's Speech;* **Actor in a Supporting Role:** Christian Bale (*The Fighter*);

Natalie Portman

Actress in a Leading Role: Natalie Portman (*Black Swan*); **Actress in a Supporting Role:** Melissa Leo (*The Fighter*); **Animated Feature Film:** Lee Unkrich (*Toy Story 3*); **Art Direction: Product Design:** Robert Stromberg **Set Decoration:** Karen O,Hara; **Movie:** Alice in Wonderland; **Cinematography:** Wally Pisher (*Inception*); **Costume Design:** Colleen Atwood (*Alice in Wonderland*); **Directing:** Tom Hooper (*The King's Speech*); **Documentary (Feature):** Charles Ferguson and Audrey Marrs (Inside Job); **Documentary (Short Subject):** Karen Goodman and Kirk Simon (Strangers No More); **Film Editing:** Angus Wall and Kirk Baxter (The Social Network); **Foreign Language Film:** Denmark (*In a Better World*); **Makeup:** Rick Baker and Dave Elsey (*The Wolfman*); **Music (Original Score):** Trent Reznor and Atticus Ross (The Social Network); **Music (Original Song):** We belong Together by Randy Newman (*Toy Story 3*); **Picture:** Iain Canning, Emile Sherman and Gareth Unwin, Producers; (*The King's Speech*); **Short Film (Animated):** Shaun Tan and Andrew Ruhemann (*The Last Thing*); **Short Film (Live Action):** Luke Matheny (*God of Love*); **Sound Editing:** Richard King (*Inception*); **Sound Mixing:** Lora Hirschberg, Gary A Rizzo and Ed Novick (*Inception*); **Visual Effects:** Paul Franklin,Chris Corbould, Andrew Lockley and Peter Bebb (*Inception*); **Writing (Adapted Screenplay):** Aaron Sorkin (The Social network); **Writing (Original Screenplay):** David Seidler (*The King's Speech*).

Tom Hooper

Hollywood Star: Simon Fuller, the British creator of hit TV show *American Idol* wins star on the Hollywood Walk of Fame.

Cannes Festival: Palm d'Or to Terrence Malick's *The Tree of Life*.

National

58th National Film Award: Best Actor: Dhanush (*Aadukalam*/Tamil) & Salim Kumar (*Adhaminde Magan Abu*/Malayalam); **Supporting Actor:** Thambi Rammayya (*Myna*/Tamil); **Supporting Actress:** Saranya (*Thenmerku Paruvakaatru*/Tamil); **Director:** Vetrimaaran (*Aadukalam*/Tamil); **Movie:** *Adhaminde Magan Abu* (Malayalam); **Male Playback Singer:** Suresh Wadekar; **Female Playback Singer:** Rekha Bharathwaj; **Lyricist:** Vairamuthu *(Thenmerku Paruvakaatru*/Tamil); **Regional Movie/Tamil :** *Thenmerku Paruvakaatru*; **Screenplay (Original):** Vetrimaaran (*Aadukalam*/ Tamil); **Choreography:** Dineshkumar (*Aadukalam*/Tamil); **Music Director:** Vishal Bharath-

Saranya

Rajani and Aiswarya

waj; **Background Score:** Isac Thomas Kottakapalli (*Adhaminde Magan Abu*/ Malayalam); **Special Effects:** *Endhiran*/ Tamil; **Art Direction:** Sabu Cyril (*Endhi-*

ran/Tamil); **Regional Movie/Hindi:** *Do Dooni Chaar;* **Cinematographer:** Madhu Ambat; **Entertaining Movie:** *Dabangg*/Hindi; **Child Artist:** Arsh Mayyar

12th IIFA Awards: Dabangg wins six trophies in the popular category. Best actro and direction Awards to Shah Rukh Khan and Karan Johar for *My Name is Khan*.

Literature

International

Scotiabank Griller Prize: Johanna Skibsrud for her novel *The Sentimentalists*. $50,000.

Costa Book Award: (Britain): Maggie O'Farrell, novelist of the year (*The Hand That First Held Mine*); Kishwar Desai for best debut novel (*Witness the Night*).

International Award (Chaudhuri Memorial) in Literature: Khaled Husseini. US $100,000.

Orange Prize for Fiction: Tea Obrehat, Serbain-American, writer for his debut novel *The Tiger's Wife*.

Music & Arts

National

Sangeet Natak Akademi Award Fellowship: Girija Devi & Nataraj Ramkrishna. $10,000.

Science & Technology

National

SASTRA-Ramanujan Award: Prof. Wei Zhang of Harvard.

TOYP World Award for Medical Innovation (Junior Chamber): Dr. Gifty Immanuel, Tuticorin - based Indian physician.

Infosys Prizes: Prof. Chandrasekhar Khare (Mathematical Sciences), Prof. Sandip Trivedi (Physical Sciences), Prof. Ashutosh Sharma (Engg. & Computer Sciences), Chetan Chitnis (Life sciences), Prof. Amita Baviskar and Prof. Nandini Sundar (Social Sciences)

Rs. 50 lakh.

Lifetime Achievement Award of Department of Atomic Energy: N. Srinivasan

Peace & Humanism

International

Confucius Peace Prize: Lien Chan, Taiwanese politician.

Lien Chan

Miscellaneous

International

Pravasi Bharatiya Samman Award 2011: Sri Lankan industrialist Mano Selvanathan.

Freedom of the City of London: Alastair Cook.

MacArthur Award for Creative and Effective Institutions: Action Research & Training for Health, Rajasthan. $350,000.

Alastair Cook

Ernst Young Awards, 2010: Entrepreneur of the Year: Dilip Sanghvi (Sun Pharma).

Lifetime Achievement Award: Brijmohan Lall Mujal (Hero Honda).

Radcliffe Institute Medal (Harvard Uni-

Pulitzer Prizes

Joseph Pulitzer was a Hungarian-born American newspaper publisher. The Pulitzer Prize for Reporting is the oldest prize given in journalism and was first awarded in 1917.

Angela Merkel

versity): Ela Bhatt, founder of SEVA.
Best Retail Bank (Asian Banker): HDFC Bank, the second largest private bank in India.
Merlin Award, 2011 (International Magicians Society): Gopinath Muthukad.

Jawaharlal Nehru Award for International Understanding: Angela Merkel

Man Booker International : Philip Roth, Portnoy's Complaint. $100,000.

Gwangju Award for Human Rights, 2011: Binayak Sen

National Spelling Bee, USA: Sukanya Roy, 14-year-old Indian American for Spelling 'cymotrichous'.

Templeton Prize, 2011: Martin Rees, British astrophysicist for career achivements affirming life's spiritual dimension. £1 m., the world's largest award to an individual.

National
Global Vision Award (Asia Society): Mukesh Ambani
SCOPE Award: Gold trophy to A.R. Choudhury, NTPC chairman.
Best Bank Award (Business World): South Indian Bank.

Rabindranath Tagore Memorial Prize (IIPM): Rampada Choudhuri. 1.15 m. Euros.
Tagore Memorial Peace Prize: Irom Chami Sharmila for her struggle for peace in Manipur. Rs. 50 lakhs.
Bharatiya Manavata Vikas Puraskar (IIPM) for Social Contribution: Binayak Sen and wife Ilina Sen. Rs. 5 lakh each.

Kanishtha Dhankar

Crystal Award: A.R. Rahman.
President's Medal of Royal College of Psychiatrists: E.S. Krishnamoorthy, Chennai.
Decent Work Research Prize of ILO: Economist Jayati Ghosh (JNU) and Prof. Eve Landon. $5000.

Miss India: Kanishtha Dhankar
Phalke Award, 2010: K. Balachander
Mercy Ravi 'Woman of Substance' Award: Sheila Dikshit
Rajiv Gandhi Khel Ratna Award, 2011: Gagan Narang

Gagan Narang

Records

Most Expensive Suit: On Dec. 9, 2010, Dormeuil Mode launched in New Delhi a suit priced at Rs. 51 lakh, the world's most expensive suit.

Most Expensive Christmas Tree: A Xmas tree costing $11 m. was unveiled at Abu Dhabi's Emirates Palace hotel in Dec. 2010. The 43-foot fanx fir has 131 ornaments including precious stones.

Rich in Wives: Ziona Chana, 66, lives in a Mountainous village in Mizoram with his 39 wives, 94 children and 33 grand children. He is the head of a local Christian religious sect 'the Chana', which allows polygamy.

The Tallest Celebrity At 7.3 ft, actor Peter Mayhew is the tallest celebrity in Hollywood. He is popular for his role as Chewbacca Wookie.

Most Expensive Fish: A 754-pound bluefin tuna was sold for $396,000 at the Tsukiji fish market auction in Tokyo, a few days before the tsunmai struck.

The Longest Sausage: Italian Aberto Della Pelle created a sausage 597.8m. long in the main street in Penne. Previous record was 392 m. made by a Romanian.

Most Premature Baby: A German woman gave birth to a one-pound baby after and 21 weeks & 5 days of pregnancy, making it the world's most premature baby ro survive the child Frieda down on Nov. 7, 2010 was only 460 gm. and measured 28 cm.

Father at 72: Ian McMean, 72, becomes Britain's oldest father, for his wife, 30 years younger to him, gives birth to a baby girl in Feb. 2011.

A Stinky Giant: A giant stinky Titan Arum has bloomed in the botanical garden of the University of Basel, Switzerland. It blossons for the first five in 17 years.

Highest Paid Child Star: Will Smith's son Jaden is the highest paid child star after earning £2 m. for 'Karate Kid'.

Jaden Smith

Oscar Awards

1928	Wings
1929	The Broadway Melody
1930	All Quiet on the Western Front
1931	Cimarron, RKO Radio
1932	Grand Hote
1933	Cavalcade
1934	It Happened One Night
1935	Mutiny on the Bounty
1936	The Great Ziegfeld
1937	The Life of Emile Zola
1938	You Can't Take It with You
1939	Gone with the Wind
1940	Rebecca
1941	How Green Was My Valley
1942	Mrs. Miniver
1943	Casablanca
1944	Going My Way
1945	The Lost Weekend
1946	The Best Years of Our Lives
1947	Gentleman's Agreement
1948	Hamlet
1949	All the King's Men
1950	All About Eve
1951	An American in Paris
1952	The Greatest Show on Earth
1953	From Here to Elemity
1954	On the Waterfront
1955	Marty
1956	Around the World in 80 Days
1957	The Bridge on the River Kwai
1958	Gigi
1959	Ben-Hur
1960	The Apartment
1961	West Side Story
1962	Lawrence of Arabia
1963	Tom Jones
1964	My Fair Lady

A scene from 'The Hurt Locker'

The Oscar

The Oscars, officially known as the Academy of Motion Picture Arts and Science Awards, were inaugurated in 1928. Members (now over 3,000) are divided into 13 branches, each branch selecting up to five nominees for awards in its area.

A scene from 'The King's Speech'

1965	The Sound of Music
1966	A Man for All Seasons
1967	In the Heat of the Night
1968	Oliver!
1969	Midnight Cowboy
1970	Patton
1971	The French Connection
1972	The Godfather
1973	The Sting
1974	The Godfather
1975	One Flew Over the Cuckoo's Nest
1976	Rocky
1977	Annie Hall
1978	The Deer Hunter
1979	Kramer vs. Kramer
1980	Ordinary People
1981	Chariots of Fire
1982	Gandhi
1983	Terms of Endearment
1984	Amadeus
1985	Out of Africa
1986	Platoon
1987	The Last Emperor
1988	Rain Man
1989	Driving Miss Daisy
1990	Dances With Wolves
1991	The Silence of the Lambs
1992	Unforgiven
1993	Schindler's List
1994	Forrest Gump
1995	Braveheart
1996	The English Patient
1997	Titanic
1998	Shakespeare in Love
1999	American Beauty
2000	Gladiator
2001	A Beautiful Mind
2002	Chicago
2003	The Lord of the Rings : The Return of the King
2004	Million Dollar Baby
2005	Crash
2006	The Departed
2007	No Country For Old Man
2008	Slumdog Millionaire
2009	The Hurt Locker
2010	The King's Speech

India: The First 10 Best Films

Feature Film : Gold Medal / Swarna Kamal

Year	Name of the Film	Language	Director
1953	Shyamchi Aai	Marathi	P.K. Atre
1954	Mirza Ghalib	Hindi	Sohrab Modi
1 955	Pather Panchali	Bengali	Satyajit Ray
1956	Kabuliwala	Bengali	Tapan Sinha
1957	Do Ankhen Barah Haath	Hindi	V. Shantharam
1958	Sagar Sangame	Bengali	Debaki Kumar Bose
1959	Apur Sansar	Bengali	Satyajit Ray
1960	Anuradha	Hindi	Hrishikesh Mukherji
1961	Bhagini Nivedita	Bengali	Bejoy Bose
1962	Dada Thakur	Bengali	Sudhir Mukherji

First Indian Film

On May 18, 1912, R.G, Torney's Pundalik was released at Coronation Cinematograph in Bombay. It was the first real attempt at an Indian feature film, but it was shot by foreign technicians and the duration of the film was only 12 minutes.

Crisis Management

Bimal Balakrishnan, PhD
Assistant Professor,
Department of Architectural Studies, University of Missouri

Natural calamities and man-made disasters call for emergency crisis management. We should have a multi-disciplinary approach to improve our understanding of the problem.

In a world that is increasingly connected by electronic media, we have seen many crises play out in real-time. These include the recent accident at the Fukushima Dai-ichi nuclear power plant, the 2008 terrorist attacks in Mumbai and the September 11 attacks in United States, the 2004 Indian Ocean tsunami, hurricane Katrina in the United States and recent earthquakes in China, Pakistan and Iran among others. While some of these are natural calamities, others are man-made. During times of crisis, citizens look up to their government for assistance as well as guidance. Responses to crisis situations involve allocation of appropriate resources over a specific geographic area and within a specific timeframe to prevent the situation from escalating. Allocation of resources must be coordinated to maintain control and ensure efficiency. We have made rapid strides in emergency crisis management in recent years. However, a critical examination of responses to recent crisis situations suggests room for further improvement. Some of the critical issues in crisis management and considerations within the Indian context are discussed below.

The Disaster Management Act (2005)

The Disaster Management Act of 2005 and the National Policy on Disaster Management provides the vision and organizational foundation for disaster management in India. The Disaster Management Act of 2005

envisioned the creation of a National Disaster Management Authority (NDMA), State Disaster Management Authorities (SDMAs) and District Disaster Management Authorities (DDMAs). Each of these authorities has access to unique expertise and resources. The DMA thus takes an integrated approach to disaster management in India integrating relevant authorities at the district, state, and national level. The National Policy on Disaster Management takes a more long-term strategic approach to disaster management. The new approach emphasizes a prevention, mitigation and preparedness-driven approach instead of a relief-centered approach that was common prior to the Disaster Management Act of 2005. The national policy identifies various institutions and agencies at the central, state and district levels and ascertains their roles in disas-

Huge Disasters	The Fukushima Daichi disaster was compared with the accident that occurred at America's Three Mile Island in 1979 and at Ukraine's Chernobyl in 1986.

ter management based on their expertise. Many details are still being worked out and many of the envisioned strategies are still to be tested. Comprehensive disaster management in India is still in a nascent stage and faces many challenges. The national policy document identifies potential calamities and lays out broad strategies to combat those. The strength of any crisis management policy lies in its ability to guide action on the ground. Some real-world challenges in crisis management are identified next.

Critical Issues and Challenges in Crisis Management

Maintaining critical infrastructure and human resources. It is easy to see the role of governmental institutions like the army, police or firefighters in crisis management. Agencies like the NDMA cannot easily identify and develop contingency plans for every organization that will be involved in crisis response and recovery acts. It is important to develop contingency plans for critical institutions, whether they are governmental or private. Various agencies that have important roles in crisis response should develop plans on their own for their continued operations during a time of crisis. It is important that these institutions decentralize operations (including human resources) and build system redundancies for their information infrastructure to ensure continuity of operations. Crisis management planning should develop strategies to ensure stability of the information and communication infrastructure for entities that are important to the nation, even though they play a limited role in immediate crisis management. For example, the economic loss that would result from lost productivity due to a crisis is substantial for a critical entity like the stock exchange. However, the cost of maintaining back up of critical data and software applications is relatively modest.

Maintaining a common operational picture

A disaster management plan does not directly translate to successful crisis management operations on the ground. One should see the national policy on disaster management as a broad strategy and crisis management as a series of tactical operations responding to conditions on the ground [4]. Effective response to a crisis situation often requires multiple agencies, each with its own hierarchical structure and organizational and operational culture. An important challenge during any crisis response is to maintain a common operational picture among the various agencies and the stakeholders. This is important to achieve the strategic goals envisioned in a given disaster management plan. A functioning telecommunication infrastructure and a clear understanding of communication processes is a necessary foundation for crisis management. This is needed to coordinate allocation of appropriate resources to control the crisis effectively. To maintain a common operational picture, the communication processes and the nature of information flow is equally important. It is critical to take into account the nature of information flows within each agency and between agencies as well as the to and fro communication between different agencies and the public. Many technological, sociological and organizational challenges have been identified with respect to communication, which hinder the formation of an effective common operational picture. These include rapid deployment of communication infrastructure, multi-agency interoperability of radio channels, issues of trust and credibility between ad-hoc response teams, inter-organizational compatibility, and compressed decision times for agencies which normally require multi level approval for decisions.

Need For Flexibility In Crisis Management Strategies

Investment in organizational design is often given greater priority than investment in resources and training for personnel involved in crisis management. Each crisis event is unique and crisis management planners tend to emphasize control over possible crisis situations through administrative structures such as those outlined in the NDMP. However, our recent experiences indicate that the interaction between urban systems (communication, transportation and physical infrastructure) and human behavior in the aftermath of a disaster is extremely complex. These interactions cannot be entirely foreseen leading to gaps between policy and practice. Crisis management is often perceived as the job of government, whether at district, state or central level. An effective management plan should take into account additional levels of granularity – household, residential neighborhoods and workplace. Each level has the capacity for specific actions to reduce risk during a disaster and should be empowered through information and training. Disaster management is often takes a top-down information communication and control with limited thoughts on bottom up information flow from victims as well as responders on the ground. Communication networks and protocol should allow for multi-directional information flow and should take into account bottom-up information and communication.

The recent national policy on disaster management appears to emphasize planning for natural disasters compared to security threats such as terrorism. Emergency situations such as the 2008 terrorist attacks in Mumbai or the serial blasts in 1993 have shown the need for coordinated efforts from first responders. While special military or paramilitary forces are often entrusted with the task of dealing with the threat from insurgents, concerted supporting action is required from police, fire fighters and emergency medical personnel. In such situations, events rapidly evolve and crisis management requires a more flexible approach. A more nimble approach through networking of organizations that engage in informed action and emphasizing continual and adaptive learning is better suited here. Shortcomings in dealing with the 2008 Mumbai terrorist attacks reveal the limitations of crisis management structures developed primarily with the view of natural disasters.

The national policy on disaster management guides the formulation of disaster management plans at the local, state and national levels. Disaster management plans should be seen as a living document reflecting the current state of knowledge regarding crisis management. The national policy gives priority to institutional capacity building for identifying and training personnel. This should be complemented by developing performance measures and benchmarks. Academic institutions and research organizations can play an important role in further improving our understanding of crisis management from multiple perspectives – organizational and behavior psychology, team cognition, logistics and supply chain management to name a few. Governmen-

> Disaster management plans should be seen as a living document reflecting the current state of knowledge regarding crisis management.

tal agencies and private foundations can provide incentives and grants to facilitate the research. Academic institutions have experts from diverse disciplines with already established inter-disciplinary connections. Academic faculty from disciplines such as architecture and structural design can also play a valuable service in post disaster assessment operations. For example, they could assist with visual inspection of building for structural safety for buildings that are partially damaged during an earthquake or a tornado.

Visual Analytics and Geo-collaboration tools

In any crisis management situation, the response team needs to maintain an overall situation awareness regarding events that are unfolding and resources at any given team's disposal. A key challenge here is the management of information to gain immediate insight. This is important for co-ordination of action, allocation of appropriate resources to the correct geographic location in a timely fashion. Enhanced communication infrastructure including cellular phones and wireless equipment often result in information overload bringing a new complexity to crisis management. In the NDMA, agencies such as the National Remote Sensing Agency are identified as key players who can bring in relevant expertise. Crisis situations often present experts from these agencies complex, non-routine challenges that require complex analytical reasoning and sense making skills. Crisis management leaders have to monitor a large number of unfolding events triggered by the crisis, recognize patterns and make resource allocation decisions. This places a huge burden on their mental capacity to process information and make meaningful decisions.

Advanced geographic information systems (GIS), remote sensing data, building information modeling (BIM) tools and interactive digital tools are all seen as powerful tools for crisis management. Integrating these tools and interactive technologies to aid analytical reasoning and decision-making during crisis situations is a challenge. Visual analytics, an emerging field, seeks to answer this specific challenge. Visual analytics is defined as "the science of analytical reasoning facilitated by visual interactive interfaces". The science of visual analytics aims to integrate advances in visual representations and interaction technologies, data visualization as well as decision and behavior sciences to support analytical reasoning and decision-making. Visual analytic techniques help to gain insight from abstract information by revealing trends and hidden patterns. It is vital that we make a long-term strategic investment in development of visual analytic tools and technologies. Emergency Operations Centers should have state-of-the-art capabilities for visual analytics for disaster management operations. One should note that social and cultural factors have a strong influence on representational conventions as well as decision-making. So the development of these tools and technologies should be rooted in the Indian context.

In summary, the National Policy on Disaster Management as envisioned in the act of 2005 outlines organizational structure for disaster management, identifies relevant agencies for specific situations and outlines the vision for capacity building. It is important to see this policy as a broad and flexible strategy that can be adapted depending on a given crisis situation. We should take a multi-dimensional, multi-disciplinary approach to improve our understanding of crisis management. We need long-term strategic investments in developing geo-collaboration and visual analytic tools to improve co-ordination and collaboration between agencies involved in crisis management. We also need to invest in both communication infrastructure and communication protocol at national, state and local levels to ensure effective management of crisis situations.

References:

http://www.ndmindia.nic.in/acts-rules/ Disaster Management Act 2005.pdf, Retrieved May 1, 2011.

http://nidm.gov.in/PDF/policies/ndm_policy2009.pdf, Retrieved May 1, 2011.

Seifert, J. W. (2002). The effects of September 11, 2001, terrorist attacks on public and private information infrastructures: a preliminary assessment of lessons learned, Government Information Quarterly, 19, 225-242.

Quarantelli, E. L. (1988). Disaster crisis management: a summary of research findings, Journal of Management Studies, 25 (4), 373-385.

Manoj, B.S., & Baker, A. H. (2007). Communication challenges in emergency response, Communications of the ACM, 50(3), 51-53.

Comfort, L. K., & Haase, T.W. (2006). Communication, coherence and collective action: The impact of hurricane Katrina on communications infrastructure, Public Works Management & Policy, 10(4), 328-343.

Comfort, L. K. (2005). Risk, security, and disaster management, Annual Review of Political Science, 8, 335-356.

Thomas, J. J., & Cook, K. A. (2005). Illuminating the Path: The Research and Development Agenda for Visual Analytics, Retrieved November 8, 2007 from HYPERLINK "http://nvac.pnl.gov/agenda.stm"http://nvac.pnl.govagenda.stm, 2006.

Nisbett, R. E. (2003). The geography of thought: How Asians and Westerners think differently...and why. New York: Free Press. ∎

Fukushima Nuclear Accident: Lessons for India

Dr K S Parthasarathi
Raja Ramanna Fellow, Department of Atomic Energy, Mumbai

India's nuclear safety is being reviewed in the context of the Japanese tragedy. Studies have been initiated to review the capability of Indian nuclear plants to withstand earthquakes and tsunamis.

Indian scientists and engineers reviewed the status of nuclear safety of Indian nuclear power plants in the light of the accident at the Fukushima nuclear power plant in Japan. Admittedly, a closer look was necessary for reactors of earlier vintage. The first two nuclear power reactors at Tarapur Atomic Power Station (TAPS 1&2) went commercial in 1969. Are these Indian reactors safe?

Safety of Indian reactors has been under constant review. When TAPS 1&2 completed 32 years of operation, Atomic Energy Regulatory Board (AERB) directed Nuclear Power Corporation of India Limited (NPCIL) to assess comprehensively the actual condition of the plant vis-à-vis the current safety requirements.

AERB reviewed the operating experience, ageing management programme and assessed the residual life of all safety related components and systems of these reactors. Subsequently, AERB included seismic re-evaluation also, as part of the review.

NPCIL and AERB used the safety report INSAG 8 titled "Common Basis for Judging Safety of Nuclear Power Plants (NPPs) Built to Earlier Standards" of International Atomic Energy Agency (IAEA) and NUREG 800 issued by US-NRC as the standard review plan along with AERB documents for the analysis

They verified whether adequate redundancy and diversity is provided for the safety systems of TAPS and considered defence-in-depth, physical and functional separation of components and common cause failure vulnerabilities.

AERB reviewed the seismic re-evaluation of structures, systems and components of TAPS 1 & 2, carried out by NPCIL using IAEA Safety Reports Series No. 28 on 'Seismic re-evaluation of existing nuclear power plants'. NPCIL remedied the shortfalls.

During the planned shutdown between October 2005 and February 2006, NPCIL implemented several safety upgrades. These included the installation of three new diesel generators of higher capacity and unit-wise segregation of power supplies to avoid common cause failures; segregation of some other shared systems such as those for shutdown cooling and fuel pool

Worst Disaster in 65 Years	It was Japan's worst disaster in 65 years after the end of the Second World War. A deadly tsunami (the word itself is Japanese) struck the country's north east coast on March 11, 2011, set off by the largest earthquake in the nation's history.

cooling; addition of an independent set Control Rod Drive pumps to strengthen the emergency feed water supply to the reactor; addition of a supplementary control room and extensive up-gradation of fire protection system.

Since NPCIL addressed the outstanding safety issues satisfactorily, AERB determined that the reactors are safe to operate and renewed their authorization for operation in February 2006.

AERB has set up a specialist committee to review the capability of Indian nuclear power plants to withstand earthquakes and other external events such as tsunami, cyclones etc..

NPCIL set up committees to review the safety of TAPS 1&2. and other reactors. As a short term measure, NPCIL will augment regular training for emergency operating procedures, mock up drills, disaster management training and make provisions for self sufficiency at site for 7 days without any external help.

As the primary containment volume to power ratio for TAPS 1&2 is ten times more than that of Fukushima-Daiichi Unit 1, pressure will build up more slowly in TAPS 1&2. Passive system for decay heat removal is adequate to cool the reactor core in 8 hours. TAPS has procedures in place to handle complete loss of power at site.

As a matter of abundant caution, NPCIL may inert the containment of TAPS with nitrogen to prevent hydrogen explosions. Hydrogen explosions due to metal water reactions caused significant damage at Fukushima.

Though the probability of occurrence of a tsunami and severe earthquake at Tarapur site is negligible, NPCIL decided to improve the reliability of power supply, raise tsunami resistant walls around emergency diesel generators and tanks, provide mobile diesel generators (DG) inside the plant, relocate station black out DG at higher elevation, and make provisions for power supply from CNG/GAS generators outside the plant through overhead cables.

NPCIL plans to provide water sources, suction from intake canal, underground raw water tank and an overhead tank away from site to ensure reliable core cooling, other measures include provision for coolant injection into feed waterlines, reactor pressure vessel, drywell and suppression pool and secondary side inventory. NPCIL will address issues related to hydrogen management and passive recombiners. Taking a cue from Fukushima, NPCIL will also review the arrangements for spent-fuel pool management

Safety of other nuclear power reactors

The designers of Indian NPPs followed seismic safety principles even when a high intensity event has a low probability of occurrence. The Nuclear Power Corporation of India Limited (NPCIL) has installed seismic sensors at all plants as stipulated by the Atomic Energy Regulatory Board (AERB)

In India, specialists examining the site will accept it for constructing a nuclear power plant only after analyzing the seismic inputs from various agencies Indian standard code IS 1893 "Criteria for earthquake resistant design of structures" categorises the country into four seismic zones and specifies the maximum possible earth quake in each zone. Forces to which the structure may be subjected to during an earthquake may be larger than those specified in the standard. The structures have a lot of reserve that is not considered in the design. All earthquakes of magnitude 8 and above occurred in zone V.

The Atomic Energy Regulatory Board (AERB) has issued a "Code Practice on Safety in Nuclear Power Plant Siting". The Code prescribes the criteria for selection of sites for nuclear power plants and addresses the impact of natural events such as earthquakes, shore line erosion, flooding etc and man-induced events such as aircraft crash, chemical explosions, toxic gas releases and oil slick.

AERB will evaluate the general seismic

| Fifth Largest Quake | The 9.00 magnitude quake which for than two minutes rocked the Tohoku region of the Honshu island, about 400 kilometers northeast of Tokyo, the capital, was the fifth-largest in the world in more than a century. It was followed by more than 40 aftershocks. |

intensity expected for earthquakes in the region by considering the seismic history and its potential as well as geological characteristics of the region. Historical data relating to the past earthquakes in the tectonic province covering an area of about 300 km radius around the site in which the proposed plant has to be located should be collected.

As per the existing norm, nuclear power plants (NPP) shall not be constructed at sites falling above Zone 4. AERB prohibits construction of NPPs at sites with a fault located within 5 km.

The designers estimate the seismic parameters for nuclear power plant structures conservatively. The analysis and design of these structures follow internationally accepted standards.

As the nuclear power reactors at Narora are at seismic zone 4, they have been designed by accepting a value of 0.3g for the peak ground acceleration. A value of 0.1 g is taken for the reactors at Rajasthan and for other reactors a peak acceleration value of 0.2 g is taken.

Nuclear power plants are the most seismically hardened structures in the country.

The nuclear power plants at Kakrapar, Narora, and Rawatbhata operated normally during the Bhuj earthquake (6.9 on the Richter scale) on January 26, 2001.These plants experienced levels of vibration much below those for which they have been designed.

Tsunami

The Madras Atomic Power Station (MAPS) withstood the tsunami disaster which hit the east coast of India on the morning of December 26, 2004. Unit -2 was operating at 215 MWe while Unit 1 was under long shut down.

The damage caused by tsunami was limited only to the peripheral areas such as damage to the cement –brick wall at the plant periphery and inundation of roads on the east side of the turbine building. After detailed review AERB permitted operation of the unit on January 1, 2005.

There was no loss of life or any significant loss of property due to tsunami. Radiation levels in and around the plant were found to be normal.Vital areas such as the reactor building, turbine and service building. switch yard, water treatment plant etc were unaffected by the tsunami

Kudankulam reactors have an elevation of 7.5 metre above the mean sea level to take care of a potential tsunami. For Prototype Fast Breeder Reactor (PFBR) being constructed at Kalpakkam, the elevation is 9 metre. For Jaitapur, the elevation above mean sea level is about 25 metre. After excavation the elevation will be 16 metre.

Specialists believe that these elevations are more than adequate to take care of potential tsunamis.

Some design features of PHWRs

On March 31, 1993, a serious fire incident occurred at the Narora Atomic Power Station. There was a "black out"(loss of all power supplies) for 17 hrs. Thermo -siphoning took place.

Thermo- siphon refers to a method of heat exchange based on natural convection which circulates liquid without the necessity of a mechanical pump. During the incident, there was no fuel failures or related consequences. Based on this experience NPCIL initiated remedial actions to prevent such incidents in all reactors.

Pressurized Heavy Water (PHWR) of 220 MW capacity has an inventory of 210 tonnes of heavy water; besides this, the calandria vault has about 500 tonnes of ordinary water. Large inventory of heavy water and light water will serve as a possible heat sink in a loss of coolant accident. Not withstanding these features, reactor designers and operators of Indian reactors and others elsewhere will review the Fukushima accident for ensuring safety of nuclear power reactors worldwide.

In the wake of the accident at the Fukushima Atomic Power Station, AERB set up a specialist committee to review the capability of Indian Nuclear Power Plants to withstand earthquakes and other external events such as tsunamis, cyclones, floods, etc. The committee will examine the aadequacy of provisions available to ensure safety in case of such events, both within and beyond design basis. NPCIL has also set up its own committee to review the safety of Indian NPPs. ■

Mayapuri Radiation Accident

On April 7, 2010 (afternoon),the Atomic Energy Regulatory Board (AERB) received a message that a 32 year old, metal scrap dealer with suspected radiation injuries was admitted to a leading hospital in Delhi. On investigation, the officers from AERB found high levels of radiation and some contaminated scrap in a scrap dealer's shop at Mayapuri, Delhi. They segregated the scrap, shielded it with available steel plates, cordoned off the area and informed the Crisis Management Group (CMG), Department of Atomic Energy (DAE).

Later investigation revealed that seven persons who handled radiation sources dismantled from a radiation device suffered radiation injuries. Their radiation doses ranged from 0.4 to 3.7 Gy.(Gy is a unit of radiation dose; the absorbed dose is one Gy when the radiation energy absorbed in material is one Joule per kg)

One person, named Rajender Prasad, aged 35, succumbed to radiation injuries on April 26, 2010; This may be the first radiation death in India. Others were discharged from the hospitals on various dates, last one being on May 24, 2010.

A team of officers of AERB, Bhabha Atomic Research Centre (BARC), Nuclear Power Corporation (NPCIL), National Disaster Response Force (NDRF) and police located the sources, identified it as Coblat-60 and recovered all sources present in the shop. The team sent them safely in a shielded container to Narora Atomic Power Station (NAPS) for secure storage. On further monitoring, the team recovered more sources on April 14.

The team carried out radiation survey in about 800 shops. On April 16, 2010 information was received that one more person has been admitted to a hospital of Delhi with localized radiation injury. The team recovered the source from the wallet of the injured person and transported it safely in a shielded container to Narora Atomic Power Station (NAPS). Scientists from AERB and the Board of Radiation and Isotope Technology (BRIT) inspected the recovered sources and source cage stored at NAPS and confirmed that the 48 slot cage and source pencils belong to a Gamma Cell which was not manufactured in India.

On April 28, 2010, an AERB officer traced the origin of the Gamma Cell (GC) with the help of local police and inputs provided by the victims admitted at the hospital in Delhi. In 1969, the Delhi University imported the gamma cell (GC 220) from Atomic Energy Canada Limited (AECL) using the funds available from the Ford Foundation Assistance Programme.

The University auctioned the GC 220, on February 26, 2010. A scrap dealer of Mayapuri, purchased it. Local workers dismantled it. GC is used basically for research and development work such as sterilization or microbiological reduction in medical and pharmaceutical supplies, preservation of foodstuffs, radiation effect studies, chemical and polymer synthesis.

Records showed that the Gamma Cell had 16 pencils; total radioactivity was 3978 Ci as on August/September 1969.(Curie-Ci-is a unit of radioactivity, In a radioactive source of one Ci 37000 million disintegrations occur every sec).

When auctioned the total radioactivity of the source was about 18.6 Ci. During May 3 and 4, 2010, Scientists from the Board of Radiation and Isotope Technology and AERB accounted the sources after inspection.

AERB issued a show cause notice to Delhi University and prohibited it from using radioactive sources. The legal process initiated by AERB is yet to conclude.

Bharat Ratna

The following are the recipients of
Bharat Ratna so far.

C. Rajagopalachari	(1954)
S. Radhakrishnan	(1954)
C.V. Raman	(1954)
Jawaharlal Nehru	(1955)
Bhagwan Das	(1955)
M. Visweswarayya	(1955)
Govind Ballabh Pant	(1957)
D.K. Karve	(1958)
B.C. Roy	(1961)
P.D. Tandon	(1961)
Rajendra Prasad	(1962)
Zakir Hussain	(1963)
P.V. Kane	(1963)
Lal Bahadur Shastri	(posthumous 1966)
Indira Gandhi	(1971)
V.V. Giri	(1975)
K. Kamaraj	(posthumous 1976)
Mother Teresa	(1980)
Vinoba Bhave	(1983)

Nelson Mandela   Amartya Sen

'Frontier Gandhi' Khan Abdul Ghafar Khan	(1987)
M.G. Ramachandran	(posthumous, 1988)
Dr. B.R. Ambedkar	(posthumous, 1990)
Dr. Nelson Mandela	(1990)
Rajiv Gandhi	(posthumous, 1991)
Sardar Vallabhbhai Patel	(posthumous, 1991)
Morarjee Desai	(1991)
J.R.D. Tata, Satyajit Ray,	(posthumous)
Maulana Abul Kalam Azad,	(1992)
Aruna Asaf Ali	(posthumous)
Gulzarilal Nanda	(1997)

APJ Abdul Kalam,
  M.S. Subbalakshmi,
  C. Subramaniam
	(1998)

Jaiprakash Narayan	(posthumous)

Amartya Sen,
  Ravi Shankar,
  Gopinath Bordoloi...(posthumous)
	(1999)

Ustad Bismillah Khan and Lata Mangeshkar (2001)	
Pandit Bhimsen Joshi	(2008)

Lata Mangeshkar   Bhimsen Joshi

Frontier Gandhi	**Frontier Gandhi Khan Adul Gaffar Khan (1890-1988), pre-eminent Pashtun leader, was a follower of Mahatma Gandhi and founder of the Khudai Khitmatgar (the Red Shirt Movement). He was the first foreigner to get the Bharat Ratna.**

Nobel Prize Winners since 2000

Physics

2000 Jack S.Kilby, U.S.; Zhores I.Alferov, Russ.

2001 Eric A. Cornell, Carl E. Wieman, U.S.; Wolfgang Ketterle, Ger.

2002 Riccardo Giacconi, Rayond Davis Jr. U.S.; Masatoshi Koshiba, Jap.

2003 Alexei A. Abrikosov, US.-Rus.; Vitaly I. Ginz-burg, Rus.; Anthony J. Leggett, U.K.-US.

2004 David J Gross, H. David Politzer, Frank Wilczek (USA)

2005 Roy Glauber, John Hall (both US), and Theodor Haensch(Germany)

2006 John C. Mather and George F. Smoot (both US)

2007 Peter Gruenberg (Germany), Albert Fert (France)

2008 Makoto Kobayashi, Toshihide Maskawa (both Jap.), Yoichiro Nambu (Jap-born US)

2009 Charles K Kao (China), Williard S Boyle (USA), George E Smith (USA)

2010 Andre Geim and Konstantin Novoselov

Andre Geim and Konstantin Novoselov

Chemistry

2000 Alan J. Heeger, U.S.; Alan G. MacDiarmid, NZ-US.; Hideki Shirakawa, Japan

2001 K. Barry Sharpless, U.S.; William S. Knowles, U.S.; Ryoji Noyori, Japan

2002 John B. Fenn, U.S., Kurt Wuthrich, Swiss, Koichi Tanaka, Jap.

2003 Peter Agre, Roderick Mackinnon, U.S.

2004 Aaron Ciechanover, Avram Hershko (both Israel), Irwin Rose (USA)

2005 Yves Chauvin (France), Robert H. Grubbs, Richard H. Schrock (both U.S.)

2006 Roger Kornberg (US)

2007 Gerhard Ertl (Germany)

2008 Osamu Shimomura (Jap), Martin Chalfie and Roger Tsien (both US)

2009 Venkataraman Ramakrishnan (US), Thomas A. Steitz (US) and Ada E. Yonath (Israel)

2010 Richard F. Heck, Ei-ichi Negishi and Akira Suzuki

Richard F. Heck   *Akira Suzuki*

Physiology or Medicine

2000 Arvid Carlsson, Swed.; Paul Greengard, U.S.; Eric R. Kandel, Aus.-U.S.

2001 Leland H. Hartwell, U.S.; R. Timothy (Tim) Hunt, Sir Paul M. Nurse, Br.

2002 Sydney Brenner, U.K.; H. Robert Howvitz, U.S.; John E. Sulston, U.K.

2003 Paul C. Lauterbur, U.S.; Sir Peter Mansfield, U.K.

2004 Richard Axel and Linda Buck (USA)

2005 BarryJ.Marshall, Robin Warren (Austral.)

They Missed It | **These authors missed the Nobel Prize for literature: Leo Tolstoy, Emile Zola, Henrik Ibsen, Marcel Proust, Mark Twain, Joseph Conrad, Maxim Gorki, Theodore Dreiser and August Strindberg.**

Robert G. Edwards *Carol Greider*   *Elizabeth H. Blackburn* *Liu Xiaobo*

2006 Andrew Fire and Craig Mello (both US)
2007 Dr. Oliver Smithies (US), Mario R. Capecchi (US), Martin Evans (Britan).
2008 Harald Zur Hausen (Germany), Francoise Barre-Sinoussi, Luc Montagnier (both France).
2009 Elizabeth H. Blackburn, Carol Greider, Jack Szostak (US).
2010 Robert G. Edwards

Literature

2000 Gao Xingjian, Chin.
2001 Sir V.S. Naipaul, Br.
2002 Imre Kertesz, Hug.
2003 John Maxwell Coetzee, S.Afr.
2004 Elfriede Jelinek (Austria)
2005 Harold Pinter (Br.)
2006 Orhan Pamuk (Turkey)
2007 Doris Lessing (Britain)
2008 Jean-Marie Gustave le Clezio (Fr.)
2009 Herta Muller (Germany)
2010 Mario Vargas Llosa

Peace

2000 Kim Dae Jung, S.Kor.

Coetzee J.M.   *Mario Vargas Llosa*

2001 UN; Kofi Annan, Ghana
2002 Jimmy Carter, U.S.
2003 Shirin Ebadi, Iran
2004 Wangari Maathai (kenya)
2005 Un International Atomic Energy Agency and its D-G Mohamed El Baradei (Egypt)
2006 Muhammad Yunus (Bangladesh) and the Grameen Bank.
2007 Al Gore (former US Vice President), and UN's Inter-governmental Panel on Climate Change.
2008 Martti Ahtissari (Fin.), former President of Finland.
2009 Barack Obama (US)
2010 Liu Xiaobo (China)

Economics

2000 James J. Heckman, DanielL.McFadden, U.S.
2001 George A. Akerlof, A.Michael Spence, Joseph E. Stiglitz, U.S.
2002 Daniel Kahneman, Vernon L.Smith, U.S.
2003 Robert F.Engle, U.S.; Clive W.J. Granger, U.K.
2004 Finn Kydland (Norway), Edward Prescott (USA)
2005 Robert Aumann (Israeli-US) and Thomas C. Schelling (US)
2006 Dr. Edmund Phelps (US)
2007 Leonid Hurwicz, Eric Maskin and Roger Myerson (US)
2008 Paul Krugman (US)
2009 Oliver Williamson and Elinor Ostrom (both U.S.)
2010 Peter A. Diamond, Dale T. Mortensen and Christopher A. Pissarides

Tagore and the Nobel

Tagore was 52 when he won the Nobel for his *Song Offerings* (*Gitanjali*). Tagore said the money would be used for the sanitation and drainage of Shantiniketan. But the bank where it was deposited closed its shutters in a few years and the money was lost.

Magsaysay Awardees From India

Year	Name or Company	Category
1958	Vinoba Bhave	CL
1959	Chintaman Deshmukh	GS
1961	Amitabha Chowdhury	JLCCA
1962	Mother Teresa	PIU
1963	Dara Khurody	CL
1963	Verghese Kurien	CL
1963	Tribhuvandas Patel	CL
1964	Welthy Fisher	PIU
1965	Jayaprakash Narayan	PS
1966	Kamaladevi Chattopadhyay	CL
1967	Satyajit Ray	JLCCA
1971	M.S. Swaminathan	CL
1974	M.S.Subbulakshmi	PS
1975	Boobli George Verghese	JLCCA
1976	Henning Holck-Larsen	PIU
1976	Sombhu Mitra	JLCCA
1977	Ela Ramesh Bhatt	CL
1979	MabelleArole	CL
1979	Rajanikant Arole	CL
1981	Gour Kishore Ghosh	JLCCA
1981	Pramod Karan Sethi	CL
1982	Manibhal Desai	PS
1982	Chandi Prasad Bhatt	CL
1982	Arun Shourie	JLCCA
1984	Rasipuram Laxman	JLCCA
1985	Murlidhar Amte	PS

Shantha Sinha

Kiran Bedi

Year	Name or Company	Category
1989	Lakshmi Chand Jain	PS
1991	K.V. Subbanna	JLCCA
1992	Ravi Shankar	JLCCA
1993	Banoo Jehangir Coyaji	PS
1994	Kiran Bedi	GS
1996	Pandurang Athavale	CL
1996	T.N. Seshan	GS
1997	Mahasweta Devi	JLCCA
1997	Mahesh Chander Mehta	PS
2000	Jockin Arputham	PIU
2000	Aruna Roy	CL
2001	Rajendra Singh	CL
2002	Sandeep Pandey	EL
2003	James Michael Lyngdoh	GS
2003	Shantha Sinha	CL
2004	Laxminarayan Ramdas	PIU
2005	V Shanta	PS
2006	Arvind Kejriwal	EL
2007	Palagummi Sainath	JLCCA
2008	Dr. Prakash Amte & Dr. Mandakini Amte	CL
2009	Deep Joshi	GS & CL
2010	Nileema Mishra & Harish Hande	PS

GS -Government Service; PS-Public Service; CL-Community Leadership; JLCCA-Journalism, Literature, and the Creative Communication Arts; PIU-Peace and International Understanding; EL-Emergent Leadership.

Neelima Mishra

Deep Joshi

Nobel Prizes

Each of the Nobel Prizes can be divided between not more than three contestants and must be awarded at least once in every five years. Each recipient gives a public lecture on a subject connected with the work within six months of the bestowal of the prize.

Jnanpith Awards

Year	Winner	Language
1965	G. Sankara Kurup	Malayalam
1966	Tara Shankar Banerjee	Bengali
1967	Dr. K.V. Puttappa	Kannada
1967	Umashankar Joshi	Gujarati
1968	Sumitranand Pant	Hindi
1969	Firaq Gorakhpuri	Urdu
1970	Dr. Viswanatha Satynarayana	Telugu
1971	Bishnu Dey	Bengali
1972	Dr. Ramdhari Singh Dinkar	Hindi
1973	Dattatreya Ramachandra Bendre	Kannada
1973	Gopinath Mohanty	Oriya
1974	Vishnu Sakharam Khandekar	Marathi
1975	P.V. Akhilandam (Akhilan)	Tamil
1976	Ashapurna Devi	Bengali
1977	Dr. K. Shivarama Karanth	Kannada
1978	S.H. Vatsyayan	Hindi
1979	Birendra Kumar Bhattacharya	Assamese
1980	S.K. Pottekkatt	Malayalam
1981	Amrita Pritam	Punjabi
1982	Mahadevi Verma	Hindi
1983	Dr. Masti Venkatesh Iyengar	Kannada
1984	Thakazhi Sivasankara Pillai	Malayalam
1985	Pannalal Patel	Gujarati

Nirmal Verma   *Rahman Rahi*

Year	Winner	Language
1986	Satchidanand Rautroy	Oriya
1987	V.V. Shirwadkar	Marathi
1988	Dr. C. Narayana Reddy	Telugu
1989	Qurratul-ain-Haider	Urdu
1990	Vinayak Krishna Gokak	Kannada
1991	Subhas Mukhopadhyay	Bengali
1992	Naresh Mehta	Hindi
1993	Sitakant Mahapatra	Oriya
1994	U. R. Anantha Murthy	Kannada
1995	M.T. Vasudevan Nair	Malayalam
1996	Mahasweta Devi	Bengali
1997	Ali Sardar Jafri	Urdu
1998	Girish Karnad	Kannada
1999	Nirmal Verma	Hindi
1999	Gurdayal Singh	Punjabi
2000	Indira Goswami	Assamese
2001	Rajendra Keshavlal Shah	Gujarati
2002	D. Jayakanthan	Tamil
2003	Vinda Karandikar	Marathi
2004	Rahman Rahi	Kashmiri
2005	Kunwar Narayan	Hindi
2006	Satya Vrat Shastri	Sanskrit
	Ravindra Kelekar	Konkani
2007	ONV Kurup	Malayalam
2008	Akhlaq Mohammed Khab	Urdu
2009 -	Amar Kant and Shrilal Shukla	Hindi
2010 -	Chandrasekhar Kambar	Kannada

Kunwar Narayan   *Indira Goswami*

The First Jnanpith — The first Jnanpith award was given to G. Sankara Kurup in 1965 for his collection of poems *Odakuzhal* in Malayalam. The Award was instituted to honour creative literary writing by any Indian in any language included in the Constitution.

Booker Prizes

1969 P.H. Newby *Something To Answer For*
1970 Bernice Rubens *The Elected Member*
1971 V.S. Naipaul *In A Free State*
1972 John Berger *G*
1973 J.G. Farrell *The Siege Of Krishnapur*
1974*Nadine Gordimer *The Conservationist*
    Stanley Middleton *Holiday*
1975 Ruth Prawer
    Jhabwala *Heat And Dust*
1976 David Storey *Saville*
1977 Paul Scott *Staying On*
1978 Iris Murdoch *The Sea, The Sea*
1979 Penelope Fitzgerald *Offshore*
1980 William Golding *Rites Of Passage*
1981 Salman Rushdie *Midnight's Children*
1982 Thomas Keneally *Schindler's Ark*
1983 J.M. Coetzee *Life And Times*
    Of Michael. K.
1984 Anita Brookner *Hotel Du Lac*
1985 Keri Hulme *The Bone People*
1986 Kingsley Amis *The Old Devils*
1987 Penelope Lively *Moon Tiger*
1988 Peter Carey *Oscar And Lucinda*
1989 Kazuo Ishiguro *The Remains*
    Of The Day
1990 A.S. Byatt *Possession*
1991 Ben Okri *The Famished Road*

Yann Martel   *Hilary Mantel*

1992*Michael Ondaatjee *The English Patient*
    Barry Unsworth *Sacred Hunger*
1993 Roddy Dodoyle *Paddy Clarke Ha Ha Ha*
1994 James Kelman *How Late It Was, How Late*
1995 Pat Barker *The Ghost Road*
1996 Graham Swift *Last Orders*
1997 Arundhathi Roy *The God Of Small Things*
1998 Ian Mcewan *Amsterdam*
1999 J.M.Coetzee *Disgrace*
2000 Margaret Atwood *The Blind Assassin*
2001 Peter Carey *True History of the Kelly Gang*
2002 Yann Martel *Life of Pi*
2003 D.B.C. Pierre *Vernon God Little*
2004 Alan Hollinghurst *The Line of Beauty*
2005 John Banville *The Sea*
2006 Kiran Desai *The Inheritance of Loss*
2007 Anne Enright *The Gathering*
2008 Aravind Adiga *The White Tiger*
2009 Hilary Mantel *Wolf Hall*
2010 Howard Jacobson *The Finkler Question*

Howard Jacobson   *DBC Pierre*

* Co-Winners

Coetzee is Unique — Joseph Michael Coetzee ((b.1946), the South African writer won the Booker Prize first in 1983 for *The Life and Time of Michael K.* and again in 1999 for *Disgrace* (it won Nobel). His novels deal with life under forms of imperialism including the apartheid.

Beauty Queens since 1999

Angola's Leila Lopez crowned Miss Universe 2011 by Ximena Navarrete

Miss Universe

Name	Year	Country
Mpule Kwelagobe	1999	Botswana
Lara Dutta	2000	India
Denise M. Quinones	2001	Puerto Rico
Oxana Fedrova	2002	Russia
Justine Pasek	2002	Panama
Amelia Vega Polanco	2003	Dominican Rep.
Jennifer Hawkins	2004	Australia
Natalie Glebova	2005	Canada
Zuleyka Rivera	2006	Puerto Rico
Riyo Mori	2007	Japan
Dayana Mendoza	2008	Venezuela
Stefania Fernandez	2009	Venezuela
Ximena Navarrete	2010	Mexico
Leila Lopez	2011	Angola

Miss World

Name	Year	Country
Yukta Mookhey	1999	India
Priyanka Chopra	2000	India
Agbani Darego	2001	Nigeria
Azra Akin	2002	Turkey
Rosanna Davison	2003	Ireland
Maria Julia Mantill Garcia	2004	Peru
Unnur Birna Vilhjalmsdottir Sanya	2005	Iceland
Tatana Kucharova	2006	Czech Republic
Zhang Zilin	2007	China
Ksenia Sukhinova	2008	Russia
Kaiane Aldorino	2009	Gibralt
Alexandria Mills	2010	United States

1. Crowned after Helen Mogan of the United Kingdom resigned.
2. Crowned after Gabriella Brum of West Germany resigned.

Lara Dutta

Rio Mori

Yukta Mookhey

Alexandria Mills

The Seven Wonders of the World

Seven monuments of the ancient world that appeared on various lists of late antiquity are known as the:

Seven Wonders of the World

1. The Colossus of Rhodes
2. The Pharos (lighthouse) at Alexandria

Iguazu Falls

The Great Wall of China

Seven Wonders of the Middle Ages

1. The Colosseum of Rome
2. The Catacombs of Alexandria
3. The Great Wall of China

3. The Hanging Gardens (and Walls) of Babylon
4. The temple of Artemis (or Diana) at Ephesus
5. The Pyramids of Khufu
6. The tomb of Mausolus at Halicarnassus
7. The statue of Zeus at Olympia.

The tradition of "Seven Wonders" has inspired succeeding generations to compile countless lists since the Alexandrian era.

Tower of Pisa

Pyramid of Khufu

4. Stonehenge
5. The Porcelain Tower (or Pagoda) of Nanking, China
6. The Leaning Tower of Pisa, Italy
7. Hagia Sophia (or Sancta Sophia) of Constantinople

Seven Natural Wonders of the World

1. The Grand Canyon, Colorado River, Arizona
2. Rio de Janeiro harbour
3. Iguassu Falls, Argentina

Hagia Sophia

Hagia Sophia means Holy Wisdom. It is a church in Istanbul, later a mosque and now a museum. The original building was completed in less than six years. It is a masterpiece of Byzantine art.

Stonehenge

4. Yosemite Valley and the Giant Sequioas of California
5. Mount Everest, on the border of Tibet and Nepal
6. The Nile River, Egypt
7. The Northern Lights, especially from northern Canada and Alaska.

Seven Wonders of Today

1. The Great Pyramid of Egypt and the adjacent Great Sphinx of Gizeh
2. Hagia Sophia, 6th century, in present-day Istanbul
3. Leaning Tower of Pisa, Italy
4. The Taj Mahal of Agra, India
5. The Washington Monument, Washington
6. The Eiffel Tower, Paris
7. The Empire State Building, New York city.

Seven New Wonders of the World,

as per list prepared by New Open World Corporation (2007) on the basis of voting.

1. The Taj Mahal (India)
2. The Great Wall of China
3. The Colosseum (Rome)
4. Pink ruins of Peta (Jordan)
5. Statue of Christ the Redeemer (Rio de Janeiro)
6. Incan ruins of Machu Picchu (Peru)

The Eiffel Tower

7. The Mayan city of Chichen Itza (Mexico)

Other compilers of 'wonder' lists include the Panama Canal, the Greek Parthenon

Machu Picchu

on the Acropolis at Athens, the medieval Mont-Saint Michel off the coast of France, St. Peter's Church in Rome, and the temples of Nikko National Park in Honshu, Japan. Famous palaces and ruins include the Moorish Alhambra of Granada, Angkor in Cambodia, Mayan ruins like Chichen Itza in Mexican Yacatan, and Egypt's Great Temple of Amon in Karnak.

The Taj Mahal

He Coined the Word 'Antibiotic' | **Selman Abraham Waksman was a Ukrainian-born U.S. biochemist whose discovery of the antibiotic streptomycin brought him the 1952 Nobel Prize for Medicine. He coined the word 'antibiotic'.**

Phalke Award Winners

Year	Name
1969	Smt. Devika Rani Roerich
1970	Shri. B.N. Sircar
1971	Shri. Prithvi Rajkapoor
1972	Shri. Pankaj Mullick
1973	Smt. Sulochana (Ruby Mayers)
1974	Shri. B.N. Reddy
1975	Shri. Dhiren Ganguly
1976	Smt. Kanan Devi
1977	Shri. Nitin Bose
1978	Shri. R.C. Boral
1979	Shri. Sohrab Modi
1980	Shri. P. Jairaj
1981	Shri. Naushad Ali
1982	Shri. L.V. Prasad
1983	Smt. Durga Khote
1984	Shri. Satyajit Ray
1985	Shri. V. Shantharam
1986	Shri. B. Nagi Reddi
1987	Shri. Raj Kapoor
1988	Shri. Ashok Kumar
1989	Smt. Lata Mangeshkar
1990	Shri. A. Nageswara Rao
1991	Shri. Bhaiji Pendharkar
1992	Shri. Bhupen Hazarika
1993	Shri. Majrooh Sultanpuri
1994	Shri. Dilipkumar

Sivaji Ganesan

K. Balachandar

1995	Dr. Rajkumar
1996	Shri. Sivaji Ganesan
1997	Shri. Kavi Pradeep
1998	Shri. B.R. Chopra
1999	Shri. Hrishikesh Mukherjee
2000	Smt. Asha Bhonsle
2001	Shri. Yash Chopra
2002	Shri. Dev Anand
2003	Shri. Mrinal Sen
2004	Shri. Adoor Gopalakrishnan
2005	Shri. Shyam Benegal
2006	Shri. Tapan Sinha
2007	Shri. Manna Dey
2008	Shri. V K Murthy
2009	Shri. D. Rama Naidu
2010	Shri. K. Balachander

British Prime Ministers since 1940

Winston Churchill (Conservative)	1940-1945
Clement R Attlee (Labour)	1945-1951
Winston Churchill (Conservative)	1951-1955
Anthony Eden (Conservative)	1955-1957
Harold Macmillan (Conservative)	1957-1963
Alec Douglas-Home (Conservative)	1963-1964
Harold Wilson (Labour)	1964-1970
Edward Heath (Conservative)	1970-1974
Harold Wilson (Labour)	1974-1976
James Callaghan (Labour)	1976-1979
Margaret Thatcher (Conservative)	1979-1990
John Major (Conservative)	1990-1997
Tony Blair (Labour)	1997-2007
Gordon Brown (Labour)	2007- 2010
David Cameroon (Conservative)	2010 -

Margaret Thatcher

Women Rulers

No	Name	Country	Year	Post
1.	Suhbaataryn Yanjmaa	Mongolia	1953	Acting President
2.	Sirimavo Bandaranaika	Sri Lanka	1960	Prime Minister
3.	Indira Gandhi	India	1966	Prime Minister
4.	Hilda Gibbs-Bynoe	Grenada	1967	Governor
5.	Golda Meir	Israel	1969	Prime Minister
6.	Maria Isabel Peron	Argentina	1974	President
7.	Elisabeth Domitien	Central African Republic	1975	Prime Minister
8.	Lucinda da Costa Gomez Matheeuws	Netherlands Antilles	1977	Prime Minister
9.	Doris Louise Johnson	Bahamas	1979	Acting Governor General
10.	Lydia Gveiler Tejada	Bolivia	1979	Acting President
11.	Maria de Lourdes Pintasilgo	Portugal	1979	Acting Prime minister
12.	Margaret Hilda Thatcher	Britain	1979	Prime Minister
13.	Song Qingling	China	1980	Honorary President
14.	Mary Eugenia Charles	Dominica	1980	Prime Minister
15.	Vigdis Finnbogadottir	Iceland	1980	President
16.	Maria Lea Pedini-Angelini	San Marino	1981	Co Captain Regent
17.	Elmira minita Gordon	Belize	1981	Governor General
18.	Gro Harlem Brundtland	Norway	1981	Prime Minister
19.	Milka Planinc	Yugoslovia	1982	Prime Minister
20.	Agatha Barbara	Malta	1982	Acting President
21.	Carmen Pereira	Guinea Bissau	1984	Acting President
22.	Maria Liberia Peters	Netherland Antilles	1984	Prime Minister
23.	Gloriana Ranocchini	San Marino	1984	Co Captain Regent
24.	Jeanne Mathilde Sauve	Canada	1984	Governor-General
25.	Corozon Aquino	Philippines	1986	President
26.	Flora Macdonald	Canada	1987	Acting Prime Minister
27.	Benazir Bhutto	Pakistan	1988	Prime Minister
28.	Herta Praulopp	Haiti	1990	President
29.	Sabine Bergmann-Pohl	German Democratic Republic	1990	President
30.	Kazimiera Prunskiene	Lithuania	1990	Prime Minister
31.	Ertha Pascal Trouillot	Haiti	1990	Acting President
32.	Ruth Nita Barrow	Barbados	1990	Governor-General
33.	Catherine Tizard	New Zeland	1990	Governor-General
34.	Mary Robinson	Ireland	1990	President
35.	Violeta Barrios De Chamorro	Nicaragua	1990	President
36.	Edith Cresson	France	1991	Prime Minister

Women at Supreme Court

Justice Ranjana Dessai is one of the three judges elevated to the Supreme Court and the second woman judge from the Bombay HC (16 years after Justice Sujatha Manohar) to join SC. Now there are two women judges in the SC.

37.	Edda Ceccoli	San Marino	1991	Co Captain Regent
38.	Khaleeda Zia	Bangladesh	1991	Prime Minister
39.	Hanna Suchocka	Poland	1992	Prime Minister
40.	Patricia Busignani	San Marino	1993	Co Captain Regent
41.	Kim Campbell	Canada	1993	Prime Minister
42.	Susanne Camelia-Roemer	Netherland Antilles	1993	Prime Minister
43.	Sylvie Kinigi	Burundi	1993	Prime Minister
44.	Agathe Uwilingiyimana	Rwanda	1993	Prime Minister
45.	Tansu Ciller	Turkey	1993	Prime Minister
46.	Reneta Indzhova	Bulgaria	1994	Acting Prime Minister
47.	Chandrika Kumaratunge	Sri Lanka	1994 -1994	Prime Minister, President
48.	Claudette werleigh	Haiti	1995	Prime Minister
50.	Sheik Hasina	Bangladesh	1996	Prime Minister
51.	Ruth Sando Perry	Liberia	1996	Acting President
52.	Rosalia Arteaga	Ecudor	1997	President
53.	Janet Jagan	Guyana	1997	Prime Minister, President
54.	Calliopa PearletteLouisy	St Lucia	1997	Governor General
55.	Mary Mc Aleese	Ireland	1997	President
56.	Pamela Gordon	Bermuda	1997	Prime Minister
57.	Jenny Shipley	New Zealand	1997	Prime Minister
58.	Anne Enger Lahnstein	Norway	1998	Acting Prime Minister
59.	Jennifer Smith	Bermuda	1998	Prime Minister
60.	Ruth Dreifuss	Switzerland	1999	President
61.	Irena Degutiene	Lithuania	1999	Acting Prime Minister
62.	Nyam-osoriyn Tuyaa	Mongolia	1999	Acting Prime Minister
63.	Rosa Zafferani	San Marino	1999	Co Captain Regent
64.	Helen Clarke	New Zeland	1999	Prime Minister
65.	Mireya Moscoso	Panama	1999	President
66.	Vaira Vike Freiberga	Latvia	1999	President
67.	Adrienne Clarkson	Canada	1999	Governor-General
68.	Maria Domenica Michelotti	San Marino	2000	Co Captain Regent
69.	Tarja Halonen	Finland	2000	President
70.	Gloria Macapagal- Arroyo	Philippines	2001	president
71.	Megawati Sukarnoputri	Indonesia	2001	President
72.	Madior Boye	Senegal	2001	Prime Minister
73.	Sian Seerpoohl Elias	New Zealand	2001	Acting Governor-General
74.	Silvia Cartwright	New Zealand	2001	Governor-General
75.	Ivy Dumont	Bahamas	2001	Acting Governor-General
76.	Chang sang	South Korea	2002	Prime Minister
77.	Maria Das Neves Ceita Baptista De Sousa	Sao Tome and Principe	2002	Prime Minister
78.	Monica Dacon	Saint Vincent And The Grenadines	2002	Governor-General
79.	Linda Babooiai	Trinidad and Tobago	2002	Acting president
80.	Natasa Micic	Serbia	2002	Acting president

Isabel Peron

The third wife of Argentina President Juan Peron, Isabel Peron was a dancer in 1955. She married Peron in 1961 and became his running mate in 1973 presidential election. She succeeded him when he died in 1974. Deposed in 1976, in exile in Spain.

81. Beatriz Merino Lucero	Peru	2003	Prime Minister
82. Anneli Tuulikki Jaattenmaki	Finland	2003	Prime Minister
83. Valeria Ciavatta	San Marino	2003	Co Captain Regent
84. Nino Burdzhanadze	Georgia	2003	Acting President
85. Luisa Dias Diogo	Mozambique	2004	Prime Minister
86. Radmila Sekerinska	Macedonia	2004	Prime Minister
87. Yuliya Tymoshenko	Ukraine	2005	Prime Minister
88. Maria do Carme Silveira	Sao Tome and Principe	2005	Prime Minister
89. Cynthia A Pratt	Bahamas	2005	Acting Prime Minister
90. Fausta Simona Morganti	San Marino	2005	Co Captain Regent
91. Angela Merkel	Germeny	2005	Chancellor
92. Michaelle Jean	Canada	2005	Governor General
93. Portia Simpson-Miller	Jamaica	2006	Prime Minister
94. Han Myung Sook	South Korea	2006	Prime Minister
95. Ellen Johnson-Sirleaf	Liberia	2006	President
96. Michelle Bachelet Jeria	Chile	2006	President
97. Emily Saidy de Jongh-Elhage	Netherlands Antilles	2006	Prime Minister
98. Micheline Calmy-Rey	Switzerland	2007	President
99. Dalia Itzik	Israel	2007	Acting president
100. Pratibha Patil	India	2007	President
101. Cristina Fernandez de Kirchner	Argentina	2007	President
102. Louise Lake-Tack	Antigua and Barbuda	2007	Governor General
103. Zinaidia Greceanii	Moldova	2008	Prime Minister
104. Michele Pierre-Louis	Haiti	2008	Prime Minister
105. Quentin Bryce	Australia	2008	Governor General
106. Assunta Meloni	San Marino	2008	CoCaptain Regent
107. Johanna Sigurdardottir	Iceland	2009	Prime Minister
108. Rose Francine Rogombe	Gabon	2009	Acting president
109. Jadranka Kosor	Croatia	2009	Prime Minister
110. Dalia Grybauskaite	Lithuania	2009	President
111. Cécile Manorohanta	Madagascar	2009	Acting Prime Minister
112. Doris Leuthard	Switzerland	2010	President
113. Roza Otunbayeva	Kyrgyzstan	2010	President
114. Laura Chinchilla Miranda	Costa Rica	2010	President
115. Kamla Persad-Bissessar	Trinidad and Tobago	2010	Prime minister
116. Mari Kiviniemi	Finland	2010	Prime minister
117. Julia Gillard	Australia	2010	Prime minister
118. Iveta Radicová	Slovakia	2010	Prime minister
119. Dilma Rousseff	Brazil	2011	President
120. Maria Luisa Berti	San Marino	2011	Co-Captain-regent
121. Atifete Jahjaga	Kosovo		President
122. Rosario Fernández			
123. Cissé Mariam Kaïdama Sidibé	Mali	2011	Prime minister
124. Yingluck Shinawatra	Thailand	2011	Prime minister
125. Helle Thorning-Schmidt	Denmark	2011	Prime minister

Corazon Aquino

Corazon Aquino, the 11th President of the Philippines, (1986-92), was the country's first woman President. She led the 1986 People Power Revolution dethroning President Marcos and restoring democracy. In 1986, she was Time Magazine's Woman of the Year.

Women Governors in India

No. Name	Period	State
1. Sarojini Naidu	15.08.1947 - 02.03.1949	United Provinces/UP
2. Padmaja Naidu	03.11.1956 - 01.06.1967	West Bengal
3. Vijayalakshmi Pandit	27.11.1962 - 05.09.1963	
	18.12.1963 - 08.10.1964	Maharashtra
4. Sharada Mukherjee	05.05.1977 - 14.08.1978	Andhra Pradesh
	14.08.1978 - 06.08.1983	Gujarat
5. Jyothi Venkatachalam	14.10.1977 - 27.10.1982	Kerala
6. Kumudben Joshi	26.11.1985 - 07.02.1990	Andhra Pradesh
7. Ram Dulari Sinha	23.02.1988 - 12.02.1990	Kerala
8. Serla Grewal	31.03.1989 - 06.02.1990	Madhya Pradesh
9. Chandrawati	19.02.1990 - 19.12.1990	Pondicherry (UT)
10. Rajendrakumari Bajpayi	02.05.1995 - 23.04.1998	Pondicherry (UT)
11. Sheila Kaul	17.11.1995 - 23.04.1996	Himachal Pradesh
12. Justice M. Fathima Beevi	25.01.1997 - 01.07.2001	Tamilnadu
13. V.S. Rama Devi	26.07.1997 - 02.12.1999	Himachal Pradesh
	02.12.1999 - 10.08.2002	Karnataka
14. Rajani Rai	23.04.1998 - 31.07.2002	Pondicherry (UT)
15. Pratibha Patil (Now President of India)	08.11.2004 - 21.06.2007	Rajasthan
16. Prabha Rau	19.07.2008 - 26.04.2010	Himachal Pradesh
17. Kamla Beniwal	28.11.2009 -	Gujarat
18. Margaret Alva	06.08.2009 -	Uttarakhand
19. Urmila Singh	25.01.2010 -	Himachal Pradesh

Women Chief Ministers In India

Name	State	Period	Party
1. Sucheta Kripalani	UP	1963 - 1967	Congress
2. Nandini Satpaty	Orissa	1972 - 1974 & 1974 - 1976	Congress
3. Sashikala Kadokar	Goa	1973 - 1977 & 1977 - 1979	Maha-Gomantak Party
4. Syeda Anwara Taimur	Assam	1980 - 1981	Congress
5. Janaki Ramachandran	TN	1988	A.I.A.D.M.K. (Janaki)
6. J. Jayalalithaa	TN	1991 - 1996, 2001, 2002 - 2006, 2011-	A.I.A.D.M.K
7. Mayawati	UP	1995, 1997, 2002 - 2003, 2007 -	B.S.P
8. Rajinder Kaur Bhattal	Punjab	1996 - 1997	Congress
9. Rabri Devi	Bihar	1997 - 1999, 2000 - 2005	R.J.D
10. Sushma Swaraj	Delhi	1998	B.J.P
11. Sheila Dixit	Delhi	1998 -	Congress
12. Uma Bharti	M.P	2003 - 2004	B.J.P
13. Vasundhara Raje	Rajasthan	2003 - 2008	B.J.P
14. Mamata Banerjee	WB	2011-	AITC

Presidents of USA since 1953

Name & (party)1	Term	Age at inaug.	Age at Death
Dwight D. Elsenhower (R)	1953-1961	62	78
John F. Kennedy (D)*	1961-1963	43	46
Lyndon B. Johnson (D)	1963-1969	55	64
Richard M. Nixon (R)**	1969-1974	56	81
Gerald R. Ford (R)	1974-1977	61	93
Jimmy Carter (D)	1977-1981	52	-
Ronald Reagan (R)	1981-1989	69	93
George H.W. Bush (R)	1989-1993	64	-
William J. Clinton (D)	1993-2001	46	-
George W. Bush (R)	2001-2009	54	-
Barack Obama	2009 -	47	

R-Republican; D-Democratic; *Assassinated in office; **Resigned Aug.9, 1974

Presidents of People's Republic of China

Presidents	Term
Mao Zedong	1949-1959
Liu Shaoqi	1959-1968
Dong Biwu	1968-1975
Zhu De	1975-1976
Song Qingling	1976-1978
Ye Jianying	1978-1983
Li Xiannian	1983-1988
YangShangkun	1988-1993
Jiang Zemin	1993-2003
Hu Jintao	2003 -

Leaders of Russia

Name	Term
USSR -General Secretaries	
Josef Stalin	1922-53
Georgiy Malenkov	1953
Nikita Khrushchev	1953-64
Leonid Brezhnev	1964-82
Yuri Andropov	1982-4
Konstantin Chernenko	1984-85
Mikhail Gorbachev	1985-91
Russian Federation -Presidents	
Boris Yeltsin	1991-99
Vladimir Putin	1999-2008
Dmitry Medvedev	2008-

Sucheta and J.B. Kripalani — **India's first woman Chief Minister was Sucheta Kripalani (1963 to 67). Her husband Acharya J.B. Kripalani was a renowned freedom fighter (born 1888) who became Congress President in 1946-47.**

Select Foreign - Born Rulers

Name	Country	Post	Born in
Carlos Menem	Argentina	President	Syria
Alberto Fujimori	Peru	President	Japan
Abdala Bucaram	Ecuador	President	Lebanon
Janet Jagan	Guyana	President	America
Adolf Hitler	Germany	Chancellor	Austria
Kenneth Kaunda	Zambia	President	Malawi
Hendrick Verwoerd	South Africa	Prime Minister	Holland
Adrene Poi Clarkson	Canada	Gov- General	Hong Kong

Presidents of France

Name	Term
Charles de Gaulle	1958-1969
Georges Pompidou	1969-1974
Valery Giscard d'Estaing	1974-1981
Francois Mitterrand	1981-1995
Jacques Rene Chirac	1995-2007
Nicolas Sarkozy	2007-

Chancellors of Federal Republic of Germany

Term	Name
1949-63	Konrad Adenauer
1963-66	Ludwig Erhard
1966-69	Kurt Georg Kiesinger
1969-74	Willy Brandt
1974-82	Helmut Schmidt
1982-98	Helmut Kohl
1998-2005	Gerhard Schroder
2005-	Ms. Angela Merkel

Pen Names

O. Henry	-	William Sydney Porter
P.D. James	-	Phyllis Dorothy James White
George Orwell	-	Eric Arthur Blair
George Eliot	-	Mary Ann or Marian Evans
John le Carre	-	David John Moore Cornwell
Lewis Caroll	-	Charles Lutwidge Dodgson
Dr Seuss	-	Theodar Seuss Geisel

Ellery Queen	-	Frederic Dannay and Man Fred B. Lee
Maxim Gorky	-	Aleksey Maksimovich Peshkov
George Sand	-	Amandine Luice Aurore Dupin
Mark Twain	-	Samuel Clemens
Moliere	-	Jean Baptiste Poquelin
Elia	-	Charles Lamb
Saki	-	Hector Hugh Munro
Voltaire	-	Francois Marie Arouet

Golda Meir — The Israeli stateswoman who was PM from 1969 to 74 - the first woman PM of the country. She was born in Ukraine. Emigrated to US and then to Palestine. Was minister of labour and foreign minister in Israel, succeeded Levi Eshkol as PM. Forced to resign.

Important Days

January 9	NRI Day
January 10	World Laughter Day
January 12	National Youth Day
January 15	Army Day
January 25	National Tourism Day, Voters Day
January 26	India's Republic Day, International Customs Day
January 30	Martyrs' Day; World Leprosy Eradication Day
February 2nd Sunday	World Marriage Day
February 24	Central Excise Day
February 28	National Science Day
March 2nd Thursday	World Kidney Day
March 2nd Monday	Commonwealth Day
March 8	International Women's Day
March 15	World Disabled Day; World Consumer Rights Day
March 18	Ordnance Factories Day (India)
March 21	World Forestry Day
March 21	International Day for the Elimination of Racial Discrimination
March 22	World Day for Water
March 23	World Meteorological Day
March 24	World TB Day
April 3	World Austism Day
April 5	International Day for Mine Awareness; National Maritime Day
April 7	World Health Day
April 17	World Haemophilia Day
April 18	World Heritage Day
April 21	Secretaries' Day
April 21	National Civil Services Day
April 22	Earth Day
April 23	World Book and Copyright Day
April 26	World Intellectual Property Day

Conquest of Everest The first Indian team ascended Mount Everest under the leadership of Commander M.S. Kohli on May 20, 1965.

May 1	Workers' Day (International Labour Day)
May 1st Sunday	World Laughter Day
May 1st Tuesday	World Asthma Day
May 3	Press Freedom Day
May, 2nd Sunday	Mother's Day
May 4	Coal Miners' Day
May 8	World Red Cross Day
May 9	World Thalassaemia Day
May 11	National Technology Day
May 12	World Hypertension Day; International Nurses Day
May 15	International Day of the Family
May 17	World Telecommunication Day
May 24	Commonwealth Day
May 25	World Thyroid Day
May 29	International Mount Everest Day (Desginated by Nepal)
May 31	Anti-tobacco Day
June 1	World Milk Day (FAO)
June 4	International Day of Innocent Children, Victims of Aggression
June 5	World Environment Day
June, 3rd Sunday	Father's Day
June 26	International Day against Drug Abuse and Illicit Trafficking, in support of victims of Torture
June 14	World Blood Donor Day
July 1	Doctor's Day
July 11	World Population Day
August 1st Sunday	International Friendship Day
August 6	Hiroshima Day
August 8	World Senior Citizen's Day
August 9	Quit India Day, Nagasaki Day
August 15	Indian Independence Day
August 18	Intl.Day of the World's Indigenous Peoples
August 19	Photography Day
August 29	National Sports Day
Paurnami Day of Shravana month	Sanskrit Day
September 2	Coconut Day

The Highest Road

The highest motorable road in the world was built in Khardungla area at 5602 mt. in Leh-Manali sector in 1988.

September 5	Teachers' Day
September 8	International Literacy Day (UNESCO)
September 15	Engineers' Day
September 16	World Ozone Day
September 21	Alzheimer's Day; Day for Peace & Non- violence (UN)
September 22	Rose Day (Welfare of cancer patients)
September 26	Day of the Deaf
September 27	World Tourism Day
October 1	International Day for the Elderly
October 2	Gandhi Jayanthi; International Day of Non-Violence
October 3	World Habitat Day
October 4	World Animal Welfare Day
October 8	Indian Air Force Day
October 9	World Post Office Day
October 10	National Post Day
October, 2nd Thursday	World Sight Day
October 13	UN International Day for Natural Disaster Reduction
October 15	World White Cane Day (guiding the blind)
October 16	World Food Day
October 24	UN Day; World Development Information Day
October 30	World Thrift Day
November 9	Legal Services Day
November 14	Children's Day; Diabetes Day
November 17	National Epilepsy Day
November 19	Citizens' Day
November 20	Universal Children's Day (UN), Africa Industrialisation Day
November 29	International Day of Solidarity with Palestinian People
December 1	World AIDS Day
December 3	World Day of the Handicapped
December 4	Navy Day
December 7	Armed Forces Flag Day
December 10	Human Rights Day; Intl. Children's Day of Broadcasting
December 18	Minorities Rights Day (India)
December 23	Kisan Divas (Farmer's Day)

Campaign Against Smoking

On New Year Day 1988, Maharashtra became the first Indian state to launch a public campaign against smoking.

India: Presidents, PMs, etc.

Presidents of India

Dr. Rajendra Prasad	1950-1962
Dr. Sarvepalli Radhakrishnan	1962-1967
Dr. Zakir Husain	1967-1969
Varahagiri Venkata Giri	May-July,1969 (Acting)
Justice Mohammed Hidayatullah	July-Aug.,1969 (Acting)
Varahagiri Venkata Giri	1969-1974
Fakhruddin Ali Ahmed	1974-1977
B. D. Jatti	Feb.-July,1977 (Acting)
Neelam Sanjiva Reddy	1977-1982
Giani Zail Singh	1982-1987
R. Venkataraman	1987-1992
Dr. Shankar Dayal Sharma	1992-1997
K.R. Narayanan	1997-2002
A.P.J. Abdul Kalam	2002-2007
Pratibha Patil	Since July 25, 2007

Vice-Presidents

Dr. Sarvepalli Radhakrishnan	1952-1962
Dr. Zakir Husain	1962-1967
Varahagiri Venkata Giri	1967-1969
Gopal Swarup Pathak	1969-1974
B. D. Jatti	1974-1979
Mohammed Hidayatullah	1979-1984
R. Venkataraman	1984-1987
Dr. Shankar Dayal Sharma	1987-1992
K. R. Narayanan	1992-1997
Krishan Kant	1997-2002
Bhairon Singh Shekhawat	2002-2007
Mohammad Hamid Ansari	Since Aug. 10, 2007

Prime Ministers

Jawaharlal Nehru	1947-1964
Gulzari Lal Nanda	May-June, 1964 (Acting)
Lal Bahadur Shastri	1964-1966
Gulzari Lal Nanda	11-24, Jan., 1966 (Acting)
Indira Gandhi	1966-1977
Morarji Desai	1977-1979
Charan Singh	1979-1980
Indira Gandhi	1980-1984
Rajiv Gandhi	1984-1989
Vishwanath Pratap Singh	1989-1990
Chandrasekhar	1990-1991
P.V. Narasimha Rao	1991-1996
Atal Bihari Vajpayee	16.5.'96-28.5.'96
H.D. Deve Gowda	1.6.'96-21.4.'97
Inder Kumar Gujral	21.4.'97- 18.3.'98
Atal Bihari Vajpayee	19.3. 1998 –13.10.1999
Atal Bihari Vajpayee	13.10.'99–May 2004
Dr.Manmohan Singh	Since May 22, 2004

Chief Justices

Harilal J. Kania	1950-1951
M. Patanjali Sastri	1951-1954
Mehar Chand Mahajan	1954-1954
B. K. Mukherjea	1954-1956
S. R. Das	1956-1959
Bhuvaneshwar Prasad Sinha	1959-1964
P. B. Gajendragadkar	1964-1966
A. K. Sarkar	Mar.-June, 1966
K. Subba Rao	1966-1967
K. N. Wanchoo	1967-1968
M. Hidayatullah	1968-1970
J. C. Shah	1970-1971
S. M. Sikri	1971-1973
A. N. Ray	1973-1977
M. H. Baig	1977-1978
Y. V. Chandrachud	1978-1985
P. N. Bhagwati	1985-1986
R. S. Pathak	1986-1989
E. S. Venkataramiah	June-Dec., 1989
Sabyasachi Mukherjee	1989-1990
Ranganath Mishra	1990-1991
K.N. Singh	1991-1991
M. H. Kania	1991-1992
Lalit Mohan Sharma	Nov.1992- Feb.1993
Manepalli Narayanrao Venkatachalliah	Feb. 1993-1994

A Woman CEC — V.S. Rama Devi, Governor of Himachal Pradesh and later of Karnataka, was Chief Election Commissioner for a brief period in 1990, the only woman to hold that position.

Aziz Mushabber Ahmedi	1994- 1997
Jagdish Sharan Verma	1997- 1998
M.M. Punchhi	Jan.-Oct., 1998
Adarsh Sein Anand	1998- 2001
S.P. Bharucha	2001-2002
B.N. Kirpal	May-Nov., 2002
G.B. Pattanaik	Nov.-Dec., 2002
V.N. Khare	Dec. 2002-May 2004
S. Rajendra Babu	May 2, '04 - June 1,'04
R.C. Lahoti	June 1, '04 - Oct. 31, '05
Y.K. Sabharwal	Nov.1, '05 - Jan. 13, '07
K. G. Balakrishnan	2007-2010
S.H. Kapadia	Since 2010-

Chief Election Commissioners

Sukumar Sen	1950-1958
K. V. K. Sundaram	1958-1967
S. P. Sen Verma	1967-1972
Dr. Nagendra Singh	1972-1973
T. Swaminathan	1973-1977
S. L. Shakdhar	1977-1982
R. K. Trivedi	1982-1985
R. V. S. Peri Sastri	1985-1990
Smt. V.S. Ramadevi	15.11.90-12.12.90
T. N. Seshan	1990 -1996
M.S. Gill	1996-mid 2001
J.M. Lingdoh	2001-2004
T.S. Krishnamurthy	2004-05
B.B. Tandon	2005-06
N. Gopalaswami	2006-09
Navin Chawla	2009 - 2010
S.Y. Quraishi	since July 30, 2010

Chiefs of Army Staff

General Maharaj Rajendra Sinhji	Apr.-May, 1955
General S. M. Srinagesh	1955-1957
General K. S. Thimayya	1957-1961
General R. N. Thapar	1961-1962
General J. N. Chaudhuri	1962-1966
General P.P. Kumaramangalam	'66-'69
General S. H. F. J. Manekshaw	1969-'72
Field Marshal S. H. F. J. Manekshaw	Jan.01.73- Jan.14.73
General G. G. Bewoor	1973-1975
General T. N. Raina	1975-1978
General O. P. Malhotra	1978-1981

Manekshaw   *Vijay Kumar Singh*

General K. V. Krishna Rao	1981-1983
General A. S. Vaidya	1983-1986
General K. Sundarjee	1986-1988
General V. N. Sharma	1988-1990
General S. F. Rodrigues	1990-1993
General Bipin Chandra Joshi	1993-1994
General Shankar Roy Chowdhury	1994- 1997
General Ved Prakash Malik	1997- 2000
General Sundarrajan Padmanabhan	2000– 2002
General Nirmal Chander Vij	2002-2005
General J.J. Singh	2005-2007
Deepak Kapoor	2007-2010
Gen. Vijay Kumar Singh	Since April 01, 2010

(General Sir Roy Bucher (1948-49), General K. M. Cariappa (1949-53) and General Maharaj Rajendra Sinhji (1953-55) served as commanders-in-chief of Indian Army. General Kariappa was conferred the rank of Field Marshal in 1986).

Chiefs of Naval Staff

Vice-Admiral R. D. Katari	1958-1962
Vice-Admiral B. S. Soman	1962-1966
Admiral A. K. Chatterjee	1966-1970
Admiral S. M. Nanda	1970-1973
Admiral S. N. Kohli	1973-1976
Admiral J. L. Cursetji	1976-1979
Admiral R. L. Pereira	1979-1982
Admiral O. S. Dawson	1982-1984
Admiral R. H. Tahiliani	1984-1987
Admiral J. G. Nadkarni	1987-1990
Admiral L. Ramdas	1990-1993
Admiral Vijay Singh Shekawat	1993-'96
Admiral Vishnu Bhagwat	1996-1998
Admiral Sushil Kumar	1999-2001
Admiral Madhvendra Singh	2001-2004

First Lady Chief Justice	Mrs. Justice Leila Seth, a judge of Delhi High Court, was sworn in as the Chief Justice of Himachal Pradesh High Court on Aug. 5, 1991. She was thus the country's first lady Chief Justice.

Admiral Arun Prakash	2004-06
Admiral Sureesh Mehta	2006 - 09
Admiral Nirmal Verma	since 31-08- 09

Chiefs of Air Staff

Air Marshal Sir Thomas Emhirst	'47-'50
Air Marshal Sir Ronald Lvelaw Chapnam	1950-1951
Air Marshal Sir Gerald Gibbs	1951-1954
Air Marshal S. Mukherjee	1954-1960
Air Marshal A. M. Engineer	1960-1964
Air Chief Marshal Arjan Singh	1964-'69
Air Chief Marshal P. C. Lal	1969-1973
Air Chief Marshal O. P. Mehra	1973-'76
Air Chief Marshal H.Moolgavkar	'76-'78
Air Chief Marshal I. H. Latif	1978-1981
Air Chief Marshal Dilbagh Singh	'81-'84
Air Chief Marshal L. K. Katre	1984-1985

Air Chief Marshal D. A. La Fontaine	1985-1988
Air Chief Marshal S. K. Mehra	1988-'91
Air Chief Marshal N.C. Suri	1991-1993
Air Chief Marshal Swarup Krishan Kaul	1993-1995
Air Chief Marshal Satish Kumar Sareen	1995-1998
Air Chief Marshal A.Y. Tipnis	1999-2001
Air Chief Marshal S. Krishnaswamy	2001-2004
Air Chief Marshal S.P. Tyagi	2004-2007
Air Chief Marshal Fali Homi Major	2007-2009
Air Chief Marshal Pradeep Vasant Naik	2009-2011
Air Chief Marshal N.A.K. Browne	Since July 31, 2011

Govt. of India : Table of Precedence

1. President
2. Vice-President
3. Prime Minister
4. Governors of States (within their respective States)
5. Former Presidents
5a. Deputy Prime Minister
6. Chief Justice of India; Speaker of Lok Sabha
7. Cabinet Ministers of the Union; Chief Ministers of States (within their respective States); Deputy Chairman, Planning Commission; Former Prime Ministers; Leaders of Opposition in Rajya Sabha and Lok Sabha
7a. Holders of Bharat Ratna decoration
8. Ambassadors Extraordinary and Plenipotentiary and High Commissioners of Commonwealth countries accredited to India. Chief Ministers of States (outside their respective States); Governors of States (outside their respective States)
9. Judges of Supreme Court
9a. Chief Election Commissioner; Comptroller & Auditor General of India

10. Deputy Chairman, Rajya Sabha; Deputy Chief Ministers of States; Deputy Speaker, Lok Sabha; Members of the Planning Commission; Ministers of State of the Union and any other Minister in the Ministry of Defence for defence matters.
11. Attorney General of India; Cabinet Secretary; Lieutenant Governors (within their respective Union Territories.
12. Chiefs of Staff holding the rank of full General or equivalent rank.
13. Envoys Extraordinary and Ministers Plenipotentiary accredited to India.
14. Chairmen and Speakers of State Legislatures within their respective States; Chief Justices of High Courts within their respective jurisdictions.
15. Cabinet Ministers in States within their respective States; Chief Ministers of Union Territories and Chief Executive Councilor, Delhi, within their respective Union Territories; Deputy Ministers of the Union.

(This is not a complete list.)

V.P. Singh Ministry	**The eleven-month-old National Front Government of Prime Minister V.P. Singh was voted out of Power in November, 1990. Lok Sabha rejected a motion of confidence by a vote of 346 to 142.**

Council of Ministers

Cabinet Ministers

Dr. Manmohan Singh: Prime Minister and also in-charge of the Ministries/Departments not specifically allocated to the charge of any Minister viz.:

Dr. Manmohan Singh

(i) Ministry of Personnel, Public Grievan-ces & Pensions;
(ii) Ministry of Planning;
(iii) Department of Atomic Energy; and
(iv) Department of Space

Shri Pranab Mukherjee: Minister of Finance

Shri Sharad Pawar: Minister of Agriculture, Minister of Food Processing Industries

Shri A. K. Antony: Minister of Defence

Shri P. Chidambaram Minister of Home Affairs

Shri S. M. Krishna: Minister of External Affairs

Shri Virbhadra Singh : Minister of Micro, Small and Medium Enterprises

Shri Vilasrao Deshmukh: Minister of Science and Technology, Minister of Earth Sciences

Shri Ghulam Nabi Azad: Minister of Health and Family Welfare

Shri Sushil Kumar Shinde: Minister of Power

Shri M. Veerappa Moily: Minister of Corporate Affairs

Dr. Farooq Abdullah: Minister of New and Renewable Energy

Shri S. Jaipal Reddy: Minister of Petroleum and Natural Gas

Shri Kamal Nath: Minister of Urban Development

Shri Vayalar Ravi: Minister of Overseas Indian Affairs, Minister of Civil Aviation

Smt. Ambika Soni: Minister of Information and Broadcasting

Shri Mallikarjun Kharge: Minister of Labour and Employment

Shri Kapil Sibal: Minister of Human Resource Development, Minister of Communications and Information Technology

Shri Anand Sharma: Minister of Commerce and Industry, Minister of Textiles

Shri C. P. Joshi: Minister of Road Transport and Highways

Kumari Selja: Minister of Housing and Urban Poverty Alleviation, Minister of Culture

Shri Subodh Kant Sahay: Minister of Tourism

Shri G. K. Vasan: Minister of Shipping

Pranab Mukherjee   *Sharad Pawar*   *A.K. Antony*   *P. Chidambaram*

S.M. Krishna   *Virbhadra Singh*   *Vilasrao Deshmukh*   *Ghulam Nabi Azad*

Sushil Kumar Shinde   *Veerappa Moily*   *Farooq Abdullah*   *Jaipal Reddy*

Kamal Nath   *Vayalar Ravi*   *Ambika Soni*   *Mallikarjuna Kharje*

Kapil Sibal   Anand Sharma   C.P. Joshi   Kumari Selja

Subodh Kant Sahay   G.K. Vasan   Pawan Kumar Bansal   Mukul Wasnik

M.K. Azhagiri   Praful Patel   Sriprakash Jaiswal   Salman Khursheed

Kishore Chandra Deo   Beni Prasad Verma   Dinesh Trivedi   Jairam Ramesh

Shri Pawan K. Bansal: Minister of Parliamentary Affairs, Minister of Water Resources

Shri Mukul Wasnik: Minister of Social Justice and Empowerment

Shri M. K. Alagiri: Minister of Chemicals and Fertilizers

Shri Praful Patel: Minister of Heavy Industries and Public Enterprises

Shri Shriprakash Jaiswal: Minister of Coal

Shri Salman Khursheed : Minister of Law and Justice, Minister of Minority Affairs

Shri V. Kishore Chandra Deo : Minister of Tribal Affairs, Minister of Panchayati Raj

Shri Beni Prasad Verma : Minister of Steel

Shri Dinesh Trivedi : Minister of Railways

Shri Jairam Ramesh : Minister of Rural Development, Minister of Drinking Water and Sanitation

Ministers of State (Independent Charge)

Shri Dinsha J. Patel: Minister of State (Independent Charge) of the Ministry of Mines

Smt. Krishna Tirath: Minister of State (Independent Charge) of the Ministry of Women and Child Development

Shri Ajay Maken : Minister of State (Independent Charge) of the Ministry of Youth Affairs and Sports

Prof. K. V. Thomas : Minister of State (Independent Charge) of the Ministry of Consumer Affairs, Food and Public Distribution

Shri Srikant Jena : Minister of State (Independent Charge) of the Ministry of Statistics and Programme Implementation and Minister of State of the Ministry of Chemicals and Fertilizers

Smt. Jayanthi Natrajan : Minister of State (Independent Charge) of the Ministry of Environment and Forests

Shri Paban Singh Ghatowar : Minister of State (Independent Charge) of the Ministry of Development of North Eastern Region and Minister of State of the Ministry of Parliamentary Affairs

Ministers of State

Shri E. Ahamed : Minister of State in the Ministry of External Affairs, Minister of State in the Ministry of Human Resource Development

Shri Mullappally Ramachandran : Minister of State in the Ministry of Home Affairs

Shri V. Narayanasamy : Minister of State in the Ministry of Personnel, Public Grievances and Pensions

Minister of State in the Prime Minister's Office

Shri Jyotiraditya Madhavrao Scindia : Minister of State in the Ministry of Com-

| First Non-Congress Government | Morarji Desai, who became the fourth Prime Minister of India on March 24, 1977 formed the first non-Congress (Janata) government in India. |

merce and Industry

Smt. D. Purandeswari : Minister of State in the Ministry of Human Resource Development

Shri K.H. Muniappa : Minister of State in the Ministry of Railways

Smt. Panabaka Lakshmi : Minister of State in the Ministry of Textiles

Shri Namo Narain Meena : Minister of State in the Ministry of Finance

Shri M.M. Pallam Raju : Minister of State in the Ministry of Defence

Shri Saugata Ray : Minister of State in the Ministry of Urban Development

Shri S.S. Palanimanickam : Minister of State in the Ministry of Finance

Shri Jitin Prasada : Minister of State in the Ministry of Road Transport and Highways

Smt. Preneet Kaur : Minister of State in the Ministry of External Affairs

Shri Harish Rawat : Minister of State in the Ministry of Agriculture , Minister of State in the Ministry of Food Processing Industries, Minister of State in the Ministry of Parliamentary Affairs

Shri Bharatsinh Solanki : Minister of State in the Ministry of Railways

Shri Mahadev S. Khandela : Minister of State in the Ministry of Tribal Affairs

Shri Sisir Adhikari : Minister of State in the Ministry of Rural Development

Shri Sultan Ahmed : Minister of State in the Ministry of Tourism

Shri Mukul Roy : Minister of State in the Ministry of Shipping

Shri Choudhury Mohan Jatua : Minister of State in the Ministry of Information and Broadcasting

Shri D. Napoleon : Minister of State in the Ministry of Social Justice and Empowerment

Dr. S. Jagathrakshakan : Minister of State in the Ministry of Information and Broadcasting

Shri S. Gandhiselvan : Minister of State in the Ministry of Health and Family Welfare

Shri Tusharbhai Chaudhary : Minister of State in the Ministry of Road Transport and Highways

Shri Sachin Pilot : Minister of State in the Ministry of Communications and Information Technology

Shri Prateek Prakashbapu Patil : Minister of State in the Ministry of Coal

Shri R.P.N. Singh : Minister of State in the Minister of Petroleum and Natural Gas, Minister of State in the Minister of Corporate Affairs

Shri Vincent Pala : Minister of State in the Ministry of Water Resources, Minister of State in the Ministry of Minority Affairs

Shri Pradeep Jain : Minister of State in the Ministry of Rural Development

Ms. Agatha Sangma : Minister of State in the Ministry of Rural Development

Shri Ashwani Kumar : Minister of State in the Ministry of Planning, Minister of State in the Ministry of Science and Technology, Minister of State in the Ministry of Earth Sciences

Shri K. C. Venugopal : Minister of State in the Ministry of Power

Shri Sudip Bandopadhyay : Minister of State in the Ministry of Health and Family Welfare

Shri Charan Das Mahant : Minister of State in the Ministry of Agriculture, Minister of State in the Ministry of Food Processing Industries

Shri Jitendra Singh : Minister of State in the Ministry of Home Affairs

Shri Milind Deora : Minister of State in the Ministry of Communications and Information Technology

AS ON : Wednesday, August 10, 2011

Indira Succeeded by Rajiv

Prime Minister Indira Gandhi was assassinated by her security guards at her residence on October 31 morning, 1984. Her son Rajiv Gandhi was sworn in as the 6th PM the same afternoon.

Blood Donation

Safe blood saves lives and improves health. 'More blood, More life' is the theme of Blood Donor Day, 2011.

Blood donation is the process when a person has blood drawn, voluntarily, and it is used for transfusions or made into medications by a process called fractionation.

Such people, who are called blood donors, are usually unpaid volunteers who give blood for a community supply. Some are paid and in some countries, there are incentives such as "paid time off work" in order to encourage donation. A donor can also have blood drawn for his/her own future use.

Donors are evaluated or screened for anything that might make their blood unsafe. They undergo stringent processes that include testing for several diseases that can be transmitted through blood transfusion. This includes the Human Immunodeficiency Virus (HIV), malaria, viral hepatitis and syphilis. Usually, a potential donor is asked about his or her medical history and subject to a short physical examination. How often a donor can give or donate blood depends on what he or she donates and the laws of the country where the donation takes place. In the United States for example, a donor must wait for about 56 days between whole blood donations.

The Red Cross says that all blood donations are tested and processed and made available for use between 24 and 48 hours after collection.

Whole blood is separated into its components (red blood cells, platelets and plasma). After processing, red cells can be stored for up to 42 days, plasma is frozen and stored for up to 12 months, while platelets have a life of five days.

A single unit of blood drawn during a whole blood donation is about 450 ml (or less than half a litre) or less than 10% of a person's total blood volume.

The body replenishes blood all the time irrespective of whether one donates or does not donate blood, so it is a myth that one loses blood after donation.

An adult who is of average size has a blood volume of about five litres.

Blood Groups

Everybody has a particular blood group which he or she inherits from his or her parents. There are two major blood type systems -- the ABO system and the Rhesus system (Rh factor) --- different combinations of which result in eight major blood types.

When a transfusion is required, it is preferable that a recipient receives blood of the same ABO and Rh type.

Let us have a look at different components of blood and what they do:

Red Blood Cells (RBC) are what give blood its colour and constitute 40-50% of its volume. Their main function is to carry oxygen from the lungs to all cells in the

Safe Storage of Blood

Before WWI, a physician had to find a compatible donor and give an immediate blood transfusion. Technological changes have made safe storage of blood and its components possible today.

body and remove waste products such as carbon dioxide. Transfusions are used to treat person with severe anaemia (such as Thalassaemia Major), those whose RBCs do not function to satisfaction, accident victims (or those who are bleeding profusely) and patients who are undergoing surgery.

Platelets

Platelets are those blood components that assist in the process of blood clotting. The primary use of platelets is in the treatment of people who suffer various forms of cancer and whose bone marrow is unable to produce an adequate number of platelets. Medical treatments like chemotherapy can decrease a person's platelet count. As platelets are stored at room temperature and have a short shelf life (mentioned above), it is very important to have a continuous stream of donations.

Plasma, the straw coloured fluid in which RBCs, white cells and platelets are suspended, is the most versatile component of blood as it can be processed into a variety of products, which in turn can be used to treat a number of conditions.

Platelet or plasma-only donations can be done every two weeks. Both plasma and platelet donations are made through a process called apheresis. It involves the use of a special cell separator or apheresis machine.

There are three types of blood donation:

Whole blood donation which includes the collection of three blood components (RBC, Plasma and Platelets) Persons with the blood group 'O negative' are needed for whole blood donations. It is the only blood group that can be given to everyone. Persons who are 'O negative' are called "universal donors".

Most people who are fit and healthy can be whole blood donors. In order to donate whole blood, a person should need to weight at least 45kg. In the case of donation of plasma or platelets by apheresis, a

---

Red Blood Cells

A global study shows that red blood cells from a donation are used in the following ways:

34% cancer and blood diseases
19% other causes of anaemia
18% surgical patients which involves open heart surgery and burn victims
13% in medical problems that include heart, stomach and kidney disease
10% in orthopaedic patients
4% in obstetrics
2% in trauma cases that include accidents
Total: 100%

---

person's body weight needs to be at least 50kg. Persons who are less than 18 years and weigh less than 50 kg, are ineligible to donate blood. The reason is that, internationally, it has been shown that young donors are at increased risk of fainting during or following blood donation.

Plasma donation: It involves donating a concentrated collection of plasma only. Persons with blood groups 'A', 'AB' and 'B' are particularly needed for plasma donations, says the Red Cross. As RBCs are returned to a donor, when one donates plasma, you can donate every two weeks.

Platelet donation: It involves donating a concentrated collection of platelets only. Persons with blood groups 'A' and 'O' are particularly needed for platelet donations, says the Red Cross. As the body replenishes platelets soon, a person can donate every two to four weeks.

Why plasma donation?

The Red Cross says that there are 17 different products that can be made from plasma donations. Some of the most needed products are Immunoglobulins --- these are preparations that contain antibodies used to protect against infectious diseases like tetanus, chicken pox and hepatitis B.

Early Physicians | Greek physician Galen showed that arteries carried blood, not air. But he was wrong in his conclusions about human anatomy. Andreas Vesalius found the errors and William Harvey gave the true picture.

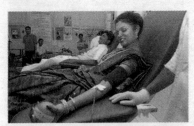

Intragam P --- a preparation containing antibodies used to boost the immune system, after a bone marrow transplant and for immune deficiency disorders. It is also used in the treatment of a number of other disorders involving the immune system.

Albumin --- used to restore blood volume in the treatment of shock or burns, and in the treatment of liver and kidney diseases.

Biostate or Factor VIII Concentrate --- used to stop or prevent bleeding in people with von Willebrand disorder and haemophilia A. These people have an inherited deficiency of von Willebrand factor or Factor VIII respectively, both of which are proteins necessary for normal blood clotting.

Plasma donation takes approximately 45 minutes, and up to 750 ml of plasma can be donated in one single plasma donation, which is greater than the amount of plasma donated in two whole blood donations. An average adult has approximately five litres of blood, three litres of which is plasma.

Why platelet donation?

Coming to platelets, they are the fragments of cells made in the bone marrow. There are about 250 million per millilitre of blood. Why do we need platelet donations? A transfusion is very important especially in conditions like leukaemia and treatments which can decrease a person's platelet count. If the number of platelets becomes too low, spontaneous bleeding can occur. Even a small amount of bleeding can be dangerous, particularly if it occurs in the brain, says the Red Cross.

World Blood Donor Day (June 14)

The World Health Organization (WHO) recognizes World Blood Donor Day on June 14 each year to promote blood donation. This is the birthday of Karl Landsteiner, the scientist who discovered the 'ABO' blood group system. In 2008, the WHO estimated that more than 81 million units of blood were being collected annually. Of this, only 38% is collected in developing countries where 82% of the world's population lives. The theme for World Blood Donor Day 2011 is [was] "More blood. More life."

The WHO says that safe blood saves lives and improves health. A decision to donate blood can save a life, or even several if blood is separated into its components — RBCs, platelets and plasma — which can be used individually for patients with specific conditions.

National Advisory Council

National Advisory Council (NAC) was set up on 4 June 2004 by Prime Minister Manmohan Singh to implement the common minimum programme of the first UPA government. It is an adivisory body comprising distinguished professionals drawn from diverse fields of development activity who serve in their individual capacities.Through the NAC, the Government has access not only to their expertise and experience but also to a larger network of research organizations, NGOs and Social Action and Advocacy Groups. The NAC would provide policy and legislative inputs to Government with special focus on social policy and the rights of the disadvantaged groups.

Chairperson: Sonia Gandhi

Members: 1). Prof M. S. Swaminathan, 2). Dr Ram Dayal Munda, 3). Dr. Narendra Jadhav, 4). Prof. Pramod Tandon, 5). Dr. Jean Dreze, 6). Ms.Aruna Roy, 7). Shri Madhav Gadgil, 8). Shri Naresh C. Saxena, 9). Dr. A. K. Shiva Kumar, 10). Shri Deep Joshi, 11). Ms. Anu Aga, 12). Ms. Farah Naqvi, 13). Shri Harsh Mander, 14).Ms Mirai Chatterjee.

Sobriquets

Places

Sobriquets	Primary Names
Bengal's Sorrow	River Damodar
City of the Golden Gate	San Francisco, USA
City of the Golden Temple	Amritsar
City of Dreaming Spires	Oxford, UK
City of Seven Hills/Eternal City	Rome
Cockpit of Europe	Belgium
Dark Continent	Africa
Emerald Island	Ireland
Empire City/City of Skyscrapers	New York, USA
Garden Ciy	Bangalore
Gate of Tears	Bab-el-mandab
Gateway of India	Bombay
Gift of the Nile	Egypt
God's Own Country	Kerala
Herring Pond	Atlantic Ocean
Holy Land	Palestine
Hermit Kingdom/Land of Morning Calm	Korea
Island of Cloves	Zanzibar
Island of Pearls	Bahrain
Key of the Mediterranean	Gibraltar
Land of Cakes	Scotland
Land of the Humming Bird	Trinidad
Land of the Kangaroo/Land of the Golden Fleece	Australia
Land of the Golden Pagoda	Myanmar (Burma)
Land of Lilies/Land of Maple/Lady of Snow	Canada
Land of the Midnight Sun	Norway
Land of the Rising Sun	Japan
Land of Thousand Lakes	Finland
Land of Thunderbolt	Bhutan
Land of the White Elephants	Thailand
Never Never Land	Prairies of N. Australia
Pink City	Jaipur
Playground of Europe	Switzerland
Queen of the Adriatic	Venice, Italy

 Early Bird The first commercial communications satellite *Intelsat I* was launched by the US in 1965 to provide high-bandwidth telecommunications service between the US and Europe. It was known as 'Early Bird'.

Queen of the Arabian Sea	Kochi
Roof of the World	Pamirs
Sick Man of Europe	Turkey
Sorrow of China/Yellow River River	Hwang Ho
Spice Garden of India	Kerala
Sugar Bowl of the World	Cuba
The Sea of Mountains	British Colombia
The Spice Island of the West	Grenada
Venice of the East	Alappuzha
Venice of the North	Stockholm, Sweden
White City	Belgrade
World's Breadbasket	Prairies of N. America
World's Loneliest Island	Tristan da Cunha

Persons

Sobriquet	Name
Adi Kavi	Valmeeki
Anna	C.N. Annadurai
Badshah Khan/Frontier Gandhi	Abdul Ghaffar Khan
Bard of Avon	William Shakespeare
Bard of Twickenham	Alexander Pope
Deenabandhu	C.F. Andrews
Deshbandhu	C.R. Das
Desert Fox	Gen. Erwin Rommel
Ike Dwight	David Eisenhower
Fuhrer	Adolf Hitler
Il Duce	Benito Mussolini
J.P., Loknayak	Jayaprakash Narayan
Kaviguru	Rabindranath Tagore
Lady with the Lamp	Florence Nightingale
Lokamanya	Bala Gangadhara Thilak
Mahamana	Madan Mohan Malaviya
Mahatma	Gandhiji
Maid of Orleans	Joan of Arc
Man of Blood and Iron	Bismarck
Netaji	Subhas Chandra Bose
Panditji	Jawaharlal Nehru
Qaid-e-Azam	Mohammed Ali Jinnah
Rajaji or 'CR'	C. Rajagopalachari
Saint of the Gutters	Mother Teresa
The Cincinnatus of the Americans	George Washington

Lawrence, Ross and Shaw

T. E. Lawrence was a British scholar and military strategist who is known as Lawrence of Arabia. He conceived the plan of supporting Arab rebellion against the Turks during WWI. After retirement he enlisted in the Air Force under the name Ross and later Shaw.

Heads of Important Offices

President of India: Smt. Pratibha Patil

Vice President: Mohammad Hamid Ansari

Prime Minister : Dr. Manmohan Singh

Chief Justice : Justice S. H. Kapadia

Speaker, Lok Sabha: Meira Kumar

Dy. Speaker, Lok Sabha: Karia Munda

Chairman, Rajya Sabha: Mohammad Hamid Ansari

Dy.Chairman, Rajya Sabha: K.Rahman Khan

Chairman, Planning Commission: Dr. Manmohan Singh

Attorney General: G.E. Vahanvati

Solicitor General: Rohinton Nariman

Comptroller and Auditor-General: Vinod Rai

Chief Election Commissioner: Dr. S.Y. Quraishi

Election Commissioners: V.S. Sampath and H S Brahma

Principal Secretary to the Prime Minister : Pulok Chatterjee

National Security Adviser: Shivashankar Menon

Principal Scientific Adviser to the Govt. : Dr. R. Chidambaram

Registrar-General & Census Commissioner: Dr. C. Chandramouli

Scientific Adviser to the Defence Minister : V.K. Saraswat

Secretary-General, Lok Sabha: T.K. Viswanathan

Secretary-General, Rajya Sabha: Dr. V.K. Agnihotri

Governor, Reserve Bank of India: Dr. D. Subbarao

Cabinet Secretary : A.K. Seth

Home Secretary : Raj Kumar Singh

Finance Secretary : Sunil Mitra

Defence Secretary: Shashi Kant Sharma

Chairman, Prime Minister's Economic Advisory Council : Dr. C. Rangarajan

Surveyor General of India: Swarna Supba Rao

Chief Vigilance Commissioner: Pradeep Kumar

Chairman, National Knowledge Commission: Sam Pitroda

Chairperson, Prasar Bharti: Smt. Mrinal Pande

Chairman, UPSC: D.P. Agrawal

Chairman, Atomic Energy Commission: Dr. Srikumar Banerjee

Chairman, CBSE : Vineet Joshi

Chairman, Central Administrative Tribunal (CAT) : Justice V.K. Bali

Chairman, Central Board of Direct Taxes: M C Joshi

Chairman, Central Board of Excise and Customs : S D Majumdar

Chairperson, Central Board of Film Certification: Ms. Leena Samson

Chairman, NABARD: Prakash Bakshi

Chairman, ABC : Vijay Darda

Chairman, Central Electricity Regulatory Authority : Pramod Deo

Chairman, Food Corporation of India: Siraj Hussain

Chairman, Foreign Inv. Promotion Board : V. Govindarajan

Chairman, Air India: Rohit Nandan

Chairman, ISRO : Dr. K. Radhakrishnan

Chairman, Law Commission: Justice P V Reddy

Chairman, Life Insurance-Corporation of India: D. K. Mehrotra (in charge)

Chairman, National Book Trust: Bipan Chandra

Chairman, National Commission on Farmers: Dr. M.S. Swaminathan

Chairman, National Commission for SCs : Dr. P L Punia

Chairman, National Commission for Backward Classes : M N Rao

Ambassador to the US — Smt. Nirupama Rao, formerly Foreign Secretary, is the new Indian Ambassador to the United States.

Important Offices: World

Director-General, UNESCO : Ms. Irina Bokova

Director-General, WHO : Dr. Margaret Chan

President, World Bank : Robert Zoellick

President, Asian Development Bank : Haruhiko Kuroda

Secretary-General, Commonwealth: Kamalesh Sharma

President, International Court of Justiice : Hisashi Owada

Director-General, WTO : Pascal Lamy

Secretary-General, ASEAN : Dr. Surin Pitsuwan

Jacques Rogge : President, International Olympic Committee

Secretary-General, SAARC : Ms. Fathimath Dhiyana Saeed

Managing Director, International Monetary Fund (IMF) : Christine Lagarde

Secretary-General, Organisation of Economic Cooperation and Development (OECD): Angel Gurria

High Commissioner, UN High Commission for Human Rights: Ms. Navanethan Pillay

Chairman, African Union: Teodoro Obiang Nguema Mbasogo

Acting Chairman, NHRC : Justice K G Balakrishnan

Chairman, Investment Commission : Ratan Tata

Chairman, Press Council of India : Justice G.W. Ray

Chairman, Press Trust of India : M P Veerendra Kumar

Chairman, Securities & Exchange Board of India : U K Sinha

Chairman, State Bank of India : Pratip Chaudhri

Chairman, University Grants Commission: Prof. Ved Prakash

Chairman, ONGC: A.K. Hazarika

Chairman, IRDA : J. Hari Narayan

Chairman, Staff Selection Commission: Dr. N.K. Raghupathy

President, Indian Council for Cultural Relations: Dr. Karan Singh

Chairman, ICHR: Basudev Chatterjee

Chairman, IFFCO :

Chairman, Indian Council of Social Science Research: Prof. Sukhudev Thorat

Chairman, Bombay Stock Exchange: Madhu Kannan

Chairman, Railway Board: Vinay Mittal

Chairman, Coir Board: V.S. Vijayaraghavan

Chairperson, Rubber Board: Sheela Thomas

Chairman, Coal India: N.C. Jha

Chairman, SAIL: C S Verma

Chairperson, Sangeet Natak Akademi: Ms. Leela Samson

Chairman, National School of Drama: Smt. Amal Allana

Chairperson, Central Social Welfare Board: Prema Cariappa

Chairperson, KVIC: Ms. Kumud Joshi

Chairperson, Children's Film Society of India: Nandita Das

Chairperson, National Commission for Women : Mamata Sharma

CMD, IDBI : R M Malla

Director, BARC : Dr. R.K. Sinha

Director, CBI : A.P. Singh

Director, VSSC : P S Veeraraghavan

Director, Intelligence Bureau: N. Sandhu

Director, Research and Analysis Wing: Sanjeev Tripathi

D-G, Border Roads Organisation: Lt. Gen. S. Ravi Sankar

D-G, BSF : Raman Srivastava

D-G, Coast Guard: Vice Admiral Anil Chopra

D-G, CRPF : K. Vijaya Kumar

D-G, CSIR : Samir K. Brahmachari

D-G, ICMR : Dr. Viswa Mohan Katoch

D-G, ASI: Dr. Gautam Sengupta

D-G, National Cadet Corps: Lt. General P.S. Bhalla

President, Assocham: Dilip Modi

President, BCCI : Shashank Manohar

President, FICCI : Harsh Mariwala

President, NASSCOM : Mr. Rajendra Pawar

President, Indian Newspaper Society : Kundan R Vyas

President, UPASI : C N Nataraj

Bollywood 2011

Overall, 2011 has been a mixed year for the Hindi film industry, though it proved that comedies continued to work. The biggest hit of 2011 during the first half was *Ready* starring Salman Khan and Asin. Produced by Eros International and directed by Anees Bazmee, *Ready* was released on June 3, and grossed Rs. 20 crore in its first week across 2000 plus screens worldwide. It has even bettered the collections of Salman Khan's last hit '*Dabangg*'.

The year 2011 began with Rajkumar Gupta directed *No one Killed Jessica* starring Vidya Balan and Rani Mukherji produced by UTV Motion pictures. It was based on the real life story of Jessica Lal murder case. Vidya Balan played the role of Jessica's elder sister, Sabrina and Rani Mukherji played a reporter. It did tremendous business at the box office.

Another film which made a good opening early this year was Samir Karnik's *Yamla Pagla Deewana* starring Dharmendra, Sunny Deol, Bobby Deol and Anupam Kher. The film was made at Rs. 20 crore. This comedy that brought the Deol troika together became a box office hit. Aamir Khan Productions *Dhobi Ghat* directed by Aamir's wife Kiran Rao also did good business at the box office.

The other films that made profits during 2011 include Vikram Bhatt's horror film *Haunted* (3D) and Rajini M.M.S directed by Pawan Kriplani. The much-hyped films like Rohan Sippy's *Dum Maro Dum* made at a budget of 20 crores and *Saat Khoon Maaf* directed by Vishal Bharadwaj (22 crore budget) did not live upto the 'hype'. Small films like the Rakeysh Omprakash Mehra produced *Teen Thay Bhai*, Balaji's *Shor In The City*, Onir's *I am* and Amole Gupte's *Stanley Ka Dabba* did not fare well. More disappointment came in the form of *Dil Toh Bachcha Hai Ji*, directed by Madhur Bhandarkar. It was his first attempt at comedy. Two other Major disappointments were Nikhil Advani's *Patiala House* and Anees Bazmee's *Thank you*.

Delhi Belly: Imran Khan and Poorna Jagannathan

Subhash Ghai made a special offer with his two small films, *Love Express* and *Cycle Kick* released respectively on June 10 and June 17. Cinegoes had a unique chance to watch both the movies on one ticket. But the idea was not successful with the audience. Indra Kumar's Double Dhamaal starring Sanjay Dutt, Riteish Deshmukh, Arshad Warsi, Jaaved Jaafri, Ashish Chowdhary, Mallika Sherawat and Kangana Ranaut which released on June 24, has got a bumper opening weekend collection of some 30 crore.

The second half of the year began with the release of much-hyped films like Puri Jagannadh's *Bhuddah........Hoga Terra Baap* starring Amitabh Bachchan, Raveena Tandan and Hema Malini, Abinay Deo's *Delhi Belly* with Imran Khan and Shehnaz Treasurywala, the thriller *Murder 2* with Emraan Hashmi and Jacqueline Fernandez and the children's film *Chillar Party*. Zoya Akhtar's multi star road movie *Zindagi Na Milegi Dobara* starring Hrithik Roshan, Farhan Akhtar, Abhay Deol, Katrina Kaif and Kalki Koechlin and Rohit Shetty's Ajay Devgan starrer *Singam* were released respectively on July 15 and July 22. Siddique's *Bodyguard* was a hit. Prakash Jha's Amitabh, Saif AliKhan, Deepika Padukone starrer *Aarakshan* was released on August 12. *Maaee* directed by Mahesh Kodiyal is the first film of Phalke award winner and noted playback singer Asha Bhosle. The 77 year old songstress plays the

A Scene from 'Singam'

role of a mother suffering from Alzheimer's who is abandoned by her only son and two daughters. Her eldest daughter has to take care of Maaee amidst work pressure and family opposition. The film was released on October 7, 2011.

Raj Kapoor Crescent

Legendary showman Rajkapoor will have a street named after him in the city of Brampton, Canada. The street is named Rajkapoor Crescent. It was inaugurated during the last week of June, in the presence of Kapoor family members.

Honorary Doctorate for Vikram

Tamil actor Vikram has been conferred with the Honorary Doctorate of Fine Arts in acting by Universita Popolare Degli Studi *Di Milano* on May 29, 2011. The University established in 1901 is also known as People's University of Milan. Vikram is the first Indian actor in the history of the European Universities to receive an honorary doctorate in Acting.

Arrival of Sequels: The production of sequels of some of the successful films is in progress in Bollywood. Among them are *Mr. India 2, Munnabhai Chale America, Kya Kool Hai Hum -2, Dhoom-3, Dabangg-2, House-*

Vikram

ful-2, Race-2, Krrish-2, Dostana-2, Murder-3, Yamla Pagla Deewana-2, Raaz-3, Delhi Belly-2, Total *Dhamaal*, Ghayal Returns and so on.

Phalke Award for K. Balachander

Tamil, Telugu, Kannada and Hindi film director and producer Kailasam Balachander has bagged the prestigious Dada Saheb Phalke Award. His directorial debut was Neerkumizhi in 1965. His major films include *Major Chandrakant, Bhama Vijayan, Ethir Neechal, Ethiroli, Kaviya Thalaivi, Velli Vizha, Arangetram, Naan Avanillai, Aval Oru Thodarkathai, Apoorva Ragangal, Aaina, Avargal, Manmatha Leelai, Moondru Mudichu, Nizhal Nijamakirathu, Thappu Thalangal, Maro Charithra, Varumayin Niram Sigappu, Thillu Mullu, Ek Duuje Ke Liye, Thanneer Thanneer, Achamillai Achamillai, Sindhu Bhairavi, Punnagai Mannan, Rudraveena, Puthu Puthu Arthangal, Azhagan, Vaaname Ellai, Duet* etc. He was the first Tamil Director to receive the Phalke Award. He brought in a change in Tamil cinema by infusing new ideas and thereby created a social thinking. He introduced several artistes like Kamalahasan, Rajni Kant, Sujatha, S.V. Sekhar and so on.

Chidananda Dasgupta (1921-2011), the most erudite Indian film critic, passed away in Kolkata on May 22, 2011. He deserves credit of pioneering the film society movement in India along with like-minded friends like Satyajit Ray and Harisadhan Dasgupta in 1947. Apart from serious in depth writing on cinema he also edited books on cinema and culture. Among his books are - *Talking About Films* (1981), The Cinema of Satyajit Ray (1980), *The Painted Face-Studies in India's Popular Cinema* (1991) and Seeing is Believing- Selected writings on Cinema (2008) that have run into several reprints and editions. He won the Best Critic award at the National level many years ago. He made several documentaries and two feature films, 'Bilet Pherat' and 'Amodini'. He wrote the mu-

Breakaway

Akshay Kumar's production venture *Breakaway* aka *Speedy Singhs* had its world premiere at the Toronto International Film Festival. The presence of Canadian PM Stephen Harper added grandeur to the occasion.

sical score for his own film '*Amodini*' and for Aparna Sen's '*Sati*'. He made history with the Lifetime Achievement Award best owed on him for Best writing at the Sixth Osian's Cinefan Festival of Asian Cinema in 2004. Film maker and Actress Aparna Sen is his eldest daughter and actress Konkona Sen Sharma is one of his grand children.

Mani Kaul (67), one of the pioneers of Indian New Wave Cinema, passed away on July 6, 2011 in Gurgaon.

A product of FTII, Kaul took up acting but soon turned to direction and bagged two National Awards for his film '*Duvidha*' in 1974, and Best Documentary Film for '*Siddeshwari*' in 1984. Kaul was one of the first Indian directors who stepped away from the style of linear, conventional storytelling. His films include *Uski Roti*, *Duvidha*, *Ashad Ka Ek Din*, *Satah Se Uthata Aadmi*, *Siddeshwari* and *Idiot*. He was a life long student of '*Dhrupad*' and sang well, too. Among his last projects was a documentary, '*A Monkey's Raincoat*' which he made in 2005. He served as the creative director of the 2009 edition of the Osian's Cinefan Festival of Asian and Arab Cinema.

Ilayaraja's 'Free' Music

The United Nations has declared the year 2011 'the International Year of Forests'. To highlight this and to spread awareness about the need to conserve and sustain our forests, writer-director R. Selvaraj has come up with a mainstream film titled *Pachchai Kudai* (Green Umberlla). Malayalam actress Nithya Das plays a tribal woman from forest.

The main attraction of the film is the mind blowing music by Isai Gnani Ilayaraja. It is surprising to note that the maestro has not accepted any amount as remuneration

for scoring the background music for *Pachchai Kudai*. Notable film maker Bharathiraja has lent his voice for the prelude. The movie will be screened only at International Film Festivals like Cannes, Toronto and so on.

Chinese Song for Tamil Movie

Veteran director Murugadoss has included a Chinese song - *Zhe Yindu Nanzi Shi Shei.....* written by Madan Karky in his Tamil film *7 Aum Arivu* starring Suriya and Shruthi Hassan. A Chinese singer has sung the song. Suriya is playing a double role - a Buddhist Monk and a scientist.

A.R. Rahman

Biography of Rahman

Nasreen Munni Kabir has written an authorized biography of maestro A.R. Rahman, the Mozart of Madras. The book is titled - *A.R. Rahman - The Spirit of Music*.

Lifetime Achievement Award for Chiru

Telugu Megastar Chiranjeevi has received a Life Time Achievement Award from Filmfare on July 2, 2011, at Hyderabad. Earlier he received Seven Filmfare awards for Best Action. The films are *Subhalekha* (1982), *Vijetha* (1985), *Aapadbhandavudu* (1992), *Mutha Maistry* (1993), *Sneham Kasam* (1999), *Indra* (2002), *Shankar Dada MBBS* (2004). He has also decided to launch a TV Channel.

Chiranjeevi

Super Heavy

Academy award winner A.R. Rahman is now set collaboration with Mick Jagger (*The Rolling Stone's Fortman*) in a super group called '*Super Heavy*'.

Ilayaraja

KIMS

Comprehensive
Cancer
Treatment
now at

KIMS PINNACLE
COMPREHENSIVE CANCER CENTER

Preventive, Medical, Surgical and Radiation Oncology

CHRYSALIS / TVM

State-of-the-art- facilities

Radiation therapy using
Linac Rapid Arc
Technology

No waiting time for Radiation
and Chemotherapy

Nuclear Medicine with
Gamma camera

Modern Chemotherapy
ward with specially
trained nurses

Brachytherapy

Highly experienced and well-qualified team led
by Prof. Jayaprakash Madhavan,
Prof. T. K Padmanabhan and Dr. Boban Thomas

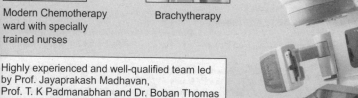

Important Addresses

President of India
Rashtrapati Bhavan, New Delhi-110004, EPABX : 23025321, Fax : 23017290 & 23017824, E-mail : presidentofindia@ rb.nic.in, Website : www.presidentofindia. nic.in

Vice President of India
6, Maulana Azad Road, New Delhi - 110011, Tel: 23016422, 23016344, Fax: 23018124, E-mail:vpindia@nic.in, E-mail: vicepresidentofindia.nic.in

Prime Minister
Office : Room No. 148 B, South Block, New Delhi, 110001, Office Tel : 23012312, Fax : 23016857, Website: www.pmindia.nic.in

Lok Sabha Speaker's Office
Parliament House Address Room No. 17, Parliament House, New Delhi-110001, +91 11 23017914 (Tel), +91 11 23017795 (Tel), +91 11 23792927 (Fax) email: speakerloksabha@sansad.nic.in

Supreme of Court of India
The Registrar, Supreme Court of India, Tilak Marg, New Delhi-110 001 (India) PABX NOS.23388922-24,23388942-44, FAX NOS.23381508,23381584,2338 4336/23384533/23384447 e-mail at : supremecourt@nic.in

Election Comission of India
Nirvachan Sadan, Ashoka Road, New Delhi-110001 Tel: 011-23717391 Fax: 011-23713412 feedback@eci.gov.in

Central Bureau of Investigation (CBI)
Block no. 4, 6th Floor, CGO Complex, Lodhi Road, New Delhi - 110003

Central Information Commision (CIC)
August Kranti Bhavan, Bhikaji Cama Place,

New Delhi - 110 066 & Old JNU Campus, New Delhi - 110 067. Phone:26161137 Fax: 26186536

National Human Rights Commission
Faridkot House,Copernicus Marg, New Delhi - 110 001. Facilitation Centre (Madad): (011) 23385368 Mobile No. 9810298900 (For complaints-24 hrs.) Fax:(011)23386521(complaints) /23384863 (Administration)/ 23382734 (Investigation) Email: covdnhrc@nic.in. (General)/ jrlaw@nic.in(For complaints) resnhrc@nic.in (Research Division) Web site: www.nhrc.nic.in

University Grant Commission (U G C)
Bahadur Shah Zafar Marg, New Delhi Pin:110 002, India E-mail: webmaster@ugc.ac.in Web: http://www. ugc.ac.in/ Tel: and Fax: EPABX Nos. 23232701/23236735/ 23239437/ 23235733/23237721/ 23232317/ 23234116/23236351/ 23230813/ 23232485 UGC reception 23239627 Fax. Nos. 23231797 / 23232783 23239659/ 23231814

Union Public Service Commission
Dholpur House, New Delhi - 110-069 Telephone No.s: 011- 23098543, 23385271 Fax: 23381125

National Commission For Women
4, Deen Dayal Upadhayaya Marg, New Delhi-110 002. Tel: 91-11-23237166, 91-11-23236988 Fax : 91-11-23236154 Complaints Cell : 91-11-23219750 Email: ncw@nic.in

National Commission For Minorities
5th Floor, Lok Nayak Bhavan, Khan Mar-

Trains of India

Indian Railways employs about 1.55 mn. people. Number of passengers daily is 13mn., trains 14,300 and railway stations 7000. The Silguri Railway Station is the only one with all Three Gauges. The states without Railway lines are Sikkim and Meghalaya.

ket, New Delhi 110 003 Tel. 24615583
Fax 24693302, 24642645, 24698410
Toll Free Number: 1800110088 E-mail:
ro-ncm@nic.in

Planning Commission of India
Yojana Bhavan, Sansad Marg, New Delhi
-110 001. E-mail: plancom@nic.in For
general queries and information Tel.:
011-23096620

Central Administrative Tribunal (CAT)
61/35 Copernicus Marg, New Delhi - 110
001, INDIA E-mail ID: cat-delhi@nic.in

Animal Welfare Board of India
13/1, Third Seaward Road, Valmiki Nagar,
Thiruvanmiyur, Chennai- 600 041.
Phone: 044-24454935, 24454958 Fax:
044-24454330 E-mail : awbi@md3.vsnl.
net.in

UPSC Calendar for Examinations - 2012

S No.	Name of Examination	Date of Notification	Last Date for Receipt of Applications	Date of Commencement of Exam	Duration of Exam
1.	Reserved for UPSC RT/Exam			08.01.12 (Sun)	1 day (Two tests)
2.	SCRA Exam, 2012	15.10.11	14.11.11 (Mon)	29.01.12 (Sun)	1 Day
3.	C.D.S. Exam.. (I) 2012	29.10.11	28.11.11 (Mon)	12.02.12 (Sun)	1 Day
4.	Reserved for UPSC RT/Exam			04.03.12 (Sun)	1 Day (Two tests)
5.	N.D.A. &N.A. Exam (I), 2012	31.12.11	20.01.12 (Mon)	15.04.12 (Sun)	1 Day
6.	Civil Services (Preliminary) Exam, 2012	04.02.12	05.03.12 (Mon)	20.05.12 (Sun)	1 Day
7.	Engineering Services Examination 2012	25.02.12	26.03.12 (Mon)	15.06.12 (Fri)	03 Days
8.	Combined Medical Services Exam,2012	03.03.12	02.04.12 (Mon)	17.06.12 (Sun)	1 Day
9.	Reserved for UPSC RT /Exam			24.06.12 (Sun)	1 Day (Two tests)
10.	Indian Forest Service Exam, 2012	31.03.12	30.04.12 (Mon)	14.07.12 (Sat)	10 Days
11.	Reserved for UPSC RT/Exam			29.07.12(Sun)	1 Day (two tests)
12.	Reserved for UPSC RT/Exam			05.08.12(Sun)	1 Day (Two tests)
13.	N.D.A. & N.A. Exam (II), 2012	05.05.12	04.06.12 (Mon)	19.08.12 (Sun)	1 Day
14.	C.D.S. Exam. (II), 2012	02.06.12	02.07.12 (Mon)	16.09.12 (Sun)	1Day
15.	Reserved for UPSC RT/Exam			23.09.12 (Sun)	1 Day (Two Tests)
16.	Civil Services (Main) Exam, 2012			05.10.12 (Fri)	21 Days
17.	Central Police Forces (AC) Exam, 2012	28.07.12	27.08.12 (Mon)	11.11.12 (Sun)	1 Day
18.	Reserved for UPSC			18.11.12 (Sun)	1 Day (Two tests)
19.	I.E.S. /I.S.S. Exam, 2012	18.08.12	17.09.12 (Mon)	01.12.12 (Sat)	3 Days
20.	Geologists' Exam, 2012	25.08.12	24.09.12 (Mon)	01.12.12 (Sat)	3 Days
21.	S.O./Steno (GD-B/GD-1) LTD. DEPTIL.COMPETITIVE EXAM	21.07.12	17.09.12 (Mon)	15.12.12 (Sat)	4 Days
22.	Reserved for UPSC RT/Exam			23.12.12 (Sun)	1 Day (Two tests)

First Superfast Train India's first superfast train is Decan Queen connecting Delhi with Pune. It was inroduced by the British in 1930.

Time Chart

Countries	(+/- IST) Hours
Afghanistan	(–) 1.30
Albania	(–) 4.30
Algeria	(–) 4.30
Antilles	(–) 9.30
Argentina	(–) 8.30
Australia	(+) 2.30/(+) 4.30
Austria	(–) 4.30
Bahamas	(–) 10.30
Bahrain	(–) 2.30
Bangladesh	(+) 0.30
Barbados	(–) 9.30
Belgium	(–) 4.30
Belize	(–) 11.30
Benin	(–) 4.30
Bermuda	(–) 9.30
Bolivia	(–) 9.30
Botswana	(–) 3.30
Brazil	(–) 8.30
Brunei	(+) 2.30
Bulgaria	(–) 2.30
Burkina Faso	(–) 5.30
Cameroon	(–) 4.30
Canada	(–) 9/14.30
Yemen Islands	(–) 10.30
Cen. African Republic	(–) 4.30
Chad	(–) 4.30
Chile	(–) 9.30
China	(+) 2.30
Colombia	(–) 10.30
Congo	(–) 4.30
Costa Rica	(–) 11.30
Cuba	(–) 10.30
Czech Republic	(–) 4.30
Denmark	(–) 4.30
Djibouti	(–) 2.30
Dominican Islands	(–) 9.30
Dominican Republic	(–) 9.30
Ecuador	(–) 10.30
Egypt	(–) 3.30
Ethiopia	(–) 2.30
Fiji	(+) 6.30
Finland	(–) 3.30
France	(–) 4.30
Gambia	(–) 5.30
Germany	(–) 4.30
Ghana	(–) 5.30
Gibralter	(–) 4.30
Greece	(–) 3.30
Grenada	(–) 9.30
Guatemala	(–) 11.30
Guyana	(–) 8.30
Haiti	(–) 10.30
Honduras	(–) 11.30
Hong Kong	(+) 2.30
Hungary	(–) 4.30
Iceland	(–) 5.30
Indonesia	(+) 1.30/3.30
Iran	(–) 2.00
Iraq	(–) 2.30
Ireland	(–) 5.30
Italy	(–) 4.30
Ivory Coast	(–) 5.30
Jamaica	(–) 10.30
Japan	(+) 3.30
Jordan	(–) 3.30
Kenya	(–) 2.30
Korea (South)	(+) 3.30
Kuwait	(–) 2.30
Lebanon	(–) 3.30
Liberia	(–) 5.30
Libya	(–) 3.30
Luxembourg	(–) 4.30
Malawi	(–) 3.30
Malaysia	(+) 2.30
Maldives	(–) 0.30
Mali	(–) 5.30
Malta	(–) 4.30
Marshall Islands	(+) 6.30
Mexico	(–) 11.30
Micronesia	(+) 3.30/5.30
Monteserat	(–) 9.30
Morocco	(–) 5.30
Mozambique	(–) 3.30
Myanmar	(+) 1.00
Namibia	(–) 3.30
Nauru	(+) 6.30
Nepal	(+) 0.00
Netherlands	(–) 4.30
New Zealand	(+) 6.30
Nicaragua	(–) 11.30
Niger	(–) 5.30
Nigeria	(–) 4.30
Norway	(–) 4.30
Oman	(–) 1.30
Pakistan	(–) 0.30
Panama	(–) 10.30
Papua New Guinea	(+) 4.30
Paraguay	(–) 9.30
Peru	(–) 10.30
Philippines	(+) 2.30
Poland	(–) 4.30
Portugal	(–) 5.30
Porto Rica	(–) 9.30
Qatar	(–) 2.30
Romania	(–) 3.30
Russia	(–)(2.30)—(+)5.30
Saudi Arabia	(–) 2.30
Senegal	(–) 5.30
Seychelles	(–) 1.30
Sierra Leone	(–) 5.30
Singapore	(+) 2.30
Somalia	(–) 2.30
Spain	(–) 4.30
Sri Lanka	(Indian Time)
Sudan	(–) 3.30
Suriname	(–) 8.30
Swaziland	(–) 3.30
Sweden	(–) 4.30
Switzerland	(–) 4.30
Syria	(–) 3.30
Taiwan	(+) 2.30
Tanzania	(–) 2.30
Thailand	(+) 1.30
Tonga	(+) 7.30
Trinidad and Tobago	(–) 9.30
Tunisia	(–) 4.30
Turkey	(–) 2.30
Uganda	(–) 2.30
United Arab Emirates	(–) 1.30
UK	(–) 5.30
Uruguay	(–) 8.30
Vanuatu	(–) 5.30
Vatican City	(–) 4.30
Venezuela	(–) 9.30
Yemen	(–) 2.30
Yugoslavia	(–) 4.30
Zaire	(–) 4.30
Zambia	(–) 3.30
Zimbabwe	(–) 2.30
USA	(4 Time Zones)
New York	(–) 10.30
Texas	(–) 11.30
Phoenix	(–) 12.30
San Francisco	(–) 13.30
Hawai (USA)	(–) 16.00

Climate Change: Do's and Don'ts

There is danger in using up resources faster than they can be replenished. Global warming is too big a threat to be ignored. How can we help improve the situation?

We live on the only planet we know has life on it. We can have life on this planet or cause massive destruction. The choice is ours:conservation is our obligation, conservation not only of human beings but other species as well.

With a population of 7 billion which is set to pass 9 billion by 2050, the Earth will find it difficult to sustain its population The rising middle class in developing countries have already started consuming at western rates. And it would take more than 5 Earths to sustain the exploding world population if everyone consumed resources at the same rate as the U.S. We could thus leave little room for wild life. We would be crowding out other species by our sheer numbers.

We are eating into the future. We are using up resources faster than they can be replenished. Spiralling food prices, soaring energy costs, tornados and other natural calamities like record-breaking monsoons, droughts...etc indicate that we have crossed some red lines. If we continue to cut more trees than we plant, put extra nitrogen into water, thicken the Earth's CO2 blanket and warm the globe, the blow will be big with adverse impact on environment, health, life support and society at large. In China's history of thousands of years the conflict between mankind and nature has never before been so fierce as it is today.

Global Warming

Even if we do manage to reduce forest loss and stop wildlife destruction, a greater threat looms on the horizon--global warm-

ing. As climate changes rapidly the territory to which species have migrated may become uninhabitable faster than they can respond. The Intergovernmental Panel on Climate Change (IPCC) has reported that warming could put as much as 70% of species at a greater risk of extinction, with Arctic animals like the polar bear potentially among the first to go.

The Planet is Warming Up

The planet is slowly warming up. The first five years of the 21st century were the hottest on record along with 1998.

Ice on land and at sea is melting faster than its normal rate. Many high altitude species are going to higher altitudes every year.

Early flowering and unseasonal rain are observed in many parts of the globe, including India.

The Human Factor

The era of cheap and plentiful oil is draw-

Life Without Water   A human being may survive without food for several days but water deprivation can kill a person within a matter of hours.

ing to an end. Burning fossil fuels is reducing Earth's oxygen levels by about 25 billion tons a year. The decline is one of the clearest evidences of the detrimental impact of human activity on nature.

Humans are the key factor in changing the chemistry and composition of atmosphere, outstripping even volcanoes, once the main source of CO2.

Climate Change

New analysis shows that climate is becoming extreme. We have to get accustomed to such extreme weather conditions as climate change intensifies. Temperature and rainfall records are being broken every year. In 2010, in Eastern Europe and Russia scorching heat claimed 50,000 lives. Temperature stayed more than 6 degree above normal for months. Two-third of the continent experienced the hottest summer in 500 years. Kuwait has seen mercury at 50 degree C. Rajasthan recorded 49 degree C. Even Canada touched 33 degree C. In Kenya, Ethiopia and Somalia millions of peo-

ple this year have little or no food because of the failure of precipitation.

The impact of climate change on rain is more important in the long run. Excess rainfall can cause deluge while scanty rain makes an area unproductive.

The number of geo-physical disasters like volcano and earthquake has remained constant while those caused by flood and storm have increased from 133 a year in 1980s to 350 a year now. It is clear that weather related disasters have been in-

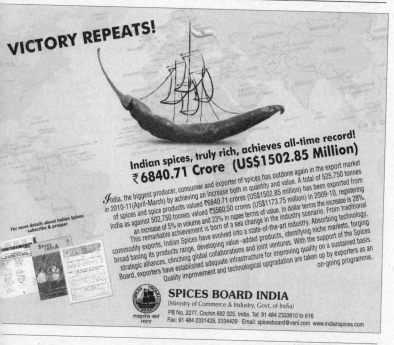

creasing especially in poor countries and they are going to get worse as climate changes further.

Nitrogen also plays a crucial role in the formation of aerosols and affects global warming. Nitrogen management has attracted the attention of climate and agricultural scientists. It is crucial in stepping up food production. But at the same time the increasing nitrogen load in the atmosphere due to human activity has lethal consequences on nature.

What can we do to reduce Global Warming?

Do's and Don'ts

- Replace your present light bulbs with electronic fluorescent lamps. They last ten times longer and consume about 75 per cent less electricity less than an ordinary bulb.
- Substitute a compact fluorescent bulb for a traditional bulbs. This will keep half a tonne of carbon dioxide out of the atmosphere. They are more expensive than an ordinary bulb, but work out much cheaper in the long run because they save electricity.
- One large ordinary bulb is more efficient than two small ones in a multi-bulb fixture. A 100 W bulb, for example, generates about as much light as two 60W bulbs, and it saves energy.
- Cut down on the use of electrical appliances.
- In summer, shut windows, blinds, curtains and doors early in the morning to keep the house cool.
- Use your water heater sparingly. Switch it off soon after your bath, for heaters are

great consumers of electricity.
- Setting your water heater too high (about 1500 F) wastes energy.
- Lower the thermostat. After all, most of us mix cold water with hot water to get the right temperature.
- If you can, install a solar water heating system in your home.
- Turn the stove off immediately after use.
- Use pressure cooks as much as possible.
- Plan well and keep ingredients ready before you start cooking.
- Keep the vessel closed while cooking and always use small, narrow-mouthed vessels.
- When the food is almost cooked, switch off the gas stove and keep the vessel closed. It will get fully cooked the heat already present.
- When you switch off the gas stove, switch off the regulator of the cyclinder as well, to prevent leaks.
- Use ISI marked stoves which use less kerosene.
- Decide what you want out of your refrigerator or freezer before opening the door.
- Don't stand and stare into the refrigerator with the door open while making up your mind.
- Check if the door is properly closed after you have finished your work.
- If your refrigerator and freezer are 5 degrees colder than necessry, their energy consumption will increase by 25%.
- The refrigerator door will not be air-tight if there is dried food stuck on the gasket. Ensure that it is always clean.
- If your refrigerator needs to be refilled with gas, it means there is a leak. Fix the leak first.
- For efficient operation, clean the condenser coils at the back or bottom of your fridge at least once a year.
- Keep your fridge full for more economical operation.
- Let foods cool to room temperature before storing.
- The easiest way to make your car more

fuel-efficient is to keep it well-tuned. A well-tuned car uses up to 9% less petrol than a poorly tuned car. If 100,000 car owners who have neglected tune-ups started getting their cars tuned up regularly, some 90 million pounds of carbon dioxide could be kept out of the atmosphere every year!

- Keep fuel filters clean. Clogged filters use more petrol.

- Check to see whether you are hauling around unnecessary weight in your car. Surprisingly, an extra hundred pounds will decrease your fuel economy by more than 1%.

- When you are buying a car, keep fuel efficiency in mind. Alternatively, equipment like power steering and automatic transmissions need a lot of energy to run.

- Inflate your tyres to the right pressure. This reduces fule consumption by 5%.

- Drive gently. Don't race the engine, accelerate and slow down gradually. All this can improve the mileage by 15%.

- Drive between 40 and 50 kmph. The faster you go the more wind resistance your vehicle will face. You can get 40% extra mileage at 40 kmph as compared to 80 kmph.

- Car sharing is an effective way of cutting down on cars and thus, on energy consumption.

- Join a car pool. Share lifts to and from work and on family outings.

- Try using the public transport systems like trains and buses.

- Better still, use a bicycle - it occupies little space, releases no pollution , and provides healthy excercise.

- Fit your car with tinted windows to help keep the temperature constant and reduce the need for airconditioning.

- Walk rather than drive wherever possible. Walking is one of the best exercises for your body.

Courtesy: Eco News, the journal of C.P.R, Environmental Education Centre.

Contributed by: **Varghese C. Thomas**

English : American & British

American	British
1. apartment	flat
2. billfold	wallet
3. automobile	car
4. bobbypin	hairgrip
5. cotton candy/ spun sugar	candyfloss
6. candy	sweets
7. closet	cupboard
8. derby	bowler hat
9. diaper	nappy
10. drapes	curtains
11. druggist	chemist, pharmacist
12. elevator	lift
13. faucet	tap
14. fall	autumn
15. fender	wing of a car, bumper
16. flashlight	torch (batter-operated)
17. furlough	absence from military duty
18. gas/gasoline	petrol
19. hood	bonnet (of a car)
20. great	very good
21. hope chest	bottom drawer
22. installment plan	hire-purchase
23. intern	junior hospital doctor/ houseman
24. kerosene	paraffin
25. kid	child
26. mortician	undertaker, funeral director
27. muffler	car silencer
28. mutual fund	unit trust
29. odometer	milometer
30. pacifier	baby's dummy
31. podiatrist	chiropodist
32. railroad	railway
33. realtor	estate agent
34. rummage sale	jumble sale
35. shot	injection
36. skillet	frying pan
37. sling shot	toy catapult
38. snap fastener	press stud
39. sidewalk	pavement
40. solitaire	(card game of) patience
41. sophomore	second year student
42. store	shop
43. stevedore, longshoreman	docker/dock worker
44. suspenders	braces
45. thumb-tack	drawing pin
46. tick-tack-toe	noughts and crosses
47. truck	lorry
48. trunk	boot of a car
49. tuxedo	men's formal dinner jacket
50. vacation	holiday
51. vest	waistcoat
52. veteran	ex-service man
53. undershirt	vest
54. zip code	pin code

Congress Presidents (Since 1960)

1960	Bangalore	Indira Gandhi
1961	Bhavnagar	N. Sanjiva Reddy
1962	New Delhi	D. Sanjivayya
1964	Bhubaneswar	K. Kamaraj
1965	Durgapur	K. Kamaraj
1966	Jaipur	K. Kamaraj
1968	Bangalore	S. Nijalingappa
1969	New Delhi	C. Subramaniam
1970	New Delhi	Jagjivan Ram
1971	Ahmedabad	D. Sanjivayya
1972	Calcutta	Shankar Dayal Sharma
1975	Chandigarh	D.K. Barooah
1976	New Delhi	Brahmananda Reddy
1978	New Delhi	Indira Gandhi
1983	Calcutta	Indira Gandhi
1984	New Delhi	Rajiv Gandhi
1985	Bombay	Rajiv Gandhi
1991	New Delhi	P.V. Narasimha Rao
1996	New Delhi	Sitaram Kesri
1998	New Delhi	Sonia Gandhi

Palindromes

Palindromes are words or phrases that read the same backwards as well as forwards. e.g. Madam, Malayalam, Not a Ton, able was i ere i saw elba.

Indian Mythological Characters

Abhimanyu: The heroic son of Arjuna, the central figure of the Mahabharata, by his wife Subhadra.

Ahalya: A Princess of the Puru dynasty, who was turned into a stone by the curse of her husband, Gautama.

Krishna

Arjuna: The third of the Pandavas.

Asvathama: Son of Drona and Krpi

Agneyi: Wife of Kuru, son of Manu.

Balabhadra (Balarama, Baladeva): The elder brother of Srikrishna and the eighth incarnation of Mahavishnu.

Bali (Mahabali): An emperor of the Asuras. He was the son of Virochana and the grandson of Prahlada.

Bharata: Son of Dasaratha

Bhima: Bhimasena, one of the five Pandavas.

Bhishma: Eighth son of Santanu, a king of the lunar dynasty and Gangadevi.

Brihaspati: The teacher of the devas (Gods)

Dasaratha: A famous king of the Ikshvaku dynasty, father of Srirama.

Dharmaputra: The eldest of the Pandavas.

Dhritarashtra: Father of the Kauravas.

Drona: The teacher in archery of the Pandavas and the Kauravas.

Duryodhana: Villain in the Mahabharata story, the eldest of the Kauravas.

Gandhari: Wife of Dhritarashtra.

Indra: Son of Kashyapa and Aditi

Indrajit: Ravana's son, Meghanada

Indrani: Wife of Indra

Karna: The eldest son of Kunti. Though he was the brother of the pandavas he joined sides with the Kauravas and became the king of Anga.

Krishna: Born in the Yadava dynasty as the son of Vasudeva and Devaki; the ninth of the incarnations of Mahavishnu.

Kunti: Wife of king Pandu and the mother of the Pandavas.

Lakshmana: Son born to Dasaratha by Sumitra.

Panchali (Draupati) : wife of the Pandavas.

Parasara: Sakti, son of Vasishta begot of his wife Adrsyanti the son named Parasara.

Parasurama: An incarnation of Mahavishnu, as man

Parvati: Wife of Siva

Prahlada: Son of Hiranyakasipu and Kayadhu.

Rama: The seventh incarnation of Mahavishnu.

Ravana: The Rakshasa king of Lanka who had ten heads.

Sarasvati: Goddess of learning

Sikhandi: Rebirth of Amba, daughter of the king of Kasi.

Siva: One of the Trinity, the other two being Brahma and Vishnu.

Urmila: Wife of Lakshmana.

Vamana: An incarnation of Mahavishnu.

Vasudeva: Father of Srikrishna.

Sarasvati

Philately

An educator named Rowland Hill of England is considered the Father of Philately. The world's first postage stamp was issued in 1840 by Great Britain. Two years later stamps were used by a private postal service in New York. Brazil and two Swiss cantons (Zurich and Geneva) were the next to issue stamps. The U.S. used its first stamps on July 1, 1847. India's first stamp appeared in 1852.

The bits of coloured paper were a curiosity and used specimens were retained by some people. Thus the hobby was born. The interest spread rapidly and everywhere men and women began hunting for used stamps of different countries. By 1850, the hobby had taken root.

Today stamp-collecting is the world's most popular hobby. It is described as 'the hobby of kids and kings'.

In recent times the study of stamps has been taken up by many. Research papers on philately are published often. There are museums of stamps and philatelic libraries, not to mention the umpteen stamp clubs. Stamp catalogues, albums and other accessories for the stamp collector are sold in large numbers every day. Philatelic exhibitions and stamp auctions are regular events in many cities. There are also journals devoted to philately and we hear about philatelic journalists. Many modern newspapers

have stamp departments to cater for the tastes of their stamp-loving readers.

India came out with its first stamp in 1852, that is only 12 years after the world's first stamp appeared. Stamp-collecting has developed to become the pastime of the thousands of young and old people today.

The first official airmail in the world was between Allahabad and Naini. On February 18, 1911 L. Pecquet flew a biplane carrying mail in connection with the United Provinces Exhibition. The golden jubilee of the event was commemorated in 1961 by India issuing three stamps. Interestingly, the first official airmails in Britain, Denmark, Italy and the USA were also begun in 1911. In 1910, mail was flown unofficially in Britain as souvenirs of the Blackpool Aviation Meeting.

Stamps to Go Online — Postal Department is planning to introduce online version of postage stamps. Copies of bar-code based receipt will be printed and used in place of postal stamps for sending mail.

Stamps for Investment

Sunil Joseph, Philatelist

Stamp-collecting is the world's most popular hobby. Now people have turned to stamps in a big way to invest money in them.

In recent months, we have witnessed a rise in the price of premium quality rare collectibles as more investors turn to our asset class as a safe haven and a means of wealth protection. The recent record set for the sale of a single stamp in the UK for £1.1 million & an India 1854 Four Anna Victoria Head inverted sold for £ 105,390, demonstrated this.

With news that banks are unlikely to pay a rate of interest that will keep up with inflation for at least the next two years, investing in tangible assets makes a lot of sense. Even more so when taking into account the tax advantages of investing in tangible assets.

Many investors turn to gold in times of panic, but it is important to consider the extent of the bull market that gold has enjoyed over the past few years. I think any downward correction here could be severe. It has happened before...

If you had invested in gold between 1980 and 1985, you would have lost 38%. Between 1995 and 2000, you would have lost 29% of your investment.

Rare collectibles on the other hand

have a long term history of never declining in value. The reason for this is simple economics. We have a declining supply as items are damaged, lost, donated to museums or tied up in long term collections. Against that, we have rising demand...

Where is this demand for collectibles coming from?

It is not widely appreciated just how big the collectibles market is. There are an estimated 200 million collectors in the world.

It is widely known that we are seeing a rising interest in collectibles from the new middle classes in the Far East. This new dimension has provided a boost to the market.

Not only that though, there are more ultra high net worth individuals in the world now than there has ever been. Some of them have got into collectibles. Notable examples include Bill Gates, Roman Abramovich and Bill Gross (the famous bond trader and avid stamp collector).

Add to that the fact that the average

A Stamp for Vegetarians

The Indian arm of the People for the Ethical Treatment of Animals (PETA) has requested the Department of Posts to issue a stamp to promote vegetarianism. Oct. 1 is the World Vegetarian Day.

collector is aged 65 plus. That demographic is rising rapidly thanks to the baby boom after World War II and people living longer. What that means is that we have an expected increase in demand for many years to come.

"No wonder financial advisers suggest adding stamps to an investor's portfolio. Investments in rare stamps can fetch annual returns of over 45%. On average, rare stamps have given returns of about 10-15% a year in recent years. They have given steady returns and occasionally".

Towards the start of this year, Dianomi Ltd undertook a wide ranging survey of almost 2,000 investors and potential investors in the UK.

The results make interesting reading.

Inflation was reported as the primary fear, with investors doing all they can to choose assets that inflation-proof their portfolios, whilst also selling gilts. As well as alternative assets, gold, silver and sectors like utilities and infrastructure are proving popular for the top investors

Two hot topics of discussion and where investors wanted free guides or reports included, "How to create a morally responsible banker" and "Guide to investments during periods of stagnation or inflation" - regrettably we can't help you with the former, but we do know that rare stamps have proven a strong hedge against inflation in the past and are proving their worth in that context once again. Their consistent growth

rates, tracked on Bloomberg in the GB30 Rarities Index, clearly demonstrate their stagnation-busting ability, particularly as a medium-term hold.

It is worth noting, therefore, that rare stamps not only hold up strongly against other asset classes, but also provide an excellent hedge against inflation. As an indicator, the last time we experienced seriously high inflation, in the period 1975 to 1980, the GB30 Rarities Index actually increased in value by 593%.

What are the top investors buying right now?

Not surprisingly, 30% of investors are buying gold and silver compared to just 19% at the same time last year and property also shows some signs of recovery with 32% buying versus 24% last year - but from Stanley Gibbons point of view, the real news is that alternative investments have surged year on year, 29% of top investors are buying alternatives (including rare stamps and coins) against 17% last year.

When you consider the continuing buoyancy of the rare stamp market and the increasing profile of rare stamps as an asset class, uncorrelated with other mainstream asset classes, this is actually no surprise.

What's happening in the rare stamp market?

Unsurprisingly also, Penny Black prices are increasing, with added interest coming from abroad (particularly China) as well as in the UK.

Further afield, both the Indian and Chinese stamp markets are booming, with Chinese stamps particularly continually breaking all sorts of records

at auction; the emergence of 5 new (philatelic) auction houses in Hong Kong in the past year points irrefutably to the region becoming a new powerhouse in stamp trading circles.

The key fact is: the stamp index has not dropped in value in any 5-year period over the past 50 years. You can now see why many financial commentators refer to our market as a "safe haven investment".

So - if you have been undecided about taking out an investment in rare stamps, now is your time to act.

Do bear in mind that although the rare stamp market continues to grow, every year.

Is it a bubble?

I think the term "bubble" is widely misused by financial commentators when referring to anything that represents a high growth market. There is validity in the concept though, that things can't go up at such high rates forever...

Ultimately, prices rise in accordance with demand against the inherent supply restrictions, which exist in the stamp world.

It stands to reason that the more expensive things get, the more collectors become priced out of the market. There will come a time when only the very wealthy have the funds available to participate in the market.

But, it is all a numbers game...

In China, there are over 20 million collectors, far more than the print runs of the stamp issues. This is in a country where wealth is rising. The Chinese elite get the importance of "tangible assets" in prudent wealth management and protection.

More and more money is flooding into the market. Naturally, this causes a supply squeeze.

It is not just the Chinese that are buying Chinese stamps...

"I would say presently that half of my buyers are from Mainland China and half are from outside China," said Louis Mangin, owner of the auction house Zurich Asia.

"Many Western-ers also buy Chinese stamps. It is seen as a diversification and investment into China."

Stamp prices in China started at very low levels. Chairman Mao banned stamp collecting, which remained in force until his death in 1976. Since then, the Chi-nese have been frantically buying back their postal heritage scattered around the world.

But, it seems that highly sought after stamps still trade at very affordable prices. From experience at auctions in China, this is the most liquid stamp market in the world, where one has never before seen so many collectors bidding in a room at one time. It staggers oneself when we see the price of a stamp going above £100,000 and there are still a dozen collectors in the game.

One day, this may become a bubble. Right now, it is a simple high growth market supported by huge and rising demand against severe supply restrictions.

investors will benefit from a "quality re-rating" when the Chinese ultimately begin to appreciate the premium rarity value of quality examples.

That is on top of the underlying growth in this asset class. The recent Merrill Lynch Wealth Report states that there are around half a million Chinese millionaires, (31% more than in 2008).

According to Barclays Capital, the Chinese account for 12% of the world's luxury goods market. The Chinese want to show off their new wealth to the world. The stamp market is just one part of this revolution.

Demand is always far in excess of the available supply in the market.....

The Chinese& Indian stamp market will remain highly lucrative for the foreseeable future. It is already the biggest and most important stamp market in the world.

To summarise the economics, you are:

Investing in a tangible asset;

In a growth market;

Not tied to the strength of the UK pound, US dollar or Euro;

Non correlated with other asset classes;

Benefits the most in times of high inflation.

A Veteran Journalist Honoured

A Commemorative stamp of ₹ 5 was brought out by the Postal Department on August 1, 2011 in honour of Shri. K.M. Mathew, Chief Editor of Malayala Manorama, 1973 - 2010, on the occasion of his first death anniversary.

Numismatics

The collection and the scientific study of coins is termed numismatics. Coin collecting is one of the oldest hobbies in the world. The use of coins in the world started in the 6th century BC. The first minted coins came from Cyme and Lydia, old cities in Asia Minor. In India the use of coins became popular in the 5th century BC in Central India. 'Rupiya' released by Sher Shah Suri (1540 – 1545) was the first Indian Rupee. In 1835 East India Company issued gold Mohur and silver Rupee coins. British India coins were in use during 1857 and 1947.Coins of Republic of India came into circulation in 1950.In 1964 Reserve Bank of India started the issue of commemorative coins to honour great personalities. The first such coin was on Nehru, the first Prime Minister of India. The latest commemorative coin issued by the India Government Mint was on Blessed Mother Teresa; a set of two coins, Rs 100 and Rs. 5. The newly issued Rupee coins (10, 5, 2 and 1) of India depict the new Rupee symbol.

Indian Coins

Coins were issued by the various Imperial dynasties and smaller middle kingdoms of India during the 1st millennium BC. In its initial stages, it consisted mainly of copper and silver coins. Broadly, coinage in India falls under the phases: Ancient, Medieval, Mughal, late pre-Colonial, British India and independent India.

Punch-marked Coins

According to the Reserve Bank of India, the first documented coinage is deemed to start with "punch marked" coins issued between the 7th and 6th centuries BC and 1st century AD. These coins derive their name because of their manufacturing technique. Most often made of silver, these bear symbols, each of which was punched on the coin with a separate punch. Metal currency was minted in India well before the Mauryan empire (322–185 BC), and as radio carbon dating indicates, before the 5th century BC. It was further enriched with the coming of Islam. The East India Company introduced uniform coinage in the 19th century. Numismatics

has been shown to be very important in determining stages in Indian history. The early coins of India (400 BC—100 A.D.) were made of silver and copper and had animal and plant symbols. But the influence of the Indo-Greek kingdom was unmistakeable.

By the 1st century BCE, tribes and dynasties and kingdoms began issuing their own coins. Kautilya's *Arthashastra* mentions the minting of coins. It also mentioned "a theory of bimetallism for coinage", which involved the use of copper and silver. The Gupta empire issued a surplus of gold coins, that showed its rulers performing rituals.Roman coins have been

The First Stamp and Coin Card

Vatican issued an interesting item, a 'stamp and coin card' on May 1, the day of the Beatification of Blessed Pope John Paul II. The stamp depicts Pope John Paul II and the coin Pope Benedict XVI.

This is the first stamp and coin card in the world and will be a precious collectors' item for stamp collectors and also for coin collectors.

Contributed by:
Prof. George John Nidhiry

found throughout India, especially in the busy maritime trading centres of South India. Arab campaigns in India led to very small silver coins being used. The coinage issued by emperors Akbar and Jahangir bore intricate Islamic calligraphy. Chinese merchant Ma Huan (1413–51) has mentioned that gold coins, known as fanam, were issued in Cochin/Kochi. Various types of coinage were issued by the East India Company until 1858. Soon there was a need to go in for a uniform imperial coinage system, which led to coinage being issued by the princely states being curtailed. With independence, India, Pakistan, and Sri Lanka issued their own coinage by 1948. Bangladesh soon followed its system on January 1, 1972.

Minting of Coins

In India, the right to mint coins lies solely with the Government of India, as given in the terms of the Coinage Act, since it was passed in 1906. Coins in denominations of 10 paise, 20 paise, 25 paise, 50 paise, one rupee, two rupees and five rupees came to be minted at the official Mints situated at Mumbai, Kolkata, Hyderabad, and Noida. However, India has issued coins minted by foreign mints during times of shortage. These were during 1857-58, 1943, 1985, 1997-2002 and these bear the mint marks of their origin. Some were minted at the Seoul Mint, the Royal Mint, London, The Heaton Press Mint, U.K., the Royal Canadian Mint, Ottawa, the Mexico Mint (Oeschger Masdach & Co,) the Moscow Mint, the Pretoria Mint (South Africa Mint Co. Pvt. Ltd.) and the Dominican Republic Mint.

The various operations are governed by the Reserve Bank of India. In 2010, the Government announced that it would be phasing out coins of 25 paise denomination and below from June 30, 2011. Currently, small coins (including 50 paise) in circulation constitute over 50% of the total volume of coins. As of March-end 2010, there were 54,738 million pieces of small coins in circulation. The value of small coins stands at Rs.1,455 crore, according to the Reserve Bank of India (RBI) annual report 2010. The total volume of coins, including small coins in circulation, increased 5.3% during 2009-10, compared with 4.7% the previous year, the apex bank has pointed out. The 10 rupee denomination showed the highest rate of growth in terms of both value and volume.

The mints of India

The East India Company set up three mints in the seventeenth and eighteenth centuries --- the Madras Mint in 1640 A.D., the Bombay Mint in 1671 A.D. and the Calcutta Mint in 1759 A.D. These mints had the latest technology incorporated in them at Bombay and Calcutta in 1829 A.D. The Madras Mint was closed in 1869. Before 1947, there were four mints, at Bombay, Calcutta, Lahore and Madras. After 1947, there are four mints, at Bombay, Calcutta, Hyderabad and Noida. The two oldest are the Alipore (Calcutta) and Bombay mints, both established in 1829 by the British Government, though the former was originally located in Calcutta and moved to its present site in 1952. The Hyderabad mint was established in 1903 by the Government of the erstwhile Nizam of Hyderabad and taken over by the Government of India in 1950. It commenced minting from 1953. The one in Noida was set up in 1986 and started minting ferritic stainless steel coins from 1988.

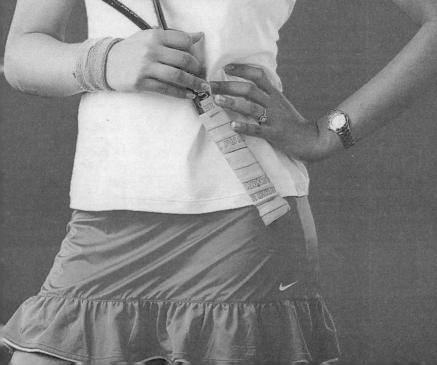

Part **14**

Sports

Pages 979 - 1024

What describes 'Indian Cricket' the best?

Aakash Chopra
Former Test Player and Columnist

Cricket in India has a colourful history. The changing face of the game is exhilarating and inspiring. The nation is becoming increasingly passionate about cricket.

Its honors, its medals, its records, its eleven illustrious men who don the Tri Color and win the country its accolades? Or its grit that has endured all to make it rise from the shadows of subjugation, stand up, challenge the odds and fight the existing hegemony and become a force to reckon with? Perhaps, each one of that, yet, nothing can lay bare its trials and tribulations, its fascinations and failures, its raw passion and its hysterics better than the unconditional love affair that each one of us has shared with it for years together. It's the people of India that make its Cricket captivating, bustling and curiously intimidating. Right from braving the harsh Indian Sun to enjoy an enthralling game of gully-cricket, queuing up long hours to buy tickets to a match, plastering bedroom walls with posters of favorite cricketing stars, getting hooked to TV and Radio sets for the latest scores, to treating every India – Pakistan encounter as 'do or die' – It's the 1.2 billion cricket fixated people of the country that work as the sole stimulus for Indian Cricket to achieve the unfathomable time and again, because for them, Cricket is not just a religion they follow, but an inherent faith they live with and swear by.

Today, as Indian Cricket stands at the crossroads of changing times, with a row of medals gleaming bright on the chest, and eyes set firmly on greater goals, the onus of protecting our rich cricket history and ensuring it does not get hidden beneath layers of newer successes lies with us. It's imperative to realize the importance of knowing the past in order to understand our present and predict our future. Where does Indian Cricket stand and what is its future? – is a crucial question that must be answered with an all-encompassing knowledge of the past. After all, legacies of excellence work as both memories of merit and inheritance of fine examples.

Palwankar Baloo

Let me begin by asking you, who would you rate India's all-time best left arm spinner? While most of you would be tempted to say Bishen Singh Bedi, who's indeed

Bishen Singh Bedi

The Origin of Cricket	Cricket originated in England among shepherds using their crooks as bats. The name came from Middle French criquet, goal stake. It was first definitively recorded in England in the late 16th century, though probably first played as early as the 1300's.

Kapil Dev

Sunil Gavaskar

been a genius, I'd still request you to ponder a bit more, delve deep in history and search for Palwankar Baloo. He belonged to the lowest rung of the prevalent Caste system of the pre-Independence times, and worked as a grounds-man in Pune Gymkhana Club in the days of the Raj. His job profile was to prepare the wickets, cut the grass and keep the ground ready for the British officers' recreational activity of playing cricket. He picked up the nuances of bowling while watching them play and soon offered his services as a net bowler too. The British officers' hunger to bat was insatiable and hence Balu was asked to bowl at as long as he could. He would be offered One Aana for every time he took an officer's wicket. And believe it or not, Balu would

Dilip Vengsarkar

always finish the month many times richer than his paltry salary as the grounds-man. His talent to bowl was then recognized and he graduated to playing competitive cricket but since the Caste system in India was at its lowest ebb, he would not be allowed to enter the dressing room or eat with the players even though he won them many a games. He went on to play for Hindus in the all-important Quadrangular in Mumbai. Yes, the first ever tournament in India was held on the basis of religion with a team each of Hindus, Muslims, Parsis and a team comprising of officers of British forces called 'The Europeans'. It was an extremely popular tournament and brought the entire city of Mumbai to a standstill for the duration of the cricket fest. India was still under the rule of the British and while the likes of Gandhi were fighting for Independence, a new breed of cricket lovers were getting increasingly involved with a sport introduced to them by their rulers. These were indeed the early beginnings of Cricket in India, a story we ought to know, for a leaf which does not know its tree, also does not know his own life story.

India was becoming increasingly passionate about cricket, as much as its western counterparts. Initially, cricket worked as a vent to our emotions, an expression of our freedom and a muted request to treat us as equals. But as time progressed, cricket became an important vehicle to assert our national identity. Post-Independence, a cricket match between India and its warring neighbor Pakistan was looked upon as war without weapons, that high the passions rode. Soon, not only Cricket but also Cricketers were pronounced National Heroes with Baloo brothers, C K Naiydu, Gavaskar and later Tendulkar acquiring Demi-God statuses.

The World Cup 1983

Yet, the watershed event that would change the dynamics of Indian and World

1983 World Cup Team

The First Century

The first century in cricket was scored on Indian soil in 1802 by Peter Vansittart for Etonians, against the Cricket Club of Calcutta.

Cricket was yet to happen. In 1983, India took the world by storm by lifting the World Cup against a much stronger West Indies, at Lord's, the Mecca of Cricket. This not only announced our arrival on the World platform, but also instilled in us a self-belief, which lacked hitherto. For kids like me, the 1983 win gave us a reason to take up cricket and idolize Kapil Dev, the people's cricketer. A nation needs heroes to pursue a particular sport and the team in 1983 gave us just that. We relinquished the status of perennial underdogs and started trading on equal terms with the then superpowers of cricket. We continued in the same vein for a while but lack of consistency proved to be our bane. While we were a dominant force at home, we were still the whipping boys overseas. Yet, we had the intent to improve and it showed eventually.

Mahender Singh Dhoni

ly started to change. In fact, the current and perhaps the best captain India has ever produced, Mahender Singh Dhoni comes from a small state unit Jharkhand. There are many such examples. While on the topic of Indian domestic structure, it's worth mentioning that the BCCI spends crores to organize cricket at all levels starting from Under 16. Every state unit except Services and Railways field their respective teams in these national age-group tournaments. The age-group tournaments are held in these categories–Under 16, Under 19, Under 22. All these matches are covered by 6 static cameras and the matches are played under ICC guidelines. The participating teams are divided into two divisions–Elite and Plate with the possibility of relegation and promotion. The matches are played in two different formats i.e. overs cricket (shorter format) and days cricket (longer format). The number of overs and days vary for different age groups. These tournaments are the feeding line for the state associations to put all the processes in place to ensure a strong team at the Ranji Trophy level.

Ranji Trophy Level

We had a rather expansive domestic structure in place with as many as 27 teams playing at the Ranji trophy level, which meant that we could choose our best XI from over 500 first class cricketers. This was and is the biggest pool of players any cricketing nation can boast of. Though all the competing teams were not forces to reckon with and rarely won the coveted title, they still played a pivotal role in producing world-class players. Initially, Mumbai, Delhi, Karnataka, Bengal, Tamil Nadu etc. remained the Indian cricket's power-centers and the majority of Indian players came from these states but things gradual-

Under-19 Level

Besides these annual domestic tournaments, BCCI remains quite active at the Under-19 level, which is in accordance to the ICC's program for the Under-19 teams. Since there's an Under–19 World Cup every alternate year, the BCCI has a program in place to keep its best Under–19 cricketers busy throughout the year. There's at least one annual International tour for Under–19 players that exposes them to their counterparts from different countries and also to alien conditions. To add to all these activities during the season, the BCCI organizes national and zonal camps at its state-

Ranji Trophy winners 2010

First Game | It is believed that cricket was played for the first time in India in Cambay of Gujarat. It was played between two groups of British sailors.

FILM
TELEVISION
NEWMEDIA
Media Education at its Best

CDIT is the Pioneer institution in Media Education and Research offering wide spectrum of courses in Media Studies. It follows advanced teaching techniques at par with the Media Education programmes world wide. The courses provide in depth knowledge, hands on training and field experience in various aspects of Media Production. CDIT produces advertisement films, documentaries and programmes for Government Departments, Educational institutions, Dooradarsan and other channels.

THE COMMUNICATION TRAINING TEAM (CTT) OF CDIT

POST GRADUATE DIPLOMA
AND CERTIFICATE COURSES

PG DIPLOMA PROGRAMMES ELIGIBILITY : ANY DEGREE

SCIENCE AND DEVELOPMENT COMMUNICATION | MULTIMEDIA DESIGN
TELEVISION AND NEW MEDIA JOURNALISM | ANIMATION FILM DESIGNING
TELEVISION PRODUCTION MANAGEMENT & MARKETING

PG CERTIFICATE PROGRAMMES ELIGIBILITY : ANY DEGREE

PHOTO JOURNALISM | TELEVISION NEWS PRESENTATION

DIPLOMA PROGRAMMES ELIGIBILITY : PLUS TWO

DIGITAL MEDIA PRODUCTION | WEB DESIGN AND DEVELOPMENT

CERTIFICATE PROGRAMMES ELIGIBILITY : SSLC/ PLUS TWO

DIGITAL STILL PHOTOGRAPHY | NON-LINEAR EDITING | VIDEOGRAPHY

be a **multifaceted**
.... **MEDIA** Professional

FOR DETAILS OF THE COURSE AND APPLICATION FORM, VISIT
www.cditcourses.org
www.cdit.org
Phone: **0471-2721917, 2384772** Fax:**0471-2721917**

CENTRE FOR DEVELOPMENT OF IMAGING TECHNOLOGY (C-DIT)

Under the Govt of Kerala   Chitranjali Hills,Thiruvallom, Thiruvananthapuaram, 695027 |
City Campus : 3rd Floor Manikanta Towers, Kowdiar,Trivandrum-695003

of-art academies during the off-season. The idea is to keep the talented cricketers not only involved throughout the year but also to monitor and streamline their progress. It was seen that our young cricketers were left to their own devices during the off-season, which was hampering their progress and these camps are a good way to bridge that gap. These camps are conducted by qualified coaches and assisted by former International cricketers to help these youngsters evolve as well-rounded sportspersons.

IPL: Commercialization of Cricket

Today, as these initiatives and processes are working well on their own, the BCCI has gone a step further to involve the corporates into the mix by introducing the Indian Premier League. Till 2008 the BCCI revenues came via broadcast rights sold to TV channels and team sponsorships, but the advent of the IPL has heralded a whole new chapter in which there is a direct participation of the corporates. These big corporate houses pay huge sums to procure a franchise and players making the BCCI and cricketers a lot richer. It wouldn't be unfair to say that the post 2008 phase has revolutionized Indian Cricket like never before. While the IPL has given a major boost to India's supremacy over World Cricket, brought to fore talented cricketers and garnered millions of supporters world-wide, it has also threatened International Cricket for the first time. Ironically, while in the pre–independence era, teams got formed on the basis of religion, today the country is being divided on the basis of states by the IPL franchises. Players are being lured by huge sums to play for their clubs and are being forced to choose between their club and country. While the Indian players escaped this dilemma, the overseas cricketers especially from not so affluent boards were in a quandary. They were repeatedly asked to either forego serious money from the IPL or betray the nation by turning their backs on them. And that brings us to the million dollar question– is the recent commercialization of cricket good? Yes and No – Firstly, cricketers have a limited shelf life and it's unrealistic to expect a flourishing career in 40s. These already short careers can further be cut short unexpectedly in

case of an injury or loss of form. While everyone appreciates and applauds when the athlete is putting up a good show, very few come to his rescue when things go wrong. And hence it's unfair to criticize the player for making hay while the sun shines. Also, the IPL has given a whole bunch of lesser-known domestic cricketers an opportunity to rub shoulders with the best in the world, showcase their talent at World Stage and earn some big money. IPL is also the only league which has the potential to make cricket a global game. The flip side of the IPL is that it has made T20 cricket the focal point of competitive cricket. If kids like me took up cricket to don the India colors, the gen-next is learning the game to play in the IPL. While there's nothing wrong with choosing one format over the other, these kids and their folks aren't smart enough to understand that pursuing only one format will make them one-trick ponies. It's imperative to learn the nuances of the game to last the distance. T20 is indeed quick fix and requires a limited skill-set but there are no shortcuts to ultimate success. The administrators must channelize the money earned from the IPL in a way that the importance of playing other formats isn't lost on the youngsters.

The Changing Face

As for now, after a wait of 28 long years, surviving several highs and lows, India's World Cup victory 2011 is surely a culmination of a long cherished dream, but more importantly, it's the beginning of another thrilling era of both eminence and dominance. There are many frontiers that still need to be conquered like winning Test series' in Australia and South Africa. The winds of change have set in to challenge the old order and jostle for space to make its mark–be it the introduction of T20, the usage of the pink ball in Test Cricket, newer rules, bats, balls, smaller grounds, technical innovations etc, the face of Cricket is changing rapidly. This is the time to tread carefully as well as embark on a new journey – the journey of accepting the change, safeguarding the old and upholding the title of the World Champions. The desire, the dream and the vision must be kept alive. ∎

News and Events

Indian Cricket's Cup of Joy

It had been a long wait. Twenty eight years in fact. In 1983 ``Kapil's Devil's'' had quite unexpectedly lifted the World Cup at Lord's. Since then six editions of the game's premier event had gone by and the best India could muster was a runner-up spot in South Africa in 2003. So many times had the Indians raised expectations only to disappoint the millions of fans the world over that the feeling was one of despondence. Would India ever win the World Cup again to make a new generation delirious? In the tenth edition of the mega event played in the sub continent the Indians finally did not falter. Starting as one of the favourites they finished second in their group to qualify easily for the knock out quarterfinals. And here at the all important stage they raised the level of their game defeating in turns Australia, Pakistan and Sri Lanka to set off celebrations that seemed to last forever.

The triumph was a big feather in MS Dhoni's cap. The charismatic Indian captain had led the team to various notable triumphs over the past few years but this was the summit. He led shrewdly and imaginatively and with his colleagues responding magnificently it turned out to be a triumph for teamwork. This was not a formidable Indian team along the lines of the West Indies of the late 70s and early 80s or Australia who had won three titles in a row

Dhoni with World Cup and Man of the Match Medal

Yuvraj Singh

from 1999. There were weaknesses in bowling and fielding but the strong batting helped to cover up. But then there were times when the much maligned bowling and fielding too rose to the occasion.

India dropped three points in group B while finishing second to South Africa. They lost to South Africa while the game against England ended in a tie. But victories over Netherlands, Ireland, Bangladesh and West Indies saw them enter the knockout stage with a degree of confidence. Australia were their next opponents but the defending champions were not the force of old and a five-wicket win with 14 balls to spare steered them into the semifinals for a unbelievably hyped up clash with Pakistan at Mohali. The prime ministers of the two countries – as well as Sonia Gandhi and Rahul Gandhi - headed the list of specta-

First Game	It is believed that cricket was played for the first time in India in Cambay of Gujarat. It was played between two groups of British sailors.

tors for this high pressure meeting of the giants. India deservedly won by 29 runs to make it to the title clash against Sri Lanka. It was for the first time that the World Cup final was being contested by two sides from the sub continent. Despite having to chase down a formidable target of 275 India did it with some degree of comfort with six wickets and ten balls to spare. Sri Lanka for the second successive edition had to be satisfied with the runners-up spot.

Compared to group B which saw a keen tussle between England, West Indies and Bangladesh for the last two places in the quarterfinals, group A was more straightforward. The presence of Zimbabwe, Canada and Kenya made the entry of Australia, New Zealand, Pakistan and Sri Lanka in the knockout stage almost inevitable. Pakistan took top spot with five wins out of six while Sri Lanka and Australia with four wins and a no result were second and third. New Zealand with four wins and two

World Cup winners celebration

defeats comfortably took the fourth spot. The quarterfinals provided one major surprise with New Zealand getting the better of South Africa who at this stage were the favourites for the title going by their impressive record in the league games. But the choker's tag returned to haunt them as they lost by 49 runs. The two remaining quarterfinals ended in ten-wicket victories with Sri Lanka routing England and Pakistan proving to be too strong for West Indies. In the semifinals

World Cup Cricket Report

Venue	Winners	Runners up	Year
England	West Indies	Australia	1975
England	West Indies	England	1979
England	India	West Indies	1983
India & Pak	Australia	England	1987
Aus & NZ	Pakistan	England	1992
Ind, Pak & SL	Sri Lanka	Australia	1996
England	Australia	Pakistan	1999
South Africa	Australia	India	2003
West Indies	Australia	Sri Lanka	2007
Ind, SL & Bang	India	Sri Lanka	2011

Sri Lanka predictably put it across New Zealand winning by five wickets.

As only to be expected there were numerous team and individual highlights during the six week long competition organized successfully by India, Sri Lanka and Bangladesh. Pride of place must go to Ireland who shocked England to prove that associate members deserved a place in the World Cup. Pride of place among the individual feats should also go to an Irishman – Kevin O'Brien who notched up the fastest century in World Cup history. In shaping his country's sensational three wicket win over England he reached three figures off just 50 balls. Among batsman Tillekeratne Dilshan took spot with an aggregate of 500 runs at an average of 62.50 and a strike rate of almost 91. But Tendulkar playing in his sixth World Cup – equaling the record set by Pakistan's Javed Miandad – was not far behind aggregating 482 runs at an average of 53.5 and a strike rate of almost 92. Among bowlers Shahid Afridi and Zaheer Khan were the standout performers. The Pakistan captain finished with 21 wickets in eight matches at an average of 12.85 with his mix of spin and guile while the Indian pace spearhead was not far behind. He also took 21 wickets in nine games at an average of almost 19. The man of the tournament award went to Yuvraj Singh who notched up an excellent double of

TAKE THE LESS TRODDEN PATH TO EXPLORE GOD'S OWN COUNTRY

KTDC presents Discover Kerala. Explore and take in the beauty of Kerala with a range of family holiday packages, tailor-made to suit your budget.

UTHARAYANAM: Discover Kerala from Kochi to Kannur.
Choose from 5-9 day packages.

DAKSHINAYANAM: Discover Kerala from Thiruvananthapuram to Kochi.
Choose from 5-8 day packages.

SUNDARA KERALAM: Explore the entire length of Kerala.
Choose from 8-13 day packages.

Special Features: **I** Choose your itinerary (start/end point) according to your convenience

KTDC Hotels & Resorts Ltd.
Mascot Square, Thiruvananthapuram 695 033, Kerala, India

For Reservations: Central Reservations Phone: 0471-2316736, 2725213
Email: centralreservations@ktdc.com **Tourist Reception Centre**
Thiruvananthapuram Phone: 0471-2330031
Tourist Reception Centre Kochi Phone: 0484-2353234

Official host to
God's Own Country
HOLIDAYS
www.ktdc.com

STARK: Tvm. 5149

362 runs and 15 wickets. He won the man of the match award four times.

IPL 4 - Another Success Story

The appetite of the Indian cricket fan is insatiable. The cynics were under the impression that they would have had their plates overfull with six weeks of World Cup fare and reckoned that the response for IPL-4 which commenced just six days after the final between India and Sri Lanka would be lukewarm. They could not have been more off the mark. The fourth edition of the tournament remained as popular as ever. Matches were well attended, fans were glued to the TV yet again and wherever one went the discussion was no more on the World Cup but all about the Super Kings and the Knight Riders, the Royals and the Chargers, the Warriors and the Tuskers.

That summed up the fascination for IPL and the Twenty20 format. Ever since its inception in 2008 the cash-rich tournament with its big names, razzle-dazzle, the Bollywood touch, the cheer leaders and rousing entertainment value has touched a chord around the cricketing world. In its fourth year it was clear that interest had not really diminished and the tournament had lost none of its cricketainment – a phrase forever linked with IPL. And while Twenty20 as a format has no doubt caught the public fancy in a big way the IPL has enhanced the scope with its emphasis on teams and cities that one can readily identify with. Sure the TRP ratings were a bit down and some of the matches drew a lukewarm response but overall IPL-4 was another success story. There were fears expressed about whether it would be a success particularly after Lalit Modi had been removed as chairman amid controversies over financial irregularities. But at the end of the 51-day competition it was clear that the average cricket fan didn't care for off the field happenings and was only concerned about the action on

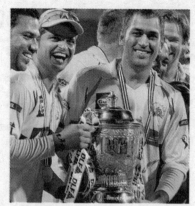

IPL 4 winners

the field.

And action there was aplenty. The addition of two new franchisees Kochi Tuskers and Pune Warriors meant that there were 74 matches instead of the 60 that were played out over each of the first three editions. And yet again the tournament did much to bring out the best of the Twenty20 format. The competition had everything – huge hits, big scores including hundreds, splendid bowling performances including hat tricks and five-wicket hauls, fluctuating fortunes among the 10 participating teams complete with the glitz and glamour always associated with the IPL.

The lead in the points table changed hands rapidly and for some time there were no clear favourites. Not unexpectedly for there was very little to choose between the teams and it was just about who performed better on the particular day. Then things started falling into place with some teams able to maintain the tempo while others were not able to do so thanks to lack of form of some players or injury problems. Finally after a fiercely competitive struggle Chennai Super Kings, Royal Challengers Bangalore, Mumbai Indians and Kolkata Knight Riders took the top four spots and

Coach for 41 Years	One of the most famous football coaches of all time was Amos Alonzo Stagg, the "grand old man of football". He coached football at the University of Chicago for 41 years, from 1892 to 1932. His coaching career continued until 1953 when he was 91. Stagg lived to 102.

made it to the qualifiers. And in a lop sided final at Chennai the home team romped to a 58-run victory over Bangalore to retain the trophy.

Among the many fine performers Chris Gayle and Lasith Malinga stood out. The tall West Indian opener joined the Bangalore outfit midway through the campaign but at the end of it all finished as the leading run getter with 608 runs at an incredible strike rate of over 183 with two hundreds and three fifties. The Sri Lankan pace bowler on his part was the leading wicket taker with 28 scalps at an average of 13.3 and an economy rate of just below six. And as usual the IPL provided the stage for comparative newcomers to make a name for themselves and none shone more than Paul Valthaty. Turning out for King's XI Punjab the right handed opening batsman took credit for the highest individual score of the tournament – an electrifying unbeaten 120 off just 63 balls with 19 fours and two sixes against Chennai besides finishing sixth on the run getters list with 463 runs at a strike rate of nearly 137.

Santosh Trophy – It's Bengal Again

The Santosh Trophy, the symbol of supremacy in National football, and Bengal have a unique relationship. Sixty-five editions of the national championship have been catalogued so far and on 31 occasions, including the latest held in Guwahati, Bengal emerged the champion. No other state has come anywhere near this number and it is unlikely that anyone will near this in the foreseeable future.

At one time such domination or winning this handsome trophy is referred to with a touch of pride by the triumphant team. But times have changed, perspectives have shifted, so much so, the very conduct of this national championship in itself is a major achievement. At a time when most of the top tournaments in the country have become non-existent, the Santosh trophy tourney remains but continues to struggle for a permanent slot in the football calendar thanks to the cash-rich I-league and the various AFC and FIFA competitions. What's more the Santosh trophy now is not a true index of the country's football talent

Messi in India

2011 September 2nd witnessed the first ever FIFA recognised international football match in India. Kolkata Salt Lake stadium hosted the historic match. It has another importance. Football's new Messiah, Lionel Messi too played here. As part of a friendly match, Argentina played against Venezuela. Argentina won the match 1-0. Though Messi couldnot shine, Nicholas Otamendi scores the solitary goal in the 67th minute. Lionel Messi made his

debut as captain of Argentina through that match. It was Alejandro Sabella's first game as coach of Argentina.

because the best, who assist the various top clubs in the I-league or are on duty for the national team, are denied permission to play in the national championship.

Be that as it may, Bengal still rules the roost. It still has borrowed talents like Branco Cardozo and Budiram Tudu (both playing for Kolkata based clubs), the stars who ensured the title-triumph with their goals in the final against Manipur. Even though Manipur, which has been rising in stature thanks to the AFC's development project, fought back to reduce the margin through Jimmy Singh, Bengal could not be denied its hour of glory yet again.

In all 31 teams took part in this year's edition and after the initial cluster-phase, the eight winners played the pre-quarterfinal knock out. The four winners from here joined last year's semi-finalists - Bengal, Goa, Punjab and Tamil Nadu - for the quarterfinal league.

The four fresh semi-finalists were Manipur, Services, Bengal and Railways with Manipur beating Services (late extra time penalty goal by Thoiba Singh) and Bengal edging Railways through Budiram Tudu's goal to decide the two finalists.

Past Winners: West Bengal 31 times; Punjab 8; Kerala 5; Goa 5; Maharashtra (earlier Bombay) 4; Karnataka (earlier Mysore) 4; Railways 3; AP 3; Services 1; Delhi 1 Manipur 1.

Salgaocar Triumph In I-League

Foreign talent continue to dominate the I-league. That an Indian (Jeje Lalpekhlua, a Mizoram native) is listed eighth in the top scorers list is ample evidence of this. Be that as it may, the latest edition proved memorable for Salgaocar, which was placed seventh on the previous occasion but catapulted to a title triumph. Observers believe a big credit had to go to its Moroccan coach Karim Bencherifa, who managed the resources in hand and whipped them up into a winning combination.

The Morrocan is not new to the I-

Jeje Lalpekhlua (blue jersey)

Ranti Martins

League. He was earlier associated with Churchill Brothers and Mohun Bagan but it was in his third change of job with Salgaocar that brought him the richest dividends. This was the Goan club's second title victory having won the 1998-99 league (then called national league). Significantly the team had outplayed what many felt was one of the favourites Dempo. For a change, Armando Colaco, currently the national coach and the man behind Dempo's famous success stories thus far could not preside over another triumph.

Many observers felt East Bengal, after its 13 consecutive wins (a feature of the initial phase of the League) had a good chance to have a tilt at the title. But consistency deserted this Kolkata team. As it happened the title was won and lost in the two late rounds in Goa. East Bengal without a few key players through suspension and injuries slid from a two-goal lead to a 2-3 loss to Salgaocar. A win would have assured East Bengal the title but it messed it up.

In the 14-team programme involving in 26 rounds and 182 matches overall,

over a period of six months, player management was the key and that was where Bencherifa scored.

A highlight of this season's league was the introduction of an India U-21 team as a replacement for Mahindra United (which

P.K. Anil Kumar

was disbanded). The idea was to give the young talents tough competition to groom them for the FIFA World Cup 2018. On the flip side was the relegation of JCT, one of the star teams of the country and a former champion. Worse was when the team owner decided later to disband the team. ONGC too slipped to relegation.

Statistics: Top scorers: Ranti Martins - Nigeria (Dempo) (Golden Boot for highest scorer) 30 goals; Onyeka Okolie Odafe -Nigeria (Churchill Brothers) silver boot (25 goals); Ryuji Sueka - Japan (Salgaocar) 18; Togay Ozbey – Aus (East Bengal) 17; Roberto Mendes Silva - Brazil (Dempo) 16; Jeje Lalpekhlua –India (Indian Arrows) 12; PK Anil Kumar – India (Viva Kerala) 11.

Standings: 1.Salgaocar 56 pts; 2. Kingfisher East Bengal 51; 3. Dempo 50; 4. Churchill Brothers 50; 5. Pune FC 36; 6.

Uruguay Regain Copa America Title

Uruguay defeated Paraguay 3-0 at the Monumental stadium in Buenos Aires to win the 2011 Copa America title in July. They regained the cup - which they had not won since 1995 – and with 15 titles became the most successful champion in the competition's history.

Uruguay dominated from the start and within the first ten minutes had six corners. It was only a matter of time before they scored and they duly went ahead in the 11th minute through Luis Suarez. Uruguay got their second goal in the 41st minute through Forlan.

In the group stage Uruguay played

Luis Suarez

out drawn out matches against Peru and Chile before beating Mexico. In all twelve teams participated in the most important football event in South America.

McDowells Mohun Bagan 34; 7. Mumbai FC 34; 8.Chirag United 29; 9. Indian Arrows 29; 10. Viva Kerala 27; 11. Air India 24, 12. HAL 24, 13. ONGC 24, 14. JCT 24 (last two relegated).

China Dominate, Good Show by India

China had announced its arrival as a major sporting force with a dazzling display at the Beijing Olympics and the country did it again in Guangzhou by dominating the Asian Games it hosted in November 2010. The fortnight long show in Guangzhou brought to view more than 10,000 athletes from 45 countries. Additionally another 4,750 team officials descended on the city along with about 60,000 volunteers.

China - in its quest to set a gold medal-winning record - had a delegation of 1,500 people, including almost 1,000 athletes. And they snapped up the medals as never before. With 199 gold medals (of the 416 at stake) including the Games' last medal in women's volleyball, China's domination was complete. South Korea was second with 76, and Japan placed next with 48.

Such was the Chinese ascendancy - sweeping diving, table tennis, basketball, beach volleyball, women's boxing and a 10-gold romp in the non-Olympic dancing events - that it found itself facing criticism for its achievements! As the Chinese delegation head, Cai Jiadong put it, "Every delegation participated at these games to ob-

tain the best possible result. Even though we were top of the medal tally, it doesn't mean we have a monopoly." He was partially right for there were a few special moments for other nations. As it happened, athletes from 36 other countries, including Myanmar and Syria, took home medals. Aside from the familiar Olympic sports, the Asian Games had a healthy bundle of traditional flavor from sepak takraw, a no-hands brand of volleyball that is popular in southeast Asia, to the Indian game of kabaddi not to forget China's own fast and furious martial art of wushu.

Beijing Olympics 2008 - silver medalists China performing

However the Games was short on world records. In facts only three were set - two in weightlifting and one in archery. That was fewer than what was obtained at the previous Games in Doha, Qatar, and prompted some criticism that the competition at Guangzhou was not as good as it should have been, considering that the participating countries represented two-thirds of the world's population. Still one notable aspect of the Games was that, as the head of the Olympic Council of Asia Al Sabah noted, taking into account the sheer size of the event, there were surprisingly few controversies.

As for India after an initial phase of no-show, competition gave way to some sterling displays of grit and gumption. India (14 gold, 17 silver, 33 bronze) finished with its best show in an Asiad with

Beijing Olympics Stadium

The Stade | Competition in the first 13 ancient Olympics consisted of only one footrace called the stade. It was a race about 200 yards (183 m.), or the length of the stadium.

64 medals overall, falling just one short of the 15 gold medals won in the inaugural Games in 1951 in New Delhi. Last time when China hosted the Games in Beijing in 1990, India had just one gold medal to show in kabaddi. To that extent this was a significant jump.

What was noteworthy was the unexpected medal-wins from disciplines like rowing, roller skating, gymnastics, archery and wushu while expectations dipped in shooting, one discipline that had fetched the bulk of medals in the CWG. A prime example was Gagan Narang, the four-gold medal winner of CWG. He could garner just two silvers. Beijing Olympics gold medallist Abhinav Bindra failed to make even a podium finish. Overall at Guangzhou the shooters' effort dwindled to one gold, three silver and four bronze medals.

Success came from Pankaj Advani (billiards), who brought up the country's first gold medal. The first surprise came in swimming when young Virdhawal Khade won a bronze in the 50m butterfly, a first from the pool for the country in 24 years (Khazan Singh won last in the 1986 Seoul Games). Tennis (two gold including Somdev Devvarman's singles gold, a first for India),

athletics (five golds including Ashwini's double), kabaddi (two golds) and boxing (two golds) pushed up India's stock.

A First In Indian Squash

Ever since the establishment of the Indian Squash Academy in Chennai, the sport has been making rapid strides in India and this has been reflected in the country's performance abroad. The latest landmark came in Colombo's Ratmalana courts when India made history by clinching the boys' title for the first time in the Asian junior team championship. The championship has been held since 1981. What made the feat additionally significant was that India had beaten arch rival and defending champion Pakistan, once considered the cradle of squash talent in the world.

One reason for the success stories in Indian squash has been the structured training that trainees at the Chennai Academy are subjected to under the watchful eyes of Maj (retd) S. Maniam, the SRFI Consultant from Malaysia and National coach Cyrus Poncha. Maniam came to India with the reputation of having turned Malaysian

Dipika's Significant Progress

For the petite Dipika Pallikal, one of India's best known names in women's squash the year brought one of her best moments in her career. Dipika who moved to senior ranks with the tag of Asian junior champion, climbed up to the 24th spot in the WISPA ranking to become the highest ranked Indian women squash player in the world and bettered it to 23 in March. She had earlier surpassed former national champion Misha Grewal's best of rank of 27 registered in 1995.

The 19-year old Chennai girl's rise to her best-ever career rankings can be attributed to her last-16 finish at the Harrow Greenwich Open in January, where she defeated compatriot Joshna Chinappa in the qualifiers before losing to Egyptian Raneem El Weleily. Dipika, who turned professional in 2006, start-

ed 2010 at 46 and ended that year at the 29th spot with the help of two WISPA titles - Nepal Open and the Indian Challenger event. The Indian girl had held the World junior No. 1 spot until she moved over to the senior ranks in September last year.

Dipika Pallikal

The rankings could keep changing depending on her performances in various tournaments but the fact remains that she has risen to the heights (read world ranking) that no other Indian woman squash player has reached till date.

India in Asian junior team squash (Boys)

1983 Singapore, India 4th
1985 Hong Kong, India 5th
1987 Karachi --- Did not take part
1989 Bahrain, India 3rd
1991 Colombo, India 3rd
1993 Singapore, India 2nd
1995 Hong Kong, India 4th
1997 Chennai, India 3rd
1999 Kuala Lumpur, India 4th
2001 Chennai, India 4th
2003 Islamabad, India 2nd
2005 Chennai, India 4th
2007 Hong Kong, India 3rd
2009 Chennai, India 2nd.

squash around to a progressive path. World Champion Nicol David, the biggest symbol of women's squash in the world today is his find.

As it happened in Sri Lanka on that January evening this year, Ramit Tandon, Abhishek Pradhan and Mahesh Mangaonkar (Vrishab Kotian did not play) outdid the tough Pakistan side. The hero was the captain Ramit and India's No 1 junior. Untested so far Ramit confirmed his growing stature by getting the better of the formidable Danish Atlas Khan, Pakistan's no.1 player, in a ninety-minute gripping tussle.

Watching Ramit play Maj Maniam said "I have not seen skills at this level amongst any Indian player in the last decade." There is thus much more to come from Tandon in the seasons ahead. The Colombo win meant India had won three of the four Asian junior titles in the year. Ravi Dixit and Dipika Pallikal had earlier garnered the respective Asian Junior individual titles. "This certainly augurs well for India squash," said Maj Maniam while Poncha felt it "was a dream that came true." All in all ten teams took part in the championship.

In a Bleak Scenario Hi Appoints Nobbs As New Foreign Coach

For the next five years the most discussed name in Indian hockey will be Michael Jack Nobbs who took over as the new foreign coach on July 3, when the preparatory camp began in Bangalore.

Nobbs' appointment came in the midst of intense debate on the need for a foreign coach to put Indian hockey back on track, so to speak, never mind the number of futile efforts made before this 57-year-old Aussie was appointed at a fee of 10,000 Australian dollars a month. Indian hockey does not need a foreign coach at all, said some, including ardent hockey lovers, the most vocal among them being former Pakistan captain and coach Tahir Zaman.

The testing job did not come easily for Nobbs. The contest began with former Indian hockey icons Dilip Tirkey and Dhanraj Pillai, a modern hero of Indian hockey expressing their wish to take on the assignment. Arjun Halappa and a few other se-

Michael Jack Nobbs

nior players supported Dhanraj. But India's disastrous performance in the Sultan Azlan Shah tournament under Indian coach Harendra Singh tilted the scales in favour of another foreign coach. Also the departure of Spaniard Jose Brasa after his contract ended following the Asian Games in 2010 with a good performance behind him, forced the hockey administration to go in for a foreign coach again.

However, Hockey India, SAI and the

Coubertin and Modern Olympics

A French aristocrat named Pierre de Coubertin was responsible for the modern version of the Olympics. In 1894 he created the International Olympic Committee, of which he became the first secretary-general.

Sports Ministry pitted Nobbs against two other strong candidates in former Dutch player-coach Rolant Oltmans, who nearly got the job and another Olympian and World Cup star Jacques Brinkman. Nobbs came

Dilip Tirkey

up trumps over his rivals primarily because the Aussie style of hockey is similar to the way the sport is played here. At least that seemed to be the view of the administrators and a five-member committee headed by former Indian captain Pargat Singh.

Nobbs however is not complacent. He has stated that the turn round in Indian

Ric Charlesworth

hockey cannot be achieved in a trice, as it were. The first task is to ensure that India qualify for the 2012 London Olympics. En route to London, the first acid test for Nobbs as chief coach would be the Asian Champions Trophy in China and then the Champions Trophy on home turf, both in September. Incidentally Nobbs is the fourth foreign coach for India, the others being German-born Gerhard Peter Rach (2004), Australian Ric Charlesworth (2008) and Jose Brasa (2009-2010).

A Triumph that Came As a Tonic for Indian Hockey

Winning a major competition is the best medicine to remove feelings of dejection and this proved to be the case for the Indian men's hockey team in September 2011. In the midst of opprobrium, it was time for some appreciation as the Michael Nobbs coached senior team won the inaugural Asian Champions Trophy tournament in Ordos, China. The tournament was the first after the Aussie took over the post and

Sandeep Singh

came as a pleasant surprise for Nobbs. "I admit I didn't expect them to win. I expected success probably a few months down the line," he said.

The victory was a shot in the arm for Indian hockey ridden as it was by controversies through the year. In a pulsating final, a charged up Indian team defeated Pakistan 4-2 in the penalty shoot out after the final ended goalless after full time and extra time. The hero of India's spectacular triumph was its young Kerala goalkeeper PK Sreejesh, who paved the way bringing off two great saves in the penalty shoot out when the scores were level at 2-2. Skipper Rajpal Singh, Danish Mujtaba, Yuvraj Walmiki and Swaranjit Singh scored for the Indians while Muhammed Rizwan and Waseem Ahmed sounded the board for Pakistan.

The Indian team began their campaign crushing China 5-0 in the opening league encounter. The team then drew with Malaysia 2-2 and beat Asian giants South Korea 5-3. But the team's entry into the final was not sure till they held Pakistan to a 2-2 draw in the final league outing.

The fillip to the team apart, the triumph ensured that Nobbs' stint as the new chief coach struck the right note. It augurs well for the future especially the all important Olympic qualifying tournament in 2012. As Nobbs put it succinctly "we can achieve much more in the months to come."

Nobbs' assistant Md Riaz, the former India captain and right half, hailed the victory as a good example of team spirit. He said

the young team did well to play attacking hockey throughout the competition. "We know where we stand now with regard to other teams." Riaz also observed that India went into the tournament without two of its key players, Sandeep Singh and Sardara Singh. This meant that there was extra pressure on the seniors Rajpal Singh, Bharat Chetri, Gurbaz Singh and Ravipal who rose to the occasion.

Maiden Davis Cup Title for Serbia

A new name was added to the Davis Cup roll of honour when Serbia became the 13th nation to be crowned champion following a 3-2 victory over France in the final at Belgrade in December 2010.

It was a meritorious performance by the Serbians who were up against nine-time champions France. Moreover few would have given them any chance of inscribing their names on the famous trophy after they were 1-2 down after the doubles. But Novak Djokovic and Viktor Troicki recorded straight set victories in the reserves singles to turn the score around in favour of the home team.

Djokovic, in imperious form, took apart Gael Monfils, who was previously unbeaten in Davis Cup play this year, winning 6-2, 6-2, 6-4 to send the tie into a deciding fifth rubber. Troicki then stepped up to meet Michael Llodra in the decider, both players having been brought in off the bench

Novak Djokovic

The touch of pink is the touch of health.

Reaching out to people across the country, we have been working to provide better, more complete and affordable healthcare. From innovative contraceptives to hospital equipment, healthcare services and pharma products to specialised healthcare programs, we're doing all it takes to make mothers and fathers and babies, and grandmothers and brothers and sisters glow with the touch of pink, the touch of good health.

www.lifecarehll.com

Hindustan Latex Limited is now **HLL Lifecare Limited**
Innovating for Healthy Generations

Gilles Simon

to replace the originally nominated Janko Tipsarevic and Gilles Simon. Troicki started brightly and never looked back. He raced through the first two sets and, despite having a minor wobble when leading by two breaks in the third, wrapped up a 6-2, 6-2, 6-3 triumph in just over two hours.

Djokovic clearly meant business when he took to the court against Monfils in the first of the reverse singles knowing that only a win would be good enough to keep Serbia's hopes alive. With the pressure of a nation firmly on his shoulders, the world No. 3 delivered a flawless display against a dangerous opponent. He dominated from the outset and didn't allow Monfils to gain a foothold in the match.

Djokovic was clearly fired up and embarked on a lap of honour before addressing the passionate Serbian fans to will them into helping teammate Troicki repeat his feat.

Troicki got off to a flying start and an out-of-sorts Llodra couldn't keep up the pace. The Frenchman had a stand-out Davis Cup year but like in the doubles he never reached the heights that he showed in previous rounds. His serve-volley game didn't translate well to the slow hard court and time after time Troicki picked him off with ease.

"This is the greatest experience in my life," said Troicki. "I still don't believe it. Seriously, I think we all did a great job this year. We truly believed that we could do it, even though we were 2 1 down."

Tipsarevic's performances in the semifinals against Czech Republic were nothing short of miraculous as he recorded wins over Tomas Berdych and Radek Stepanek, but it was Djokovic who provided the consistency in every tie. He prioritized Davis Cup throughout the year and reaped the rewards, reaching hero status by remaining unbeaten for Serbia in singles throughout the campaign.

In the final France took a 1-0 lead when Monfils defeated Tipsarevic 6-1, 7-6, 6-0 before Djokovic leveled matters for Serbia with a 6-3, 6-1, 7-5 win over Simon. The doubles was a cliff hanger before Arnaud Clement and Llodra came back from the brink to defeat Nenad Zimonjic and Troicki 3-6, 6-7, 6-4, 7-5, 6-4 and set the stage for the thrilling fare on the final day.

Volleyball seeks New Profile with IVL

To say that the Indian Premier League (IPL) revolutionized cricket would be an understatement. It changed the way audiences lapped up the game. On similar lines, in an attempt to popularize volleyball, the Volleyball Federation of India came up with the idea of launching the Indian Volley League (IVL) in 2011. The first edition got underway in Bangalore on May 28 and ended on June 1. After the Chennai (June 4 to 8) and Yanam (June 12 to 16) legs, the tournament concluded with the finale at Hyderabad from June 20 to 24.

Around 60 of the country's best spikers were chosen in six teams --- Karnataka Bulls, Chennai Spikers, Maratha Warriors, Yanam Tigers, Hyderabad and Kerala. The Chennai Spikers team was the best in the inaugural IVL as they emerged victorious in three of the four legs (Chennai, Yanam and Hyderabad). Maratha Warriors, who won the first leg at Bangalore, flattered to deceive as their performance dipped in the subsequent legs (where they finished sixth, sixth and fifth) and ended up fifth in the overall standings. Hyderabad Chargers did

One Bronze Each	In 1996, the US won 101 Olympic medals. Germany stood second (65) and Russia third (63). Nine countries won only a Bronze medal each: India, Israel, Lithuania, Mexico, Mongolia, Mozambique, Puerto Rico, Tunisia and Uganda.

well to finish overall second followed by Yanam Tigers.

The IVL was conceived as a tournament that would bring together the top players in the country to be part of various teams so that the spectators would get to see high-quality volleyball at various centres/venues. On the IVL Committee were V Ravikanth Reddy, former captain of the Indian team and an Arjuna Awardee as its chairman, Nanda Kumar as secretary and renowned

IVL 2011 Overall Ranking

1. Chennai Spikers
2. Hyderabad Chargers
3. Yanam Tigers
4. Karnataka Bulls
5. Maratha Warriors
6. Kerala Killers

coach GE Sridharan as co-ordinator. The success of the inaugural edition is expected to give the sport in India a fillip and may also pave the way for an expanded league in the years to come.

India disappoint, Aussies Regain Azlan Shah title

It is probably one of the most popular and important events in the international hockey calendar. The annual Sultan Azlan Shah Cup tournament held at Ipoh, Malaysia, usually has the top sides vying for honours. The 2011 edition saw world champions Australia regaining the title defeating Pakistan in the final. India finished sixth in the tournament, losing 1-2 to Korea in the classification match for fifth and sixth place. Earlier, in the round-robin competition, the Indians placed fifth with seven points from six games. It was a mixed performance by the Indians and the highlight of their campaign was the encounter against arch-rival Pakistan, which they lost 3-1. The victory sequence conjured up by the Indians since the World Cup last year, came to an end with this defeat to Pakistan.

The final was a close contest with Australia beating Pakistan 3-2 via a golden goal to win the 20th edition of the tournament. It was Australia's sixth title since the inception of the tournament. Australia drew first blood in the 11th minute when Christopher Ciriello converted a penalty corner. Pakistan restored parity, off their second penalty corner in the 31st minute. Waseem Ahmad trapped the ball before squaring it to Sohail Abbas who scored with a powerful flick. Glenn Turner scored in the 44th minute to put Australia ahead 2-1. Shakeel then went on one of his solo runs in the 62nd minute, leaving defenders in his wake and gave a pass to Muhd Waqas whose shot was saved by Bazeley. Rehan Butt however squeezed the rebound over the line and Pakistan were on level terms. Ciriello sent the ball into the net in the 83rd minute to give Australia the golden goal and the title.

A lot was expected of India, who normally do well at Ipoh, but they flattered to deceive, unable to put it across rivals when it mattered most. Starting with a defeat at the hands of Korea, India bounced back to beat Britain 3-1 before holding a formidable Australia to a 1-1 draw. A thumping 5-2 win over host Malaysia put them back in contention but they fluffed their chances with that loss to Pakistan. Worse

Individual Awards

Best Attacker: Prabhakaran (Chennai Spikers)

Best Universal: Gurvinder Singh (Hyderabad Chargers)

Best Blocker: Navjit Singh (Chennai Spikers)

Best Setter: KJ Kapil Dev (Chennai Spikers)

Best Libero: Vinod Negi (Hyderabad Chargrers)

Best Server: Sanjay Kumar (Karnataka Bulls)

Most Valuable Player: Gurvinder Singh (Hyderabad Chargers).

was to come when the Indians, led by Arjun Halappa , were routed 7-3 by New Zealand, which led to the team battling for the bottom spots.

The tournament which began in 1983 as a biennial contest became an annual event after 1998, following its growth and popularity. The tournament is named after the ninth Yang di-Pertuan Agong (King) of Malaysia, Sultan Azlan Shah, an avid hockey fan.

Force India Gathering Steam but not Enough

The year 2011 was a mixed one for the Force India team in Formula One. After 11 races, its two drivers Adrian Sutil and Paul di Resta had logged 18 and eight points, respectively but with a few races still left they seemed to be picking up steam after a rather stuttering start.

In the German GP at Nurburgring, Sutil surged to a notable sixth-place finish to

lap up eight points. This came as a relief after the team only managed 10 points from 10 races earlier. Though he finished a disappointing 14th in the subsequent race at Hungaroring in the Hungarian GP, Sutil

Adrian Sutil

was expecting to finish the season strongly and garner more points.

Early in the season, Sutil had a wonderful race at Monte Carlo finishing seventh which brought him six points. However, after that high, things went wrong as he couldn't manage a top-10 finish in any of the GP races in Canada, Europe and Britain (Silverstone).

His teammate di Resta, after a year of discontent, finally hit the straps with a strong seventh-place finish in the Hungarian GP which brought him six points. This was expected to give him lot of confidence going into the final stretch of the season. The talented British driver, who was drafted into the Force India team in place of Tonio Liuzzi, was highly regarded by many, but he struggled to make an impact in the F1 circuit. A seventh-place finish in his short F1 career came as a morale-booster for di Resta, who was looking to finish the up-

Formula One race

coming races, gunning for some points on the way.

Force India team principal Vijay Mallya was of the view that the team was beginning to show its true potential in 2011 after a slow start. In the first nine races of the season, Force India took just 12 points. Sutil finished a season's best sixth in Germany before Paul di Resta took the best result of his nascent career with a seventh place finish in Hungary.

Force India has come some way since its journey in F1 began, after taking over an existing F1 team. There have been some fine performances apart from being India's face in the high-profile Formula One circuit, albeit without an Indian driver. Hopefully things can only get better for the team from here on as the drivers seek to break new barriers.

With the Best Compliments from

Ganesh Travels

**RECOGNISED BY GOVERNMENT OF INDIA
ALL TYPES OF A/C, NON A/C CARS & VANS
WITH ROADWORTHY CONDITION & TRUSTWORTHY DRIVERS**

Round the Clock Personalised Service

HEAD OFFICE

35/1, P C O ROAD, EGMORE, CHENNAI 600 008
PHONE: 28190202, 28190303, 28190404, 28190505
ACCOUNTS © 28194243, TELEFAX: 28190990

BRANCH

7, VGP MURPHY SQUARE, GST ROAD
ST. THOMAS MOUNT,
CHENNAI-600 016
PHONE: 22327300

BANGALORE

9, PAMPAMAHAKAVI ROAD, SHANKARAPURAM,
BANGALORE - 560 004
PHONE: 26507766, 26507788, 26620022
TELEFAX: 26509171.

BRANCH

712/1, MUNIYELLAPPA GARDEN, KODIHALLI,
BANGALORE - 560 017
PHONE: 25255111, 25276969

People in Sports

A Mixed Year for Viswanathan Anand

Viswanathan Anand had a mixed year. For a start he must be disappointed that he will not be defending his world championship title on his home turf of Chennai against his challenger Israel's Boris Gelfand. The International Chess Federation (FIDE) allotted the prestigious contest to Moscow which came up with a higher bid vis-a-vis Chennai's.

Anand

When the AICF put up its bid it approached Tamil Nadu Chief Minister J Jayalalithaa along with the FIDE President Kirsan Illyumzhinov and FIDE vice president DV Sundar along with the newly elected AICF President JCD Prabhakaran who is also an MLA of the ruling AIADMK government which offered all monetary help so that Anand could defend his title in Chennai, widely acknowledged as the cradle of Indian chess.

However the year began on a joyful note for the reigning king of the game of 64 squares as Anand and his wife Aruna became proud parents of a baby boy who was born in Chennai. On the chess board Anand finished in second place following a draw with Ian Nepomniachtchi of Russia in the final round of the 73rd Tata Steel chess tournament in his first outing of the year. Anand however drew consolation from the fact that he would be the No 1 ranked player all over again overtaking world number one Magnus Carlsen of Norway. Hikaru Nakamura of United States won the title after drawing his final round game with Wang Hao of China. The American not only performed way beyond his rating of 2751 but also finished ahead of the world's top four ranked players. Anand got the better position with his black pieces but could not find a breakthrough as Nepomniachtchi simply got into an impregnable position in the endgame arising out of a Sicilian Defense game. The Indian ace settled for a draw in 37 moves.

"Disappointing," was Anand's verdict after the final results were out. However, Anand registered a comprehensive 4.5-1.5 victory over Spain's Alexei Shirov to claim the Leon Masters rapid chess title for the eighth time at Leon in June. In the run up to the world title match against Gelfand, Anand was slated to play a few Grand Master tournaments.

Humpy Hoping to Wear World Crown in 2011

Among the several talented chess players and perhaps the most popular Indian after Vishy Anand on the global stage is Koneru Humpy from Andhra Pradesh.

The 24-year-old who has been performing consistently for the last ten years was all set to challenge World Champion Hou Yifan (China) for the world crown in the finale to be held at Tirana, Albania in November 2011.

In a long career, Humpy has won many tournaments, but this title has been eluding her. After five failed attempts, she finally qualified to play a Women's World

The King is Dead	Chess is derived from Chaturanga, an Indian war game. The game reached Europe in about the 10th century. Its English name comes from the Persian shah meaning king. The term checkmate come from the Persian shah mat meaning The king is dead.

Koneru Humpy

Championship final. In March 2011, she won the Doha FIDE Grand Prix and qualified as the challenger from the GP series. She lost two semifinal contests in the last three years, both to Hou Yifan, a Chinese prodigy whom she faces again in the upcoming title match.

A determined lass, Humpy is hoping that it will be third time lucky when she takes on her Chinese rival in the Albanian capital. At the age of 15 years and one month she became the youngest grandmaster. In October 2007, she became the second woman player ever after Judit Polgar of Hungary, to cross the 2600-Elo mark on the FIDE World Rating List.

Among her proud moments were the Doha Asian Games 2006 when she did the nation proud by bagging two gold medals in the Individual as well as Team event.

It has been a glittering career with several achievements and trophies and though a relatively quiet first half of 2011 apart from qualifying for the world championship clash, she is eager to become the best woman chess player in the world.

Hari & Harika – Awesome twosome

With world champion Viswanathan Anand leading India's charge in the game at the global level, chess has spread rather well, spawning several other talented players in various parts of the country with several even going on to achieve international glory.

In that list are two gifted players from Andhra Pradesh -- Pentyala Harikrishna and Dronavalli Harika. They won the titles in the Asian Chess Championship held at Masshad, Iran in 2011 while Harika during

the year also achieved the GM title becoming only the second Indian woman after Koneru Humpy to attain this honour.

Harikrishna pulled off a sensational final round win over Zhao Jun of China with the black pieces to tie for first place and pip leader Yu Yangyi of China on the tiebreak. Incidentally, another Indian Krishnan Sasikiran (seeded second), who was among the pre-tournament favourites, finished sixth. Harikrishna also qualified for the World Cup thanks to the triumph. It was a memorable triumph for Harikrishna, who had won the gold medal at the 2006 Asian Games.

Dronavalli Harika

Harika, who was the top seed, also completed her victory in the final round. She scored 6.5 points from nine rounds and finished strongly with a 4/5 score to win by a clear margin. Another Indian player Eesha Karvade took the bronze medal.

Significantly, India won the gold and the bronze medal while Asian powerhouse China missed the podium with Vietnam taking the silver medal in the women's section.

This was an important win for Harikrish-

Eesha Karvade

na at this point of his career. It came after a long gap and, importantly, in a very tough event in which 30 Grandmasters took part. Also, the best of Indian men's chess, barring Anand took part in the tournament.

Much has been expected of the former World junior champion (he won in 2004) but he flattered to deceive after some initial encouraging exploits. The Andhra youngster had won multiple titles since capturing the world under-10 title in 1996. Subsequently he became a GM in 2001. At 15, he was the youngest Indian GM in history. In 2004, he became the World Junior Champion, the first Indian to do so since Anand in 1987.

In 2005, Harikrishna did well tying for first place in the Bermuda International, a Category 17 event. Later, he followed that up by winning a series of strong Category 15 and 16 events – the Sanjin Hotel Cup (2005), Crown Group of 9th Essent Hoogeveen (2005), Reykjavik Open (2006) and Marx Gyorgy Memorial (2006). In August 2006, he beat Naiditsch in Mainz to become Chess960 World Junior Champion and also recaptured the Gyorgy Marx Memorial title in 2007.

Harikrishna's rise was rather spectacular but he faded into the background after a few years of stupendous performances. It is said that lack of sponsorship/funds bogged him down. Now that he is back to winning ways with a triumph in the Asian championship, one can expect the talented 25-year-old to bounce back strongly and translate potential into victories and take forward the legacy of the incomparable Anand.

The 20-year-old Harika, another promising talent to emerge from Andhra Pradesh in the women's game after Humpy, grabbed the GM title with a fine performance at the 1st Hangzhou Women Grandmaster Chess Tournament in China in July. Harika pocketed a total of 5.5 points, following seven draws and two wins, to finish at a commendable third position. It may be noted that leading women players competed in the round-robin event. Harika had held double norms for GM title and already had bagged the titles of Woman Grandmaster and International Master previously. A former World Junior champion, Harika had earlier won the Asian Individual Chess Championships and the South African Open.

A multiple winner in the age-group events at the international level, Harika has been a consistent performer and has the ability to take on the best and beat them too. The 2011 Asian champion had won the girls title at the World Junior Chess Championship at Gaziantep Turkey, in 2008.

With stars like Harikrishna and Harika among several others, the future of Indian chess is very bright.

Rare double for Alok Kumar

A rare double is a special occasion for a sportsperson. 2011 was indeed special for one of the giants of cue sports in India, Punjab's Alok Kumar who has been at the forefront in India's prowess in billiards, snooker and 8 ball pool games.

Alok Kumar

At Kish Island in Iran on April 14, the lanky and soft spoken Alok blanked Praput Chaithanasukan of Thailand 6-0 to win the coveted Asian billiards title at the Olympic

Pankaj Advani

Stadium. Alok thus become the first player to achieve the rare feat of winning both the Asian billiards and snooker titles. Back in 2004 in Jordan, Alok had lifted the Asian snooker title defeating his compatriot Pankaj Advani in the final.

In a best of 11 games 100 points format, Alok showed grit and determination and on his first visit to the table compiled an immaculate break of 93 to go ahead 1-0. He was fast and furious in the following two frames also as he completely rattled his opponent with breaks of 84 and 85 in the second and third games respectively to go ahead 3-0 in just 25 minutes of play.

It was amazing to see the man who had won the 8-ball and 9-ball National Pool title only a week back adjusting so well in a completely different game that requires touch play. Inarguably the best all-round player of the country, Alok once again showed his versatility in the fourth game as he prevailed over his opponent with tactical play. The fifth game saw Alok unfolding a vast repertoire of strokes to recover from difficult situations and outwitted Praput by compiling yet another good run of 73 points to go ahead 5-0. In the sixth though Praput showed signs of recovery by scoring 57 points. But it was too little too late as Alok put the icing on the cake with a clinically precise 'postman's knock' break of 76 played at the top of the table to win 6-0.

In a dream run, Alok brushed aside challenges from three former world champions Pankaj Advani (India), Peter Gilchrist (Singapore) and Praprut Chaithanasukan (Thai-

land) in the quarter final, semifinal and final respectively.

Saina slips but Doubles Pair shows Promise

Badminton star Saina Nehwal ended 2010 with the Commonwealth Games gold medal and the Hong Kong Open. It was to that extent a memorable year for this Hyderabad based girl whose stupendous performances on the international plane brought memories of Prakash Padukone at his peak. However her aim of touching the number one rank in the World did not materialise. Worse, a dip in form in the new year coupled with an ankle injury actually saw her slide to No 6. There was much expectations that the World championship in London in August would see her in a new light. But like the previous two editions,

Saina Nehwal

Saina fell at the last eight stage. However Saina continues to be the shining star of Indian badminton and surely there is much more to come from this petite player.

Meanwhile two others, the doubles pair of Jwala Gutta and Ashwini Ponnappa, have demanded attention after their 'first for an Indian' show in the London World championship. Jwala and Ashwini became the first Indian doubles pair to reach the semi-final of the WBC and in doing so the Commonwealth Games gold medallists amply demonstrated their great talent. The

| Boxing | When done professionally, for a purse, boxing is also called prize-fighting. Sometimes it is called pugilism, after the Latin word for a boxer. Boxing has existed for 6000 years. It gained popularity in the Middle East and Africa and spread throughout the world. |

Jwala Gutta

jump and followed it up with a bronze in the triple jump in the Asian Athletics Championships held at Kobe, Japan, in July.

Seen by many as one of the finest Indian prospects in the long jump since Anju Bobby George, Mayookha's showing and the medals at Kobe will give new hope for athletics fans in the wake of the sport being in the news for the wrong reasons for some time.

After finishing seventh in the long jump at the 2010 Asian Games, Mayookha fared better at the 2011 National Games in February 2011, taking a long and triple jump double ahead of MA Prajusha. She became the first Indian woman to breach the 14-m mark when she bagged a bronze medal in the third and final leg of the Asian Athletics Grand Prix in Wujiang, China.

M.A. Prajusha

duo could win only a bronze but there is promise that the pair, now ranked 21st in the World will go far.

It was only in 2009 that the two came together after Jwala and Shruti Kurien split. Jwala and Shruti were unbeatable in the national circuit and even won an international title (Bulgarian GP). Now in the short time thereafter Jwala and Ashwini have gone further after their London show. Considering doubles has never been India's strong point, this fresh pair have raised hopes of erasing that shortcoming.

Mayookha who leapt into the limelight some five years ago had an eminently forgettable Commonwealth Games in Delhi in 2010 and Asian Games at Guangzhou. She finished sixth and seventh respectively. But she turned things around at Wujiang. Then, in Bangalore, she rewrote Anju George's inter-State meet record in the long jump. Mayookha is said to be an admirer of badminton ace Saina Nehwal, for her determination to measure up to the Chinese juggernaut that has dominated women's Olympic sports over the last decade.

After Anju it's Mayookha

Things were not rosy for Indian athletics in the middle of the year (2011) after the highs of the achievements in the Commonwealth Games in 2010. The dope scandal that broke out in the sport dented the athletes' image to a great extent. However, the performance of long jumper Mayookha Johny warmed the hearts of the fans. She won a gold medal in the long

Anju Bobby George

Mayookha was born on 9 August 1988 in Kozhikode, Kerala. Her father MD Johny was a bodybuilder and a former Mr Bombay, She first came into prominence in the Kerala State Athletic Championship at Thrissur in 2006 when she won a gold in the long jump and triple jump in the under-20 category. Significantly, in the triple jump event she beat the more experienced MA Prajusha and Tincy Mathew.

| Lazlo Papp | In 1948 London Olympics, Lazlo Papp of Hungary won his first of three gold medals. In 1956 (Melbourne) he became the first Olympic boxer to win three medals. |

With her wonderful efforts in Kobe, Mayookha qualified for 2012 Olympics in triple jump, going past the 2012 London Olympics Games 'B' qualifying standard of 14.10m.

The mercurial talent who holds great hope for Indian athletics has set her sights on Olympic glory.

Mayookha's Gold Highlight of India's Showing

Mayookha Johny's gold medal success was the highlight of India's show in the 19th Asian Athletics Championship in Kobe (Japan) in July. As a leading force, Japan outshone the rest by topping the medals tally securing 11 gold, 10 silver and 11 bronze medals and in the process pushed the other power-house China to the second spot (10-12-5).

India ended its campaign with 11 medals (1 gold, 2 silver and 8 bronze medals).

Mayookha Johny

The 22-year old Mayookha, an ONGC athlete who hails from Kerala leapt 6.56m in women's long jump for the gold. Mayookha also won a bronze with a 14.11 m effort in the triple jump, something that helped rewrite the national record. The Indian thus earned berths for the World championship in Daegu.

It was Vikas Gowda who opened India's

Vikas Gowda

medal quest with a silver medal in discus throw. Gowda's 61.58m on the fifth attempt was far below his best.

Career Best Ranking for Somdev

It was a mixed year for Indian tennis. The Indian team went down 1-4 to holders Serbia in the first round of the Davis Cup and awaited a qualifier against Japan in September. The winner of that tie would be back in the World Group. In the meantime the standard bearers of Indian tennis also had their ups and downs. As usual

Somdev Devvarman

the hopes centered around Somdev Devvarman and Sania Mirza in the singles and the experienced duo of Mahesh Bhupathi and Leander Paes in the doubles while the duo had their own partners in the mixed doubles. The highlight was Paes and Bhupathi making the final of the Australian Open where they lost 3–6, 4–6 to the Bryan brothers Bob and Mike. They also won three ATP Tour titles.

Somdev performed commendably and by August end enjoyed a career best ranking of 62 after beginning the year at 108.

Sania Mirza also could look back on the year with some satisfaction though as in Somdev's case she made little headway in

the singles event of the Grand Slams. But she reached a ranking of 62 – her best in years - and made considerable progress in the doubles. In August she won her third WTA doubles title of the season and 12th overall Sania clinched the 11th spot in the doubles.

Bhaichung Bhutia calls it a day

At the age of 16 he had sent ripples around in football settings with his deft ball play and after 16 years as a member of the Indian national squad he has left a legion

Bhaichung Bhutia

of football fans stunned by his decision to step down. That is Bhaichung Bhutia, a versatile footballer,

The golden goal he earned for Bengal for its 25th Santosh trophy title in Chennai in 1995 was simply a moment of genius as many stalwarts who were to witness the act said. For long Indian football was dominated by two names – Bhutia and IM Vijayan.

This indomitable pair became a part of Indian football folklore and for this a big credit has to go to the Uzbek coach Rustom Akramov who turned Bhutia into a striker from his original position of a midfielder.

Over 100 international matches and decorated with Arjuna Award and Padma Shri, Bhutia also had the distinction of being the highest paid footballer in India. Bhutia has invested a lot in the United Sikkim football club and is bent on making this one of the premier clubs in Indian football.

| Ocean to Sky | Edmund Hillary's Ocean to Sky 2525 km. long expedition on jet-boats started from Haldia to the Himalayas up the Ganga on August 25, 1977. The expedition was abandoned at Nandaprayag on Sept. 28. |

ICC Awards 2010-2011

Jonathan Trott

The awardees: Sir Garfield Sobers **Trophy for Cricketer of the Year:** Jonathan Trott (England); **Women's Cricketer of the Year:** Stafanie Taylor (West Indies); **Test Cricketer of the Year:** Alastair Cock (England); **ODI Player of the Year:** Sangakkara; **Emerging Player:** Devendra Bishoo (West Indies); Emerging Player: Devendra Bishoo (West Indies); **Spirit of Cricketer Award:** M.S. Dhoni (India); **ICC Associate Cricketer:** Ryan ten Doeschate (Netherlands); **T20 Performance of the Year:** Tim Southee (New Zealand); **Umpire of the Year:** Aleem Dar (Pakistan); **People's Choice Award:** Kumar Sangakkara (Sri Lanka).

ICC Test Team of the Year: Kumar Sangakkara (capt.), Alastair Cook, Hashim Amla, Jonathan Trott, Sachin Tendulkar, A,B. de Villiers, Jacques Kallis, Stuart Broad, Graeme Swann, Dale Steyn and James Anderson; **12th man**: Zaheer Khan.

National Sports Awards 2011

The awardees

Rajiv Gandhi Khel Ratna Award: Gagan Narang (shooting)

Arjuna award: Rahul Banerjee (archery), Preeja Sreedharan, Vikas Gowda (athletics), G. Jwala (badminton), Suranjoy Singh (boxing), Zaheer Khan (cricket), Sunil Chhetri (football), Ashish Kumar (gymnastics), Rajpal Singh (hockey), Rakesh Kumar, Tejeswini Bai (Kabaddi), Tejaswini Swant (shooting), Veerdhawal Khade (swimming). Somdev Devvaman (tennis), Sanjay Kumar (volleyball), Ravinder Singh (wrestling), K. Ravi Kumar (weightlifting); W. Sandhyarani Devi (wushu), Prasatha Karamakar (swimming-paralympics).

Dronacharya award: I. Venkateswara Rao (boxing), Devendra Kumar Rathore (gym-

Sandhyarani Devi

nastics), Ramphal (wrestling), Dr. Kuntal Roy (athletics), Rajinder Singh (hockey).

Dhyan Chand award: Shabbir Ali (football), Sushil Kohil (swimming), Rajkumar (wrestling).

| A Grand Slam | David Hampleman Adams is the first man to complete the Adventurer's Grand Slam, a Herculean series of 11 mountaineering and polar exploration tasks. |

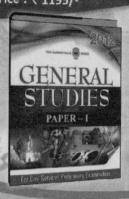

World Outdoor Records - Men

Discipline	Perf	Athlete	Nat	Venue	Date
100 Metres	9.58	Usain Bolt	JAM	Berlin	16/08/2009
200 Metres	19.19	Usain Bolt	JAM	Berlin	20/08/2009
400 Metres	43.18	Michael Johnson	USA	Sevilla	26/08/1999
800 Metres	1:41.01	David Lekuta Rudisha	KEN	Rieti	29/08/2010
1000 Metres	2:11.96	Noah Ngeny	KEN	Rieti	05/09/1999
1500 Metres	3:26.00	Hicham El Guerrouj	MAR	Roma	14/07/1998
One Mile	3:43.13	Hicham El Guerrouj	MAR	Roma	07/07/1999
2000 Metres	4:44.79	Hicham El Guerrouj	MAR	Berlin	07/09/1999
3000 Metres	7:20.67	Daniel Komen	KEN	Rieti	01/09/1996
5000 Metres	12:37.35	Kenenisa Bekele	ETH	Hengelo	31/05/2004
10,000 Metres	26:17.53	Kenenisa Bekele	ETH	Bruxelles	26/08/2005
10 Kilometres	26:44	Leonard Patrick Komon	KEN	Utrecht	26/09/2010
15 Kilometres	41:13	Leonard Patrick Komon	KEN	Nijmegen	21/11/2010
20,000 Metres	56:26.0	Haile Gebrselassie	ETH	Ostrava	27/06/2007
20 Kilometres	55:21	Zersenay Tadese	ERI	Lisboa	21/03/2010
One Hour	21.285	Haile Gebrselassie	ETH	Ostrava	27/06/2007
Half Marathon	58:23	Zersenay Tadese	ERI	Lisboa	21/03/2010
25,000 Metres	1:12:25.0	Moses Cheruiyot Mosop	KEN	Eugene, OR	03/06/2011
25 Kilometres	1:11:50	Samuel Kiplimo Kosgei	KEN	Berlin	09/05/2010
30,000 Metres	1:26:47.4	Moses Cheruiyot Mosop	KEN	Eugene, OR	03/06/2011
30 Kilometres	1:27:49	Haile Gebrselassie	ETH	Berlin	20/09/2009
Marathon	2:03:59	Haile Gebrselassie	ETH	Berlin	28/09/2008
100 Kilometres	6:13:33	Takahiro Sunada	JPN	Tokoro	21/06/1998
3000 Metres Steeplechase	7:53.63	Saif Saaeed Shaheen	QAT	Bruxelles	03/09/2004
110 Metres Hurdles	12.87	Dayron Robles	CUB	Ostrava	12/06/2008
400 Metres Hurdles	46.78	Kevin Young	USA	Barcelona	06/08/1992
High Jump	2.45	Javier Sotomayor	CUB	Salamanca	27/07/1993
Pole Vault	6.14	Sergey Bubka	UKR	Sestriere	31/07/1994
Long Jump	8.95	Mike Powell	USA	Tokyo	30/08/1991
Triple Jump	18.29	Jonathan Edwards	GBR	Göteborg	07/08/1995
Shot Put	23.12	Randy Barnes	USA	Los Angeles (Westwood), CA	0/05/1990
Discus Throw	74.08	Jürgen Schult	GDR	Neubrandenburg	6/06/1986
Hammer Throw	86.74	Yuriy Sedykh	URS	Stuttgart	30/08/1986
Javelin Throw	98.48	Jan Zelezný	CZE	Jena	25/05/1996
Decathlon	9026	Roman Šebrle	CZE	Götzis	27/05/2001

World Outdoor Records - Women

Discipline	Perf	Athlete	Nat	Venue	Date
100 Metres	10.49	Florence Griffith-Joyner	USA	Indianapolis, IN	16/07/1988
200 Metres	21.34	Florence Griffith-Joyner	USA	Seoul	29/09/1988
400 Metres	47.60	Marita Koch	GDR	Canberra	06/10/1985
800 Metres	1:53.28	Jarmila Kratochvílová	TCH	München	26/07/1983
1000 Metres	2:28.98	Svetlana Masterkova	RUS	Bruxelles	23/08/1996
1500 Metres	3:50.46	Yunxia Qu	CHN	Beijing	11/09/1993
One Mile	4:12.56	Svetlana Masterkova	RUS	Zürich	14/08/1996
2000 Metres	5:25.36	Sonia O'Sullivan	IRL	Edinburgh	08/07/1994
3000 Metres	8:06.11	Junxia Wang	CHN	Beijing	13/09/1993
5000 Metres	14:11.15	Tirunesh Dibaba	ETH	Oslo (Bislett)	06/06/2008
10,000 Metres	29:31.78	Junxia Wang	CHN	Beijing	08/09/1993
10 Kilometres	30:21	Paula Radcliffe	GBR	San Juan, PUR	23/02/2003
15 Kilometres	46:28	Tirunesh Dibaba	ETH	Nijmegen	15/11/2009
20,000 Metres	1:05:26.6	Tegla Loroupe	KEN	Borgholzhausen	03/09/2000
20 Kilometres	1:02:36	Mary Jepkosgei Keitany	KEN	Ras Al Khaimah	18/02/2011
One Hour	18.517	Dire Tune	ETH	Ostrava	12/06/2008
Half Marathon	1:05:50	Mary Jepkosgei Keitany	KEN	Ras Al Khaimah	18/02/2011
25,000 Metres	1:27:05.9	Tegla Loroupe	KEN	Mengerskirchen	21/09/2002
25 Kilometres	1:19:53	Mary Jepkosgei Keitany	KEN	Berlin	09/05/2010
30,000 Metres	1:45:50.0	Tegla Loroupe	KEN	Warstein	06/06/2003
30 Kilometres	1:38:49	Mizuki Noguchi	JPN	Berlin	25/09/2005
Marathon	2:15:25	Paula Radcliffe	GBR	London	13/04/2003
100 Kilometres	6:33:11	Tomoe Abe	JPN	Yubetsu	25/06/2000
3000 Metres Steeplechase	8:58.81	Gulnara Galkina	RUS	Beijing (National Stadium)	17/08/2008
100 Metres Hurdles	12.21	Yordanka Donkova	BUL	Stara Zagora	20/08/1988
400 Metres Hurdles	52.34	Yuliya Pechenkina	RUS	Tula	08/08/2003
High Jump	2.09	Stefka Kostadinova	BUL	Roma	30/08/1987
Pole Vault	5.06	Elena Isinbaeva	RUS	Zürich	28/08/2009
Long Jump	7.52	Galina Chistyakova	URS	Leningrad	11/06/1988
Triple Jump	15.50	Inessa Kravets	UKR	Göteborg	10/08/1995
Shot Put	22.63	Natalya Lisovskaya	URS	Moskva	07/06/1987
Discus Throw	76.80	Gabriele Reinsch	GDR	Neubrandenburg	09/07/1988
Hammer Throw	79.42	Betty Heidler	GER	Halle	21/05/2011
Javelin Throw	72.28	Barbora Špotáková	CZE	Stuttgart	13/09/2008
Heptathlon	7291	Jackie Joyner-Kersee	USA	Seoul	24/09/1988
(12.69/0.5 - 1.86 - 15.80 - 22.56/1.6 / 7.27/0.7 - 45.66 - 2:08.51)					
Decathlon	8358	Austra Skujyte	LTU	Columbia, MO	15/04/2005

Sports Diary 2011

Jan 01. Magnus Carlsen (Norway) regains No.1 spot in world chess ranking released by FIDE. Viswanathan Anand loses first rank, moves to second position **04**. Sujit Kuttan from Kerala is the fastest in 56th National School Meet at Pune. Priyanka S Kalagi (Karnataka) is the fastest female athlete • • **06**. Kerala triumphs in National School Meet. With 40 gold, 17 silver and 24 bronze Kerala claims championship for the 14th consecutive term. Haryana and Maharashtra win second and third positions • Cape Town test ends in a draw. Series levelled 1-1. Jacques Kallis declared Man of the match and Man of the series • **07**. England lifts Ashes, winning the series 3-1. England wins third test at Sydney • **08**. Auction for

Gautam Gambhir

fourth season of IPL. Kolkata Knight Riders fetches Gautam Gambhir for a record 11.04 crore rupees • **09**. India wins the lone Twenty20 match against South Africa by 21 runs in Durban • Sachin Tendulkar is the longest playing cricketer in one day matches surpassing the record held by Javed Miandad • **15**. Rajasthan lifts Ranji Trophy for the first time. • India wins second ODI against South Africa • **29**. Japan wins Asian Cup football beating Australia 1-0 in the finals at Doha • Kim Clijsters is the Australian Open women's champion • **30**. Serbian Novak Djokovic claims Australian Open men's singles. Novak beats Andy Murray 6-4, 6-2, 6-3 in the finals • **31**. Caroline Wozniacki of Denmark retains her No. 1 spot in world tennis.

Asian Cup 2011

Feb 05. South Zone claims Duleep Trophy. In the finals at Vishakapatanam • **07**. Rafael Nadal (tennis, Spain) bags Laureus World Sportsman of the year 2010 award. Lindsey Vonn (alpine skiing, US) wins Sportswoman of the year award. Spain football team named Team of the year • **13**. 34th National Games begins in Jharkhand • **14**. Ronaldo confirmed his retirement from football • **16**. Lance Armstrong announces retirement • **19**. India makes a winning start in 2011 world cup tournament. India defeats Bangladesh by 87 runs in Mirpur. Virender Sehwag with 175 runs is the Man of the match • Sachin Tendulkar becomes the most capped ODI player (445 matches) when he overtook Sanath Jayasurya. Sachin equals Javed Miandad's record for most ap-

Novak Djokovic

The Unique Owens | Born as the son of a share cropper and grandson of a slave in rural Alabama, Jesse Owens was the only athlete to have set world records in multiple events in one day. His long jump mark lasted until fellow American Ralph Boston broke it in 1960.

pearances in world cup (six consecutive tournament appearances) • **25.** National Games concludes. Services with 69 gold, 50 silver and 42 bronze secures first position. • Ed Joyce (Ireland) becomes the first player to represent two nations in cricket

Rafael Nadal

world cup after Kepler Wessels and Anderson Cummins • Australia becomes the first nation to record 25 successive victories in world cup. • **26.** Novak Kjokovic wins Dubai Open • **27.** India-England match in world cup ends in a tie. Sachin Tendulkar registers his fifth world cup century • **28.** Canada's Nitish Roenik Kumar becomes the youngest player in cricket world cup when he played against Zimbabwe.

March 06. India beats Ireland by five wickets in Bangalore. Yuvraj Singh becomes the first cricketer to take five wickets and score a 50 in a world cup match • **09.** India wins over Netherlands by five wickets. Sachin Tendulkar completes 2000 runs in world cup. Man of the match- Yuvraj Singh • **12.** India defeated at the hands of South Africa. India lost the match by three wickets • **19.** After 12 years, 34 matches and 3 titles, Australia lose a world cup match. Pakistan wins by four wickets at Colombo • Ricky Ponting becomes the most led captain (28 matches) in world cup • **20.** Saina Nehwal wins Swiss Open Grand Prix Golden badminton beating Sung Ji Hyun 21-13, 21-14 in the finals at Basel • **24.** India enters semi-finals of world cup beating reigning champions Australia by five wickets. Man of the match- Yuvraj Singh. Sachin Tendulkar completes 18, 000 runs in ODI • **28.** F 1 racing 2011 season begins with Australian GP. Red Bull's Sebastian Vettel wins in Melbourne • **29.** Sri Lanka enters finals

of world cup. In Colombo, the hosts beat New Zealand by five wickets. Man of the match- Kumar Sangakkara • Ricky Ponting gives up captaincy following Australia's world cup exit.

April 02. India wins world cup in style. Beats Sri Lanka by six wickets in the final at Mumbai Wankhede stadium. Score: Sri Lanka - 274/6, India - 277/4. Man of the match- M. S. Dhoni. Player of the tournament-Yuvraj Singh • Mahesh Bhupathi-Leander Paes duo clinches Sony Ericsson Open men's doubles in Miami. The Indian players becomes No. 1 in the ATP World Tour doubles team rankings • **08.** 4th season of IPL begins. In the first match, Chennai Super Kings beats Kolkata Knight Riders by two runs at Chennai • **10.** Sebastian Vettel once again triumphs. The 23 year old won the Malaysian Grand Prix, his second consecutive win in the season • **11.** Sania Mirza - Elena Vesnina duo clinches Family Circle Cup doubles at Charleston, their second WTA title together • Australian Shane Watson smashes 15 sixes, a record in a ODI match. He attained the record in Dhaka against Bangladesh • **13.** Sachin Tendulkar named Wisden's Leading Cricketer in the world for the year 2010 • **17.** Lewis Hamilton (McLaren) wins Chinese Grand Prix • Rafael Nadal lifts his seventh straight Monte Carlo Masters title • **19.** Abhijeet Gupta wins Dubai International Open chess title. • **22.** Sri Lankan fast bowler Lesith Malinga

Mahesh Bhupathi and Leander Paes

When Men Donned Swimsuits The first Miss America pagent in Sept. 1921 was hosted by arms-industry heir Hudson Maxim Only 8 contestants participated representing towns. The contest featured a 'bathing revue' but no talent. Even the all-male orchestra donned swimsuits.

announces retirement • **27.** Duncan Fletcher appointed coach of Indian cricket.

May 07. 65th Santosh Trophy Nationals kick starts in Assam • **09.** Mary Kom (48 kg) wins gold in Asian Cup womens boxing championship in Haikou, China • **10.** P. Harikrishna and D. Harika bags the Open and women's title in Asian chess championship at Mashhad, Iran • **13.** Indian ODI and Twenty 20 squad for West Indies tour announced. Gautam Gambhir to lead, Suresh Raina his deputy • **14.** Manchester United bags their 19th English Premier League title, a record in the history of the tournament. They surpassed Liverpool's record of 18 English Premier titles. United made a draw (1-1) with Blackburn Rovers at Ewood Park, London to become the winner • Manchester City lifts FA Cup. Beats Stoke City 1-0 in the finals at Wembley • Sachin Tendulkar bags Poly Umrigar Award for 2009-10 • **15.** Australia wins Sultan Azlan Shah Cup beating Pakistan (3-2) through a golden goal in extra time in the finals at Ipoh. India finishes sixth • 16. Annu Raj Singh earns a silver in women's 10m air pistol, in the ISSF shooting World Cup in Fort Benning, US and earns an olympic quota place • **18.** Rahi Sarnobat clinches bronze medal in the women's 25m sport pistol, in the ISSF shooting World Cup in Fort Benning, US and earns an olympic quota place • Australian cricketer Stuart Clark announces retirement from international cricket • Rajasthan Royals captain Shane Warne fined Rs. 50,000 in relation to a complaint, regarding an incident that occured after the IPL match against Royal Challengers in Jaipur on May 11 • **20.** Shane Warne retires from cricket • Seventeen year old school boy Arjun Vajpai becomes the youngest in the world to ascent Mount Lhotse, the fourth highest peak • **21.** Vijay Kumar wins silver in 25m rapid fire pistol event in the shooting World Cup in Fort Benning and earns 2012 olym-

Chennai Super Kings (IPL)

pic berth • Former New Zealand cricketer Adam Parore scales Mount Everest • **22.** Its Sebastian Vettel again, wins Spanish GP in style • **28.** Chennai Super Kings are the IPL season 4 champions. Beats Royal Challengers Bangalore by 58 runs in Chennai. Man of the match- Murali Vijay, Man of the series- Chris Gayle • Barcelona claims European Champions League football title beating Manchester United 3-1 in the finals at Wembley • **29.** China wins Sudirman Cup defeating Denmark 3-0 in Qingdao, China • Sebastian Vettel (Red Bull-Renault) triumphs in Monaco GP • Mayookha Johny became the first Indian woman to breach

the 14m mark barrier in triple jump while creating a new national record (14.02m), winning a bronze in the third and final leg of the Asian Grand Prix series at Wujiang, China • **30.** Bengal lifts Santosh Trophy. In the finals of the 65th National Championships, Bengal beat Manipur 2-1 to claim their 31st title • Salgaocar clinches I-League title after a 2-0 victory over JCT in Ludhiana. The Goan team finished top of the table with 56 points from 26 matches.

Sebastian Vettel

The Stanley Cup The name Stanley Cup comes from Lord Stanley Preston, a governor general of Canada who purchased a silver trophy in 1893 to be awarded to the best amateur hockey team of Canada.

June 01. Sepp Blatter re-elected President of FIFA • **04.** India-West Indies cricket series begins with a Twenty20 International at Port-of-Spain. The visiting side defeats the host by 16 runs. Man of the match-S. Badrinath • Li Na clinches French Open women's singles, becoming the first Asian to win a Grand Slam singles title • **05.** Rafael Nadal claims his sixth French Open singles title, equalling Bjorn Borg's record of six French titles. Nadal defeats Roger Federer 7-5, 7-6 (7), 5-7, 6-1 in the final clash • **06.** India-West Indies ODI series begins in Port of Spain. India wins first match by four wickets. Man of the match- Rohit Sharma • **07.** Brazilian footballer Ronaldo ended his international career with a 15 minute appearance as a substitute in Brazil's 1-0 win over Romania in a friendly match at Sao Paulo • **08.** India wins second ODI of the series against West Indies. At Port-of-Spain, India beat the host by seven wickets with 20 balls remaining through D/L method. Man of the match- Virat Kohli • **11.** India clinches ODI series against West Indies with a 3-0 lead. At St. Johns, Antigua the touring side beat the host by three wickets in the third match of the series. Man of the match- Rohit Sharma • 51st senior inter-state athletics championship begins in Bangalore. Shameermon and P. K. Priya (both Kerala) fastest • Jenson Button (McLaren) clinches Canadian GP, his first win of the season • **13.** West Indies beats India by 103 runs at Antigua in the fourth ODI. Man of the match- Anthony Martin •**14.** Kerala with 13 gold, seven silver and seven bronze bags overall title in the 51st senior inter-state athletics championship at Bangalore. Punjab and Tamil Nadu in second and third positions. Sajeesh

Sepp Blatter

Joseph and Mayookha Johny (both Kerala) adjudged best men and women athlete respectively • **16.** West Indies wins last ODI of the series by seven wickets. India wins series 3-2. Man of the match- Andre Russell. Man of the series- Rohit Sharma • **20.** India- West Indies test series begins in Kingston • Punjab based JCT club disbands its team from professional football citing lack of public interest in the game in India • **23.** India wins Kingston test by 63 runs. Man of the match- Rahul Dravid • **24.** Chennai Spikers emerges champion in the inaugural edition of Indian Volley League. Hyderabad Chargers in second spot • **25.** Mexico lifts CONCACAF Gold cup beating USA 4-2 in the finals • Kerala bags D. V. Subba Roy Trophy inter state cricket tournament. Scores: Kerala - 376 , Madhya Pradesh - 214 • **26.** Sebastian Vettel (Red Bull - Renault) clinches European GP in Valencia,

Rohit Sharma

Spain, his sixth win of the season • Anaka Alankamony wins the girl's Under - 19 title at the 18th Asian Junior squash championships in Amman • Yihan Wang of China takes Indonesia Open Super Series badminton. Saina Nehwal is the runner up • **28.** Sanath Jayasurya plays his last international cricket match, an ODI against England • India- Windies second test match begins in Kensington Oval, Bridgetown, Barbados.

World Footballers, 1991-2000	Lother Matthaus (1991), Marco Van Basten (1992), Roberto Baggio (1993), Romario (1994), George Weah (1995), Ronaldo (1996 & 1997), Zinedine Zidane (1998 & 2000) and Rivaldo (1999) are World Footballers, 1991 - 2000.

V. V. S. Laxman touches 8000 run mark in test cricket.

July 01. Kick off to 43rd Copa America football. Argentina meets Bolivia at La Plata, Buenos Aires in the inaugural match. First match ends in draw (1-1) • **02.** Bridgetown test ends in a draw. Ishant Sharma who captured 10 wickets from both innings declared Man of the Match. Ishant becomes the first Indian to claim 10 wickets in a test in the Carribean • Petra Kvitova (Czech Republic) wins her first Grand Slam title when she stunned former champion Maria Sharapova 6-3, 6-4 in the Wimbledon women's singles • **03.** Serbian Novak Djokovic captures his first Wimbledon title with a beautiful 6-4, 6-1, 1-6, 6-3 victory over defending champion Rafael Nadal.

Ishant Sharma

Novak becomes the first Serbian to claim The Championship. • **04.** Novak Djokovic ranked World No. 1 in ATP rankings. Denmark's Caroline Wozniacki tops WTA rankings • **06.** Last match of India- West Indies test series begins in Roseau, Dominica • **07.** Mayookha Johny claims gold in long jump on the opening day of 19th Asian athletics championships in Kobe, Japan. Vikas Gowda (Discus) wins silver and Preeja Sreedharan wins bronze in 10, 000m race • Harbhajan Singh completes 400 test wickets • **08.** M. S. Dhoni touches 3000 runs in test cricket, becoming the first Indian wicketkeeper to achieve the feat • Decathlete Bharat Inder Singh, discus thrower Harwant Kaur and athlete O. P. Jaisha adds three bronze medals to India's collection on the second day of the 19th Asian athletics championships. Su Bingtan (China) and Guzel Khubbieva (Uzbekistan) emerges fastest • **09.** Mayookha Johny wins bronze

O.P. Jaisha

in triple jump, posting a national record of 14.10m in Asian Athletics Championships. Om Prakash Karhana secures a bronze in shot put event • 2006 world cup winning captain Fabio Cannavaro announces retirement on medical advice • **10.** Roseau test ends in a draw. India wins test series (1-0) against West Indies. Man of the match - Shivnarine Chanderpaul. Ishant Sharma who took 23 wickets from three tests declared Man of the series • Fernando Alonso (Ferrari) wins British GP at Silverstone • 19th Asian Athletics Championships concludes. Japan tops medal tally with 11 gold, 10 silver and 11 bronze. China and Bahrain in second and third spots. India with a gold, two silver and eight bronze moves to eighth position. Sudha Singh wins silver in steeplechase. Tintu Luka and Ghamanda Ram (800 m) takes bronze • Indian women's team comprising Laishram Bombayla Devi, Deepika Kumari and Chekrovolu Swuro wins silver in recurve event final in the Archery World Championship at Turin • **11.** India retains No. 1 position in ICC's test cricket ranking • **12.** Ronjan Sodhi takes a bronze medal in double trap in the shotgun World Cup in Maribor, Slovenia. **17.** Japan clinches women's football world cup. Beats US 3-1 on a penalty shoot out after the final had finished 2-2 in extra time • **18.** ICC chooses all-time greatest Test team through an online poll. Four Indians - Sachin Tendulkar, Kapil Dev, Sunil Gavaskar and Virender Sehwag make into the list. The poll was con-

Fernando Alonso

Sachin Tendulkar

ducted as part of the build-up to the India-England Test match at Lord's to celebrate the 2000th cricket test • **21.** Historic test match at Lords. India- England test series begins. It was the 2000th match in the history of Test cricket. The match also marks the 100th Test between India and England. Indian coach Duncan Fletcher becomes the first coach to complete hundred test matches as a national coach • 24. Uruguay lifts Copa America. Uruguay defeats Paraguay 3-0 in Buenos Aires to win a record 15th title • Lewis Hamilton (McLaren) wins German GP • Cadel Evans becomes the first Australian to win the Tour de France • **25.** England wins the historic Lords test by 196 runs. Man of the match- Kevin Pietersen • **29.** Second test between India and England begins in Trent Bridge, Nottingham. Rahul Dravid becomes the first player other than a wicket keeper to take 400 catches in international cricket (ODI plus test) when he caught Matt Prior • **30.** English bowler Stuart Broad gets hat-trick in Nottingham test. Broad's feat is the 39th hat-trick in test cricket • **31**. McLaren's Jenson Button completes his 200th GP with a super win in Hungarian Grand Prix.

Aug 01. Ronjan Sodhi is World No. 1 in double trap the rankings released by ISSF • **02.** Tintu Luka wins 800m in the Folksam Grand Prix meet at Karlstad • **04.** Zimbabwe marks their return to test cricket after six years, coring 264/2 against Bangladesh at Harare on the first day • **06**. Former South African cricketer Norman Gordon becomes the first Test player ever to reach 100 years of age. • **08.** Ajantha Mendis becomes the first cricketer in T20 international to take six wickets in a match-against Australia in Pallekele • **10.** Third test between India and England in Birmingham • **12.** Jwala Gutta-Ashwini Ponappa duo creates history in London by becoming the first Indian woman pair to reach the semifinals of World badminton Championships • **13.** England is the new No. 1 team in test rankings. Indiav beaten by England in Birmingham test. • Krishna Punia wins discus title in the Portland annual athletics meet in US • Jwala Gutta-Ashwini Ponappa duo gets bronze in World badminton Championships. Karan Rastogi wins singles in the ITF men's Futures tennis at Astana • **14.** Tintu Luka second in the 800m, Flanders Cup at Belgium. 800m specialist in men's section Ghamanda Ram (men's)has 2nd position • Lin Dan and Wang Yihan (both China) win World badminton Championship in men's and women's respectively • **16.** Rajpal Singh to lead Indian hockey in the maiden Asian Champions Trophy in Ordos, China • **18.** Last test of the India-England series begins at the Kia Oval • **21.** Bhupathi-Paes pair wins Cincinnati Masters Doubles. Andy Murray wins ATP's singles. Maria Sharapova lifts Cincinnati WTA title • **20.** Brazil lifts FIFA Under-20 football world cup, beating Portugal • **21.** Rahul Dravid becomes the first player ever to face 30,000 deliveries (5000 overs) in test cricket • **22.** England makes a clean 4-0 sweep in the

Karan Rastogi

Sister Prodigies **Susan, Sofia and Judith Polgar are three Hungarian sisters who have taken the chess world by storm.**

Deepika Kumari

test series against India. English team defeats India by innings and eight runs in the last and fourth test. India slips to 3rd position in test rankings. Man of the match-Ian Bell • **24.** Legendary Indian footballer Baichung Bhutia announces retirement • **27.** World athletics championships begins in Daegu, South Korea • India wins the Presidents Cup international volleyball tournament beating Tunisia at Almaty • **28.** Jamaican Yohan Blake fastest in World athletics championships. Usain Bolt disqualified for false start. Oscar Pistorius becomes the first amputee athlete to compete in World athletics championships • Deepika Kumari wins the junior recurve individual women's gold medal in Legnica, Poland • Sebastian Vettel (Red Bull) clinches Belgium GP • **29.** Carmelita Jeter of US is the fastest woman in World athletics championships • Discus thrower Vikas Gowda becomes the first Indian male athlete and the 4th Indian to have entered the final of an individual event in the WA championships • **30.** Inaugural edition of President's Trophy Boat Race at Ashtamudi Lake, Kollam • **31.** India defeated by England in the lone Twenty 20 of their English tour. English team wins by six wickets at Manchester.

Sept 02. Argentina takes on Venezuela in a friendly match at Salt Lake sta-

dium in first FIFA match. Argentina wins. Lionel Messi makes his debut as captain of Argentina. Alejandro Sabella takes over his first game as coach of Argentina • **03.** Inaugural edition of Asian Champions Trophy hockey begins in Ordos, China. India beats host 5-0 • Ricky Ponting becomes the first player to play in 100 Test wins • First ODI of India-England series washed off by rain • **04.** World athletics championships concludes: US with 12-8-5 tops the medal tally. Russia comes 2nd, Kenya 3rd • Japan holds India 1-1 in Asian Champions Trophy hockey • **06.** India faces 7 wicket defeat in the second one dayer against England. Alastair Cook is the Man of the match at Southampton • India beats South Korea in Asian Champions, 5-3 • India loses right to host 2011 Mens Champions Trophy • **07.** India drew with Malaysia 2-2 in Asian Champions Trophy hockey • **09.** India faces a 3 wicket in the third ODI against England. England leads series 2-0 • **10.** Indian women's recurve archery team wins gold in the final of the World Cup 215-204 • 51st National Open athletics championship begins at Salt Lake Stadium, Kolkata • South Korea wins women's Asian Champions Trophy hockey

Samantha Stosur

tournament beating China. • **11.** India bags inaugural Asian Champions Trophy hockey. Beats Pak 4-2 • England clinches ODI series against India • Australia's Samantha Stosur wins US Open women's title, claiming her maiden Grand Slam. Serena William is the runner-up. Samantha becomes the first

Australian woman to claim a Slam since Evonne Goolagong won Wimbledon in 1980 • Manish (Haryana) and Asha Roy (Bengal) fastest in National Open athletics • Red Bull's Sebastian Vettel victorious in Italian Grand Prix • Dipika Pallikal wins $9,000 Orange County squash Open, a WISPA event in Irvine, California. She defeated Egypt's Yathreb Adel 11-6, 12-10, 11-9 for the title • **12.** Serbian Novak Djokovic claims US Open men's singles, his third Grand Slam of 2011. Novak beats Rafael Nadal in the finals • ICC's annual awards announced. English player Jonathan Trott bagged the Sir Garfield Sobers Trophy for Cricketer of the Year award. Alastair Cook is the Test Player of the Year and Kumar Sangakkara is the ODI player • Sania Mirza got into the doubles top-10 for the first time in her career • **13.** 51st National Open athletics concludes. Railways with 17 gold, 13 silver and eight bronze tops the medal tally. ONGC and Services in second and third spot. Arpinder Singh (Punjab) is the best male athlete and Mayookha Johny (ONGC) is the best female athlete • **16.** Team India returns empty handed after a worst English season. England wins the last one day at Cardiff to clinch ODI series 3-0. India defeated by six wicket via D/L method in a rain hit match. Rahul Dravid plays his last ODI match • Japan takes a 2-0 lead against India on the opening day of Davis Cup World Group play-off tie in Tokyo. Somdev Devvarman and Rohan Bopanna looses their singles matches • **17.** India wins doubles match of Davis Cup World Group play-off tie against Japan. Mahesh Bhupathi- Rohan Bopanna duo wins 7-5, 3-6, 6-3, 7-6 • **18.** India defeated 1-4 in Davis Cup World Group play-off tie against Japan. Vishnu Vardhan and Rohan Bopanna looses in reverse singles. India relegated to the Asia/Oceania Zone Group 1 • **19.** N. Srinivasan takes over as President of BCCI. Sanjay Jagdale is the new Secretary • Peter Svidler wins World Cup chess championship at Khanty Mansiysk, Russia. Svidler defeated BCCI terminates the contract of IPL franchise Kochi Tuskers Kerala for non payment of bank guarnatee • **22.** 'Tiger' Pataudi passed away in New Delhi. Former Indian captain Mansur Ali Khan Pataudi, 70 years, was battling a lung infection for the

last few months • **23.** Champions League T20 cricket begins in Bangalore. In the first match, Warriors from South Africa makes a last ball victory over Royal Challengers Bangalore • Vinod Kambli announces retirement from first class cricket • **25.** Its Sebastian Vettel again. Vettel continues supreme at Singapore GP too • Kenya's Patrick Makau sets new world record in Marathon. He finished the race in 2hr 03 min 38 sec in the Berlin Marathon • Deepika Kumari settles for a silver in the Archery World Cup final in Istanbul • **27.** International Hockey Federation (FIH) asks Sports Ministry to resolve the issues related to governance of hockey in India. A letter written by FIH, warns India's participation in major international tournaments may be jeopardised if issues were not solved • **29.** Salgaocar lifts Federation Cup thrashing East Bengal 3-1 in the finals at Kolkata.

| **Oct. 04.** | Ronjan Sodhi defends the double trap gold in the World Cup Finals in Al Ain, UAE • Rare distinction for Shikhar Dhawan and Abhinav Mukund in Irani Trophy. Rest of India's Shikhar Dhawan |

Sania Mirza

becomes the first to hit a century in each innings in Irani Trophy. Mukund became the first to score century three-in-a-row in consecutive Irani Trophy matches. They achieved the feat in Jaipur, while playing against Rajasthan on the fourth day of the contest • **05.** Rest of India clinches Irani Trophy for the sixth consecutive time. ROI thrashed Ranji Trophy winners Rajasthan by a margin of 400 runs in Jaipur. Shikhar Dhawan who scored a century in both innings adjudged Man of the match.

By **Anil Philip**

Obituary

World

2010 November 3. Viktor Chernomyodin, 72, former Russian Prime Minister • **6.** Jill Clayburgh, 66, actress. *An Unmarried Woman* • **9.** Emilio Massera, 85, Argentinian military junta leader, 1976-83 • **29.** Leslie Nielsen, 84, veteran TV and movie actor.

Viktor Chernomyodin

December 14. Richard Holbrooke, 69, President Obama's Special Representative for Afghanistan and Pakistan •**15** Walter Haeusserneann, 96, Nazi Germany's famous rocket scientist •**17.** Blake Edwards, 88, Oscar-winning director. *Pink Panther* movies, *Breakfast at Tiffany's* • **19.** Tommaso Padoa Schioppa,70, Italian economist, one of the intellectual architects of Euro • **26.** Carlos Andres Perez, 88, former Venezuelan President • **27.** Teena Marie, 54, US R&B singer • Elisabeth Beresford, 86, novelist and journalist.

2011 January 3. Pete Postlethwaite, 64, Oscar-nominated actor •**07.** Vang Pao, 81, former Laotian general •**16.** Susannah York, 72, actress •**29.** Szeto Wah, 79, Hong Kong democracy icon •**31.** John Barry, 77, British film composer, wrote music for several Bond movies, five Oscars.

February 28. Frank Buckles, 110, The last US veteran of WWI

March 1. Jane Russell, 89, screen siren of choice for a generation of American troops at war. • **04.** Sir Anthony Hayward, 83, the last British chairman of Shaw Wallace Group and President, Assocham • **05.** K.P. Bhattarai, 87, fomer Nepal PM • **06.** Alberto Grnnado,88, who was Che Grevara's motorcycle trip companions on a 1952 journey of discovery across Latin America • **12.** Biren De, 85, one of the pioneers of neo-Tantrik art • **14.** Owsley Stanley, 76, who supplied LSD to the 1960s flower power generation • **19.** Warren Christopher, 85, Ex-US Secretary of State • **20.** Bob Christo, 72, Australian born actor • **23.** Elizabeth Taylor, 71, a legendary Hollywood beauty, winner of two Oscars, was married 8 times • **25.** Lanford Wilson, 73, playwright, *Talley's Folly* • **28.** Harry Wesley Coover, 94, Super Glue inventor

April 6. Trevor Chesterfield, cricket journalist • **13.** Lewis Binford, 80, founder of the New Archaeology Movement • **14.** Sidney Harman, 92, 'Newsweek' chief and audio pioneer • **19.** Pietro Ferrero, 47, Italian chocolate tycoon •

20. Elizabeth Sladen, 63, actress. Best known for role in 'Doctor Who' • **24.** Norway, Gombu, the youngest on Edmund Hillary's Everest team • **24.** Norio Ohga, 81, credited with developing CDs, chairman, Sony.

Nawang Gombu

May 5. Claude Choules, 110, the last surviving combat veteran of WWI • **7.** Seve Ballesteros, 54, one of golf's greatest players • **09.** Dana Wynter, 79, film star (*Invasion Body Snatchers*) • **22.** Joseph Brooks, Academy award-winning song writer.

June 12. Esmond Kentis, 94, former West Indies Test cricketer.

July 4. Dr. Jack Kevorkian, 93, known as Dr. Death, stood for euthanasia **06.** Cy Twonbly, 83, American painter renowned for his large-scale scribbled canvases • **16.** Travis Bean, 83, innovative guitar-maker • **24.** Amy Winehouse, 27, singer • **25.** Lindo Christian, 87, first Bond girl • **26.** Robert Ettinger, pioneer of the cryonics movement.

Aug 08. Nancy Wake, 98, Australian spy, most decorated service woman for role in French resistance in WWII.

Sept 04. Julio Casas Regueiro, 75, Defence Minister of Cuba • **14.** Sa Parante, 70, Brazilian scientist, inventor of bidiesel • **20.** Dolores Hope, 102, wife of the late Bob Hope - the entertainer • **26.** Wangari Maathai,71, Kenyan environmentalist and Nobel laureate.

Wangari Maathai

Oct 05. Steve Jobs, 56, founder and former CEO of Apple the visionary co-founder of Apple who helped

India

2010 November 6. Siddhartha Shankar Ray, 90, former West Bengal Chief Minister, Governor of Punjab, Union Minister, Ambassador to USA • **14.** L.C. Jain, 85, Gandhian, Magsaysay Award winner • **16.** Acharya Narendra Bhushan, 73, Vedic scholar.

Siddhartha Shankar Ray

December 19. Murali Kuttan, 57, Asian Games medal-

ist • **23.** K. Karunakaran, 93, Congress stalwart, four-time Chief Minister of Kerala • **24.** Swarnaprava Mahanta, 86, former Assam minister • **30.** K.G. Kannabiran, 81, civil rights activist • **30.** Vettath Balakrishna Eradi, 88, former Supreme Court judge .

2011 January 3. Suchitra Misra, 86, Rabeendra Sangeet exponent • **12.** A. Sivasailam, 76, industrialist • **24.** Pandit Bhimsen Joshi, 88, the doyen of Hindustani classical music, Bharat Ratna awardee.

February 2. K. Subramanyam, 82, pre-eminent security and foreign policy thinker • **12.** Vipindas, 72, cinematographer • **15.** Lt. Col. Man Bahadur Rai, 95, the oldest Ashok Chakra recipient • **19.** Suresh Babu, 58, Olympian • **20.** Malaysia Vasudevan,

Anant Pai

playback singer • Parvathi Ammal, 81, mother of slain LTTE leader Velupillai • **21** Aranmula Ponnamma, 96, Malayalam film actress, over 500 films • **24.** Anant Pai, 82, Man with passion for comics who was behind *Amar Chitra Kathas* and children's magazine *Tinkle*.

March 4. Arjun Singh, 81, veteran Congress leader, former HRD Minister, Chief Minister of M.P. three times • **26.** Dr. P. K.R. Warrier, 90, cardio-thoracic surgeon, social activist • **28.** P.C. Mathew, I.C.S., 97, one of the last surviving members of I.C.S

Arjun Singh

April 1. Cardinal Mar Varkey Vithayathil, 84, Syro-Malabar Church's Major Archbishop • **06.** Sujatha, 58, Tamil & Malayalam films • **17.** Brig. Bhawani Singh, 80, former Maharaja of Jaipur • **20.** B.K. Shekhar, 51, BJP leader • **24.** Satya Sai Baba, 85, the godman of Putta Parthi worshipped by lakhs • **29.** Abdul Hamid, 83, Urdu fiction writer, in Lahore • Narayan Athavale, Marathi litterateur.

May 4. Dorjee Khandu, CM of Arunachal Pradesh (killed in helicopter crash) • **15.** Mahendra Singh Tikait, 76, the farmer leader of many peasant struggles • **23.** Chidananda Dasgupta,

Dorjee Khandu

91, film critic, pioneer of film society movement, father of Aparna Sen • N. Mariyam Pichai, Tamil Nadu minister • Mala Sen, 64, writer of Shekhar Kapoor's film *Bandit Queen* • **25.** Ustad Meh-

mood Dhaulpuri, harmonium maestro.

June 1. Kamalakshi Amma ('Katha'), 83, wife of Jnanpith laureate Thazhazhi • **3.** Bhajan Lal, 81, former Haryana CM • **9.** M F Hussain, 95, India's most celebrated painter worldwide, in London. On self-imposed exile. A Qatari citizen. Padma Vibhushan. • **21.** Dr. Suresh Tendulkar, 72, economist, taught at DSE • **25.** Saurav Kumar Chaliha, 81, Assamese short story writer, Sahitya Akademi Award.

July 4. Ravindran (Chintha Ravi), 65, writer, film director • **4.** B.S.S. Rao, 82, art critic • **6.** Mani Kaul, 66, film maker, one of the pioneers of new Indian cinema, *Uski Roti, Duvidha, Idiot* • **9.** Justice K.K. Narendran, 88, former Kerala High Court judge • **9.** Sadhana Amte, 85, wife of the late Baba Amte • **15.** Swami Athuradas, 99, promoted western homoeopathy and native medicine treatment • **18.** B.D. Garga, 86, film historian.

Malliyoor

August 2. *Bhagawathahamsom* Malliyoor Sankaran Namboodiri, 91, saintly Bhagawatham exponent • **7.** Archbishop Dr. Cornelius Elanjickal, Kochi, 93 • **10.** Dr. P.C. Alexander, 90, formerly Principal Private Secretary to Ms. Indira Gandhi and Rajiv Gandhi, Governor of Maharashtra and Tamil Nadu, High Commissioner to UK, UN expert, Rajya Sabha member • **11.** Kuzhur Narayana Marar, 91, percussionist maestro • **14.** Shammi Kapoor, 79, veteran actor, leading star of the 60s • **20.** M.K. Pandhe, 86, CPM politburo member, trade unionist.

P.C. Alexander

September 04. Sumant Misra, 88, one of the legends of Indian tennis • **04.** Jagmohan Mudhra, 62, Hollywood-based film maker • **13.** Gautam Rajadhyaksha, 62, veteran Bollywood photographer • **22.** Mansur Ali Khan Pataudi, 70, one of the greatest Indian cricket captains. Played 46 Tests for India, 40 as captain, scoring 2793 runs for an average of 34.91 • **23.** Vasant Sathe, 86, Congress veteran and former Union Minister.

Vasant Sathe

October 04. Bhagawat Jha Azad, 89, former Bihar CM, 6 time LS member.

Stop Press

Corrections and additional information

Page 516:

Literates and literacy rates by sex : 2011

	*Persons	Males	Females
A & N Is.	0.293	0.164	0.129
Arunachal Pradesh	0.789	0.454	0.335
Dadra & Nagar Haveli	0.228	0.144	0.083
Daman & Diu	0.188	0.124	0.064
Lakshadweep	0.052	0.028	0.024
Mizoram	0.847	0.438	0.408
Nagaland	1.357	0.731	0.625
Puducherry	0.966	0.502	0.464
Sikkim	0.449	0.253	0.195

* (in Millions)

All the total figures in the Literacy Table are given in Million

New Governors: Jharkand-Syed Ahmed, Kerala - MOH Farook Maricar, Madhya Pradesh - Ram Naresh Yadav, Mizoram - Vakkom Purushothaman, Tamil Nadu - Konijeti Rosaiah

Page 513: 10 Most Populated Nations: Please read the Number 1 (yellow) as Others, 2 (Purple) as China, and Others (dark green) as India

Page 543-544: Haryana: Rewari is a major railway junction. It is also connected by three national highways: NH8, NH71 & NH71B

Page 569: Kerala: In the later part of first para starting from "93.91 'Density: 96.02', 'Decadal growth rate: 91.98%'" is a mistake.

Cover Story: Gaddafi is also spelt as Qaddafi.

World: Presidents - Haiti : Michel Martelly, **Latvia :** Andris Berzins, **Sao Tome and Principe :** Manuel Pinto da Costa, **Vietnam :** Truong Tan Sang, **Zambia :** Michael Sata

Prime Ministers - Denmark : Helle Thorning-Schmidt, **Haiti :** Garry Conille, **Japan :** Yoshihiko Noda, **Libya :** Mahmoud Jibril, **Rwanda :** Pierre Damien Habumuremyi, **Sao Tome and Principe :** Patrice Trovoada

Awards & Honours

Mo Ibrahim Prize: The $ 5mn. Prize for good African governance: Pedro Verona Pires, 77, former President of Cape Verde.

Index

We are living in
an age of **Knowledge explosion**
an era when knowledge rules the world

- Shalom Residential Public School imparts qualitative English Medium education and makes a difference in the field of education.

- The school is not a mere centre of information, but a centre of character formation.

- Ensuring the spread of education across different sectors of the society

- Talented and trained teachers take care of the students.

- Social equality and economic development go hand in hand.

- Imparts value-based education.

- Classes from Pre-Kinder Garten to IXth Std.

- Value-based & child oriented education International standards

- Low Student-Teacher Ratio

- A safe, secure and global study environment

- Optimum value for money

- Separate Hostel Facility for Boys & Girls

- Plans to offer IB accreditation

SHALOM RESIDENTIAL PUBLIC SCHOOL
Shalom Nagar, Chittur, **PALAKKAD - 678101, Kerala.**
Tel: **04923-222206 / 224207.** email: shalomschoolchittur@gmail.com

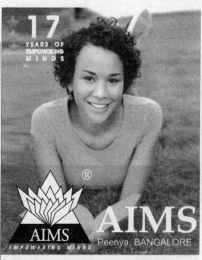

India's Unique Identity Card
Government of India

For Aadhar registration, you must bring any one of the following documentary proof with regard to identification and address, which are available with you

Ration Card - Public distribution system

Voter's Identity Card

Driving Licence

Bank Statement / Pass Book

M G. Job Guarantee Card

Pan Card

LPG (Gas) Pass Book

National Survey Register - Temporary Identity Number (Tin Number)

Aadhar Centers will be opened at the following places:-
Nearest Akshaya Centers, Panchayath Office, Local Self Government Institution or Other Government Offices.
For more details please contact District Government Administration.

Unique Identity will help ease you way

◄ A prestigious Gift from Government - Aadhar
◄ For getting benefits from Government - Aadhar will help you
◄ Non destructible Identity - Easy assurance

Aadhar
Right of Common People
Toll Free Phone No. 📞 1800 180 1947